APA Handbook of

Personality and
Social Psychology

APA Handbooks in Psychology® Series

APA Handbook of Industrial and Organizational Psychology—three volumes
  Sheldon Zedeck, Editor-in-Chief

APA Handbook of Ethics in Psychology—two volumes
  Samuel J. Knapp, Editor-in-Chief

APA Educational Psychology Handbook—three volumes
  Karen R. Harris, Steve Graham, and Tim Urdan, Editors-in-Chief

APA Handbook of Research Methods in Psychology—three volumes
  Harris Cooper, Editor-in-Chief

APA Addiction Syndrome Handbook—two volumes
  Howard J. Shaffer, Editor-in-Chief

APA Handbook of Counseling Psychology—two volumes
  Nadya A. Fouad, Editor-in-Chief

APA Handbook of Behavior Analysis—two volumes
  Gregory J. Madden, Editor-in-Chief

APA Handbook of Psychology, Religion, and Spirituality—two volumes
  Kenneth I. Pargament, Editor-in-Chief

APA Handbook of Testing and Assessment in Psychology—three volumes
  Kurt F. Geisinger, Editor-in-Chief

APA Handbook of Multicultural Psychology—two volumes
  Frederick T. L. Leong, Editor-in-Chief

APA Handbook of Sexuality and Psychology—two volumes
  Deborah L. Tolman and Lisa M. Diamond, Editors-in-Chief

APA Handbook of Personality and Social Psychology—four volumes
  Mario Mikulincer and Phillip R. Shaver, Editors-in-Chief

APA Handbooks in Psychology

APA Handbook of
Personality and Social Psychology

VOLUME 3
Interpersonal Relations

Mario Mikulincer and Phillip R. Shaver, *Editors-in-Chief*
Jeffry A. Simpson and John F. Dovidio, *Associate Editors*

American Psychological Association • Washington, DC

Published by
American Psychological Association
750 First Street, NE
Washington, DC 20002-4242
www.apa.org

To order
APA Order Department
P.O. Box 92984
Washington, DC 20090-2984
Tel: (800) 374-2721; Direct: (202) 336-5510
Fax: (202) 336-5502; TDD/TTY: (202) 336-6123
Online: www.apa.org/pubs/books/
E-mail: order@apa.org

In the U.K., Europe, Africa, and the Middle East, copies may be ordered from
American Psychological Association
3 Henrietta Street
Covent Garden, London
WC2E 8LU England

AMERICAN PSYCHOLOGICAL ASSOCIATION STAFF
Gary R. VandenBos, *Publisher*
Julia Frank-McNeil, *Senior Director, APA Books*
Theodore J. Baroody, *Director, Reference, APA Books*
Patricia Mathis, *Reference Editorial Manager, APA Books*

Typeset in Berkeley by Cenveo Publisher Services, Columbia, MD

Printer: Edwards Brothers, Inc., Lillington, NC
Cover Designer: Naylor Design, Washington, DC

Library of Congress Cataloging-in-Publication Data

APA handbook of personality and social psychology / Mario Mikulincer
and Phillip R. Shaver, Editors-in-Chief. — First edition.
    volumes; cm. — (APA handbooks in psychology)
  Includes bibliographical references and index.
  ISBN 978-1-4338-1699-4 — ISBN 1-4338-1699-7
  1. Personality. 2. Social psychology. I. Mikulincer, Mario. II. Shaver, Phillip R.
III. American Psychological Association.
  BF698.A647 2014
  155.2—dc23
                        2013039784

British Library Cataloguing-in-Publication Data
A CIP record is available from the British Library.

Printed in the United States of America
First Edition

http://dx.doi.org/10.1037/14344-000

This book is dedicated to my family—Cindy, Chris, Natalie, Susan, and Ryan—for their love and inspiration.
—*Jeffry A. Simpson*

This book is dedicated to my students, who have helped and inspired me throughout my career and who have taught me (and continue to teach me) so much.
—*John F. Dovidio*

Contents

Editorial Board

Contributors

Hillie Aaldering, MS, Department of Psychology, University of Amsterdam, the Netherlands

Dominic Abrams, PhD, School of Psychology, University of Kent, Canterbury, England

Joshua M. Ackerman, PhD, Sloan School of Management, Massachusetts Institute of Technology, Cambridge

Christopher R. Agnew, PhD, Department of Psychological Sciences, Purdue University, West Lafayette, IN

John Antonakis, PhD, Department of Organizational Behavior, University of Lausanne, Switzerland

Jens B. Asendorpf, PhD, Department of Psychology, Humboldt University Berlin, Germany

Adam A. Augustine, PhD, Department of Clinical and Social Sciences in Psychology, University of Rochester, Rochester, NY

Özlem Ayduk, PhD, Department of Psychology, University of California, Berkeley

Renée Baillargeon, PhD, Department of Psychology, University of Illinois at Urbana-Champaign

Benjamin Baird, Doctoral Candidate, Department of Psychological and Brain Sciences, University of California, Santa Barbara

Daniel Balliet, PhD, Department of Social and Organizational Psychology, VU University Amsterdam, the Netherlands

Manuela Barreto, PhD, School of Psychology, University of Exeter, England; and Lisbon University Institute (CIS/ISCTE-IUL), Lisbon, Portugal

Kim Bartholomew, PhD, Department of Psychology, Simon Fraser University, Burnaby, British Columbia, Canada

Lucy A. Bates, PhD, Centre for Social Learning and Cognitive Evolution, University of St. Andrews, Fife, Scotland

Roy F. Baumeister, PhD, Department of Psychology, Florida State University, Tallahassee

Lindsey A. Beck, PhD, Department of Communication Sciences and Disorders, Emerson College, Boston, MA

Lane Beckes, PhD, Department of Psychology, University of Virginia, Charlottesville

Verónica Benet-Martínez, PhD, ICREA and Universitat Pompeu Fabra, Barcelona, Spain

Lin Bian, Doctoral Candidate, Department of Psychology, University of Illinois at Urbana-Champaign

This contributor listing includes chapter authors across all four volumes.

Rezarta Bilali, PhD, Department of Applied Psychology, New York University, New York

Irene V. Blair, PhD, Department of Psychology and Neuroscience, University of Colorado, Boulder

Eugene Borgida, PhD, Department of Psychology, University of Minnesota, Minneapolis

Pablo Briñol, PhD, Facultad de Psicología, Universidad Autónoma de Madrid, Spain

David M. Buss, PhD, Department of Psychology, University of Texas, Austin

Richard W. Byrne, PhD, Centre for Social Learning and Cognitive Evolution, University of St. Andrews, Fife, Scotland

Lorne Campbell, PhD, Department of Psychology, University of Western Ontario, London, Ontario, Canada

W. Keith Campbell, PhD, Department of Psychology, University of Georgia, Athens

Amy Canevello, PhD, Department of Psychology, University of North Carolina, Charlotte

Rodrigo J. Carcedo, PhD, Department of Developmental and Educational Psychology, University of Salamanca, Spain

Charles S. Carver, PhD, Department of Psychology, University of Miami, Coral Gables, FL

Tomas Chamorro-Premuzic, PhD, Department of Psychology, University College London, England; and Department of Psychology, New York University, New York

Sapna Cheryan, PhD, Department of Psychology, University of Washington, Seattle

James A. Coan, PhD, Department of Psychology, University of Virginia, Charlottesville

Rebecca J. Cobb, PhD, Department of Psychology, Simon Fraser University, Burnaby, British Columbia, Canada

Dov Cohen, PhD, Department of Psychology, University of Illinois at Urbana-Champaign

Jennifer Crocker, PhD, Department of Psychology, Ohio State University, Columbus

Alyssa Croft, MA, Department of Psychology, University of British Columbia, Vancouver, Canada

William Cupach, PhD, School of Communication, Illinois State University, Normal

Nilanjana Dasgupta, PhD, Department of Psychology, University of Massachusetts, Amherst

Carsten K. W. de Dreu, PhD, Department of Psychology, University of Amsterdam, the Netherlands

Roland Deutsch, PhD, Department of Psychology, Technische Universitaet Dresden, Germany

Colin G. DeYoung, PhD, Department of Psychology, University of Minnesota, Minneapolis

Lisa M. Diamond, PhD, Department of Psychology, University of Utah, Salt Lake City

Ed Diener, PhD, Department of Psychology, University of Illinois at Urbana-Champaign

M. Brent Donnellan, PhD, Department of Psychology, Michigan State University, East Lansing

Bruce P. Doré, Doctoral Candidate, Department of Psychology, Columbia University, New York, NY

David Dunning, PhD, Department of Psychology, Cornell University, Ithaca, NY

Donald G. Dutton, PhD, Department of Psychology, University of British Columbia, Vancouver, British Columbia, Canada

Alice H. Eagly, PhD, Department of Psychology, Northwestern University, Evanston, IL

Paul W. Eastwick, PhD, Department of Human Development and Family Sciences, University of Texas, Austin

Nicholas R. Eaton, PhD, Department of Psychology, State University of New York, Stony Brook

Jiska Eelen, PhD, Amsterdam School of Communication Research, University of Amsterdam, the Netherlands

Victoria M. Esses, PhD, Department of Psychology, University of Western Ontario, London, Ontario, Canada

Allison K. Farrell, Doctoral Candidate, Department of Psychology, University of Minnesota, Minneapolis

Beverley Fehr, PhD, Department of Psychology, University of Winnipeg, Manitoba, Canada

Diane Felmlee, PhD, Department of Sociology, Pennyslvania State University, University Park

Eli J. Finkel, PhD, Departments of Psychology and Management and Organizations (MORS), Northwestern University, Evanston, IL

Susan T. Fiske, PhD, Department of Psychology and Woodrow Wilson School of Public and International Affairs, Princeton University, Princeton, NJ

Julie Fitness, PhD, Department of Psychology, Macquarie University, Sydney, New South Wales, Australia

Gráinne M. Fitzsimons, PhD, Department of Psychology and Fuqua School of Business, Duke University, Durham, NC

William Fleeson, PhD, Department of Psychology, Wake Forest University, Winston-Salem, NC

Rob Foels, PhD, Department of Psychology, Richard Stockton College, Galloway, NJ

Marc A. Fournier, PhD, Department of Psychology, University of Toronto Scarborough, Ontario, Canada

R. Chris Fraley, PhD, Department of Psychology, University of Illinois at Urbana-Champaign

David C. Funder, PhD, Department of Psychology, University of California, Riverside

Adam D. Galinsky, PhD, Management Department, Columbia University, New York, NY

Patrick Gallagher, PhD, Altisource, Winston-Salem, NC

Danielle Gaucher, PhD, Department of Psychology, University of Winnipeg, Manitoba, Canada

Brittany Gentile, PhD, Department of Psychology, University of Georgia, Athens

Erik J. Girvan, JD, PhD, School of Law, University of Oregon, Eugene

Jack Glaser, PhD, Richard and Rhoda Goldman School of Public Policy, University of California, Berkeley

Marci E. J. Gleason, PhD, Department of Human Development and Family Sciences, University of Texas, Austin

Samuel D. Gosling, PhD, Department of Psychology, University of Texas, Austin

Jeff Greenberg, PhD, Department of Psychology, University of Arizona, Tucson

Vladas Griskevicius, PhD, Carlson School of Management, University of Minnesota, Minneapolis

Ana Guinote, PhD, Department of Cognitive, Perceptual, and Brain Sciences, University College, London, England

Leila Guller, MS, Department of Psychology, University of Kentucky, Lexington

Samer Halabi, PhD, School of Behavioral Sciences, Tel-Aviv Jaffa Academic College, Jaffa, Israel

William Hall, MA, Department of Psychology, University of British Columbia, Vancouver, Canada

David L. Hamilton, PhD, Department of Psychological and Brain Sciences, University of California, Santa Barbara

Leah Hamilton, PhD, Department of Management, Mount Royal University, Calgary, Alberta, Canada

Martie G. Haselton, PhD, Department of Communication Studies, University of California, Los Angeles

Nick Haslam, PhD, School of Psychological Sciences, University of Melbourne, Parkville, Victoria, Australia

S. Alexander Haslam, PhD, School of Psychology, University of Queensland, Brisbane, St. Lucia, Australia

Zijing He, PhD, Department of Psychology, Sun Yat-sen University, Guangzhou, Guangdong, China

Todd F. Heatherton, PhD, Department of Psychological and Brain Sciences, Dartmouth College, Hanover, NH

Vicki S. Helgeson, PhD, Department of Psychology, Carnegie Mellon University, Pittsburgh, PA

Sarah D. Herrmann, Doctoral Candidate, Department of Psychology, Arizona State University, Tempe

E. Tory Higgins, PhD, Department of Psychology, Columbia University, New York, NY

Patrick L. Hill, PhD, Department of Psychology, Carleton University, Ottawa, Ontario, Canada

Aline Hitti, PhD, Department of Psychology, Tulane University, New Orleans, LA

Sara D. Hodges, PhD, Department of Psychology, University of Oregon, Eugene

Robert Hogan, PhD, Hogan Assessment Systems, Fernandina Beach, FL

Ryan Y. Hong, PhD, Department of Psychology, National University of Singapore

E. J. Horberg, PhD, Department of Psychology, Stanford University, Stanford, CA

Rick H. Hoyle, PhD, Department of Psychology and Neuroscience, Duke University, Durham, NC

William Ickes, PhD, Department of Psychology, University of Texas, Arlington

Masumi Iida, PhD, School of Social and Family Dynamics, Arizona State University, Tempe

Priya A. Iyer-Eimerbrink, PhD, Department of Psychiatry, Indiana University School of Medicine, Indianapolis

Lauri A. Jensen-Campbell, PhD, Department of Psychology, University of Texas, Arlington

Kyong-sun Jin, Doctoral Candidate, Department of Psychology, University of Illinois at Urbana-Champaign

John T. Jost, PhD, Department of Psychology, New York University, New York

Benjamin R. Karney, PhD, Department of Psychology, University of California, Los Angeles

Liam C. Kavanagh, Doctoral Candidate, Department of Psychology, University of California, San Diego

Aaron C. Kay, PhD, Fuqua School of Business and Department of Psychology and Neuroscience, Duke University, Durham, NC

Dacher Keltner, PhD, Department of Psychology, University of California, Berkeley

Melanie Killen, PhD, Department of Human Development and Quantitative Methodology, University of Maryland, College Park

Laura A. King, PhD, Department of Psychological Sciences, University of Missouri, Columbia

Jennifer M. Knack, PhD, Department of Psychology, Clarkson University, Potsdam, NY

Robert F. Krueger, PhD, Department of Psychology, University of Minnesota, Minneapolis

Virginia S. Y. Kwan, PhD, Department of Psychology, Arizona State University, Tempe

Mark J. Landau, PhD, Department of Psychology, University of Kansas, Lawrence

Natalia Lapshina, MA, Department of Psychology, University of Western Ontario, London, Ontario, Canada

Randy J. Larsen, PhD, Department of Psychology, Washington University, St. Louis, MO

Howard Lavine, PhD, Department of Political Science, University of Minnesota, Minneapolis

Colin Wayne Leach, PhD, Department of Psychology, University of Connecticut, Storrs

Mark R. Leary, PhD, Department of Psychology and Neuroscience, Duke University, Durham, NC

Jenna Lee-Dussud, PhD, Department of Psychology, University of Washington, Seattle

John M. Levine, PhD, Department of Psychology, University of Pittsburgh, Pittsburgh, PA

Karyn L. Lewis, Doctoral Candidate, Department of Psychology, University of Oregon, Eugene

Milton Lodge, PhD, Department of Political Science, State University of New York, Stony Brook

Timothy J. Loving, PhD, Department of Human Development and Family Sciences, University of Texas, Austin

Richard E. Lucas, PhD, Department of Psychology, Michigan State University, East Lansing

Diane M. Mackie, PhD, Department of Psychological and Brain Sciences, University of California, Santa Barbara

Joe C. Magee, PhD, Department of Management and Organizations, New York University, New York

Erika Manczak, Doctoral Candidate, Department of Psychology, Northwestern University, Evanston, IL

E. J. Masicampo, PhD, Department of Psychology, Wake Forest University, Winston-Salem, NC

Dan P. McAdams, PhD, Department of Psychology, Northwestern University, Evanston, IL

Stelian Medianu, MS, Department of Psychology, University of Western Ontario, London, Ontario, Canada

Rodolfo Mendoza-Denton, PhD, Department of Psychology, University of California, Berkeley

Sandra Metts, PhD, School of Communication, Illinois State University, Normal

Sarah Molouki, MA, Booth School of Business, University of Chicago, Chicago, IL

Joann M. Montepare, PhD, The RoseMary B. Fuss Center for Research on Aging and Intergenerational Studies, Lasell College, Newton, MA

D. S. Moskowitz, PhD, Department of Psychology, McGill University, Montreal, Quebec, Canada

Michael D. Mrazek, Doctoral Candidate, Department of Psychological and Brain Sciences, University of California, Santa Barbara

Kelly Lynn Mulvey, PhD, Department of Educational Studies, University of South Carolina, Columbia

Arie Nadler, PhD, School of Psychological Sciences, Tel Aviv University, Ramat-Aviv, Israel

Steven L. Neuberg, PhD, Department of Psychology, Arizona State University, Tempe

Paula Niedenthal, PhD, Department of Psychology, University of Wisconsin, Madison

Bernard A. Nijstad, PhD, Department of Human Resource Management and Organizational Behaviour, University of Groningen, the Netherlands

Kevin N. Ochsner, PhD, Department of Psychology, Columbia University, New York, NY

M. Minda Oriña, PhD, Department of Psychology, St. Olaf College, Northfield, MN

Elizabeth Page-Gould, PhD, Department of Psychology, University of Toronto, Ontario, Canada

Stefano Pagliaro, PhD, Department of Psychology, Seconda Università di Napoli, Italy

Sampo V. Paunonen, PhD, Department of Psychology, University of Western Ontario, London, Ontario, Canada

Lars Penke, PhD, Georg Elias Müller Institute of Psychology, Georg August University, Göttingen, Germany

Elise J. Percy, PhD, Department of Psychology, University of Western Ontario, London, Ontario, Canada

Daniel Perlman, PhD, Department of Human Development and Family Studies, University of North Carolina, Greensboro

Richard E. Petty, PhD, Department of Psychology, Ohio State University, Columbus

Paula R. Pietromonaco, PhD, Department of Psychology, University of Massachusetts, Amherst

Jennifer C. Pink, Master's Candidate, Department of Psychology, University of Western Ontario, London, Ontario, Canada

Michael J. Platow, PhD, Research School of Psychology, The Australian National University, Canberra, Australia

Victoria C. Plaut, PhD, School of Law, University of California, Berkeley

Felicia Pratto, PhD, Department of Psychology, University of Connecticut, Storrs

Emily Pronin, PhD, Department of Psychology, Princeton University, Princeton, NJ

Tom Pyszczynski, PhD, Department of Psychology, University of Colorado, Colorado Springs

Ted Reichborn-Kjennerud, MD, Norwegian Institute of Public Health, University of Oslo, Norway

Stephen D. Reicher, PhD, School of Psychology, University of St. Andrews, Fife, Scotland

Jennifer A. Richeson, PhD, Department of Psychology and Institute for Policy Research, Northwestern University, Evanston, IL

Brent W. Roberts, PhD, Department of Psychology, University of Illinois at Urbana-Champaign

Richard W. Robins, PhD, Department of Psychology, University of California, Davis

Michael D. Robinson, PhD, Department of Psychology, North Dakota State University, Fargo

Alexander J. Rothman, PhD, Department of Psychology, University of Minnesota, Minneapolis

Derek D. Rucker, PhD, Department of Marketing, Northwestern University, Evanston, IL

Gerard Saucier, PhD, Department of Psychology, University of Oregon, Eugene

Özüm Saygi, MS, Department of Psychology, University of Amsterdam, the Netherlands

David A. Sbarra, PhD, Department of Psychology, University of Arizona, Tucson

Mark Schaller, PhD, Department of Psychology, University of British Columbia, Vancouver, Canada

Toni Schmader, PhD, Department of Psychology, University of British Columbia, Vancouver, Canada

Abigail A. Scholer, PhD, Department of Psychology, University of Waterloo, Ontario, Canada

Jonathan W. Schooler, PhD, Department of Psychological and Brain Sciences, University of California, Santa Barbara

Julia Schüler, PhD, Institute of Sport Science, University of Bern, Switzerland

Norbert Schwarz, PhD, Department of Psychology and Marshall School of Business, University of Southern California, Los Angeles

Rose M. Scott, PhD, School of Social Sciences, Humanities, and Arts, University of California, Merced

Suzanne C. Segerstrom, PhD, Department of Psychology, University of Kentucky, Lexington

Peipei Setoh, Doctoral Candidate, Department of Psychology, University of Illinois at Urbana-Champaign

Kennon M. Sheldon, PhD, Department of Psychological Sciences, University of Missouri, Columbia

J. Nicole Shelton, PhD, Department of Psychology, Princeton University, Princeton, NJ

Steven J. Sherman, PhD, Department of Psychological and Brain Sciences, Indiana University, Bloomington

Rebecca L. Shiner, PhD, Department of Psychology, Colgate University, Hamilton, NY

Yuichi Shoda, PhD, Department of Psychology, University of Washington, Seattle

Jeffry A. Simpson, PhD, Department of Psychology, University of Minnesota, Minneapolis

Stephanie Sloane, Doctoral Candidate, Department of Psychology, University of Illinois at Urbana-Champaign

Eliot R. Smith, PhD, Department of Psychological and Brain Sciences, Indiana University, Bloomington

Gregory T. Smith, PhD, Department of Psychology, University of Kentucky, Lexington

Timothy W. Smith, PhD, Department of Psychology, University of Utah, Salt Lake City

Brittany C. Solomon, Doctoral Candidate, Department of Psychology, Washington University, St. Louis, MO

Susan C. South, PhD, Department of Psychological Sciences, Purdue University, West Lafayette, IN

Susan Sprecher, PhD, Department of Sociology and Anthropology, Illinois State University, Normal

Sanjay Srivastava, PhD, Department of Psychology, University of Oregon, Eugene

Sarah C. E. Stanton, Doctoral Candidate, Department of Psychology, University of Western Ontario, London, Ontario, Canada

Chadly Stern, Doctoral Candidate, Department of Psychology, New York University, New York

Flannery G. Stevens, PhD, Eccles School of Business, University of Utah, Salt Lake City

Nan L. Stevens, PhD, Behavioural Science Institute, Radboud University Nijmegen, the Netherlands

Fritz Strack, PhD, Department of Psychology, Universitaet Würzburg, Germany

Daniel Sullivan, PhD, Department of Psychology, University of Arizona, Tucson

Courtney Bearns Tablante, Doctoral Candidate, Department of Psychology, Princeton University, Princeton, NJ

Shelley E. Taylor, PhD, Department of Psychology, University of California, Los Angeles

R. Scott Tindale, PhD, Department of Psychology, Loyola University of Chicago, Chicago, IL

Kaitlin Toner, PhD, Institute for Energy and Environment, Vanderbilt University, Nashville, TN

Linda R. Tropp, PhD, Department of Psychology, University of Massachusetts, Amherst

Timothy J. Trull, PhD, Department of Psychological Sciences, University of Missouri, Columbia

Jean M. Twenge, PhD, Department of Psychology, San Diego State University, San Diego, CA

Tom R. Tyler, PhD, Law School and Department of Psychology, Yale University, New Haven, CT

Michelle R. vanDellen, PhD, Department of Psychology, University of Georgia, Athens

Laura E. VanderDrift, PhD, Department of Psychology, Syracuse University, Syracuse, NY

Anita L. Vangelisti, PhD, Department of Communication Studies, University of Texas, Austin

Paul A. M. Van Lange, PhD, Department of Social and Organizational Psychology, VU University Amsterdam, the Netherlands

Martijn van Zomeren, PhD, Department of Social Psychology, University of Groningen, the Netherlands

Simine Vazire, PhD, Department of Psychology, Washington University, St. Louis, MO

Kathleen D. Vohs, PhD, Marketing Department, University of Minnesota, Minneapolis

Dylan D. Wagner, PhD, Department of Psychological and Brain Sciences, Dartmouth College, Hanover, NH

Nate Way, PhD, Department of Psychological and Brain Sciences, University of California, Santa Barbara

Donna D. Whitsett, PhD, Department of Psychology, University of Washington, Seattle

Thomas A. Widiger, PhD, Department of Psychology, University of Kentucky, Lexington

Joseph Wielgosz, Doctoral Candidate, Department of Psychology, University of Wisconsin, Madison

Benjamin M. Wilkowski, PhD, Department of Psychology, University of Wyoming, Laramie

Paula G. Williams, PhD, Department of Psychology, University of Utah, Salt Lake City

Nicole L. Wilson, PhD, Department of Psychology, University of Washington, Seattle

Piotr Winkielman, PhD, Department of Psychology, University of California, San Diego

Di Wu, PhD, Department of Psychology, Cedarville University, Cedarville, OH

Tal Yarkoni, PhD, Department of Psychology, University of Texas, Austin

Vivian Zayas, PhD, Department of Psychology, Cornell University, Ithaca, NY

Leslie A. Zebrowitz, PhD, Department of Psychology, Brandeis University, Waltham, MA

Noam Zerubavel, Doctoral Candidate, Department of Psychology, Columbia University, New York, NY

Volume 3 Introduction: Past, Present, and Future Directions in the Science of Interpersonal Relations

In a now classic definition of our field, Gordon Allport (1954) proposed that "social psychology is the scientific attempt to explain how the thoughts, feelings, and behaviors of individuals are influenced by the actual, imagined, or implied presence of other human beings" (p. 5). At its core, Allport's definition focuses on how social interaction (which for present purposes also encompasses the imagined or implied presence of others) influences the way in which people think, feel, and behave in the context of relationships in their daily lives. Relationships, therefore, reside at the intellectual heart of our field, not only because they serve as the main context in which most important forms of social influence occur in daily life but also because their nature and quality shape how individuals think, feel, and act as they navigate through their social worlds. The 22 excellent chapters in this volume reveal and elucidate the critical role that different types of relationships—especially close and intimate ones—play in people's daily lives.

When planning this volume, we (the editors) wanted to showcase some of the leading theoretical and empirical work that has been conducted in the rapidly expanding field of interpersonal relationships. We also wanted to identify a few of the most significant and potentially promising new directions for future research in various areas. After surveying the field, we identified seven broad areas in which especially good, interesting, and promising relationship-relevant research was occurring. These areas are organized around seven major themes: (a) major theoretical approaches, (b) biological–health approaches, (c) attraction–relationship development, (d) motivation–emotion, (e) communication–support–power, (f) friendship and love–sexuality, and (g) relationship maintenance–dissolution. The authors invited to write chapters for the volume were chosen in part to represent the diverse array of disciplines within relationship science, including clinical psychology, health psychology, social and personality psychology, family social science, communication studies, sociology, neuroscience, human sexuality, and marketing. We wanted to assemble authors from a broad array of disciplines so that wider swaths of the theoretical and empirical literature in relationship science would be covered.

The authors were given a set of instructions before writing their chapters. We requested that each chapter be structured to accomplish three goals: (a) highlighting the most important principles, ideas, and findings relevant to the topic of the chapter; (b) identifying the most important and novel emerging themes or issues relevant to the topic; and (c) proposing new, promising directions for future research. We felt that addressing this third goal was particularly important because we want this book to serve as a roadmap for future theory and research on the topics covered in each chapter. Especially for young scholars or for those approaching a specific topic or area for the first time, it can be difficult to know the best directions in which the next generation of theory and research should head. We hope the roadmaps that appear toward the end of each chapter will make these intellectual journeys a little easier, a little less circuitous, and much more productive.

To give you—the reader—an overview of what is to come, I now briefly summarize each of the chapters, which are organized by the seven major themes mentioned earlier.

MAJOR THEORETICAL APPROACHES

One prominent theme in relationship science is the need to further develop and integrate existing theories and models that address critical relationship processes and outcomes (Holmes, 2012; Reis, 2007). The first major section of this volume, therefore, contains chapters that present four major theoretical approaches, each of which has important implications for relationships.

In Chapter 1, "Evolution and Close Relationships," Griskevicius, Haselton, and Ackerman suggest that our ancestors faced a stable set of challenges to survival and reproduction throughout evolutionary history, which included finding and retaining a suitable mate, caring for kin, forming and maintaining coalitions, and achieving status in different groups. They propose that different types of relationships were associated with these different evolutionary challenges (e.g., mate attraction with young romantic couples, mate retention with more established couples, kin care with family members, coalition formation with friends and coworkers). Moreover, each ancestral challenge might have presented unique evolutionary opportunities and costs. Griskevicius et al. thus propose that different types of relationships are linked to different relationship-specific modes of thinking and decision making.

Pietromonaco and Beck, in Chapter 2, "Attachment Processes in Adult Romantic Relationships," provide a broad overview of attachment theory and research, focusing primarily on adult romantic attachment. They review and evaluate research examining how attachment orientations shape the way in which people experience and regulate emotions, how they perceive their romantic partners and relationships, how they behave toward their partners, and how they initiate relationships, maintain them, and react when they end. They conclude by presenting a person-in-context model of attachment processes, discuss how romantic partners can foster change versus stability in each other's attachment representations, speculate about how attachment orientations might statistically interact with certain personality traits to predict novel relationship outcomes, and ponder how attachment orientations may affect the health status of both relationship partners.

In Chapter 3, "Interdependence Theory," Van Lange and Balliet offer a historical overview of interdependence theory and discuss four basic principles of the theory: structure (the current situation individuals are in), transformation (how individuals construe the situation), interaction (the characteristics of both individuals [partners] and the objective features of the situation), and adaptation (how repeated social interactions with a partner result in stable orientations to adopt certain transformations in similar situations with the partner). The authors then illustrate each of these principles by discussing research on power and dependence, cooperation and conflict, trust and distrust, attribution and self-presentation, and stereotyping and information seeking. They conclude the chapter by identifying several major implications of interdependence theory.

Finally, in Chapter 4, "Relationships and the Self: Egosystem and Ecosystem," Crocker and Canevello suggest that many scholars assume that people desire relationships to satisfy their own personal needs and goals. As a result, people make sacrifices and compromises to keep their partners happy so they can continue to receive relationship benefits. The authors claim that this self-centered view of relationships reflects egosystem motivation, and they go on to propose a second ecosystem motivation in which people forego their self-interest and come to care deeply about the best interests of their partners. After describing this alternative motivation, Crocker and Canevello evaluate various romantic relationship principles from this ecosystem perspective. They also discuss variables that might predict whether egosystem or ecosystem principles are likely to characterize certain relationships at particular points of development.

BIOLOGICAL APPROACHES AND HEALTH

Two other rapidly expanding areas within relationship science are relationship neuroscience and the connection between relationship quality and health (Simpson & Campbell, 2013). This development has been facilitated by new and affordable technologies, by the changing funding priorities of federal grant agencies, and by new relationship scholars who are receiving advanced training in the health sciences. Thus, the second major section of this volume contains chapters that showcase recent discoveries in both relationship neuroscience and relationships and health.

In Chapter 5, "Relationship Neuroscience," Beckes and Coan focus on how the thoughts, feelings, and behaviors that people exhibit in different relationship contexts are tied to what is happening at a neurobiological level. The authors discuss the many challenges associated with conducting relationship neuroscience research, including how to interpret complicated findings. They then review the relationship neuroscience literature, focusing on the neural substrates of self-representation, the representation of others, empathy, emotion regulation, sex, caregiving, and attachment. While doing so, they review neuroscientific conceptions of emotion and sociality such as the somatic marker hypothesis, theories of subjective experience, the tend-and-befriend model, and models that explain similarities between the physical and social pain circuits. They focus considerable attention on social baseline theory and shared-systems approaches to empathy. Beckes and Coan conclude by discussing the economy of action, prediction, perception–action linkages, rerepresentation processes, and sociality.

Addressing relationships and health, Loving and Sbarra begin Chapter 6, "Relationships and Health," by noting that there is a strong connection between having good relationships and having positive physical and mental health outcomes, with negative relationship events forecasting poorer health outcomes. The authors structure their review of the relationships and health literature around normative romantic relationship development processes, examining research that has used both objective health markers and biomarkers of health, such as mental illness and depression. They call for more experimental studies of physical health outcomes to shed additional light on the most plausible mediators that link relationship processes to physical and mental health outcomes.

ATTRACTION AND RELATIONSHIP DEVELOPMENT

The study of interpersonal relationships in social psychology began by focusing on the basic determinants of attraction in new and emerging relationships (Berscheid, 1985). The field moved into the study of established dyads after the publication of Kelley et al.'s seminal book *Close Relationships* in 1983. Nevertheless, interpersonal attraction remains a central and vibrant topic in relationship science, partly because the conditions under which a relationship begins can strongly affect how it develops, how and why it is (or is not) well maintained, and whether or not it eventually dissolves. The third major section of the book contains three chapters that tackle initial attraction and relationship development.

Chapter 7 by Finkel and Eastwick, "Interpersonal Attraction: In Search of a Theoretical Rosetta Stone," reviews theory and research on interpersonal attraction processes. Finkel and Eastwick first discuss three metatheoretical perspectives—the domain-general reward perspective, the domain-specific evolutionary perspective, and the attachment perspective—that explain the bulk of current interpersonal attraction results. They then review the vast interpersonal attraction literature within these metatheories. They suggest that the instrumentality principle—the notion that people become attracted to others when others help them achieve their most important goals—could be the unifying principle of interpersonal attraction. Finkel and Eastwick also propose that once people have achieved an important goal, they should be less attracted to partners who initially were instrumental in helping them attain that goal.

Sprecher, Felmlee, Metts, and Cupach, in Chapter 8, "Relationship Initiation and Development," examine the environmental context of potential relationships and how proximity and certain situations often combine initially to propel two individuals into a relationship. They then discuss internal factors that contribute to relationship development, such as whether a person is ready to start a new relationship and the role that mutual attraction plays in this process. The authors then review the signals that people use to convey interest in forming a relationship, which can lead to later relationship phases and turning points that further cement relationship bonds. They also discuss how self-disclosure, certain intensification strategies, and sexual intimacy all affect relationship development processes. After this, they address problematic relationship initiation experiences, focusing on deception, unwanted relationship advances, and stalking. They conclude by discussing third-party assistance in relationship initiation.

Finally, in Chapter 9, "Ideal Mate Standards and Romantic Relationships," Campbell, Pink, and Stanton review how ideal mate standards affect interpersonal attraction, relationship initiation, and relationship maintenance. They discuss what ideal mate standards (preferences) are, how they develop, and what many people want in short-term and long-term romantic relationships. Guided by the ideal standards model, they then discuss how perceived discrepancies (e.g., ideal partner vs. actual partner disparities) affect the evaluation and maintenance of established relationships. Campbell et al. next address a debate in the literature about the association between self-reported ideal mate preferences and mate choice, focusing on whether and when ideal mate preferences influence actual mate selection. They conclude by speculating about when certain ideal standards should govern relationship processes most strongly and how ideals can change over time.

MOTIVATION, EMOTION, AND INTERSUBJECTIVITY

Close relationships are one of the most fertile contexts in which powerful motivations and intense emotions are experienced, expressed, and acted on (Berscheid, 1983). Because of the strong interdependence that exists in close relationships, close relationship partners are not only more likely to experience strong motivations and feel intense negative and positive emotions, they can also intensify or diminish the motivations and emotions experienced by their partners, depending on how they behave in the relationship. For this reason, the fourth major section of the book is devoted to the interrelated and often interlocking concepts of motivation, emotion, and intersubjectivity in relationships.

In Chapter 10, "Goal Pursuit in Relationships," Fitzsimons and vanDellen open by explaining that most goal pursuit occurs in social contexts with friends, coworkers, family, and romantic partners. They then review research on how goal pursuit is both affected by and affects these relationships in various ways. Then Fitzsimons and vanDellen describe a transactive self-regulation model, which highlights relations among the personal and interpersonal goal pursuits enacted by relationship partners. According to this model, self-regulation is an interdependent process instead of an independent one. The authors then use this model to interpret research findings concerning goal pursuit in various relationship contexts. While doing so, they cover aspects of interpersonal goal priming, goal contagion, social support, the motivating impact of successful others, the effects of regulatory resources and strategic motivational orientations on relationship processes, and the effects of relationship processes on self-regulation.

The next chapter, "Emotions in Relationships," by Fitness focuses directly on relationship-related emotional processes. Fitness provides an integrative summary of what is known about emotions within relationships. She begins by reviewing emotion theory from an evolutionary–social psychological perspective, emphasizing the information and communication functions that different emotions serve. Fitness then reviews the cognitive appraisal approach to emotion elicitation, including how the personalities and attachment histories of each relationship partner affect emotion appraisals and experiences. Next, Fitness discusses the importance of good emotion communication and regulation for maintaining healthy relationships, with an emphasis on the intrapersonal and interpersonal costs of emotional suppression. Fitness concludes the chapter by reviewing the important role of positive emotions in adaptive relationship functioning, highlighting positive emotions such as joy, interest, love, compassion, and gratitude and encouraging more theoretically integrative research on emotions in relationships.

Hodges, Lewis, and Ickes, in Chapter 12, "The Matter of Other Minds: Empathic Accuracy and the Factors That Influence It," address empathic accuracy in relationships. After defining what empathic accuracy is, they focus on three sources of variance in empathic accuracy performance in relationships: the characteristics of perceivers that predict better empathic accuracy, the factors that contribute to the readability of the target, and how characteristics of the perceiver and target statistically interact to predict empathic accuracy in a particular social situation. They then examine whether higher levels of empathic accuracy are essential for good social and interpersonal outcomes, which target variables still need to be investigated, and how the nature of the relationship between the target and the perceiver should affect empathic accuracy levels.

SUPPORT, COMMUNICATION, AND POWER

As mentioned, communication and social influence lie at the heart of not only relationships but social psychology as well (Allport, 1954). Indeed, the defining feature of a close relationship is that partners strongly influence each other's thoughts, feelings, and behaviors over time and in different social contexts (see Kelley et al., 1983). Studying relationship processes, therefore, requires a different way of conceptualizing these intrinsically interpersonal variables. More specifically, because a relationship exists between two people, the patterns of interconnection between partners within a relationship must be measured and modeled appropriately. The fifth section of the book examines these issues: communication, support, and influence between partners in relationships.

In Chapter 13, "Social Support," Gleason and Iida note that the study of social support has relied heavily on retrospective reports of received support and its perceived availability. They point out that some past research has concluded that social support tends to be beneficial for most recipients. However, recent research investigating recipients' responses to enacted support has indicated that it has either no effects or negative effects on many support recipients. The authors discuss why enacted support often fails to alleviate recipients' distress; they focus on the motivation, timing, content, and skills of enacted support along with the characteristics of support receivers and support providers. Gleason and Iida then address some of the negative effects of support provision on the support provider.

Vangelisti's Chapter 14, "Communication in Personal Relationships," explains that communication in relationships is important because it both shapes and reflects how partners perceive, think, feel, and behave toward one another. Five properties of communication are then described (interdependence, reflexivity, complexity, ambiguity, and indeterminancy), and theories and research on these properties are reviewed. These properties can be understood at both an individual and a dyadic level. At the individual level, Vangelisti reviews the basic cognitive and emotional patterns that affect and are affected by communication processes. At the dyadic level, she evaluates couple types and certain behavioral sequences associated with different relationship outcomes.

In Chapter 15, "Power and Social Influence in Relationships," Simpson, Farrell, Oriña, and Rothman provide an overview of theory and research on power and social influence in relationships. Although most prior research has investigated interactions between strangers, the authors note that attention is shifting to how and why different kinds of social influence strategies and tactics are more or less effective in established relationships and how power differences between relationship partners predict various relationship outcomes. Simpson et al. begin by reviewing the theoretical literature on power and social influence, focusing on influence agents (those attempting to persuade their partners) and influence targets (those being persuaded). Next, they review research on the use and effectiveness of different power and influence strategies and tactics in established relationships. Following this, they unveil a new process model—the dyadic power–social influence model—that specifies how the use of different influence strategies and tactics, in combination with the power dynamics in a given relationship, affect different personal and relational outcomes. They conclude the chapter by speculating about how power develops and is used at different stages of relationship development.

Finally, in Chapter 16, "Power: Past Findings, Present Considerations, and Future Directions," which outlines power as a basic and pervasive individual difference variable, Galinsky, Rucker, and Magee offer a primer on the social psychology of power. They begin by providing a clear definition of power and then discuss both the antecedents (manipulations and measures) and the consequences of power along with several variables that reliably moderate power outcomes. Galinsky et al. then review different theories of how power can guide and affect different types of social behavior. They conclude the chapter by discussing novel and emerging themes in the study of power, making several important points that both new and seasoned power scholars will appreciate.

FRIENDSHIP, LOVE, AND SEXUALITY

This section of the book deals with the topics of friendship, different types of love in relationships, and sexuality, with a special focus on nonheterosexual relationships. Each of these topics is central to the study of close relationships (see Diamond, 2003; Fehr, 1996), and each chapter provides a detailed theoretical and empirical overview of these core topics.

In Chapter 17, "Friendship," Perlman, Stevens, and Carcedo summarize what is known about friendships. They begin by discussing friendship qualities, including the types of friendships people typically have and how friendships differ from other types of relationships. Next, Perlman et al. indicate how and why friendships are initiated, maintained, and sometimes dissolved. They then turn to the nature of friendships, including how and why friendships are similar or different at different points in a person's life and how gender affects the nature of friendships in childhood and adulthood. After this, the authors review work on friendship and well-being, revealing that not having close friendships has several major disadvantages. They conclude the chapter by discussing the future of friendships, especially networked individualism, a pattern of friendship that has become more common with recent changes in communication technology.

In Chapter 18, "Love: Conceptualization and Experience," Fehr summarizes what is known about love from a social psychological perspective. She addresses how people view and define love, what is currently known about gender and cultural differences in conceptions of love, and how conceptions of love affect relationship satisfaction and stability. After this, Fehr reviews how individuals actually experience love in relationships, including the neurological correlates of love and its developmental course across time as relationships develop. She concludes the chapter by surmising how different forms of love influence relationship satisfaction, commitment, and deterioration.

Diamond provides a comprehensive review of human sexuality in Chapter 19, "Sexuality and Same-Sex Sexuality in Relationships." She explains the role that sexual behavior plays in couple functioning; the variables that predict sexual satisfaction; the challenges posed by self or partner illness, disability, or sexual dysfunction; and the protective health benefits of good sex and the positive aspects of sexuality. She also evaluates the relationship dynamics of same-sex couples, including issues of sexual stigmatization and marginalization, legal recognition, gender differences, and sexual norms and practices.

MAINTENANCE, STRIFE, AND DISSOLUTION

The final section of the book considers how relationships are maintained and how and why they occasionally dissolve despite the good intentions of well-meaning partners. Traditionally, a considerable amount of research in relationship science has focused on these significant topics, particularly within clinical and social psychology and the family social sciences (see Bradbury, Fincham, & Beach, 2000).

In Chapter 20, "Why Marriages Change Over Time," Karney addresses how and why marriages often change over time, even though most spouses want to preserve their initial levels of happiness. Karney opens the chapter by discussing the nature of change in marriage and then addresses what changes and how different features of marriage tend to shift over time. He presents a model outlining how marital change occurs, focusing on how and why spouses' marital evaluations typically decline. He then reviews evidence showing that spouses' specific perceptions of their marriage are more susceptible to change than are their global evaluations of their marriage. Karney proposes that change at a global level is often attributable to either an accumulation of specific negative perceptions or limits on spouses' ability or a motivation to assimilate negative perceptions into their global marital views.

In Chapter 21, "Relationship Maintenance and Dissolution," Agnew and VanderDrift suggest that relationships can be conceptualized on an independence–interdependence continuum, and they suggest that relationship maintenance processes sustain partners' interdependence. They then review past research on relationship maintenance from this perspective. The authors discuss maintenance processes that keep interdependent partners happy and stable (stability promotion processes), that increase partners' level of interdependence (interdependence promotion processes), and that deal with threats to the relationship (threat-induced processes). They conclude by reviewing the positive and negative consequences of not maintaining relationships and the variables that forecast relationship dissolution.

Finally, in Chapter 22, "Established and Emerging Perspectives on Violence in Intimate Relationships," Bartholomew, Cobb, and Dutton address classic and recent perspectives on the causes of violence in intimate relationships. They first review feminist perspectives on how the patriarchal system contributes to men's violence against women. After this, they discuss psychological perspectives on the background and personality variables that place certain individuals at risk for becoming violent toward their partners. Bartholomew et al. then review interactional perspectives that focus on the relational and situational contexts in which partner violence arises. They first discuss how partner abuse may be elicited by a confluence of different partner characteristics and how certain combinations of partner characteristics can emerge over time. They then review the social contexts that often elicit abuse, including those that inhibit and disinhibit aggression. They conclude by describing a multifactor model that integrates different approaches and by discussing how these perspectives might be used to prevent and treat partner abuse.

CONCLUSION

When we (the editors) were planning this book, we hoped that the envisioned chapters would provide broad and comprehensive coverage of the most important theories, models, principles, and research findings relevant to the topic addressed by each chapter. We also hoped that the authors of each chapter would provide clear and useful roadmaps for researchers interested in each topic to follow in the coming decade. We could not be happier with what the chapter authors have delivered. And we believe that you—the reader—will agree.

Jeffry A. Simpson
Associate Editor

References

Allport, G. W. (1954). The historical background of social psychology. In G. Lindzey & E. Aronson (Eds.), *Handbook of social psychology* (Vol. 1, pp. 1–46). New York, NY: Random House.

Berscheid, E. (1983). Emotion. In H. H. Kelley et al. (Eds.), *Close relationships* (pp. 110–168). San Francisco, CA: Freeman.

Berscheid, E. (1985). Interpersonal attraction. In G. Lindzey & E. Aronson (Eds.), *The handbook of social psychology* (pp. 413–484). New York, NY: Random House.

Bradbury, T. N., Fincham, F. D., & Beach, S. R. H. (2000). Research on the nature and determinants of marital satisfaction: A decade in review. *Journal of Marriage and the Family, 62,* 964–980. doi:10.1111/j.1741-3737.2000.00964.x

Diamond, L. M. (2003). What does sexual orientation orient? A biobehavioral model distinguishing romantic love and sexual desire. *Psychological Review, 110,* 173–192. doi:10.1037/0033-295X.110.1.173

Fehr, B. (1996). *Friendship processes.* New York, NY: Sage.

Holmes, J. G. (2012). The future of relationship science. In L. Campbell, J. G. LaGuardia, J. M. Olson, & M. P. Zanna (Eds.), *The science of the couple: The Ontario symposium* (Vol. 12, pp. 231–253). New York, NY: Taylor & Francis.

Kelley, H. H., Berscheid, E., Christensen, A., Harvey, J. H., Huston, T. L., Levinger, G., … Peterson, D. R. (1983). *Close relationships.* New York, NY: Freeman.

Reis, H. T. (2007). Steps toward the ripening of relationship science. *Personal Relationships, 14,* 1–23. doi:10.1111/j.1475-6811.2006.00139.x

Simpson, J. A., & Campbell, L. (Eds.). (2013). *The Oxford handbook of close relationships.* New York, NY: Oxford University Press.

PART I

MAJOR THEORETICAL APPROACHES

CHAPTER 1

EVOLUTION AND CLOSE RELATIONSHIPS

Vladas Griskevicius, Martie G. Haselton, and Joshua M. Ackerman

Throughout history, humans have faced critical challenges that included finding a mate, keeping that mate, caring for kin, forming coalitions, and gaining some status. Solving each of these ancestral challenges involved forming a different type of social relationship. An evolutionary perspective suggests that there is a set of fundamentally different types of close relationships associated with different evolutionary challenges. These types include (a) mate attraction (e.g., dating couples), (b) mate retention (e.g., married couples), (c) kin care (e.g., family members), (d) coalition formation (e.g., friends), and (e) status (e.g., workplace relationships). Each type of ancestral challenge is associated with different kinds of evolutionary opportunities and costs, suggesting that different types of relationships may be governed by a different relationship-specific psychology. In this chapter, we review the principles of evolutionary psychology and their implications for close relationships.

Although some animals spend most of their lives as hermits, humans have always lived in groups. The human brain has evolved for social relationships (Kenrick, Griskevicius, Neuberg, & Schaller, 2010; Kenrick, Neuberg, & White, in press). But although people are born ready to love and relate to other people, relationships differ in several important ways. For example, the words *I love you* can be spoken by a parent to a newborn baby, by a young man to a woman he met yesterday at a beach resort in Mexico, and by a heterosexual woman to her best female friend. Yet parental love is not the same as romantic love, which is still different from platonic love between friends.

In this chapter, we consider social relationships from an evolutionary perspective. This perspective contends that, throughout history, humans have faced a set of core ancestral challenges, which include attracting a mate, keeping that mate, caring for kin, forming coalitions, and attaining status. An evolutionary perspective suggests that each type of challenge can be solved by forming different types of relationships. These relationship types include (a) dating couples, (b) married couples, (c) family members, (d) friends, and (e) coworkers (see Table 1.1). Each type of relationship is associated with different kinds of evolutionary opportunities and costs, meaning that people need different things from different types of intimate others and must provide different things to those intimate others. These needs and provisions vary systematically depending on the type of relationship.

In this chapter, we first briefly review what it means to take an evolutionary perspective, reviewing some foundational principles. We then discuss each of the five types of relationships, reviewing relevant theory and findings. Finally, we discuss emerging themes and future directions in the study of social relationships from an evolutionary perspective.

AN EVOLUTIONARY APPROACH TO RELATIONSHIPS

A modern evolutionary approach is based on the seminal work of Charles Darwin. This approach suggests that, just as the forces of natural selection can

http://dx.doi.org/10.1037/14344-001
APA Handbook of Personality and Social Psychology: Vol. 3. Interpersonal Relations, M. Mikulincer and P. R. Shaver (Editors-in-Chief)

TABLE 1.1

Relationship Types and Associated Evolutionary Opportunities and Threats

Relationship domain	Typical dyads	Relationship tasks	Key evolutionary theories	Relationship opportunities	Relationship threats	Relationship-specific sensitivities
Mate attraction	Dating couple	Attract desirable romantic partner	Intersexual selection, parental investment, strategic pluralism, sexual strategies	Sexual and reproductive access, resource access	Abandonment after pregnancy, sexually transmitted diseases, partner deception	Sensitivity to partner's mate value, sexual strategy, honest costly signaling, other mating opportunities
Mate retention	Married couple	Preserve alliance with romantic partner	Attachment theory, strategic interference theory	Long-term parental alliance, instrumental and emotional support	Sexual infidelity, resource infidelity, cuckoldry	Sensitivity to partner's change in relative mate value, cues to infidelity, mate poaching, infertility, mating ecology
Kin care	Parent–child, siblings	Successfully raise children and care for relatives	Kin selection, parent–offspring conflict	Inclusive fitness, account-free resource sharing, cooperative breeding	High costs of close kin, parasitism of kinship, inbreeding	Sensitivity to kin member's relatedness, age, sex, ability, need, health, and other cues to enhancing inclusive fitness
Coalition	Friends, teammates	Develop and maintain cooperative alliances	Reciprocal altruism, social contract theory, intergroup conflict	Shared resources, material support, instrumental support, protection	Free-riding cheaters, excessive demands, social rejection, stigmatization	Sensitivity to equity and unfair exchanges, trustworthiness, rejection, competence, group power
Status	Worker–boss, coworkers	Gain and maintain social prestige and power	Intrasexual selection, dominance hierarchy	Reputation-enhancing alliances, moving up status hierarchies	Loss of reputation, respect, and power	Sensitivity to position in hierarchies, leadership cues in others, other status opportunities

shape morphological features, so too can those forces shape psychological and behavioral tendencies. An evolutionary approach maintains that human and nonhuman animals inherit brains and bodies equipped to behave in ways that are fitted to the demands of the environments within which their ancestors evolved. Just as human morphological features—opposable thumbs, larynxes, and upright postures—have been shaped by evolutionary pressures, humans inherited brains specially designed to solve recurrent problems in the ancestral world (L. Barrett, Dunbar, & Lycett, 2002; Buss, 1995; Neuberg, Kenrick, & Schaller, 2010; Tooby & Cosmides, 1992). For example, along with the larynx, humans also inherited a brain designed to easily learn to communicate using language. Although the specific words and sounds of a language might differ across cultures, all languages share an underlying universal structure as a result of the evolved human mechanisms for language (Pinker, 1994). Next, we review two key distinguishing features of a modern evolutionary approach.

The Mind Evolved to Solve Adaptive Problems of the Ancestral Past

An evolutionary approach does not assume that humans or other organisms inherit the capacity to determine in advance which behaviors will enhance fitness. People do not proceed through life deliberating the reproductive consequences of each decision. Instead, natural selection, operating over millennia, endows individuals with a psychology designed to increase the probability of solving recurrent adaptive challenges. All of our ancestors confronted a set of problems that had to be solved to survive and reproduce, such as making friends, gaining status, attracting a mate, keeping a mate, and caring for family. The brain is designed to solve adaptive challenges, whereby the cumulative solutions to these challenges together enhanced fitness over evolutionary history.

Although the modern environment is in many ways different from ancestral environments, humans still encounter problems the brain is designed to solve. Each problem has always been uniquely different. Solutions to one problem failed to successfully solve other problems. For example, solutions to the adaptive problems of attracting a mate (e.g., approaching genetically fit individuals) generally could not be used as solutions to the adaptive problem of gaining status (e.g., approaching people with power or prestige). Because different evolutionary problems required qualitatively different solutions, an evolutionary psychological perspective suggests that the brain houses multiple domain-specific psychological mechanisms geared toward solving different adaptive problems (H. Barrett & Kurzban, 2006; Tooby & Cosmides, 1992).

The domain-specific view of the mind is importantly different from the domain-general view that dominated the social sciences in the 20th century. This traditional view posits that the brain has a single executive system operating according to a few domain-general rules such as seek rewards, avoid punishments, or maximize utility. Such views

initially appeal to parsimony, but an abundance of research on learning and cognition in both animals and humans challenged views of the brain that are completely domain general. Zoologists, biologists, and ecologists have uncovered a wealth of specialized behavioral and cognitive mechanisms in animals peculiarly suited to solving different types of adaptive challenges (Garcia & Koelling, 1966; Wilcoxon, Dragoin, & Kral, 1971). For example, birds use distinct, domain-specific neuropsychological systems for learning and remembering information about species songs, poisonous foods, and spatial position of food caches (Sherry & Schachter, 1987). Similarly, humans use distinct, domain-specific systems and neural architectures for dealing with different types of adaptive problems (H. Barrett & Kurzban, 2006; S. B. Klein, Cosmides, Tooby, & Chance, 2002). Thus, because different types of social relationships helped to solve fundamentally different types of adaptive challenges, an evolutionary perspective posits that different types of social relationships function according to different rules—in the ancestral past and today.

Multiple Levels of Explanation for Behavior

An evolutionary perspective draws an important distinction between ultimate and proximate explanations for behavior (see Tinbergen, 1963). Psychologists have typically been concerned with proximate explanations for behavior, which focus on the relatively immediate triggers (causes) of action. For example, when considering why so many people seek romantic relationships, the primarily proximate reasons often include sex, companionship, love, happiness, pleasure, resources, and support. An evolutionary approach, however, also asks why people evolved to want sex, companionship, and love and why these things provide so much pleasure in the first place. The ultimate reason why so many people enter romantic relationships is because they enhanced our ancestors' reproductive fitness during evolutionary history.

Proximate and ultimate explanations are not in competition with each other. Instead, they are complementary. Because human behavior is the product of brain activity and the brain is an evolved organ, behaviors are likely to have both ultimate and proximate explanations. For example, people seek romantic relationships because they provide pleasure (a proximate reason) and because they enhanced reproductive fitness in ancestral environments (an ultimate reason). Both of these explanations are correct. Each one provides insights into the same behaviors, but at different levels of analysis (see Simpson & Gangestad, 2001).

Sometimes the connections between the different levels of analysis are obvious. But connections between different levels of analysis are not always obvious. Consider why birds migrate each year. A proximate explanation is that birds migrate because days are getting shorter—the immediate cue triggering migration. The ultimate reason for such migration, however, is survival and reproduction: The distribution of desirable food and mating sites varied seasonally throughout the evolutionary history of birds. There are two key implications here: (a) Animals, including humans, need not be consciously aware of the ultimate functions of their behaviors that were forged over evolutionary time and (b) the connection between ultimate functions and immediate goals is often indirect and nonobvious.

An explanation at one level of analysis must be compatible with explanations at other levels. Positing a proximate mechanism that would have reliably led people to make functionally maladaptive decisions (such as Freud's death instinct) is problematic (Tooby & Cosmides, 1992). Evolutionary psychologists typically advance hypotheses about links between proximate mechanisms and ultimate functions. In deriving those hypotheses, however, psychologists adopting an evolutionary perspective attempt to take into account pertinent findings from evolutionary biology and anthropology. Psychologists can derive hypotheses about proximate causes and development without thinking in evolutionary terms, but disregarding evidence and theory derived from research on other cultures and other species can lead to hypotheses that are incompatible with other levels of analysis. For example, psychologists during the last century often assumed that most sex differences in social behavior (such as differences in violent aggression) were products of

U.S. culture, unaware that similar differences were found in other cultures across time, and even in other species (see Daly & Wilson, 1988; Kenrick, Trost, & Sundie, 2004).

To achieve compatibility between levels of explanation, evolutionarily minded researchers often adopt an engineering focus to detail the functioning of potentially adaptive behaviors at multiple causal levels. Tooby and Cosmides (1992) recommended five central components of an adaptation analysis: (a) identification of an adaptive target (a proposed biologically successful outcome), (b) background conditions (a description of the relevant ancestral environment in which the feature likely emerged), (c) a design (a detailed depiction of the components and boundaries of the feature), (d) a performance examination (a description of the actions and outcomes of the feature), and (e) a performance evaluation (an assessment of how well the design has met the adaptive target). An analysis such as this one highlights both ultimate function and proximate mechanism as well as their necessary interplay.

Foundational Principles

At its core, an evolutionary approach is concerned with how various behaviors and mental constructs facilitated reproductive success. This success arises from differential reproduction (either by outproducing conspecifics or inhibiting those conspecifics' own production), and thus an evolutionary approach involves many principles related to aspects of reproduction. Before turning to the specific domains that make up human relationship psychology, we introduce some foundational principles that have broad relevance to multiple relationship domains.

Inclusive fitness.   A key, often misunderstood aspect of an evolutionary perspective is that it is focused on reproductive success at the genetic level, not at the level of the individual. Thus, what matters is the aggregate success of individuals who have genes in common. *Inclusive fitness* refers to the mechanisms that might facilitate this aggregate success, such as those for biological kin recognition and altruism among genetic relatives (Hamilton, 1964; Lieberman, Tooby, & Cosmides,

2007; Park & Ackerman, 2011). Inclusive fitness theory does not predict that people always prefer or help their relatives; rather, it predicts that psychological mechanisms that tended to increase the reproductive success of relatives will evolve. These mechanisms, of course, function at a proximate level and are susceptible to erroneous or novel inputs, which can produce behaviors that seem maladaptive despite their foundation in inclusive fitness. Interestingly, this theory also predicts non-affiliative tendencies between relatives that might impair genetic success, such as incest aversion (Westermarck, 1891).

Parental investment. After conceiving offspring, organisms face the issue of whether or not to invest in the development of that offspring. This investment typically carries costs such as limiting future reproduction opportunities and loss of resources that might be used for the self or for others (such as other genetic relatives). Parents engage in investment because it supports the physical and mental maturation of offspring, which in turn promotes future genetic propagation (of shared genes). The "decision" of how much to invest, typically made unconsciously, is rooted in the cost–benefit trade-offs that parents face as a function of factors such as what resources parents have, what offspring need (e.g., owing to their health or environmental pressures), what relatives need (e.g., other offspring), and the likelihood that a parent shares genes with the offspring.

More important, organisms face these trade-offs not only after conception but before conception as well. Some costs can be predicted in advance, and organisms often act to minimize them. With mammals, there is a natural division in parental investment because females gestate the young within their bodies (for almost 2 years in the case of elephants and for 9 months in the case of humans), and they then nurse them afterward (sometimes for several years). Thus, females have a higher minimal obligatory parental investment than do males (Trivers, 1972). Males could, in theory, contribute little more than sperm to their offspring, which is the typical pattern for more than 90% of mammalian species (Geary, 2000).

Sexual selection. The established differences in prospective costs for females and males set the stage for a number of additional behavioral sex differences. Within a species, the sex that invests less in offspring tends to compete for mating opportunities with the higher investing sex. Because mammalian females nearly always pay a higher price for reproduction, whereas males might contribute little or nothing to offspring care, females are relatively more selective in their choice of mates (Trivers, 1972). This reflects sexual selection, which refers to the relative success of traits that assist in mating (by helping to either attract the opposite sex or compete with one's own sex for mates). Darwin developed the idea of sexual selection to address the fact that one sex is often larger, more colorful, and more competitive than the other (i.e., sexually dimorphic). A peacock's bright feathers increase his chances of attracting peahens as mates while at the same time making him more susceptible to detection by predators. The increased developmental effort necessary to produce these feathers, and the associated increased risk of predation, make such indicators honest or costly signals (Grafen, 1990; Zahavi, 1975). Females do not need ostentatious ornamentation displays to the same extent as males because they make a higher investment in offspring and, therefore, are choosier about their mating partners, who must compete with other males to be chosen as mates.

Male investment, however, varies across species. To the extent that male investment in offspring increases, the degree of sexual dimorphism is reduced, as in many bird species in which both parents devote effort to nest building and offspring care (Cockburn, 2006). In rare cases, a male actually invests more resources in the offspring than does the female, as in the case of bird species such as phalaropes—a type of sandpiper—in which the female leaves the male to tend the eggs while she searches for another mating opportunity (Colwell & Oring, 1989). Consistent with parental investment theory, sex differences in morphology and behavior reverse for such species (see Trivers, 1985).

Because all the usual mammalian constraints on gestation and nursing apply to humans, several broad sex differences—greater female mating selectivity and greater male intrasexual competition—also apply to humans (e.g., Clark & Hatfield, 1989; Wilson & Daly, 1985). One indirect consequence of greater female selectivity is slower sexual maturity in males (Geary, 1998). The reason for the maturational delay among males in dimorphic species is that it takes longer for males to reach a size at which they can successfully compete with other males for females. In line with this observation, human males typically reach sexual maturity much later than females, and they attain a somewhat larger size than do females.

TYPES OF CLOSE RELATIONSHIPS AND ASSOCIATED ANCESTRAL CHALLENGES

As noted earlier, throughout history humans have faced a set of core ancestral challenges, each of which can be solved by forming different types of relationships. These evolutionary challenges include (a) mate attraction (e.g., dating couples), (b) mate retention (e.g., married couples), (c) coalition formation (e.g., friends), (d) status (e.g., workplace relationships), and (e) kin care (e.g., family members; see Table 1.1). In this section, we discuss how each type of challenge is associated with different kinds of evolutionary opportunities and costs, which have important ramifications for the workings of relationships that help solve different evolutionary challenges.

Dating Couples: Challenge of Mate Attraction

Differential reproduction is at the center of natural selection. Hence, decisions about mating are, from a functional perspective, crucially important. Evolution-inspired research on mate selection has been abundant. Selecting a mate involves three separable questions:

1. Which type of relationship is the partner being considered for (e.g., short term vs. long term)?
2. What are the characteristics of the potential mate (e.g., his or her physical attractiveness and social status)?
3. How does the potential mate's characteristics meet one's desires and needs?

The characteristics desired in a short-term mate are different from those desired in a long-term mate (e.g., Buss & Schmitt, 1993; Fletcher, Tither, O'Loughlin, Friesen, & Overall, 2004; N. Li & Kenrick, 2006). Because of differences in obligatory parental investment (with women being required to invest more in potential offspring), men and women differ in their preferences for both types of relationship and the characteristics they desire in a mate (e.g., Kenrick, Sadalla, Groth, & Trost, 1990; Shackelford, Goetz, LaMunyon, Quintus, & Weekes-Shackelford, 2004; Wiederman & Hurd, 1999). Sex differences are also found in the criteria for mate choice, with women prioritizing status and resources more than men and men prioritizing physical attractiveness more than women (Buss, 1989; Kenrick, Groth, Trost, & Sadalla, 1993; N. Li & Kenrick, 2006). Human males and females often cooperate in raising offspring, and raising offspring requires some similar characteristics in men and women (e.g., cooperativeness, generosity, sense of humor). Consequently, the sex differences in mate selection criteria exist alongside a number of sex similarities (Kenrick et al., 1990, 1993; N. Li & Kenrick, 2006).

Romantic relationship preferences. In humans, romantic relationship preferences are often characterized along the dimension of short-term and long-term relationships. People tend to seek out romantic partners for short-term romantic (typically sexual) encounters, or they look for more longer term relationships that are more likely to provide stability, support, and parental investment. The short-term approach tends to be marked by increased openness to multiple mating partners. The long-term approach is characterized by sexual exclusivity (lack of openness) or the existence of extrapair liaisons (some degree of openness to certain kinds of partners). A great deal of within-sex variation exists in human mating strategies, with both men and women varying in their courtship strategies in ways linked to either different developmental trajectories (Belsky, Steinberg, & Draper, 1991) or local environmental conditions (Gangestad & Simpson, 2000). Men who adopt an unrestricted (sexually open) mating strategy, for example, are larger, more physically attractive, and more competitive on average than men who adopt a restricted strategy, characterized by higher investment and greater monogamy (Boothroyd, Jones, Burt, DeBruine, & Perrett, 2008; Thornhill & Gangestad, 1994).

Compared with people who have a restricted orientation, individuals with an unrestricted orientation have relatively more partners in the past, including one-night stands, and are more likely to view their opposite-sex friends as potential sexual partners (Bleske-Rechek & Buss, 2001). They also intend to have relatively more partners in the future, begin having sex earlier in any given relationship, are more likely to carry on multiple relationships at one time, and feel less investment in, commitment to, love for, and interdependence with their current partners (Simpson & Gangestad, 1992).

Ecological and cultural factors influence tendencies toward restricted versus unrestricted mating, but men are universally more inclined toward unrestrictedness (Schmitt, 2003). Numerous studies have demonstrated that women are more reticent about entering short-term relationships and more selective about the minimum characteristics they will accept in a partner for such relationships (e.g., Clark & Hatfield, 1989; Kenrick et al., 1990; Schmitt et al., 2012). When asked about their regrets in life, men are much more likely to wish they had slept with more partners, whereas women wish they had tried harder to avoid getting involved with losers (Roese et al., 2006). When asked about casual sex experiences in the past, women are far more likely than men to say that they regret them (Galperin et al., 2013). One survey of 16,288 people from around the world suggested that the sex difference in the desire for sexual variety is universal and medium to large in magnitude (*d*s ranging from 0.31 to 1.20; Schmitt, 2003).

The sex difference in interest in casual sex has implications for other aspects of relationships. For example, people sometimes deceive others about the extent of their interest in forming a long-term relationship to induce a partner to have sex. Women tend to be bothered much more than men by such deception (sex differences *d*s ranging from 0.67 to 1.69; Haselton, Buss, Oubaid, & Angleitner, 2005). Compared with men, women are also more skeptical about interpreting a man's compliments, gifts,

touch, and even confessions of love as evidence of commitment (Ackerman, Griskevicius, & Li, 2011; Haselton & Buss, 2000). Because women are reticent about sexual opportunities, men tend not to miss possible signs of sexual interest (Haselton & Buss, 2000; Haselton & Funder, 2006). Compared with women, men are more likely to interpret a woman's compliments, gifts, touch, and love confessions as a signal of true sexual desire (Ackerman et al., 2011; Haselton, 2003; Haselton & Buss, 2000). In one study, college students were asked to judge whether faces in photographs showed subtle signs of suppressing any underlying feelings. In reality, all the faces had been carefully picked to be emotionally neutral. After watching a film clip that put them into a romantic frame of mind, men projected their sexual feelings onto the photos, but only the photos of beautiful women. Women's romantic feelings, however, did not cloud their judgments (Maner et al., 2005).

Romantic partner preferences. Just as people prefer different types of romantic relationships, they also seek different types of romantic partners. Sometimes this search is tied to their particular relationship preferences. For example, unrestricted people tend to choose partners who are socially visible and attractive (Simpson & Gangestad, 1992). Restricted individuals prefer partners with traits linked to good parenting, such as responsibility, affection, stability, and faithfulness (Simpson & Gangestad, 1992). The preference for certain partner characteristics is also tied to other individual and ecological factors. One of the most prevalent of these in the research literature has been an individual's biological sex (Gangestad & Simpson, 2000).

Women's relative preference for status. The sex difference in minimal obligatory parental investment leads female mammals to be more choosy when picking mates, and it leads males to compete with one another to demonstrate their relative viability and superiority as mates. This generalization applies to humans as well. Despite the fact that human males contribute to offspring care, human females still make a higher physiological investment in gestation and nursing, and they typically provide more direct care for children than do men.

Because men do not contribute resources directly from their bodies to the offspring, evolutionary theorists argue that ancestral women sought high-status men who could provide resources and protection (Gangestad & Simpson, 2000; Gangestad & Thornhill, 1998).

Numerous studies have found that women place more emphasis on status than do men when selecting partners. For example, in one study, women preferred a physically unattractive but well-dressed man to a handsome burger flipper (Townsend & Levy, 1990). Another study found that women were more attracted to a man who made money in business over one who just got lucky, suggesting that it is the ability to generate future resources that is attractive to women (Hanko, Master, & Sabini, 2004). Women's singles ads are, compared with men's, more likely to require status or wealth in a man; conversely, men taking out singles advertisements are more likely to advertise any status or wealth they possess (Rajecki, Bledsoe, & Rasmussen, 1991; Wiederman, 1993). Women also respond more to men who advertise their income and education levels, whereas men reading women's ads pay little attention to a woman's status (Baize & Schroeder, 1995). A study of 37 different cultures found the same trends around the world (Buss, 1989). Similar to American women, Japanese, Zambian, and Yugoslavian women rate good financial prospects in a mate as more important than do men in those countries (Buss, 1989). Women around the world also tend to seek and to marry somewhat older men, who generally have more resources and social status (Buss, 1989; Kenrick & Keefe, 1992).

Men compete for women's attention not only by fighting and struggling for social status but also by signaling that they have desirable characteristics such as attractiveness, health, intelligence, sense of humor, and creativity (e.g., Griskevicius et al., 2006; Maner & Ackerman, 2013). Wilbur and Campbell (2011) found that, in dating contexts, men report being more likely to show off their sense of humor, whereas women evaluate men as potential partners on these kinds of displays. These researchers also found that women evaluate nonhumorous online dating profiles as much less desirable (men also preferred a partner with a good sense of humor, but not

as strongly as women). In a related study, Bressler, Martin, and Balshine (2006) found that women prefer men who demonstrate their sense of humor, whereas men prefer women who are receptive to their own humor.

Men's relative preference for reproductive resources.   Given women's provision of direct physical resources to their offspring, it would have been advantageous for ancestral men to seek out cues of health and reproductive potential, such as youth and physical attractiveness, in their mates (Pawlowski & Dunbar, 1999). Indeed, men's age preferences in mates are consistent with the general tendency for men to prioritize cues to fertility over cues to status. Women's fertility peaks in their mid-20s (Dunson, Colombo, & Baird, 2002). Older men tend to be attracted to younger women, men in their 20s are attracted to women around their own age, and teenage men are attracted to slightly older women (Buunk, Dijkstra, Fetchenhauer, & Kenrick, 2002; Kenrick & Keefe, 1992).

As we noted, men advertise, and women request, financial resources in singles advertisements. On the other side of the bargain, men evaluating potential dates place more emphasis on physical appearance (N. Li, Bailey, Kenrick, & Linsenmeier, 2002; Shaw & Steers, 2001). Other findings have suggested that being seen with a physically attractive member of the opposite sex improves the social impression made by a man but has no effect on the impression made by a woman (Sigall & Landy, 1973). Indeed, to say that a man is physically attractive is to say he shows signs of social dominance, such as a strong chin and mature features, whereas a physically attractive woman shows signs not of dominance but of youthfulness and fertility (Singh, 1993).

Both sexes would be most happy with a partner who is high on all desirable dimensions—physically attractive, wealthy, charming, agreeable, and so on (Fletcher, Simpson, Thomas, & Giles, 1999). However, most people are not in a position to attract a partner who is perfect in every way, so they must compromise and make trade-offs. When forced to compromise in choosing a long-term partner, men and women make very different choices. Women prioritize social status and give up good looks;

men prioritize attractiveness and give up wealth (N. Li et al., 2002). In choosing a casual sexual partner, however, women shift their priority to physical attractiveness (Fletcher et al., 2004; N. Li & Kenrick, 2006).

Hormonal effects on mating strategies. Several decades ago, many scientists believed that hormonal influences were irrelevant to human sexual behavior (e.g., Simon & Gagnon, 1984). However, numerous studies have refuted that viewpoint and suggested that sex hormones have many of the same functions in humans as they do in other mammals (Leitenberg & Henning, 1995; Regan & Berscheid, 1999). For instance, injecting testosterone into men who have malfunctioning testes leads them to increase their sexual fantasies, and stopping the injections leads to a drop in fantasies (Regan & Berscheid, 1999). Likewise, injections of testosterone increase sexual desire and fantasy in women (Sherwin, Gelfand, & Brender, 1985). Men involved in short-term relationships have higher levels of testosterone, whereas married men have lower levels (Gray et al., 2004). Increases in testosterone might also facilitate intrasexual competition for mates (Mazur & Booth, 1998), supporting the view that this hormone is intricately involved in many aspects of sexuality and initial mating effort.

Several findings have also suggested that the rules of mate selection change when women are in the ovulatory phase of their menstrual cycles and, hence, are most fertile (e.g., Pillsworth & Haselton, 2006b; Thornhill & Gangestad, 2008). At these times, women show increased preferences for men with sexy traits such as masculine faces (DeBruine et al., 2010) and competitive behavior (Gangestad, Simpson, Cousins, Garver-Apgar, & Christensen, 2004). Additionally, women report greater attraction to men other than their primary partners, particularly when their primary partners lack the sexy traits these women prefer most strongly near ovulation (Gangestad, Thornhill, & Garver-Apgar, 2005; Haselton & Gangestad, 2006; Pillsworth & Haselton, 2006a).

Other factors affecting variation in mating strategies. Other findings have suggested that variations in mating strategies can influence the characteristics people seek out in others. Unrestricted

women—who are inclined to have short-term sexual relationships—tend to prefer masculine men (Waynforth, Delwadia, & Camm, 2005). When women are considering men for short-term sexual relationships, they are similar to men in that they give priority to physical attractiveness over other characteristics that might be more desirable in a long-term mate (Fletcher et al., 2004; N. Li & Kenrick, 2006). These findings suggest that some women some of the time play an alternative mating strategy of seeking a man whose characteristics indicate good genes, even if that means compromising on getting a man who will stay around and invest in offspring (see Gangestad & Simpson, 2000).

Correlational evidence has shown that women who state they are in control of their own resources, and presumably less dependent on a man for assistance with offspring care, place greater emphasis on attractiveness in mates than women who do not feel in control of their own resources (Moore, Cassidy, Law Smith, & Perrett, 2006). Recent experimental research has shown that women placed in positions of power over a male stranger have more sexual thoughts and perceive greater sexual interest from the man (Kunstman & Maner, 2011). Together, these findings suggest that women in nontraditional gender roles—perhaps those women high in occupational prestige—display a mating psychology shifted toward that of men.

Finally, research has also pointed to variation in the basic process of mate attraction (Maner & Ackerman, 2013). People are typically assumed to seek out and interact with mate prospects in interpersonal bubbles, away from third-party influences. When social environments are taken into account, research has almost exclusively considered third parties as potential competitors (e.g., Buss, 1989; Maner, Miller, Rouby, & Gailliot, 2009; Shackelford, Goetz, Buss, Euler, & Hoier, 2005). Yet, cross-species findings have indicated that animals sometimes cooperate in their courtship pursuits (e.g., Krakauer, 2005; Smuts & Smuts, 1993). Some evidence has suggested that people do so as well, with women cooperating more strongly to build mating quality control thresholds and barriers to unwanted advances and men cooperating more strongly to overcome these thresholds and interpersonally break down these barriers (Ackerman & Kenrick, 2009; Bleske-Rechek & Buss, 2001).

Married Couples: Challenge of Mate Retention

Once a romantic couple forms, relationship cognition shifts from a mate attraction mindset to a mate retention mindset. Clearly, continuing to perform many of the behaviors and decisions that attracted romantic partners would damage one's chances of maintaining a long-term relationship. For example, a man who spent lavishly to display status and attract women might undermine his long-term relationship success by persisting in this behavior after marriage. Instead, other problems emerge in this relationship domain, including maintenance of bonds, dealing with the threat of infidelity, and, potentially, child care.

The joint care of two parents was probably crucial to the survival of human children throughout evolutionary history (Hrdy, 1999). As a point of comparison, newborn chimpanzees are able to hold onto their mothers' backs as their mothers forage for food in the forest, they are weaned at about 4 years of age, and they are self-sufficient by about 5 years of age. Chimpanzee mothers have only one offspring about every 5.5 years, rarely caring for more than one dependent offspring at a time (Lancaster, Kaplan, Hill, & Hurtado, 2000). In contrast, human children are born helpless. They are unable to lift their own heads or unfold their hands until almost the 3rd month of life, they often share parental care with dependent siblings, and they remain dependent on their caregivers for a much longer period of time than any other primate offspring. Among modern hunter-gatherers, children cannot personally acquire as many calories as they need to consume to survive until approximately age 15 (Hill & Hurtado, 1996; Lee & Kramer, 2002). The needs of human children might explain the fact that, across cultures, men and women fall in love (Jankowiak & Fisher, 1992) and form long-term cooperative relationships in which both parents contribute to the offspring's welfare (Daly & Wilson, 1983; Geary, 1998). A key adaptive problem for both sexes is maintaining these mating bonds with desirable and cooperative partners (Buss, 2007; Hazan & Diamond, 2000).

The process of maintaining these bonds might have exploited existing physiological systems designed for attachment between mammalian mothers and infants (Brown & Brown, 2006; Hazan & Shaver, 1994). The hormone oxytocin is secreted in greater quantities by women, and it is believed to promote maternal bonding (Feldman, Weller, Zagoory-Sharon, & Levine, 2007). Oxytocin is also linked to sexual receptivity, increased genital lubrication in women, and orgasm in both sexes (Salonia et al., 2005). Other neuropsychological evidence has suggested that oxytocin might play a role in connecting love and sex, explaining why the two are more closely interconnected for women than for men (Diamond, 2004).

Certain lower order processes might also facilitate mate retention. Attention to desirable alternative partners can lower relationship commitment (Kenrick, Neuberg, Zierk, & Krones, 1994), and some research has suggested that people maintain commitments partly by changing their visual attention to and perceptions of attractive alternatives (Gonzaga, Haselton, Smurda, Davies, & Poore, 2008; Johnson & Rusbult, 1989; Lydon, Fitzsimmons, & Naidoo, 2003; Maner, Rouby, & Gonzaga, 2008). In one study of this phenomenon, Simpson, Gangestad, and Lerma (1990) asked students to judge advertisements from magazines such as *Cosmopolitan, Gentleman's Quarterly,* and *Time.* Included in the series were several photographs of attractive members of the opposite sex. College men and women involved in dating relationships, in contrast to those not involved, found the models significantly less physically and sexually attractive. In another study, participants saw a profile of a highly attractive member of the opposite sex and learned that this person was currently available (Lydon et al., 1999). Half were also told that this person had expressed a romantic interest in them. How participants responded depended on how committed they were to their current relationship. When the attractive person expressed romantic interest, less committed participants increased in their attraction to the person, but more committed participants became less attracted to the person. These findings indicate that being in a loving relationship leads to a defensive change in perception—seeing potentially threatening alternatives as less desirable. Benefiting long-term bonds, this inattention to attractive alternatives can make people more content with the relationship they currently have (R. S. Miller, 1997).

Threat of infidelity. On a less rosy side, relationship maintenance also involves defending against incursions by interlopers, competitors who might be romantically attracted to one's partner (Shackelford & Goetz, 2007). The threat of infidelity can elicit an array of changes in behavior, such as increased visual attention to potential interlopers (Maner et al., 2009) and feelings of sexual jealousy if others have desirable characteristics, such as dominance in a man and physical attractiveness in a woman (Buunk & Dijkstra, 2005). Men and women are highly sensitive to what the other sex finds desirable, with jealous women paying more attention to a potential rival's waist, hips, and hair and men checking out a rival's shoulders (Buunk & Dijkstra, 2005). If one's romantic partner seems to be showing interest in, or involvement with, potential interlopers, more extensive, defensive responses might occur, including emotional and physical violence directed either at the partner (Shackelford et al., 2005) or at the potential mate poacher (Campbell & Ellis, 2005).

Additionally, there is a sex difference in the dangers posed by infidelity linked to life history differences between men and women. Women bear children and are always absolutely sure that a given child is their own biological offspring. For men, it is less clear; indeed, a recent meta-analysis reported that approximately 1 in 25 children are genetically unrelated to their purported birth fathers (Bellis, Hughes, Hughes, & Ashton, 2005). If a man's partner was unfaithful, he might unknowingly invest substantial resources in raising another person's child—an act that had high fitness costs throughout evolutionary history. Given the possibility of paternal uncertainty, men might be particularly prone to jealousy about a partner's sexual liaisons. Conversely, because the father's resources and support are often critical to raising a child successfully (Geary, 2000; Steiglitz, Gurven, Kaplan, & Winking, 2012), a woman stands to lose considerably if her partner falls in love with another woman.

This problem of paternal investment suggests that women might be especially concerned about a male partner's emotional rather than sexual attachments.

To test these ideas, Buss, Larsen, Westen, and Semmelroth (1992) asked subjects to imagine either that their long-term partner was falling in love and forming a deep emotional attachment to another person or having sexual intercourse with that person. The majority of the men reported they would be more distressed by the sexual infidelity. However, approximately 80% of the women said they would be more upset by the emotional attachment. Similar sex differences in the triggers of jealousy have since been found in Korea, Japan, Germany, the Netherlands, and Sweden (Buss et al., 1992; Buunk, Angleitner, Oubaid, & Buss, 1996).

However, there has been controversy about the extent of the sex difference in jealousy and its theoretical meaning. Some psychologists have argued that the sex difference depends on the particular method used to measure jealousy (e.g., DeSteno, Bartlett, Braverman, & Salovey, 2002), but other researchers have found the same sex difference using very different methods (Pietrzak, Laird, Stevens, & Thompson, 2002; Shackelford, LeBlanc, & Drass, 2000). In another critique of the paternal uncertainty hypothesis, Harris (2003) argued that the sex difference in jealousy-linked homicides is simply another manifestation of the general tendency of men to be more violent than women. Consistent with this idea, she reported cross-cultural data demonstrating that although women are less likely to kill, 16% of killings by women are motivated by jealousy, compared with about 12% of killings by men. Most psychologists involved in this controversy agree that jealousy is a powerful emotion that is likely to have some adaptive function, but they disagree about whether there is a specific sex difference in the triggers for jealousy per se. One alternative is that both sexes are equally upset by either sexual or emotional infidelity because, ancestrally, the survival of human infants required a close bond between both parents (DeSteno et al., 2002; Harris, 2003). Challenging the idea that the sexes are equal in their responses to infidelity, a recent meta-analysis of the published and unpublished literature has shown that sex differences in responses to hypothetical jealousy scenarios and experienced jealousy events are robust and consistent across the methodologies used to investigate them (Sagarin et al., 2012).

Monogamy and polygyny across cultures. The vast majority of human societies allow a man to marry multiple wives, whereas only about half of 1% allow polyandrous unions between a woman and multiple men. Regardless of whether a society permits polygamy or not, most of the marriages in all societies are monogamous. If our species is generally inclined toward monogamy, though, why are any societies and any marriages within those societies nonmonogamous?

Traditional Tibetans are one of the world's few polyandrous societies, with one woman often marrying a group of brothers. The harsh conditions of life in the high Himalayan desert have made it difficult for a single man and woman to survive alone. Tibetan families in which one man marries one woman have fewer surviving children than do families in which brothers pool their resources and share a wife (Crook & Crook, 1988). By sharing one wife, brothers can preserve the family estate, which would not support even one family if it were subdivided each generation. If all the children are girls, the polyandrous pattern switches to a polygynous one, with several sisters marrying one man and passing the family estate on to the sons from that marriage. Hence, Tibetan polyandry appears to be an economically based strategy by which a limited pool of resources must be channeled into a very focused family line.

Economic resources may also explain the link between social status and polygynous marriage. Men are especially likely to take multiple wives when several conditions converge: (a) a steep social hierarchy, (b) a generally rich environment so one family can accumulate wealth, and (c) occasional famines so the poor face the possible danger of starvation (Crook & Crook, 1988). Under these circumstances, a woman who joins a large, wealthy family reaps benefits, even if she must share her husband with other women. Compared with marrying a poorer man with no additional wives, marrying into a wealthy family can provide a more satisfactory

buffer against famine along with the chance of greater wealth for children in times of plenty. Interestingly, this is the same pattern found in birds such as the indigo bunting: Males who attract more than one female are those that control resource-rich territories (Orians, 1969).

Friendships: Challenge of Coalition Formation

Despite the dangers of physical violence or disease posed by other people (Ackerman, Huang, & Bargh, 2012), human beings have evolved to seek out the company of others. Unlike some other species—for example, our close relatives the orangutans, who live relatively solitary lives outside the mating season—our hunter-gatherer ancestors lived in groups, as did most of the primates from which they evolved (Lancaster, 1975). The desire to maintain in-group relationships through stable interpersonal bonds is a human universal (Baumeister & Leary, 1995) and perhaps a survival strategy (Caporael, 1997). Forming connections with others was sufficiently important to human survival in our ancestral past that responses to social rejection are linked to the same brain regions that are involved in responses to physical threat (Eisenberger & Cole, 2012; Eisenberger, Lieberman, & Williams, 2003).

The inclination to form groups and befriend others, however, involves certain trade-offs. Affiliation and coalition formation can entail costs such as wanton trust, intragroup competition over local resources, socially transmitted diseases, exploitation by fellow group members, and obligations to engage in intergroup competition. However, these costs are often balanced by many benefits: Humans everywhere profit from sharing extensive resources, knowledge, and parenting chores with other group members (Henrich & Boyd, 1998). Moreover, ancestrally, one's closest friends were usually genetic relatives, which remains the case in many contemporary societies (Daly, Salmon, & Wilson, 1997). These shared genetic interests make it easier to cooperate with close kin and more costly to compete with them (Kenrick, Sundie, & Kurzban, 2008). Cooperative relationships with nonkin are more likely to be marked by attention to reciprocity than are those with immediate relatives, although they might both be reinforced by similar proximate psychological mechanisms, such as physical resemblance or nearby residence.

Affiliation is centrally linked to other social motives. For example, to gain status or acquire mates, one must first affiliate with other people. Activating social motives can also activate affiliatively linked behaviors. Similar to the members of most other social species, human beings are safer in groups, and activating self-protective motives increases people's tendencies to conform to other people's opinions rather than to stand out from the crowd (Griskevicius, Goldstein, Mortensen, Cialdini, & Kenrick, 2006; Griskevicius, Goldstein, et al., 2009). This desire for inclusion is also strong in people who face dangers, such as the possibility of physical harm, that stem from social rejection. For instance, people who feel rejected have greater interest in making new friends, have an increased desire to work with others, and are more positive in their impressions of other people (Maner, DeWall, Baumeister, & Schaller, 2007).

As noted earlier, affiliation motives are also linked to certain mate attraction behaviors. For example, compared with women, men are more likely to help their same-sex friends break down social barriers in the pursuit of attractive members of the opposite sex (Ackerman & Kenrick, 2009). Women also use their friends to meet attractive members of the opposite sex, but they are even more likely to use friends to help them avoid someone they are not interested in dating. These findings fit well within the broader perspective of differential parental investment; whereas both sexes are interested in finding mates, the potential costs of an undesirable mate are often substantially higher for women than for men.

On average, women tend to be more affiliative than men. Indeed, compared with men, women tend to be more agreeable, more empathic, more skilled in nonverbal communication, and better at smoothing interactions in social groups (Bank & Hansford, 2000; K. J. K. Klein & Hodges, 2001). Women are also more attentive to their friends and more direct in showing their appreciation of other people (Carli, 1989; Helgeson, Shaver, & Dyer, 1987). In essence, women might be more likely to treat friends as they

treat their own kin, whereas men might be more likely to treat friends as they treat mere acquaintances. Ackerman, Kenrick, and Schaller (2007) found that this was true both for attributions of credit for a team's success (where kin and friends of women were given more credit than the self) and for aversion to sexual contact (where kin and friends of women were relatively undesirable compared with strangers). Moreover, when women are under stress, they are more likely to seek support than men (Tamres, Janicki, & Helgeson, 2002). Women also nonverbally invite support and intimacy by smiling substantially more than men do (LaFrance, Hecht, & Paluck, 2003). In response to threat, Taylor et al. (2000) have argued that females, compared with males, are more likely to adopt a tend-and-befriend rather than a fight-or-flight response. Whereas males under stress are more likely to secrete androgens (associated with aggressive behavior), females under stress are more likely to secrete oxytocin (associated with nurturing maternal behaviors and attachment). Taylor et al. interpreted these findings in evolutionary terms, suggesting that ancestral male and female mammals would have been better served by having different responses to stress. For females, fighting or running away would probably have endangered their offspring, who are more dependent on their mothers than their fathers for care.

These sex differences are not absolute, and there are important functional qualifications to the generalization that females are more affiliative. For example, Geary and Flinn (2002) have pointed out that men also depend on other group members, so that tending and befriending should play a part in male responses to stress in certain contexts. When competition with out-groups is salient, in fact, men are more likely than women to make cooperative choices that favor the group good (Van Vugt, De Cremer, & Janssen, 2007).

Benenson and colleagues have conducted a number of evolution-based studies of male and female friendships. One series of studies found that boys, compared with girls, receive relatively more benefits from friends relative to their kin (Benenson, Saelen, Markovits, & McCabe, 2008). Among humans' close primate relatives, some functionally relevant variations in sex differences parallel this finding. For example, male (but not female) chimpanzees form alliances with members of the same sex to hunt and fight with other groups, activities that do not occur in bonobos. Humans are similar to chimps in engaging in hunting, meat sharing, and intergroup aggression. Benenson et al. (2008) reviewed a number of findings suggesting that human males form alliances with large groups of other males, whereas females are more likely to associate with one another either one at a time or in small cliques. They also noted that human males are, compared with females, more concerned with their friends' skills (e.g., intelligence, athleticism, financial potential, creativity) and their friends' social connections. In their own research, Benenson et al. found that boys at all ages want less help from their parents than do girls. Although children of both sexes receive more material and social support from their parents than from other sources, boys rely on their same-sex friends for a greater percentage of their social support than girls do.

Coworkers: Challenge of Status

The status domain involves gaining access to the indicators of social power used to categorize and regulate social interactions (Barkow, 1989; Eibl-Eibesfeldt, 1989). Around the world, dominant versus submissive is one of the two primary dimensions on which people categorize members of their groups (White, 1980). Indeed, all group-living primates form dominance hierarchies, and higher ranking members of those hierarchies tend to prosper (Fiske, 2010). In nonhuman animals, high status translates into more access to resources such as food, mates, or a place at the waterhole (Van Vugt, Hogan, & Kaiser, 2008). As with other animals, higher status also results in benefits for both men and women because it often translates into the receipt of favors.

Van Vugt et al. (2008) have analyzed leadership in evolutionary terms, arguing that leadership evolved for coordination, movement, peacekeeping, and intergroup conflict. Although leaders serve the group's interests, they are also often motivated by personal gains, such as preferred access to resources and mates, leading to the potential for exploitation.

Van Vugt et al. claimed that modern organizations are often mismatched with evolved leadership psychology in that ancestral groups were probably more democratic and egalitarian, whereas modern groups are more hierarchical, opening the potential for despotic rule. They argued that this is tied to the fact that the majority of employees in modern organizations report that their immediate supervisors are the most stressful aspect of their jobs. However, some evidence has suggested that despotic self-interest emerges primarily when high-status positions are unstable and mainly for people high in a desire for dominance (Maner & Mead, 2010).

Other animals gain and maintain status primarily by force—by being willing and able to carry out acts of aggression against other members of their groups. This is sometimes true for humans, as in the case of gang leaders and military dictators, but humans can also achieve status through prestige—by earning others' respect without using force or power (Henrich & Gil-White, 2001). In the modern world, one can gain status by having access to desirable information and using that information for the good of others. This highlights a central trade-off associated with status—that respect does not come for free (Van Vugt et al., 2008). Leaders have to give to the group more than do followers. On the positive side, although other animals generally give a wide berth to dominant individuals in their groups, humans strive to get close to those who have high prestige.

Besides having access to other resources, status also has an additional benefit for human males in increasing their access to mates (Betzig, 1992; N. Li & Kenrick, 2006; Turke & Betzig, 1985), which helps to explain why men are often more willing to take social and physical risks to attain status, a proclivity that is enhanced when mating motives are made salient (Griskevicius et al., 2006; Griskevicius, Tybur, et al., 2009; Wilson & Daly, 1985). This fact has several consequences for behavior in social settings. For example, Griskevicius, Cialdini, and Kenrick (2006) put men and women in a mating frame of mind by having them imagine an ideal date with a dream partner. Thinking about mating led men, but not women, to show off in several ways. For instance, men in a mating frame of mind gave more creative and interesting answers on various tests of their creative ability. In another series of studies, men thinking about mating were more likely to give opinions that went against those of other group members. Women in a mating frame of mind, however, were more likely to conform than were women in a control condition (Griskevicius et al., 2006). Other studies have indicated that mating-related cues increase competitiveness and riskiness in men. For example, young men at a skateboard park who were exposed to an attractive woman made more risky moves, a tendency that was linked to increases in testosterone (Roney & Von Hippel, 2010). In another series of studies, the classic behavioral economic bias toward risk aversion was reduced or reversed in men under a mating motivation (Y. Li, Kenrick, Griskevicius, & Neuberg, 2012). In a related vein, activating status-related motivation increases men's tendency to respond to put-downs with direct aggression (Griskevicius, Tybur, et al., 2009).

Simpson, Gangestad, Christensen, and Leck (1999) studied competition for mates directly, bringing people into the lab and asking them to compete for attractive partners. They found that more physically symmetrical men with an unrestricted sociosexual orientation were more likely to use direct competitive tactics than were less symmetrical and restricted men. These sexy men tried to dominate their opponent with statements to the attractive women such as "You'd have a lot more interesting time with me than with that other guy." Restricted men took a softer approach, focusing on their own positive qualities and presenting themselves as nice guys. Women, however, were less likely to try to dominate their female opponents.

Another series of studies examined how mating competitors influence one's self-assessments. In one study (Gutierres, Kenrick, & Partch, 1999), participants were shown profiles of eight members of their own sex who had presumably signed up for a campus dating service. In some cases, the other students were all highly socially dominant. One was a former editor of a university newspaper who had published articles in *Runner's World* on what it takes to achieve excellence, and another was a youthful proprietor of a successful business. In other cases, the profiled students were low in social dominance (one listed a letter to the editor of the campus newspaper as his or her major accomplishment). Attached to each profile was a photograph. Half of the students saw very attractive members of their sex who were actually models from a local agency. The other half saw average-looking people. When later asked to rate their own desirability as a marriage partner, the men downgraded themselves after seeing a pool of potential competitors full of socially dominant, high-roller types. The women, however, were affected by the other women's physical attractiveness, downgrading their own mate value when the other women were all good-looking.

The links between male reproductive success and status help explain the tendency for men to compete more for leadership positions (Kenrick et al., 2004). Despite men's thirst for leadership, they do not necessarily make better leaders in modern organizations (Van Vugt et al., 2008). Women might be more effective at what is called social–emotional leadership, whereas men might be more effective at task leadership. Additionally, Van Vugt and Spisak (2008) found that men were more likely to be chosen as group leaders when conflict with other groups was salient, but women were overwhelmingly preferred when getting along with other group members was salient.

Family Members: Challenge of Kin Care

Kin care refers to the manner in which people manage relationships with biologically related others. Biological kinship involves a different type of interpersonal tie, characterized by unique psychological mechanisms, than the typical affiliative relationship (Park & Ackerman, 2011). From an inclusive fitness perspective (Hamilton, 1964), people should be more inclined to deliver benefits to kin than nonkin. Research with species ranging from ground squirrels to humans has suggested lower thresholds for engaging in various types of cooperative behavior among neighbors who are closely related (e.g., Burnstein, Crandall, & Kitayama, 1994; Sherman, 1981). For example, analysis of inheritance payouts has shown that kin are preferred over nonkin, and genetically closer kin are preferred over genetically distant kin. On the basis of such considerations, Daly et al. (1997) posited that there exists "a relationship specific kinship psychology, in which specialized motivational and information processing devices cope with the peculiar demands of being a mother, a father, an offspring, a sibling, a grandparent or a mate" (p. 266).

Parental care is critical to the survival of human offspring (Geary, 2000). The bond between a mammalian mother and her offspring serves an obvious purpose—it helps the offspring survive (Bowlby, 1969). For 90% of mammals, the adult male is out of the attachment loop, contributing little more than sperm to his offspring (Geary, 2000). Human males, though, are different—they normally show a great deal of interest in, and care for, their offspring. Social and developmental psychologists have conducted a great deal of research applying Bowlby's (1969) attachment theory to adult relationships (e.g., Hazan & Shaver, 1994; Simpson & Rholes, 2012; see Chapter 2, this volume). As Shaver, Hazan, and Bradshaw (1988) noted, Bowlby distinguished the attachment system from the caregiving and sexuality systems. The caregiving system, although less explored, is most relevant to kin care.

Emerging evidence has indicated that hormones associated with the birth of a child might trigger adaptations for parental care (Eibl-Eibesfeldt, 1989; Hahn-Holbrook, Holt-Lunstad, Holbrook, Coyne, & Lawson, 2011) and even permanently reorganize brain systems involved in parenting (Glynn & Sandman, 2011). For example, gray matter increases in brain regions associated with maternal motivation, and mothers with the largest increases have the most positive feelings about their infants (Kim et al., 2010). Breastfeeding hormones, such as prolactin and oxytocin, might trigger maternal adaptations for defending offspring. In one study, immediately after feeding their infant, breastfeeding and bottle-feeding mothers were given the opportunity to deliver noise blasts to a female confederate who had been rude to them (Hahn-Holbrook et al., 2011). Breastfeeding moms experienced smaller increases in blood pressure in response to the rude confederate, but they delivered louder blasts than bottle-feeding moms. Like mama bears, new mothers awash in postpartum hormones might be especially bold when confronted by an aggressor. Fathers also experience changes in hormones surrounding the birth of children.

Men's prolactin levels are higher at the end of their partner's pregnancy and correlate with more male pregnancy (couvade) symptoms (Storey, Walsh, Quinton, & Wynne-Edwards, 2000). Higher prolactin levels in fathers are associated with increased father–infant play (Gordon, Zagoory-Sharon, Leckman, & Feldman, 2010) and more alertness and positive responses to infant cries (Fleming, Gorter, Stallings, & Steiner, 2002; Storey et al., 2000).

Although many important proximate processes are involved in kin care (e.g., kin recognition, kin conflict; Park & Ackerman, 2011), perhaps the most critical issue involves the decision of whether to actively support a relative. The motivation to nurture offspring is not a constant across all parents. Evolutionary theorists have hypothesized that decisions about caring for any particular offspring are contingent on various factors that affect payoffs for their parental investment (Daly & Wilson, 1980; Hrdy, 1999). Because both men and women face inherent constraints on reproduction, the trade-offs involved in allocating scarce resources across all available genetic offspring differ depending on factors such as life history stage and the age range of individuals involved; investment in one genetic outlet cannot be invested in another outlet, including potential future offspring (Trivers, 1972). For example, a child produced by a young parent is, in essence, in competition with that parent's yet-to-be-born offspring for resources. If a child is born to a parent approaching the end of his or her reproductive life span, however, there are fewer opportunity costs for investing in that offspring, making present investment more likely. Parents and children are as genetically related as full siblings, sharing 50% of their genes ($r = .5$), yet parents tend to invest more in their children than siblings do in each other for several reasons. For example, the benefit to young individuals is likely to be greater than the marginal benefit of investment in older adults, and children have greater remaining reproductive value relative to full siblings if those siblings are older and have other access to resources.

The fact that men can produce offspring much later in their lives than women leads to another asymmetry. On one hand, once past their reproductive period, women have no opportunity costs associated with future direct offspring. Men, on the other hand, who have the possibility of future offspring during most of their life span, almost always have opportunity costs associated with investing in current offspring, including potential investment in finding an additional mate and investing in additional descendants. Very broadly, this leads to the prediction that women should be inclined to invest more in current offspring than are men.

Finally, parents' willingness to invest resources in a given child might be in conflict with the desire that child has for being invested in. This parent–offspring conflict should be mediated by the existence of other children and by the reproductive viability of those children (Trivers, 1974). Even though a child and his or her (full) sibling are, similar to the child and his or her parent, related to one another by $r = .5$, there is a conflict of interest regarding a parent's investment in a given child. As Trivers (1974) observed, a parent will generally be motivated to invest similarly in multiple children, each of whom is related 50% to that parent. However, each child is related to him- or herself 100%, so the child should be motivated to demand more than an equal share of the parents' resources because any resources diverted to siblings are lost "income."

A straightforward evolutionary prediction is that parental care will be strengthened by cues to genetic relatedness. Mothers are typically certain about their relationship to their children, whereas fathers are not. Fathers suffer the possible fitness costs of mistakenly investing in a child who is not their genetic relative when that investment could have been directed to the care of genetically related children or to the acquisition of other mates. On the basis of a review of the literature on paternal certainty, Kurland and Gaulin (2005) estimated that the average rate of paternity certainty in the general population is 90%.

Paternity uncertainty can produce decreased investment from a range of sources. Human beings, similar to many bird species, frequently assist their parents in raising younger offspring, a phenomenon known as cooperative breeding (Emlen, 1982). Humans also receive substantial amounts of care

from grandparents, a factor that could have been a substantial force in human evolution (Hawkes, O'Connell, Blurton Jones, Alvarez, & Charnov, 1998). On average, the most grandparental care comes from the mother's mother (i.e., the maternal grandmother of the child), which might be attributable to greater maternal certainty than paternal certainty (Euler & Weitzel, 1996). Maternal grandmothers have no uncertain genetic links to their grandchildren, and several studies have indicated that mothers' mothers are, in fact, the grandparents who invest most in such offspring. Fathers' fathers (i.e., paternal grandfathers), however, have two uncertain links, and paternal grandfathers are generally the least investing grandparents. However, Laham, Gonsalkorale, and von Hippel (2005) found that the reduction in investment by paternally linked grandparents is modified by the existence of other grandchildren. If a paternal grandmother has grandchildren by both her daughter and her son, her investment in the son's offspring is reduced. If, however, she has only sons, then she invests relatively more in those grandchildren, presumably because there is no competition for her investment that would yield a higher payoff for investing in one child relative to another.

A final issue involving parental uncertainty concerns nonbiological kin care. Children are often raised in either step- or adoptive families that might feature some proximate cues to genetic relatedness (e.g., coresidence) but may lack many others (e.g., physical similarity). These families (and other similar relationships) might reinforce feelings of genetic relatedness, known as psychological kinship (Bailey, 1988). However, such mechanisms are not always successful. Daly and Wilson (1988) have demonstrated that children suffer disproportionately more neglect and intentional aggression from stepparents. Some data have shown that forms of infanticide are 100 times more likely to occur by stepfathers than by genetic fathers (Daly & Wilson, 2001). Further evidence has suggested that adoptive children might not face the same neglect as stepchildren. Gibson (2009) showed that, despite the greater negative outcomes for adoptive children, they are more likely to receive parental support than stepchildren. One possible explanation for the differences in adoptive and stepfamilies is that adoptive families generally result from prolonged parenting effort (e.g., a strong desire to be a parent), whereas stepfamilies might result from prolonged mating effort on the part of stepparents (e.g., mating and remating, which results in a stepfamily; Gibson, 2009).

EMERGING THEMES AND FUTURE DIRECTIONS

An evolutionary perspective brings several important themes to the study of close relationships. One is the idea that the cognitive and affective processes involved in different types of relationships are qualitatively different. From this perspective, the feelings and thoughts people have about romantic partners are governed by a different system from those governing feelings and thoughts about children, which are qualitatively different from those governing feelings and thoughts about friends, coworkers, and strangers. Relationship research from an evolutionary perspective has in recent years focused heavily on romantic relationships, and although research has been done on other types of relationships, it is rare that different types of relationships are compared in a functional light. There are likely to be many interesting empirical advances that could come from contrasting different types of relationships in terms of their evolved functions (e.g., Ackerman et al., 2007; Haselton & Galperin, 2013). Yet many questions remain about precisely how relationships between friends, lovers, family members, and coworkers are similar and different. Answering these questions will involve connecting a functional evolutionary level of analysis with a focus on more proximate mechanisms and processes. For example, to what extent are there different brain systems that come into play for some types of relationships, and to what extent is there sharing of neural circuitry?

The study of relationships and the developmental trajectories of relationships through perspectives such as life history theory is another largely unexplored area with a number of interesting implications for relationships research. For example, how do the various trade-offs involved in relationships with kin, mates, friends, strangers, and other group members change over the life span? How are responses to threats and opportunities affected by functionally relevant aspects of the environment, such as sex ratios (i.e., the number of men relative to women in the local environment), the amount of resources readily available, and the manner in which these resources are distributed across people or locations? Griskevicius and his colleagues have begun to examine these questions in several lines of research. For example, Griskevicius, Delton, Robertson, and Tybur (2011) primed people to view the future as threatening and found that this altered their reproductive plans in systematic ways predicted by life history theory. People who came from lower class backgrounds—in which resources had likely been scarce and unpredictable in their availability—responded to such threats by planning to reproduce early, whereas those from middle- and upper-class backgrounds—in which resources had been sufficient and predictably available—responded in the opposite way. The same team of researchers also found that (real and perceived) variations in sex ratios influenced financial decisions (Griskevicius et al., 2012).

Another emerging but understudied area is the changes in human social behavior associated with reproductively crucial events surrounding pregnancy and the birth of children, areas almost completely untouched by social psychologists. For example, an evolutionary perspective leads to predictions about how pregnancy will shift women's perceptions of the threats and opportunities afforded by others (Navarrete, Fessler, & Eng, 2007). In addition, the weight of the literature on mate choice is far larger than that on the later transition to parenthood for couples. However, the transition to parenthood was an event likely to be as important or more important to fitness in the ancestral past (Simpson, Rholes, Campbell, Tran, & Wilson, 2003). Little research in this area has been explicitly guided by evolutionary theorizing.

Microlevel Causes: Hormones and Genes

One of the most active areas of research taking an evolutionary perspective considers the role of hormones on behavioral outcomes. Much of this work highlights the roles that different hormones play in linking fundamental goals, cognitive and affective processes, and behaviors within different types of relationships. As noted earlier, a number of interesting findings have suggested functionally sensible relations between hormones such as testosterone and oxytocin and social relationships. Nevertheless, much research remains to be done on these topics. Exactly how, for example, do the different motivational systems we have discussed connect with specific hormones, or hormone profiles, in influencing relationship decisions?

A burgeoning research area involves the role of hormonal fluctuations across the menstrual cycle on psychological outcomes (e.g., Haselton & Gildersleeve, 2011; Thornhill & Gangestad, 2008). Such outcomes reflect adaptive changes in response to changing levels of fertility. These changes include hormone shifts (e.g., of estrogens) around the period of ovulation, and these fluctuations are accompanied by behavioral changes in both women and, correspondingly, men.

Many of these behavioral effects promote or inhibit aspects of romantic involvement (e.g., sexual attraction, intrasexual competition) depending on the stage of the cycle. Indeed, because fertility is essential for reproduction, a straightforward evolutionary prediction is that women possess adaptations designed to promote sexual attraction and mating behavior with mates who display cues of genetic fitness during the period just before ovulation when fertility is highest (e.g., DeBruine et al., 2010). In women, ovulation coincides with increased motivation to engage in activities associated with mate attraction, such as attending social gatherings (Haselton & Gangestad, 2006), wearing more attractive or sexy clothing (Durante, Li, & Haselton, 2008; Haselton, Mortezaie, Pillsworth, Bleske-Recheck, & Frederick, 2007), and enhancing the attractiveness of their voices by raising their pitch (Bryant & Haselton, 2009). Women's preferences for romantic partner characteristics also shift during this period to prioritize indicators of good genes, such as masculinity, social dominance, and physical symmetry (e.g., Gangestad et al., 2004, 2005; Penton-Voak et al., 1999), and their attention appears to automatically orient to such men (Anderson et al., 2010). Some of this behavior could be designed to promote

romantic activity, but it might also improve women's chances at besting their romantic rivals (Durante, Griskevicius, Hill, Perilloux, & Li, 2011). Near ovulation, women also strategically avoid certain kinds of men, including out-group men who might have posed greater sexual coercion threats ancestrally (Navarrete, Fessler, Santos Fleischman, & Geyer, 2009). In a recent study examining women's pattern of cell phone use reflected in their monthly phone bills, women nearing ovulation decreased their calls to those men with whom, in theory, they should be least interested in affiliating when fertile: their fathers (Lieberman, Pillsworth, & Haselton, 2011).

Men also alter their behavior in the presence of ovulating women. From an evolutionary perspective, men should benefit from preferentially devoting mating efforts to highly fertile women. However, unlike females of many other primate species who have sexual swellings, human females do not display obvious outward signs of ovulation. Emerging evidence has suggested that, although cues of ovulation in humans might be subtle and operate below the level of conscious awareness, men respond differently to women who are near ovulation. One cue to which men respond involves olfaction—the scent of women during their peak period of fertility. In many animals, chemosensory signaling serves as a principal avenue by which female fertility shapes male mating behaviors (Ziegler, Schultz-Darken, Scott, Snowdon, & Ferris, 2005). In a recent study in humans, for example, researchers collected underarm samples on high- and low-fertility days of the cycle using cotton gauze affixed to women's underarms with surgical tape. Later, men smelled pairs of high- and low-fertility samples presented in plastic squeeze bottles. Men preferred the odors of women close to ovulation and rated those odors as more pleasant smelling than the odors of women at other points in their cycle (Gildersleeve, Haselton, Larson, & Pillsworth, 2012). These olfactory cues might directly stimulate hormonal changes in men. For example, S. L. Miller and Maner (2011) asked undergraduate male participants to smell T-shirts, some of which had been worn by women on a high-fertility day of the cycle. Saliva samples showed that men who had smelled the T-shirt of an ovulating woman had higher levels of testosterone, a hormone associated with sexual desire and mating behavior, than men who smelled shirts worn by women on a low-fertility day or unworn shirts. Other studies have shown that men also respond to ovulatory cues by perceiving greater sexual interest on the part of women and by increasing their own level of risk-taking behavior when interacting with a woman near ovulation as opposed to other cycle phases (S. L. Miller & Maner, 2011). Last, men in lapdance clubs part with more cash after a dance from a woman who is ovulating than after a dance from a woman who is not (G. Miller, Tybur, & Jordan, 2007).

In addition to hormonal effects on close relationships, recent technological and theoretical advances have made it possible to begin examining the ways in which genes interact with social experiences to influence social behavior and cognition. Robinson, Fernald, and Clayton (2008) have tracked the specific hormonal and genetic changes that unfold in male cichlid fish when a dominant male is removed from the group. As soon as a dominant male is removed, another male who was previously subordinate starts to behave in a more dominant fashion, begins building new neural structures in his brain, and becomes more colorful. These effects are linked to the activation of a specific transcription factor–encoding gene (*egr*1) involved in social behaviors across a wide range of species, including song recognition in zebra finches and mothering in rats. Other researchers working in the new area of social genomics have begun to examine parallel links between social experience and gene expression in human beings. For example, human genes are turned on and off by stressful experiences linked to relationships (such as loneliness). These experiences can change the molecular structure of human cells and, therefore, the structure of humans' brains and bodies in ways that unfold over hours, days, months, and lifetimes (Cole, 2009). One fascinating shift in gene expression is that social connectedness appears to upregulate the expression of genes facilitating viral defense, whereas social isolation (loneliness) upregulates the physiologically taxing expression of inflammatory responses facilitating bacterial defense (Cole, 2009). These responses could reflect evolved responses to increased risk of viral transmission among socially connected people

and increased risk of physical injury of people who are rejected from their social groups and forced to get by on their own (and the associated risk of bacterial infection as a consequence of those injuries). The latter of these might not have been functional in harsh ancestral conditions (and perhaps even in the modern world), where a person can be socially isolated and miserable but safe from physical harm from predatory animals, forces of nature, or hostile out-group members. Inflammation is a major source of illness, including heart disease (G. E. Miller & Blackwell, 2006). This work therefore provides clues about mismatches between ancestral conditions and modern environments that can have negative health consequences, and it suggests possible social psychological interventions.

Macrolevel Causes: Culture and Geography

Another set of fascinating questions involves the relations between these various biological processes and cultural influences on behavior. The tendency within psychology has been to regard cultural influences as being largely independent of biological influences, but new research and theory have challenged that assumption (e.g., Kenrick, Nieuweboer, & Buunk, 2010; Kitayama & Uskul, 2011). Many important questions exist about how cultural influences are shaped by, and in turn shape, universal human social motivational systems as they relate to different types of relationships.

One fascinating and active area of research with cultural implications is the influence of pathogens and contagious disease–causing organisms on relationship psychology. A number of recent studies have indicated that human sociality is heavily influenced by the concentration and virulence of infectious disease agents (e.g., bacteria, viruses). A long history of exposure to such agents has led to the evolution of pathogen-combating adaptations, represented in both the physical immune system and the more recently investigated behavioral immune system (Schaller, 2011; Schaller & Park, 2011). The threat of pathogens can vary across situations (e.g., being around sick people, eating contaminated food) but also across cultures (e.g., hot, wet locales have higher pathogen loads). Infection can damage physical, biological, and neural functioning (e.g., Møller, Gangestad, & Thornhill, 1999; Tooby, 1982).

The behavioral adaptations people seem to possess include a number of traits and predispositions that reduce the potential for infection. For example, people facing either temporary cues to disease or living in areas bearing higher pathogen loads show decreased extraversion, agreeableness, and openness to experience, all traits that may elevate the chances of infection exposure (Duncan, Schaller, & Park, 2009; Mortensen, Becker, Ackerman, Neuberg, & Kenrick, 2010; Schaller & Murray, 2008; Thornhill, Fincher, Murray, & Schaller, 2010). At a macro level, increasing levels of parasite stress are associated with a wide range of culturally relevant features, including heightened religiosity, stronger familial ties, collectivism, aversion to non-normative behavior, and social conservatism (Fincher & Thornhill, 2012; Fincher, Thornhill, Murray, & Schaller, 2008; Murray, Trudeau, & Schaller, 2011; Schaller, 2011; Thornhill, Fincher, & Aran, 2009). At the level of individual social interactions, research has suggested that disease cues, primes, individual sensitivities, and even recent illness can direct interpersonal attention and trigger avoidant cognitive and motor responses (Ackerman et al., 2009; S. L. Miller & Maner, 2011; Mortensen et al., 2010). People concerned about the possibility of disease are also less likely to endorse sexually unrestricted and promiscuous behavior (Duncan et al., 2009). Recent work in this area has shown that such cues strongly influence prejudicial attitudes and behavior on the basis of the notion that prejudices facilitate avoidance of people who might carry unfamiliar pathogens. These prejudices involve not only veridical disease signals but also "abnormalities" that might be heuristically linked to disease, including obesity, old age, and out-group membership (e.g., Park, Faulkner, & Schaller, 2003; Park, Schaller, & Crandall, 2007). Demonstrating the close link between such features and disease, experimental immunity interventions (e.g., immunizations, hand washing) can alleviate prejudicial attitudes (Huang, Sedlovskaya, Ackerman, & Bargh, 2011). Research on these topics is emerging rapidly, yet much more remains to be done to link disease-related cognition and behavior to close and in-group relationships.

CONCLUSION

Humans are social animals, with brains designed by evolutionary processes to manage different kinds of relationships and the distinct challenges and opportunities these types of relationships afford. We have reviewed a small portion of the literature touching on an evolutionary approach to relationship science. The contributions of the evolutionary approach to this point are clear—in terms of novel hypotheses generated and tested, new phenomena discovered, and a wide range of findings that are better integrated. Its future promise is also clear. It highlights the importance of appreciating from the start that different types of relationships are likely to be processed and managed by somewhat distinct psychological systems and of conceptualizing relationships in terms of their relevance to fundamental social goals and their ultimate evolutionary functions. It provides a natural framework for linking the psychological and behavioral to the physiological and genetic on one hand and to the ecological and cultural on the other. It also provides a way of bridging research on relationships not only to other areas of psychology but also to its neighboring social and biological sciences.

References

Ackerman, J. M., Becker, D. V., Mortensen, C. R., Sasaki, T., Neuberg, S. L., & Kenrick, D. T. (2009). A pox on the mind: Disjunction of attention and memory in processing physical disfigurement. *Journal of Experimental Social Psychology, 45*, 478–485. doi:10.1016/j.jesp.2008.12.008

Ackerman, J. M., Griskevicius, V., & Li, N. P. (2011). Let's get serious: Communicating commitment in romantic relationships. *Journal of Personality and Social Psychology, 100*, 1079–1094. doi:10.1037/a0022412

Ackerman, J. M., Huang, J. Y., & Bargh, J. A. (2012). Evolutionary perspectives on social cognition. In S. T. Fiske & C. N. Macrae (Eds.), *The Sage handbook of social cognition* (pp. 451–473). Thousand Oaks, CA: Sage. doi:10.4135/9781446247631.n23

Ackerman, J. M., & Kenrick, D. T. (2009). Cooperative courtship: Helping friends raise and raze relationship barriers: How men and women cooperate in courtship. *Personality and Social Psychology Bulletin, 35,* 1285–1300. doi:10.1177/0146167209335640

Ackerman, J. M., Kenrick, D. T., & Schaller, M. (2007). Is friendship akin to kinship? *Evolution and Human Behavior, 28,* 365–374. doi:10.1016/j.evolhumbehav.2007.04.004

Anderson, U. S., Perea, E. F., Becker, D. V., Ackerman, J. M., Shapiro, J. R., Neuberg, S. L., & Kenrick, D. T. (2010). I only have eyes for you: Ovulation redirects attention (but not memory) to attractive men. *Journal of Experimental Social Psychology, 46,* 804–808. doi:10.1016/j.jesp.2010.04.015

Bailey, K. G. (1988). Psychological kinship: Implications for the helping professions. *Psychotherapy: Theory, Research, Practice, Training, 25,* 132–141. doi:10.1037/h0085309

Baize, H. R., & Schroeder, J. E. (1995). Personality and mate selection in personal ads: Evolutionary preferences in a public mate selection process. *Journal of Social Behavior & Personality, 10,* 517–536.

Bank, B. J., & Hansford, S. L. (2000). Gender and friendship: Why are men's best same-sex friendships less intimate and supportive? *Personal Relationships, 7,* 63–78. doi:10.1111/j.1475-6811.2000.tb00004.x

Barkow, J. H. (1989). *Darwin, sex, and status: Biological approaches to mind and culture.* Toronto, Ontario, Canada: University of Toronto Press.

Barrett, H. C., & Kurzban, R. (2006). Modularity in cognition: Framing the debate. *Psychological Review, 113,* 628–647. doi:10.1037/0033-295X.113.3.628

Barrett L., Dunbar, R., & Lycett, J. (2002). *Human evolutionary psychology.* London, England: Palgrave.

Baumeister, R. F., & Leary, M. R. (1995). The need to belong: Desire for interpersonal attachments as a fundamental human motivation. *Psychological Bulletin, 117,* 497–529. doi:10.1037/0033-2909.117.3.497

Bellis, M. A., Hughes, K., Hughes, S., & Ashton, J. R. (2005). Measuring paternal discrepancy and its public health consequences. *Journal of Epidemiology and Community Health, 59,* 749–754. doi:10.1136/jech.2005.036517

Belsky, J., Steinberg, L., & Draper, P. (1991). Childhood experience, interpersonal development, and reproductive strategy: An evolutionary theory of socialization. *Child Development, 62,* 647–670. doi:10.2307/1131166

Benenson, J. F., Saelen, C., Markovits, H., & McCabe, S. (2008). Sex differences in the value of parents versus same-sex peers. *Evolutionary Psychology, 6,* 13–28.

Betzig, L. (1992). Roman polygyny. *Ethology and Sociobiology, 13,* 309–349. doi:10.1016/0162-3095(92)90008-R

Bleske-Rechek, A. L., & Buss, D. M. (2001). Opposite-sex friendship: Sex differences and similarities in initiation, selection, and dissolution. *Personality and Social Psychology Bulletin, 27,* 1310–1323.

Bowlby, J. (1969). *Attachment and loss.* New York, NY: Basic Books.

Bressler, E. R., Martin, R. A., & Balshine, S. (2006). Production and appreciation of humor as sexually selected traits. *Evolution and Human Behavior, 27,* 121–130. doi:10.1016/j.evolhumbehav.2005.09.001

Brown, S. L., & Brown, R. M. (2006). Selective investment theory: Recasting the functional significance of close relationships. *Psychological Inquiry, 17,* 1–29. doi:10.1207/s15327965pli1701_01

Bryant, G. A., & Haselton, M. G. (2009). Vocal cues of ovulation in human females. *Biology Letters, 5,* 12–15. doi:10.1098/rsbl.2008.0507

Burnstein, E., Crandall, C., & Kitayama, S. (1994). Some neo-Darwinian rules for altruism: Weighing cues for inclusive fitness as a function of the biological importance of the decision. *Journal of Personality and Social Psychology, 67,* 773–789. doi:10.1037/0022-3514.67.5.773

Buss, D. M. (1989). Sex differences in human mate preferences: Evolutionary hypotheses tested in 37 cultures. *Behavioral and Brain Sciences, 12,* 1–49. doi:10.1017/S0140525X00023992

Buss, D. M. (1995). Evolutionary psychology: A new paradigm for psychological science. *Psychological Inquiry, 6,* 1–30.

Buss, D. M. (2007). *Evolutionary psychology: The new science of mind* (3rd ed.). Boston, MA: Allyn & Bacon.

Buss, D. M., Larsen, R. J., Westen, D., & Semmelroth, J. (1992). Sex differences in jealousy: Evolution, physiology, and psychology. *Psychological Science, 3,* 251–255.

Buss, D. M., & Schmitt, D. (1993). Sexual strategies theory: An evolutionary perspective on human mating. *Psychological Review, 100,* 204–232. doi:10.1037/0033-295X.100.2.204

Buunk, B. P., Angleitner, A., Oubaid, V., & Buss, D. M. (1996). Sex differences in jealousy in evolutionary and cultural perspective: Tests from the Netherlands, Germany, and the United States. *Psychological Science, 7,* 359–363. doi:10.1111/j.1467-9280.1996.tb00389.x

Buunk, B. P., & Dijkstra, P. (2005). A narrow waist versus broad shoulders: Sex and age differences in the jealousy-evoking characteristics of a rival's body build. *Personality and Individual Differences, 39,* 379–389. doi:10.1016/j.paid.2005.01.020

Buunk, B. P., Dijkstra, P., Fetchenhauer, D., & Kenrick, D. T. (2002). Age and gender differences in mate selection criteria for various involvement levels. *Personal Relationships, 9,* 271–278. doi:10.1111/1475-6811.00018

Campbell, L., & Ellis, B. J. (2005). Commitment, love, and mate retention. In D. M. Buss (Ed.), *The handbook of evolutionary psychology* (pp. 419–442). Hoboken, NJ: Wiley.

Caporael, L. R. (1997). The evolution of truly social cognition: The core configurations model. *Personality and Social Psychology Review, 1*, 276–298. doi:10.1207/s15327957pspr0104_1

Carli, L. L. (1989). Gender differences in interaction style and influence. *Journal of Personality and Social Psychology, 56*, 565–576.

Clark, R. D., & Hatfield, E. (1989). Gender differences in receptivity to sexual offers. *Journal of Psychology & Human Sexuality, 2*, 39–55. doi:10.1300/J056v02n01_04

Cockburn, A. (2006). Prevalence of different modes of parental care in birds. *Proceedings of the Royal Society B: Biological Sciences, 273*, 1375–1383. doi:10.1098/rspb.2005.3458

Cole, S. W. (2009). Social regulation of human gene expression. *Current Directions in Psychological Science, 18*, 132–137. doi:10.1111/j.1467-8721.2009.01623.x

Colwell, M. A., & Oring, L. W. (1989). Extra-pair mating in the spotted sandpiper: A female mate acquisition tactic. *Animal Behaviour, 38*, 675–684. doi:10.1016/S0003-3472(89)80013-2

Crook, J. H., & Crook, S. J. (1988). Tibetan polyandry: Problems of adaptation and fitness. In L. Betzig, M. Borgerhoff-Mulder, & P. Turke (Eds.), *Human reproductive behavior: A Darwinian perspective* (pp. 97–114). Cambridge, MA: Cambridge University Press.

Daly, M., Salmon, C., & Wilson, M. (1997). Kinship: The conceptual hole in psychological studies of social cognition and close relationships. In J. A. Simpson & D. T. Kenrick (Eds.), *Evolutionary social psychology* (pp. 265–296). Mahwah, NJ: Erlbaum.

Daly, M., & Wilson, M. (1980). Discriminative parental solicitude: A biological perspective. *Journal of Marriage and the Family, 42*, 277–288. doi:10.2307/351225

Daly, M., & Wilson, M. (1988). *Homicide*. New York, NY: Aldine de Gruyter.

Daly, M., & Wilson, M. (2001). An assessment of some proposed exceptions to the phenomenon of nepotistic discrimination against stepchildren. *Annales Zoologici Fennici, 39*, 287–296.

Daly, M., & Wilson, M. I. (1983). *Sex, evolution and behavior: Adaptations for reproduction* (2nd ed.). Boston, MA: Willard Grant Press.

DeBruine, L., Jones, B. C., Frederick, D. A., Haselton, M. G., Penton-Voak, I. S., & Perrett, D. I. (2010). Evidence for menstrual cycle shifts in women's preferences for masculinity: A response to Harris (in press). Menstrual cycle and facial preferences reconsidered. *Evolutionary Psychology, 8*, 768–775.

DeSteno, D., Bartlett, M., Braverman, J., & Salovey, P. (2002). Sex differences in jealousy: Evolutionary mechanism or artifact of measurement? *Journal of Personality and Social Psychology, 83*, 1103–1116. doi:10.1037/0022-3514.83.5.1103

Diamond, L. M. (2004). Emerging perspectives on distinctions between romantic love and sexual desire. *Current Directions in Psychological Science, 13*, 116–119. doi:10.1111/j.0963-7214.2004.00287.x

Duncan, L. A., Schaller, M., & Park, J. H. (2009). Perceived vulnerability to disease: Development and validation of a 15-item self-report instrument. *Personality and Individual Differences, 47*, 541–546. doi:10.1016/j.paid.2009.05.001

Dunson, D. B., Colombo, B., & Baird, D. D. (2002). Changes with age in the level and duration of fertility in the menstrual cycle. *Human Reproduction, 17*, 1399–1403. doi:10.1093/humrep/17.5.1399

Durante, K. M., Griskevicius, V., Hill, S. E., Perilloux, C., & Li, N. P. (2011). Ovulation, female competition, and product choice: Hormonal influences on consumer behavior. *Journal of Consumer Research, 37*, 921–934. doi:10.1086/656575

Durante, K. M., Li, N. P., & Haselton, M. G. (2008). Changes in women's choice of dress across the ovulatory cycle: Naturalistic and laboratory task-based evidence. *Personality and Social Psychology Bulletin, 34*, 1451–1460. doi:10.1177/0146167208323103

Eibl-Eibesfeldt, I. (1989). *Human ethology*. New York, NY: Aldine de Gruyter.

Eisenberger, N. I., & Cole, S. W. (2012). Social neuroscience and health: Neuropsychological mechanisms linking social ties with physical health. *Nature Neuroscience, 15*, 669–674.

Eisenberger, N. I., Lieberman, M. D., & Williams, K. D. (2003). Does rejection hurt? An fMRI study of social exclusion. *Science, 302*, 290–292. doi:10.1126/science.1089134

Emlen, S. T. (1982). The evolution of helping. I. An ecological constraints model. *American Naturalist, 119*, 29–39. doi:10.1086/283888

Euler, H. A., & Weitzel, B. (1996). Discriminative grandparental solicitude as reproductive strategy. *Human Nature, 7*, 39–59.

Feldman, R., Weller, A., Zagoory-Sharon, O., & Levine, A. (2007). Evidence for a neuroendocrinological foundation of human affiliation: Plasma oxytocin levels across pregnancy and the postpartum period predict mother-infant bonding. *Psychological Science, 18*, 965–970. doi:10.1111/j.1467-9280.2007.02010.x

Fincher, C. L., & Thornhill, R. (2012). Parasite-stress promotes in-group assortative sociality: The cases of strong family ties and heightened religiosity. *Behavioral and Brain Sciences, 35*, 61–79. doi:10.1017/S0140525X11000021

Fincher, C. L., Thornhill, R., Murray, D. R., & Schaller, M. (2008). Pathogen prevalence predicts human cross-cultural variability in individualism/collectivism. *Proceedings of the Royal Society B: Biological Sciences, 275*, 1279–1285. doi:10.1098/rspb.2008.0094

Fleming, A. S., Gorter, C., Stallings, J., & Steiner, M. (2002). Testosterone and prolactin are associated with emotional responses to infant cries in new fathers. *Hormones and Behavior, 42*, 399–413. doi:10.1006/hbeh.2002.1840

Fletcher, G. J. O., Simpson, J. A., Thomas, G., & Giles, L. (1999). Ideals in intimate relationships. *Journal of Personality and Social Psychology, 76*, 72–89. doi:10.1037/0022-3514.76.1.72

Fletcher, G. J. O., Tither, J. M., O'Loughlin, C., Friesen, M., & Overall, N. (2004). Warm and homely or cold and beautiful? Sex differences in trading off traits in mate selection. *Personality and Social Psychology Bulletin, 30*, 659–672. doi:10.1177/0146167203262847

Galperin, A., Haselton, M. G., Frederick, D. A., Poore, J., von Hippel, W., Gonzaga, G., & Buss, D. M. (2013). Sexual regret: Evidence for evolved sex differences. *Archives of Sexual Behavior, 42*, 1145–1161. doi:10.1007/s10508-012-0019-3

Gangestad, S. W., & Simpson, J. A. (2000). The evolution of human mating: Trade-offs and strategic pluralism. *Behavioral and Brain Sciences, 23*, 573–587. doi:10.1017/S0140525X0000337X

Gangestad, S. W., Simpson, J. A., Cousins, A. J., Garver-Apgar, C. E., & Christensen, P. N. (2004). Women's preferences for male behavioral displays change across the menstrual cycle. *Psychological Science, 15*, 203–207. doi:10.1111/j.0956-7976.2004.01503010.x

Gangestad, S. W., & Thornhill, R. (1998). Menstrual cycle variation in women's preference for the scent of symmetrical men. *Proceedings of the Royal Society of London B, 265*, 927–933.

Gangestad, S. W., Thornhill, R., & Garver-Apgar, C. E. (2005). Women's sexual interests across the ovulatory cycle depend on primary partner fluctuating asymmetry. *Proceedings of the Royal Society B: Biological Sciences, 272*, 2023–2027. doi:10.1098/rspb.2005.3112

Garcia, J., & Koelling, R. A. (1966). Relation of cue to consequence in avoidance learning. *Psychonomic Science, 4*, 123–124.

Geary, D. C. (1998). *Male, female: The evolution of human sex differences.* Washington, DC: American Psychological Association. doi:10.1037/10370-000

Geary, D. C. (2000). Evolution and the proximate expression of human paternal investment. *Psychological Bulletin, 126*, 55–77. doi:10.1037/0033-2909.126.1.55

Geary, D. C., & Flinn, M. V. (2002). Sex differences in behavioral and hormonal response to social threat: Commentary on Taylor et al. *Psychological Review, 109*, 745–750, 2000. doi:10.1037/0033-295X.109.4.745

Gibson, K. (2009). Differential parental investment in families with both adopted and genetic children. *Evolution and Human Behavior, 30*, 184–189. doi:10.1016/j.evolhumbehav.2009.01.001

Gildersleeve, K. A., Haselton, M. G., Larson, C. M., & Pillsworth, E. G. (2012). Body odor attractiveness as a cue of impending ovulation in women: Evidence from a study using hormone-confirmed ovulation. *Hormones and Behavior, 61*, 157–166. doi:10.1016/j.yhbeh.2011.11.005

Glynn, L. M., & Sandman, C. A. (2011). Prenatal origins of neurological development: A critical period for fetus *and* mother. *Current Directions in Psychological Science, 20*, 384–389. doi:10.1177/0963721411422056

Gonzaga, G., Haselton, M. G., Smurda, J., Davies, M. S., & Poore, J. C. (2008). Love, desire, and the suppression of thoughts of romantic alternatives. *Evolution and Human Behavior, 29*, 119–126. doi:10.1016/j.evolhumbehav.2007.11.003

Gordon, I., Zagoory-Sharon, O., Leckman, J. K., & Feldman, R. (2010). Prolactin, oxytocin, and the development of paternal behavior across the first six months of fatherhood. *Hormones and Behavior, 58*, 513–518. doi:10.1016/j.yhbeh.2010.04.007

Grafen, A. (1990). Biological signals as handicaps. *Journal of Theoretical Biology, 144*, 517–546. doi:10.1016/S0022-5193(05)80088-8

Gray, P. B., Chapman, J. F., Burnham, T. C., McIntyre, M. H., Lipson, S. F., & Ellison, P. T. (2004). Human male pair bonding and testosterone. *Human Nature, 15*, 119–131. doi:10.1007/s12110-004-1016-6

Griskevicius, V., Cialdini, R. B., & Kenrick, D. T. (2006). Peacocks, Picasso, and parental investment: The effects of romantic motives on creativity. *Journal of Personality and Social Psychology, 91*, 63–76. doi:10.1037/0022-3514.91.1.63

Griskevicius, V., Delton, A. W., Robertson, T. E., & Tybur, J. M. (2011). Environmental contingency in life history strategies: Influence of mortality and socioeconomic status on reproductive timing. *Journal of Personality and Social Psychology, 100*, 241–254. doi:10.1037/a0021082

Griskevicius, V., Goldstein, N., Mortensen, C., Cialdini, R. B., & Kenrick, D. T. (2006). Going along versus going alone: When fundamental motives facilitate strategic (non)conformity. *Journal of Personality and Social Psychology, 91*, 281–294. doi:10.1037/0022-3514.91.2.281

Griskevicius, V., Goldstein, N. J., Mortensen, C. R., Sundie, J. M., Cialdini, R. B., & Kenrick, D. T. (2009). Fear and loving in Las Vegas: Evolution, emotion, and persuasion. *Journal of Marketing Research, 46*, 384–395. doi:10.1509/jmkr.46.3.384

Griskevicius, V., Tybur, J. M., Ackerman, J. M., Delton, A. W., Robertson, T. E., & White, A. E. (2012). The financial consequences of too many men: Sex ratio effects on saving, borrowing, and spending. *Journal of Personality and Social Psychology, 102,* 69–80. doi:10.1037/a0024761

Griskevicius, V., Tybur, J. M., Gangestad, S. W., Perea, E. F., Shapiro, J. R., & Kenrick, D. T. (2009). Aggress to impress: Hostility as an evolved context-dependent strategy. *Journal of Personality and Social Psychology, 96,* 980–994. doi:10.1037/a0013907

Gutierres, S. E., Kenrick, D. T., & Partch, J. (1999). Contrast effects in self assessment reflect gender differences in mate selection criteria. *Personality and Social Psychology Bulletin, 25,* 1126–1134. doi:10.1177/01461672992512006

Hahn-Holbrook, J., Holt-Lunstad, J., Holbrook, C., Coyne, S. M., & Lawson, E. T. (2011). Maternal defense: Breast feeding increases aggression by reducing stress. *Psychological Science, 22,* 1288–1295. doi:10.1177/0956797611420729

Hamilton, W. D. (1964). The genetical evolution of social behavior: I & II. *Journal of Theoretical Biology, 7,* 1–16. doi:10.1016/0022-5193(64)90038-4

Hanko, K., Master, S., & Sabini, J. (2004). Some evidence about character and mate selection. *Personality and Social Psychology Bulletin, 30,* 732–742. doi:10.1177/0146167204263967

Harris, C. R. (2003). A review of sex differences in sexual jealousy, including self-report data, psychophysiological responses, interpersonal violence, and morbid jealousy. *Personality and Social Psychology Review, 7,* 102–128. doi:10.1207/S15327957PSPR0702_102-128

Haselton, M. G. (2003). The sexual overperception bias: Evidence of a systematic bias in men from a survey of naturally occurring events. *Journal of Research in Personality, 37,* 34–47. doi:10.1016/S0092-6566(02)00529-9

Haselton, M. G., & Buss, D. M. (2000). Error management theory: A new perspective on biases in cross-sex mind reading. *Journal of Personality and Social Psychology, 78,* 81–91. doi:10.1037/0022-3514.78.1.81

Haselton, M. G., Buss, D. M., Oubaid, V., & Angleitner, A. (2005). Sex, lies, and strategic interference: The psychology of deception between the sexes. *Personality and Social Psychology Bulletin, 31,* 3–23. doi:10.1177/0146167204271303

Haselton, M. G., & Funder, D. C. (2006). The evolution of bias and accuracy in social judgment. In M. Schaller, J. Simpson, & D. T. Kenrick (Eds.), *Evolution and social psychology* (pp. 15–29). New York, NY: Psychology Press.

Haselton, M. G., & Galperin, A. (2013). Error management in relationships. In J. A. Simpson & L. Campbell (Eds.), *The Oxford handbook of close relationships* (pp. 234–254). New York, NY: Oxford University Press.

Haselton, M. G., & Gangestad, S. W. (2006). Conditional expression of women's desires and men's mate guarding across the ovulatory cycle. *Hormones and Behavior, 49,* 509–518. doi:10.1016/j.yhbeh.2005.10.006

Haselton, M. G., & Gildersleeve, K. (2011). Can men detect ovulation? *Current Directions in Psychological Science, 20,* 87–92. doi:10.1177/0963721411402668

Haselton, M. G., Mortezaie, M., Pillsworth, E. G., Bleske-Recheck, A. E., & Frederick, D. A. (2007). Ovulation and human female ornamentation: Near ovulation, women dress to impress. *Hormones and Behavior, 51,* 40–45. doi:10.1016/j.yhbeh.2006.07.007

Hawkes, K., O'Connell, J. F., Blurton Jones, N. G., Alvarez, H., & Charnov, E. L. (1998). Grandmothering, menopause, and the evolution of human life histories. *Proceedings of the National Academy of Sciences, USA, 95,* 1336–1339. doi:10.1073/pnas.95.3.1336

Hazan, C., & Diamond, L. M. (2000). The place of attachment in human mating. *Review of General Psychology, 4,* 186–204. doi:10.1037/1089-2680.4.2.186

Hazan, C., & Shaver, P. R. (1994). Attachment as an organizational framework for research on close relationships. *Psychological Inquiry, 5,* 1–22. doi:10.1207/s15327965pli0501_1

Helgeson, V. S., Shaver, P., & Dyer, M. (1987). Prototypes of intimacy and distance in same-sex and opposite-sex relationships. *Journal of Social and Personal Relationships, 4,* 195–233.

Henrich, J., & Boyd, R. (1998). The evolution of conformist transmission and between-group differences. *Evolution and Human Behavior, 19,* 215–241. doi:10.1016/S1090-5138(98)00018-X

Henrich, J., & Gil-White, F. J. (2001). The evolution of prestige: Freely conferred deference as a mechanism for enhancing the benefits of cultural transmission. *Evolution and Human Behavior, 22,* 165–196. doi:10.1016/S1090-5138(00)00071-4

Hill, K., & Hurtado, A. M. (1996). *Ache life history: The ecology and demography of a foraging people.* New York, NY: Aldine de Gruyter.

Hrdy, S. B. (1999). *Mother nature: A history of mothers, infants, and natural selection.* New York, NY: Pantheon.

Huang, J. Y., Sedlovskaya, A., Ackerman, J. M., & Bargh, J. A. (2011). Immunizing against prejudice: Effects of disease protection on out-group attitudes. *Psychological Science, 22,* 1550–1556. doi:10.1177/0956797611417261

Jankowiak, W., & Fisher, E. (1992). A cross-cultural perspective on romantic love. *Ethnology, 31,* 149–155. doi:10.2307/3773618

Johnson, D. J., & Rusbult, C. E. (1989). Resisting temptation: Devaluation of alternative partners as a means of maintaining commitment in close relationships. *Journal of Personality and Social Psychology, 57,* 967–980. doi:10.1037/0022-3514.57.6.967

Kenrick, D. T., Griskevicius, V., Neuberg, S. L., & Schaller, M. (2010). Renovating the pyramid of needs: Contemporary extensions built upon ancient foundations. *Perspectives on Psychological Science, 5,* 292–314. doi:10.1177/1745691610369469

Kenrick, D. T., Groth, G. E., Trost, M. R., & Sadalla, E. K. (1993). Integrating evolutionary and social exchange perspectives on relationship: Effects of gender, self-appraisal, and involvement level on mate selection criteria. *Journal of Personality and Social Psychology, 64,* 951–969. doi:10.1037/0022-3514.64.6.951

Kenrick, D. T., & Keefe, R. C. (1992). Age preferences in mates reflect sex differences in human reproductive strategies. *Behavioral and Brain Sciences, 15,* 75–91. doi:10.1017/S0140525X00067595

Kenrick, D. T., Neuberg, S. L., & White, A. E. (in press). Evolutionary approaches to relationships. In J. A. Simpson & L. Campbell (Eds.), *Oxford handbook of close relationships.* New York, NY: Oxford University Press.

Kenrick, D. T., Neuberg, S. L., Zierk, K., & Krones, J. (1994). Evolution and social cognition: Contrast effects as a function of sex, dominance, and physical attractiveness. *Personality and Social Psychology Bulletin, 20,* 210–217. doi:10.1177/0146167294202008

Kenrick, D. T., Nieuweboer, S., & Buunk, A. P. (2010). Universal mechanisms and cultural diversity: Replacing the blank slate with a coloring book. In M. Schaller, S. Heine, A. Norenzayan, T. Yamagishi, & T. Kameda (Eds.), *Evolution, culture, and the human mind* (pp. 257–271). Mahwah, NJ: Erlbaum.

Kenrick, D. T., Sadalla, E. K., Groth, G., & Trost, M. R. (1990). Evolution, traits, and the stages of human courtship: Qualifying the parental investment model. *Journal of Personality, 58,* 97–116. doi:10.1111/j.1467-6494.1990.tb00909.x

Kenrick, D. T., Sundie, J. M., & Kurzban, R. (2008). Cooperation and conflict between kith, kin, and strangers: Game theory by domains. In C. Crawford & D. Krebs (Eds.), *Foundations of evolutionary psychology* (pp. 353–370). New York, NY: Erlbaum.

Kenrick, D. T., Trost, M. R., & Sundie, J. M. (2004). Sex roles as adaptations: An evolutionary perspective on gender differences and similarities. In A. H. Eagly, A. E. Beall, & R. J. Sternberg (Eds.), *The psychology of gender* (pp. 65–91). New York, NY: Guilford Press.

Kim, P., Leckman, J. F., Mayes, L. C., Feldman, R., Wang, X., & Swain, J. E. (2010). The plasticity of human maternal brain: Longitudinal changes in brain anatomy during the early postpartum period. *Behavioral Neuroscience, 124,* 695–700. doi:10.1037/a0020884

Kitayama, S., & Uskul, A. K. (2011). Culture, mind, and the brain: Current evidence and future directions. *Annual Review of Psychology, 62,* 419–449. doi:10.1146/annurev-psych-120709-145357

Klein, K. J. K., & Hodges, S. D. (2001). Gender differences, motivation and empathic accuracy: When it pays to understand. *Personality and Social Psychology Bulletin, 27,* 720–730. doi:10.1177/0146167201276007

Klein, S. B., Cosmides, L., Tooby, J., & Chance, S. (2002). Decisions and the evolution of memory: Multiple systems, multiple functions. *Psychological Review, 109,* 306–329. doi:10.1037/0033-295X.109.2.306

Krakauer, A. H. (2005). Kin selection and cooperative courtship in wild turkeys. *Nature, 434,* 69–72. doi:10.1038/nature03325

Kunstman, J. W., & Maner, J. K. (2011). Sexual overperception: Power, mating motives, and biases in social judgment. *Journal of Personality and Social Psychology, 100,* 282–294. doi:10.1037/a0021135

Kurland, J. A., & Gaulin, S. (2005). Cooperation and conflict among kin. In D. M. Buss (Ed.), *Handbook of evolutionary psychology* (pp. 447–482). New York, NY: Wiley.

LaFrance, M., Hecht, M. A., & Paluck, E. L. (2003). The contingent smile: A meta-analysis of sex differences in smiling. *Psychological Bulletin, 129,* 305–334. doi:10.1037/0033-2909.129.2.305

Laham, S. M., Gonsalkorale, K., & von Hippel, W. (2005). Darwinian grandparenting: Preferential investment in more certain kin. *Personality and Social Psychology Bulletin, 31,* 63–72. doi:10.1177/0146167204271318

Lancaster, J. B. (1975). *Primate behavior and the emergence of human culture.* New York, NY: Holt, Rinehart, & Winston.

Lancaster, J. B., Kaplan, H., Hill, K., & Hurtado, A. M. (2000). The evolution of life history, intelligence, and diet among chimpanzees and human foragers. In F. Tonneau & N. S. Thompson (Eds.), *Perspectives in ethology: Evolution, culture, and behavior* (Vol. 13, pp. 47–72). New York, NY: Plenum Press. doi:10.1007/978-1-4615-1221-9_2

Lee, R. D., & Kramer, K. L. (2002). Children's economic roles in the Maya family life cycle: Cain, Caldwell, and Chayanov revisited. *Population and Development Review, 28,* 475–499. doi:10.1111/j.1728-4457.2002.00475.x

Leitenberg, H., & Henning, K. (1995). Sexual fantasy. *Psychological Bulletin, 117,* 469–496. doi:10.1037/0033-2909.117.3.469

Li, N. P., Bailey, J. M., Kenrick, D. T., & Linsenmeier, J. A. (2002). The necessities and luxuries of mate preferences: Testing the trade-offs. *Journal of Personality and Social Psychology, 82,* 947–955. doi:10.1037/0022-3514.82.6.947

Li, N. P., & Kenrick, D. T. (2006). Sex similarities and differences in preferences for short-term mates: What, whether, and why. *Journal of Personality and Social Psychology, 90*, 468–489. doi:10.1037/0022-3514.90.3.468

Li, Y. J., Kenrick, D. T., Griskevicius, V., & Neuberg, S. L. (2012). Decision biases and fundamental motivations: Loss aversion, mating, and self-protection. *Journal of Personality and Social Psychology, 102*, 550–561.

Lieberman, D., Pillsworth, E. G., & Haselton, M. G. (2011). Kin affiliation across the ovulatory cycle: Females avoid fathers when fertile. *Psychological Science, 22*, 13–18. doi:10.1177/0956797610390385

Lieberman, D., Tooby, J., & Cosmides, L. (2007). The architecture of human kin detection. *Nature, 445*, 727–731. doi:10.1038/nature05510

Lydon, J. E., Fitzsimmons, G. M., & Naidoo, L. (2003). Devaluation versus enhancement of attractive alternatives: A critical test using the calibration paradigm. *Personality and Social Psychology Bulletin, 29*, 349–359. doi:10.1177/0146167202250202

Lydon, J., Meana, M., Sepinwall, D., Richards, N., & Mayman, S. (1999). The commitment calibration hypothesis: When do people devalue attractive alternatives? *Personality and Social Psychology Bulletin, 25*, 152–161.

Maner, J. K., & Ackerman, J. M. (2013). Love is a battlefield: Romantic attraction, intrasexual competition, and conflict between the sexes. In J. A. Simpson & L. Campbell (Eds.), *Oxford handbook of close relationships* (pp. 137–160). New York, NY: Oxford University Press.

Maner, J. K., DeWall, C. N., Baumeister, R. F., & Schaller, M. (2007). Does social exclusion motivate interpersonal reconnection? Resolving the "porcupine problem." *Journal of Personality and Social Psychology, 92*, 42–55. doi:10.1037/0022-3514.92.1.42

Maner, J. K., Kenrick, D. T., Becker, D. V., Robertson, T. E., Hofer, B., Neuberg, S. L., . . . Schaller, M. (2005). Functional projection: How fundamental social motives can bias interpersonal perception. *Journal of Personality and Social Psychology, 88*, 63–78. doi:10.1037/0022-3514.88.1.63

Maner, J. K., & Mead, N. (2010). The essential tension between leadership and power: When leaders sacrifice group goals for the sake of self-interest. *Journal of Personality and Social Psychology, 99*, 482–497. doi:10.1037/a0018559

Maner, J. K., Miller, S. L., Rouby, D. A., & Gailliot, M. T. (2009). Intrasexual vigilance: The implicit cognition of romantic rivalry. *Journal of Personality and Social Psychology, 97*, 74–87. doi:10.1037/a0014055

Maner, J. K., Rouby, D. A., & Gonzaga, G. C. (2008). Automatic attention to attractive alternatives: The evolved psychology of relationship maintenance. *Evolution and Human Behavior, 29*, 343–349. doi:10.1016/j.evolhumbehav.2008.04.003

Mazur, A., & Booth, A. (1998). Testosterone and social dominance in men. *Behavioral and Brain Sciences, 21*, 353–363. doi:10.1017/S0140525X98001228

Miller, G., Tybur, J. M., & Jordan, B. D. (2007). Ovulatory cycle effects on tip earnings by lap dancers: Economic evidence for human estrus? *Evolution and Human Behavior, 28*, 375–381. doi:10.1016/j.evolhumbehav.2007.06.002

Miller, G. E., & Blackwell, E. (2006). Turning up the heat: Inflammation as a mechanism linking chronic stress, depression, and heart disease. *Current Directions in Psychological Science, 15*, 269–272. doi:10.1111/j.1467-8721.2006.00450.x

Miller, R. S. (1997). Inattentive and contented: Relationship commitment and attention to alternatives. *Journal of Personality and Social Psychology, 73*, 758–766. doi:10.1037/0022-3514.73.4.758

Miller, S. L., & Maner, J. K. (2011). Ovulation as a mating prime: Subtle signs of female fertility influence men's mating cognition and behavior. *Journal of Personality and Social Psychology, 100*, 295–308. doi:10.1037/a0020930

Møller, A. P., Gangestad, S. W., & Thornhill, R. (1999). Nonlinearity and the importance of fluctuating asymmetry as a predictor of fitness. *Oikos, 86*, 366–368. doi:10.2307/3546453

Moore, F. R., Cassidy, C., Law Smith, M. J., & Perrett, D. I. (2006). The effects of female control of resources on sex-differentiated mate preferences. *Evolution and Human Behavior, 27*, 193–205. doi:10.1016/j.evolhumbehav.2005.08.003

Mortensen, C. R., Becker, D. V., Ackerman, J. M., Neuberg, S. L., & Kenrick, D. T. (2010). Infection breeds reticence: The effects of disease salience on self-perceptions of personality and behavioral avoidance tendencies. *Psychological Science, 21*, 440–447. doi:10.1177/0956797610361706

Murray, D. R., Trudeau, R., & Schaller, M. (2011). On the origins of cultural differences in conformity: Four tests of the pathogen prevalence hypothesis. *Personality and Social Psychology Bulletin, 37*, 318–329. doi:10.1177/0146167210394451

Navarrete, C. D., Fessler, D. M. T., & Eng, S. J. (2007). Elevated ethnocentrism in the first trimester of pregnancy. *Evolution and Human Behavior, 28*, 60–65. doi:10.1016/j.evolhumbehav.2006.06.002

Navarrete, C. D., Fessler, D. M. T., Santos Fleischman, D., & Geyer, J. (2009). Race bias tracks conception risk across the menstrual cycle. *Psychological Science, 20*, 661–665. doi:10.1111/j.1467-9280.2009.02352.x

Neuberg, S. L., Kenrick, D. T., & Schaller, M. (2010). Evolutionary social psychology. In S. T. Fiske,

D. T. Gilbert, & G. Lindzey (Eds.), *Handbook of social psychology* (5th ed., Vol. 2, pp. 761–796). New York, NY: Wiley.

Orians, G. H. (1969). On the evolution of mating systems in birds and mammals. *American Naturalist, 103,* 589–603. doi:10.1086/282628

Park, J. H., & Ackerman, J. M. (2011). Passion and compassion: Psychology of kin relations within and beyond the family. In C. Salmon & T. Shackelford (Eds.), *Oxford handbook of evolutionary family psychology* (pp. 329–344). New York, NY: Oxford University Press. doi:10.1093/oxfordhb/9780195396690.013.0019

Park, J. H., Faulkner, J., & Schaller, M. (2003). Evolved disease-avoidance processes and contemporary antisocial behavior: Prejudicial attitudes and avoidance of people with physical disabilities. *Journal of Nonverbal Behavior, 27,* 65–87. doi:10.1023/A:1023910408854

Park, J. H., Schaller, M., & Crandall, C. S. (2007). Pathogen-avoidance mechanisms and the stigmatization of obese people. *Evolution and Human Behavior, 28,* 410–414. doi:10.1016/j.evolhumbehav.2007.05.008

Pawlowski, B., & Dunbar, R. I. M. (1999). Withholding age as putative deception in mate search tactics. *Evolution and Human Behavior, 20,* 53–69. doi:10.1016/S1090-5138(98)00038-5

Penton-Voak, I. S., Perrett, D. I., Castles, D., Burt, M., Koyabashi, T., & Murray, L. K. (1999). Female preference for male faces changes cyclically. *Nature, 399,* 741–742. doi:10.1038/21557

Pietrzak, R. H., Laird, J. D., Stevens, D. A., & Thompson, N. S. (2002). Sex differences in human jealousy: A coordinated study of forced-choice, continuous rating-scale, and physiological responses on the same subjects. *Evolution and Human Behavior, 23,* 83–94. doi:10.1016/S1090-5138(01)00078-2

Pillsworth, E. G., & Haselton, M. G. (2006a). Male sexual attractiveness predicts differential ovulatory shifts in female extra-pair mate attraction and male mate retention. *Evolution and Human Behavior, 27,* 247–258. doi:10.1016/j.evolhumbehav.2005.10.002

Pillsworth, E. G., & Haselton, M. G. (2006b). Women's sexual strategies: The evolution of long-term bonds and extra-pair sex. *Annual Review of Sex Research, 17,* 59–100.

Pinker, S. (1994). *The language instinct.* New York, NY: Harper Collins.

Rajecki, D. W., Bledsoe, S. B., & Rasmussen, J. L. (1991). Successful personal ads: Gender differences and similarities in offers, stipulations, and outcomes. *Basic and Applied Social Psychology, 12,* 457–469. doi:10.1207/s15324834basp1204_6

Regan, P. C., & Berscheid, E. (1999). *Lust: What we know about human sexual desire.* Thousand Oaks, CA: Sage.

Robinson, G. E., Fernald, R. D., & Clayton, D. F. (2008). Genes and social behavior. *Science, 322,* 896–900. doi:10.1126/science.1159277

Roese, N. J., Pennington, G. L., Coleman, J., Janicki, M., Li, N. P., & Kenrick, D. T. (2006). Sex differences in regret: All for love or some for lust? *Personality and Social Psychology Bulletin, 32,* 770–780. doi:10.1177/0146167206286709

Roney, R., & Von Hippel, W. (2010). The presence of an attractive woman elevates testosterone and physical risk taking in young men. *Social Psychological and Personality Science, 1,* 57–64.

Sagarin, B. J., Martin, A. L., Coutinho, S. A., Edlund, J. E., Patel, L., Skowronski, J. J., & Zengel, B. (2012). Sex differences in jealousy: A meta-analytic examination. *Evolution and Human Behavior, 33,* 595–614. doi:10.1016/j.evolhumbehav.2012.02.006

Salonia, A., Nappi, R. E., Pontillo, M., Daverio, R., Smeraldi, A., Briganti, A., . . . Montorsi, F. (2005). Menstrual cycle-related changes in plasma oxytocin are relevant to normal sexual function in health women. *Hormones and Behavior, 47,* 164–169. doi:10.1016/j.yhbeh.2004.10.002

Schaller, M. (2011). The behavioural immune system and the psychology of human sociality. *Philosophical Transaction of the Royal Society B: Biological Sciences, 366,* 3418–3426.

Schaller, M., & Murray, D. R. (2008). Pathogens, personality, and culture: Disease prevalence predicts worldwide variability in sociosexuality, extraversion, and openness to experience. *Journal of Personality and Social Psychology, 95,* 212–221. doi:10.1037/0022-3514.95.1.212

Schaller, M., & Park, J. H. (2011). The behavioral immune system (and why it matters). *Current Directions in Psychological Science, 20,* 99–103. doi:10.1177/0963721411402596

Schmitt, D. P. (2003). Universal sex differences in the desire for sexual variety: Tests from 52 nations, 6 continents, and 13 islands. *Journal of Personality and Social Psychology, 85,* 85–104. doi:10.1037/0022-3514.85.1.85

Schmitt, D. P., Jonason, P. K., Byerley, G. J., Flores, S. D., Illbeck, B. E., O'Leary, K. N., & Qudrat, A. (2012). A reexamination of sex differences in sexuality: New studies. *Current Directions in Psychological Science, 21,* 135–139. doi:10.1177/0963721412436808

Shackelford, T. K., & Goetz, A. T. (2007). Adaptation to sperm competition in humans. *Current Directions in Psychological Science, 16,* 47–50. doi:10.1111/j.1467-8721.2007.00473.x

Shackelford, T. K., Goetz, A. T., Buss, D. M., Euler, H. A., & Hoier, S. (2005). When we hurt the ones we love: Predicting violence against women from men's mate retention. *Personal Relationships, 12*, 447–463. doi:10.1111/j.1475-6811.2005.00125.x

Shackelford, T. K., Goetz, A. T., LaMunyon, C. W., Quintus, B. J., & Weekes-Shackelford, V. A. (2004). Sex differences in sexual psychology produce sex-similar preferences for a short-term mate. *Archives of Sexual Behavior, 33*, 405–412. doi:10.1023/B:ASEB.0000028893.49140.b6

Shackelford, T. K., LeBlanc, G. J., & Drass, E. (2000). Emotional reactions to infidelity. *Cognition and Emotion, 14*, 643–659. doi:10.1080/02699930050117657

Shaver, P. R., Hazan, C., & Bradshaw, D. (1988). Love as attachment: The integration of three behavioral systems. In R. J. Sternberg & M. L. Barnes (Eds.), *The psychology of love* (pp. 68–99). New Haven, CT: Yale University Press.

Shaw, J. I., & Steers, W. N. (2001). Gathering information to form an impression: Attribute categories and information valence. *Current Research in Social Psychology, 6*, 1–17.

Sherman, P. W. (1981). Kinship, demography, and Belding's ground squirrel nepotism. *Behavioral Ecology and Sociobiology, 8*, 251–259. doi:10.1007/BF00299523

Sherry, D. F., & Schacter, D. L. (1987). The evolution of multiple memory systems. *Psychological Review, 94*, 439–454. doi:10.1037/0033-295X.94.4.439

Sherwin, B. B., Gelfand, M. M., & Brender, W. (1985). Androgen enhances sexual motivation in females: A prospective, crossover study of sex steroid administration in the surgical menopause. *Psychosomatic Medicine, 47*, 339–351.

Sigall, H., & Landy, D. (1973). Radiating beauty: Effects of having a physically attractive partner on person perceptions. *Journal of Personality and Social Psychology, 28*, 218–224. doi:10.1037/h0035740

Simon, W., & Gagnon, J. H. (1984). Sexual scripts. *Bulletin of the Psychonomic Society, 22*, 53–60. doi:10.1007/BF02701260

Simpson, J. A., & Gangestad, S. W. (1992). Sociosexuality and romantic partner choice. *Journal of Personality, 60*, 31–51. doi:10.1111/j.1467-6494.1992.tb00264.x

Simpson, J. A., & Gangestad, S. W. (2001). Evolution and relationships: A call for integration. *Personal Relationships, 8*, 341–355. doi:10.1111/j.1475-6811.2001.tb00044.x

Simpson, J. A., Gangestad, S. W., Christensen, P. N., & Leck, K. (1999). Fluctuating asymmetry, sociosexuality, and intrasexual competitive tactics. *Journal of Personality and Social Psychology, 76*, 159–172. doi:10.1037/0022-3514.76.1.159

Simpson, J. A., Gangestad, S. W., & Lerma, M. (1990). Perception of physical attractiveness: Mechanisms involved in the maintenance of romantic relationships. *Journal of Personality and Social Psychology, 59*, 1192–1201. doi:10.1037/0022-3514.59.6.1192

Simpson, J. A., & Rholes, W. S. (2012). Adult attachment orientations, stress, and romantic relationships. In P. G. Devine & A. Plant (Eds.), *Advances in experimental social psychology* (Vol. 45, pp. 279–328). doi:10.1016/B978-0-12-394286-9.00006-8

Simpson, J. A., Rholes, W. S., Campbell, L., Tran, S., & Wilson, C. L. (2003). Adult attachment, the transition to parenthood, and depressive symptoms. *Journal of Personality and Social Psychology, 84*, 1172–1187. doi:10.1037/0022-3514.84.6.1172

Singh, D. (1993). Adaptive significance of female physical attractiveness: Role of waist-to-hip ratio. *Journal of Personality and Social Psychology, 65*, 293–307. doi:10.1037/0022-3514.65.2.293

Smuts, B. B., & Smuts, R. W. (1993). Male aggression and sexual coercion of females in nonhuman primates and other mammals: Evidence and theoretical implications. *Advances in the Study of Behavior, 22*, 1–63. doi:10.1016/S0065-3454(08)60404-0

Steiglitz, J., Gurven, M., Kaplan, H., & Winking, J. (2012). Infidelity, jealousy, and wife abuse among Tsimane-forager farmers: Testing evolutionary hypotheses of marital conflict. *Evolution and Human Behavior, 33*, 438–448.

Storey, A. E., Walsh, C. J., Quinton, R. L., & Wynne-Edwards, K. E. (2000). Hormonal correlates of paternal responsiveness in new and expectant fathers. *Evolution and Human Behavior, 21*, 79–95. doi:10.1016/S1090-5138(99)00042-2

Tamres, L. K., Janicki, D., & Helgeson, V. S. (2002). Sex differences in coping behavior: A meta-analytic review and an examination of relative coping. *Personality and Social Psychology Review, 6*, 2–30. doi:10.1207/S15327957PSPR0601_1

Taylor, S. E., Klein, L. C., Lewis, B. P., Gruenewald, T. L., Gurung, R. A. R., & Updegraff, J. A. (2000). Biobehavioral responses to stress in females: Tend-and-befriend, not fight-or-flight. *Psychological Review, 107*, 411–429. doi:10.1037/0033-295X.107.3.411

Thornhill, R., Fincher, C. L., & Aran, D. (2009). Parasites, democratization, and the liberalization of values across contemporary countries. *Biological Reviews, 84*, 113–131.

Thornhill, R., Fincher, C. L., Murray, D. R., & Schaller, M. (2010). Zoonotic and non-zoonotic diseases in relation to human personality and societal values: Support for the parasite-stress model. *Evolutionary Psychology, 8*, 151–169.

Thornhill, R., & Gangestad, S. W. (2008). *The evolutionary biology of human female sexuality*. New York, NY: Oxford University Press.

Tinbergen, N. (1963). On aims and methods of ethology. *Zeitschrift für Tierpsychologie, 20*, 410–433. doi:10.1111/j.1439-0310.1963.tb01161.x

Tooby, J. (1982). Pathogens, polymorphism, and the evolution of sex. *Journal of Theoretical Biology, 97*, 557–576. doi:10.1016/0022-5193(82)90358-7

Tooby, J., & Cosmides, L. (1992). The psychological foundations of culture. In J. H. Barkow, L. Cosmides, & J. Tooby (Eds.), *The adapted mind* (pp. 19–136). New York, NY: Oxford University Press.

Townsend, J. M., & Levy, G. D. (1990). Effects of potential partners' physical attractiveness and socioeconomic status on sexuality and partner selection. *Archives of Sexual Behavior, 19*, 149–164. doi:10.1007/BF01542229

Trivers, R. L. (1972). Parental investment and sexual selection. In B. Campbell (Ed.), *Sexual selection and the descent of man 1871–1971* (pp. 136–179). Chicago, IL: Aldine.

Trivers, R. L. (1974). Parent-offspring conflict. *American Zoologist, 14*, 249–264.

Trivers, R. L. (1985). *Social evolution*. Menlo Park, CA: Benjamin/Cummings.

Turke, P. W., & Betzig, L. L. (1985). Those who can do: Wealth, status, and reproductive success on Ifaluk. *Ethology and Sociobiology, 6*, 79–87. doi:10.1016/0162-3095(85)90001-9

Van Vugt, M., De Cremer, D., & Janssen, D. P. (2007). Gender differences in cooperation and competition: The male-warrior hypothesis. *Psychological Science, 18*, 19–23. doi:10.1111/j.1467-9280.2007.01842.x

Van Vugt, M., Hogan, R., & Kaiser, R. B. (2008). Leadership, followership, and evolution: Some lessons from the past. *American Psychologist, 63*, 182–196. doi:10.1037/0003-066X.63.3.182

Van Vugt, M., & Spisak, B. R. (2008). Sex differences in the emergence of leadership during competitions within and between groups. *Psychological Science, 19*, 854–858. doi:10.1111/j.1467-9280.2008.02168.x

Waynforth, D., Delwadia, S., & Camm, M. (2005). The influence of women's mating strategies on preference for masculine facial architecture. *Evolution and Human Behavior, 26*, 409–416. doi:10.1016/j.evolhumbehav.2005.03.003

Westermarck, E. (1891). *The history of human marriage*. London, England: Macmillan.

White, G. M. (1980). Conceptual universals in interpersonal language. *American Anthropologist, 82*, 759–781. doi:10.1525/aa.1980.82.4.02a00030

Wiederman, M. W. (1993). Evolved gender differences in mate preferences: Evidence from personal advertisements. *Ethology & Sociobiology, 14*, 331–351. doi:10.1016/0162-3095(93)90003-Z

Wiederman, M. W., & Hurd, C. (1999). Extradyadic involvement during dating. *Journal of Social and Personal Relationships, 16*, 265–274. doi:10.1177/0265407599162008

Wilbur, C. J., & Campbell, L. (2011). Humor in romantic contexts: Do men participate and women evaluate? *Personality and Social Psychology Bulletin, 37*, 918–929. doi:10.1177/0146167211405343

Wilcoxon, H. C., Dragoin, W. B., & Kral, P. A. (1971). Illness-induced aversions in rat and quail: Relative salience of visual and gustatory cues. *Science, 171*, 826–828. doi:10.1126/science.171.3973.826

Wilson, M., & Daly, M. (1985). Competitiveness, risk-taking, and violence: The young male syndrome. *Ethology and Sociobiology, 6*, 59–73. doi:10.1016/0162-3095(85)90041-X

Zahavi, A. (1975). Mate selection: Selection for a handicap. *Journal of Theoretical Biology, 53*, 205–214. doi:10.1016/0022-5193(75)90111-3

Ziegler, T. E., Schultz-Darken, N. J., Scott, J. J., Snowdon, C. T., & Ferris, C. F. (2005). Neuroendocrine response to female ovulatory odors depends upon social condition in male common marmosets (*Callithrix jacchus*). *Hormones and Behavior, 47*, 56–64. doi:10.1016/j.yhbeh.2004.08.009

CHAPTER 2

ATTACHMENT PROCESSES IN ADULT ROMANTIC RELATIONSHIPS

Paula R. Pietromonaco and Lindsey A. Beck

We begin this chapter with an overview of attachment theory, including the main tenets of Bowlby's (1969) original theory as well as later extensions to adult romantic relationships. We provide an updated theoretical statement that incorporates Bowlby's original theory and Hazan and Shaver's (1987) provocative extension to adult romantic relationships as well as additional theoretical revisions from more than 2 decades of theoretical development and empirical findings. We review and evaluate research following from attachment theory that has demonstrated that attachment shapes (a) how people experience and regulate emotion, (b) how they think about their romantic relationships, (c) their motives and goals in those relationships, (d) how they behave and interact with their partners (e.g., how they provide and seek support), and (e) how they initiate and maintain relationships and respond to relationship dissolution or loss. Finally, we discuss several emerging themes and promising directions for future research, including expanding on a person-in-context approach to attachment processes, investigating how partners may promote change or stability in each other's attachment representations, exploring interactions between attachment and temperament or personality, and examining the implications of attachment for both partners' health-related processes and outcomes.

Attachment theory is a broad, comprehensive theory that provides an evolutionary, biologically based account for why humans form and maintain close emotional bonds with others. Bowlby (1969, 1973, 1979, 1980) originally proposed that the attachment behavioral system functions to protect infants from harm and increase their likelihood of survival by keeping them close to caregivers and leading them to seek proximity and contact when they encounter potentially threatening or dangerous situations. Comfort and contact with a caregiver helps infants regulate feelings of distress and reestablish a sense of emotional well-being, or "felt security" (Sroufe & Waters, 1977). As this sequence of events implies, a primary function of the attachment behavioral system is to regulate feelings of distress: The perception of threat pushes infants closer to their attachment figure, who will typically provide comfort and safety, leading infants to experience emotional relief (Mikulincer & Shaver, 2007). Through interactions of this sort, individuals develop internal working models (mental representations) of themselves in relation to important others that are thought to guide attachment processes from infancy through adulthood (Bowlby, 1973; Mikulincer & Shaver, 2007; Pietromonaco & Barrett, 2000).

Bowlby's original attachment theory focused on the infant–caregiver bond and, not surprisingly, the majority of research following from it initially examined attachment processes in infants and children. Bowlby recognized, however, that attachment processes are implicated in relationships throughout the life span, noting the

Preparation of this chapter was facilitated by National Cancer Institute Grant R01CA133908 to Paula Pietromonaco.

http://dx.doi.org/10.1037/14344-002
APA Handbook of Personality and Social Psychology: Vol. 3. Interpersonal Relations, M. Mikulincer and P. R. Shaver (Editors-in-Chief)

significance of attachment processes from cradle to grave (Bowlby, 1979). Building on this idea and the broader theory, Hazan and Shaver (1987) proposed that the emotional bonds between romantic partners resemble those between infants and caregivers and that adult romantic relationships serve attachment functions. This seminal article provided the impetus for thousands of studies examining attachment in adult relationships, including those with dating partners, spouses, friends, siblings, and others (see Mikulincer & Shaver, 2007). A large body of research has yielded widespread empirical support for attachment processes in adult relationships as well as revisions and extensions of attachment theory (e.g., Collins & Feeney, 2010; Fraley & Shaver, 2000; Mikulincer & Shaver, 2007; Pietromonaco & Barrett, 2000; Simpson & Rholes, 1994).

This chapter focuses on work within social and personality psychology that has examined attachment processes in adult romantic relationships. Although other adult relationships (e.g., with parents, siblings, friends, children) can serve attachment functions in adulthood, we focus on romantic partners because they are often the primary attachment figure for adults (see Doherty & Feeney, 2004). Furthermore, the majority of research on romantic attachment has been conducted within social and personality psychology, and accordingly we emphasize this literature (for related developmental work, see Mikulincer & Shaver, 2007). Our review is organized around the ideas that the attachment system functions to regulate negative affect when individuals are faced with an actual or perceived threat and that attachment-related processes, including affective, cognitive, motivational, and support seeking and caregiving, operate to reduce distress and restore feelings of emotional well-being. We first discuss core principles of attachment theory and its extensions. We next review research examining attachment in relation to affective, cognitive, motivational, and support processes and then discuss how these attachment-related processes are implicated in relationship formation, functioning, and stability. Finally, we discuss selected emerging themes and promising directions for future research.

ATTACHMENT THEORY: BASIC PRINCIPLES

Attachment theory emphasizes both normative attachment processes fundamental to the human experience (e.g., seeking an attachment figure for protection when danger looms) and individual differences in attachment processes based on each person's history of experiences with caregivers (e.g., consistently responsive caregivers or inconsistent or neglectful caregivers).

Normative Features of Attachment Processes

Some features of the attachment system are thought to be normative because they are typical for all people from infancy through adulthood (Mikulincer & Shaver, 2007). In this section, we discuss the attachment behavioral system and its normative functions as well as several related behavioral systems, including those that focus on caregiving, sexual behavior, and exploration.

Attachment behavioral system. The attachment behavioral system is conceptualized as a biologically based, innate system that serves to protect individuals by keeping them close to caregivers in the face of danger or threat (Bowlby, 1969). The perception of threat is key in evoking attachment processes (Bowlby, 1980; Simpson & Rholes, 1994; Simpson, Rholes, & Phillips, 1996). Any situation that threatens an attachment bond (e.g., physical danger, illness, failure, rejection, loss of a loved one, conflict), whether real or imagined, can activate attachment behaviors (e.g., clinging, crying, attention getting) that are designed to reestablish and maintain the bond (see Mikulincer & Shaver, 2007). The attachment system promotes infants' survival by fostering safety, and it enables individuals of any age who feel threatened to reestablish security through contact and comfort from an attachment figure. Bowlby (1988) argued that turning to one's attachment figure is a normative and healthy response to adversity and threat.

Affect and affect regulation. The attachment system serves not only to protect individuals from physical harm but also to help them regulate negative feelings and restore a sense of calm, or felt security (Bowlby, 1973; Sroufe & Waters, 1977). This affect regulation function is evident when distressed infants seek proximity to their caregivers and when caregivers respond by providing comfort and reassurance, thereby helping infants regulate negative affect and regain felt security. Paralleling the process observed in children, adults who are distressed in response to a threat may seek out an attachment figure (e.g., their spouse) in an attempt to restore emotional well-being, and adult partners typically respond by providing care through reassurance, comfort, and concrete support (Collins & Feeney, 2010; Simpson & Rholes, 1994). Thus, the attachment relationship serves as a regulatory system in which a distressed individual seeks out a relationship partner, who in turn responds in ways that will either facilitate or inhibit the distressed person's efforts to cope with and alleviate negative feelings. Although this process often involves assistance from an actual partner, adults may also imagine or recall a partner's supportive and soothing responses at times when their attachment figure is not readily accessible (e.g., Bowlby, 1969; Mikulincer & Shaver, 2007).

Recent groundbreaking research has provided evidence that affect and affect regulation processes may be fundamental in the normative development of attachment bonds (Beckes, Simpson, & Erickson, 2010). This research demonstrated that, in the context of threat, a responsive person becomes automatically associated with attachment-related feelings of security. By combining ideas from attachment theory with a neurobiological model of an integrative emotional system (Nelson & Panksepp, 1998), Beckes et al. (2010) reasoned that threat triggers the separation–distress subsystem, producing a need for support and reassurance; if another person is responsive, then the comfort subsystem becomes activated, thereby downregulating distress. In this work, participants first completed a training phase in which either a fear-inducing unconditioned stimulus (e.g., a picture of a snake about to strike) or a neutral stimulus (e.g., a rolling pin) was presented below conscious awareness and paired with a conditioned stimulus (e.g., a smiling face). During a subsequent test phase, smiling faces that had been paired with the fear-inducing stimulus

(but not the neutral one) facilitated participants' responses to attachment-related security words but not to non–attachment-related positive words. This research points to a normative process in which people implicitly form attachment bonds through the pairing of a fear-provoking event with a responsive person. If the formation of attachment bonds indeed follows such a process, then this evidence suggests that affect-based processes are integral to attachment bonds and associated attachment-related expectations, beliefs, and goals (see Pietromonaco & Barrett, 2000; Pietromonaco, Barrett, & Powers, 2006).

Related behavioral systems. Bowlby (1969, 1973, 1980) proposed that other behavioral systems (e.g., caregiving, sexual behavior, exploration) work together with the attachment system (see also Mikulincer & Shaver, 2007). For example, the caregiving system leads individuals to be attuned to their relationship partner's distress signals, and it typically triggers behaviors that will protect, support, and promote the well-being of the relationship partner. In adults, the sexual behavior system promotes reproduction, but it also can operate with other behavioral systems. For example, sexual behavior can interconnect with caregiving (e.g., sex may provide comfort) and can strengthen an attachment bond (Davis, Shaver, & Vernon, 2004). Exploration of the environment (e.g., working, playing, pursuing personal goals) is also facilitated when individuals are confident that their attachment figure will be available and responsive if the need arises (e.g., Collins & Feeney, 2010).

Internal Working Models

Internal working models are dynamic, affectively charged representations that include event-related details of attachment-related experiences, the affect associated with those experiences, and—more important—generalized expectations, beliefs, and feelings about whether attachment figures will be sufficiently responsive, available, and reliable and whether the self is worthy of receiving such care (Bowlby, 1973; Bretherton, 1985; Collins, Guichard, Ford, & Feeney, 2004; Mikulincer & Shaver, 2007; Pietromonaco & Barrett, 2000). Furthermore, working models are assumed to include both explicit, consciously accessible knowledge and implicit, less consciously accessible knowledge (Bowlby, 1980; Bretherton, 1985, 1990; Collins et al., 2004; Mikulincer & Shaver, 2007).

Although working models were originally discussed in the context of individuals' earliest attachment relationships (e.g., with a parent), theorists have suggested that they can be revised over the life course as attachment figures shift from parents or childhood caregivers to other important relationship partners such as peers, dating partners, or spouses (Bowlby, 1973; Hazan & Shaver, 1987; see also Hazan & Zeifman, 1994). Within any given relationship, working models tend to be stable, reflecting consistencies in how relationship partners interact with each other as well as tendencies for people to interpret relational events in ways that fit with their existing mental representations (Ainsworth, 1989; Bowlby, 1973; Hazan & Shaver, 1987). Attachment representations based on earlier relationships may also have enduring effects on later representations (e.g., Fraley, 2002; Fraley & Brumbaugh, 2004), although the extent of this influence is open to debate (e.g., Fraley & Brumbaugh, 2004; Fraley, Vicary, Brumbaugh, & Roisman, 2011). The idea that people have multiple representations corresponding to different attachment relationships fits with extensions of attachment theory that suggest that working models may be multifaceted and organized within a complex network of associations, from generalized representations that may provide a default model for close relationships to more specific representations for particular relationship partners across the life course (parents, friends, romantic partners; Collins et al., 2004; Pietromonaco & Barrett, 2000).

Individual Differences in Working Models

Through recurring interactions with caregivers, individuals develop working models and associated attachment styles that reflect the nature of those experiences. As a result, individuals differ in the content of their working models, as evidenced in their attachment patterns. Early work examining infants' attachment patterns with their caregivers revealed three types of attachment styles: secure, anxious–ambivalent, and avoidant (e.g., Ainsworth, Blehar, Waters, & Wall, 1978). These categorizations were based on behavioral observations of 12- to 18-month-old babies in a laboratory situation (the Strange Situation) in which babies were separated from their caregiver, left with a stranger, and reunited with their caregiver. Secure babies were easily comforted and calmed in this situation, suggesting a history of responsiveness and warmth from their caregiver. Anxious–ambivalent babies were hard to comfort, more likely to protest, and more likely to show approach–avoidance behavior (e.g., crying, clinging, pushing away), all behaviors assumed to reflect a history of inconsistent responsiveness and warmth. Avoidant babies resisted contact, distancing themselves from the caregiver, a pattern that may develop when caregivers are distant and neglect or reject infants' demands for attention. A critical point is that these attachment behavior patterns are assumed to reflect infants' underlying working models and the history of attachment-related experiences on which they are built. In line with this idea, a meta-analysis (van IJzendoorn, 1995) indicated that parents' state of mind with respect to attachment (as reflected in their responses to the Adult Attachment Interview; see Hesse, 1999) is associated with their own sensitivity and responsiveness to infants' attachment signals during infant–caregiver interactions as well as with their infants' attachment classification in the Strange Situation.

Working models based on the parent–child bond need to be considered in the context of adult attachment because, to some extent, they establish a basis for working models with other important attachment figures throughout life (e.g., peers, romantic partners). Of course, working models are likely to evolve with age as cognitive abilities become more complex, as individuals gain experience in new and different relationships, and as life circumstances change (Bowlby, 1969; Bretherton, 1990; Fraley, 2002; Vaughn, Egeland, Sroufe, & Waters, 1979). At a conceptual level, attachment styles in romantic relationships parallel those in parent–child relationships, although measures of attachment in adults differ considerably from those used to assess attachment in children. Adult attachment is typically measured via self-report in the social and personality literature, in contrast to behavioral (e.g., observations in the Strange Situation) and interview assessments (e.g., the Adult Attachment Interview) typically used in the developmental literature (see Mikulincer & Shaver, 2007). Early measures of attachment style in adults mapped onto the three (secure, anxious–ambivalent, avoidant; Hazan & Shaver, 1987) or four (secure, preoccupied–anxious, fearful–avoidant, dismissing avoidant; Bartholomew & Horowitz, 1991) categories identified in babies. Subsequent research has demonstrated that attachment styles in adults are best captured by two dimensions: anxiety and avoidance (Fraley, Waller, & Brennan, 2000). People high in anxiety desire excessive closeness, worry about their partner not being responsive or abandoning them, and often see themselves as unworthy of love. People high in avoidance are uncomfortable with closeness and reluctant to rely on others, preferring to maintain emotional distance and self-reliance.[1]

As suggested by Mikulincer and Shaver's (2007) control systems model of attachment dynamics, anxious versus avoidant individuals rely on different affect regulation strategies to deal with threat or danger. Anxious individuals expect that their attachment figures will be insufficiently available and therefore need to draw attention to their distress. The result is a pattern of hyperactivation in response to threat in which anxiously attached individuals display heightened distress and persistently seek proximity and reassurance from attachment figures. In contrast, avoidant individuals anticipate that attachment figures will not be available or responsive. As a consequence, they show a pattern of deactivation in response to threat in which they minimize distress, turn their attention away from the threat, and overly rely on themselves. Secure individuals are confident that their attachment figures will be available when they need them, and they are able to reestablish felt security and emotional well-being by turning to their partner (or to an internalized representation of their partner).

ATTACHMENT PROCESSES AND AFFECT REGULATION

A large literature has examined the links between attachment style and affective, cognitive, motivational, and behavioral responses (see Mikulincer & Shaver, 2007). Many of these associations reflect differences in the extent to which people with different attachment styles experience distress and how they attempt to regulate those feelings. In the next sections, we first review and evaluate representative studies that demonstrate connections between attachment and affective responses; second, we turn to studies examining cognitive, motivational, and social support processes that are implicated in the regulation of affect; third, we examine the consequences of these chronic attachment patterns and associated affect regulation strategies for relationship processes and outcomes (e.g., satisfaction, stability).

Affective Responses

The pattern of hyperactivation associated with anxious–ambivalence suggests that anxious individuals will show exaggerated emotional reactions, whereas the pattern of deactivation associated with avoidance suggests blunted emotional reactions (Mikulincer & Shaver, 2007). Consistent with the idea of hyperactivation, people with a more anxious attachment style evidence greater affective reactivity and distress in response to aversive situations (e.g., Bartholomew & Horowitz, 1991; Hazan & Shaver, 1987; Pietromonaco & Barrett, 1997; Simpson, Rholes, & Nelligan, 1992). They report more intense emotions (Collins & Read, 1990; Pietromonaco & Barrett, 1997; Pietromonaco & Carnelley, 1994), frequent emotional ups and downs (Hazan & Shaver, 1987), high emotional expressiveness (Bartholomew & Horowitz, 1991), and high anxiety and impulsiveness (Shaver & Brennan, 1992). Anxiously attached individuals tend to respond with more intense anger and hostility (e.g., Dutton, Saunders, Starzomski, & Bartholomew, 1994;

[1]To aid in interpreting research findings based on earlier measures using four attachment prototypes (Bartholomew & Horowitz, 1991), note that the anxiety and avoidance dimensions map onto preoccupied attachment when anxiety is high and avoidance is low, fearful–avoidance when both anxiety and avoidance are high, dismissing avoidance when anxiety is low and avoidance is high, and secure attachment when both anxiety and avoidance are low.

Mikulincer, 1998b) and heightened feelings of rejection and negative feelings about the self in response to a hurtful interpersonal experience (Cassidy, Shaver, Mikulincer, & Lavy, 2009). They also report greater pain (J. A. Feeney & Ryan, 1994) and experience greater sensitivity to pain induced via laboratory tasks (Meredith, Strong, & Feeney, 2006; Wilson & Ruben, 2011). Furthermore, they appear highly sensitive to emotional cues; for example, more anxious individuals are quicker to notice changes in emotional expressions than are less anxious individuals (Fraley, Niedenthal, Marks, Brumbaugh, & Vicary, 2006).

In contrast to anxious individuals, avoidant individuals tend to report dampened emotionality (Pietromonaco & Barrett, 1997), and interviewers rate them as less emotionally expressive than other individuals (Bartholomew & Horowitz, 1991, Study 1). They are also more able to suppress their feelings (Fraley & Shaver, 1997) and to tolerate pain (Wilson & Ruben, 2011). Avoidant individuals, however, do not always show diminished emotional reactions, suggesting that deactivating strategies are not always effective. Avoidant individuals exhibit heightened distress in situations involving severe, chronic stress, such as caring for an infant with a severe coronary heart defect (Berant, Mikulincer, & Shaver, 2008) or when task demands inhibit their ability to control responses (Mikulincer, Dolev, & Shaver, 2004). Furthermore, both attachment anxiety and avoidance have been associated with depressive symptoms (e.g., Carnelley, Pietromonaco, & Jaffe, 1994; Cooper, Shaver, & Collins, 1998; Davila, 2001; Simpson, Rholes, Campbell, Tran, & Wilson, 2003; Wei, Mallinckrodt, Larson, & Zakalik, 2005), which may arise in reaction to chronic or uncontrollable stress.

In addition, recent work has suggested that the link between each type of attachment insecurity and depression depends on whether situational contingencies evoke threats relevant to anxiety (e.g., fear of abandonment, rejection) or to avoidance (e.g., fear of losing autonomy). For example, a study examining couples over the first 2 years of the transition to parenthood found that, for anxious individuals, depression symptoms depended on concerns about partner responsiveness and abandonment

(Rholes et al., 2011). When anxious individuals perceived that their partner provided less support, wives' depression remained high over time and husbands' depression levels increased. The opposite pattern occurred for anxious individuals who perceived more support: In this case, both women and men showed a decline in depressive symptoms. In contrast, for avoidant individuals, depression varied as a function of their concerns about autonomy. For example, avoidant individuals experienced higher initial depression that increased over time when they perceived that the baby interfered with their ability to freely spend time with their partner, but avoidant individuals who did not perceive interference showed lower initial symptoms that decreased over time.

Another study illustrating the importance of attachment-related situational contingencies examined adults' negative and positive affect after daily interpersonal interactions with a variety of relationship partners (e.g., romantic, friends, coworkers; Sadikaj, Moskowitz, & Zuroff, 2011). All participants reported greater negative affect after interactions in which they perceived that their partner had behaved less agreeably than after those in which they perceived that their partner had behaved more agreeably, but this association was significantly stronger for individuals high in attachment anxiety than for those low in attachment anxiety. A partner's more or less agreeable behavior may intensify affective reactions for anxious individuals because it conveys acceptance or rejection. Avoidant individuals, however, may be less reactive to these cues because they are less concerned about approval from others. In line with this idea, individuals higher in avoidance showed a smaller association between perceptions of their partners' less agreeable behavior and negative and positive affect than did those lower in avoidance. Furthermore, the effects of attachment style were more pronounced for interactions with romantic partners, which is noteworthy because romantic partners are most likely to serve adults' attachment needs. Both of these studies (Rholes et al., 2011; Sadikaj et al., 2011) highlighted the importance of situational contingencies relevant to anxiety or avoidance in understanding connections between attachment and negative affective reactions.

An emerging literature has begun investigating links between romantic attachment and physiological responses (Diamond, 2001; Diamond & Fagundes, 2010), which are particularly important given that attachment is closely linked to biological and neural mechanisms implicated in affective reactions (e.g., Carter, 1998; Schore, 2001; Siegel, 2001). Furthermore, because physiological responses are automatic and occur below conscious awareness, they can provide different insights into affective responses than those revealed through more consciously controlled self-reports of affect.

A small literature has suggested that attachment insecurity is associated with heightened or dysregulated patterns of activation in the autonomic nervous system and the hypothalamic–pituitary–adrenal (HPA) axis. For example, participants high in either attachment anxiety or avoidance have shown increased heart rate and blood pressure when they were separated from their romantic partner during a stress task (Carpenter & Kirkpatrick, 1996; B. C. Feeney & Kirkpatrick, 1996) or when they imagined themselves in anger-evoking scenarios involving their romantic partner (Mikulincer, 1998b). Attachment insecurity (anxiety, avoidance, or both) has also been linked to greater HPA activation (assessed via cortisol) in response to stress (Brooks, Robles, & Dunkel Schetter, 2011; Diamond, Hicks, & Otter-Henderson, 2008; Powers, Pietromonaco, Gunlicks, & Sayer, 2006; Quirin, Pruessner, & Kuhl, 2008; for a review see Pietromonaco, DeBuse, & Powers, 2013). For instance, research examining the cortisol responses of members of 124 dating couples (Powers et al., 2006) to a conflict discussion found that more anxiously attached men showed heightened cortisol levels in reaction to the discussion and slower recovery rates; more avoidantly attached women showed heightened cortisol levels before and during the discussion but rapid recovery rates when the discussion ended. In addition, men whose dating partners were more secure showed less cortisol reactivity and quicker recovery than men who had more insecure (anxious, avoidant, or both) dating partners. A smaller study of 30 dating couples (Brooks et al., 2011) similarly revealed that more anxious men evidenced higher cortisol reactivity during discussions of both a relationship conflict and their own personal concerns; women, however, showed greater cortisol

reactivity only when their partner was more avoidant. Although a number of differences between the studies (e.g., in sample size, number of cortisol samples, measures of reactivity and recovery) could account for the somewhat different findings, both studies indicated that men's attachment anxiety predicts their physiological stress in relationship discussions and that one partner's attachment style may be important in predicting the other's physiological stress. In addition, research examining individuals' daily cortisol levels before, during, and after a 4- to 7-day separation when their marital partner was traveling has also shown a link between attachment anxiety and cortisol reactivity (Diamond et al., 2008); attachment anxiety was associated with higher cortisol during the separation, an event that should be especially stress inducing for anxious individuals.

A recent study highlights the importance of the interplay between partners' attachment styles in shaping cortisol responses (Beck, Pietromonaco, DeBuse, Powers, & Sayer, 2013). This study found that newlywed couples including an anxiously attached wife and an avoidantly attached husband, compared to couples with other attachment pairings (e.g., an anxious wife with a nonavoidant husband), showed distinctive cortisol reactivity patterns in anticipating a conflict discussion as well as less constructive behavior during the discussion.

These studies focused on cortisol responses during an acute stressor, but cortisol patterns in general are of interest because cortisol at awakening and over the course of the day has been linked to depression, with flatter patterns associated with greater depression (e.g., Bhattacharyya, Molloy, & Steptoe, 2008; Hsiao et al., 2010). In a study of cortisol patterns after awakening, more anxiously attached working women showed less of an increase in cortisol after awakening (i.e., a flatter pattern from time of awakening to 75 minutes later) than did less anxious women, suggesting dysregulated HPA activation for more anxious women (Quirin et al., 2008).

Overall, the few available studies have suggested that attachment insecurity, especially anxiety, is associated with different, and perhaps dysregulated, physiological responses than attachment security. However, considerable variation exists in the samples (young or dating couples, married couples, working women), measures (e.g., blood pressure, acute cortisol, diurnal cortisol), and methods (after lab interactions, separations, or nonrelational stress) and thus any conclusions are necessarily tentative. There are also hints that one partner's attachment style may influence the other's physiological stress reactions. Given the potential for partners to influence each other's physiological responses and downstream health outcomes (see Pietromonaco, Uchino, & Dunkel Schetter, 2013; Sbarra & Hazan, 2008), this issue represents an important avenue for future research. One direction is suggested by prior work indicating that behavioral patterns play a key role in partners' physiological reactions: Specifically, wives' cortisol levels were higher when they engaged in negative behavior from which their husbands withdrew (Kiecolt-Glaser et al., 1996; see also Beck, Pietromonaco, DeBuse, et al., 2013). Research on attachment and physiological responses has not incorporated an analysis of couples' behavior patterns, but investigating the interplay among attachment, behavior, and physiological reactions may help clarify this link.

Taken together, this literature suggests different patterns of affective reactivity for anxiously and avoidantly attached individuals. Anxious individuals are more likely to experience intense subjective feelings of distress, and they may also show physiological dysregulation. In contrast, avoidant individuals generally report blunted affective reactions, although they evidence distress in situations in which stress is severe or chronic or when they do not have the cognitive resources to cope, and sometimes in their less consciously controlled (e.g., physiological) responses. As we discuss in the next sections, the regulation of attachment-related affect can occur through cognitive processes such as attention, memory, and interpretation; through the pursuit of relational goals; and through relationship processes (e.g., support).

Cognitive Processes

Internal working models are thought to guide people's attention to and memory for relational information and to provide a lens for interpreting relational information (for a review, see Dykas & Cassidy, 2011). These processes should work in the interest of confirming individuals' attachment-related expectations, beliefs, and goals and regulating feelings of distress. For avoidant individuals, cognitive processes

should promote distance from others and serve to maintain self-reliance as a way of protecting them from potential attachment-related distress. For anxious individuals, cognitive processes should maintain proximity to others in the interest of achieving reassurance and security. We examine these propositions with regard to how people attend to, remember, and interpret attachment-relevant information.

Attention.   Although relatively few studies have examined how attachment is associated with attentional processes, the findings generally suggest that avoidant individuals turn their attention away from relationship-relevant emotional information (e.g., Dewitte, 2011; Dewitte, Koster, De Houwer, & Buysse, 2007; Edelstein & Gillath, 2008; Fraley, Garner, & Shaver, 2000; Rholes, Simpson, Tran, Martin, & Friedman, 2007). For example, recent work investigated the connection between attachment and attention using a task designed to evaluate the inhibition of attention (Dewitte, 2011). This research found that individuals higher in attachment avoidance (but not anxiety) inhibited attention to negative relational information (angry or sad faces) but not to positive relational information (happy faces). This inhibitory process may allow avoidant individuals to prevent distress that may be triggered by such information (Dewitte, 2011). Similarly, in work using an emotional Stroop task, people who were highly avoidant and not under cognitive load attended less to attachment-related emotional words; attachment anxiety, however, was unrelated to attention patterns (Edelstein & Gillath, 2008). More important, avoidant individuals did not attend less to emotional material that was not attachment related. Furthermore, these effects held only for avoidant individuals who were currently in a romantic relationship, presumably because the relationship context heightened their need to apply defensive, self-protective strategies to regulate affect. In addition, avoidant individuals evidenced attentional biases only when they were not under cognitive load; performing a simultaneous difficult cognitive task interfered with their ability to turn their attention away from attachment-related information.

Anxious attachment has not been consistently associated with attentional biases in studies examining attention to generic attachment-related words (e.g., Edelstein & Gillath, 2008) or faces (e.g., Dewitte, 2011; see also Dykas & Cassidy, 2011). However, in studies in which individuals were exposed to the names of their own attachment figures, people higher in attachment anxiety (but not those higher in avoidance) were more likely to respond in ways indicating greater selective attention to their attachment figure; surprisingly, this effect occurred in threatening and in positive contexts (Dewitte, De Houwer, Koster, & Buysse, 2007) and in threatening and neutral contexts (Mikulincer, Gillath, & Shaver, 2002). These findings raise the possibility that anxious individuals' tendency to monitor the availability of their attachment figure may become chronic, such that they do so even in situations in which no clear threat exists.

These findings support the idea that avoidant people divert attention from information that could activate the attachment system, allowing them to prevent attachment-related distress (Bowlby, 1980). Although attentional effects are less consistent for anxious individuals, they appear to be vigilant to information about the availability of their own attachment figures.

Memory.   Studies have consistently revealed that avoidant individuals have difficulty remembering attachment-related information (e.g., Edelstein, 2006; Fraley & Brumbaugh, 2007; Mikulincer & Orbach, 1995; Simpson, Rholes, & Winterheld, 2010), which again may help to regulate negative affect by preventing it. For example, more avoidant individuals showed deficits in working memory when the task included both positive and negative attachment-related words but not when it included non–attachment-related emotional or nonemotional words; however, attachment anxiety was unrelated to working memory capacity (Edelstein, 2006).

People may also reconstruct their memories in ways that support their preferred affect regulation strategies of seeking closeness or distance. In a study examining this idea, couples discussed a major disagreement in their relationship and rated how supportive and distant or disengaged they had been during the discussion both immediately afterward and 1 week later (Simpson et al., 2010). This work is note-worthy because couple members remembered their perceptions of their own actual relationship behavior, which is likely to be more emotionally significant and relevant than the standardized stimuli (e.g., attachment-related words) typically used in other studies. As expected, more avoidant individuals remembered being less supportive, whereas more anxious individuals remembered being less distant. In each case, individuals remembered their behavior in a way that confirmed their attachment-related beliefs and goals and that was congruent with their preferred approach to regulating distress. Moreover, these reconstructive memory biases occurred only when individuals appeared more distressed (as rated by observers) during the actual discussion, supporting the idea that these biases serve to regulate negative affect.

Other work also has distinguished between the type of information most likely to be remembered by those high in attachment avoidance versus anxiety (Ein-Dor, Mikulincer, & Shaver, 2011). Ein-Dor et al. (2011) proposed that anxious individuals are most likely to remember information related to quickly detecting danger and warning others while staying close to them (a sentinel schema) because such information is adaptive for those who are apt to experience intense distress in response to threat and to turn to others for help with affect regulation. In contrast, Ein-Dor et al. suggested that avoidant individuals are most likely to remember information related to taking rapid and independent action to protect themselves (a rapid fight–flight schema) because such information is adaptive for individuals who seek to protect themselves from distress and whose primary affect regulation strategy is to rely on themselves and maintain distance from others. Results indicated that attachment anxiety predicted more accurate and rapid recognition memory for information related to danger (Study 2), and attachment avoidance predicted more rapid recognition of sentences related to fight–flight (Study 3). Furthermore, in recalling information from a story with sentinel-based and neutral information, anxious people were more likely to make inferences (e.g., elaborations) congruent with a sentinel schema (Study 4). In contrast, after hearing a story with fight–flight and neutral information, avoidant people were more likely to make inferences congruent with a rapid fight–flight schema (Study 5). This work, together with the Simpson et al. (2010) study, argues for examining how the specific content of working models (e.g., content related to intimacy, distance, or strategies used in response to threat), beyond the global positive or negative valence of that content, might bias memories in ways that confirm and perpetuate attachment-related expectations, beliefs, and goals and that allow for the regulation of negative feelings.

Interpretation. The evidence has generally indicated that secure individuals are inclined to give their partners the benefit of the doubt and interpret negative events in less relationship-threatening ways, whereas insecure individuals are more inclined to assign a negative interpretation. In studies of attribution patterns, individuals typically read hypothetical scenarios in reference to a partner (either imagined or their own) who performs either negative or positive attachment-related behaviors. Across several studies, anxious individuals were more likely to explain a partner's negative behavior in more pessimistic, relationship-threatening terms (Collins, 1996; Collins, Ford, Guichard, & Allard, 2006; Gallo & Smith, 2001; Pearce & Halford, 2008). In addition, anxious individuals selected more pessimistic interpretations to explain their partner's negative or positive behavior, especially if they were less satisfied in their current romantic relationship (Collins et al., 2006). Attachment avoidance has been less consistently associated with pessimistic attributions, with some studies finding that avoidance predicts more negative (or less positive) attributions and others showing no association. Other work has indicated that insecure individuals (both anxious and avoidant) are more likely to interpret ambiguous feedback from romantic partners in a negative light (Collins & Feeney, 2004) and to assign greater hostile intent to romantic partners' ambiguous behavior (Mikulincer, 1998b). These findings suggest that insecure individuals will have greater difficulty with affect regulation because they are inclined to construe partners' behaviors in more pessimistic terms, thereby maintaining their own distress. Furthermore, their partners may become frustrated if the insecure person's distress persists, leading them to withdraw or even become hostile.

In general, research on cognitive processes is consistent with the idea that working models guide people's attention, memory, and interpretation of attachment-relevant information. However, few studies have examined how attachment style contributes to attention and memory, and even fewer have investigated these processes in the context of actual relationships in which people are more likely to experience intense affect and involvement (e.g., Simpson et al., 2010). For example, one critical future direction would be to examine attentional and memory biases as they occur in actual relationships and the conditions under which they enhance or impair individuals' ability to regulate feelings of distress.

Goal-Directed Processes

At a normative level, working models are organized around the overarching goal to achieve felt security (Ainsworth, 1989; Sroufe & Waters, 1977). When individuals experience a threat, they will engage in behaviors in an attempt to restore felt security. Some evidence has supported this normative process and suggested that it occurs automatically and effortlessly: When people were primed below conscious awareness (i.e., subliminally) with the name of a security-promoting attachment figure, they reported greater willingness to disclose personal information and to seek support, and they were faster to respond to goal-related words such as *comfort* and *support,* suggesting increased accessibility of these constructs (Gillath et al., 2006).

How people attempt to achieve felt security, however, will vary as a function of their attachment-relevant experiences and resulting attachment styles (see Pietromonaco & Barrett, 2000). Avoidant individuals (especially dismissing avoidant individuals) have chronic interpersonal goals to maintain independence and distance and to protect themselves from attachment-related distress. Anxious individuals (especially preoccupied ones) chronically strive for intimacy and closeness and are most likely to turn to others for reassurance to regulate their negative feelings. People who are more secure may hold a variety of interpersonal goals (e.g., for support, independence, self-protection), but they apply these goals more flexibly and appropriately, depending on the demands of the situation. Content analyses of dating partners' conversations about their relationships support these ideas: Secure people focus on achieving balance between intimacy and independence, whereas avoidant people focus on restricting intimacy and anxious people focus on enhancing intimacy (J. A. Feeney, 1999; J. A. Feeney & Noller, 1991).

Consistent with this reasoning, anxious individuals are more likely to excessively seek reassurance in their relationships (Davila, 2001; Eberhart & Hammen, 2009) and to seek information about their dating partner's personal thoughts and to evaluate such knowledge as more important (Rholes et al., 2007). Individuals higher in attachment anxiety are more likely to pursue approach goals (relevant to sex or sacrificing) to obtain intimacy and closeness as well as avoidance goals to prevent rejection in their relationships (Impett & Gordon, 2010; Impett, Gordon, & Strachman, 2008). This pursuit of both approach and avoidance goals in the service of maintaining a relationship may illuminate recent findings showing that, on both implicit and explicit measures, anxious individuals evidenced dual motivations to approach and avoid a romantic partner (Mikulincer, Shaver, Bar-On, & Ein-Dor, 2010). These dual motivations make sense if anxious individuals use both in the broader interest of maintaining their relationship and closeness over the longer term. Other work has indicated that, for anxious individuals, intimacy goals are closely tied to their feelings for their partners, suggesting their importance for the quality of anxious individuals' relationships (Pietromonaco & Barrett, 2006); after interactions in which anxious (preoccupied) individuals believed that their partner had behaved in ways that fulfilled intimacy-related needs (i.e., understood them, cared for them, approved of them), they valued their partner more.

In contrast, avoidant individuals prefer to seek distance and escape closeness. They are less likely to pursue approach goals that might push them toward intimacy with their romantic partner (Impett & Gordon, 2010; Impett et al., 2008), less likely to seek personal information about a dating partner, and more likely to downplay the importance of such knowledge (Rholes et al., 2007). Avoidant individuals even distance themselves in situations in which people typically seek closeness and comfort. When avoidant women appeared distressed about an upcoming stressful task, they sought less support

and comfort from their dating partner; in contrast, when secure women were distressed, they sought more support (Simpson et al., 1992).

Social Support Processes

Interactions involving seeking, perceiving, and providing support are central in helping individuals reestablish emotional well-being when they encounter threatening situations (e.g., see Collins & Feeney, 2010). Partners need to effectively solicit support when needed and to accurately detect when their partner is offering comfort; as caregivers, individuals need to be attuned to their partner's needs and, when appropriate, be responsive, caring, and available. Attachment styles have been linked to chronic differences in these support-related processes.

Support seeking. Attachment theory suggests that the ability to effectively use a secure base (i.e., the relationship partner who serves as an attachment figure) to restore emotional equilibrium requires providing a clear and consistent signal to the partner (Crowell, Treboux, & Waters, 2002). Securely attached people are more likely to attempt to solicit support and to do so in ways that are constructive and effective; in contrast, insecure people are less likely to actively seek support, and when they do, they use indirect, less effective means such as sulking or crying (e.g., Collins & Feeney, 2000; Fraley & Shaver, 1998; Simpson et al., 1992). Studies of dating couples have found that more avoidant individuals solicited less support from their partner when discussing a problem, even when the problem was a major source of stress (Collins & Feeney, 2000) and that avoidant women who showed more distress when anticipating a stressor were less likely to seek support from their partner (Simpson et al., 1992). Avoidant individuals were also less likely to seek proximity or support when they were about to be separated from their romantic partner at the airport (Fraley & Shaver, 1998). Although anxious individuals are more likely than secure individuals to want partners to help them regulate their distress (Pietromonaco & Barrett, 2006), they do not actually seek more support in experimental studies than those lower in anxiety (Collins & Feeney, 2000).

he explanation for this inconsistency is that anxious individuals both desire support and fear rejection and abandonment, and these latter worries may prevent them from directly seeking support (Mikulincer & Shaver, 2007). This work suggests that whether people seek support will vary depending on their attachment style, and thus their partner's knowledge of their style and ability to detect and respond sensitively to their distress is apt to be important in helping threatened individuals regulate distress and cope in a crisis.

Perceptions of support and responsiveness. To benefit from a partner's responsiveness, individuals must accurately perceive a partner's supportive attempts. People who are more securely attached generally expect support to be available if it is needed, and they are more likely to view support attempts as effective (for reviews, see Collins & Feeney, 2010; Mikulincer & Shaver, 2007). In experimental studies manipulating the quality of support from a partner, participants received notes ostensibly from their dating partner that conveyed either ambiguous or clear-cut support; insecure individuals were more likely than secure individuals to perceive the ambiguous notes in a negative light, although secure and insecure individuals did not differ in their evaluations of the highly supportive notes (Collins & Feeney, 2004, Study 1). Similarly, in a follow-up study in which participants wrote their own notes, insecure individuals perceived their partner's note as less supportive when the note was somewhat ambiguous in conveying support than did secure individuals (Collins & Feeney, 2004, Study 2).

Insecure individuals also differ from secure individuals in their perceptions of daily support from a dating partner (Campbell, Simpson, Boldry, & Kashy, 2005). At the end of each of 14 days, dating partners described the most supportive experience in their relationship (if one had occurred) for that day and rated its implications for the future longevity of the relationship and the degree to which it was a positive experience. Although attachment style was not related to the number of supportive events reported, it did predict different perceptions of these events. When anxiously attached individuals reported a supportive daily experience, they were more optimistic about its implications for the longevity of their relationship, suggesting that their relationship perceptions may depend heavily on what happens on a particular day. When avoidant individuals reported a supportive daily experience in their relationship, they viewed it as a less positive experience, which was attributed to their discomfort with interdependence.

These examples, together with other research (see Collins & Feeney, 2010; Mikulincer & Shaver, 2007), suggest that insecurely attached individuals are less likely to experience emotional relief when partners provide support. Insecure individuals may not interpret a partner's gesture as supportive or pleasant, or their perceptions may be more variable depending on their most recent interactions. We are aware of only one study that has examined whether particular kinds of support (e.g., emotional, instrumental) might be more or less effective in helping insecure individuals modulate distress (Simpson, Winterheld, Rholes, & Oriña, 2007). Simpson, Winterheld, et al. (2007) found that young adults' attachment to parents (assessed by the Adult Attachment Interview) predicted the extent to which they were calmed by different kinds of support from their dating partner; individuals showing secure attachment to parents were more calmed after their romantic partner provided emotional support during a conflict interaction, whereas dismissing avoidant individuals were more calmed after receiving instrumental (concrete, rational advice) support. These patterns in young dating couples were linked specifically to attachment to parents and not to self-reported romantic attachment style; however, it is possible that romantic attachment would predict links between one partner's use of a particular form of caregiving and the other's distress relief in more established couples (e.g., married couples) in which partners are more likely to serve as primary attachment figures.

Providing support and being responsive. Because the attachment and caregiving systems are intertwined in adults, attachment styles are associated not only with attachment-related thoughts, feelings, and behaviors but also with the provision of care and support to close partners (Collins & Feeney, 2010).

Secure individuals are better equipped than insecure individuals to help their partners regulate distress (Carnelley, Pietromonaco, & Jaffe, 1996; Collins & Feeney, 2000; B. C. Feeney & Collins, 2001; Simpson et al., 1992; Simpson, Rholes, Oriña,& Grich, 2002). Secure adults are more sensitive to their partner's signals, and they are more cooperative and less controlling in responding to their partner (B. C. Feeney & Collins, 2001; Kane et al., 2007). Securely attached women also respond more flexibly to their partner's needs, providing more support when their partner desires it and less support when he or she does not (Simpson et al., 2002).

In contrast, insecure adults are more likely to offer ineffective support and care (see Collins & Feeney, 2010). For example, in one study, dating couples were videotaped while one partner disclosed a personal problem to the other (Collins & Feeney, 2000). When caregiving partners were high in attachment anxiety, they were less responsive, offered less instrumental support, and displayed more negative behavior (e.g., minimizing the problem, blaming the discloser for the problem) to the disclosing partner. In other work, women who expected to undergo a stressful procedure were videotaped while they waited with their dating partner (Rholes, Simpson, & Oriña, 1999; Simpson et al., 1992). Secure men provided more emotional support and anticipated their partner's needs, but avoidant men provided less support as their partner's distress increased (Simpson et al., 1992); avoidant men were also more likely to show anger toward their distressed partner (Rholes et al., 1999). These findings suggest that being in a relationship with an insecurely attached partner may reduce one's ability to regulate distress, which may interfere with maintaining a satisfying relationship over time.

ATTACHMENT PROCESSES AND RELATIONSHIP FUNCTIONING AND STABILITY

Attachment-related differences in affective, cognitive, motivational, and support-related processes can directly serve affect regulation functions, but they can also contribute to how individuals form new relationships, how they function as relationships become more established, and how they maintain relationships over time.

Relationship Initiation

Even the earliest romantic encounters can activate attachment-related processes. Such encounters often are emotionally salient: They raise concerns about care and regard, acceptance and rejection. Some findings (Brumbaugh & Fraley, 2006) support the idea that working models of attachment are implicated in relationship initiation processes. Specifically, people transferred their attachment expectations to potential romantic partners; anxious individuals expected to feel anxious toward potential partners, and avoidant individuals expected to feel avoidant toward potential partners, even when those partners did not resemble their past partners.

Normative processes in partner preference. Most people desire mutually satisfying romantic relationships and are therefore apt to prefer secure partners who offer the best opportunity to form a secure attachment bond (e.g., Chappell & Davis, 1998; Klohnen & Luo, 2003). Across studies in which people read about potential romantic partners, people of all attachment styles viewed secure partners as more attractive than insecure partners (Frazier, Byer, Fischer, Wright, & DeBord, 1996; Klohnen & Luo, 2003; Latty-Mann & Davis, 1996), reported fewer negative emotions and more positive emotions when they imagined relationships with secure partners (Chappell & Davis, 1998; Pietromonaco & Carnelley, 1994), and preferred to date secure partners (Chappell & Davis, 1998).

Although people prefer secure partners in general, they also distinguish between avoidant and anxious partners. People evaluate and react to anxious partners more favorably than to avoidant partners (Chappell & Davis, 1998; Frazier et al., 1996; Klohnen & Luo, 2003; Latty-Mann & Davis, 1996; Pietromonaco & Carnelley, 1994). Klohnen and Luo (2003) proposed that the anxiety dimension of attachment may be less important to preferences during initial romantic encounters than the avoidance dimension. This reasoning is supported by evidence that the statelike experience of attachment anxiety is a normative part of relationship initiation that has functional implications for developing relationships because it motivates people to communicate interest and care for potential romantic partners (Eastwick & Finkel, 2008). This normative process may help explain why people evaluate potential partners with anxious qualities as more desirable than those with avoidant qualities during the early stages of relationships.

Individual difference processes in partner preference. Individuals' own attachment orientations also predict their preferences for potential romantic partners. Insecure people view insecure potential partners as more attractive than do secure people (Frazier et al., 1996; Klohnen & Luo, 2003; Latty-Mann & Davis, 1996), even though both secure and insecure people view secure potential partners as more attractive overall. Some work (Frazier et al., 1996; Klohnen & Luo, 2003; Latty-Mann & Davis, 1996) has found similarity between insecure people's attachment orientations and their partner preferences, such that avoidant individuals are more attracted to partners high in avoidance (i.e., avoidant or fearful) and anxious individuals are more attracted to partners high in anxiety (i.e., anxious or fearful). Other work (e.g., Pietromonaco & Carnelley, 1994) has found complementary patterns, such that avoidant individuals prefer anxious partners, perhaps because these partners confirm their expectations of others as needy and dependent and their expectations of themselves as self-reliant and independent. Both patterns of partner preference have implications for relationship well-being and emotional health because relationships with insecure partners tend to function less well than those with secure partners.

People's attachment orientations not only guide their preferences for relationship partners but they also contribute to how people initiate relationships. For example, people higher in attachment avoidance seek less information about potential partners when deciding whom to date than do those lower in avoidance (Aspelmeier & Kerns, 2003), which indicates that avoidant individuals may avoid exploring relational information. Indeed, when given the opportunity, avoidant individuals evade situations that provide information about others' relational

interest in them. Avoidant individuals, but not others, prefer social situations that do not provide feedback about how another person feels about them, and people who are experimentally primed to feel avoidant are also less likely than those primed to feel secure or anxious to choose to receive feedback about how another person feels about them (Beck & Clark, 2009). By restricting information seeking, avoidant individuals can manage potential distress by maintaining relational distance. Such strategies, however, can prevent them from receiving clear feedback that a partner likes them, which is a powerful determinant of reciprocating liking and presumably of developing close relationships, or from detecting that a partner does not reciprocate interest and that the relationship may not be worth pursuing.

Taken together, the research has consistently found that people seek attachment security in potential romantic partners, regardless of their own attachment style. Entering a relationship with a secure partner who is better able to provide sensitive and responsive care may enhance insecure individuals' ability to regulate distress. At the same time, insecure people are more attracted to insecure potential partners than are secure people, and entering such relationships may impair their ability to effectively regulate feelings of distress. For example, insecure individuals' generally ineffective affect regulation strategies may interact with an insecure partner's difficulty with supportively responding to their distress, further exacerbating feelings of distress and interfering with attempts to restore felt security.

Self-presentation and self-disclosure. Self-presentation and self-disclosure processes are especially important during the early stages of romantic relationships. People are often uncertain about whether a potential partner will reciprocate romantic interest, so they may be particularly focused on securing that person's approval and regard (e.g., Swann, De La Ronde, & Hixon, 1994). During relationship initiation, people may be especially concerned about presenting themselves as desirable partners (Beck & Clark, 2010; Clark & Beck, 2011), but individual differences in attachment may facilitate or inhibit self-presentation. Because almost everyone would prefer a relationship with a secure partner, people who present themselves in a way that reflects attachment security—such as being supportive, responsive, and comfortable with balancing relational closeness and distance—convey that they would be a desirable partner.

Of course, presenting oneself as a desirable relationship partner may be easier for secure individuals because it is consistent with authentic self-presentation. In contrast, avoidant people may present an overly positive view of themselves to seem self-reliant and independent (Mikulincer, 1998a), which may communicate that they are not really interested in a relationship. In contrast, anxious people may present an overly negative view of themselves to elicit support and compassion (Mikulincer, 1998a), which may convey that they would be a needy or demanding relationship partner. Both of these self-presentation strategies can hinder rather than promote relationship development. At the same time, recent research (Brumbaugh & Fraley, 2010) has suggested that insecure individuals may use compensatory strategies to present themselves as desirable partners. For example, anxious individuals may present themselves as warm and engaging when interacting with potential romantic partners, and both anxious individuals and avoidant individuals may present themselves as humorous. These positive qualities may help insecure people win over potential romantic partners, at least in the early stages of relationships.

The pace at which people share personal information and their responsiveness to their partners' disclosures contribute to relationship development. The early stages of relationships involve initially low levels of self-disclosure that gradually increase over time (Altman & Taylor, 1973). During these early stages, immediate disclosure of personal feelings and concerns may be perceived as neediness. As the relationship develops, however, failure to self-disclose can be perceived as a lack of investment or as disinterest in one's partner and the relationship.

Secure attachment can facilitate self-disclosure through responsiveness, sensitivity, and reciprocation of romantic partners' disclosures. Secure people synchronize their own disclosures with those of their partners, which promotes partners' self-disclosure and assuages concerns about vulnerability and rejection (Grabill & Kerns, 2000; Keelan, Dion, & Dion, 1998; Mikulincer & Nachshon, 1991). In addition, secure people reveal more intimate information to high-disclosing partners than to low-disclosing partners (Mikulincer & Nachshon, 1991) and are more responsive to their partners' disclosures (Grabill & Kerns, 2000; Keelan et al., 1998). These behaviors can support the development of intimacy and trust.

In contrast, insecure individuals can behave in ways that disrupt self-disclosure. Avoidant people disclose information to dating partners less frequently than do secure people (Bradford, Feeney, & Campbell, 2002). In contrast, anxious people tend to disclose personal information indiscriminately—often before such disclosures are appropriate—and are not very responsive to their partners' disclosures, perhaps because of intense self-focus (Grabill & Kerns, 2000; Mikulincer & Nachshon, 1991). They share more negative information with dating partners and report more dissatisfaction with their interactions (Bradford et al., 2002). Ironically, the more interested anxious individuals are in a potential romantic partner, the less interest they actually express (Vorauer, Cameron, Holmes, & Pearce, 2003), which may further interfere with self-disclosure.

Working models of attachment, as well as associated affect regulation strategies, appear to be implicated in relationship initiation processes. Insecure individuals may self-present and self-disclose to potential partners in ways that support their affect regulation goals. Avoidant individuals often present themselves as self-reliant and disclose little information to their partners, which can serve to protect them from attachment-related distress by promoting distance from others. In contrast, anxious individuals may present an overly negative view of themselves to elicit support and compassion from others. They may also disclose personal information freely (often before their partner feels comfortable with such disclosures), both of which may represent attempts to attain closeness in the interest of achieving reassurance and security.

Relationship Maintenance

People's attachment-related desires for closeness and distance and their ability to balance their own needs with those of their partner can contribute to the development of intimacy and commitment in romantic relationships. Secure individuals consistently evidence more intimate relationships than do insecure individuals (e.g., J. A. Feeney & Noller, 1991; Hazan & Shaver, 1987; Mikulincer & Erev, 1991; Treboux, Crowell, & Waters, 2004), yet insecure individuals differ in their desire for intimacy. Anxious people tend to desire greater intimacy than they report having, perhaps because they cannot achieve the intense intimacy they want or because their desire for excessive closeness pushes away their partner (Mikulincer & Erev, 1991). In contrast, avoidant people report low levels of both the intimacy they have and the intimacy they want. Interestingly, avoidant individuals believe that their partner feels less intimacy than he or she actually does (Mikulincer & Erev, 1991) and are less likely to perceive their partner as responsive (Beck, Pietromonaco, DeVito, Powers, & Boyle, 2013), which may be affect regulation strategies that allow them to keep their partner at a distance and to maintain independence.

People's commitment to their relationships follows a similar pattern: Secure individuals experience greater commitment as well as greater intimacy in their relationships. A prospective study of relationship formation found that avoidant individuals were less likely to initiate committed dating relationships than were secure individuals (Schindler, Fagundes, & Murdock, 2010), and other work has suggested that avoidant individuals begin new relationships with elaborate scripts for commitment aversion that lead them to expect their relationships to fail (Birnie, McClure, Lydon, & Holmberg, 2009). Furthermore, the many studies on commitment in dating and marital relationships have consistently found that attachment security predicts greater commitment, often for both partners (e.g., Keelan, Dion, & Dion, 1994; Pistole, Clark, & Tubbs, 1995; Simpson, 1990). For example, secure individuals maintained high commitment to their dating partners over 4 months, whereas anxious and avoidant individuals decreased their commitment to their partners over the same time period (Keelan et al., 1994).

Anxious and avoidant people, however, differ considerably in their desire for commitment, just as they differ in their desire for intimacy. Anxious individuals are more likely to want a highly committed relationship than are avoidant individuals (J. A. Feeney & Noller, 1990), and these desires are reflected in their behavior. For example, anxious husbands spent significantly less time dating their partner before getting married (19 months) than did avoidant (46 months) or secure (49 months; Senchak & Leonard, 1992) husbands. An important consequence is that anxious people may commit to a relationship before they truly know their partner, making them more likely to become involved with an uncaring, uncommitted partner who cannot fulfill their needs for security (Morgan & Shaver, 1999). Furthermore, the partners of insecure individuals evidence less commitment than those of secure individuals (Kirkpatrick & Davis, 1994; Mikulincer & Erev, 1991; Simpson, 1990), which may further frustrate anxious individuals' desires for commitment and their attempts to regulate distress by drawing closer to their partner.

Relationship Satisfaction

From an attachment perspective, relationship satisfaction should be enhanced when partners offer a safe haven of support and security, are dependable and available, and provide a secure base from which each partner can explore and grow (Collins & Feeney, 2010). Attachment insecurity consistently predicts relationship dissatisfaction for men and women (e.g., Campbell et al., 2005; Davila, Karney, & Bradbury, 1999; J. A. Feeney, 2002; Shaver, Schachner, & Mikulincer, 2005), even when other personality characteristics (e.g., depression, self-esteem, Big Five traits; Carnelley et al., 1994; Jones & Cunningham, 1996; Noftle & Shaver, 2006; Shaver & Brennan, 1992) have been taken into account. Gender, however, plays a role in this association: Whereas both avoidance and anxiety predict women's relationship satisfaction, avoidance more consistently predicts men's relationship satisfaction than does anxiety. Mikulincer and Shaver (2007) offered two possible explanations for this pattern: Avoidance may intensify (or be intensified by) male gender role norms of self-reliance and emotional restraint, or women may be especially dissatisfied with avoidant men, leading them to communicate their feelings to their partners which, in turn, lowers men's satisfaction.

Studies with prospective and daily diary designs reduce the possibility that links between insecure attachment and relationship satisfaction may result from dissatisfaction leading to lower attachment security, rather than vice versa. For example, one such study found that higher levels of anxiety and avoidance during the first 6 months of marriage led to declines in marital satisfaction over 2 years (Davila et al., 1999). These findings also revealed a reciprocal relationship between insecure attachment and relationship dissatisfaction, which suggests that they may influence one another over time. Several diary studies ranging from 1 to 3 weeks in length have also indicated that insecure attachment predicts less daily relationship satisfaction (Campbell et al., 2005; J. A. Feeney, 2002; Shaver et al., 2005). For example, individuals high in attachment anxiety were more reactive to day-to-day changes in their partners' behaviors; they responded to their partners' positive behaviors (e.g., support) with increased relationship satisfaction and to partners' negative behaviors (e.g., conflict) with decreased satisfaction (Campbell et al., 2005; J. A. Feeney, 2002). Campbell et al. (2005) suggested that this intense focus on day-to-day relationship events may explain why anxious individuals and their partners experience less relationship satisfaction; their relationships should feel more turbulent and less stable because they are focused on daily events rather than on long-term experiences.

In contrast, attachment security can enhance relationship satisfaction, particularly during times of stress and life transitions. For instance, one study found that women with prolonged infertility problems experienced lower relationship satisfaction than women with more recent infertility problems, but these effects were primarily for anxious women; secure women were better able to maintain relationship satisfaction (Amir, Horesh, & Lin-Stein, 1999). Similarly, when anxious women—but not secure women—perceived low levels of support from their spouse 6 weeks before the birth of their first child, both they and their partner experienced declines in

relationship satisfaction 6 months later (Rholes, Simpson, Campbell, & Grich, 2001). Taken together, this research has suggested that attachment security serves as a resource for individuals and their partners by preserving relationship satisfaction during times of life stress.

Relationship Stability

Individual differences in attachment also contribute to people's ability to maintain stable, enduring romantic relationships. Secure people have longer, more stable relationships than insecure people (e.g., J. A. Feeney & Noller, 1990; Hill, Young, & Nord, 1994). Furthermore, insecure attachment predicts relationship dissolution in dating couples (Duemmler & Kobak, 2001; Kirkpatrick & Hazan, 1994; Shaver & Brennan, 1992) and divorce in married couples (e.g., Birnbaum, Orr, Mikulincer, & Florian, 1997; Crowell & Treboux, 2001; Hill et al., 1994).

More important, anxious and avoidant people may experience relationship dissolution in different ways. Avoidant individuals may want to leave their relationship as soon as they feel distressed (Kirkpatrick & Hazan, 1994), consistent with their strategy of regulating affect by turning attention away from a threat. Anxious individuals, however, may break up and reunite with the same partner, sometimes more than once (Kirkpatrick & Hazan, 1994), consistent with their attempts to regulate affect by seeking closeness. Attachment anxiety may also lead to reluctance to leave romantic relationships, even when those relationships are no longer fulfilling. For example, a longitudinal study of dating couples revealed that when people's partners failed to help them meet their needs for autonomy and relatedness, individuals low in anxiety—but not those high in anxiety—experienced less commitment to their relationships at the beginning of the study, deteriorating commitment over time, and a higher risk of break up (Slotter & Finkel, 2009). These findings suggest that anxious people may maintain their romantic relationships even when their partner does not fulfill their psychological needs. Similarly, a 4-year longitudinal study of newlywed couples found that spouses who were in unhappy marriages had the highest levels of attachment anxiety—both initially and over time—compared with spouses in happy marriages and spouses who were divorced (Davila & Bradbury, 2001). Thus, spouses' attachment anxiety may contribute to both dissatisfaction and stability in their marriage.

Relationship Dissolution and Loss

Many theorists (e.g., Bowlby, 1980; Fraley & Shaver, 1999; Mikulincer & Shaver, 2007; Sbarra & Hazan, 2008; Weiss, 2001) have asserted that distress in response to separation from an attachment figure is the most powerful indicator of an attachment relationship and, in turn, that separation or loss of an attachment figure disturbs the sense of felt security. Sbarra and Hazan (2008) provided a provocative extension by arguing that the loss of a long-term romantic relationship leads people to lose the very person who helped them maintain psychophysiological homeostasis, which centers on the sense of felt security; this disturbance in homeostasis can result in biobehavioral dysregulation, ranging from mild psychophysiological arousal to an extreme stress response, which can be attenuated by reestablishing felt security.

In addition to these normative responses, people's attachment orientations predict how they respond to relationship dissolution and loss. Attachment security facilitates emotional recovery and adjustment in both dating and married couples (e.g., Birnbaum et al., 1997; Davis, Shaver, & Vernon, 2003; J. A. Feeney & Noller, 1992; Moller, Fouladi, McCarthy, & Hatch, 2003; Moller, McCarthy, & Fouladi, 2002; Pistole, 1995; Sbarra, 2006; Sbarra & Emery, 2005; Sprecher, Felmlee, Metta, Fehr, & Vanni, 1998). In contrast, attachment insecurity can interfere with the recovery process, in part because insecure individuals may use less effective affect regulation strategies than secure individuals when coping with relationship dissolution.

Consistent with their attempts to regulate distress under other conditions of threat, avoidant individuals tend to rely on distancing strategies, anxious individuals tend to rely on emotion-focused strategies, and secure individuals tend to rely on social coping strategies (e.g., Birnbaum et al., 1997; Davis et al., 2003). For example, an Internet survey with more than 5,000 respondents (Davis et al., 2003) found that secure individuals were more likely to

react to romantic breakups with social coping strategies, such as turning to family and friends as safe havens of support. In contrast, anxious individuals were more likely to react with dysfunctional coping strategies, emotional and physical distress, angry behavior, disrupted behavior at school and work, attraction to and preoccupation with their former partner, perseveration about the breakup, and attempts to reunite with their former partner. These strategies reflect anxious individuals' attempts to regulate affect by seeking closeness and reassurance from their attachment figure (even when it may no longer be appropriate to do so) as well as their heightened affective reactivity to distress. Finally, avoidant individuals were more likely to react with self-reliant and avoidant coping strategies, such as avoiding new romantic relationships or failing to seek support, which are consistent with their attempts to regulate distress by suppressing negative emotions and turning their attention away from attachment-related threats.

How avoidant people react to relationship dissolution may depend on the nature of the relationship. Although avoidant individuals may respond to the dissolution of dating relationships with decreased distress (e.g., Davis et al., 2003; Simpson, 1990) and increased relief (e.g., J. A. Feeney & Noller, 1992), they may respond to the dissolution of marital relationships with increased distress. For example, one study found that both avoidant and anxious individuals responded to divorce with increased distress and decreased well-being compared with secure individuals (Birnbaum et al., 1997); although avoidant people believed they could cope, they also viewed divorce as a threat and displayed ineffective coping strategies that led to their increased distress and decreased well-being. Birnbaum et al. (1997) suggested that avoidant individuals may be able to regulate their distress when a more casual dating relationship ends, but they may not be able to do so when a long-term attachment relationship ends, as in the case of divorce. These findings fit with other work showing that avoidant individuals' defensive distancing strategies may break down under severe or chronic stress or under high cognitive demand (e.g., Berant et al., 2008; Mikulincer et al., 2004), any of which may apply when individuals are faced with reorganizing their lives, identities, and interpersonal connections in the aftermath of divorce.

Attachment-related processes play a critical role in people's ability to maintain long-term, mutually satisfying romantic relationships, which in turn can influence their ability to manage distress. Attachment security predicts a host of positive relationship outcomes, such as responsive caregiving and enhanced relationship satisfaction, even in the face of stress. In contrast, attachment insecurity appears to interfere with healthy relationship functioning.

EMERGING THEMES AND FUTURE DIRECTIONS

Although research over the past 25 years has yielded a great deal of knowledge about attachment-related processes in adults, there is still much to learn. We focus here on four emerging themes that are particularly likely to lead to novel insights into attachment processes and their implications for affect regulation (for additional emerging themes, see Simpson & Rholes, 2010). We call for research that (a) incorporates a person-in-context approach in investigating attachment processes in romantic couples, (b) investigates the processes through which adult romantic partners may promote change or stability in each other's attachment representations, (c) tests the interactive effects of attachment and temperament or personality, and (d) identifies the processes (e.g., behavioral, biological) through which attachment may influence individuals' health-related processes and outcomes as well as those of their partners.

Person-in-Context Effects

An emergent theme in the literature is that the effects of adult attachment styles often depend on the situational context. In many studies, individuals' attachment styles interact with aspects of the situation to enhance or attenuate their reactions. For example, avoidant individuals divert their attention from emotionally threatening words but only for attachment-relevant words (Edelstein & Gillath, 2008); insecure individuals show reconstructive memory biases congruent with their preferred affect regulation strategies only when the to-be-remembered event was distressing (Simpson et al., 2010); and

anxious individuals evidence poorer emotional outcomes only when they also perceived an attachment-relevant threat (less support from their spouse [Rholes et al., 2011] or less agreeable behavior from their partner [Sadikaj et al., 2011]). These studies and others make salient that different situations may be threatening for different people. Anxious individuals are likely to be threatened in situations in which support is insufficient or partners are rejecting, whereas avoidant individuals are apt to be threatened when situations promote intimacy and closeness. Not all studies, however, have found context effects (e.g., Mikulincer et al., 2002), so it would be important to further specify the contingencies under which stress activates the attachment system for people with different attachment styles.

In addition, the characteristics of both partners and the relationship are critical features of the situation. Attachment relationships are dyadic, and any examination of attachment styles must take into account not only individuals' own characteristics but also those of their partner and the potential interaction between the two. Although some attachment research has incorporated a dyadic approach, more work along these lines would better capture how the relationship context might predict outcomes for both partners. For example, it would be important to know which partner characteristics and behaviors might enhance or impair individuals' ability to engage in constructive problem solving, cope with stress, or benefit from a partner's attempts to soothe them (e.g., see Beck, Pietromonaco, DeBuse, et al., 2013; Simpson, Winterheld, et al., 2007). Furthermore, little work has examined how dyadic processes might shape what partners attend to and remember, yet these processes are likely pivotal in whether working models remain stable or change.

Stability and Change in Attachment Representations in Adulthood

Bowlby (1973) theorized that working models developed early in life guide how the attachment system functions in close relationships throughout the life course, an idea with important implications for affective, support, and maintenance processes in adult relationships. Bowlby (1973) also suggested that working models become increasingly stable from infancy to adulthood, in part because people attend to, remember, interpret, and behave in their interactions in ways that reinforce their relationship expectations and beliefs. This assumption of continuity and stability in attachment representations from infancy through adulthood is a central tenet of attachment theory, yet it has remained an open question owing to a lack of quantitative predictions about what, exactly, constitutes attachment stability or change over the life course. Fraley and Brumbaugh (2004), for example, noted that a stability coefficient of .30 suggests some degree of attachment stability but that it is unclear whether this value strengthens arguments for attachment stability or attachment change. Consequently, longitudinal studies on attachment from infancy to young adulthood and on attachment during adulthood have provided ambiguous support for assumptions of stability because of variations in the findings as well as differences in researchers' interpretations of these findings. For example, some studies of attachment from infancy to young adulthood have found moderate to high levels of stability (e.g., Waters, Merrick, Treboux, Crowell, & Albersheim, 2003), whereas others have found little to no stability (e.g., Lewis, Feiring, & Rosenthal, 2000). Furthermore, some researchers examining attachment in adults have interpreted their results as evidence of instability in adult attachment style (e.g., Baldwin & Fehr, 1995; Davila, Burge, & Hammen, 1997; Kirkpatrick & Hazan, 1994), whereas others have interpreted similar results as evidence of stability (e.g., Keelan et al., 1994; Klohnen & Bera, 1998; Scharfe & Bartholomew, 1994; Shaver & Brennan, 1992).

Two meta-analyses have addressed these conflicting interpretations of attachment stability from infancy to young adulthood and throughout adulthood. One meta-analysis on attachment stability from infancy to young adulthood (Fraley, 2002) used 27 samples that collected test–retest data on parent–child attachment at 12 months and at later ages, whereas another meta-analysis on attachment stability during adulthood (Fraley & Brumbaugh, 2004) used 34 samples that collected test–retest data on either parent–child or romantic attachment

among adults. Attachment patterns were more stable in adulthood ($r = .54$; Fraley & Brumbaugh, 2004) than in childhood ($r = .39$; Fraley, 2002). In both cases, the researchers concluded that the findings supported a prototype model of attachment, such that a stable, latent pattern of attachment endures over time and underlies changes in attachment (e.g., Sroufe, Egeland, Carlson, & Collins, 2005; Sroufe, Egeland, & Kreutzer, 1990).

More important, Fraley (2002) noted that although early attachment representations should influence adult attachment in romantic relationships, none of the studies examining attachment through young adulthood specifically assessed attachment to romantic partners. Indeed, few studies have explicitly examined the link between early attachment representations and adult romantic attachment. However, recent longitudinal work (Zayas, Mischel, Shoda, & Aber, 2011) has shown that the quality of maternal caregiving at age 18 months predicts adults' attachment style at age 22 years. When mothers showed more sensitive caregiving, individuals were less avoidant and less anxious in their romantic relationships and less avoidant in their adult relationships with friends. In contrast, when mothers showed more controlling caregiving, individuals were more avoidant and more anxious with romantic partners and more avoidant in their relationships with friends. These findings suggest that early caregiving experiences—a central component of working models—shape adult attachment patterns in friendships and romantic relationships, supporting the idea that a stable, latent pattern of attachment endures from infancy through adulthood (cf. Simpson, Collins, Tran, & Haydon, 2007).

Theorists (e.g., Bowlby, 1973; Fraley, 2002; Fraley & Brumbaugh, 2004; Mikulincer & Shaver, 2007; Sroufe et al., 1990; Waters et al., 2003) have also acknowledged the possibility that change in attachment style occurs through experiences that challenge existing attachment representations. These experiences could include negative interactions (e.g., involving rejection, criticism) or relationship dissolution for secure individuals and positive interactions (e.g., involving acceptance, support) or maintaining a satisfying relationship for insecure individuals (e.g., Mikulincer & Shaver, 2007). In fact, Bowlby's (1988) model of therapeutic change assumes that insecure attachment representations can be revised in adulthood through the therapist–patient relationship, and related clinical interventions explicitly target attachment-related beliefs and behaviors in couples (e.g., emotionally focused therapy; e.g., Johnson, 2004). These ideas raise the provocative question of whether relationship partners can shape one another's attachment style over time in adulthood.

A few studies have examined the possibility that experiences with relationship partners can challenge existing attachment representations and, in turn, change people's attachment orientations. Some work has suggested that attachment-related life transitions—such as initiating a new romantic relationship, dissolving an existing romantic relationship, or becoming a parent—can produce changes in one's attachment style. For example, longitudinal research on dating couples has found that relationship problems or break-ups lead to lower levels of attachment security (e.g., Kirkpatrick & Hazan, 1994; Ruvolo, Fabin, & Ruvolo, 2001), whereas the initiation (e.g., Kirkpatrick & Hazan, 1994) or maintenance of a romantic relationship (Ruvolo et al., 2001) leads to higher levels of attachment security. Similarly, longitudinal studies of newlyweds have shown that people generally become more secure as they transition to marriage (Crowell et al., 2002; Davila et al., 1999). Other work, however, has not found links between attachment-related experiences and attachment style change (Davila & Cobb, 2003; Davila et al., 1997; Scharfe & Bartholomew, 1994).

Davila and Cobb (2004) suggested that people's subjective perceptions of attachment-related events may underlie the inconsistencies in studies of attachment change. They argued that whether a given experience influences attachment representations may depend on whether people perceive that experience as challenging their working models of attachment. Recent research has provided preliminary support for this perspective; for example, newlyweds became more secure over time when they perceived their marriage as satisfying (Davila et al., 1999). Furthermore, a longitudinal study of the transition to parenthood (Simpson, Rholes,

Campbell, & Wilson, 2003) found associations between changes in attachment style and spouses' perceptions of support. Wives became more anxiously attached during the transition to parenthood when they perceived their husbands as less supportive and more rejecting during pregnancy, whereas wives became more avoidant when they sought less support during pregnancy and when their husbands were more avoidant. In contrast, husbands became less avoidant when they perceived themselves as giving more support to their wives during pregnancy. Taken together, these findings suggest that attachment-related experiences may work through subjective perceptions of events to produce attachment style change. Additional prospective longitudinal studies that assess partners' attachment orientations and subjective perceptions at multiple time points will help shed light on whether relationship partners shape one another's attachment style over time.

Interconnections Among Attachment Style, Temperament, and Personality

A persistent question is whether links among attachment style, affect regulation, and relationship processes could be explained by associated temperament, personality, and genetic factors. In the developmental literature, this issue has been a long-standing source of controversy, but the evidence has generally suggested that temperament and attachment are not identical (see Mikulincer & Shaver, 2007; Vaughn & Shin, 2011). Similarly, in adults, attachment dimensions have been associated with personality traits such as the Big Five factors (e.g., Brennan & Shaver, 1992; Noftle & Shaver, 2006; see Mikulincer & Shaver, 2007), which are assumed to reflect underlying temperamental or genetic predispositions (e.g., Loehlin, McCrae, Costa, & John, 1998) and genetic influences (e.g., Donnellan, Burt, Levendosky, & Klump, 2008; Gillath, Shaver, Baek, & Chun, 2008). Anxious attachment is moderately associated with greater neuroticism (a tendency to experience negative emotions), and avoidance is associated with less extraversion and conscientiousness, although the magnitude of these associations is typically small (e.g., Noftle & Shaver, 2006). When adult attachment researchers have controlled for personality variables such as neuroticism, attachment dimensions have remained significant predictors of relationship-related outcomes (e.g., stability of attachment representations [Fraley et al., 2011], relationship quality [Noftle & Shaver, 2006], attachment-related memory biases [Simpson et al., 2010], perceived support and depression [Simpson, Rholes, Campbell, Tran, & Wilson, 2003]), suggesting that broad personality factors are not redundant with adult attachment style.

Although controlling for temperament and personality variables offers some assurance that attachment style produces unique effects, little work in the adult literature has investigated how temperament and personality might modulate the links between attachment style and relationship processes and outcomes. The developmental literature has suggested that temperament may create a contextual push toward attachment security or insecurity; for example, infants with more difficult temperaments (e.g., high irritability) appear more likely to become insecurely attached when they live under adverse conditions (i.e., under economic strain; see Susman-Stillman, Kalkose, Egeland, & Waldman, 1996). Temperament can also interact with attachment, as illustrated by findings that infants with a fearful temperament experience heightened cortisol reactivity to stress only when they are also insecurely attached (Gunnar, Brodersen, Nachmias, Buss, & Rigatuso, 1996). Furthermore, temperament and environments may interact such that some people may fare poorly under adverse conditions but blossom under beneficial ones; the differential susceptibility hypothesis suggests that children with difficult temperaments may be more likely to develop insecure attachments under adverse conditions, but they may also be more likely to become securely attached under favorable conditions (Belsky & Pluess, 2009).

Few studies in the adult attachment literature, however, have explored how temperament might interact with either contextual factors (e.g., stressful circumstances, partner characteristics) or individuals' attachment style in ways that influence individual and relationship outcomes (but see Laurent & Powers, 2007). Little theory exists on how adult

attachment and temperament might interact to predict such outcomes. For example, anxious attachment combined with high neuroticism may be associated with quite different reactions to relationship conflict (e.g., greater emotional intensity, hostility) than anxious attachment combined with low neuroticism. Another possibility is that secure attachment protects individuals from the negative psychological and interpersonal outcomes that accompany high neuroticism (e.g., Donnellan, Assad, Robins, & Conger, 2007). In addition, the notion of differential susceptibility (Belsky & Pluess, 2009) suggests that people who are temperamentally more susceptible to environmental influences, both good and bad, may be those most likely to benefit from a relationship with a secure romantic partner or from interventions to enhance security (e.g., Carnelley & Rowe, 2007), but this intriguing idea has yet to be examined in adults. Research that considers the joint effects of attachment and temperament or personality across both adverse and beneficial situations will enhance our understanding of the complex interplay among environmental, biological, and genetic factors in attachment processes in adulthood.

Attachment and Health

A wealth of evidence has indicated that being in a supportive relationship predicts better health (e.g., Cohen, 2004; Uchino, 2009) and that the lack of close relationships is associated with an increased risk of mortality from cardiovascular and other diseases (see Holt-Lunstad, Smith, & Layton, 2010). Much more needs to be known, however, about the processes through which close relationships translate into better or worse health outcomes, and attachment theory offers a highly relevant and rich framework for generating hypotheses to address this gap (see Pietromonaco et al., 2013). Despite the relevance of attachment theory for understanding the link between relationships and health, little is known about how attachment processes in adult relationships might contribute to physical health outcomes over the life course. Work so far has focused primarily on connections between individuals' attachment styles and their own health outcomes. For example, insecure attachment (anxiety, avoidance, or both) has been linked to risky health behaviors (e.g., drug use, risky sexual behavior, alcohol use, poor diet; Cooper et al., 1998; J. A. Feeney, Peterson, Gallois, & Terry, 2000), less adherence to treatment regimens (e.g., Ciechanowski, Katon, Russo, & Walker, 2001), and more problematic interactions with health care providers (e.g., Maunder et al., 2006; Noyes et al., 2003). Anxious attachment has been also associated with heightened reactions to experimentally induced pain (Wilson & Ruben, 2011) and poorer ability to cope with chronic pain (Meredith et al., 2006). In addition, recent longitudinal evidence has indicated that individuals who were classified as insecurely attached at age 12–18 months in the Strange Situation were more likely to experience health problems in their early 30s (i.e., 30 years later). It is important to note that these effects held even after the researchers statistically controlled for a variety of known predictors of health problems, such as participants' current body mass index, socioeconomic status, life stress, and perceived social support (Puig, Englund, Collins, & Simpson, 2013).

The next generation of studies on attachment and health needs to identify the mechanisms through which individuals' attachment orientations contribute to health outcomes or, as noted by Simpson and Rholes (2010), how attachment gets under the skin. Emerging work has suggested that adult attachment insecurity is associated with physiological responses that have been linked with poorer health outcomes, such as dysregulated HPA patterns in insecurely attached young adults (Brooks et al., 2011; Powers et al., 2006) and greater inflammatory responses to conflict in avoidant spouses (Gouin et al., 2009). Many questions remain, however, about the conditions under which these attachment-related physiological responses are most likely to influence health (e.g., responses to acute stress, diurnal response patterns), the patterns of those responses (e.g., whether responses are heightened vs. dampened), and what constellations of physiological markers (e.g., cortisol, oxytocin) and responses across different systems (e.g., HPA, autonomic nervous system) are associated with better or worse health outcomes (see Diamond & Fagundes, 2010). Furthermore, we are not aware of any work

that has shown that attachment style predicts physiological responses, which in turn lead to adverse health outcomes over time. Such mediation models need to be tested to establish whether attachment patterns predict longer term health outcomes through physiological mechanisms (e.g., through HPA dysregulation). Additionally, we need to understand whether physiological changes that may occur as a function of early relationship experiences (e.g., Repetti, Taylor, & Seeman, 2002; Taylor, Lerner, Sage, Lehman, & Seeman, 2004) also shape physiological responses in adult relationships, whether physiological changes resulting from early experiences can be modulated by later relationship experiences (e.g., a relationship with a secure partner), and how physiological response patterns linked to both early and later relationship experiences contribute to health and disease outcomes.

Most research on attachment and physical health has emphasized attachment as an individual difference variable detached from the relationship context, offering little insight into how attachment processes within dyadic relationships might influence health and disease outcomes over time. The affect regulation functions of attachment relationships suggest that how partners respond to each other will be critical in understanding connections between attachment and health. For example, do security-enhancing interactions with a romantic partner reduce health risks for cardiovascular disease, cancer, or diabetes, and if so, how? Do such interactions increase the likelihood that individuals can initiate and sustain difficult behavioral changes (e.g., losing weight, quitting smoking), follow challenging medical regimens (e.g., diabetes care), or cope with a chronic and potentially life-threatening disease such as cancer? And how are these processes affected by the attachment orientations of each partner or by the combination of attachment styles within a couple (e.g., a secure–secure pair or an anxious–avoidant pair)?

In particular, questions about whether and how romantic partners influence each other's physiological responses need to be considered, given the possible mediating role of physiological processes in the link between attachment and health. For example, some theorists have argued that coregulation, defined as the dynamic, reciprocal maintenance of psychophysiological homeostasis or equilibrium between partners, is an essential feature of attachment relationships (e.g., Butler & Randall, 2013; Diamond, 2001; Sbarra & Hazan, 2008). Research on coregulation in adult relationships is just beginning (e.g., Diamond et al., 2008), and we need to understand how these processes operate at the normative level in adult romantic relationships as well as how they may be moderated by individual (and couple) differences in attachment style. If partners regularly influence each other's physiological responses (e.g., cortisol levels, immune functioning), then we will need to ask how their interconnected physiological patterns predict health risks for each partner as well as health and disease outcomes over time.

CONCLUSION

Our overview of the large and growing literature on adult romantic attachment indicates that attachment-related processes, including affective, cognitive, motivational, and support processes, operate in the interest of managing distress and restoring feelings of security. Furthermore, these processes contribute to and shape a variety of relationship processes, from relationship initiation to breakup. Knowledge about attachment processes in romantic relationships has progressed significantly on both theoretical and empirical fronts since Hazan and Shaver's (1987) original extension of Bowlby's (1969, 1973, 1979, 1980) attachment theory. Our goal in evaluating this literature was to identify several emerging themes that will lead to further innovative and exciting research. We have suggested several future directions that we believe will enhance knowledge about attachment processes in romantic relationships: (a) emphasizing the interplay between individuals' working models and situational activators (taking a person-in-context approach), (b) further elaborating the conditions under which partners influence each other's attachment representations, (c) exploring interactions between attachment and temperament or personality, and (d) examining how attachment processes might influence couple members' health-related processes and outcomes.

Research addressing these issues will help us better understand how attachment processes in romantic relationships contribute to people's long-term emotional and physical health and well-being.

References

Ainsworth, M. S. (1989). Attachments beyond infancy. *American Psychologist, 44,* 709–716. doi:10.1037/0003-066X.44.4.709

Ainsworth, M. S., Blehar, M. C., Waters, E., & Wall, S. (1978). *Patterns of attachment: A psychological study of the strange situation.* Hillsdale, NJ: Erlbaum.

Altman, I., & Taylor, D. A. (1973). *Social penetration: The development of interpersonal relationships.* New York, NY: Holt, Rinehart, & Winston.

Amir, M., Horesh, N., & Lin-Stein, T. (1999). Infertility and adjustment in women: The effects of attachment style and social support. *Journal of Clinical Psychology in Medical Settings, 6,* 463–479. doi:10.1023/A:1026280017092

Aspelmeier, J. E., & Kerns, K. A. (2003). Love and school: Attachment/exploration dynamics in college. *Journal of Social and Personal Relationships, 20,* 5–30.

Baldwin, M. W., & Fehr, B. (1995). On the instability of attachment style ratings. *Personal Relationships, 2,* 247–261. doi:10.1111/j.1475-6811.1995.tb00090.x

Bartholomew, K., & Horowitz, L. M. (1991). Attachment styles among young adults: A test of a four-category model. *Journal of Personality and Social Psychology, 61,* 226–244. doi:10.1037/0022-3514.61.2.226

Beck, L. A., & Clark, M. S. (2009). Choosing to enter or avoid diagnostic social situations. *Psychological Science, 20,* 1175–1181. doi:10.1111/j.1467-9280.2009.02420.x

Beck, L. A., & Clark, M. S. (2010). What constitutes a healthy communal marriage and why relationship stage matters. *Journal of Family Theory and Review, 2,* 299–315. doi:10.1111/j.1756-2589.2010.00063.x

Beck, L. A., Pietromonaco, P. R., DeBuse, C. J., Powers, S. I., & Sayer, A. G. (2013). Spouses' attachment pairings predict neuroendocrine, behavioral, and psychological responses to marital conflict. *Journal of Personality and Social Psychology, 105,* 388–424. doi:10.1037/a0033056

Beck, L. A., Pietromonaco, P. R., DeVito, C. C., Powers, S. I., & Boyle, A. M. (2013). Congruence between spouses' perceptions and observers' ratings of responsiveness: The role of attachment avoidance. *Personality and Social Psychology Bulletin.* Advance online publication. doi:10.1177/0146167213507779

Beckes, L., Simpson, J. A., & Erickson, A. (2010). Of snakes and succor: Learning secure attachment associations with novel faces via negative stimulus pairings. *Psychological Science, 21*, 721–728. doi:10.1177/0956797610368061

Belsky, J., & Pluess, M. (2009). Beyond diathesis stress: Differential susceptibility to environmental influences. *Psychological Bulletin, 135*, 885–908. doi:10.1037/a0017376

Berant, E., Mikulincer, M., & Shaver, P. R. (2008). Mothers' attachment style, their mental health, and their children's emotional vulnerabilities: A 7-year study of children with congenital heart disease. *Journal of Personality, 76*, 31–66. doi:10.1111/j.1467-6494.2007.00479.x

Bhattacharyya, M. R., Molloy, G. J., & Steptoe, A. (2008). Depression is associated with flatter cortisol rhythms in patients with coronary artery disease. *Journal of Psychosomatic Research, 65*, 107–113. doi:10.1016/j.jpsychores.2008.03.012

Birnbaum, G. E., Orr, I., Mikulincer, M., & Florian, V. (1997). When marriage breaks up: Does attachment style contribute to coping and mental health? *Journal of Social and Personal Relationships, 14*, 643–654. doi:10.1177/0265407597145004

Birnie, C., McClure, M. J., Lydon, J. E., & Holmberg, D. (2009). Attachment avoidance and commitment aversion: A script for relationship failure. *Personal Relationships, 16*, 79–97. doi:10.1111/j.1475-6811.2009.01211.x

Bowlby, J. (1969). *Attachment and loss: Vol. 1. Attachment.* New York, NY: Basic Books.

Bowlby, J. (1973). *Attachment and loss: Vol. 2. Separation: Anxiety and anger.* New York, NY: Basic Books.

Bowlby, J. (1979). *The making and breaking of affectional bonds.* London, England: Tavistock.

Bowlby, J. (1980). *Attachment and loss: Vol. 3. Sadness and depression.* New York, NY: Basic Books.

Bowlby, J. (1988). *A secure base: Clinical applications of attachment theory.* London, England: Routledge.

Bradford, S. A., Feeney, J. A., & Campbell, L. (2002). Links between attachment orientations and dispositional and diary-based measures of disclosure in dating couples: A study of actor and partner effects. *Personal Relationships, 9*, 491–506. doi:10.1111/1475-6811.00031

Bretherton, I. (1985). Attachment theory: Retrospect and prospect. *Monographs of the Society for Research in Child Development, 50*, 3–35. doi:10.2307/3333824

Bretherton, I. (1990). Open communication and internal working models: Their role in the development of attachment relationships. In R. A. Thompson (Ed.), *Nebraska Symposium on Motivation* (Vol. 36, pp. 57–113). Lincoln: University of Nebraska Press.

Brooks, K. P., Robles, T. F., & Dunkel Schetter, C. (2011). Adult attachment and cortisol responses to discussions with a romantic partner. *Personal Relationships, 18*, 302–320. doi:10.1111/j.1475-6811.2011.01357.x

Brumbaugh, C. C., & Fraley, R. C. (2006). Transference and attachment: How do attachment patterns get carried forward from one relationship to the next? *Personality and Social Psychology Bulletin, 32*, 552–560. doi:10.1177/0146167205282740

Brumbaugh, C. C., & Fraley, R. C. (2010). Adult attachment and dating strategies: How do insecure people attract mates? *Personal Relationships, 17*, 599–614. doi:10.1111/j.1475-6811.2010.01304.x

Butler, E. A., & Randall, A. K. (2013). Emotional coregulation in close relationships. *Emotion Review, 5*, 202–210.

Campbell, L., Simpson, J. A., Boldry, J., & Kashy, D. A. (2005). Perceptions of conflict and support in romantic relationships: The role of attachment anxiety. *Journal of Personality and Social Psychology, 88*, 510–531. doi:10.1037/0022-3514.88.3.510

Carnelley, K. B., Pietromonaco, P. R., & Jaffe, K. (1994). Depression, working models of others, and relationship functioning. *Journal of Personality and Social Psychology, 66*, 127–140. doi:10.1037/0022-3514.66.1.127

Carnelley, K. B., Pietromonaco, P. R., & Jaffe, K. (1996). Attachment, caregiving, and relationship functioning in couples: Effects of self and partner. *Personal Relationships, 3*, 257–278. doi:10.1111/j.1475-6811.1996.tb00116.x

Carnelley, K. B., & Rowe, A. C. (2007). Repeated priming of attachment security influences later views of self and relationships. *Personal Relationships, 14*, 307–320. doi:10.1111/j.1475-6811.2007.00156.x

Carpenter, E. M., & Kirkpatrick, L. A. (1996). Attachment style and presence of a romantic partner as moderators of psychophysiological responses to a stressful laboratory situation. *Personal Relationships, 3*, 351–367. doi:10.1111/j.1475-6811.1996.tb00121.x

Carter, C. S. (1998). Neuroendocrine perspectives on social attachment and love. *Psychoneuroendocrinology, 23*, 779–818. doi:10.1016/S0306-4530(98)00055-9

Cassidy, J., Shaver, P. R., Mikulincer, M., & Lavy, S. (2009). Experimentally induced security influences responses to psychological pain. *Journal of Social and Clinical Psychology, 28*, 463–478. doi:10.1521/jscp.2009.28.4.463

Chappell, K. D., & Davis, K. E. (1998). Attachment, partner choice, and perception of romantic partners: An experimental test of the attachment-security hypothesis. *Personal Relationships, 5*, 327–342. doi:10.1111/j.1475-6811.1998.tb00175.x

Ciechanowski, P. S., Katon, W. J., Russo, J. E., & Walker, E. A. (2001). The patient-provider relationship: Attachment theory and adherence to treatment in diabetes. *American Journal of Psychiatry, 158*, 29–35. doi:10.1176/appi.ajp.158.1.29

Clark, M. S., & Beck, L. A. (2011). Initiating and evaluating close relationships: A task central to emerging adults. In F. D. Fincham & M. Cui (Eds.), *Romantic relationships in emerging adulthood* (pp. 190–212). New York, NY: Cambridge University Press.

Cohen, S. (2004). Social relationships and health. *American Psychologist, 59,* 676–684. doi:10.1037/0003-066X.59.8.676

Collins, N. L. (1996). Working models of attachment: Implications for explanation, emotion, and behavior. *Journal of Personality and Social Psychology, 71,* 810–832. doi:10.1037/0022-3514.71.4.810

Collins, N. L., & Feeney, B. C. (2000). A safe haven: An attachment theoretical perspective on support seeking and caregiving in intimate relationships. *Journal of Personality and Social Psychology, 78,* 1053–1073. doi:10.1037/0022-3514.78.6.1053

Collins, N. L., & Feeney, B. C. (2004). Working models of attachment shape perceptions of social support: Evidence from experimental and observational studies. *Journal of Personality and Social Psychology, 87,* 363–383. doi:10.1037/0022-3514.87.3.363

Collins, N. L., & Feeney, B. C. (2010). An attachment theoretical perspective on social support dynamics in couples: Normative processes and individual differences. In K. Sullivan & J. Davila (Eds.), *Support processes in intimate relationships* (pp. 89–120). New York, NY: Oxford University Press. doi:10.1093/acprof:oso/9780195380170.003.0004

Collins, N. L., Ford, M. B., Guichard, A. C., & Allard, L. M. (2006). Working models of attachment and attribution processes in intimate relationships. *Personality and Social Psychology Bulletin, 32,* 201–219. doi:10.1177/0146167205280907

Collins, N. L., Guichard, A. C., Ford, M. B., & Feeney, B. C. (2004). Working models of attachment: New developments and emerging themes. In W. S. Rholes & J. A. Simpson (Eds.), *Adult attachment: Theory, research, and clinical implications* (pp. 196–239). New York, NY: Guilford Press.

Collins, N. L., & Read, S. J. (1990). Adult attachment, working models and relationship quality in dating couples. *Journal of Personality and Social Psychology, 58,* 644–663. doi:10.1037/0022-3514.58.4.644

Cooper, M. L., Shaver, P. R., & Collins, N. L. (1998). Attachment styles, emotion regulation, and adjustment in adolescence. *Journal of Personality and Social Psychology, 74,* 1380–1397. doi:10.1037/0022-3514.74.5.1380

Crowell, J., & Treboux, D. (2001). Attachment security in adult partnerships. In C. Clulow (Ed.), *Adult attachment and couple psychotherapy: The "secure base" in practice and research* (pp. 28–42). New York, NY: Brunner-Routledge.

Crowell, J. A., Treboux, D., & Waters, E. (2002). Stability of attachment representations: The transition to marriage. *Developmental Psychology, 38,* 467–479. doi:10.1037/0012-1649.38.4.467

Davila, J. (2001). Refining the association between excessive reassurance seeking and depressive symptoms: The role of related interpersonal constructs. *Journal of Social and Clinical Psychology, 20,* 538–559. doi:10.1521/jscp.20.4.538.22394

Davila, J., & Bradbury, T. N. (2001). Attachment insecurity and the distinction between unhappy spouses who do and do not divorce. *Journal of Family Psychology, 15,* 371–393. doi:10.1037/0893-3200.15.3.371

Davila, J., Burge, D., & Hammen, C. (1997). Why does attachment style change? *Journal of Personality and Social Psychology, 73,* 826–838. doi:10.1037/0022-3514.73.4.826

Davila, J., & Cobb, R. J. (2003). Predicting change in self-reported and interviewer-assessed adult attachment: Tests of the individual difference and life stress models of attachment change. *Personality and Social Psychology Bulletin, 29,* 859–870. doi:10.1177/0146167203029007005

Davila, J., & Cobb, R. J. (2004). Predictors of change in attachment security during adulthood. In W. S. Rholes & J. A. Simpson (Eds.), *Adult attachment: Theory, research, and clinical implications* (pp. 133–156). New York, NY: Guilford Press.

Davila, J., Karney, B. R., & Bradbury, T. N. (1999). Attachment change processes in the early years of marriage. *Journal of Personality and Social Psychology, 76,* 783–802. doi:10.1037/0022-3514.76.5.783

Davis, D., Shaver, P. R., & Vernon, M. L. (2003). Physical, emotional, and behavioral reactions to breaking up: The roles of gender, age, emotional involvement, and attachment style. *Personality and Social Psychology Bulletin, 29,* 871–884. doi:10.1177/0146167203029007006

Davis, D., Shaver, P. R., & Vernon, M. L. (2004). Attachment style and subjective motivations for sex. *Personality and Social Psychology Bulletin, 30,* 1076–1090. doi:10.1177/0146167204264794

Dewitte, M. (2011). Adult attachment and attentional inhibition of interpersonal stimuli. *Cognition and Emotion, 25,* 612–625. doi:10.1080/02699931.2010.508683

Dewitte, M., De Houwer, J., Koster, E. H. W., & Buysse, A. (2007). What's in a name? Attachment-related attentional bias. *Emotion, 7,* 535–545. doi:10.1037/1528-3542.7.3.535

Dewitte, M., Koster, E. H. W., De Houwer, J., & Buysse, A. (2007). Attentive processing of threat and adult attachment. *Behaviour Research and Therapy, 45,* 1307–1317. doi:10.1016/j.brat.2006.11.004

Diamond, L. (2001). Contributions of psychophysiology to research on adult attachment: Review and recommendations. *Personality and Social Psychology Review, 5,* 276–295. doi:10.1207/S15327957PSPR0504_1

Diamond, L. M., & Fagundes, C. P. (2010). Psychobiological research on attachment. *Journal of Social and Personal Relationships, 27,* 218–225. doi:10.1177/0265407509360906

Diamond, L. M., Hicks, A. M., & Otter-Henderson, K. D. (2008). Every time you go away: Changes in affect, behavior, and physiology associated with travel-related separations from romantic partners. *Journal of Personality and Social Psychology, 95,* 385–403. doi:10.1037/0022-3514.95.2.385

Doherty, N. A., & Feeney, J. A. (2004). The composition of attachment networks throughout the adult years. *Personal Relationships, 11,* 469–488. doi:10.1111/j.1475-6811.2004.00093.x

Donnellan, M. B., Assad, K. K., Robins, R. W., & Conger, R. D. (2007). Do negative interactions mediate the effects of negative emotionality, communal positive emotionality, and constraint on relationship satisfaction? *Journal of Social and Personal Relationships, 24,* 557–573. doi:10.1177/0265407507079249

Donnellan, M. B., Burt, S. A., Levendosky, A. A., & Klump, K. L. (2008). Genes, personality, and attachment in adults: A multivariate behavioral genetic analysis. *Personality and Social Psychology Bulletin, 34,* 3–16. doi:10.1177/0146167207309199

Duemmler, S. L., & Kobak, R. (2001). The development of commitment and attachment in dating relationships: Attachment security as relationship construct. *Journal of Adolescence, 24,* 401–415. doi:10.1006/jado.2001.0406

Dutton, D. G., Saunders, K., Starzomski, A. J., & Bartholomew, K. (1994). Intimacy-anger and insecure attachment as precursors of abuse in intimate relationships. *Journal of Applied Social Psychology, 24,* 1367–1386. doi:10.1111/j.1559-1816.1994.tb01554.x

Dykas, M. J., & Cassidy, J. (2011). Attachment and the processing of social information across the life span. *Psychological Bulletin, 137,* 19–46. doi:10.1037/a0021367

Eastwick, P. W., & Finkel, E. J. (2008). The attachment system in fledgling relationships: An activating role for attachment anxiety. *Journal of Personality and Social Psychology, 95,* 628–647. doi:10.1037/0022-3514.95.3.628

Eberhart, N. K., & Hammen, C. L. (2009). Interpersonal predictors of stress generation. *Personality and Social Psychology Bulletin, 35,* 544–556. doi:10.1177/0146167208329857

Edelstein, R. S. (2006). Attachment and emotional memory: Investigating the source and extent of avoidant memory deficits. *Emotion, 6,* 340–345. doi:10.1037/1528-3542.6.2.340

Edelstein, R. S., & Gillath, O. (2008). Avoiding interference: Adult attachment and emotional processing biases. *Personality and Social Psychology Bulletin, 34,* 171–181. doi:10.1177/0146167207310024

Ein-Dor, T., Mikulincer, M., & Shaver, P. R. (2011). Attachment insecurities and the processing of threat-related information: Studying the schemas involved in insecure people's coping strategies. *Journal of Personality and Social Psychology, 101,* 78–93. doi:10.1037/a0022503

Feeney, B. C., & Collins, N. L. (2001). Predictors of caregiving in adult intimate relationships: An attachment theoretical perspective. *Journal of Personality and Social Psychology, 80,* 972–994. doi:10.1037/0022-3514.80.6.972

Feeney, B. C., & Kirkpatrick, L. A. (1996). The effects of adult attachment and presence of romantic partners on physiological responses to stress. *Journal of Personality and Social Psychology, 70,* 255–270. doi:10.1037/0022-3514.70.2.255

Feeney, J. A. (1999). Issues of closeness and distance in dating relationships: Effects of sex and attachment style. *Journal of Social and Personal Relationships, 16,* 571–590. doi:10.1177/0265407599165002

Feeney, J. A. (2002). Attachment, marital interaction, and relationship satisfaction: A diary study. *Personal Relationships, 9,* 39–55. doi:10.1111/1475-6811.00003

Feeney, J. A., & Noller, P. (1990). Attachment style as a predictor of adult romantic relationships. *Journal of Personality and Social Psychology, 58,* 281–291. doi:10.1037/0022-3514.58.2.281

Feeney, J. A., & Noller, P. (1991). Attachment style and verbal descriptions of romantic partners. *Journal of Social and Personal Relationships, 8,* 187–215. doi:10.1177/0265407591082003

Feeney, J. A., & Noller, P. (1992). Attachment style and romantic love: Relationship dissolution. *Australian Journal of Psychology, 44,* 69–74. doi:10.1080/00049539208260145

Feeney, J. A., Peterson, C., Gallois, C., & Terry, D. J. (2000). Attachment style as a predictor of sexual attitudes and behavior in late adolescence. *Psychology and Health, 14,* 1105–1122. doi:10.1080/08870440008407370

Feeney, J. A., & Ryan, S. M. (1994). Attachment style and affect regulation: Relationships with health behavior and family experiences of illness in a student sample. *Health Psychology, 13,* 334–345. doi:10.1037/0278-6133.13.4.334

Fraley, R. C. (2002). Attachment stability from infancy to adulthood: Meta-analysis and dynamic modeling of developmental mechanisms. *Personality and Social Psychology Review, 6,* 123–151. doi:10.1207/S15327957PSPR0602_03

Fraley, R. C., & Brumbaugh, C. C. (2004). A dynamical systems approach to understanding stability and change in attachment security. In W. S. Rholes & J. A. Simpson (Eds.), *Adult attachment: Theory, research, and clinical implications* (pp. 86–132). New York, NY: Guilford Press.

Fraley, R. C., & Brumbaugh, C. C. (2007). Adult attachment and preemptive defenses: Converging evidence on the role of defensive exclusion at the level of encoding. *Journal of Personality, 75,* 1033–1050. doi:10.1111/j.1467-6494.2007.00465.x

Fraley, R. C., Garner, J. P., & Shaver, P. R. (2000). Adult attachment and the defensive regulation of attention and memory: Examining the role of preemptive and postemptive defensive processes. *Journal of Personality and Social Psychology, 79,* 816–826. doi:10.1037/0022-3514.79.5.816

Fraley, R. C., Niedenthal, P. M., Marks, M. J., Brumbaugh, C. C., & Vicary, A. (2006). Adult attachment and the perception of emotional expressions: Probing the hyperactivating strategies underlying anxious attachment. *Journal of Personality, 74,* 1163–1190. doi:10.1111/j.1467-6494.2006.00406.x

Fraley, R. C., & Shaver, P. R. (1997). Adult attachment and the suppression of unwanted thoughts. *Journal of Personality and Social Psychology, 73,* 1080–1091. doi:10.1037/0022-3514.73.5.1080

Fraley, R. C., & Shaver, P. R. (1998). Airport separations: A naturalistic study of adult attachment dynamics in separating couples. *Journal of Personality and Social Psychology, 75,* 1198–1212. doi:10.1037/0022-3514.75.5.1198

Fraley, R. C., & Shaver, P. R. (1999). Loss and bereavement: Attachment theory and recent controversies concerning "grief work" and the nature of detachment. In J. Cassidy & P. R. Shaver (Eds.), *Handbook of attachment: Theory, research, and clinical applications* (pp. 735–759). New York, NY: Guilford Press.

Fraley, R. C., & Shaver, P. R. (2000). Adult romantic attachment: Theoretical developments, emerging controversies, and unanswered questions. *Review of General Psychology, 4,* 132–154. doi:10.1037/1089-2680.4.2.132

Fraley, R. C., Vicary, A. M., Brumbaugh, C. C., & Roisman, G. I. (2011). Patterns of stability in adult attachment: An empirical test of two models of continuity and change. *Journal of Personality and Social Psychology, 101,* 974–992. doi:10.1037/a0024150

Fraley, R. C., Waller, N. G., & Brennan, K. A. (2000). An item response theory analysis of self-report measures of adult attachment. *Journal of Personality and Social Psychology, 78,* 350–365. doi:10.1037/0022-3514.78.2.350

Frazier, P. A., Byer, A. L., Fischer, A. R., Wright, D. M., & DeBord, K. A. (1996). Adult attachment style and partner choice: Correlational and experimental findings. *Personal Relationships, 3,* 117–136. doi:10.1111/j.1475-6811.1996.tb00107.x

Gallo, L. C., & Smith, T. W. (2001). Attachment style in marriage: Adjustment and responses to interaction. *Journal of Social and Personal Relationships, 18,* 263–289. doi:10.1177/0265407501182006

Gillath, O., Mikulincer, M., Fitzsimons, G. M., Shaver, P. R., Schachner, D. A., & Bargh, J. A. (2006). Automatic activation of attachment-related goals. *Personality and Social Psychology Bulletin, 32,* 1375–1388. doi:10.1177/0146167206290339

Gillath, O., Shaver, P. R., Baek, J.-M., & Chun, D. S. (2008). Genetic correlates of adult attachment style. *Personality and Social Psychology Bulletin, 34,* 1396–1405. doi:10.1177/0146167208321484

Gouin, J.-P., Glaser, R., Loving, T. J., Malarkey, W. B., Stowell, J., Houts, C., & Kiecolt-Glaser, J. (2009). Attachment avoidance predicts inflammatory responses to marital conflict. *Brain, Behavior, and Immunity, 23,* 898–904. doi:10.1016/j.bbi.2008.09.016

Grabill, C. M., & Kerns, K. A. (2000). Attachment style and intimacy in friendship. *Personal Relationships, 7,* 363–378. doi:10.1111/j.1475-6811.2000.tb00022.x

Gunnar, M. R., Brodersen, L., Nachmias, M., Buss, K., & Rigatuso, J. (1996). Stress reactivity and attachment security. *Developmental Psychobiology, 29,* 191–204. doi:10.1002/(SICI)1098-2302(199604)29:3<191::AID-DEV1>3.0.CO;2-M

Hazan, C., & Shaver, P. (1987). Romantic love conceptualized as an attachment process. *Journal of Personality and Social Psychology, 52,* 511–524. doi:10.1037/0022-3514.52.3.511

Hazan, C., & Zeifman, D. (1994). Sex and the psychological tether. In D. Perlman & K. Bartholomew (Eds.), *Advances in personal relationships* (Vol. 5, pp. 151–180). London, England: Jessica Kingsley.

Hesse, E. (1999). The Adult Attachment Interview: Historical and current perspectives. In J. Cassidy & P. R. Shaver (Eds.), *Handbook of attachment: Theory, research, and clinical applications* (pp. 395–433). New York, NY: Guilford Press.

Hill, E. M., Young, J. P., & Nord, J. L. (1994). Childhood adversity, attachment, security, and adult relationships: A preliminary study. *Ethology and Sociobiology, 15,* 323–338. doi:10.1016/0162-3095(94)90006-X

Holt-Lunstad, J., Smith, T. B., & Layton, B. (2010). Social relationships and mortality: A meta-analysis. *PLoS Medicine, 7,* e1000316. doi:10.1371/journal.pmed.1000316

Hsiao, F.-H., Yang, T.-T., Ho, R. T. H., Jow, G.-M., Ng, S.-M., Chan, C. L. W., . . . Wang, K.-C. (2010). The self-perceived symptom distress and health-related conditions associated with morning to evening diurnal cortisol patterns in outpatients with major depressive disorder. *Psychoneuroendocrinology, 35,* 503–515. doi:10.1016/j.psyneuen.2009.08.019

Impett, E. A., & Gordon, A. M. (2010). Why do people sacrifice to approach rewards versus to avoid costs? Insights from attachment theory. *Personal Relationships, 17,* 299–315. doi:10.1111/j.1475-6811.2010.01277.x

Impett, E. A., Gordon, A. M., & Strachman, A. (2008). Attachment and daily sexual goals: A study of dating couples. *Personal Relationships, 15*, 375–390. doi:10.1111/j.1475-6811.2008.00204.x

Johnson, S. M. (2004). *The practice of emotionally focused couple therapy: Creating connection* (2nd ed.). New York, NY: Brunner-Routledge.

Jones, J. T., & Cunningham, J. D. (1996). Attachment styles and other predictors of relationship satisfaction in dating couples. *Personal Relationships, 3*, 387–399. doi:10.1111/j.1475-6811.1996.tb00123.x

Kane, H. S., Jaremka, L. M., Guichard, A. C., Ford, M. B., Collins, N. L., & Feeney, B. C. (2007). Feeling supported and feeling satisfied: How one partner's attachment style predicts the other partner's relationship experiences. *Journal of Social and Personal Relationships, 24*, 535–555. doi:10.1177/0265407507079245

Keelan, J. P. R., Dion, K. K., & Dion, K. L. (1998). Attachment style and relationship satisfaction: Test of a self-disclosure explanation. *Canadian Journal of Behavioural Science, 30*, 24–35. doi:10.1037/h0087055

Keelan, J. P. R., Dion, K. L., & Dion, K. K. (1994). Attachment style and heterosexual relationships among young adults: A short-term panel study. *Journal of Social and Personal Relationships, 11*, 201–214. doi:10.1177/0265407594112003

Kiecolt-Glaser, J. K., Newton, T., Cacioppo, J. T., MacCallum, R. C., Glaser, R., & Malarkey, W. B. (1996). Marital conflict and endocrine function: Are men really more physiologically affected than women? *Journal of Consulting and Clinical Psychology, 64*, 324–332.

Kirkpatrick, L. A., & Davis, K. E. (1994). Attachment style, gender, and relationship stability: A longitudinal analysis. *Journal of Personality and Social Psychology, 66*, 502–512.

Kirkpatrick, L. A., & Hazan, C. (1994). Attachment styles and close relationships: A four-year prospective study. *Personal Relationships, 1*, 123–142.

Klohnen, E. C., & Bera, S. (1998). Behavioral and experiential patterns of avoidantly and securely attached women across adulthood: A 31-year longitudinal perspective. *Journal of Personality and Social Psychology, 74*, 211–223.

Klohnen, E. C., & Luo, S. (2003). Interpersonal attraction and personality: What is attractive—Self similarity, ideal similarity, complementarity, or attachment security? *Journal of Personality and Social Psychology, 85*, 709–722.

Latty-Mann, H., & Davis, K. E. (1996). Attachment theory and partner choice: Preference and actuality. *Journal of Social and Personal Relationships, 13*, 5–23.

Laurent, H., & Powers, S. (2007). Emotion regulation in emerging adult couples: Temperament, attachment, and HPA response to conflict. *Biological Psychology, 76*, 61–71.

Lewis, M., Feiring, C., & Rosenthal, S. (2000). Attachment over time. *Child Development, 71*, 707–720.

Loehlin, J. C., McCrae, R. R., Costa, P. T., & John, O. P. (1998). Heritabilities of common and measure-specific components of the Big Five personality factors. *Journal of Research in Personality, 32*, 431–453.

Maunder, R. G., Panzer, A., Viljoen, M., Owen, J., Human, S., & Hunter, J. J. (2006). Physicians' difficulty with emergency department patients is related to patients' attachment style. *Social Science and Medicine, 63*, 552–562.

Meredith, P., Strong, J., & Feeney, J. (2006). Adult attachment, anxiety, and pain self-efficacy as predictors of pain intensity and disability. *Pain, 123*, 146–154.

Mikulincer, M. (1998a). Adult attachment style and affect regulation: Strategic variations in self-appraisals. *Journal of Personality and Social Psychology, 75*, 420–435.

Mikulincer, M. (1998b). Adult attachment style and individual differences in functional versus dysfunctional experiences of anger. *Journal of Personality and Social Psychology, 74*, 513–524.

Mikulincer, M., Dolev, T., & Shaver, P. R. (2004). Attachment-related strategies during thought-suppression: Ironic rebounds and vulnerable self-representations. *Journal of Personality and Social Psychology, 87*, 940–956.

Mikulincer, M., & Erev, I. (1991). Attachment style and the structure of romantic love. *British Journal of Social Psychology, 30*, 273–291.

Mikulincer, M., Gillath, O., & Shaver, P. R. (2002). Activation of the attachment system in adulthood: Threat-related primes increase the accessibility of mental representations of attachment figures. *Journal of Personality and Social Psychology, 83*, 881–895.

Mikulincer, M., & Nachshon, O. (1991). Attachment styles and patterns of self-disclosure. *Journal of Personality and Social Psychology, 61*, 321–331.

Mikulincer, M., & Orbach, I. (1995). Attachment styles and repressive defensiveness: The accessibility and architecture of affective memories. *Journal of Personality and Social Psychology, 68*, 917–925.

Mikulincer, M., & Shaver, P. R. (2007). *Attachment in adulthood: Structure, dynamics, and change.* New York, NY: Guilford Press.

Mikulincer, M., Shaver, P. R., Bar-On, N., & Ein-Dor, T. (2010). The pushes and pulls of close relationships:

Attachment insecurities and relational ambivalence. *Journal of Personality and Social Psychology, 98,* 450–468.

Moller, N. P., Fouladi, R. T., McCarthy, C. J., & Hatch, K. D. (2003). Relationship of attachment and social support to college students' adjustment following a relationship breakup. *Journal of Counseling and Development, 81,* 354–369.

Moller, N. P., McCarthy, C. J., & Fouladi, R. T. (2002). Earned attachment security: Its relationship to coping resources and stress symptoms among college students following relationship breakup. *Journal of College Student Development, 43,* 213–230.

Morgan, H. J., & Shaver, P. R. (1999). Attachment processes and commitment to romantic relationships. In J. M. Adams & W. H. Jones (Eds.), *Handbook of interpersonal commitment and relationship stability* (pp. 109–124). Dordrecht, the Netherlands: Kluwer Academic.

Nelson, E. E., & Panksepp, J. (1998). Brain substrates of infant-mother attachment: Contributions of opioids, oxytocin, and norepinephrine. *Neuroscience and Biobehavioral Reviews, 22,* 437–452.

Noftle, E. E., & Shaver, P. R. (2006). Attachment dimensions and the Big Five personality traits: Associations and comparative ability to predict relationship quality. *Journal of Research in Personality, 40,* 179–208.

Noyes, R., Jr., Stuart, S. P., Langbehn, D. R., Happel, R. L., Longley, S. L., Muller, B. A., & Yagla, S. J. (2003). Test of an interpersonal model of hypochondriasis. *Psychosomatic Medicine, 65,* 292–300.

Pearce, Z. J., & Halford, W. K. (2008). Do attributions mediate the association between attachment and negative couple communication? *Personal Relationships, 15,* 155–170.

Pietromonaco, P. R., & Barrett, L. F. (1997). Working models of attachment and daily social interactions. *Journal of Personality and Social Psychology, 73,* 1409–1423.

Pietromonaco, P. R., & Barrett, L. F. (2000). Internal working models: What do we really know about the self in relation to others? *Review of General Psychology, 4,* 155–175.

Pietromonaco, P. R., & Barrett, L. F. (2006). What can you do for me? Attachment style and motives underlying esteem for partners. *Journal of Research in Personality, 40,* 313–338.

Pietromonaco, P. R., Barrett, L. F., & Powers, S. A. (2006). Adult attachment theory and affective reactivity and regulation. In J. Simpson, D. Snyder, & J. Hughes (Eds.), *Emotion regulation in families and close relationships: Pathways to dysfunction and health* (pp. 57–74). Washington, DC: American Psychological Association.

Pietromonaco, P. R., & Carnelley, K. B. (1994). Gender and working models of attachment: Consequences for perceptions of self and romantic relationships. *Personal Relationships, 1,* 63–82.

Pietromonaco, P. R., DeBuse, C. J., & Powers, S. I. (2013). Does attachment get under the skin? Adult romantic attachment and cortisol responses to stress. *Current Directions in Psychological Science, 22,* 63–68. doi:10.1177/0963721412463229

Pietromonaco, P. R., Uchino, B., & Dunkel Schetter, C. (2013). Close relationship processes and health: Implications of attachment theory for health and disease. *Health Psychology, 32,* 499–513.

Pistole, M. C. (1995). College students' ended love relationships: Attachment style and emotion. *Journal of College Student Development, 36,* 53–60.

Pistole, M. C., Clark, E. M., & Tubbs, A. L. (1995). Love relationships: Attachment style and the investment model. *Journal of Mental Health Counseling, 17,* 199–209.

Powers, S. I., Pietromonaco, P. R., Gunlicks, M., & Sayer, A. (2006). Dating couples' attachment styles and patterns of cortisol reactivity and recovery in response to a relationship conflict. *Journal of Personality and Social Psychology, 90,* 613–628.

Puig, J., Englund, M. M., Collins, W. A., & Simpson, J. A. (2013). Predicting adult physical illness from infant attachment: A prospective longitudinal study. *Health Psychology, 32,* 409–417.

Quirin, M., Pruessner, J. C., & Kuhl, J. (2008). HPA system regulation and adult attachment anxiety: Individual differences in reactive and awakening cortisol. *Psychoneuroendocrinology, 33,* 581–590.

Repetti, R. L., Taylor, S. E., & Seeman, T. E. (2002). Risky families: Family social environments and the mental and physical health of offspring. *Psychological Bulletin, 128,* 330–366.

Rholes, W. S., Simpson, J. A., Campbell, L., & Grich, J. (2001). Adult attachment and the transition to parenthood. *Journal of Personality and Social Psychology, 81,* 421–435.

Rholes, W. S., Simpson, J. A., Kohn, J. L., Wilson, C. L., Martin, A. M., Tran, S., & Kashy, D. A. (2011). Attachment orientations and depression: A longitudinal study of new parents. *Journal of Personality and Social Psychology, 100,* 567–586.

Rholes, W. S., Simpson, J. A., & Oriña, M. (1999). Attachment and anger in an anxiety-provoking situation. *Journal of Personality and Social Psychology, 76,* 940–957.

Rholes, W. S., Simpson, J. A., Tran, S., Martin, A. M., III, & Friedman, M. (2007). Attachment and information seeking in romantic relationships. *Personality and Social Psychology Bulletin, 33,* 422–438.

Ruvolo, A. P., Fabin, L. A., & Ruvolo, C. M. (2001). Relationship experiences and change in attachment characteristics of young adults: The role of relationship breakups and conflict avoidance. *Personal Relationships, 8,* 265–281.

Sadikaj, G., Moskowitz, D. S., & Zuroff, D. C. (2011). Attachment-related affective dynamics: Differential reactivity to others' interpersonal behavior. *Journal of Personality and Social Psychology, 100,* 905–917.

Sbarra, D. A. (2006). Predicting the onset of emotional recovery following nonmarital relationship dissolution: Survival analyses of sadness and anger. *Personality and Social Psychology Bulletin, 32,* 298–312.

Sbarra, D. A., & Emery, R. E. (2005). The emotional sequelae of nonmarital relationship dissolution: Analysis of change and intraindividual variability over time. *Personal Relationships, 12,* 213–232.

Sbarra, D. A., & Hazan, C. (2008). Coregulation, dysregulation, self-regulation: An integrative analysis and empirical agenda for understanding adult attachment, separation, loss, and recovery. *Personality and Social Psychology Review, 12,* 141–167.

Scharfe, E., & Bartholomew, K. (1994). Reliability and stability of adult attachment patterns. *Personal Relationships, 1,* 23–43.

Schindler, I., Fagundes, C. P., & Murdock, K. W. (2010). Predictors of romantic relationship formation: Attachment style, prior relationships, and dating goals. *Personal Relationships, 17,* 97–105.

Schore, A. N. (2001). Effects of a secure attachment relationship on right brain development, affect regulation, and infant mental health. *Infant Mental Health Journal, 22,* 7–66.

Senchak, M., & Leonard, K. E. (1992). Attachment styles and marital adjustment among newlywed couples. *Journal of Social and Personal Relationships, 9,* 51–64.

Shaver, P. R., & Brennan, K. A. (1992). Attachment styles and the "Big Five" personality traits: Their connections with each other and with romantic relationship outcomes. *Personality and Social Psychology Bulletin, 18,* 536–545.

Shaver, P. R., Schachner, D. A., & Mikulincer, M. (2005). Attachment style, excessive reassurance seeking, relationship processes, and depression. *Personality and Social Psychology Bulletin, 31,* 343–359.

Siegel, D. J. (2001). Toward an interpersonal neurobiology of the developing mind: Attachment, "mind sight," and neural integration. *Infant Mental Health Journal, 22,* 67–94.

Simpson, J. A. (1990). Influence of attachment styles on romantic relationships. *Journal of Personality and Social Psychology, 59,* 971–980.

Simpson, J. A., Collins, W. A., Tran, S., & Haydon, K. C. (2007). Attachment and the experience and expression of emotions in adult romantic relationships: A developmental perspective. *Journal of Personality and Social Psychology, 92,* 355–367.

Simpson, J. A., & Rholes, W. S. (1994). Stress and secure base relationships in adulthood. In K. Bartholomew & D. Perlman (Eds.), *Attachment processes in adulthood* (pp. 181–204). London, England: Jessica Kingsley.

Simpson, J. A., & Rholes, W. S. (2010). Attachment and relationships: Milestones and future directions. *Journal of Social and Personal Relationships, 27,* 173–180.

Simpson, J. A., Rholes, W. S., Campbell, L., Tran, S., & Wilson, C. L. (2003). Adult attachment, the transition to parenthood, and depressive symptoms. *Journal of Personality and Social Psychology, 84,* 1172–1187.

Simpson, J. A., Rholes, W. S., Campbell, L., & Wilson, C. L. (2003). Changes in attachment orientations across the transitions to parenthood. *Journal of Experimental Social Psychology, 39,* 317–331.

Simpson, J. A., Rholes, W. S., & Nelligan, J. S. (1992). Support seeking and support giving within couples in an anxiety-provoking situation: The role of attachment styles. *Journal of Personality and Social Psychology, 62,* 434–446.

Simpson, J. A., Rholes, W. S., Oriña, M., & Grich, J. (2002). Working models of attachment, support giving, and support seeking in a stressful situation. *Personality and Social Psychology Bulletin, 28,* 598–608.

Simpson, J. A., Rholes, W. S., & Phillips, D. (1996). Conflict in close relationships: An attachment perspective. *Journal of Personality and Social Psychology, 71,* 899–914.

Simpson, J. A., Rholes, W. S., & Winterheld, H. A. (2010). Attachment working models twist memories of relationship events. *Psychological Science, 21,* 252–259.

Simpson, J. A., Winterheld, H. A., Rholes, W. S., & Oriña, M. M. (2007). Working models of attachment and reactions to different forms of caregiving from romantic partners. *Journal of Personality and Social Psychology, 93,* 466–477.

Slotter, E. B., & Finkel, E. J. (2009). The strange case of sustained dedication to an unfulfilling relationship: Predicting commitment and breakup from attachment anxiety and need fulfillment within relationships. *Personality and Social Psychology Bulletin, 35,* 85–100.

Sprecher, S., Felmlee, D., Metts, S., Fehr, B., & Vanni, D. (1998). Factors associated with distress following the breakup of a close relationship. *Journal of Social and Personal Relationships, 15,* 791–809.

Sroufe, L. A., Egeland, B., Carlson, E. A., & Collins, W. A. (2005). *The development of the person: The Minnesota study of risk and adaptation from birth to adulthood.* New York, NY: Guilford Press.

Sroufe, L. A., Egeland, B., & Kreutzer, T. (1990). The fate of early experience following developmental change: Longitudinal approaches to individual adaptation in childhood. *Child Development, 61,* 1363–1373.

Sroufe, L. A., & Waters, E. (1977). Attachment as an organizational construct. *Child Development, 48,* 1184–1199.

Susman-Stillman, A., Kalkoske, M., Egeland, B., & Waldman, I. (1996). Infant temperament and maternal sensitivity as predictors of attachment security. *Infant Behavior and Development, 19,* 33–47.

Swann, W. B., De La Ronde, C., & Hixon, J. G. (1994). Authenticity and positivity strivings in marriage and courtship. *Journal of Personality and Social Psychology, 66,* 857–869.

Taylor, S. E., Lerner, J. S., Sage, R. M., Lehman, B. J., & Seeman, T. E. (2004). Early environment, emotions, responses to stress, and health. *Journal of Personality, 72,* 1365–1393.

Treboux, D., Crowell, J. A., & Waters, E. (2004). When "new" meets "old": Configurations of adult attachment representations and their implications for marital functioning. *Developmental Psychology, 40,* 295–314.

Uchino, B. N. (2009). Understanding the links between social support and physical health: A lifespan perspective with emphasis on the separability of perceived and received support. *Perspectives in Psychological Science, 4,* 236–255.

van IJzendoorn, M. H. (1995). Adult attachment representations, parental responsiveness, and infant attachment: A meta-analysis on the predictive validity of the Adult Attachment Interview. *Psychological Bulletin, 117,* 387–403.

Vaughn, B. E., Egeland, B. R., Sroufe, L. A., & Waters, E. (1979). Individual differences in infant-mother attachment at 12 and 18 months: Stability and change in families under stress. *Child Development, 50,* 971–975.

Vaughn, B. E., & Shin, N. (2011). Attachment, temperament, and adaptation: One long argument. In D. Cicchetti & G. I. Roisman (Eds.), *The origins and organization of adaptation and maladaptation* (pp. 55–107). Hoboken, NJ: Wiley.

Vorauer, J. D., Cameron, J. J., Holmes, J. G., & Pearce, D. G. (2003). Invisible overtures: Fears of rejection and the signal amplification bias. *Journal of Personality and Social Psychology, 84,* 793–812.

Waters, E., Merrick, S., Treboux, D., Crowell, J., & Albersheim, L. (2003). Attachment security in infancy and early adulthood: A twenty-year longitudinal study. In M. E. Hertzig & E. A. Farber (Eds.), *Annual progress in child psychiatry and child development: 2000–2001* (pp. 63–72). New York, NY: Brunner-Routledge.

Wei, M., Mallinckrodt, B., Larson, L. A., & Zakalik, R. A. (2005). Attachment, depressive symptoms, and validation from self versus others. *Journal of Counseling Psychology, 52,* 368–377.

Weiss, R. S. (2001). Grief, bonds, and relationships. In M. S. Stroebe, R. O. Hansson, W. Stroebe, & H. Schut (Eds.), *Handbook of bereavement research: Consequences, coping, and care* (pp. 47–62). Washington, DC: American Psychological Association.

Wilson, C. L., & Ruben, M. A. (2011). A pain in her arm: Romantic attachment orientations and the tourniquet task. *Personal Relationships, 18,* 242–265.

Zayas, V., Mischel, W., Shoda, Y., & Aber, J. L. (2011). Roots of adult attachment: Maternal caregiving at 18 months predicts adult peer and partner attachment. *Social Psychological and Personality Science, 2,* 289–297. doi:10.1177/1948550610389822

CHAPTER 3

INTERDEPENDENCE THEORY

Paul A. M. Van Lange and Daniel Balliet

One of the classic theories in the social and behavioral sciences is interdependence theory, originally developed by John Thibaut and Harold Kelley (1959). Over the past decades, this theory has been extended, first by Kelley and Thibaut (1978) and then by others (e.g., Kelley et al., 2003), into a comprehensive theory of social interaction. In this chapter, we provide a history and overview of interdependence theory and discuss the primary features of the theory, including (a) the principle of structure (the situation); (b) the principle of transformation, or what people make of the situation; (c) the principle of interaction, being determined by the interacting people and (objective features) of the situation; and (d) the principle of adaptation, suggesting that repeated social interaction experiences yield adaptations that are reflected in relatively stable orientations to adopt particular transformations in similar situations. These principles are illustrated by research on topics such as power and dependence, cooperation and conflict, trust and distrust, attribution and self-presentation, and stereotyping and information seeking. We conclude by outlining broader implications of interdependence theory as well as issues for future research, such as understanding the intricate relation between material and personal outcomes or articulating how interdependence theory helps us to understand the social mind.

Human life is inherently social. Much of it unfolds in the context of dyadic or group interactions; numerous human traits have their origins in interpersonal experiences, and the source of many powerful norms can be identified in the interdependent situations for which those norms are adaptations. One essential feature of social experience is the interdependence of interacting people. As Lewin (1948) noted,

> The essence of a group is not the similarity or dissimilarity of its members, but their interdependence. . . . A change in the state of any subpart changes the state of any other subpart. . . . Every move of one member will, relatively speaking, deeply affect the other members, and the state of the group. (pp. 84–88)

Therefore, to fully comprehend human behavior it is essential that one understand the nature and meaning of interpersonal interdependence, defined as the process by which interacting people influence one another's experiences (i.e., the effects individuals have on other people's thoughts, emotions, motives, behavior, and outcomes).

Kurt Lewin is a natural starting point for a variety of themes within social psychology, and interdependence is no exception. In fact, one could claim that he is the founder of an interdependence perspective on social psychology in that he was to first to define groups in terms of interdependence. As we show, his influence on interdependence theory, as originally developed by Thibaut and Kelley (1959), was quite pronounced and enduring. However, other frameworks were also inspired by Lewin's emphasis on group productivity, cooperation, conflict, membership,

http://dx.doi.org/10.1037/14344-003
APA Handbook of Personality and Social Psychology: Vol. 3. Interpersonal Relations, M. Mikulincer and P. R. Shaver (Editors-in-Chief)

leadership, and the like. A case in point is Deutsch's (1949, 1973) theory of cooperation and competition, in which he conceptualized promotive and contrient interdependence, referring to situations in which there are corresponding interests and conflicting interests, respectively. Also inspired by Lewin's emphasis on the relation between interpersonal and intrapersonal processes, Deutsch (1982) outlined the cognitive, motivational, moral, and action orientations that may be energized by promotive versus contrient interdependence.

The concept of interdependence is very broad, and in principle it could include nearly all classic themes in social psychology, especially those that emphasize social interaction. To illustrate, many domains in the *Handbook of Social Psychology* (S. T. Fiske, Gilbert, & Lindzey, 2010) have a direct and pronounced link with interdependence; examples include the chapters on person perception, emotion, personality in social psychology, evolutionary social psychology, morality, aggression, affiliation, close relationships, justice, status and power, social conflict, intergroup bias, social justice, influence and leadership, group behavior and performance, and cultural psychology. The domains of intrapersonal processes are especially relevant to interdependence, such as person perception, attribution, self-presentation, emotion, and personality processes related to social situations.

Given the breadth of the concept of interdependence, a question arises: Where does one begin? What should be covered, what less so, and what not at all? Clearly, we need a comprehensive review of the concept's history, but we also need a theoretical orientation and we need a focus that gets to the heart of interdependence. In our view, interdependence theory, as developed by Thibaut and Kelley (1959; Kelley & Thibaut, 1978), is the most comprehensive theoretical framework for understanding interdependence and social interaction. This is one reason why we use the constructs and principles of this theory to delineate the primary features of interdependence phenomena, as well as why we use this theory to describe the historical development of the interdependence research domain over the past several decades.

At the outset, we should acknowledge that several theoretical frameworks were developed around the same time, and these frameworks influenced interdependence theory in many ways, just as interdependence theory influenced them. We already alluded to the work of Deutsch, but we should also note that in the domain of social dilemmas alone, goal-expectation theory (Pruitt & Kimmel, 1977), structural goal-expectation theory (Yamagishi, 1986), the individual–group discontinuity model (Insko & Schopler, 1998), various formulations of game theory (e.g., Schelling, 1960/1980), and theories of direct reciprocity (Axelrod, 1984) and indirect reciprocity (Nowak & Sigmund, 2005) are important complementary frameworks.

In other social science domains, there are various complementary frameworks, such as the need-to-belong model (Baumeister & Leary, 1995), the investment model of commitment processes (Rusbult & Agnew, 2010), the model of communal (and exchange) orientations (in close relationships; Clark & Mills, 2012), the empathy–altruism model (explaining altruism and prosocial behavior; Batson, 1998), realistic conflict theory (applied to intergroup processes by Sherif, Harvey, White, Hood, & Sherif, 1961), and the dual-concern model (applied in the domains of negotiation and bargaining; Pruitt & Rubin, 1986). If we go a small step further by bringing to models of the mind and theories of justice the notions of aggression, prosocial behavior, and intergroup relations, it is clear that the concept of interdependence is used beyond the traditional boundaries of social psychology (e.g., markets as studied by economists, social preferences, international relations; for a review, see Gintis, Bowles, Boyd, & Fehr, 2005). The list of such topics and research domains is immense.

For three reasons, we have decided to discuss the domains of interdependence touched on in the tradition of Kelley and Thibaut's (1978) interdependence theory. First, as noted earlier, interdependence theory is one of the most comprehensive theories, with implications for a wide variety of topics. This is so because the theory advances a comprehensive taxonomy of situations from which one can understand a variety of psychological processes, behaviors, and social interactions. Second, interdependence theory relates comfortably to the many complementary theories and models developed around the same time that it was being developed. Third, interdependence theory is an excellent example of cumulative science; the theory has been continuously refined and extended while retaining the solid foundation provided by Kelley and Thibaut.

INTERDEPENDENCE THEORY

Interdependence theory was originally proposed by Thibaut and Kelley in their 1959 book titled *The Social Psychology of Groups*. Although Kelley and Thibaut referred to their theory as a theory of interdependence in 1978 in their book *Interpersonal Relations: A Theory of Interdependence*, the 1959 Thibaut and Kelley book should be regarded as the birthplace of the theory. The theoretical foundation—especially the notion of interdependence and several other key concepts—was advanced in 1959, and the 1978 book built on it in several important ways without changing the fundamental principles advanced earlier. Interdependence theory grew out of two previous classic theories—exchange theory and game theory—both of which were innovative and important frameworks for understanding interpersonal relations and group dynamics.

In the 1998 edition of the *Handbook of Social Psychology*, in his chapter on the historic development of social psychology, Ned Jones made the following prediction about interdependence theory: "Given the elegance and profundity of this analysis . . . there is good reason that its impact will be durable" (p. 30). Now, more than a decade later, it is clear that interdependence theory has influenced successive generations of scientists for more than 50 years. It is especially interesting to see that it has stimulated research in various domains of social psychology, including research focusing on within-person processes such as affect and cognition, as well as between-person processes such as behavior and interactions in dyads and groups. Since the time of Thibaut and Kelley (1959) and Kelley and Thibaut (1978), interdependence theory and its key concepts and principles have been used to analyze group dynamics, power and dependence, social comparison, conflict and cooperation, attribution

and self-presentation, trust and distrust, emotions, love and commitment, coordination and communication, risk and self-regulation, performance and motivation, social development, and neuroscientific models of social interaction (for reviews, see Kelley et al., 2003; Rusbult & Van Lange, 2003; Van Lange, De Cremer, Van Dijk, & Van Vugt, 2007).

To understand and appreciate the historical development of interdependence theory, it is important to discuss its core concepts and principles. Here, we discuss (a) interdependence structure, its importance, and the key dimensions of interdependence structure; (b) interdependence processes, with a strong emphasis on the concept of transformation; (c) social interaction (which results from the structure of the social situation and the people involved); and (d) adaptation. The principles relevant to structure, processes, interaction, and adaptation are briefly summarized in Exhibit 3.1. After reviewing the core concepts and principles, we provide a brief history of interdependence theory. We then outline several implications of interdependence theory for understanding various social psychological phenomena, such as self-regulation, trust, and intergroup processes. (Some of our sections are based on earlier writings, especially Rusbult & Van Lange, 2003; Van Lange et al., 2007; Van Lange & Rusbult, 2012.)

INTERDEPENDENCE STRUCTURE

Interdependence theory uses two formal tools to represent the outcomes of interactions—matrices and transition lists (Kelley, 1984; Kelley & Thibaut, 1978). The purpose of these formal representations is to specify precisely the character of situation structure—to describe the ways in which people can affect one another's outcomes during the course of an interaction. To predict what will transpire in an interaction between two people, one must consider (a) what situation they confront (e.g., are their interests at odds, does one hold greater power?); (b) what we call Person A's needs, thoughts, and motives with respect to this interaction (i.e., which traits or values are activated; how does Person A feel about Person B?); and (c) Person B's needs, thoughts, and motives with respect to this

---

**Exhibit 3.1
Overview of Interdependence Theory's Basic
Assumptions**

---

1. **The Principle of Structure (The Situation)**
   Understanding the interdependence features of a situation is essential to understanding psychological processes (motives, cognition, and affect), behavior, and social interaction. The features are formalized in a taxonomy of situations, based on degree of dependence, mutuality of dependence, covariation of interests, bases of dependence, temporal structure, and information availability.

2. **The Principle of Transformation (What People Make of the Situation)**
   Interaction situations may be subject to transformations by which an individual considers the consequences of his or her own (and other's) behavior in terms of outcomes for self and other and in terms of immediate and future consequences.
   Transformation is a psychological process that is guided by interaction goals, which may be accompanied and supported by affective, cognitive, and motivational processes.

3. **The Principle of Interaction (Sabi: I = F [A, B, S])**
   Interaction is a function of two persons (Persons A and B) and (objective properties) of the Situation. The Situation may activate particular motives, cognitions, and affects in Persons A and B, which ultimately, through their mutual behavioral responses, produce a particular pattern of interaction.

4. **The Principle of Adaptation**
   Repeated social interactions yield adaptations that are reflected in relatively stable orientations to adopt particular transformations. These adaptations are probabilistic and reflect (a) differences in orientation between people across partners and situations (dispositions), (b) orientations that people adopt to a specific interaction partner (relationship-specific orientations), and (c) rule-based inclinations that are shared by many people within a culture to respond to a particular class of situation in a specific manner (social norms).

Note. From *Handbook of the History of Social Psychology* (p. 353), by A. W. Kruglanski and W. Stroebe (Eds.), 2012, London, England: Psychology Press. Copyright 2012 by Taylor & Francis Group. Reprinted with permission.

interaction. In the following examples, we replace *Person A* and *Person B* with *John* and *Mary*, two names that have often been used to illustrate the formal logic of interdependence theory.

The precise outcomes of an interaction—for example, the degree to which John and Mary experience it as satisfying—depend on whether the interaction gratifies (vs. frustrates) important needs, such as those for security, belongingness, and exploration (cf. Baumeister & Leary, 1995; S. T. Fiske, 2004; Reis, Collins, & Berscheid, 2000). An interaction yields not only concrete outcomes, or immediate experiences of pleasure versus displeasure, but also symbolic outcomes, or experiences that rest on the broader implications of the interaction (e.g., Rusbult & Van Lange, 2003). For example, if John and Mary disagree about where to dine, yet John suggests Mary's favorite restaurant, Mary not only enjoys the concrete benefits of good food and wine but also enjoys the symbolic pleasure of perceiving that John is responsive to her needs.

By analyzing how each person's possible behaviors would affect each person's outcomes, one can discern the structure of a situation with respect to the degree and type of interdependence, examining (a) actor control—the impact of each person's actions on his or her own outcomes; (b) partner control—the impact of each person's actions on the partner's outcomes; and (c) joint control—the impact of the partners' joint actions on each person's outcomes. By examining, in the interdependence matrix, the across-cell association between outcomes, one can discern covariation of interests, or the extent to which the partners' outcomes are correlated. These features of an interaction define four structural dimensions, and two additional dimensions have been identified more recently (all six are described later; see also Kelley et al., 2003). Most situations are defined by their properties with respect to two or more dimensions. One key advantage of interdependence theory is its ability to outline the interdependence structure of many commonly encountered social situations and to define similarities and differences between those situations. For example, the prisoner's dilemma, hero, and chicken situations (discussed by game theorists) all involve moderate and mutual dependence along with moderately conflicting interests, but they differ in the magnitude of actor control, partner control, and joint control, as well as in their implications for interaction.

All conceivable combinations of the six properties define a very large number of patterns. However, we can identify at least 20 to 25 prototypical situations (Kelley et al., 2003). Everyday situations resemble these abstract patterns, having common interpersonal problems and opportunities. For example, the twists-of-fate situation is one in which each partner, at some point, might unexpectedly find himself or herself in a position of extreme unilateral dependence; this sort of situation is characteristic of health crises and other reversals of fortune. The prisoner's dilemma, however, is a situation in which each person's outcomes are more powerfully influenced by the partner's actions than by his or her own actions. This sort of situation is characteristic of interactions involving mutual sacrifice, trading favors, and free-riding. Everyday situations that share the same abstract pattern have parallel implications for motivation, cognition, and interaction.

Importance of Interdependence Structure

Why should one care about interdependence structure? To begin with, structure in itself reliably influences behavior. For example, situations with structure resembling the threat situation reliably yield demand–withdraw patterns of interaction—demands for change on the part of the lower power partner, met by withdrawal and avoidance on the part of the higher power partner (Holmes & Murray, 1996). Situations with structure resembling the chicken situation reliably yield interactions centering on establishing dominance and sustaining one's reputation (Nisbett & Cohen, 1996). Also, research on behavior in the prisoner's dilemma situation has found that people are more likely to behave cooperatively as the structure of outcomes changes, such that there is less conflict between self's and other's interests (Komorita, Sweeney, & Kravitz, 1980). In short, the structure of situations often directly shapes behavior above and beyond the specific goals and motives of interacting individuals.

Moreover, specific structural patterns present specific sorts of problems and opportunities, and therefore they (a) logically imply the relevance of specific goals and motives and (b) permit the expression of those goals and motives. The Gibsonian term *affordance* (Gibson, 1977) nicely describes what a situation makes possible or may activate (see Table 3.1, which provides an overview of possible affordances). For example, situations with uncertain information afford misunderstanding and invite reliance on generalized schemas regarding partners and situations; generalized schemas carry less weight when information is more complete. In short, situation structure matters because it is the interpersonal reality within which motives are activated, toward which cognition is oriented, and around which interaction unfolds.

Dimensions of Interdependence Structure

We assume that the structure of interdependence is best described in terms of dimensions representing a continuum with extremes and intermediate values (e.g., low to high levels of dependence, degree of conflicting versus corresponding interest). In theory, this taxonomic scheme allows one to locate any specific situation in this six-dimensional framework. More practically, it is possible to describe situations in terms of their standing (e.g., high vs. low) in these dimensions. So, what constitute the six dimensions of interdependence structure?

Level of dependence. This dimension refers to the degree to which an actor relies on an interaction partner, in that his or her outcomes are influenced by the partner's actions. If Mary can obtain good outcomes irrespective of John's actions (high actor control), she is independent; she is dependent to the extent that John can (a) unilaterally determine her pleasure versus displeasure (partner control) or (b), in combination with Mary's actions, determine her pleasure versus displeasure (joint control). Increasing dependence tends to cause increased attention to situations and partners, more careful and differentiated cognitive activity (e.g., deep processing rather than shallow processing, tendencies toward information seeking), and perseverance in interaction (e.g., S. T. Fiske, 1993; Rusbult, 1983). As noted in Table 3.1, dependence affords thoughts and motives centering on comfort versus discomfort with dependence and independence. For example, high-dependence situations will activate Mary's trait-based reluctance to rely on others, her discomfort with dependence will strongly shape her behavior, and her discomfort will be particularly evident to others; in low-dependence situations, this trait will be less visible and less relevant for her behavior.

Mutuality of dependence.   This dimension refers to whether two people are equally dependent on one another. Nonmutual dependence entails differential power: When Mary is more dependent, John holds greater power. The less dependent partner tends to exert greater control over decisions and resources, whereas the more dependent partner carries the greater burden of interaction costs (sacrifice, accommodation) and is more vulnerable to possible abandonment, and threats and coercion are possible (e.g., Attridge, Berscheid, & Simpson, 1995; Murray, Holmes, & Collins, 2006). Interactions with mutual dependence tend to feel safer and are more stable and affectively serene (less anxiety, guilt). Situations with nonmutual dependence afford the expression of comfort rather than discomfort with another having control over one's outcomes (e.g., feelings of vulnerability on the part of the dependent partner) along with comfort versus discomfort with one's having control over the other's outcomes (e.g., feelings of responsibility; see Table 3.1). For example, unilateral dependence will activate John's insecurity, and his insecurity will powerfully shape his behavior and be visible to others; in mutual dependence situations, his insecurity will be less visible and less relevant to predicting his behavior.

Basis of dependence.   This dimension refers to the ways in which partners influence each other's outcomes—the relative importance of partner versus joint control as a source of dependence. With partner control, the actor's outcomes rest in the partner's hands, so interaction may involve promises or threats as well as reliance on moral norms ("this is how decent people behave"); common interaction patterns may include unilateral action (when partner control is nonmutual) or tit-for-tat or turn-taking (when partner control is mutual; e.g., Clark, Dubash, & Mills, 1998; A. P. Fiske, 1992). In contrast, joint control entails contingency-based coordination of action, such that ability-relevant traits become more important, including intelligence, initiative taking, and strategic skills; rules

of conventional behavior carry more weight than moral norms ("This is the normal way to behave"; e.g., Turiel, 1983). That is, joint control often calls for coordination (e.g., in traffic), but coordination is sometimes quite challenging for dyads and especially for larger groups. A case in point is the productivity loss resulting from suboptimal coordination during brainstorming sessions (e.g., Stroebe & Diehl, 1994). The basis-of-dependence dimension affords the expression of dominance (vs. submissiveness) and assertiveness (vs. passivity), as well as the use of ability and skills such as social intelligence (see Table 3.1).

Covariation of interests.   This dimension concerns whether partners' outcomes correspond or conflict—whether partners' joint activities yield similarly gratifying outcomes for John and Mary. Covariation ranges from perfectly corresponding patterns (coordination) through mixed-motive patterns to perfectly conflicting patterns (zero-sum). Given corresponding interests, interaction is easy: John and Mary simply pursue their own interests, simultaneously producing good outcomes for both. In contrast, situations with conflicting interests tend to generate negative cognitions and emotions (greed, fear) and yield more active and differentiated information-seeking and self-presentation efforts ("Can Mary be trusted?"; e.g., Van Lange, Rusbult, et al., 1997). Situations that arouse conflicting interests afford the expression of cooperation versus competition and trust versus distrust (see Table 3.1). In such situations, John may demonstrate his prosocial motives as well as his trust in Mary. This dimension was noticed independently by Deutsch (1949, 1973), who used the terms *promotive* and *contrient interdependence*.

Temporal structure.   Temporal structure is the fifth important structural dimension, one that highlights dynamic and sequential processes. As a result of interaction, certain subsequent behaviors, outcomes, or situations may be made available, and others may be eliminated. John and Mary may be passively moved from one situation to another, or they may be active agents in seeking such movement. Extended situations involve a series of steps before reaching a goal (e.g., investments leading

---

TABLE 3.1

Six Dimensions of Situational Structure and Their Affordances

Situation dimension	Relevant motives
1. Level of dependence	Comfort versus discomfort with dependence
	Comfort versus discomfort with independence
2. Mutuality of dependence	Comfort versus discomfort with vulnerability (as dependent)
	Comfort versus discomfort with responsibility (as power holder)
3. Basis of dependence	Dominance (leading) versus submissiveness (following)
	Assertiveness versus passivity
4. Covariation of interests	Prosocial versus self-interested motives (rules for self)
	Trust versus distrust of partner motives (expectations about others)
5. Temporal structure	Dependability versus unreliability
	Loyalty versus disloyalty
6. Information availability	Openness versus need for certainty
	Optimism versus pessimism

Note. From *Handbook of the History of Social Psychology* (p. 347), by A. W. Kruglanski and W. Stroebe (Eds.), 2012, London, England: Psychology Press. Copyright 2012 by Taylor & Francis Group. Reprinted with permission.

---

to a desirable outcome). *Situation selection* refers to movement from one situation to another, bringing partners to a new situation that differs from the prior situation in terms of behavioral options or outcomes. For example, Mary may seek situations entailing less interdependence, or John may confront the juncture between a present relationship and an alternative relationship by derogating tempting alternatives (e.g., Johnson & Rusbult, 1989; Miller, 1997). Temporally extended situations afford the expression of self-control, delay of gratification, and the inclination to stick with it, raising the issues of dependability versus unreliability and loyalty versus disloyalty (e.g., Balliet, Li, & Joireman, 2011; Mischel, 2012; Rusbult, Verette, Whitney, Slovik, & Lipkus, 1991; see Table 3.1).

Information availability. The final structural dimension concerns information availability: Do John and Mary possess certain versus uncertain information about (a) the impact of each of their actions on both partners' outcomes, (b) the goals and motives guiding each person's actions, and (c) the opportunities that will be made available (or eliminated) as a consequence of their actions? Certain information is critical in novel or risky situations and in interactions with unfamiliar partners. Accordingly, partners engage in a good deal of information exchange during the course of interaction,

engaging in attributional activity to understand one another and the situation (e.g., Collins & Miller, 1994). People may also use representations of prior interaction partners to fill in the informational gaps in interactions with new partners, or they may develop frozen expectations that reliably color their perceptions of situations and partners (e.g., Andersen & Chen, 2002; Holmes, 2000). For example, people may generally rely on the belief that most people are (rationally) self-interested, which may in turn help them to fill in the blanks when faced with incomplete information about another person's actions (Vuolevi & Van Lange, 2010). As another example, people who are avoidant with respect to attachment may perceive a wide range of situations as risky, anticipate that partners are likely to be unresponsive, and readily forecast problematic interactions. Thus, uncertain information affords, among other things, the expression of openness versus a need for certainty, as well as optimism versus pessimism (see Table 3.1).

Recall that interaction, which can be represented with the equation $I = f(S, A, B)$, is shaped not only by interdependence structure (S), but also by partners' needs, thoughts, and motives in relation to one another (A and B) in the context of the situation in which their interaction unfolds. Thus, we must add to our structural analysis a complementary analysis of how John and Mary react to the situations they encounter. How do they construe specific situations? How do they respond on the basis of considerations other than tangible self-interest? What role do mental events and habits play in shaping this process, and how do partners seek to understand and predict one another? How do people develop relatively stable tendencies to react to specific situations in specific ways?

INTERDEPENDENCE PROCESSES: TRANSFORMATION

To describe how situation structure affects motivation, interdependence theory distinguishes between (a) the given situation—preferences based on self-interest (the "virtual structure" of a situation)—and (b) the effective situation—preferences based on broader considerations, including concern for the partner's interests, long-term goals, or strategic considerations (Kelley & Thibaut, 1978; Van Lange & Joireman, 2008). Psychological transformation refers to the shift in motivation from given to effective preferences. People typically behave on the basis of transformed preferences—considerations other than immediate self-interest. However, they sometimes behave on the basis of given preferences; this is likely in simple situations for which no broader considerations are relevant, when people lack the motivation or ability to take broader considerations into account, or in situations involving time pressure or constrained cognitive capacity (Finkel & Rusbult, 2008).

Transformations are often conceptualized as decision rules that a person (often implicitly) adopts during interactions (Kelley et al., 2003; Murray & Holmes, 2009; Van Lange et al., 2007). People may follow rules that involve sequential or temporal considerations, such as waiting to see how the partner behaves or adopting strategies such as tit-for-tat or turn-taking. Other rules reflect differential concern for one's own and a partner's outcomes, including altruism, which maximizes the partner's outcomes; cooperation, which maximizes combined outcomes; competition, which maximizes the relative difference between one's own and one's partner's outcomes; and individualism, which maximizes one's own outcomes irrespective of one's partner's outcomes.

Transformation is particularly likely to occur when a given situation structure dictates one kind of behavior, but personal traits or values dictate another kind. When people act on the basis of transformed preferences, it is possible to discern their personal traits and motives. For example, when Mary helps John with yard work rather than going out with her friends, she communicates concern for his welfare. The transformation process is thus the point at which the rubber meets the road, or the point at which intrapersonal processes—cognition, affect, and motivation—operate on specific situations in such a manner as to reveal a partner's unique self.

Cognition, Affect, and Habit

Human intelligence is clearly social. Cognitively and affectively, people are well prepared to construe the world in terms of interdependence (Rusbult & Van Lange, 2003). Mental events are geared toward discerning what a situation is about, evaluating that structure in terms of one's own needs and motives, perceiving the partner's needs and predicting his or her motives, and forecasting implications for future interactions (e.g., Kelley, 1984). Situation structure partially shapes cognition and affect. For example, the prisoner's dilemma situation entails a choice between benefiting the partner at low cost to oneself and benefiting oneself at substantial cost to the partner. The characteristic blend of fear and greed that is afforded by this situation is an indicator of the essential opportunities and constraints offered by this kind of situation.

The transformation process is often driven by the thoughts and feelings that a situation affords. For example, Mary is likely to exhibit a self-centered or antisocial transformation when she experiences greedy thoughts and desires ("It'd be nice to take a free ride") or feels fearful about John's motives ("Will he exploit me?"). Cognition and emotion are also shaped by distal causes—by the values, goals, and dispositions that are afforded by the situation. For example, Mary's reaction to situations with conflicting interests will be colored by the value she places on fairness, loyalty, or communal norms (vs. greed), as well as by whether she trusts John (or, alternatively, fears him). Thus, the mental events that underlie transformations are adapted to situation structure and take forms that are relevant to that structure.

At the same time, the transformation process does not necessarily rest on extensive mental activity. As a consequence of adaptation to repeatedly encountered patterns, people develop habitual tendencies to react to specific situations in specific ways, such that transformation often transpires with little or no conscious thought (e.g., Agnew, Van Lange, Rusbult, & Langston, 1998; Balliet, Li, & Joireman, 2011; Perunovic & Holmes, 2008). For example, after repeated interactions in situations with a prisoner's dilemma structure, John and Mary may automatically exhibit mutual cooperation, with little or no cognition or affect. Mediation by explicit conscious cognitive processes is more probable in novel situations with unknown implications, in risky situations with the potential for harm, and in interactions with unfamiliar partners.

Communication, Attribution, and Self-Presentation

During the course of an interaction, partners convey their goals, values, and dispositions through both direct and indirect means. Communication entails self-presentation on the part of one person and attribution on the part of the other. As noted earlier, the material for self-presentation and attribution resides in the disparity between the given and effective situations, because deviations from self-interested behavior reveal an actor's goals and motives (e.g., Balliet, Mulder, & Van Lange, 2011; Rusbult & Van Lange, 2003). Thus, the ability to communicate self-relevant information is limited by interdependence structure—that is, specific situations afford the display of specific motives. For example, it is difficult for people to convey trustworthiness (or to discern it) in situations with correspondent interests, because in these situations, trustworthy behavior aligns with self-interested behavior (see Balliet & Van Lange, 2013; Simpson, 2007a).

People engage in attributional activity to understand the implications of a partner's actions, seeking to predict future behavior and to explain prior behavior in terms of situation structure or underlying dispositions. Expectations are not particularly

accurate in interactions with new partners because they are necessarily based on probabilistic assumptions about how the average person would react in a given situation. In longer term relationships, expectations can also be based on knowledge of how a partner has behaved in a variety of situations. The term *self-presentation* refers to people's attempts to communicate their motives and dispositions to one another. Of course, self-presentation may sometimes be geared toward concealing one's true preferences and motives. Moreover, given that people do not always hold complete information about their partners' given outcomes, they may sometimes mistakenly assume that a partner's behavior reflects situation structure rather than psychological transformation. For example, Mary's loyalty or sacrifice may not be visible if John fails to recognize the costs she incurred.

INTERACTION = f (S, A, B)

Social interaction is at the heart of interdependence theory, but what precisely does social interaction mean in the theory? First, it means that interactions are defined in terms of people and situations (Kelley et al., 2003). Specifically, for a dyad, social interaction is defined as Interaction = f (S, A, B), meaning that social interaction should be understood as a function of the situation, Person A, and Person B. This model is sometimes referred to as SABI, whereby situation, Person A, and Person B produce interaction.

A key component of interaction is the situation, which affords various orientations that may underlie and explain individual behavior in that situation. For example, a social dilemma focuses on the conflict between self-interest and collective interest, thereby affording selfishness (the direct pursuit of one's own outcomes) and cooperation (the pursuit of collective outcomes). More important, however, by examining interactions, one also sees that orientations such as equality become important. For example, equality as an instance of fairness may become important because of influences regarding the self, or Person A (e.g., I hold a prosocial orientation and thus wish to pursue equality in outcomes); because of partner influences (e.g., Partner B holds a competitive orientation by which equality becomes very salient); or because the situation involves inequality (e.g., one partner has greater outcomes than the other when the interaction begins). Similarly, altruism can be activated by the self, the partner, and the situation; because there is interindividual variability in empathy (e.g., dispositional empathy; Davis, 1983), empathy may be more strongly activated by some partners than by others (e.g., one's child vs. a stranger), and some situations are especially likely to call for empathy (e.g., when a partner suffers from a bad event and is strongly dependent on one's help).

Second, a social interaction analysis is fairly inclusive, in that it allows one to focus on distal and proximal determinants of social interactions. Examples of distal determinants are personality variables (e.g., differences in prosocial, individualistic, and competitive orientations; Van Lange, Otten, De Bruin, & Joireman, 1997), relational variables (e.g., differences in trust in the partner; differences in relational commitment; e.g., Rusbult & Van Lange, 2003), and situational variables (e.g., climates of trust vs. distrust, group size; Dovidio, 1984; Kerr & Tindale, 2004). Examples of proximal mechanisms (which are often both a determinant and a consequence of social interactions) are emotions (e.g., feelings of guilt, feelings of shame) and cognitions (e.g., how the situation is defined, especially in terms of norms and roles; Van Lange et al., 2007). For example, prosocial individuals may believe that others tend to be prosocial, individualistic, or competitive, whereas competitors tend to believe that most or all others are competitive (Kelley & Stahelski, 1970). Such beliefs may be rooted in social interaction experiences, with prosocial people often developing interactions involving mutual cooperation or mutual noncooperation and competitors often developing interactions involving mutual noncooperation. The latter experiences confirm their belief that all people are competitive, even though in many cases the competition may have resulted from their own actions, a perfect example of a self-fulfilling prophecy (Kelley & Stahelski, 1970). In other words, beliefs can affect interaction outcomes, which can in turn affect beliefs.

Third, a social interaction analysis is also important from the perspective of observation and learning. Social interactions are largely observable to oneself, to the other, and to third parties who may not be involved (e.g., observers). As such, the manner in which a social interaction unfolds (e.g., two people en route to cooperation vs. two people en route to noncooperation because of one person's lack of cooperation) serves important communicative purposes—for both the interactants and the observers. The interactants may signal their boundaries of cooperation (e.g., by communicating threats and promises) and learn from their actions (e.g., "Next time, I will more carefully examine his responses to my cooperative initiatives"). Observers may learn as well, an example being children copying and learning from interactions between their parents. The point is that social experiences will often provide the basis for the development of a particular personality style. For example, people raised in larger families may be more likely to develop an orientation of equality because the situations they have typically entered were more likely to call for sharing (e.g., they may quickly learn that not sharing is a dysfunctional way to try to solve social dilemmas; Van Lange et al., 1997).

Finally, a social interaction analysis highlights interpersonal orientations, the preferences people have regarding the ways in which outcomes are allocated to themselves and others. At least six important orientations, or decision rules, can be meaningfully distinguished: altruism, cooperation, equality, individualism, competition, and aggression. We do not review them in detail here because they were discussed earlier in this chapter (for a comprehensive review, see Van Lange et al., 2007).

Interdependence theory is one of the few social psychological theories to provide a comprehensive analysis with a strong orientation toward conceptualizing interpersonal structure and processes (Kelley et al., 2003; Kelley & Thibaut, 1978; Thibaut & Kelley, 1959). Moreover, the theory has shown how intrapersonal motivational processes can be traced back to interpersonal structures and processes. Analogous to contemporary physics—in which the relations between particles are as meaningful as the particles themselves—in interdependence theory, between-person relations are as meaningful as the individuals themselves (Rusbult & Van Lange,

2003). Indeed, concepts such as coordination, trust, cooperation, communication, and commitment can be understood only in terms of social interaction, and many of the needs, motives, and processes that receive considerable attention in contemporary social psychology—such as the need to belong, uncertainty management, and self-regulation—are often oriented toward the threats and opportunities of social interaction.

ADAPTATION

When people initially encounter a specific situation, the problems and opportunities inherent in the situation will often be unclear. Hence, Mary may systematically analyze the situation and actively reach a decision about how to behave, or she may simply react on the basis of impulse. Either way, experience is acquired. If her choice yields good outcomes, she will react similarly in future situations with parallel structure; if her choice yields poor outcomes, she will modify her behavior in future situations with parallel structure. Adaptation describes the process by which repeated experiences in situations with similar structure give rise to habitual response tendencies that on average yield good outcomes. Adaptations may be embodied in (a) interpersonal dispositions, (b) relationship-specific motives, or (c) social norms (Rusbult & Van Lange, 2003).

Interpersonal dispositions are actor-specific inclinations to respond to particular classes of situations in a specific manner across diverse partners (Kelley, 1983). Dispositions emerge because over the course of development different people experience different histories with different partners, confronting different sorts of interaction opportunities and problems. As a result of adaptation, John and Mary acquire dispositional tendencies to perceive situations and partners in specific ways, and specific sorts of transformations come to guide their behavior. Thus, the self is the sum of one's adaptations to previous situations and partners (such adaptations are also affected by needs and motives that are biologically based). For example, if John's mother used her power in a benevolent manner, gratifying his childhood needs and serving as a secure base from which he could explore, John will have developed trusting and secure expectations

about dependence (for a review, see Fraley & Shaver, 2000; Mikulincer & Shaver, 2007).

Relationship-specific motives are inclinations to respond to particular classes of situation in a specific manner with a specific partner (Rusbult & Van Lange, 2003). For example, commitment emerges as a result of dependence on a partner, and it is strengthened by satisfaction (John gratifies Mary's most important needs), poor alternatives (Mary's needs could not be gratified independent of her relationship), and high investments (important resources are bound to her relationship). Commitment colors emotional reactions to interaction (feeling affection rather than anger) and gives rise to habits of thought that support sustained involvement (use of plural pronouns; e.g., Agnew et al., 1998). In turn, benevolent thoughts encourage prosocial transformations. For example, strong commitment promotes prosocial acts such as sacrifice, accommodation, and forgiveness (e.g., Finkel, Rusbult, Kumashiro, & Hannon, 2002; Rusbult et al., 1991; Van Lange et al., 1997).

Social norms are rule-based, socially transmitted inclinations to respond to particular classes of situation in a specific manner (Thibaut & Kelley, 1959). For example, most societies develop rules regarding acceptable behavior in specific types of situation; rules of civility and etiquette regulate behavior in such a manner as to yield harmonious interaction. Partners frequently follow agreed-on rules regarding resource allocation, such as equity, equality, or need (Deutsch, 1975). Such rules may govern a wide range of interactions or may be relationship specific (e.g., communal norms in close relationships; Clark et al., 1998; A. P. Fiske, 1992). Norms not only govern behavior but also shape cognition (or lack thereof). For example, in interactions guided by communal norms, partners neither monitor nor encode the extent of each person's (short-term) contributions to the other's welfare.

HISTORICAL DEVELOPMENT OF INTERDEPENDENCE THEORY

Obviously, the history of interdependence theory was strongly affected by a long-standing collaboration (and friendship) between Harold Kelley and John

Thibaut. A broad outline of the history of interdependence theory is provided in Exhibit 3.2, which reveals that the theory is an excellent example of one that made progress thanks to a firm foundation on which others can build and erect bridges to and from other fields and disciplines (Van Lange & Rusbult, 2012). The theory's key assumptions remained largely intact while new principles were added over a period of 50 years.

Thibaut and Kelley (1959)

This initial book was rooted in the theorizing and topical interests of Kurt Lewin (1935, 1936, 1952), who was interested in the scientific study of individuals in group situations, with a focus on issues such as group productivity, communication, group membership, and cooperation and conflict. Throughout their impressive careers, Kelley and Thibaut were inspired by Lewin's emphasis on the importance of theory, the value of experimentation for clarifying and testing ideas, the interrelatedness of people and environments, and the importance of understanding individuals in group contexts and cultural contexts.

Although the inspiration of Lewin is quite clear in Kelley and Thibaut's 1959 book, what made the book truly exceptional at the time was that it combined insights and principles derived from two

---

Exhibit 3.2
Brief Historical Overview of Interdependence Theory

1959

Thibaut, J. W., & Kelley, H. H. (1959). *The Social Psychology of Groups*. New York, NY: Wiley.

- provides social exchange analysis of interactions and relationships between individuals in dyads and small groups;
- uses games as a conceptual tool and focuses on the analysis of dependence, power, rewards, costs, needs, and outcomes in exchange relations; and
- introduces new concepts such as comparison level and comparison level of alternatives (CL and CL-alt) to understand relationship satisfaction and stability.

1978

Kelley, H. H., & Thibaut, J. W. (1978). *Interpersonal Relations: A Theory of Interdependence*. New York, NY: Wiley.

- provides a comprehensive analysis of interaction situations in terms of four dimensions: degree of dependence, mutuality of dependence, correspondence of outcomes, and basis of dependence;
- introduces transformation of the given to the effective matrix, thereby formalizing interaction goals broader than immediate self-interest; and
- adopts a functional analysis of transformations, thereby recognizing social learning of transformation rules and their functional value for particular domains of situations.

2003

Kelley, H. H., Holmes, J. W., Kerr, N. L., Reis, H. T., Rusbult, C. E., & Van Lange, P. A. M. (2003). *An Atlas of Interpersonal Situations*. New York, NY: Cambridge.

- provides an overview of 21 basic interaction situations, analyzed in terms of interdependence features, the psychological processes they afford, and the interaction processes they may evoke; and
- extends the taxonomy of situations by adding two additional dimensions to yield six in all, including (a) degree of dependence, (b) mutuality of dependence, (c) basis of dependence, (d) covariation of interest (formerly referred to as correspondence of outcomes), (e) temporal structure, and (f) information availability.

At Present And In The Future

- integrates interdependence theory with principles of evolutionary theory to conceptualize adaptation as a function of situational structure;
- extends taxonomy by considering differences in outcomes: material versus personal;
- extends interdependence theory to include neuroscientific approaches to understanding the social mind; and
- furthers the application of interdependence theory to group processes and relationships between groups.

Note. From *Handbook of the History of Social Psychology* (p. 342), by A. W. Kruglanski and W. Stroebe (Eds.), 2012, London, England: Psychology Press. Copyright 2012 by Taylor & Francis Group. Reprinted with permission.

theories that were very innovative and influential at the time. The 1959 book was inspired by social exchange theory (in particular, Homans, 1950) and by game theory and decision theory (in particular, a highly influential book by Luce & Raiffa, 1957).

Social exchange theory grew out of economics, sociology, and behaviorist psychology and focused on the exchange of goods, both material and nonmaterial, such as approval or prestige. Homan (1950) listed eleven propositions, including one emphasizing that people who get much from others are under pressure to give much to them. This process of influence tends to work out at equilibrium to a balance in the exchanges. Later, Mills and Clark (1982) extended exchange theory by advancing the thesis that people also develop and maintain communal relationships or orientations, whereby they respond to others' needs rather than to the balance of exchange. Nevertheless, the key assumptions of social exchange theory were important and helped social psychologists understand social interactions in dyads and groups. For Thibaut and Kelley at the time, the notion of exchange formed an excellent basis for analyzing the situations in which people might affect each other's outcomes.

Game theory was primarily rooted in computer science, economics, and mathematics. It provided many of the tools—for example, outcome matrices—that Thibaut and Kelley used to analyze social situations and interactions. Outcome matrices are mathematically precise representations of the intricacies of exchanges. They can be used as conceptual tools for analyzing situations in terms of several features, such as the degree of corresponding versus conflicting preferences. Moreover, outcome matrices can be used as empirical tools for the study of human cooperation. The frequently studied prisoner's dilemma is rooted in game theory, as are games that have been more recently developed, such as the ultimate bargaining game, the dictator game, and the trust game—games that have attracted numerous scientists across different disciplines.

Kelley and Thibaut used outcome matrices as empirical tools in their work on coordination, cooperation, competition, and bargaining. An article by Kelley and Stahelski (1970) was a classic contribution that provided evidence for an important social

psychological process—the self-fulfilling prophecy—in the context of a prisoner's dilemma game. It showed that competitors tended to elicit self-centered behaviors from others because they acted on their belief that everybody is selfish; that is, their own selfish behavior provoked selfish behavior in a partner, thereby seeming to support the initial belief about other people's motives. However, Thibaut and Kelley used game theory primarily as a conceptual tool, to conceptualize patterns of exchange and coordination between interaction partners. They thought that outcome matrixes, and especially the ways in which they can be analyzed (in terms of the features of interdependence), provided a powerful representation of interdependence. Also, even though many of their contemporaries had similar interests in the social psychology of groups, there was no formal conceptualization to analyze group situations (Kelley, 1984).

Hence, Thibaut and Kelley (1959) analyzed social interactions in dyads and small groups in terms of patterns of social exchange, thereby using games as the conceptual tool to delineate the patterns of interdependence, such as rewards and costs and power and dependence. They also introduced new concepts such as comparison level, a reference point determined by quality of outcomes evaluated in light of one's global expectations, and comparison level for alternatives, a reference point based on the quality of outcomes relative to those that can be obtained with alternative partners (or without any partner). Their analyses using these two concepts allowed them to distinguish clearly between satisfaction and dependence. This book was a great success and a must-read for any social psychologist at that (or any) time (see Jones, 1998).

Kelley and Thibaut (1978)

Nearly 2 decades after their first book was published, Kelley and Thibaut (1978) modestly expressed the belief that their methods of analysis—in terms of interdependence—might now meet the standards for a genuine theory. Although its origins were captured in the 1959 book, interdependence theory was now formally born. (Kelley and Thibaut were careful scientists who reserved the label of *theory* only for those kinds of conceptual analysis that would pass stringent tests of scientific rigor—probably defined by them in terms of clear logic and wide breadth of relevance.) In that book, they presented interdependence theory, and it immediately became clear that many years were devoted to very basic theoretical issues.

One decision they faced was whether behavior was primarily based on the given matrix (i.e., on the basis of immediate self-interest) or whether the theory should be extended to include broader considerations. Informed by research conducted during the 1960s and 1970s, they chose the second option and provided a logical framework for a number of fundamental transformations, which they labeled *MaxJoint* (enhancement of joint outcomes), *MinDiff* (minimization of absolute differences in outcomes for self and others), *MaxRel* (maximization of relative advantage over other's outcomes), and the like. These transformations were influenced by the work of Messick and McClintock (e.g., Messick & McClintock, 1968), and many others around the world, who had already provided empirical evidence for some transformations on the basis of research using experimental games as empirical tools. Kelley and Thibaut (1978) also outlined other types of transformation, which are based on people responding to both present contingencies and implications of present behavior for the future. A key difference from the earlier book was that the new one emphasized the value of various transformations. The book was an attempt to answer the question "What do people make of situations?" (see also Kelley et al., 2003).

In the 1978 book, interdependence theory was expanded to encompass (a) a formal analysis of the objective properties of a situation (resulting in a taxonomy of situations); (b) a conceptualization of psychological processes in terms of transformations, including motives, cognitions, and affect (what people make of the situation); and (c) behavior and social interaction resulting from both the objective properties of the situation and what both people made of it. Moreover, they emphasized adaptation and learning as longer term orientations that may grow out of experience. Inspired by the work of Messick and McClintock(1968) and their own research (Kelley & Stahelski, 1970), Kelley and

Thibaut(1978) also suggested that people might differ in their transformational tendencies. These adaptations were later conceptualized in terms of dispositions, relationship-specific motives, and social norms (Rusbult & Van Lange, 2003).

Over time, numerous investigators were inspired by the logic of interdependence theory—its assumptions, reasoning, and focus. Logic is one thing, but the theory also appeared to have considerable breadth. Researchers found it useful in conceptualizing phenomena as diverse as altruism, attribution, coordination, conflict, cooperation, competition, delay of gratification, exchange, investments, fairness, justice, love, power, prosocial behavior, trust, sacrifice, self-presentation, stereotyping, and hostility and aggression in the context of dyads, ongoing relationships (close or not), and groups (small and larger, ongoing or temporary). Also, researchers studying environmental issues, organizational issues, and political issues fruitfully used principles from interdependence theory (for a comprehensive review, see Rusbult & Van Lange, 2003; Van Lange & Joireman, 2008).

Kelley et al. (2003)

In the meantime, it became increasingly clear that people with various topical interests were intrigued by interdependence theory. After a Society of Experimental Social Psychology/European Association of Experimental Social Psychology conference in Washington, DC, in 1995 a group of six people, who worked individually on complementary topics, decided to work together on interdependence theory. This resulted in a 6-year collaboration that resulted in the publication of *An Atlas of Interpersonal Situations* (Kelley et al., 2003). This book extended Kelley and Thibaut(1978) in important ways, perhaps most notably by analyzing 21 situations and adding two dimensions to the four dimensions of interdependence that Kelley and Thibaut had previously identified. The added dimensions were (a) temporal structure and (b) information availability. There is little doubt about the relevance and necessity of these two dimensions, which we informally referred to as *time* and *information*. We now discuss the merits and implications of these two dimensions in turn, with reference to two research topics, persistence and generosity.

TEMPORAL STRUCTURE: THE TIME DIMENSION

Temporal structure is a key feature of interdependence situations and is essential to understanding social interaction. Although time was not strongly conceptualized by interdependence theorists until 2003, it was a key variable in several lines of research. For example, the work of Mischel and colleagues (Mischel, 2012; Mischel, Shoda, & Rodriguez, 1989) on delay of gratification focused on a situation in which people (children) needed to exercise control by resisting the temptation of direct reward to receive larger rewards in the future. In general, investment situations are often ones in which a person needs to accept present costs to build for the future. What is often observed in such situations is that people engage in temporal discounting (devaluing future outcomes) and that it takes effort to forgo short-term interests (Joireman, Balliet, Sprott, Spangenberg, & Schultz, 2008).

Temporal structure has also been considered important in the development of cooperation. For example, it has been noted that people are more likely to cooperate if they know they are going to be interdependent for many interaction situations. In his analysis of the so-called tit-for-tat strategy, the political scientist Axelrod (1984) coined the phrase *the shadow of the future* to suggest that people often cooperate because they foresee future rewards for cooperation and future costs or punishments for noncooperation, therefore encouraging a longer term perspective on the immediate situation. Also, game theorists have outlined that although noncooperation is rational in a social dilemma involving a single trial, cooperation is rational in a repeated-interaction social dilemma situation (Rapoport, 1990). Kelley and Thibaut (1978) noted that a concern with long-term self-interest might promote cooperation at the outset of a series of interactions (e.g., sequential transformations). It is therefore not surprising that scientists have distinguished between two temporal orientations, present and future, that seem to predict many behaviors in situations in which short- and long-term interests are at odds (e.g., Joireman, Anderson, & Strathman, 2003; Joireman, Shaffer, Balliet, & Strathman, 2012;

Van Lange, Klapwijk, & Van Munster, 2011). Research on social interactions in the laboratory have often focused on longer term concerns within the scope of a single experimental session, or even multiple sessions over a semester. Yet the time dimension is especially relevant to interactions that involve longer time periods.

An interesting case in point is persistence, for example in jobs or relationships. Traditionally, persistence has been explained by reference to positive affect: People persevere in specific endeavors because they have positive explicit or implicit attitudes about the endeavor; people persevere in specific jobs or relationships because they feel satisfied with them (e.g., Ajzen, 1991; Greenwald, McGhee, & Schwartz, 1998). The affect construct has been operationally defined in terms of satisfaction level, positive attitudes, liking, or attraction. An important challenge to this "feel-good" model of persistence ("so long as it feels good, I'll stick with it") is found in situations in which people persevere despite the existence of negative affect. Clearly, people sometimes persevere even though they hold negative attitudes about certain aspects of an endeavor; they sometimes stick with jobs or marriages despite feelings of dissatisfaction. Persistence in an abusive relationship is a particularly telling example: Surely people do not persist because they are delighted with such relationships. Some authors have sought to account for such inexplicable persistence in terms of traits such as low self-esteem or learned helplessness (e.g., Aguilar & Nightingale, 1994; Walker, 2000). That is, persistence is assumed to be an actor effect—people persevere because of something peculiar or unhealthy about themselves.

In contrast, an interdependence analysis explains persistence more broadly, by reference to the nature of an actor's dependence. To the extent that people are more dependent on their jobs or relationships, they are more likely to persist in them; the greater their dependence on a distal goal, the more likely they are to persist in pursuit of that goal. In relationships, dependence is strengthened by increasing satisfaction (are important needs gratified?) but also by declining alternatives (could important needs be gratified elsewhere?) and increasing investments (are important resources linked to persisting?

[Rusbult, Coolsen, Kirchner, & Clarke, 2006]). For example, Mary may persevere in an abusive relationship not necessarily because she has low self-esteem or has acquired a pattern of learned helplessness but rather for reasons related to structural dependence—because she is heavily invested in remaining with her partner (e.g., she is married to John or has young children with him) or has poor alternatives (e.g., she has no driver's license or faces poor employment opportunities; Rusbult & Martz, 1995).

Why should scientists favor an interdependence-based analysis of persistence? For one thing, positive affect is not particularly reliable—affect ebbs and flows even in the most satisfying jobs and relationships, making feeling good an insufficient reason to sustain long-term persistence. In addition, actor-based explanations are limited in light of evidence for dependence-based causes of persistence (e.g., Mary may have invested too much to quit). Moreover, interdependence-based explanations imply unique intervention strategies. For example, if one seeks to enhance Mary's freedom to persist versus cease her involvement with John, an actor-based explanation might favor psychotherapy geared toward raising self-esteem or eliminating learned helplessness. In contrast, an interdependence-based explanation might inspire interventions designed to reduce (unilateral) dependence—for example, improving the quality of Mary's economic alternatives through education, driving lessons, or job training. Even in therapy, the focus may be not only on fluctuations in satisfaction but also on the interpersonal causes that might account for it in combination with implications for the future of the relationship. This interdependence-based analysis differs from actor-based approaches in trying to change patterns of dependence and independence rather than trying to change only one or both individuals in the relationship.

INFORMATION AVAILABILITY: THE INFORMATION DIMENSION

Information, especially when it is lacking, is essential for understanding social interaction. Information was addressed by Kelley and Thibaut(1978),

especially in their analysis of self-presentation and attribution. People often want to present themselves favorably (i.e., provide favorable information about themselves) and often realize when they do not (e.g., when their actions harm others). People also want to know what their interaction partners are thinking, wanting, and so on (resulting in information seeking and attributions about the partner's motives and intentions). As explained earlier, these processes often involve noticing differences between the given matrix and the effective matrix (personality, motives, intentions, etc. are revealed in perceived disparities between the given matrix and the effective matrix). However, self-presentation and attribution processes had always been conceptualized (and examined) largely in the context of situations in which people had complete information about (a) one another's preferences (e.g., implicitly assuming that one knows how one's partner's outcomes are influenced when one considers attending a third professional conference within a few months) and (b) whether the outcomes one experiences are always a product of the other's intended actions (e.g., noise, fatigue, and unintended errors can affect another person's actions and outcomes).

It is far more common for people to have incomplete information about others' motives and preferences. One often does not precisely know how much another person enjoys a particular joint activity (e.g., when considering which movie or concert to attend), how much the person hates it when the partner leaves dirty dishes in the kitchen sink, or how much a colleague appreciates a compliment on his or her new scientific paper. Also, external interference and unintended errors are bound to occur in many social interaction situations. For example, when one is waiting for quite some time for a reply to one's e-mail, it may be that the other is either unable (e.g., server breakdown) or unwilling (e.g., gave low priority to the e-mail) to reply, and the differences between these causes are important for the future of the relationship. Similarly, when one arrives late for an appointment, it is often hard to tell whether there were external constraints (e.g., an unforeseen traffic jam) or not. Thus, the addition of information availability to the dimensions of interdependence structure makes interdependence theory more comprehensive and opens new lines of research.

An interesting case in point is research on the functionality of interpersonal generosity in the prisoner's dilemma. Traditional analyses of situations with this structure have revealed that people enjoy superior outcomes over a long span of interactions if they behave on the basis of *quid pro quo*, or tit-for-tat (Axelrod, 1984): If an interaction partner cooperates, one should also cooperate; if a partner competes, one should also compete. But how effective is tit-for-tat when information is limited—for example, when people are aware of how a partner's behavior affects their own outcomes but are not aware of situational constraints that may have shaped the partner's actions? An interdependence analysis suggests that misunderstanding is often rooted in noise, or discrepancies between intended outcomes and actual outcomes resulting from a partner's unintended errors (Kollock, 1993). For example, when John fails to receive a response to an e-mail message he sent to Mary, it may be because of a network breakdown in Mary's workplace rather than Mary's disregard for his well-being. Noise is ubiquitous in everyday interaction; the external world is not error free (e.g., networks sometimes crash), and people cannot lead error-free lives (e.g., Mary may accidentally delete John's e-mail message in her daily automatic spam-purge).

Given that tit-for-tat entails reciprocating a partner's actual behavior, not his or her intended behavior, responding in kind serves to reinforce and exacerbate accidents. If the accident involves unintended good outcomes, the consequences may be positive. If the accident entails unintended negative outcomes, however, the consequences may be damaging. For example, when Mary's actions cause John to suffer poor outcomes, he may respond with tit-for-tat, enacting a behavior that will cause her to have poor outcomes. In turn—and despite the fact that she did not initially intend to harm John—Mary will react to John's negative behavior with tit-for-tat, causing him to suffer poor outcomes. John and Mary will then enter into a pattern of negative reciprocity, and they may become trapped in an extended and perhaps escalating echo process from which they cannot readily escape.

Indeed, research has confirmed that negative noise has detrimental effects when people follow a strict reciprocity rule: Partners form more negative impressions of one another, and both people suffer poorer outcomes (Van Lange, Ouwerkerk, & Tazelaar, 2002). In contrast, a more generous tit-for-tat-plus-one strategy (giving the partner a bit more than is received from the partner) yields better outcomes—noise does not negatively affect partners' impressions of one another or the outcomes each receives over the course of an extended interaction. Indeed, in the presence of negative noise, a generous strategy yields better outcomes for both people than does tit-for-tat (for more extended evidence, see Klapwijk & Van Lange, 2009). Such findings are reminiscent of the literature on interactions in close relationships, in which partners have been shown to enjoy better outcomes in conflictual interactions when one or both partners accommodate or forgive (e.g., Karremans & Van Lange, 2009; Rusbult et al., 1991).

The societal implications of this interdependence analysis are quite powerful. They suggest concrete advice for people entering new situations at school, in organizations, or wherever else people interact in dyads or small groups. Under circumstances of imperfect information (which are very common), it helps to give people the benefit of the doubt, to reserve judgment, and to be more generous than a tit-for-tat strategy would advise. The research findings on this topic may also be especially relevant to e-mail and other forms of electronic communication because these devices are quite noisy and tend to be less effective than face-to-face communication in generating cooperation (Balliet, 2010).

BROADER RELEVANCE OF INTERDEPENDENCE THEORY

To comprehend the utility of interdependence concepts, it is important to see them in action—to perceive the theoretical, empirical, and societal benefits of these concepts in advancing the understanding of specific psychological phenomena. We suggest that more recent formulations of interdependence theory are especially useful for understanding relationship persistence and stability, as well as interpersonal generosity. However, the recent formulations of interdependence are also relevant to issues that (a) may seem less obvious from an interdependence perspective, such as understanding goal pursuit; (b) may be somewhat controversial, such as the origins of trust; or (c) may have been overlooked in past research.

Understanding Goal Pursuit

Goals are end states that give direction to behavior, either as overarching life plans or as aims of simple everyday endeavors. Traditional models of goal pursuit have used intrapersonal explanations, examining individual-level processes such as goal plan–directed behavior, self-regulation, or goal–behavior disparities (e.g., Carver & Scheier, 1998; Mischel, 2011). The success of goal pursuit has been argued to rest on actor-level variables such as goals, traits, skills, and motives. Notable approaches in this tradition are regulatory focus and regulatory fit theories (Higgins, 2012), which suggest that people are more likely to achieve goals when they approach them in a manner that fits their regulatory orientation; that is, when they approach promotion or ideal-self goals to accomplish something in an eager manner and approach prevention or ought-self goals to remain safe from a threat in a vigilant manner.

An interdependence analysis shares some of these assumptions but extends them in interesting directions. Research has indicated that, in ongoing relationships, people enjoy greater movement toward their ideal selves not only when (a) they themselves possess a strong promotion orientation (actor control) but also when (b) their partners possess a strong promotion orientation (partner control). (Corresponding negative associations are evident for a prevention orientation; Righetti, Rusbult, & Finkenauer, 2010.) Indeed, partners with a strong promotion orientation support an actor's movement toward his or her ideal self because they more reliably elicit key components of the actor's ideal-related eagerness. Recent work has also demonstrated benefits for goal achievement deriving from a form of interpersonal regulatory fit: Above and beyond actor and partner effects, there is evidence for a joint control effect, such that actor–partner commonality in promotion orientation

favors each person's movement toward goals (Righetti, Finkenauer, & Rusbult, 2011). Thus, the fact that goal pursuit and attainment are powerfully and reliably influenced by interdependence processes suggests that there is much to recommend an interdependence analysis of goal pursuit. Interdependence matters.

Understanding Trust

Our second example illustrates an important interdependence assertion: A sophisticated understanding of human behavior frequently involves analyzing processes that are temporally extended and entail across-partner influence. A case in point is trust. Traditional explanations of trust characterize it as a trait-based phenomenon or a frozen expectation—a generalized belief that others will behave in a benevolent rather than a malevolent manner (e.g., Fraley & Shaver, 2000; Rotter, 1980). As noted earlier, individual differences in trust may be viewed as results of different developmental histories: If John experiences others' benevolence in his early interactions, he will develop a generalized tendency to trust others; if John receives insensitive or ruthless treatment, he will develop a generalized tendency not to trust others.

An interdependence analysis shares many of these assumptions (Holmes & Rempel, 1989; Wieselquist, Rusbult, Foster, & Agnew, 1999). Indeed, as a consequence of differing interaction histories, people can develop generalized, trait-based tendencies toward trust or distrust—just as such histories may help to account for differences in prosocial, individualistic, and competitive orientations (Van Lange et al., 1997). Beyond that, however, trust may also be a relationship-specific adaptation. If Mary is reliably responsive to John's needs and is genuinely concerned with his well-being, he will come to trust her; if she is unresponsive and indifferent to his needs, he will not trust her. Thus, trust is as much a partner effect as an actor effect—John's experience of trust in Mary may be as much a reflection of Mary's contemporary behavior as a consequence of his own childhood interactions.

For example, actors become more trusting when they observe a partner engage in prorelationship acts in diagnostic situations—for example, situations that arouse conflicting interests (self vs. partner vs. relationship; Holmes & Rempel, 1989; Simpson, 2007b; Van Lange & Rusbult, 2012). As noted earlier, strong commitment is one important cause of costly prorelationship acts such as accommodation, forgiveness, and sacrifice (e.g., Rusbult et al., 1991; Van Lange et al., 1997). As such, actor trust is the converse of partner commitment—John's trust in Mary is a gauge of the strength of her commitment to him. Moreover, research has revealed that as actors develop greater trust in their partners, they become increasingly dependent on and committed to their relationships, which in turn promotes further prorelationship acts. These acts are in turn perceived by the partner, thereby strengthening the partner's trust, and so on, in a pattern of mutual cyclical growth (Rusbult & Agnew, 2010; Wieselquist et al., 1999).

We suggest that this interdependence theoretic analysis provides a deeper understanding of trust than trait-oriented approaches. For one thing, it is a powerful predictive model—in accounting for dependence, commitment, prorelationship acts, and trust, interdependence variables account for substantially more unique variance (more than 30%) than do prominent actor-based variables (e.g., attachment style accounts for less than 5% of the variance; Wieselquist et al., 1999). That is, in ongoing relationships, partners' actions are more important than are each person's trait-based, frozen expectations. Second, whereas trait-based explanations place responsibility for present behavior entirely in the hands of the actor, an interdependence-based explanation suggests that contemporary trust phenomena rest in both John's and Mary's hands. Third, the model highlights the fact that trust is not merely in the mind of the perceiver—there is a reality component to trust, in that Mary's actual trustworthiness plays a crucial role in shaping John's trust in her. Fourth, the model is dynamic and truly interpersonal, explaining how each person's motives and actions influence the partner's motives and actions in a dynamic, cyclical process. As such, the model illustrates the interdependence theoretic goal of explaining behavior via an analysis of processes that are temporally extended and entail across-partner influence.

Understanding Intergroup Relations

Most group phenomena are more complex than dyadic phenomena and often too complex for a comprehensive analysis, which is probably why Thibaut and Kelley often did not go beyond the triad. Nevertheless, the logic provided by interdependence theory has considerable potential for analyzing intergroup relations.

One important issue is the analysis of intergroup relations. Sometimes groups face high correspondence of outcomes, in that they both (or all) are pursuing the same goal and need each other in that pursuit. For example, neighboring countries help each other to control the import and use of hard drugs. Under such circumstances, the countries may develop congenial relationships, especially when they hold similar views about the policies that need to be used. In other cases, groups may have moderately corresponding outcomes when pursuing a goal that is quite costly to each group. For example, countries want to control global warming, but they differ in their interest or views as to how much to contribute to the effort. Under such circumstances, groups are faced with social dilemmas (in the intergroup context, a conflict between in-group interest and common, superordinate interests), and they often exhibit considerably less cooperation than do individuals in similar situations (Insko & Schopler, 1998). The primary reasons for this have to do with the affordances of the interdependence situation. For example, some degree of conflicting interest poses a greater challenge to trust (and enhances competitive motivation more) in interactions between groups than in ones between individuals (for meta-analytic reviews, see Balliet & Van Lange, 2013; Wildschut, Pinter, Vevea, Insko, & Schopler, 2003). A good deal of evidence has shown that an interdependence approach complements other approaches (such as social identity and self-categorization approaches) in predictions of intergroup relations.

A strong concern with receiving better outcomes—and not getting worse outcomes—than other groups often conflicts with good outcomes for the collective (de Dreu, 2010). However, competition can sometimes be a powerful means to cooperation. It takes an interdependence approach to analyze the patterns of interdependence among (a) the individual and his or her group, (b) the individual and the collective, and (c) the group and the collective (see Bornstein, 1992; Halevy, Bornstein, & Sagiv, 2008; Wit & Kerr, 2002). For example, a soldier (i.e., an individual) who fights forcefully often serves the group (i.e., his or her country) but not necessarily the world (i.e., the entire collective). In such multi-layered social dilemmas, competition can be quite beneficial. When there are two (or more) well-defined groups making up the entire collective, competition between the groups can sometimes benefit the entire collective. The competition should deal with a broadly desired goal. For example, the Netherlands has a contest between cities for the title "Cleanest City." As another example, two departments at a university may do better (yielding greater research output and enhanced teaching) if the university provides extra resources only for excellent departments. Indeed, organizations often use competition as a means to promote better outcomes at the organizational level.

FUTURE ISSUES IN INTERDEPENDENCE THEORY

The utility of interdependence theory goes beyond the illustrations we have discussed. Moreover, certain topics may well become important themes in the future development of interdependence theory.

Understanding Situation Selection

The typology of situations proffered by interdependence theory should be used in classic domains of personality psychology, such as situation selection and Person × Situation interactions (cf. Mischel & Shoda, 1995; Snyder & Cantor, 1998). We can illustrate this point using the example of situation selection. Clearly, life entails more than simply responding to the discrete situations with which one is confronted. Interactions and relationships unfold through situation selection—people change the structure of existing situations and choose to enter new situations. Situation selection brings the actor, the partner, or the pair (or even an entire group) to a situation that differs from the previous situation in terms of outcomes, behavioral options, or both. For

example, deciding whether to attend a conference, to sit close or not so close to an interaction partner, to quit working on a project, or to change the conversation topic illustrates situation selection.

The concept of situation selection has received relatively little attention in psychology. Although classic writings by Lewin (1935, 1936) and Festinger (1950) included concepts such as movement and locomotion, those theorists focused primarily on movement and change within the context of a specific situation rather than movement among situations. Situation selection has received somewhat greater attention over the past few decades (e.g., Buss, 1987; Mischel, 2004; Snyder & Cantor, 1998), but contemporary approaches are mute with respect to the sorts of situations that people select. Given that interdependence theory offers a well-articulated taxonomy of situations, it can help to understand and predict the types of situations that people are likely to select.

For example—and relevant to the dependence dimension of interdependence structure—people may sometimes engage in situation selection geared toward modifying dependence, either reducing dependence (e.g., maximizing one's personal income) or enhancing dependence (e.g., making eye contact to signal interest). For example, depending on their levels of attachment security or insecurity, people may ask for support from a partner or not and spontaneously provide support or not (e.g., Simpson, Rholes, & Nelligan, 1992). Needs, thoughts, and motives centering on independence, vulnerability, and responsibility are likely to explain situation selection involving changes in dependence (see Table 3.1). Relevant to covariation of interests, it seems clear that people often seek to reduce conflict by engaging in situation selection that increases correspondence (e.g., identifying integrative solutions), and people may sometimes seek enhanced conflict of interests (e.g., picking a fight, playing games). Needs, thoughts, and motives centering on trust and prosocial motives are likely to explain situation selection involving changes in covariation of interests. Relevant to the temporal dimension, people may seek to restrict (e.g., "I'm outta here!") versus extend the duration of their involvement in a specific situation (e.g., long-term investment in a career), and they may likewise seek to limit (e.g., abstaining from investment in a relationship) or extend the extent of their involvement with a specific partner (e.g., committing to the relationship for better or for worse). Needs, thoughts, and motives centering on reliability, dependability, and loyalty are likely to explain situation selection involving temporal structure. With respect to the information dimension, people may sometimes seek out or provide information to enhance information certainty (e.g., making oneself clear). People may also seek out or create attributionally ambiguous situations, allowing them to hide important properties of the situation or themselves (e.g., disguising one's intentions or incompetence). Needs, thoughts, and motives centering on openness, flexibility, and optimism are likely to explain situation selection involving changes in information certainty (see Table 3.1).

Thus, it is one thing to recognize that people are not slaves of situational forces, that they select and modify situations in explicit or subtle ways. It is quite another thing to predict the character of situation selection. Interdependence theory provides insight in this respect, in that the dimensions underlying situations should reliably activate and afford specific sorts of goals and motives. Situation selection is often functional, in that it helps to gratify specific needs or promotes long-term outcomes (Snyder & Cantor, 1998). Of course, situation selection may also initiate or sustain self-defeating processes. For example, shy children may avoid interaction, which in turn may limit their opportunities for overcoming shyness. The interdependence theory typology of situations can be used to extend predictive specificity in classic psychological domains, including not only the problem of specificity in predicting how traits relate to situation selection but also specificity in predicting Person × Situation interactions (cf. Mischel & Shoda, 1995; Snyder & Cantor, 1998). As such, an interdependence theoretic analysis can advance precise predictions about the inextricable link between people and situations.

Understanding Material Versus Personal Outcomes

Interdependence theory focuses on outcomes as the primary concept that shapes patterns of interdependence. Indeed, outcomes are exceptionally useful in delineating the specific properties of interdependence—that is, the situation (the structure) to which two or more people adapt. Also, interdependence theory has used outcomes to define the ways in which people adapt to patterns of interdependence. For example, transformations such as maximization of joint outcomes, equality in outcomes, and the like are all transformation of outcomes. Although it is reasonable that much of human motivation and adaptation is influenced by outcomes in a general sense, we suggest that it is theoretically enriching to distinguish between material outcomes and personal outcomes. Material outcomes are results of actions and interactions that have a high degree of universality and often reflect the high degree of similarity between people: Most of them appreciate money, free time, or activities they consider enjoyable (a particular movie) and so on, and such material outcomes are often translated by society into monetary value (e.g., income decline for a day not working). Personal outcomes are results of actions and interactions that are more particularistic to the self and often reflect some degree of dissimilarity between people; for example, people may differ in their desires for social approval, status, and positive reputation.

The general distinction between material and personal outcomes is rooted in the classic work of Foa and Foa (1980) and is worth emphasizing for a variety of reasons. First, differences between material and personal outcomes underlie transformations. For example, people behave more cooperatively toward others if the other's outcomes are displayed in self-related emotions (e.g., facial expressions that systematically differ in terms of sadness vs. happiness) rather than monetary values (Grzelak, Poppe, Czwartosz, & Nowak, 1988). Also, interpersonal harm in the form of personal outcomes (e.g., insulting one's child in response to bad behavior) may often be considered more psychologically aversive or more morally inappropriate than interpersonal harm in the form of material outcomes (e.g., being given less allowance in response to bad behavior). In the context of groups, people pursue good outcomes for themselves but are often willing to forgo such material outcomes if they can gain in reputation (an outcome that is particularistic to the self). For example, reputation as a cooperative member increases one's status in a group, which is essential for understanding why people often keep track of one another's behavior and translate it into reputation and why patterns of cooperation develop and persist even in fairly sizable groups (Nowak & Sigmund, 2005). Generally speaking, the distinction between material and personal outcomes is essential because it underlies transformations, seems intimately connected to cognition and affect, and resonates well with evolutionary approaches to human cooperation, which distinguish between (material) outcomes and reputation.

Understanding the Social Mind

We suggest that interdependence theory should be exceedingly helpful in understanding when and why particular neurological networks, hormonal responses, and complementary physiological responses are activated. These biological responses will often be adaptive, given the qualities of both people and the situation—that is, when viewed in terms of the SABI model discussed earlier. For example, on the observer's side, responses related to anger are probably best understood when carefully analyzing another person's violation of a norm in situations in which people are likely to have somewhat conflicting preferences (e.g., Singer et al., 2006; Yamagishi et al., 2009). It is especially striking that people with prosocial orientations tend to react very automatically to a violation of equality, revealing activation in the amygdala (Haruno & Frith, 2010). Such findings provide neuroscientific evidence in support of the integrative model approach to relationships, which states that a prosocial orientation involves not only the tendency to enhance joint outcomes but also the tendency to enhance equality of outcomes (Van Lange, 1999). These differences in turn might account for the finding that prosocial individuals are more likely to vote for liberal, left-wing political parties than individualists and competitors, who are more likely to vote for conservative, right-wing political parties (Van Lange, Bekkers, Chirumbolo, & Leone, 2012). On the actor's side, feelings of guilt might be evoked in situations in which an actor violates such norms

(e.g., Pinter et al., 2007). In a related vein, interdependence theory could be extended to capture emotional responses and affect, especially those that give direction to people's social interactions. Emotions such as empathy, gratitude, or anger are clearly of great interest to understanding the affective underpinnings of motives (such as altruism), human behavior, and social interactions (e.g., Batson, 1998; Van Lange, 2008). Finally, phenomena such as self-regulation (and affect regulation and self-control) in the interpersonal domain will involve inhibition of the temptation to be selfish and the imposition of self-restraint, which can be studied at both behavioral and physiological levels.

Benefits of a Taxonomic Approach: Future Theoretical Developments

A unique and exceptionally important contribution of interdependence theory is the advancement of a taxonomy of situations. Indeed, very few theories in social psychology advance a taxonomy of situations, even though social psychology as a field is strongly concerned with situational influence or influences from the social environment (see also Reis, 2008). We believe that the dimensions of temporal structure and information availability that have recently been added to interdependence theory (Kelley et al., 2003) will prove important to several topics in psychological science and beyond.

First, much research and theory in social psychology focuses on processes in an attempt to understand "system questions," such as how cognition and affect influence each other and how the mind can be characterized as a dual-process system (implicit and explicit, automatic and controlled, impulsive and reflective, etc.). We suggest that interdependence theory provides a much-needed taxonomy of situations that will help us to understand when (i.e., the situations in which) particular systems are activated. For example, forms of dependence call for trust, especially when there is a conflict of interest, and limited time may set into motion a hot system whereby impulses and gut feelings, rather than systematic thought, drive behavior (Hertel, Neuhof, Theuer, & Kerr, 2000; Kruglanski & Webster, 1996). An excellent case in point is the analysis of relations between the powerful and the powerless in organizations (S. T. Fiske, 1993). Because the latter are strongly dependent on the former, it becomes important to engage in deep, systematic processing to reach accurate conclusions about the motives and attributes of the powerful. In contrast, the powerful are less dependent on the powerless (and there are often many of the latter), so the powerful may use shallower, more heuristic processing when forming impressions of the powerless. Accordingly, the powerful are more likely to fall prey to stereotypic information (S. T. Fiske, 1993).

Second, a taxonomic approach is essential to understanding basic evolutionary issues. Because evolutionary theory focuses on the question of how common human characteristics interact with the social environment, it is essential to have the theoretical tools needed to analyze social situations in terms of their key adaptation-relevant features (e.g., Schaller, Kenrick, & Simpson, 2006; Tooby & Cosmides, 2005; Van Vugt, 2006). Interdependence theory shares some assumptions with evolutionary approaches. One shared assumption is that the social context is fundamental to understanding human behavior (Kelley & Thibaut, 1978). Interdependence theory, by providing a systematic analysis of situations, may contribute to evolutionary theorizing about possible human adaptations for common problems and challenges that arise in social contexts. Specifically, interdependence theory can specify key properties of social situations for which humans have evolved adaptations, such as dependence, conflicting interests, information availability, and so on. Interdependence theory may also provide insights into contingency rules of the if–then form, which are important in contemporary personality theories (Mischel & Shoda, 1999; see Murray & Holmes, 2009; Reis, 2008).

CONCLUSION

Historically, one primary inspiration to the emerging and rapidly growing discipline of social psychology was the realization that it takes both personality and situation to explain human behavior. The well-known formula proposed by Lewin, $B = f(P, E)$—behavior is a function of person and situation—was extended by interdependence theorists into a formula for dyadic social interaction (I), which is a function of the situation (S) and the two people in the situation (A, B), hence, $I = f(S, A, B)$. In both formulas, the situation is essential. Therefore, it is surprising that not much theorizing in social psychology is provided an analysis of situations. By providing a taxonomy of interpersonal situations, interdependence theory has served that role from the very beginning and extended it to provide a more comprehensive taxonomy of situations. The addition of new dimensions (temporal structure and information availability) to the well-established ones (dependence, mutuality of dependence, basis of dependence, covariation of interest) should be essential in understanding (a) the motives and skills that are relevant to time in a general sense (e.g., investment, delay of gratification, consideration of future consequences, as well as issues of self-regulation and self-control) and (b) the nature and mechanics of (implicit) theories that people bring to bear on situations when they have limited information. The current taxonomy provided by interdependence theory is quite comprehensive, but future conceptual work may extend it by identifying other features of interdependence (such as the degree to which outcomes are material vs. personal).

For more than 50 years, since Thibaut and Kelley's 1959 book, interdependence theory has been successfully elaborated, tested, and applied to an increasing number of important social phenomena, hence providing a model of cumulative social science. It really has helped theorists and researchers to define situations that interacting partners face or might face (the given interdependence situation), what they make of it (the transformation process) in terms of cognition and emotion, and how the structure and the processes shape human behavior and social interactions. This also helps to explain why interdependence theory has been well appreciated for more than 5 decades, why it has grown, why it is one key example of cumulative science, and why interdependence theory has been used to understand so many issues—group dynamics, power and dependence, social comparison, conflict and cooperation, attribution and self-presentation, trust and distrust, emotions, love and commitment, coordination and communication, risk and self-regulation, performance and motivation, social development, and neuroscientific models of social interaction. Given its long-standing history of 50 years, many of us are looking forward to the theoretical contributions and implications of interdependence theory over the next 50 years.

References

Agnew, C. R., Van Lange, P. A. M., Rusbult, C. E., & Langston, C. A. (1998). Cognitive interdependence: Commitment and the mental representation of close relationships. *Journal of Personality and Social Psychology, 74,* 939–954. doi:10.1037/0022-3514.74.4.939

Aguilar, R. J., & Nightingale, N. N. (1994). The impact of specific battering experiences on the self-esteem of abused women. *Journal of Family Violence, 9,* 35–45. doi:10.1007/BF01531967

Ajzen, I. (1991). The theory of planned behavior. *Organizational Behavior and Human Decision Processes, 50,* 179–211. doi:10.1016/0749-5978(91)90020-T

Andersen, S. M., & Chen, S. (2002). The relational self: An interpersonal social-cognitive theory. *Psychological Review, 109,* 619–645. doi:10.1037/0033-295X.109.4.619

Attridge, M., Berscheid, E., & Simpson, J. A. (1995). Predicting relationship stability from both partners versus one. *Journal of Personality and Social Psychology, 69,* 254–268. doi:10.1037/0022-3514.69.2.254

Axelrod, R. (1984). *The evolution of cooperation.* New York, NY: Basic Books.

Balliet, D. (2010). Communication and cooperation in social dilemmas: A meta-analytic review. *Journal of Conflict Resolution, 54,* 39–57. doi:10.1177/0022002709352443

Balliet, D., Li, N. P., & Joireman, J. (2011). Relating trait self-control and forgiveness among prosocials and proselfs: A test of compensatory and synergistic models. *Journal of Personality and Social Psychology, 101,* 1090–1105. doi:10.1037/a0024967

Balliet, D., Mulder, L. B., & Van Lange, P. A. M. (2011). Reward, punishment, and cooperation: A meta-analysis. *Psychological Bulletin, 137,* 594–615. doi:10.1037/a0023489

Balliet, D., & Van Lange, P. A. M. (2013). Trust, conflict, and cooperation: A meta-analysis. *Psychological Bulletin, 139,* 1090–1112.

Batson, C. D. (1998). Altruism and prosocial behavior. In D. T. Gilbert, S. T. Fiske, & G. Lindzey (Eds.), *The handbook of social psychology* (pp. 282–316). New York, NY: McGraw-Hill.

Baumeister, R. F., & Leary, M. R. (1995). The need to belong: Desire for interpersonal attachments as a fundamental human motivation. *Psychological Bulletin, 117,* 497–529. doi:10.1037/0033-2909.117.3.497

Bornstein, G. (1992). The free rider problem in intergroup conflicts over step-level and continuous public goods. *Journal of Personality and Social Psychology, 62,* 597–606. doi:10.1037/0022-3514.62.4.597

Buss, D. M. (1987). Selection, evocation, and manipulation. *Journal of Personality and Social Psychology, 53,* 1214–1221. doi:10.1037/0022-3514.53.6.1214

Carver, C. S., & Scheier, M. F. (1998). *On the self-regulation of behavior.* New York, NY: Cambridge University Press.

Clark, M. S., Dubash, P., & Mills, J. (1998). Interest in another's consideration of one's needs in communal and exchange relationships. *Journal of Experimental Social Psychology, 34,* 246–264. doi:10.1006/jesp.1998.1352

Clark, M. S., & Mills, J. (2012). A theory of communal (and exchange) relationships. In P. A. M. Van Lange, A. W. Kruglanski, & E. T. Higgins (Eds.), *Handbook of theories of social psychology* (Vol. 2, pp. 232–250). Thousand Oaks, CA: Sage.

Collins, N. L., & Miller, L. C. (1994). Self-disclosure and liking: A meta-analytic review. *Psychological Bulletin, 116,* 457–475. doi:10.1037/0033-2909.116.3.457

Davis, M. H. (1983). The effects of dispositional empathy on emotional reactions and helping: A multidimensional approach. *Journal of Personality, 51,* 167–184. doi:10.1111/j.1467-6494.1983.tb00860.x

de Dreu, C. K. W. (2010). Social conflict: The emergence and consequences of struggle and negotiation. In S. T. Fiske, D. T. Gilbert, & G. Lindzey (Eds.), *Handbook of social psychology* (5th ed., Vol. 2, pp. 983–1023). New York, NY: Wiley.

Deutsch, M. (1949). A theory of cooperation and competition. *Human Relations, 2,* 129–152. doi:10.1177/001872674900200204

Deutsch, M. (1973). *The resolution of conflict: Constructive and destructive processes.* New Haven, CT: Yale University Press. doi:10.1177/000276427301700206

Deutsch, M. (1975). Equity, equality, and need: What determines which value will be used as the basis of distributive justice? *Journal of Social Issues, 31,* 137–149. doi:10.1111/j.1540-4560.1975.tb01000.x

Deutsch, M. (1982). Interdependence and psychological orientation. In V. Derlega & J. L. Grzelak (Eds.), *Cooperation and helping behavior* (pp. 16–41). New York, NY: Academic Press.

Dovidio, J. F. (1984). Helping behavior and altruism: An empirical and conceptual overview. In L. Berkowitz (Ed.), *Advances in experimental social psychology*

(Vol. 17, pp. 361–427). New York, NY: Academic Press. doi:10.1016/S0065-2601(08)60123-9

Festinger, L. (1950). Informal social communication. *Psychological Review, 57,* 271–282.

Finkel, E. J., & Rusbult, C. E. (2008). Prorelationship motivation: An interdependence theory analysis of situations with conflicting interests. In J. Y. Shah & W. L. Gardner (Eds.), *Handbook of motivation science* (pp. 547–560). New York, NY: Guilford Press.

Finkel, E. J., Rusbult, C. E., Kumashiro, M., & Hannon, P. A. (2002). Dealing with betrayal in close relationships: Does commitment promote forgiveness? *Journal of Personality and Social Psychology, 82,* 956–974. doi:10.1037/0022-3514.82.6.956

Fiske, A. P. (1992). The four elementary forms of sociality: Framework for a unified theory of social relations. *Psychological Review, 99,* 689–723. doi:10.1037/0033-295X.99.4.689

Fiske, S. T. (1993). Controlling other people: The impact of power on stereotyping. *American Psychologist, 48,* 621–628. doi:10.1037/0003-066X.48.6.621

Fiske, S. T. (2004). *Social beings: A core motives approach to social psychology.* New York, NY: Wiley.

Fiske, S. T., Gilbert, D. T., & Lindzey, G. (Eds.). (2010). *Handbook of social psychology* (5th ed.). New York, NY: Wiley.

Foa, E. B., & Foa, U. G. (1980). Resource theory: Interpersonal behavior as social exchange. In K. J. Gergen, M. S. Greenberg, & R. H. Willis (Eds.), *Social exchange: Advances in theory and research* (pp. 77–94). New York, NY: Plenum Press. doi:10.1007/978-1-4613-3087-5_4

Fraley, R. C., & Shaver, P. R. (2000). Adult romantic attachment: Theoretical developments, emerging controversies, and unanswered questions. *Review of General Psychology, 4,* 132–154. doi:10.1037/1089-2680.4.2.132

Gibson, J. J. (1977). The theory of affordances. In R. Shaw & J. Bransford (Eds.), *Perceiving, acting, and knowing: Toward an ecological psychology* (pp. 67–82). Hillsdale, NJ: Erlbaum.

Gintis, H., Bowles, S., Boyd, R., & Fehr, E. (Eds.). (2005). *Moral sentiments and material interests: The foundations of cooperation in economic life.* Cambridge, MA: MIT Press.

Greenwald, A. G., McGhee, D. E., & Schwartz, J. L. K. (1998). Measuring individual differences in implicit cognition: The Implicit Association Test. *Journal of Personality and Social Psychology, 74,* 1464–1480. doi:10.1037/0022-3514.74.6.1464

Grzelak, J. L., Poppe, M., Czwartosz, Z., & Nowak, A. (1988). "Numerical trap": A new look at outcome representation in studies on choice behavior. *European Journal of Social Psychology, 18,* 143–159. doi:10.1002/ejsp.2420180206

Halevy, N., Bornstein, G., & Sagiv, L. (2008). "In-group love" and "out-group hate" as motives for individual participation in intergroup conflict: A new game paradigm. *Psychological Science, 19,* 405–411. doi:10.1111/j.1467-9280.2008.02100.x

Haruno, M., & Frith, C. D. (2010). Activity in the amygdala elicited by unfair divisions predicts social value orientation. *Nature Neuroscience, 13,* 160–161. doi:10.1038/nn.2468

Hertel, G., Neuhof, J., Theuer, T., & Kerr, N. (2000). Mood effects on cooperation in small groups: Does positive mood simply lead to more cooperation? *Cognition and Emotion, 14,* 441–472. doi:10.1080/026999300402754

Higgins, E. T. (2012). Regulatory focus theory. In P. A. M. Van Lange, A. W. Kruglanski, & E. T. Higgins (Eds.), *Handbook of theories of social psychology* (Vol. 1, pp. 483–504). Thousand Oaks, CA: Sage.

Holmes, J. G. (2000). Social relationships: The nature and function of relational schemas. *European Journal of Social Psychology, 30,* 447–495. doi:10.1002/1099-0992(200007/08)30:4<447::AID-EJSP10>3.0.CO;2-Q

Holmes, J. G., & Murray, S. L. (1996). Conflict in close relationships. In E. T. Higgins & A. Kruglanski (Eds.), *Social psychology: Handbook of basic principles* (pp. 622–654). New York, NY: Guilford Press.

Holmes, J. G., & Rempel, J. K. (1989). Trust in close relationships. In C. Hendrick (Ed.), *Review of personality and social psychology* (Vol. 10, pp. 187–220). London, England: Sage.

Homans, G. C. (1950). *The human group.* New York, NY: Harcourt, Brace & World.

Insko, C. A., & Schopler, J. (1998). Differential distrust of groups and individuals. In C. Sedikides, J. Schopler, & C. A. Insko (Eds.), *Intergroup cognition and intergroup behavior: Toward a closer union* (pp. 75–107). Hillsdale, NJ: Erlbaum.

Johnson, D. J., & Rusbult, C. E. (1989). Resisting temptation: Devaluation of alternative partners as a means of maintaining commitment in close relationships. *Journal of Personality and Social Psychology, 57,* 967–980. doi:10.1037/0022-3514.57.6.967

Joireman, J., Anderson, J., & Strathman, A. (2003). The aggression paradox: Understanding links among aggression, sensation seeking, and the consideration of future consequences. *Journal of Personality and Social Psychology, 84,* 1287–1302. doi:10.1037/0022-3514.84.6.1287

Joireman, J., Balliet, D., Sprott, D., Spangenberg, E., & Schultz, J. (2008). Ego depletion, consideration of future consequences, and decision-making preferences: Implications for the self-regulation of behavior. *Personality and Individual Differences, 45,* 15–21. doi:10.1016/j.paid.2008.02.011

Joireman, J., Shaffer, M., Balliet, D., & Strathman, A. (2012). Promotion orientation explains why future-oriented people exercise and eat healthy: Evidence from a two-factor consideration of future consequences-14 scale. *Personality and Social Psychology Bulletin, 38,* 1272–1287.

Jones, E. J. (1998). Major developments in five decades of social psychology. In D. Gilbert, S. Fiske, & G. Lindzey (Eds.), *Handbook of social psychology* (4th ed., Vol. 2, pp. 3–57). Boston, MA: McGraw-Hill.

Karremans, J. C., & Van Lange, P. A. M. (2009). Forgiveness in personal relationships: Its malleability and powerful consequences. *European Review of Social Psychology, 19,* 202–241. doi:10.1080/10463280802402609

Kelley, H. H. (1983). The situational origins of human tendencies: A further reason for the formal analysis of structures. *Personality and Social Psychology Bulletin, 9,* 8–30. doi:10.1177/0146167283091003

Kelley, H. H. (1984). The theoretical description of interdependence by means of transition lists. *Journal of Personality and Social Psychology, 47,* 956–982. doi:10.1037/0022-3514.47.5.956

Kelley, H. H., Holmes, J. G., Kerr, N. L., Reis, H. T., Rusbult, C. E., & Van Lange, P. A. M. (2003). *An atlas of interpersonal situations.* New York, NY: Cambridge University Press.

Kelley, H. H., & Stahelski, A. J. (1970). Social interaction basis of cooperators' and competitors' beliefs about others. *Journal of Personality and Social Psychology, 16,* 66–91. doi:10.1037/h0029849

Kelley, H. H., & Thibaut, J. W. (1978). *Interpersonal relations: A theory of interdependence.* New York, NY: Wiley.

Kerr, N. L., & Tindale, R. S. (2004). Small group decision making and performance. *Annual Review of Psychology, 55,* 623–655. doi:10.1146/annurev.psych.55.090902.142009

Klapwijk, A., & Van Lange, P. A. M. (2009). Promoting cooperation and trust in "noisy" situations: The power of generosity. *Journal of Personality and Social Psychology, 96,* 83–103. doi:10.1037/a0012823

Kollock, P. (1993). "An eye for an eye leaves everyone blind": Cooperation and accounting systems. *American Sociological Review, 58,* 768–786. doi:10.2307/2095950

Komorita, S. S., Sweeney, J., & Kravitz, D. A. (1980). Cooperative choice in the *N*-person prisoner's dilemma situation. *Journal of Personality and Social Psychology, 38,* 504–516. doi:10.1037/0022-3514.38.3.504

Kruglanski, A. W., & Stroebe, W. (Eds.). (2012). *Handbook of the history of social psychology.* London, England: Psychology Press.

Kruglanski, A. W., & Webster, D. M. (1996). Motivated closing of the mind: "Seizing" and "freezing." *Psychological Review, 103,* 263–283. doi:10.1037/0033-295X.103.2.263

Lewin, K. (1935). *A dynamic theory of personality.* New York, NY: McGraw-Hill.

Lewin, K. (1936). *Principles of topological psychology.* New York, NY: McGraw-Hill. doi:10.1037/10019-000

Lewin, K. (1948). *Resolving social conflicts: Selected papers on group dynamics* (Gertrude W. Lewin, Ed.). New York, NY: Harper & Row.

Lewin, K. (1952). *Field theory in social sciences: Selected theoretical papers.* New York, NY: Harper.

Luce, R. D., & Raiffa, H. (1957). *Games and decisions: Introduction and critical survey.* London, England: Wiley.

Messick, D. M., & McClintock, C. G. (1968). Motivational bases of choice in experimental games. *Journal of Experimental Social Psychology, 4,* 1–25. doi:10.1016/0022-1031(68)90046-2

Mikulincer, M., & Shaver, P. R. (2007). *Attachment in adulthood: Structure, dynamics, and change.* New York, NY: Guilford Press.

Miller, R. S. (1997). Inattentive and contented: Relationship commitment and attention to alternatives. *Journal of Personality and Social Psychology, 73,* 758–766. doi:10.1037/0022-3514.73.4.758

Mills, J., & Clark, M. S. (1982). Exchange and communal relationships. In L. Wheeler (Ed.), *Review of personality and social psychology* (pp. 121–144). Beverly Hills, CA: Sage.

Mischel, W. (2004). Toward an integrative science of the person. *Annual Review of Psychology, 55,* 1–22. doi:10.1146/annurev.psych.55.042902.130709

Mischel, W. (2012). Self-control theory. In P. A. M. Van Lange, A. W. Kruglanski, & E. T. Higgins (Eds.), *Handbook of theories of social psychology* (Vol. 2, pp. 1–22). Thousand Oaks, CA: Sage.

Mischel, W., & Shoda, Y. (1995). A cognitive-affective system theory of personality: Reconceptualizing situations, dispositions, and invariance in personality structure. *Psychological Review, 102,* 246–268. doi:10.1037/0033-295X.102.2.246

Mischel, W., Shoda, Y., & Rodriguez, M. L. (1989). Delay of gratification in children. *Science, 244,* 933–938. doi:10.1126/science.2658056

Murray, S. L., & Holmes, J. G. (2009). The architecture of interdependent minds: A motivation-management theory of mutual responsiveness. *Psychological Review, 116,* 908–928. doi:10.1037/a0017015

Murray, S. L., Holmes, J. G., & Collins, N. L. (2006). Optimizing assurance: The risk regulation system in relationships. *Psychological Bulletin, 132,* 641–666. doi:10.1037/0033-2909.132.5.641

Nisbett, R. E., & Cohen, D. (1996). *Culture of honor: The psychology of violence in the south.* Boulder, CO: Westview Press.

Nowak, M. A., & Sigmund, K. (2005). Evolution of indirect reciprocity. *Nature, 437,* 1291–1298. doi:10.1038/nature04131

Perunovic, M., & Holmes, J. G. (2008). Automatic accommodation: The role of personality. *Personal Relationships, 15,* 57–70. doi:10.1111/j.1475-6811.2007.00184.x

Pinter, B., Insko, C. A., Wildschut, T., Kirchner, J. L., Montoya, R. M., & Wolf, S. T. (2007). Reduction of the interindividual-intergroup discontinuity: The role of leader accountability and proneness to guilt. *Journal of Personality and Social Psychology, 93,* 250–265. doi:10.1037/0022-3514.93.2.250

Pruitt, D. G., & Kimmel, M. J. (1977). Twenty years of experimental gaming: Critique, synthesis, and suggestions for the future. *Annual Review of Psychology, 28,* 363–392. doi:10.1146/annurev.ps.28.020177.002051

Pruitt, D. G., & Rubin, J. Z. (1986). *Social conflict: Escalation, stalemate, and settlement.* New York, NY: McGraw-Hill.

Rapoport, A. (1990). *Experimental studies of interactive decisions.* Dordrecht, the Netherlands: Kluwer Academic. doi:10.1007/978-94-009-1992-1

Reis, H. T. (2008). Reinvigorating the concept of situation in social psychology. *Personality and Social Psychology Review, 12,* 311–329. doi:10.1177/1088868308321721

Reis, H. T., Collins, W. A., & Berscheid, E. (2000). The relationship context of human behavior and development. *Psychological Bulletin, 126,* 844–872. doi:10.1037/0033-2909.126.6.844

Righetti, F., Finkenauer, C., & Rusbult, C. E. (2011). The benefits of interpersonal regulatory fit for individual goal pursuit. *Journal of Personality and Social Psychology, 101,* 720–736. doi:10.1037/a0023592

Righetti, F., Rusbult, C. E., & Finkenauer, C. (2010). Regulatory focus and the Michelangelo phenomenon: How close partners promote one another's ideal selves. *Journal of Experimental Social Psychology, 46,* 972–985. doi:10.1016/j.jesp.2010.06.001

Rotter, J. B. (1980). Interpersonal trust, trustworthiness, and gullibility. *American Psychologist, 35,* 1–7. doi:10.1037/0003-066X.35.1.1

Rusbult, C. E. (1983). A longitudinal test of the investment model: The development (and deterioration) of satisfaction and commitment in heterosexual involvements. *Journal of Personality and Social Psychology, 45,* 101–117. doi:10.1037/0022-3514.45.1.101

Rusbult, C. E., & Agnew, C. R. (2010). Prosocial motivation and behavior in close relationships. In M. Mikulincer & P. R. Shaver (Eds.), *Prosocial motives, emotions, and behavior: The better angels of our nature* (pp. 327–345). Washington, DC: American Psychological Association. doi:10.1037/12061-017

Rusbult, C. E., Coolsen, M. K., Kirchner, J. L., & Clarke, J. (2006). Commitment. In A. Vangelisti & D. Perlman (Eds.), *Handbook of personal relationships* (pp. 615–635). New York, NY: Cambridge University Press.

Rusbult, C. E., & Martz, J. M. (1995). Remaining in an abusive relationship: An investment model analysis of nonvoluntary commitment. *Personality and Social Psychology Bulletin, 21,* 558–571. doi:10.1177/0146167295216002

Rusbult, C. E., & Van Lange, P. A. M. (2003). Interdependence, interaction, and relationships. *Annual Review of Psychology, 54,* 351–375. doi:10.1146/annurev.psych.54.101601.145059

Rusbult, C. E., Verette, J., Whitney, G. A., Slovik, L. F., & Lipkus, I. (1991). Accommodation processes in close relationships: Theory and preliminary empirical evidence. *Journal of Personality and Social Psychology, 60,* 53–78. doi:10.1037/0022-3514.60.1.53

Schaller, M., Kenrick, D., & Simpson, J. (Eds.). (2006). *Evolution and social psychology.* New York, NY: Psychology Press.

Schelling, T. (1980). *The strategy of conflict.* Cambridge, MA: Harvard University Press. (Original work published 1960)

Sherif, M., Harvey, O. J., White, B. J., Hood, W. R., & Sherif, C. W. (1961). *Intergroup conflict and cooperation: The Robbers Cave experiment.* Norman: University of Oklahoma Book Exchange.

Simpson, J. A. (2007a). Foundations of interpersonal trust. In A. W. Kruglanski & E. T. Higgins (Eds.), *Social psychology: Handbook of basic principles* (2nd ed., pp. 587–607). New York, NY: Guilford Press.

Simpson, J. A. (2007b). Psychological foundations of trust. *Current Directions in Psychological Science, 16,* 264–268. doi:10.1111/j.1467-8721.2007.00517.x

Simpson, J. A., Rholes, W. S., & Nelligan, J. S. (1992). Support seeking and support giving within couples in an anxiety-provoking situation: The role of attachment styles. *Journal of Personality and Social Psychology, 62,* 434–446. doi:10.1037/0022-3514.62.3.434

Singer, T., Seymour, B., O'Doherty, J., Klaas, E. S., Dolan, J. D., & Frith, C. (2006). Empathic neural responses are modulated by the perceived fairness of others. *Nature, 439,* 466–469. doi:10.1038/nature04271

Snyder, M., & Cantor, N. (1998). Understanding personality and social behavior: A functionalist strategy. In D. T. Gilbert, S. T. Fiske, & G. Lindzey (Eds.), *The handbook of social psychology* (pp. 635–679). New York, NY: McGraw-Hill.

Stroebe, W., & Diehl, M. (1994). Why groups are less effective than their members: On productivity loss in idea-generating groups. *European Review of Social Psychology, 5*, 271–304.

Thibaut, J. W., & Kelley, H. H. (1959). *The social psychology of groups.* New York, NY: Wiley.

Tooby, J., & Cosmides, L. (2005). Conceptual foundations of evolutionary psychology. In D. M. Buss (Ed.), *The handbook of evolutionary psychology* (pp. 5–67). Hoboken, NJ: Wiley.

Turiel, E. (1983). *The development of social knowledge: Morality and convention.* Cambridge, England: Cambridge University Press.

Van Lange, P. A. M. (1999). The pursuit of joint outcomes and equality in outcomes: An integrative model of social value orientation. *Journal of Personality and Social Psychology, 77*, 337–349. doi:10.1037/0022-3514.77.2.337

Van Lange, P. A. M. (2008). Does empathy trigger only altruistic motivation—How about selflessness and justice? *Emotion, 8*, 766–774. doi:10.1037/a0013967

Van Lange, P. A. M., Bekkers, R., Chirumbolo, A., & Leone, L. (2012). Are conservatives less likely to be prosocial than liberals? From games to ideology, political preferences and voting. *European Journal of Personality, 26*, 461–473.

Van Lange, P. A. M., De Cremer, D., Van Dijk, E., & Van Vugt, M. (2007). Self-interest and beyond: Basic principles of social interaction. In A. W. Kruglanski & E. T. Higgins (Eds.), *Social psychology: Handbook of basic principles* (pp. 540–561). New York, NY: Guilford Press.

Van Lange, P. A. M., & Joireman, J. A. (2008). How can we promote behaviour that serves all of us in the future. *Social Issues and Policy Review, 2*, 127–157. doi:10.1111/j.1751-2409.2008.00013.x

Van Lange, P. A. M., Klapwijk, A., & Van Munster, L. (2011). How the shadow of the future might promote cooperation. *Group Processes and Intergroup Relations, 14*, 857–870. doi:10.1177/1368430211402102

Van Lange, P. A. M., Otten, W., De Bruin, E. M. N., & Joireman, J. A. (1997). Development of prosocial, individualistic, and competitive orientations: Theory and preliminary evidence. *Journal of Personality and Social Psychology, 73*, 733–746. doi:10.1037/0022-3514.73.4.733

Van Lange, P. A. M., Ouwerkerk, J. W., & Tazelaar, M. J. A. (2002). How to overcome the detrimental effects of noise in social interaction: The benefits of generosity. *Journal of Personality and Social Psychology, 82*, 768–780. doi:10.1037/0022-3514.82.5.768

Van Lange, P. A. M., & Rusbult, C. E. (2012). Interdependence theory. In P. A. M. Van Lange, A. W. Kruglanski, & E. T. Higgins (Eds.), *Handbook of theories of social psychology* (Vol. 2, pp. 251–272). Thousand Oaks, CA: Sage. doi:10.4135/9781446249222.n39

Van Lange, P. A. M., Rusbult, C. E., Drigotas, S. M., Arriaga, X. B., Witcher, B. S., & Cox, C. L. (1997). Willingness to sacrifice in close relationships. *Journal of Personality and Social Psychology, 72*, 1373–1395. doi:10.1037/0022-3514.72.6.1373

Van Vugt, M. (2006). Evolutionary origins of leadership and followership. *Personality and Social Psychology Review, 10*, 354–371. doi:10.1207/s15327957pspr1004_5

Vuolevi, J. H. K., & Van Lange, P. A. M. (2010). Beyond the information given: The power of the belief in self-interest. *European Journal of Social Psychology, 40*, 26–34.

Walker, L. (2000). *The battered woman syndrome* (2nd ed.). New York, NY: Springer.

Wieselquist, J., Rusbult, C. E., Foster, C. A., & Agnew, C. R. (1999). Commitment, pro-relationship behavior, and trust in close relationships. *Journal of Personality and Social Psychology, 77*, 942–966. doi:10.1037/0022-3514.77.5.942

Wildschut, T., Pinter, B., Vevea, J. L., Insko, C. A., & Schopler, J. (2003). Beyond the group mind: A quantitative review of the interindividual-intergroup discontinuity effect. *Psychological Bulletin, 129*, 698–722. doi:10.1037/0033-2909.129.5.698

Wit, A. P., & Kerr, N. L. (2002). "Me vs. just us vs. us all": Categorization and cooperation in nested social dilemmas. *Journal of Personality and Social Psychology, 83*, 616–637. doi:10.1037/0022-3514.83.3.616

Yamagishi, T. (1986). The structural goal/expectation theory of cooperation in social dilemmas. In E. Lawler (Ed.), *Advances in group processes* (Vol. 3, pp. 51–87). Greenwich, CT: JAI Press.

Yamagishi, T., Horita, Y., Takagishi, H., Shinada, M., Tanida, S., & Cook, K. S. (2009). The private rejection of unfair offers and emotional commitment. *Proceedings of the National Academy of Sciences, USA, 106*, 11520–11523. doi:10.1073/pnas.0900636106

CHAPTER 4

RELATIONSHIPS AND THE SELF: EGOSYSTEM AND ECOSYSTEM

Jennifer Crocker and Amy Canevello

Most social scientists assume that people are fundamentally self-interested, that they do what they perceive to be advantageous to themselves (Miller, 1999). Unsurprisingly, this view pervades research on the self, in which people are depicted as self-enhancing and self-protective, seeking validation and affirmation, and taking credit for successes but dodging blame for failures. Perhaps more surprising, this view also pervades a great deal of research on relationships, which presumably involve shared bonds between people and feelings such as closeness, caring, affection, or love. Many researchers assume that people in relationships, as in the rest of their lives, are fundamentally self-centered and self-serving. In this view, people want to be in relationships to promote their own ends, they use relationship partners to satisfy their own needs, and they sacrifice and compromise in relationships to keep their relationship partners happy so they can continue to reap benefits the relationship brings them. Being desired, idealized, and accepted by another person are peak relationship experiences, whereas being unwanted, criticized, or rejected are ultimate downers.

Although this view surely describes many relationships at least some of the time, we believe that it is at best incomplete and at worst wildly misleading as a depiction of the self in relationships. In this chapter, we begin by articulating the self-centered view of relationships that dominates much research and theory on relationships and the self. Consistent with our previous work, we call this orientation to relationships *egosystem motivation* (Crocker, 2008;

Crocker & Canevello, 2008, 2012b; Crocker, Olivier, & Nuer, 2009). We first describe this system in general terms that apply to most, if not all, types of relationships. Then, because romantic relationships are the focus of a great deal of interest and research, we describe the principles of romantic relationships driven by egosystem motivation.

We next describe an emerging alternate view, in which people have the capacity to transcend self-interest and care deeply about people and things beyond themselves, which we call *ecosystem motivation* (Crocker, 2008; Crocker & Canevello, 2008, 2012b; Crocker et al., 2009). In relationships, people driven by ecosystem motivation seek to promote the well-being of the relationship partner not out of selfish motives to obtain benefits in return, but because they care about the partner or because both people care about the well-being of someone or something beyond themselves. We describe this perspective in general terms and then consider the principles of romantic relationships from the ecosystem perspective. We consider factors that predict which set of principles—those of the egosystem or those of the ecosystem—will best describe a particular relationship at a particular moment. We then suggest a number of issues for future research.

SELF AND RELATIONSHIPS MOTIVATED BY THE EGOSYSTEM

The egosystem is a motivational system centered on the self; in this system, people are primarily concerned with ensuring that their own needs are met

http://dx.doi.org/10.1037/14344-004
APA Handbook of Personality and Social Psychology: Vol. 3. Interpersonal Relations, M. Mikulincer and P. R. Shaver (Editors-in-Chief)

and their desires satisfied (Crocker & Canevello, 2012a). The important quality of relationships in the egosystem is that people strive for benefits that flow to the self from relationship partners. In this system, people are not particularly concerned about others' well-being. Accordingly, people with egosystem motivation in relationships prioritize their own needs and desires over those of other people. They are self-involved, focusing on what being in the relationship or the quality of the relationship says about them, in their own eyes and in the eyes of others. They aim to maximize their gains and minimize their losses in the relationship and in their interactions with relationship partners. They tend to view outcomes as zero-sum in nature, such that satisfaction of the needs and desires of one person must necessarily come at the expense of others (Crocker & Canevello, 2012a).

In this system, other people matter only if they can potentially satisfy or thwart one's own needs and desires. To the extent that others matter, they are viewed as an obstacle to be overcome or as a means to an end. In this system, people do not expect others to care much about their well-being for its own sake. They feel at the mercy of relationship partners because they must induce others to help them get their needs met (Crocker & Canevello, 2012a). Accordingly, when people are driven by egosystem motivation, they attempt to control others through persuasion, negotiation, ingratiation, manipulation, or intimidation (Crocker & Canevello, 2012a). In interpersonal contexts, they typically have self-image goals; that is, they try to get others to view them as having desired qualities, and as not having undesired qualities, so that others will give them what they want. They focus on proving themselves to others and obtaining validation that relationship partners recognize their positive qualities (Crocker, 2008; Crocker & Canevello, 2012a; Crocker et al., 2009).

Because relationship events in the egosystem implicate the self, emotions in these relationships tend to involve high arousal. Acceptance and validation from relationship partners elicit self-conscious emotions such as pride and boosts to self-esteem, whereas rejection and criticism elicit shame or humiliation. Furthermore, basic emotions such as

anger, fear, sadness, and happiness are self-referent; in the egosystem, one might feel anger at being treated unfairly by a relationship partner, fear of a relationship partner's negative judgment, sadness about the loss of a relationship partner, and elation or joy when obtaining desired outcomes from a relationship partner.

At the same time, relationships in the egosystem tend to elicit ambivalent feelings. Because people in this system tend to have a zero-sum view of relationships, positive events for the self are assumed to have negative implications for relationship partners, and vice versa. Thus, relationships in the egosystem inherently put people between the proverbial rock and a hard place, because although people want outcomes for themselves, they or the relationship may pay for the cost this extracts from others. Consequently, relationships in the egosystem tend to involve feeling afraid, conflicted, and confused (Crocker & Canevello, 2008).

Note that in the egosystem behavior is not completely selfish; people sometimes sacrifice or give to their relationship partners. The important question is why. In this system, people give, sacrifice, and support relationship partners as a loan or an investment, to obtain something in return from the partners (Van Lange et al., 1997). They might give expecting their partners to reciprocate, as when people say "I love you" to get the other person to say it in return. They might trade, giving in one area to obtain what they want in another area. They might give to keep their partner from leaving, to induce feelings of gratitude in their partner, to become indispensable to their partner, or to create a bank of favors or good will they can draw on so their selfish behaviors do not destroy the relationship and therefore the benefits they obtain (Batson, 1979; Murray, Aloni, et al., 2009; Murray, Leder, et al., 2009). In the egosystem, people might sometimes give and not want their partner to reciprocate because they prefer to hold the moral high ground and be seen as the good person in the relationship.

Paradoxically, egosystem motivation in close relationships does not necessarily result in increased benefits for the self, in part because relationship partners appear to sense the selfish intentions behind giving in the egosystem (Crocker & Canevello,

2008, 2012a). In general, egosystem motivation may lead people to adopt relatively short-term and narrowly self-interested perspectives in their relationships. Thus, in the egosystem people may not think about the long-term consequences of their behaviors for the sustainability of relationships over time.

RELATIONSHIPS IN THE ECOSYSTEM

Although people often care about satisfying their own needs and desires without regard for others, they also have the capacity for empathy, compassion, and generosity motivated by caring about the well-being of others (Mikulincer & Shaver, 2010). Although selfish motives underlie some altruistic behavior, people sometimes genuinely care about others' well-being (Batson, 1998; S. L. Brown, Brown, & Penner, 2012; Mikulincer & Shaver, 2010). The ability to transcend one's own self-interest and to care about something besides one's own ego and desires has important implications for understanding relationships and how they function. Only recently, however, have self researchers begun to explore systematically the capacity to transcend egotism and self-interest (e.g., Wayment & Bauer, 2008). Similarly, although caring for others has long been recognized as an important aspect of attachment relationships, particularly between parents and children, the study of a motivational system that promotes unselfish caregiving in other types of relationships is a recent development (e.g., S. L. Brown et al., 2012; Mikulincer & Shaver, 2010).

We draw on the biological notion of an ecosystem as a metaphor for a motivational system in which the self is part of a larger whole, a system of separate individuals whose actions nonetheless have consequences for others, with repercussions for the entire system that ultimately affect the ability of everyone to satisfy their needs (Crocker et al., 2009). In the interpersonal ecosystem, people see themselves and their own needs and desires as part of a larger system of interconnected people, each of whom also has needs and desires (Crocker & Canevello, 2012a). In this system, the well-being of one depends on the well-being of others and the entire system, not because others overlap mentally

with the self or are included in the self but because people who are separate and distinct and who have their own needs and desires nonetheless influence each other's well-being. The needs and desires of others are just as important and valid as the needs and desires of the self. This does not mean that in the ecosystem people treat everyone equally, feel responsible for satisfying everyone else's needs, or necessarily expend significant amounts of effort, expense, or time to ensure that everyone else's needs are met.

In the ecosystem, people care about others' well-being and assume that at least some other people care about their well-being for its own sake (Crocker & Canevello, 2012a). In this system, people trust that their own needs will be met in collaboration with their social environment, not as the result of an exchange of benefits or a successful investment but because others care about their well-being. Consequently, they do not need to manipulate, persuade, or convince others to help them satisfy their needs and desires. They recognize that satisfying their own needs and desires at the expense of others inevitably has costs to the system and ultimately themselves. Accordingly, they search for ways to get their needs met in collaboration with other people or in ways that do not harm others. People tend to feel cooperative with others and view desired outcomes as having a non–zero-sum or win–win quality. That is, they assume that success for one person need not detract from others (Crocker & Canevello, 2008). Because others care about the self, giving to others need not be costly to the self.

In this system, people feel at the source in relationships because they view themselves as the starting point in their relationships, responsible for creating relationships that are good for others as well as the self (Crocker & Canevello, 2012a). Thus, compatible with Ghandi's admonition to "be the change you want to see in the world," being at the source means "it starts with me." Accordingly, when people are driven by ecosystem motivation, they take others' needs and desires into account, considering the impact of their decisions and behaviors on people they care about (Crocker & Canevello, 2012a). In interpersonal contexts, they typically have compassionate goals; that is, they focus on being supportive and constructive toward others and on making a contribution (Crocker, 2008; Crocker & Canevello, 2012a; Crocker et al., 2009).

Relationships in the ecosystem typically elicit calm, peaceful feelings (Crocker & Canevello, 2008). Because in the ecosystem people care about others and not just themselves, they are not ego involved in events; they do not view relationship events as primarily implicating the self, diagnostic of their worth and value. Their primary concern is not how events in the relationship affect satisfaction of their own needs and desires. Consequently, in the ecosystem people are less likely to experience self-relevant emotions such as self-focused pride, shame, or humiliation, and they are more likely to experience other-directed, low-arousal emotions such as compassionate love (Sprecher & Fehr, 2005), gratitude (Tsang, 2006), and empathic concern (Batson, 1987). Acceptance and validation from relationship partners elicit humility (Exline, 2008; Tangney, 2009), whereas rejection and criticism may elicit sadness but not ego-involved emotions such as jealousy, humiliation, or shame. Furthermore, because people care about the well-being of others, basic emotions such as anger, fear, sadness, and happiness are more likely to be other-referent; in the ecosystem, one might feel anger when a relationship partner is treated unfairly, fear that a relationship partner will be hurt, sadness for a relationship partner's loss, and happiness or joy when a relationship partner obtains desired outcomes. Because people in this system tend to have a non–zero-sum view of relationships, positive events for the self are not assumed to have negative implications for relationship partners and vice versa (Crocker & Canevello, 2008). Thus, relationships in the ecosystem lead people to feel aligned with others and cooperative rather than competitive (Crocker & Canevello, 2008).

In the ecosystem, people are not completely selfless, self-sacrificing, or self-disparaging. The sustainable alternative to the selfish egosystem is not selflessness, costly altruism, or self-sacrifice; it is contributing or giving that is good for others and the self. Selflessness is unsustainable over time because it is bad for oneself and therefore bad for one's interpersonal ecosystem. Apparent selflessness or self-sacrifice often serves egoistic ends, such as demonstrating one's generosity to others, earning respect or admiration, or making others feel indebted (Cialdini, Brown, Lewis, Luce, & Neuberg, 1997). Unmitigated communion, or excessive concern for others in relationships, is often driven by the desire to boost self-esteem or keep others close by demonstrating that one is indispensable (Fritz & Helgeson, 1998). Again, the important question is why people sacrifice or give to their partners (Konrath, Fuhrel-Forbis, Lou, & Brown, 2012). In the ecosystem, people give, sacrifice, and support relationship partners freely, trusting that their own needs will be met in collaboration with others. Although needs may sometimes be met by the partner, they can also be in collaboration with others in the interpersonal ecosystem. Giving is not a loan or an investment, to obtain something in return from others. In the ecosystem, people do not give to get others to reciprocate, as a trade, or to keep their partner from leaving. Giving in the ecosystem is not to hold the moral high ground or prove something about the self. People give voluntarily, with no strings attached, with the intention to promote the well-being of others (e.g., Feeney & Collins, 2003).

Paradoxically, ecosystem motivation in close relationships seems to result in increased benefits for the self, in part because giving directly benefits the self and in part because relationship partners appear to sense the caring intentions behind giving in the ecosystem (Crocker & Canevello, 2008, 2012a). In general, ecosystem motivation may lead people to adopt relatively long-term views of relationships, in which they consider the consequences of their behaviors for the sustainability of relationships over time.

CATEGORIZING RELATIONSHIP THEORIES AS EGOSYSTEM OR ECOSYSTEM

If, as we hypothesize, there are two sets of fundamental principles of relationships—one governing relationships in the egosystem and the other governing relationships in the ecosystem—then it becomes important to understand which relationship theories, programs of research, and empirical findings link to which set of principles. The distinction between egosystem and ecosystem motivations in relationships is not about what people do but about why they do it; in the egosystem, people are primarily concerned with satisfaction of their own needs and desires, whereas in the ecosystem people care about the well-being of others—with an emphasis on the emotional bond of caring. In our reading of the literature, researchers are often vague about this issue, or their work is misinterpreted.

One of many examples concerns research on the distinction between communal and exchange relationships. Clark and Mills (e.g., Clark, Mills, & Powell, 1986) proposed that the giving and receipt of benefits in relationships can be governed either by exchange norms, in which benefits are given with the expectation of receiving equal benefits in return, or by communal norms, in which benefits are given noncontingently to promote the well-being of the partner.

The focus on norms governing receipt of benefits in both the original qualitative distinction between communal and exchange relationships and the subsequent research on variation in communal strength is often interpreted as meaning that exchange relationships are selfish, whereas communal relationships are selfless (Clark, 2011). However, as Clark (2011) pointed out, people can have selfish motivations in a communal relationship, and they can have selfless motivations in an exchange relationship. The desire for a communal relationship leads people to focus on what their partners do for them and monitor their partner's responsiveness to their needs (Clark, Dubash, & Mills, 1998). Indeed, people may desire a communal relationship with another person because they believe such a relationship is the best way to satisfy their own needs; they are willing to attend to the needs of their partner to obtain the benefits of being in a communal relationship. The Communal Orientation Scale, which assesses individual differences in the tendency to adopt communal norms in relationships, includes items such as "It bothers me when other people neglect my needs" and "I expect people I know to be responsive to my needs and feelings," consistent with the idea that people may have a communal orientation as a strategy for getting their own needs met (Clark, Oullette, Powell, & Milberg, 1987).

Likewise, the strength of a communal relationship is operationalized as how much cost people will incur in terms of time, money, or effort to benefit another person; the scale is not a measure of how much people care about the other person or are willing to give noncostly emotional support (Mills, Clark, Ford, & Johnson, 2004).

By the same reasoning, exchange relationships are not inherently selfish or motivated by the egosystem. There is nothing inherently selfish about wanting to pay a fair price for goods one purchases in an exchange relationship; in the ecosystem, people may want a seller to obtain a fair price and make a decent living because they care about the seller's well-being and so the relationship can be sustained over time. They may consider the well-being of those who produce or distribute goods they purchase, the impact of production and distribution on the environment, and other factors that affect the well-being of others and the sustainability of the interpersonal ecosystem. We do not suggest that communal relationships are always motivated by the egosystem or exchange relationships by the ecosystem; in general, communal strength correlates positively with love and caring. Sharing, however, is not the same thing as caring; sometimes responding to the needs of others is governed by strong communal norms because people feel obligated and not because they feel love, as when adult children feel resentful yet obligated to respond to their aging parents' needs. Sometimes people care about the well-being of those with whom they have exchange relationships. The norms that apply to a particular relationship do not necessarily govern whether people in that relationship have egosystem or ecosystem motivations.

We use the communal–exchange distinction to illustrate a broader point about the confusion that can arise in relationship theories, in part because Clark herself has attempted to clarify this same confusion (Clark, 2011). Many other theories and programs of research have been vague either in their conceptualization or in others' interpretations as to whether people prioritize their own well-being in their close relationships over that of their relationship partners or whether they take others' well-being into account because they care about them.

Examining close relationships through the lens of egosystem and ecosystem motivational systems may clarify the psychology of relationships.

ROMANTIC RELATIONSHIPS IN THE EGOSYSTEM: IT'S ABOUT ME

Egosystem motivation shapes the quality of romantic relationships in all their stages, from initial attraction and drawing close, through the thrill of falling in love, to maintaining the relationship, to relationship breakdown and dissolution.

Attraction: Impression Management and Self-Presentation

In the egosystem, people want to be in a romantic relationship for the benefits it can provide them. These benefits may range from tangible benefits such as financial advantages (Drigotas & Rusbult, 1992; Rusbult, Drigotas, & Verette, 1994) and access to an attractive sexual partner (Drigotas & Rusbult, 1992; Rusbult et al., 1994) to intangible benefits such as feelings of security and belonging, meeting normative expectations that one should be in a relationship (DePaulo & Morris, 2006), basking in the reflected glory of the partner's accomplishments (Tesser, 1988), and a boost in self-esteem (Sanchez & Kwang, 2007).

Accordingly, the initial goal of a relationship is to attract the most desirable partner one can and win his or her love and affection (Fletcher, Simpson, & Thomas, 2000). To attract a partner, people want to ensure that potential partners see them as having desirable qualities and as not having undesirable qualities. Self-presentation can help people accomplish interpersonal goals that depend on influencing or controlling the responses other people have to them (Schlenker, 2003). Consequently, in the initial stages of romantic relationships in the egosystem, people present themselves in the best possible light, acting in ways that ensure that potential partners notice their positive qualities and do not see them as having negative qualities. People get their game face on, put their best foot forward, and are on their best behavior. For example, to appear more feminine, women eat less when getting acquainted with a desirable man than when getting acquainted with a less desirable man or a woman (Mori, Chaiken, & Pliner, 1987; Pliner & Chaiken, 1990). The qualities considered attractive or desirable can vary; different people might want to ensure that potential partners see them as physically attractive, outdoorsy, kind, or accommodating. When attempting to attract a specific partner, self-presentations may be tailored to the preferences of the prospect. For example, women expecting to interact with a socially desirable man who held traditional attitudes toward women described themselves as possessing more stereotypic feminine attitudes and traits than women expecting to interact with a man with less traditional views (Zanna & Pack, 1975).

There are limits to the images people can successfully present to others (Schlenker, 2003). Although anyone can describe him- or herself as tall, attractive, and physically fit on an Internet dating service, many gross misrepresentations will quickly be uncovered in face-to-face meetings. Most self-presentation involves efforts to convey roughly accurate but slightly improved, polished, or glorified images of oneself (Greenwald & Breckler, 1985).

The initial attraction stage of romantic relationships in the egosystem creates several types of risk. First, one could fail to attract desirable partners for a variety of reasons: because one lacks qualities others desire, one's self-presentation skills are lacking, or the people one desires are unavailable or unobtainable. The risk of failing to attract someone desirable is what the failure says about oneself—that one is unattractive and undesirable—and the consequent blow to self-esteem (Sanchez, Good, Kwang, & Saltzman, 2008; Sanchez & Kwang, 2007).

Second, one could be fooled by a prospective partner's self-presentation and drawn into a relationship with a person with serious flaws, perhaps forgoing more attractive alternatives in the process. Because both partners likely have the same aim to attract the most desirable mate possible, by presenting themselves in a positive light each risks being duped by the other, believing the other person has qualities he or she does not, in fact, have. Consequently, each must verify that the self-presentations of the prospective partner are based on fact rather than fiction. They may ask mutual acquaintances, do Internet research, or even hire a private investigator to verify that a prospective partner has the desirable qualities he or she claims. Efforts to verify the claims of potential partners can be time consuming, expensive, and unreliable; for example, friends will often aid and abet self-presentations, whereas exes may have axes to grind, making them less than ideal references (Schlenker & Britt, 1999). At the same time, however, when a prospective partner appears to offer important benefits (e.g., when the partner is very attractive, wealthy, or powerful), people may be motivated to discount or overlook potential partners' shortcomings even at this early stage (Kunda, 1990). For example, the fact that a prospective partner's previous two marriages ended in divorce after extramarital affairs may be discounted ("It will be different with me") or the seriousness of a gambling or alcohol problem diminished because of the benefits that could be gained in the relationship. Thus, even in the initial attraction stage, potential partners may collude to support each other's self-presentations and overlook flaws that pose significant problems to a relationship.

Third, prospective partners might see through one's own self-presentations. Prospective partners who discover one's foibles and flaws might lose interest or conclude that they could do better with another person, leading to rejection. Consequently, initial stages of relationships in the egosystem involve pressure to be at one's best and concomitant anxiety that one might not be able to sustain the illusion. Although concern about having one's flaws revealed may encourage people to be their best selves, with potentially lasting consequences (see Schlenker, 2003, for a review), self-presentation interferes with getting to know and being known by the other person beyond a superficial level. Initial attraction in the egosystem, then, is less about attraction between two authentic human beings and more about attraction between two constructed images.

Drawing Close: Risk Regulation

Once people have attracted the interest of a potential partner, to obtain many of the benefits of romantic relationships they must draw close to one another. In the egosystem, closeness may involve inclusion of the relationship partner in representations of the self, thus expanding the resources available to the self (Aron, Aron, & Smollan, 1992). In close relationships in the egosystem, one's happiness depends on one's partner (Rusbult & Van Lange, 2003). A key predictor of closeness is perceived partner responsiveness to the self—that is, the degree to which people believe that their partner understands who they are, cares about them, and validates central, core features of the self (Reis, Clark, & Holmes, 2004).

How, then, do relationships in the egosystem evolve from attracting a partner through self-presentation of desired images to a degree of closeness based on the perception that one's partner understands, cares about, and validates central features of the self? The risk regulation model describes the dilemma of this phase of romantic relationships in the egosystem (Murray, Holmes, & Collins, 2006). According to the risk regulation model, people obtain many of the psychological benefits of relationships, such as feelings of belonging and connectedness, only when they become emotionally close to their partners. Closeness, however, requires vulnerability; people must "behave in ways that give a partner power over their outcomes and emotions and think in ways that invest great value and importance in the relationship" (Murray et al., 2006, p. 641). These behaviors both increase the potential for rejection in the short term and intensify the pain of rejection if and when it occurs in the long term.

According to the risk regulation model, people resolve this dilemma by monitoring the regard their partner has for them and acting in ways that increase vulnerability and closeness only when they are confident that they will not be rejected. When they perceive that their partner's regard is waning, people increase psychological distance from their partners to protect themselves from the pain of rejection. Relationships in the egosystem begin with mistrust; partners must earn the trust that permits vulnerability and closeness. Trust develops as a result of diagnostic situations, when people perceive that their partners behave in ways that benefit the relationship, departing from their direct self-interest for the good of the relationship (e.g., Simpson, 2007; Wieselquist, Rusbult, Foster, & Agnew,

1999). Ultimately, if their partner passes repeated tests by responding to vulnerability and self-disclosures with understanding, caring, and validation and signals his or her positive regard, people will gradually allow their weaknesses and shortcomings to be known by their partners, creating intimacy and closeness.

Despite this increasing vulnerability, however, in the egosystem people continue to want their partners to idealize them; that is, they want their partners to regard them more highly than they regard themselves (Murray, Holmes, & Griffin, 2000). This creates a Catch-22 situation—people want to be close and vulnerable to their partners but fear that revealing their weaknesses might undermine the idealized images their partners have of them.

Several aspects of the risk regulation model prompt us to suggest that it characterizes relationships in the egosystem. First, the focus of the model is on obtaining benefits and avoiding risk for the self; in this model, people are preoccupied with their own needs and desires. Second, although people may give support to their partners, they do so only when they are confident that their partner will not reject them, and they do so to obtain benefits for the self. Third, the key mechanism that regulates closeness versus distance in relationships is perceived partner regard. Thus, the image partners have of the self is a constant concern. Fourth, in the risk regulation model people feel at the mercy of their partners. People cannot allow themselves to be vulnerable in ways that create closeness until their partners have proven their trustworthiness and signaled their regard and caring. The worst thing that can happen in relationships is the pain of being rejected by a partner after one has allowed oneself to be vulnerable, so one's happiness is in the hands of one's partner.

Love: Desire and the Ego High

When people present themselves successfully, attract a romantic partner, and draw close while regulating the risks of dependency, they may fall in love. Although falling in love can be a mutual experience between partners, it has two separable aspects—loving another and being loved. In the egosystem, both aspects of love center on oneself.

Loving.   Passionate love has been described as "a state of intense longing for union with another" (Hatfield & Walster, 1978, p. 9). In the egosystem, loving another person involves desire—not necessarily sexual desire (Diamond, 2003; Gonzaga, Turner, Keltner, Campos, & Altemus, 2006), but the desire of wanting to win, possess, or acquire the loved one.

The distinction between wanting and liking proposed by addiction researchers is useful when characterizing love in the egosystem (Berridge, 2004a, 2004b; Berridge & Robinson, 1995; Robinson & Berridge, 2003). In this research, *liking* refers to activation of pleasure systems in the brain, whereas *wanting* refers to the attributed incentive value of the object of desire, which drives the desire to consume it. Although liking and wanting often coincide, they are potentially separable: One can derive pleasure from a sunset but not want to consume it, and one can want to consume cake without deriving pleasure from it. We suggest that loving someone in the egosystem involves wanting the person but not necessarily liking him or her.

Consistent with the idea that passionate love in the egosystem is like an addiction, passionate love shares some similarities with addiction to substances, including euphoria and unrestrained desire in the presence of the loved one; desperation, anhedonia, and sleep disturbance when separated from the loved one; focused attention on and intrusive thoughts about the loved one; and maladaptive patterns of behavior leading to distress and pursuit of the loved one despite knowledge of adverse consequences (see Reynaud, Karila, Blecha, & Benyamina, 2010, for a review). Some studies have indicated that passionate love and substance dependence involve similar brain regions and neurotransmitters. These addictive qualities of passionate love in the egosystem may explain why it is usually unsustainable (Acevedo & Aron, 2009).

Being loved.   When passionate love is reciprocated, people experience the emotional high of winning their partner's love and affection. In the egosystem, falling in love—that is, winning the love and affection of a partner one desires—indicates that one is desirable and loveable, hence raising self-esteem

(Aron, Paris, & Aron, 1995). Indeed, no other life event may have the same potential for boosting self-esteem as winning the love of a desired partner because the degree of acceptance is very high and the entire self is validated. To be sure, people differ in how much their self-esteem is contingent on being in a relationship (Sanchez & Kwang, 2007) and on having that relationship go well (Knee, Canevello, Bush, & Cook, 2008). However, if self-esteem is an indicator of perceived relational value, as sociometer theory suggests (Leary & Baumeister, 2000), being loved by a desired partner is likely an important self-esteem boost for nearly everyone. Falling in love should boost one's relational value in the eyes of other people as well. Particularly if the partner is considered desirable by others, winning the partner's love is a sure signal that one has value as a romantic relationship partner.

Beyond boosting self-esteem, falling in love also appears to expand the contents of the self-concept. Seeing the self through the eyes of a loving partner, people may see qualities in themselves they did not know they had or did not appreciate before. In addition, according to self-expansion theory, "a close relationship involves integrating, to some extent, other's resources, perspectives, and characteristics into the self" (Aron et al., 1995, p. 1103). Thus, people gain in numerous ways when they are loved by another.

Once people win the love and affection of a partner, their motivation to have positive illusions about their partner increases. Whereas people trying to attract a desirable partner may want to know the reality behind the partner's self-presentation, once they have won the partner's love and affection they should be highly motivated to see that person in the most desirable ways possible (Murray, Holmes, & Griffin, 1996a, 1996b). After all, being loved by someone with many highly desirable qualities should be a greater boost to self-esteem and one's public image than being loved by someone with obvious flaws and foibles.

Satisfaction and Commitment: Negotiating Conflicting Goals and Desires

Once people have attracted a partner, drawn close, and perhaps fallen in love, they may be sufficiently satisfied with the relationship that they commit to it. In the egosystem, relationship satisfaction depends on the degree to which the relationship gratifies one's own important needs and desires; commitment refers to the desire for the relationship to last a long time (Rusbult, Martz, & Agnew, 1998). Satisfaction is an important, but not the only, predictor of commitment to a relationship. According to the investment model, commitment to the relationship develops as a result of high levels of satisfaction, the absence of available alternatives (i.e., other potential partners who could more effectively gratify one's important needs and desires), and high levels of investment of resources (e.g., personal identity, effort, or material possessions) that would be lost or reduced if one were not in the relationship (Rusbult et al., 1994, 1998). Thus, in the egosystem people might remain committed to a relationship even though an available alternative would provide them more benefits if they have invested significant resources in the current relationship.

Love and commitment involve interdependence; each partner has the capacity to influence the happiness of the other, for better or worse (Kelley & Thibaut, 1978; Rusbult & Van Lange, 2003; Thibaut & Kelley, 1959). A variety of conflicts of interest may develop that could threaten the relationship and therefore the benefits people obtain from it. One such conflict of interest is a potential threat to self-esteem or self-evaluation when people are outperformed by their partner in an important, self-defining domain (Tesser, 1988). A second type of conflict of interest involves incompatibility of preferences, goals, and desires, so when one partner gets what he or she wants, the other necessarily does not (Rusbult & Van Lange, 2003). Third, one's relationship partner may behave badly, acting in ways that seem inconsiderate or annoying (Yovetich & Rusbult, 1994). The most serious type of conflict involves acts of betrayal, in which one partner humiliates or degrades the other partner (Finkel, Rusbult, Kumashiro, & Hannon, 2002).

Conflicts of interest such as these challenge relationships in the egosystem because they interfere with the gratification of needs and desires on which relationship satisfaction depends. People can respond to these conflicts in ways that promote their direct self-interest, for example by attempting to outperform their partner or sabotaging the partner's performance (Tesser, 1988); by insisting that their own needs and desires are met, even at the expense of their partner; by criticizing their partner's annoying behaviors; or by retaliating against the partner in the case of betrayal. These responses promote self-interest in the immediate situation but have high costs to the relationship over time (Rusbult & Agnew, 2010). Alternatively, people can undergo what Rusbult and Van Lange (2003) called a *transformation of motivation*, prioritizing the survival of the relationship over direct and immediate self-interest. For example, people can respond to conflicts of goals and desires with sacrifice (e.g., compromising or deferring to their partner's wishes), to bad behavior from their partner with conciliation and accommodation (e.g., ignoring the bad behavior), and to betrayal with forgiveness (Rusbult & Agnew, 2010).

Because sacrifice, accommodation, and forgiveness do not effectively resolve the original conflict, relationship satisfaction may decline over time despite these prorelationship responses and the trust they engender (Wieselquist et al., 1999). People may sustain their commitment despite their decreased satisfaction after conflicts of interest by convincing themselves that their relationship is superior to other relationships (Rusbult, Lange, Wildschut, Yovetich, & Verette, 2000) or by ignoring or devaluing alternative relationship partners (Johnson & Rusbult, 1989).

According to Rusbult and Agnew (2010), sacrifice, accommodation, and forgiveness are constructive responses to conflicts because they promote the survival of the relationship. The more committed people are to a relationship, the more likely they are to respond to conflicts with prorelationship behaviors. Although these responses might be considered prosocial in this sense, their association with commitment implicates the egosystem, in our opinion. Because commitment in this research is a product of satisfaction (i.e., people believe their needs and desires are gratified by the relationship), lack of better alternative relationships, and investment (i.e., the resources people stand to lose if the relationship ends), associations of prorelationship behaviors with commitment suggest that they are typically driven by concern with one's own needs and desires. The transformation of motivation that precedes these prorelationship behaviors is not typically a shift away from egosystem motivation but rather a shift from one's immediate, narrow self-interest in the specific situation to one's larger self-interest as a partner in the relationship over time.

Breaking Up: Leaving and Being Left

In the egosystem, relationship breakups happen when one of the relationship partners determines that the benefits he or she would gain from breaking up outweigh the costs. People are more likely to choose to leave a relationship when their dependence and investment are low. That is, people are more likely to choose to leave when they do not stand to lose resources (Rusbult et al., 1994, 1998) and when their important needs can be better met elsewhere than in their current relationship (Drigotas & Rusbult, 1992). Commitment to the relationship (i.e., the desire for the relationship to last), which includes need gratification, availability of alternatives, and investment, is a strong predictor of decisions to stay in the relationship rather than leave it (Rusbult et al., 1994).

Whereas the investment model predicts who will choose to leave and who will choose to stay in relationships in the egosystem, other researchers have focused on the reactions of the person who is left. Just as falling in love is one of the most significant self-esteem boosts people can experience, involuntarily being left, particularly for another person, provides a clear signal that one lacks sufficient relational value to hold onto a partner. This is one of the most significant blows to self-esteem people can experience (Leary & Baumeister, 2000). People whose self-esteem is invested in having a good relationship, or simply in being in a relationship, are particularly vulnerable to feelings of worthlessness when a relationship breaks up (Knee et al., 2008; Park, Sanchez, & Brynildsen, 2011a). Romantic jealousy is related to both the self-esteem threat of potentially being left for another and the loss of relationship benefits (Mathes, Adams, & Davies, 1985; Sharpsteen, 1995; White, 1981). Even those whose self-esteem is not particularly invested in being in a good relationship experience a loss of benefits, ranging from financial and material benefits to companionship and social support (Drigotas & Rusbult, 1992). Not surprisingly, the person who is left is more dependent on the relationship for satisfaction of important needs than the person who leaves. Perhaps more surprising, people who are left feel just as dependent on their partners as people in relationships that do not break up (Drigotas & Rusbult, 1992). In addition to dependency on a partner for satisfaction of important needs, greater investment of time, effort, and material resources in the relationship should make being left particularly painful. When people feel close to a relationship partner and include the other in mental representations of themselves (Aron, Aron, Tudor, & Nelson, 1991), believe that their partner brings out the best in them (Rusbult, Kumashiro, Kubacka, & Finkel, 2009), or believe that their partner knows them intimately, being left should hurt even more.

Research on social exclusion has demonstrated that the self-threat of being rejected has a wide range of negative effects beyond loss of self-esteem and increased negative emotions. Social exclusion can lead to failures of self-control (Baumeister, DeWall, Ciarocco, & Twenge, 2005), decreased prosocial behavior (Twenge, Baumeister, DeWall, Ciarocco, & Bartels, 2007), distorted perceptions of time, meaninglessness, decreased self-awareness (Twenge, Catanese, & Baumeister, 2003), and increased self-destructive behavior (Twenge, Catanese, & Baumeister, 2002). Even the threat of being alone later in one's life leads to the temporary loss of cognitive capacities (Baumeister, Twenge, & Nuss, 2002). Destructive impulses may be directed against the self, as in risk taking, drinking, or suicide attempts (Baumeister, 1997; Baumeister & Scher, 1988; Leith & Baumeister, 1996), or against the rejecting partner, as in stalking or physical violence (Twenge, Baumeister, Tice, & Stucke, 2001). Although most of the relevant research has not focused specifically on romantic rejection, it seems plausible that romantic rejection is more threatening to self-esteem and therefore has more negative effects than exclusion from a group of strangers in a laboratory experiment (Leary, Tambor, Terdal, & Downs, 1995) or ostracism in a game of cyberball with computer avatars (van Beest & Williams, 2006). Whether destructive impulses are directed toward the self or toward the rejecting partner, destructive responses to romantic rejection can exact a high toll.

Destructive responses to rejection are particularly likely for relationships in the egosystem. Findings have indicated that people with a more fragile sense of self-worth are particularly likely to respond in counterproductive, destructive, and ultimately self-destructive ways, suggesting that these destructive responses are driven by ego involvement in the relationship, in one form or another. For example, destructive or counterproductive responses to rejection have been linked to individual differences in narcissism (Twenge & Campbell, 2003), fragile egotism (Baumeister, Smart, & Boden, 1996), relationship-contingent self-esteem (Park, Sanchez, & Brynildsen, 2011b), shame proneness (Tangney, Wagner, Hill-Barlow, Marschall, & Gramzow, 1996), and rejection sensitivity (Downey, Feldman, & Ayduk, 2000; Downey, Freitas, Michaelis, & Khouri, 1998).

Although most research has focused on destructive responses to rejection, rejection can increase the desire to affiliate with new partners (Maner, DeWall, Baumeister, & Schaller, 2007). This finding might explain why some people enter rebound relationships right after a breakup—they need the connection to feel that they belong.

Summary

To this point, we have described a number of widely accepted principles of romantic relationships. The theories and findings summarized so far represent, for the most part, the established and accepted wisdom of relationship researchers, self researchers, or both. These principles of relationships all view romantic relationships as a means to gratify one's own needs and desires, whether for companionship and support, material well-being, self-esteem, or other desirable outcomes. The needs and desires of others, including relationship partners, are secondary and are taken into account only because maintaining the benefits of being in the relationship require it.

We do not mean to suggest that all relationships in the egosystem are the same. Just as "every unhappy family is unhappy in its own way" (as Tolstoy wrote), every relationship may have its own egosystem dynamics. Relationship researchers have noted a variety of ways in which people differ in their characteristic approaches to relationships. For example, people can have approach and avoidance reasons for sacrificing in their relationships (Impett, Gable, & Peplau, 2005; Impett et al., 2010) and anxious or avoidant styles of attachment insecurity (Mikulincer & Shaver, 2003). Other researchers have documented that trait self-esteem moderates how people manage risk and opportunity in relationships (Forest & Wood, 2011; Murray et al., 2000; Wood & Forest, 2011).

While acknowledging the reality of these differences and the consequences they have for relationships, we suggest that each of these distinctions describes two sides of the same coin rather than fundamentally different paradigms in relationships. For example, both the self-protection of people low in self-esteem and the self-enhancement of people with high self-esteem reflect, first and foremost, a concern with self-esteem. Both sacrificing in relationships to keep one's partner happy and sacrificing to avoid making one's partner angry represent accommodation in conflict situations to continue obtaining the benefits of the relationship. Similarly, anxious and avoidant attachment styles represent different ways of coping with concern that one's own needs will not be met in a relationship. Again, our point is not that these style differences are unimportant but that they represent different ways of managing relationships in the egosystem.

ROMANTIC RELATIONSHIPS IN THE ECOSYSTEM: IT'S ABOUT MORE THAN ME

Because the idea of relationships in the ecosystem is a newly emerging perspective on self and relationships, little research has examined how ecosystem motivation shapes the quality of romantic relationships in all stages. Thus, the following sections articulate hypotheses about romantic relationships in the ecosystem, citing supportive evidence when possible.

Attraction: Getting to Know Each Other

Although people with ecosystem motivation may want to be in a relationship, their main goal is not to attract the person who can best satisfy their own needs and desires but rather to find a person whose joys and sorrows they want to share and whose well-being they want to support. Consequently, we hypothesize that the initial stage of relationships in the ecosystem focuses on getting to know each other—not only strengths and aspirations, but also foibles and challenges. Because in the ecosystem one's own needs and desires are neither more nor less important than others', people seek romantic relationships that are good for both partners. Thus, in the ecosystem, people should not be attracted to partners simply because of the physical, material, or emotional resources potential partners have or because potential partners are needy and can be rescued, but rather because they want to contribute to their partner's well-being and the potential partner wants to contribute to their well-being.

The Michelangelo phenomenon, in which relationship partners help each other move toward their ideal selves (Drigotas, Rusbult, Wieselquist, & Whitton, 1999; Rusbult, Finkel, & Kumashiro, 2009; Rusbult, Kumashiro, et al., 2009), may provide an example of this good-for-each-other aspect of relationships in the ecosystem. People are more attracted to potential partners when the partner's actual qualities resemble their own ideal selves (Rusbult, Kumashiro, et al., 2009), consistent with either egosystem or ecosystem motivation. In ecosystem relationships, we expect that people are also more attracted to potential partners when the potential partner's ideal self is inspiring to them; that is, they want to help the potential partner more toward his or her ideal self.

We hypothesize that relationships in the ecosystem are built on honesty and openness rather than self-presentation. Creating a relationship in which both partners take each other's needs and desires into account requires that people be honest and open about their own needs and desires. Furthermore, in this system people acknowledge the ways in which they and their potential partner fall short of ideal. They share their hopes and dreams and perhaps also their fears. Thus, in contrast to relationships in the egosystem, relationships in the ecosystem begin with disclosure of emotionally significant self-relevant information.

Research on the Michelangelo phenomenon has indirectly highlighted this aspect of initial attraction in the ecosystem (Rusbult, Kumashiro, et al., 2009). Specifically, the finding that people are attracted to potential partners who can help them move closer to their ideal selves suggests that these people are willing to acknowledge that they fall short of their ideal selves in some regards. Similarly, the finding that partners who possess key components of one another's ideal selves are more likely to believe in one another's potential and challenge one another suggests that in these relationships people recognize some of their partner's imperfections, and they try to support their partner to move closer to his or her ideal (Rusbult, Kumashiro, et al., 2009).

Thus, romantic relationships in the ecosystem are built on vulnerability—acknowledging one's own and the potential partner's imperfections, seeing the potential in one another, and wanting to support each other to move toward each other's ideal self. Because in the ecosystem people tend to be at the source of what they want to experience in relationships rather than at the mercy of their partners, we expect that in these relationships people view themselves as the starting point of the openness, honesty, and vulnerability they want in their relationships; they do not wait for potential partners to reveal their imperfections, hopes, and fears before revealing their own.

The initial attraction stage of romantic relationships in the ecosystem involves some of the same risks as relationships in the egosystem. Specifically, as with relationships in the egosystem, one could fail to find a partner. Because people may disclose more emotionally significant self-relevant information early on in the relationship, rejection by a partner is not rejection of an image one has constructed of the self but rather rejection of one's authentic self, which can hurt. However, the conclusions people draw from rejection in the ecosystem differ from the conclusions they draw in the egosystem. In the egosystem, relationships validate self-esteem and relational value; rejection implies that one has low relational value and can pose a devastating blow to self-esteem. In the ecosystem, people seek a relationship that is good for both people; rejection implies that the relationship was not good for the other

person, so it was not the relationship one desired. The risk of failing to find a suitable partner is the disappointment of not having someone with whom to share one's hopes and fears and with whom to create a mutually supportive relationship. Although the failure to find a relationship partner may be sad and disappointing, it should not pose a devastating blow to self-esteem.

Furthermore, as in the egosystem, people could be fooled by a prospective partner's self-presentation. Thus, one person may take the risk to reveal his or her imperfections, hopes, and fears, whereas a potential partner engages in self-presentation. This sort of mismatch of goals should be relatively easy to detect, however, because the risks one person takes by revealing imperfections would not be reciprocated by the other, and neither person should find this situation appealing.

Drawing Close: Creating a Trusting and Supportive Relationship

In the ecosystem, closeness involves knowing each other and caring about each other's well-being rather than acquiring the other's resources as a result of including the other in the self (Aron et al., 1992). Relationships in the ecosystem are not built on self-presentation and image management but rather on vulnerability and honesty, which create the possibility for potential partners to know and care about each other. Consequently, drawing close in the ecosystem is simpler and less problematic (Canevello & Crocker, 2010; Crocker & Canevello, 2008).

In contrast to the egosystem, in which drawing close involves increasingly depending on the other for gratification of one's needs and desires (Rusbult et al., 1994), in the ecosystem drawing close involves creating a mutually trusting, supportive, and responsive relationship (Canevello & Crocker, 2010; Clark & Monin, 2006; Crocker & Canevello, 2008; Feeney & Collins, 2003). Self-esteem comes not from the perceived regard of partners or assessments of one's desirability to others but rather from giving support and being responsive to partners and knowing that one can make a positive contribution to another's well-being and support him or her to develop real potential. In roommate relationships, for example, increases in students' self-esteem over the first semester of college are not predicted by how responsive they perceive their roommates to be but instead by how responsive students are to their roommates (Canevello & Crocker, 2011). Thus, self-esteem may reflect different aspects of perceived relational value in the ecosystem and the egosystem. Whereas in the egosystem perceived relational value depends on the desired images one has constructed in others' eyes, in the ecosystem it depends on knowing that one can contribute, making a positive difference for others. Although others may develop desired images of the self, one's own self-esteem does not depend on this happening.

Of course, growing close is not assured in romantic relationships in the ecosystem; sometimes as partners get to know each other well, they may conclude that their hopes and dreams are not compatible, or they may not wish to help each other move toward ideal selves they find uninspiring. Because the primary concern of relationships in the ecosystem is promoting the well-being of the partner in ways that are mutually beneficial, the failure to draw close may be sad and disappointing but not devastating to self-esteem.

Because people are less ego involved in relationships in the ecosystem, they should feel less need to regulate the risk of rejection by testing whether their partner can be trusted not to hurt them before they open up to the partner. Because they care about their partner's well-being and view themselves as the starting point of constructive relationship processes, they aim to create supportive, responsive relationships by giving support to their partner and responding to their partners' needs (Canevello & Crocker, 2010; Crocker & Canevello, 2008). Their partners are likely to notice this supportive, responsive behavior and reciprocate by being supportive and responsive in return (Canevello & Crocker, 2010; Crocker & Canevello, 2008; Gable & Reis, 2006; Lemay, Clark, & Feeney, 2007). Although partners are not guaranteed to reciprocate with increased support and responsiveness, research on college roommates has indicated that people who perceive that a relationship partner has become more supportive and responsive give more support and responsiveness in return (Canevello & Crocker, 2010; Crocker & Canevello, 2008).

Through this process of caring about their partner's well-being and creating upward spirals of support and responsiveness in the relationship, people develop increased trust (Crocker & Canevello, 2008). In contrast to the egosystem, in which trust is initially low and partners must earn trust by acting against their own self-interest for the good of the relationship (Wieselquist et al., 1999), in the ecosystem relationships begin with trust. This is not to suggest that people with ecosystem motivation trust blindly; rather, if partners in diagnostic situations act on their direct self-interest in ways that are bad for the self or harm the relationship, then trust will decline (e.g., Simpson, 2007; Wieselquist et al., 1999). Whereas trust in the egosystem depends on partners proving their trustworthiness, in the ecosystem people are the starting point of trust, creating trust by caring about their partner's well-being. Over time, closeness increases for both partners (Canevello & Crocker, 2010). Furthermore, when people notice that their partners have become more responsive, they tend to develop increased compassionate goals toward their partners—that is, they want to be supportive and constructive toward their partners (Canevello & Crocker, 2010). Thus, one partner's compassionate goals elicit increases in the other partner's compassionate goals over time.

Love: Affection and Caregiving

When people find someone whose hopes and dreams they find inspiring and want to support, they may fall in love. In the ecosystem, loving another centers on caring about the other; being loved indicates the opportunity to create a mutually caring and supportive relationship.

Loving. Loving another person in the ecosystem means caring—developing affectional bonds that promote wanting the best for the other; wanting to encourage the other's growth, aspirations, and well-being; and wanting to give to the loved one (S. L. Brown & Brown, 2006; Shaver & Hazan, 1988; Shaver, Mikulincer, & Shemesh-Iron, 2010). Thus, love in the ecosystem has elements of compassionate love (Sprecher & Fehr, 2005;

Underwood, 2002). To love in the ecosystem does not require that one win or possess the other, only that one feel an emotional bond that inspires giving. Again, the distinction between wanting and liking is useful (Berridge, 2004b). Thoughts of the loved one, or being in the presence of the loved one, should involve liking more than wanting—that is, the loved one should activate pleasure systems without necessarily activating the motivation to acquire or consume. Consistent with this idea, compassionate love relates more strongly to life satisfaction than does passionate love (Kim & Hatfield, 2004) and does not lead to the intense emotional highs and lows characteristic of passionate love (Underwood, 2002).

Accumulating research findings have indicated that feelings of love in the ecosystem enable people to transcend self-interest (S. L. Brown & Brown, 2006; S. L. Brown et al., 2012; Shaver et al., 2010). Love in the ecosystem activates the caregiving behavioral system (Gonzaga, Keltner, Londahl, & Smith, 2001; Gonzaga et al., 2006; Shaver & Hazan, 1988; Shaver et al., 2010). Because love involves caring about someone other than oneself and wanting to promote the well-being of others in ways that are good for the self, it fosters personal growth (Aron & Aron, 1986). In roommate dyads, feelings of love and connection are linked to the desire to be supportive and constructive (Crocker & Canevello, 2008). Reflecting on important values induces feelings of love and connection, which reduce defensive responses to self-threatening health information (Crocker, Niiya, & Mischkowski, 2008).

Being loved. In the ecosystem, being loved means being cared for by a partner who is supportive and responsive (Berscheid, 2010; Collins & Feeney, 2000; Cutrona, 1996; Feeney & Collins, 2001, 2003; Post, Underwood, Schloss, & Hurlbut, 2002; Sprecher & Fehr, 2005). Being loved affords the opportunity to create a mutually supportive and caring relationship. Perhaps the most important aspect of love in the ecosystem is that people do not wait for another person to love them before they give love; love cannot be earned, won, or stolen. Rather, people create love in the ecosystem by giving

it freely. When freely given, and accompanied by caring, constructive, supportive behavior, others may reciprocate with love and affection.

Satisfaction and Commitment: Negotiating Conflicting Goals and Desires

Once people have found a partner, drawn close, and perhaps fallen in love, they may become committed. In the ecosystem, commitment refers not to the desire for the relationship to last a long time (Rusbult et al., 1998) but rather to the intention to make the relationship good for both partners. Relationship satisfaction depends on the degree to which the relationship is good for both partners—that is, whether partners are mutually supportive and responsive and the relationship promotes the growth and well-being of both partners (Canevello & Crocker, 2010). Thus, commitment is the starting point of need satisfaction, not the outcome. The availability of attractive alternative partners is irrelevant to this form of commitment because people view themselves as the starting point of relationship quality. Thus, in the ecosystem people will not likely remain committed to a relationship that remains bad—that is, not supportive and constructive—for either or both partners.

As in the egosystem, love and commitment in the ecosystem involve interdependence; each partner has the capacity to influence the happiness of the other, for better or worse (Kelley & Thibaut, 1978; Rusbult & Van Lange, 2003; Thibaut & Kelley, 1959). If both partners are committed to making the relationship good and care for each other's well-being, then conflicts of interest should be relatively infrequent. The success of one partner should not threaten the self-esteem of the other, even when the partner's success occurs in domains that define the self. Incompatibility of preferences, goals, and desires should be less likely, because people have presumably chosen partners whose important goals they wish to support. When differences in goals, desires, and preferences arise, in the ecosystem people search for solutions that are good for both, or at least not harmful to one partner; they do so not to avoid conflict or keep their partner in the relationship but rather because they care about their partner's well-being. Partners should be less likely to behave badly, acting in ways that are intentionally inconsiderate or annoying. Acts of betrayal, in which one partner humiliates or degrades the other, should be quite rare.

Should conflicts arise, people prioritize both partners' needs equally. Therefore, people will not sacrifice for their partners in ways that harm themselves, nor will they insist on getting their own way if doing so would harm their partners. People in these relationships will not respond to bad behavior with conciliation and accommodation, which may allow the bad behavior to continue and harm one or both partners. Instead, we suggest that they address the issue in a vulnerable, exploratory, and constructive way, attempting to understand the situation from the other's point of view and explaining how it harms them. Similarly, we suggest that in relationships in the ecosystem, people do not simply forgive betrayals. Rather, their commitment to make the relationship good for both people leads them to explore the root causes of the betrayal, including each partner's responsibility for the situation, and address them.

Breaking Up: Leaving and Being Left

In the ecosystem, relationship breakups happen when people determine that the relationship is not good for one or both of the relationship partners, despite commitment to make the relationship good. Thus, we suggest that the distinction between relationships in the egosystem and those in the ecosystem is not whether the relationship lasts or breaks up, but rather the reasons people have for leaving versus staying and how compassionate they are when breaking off a relationship. Because people care about their partner's well-being and their own, and perhaps still love each other, they should feel sad but accepting if the relationship breaks up when it is bad for one or both of the partners, regardless of who initiated the breakup. People who initiate a breakup should consider their partner's well-being without sacrificing their own well-being in the process (Sprecher, Zimmerman, & Abrahams, 2010). Both partners may continue to care about each other after the breakup, and both care about people or things beyond the dyadic relationship. For example, in

relationships in the ecosystem, a couple with children would presumably continue to care about one another's well-being because they both care about the well-being of their children.

Because relationships in the ecosystem are not primarily reflections on the self, breakups should not devastate the self-esteem of the leaver or the one left. Consequently, we predict that self-control failures and destructive impulses are far less likely to follow breakups of relationships in the ecosystem.

Summary

The principles of relationships in the ecosystem differ in a number of ways from the principles of relationships in the egosystem, at every stage of relationship formation, maintenance, and dissolution. Most important, whereas in the egosystem people focus primarily on how well the relationship gratifies their own needs and desires, in the ecosystem they give equal priority to their own needs and those of relationship partners. Consequently, people tend to have non–zero-sum beliefs about the connection between their own well-being and that of their partner. Second, in the ecosystem people feel at the source of constructive relationship processes rather than at the mercy of their relationship partner. Thus, they create vulnerability, trust, and love by giving them freely rather than waiting for their partner to earn them. Third, closeness and love involve affectional bonds that inspire giving to promote the well-being of the relationship partner instead of dependence on the other to gratify one's own important needs and desires. Commitment involves the intention to make the relationship good for the self and the partner rather than determination to make the relationship last, no matter what. Thus, whereas in the egosystem people may stay in relationships that are bad for them or for their partner (or both) because they lack alternatives that would be more gratifying or because they stand to lose resources if the relationship ends, in the ecosystem people will end a relationship if it is harmful to one or both partners and they cannot make it good. Because the self and other are not merged, the self is not lost when the relationship breaks up, so breakups should not devastate self-esteem.

REMAINING ISSUES

We have suggested that the principles governing relationships depend on what motivational system is activated. Relationships motivated by the egosystem follow a set of principles in which the needs of the self take priority over the needs of relationship partners, whereas relationships motivated by the ecosystem follow a different set of principles in which people care about the well-being of relationship partners and give equal priority to the needs of the self and the partner. This framework raises a number of issues for research.

The Shift

Readers may be tempted to characterize their own relationships, or those of their friends and family, as following the principles of the egosystem or the ecosystem. Surely people and relationships differ in how frequently they follow the principles of one system or another (Canevello & Crocker, 2010; Crocker & Canevello, 2008; Feeney & Collins, 2003; Shaver et al., 2010). However, both people and relationships can shift from one motivational system to the other, with important consequences for relationships (Canevello & Crocker, 2010; Crocker & Canevello, 2008; Feeney & Collins, 2003; Mikulincer & Shaver, 2005; Mikulincer, Shaver, Gillath, & Nitzberg, 2005; Shaver et al., 2010). For example, research has suggested that when attachment security increases, people become more compassionate and more helpful (Mikulincer et al., 2005; Shaver et al., 2010). However, threats to self-esteem decrease concern with the well-being of others (Twenge et al., 2007; Vohs & Heatherton, 2001). Negative emotions such as anxiety and depression predict decreased intentions to be supportive toward close relationship partners (Crocker, Canevello, Breines, & Flynn, 2010). Taken together, findings such as these suggest that ecosystem motivation is activated when people trust that their needs can be met in collaboration with their social environment (including, but not limited to, their relationship partners), whereas egosystem motivation is activated when people lose this trust (Crocker & Canevello, 2012a; Crocker et al., 2009). Individual differences such as insecure attachment styles and low self-esteem, situational threats to need satisfaction such as stress and self-image threats, and relationship factors such as contagion of interpersonal goals all shape whether a relationship is governed at a particular moment by the principles of the egosystem or those of the ecosystem.

For both theoretical and practical reasons, one of the most important issues still to be resolved is whether people can choose to shift from one motivational system to the other. That is, can people choose to be motivated by the ecosystem even when they are dispositionally insecure, they are situationally threatened, or their relationship partner is governed by the egosystem? We suggest that when people understand that the principles of the egosystem lead to negative outcomes for themselves, the people they care about, and their relationships, they can choose to respond from the psychological space of the ecosystem instead of the egosystem.

Exploitation

One concern for many people is whether they will be exploited if they are motivated by caring for the well-being of others. It seems logical that people with the impulse to give freely could be taken advantage of (e.g., S. L. Brown & Brown, 2006). However, in the egosystem commitment refers to the intention to make the relationship last, so people will accommodate bad behavior and forgive betrayals, whereas in the ecosystem giving is typically reciprocated (Canevello & Crocker, 2010; Crocker & Canevello, 2008). Thus, it seems possible that exploitation is just as much, or even more, a risk in relationships in the egosystem.

Generalizing to Other Types of Relationships

We have elaborated the idea that there are two sets of fundamental principles of relationships—one describing relationships in the egosystem and the other describing relationships in the ecosystem, using romantic relationships as an illustration. However, we see no reason why this distinction, and many if not all of the fundamental principles we describe, cannot apply to other types of relationships as well. For example, in our own research we have begun to apply this distinction to work relationships; one can easily imagine, for example, that relationships between peers or between supervisor and subordinate could be characterized as following egosystem or ecosystem principles. In our own work, we have demonstrated the utility of this perspective in understanding relationships of roommate dyads in the first semester of college.

Cultural Differences

Although the distinction between egosystem and ecosystem motivation in relationships may be important in the U.S. and other Western cultures, the relevance of this distinction in non-Western cultures characterized by interdependent selves remains unclear. Interdependent self-construals are flexible, variable self-conceptions that emphasize external, public features such as statuses, belonging and fitting in, occupying one's proper place, and indirectness in communication (Singelis, 1994). In cultures that emphasize interdependence, the self is defined within specific social contexts, connected to and overlapping with others (Markus & Kitayama, 1991). People in collectivistic cultures such as Japan tend to give priority to communal goals over personal goals (Yamaguchi, 1994) and to value empathy (Tobin, Wu, & Davidson, 1989). These findings suggest that people in collectivist cultures may generally have ecosystem motivations in relationships; egosystem motivation may be less important in collectivist cultures because people assume that their needs will be met in collaboration with others.

However, research in one collectivist culture, Japan, shows that the Japanese do enhance their positive self-images (J. D. Brown & Kobayashi, 2002; Kurman, 2003; Sedikides, Gaertner, & Vevea, 2005; Takata, 2003) and validate their self-worth indirectly through others (Dalsky, Gohm, Noguchi, & Shiomura, 2008). Research on the concept of face suggests that maintaining and restoring public images of the self are crucial elements of Japanese interactions (Hamamura & Heine, 2008; Heine, 2005). These findings suggest that people in collectivist cultures do care about impression management and have egosystem motivation in relationships, even if the specific

form of egosystem motivation varies by culture. For example, people in collectivist cultures may not only give priority to communal goals over personal goals, they may also want to manage others' impressions of them as appropriately prioritizing collective goals to ensure that others have high regard for them. Thus, even in collectivist cultures characterized by interdependent selves, people may have either egosystem or ecosystem motivation in their close relationships (Niiya, Crocker, & Mischkowski, 2013).

CONCLUSION

As do other social scientists, relationship scientists typically assume that people are fundamentally self-interested; they do what they perceive to be advantageous to themselves (Miller, 1999). Although people are surely capable of being self-interested in their close relationships, people also have the capacity to transcend self-interest and to care deeply about people and things beyond themselves. This capacity extends to close relationships, in which people driven by ecosystem motivation seek to promote the well-being of others not out of selfish motives to obtain benefits in return, but because they care about them or because both people care about the well-being of someone or something beyond themselves. They create mutually supportive relationships because they care about their partners, and they dissolve them when the relationship is bad for one or both of them.

Although research on ecosystem motivation in relationships is relatively scarce, existing research has suggested that relationships in the ecosystem are qualitatively different, following a different set of governing principles than relationships in the egosystem. We suggest that relationship researchers more clearly articulate their assumptions about the motivations guiding the phenomena they study. Identifying the conditions under which relationship behaviors are driven by one motivational system or another, the consequences of these systems for relationships and the people in them, and whether people can choose to shift from one system or another are urgent priorities for future research.

References

Acevedo, B. P., & Aron, A. (2009). Does a long-term relationship kill romantic love? *Review of General Psychology, 13,* 59–65. doi:10.1037/a0014226

Aron, A., & Aron, E. N. (1986). *Love as the expansion of self: Understanding attraction and satisfaction.* New York, NY: Hemisphere.

Aron, A., Aron, E. N., & Smollan, D. (1992). Inclusion of Other in the Self Scale and the structure of interpersonal closeness. *Journal of Personality and Social Psychology, 63,* 596–612. doi:10.1037/0022-3514.63.4.596

Aron, A., Aron, E. N., Tudor, M., & Nelson, G. (1991). Close relationships as including other in the self. *Journal of Personality and Social Psychology, 60,* 241–253.

Aron, A., Paris, M., & Aron, E. N. (1995). Falling in love: Prospective studies of self-concept change. *Journal of Personality and Social Psychology, 69,* 1102–1112. doi:10.1037/0022-3514.69.6.1102

Batson, C. D. (1979). Helping under conditions of common threat: Increased "we-feeling" or ensuring reciprocity. *Social Psychology Quarterly, 42,* 410–414. doi:10.2307/3033812

Batson, C. D. (1987). Prosocial motivation: Is it ever truly altruistic? In L. Berkowitz (Ed.), *Advances in experimental social psychology* (Vol. 20, pp. 65–122). San Diego, CA: Academic Press. doi:10.1016/S0065-2601(08)60412-8

Batson, C. D. (1998). Altruism and prosocial behavior. In D. Gilbert, S. T. Fiske, & G. Lindzey (Eds.), *The handbook of social psychology* (4th ed., Vol. 2, pp. 282–316). New York, NY: McGraw-Hill.

Baumeister, R. F. (1997). Esteem threat, self-regulatory breakdown, and emotional distress as factors in self-defeating behavior. *Review of General Psychology, 1,* 145–174. doi:10.1037/1089-2680.1.2.145

Baumeister, R. F., DeWall, C. N., Ciarocco, N. J., & Twenge, J. M. (2005). Social exclusion impairs self-regulation. *Journal of Personality and Social Psychology, 88,* 589–604. doi:10.1037/0022-3514.88.4.589

Baumeister, R. F., & Scher, S. J. (1988). Self-defeating behavior among normal individuals: Review and analysis of common self-destructive tendencies. *Psychological Bulletin, 104,* 3–22. doi:10.1037/0033-2909.104.1.3

Baumeister, R. F., Smart, L., & Boden, J. M. (1996). Relation of threatened egotism to violence and aggression: The dark side of high self-esteem. *Psychological Review, 103,* 5–33. doi:10.1037/0033-295X.103.1.5

Baumeister, R. F., Twenge, J. M., & Nuss, C. K. (2002). Effects of social exclusion on cognitive processes: Anticipated aloneness reduces intelligent thought. *Journal of Personality and Social Psychology, 83,* 817–827. doi:10.1037/0022-3514.83.4.817

Berridge, K. C. (2004a). Motivational concepts inbehavioral neuroscience. *Physiology and Behavior, 81,* 179–209. doi:10.1016/j.physbeh.2004.02.004

Berridge, K. C. (2004b). Pleasure, unfelt feelings, and irrational desire. In A. S. R. Manstead, N. H. Frijda, & A. H. Fischer (Eds.), *Feelings and emotions: The Amsterdam symposium* (pp. 243–262). Cambridge, England: Cambridge University Press. doi:10.1017/CBO9780511806582.015

Berridge, K. C., & Robinson, T. E. (1995). The mind of an addicted brain: Neural sensitization of wanting versus liking. *Current Directions in Psychological Science, 4,* 71–76. doi:10.1111/1467-8721.ep10772316

Berscheid, E. (2010). Love in the fourth dimension. *Annual Review of Psychology, 61,* 1–25. doi:10.1146/annurev.psych.093008.100318

Brown, J. D., & Kobayashi, C. (2002). Self-enhancement in Japan and America. *Asian Journal of Social Psychology, 5,* 145–168. doi:10.1111/1467-839X.00101

Brown, S. L., & Brown, R. M. (2006). Selective investment theory: Recasting the functional significance of close relationships. *Psychological Inquiry, 17,* 1–29. doi:10.1207/s15327965pli1701_01

Brown, S. L., Brown, R. M., & Penner, L. A. (Eds.). (2012). *Moving beyond self-interest: Perspectives from evolutionary biology, neuroscience, and the social sciences.* New York, NY: Oxford University Press.

Canevello, A., & Crocker, J. (2010). Creating good relationships: Responsiveness, relationship quality, and interpersonal goals. *Journal of Personality and Social Psychology, 99,* 78–106. doi:10.1037/a0018186

Canevello, A., & Crocker, J. (2011). Interpersonal goals, others' regard for the self, and self-esteem: The paradoxical consequences of self-image and compassionate goals. *European Journal of Social Psychology, 41,* 422–434. doi:10.1002/ejsp.808

Cialdini, R. B., Brown, S. L., Lewis, B. P., Luce, C., & Neuberg, S. L. (1997). Reinterpreting the empathy–altruism relationship: When one into one equals oneness. *Journal of Personality and Social Psychology, 73,* 481–494. doi:10.1037/0022-3514.73.3.481

Clark, M. S. (2011). Communal relationships can be selfish and give rise to exploitation. In R. M. Arkin (Ed.), *Most underappreciated: 50 prominent social psychologists describe their most unloved work* (pp. 77–81). New York, NY: Oxford University Press.

Clark, M. S., Dubash, P., & Mills, J. (1998). Interest in another's consideration of one's needs in communal and exchange relationships. *Journal of Experimental Social Psychology, 34,* 246–264. doi:10.1006/jesp.1998.1352

Clark, M. S., Mills, J., & Powell, M. C. (1986). Keeping track of needs in communal and exchange relationships. *Journal of Personality and Social Psychology, 51,* 333–338. doi:10.1037/0022-3514.51.2.333

Clark, M. S., & Monin, J. K. (2006). Giving and receiving communal responsiveness as love. In R. J. Sternberg & K. Weis (Eds.), *The new psychology of love* (pp. 200–221). New Haven, CT: Yale University Press.

Clark, M. S., Oullette, R., Powell, M. C., & Milberg, S. (1987). Recipient's mood, relationship type, and helping. *Journal of Personality and Social Psychology, 53,* 94–103. doi:10.1037/0022-3514.53.1.94

Collins, N. L., & Feeney, B. C. (2000). A safe haven: An attachment theory perspective on support seeking and care giving in close relationships. *Journal of Personality and Social Psychology, 78,* 1053–1073. doi:10.1037/0022-3514.78.6.1053

Crocker, J. (2008). From egosystem to ecosystem: Implications for learning, relationships, and well-being. In H. A. Wayment & J. J. Brauer (Eds.), *Transcending self-interest: Psychological explorations of the quiet ego* (pp. 63–72). Washington, DC: American Psychological Association. doi:10.1037/11771-006

Crocker, J., & Canevello, A. (2008). Creating and undermining social support in communal relationships: The role of compassionate and self-image goals. *Journal of Personality and Social Psychology, 95,* 555–575. doi:10.1037/0022-3514.95.3.555

Crocker, J., & Canevello, A. (2012a). Consequences of self-image and compassionate goals. In P. G. Devine & E. A. Plant (Eds.), *Advances in experimental social psychology* (Vol. 45, pp. 229–277). New York, NY: Elsevier.

Crocker, J., & Canevello, A. (2012b). Egosystem and ecosystem: Motivational perspectives on caregiving. In S. E. Brown, M. Brown, & L. A. Penner (Eds.), *Moving beyond self-interest: Perspectives from evolutionary biology, neuroscience, and the social sciences* (pp. 211–223). New York, NY: Oxford University Press.

Crocker, J., Canevello, A., Breines, J. G., & Flynn, H. (2010). Interpersonal goals and change in anxiety and dysphoria in first-semester college students. *Journal of Personality and Social Psychology, 98,* 1009–1024. doi:10.1037/a0019400

Crocker, J., Niiya, Y., & Mischkowski, D. (2008). Why does writing about important values reduce defensiveness? Self-affirmation and the role of positive other-directed feelings. *Psychological Science, 19,* 740–747. doi:10.1111/j.1467-9280.2008.02150.x

Crocker, J., Olivier, M.-A., & Nuer, N. (2009). Self-image goals and compassionate goals: Costs and benefits. *Self and Identity, 8,* 251–269. doi:10.1080/15298860802505160

Cutrona, C. E. (1996). *Social support in couples: Marriage as a resource in times of stress.* Thousand Oaks, CA: Sage.

Dalsky, D., Gohm, C. L., Noguchi, K., & Shiomura, K. (2008). Mutual self-enhancement in Japan and the United States. *Journal of Cross-Cultural Psychology, 39,* 215–223. doi:10.1177/0022022107313863

DePaulo, B. M., & Morris, W. L. (2006). The unrecognized stereotyping and discrimination against singles. *Current Directions in Psychological Science, 15,* 251–254. doi:10.1111/j.1467-8721.2006.00446.x

Diamond, L. M. (2003). What does sexual orientation orient? A biobehavioral model distinguishing romantic love and sexual desire. *Psychological Review, 110,* 173–192. doi:10.1037/0033-295X.110.1.173

Downey, G., Feldman, S., & Ayduk, O. (2000). Rejection sensitivity and male violence in romantic relationships. *Personal Relationships, 7,* 45–61. doi:10.1111/j.1475-6811.2000.tb00003.x

Downey, G., Freitas, A. L., Michaelis, B., & Khouri, H. (1998). The self-fulfilling prophecy in close relationships: Rejection sensitivity and rejection by romantic partners. *Journal of Personality and Social Psychology, 75,* 545–560. doi:10.1037/0022-3514.75.2.545

Drigotas, S. M., & Rusbult, C. E. (1992). Should I stay or should I go? A dependence model of breakups. *Journal of Personality and Social Psychology, 62,* 62–87. doi:10.1037/0022-3514.62.1.62

Drigotas, S. M., Rusbult, C. E., Wieselquist, J., & Whitton, S. W. (1999). Close partner as sculptor of the ideal self: Behavioral affirmation and the Michelangelo phenomenon. *Journal of Personality and Social Psychology, 77,* 293–323. doi:10.1037/0022-3514.77.2.293

Exline, J. J. (2008). Taming the wild ego: The challenge of humility. In H. A. Wayment & J. J. Bauer (Eds.), *Transcending self-interest: Psychological explorations of the quiet ego* (pp. 53–62). Washington, DC: American Psychological Association. doi:10.1037/11771-005

Feeney, B. C., & Collins, N. L. (2001). Predictors of caregiving in adult intimate relationships: An attachment theoretical perspective. *Journal of Personality and Social Psychology, 80,* 972–994. doi:10.1037/0022-3514.80.6.972

Feeney, B. C., & Collins, N. L. (2003). Motivations for caregiving in adult intimate relationships: Influences on caregiving behavior and relationship functioning. *Personality and Social Psychology Bulletin, 29,* 950–968. doi:10.1177/0146167203252807

Finkel, E. J., Rusbult, C. E., Kumashiro, M., & Hannon, P. A. (2002). Dealing with betrayal in close relationships: Does commitment promote forgiveness? *Journal of Personality and Social Psychology, 82,* 956–974. doi:10.1037/0022-3514.82.6.956

Fletcher, G. J. O., Simpson, J. A., & Thomas, G. (2000). Ideals, perceptions, and evaluations in early relationship development. *Journal of Personality and Social Psychology, 79*, 933–940. doi:10.1037/0022-3514.79.6.933

Forest, A. L., & Wood, J. V. (2011). When partner caring leads to sharing: Partner responsiveness increases expressivity, but only for individuals with low self-esteem. *Journal of Experimental Social Psychology, 47*, 843–848. doi:10.1016/j.jesp.2011.03.005

Fritz, H. L., & Helgeson, V. S. (1998). Distinctions of unmitigated communion from communion: Self-neglect and overinvolvement with others. *Journal of Personality and Social Psychology, 75*, 121–140. doi:10.1037/0022-3514.75.1.121

Gable, S. L., & Reis, H. T. (2006). Intimacy and the self: An iterative model of the self and close relationships. In P. Noller & J. A. Feeney (Eds.), *Close relationships: Functions, forms and processes* (pp. 211–225). Hove, England: Psychology Press.

Gonzaga, G. C., Keltner, D., Londahl, E. A., & Smith, M. D. (2001). Love and the commitment problem in romantic relations and friendship. *Journal of Personality and Social Psychology, 81*, 247–262. doi:10.1037/0022-3514.81.2.247

Gonzaga, G. C., Turner, R. A., Keltner, D., Campos, B., & Altemus, M. (2006). Romantic love and sexual desire in close relationships. *Emotion, 6*, 163–179. doi:10.1037/1528-3542.6.2.163

Greenwald, A. G., & Breckler, S. J. (1985). *To whom is the self presented? The self and social life* (pp. 126–145). New York, NY: McGraw Hill.

Hamamura, T., & Heine, S. J. (2008). The role of self-criticism in self-improvement and face maintenance among Japanese. In E. C. Chang (Ed.), *Self-criticism and self-enhancement: Theory, research, and clinical implications* (pp. 105–122). Washington, DC: American Psychological Association. doi:10.1037/11624-007

Hatfield, E., & Walster, G. W. (1978). *A new look at love.* Lanham, MD: University Press of America.

Heine, S. J. (2005). Where is the evidence for pancultural self-enhancement? A reply to Sedikides, Gaertner, and Toguchi (2003). *Journal of Personality and Social Psychology, 89*, 531–538. doi:10.1037/0022-3514.89.4.531

Impett, E. A., Gable, S. L., & Peplau, L. A. (2005). Giving up and giving in: The costs and benefits of daily sacrifice in intimate relationships. *Journal of Personality and Social Psychology, 89*, 327–344.

Impett, E. A., Gordon, A. M., Kogan, A., Oveis, C., Gable, S. L., & Keltner, D. (2010). Moving toward more perfect unions: Daily and long-term consequences of approach and avoidance goals in romantic relationships. *Journal of Personality and Social Psychology, 99*, 948–963. doi:10.1037/a0020271

Johnson, D. J., & Rusbult, C. E. (1989). Resisting temptation: Devaluation of alternative partners as a means of maintaining commitment in close relationships. *Journal of Personality and Social Psychology, 57*, 967–980. doi:10.1037/0022-3514.57.6.967

Kelley, H. H., & Thibaut, J. W. (1978). *Interpersonal relations.* New York, NY: Wiley.

Kim, J., & Hatfield, E. (2004). Love types and subjective well-being: A cross cultural study. *Social Behavior and Personality, 32*, 173–182. doi:10.2224/sbp.2004.32.2.173

Knee, C. R., Canevello, A., Bush, A. L., & Cook, A. (2008). Relationship-contingent self-esteem and the ups and downs of romantic relationships. *Journal of Personality and Social Psychology, 95*, 608–627. doi:10.1037/0022-3514.95.3.608

Konrath, S., Fuhrel-Forbis, A., Lou, A., & Brown, S. L. (2012). Motives for volunteering are associated with mortality risk in older adults. *Health Psychology, 31*, 87–96.

Kunda, Z. (1990). The case for motivated reasoning. *Psychological Bulletin, 108*, 480–498. doi:10.1037/0033-2909.108.3.480

Kurman, J. (2003). Why is self-enhancement low in certain collectivist cultures? An investigation of two competing explanations. *Journal of Cross-Cultural Psychology, 34*, 496–510. doi:10.1177/0022022103256474

Leary, M. R., & Baumeister, R. F. (2000). The nature and function of self-esteem: Sociometer theory. In M. Zanna (Ed.), *Advances in experimental social psychology* (Vol. 32, pp. 1–62). San Diego, CA: Academic Press. doi:10.1016/S0065-2601(00)80003-9

Leary, M. R., Tambor, E. S., Terdal, S. K., & Downs, D. L. (1995). Self-esteem as an interpersonal monitor: The sociometer hypothesis. *Journal of Personality and Social Psychology, 68*, 518–530. doi:10.1037/0022-3514.68.3.518

Leith, K. P., & Baumeister, R. F. (1996). Why do bad moods increase self-defeating behavior? Emotion, risk-taking, and self-regulation. *Journal of Personality and Social Psychology, 71*, 1250–1267. doi:10.1037/0022-3514.71.6.1250

Lemay, E. P., Jr., Clark, M. S., & Feeney, B. C. (2007). Projection of responsiveness to needs and the construction of satisfying communal relationships. *Journal of Personality and Social Psychology, 92*, 834–853. doi:10.1037/0022-3514.92.5.834

Maner, J. K., DeWall, C. N., Baumeister, R. F., & Schaller, M. (2007). Does social exclusion motivate interpersonal reconnection? Resolving the "porcupine problem." *Journal of Personality and Social Psychology, 92*, 42–55. doi:10.1037/0022-3514.92.1.42

Markus, H. R., & Kitayama, S. (1991). Culture and the self: Implications for cognition, emotion, and motivation. *Psychological Review, 98*, 224–253. doi:10.1037/0033-295X.98.2.224

Mathes, E. W., Adams, H. E., & Davies, R. M. (1985). Jealousy: Loss of relationship rewards, loss of self-esteem, depression, anxiety, and anger. *Journal of Personality and Social Psychology, 48*, 1552–1561. doi:10.1037/0022-3514.48.6.1552

Mikulincer, M., & Shaver, P. R. R. (2003). The attachment behavioral system in adulthood: Activation, psychodynamics, and interpersonal processes. In M. P. Zanna (Ed.), *Advances in experimental social psychology* (Vol. 35, pp. 53–152). San Diego, CA: Academic Press. doi:10.1016/S0065-2601(03)01002-5

Mikulincer, M., & Shaver, P. R. (2005). Attachment security, compassion, and altruism. *Current Directions in Psychological Science, 14*, 34–38. doi:10.1111/j.0963-7214.2005.00330.x

Mikulincer, M., & Shaver, P. R. (Eds.). (2010). *Prosocial motives, emotions, and behavior: The better angels of our nature.* Washington, DC: American Psychological Association. doi:10.1037/12061-000

Mikulincer, M., Shaver, P. R., Gillath, O., & Nitzberg, R. A. (2005). Attachment, caregiving, and altruism: Boosting attachment security increases compassion and helping. *Journal of Personality and Social Psychology, 89*, 817–839. doi:10.1037/0022-3514.89.5.817

Miller, D. T. (1999). The norm of self-interest. *American Psychologist, 54*, 1053–1060. doi:10.1037/0003-066X.54.12.1053

Mills, J., Clark, M. S., Ford, T. E., & Johnson, M. (2004). Measurement of communal strength. *Personal Relationships, 11*, 213–230. doi:10.1111/j.1475-6811.2004.00079.x

Mori, D., Chaiken, S., & Pliner, P. (1987). "Eating lightly" and the self-presentation of femininity. *Journal of Personality and Social Psychology, 53*, 693–702. doi:10.1037/0022-3514.53.4.693

Murray, S. L., Aloni, M., Holmes, J. G., Derrick, J. L., Stinson, D. A., & Leder, S. (2009). Fostering partner dependence as trust insurance: The implicit contingencies of the exchange script in close relationships. *Journal of Personality and Social Psychology, 96*, 324–348. doi:10.1037/a0012856

Murray, S. L., Holmes, J. G., & Collins, N. L. (2006). Optimizing assurance: The risk regulation system in relationships. *Psychological Bulletin, 132*, 641–666. doi:10.1037/0033-2909.132.5.641

Murray, S. L., Holmes, J. G., & Griffin, D. W. (1996a). The benefits of positive illusions: Idealization and the construction of satisfaction in close relationships. *Journal of Personality and Social Psychology, 70*, 79–98. doi:10.1037/0022-3514.70.1.79

Murray, S. L., Holmes, J. G., & Griffin, D. W. (1996b). The self-fulfilling nature of positive illusions in romantic relationships: Love is not blind, but prescient. *Journal of Personality and Social Psychology, 71*, 1155–1180. doi:10.1037/0022-3514.71.6.1155

Murray, S. L., Holmes, J. G., & Griffin, D. W. (2000). Self-esteem and the quest for felt security: How perceived regard regulates attachment processes. *Journal of Personality and Social Psychology, 78*, 478–498. doi:10.1037/0022-3514.78.3.478

Murray, S. L., Leder, S., MacGregor, J. C. D., Holmes, J. G., Pinkus, R. T., & Harris, B. (2009). Becoming irreplaceable: How comparisons to the partner's alternatives differentially affect low and high self-esteem people. *Journal of Experimental Social Psychology, 45*, 1180–1191. doi:10.1016/j.jesp.2009.07.001

Niiya, Y., Crocker, J., & Mischkowski, D. (2013). Compassionate and self-image goals in the United States and Japan. *Journal of Cross-Cultural Psychology, 44*, 389–405.

Park, L. E., Sanchez, D. T., & Brynildsen, K. (2011a). Maladaptive responses to relationship dissolution: The role of relationship contingent self-worth. *Journal of Applied Social Psychology, 41*, 1749–1773. doi:10.1111/j.1559-1816.2011.00769.x

Park, L. E., Sanchez, D. T., & Brynildsen, K. (2011b). Maladaptive responses to romantic breakup: The role of relationship-contingent self-worth. *Journal of Applied Social Psychology, 41*, 1749–1773. doi:10.1111/j.1559-1816.2011.00769.x

Pliner, P., & Chaiken, S. (1990). Eating, social motives, and self-presentation in women and men. *Journal of Experimental Social Psychology, 26*, 240–254. doi:10.1016/0022-1031(90)90037-M

Post, S. G., Underwood, L. G., Schloss, J. P., & Hurlbut, W. B. (2002). *Altruism and altruistic love: Science, philosophy, and religion in dialogue.* New York, NY: Oxford University Press. doi:10.1093/acprof:oso/9780195143584.001.0001

Reis, H. T., Clark, M. S., & Holmes, J. G. (2004). Perceived partner responsiveness as an organizing construct in the study of intimacy and closeness. In D. Mashek & A. P. Aron (Eds.), *Handbook of closeness and intimacy* (pp. 201–225). Mahwah, NJ: Erlbaum.

Reynaud, M., Karila, L., Blecha, L., & Benyamina, A. (2010). Is love passion an addictive disorder? *American Journal of Drug and Alcohol Abuse, 36*, 261–267. doi:10.3109/00952990.2010.495183

Robinson, T. E., & Berridge, K. C. (2003). Addiction. *Annual Review of Psychology, 54*, 25–53. doi:10.1146/annurev.psych.54.101601.145237

Rusbult, C. E., & Agnew, C. R. (2010). Prosocial motivation and behavior in close relationships. In M. Mikulincer & P. R. Shaver (Eds.), *Prosocial motives, emotions, and behavior: The better angels of our nature* (pp. 327–345). Washington, DC: American Psychological Association. doi:10.1037/12061-017

Rusbult, C. E., Drigotas, S. M., & Verette, J. (1994). The investment model: An interdependence analysis of commitment processes and relationship maintenance phenomena. In D. J. Canary & L. Stafford (Eds.), *Communication and relational maintenance* (pp. 115–139). San Diego, CA: Academic Press.

Rusbult, C. E., Finkel, E. J., & Kumashiro, M. (2009). The Michelangelo phenomenon. *Current Directions in Psychological Science, 18*, 305–309. doi:10.1111/j.1467-8721.2009.01657.x

Rusbult, C. E., Kumashiro, M., Kubacka, K. E., & Finkel, E. J. (2009). "The part of me that you bring out": Ideal similarity and the Michelangelo phenomenon. *Journal of Personality and Social Psychology, 96*, 61–82. doi:10.1037/a0014016

Rusbult, C. E., Lange, P. A. M. V., Wildschut, T., Yovetich, N. A., & Verette, J. (2000). Perceived superiority in close relationships: Why it exists and persists. *Journal of Personality and Social Psychology, 79*, 521–545. doi:10.1037/0022-3514.79.4.521

Rusbult, C. E., Martz, J. M., & Agnew, C. R. (1998). The Investment Model Scale: Measuring commitment level, satisfaction level, quality of alternatives, and investment size. *Personal Relationships, 5*, 357–387. doi:10.1111/j.1475-6811.1998.tb00177.x

Rusbult, C. E., & Van Lange, P. A. M. (2003). Interdependence, interaction and relationships. *Annual Review of Psychology, 54*, 351–375. doi:10.1146/annurev.psych.54.101601.145059

Sanchez, D. T., Good, J. J., Kwang, T., & Saltzman, E. (2008). When finding a mate feels urgent: Why relationship contingency predicts men's and women's body shame. *Social Psychology, 39*, 90–102. doi:10.1027/1864-9335.39.2.90

Sanchez, D. T., & Kwang, T. (2007). When the relationship becomes her: Revisiting women's body concerns from a relationship contingency perspective. *Psychology of Women Quarterly, 31*, 401–414. doi:10.1111/j.1471-6402.2007.00389.x

Schlenker, B. R. (2003). Self-presentation. In M. R. Leary & J. P. Tangney (Eds.), *Handbook of self and identity* (pp. 492–518). New York, NY: Guilford Press.

Schlenker, B. R., & Britt, T. W. (1999). Beneficial impression management: Strategically controlling information to help friends. *Journal of Personality and Social Psychology, 76*, 559–573. doi:10.1037/0022-3514.76.4.559

Sedikides, C., Gaertner, L., & Vevea, J. L. (2005). Pancultural self-enhancement reloaded: A meta-analytic reply to Heine (2005). *Journal of Personality and Social Psychology, 89*, 539–551. doi:10.1037/0022-3514.89.4.539

Sharpsteen, D. J. (1995). The effects of relationship and self-esteem threats on the likelihood of romantic jealousy. *Journal of Social and Personal Relationships, 12*, 89–101. doi:10.1177/0265407595121006

Shaver, P. R., & Hazan, C. (1988). A biased overview of the study of love. *Journal of Social and Personal Relationships, 5*, 473–501. doi:10.1177/0265407588054005

Shaver, P. R., Mikulincer, M., & Shemesh-Iron, M. (2010). A behavioral-systems perspective on prosocial behavior. In M. Mikulincer & P. R. Shaver (Eds.), *Prosocial motives, emotions, and behavior: The better angels of our nature* (pp. 72–91). Washington, DC: American Psychological Association. doi:10.1037/12061-004

Simpson, J. A. (2007). Psychological foundations of trust. *Current Directions in Psychological Science, 16*, 264–268. doi:10.1111/j.1467-8721.2007.00517.x

Singelis, T. M. (1994). The measurement of independent and interdependent self-construals. *Personality and Social Psychology Bulletin, 20*, 580–591. doi:10.1177/0146167294205014

Sprecher, S., & Fehr, B. (2005). Compassionate love for close others and humanity. *Journal of Social and Personal Relationships, 22*, 629–651. doi:10.1177/0265407505056439

Sprecher, S., Zimmerman, C., & Abrahams, E. M. (2010). Choosing compassionate strategies to end a relationship: Effects of compassionate love for partner and the reason for the breakup. *Social Psychology, 41*, 66–75. doi:10.1027/1864-9335/a000010

Takata, T. (2003). Self-enhancement and self-criticism in Japanese culture. An experimental analysis. *Journal of Cross-Cultural Psychology, 34*, 542–551. doi:10.1177/0022022103256477

Tangney, J. P. (2009). Humility. In S. J. Lopez & C. R. Snyder (Eds.), *Oxford handbook of positive psychology* (2nd ed., pp. 483–490). New York, NY: Oxford University Press. doi:10.1093/oxfordhb/9780195187243.013.0046

Tangney, J. P., Wagner, P. E., Hill-Barlow, D., Marschall, D. E., & Gramzow, R. (1996). Relation of shame and guilt to constructive versus destructive responses to anger across the lifespan. *Journal of Personality and Social Psychology, 70*, 797–809. doi:10.1037/0022-3514.70.4.797

Tesser, A. (1988). Toward a self-evaluation maintenance model of social behavior. In L. Berkowitz (Ed.), *Advances in experimental social psychology* (Vol. 21, pp. 181–227). San Diego, CA: Academic Press. doi:10.1016/S0065-2601(08)60227-0

Thibaut, J. W., & Kelley, H. H. (1959). *The social psychology of groups*. New York, NY: Wiley.

Tobin, J. J., Wu, D. Y. H., & Davidson, D. H. (1989). *Preschool in three cultures: Japan, China, and the United States*. New Haven, CT: Yale University Press.

Tsang, J.-A. (2006). Gratitude and prosocial behaviour: An experimental test of gratitude. *Cognition and Emotion, 20*, 138–148. doi:10.1080/02699930500172341

Twenge, J. M., Baumeister, R. F., DeWall, C. N., Ciarocco, N. J., & Bartels, J. M. (2007). Social exclusion decreases prosocial behavior. *Journal of Personality and Social Psychology, 92,* 56–66. doi:10.1037/0022-3514.92.1.56

Twenge, J. M., Baumeister, R. F., Tice, D. M., & Stucke, T. S. (2001). If you can't join them, beat them: Effects of social exclusion on aggressive behavior. *Journal of Personality and Social Psychology, 81,* 1058–1069. doi:10.1037/0022-3514.81.6.1058

Twenge, J. M., & Campbell, W. K. (2003). "Isn't it fun to get the respect that we're going to deserve?" Narcissism, social rejection, and aggression. *Personality and Social Psychology Bulletin, 29,* 261–272. doi:10.1177/0146167202239051

Twenge, J. M., Catanese, K. R., & Baumeister, R. F. (2002). Social exclusion causes self-defeating behavior. *Journal of Personality and Social Psychology, 83,* 606–615. doi:10.1037/0022-3514.83.3.606

Twenge, J. M., Catanese, K. R., & Baumeister, R. F. (2003). Social exclusion and the deconstructed state: Time perception, meaninglessness, lethargy, lack of emotion, and self-awareness. *Journal of Personality and Social Psychology, 85,* 409–423. doi:10.1037/0022-3514.85.3.409

Underwood, L. (2002). The human experience of compassionate love: Conceptual mapping and data from selected studies. In S. G. Post, L. G. Underwood, J. P. Schloss, & W. B. Hurlbut (Eds.), *Altruism and altruistic love* (pp. 72–88). New York, NY: Oxford University Press. doi:10.1093/acprof:oso/9780195143584.003.0009

van Beest, I., & Williams, K. D. (2006). When inclusion costs and ostracism pays, ostracism still hurts. *Journal of Personality and Social Psychology, 91,* 918–928. doi:10.1037/0022-3514.91.5.918

Van Lange, P. A. M., Rusbult, C. E., Drigotas, S. M., Arriaga, X. B., Witcher, B. S., & Cox, C. L. (1997). Willingness to sacrifice in close relationships. *Journal of Personality and Social Psychology, 72,* 1373–1395. doi:10.1037/0022-3514.72.6.1373

Vohs, K. D., & Heatherton, T. F. (2001). Self-esteem and threats to self: Implications for self-construals and interpersonal perceptions. *Journal of Personality and Social Psychology, 81,* 1103–1118. doi:10.1037/0022-3514.81.6.1103

Wayment, H., & Bauer, J. J. (Eds.). (2008). *Transcending self-interest: Psychological explorations of the quiet ego.* Washington, DC: American Psychological Association. doi:10.1037/11771-000

White, G. L. (1981). A model of romantic jealousy. *Motivation and Emotion, 5,* 295–310. doi:10.1007/BF00992549

Wieselquist, J., Rusbult, C. E., Foster, C. A., & Agnew, C. R. (1999). Commitment, pro-relationship behavior, and trust in close relationships. *Journal of Personality and Social Psychology, 77,* 942–966. doi:10.1037/0022-3514.77.5.942

Wood, J. V., & Forest, A. L. (2011). Seeking pleasure and avoiding pain in interpersonal relationships. In M. D. Alicke & C. Sedikides (Eds.), *Handbook of self-enhancement and self-protection* (pp. 258–278). New York, NY: Guilford Press.

Yamaguchi, S. (1994). Collectivism among the Japanese: A perspective from the self. In U. Kim, H. C. Triandis, Ç. Kâ itçiba i, S.-C. Choi & G. Yoon (Eds.), *Individualism and collectivism: Theory, method, and applications* (pp. 175–188). Thousand Oaks, CA: Sage.

Yovetich, N. A., & Rusbult, C. E. (1994). Accommodative behavior in close relationships: Exploring transformation of motivation. *Journal of Experimental Social Psychology, 30,* 138–164. doi:10.1006/jesp.1994.1007

Zanna, M. P., & Pack, S. J. (1975). On the self-fulfilling nature of apparent sex differences in behavior. *Journal of Experimental Social Psychology, 11,* 583–591. doi:10.1016/0022-1031(75)90009-8

PART II

BIOLOGICAL APPROACHES
AND HEALTH

CHAPTER 5

RELATIONSHIP NEUROSCIENCE

Lane Beckes and James A. Coan

The study of interpersonal relationships is now a part of the burgeoning field of social neuroscience (cf. Coan, Beckes, & Allen, 2013; Coan, Schaefer, & Davidson, 2006). Social proximity and close interpersonal relationships are critical for optimal human brain functioning (Beckes & Coan, 2011). Positive relationships are now well known to benefit health and well-being (House, Landis, & Umberson, 1988; Holt-Lunstad, Smith, & Layton, 2010; Robles & Kiecolt-Glaser, 2003; Uchino, Cacioppo, & Kiecolt-Glaser, 1996; Uvnäs-Moberg, 1998). However, the neural mechanisms linking relationships to health and well-being are not well understood.

In this chapter, we review much of the latest research on the neural correlates of social relationships and attempt to integrate much of it into a set of basic principles. First, we discuss issues relating to neural modularity and the interpretation of neuroscientific findings. Second, we discuss how the brain manages self-representation, other-representation, and their overlap in neural circuitry. Third, we review and discuss the literature on behavioral systems and their instantiation in neural activity. Fourth, we outline and discuss some proposed principles of relationship neuroscience and briefly describe social baseline theory (SBT; Beckes & Coan, 2011). We conclude with proposals for the future of relationship neuroscience.

MODULARITY AND INTERPRETATION

A persistent problem in the neurosciences concerns the functional specificity of neural circuits (cf. Bunzl,

Hanson, & Poldrack, 2010; Fodor, 1983; Kanwisher, 2010). The oversimplified version of this debate pits those who believe the brain is composed of discrete functional modules against those who believe the brain is more functionally generalized in its design. The question of whether specific psychological functions can be located in specific neural circuits has been a core debate in the brain sciences since the early 1800s (see Kanwisher, 2010). Perhaps the most egregious mistake one can make in interpreting brain data is to assume that whatever regions are active during a given psychological task are intrinsic to whatever construct one is exploring. Most readers have probably seen such inferential errors in popular press write-ups. For example, one article (Zinkova, 2009) suggested that "researchers have identified four regions of the brain that are believed to form the love circuit" (p. 1). These identified regions are associated with reward processing and are part of the dopamine-rich ventral striatum, but they are not part of a "love" circuit in any meaningful sense.

Despite these difficulties, much of the brain is at least weakly modular (cf. Kanwisher, 2010; Karmiloff-Smith, 2010). For example, much of the processing of different sensory modalities is done in distinct regions of the brain. The difficulty arises when discussing higher order psychological constructs, which are more likely to emerge out of the interaction of multiple neural networks. *Emergence,* in this context, refers to a relatively irreducible quality that arises out of the interaction and integration of signals from multiple systems (as in a gestalt; see Coan, 2010b, for a detailed discussion). Activation

http://dx.doi.org/10.1037/14344-005
APA Handbook of Personality and Social Psychology: Vol. 3. Interpersonal Relations, M. Mikulincer and P. R. Shaver (Editors-in-Chief)

across such networks can frequently be understood as indexing processing that is critically related to a psychological construct. For example, theory-of-mind tasks consistently activate regions such as the superior temporal sulcus (STS; cf. Allison, Puce, & McCarthy, 2000; Grossman & Blake, 2002; Pelphrey, Morris, Michelich, Allison, & McCarthy, 2005; Morris, Pelphrey, & McCarthy, 2008) and the temporoparietal junction (Saxe & Kanwisher, 2003), even though it is unlikely that either the STS or the temporoparietal junction can be construed as theory-of-mind circuits per se.

It is important to emphasize that this problem of identifying the function of a given brain region and associating it with a specific conceptual process is difficult, rarely intuitive, and frequently impossible if one hopes to find one simple process that exists in either the psychological or the lay lexicon. Thus, we urge readers to keep in mind that functional descriptions of specific brain regions are approximations at best and subject to change with further evidence. A good example is the emerging understanding of the amygdala. Early investigations focused on its role in fear and fear conditioning (cf. Davis, 1992; Ledoux, 2000), with it often being referred to as the "fear center" in popular media (e.g., Walker, 2010). Subsequently, it has been found to be sensitive to positive stimuli in some contexts (Hamann, Ely, Hoffman, & Kilts, 2002) and strongly associated with vigilance to ambiguous stimuli (Davis & Whalen, 2001). More recently, Ralph Adolphs (2010) has marshaled compelling evidence that the amygdala is best characterized as sensitive to the biological relevance, salience, and value of stimuli, and it may be critical for determining the biological value of ambiguous stimuli. Thus, our understanding of the function of individual regions of the brain is ongoing and complex.

SELF-EXPANSION, SELF–OTHER OVERLAP, AND EMPATHY

Over the past decade, social neuroscience has taken on the question of how people understand the minds of others and how that understanding is related to the self (cf. Lamm, Batson, & Decety, 2007; Lamm, Meltzoff, & Decety, 2010; Singer &

Lamm, 2009; Singer et al., 2004; see also Keysers & Gazzola, 2009). One of the interesting outcomes of this research is evidence that, during empathic tasks, the "self" and "other" are processed similarly and in regions implicated in processing social information more generally (e.g., Singer et al., 2006). Such findings were anticipated by earlier research on relationships. For example, self-expansion theory (cf. Aron & Aron, 1996) posits that self-concepts and self-representations become more intertwined with people's representations of others as they grow closer to them. In the following section, we explore research dedicated to understanding how the brain constructs the self, how the brain understands others, and how those two processes converge as relationships develop.

Self-Expansion and Self–Other Overlap in Relationship and Social Psychological Theory

Theorists have long argued that the self is at least partially defined by one's social relationships (Andersen & Chen, 2002; Aron & Aron, 1996). Self-expansion theory (Aron & Aron, 1996) suggests that love is the process or output of a motivation to expand the self. The theory has largely been promoted as a heuristically useful metaphor that describes the intertwining of the self with the other in an intuitively accessible manner. Although aspects of the model lack formal specification and, therefore, falsifiability, it has inspired considerable research and has led to meaningful insights. Inspired by George Lakoff's (Lakoff & Johnson, 1999) ideas regarding embodied metaphors, the model was designed as a heuristic for guiding research about how the self becomes entangled with others in memory. In many ways, self-expansion theory presaged the explosion in embodiment research, which provides evidence for the idea that people understand themselves, others, and the world through embodied cognitive and affective representations (cf. Damasio, 1999; Niedenthal, 2007). At its core, the model proposes three ideas:

> 1) people seek to expand the self, 2) one way they seek to do so is by attempting to include others in the self through close

relationships, 3) people seek situations and experiences that have become associated with experiences of expansion of the self. (Aron & Aron, 1996, p. 49)

Aron, Aron, Tudor, and Nelson (1991) have found that close others are more likely to be treated like the self in resource distribution scenarios, and attributions for the self versus the other are more similar for close others. Furthermore, self–other confusion in memory is more common with close others (Aron & Fraley, 1999; Mashek, Aron, & Boncimino, 2003). The Inclusion of the Other in the Self (IOS) Scale (Aron, Aron, & Smollan, 1992), which allows people to identify how close they subjectively feel to another by choosing one of a series of progressively overlapping circles, measures psychological closeness quite well. It is, perhaps, the best measure of relationship closeness in predictive terms, with the possible exception of the Relationship Closeness Inventory (Berscheid, Snyder, & Omoto, 1989, 2004), an extensive self-report measure of closeness-related behaviors.

Although it is difficult to determine how the model could be tested neuroscientifically, Aron and Aron (1996) provided some general hypotheses that are promising in terms of advancing the understanding of self–other dynamics. For example, they argued that it is difficult to imagine why people would behave in truly altruistic ways toward others (i.e., sacrificing the self for another) unless one considers that self-expansion theory predicts that the other is a part of the self. In this sense, selfless acts are more likely given that the other person is simply an extension of the self. Testing such hypotheses would require operationalization of self–other overlap or inclusion of other in the self that mapped onto neural activity to be useful for neuroscientists, but as we discuss, recent research on empathy is building some potential ways to test these ideas more directly. We now discuss what is already known about the neural representation of the self and others.

Neural Representations of the Self

Many socially relevant brain processes are supported by neural substrates that represent the body, the subjective self, the agentic self, and the self's various feeling states, including emotions and sensations. Two contemporary theories represent the state of the art in understanding the neural manifestation of the self, each of which is highly compatible with the other. In this section, we discuss Antonio Damasio's (1994) somatic marker hypothesis and Bud Craig's (2002, 2009) theory regarding meta-representation of the self in the anterior insular cortex (AIC).

Somatic marker hypothesis. This theoretical formulation of decision making and reasoning (e.g., Damasio, 1994; Bechara & Damasio, 2004) argues that emotion and affective states are a critical foundation for decision making. Emotions are created through unified changes in somatic states (physiological states of the body such as heart rate changes, musculoskeletal action, and endocrine release), the release of neurotransmitters and neuromodulators such as dopamine or serotonin, the activation of somatosensory maps in regions such as the insula, and the modification of signals being transmitted from the body to regions of the brain involved in somatosensory processing. Affective stimuli, according to this theory, are frequently distinguished as either primary or secondary inducers. Primary inducers elicit an automatic and obligatory somatic response in the individual and are innate response elicitors (e.g., food, snakes, soothing touch), learned elicitors such as conditioned stimuli (e.g., a type of food that has been associated with illness and vomiting), or stimuli of sufficiently strong affective value to warrant explicit knowledge (e.g., learning that your bank account has been cleared of money by an imposter). Secondary inducers are usually a memory or thought that elicits an emotional response, such as remembering a car accident or imagining learning that one has a terminal illness. It is argued that states elicited by primary inducers are mediated through the amygdala, whereas secondary inducers are primarily associated with the ventromedial prefrontal cortex (vmPFC).

In this formulation, information regarding primary inducers is sent from sensory receptors to the amygdala through either sensory cortex or a more direct thalamic pathway. The amygdala sends this information to effector structures such as the hypothalamus, the ventral striatum, and brain stem nuclei (e.g., the periaqueductal gray), which trigger changes in peripheral physiological systems such as muscles involved in facial expressions, approach or avoidance behaviors, and endocrine and cardiovascular systems. The somatic states induced by changes in the body are then signaled back to regions in the brain stem such as the parabrachial nucleus of the brain stem, which then relays somatic patterns to somatosensory-related cortices including the insula, primary and secondary somatosensory cortices, and cingulate cortex. Secondary inducers are generated largely by vmPFC, which can couple memories encoded in higher order association cortices with effector structures that initiate somatic states, such as the amygdala, and neural regions that process the somatic states, such as those in the brain stem (e.g., parabrachial nucleus of the brain stem) and cortical somatosensory regions (e.g., primary somatosensory cortex, insula).

The vmPFC plays a critical role in activating regions in the brain stem and hypothalamus, which act in turn to "rerepresent" or model the somatic states as they were originally experienced. This process, in which the peripheral effects are not occurring directly in the body, has been described as the *as-if body loop*. This as-if loop mimics the original somatic state, even in the absence of that state in the body. The vmPFC can trigger such as-if body loop processes to select for and attend to different alternatives for potential action. For example, the vmPFC can use memory to trigger somatic representations of the body from previous experiences, often in rapid succession, and use rerepresentations of earlier experiences to make decisions about appropriate responses given situational goals and constraints. In this way, emotional information is used to select responses to external stimuli and internal states, biasing and frequently improving decision making.

Anterior insula and human awareness.   Bud Craig (2002, 2009) has presented a similar model, emphasizing insular cortex involvement in human awareness and self-representation. He notes that the posterior insula receives interoceptive information about the body (information about the state of the body, including heart rate, pain, temperature, etc.) and forwards it to the AIC to be integrated

with other sources of neural information. Subjective reports of bodily feelings are most strongly associated with the AIC and the adjacent orbitofrontal cortex (OFC), suggesting that the insula contains a somatotopic rerepresentation or model of the body. This rerepresentation can be influenced by a host of factors over and above those associated with sensory afferent information. Moreover, it is this integrated and modified rerepresentation of the body that is subjectively experienced in consciousness, which leads to a subjective sense of one's body as one's self.

One critical feature of the structural organization of the insula is its unique access to peripheral information as represented by a phylogenetically new afferent pathway from the brain stem (i.e., lamina I and solitary nucleus) to the insula, a pathway seen only in higher order primates. This pathway allows for a direct representation of the body's homeostatic physiological state in the posterior insula. The mid-insula then creates a rerepresentation of the body state that includes representations of emotionally salient stimuli from higher cortical areas, the amygdala, the ventral striatum and nucleus accumbens, and the temporal pole. At this point, the self-representation in the amygdala includes the homeostatic state of the body, emotionally relevant environmental stimuli, and motivational impulses. Finally, all salient information is rerepresented with the homeostatic conditions of the body, its fit in the environment (or the degree to which the individual is able to achieve goals and meet basic needs), important social features of the environment, and the person's current motivational state in the AIC and the junction between the AIC and the frontal operculum. One can view all of this as a meta-representation of the self-in-context or, as Craig (2009) argued, a meta-representation of the "global emotional moment" or "an image of 'the material me'" (p. 67).

Self-in-context.   Despite these insightful and useful accounts of the neural basis of the self, self-representation is likely to be highly context dependent, and elements of self-representation may be difficult, if not impossible, to extract from prevailing physical, psychological, and social circumstances. This idea should be familiar to social psychologists, who study the social-cognitive underpinnings of the self. For example, Markus and colleagues (e.g., Markus & Kunda, 1986; Markus & Wurf, 1987) have proposed that people hold working self-concepts that are sensitive to the current social environment. Thus, neural processing of the self may similarly shift as a function of context. One context that has received much attention in the neurosciences is the self when threatened with or experiencing some sort of physical or social pain. As we discuss in depth shortly, this domain of research is particularly useful for making self–other comparisons because threatening and painful contexts have been extensively explored both when individuals are the targets of threat or pain and when other people are the targets of threat or pain. The neural literature on empathy has provided a window through which self–other comparisons can be made within a specific context. This context provides an opportunity for exploring the neural evidence for relationship theories that posit greater overlap in self and other representations as a function of closeness, interdependence, identification, or other social cues of similarity or group membership.

A common pattern of neural activity is typically identified during threat and pain (cf. Coan, Schaefer, & Davidson, 2006; Dalton, Kalin, Grist, & Davidson, 2005; Price, 2000). This pattern includes subcortical and midbrain regions involved in motivation and affect, such as the periaqueductal gray, amygdala, putamen, caudate, hypothalamus, and thalamus; cortical regions involved in problem-solving, goal and motor planning, somatosensation, self-regulation, emotional processing, interoception, and rerepresentation processes in regions such as the OFC and vmPFC, anterior cingulate cortex, posterior cingulate cortex, insula, and superior, medial, and inferior frontal gyri; and parietal regions such as the angular and supramarginal gyri. These neural regions are activated by threats of shock and can be thought of as constituting a threat matrix. It is important to note that none of these regions processes threats exclusively. Each of these brain regions responds to a different aspect of the threat, and most or all of them are involved in a host of non–threat-related processes.

Fascinatingly, many of the regions involved in responding to threat are also involved in processing self-focus. Similar to threat responding, the self is a complicated concept that is not easily mapped onto a simple (or a single) neural substrate. Despite this complexity, the models we have described give one some sense of what neural substrates might most closely match what psychologists and philosophers often mean by the term *the self*. William James (1890) made a distinction between the "me" self, or the self as known, and the "I" self, or the self as knower. It is difficult to link James's selves to neural substrates, but it is possible to think of the vmPFC and the AIC as representing two aspects of the self that directly relate to the distinction between the "I" and the "me," respectively. The vmPFC seems to act as a decision maker, a selector of actions. In a sense, this region can be thought of as a candidate region for a neural "I" that acts on the world. The AIC, alternatively, represents the body and its fit in the environment and a sense of self that is most closely aligned with the "me." More important, both of these conceptualizations of the self suggest that both the agentic self and the material self are rerepresentations that summarize the activity of distributed neural activity related to a variety of interoceptive, motivational, perceptual, affective, and cognitive processes. The neural processes and regions involved in these different representations of the self are critical in a variety of social and relationship-based cognitive, motivational, and affective processes. As such, it will be useful to consider how frequently areas involved in self-representation are also involved in the representation of close others and how closeness and other social factors change the degree to which contextualized representation is more or less similar between the self and other.

Neural Representations of Others

Social perception has been studied in numerous ways by those using neuroscience methods. Here, we only briefly review social perception research. Instead, we focus on the portions of the literature that are more directly applicable to self-expansion and related theories (e.g., Andersen & Chen, 2002; Aron & Aron, 1996; Brewer & Gardner, 1996), which address the way in which self-representations overlap with other-representations. We emphasize, however, that important ideas may also emerge from the social perception literature. Indeed, we would not be surprised if lower level social perception processes capture and explain important psychological and interpersonal dynamics that one might not expect to be linked to more basic social perception processes.

A tremendous amount of research has investigated how people understand the minds and intentions of others, an area of inquiry commonly called *theory of mind* (cf. Allison et al., 2000; Frith & Frith, 1999; Saxe & Kanwisher, 2003). Multiple brain systems are involved in understanding the mental states of others, including the STS, which appears to decode biological motion and implied biological motion (e.g., Allison et al., 2000), and the temporoparietal junction, located in the same general region of the brain as the STS, which Saxe and Kanwisher (2003) have argued is involved in reasoning about the content of others' mental states. Also involved is the amygdala, which is associated with emotional perception (e.g., Adolphs, 2002, 2010; Whalen et al., 2009) and determination of the trustworthiness of others (Engell, Haxby, & Todorov, 2007; Koscik & Tranel, 2011; Platek, Krill, & Wilson, 2009).

Allison et al. (2000) proposed a model of the neural control of social cognition in which the STS plays an early role in detecting biologically relevant cues and integrating object recognition with spatial location and movement (cf. Ungerleider & Haxby, 1994). The STS forwards this information to the amygdala and OFC, which determine the biological and affective value of the stimulus (cf. Adolphs, 1999). Subsequently, the PFC uses this integrated information to make decisions, deploy resources such as attention, and engage other systems in the brain (cf. Miller & Cohen, 2001). This general-purpose theory of mind and social cognition network, however, is not the only system involved in social cognition or the process by which people understand the mental states of others. Indeed, another intensely studied system that appears to be critical in some instances of social cognition is an empathy network (cf. Singer & Lamm, 2009).

Neural networks supporting empathy. According to de Vignemont and Singer (2006), empathy occurs when

> (i) one is in an affective state; (ii) this state is isomorphic to another person's affective state; (iii) this state is elicited by the observation or imagination of another person's affective state; (iv) one knows that the other person is the source of one's own affective state. (p. 435)

It is important to note that there are other classes of affective and cognitive response to the affective states of others, including emotional contagion (Hatfield, Cacioppo, & Rapson, 1994), sympathy, empathic concern, and compassion. Empathic concern, sympathy, and compassion are all seen as lacking affective isomorphism (*isomorphism* refers to a similarity in form with a one-to-one match in individual components or elements), and emotional contagion occurs when the isomorphic emotional state is not attributed to the other person. Therefore, Singer and Lamm (2009) have argued that these types of processes do not constitute empathy in a strict sense. Most neuroscience investigations of these processes have focused exclusively on empathy.

Moreover, most studies on empathy have investigated empathy within a negatively valenced context. A thorough reading of the literature suggests that most of these studies use either painful or threatening stimuli applied to someone other than the participant to elicit empathic responses, or they show images of others expressing or experiencing pain or fear. A groundbreaking study by Tania Singer et al. (2004) subjected participants and their romantic partners to a painful stimulus and then examined which regions of the participants' brains were active when both they and their partners were in pain. They found substantial spatial overlap in the neural response to self-pain and other-pain in regions typically associated with affective processing, including the AIC and the anterior cingulate cortex. Additionally, they noted that the extent of activation in parts of this network was positively associated with participants' self-reports of empathy. This finding, that many of the same brain structures commonly activated in the firsthand experience of pain and threat are also active in vicarious experience of pain and threat, has been replicated numerous times (e.g., Beckes, Coan, & Hasselmo, 2013; Lamm et al., 2007, 2010).

Subsequent research has begun to define the boundary conditions and generalizability of this effect. For example, children show the same pattern of empathic response as adults (Decety, Michalska, & Akitsuki, 2008), and adults process the unusual pain of others (pain the participant has never experienced personally) in these same general regions (Lamm et al., 2010). Despite this general pattern, Lamm et al. (2010) found that empathy for unusual pain elicited a weaker response in participants. Other studies have found similarly weakened empathic responses to the pain in AIDS patients believed to have contracted the disease through illegal drug use (Decety, Echols, & Correll, 2010) and to the pain of others who are perceived to have behaved in an unfair manner in an economic game (Singer et al., 2006). Additionally, vicarious pain responses to displays of chronic pain are weaker than those to displays of acute pain (Saarela et al., 2007), and inferior parietal activations (e.g., supramarginal and angular gyri) are greater for similar targets than for dissimilar targets.

State-of-the-art research has suggested that empathy is supported by shared networks of activity, meaning that self-related processing occurs in very similar regions to other-related processing in situations that invoke an empathic response. Singer and Lamm (2009) argued for a dual-component-style model composed of subcortical regions that are involved in motivational affective processing, such as the amygdala or ventral striatum, and another component composed of areas involved in integrative and higher level processing (e.g., goals, interoception, planning) such as anterior cingulate cortex, OFC, prefrontal cortex (PFC), AIC, inferior and superior frontal regions, supplementary motor cortex, and somatosensory components (e.g., Singer & Lamm, 2009). Interestingly, one of the few studies to investigate empathy in a positive context found that highly pleasant smells experienced vicariously are represented in the AIC and adjacent frontal operculum (Jabbi, Swart, & Keysers, 2007).

Self–other overlap.   There are several ways to interpret the empathy literature in terms of support for psychological theories that argue for intertwining self–other representations. First, however, it is important to note the interesting consistency with which other-threat activations are topographically similar to self-threat activations. To extend this observation further, the areas identified as self-relevant in the somatic marker hypothesis (Damasio, 1994) and Craig's (2009) AIC self-representation theory are heavily included in those regions identified as part of the putative empathy network (as well as the threat matrix). Indeed, the AIC is almost always detected as active in empathy studies during vicarious emotional experience. Does this mean that people are including others in the self when they are empathizing? Perhaps, but it is not so simple. Frequently, these results are discussed in terms of whether they represent simulation (cf. Gallese & Goldman, 1998) of the state of others, an idea that is heavily debated (cf. Decety, 2011). Complicating matters, there is ambiguity regarding what simulation even means. For example, it may be that the brain simply uses self-related processes, including embodied representations, to calculate or understand the current emotional state of others (Jacob, 2008) rather than actually treating others as if they were similar to, or an extension of, the self. Additionally, the method used to identify overlapping brain regions in empathy tasks is more descriptive than quantitative. For example, the fact that the same brain region is recruited to process the self and others is not direct evidence for self–other overlap as is often meant in social psychological terms. Rather, it would be better evidence to find that not only the location of activity is similar but also the degree of activation is more similar within individuals in those regions when the other is a significant other than when the other is a random stranger. This would give stronger credence to the idea that people are treating close others as if they are the self than most studies to date can claim.

The current evidence suggests that this network of regions is involved in processing threat and pain in both the self and others but is not engaged when the other appears to be unworthy of empathy for one reason or another (i.e., selfishness or acting in ways that invite the painful or threatening circumstance). In our view, this constitutes weak evidence—but evidence nonetheless—for what relationship-oriented theories of self–other overlap predict. We are currently developing analytical approaches that may shed light on these types of issues more directly. For example, we recently collected functional images of brain function during a threat-of-shock task in which participants experienced a threat directly, a friend of participants experienced the threat, and a stranger experienced the threat (Coan et al., 2013). Group-level analyses revealed the typical pattern of activation found in empathy studies in which the threat matrix was active in all three conditions. Using a covariate approach, however, we found that self-threat activity was significantly correlated with friend-threat activity in a variety of threat-responsive regions, but few similar correlations between self-threat and stranger-threat were found (an exception being the right OFC). Moreover, we observed that higher scores on Aron et al.'s (1992) IOS measure corresponded with increased activity in the AIC and inferior frontal cortex for threatened friends but not for threatened strangers. Thus, under threatening conditions, self-focused processing is highly similar to friend-focused but not stranger-focused processing.

These observations suggest that relationship closeness binds self- and other-representations in the brain and that the inclusion of the other in the self may be significantly more than merely metaphor. We are now attempting to create an individual difference variable indexing the degree to which self-threat activation is synchronized with other-threat activation (see Levinson & Gottman, 1983, for an example of psychophysiological measures of synchrony). Indeed, initial analyses of these results have suggested that important relationship factors in early life are associated with the likelihood that participants experience correlations in self-threat response and other-threat response and that such measures covary with self-reported empathy in predictable ways (Coan et al., 2013). Such novel measurement approaches increase the links between social neuroscience and previous studies of relationships grounded in more social psychological traditions. One exciting opportunity is to explore whether such measurement approaches produce evidence for or against the hypothesis that greater degrees of self–other entanglement lead to greater prosocial behavior, motivation, or both.

In the next section, we discuss a set of highly related domains of interpersonal behavior and relationship phenomena that have been extensively documented at the neural level. Although the terminology used in neuroscience and social psychology is different and the underlying theories differ conceptually in important ways, neuroscience has learned much about the basic behavioral systems associated with attachment, caregiving, and sex. In these domains, the integration of neuroscience, relationship science, and social psychology is reaching a tipping point at which the field is becoming highly integrated.

SEX, CAREGIVING, AND ATTACHMENT

John Bowlby's (e.g., 1969/1982) attachment theory has been hugely influential across psychological disciplines (see Cassidy & Shaver, 2008). With this theory, Bowlby introduced the concept of the attachment system as the primary motivator for the bonds that tie children to their parents. By *attachment system*, Bowlby meant the coordination and action of multiple component processes and instincts. The proximal function of each attachment instinct in children is the maintenance of proximity to the child's primary caregiver, usually the child's mother. What begins as individual instinctive behaviors serving the same general function eventually become coordinated into "sophisticated goal-corrected systems" (Bowlby, 1969/1982, p. 180), which effectively coordinate a variety of behaviors, such as suckling, clinging, crying, and following to reach the desired end state (i.e., closer proximity to the caregiver).

Bowlby (1969/1982) theorized that evolutionary pressures conferred on humans and other species a finite number of goal-corrected behavior systems. These systems involved instinctive programs that promoted successful attainment of a given organism's physiological, social, and psychological goals, including the avoidance of danger. In other words, these systems motivate and organize behavior to achieve a specific adaptive goal. Over time, these systems become goal corrected through feedback mechanisms that indicate the organism's relative success or failure at achieving that goal. By adulthood, these instinctive programs have, at least in humans, been tuned by complex cognitive and behavioral learning histories. As a consequence, adults rarely exhibit the kind of obvious instinctive behavior one commonly sees in infants and small children. However, such instinctual motivations still influence behavior toward the attainment of the same functional goals necessary for the basic fulfillment of all organisms' evolutionary mandates: survival, growth, reproduction, and rearing (see Kaplan & Gangestad, 2005; Simpson & Belsky, 2008, for a discussion of life history theory). A key conceptual argument made by Bowlby is that these behavioral systems are activated by certain environmental stimuli and physiological states (e.g., hormone levels) and terminated by a complementary set of stimuli and states. In the current psychological lexicon, activation of a behavioral system might be associated with the initiation of appetitive or aversive anticipatory motivational states that either compel the organism to approach or avoid some specific outcome. Alternatively, termination of a behavioral system might be associated with the consummatory act of achieving the goal. The separation of anticipatory and consummatory processes has been critical in research on reward, a feature particularly well studied in research on the neuroscience of sex.

Bowlby (1969/1982) did not intend to describe the action of only the attachment behavioral system; he also argued for the existence of other behavioral systems governing other behaviors such as caregiving and sexual behavior. In many ways, his behavioral systems approach was an attempt at integrating evolutionary biology (particularly ethological approaches), behaviorism, and psychodynamics (particularly relating to the importance and influence of early experience on personality and development), representing one of a few attempts at a grand theory of relationships (see Berscheid, 1995). Since Bowlby's seminal work, other theorists have argued that love emerges in various ways out of the attachment, caregiving, and sexual systems (e.g., Berscheid, 2006b; Hazan & Shaver, 1987; Hazan &

Zeifman, 1994; Mikulincer, 2006), highlighting the broad reach and impact that attachment theory has had on contemporary psychological approaches to interpersonal relationships. In the next section, we discuss what neuroscience has gleaned about how the brain manages attachment, caregiving, and sex. First, we discuss the difference between behavioral systems and neural systems, after which we discuss various neural components that are important component processes underlying attachment, caregiving, and sex. We conclude with a discussion of how neuroscientific approaches can shed light on these ideas and theories more broadly.

Neural Systems Versus Behavioral Systems

One may be tempted to assume that Bowlby (1969/1982) hypothesized that behavioral systems are instantiated in the brain in a modular fashion. A close reading of Bowlby, however, suggests that a strict modular interpretation of behavioral systems, such as that proposed by Fodor (1983), would be incompatible with his view that behavioral systems are composed of numerous instinctive responses that organize or develop and are strongly influenced by learning. It would also be a mistake to assume that behavioral systems have any dedicated and discrete instantiation in the brain. Rather, the brain is most likely composed of neural systems that are involved in components of each behavioral system (cf. Coan, 2008). For example, if one were looking for the attachment behavioral system per se in the brain, one would find little evidence of it. However, there is a rich neuroscientific literature related to detecting and learning the stimulus characteristics of another person, behavioral responses to separation, reward processes, stress responses, and a multitude of other processes involved in interpersonal behavior. Much is known about how the brain handles many of these processes. Moreover, many of the same neural systems involved in the action of one putative behavioral system are also involved in the action of other behavioral systems.

Neural systems are a collection of integrated neurons that form a circuit. Any given system may be manifested physically as a local bundle of neurons in the same general spatial location or as a distributed network of neurons located throughout the brain. The activity of these systems can result in varied behavior depending on the interaction of different systems in coordination. It is unlikely that any one of these systems neatly corresponds to the large diversity of potential attachment behaviors (e.g., proximity seeking, affect regulation) or representations (e.g., working models). Instead, many of these systems are engaged in processes for which researchers currently have an impoverished vocabulary to accurately describe. Indeed, description may be possible only mathematically (although the sheer size and computational power of the brain makes accurate mathematical modeling excessively difficult and hard to imagine as it is applied to complex behaviors and processes). For example, the dorsolateral PFC is known to be typically active during threatening tasks (e.g., Coan, Schaefer, & Davidson, 2006), but it is unlikely that the dorsolateral PFC is a threat region. It is also known to be involved in executive processes (cf. Miller & Cohen, 2001), including (but certainly not limited to) effortful emotion regulation (Ochsner, Bunge, Gross, & Gabrielli, 2002). As such, its involvement in responses to threat cues may support emotion regulation demands that facilitate other situational goals, such as not embarrassing oneself. With this in mind, one can think of the overall matrix of brain regions activated by a specific stimulus as reflecting the number of unique problems associated with that stimulus, as opposed to reflecting only responses to that stimulus per se.

Likely Components of an Attachment Behavioral System

Any attachment system is likely composed of numerous neural systems involved in different aspects of attachment thoughts, feelings, and behaviors. One might hypothesize, for example, that attachment uses the components necessary for recognizing attachment figures, anticipating reward, or receiving comfort from contact with them; social perception; motivated support seeking during stress; and processes involved in emotion regulation. Thus, it is reasonable to hypothesize that out of the action of these many processes emerges what looks like a singular attachment system.

Familiarity. Familiarity may be the core of interpersonal relationships. Robert Zajonc (1968, 1980, 2001) demonstrated the power of mere exposure on preferences, showing that even slight familiarity with a stimulus makes one's evaluations of that stimulus more positive. Determining who is familiar and who is not familiar is critical for attachment and caregiving processes, and social animals appear to be very sensitive to learning the identity of their mothers, usually within hours after birth (e.g., DeCasper & Fifer, 1980; Lorenz, 1981). Several neural structures have been implicated in the detection of social familiarity, including the retrosplenial cortex and posterior cingulate cortex (Shah et al., 2001), as well as the neuropeptides oxytocin and vasopressin (cf. Winslow & Insel, 2004). One important feature of the neural processing of familiarity relates to the overall developmental trajectory of the brain and the importance of caregiving in species that give birth to altricial young. Because altricial young have a better chance of survival if they maintain proximity to their parents, even when parents are abusive or neglectful (Hofer, 2006; Moriceau & Sullivan, 2005), some aspects of brain development seem to result in more rapid and contextually insensitive bonding in infancy.

Familiarity and bonding in infants is sensitive to the interaction between the locus coerulus and the amygdala. For example, norepinephrine released by the locus coerulus plays a moderating (but not direct) role in adult bonding (Cahill, Prins, Weber, & McGaugh, 1994), whereas in infants it is necessary and sufficient for bonding (Sullivan, 2003). Because the locus coerulus releases high amounts of norepinephrine in early life, the sensory characteristics of caregivers get learned very rapidly. Furthermore, the amygdala, important in aversive conditioning (Sullivan, 2003), is underdeveloped at this point, creating a combination of amnesia to negative interactions with a caregiver and highly acute memory for positive interactions with the caregiver, thus leading to a virtually unconditional preference for familiar stimuli. The amygdala also appears to be critical for the encoding of emotionally salient information (Hamman, Ely, Grafton, & Kilts, 1999), and it has strong connections with the hippocampus, which is critical for long-term memory consolidation (Brasted, Bussey, Murray, & Wise, 2003; Kennedy & Shapiro, 2004). Early in development, this connection between the amygdala and the hippocampus is particularly underdeveloped (Herschkowitz, 2000), potentially adding to the contextual insensitivity in infant bonding.

Anticipatory reward and incentive salience. A tremendous amount of relationship behavior is intimately tied to motivation and emotion. To bond with another person, aversive tendencies must be tempered, and approach tendencies need to be increased. Several neurochemicals are involved in this process, and each seems to have a more or less distinct role in social motivation and reward. It is useful to keep in mind the distinction between anticipatory reward and consummatory reward, or—as Bowlby (1969/1982) might have thought about it—activation and termination processes.

The type of reward process most closely associated with excitement, fun, and desire is anticipatory. It is dominated in large part by dopamine transmitters and is thought to be responsible for motivating goal-based behavior (e.g., Berridge, 2007; Depue & Collins, 1999). The dopamine system is rooted in the ventral tegmental area (VTA) and substantia nigra and is directly connected to as many as 30 different neural systems (Le Moal & Simon, 1991). The dopamine circuits most strongly associated with anticipatory reward are the ventral and dorsal strata. Whereas the dorsal striatum seems to be most strongly associated with decision making (cf. Balleine, Delgado, & Hikosaka, 2007) and the ventral striatum appears to be most strongly associated with the emotional and motivational (cf. Costa, Lang, Sabatinelli, Versace, & Bradley, 2010) aspects of goal-directed behavior, Berridge and Robinson (1998) argue that dopamine's primary role in these systems is to signal incentive salience. Incentive salience essentially translates into the feeling of wanting something or desiring it. Thus, dopamine plays little role in the hedonic pleasure a given stimulus produces (other than moderating the hedonic value of stimuli through anticipatory arousal), but rather plays a role in the motivation to obtain the stimulus. The ventral striatum is largely defined by a connection between the VTA and the nucleus

accumbens and shared projections with the amygdala and the PFC. The dorsal striatum, alternatively, is mainly composed of the VTA and its projections to the caudate and putamen.

Evidence has supported a functional role for dopamine circuits in maternal and caregiving behavior. For example, Mattson and Morrell (2005) have found that the ventral striatum is involved in approach behaviors associated with caregiving. In rats, conditioned preferences and maternal behaviors such as licking and grooming seem to require dopamine activity (e.g., Fleming, Korsmit, & Deller, 1994; Keer & Stern, 1999; Numan et al., 2005). Moreover, functional MRI (fMRI) studies of human mothers have indicated striatum activity when mothers view photos of their infants (Bartels & Zeki, 2004).

Dopamine is also strongly implicated in sexual behavior. For example, human and rat males administered with dopamine have been observed to obtain spontaneous erections (Lal et al., 1987; Melis, Argiolas, & Gessa, 1987). Furthermore, blockade of dopamine via antagonists decreases sexual desire and response (Pfaus & Phillips, 1991; cf. Pfaus, Kippen, & Coria-Avila, 2003). Similarly, females who are depleted of dopamine are less sexually responsive (Neckameyer, 1998) and regain responsiveness after administration of a dopamine metabolite, L-3,4-dihydroxyphenylalanine.

Several fMRI studies have also supported the conclusion that dopamine is involved in sexual behavior. For example, during studies in which participants view pictures of people with whom they are in love, various dopamine-rich structures, such as the caudate, putamen, and VTA, are more active than in control conditions (e.g., Acevedo, Aron, Fisher, & Brown, 2012; Aron et al., 2005; Bartels & Zeki, 2000; Fisher, Aron, & Brown, 2006). Moreover, participants viewing images of former partners who recently terminated their relationship show a similar pattern (Fisher, Brown, Aron, Strong, & Mashek, 2010), and the names of romantic partners also seem to activate these dopamine circuits (Ortigue, Bianchi-Demicheli, de C. Hamilton, & Grafton, 2007). Pfaus (1996, 1999) argued that the dopamine system, consistent with an incentive-salience interpretation, is primarily involved in the arousal, excitement, and anticipatory phase of sexual activity. Although there is no clear point at which one can say there is a shift from the anticipatory phase to the consummatory phase in sex, it seems clear that dopamine controls excitement, whereas orgasm and its associated euphoria are more associated with endogenous opioids, which are discussed next.

Perhaps one of the most important ways the dopamine system is involved in various relationship processes is that it is particularly sensitive to cues that predict reward (Schultz, Dayan, & Montague, 1997) and is involved in conditioned learning (Depue & Collins, 1999). Because of these features, the dopamine system learns to respond to cues that lovers, caregivers, and other relationship partners are nearby and the likelihood the person can garner the unconditioned reward of various types of social contact from them. Thus, the dopamine system may be important in ramping up motivation to approach these relationship partners and to behave in ways that increase the predictability and likelihood of getting social rewards (cf. Coan, 2008).

Organization, sensitization, and perception. Oxytocin, and its sibling molecule vasopressin, are neuropeptides that modulate the function of a wide range of brain systems. Oxytocin has been implicated in the functioning of various interpersonal behaviors. Its role in social bonding has also been extensively studied (e.g., Borman-Spurrell, Allen, Hauser, Carter, & Cole-Detke, 1995; Carter, 2003; Insel & Fernald, 2004; Young & Wang, 2004), yet there are gaps in researchers' understanding of oxytocin that are only beginning to be filled by theory and research.

As part of caregiving, oxytocin is associated with milk letdown (Capuco & Akers, 2009) and may have been exapted over evolutionary time to facilitate bonding in various types of relationships. Oxytocin, along with several other hormones such as progesterone, prolactin, and estrogen, is associated with increased basal levels in women in response to pregnancy and birth (e.g., Gonzalez, Atkinson, & Fleming, 2009; Numan, Fleming, & Levy, 2006; Panksepp, 1998). Oxytocin has been implicated in animals with the initiation of maternal behavior in

conjunction with these other hormones (e.g., Keverne & Kendrick, 1991; Panksepp, 1998; Pereira, Seip, Morrell, & Bridges, 2008). However, evidence from rat and sheep models indicates that administering oxytocin directly into the ventricular system is sufficient for the onset of maternal behavior (Keverne & Kendrick, 1994; Pedersen, Ascher, Monroe, & Prange, 1982).

Oxytocin also appears to play an important role in sexual behavior. For example, using an oxytocin antagonist to block the binding of oxytocin to receptor sites leads to a decrease in erectile response in males (Melis, Spano, Succu, & Argiolas, 1999). In addition, oxytocin is associated with increased epinephrine in the blood, which correlates with arousal reports in men (Burri, Heinrichs, Schedlowski, & Kruger, 2008). Numerous animal studies have also found that oxytocin facilitates and supports sexual behavior (Argiolas & Gessa, 1991; Argiolas & Melis, 2005; Carter, 1992, 1998; Cushing & Carter, 2000) in various ways.

Monogamous prairie voles have been the animal model of choice in studying oxytocin's and vasopressin's role in pair bonding (e.g., Carter, Grippo, Pournajafi-Nazarloo, Ruscio, & Porges, 2008; Carter & Keverne, 2002). This research has indicated that both oxytocin and vasopressin are critical in organizing a variety of social behaviors (Carter et al., 2008), including general affiliative behavior (Cho, DeVries, Williams, & Carter, 1999), pair bonding, and stranger aggression (e.g., Argiolas, 1999; Carter, 1992; Williams, Catania, & Carter, 1992; Winslow, Hastings, Carter, Harbaugh, & Insel, 1993). For example, central administration of oxytocin promotes pair bonding, and antagonists prevent pair bonding (Cho et al., 1999; Williams, Insel, Harbaugh, & Carter, 1994; Winslow et al., 1993). Furthermore, blocking vasopressin in male voles reduces stranger aggression and mating behavior (Winslow et al., 1993). Its role in pair bonding and other interpersonal behaviors does not seem to end there; rather, oxytocin has been implicated in processes as basic as social perception, including social recognition (e.g., Dantzer & Bluthé, 1992; Dluzen, Muraoka, & Landgraf, 1998), biological motion detection (e.g., Jack, Connelly, & Morris, 2012), and trust (Kosfeld, Heinrichs, Zak, Fischbacher,

& Fehr, 2005; Zak, Stanton, & Ahmadi, 2007). Indeed, nasal administration of oxytocin promotes more trusting behavior in economic games (e.g., Kosfeld et al., 2005; Zak et al., 2007), and higher blood measures of oxytocin concentration predict more trusting behavior (Zak, Kurzban, & Matzner, 2005). It is important, however, that oxytocin seems to make people selectively trusting, but not gullible (Mikolajczak et al., 2010); it is not the trust peptide but has a more restricted role than making people indiscriminantly trustful of others.

Shelley Taylor's (2006; Taylor et al., 2000) tend-and-befriend model and related research are beginning to uncover other functional roles of oxytocin in relationship behavior. This model is based on the premise that when under duress, people are motivated to befriend others and tend to the needs of others. According to this theory, relationship stress induces oxytocin release, which motivates affiliative behavior. Current evidence has suggested that the link between stress and oxytocin is relationship specific. For example, women experiencing relationship conflict or emotional distance from their partner have higher plasma oxytocin levels (Taylor, 2006), which stands in contrast to evidence that oxytocin reduces the stress response (Heinrichs, Baumgartner, Kirschbaum, & Ehlert, 2003; Light et al., 2000) in some contexts. This apparently conflicting evidence, however, may suggest that oxytocin is more important for organizing affiliative behavior, sensitizing reward systems to social rewards, and promoting social perception. Thus, it may serve a motivational role, but in more of an organizational manner rather than promoting anticipatory reward per se. Oxytocin does not seem to fit the role of a general approach substrate, nor does it seem to fit the role of consummatory reward, as indicated by its context-dependent positive association with the stress response, but it may indicate something more akin to social receptivity (cf. Kemp & Guastella, 2011). As such, it seems likely that oxytocin plays a general role in organizing affiliative behavior and promoting bonding, perhaps heightening the sensitivity of the dopamine system and endogenous opioids.

Consummatory reward. The neurobiological substrates of consummatory reward are most strongly associated with the endogenous opioids (e.g., Levine, Morley, Gosnell, Billington, & Bartness, 1985). Endogenous opioids have strong addictive (e.g., Kreek, 1996) and analgesic properties (e.g., Kealey, 1995), suggesting that although rewarding, they are also involved in signaling safety and comfort rather than excitement and anticipation. Consummatory reward serves to (a) increase the likelihood that the organism will reproduce rewarding feelings in the future and (b) signal that a goal is being or has been met. In this sense, opioids are critical in the termination phase of goal-directed behavior. They become more dominant the closer one gets to satiety, and once sated, they may deactivate motivational circuits, signaling to the rest of the brain to relax because everything is going well.

This may explain why opioids do not have a simple relation with sexual behavior, where they simultaneously act as a strong sexual reward substrate but also diminish motivation to engage in sexual behavior (cf. Pfaus & Gorzalka, 1987). Chronic opiate use is associated with decreased sexual behavior despite its responsibility for the euphoric feelings associated with orgasm (cf. Pfaus & Gorzalka, 1987). Indeed, the use of opioids has been consistently associated with sexual dysfunction from low motivation to erectile dysfunction (e.g., Cushman, 1972; Greenberg, 1984; Jones & Jones, 1977). Blocking opioid binding with an antagonist, alternatively, seems to heighten various aspects of the sexual response and can result in spontaneous erections (e.g., Graber, Blake, Gartner, & Wilson, 1984; Holister, 1975; Mendelson, Ellingboe, Keuhnle, & Mello, 1978). This puzzling set of facts is in apparent contrast with the fact that opioid binding increases over the course of a sexual episode (e.g., Szechtman, Hershkowitz, & Simantov, 1981; Whipple & Komisaruk, 1985) and is critical for sex-related bonding to occur (cf. Pfaus, 2009).

Panksepp and colleagues (e.g., Panksepp, 1981; Nelson & Panksepp, 1998; Panksepp, Nelson, & Bekkedal, 1997) have argued that social bonds have highly similar characteristics to opioid dependence. Although Panksepp has not argued for a strict conceptualization of social attachments as emerging only from the opioid system, he and his colleagues have noted that opioid mechanisms appear to play a critical role in social bonds. Key points of evidence for this idea come from the fact that opioids are released during various types of social contact (Keverne, Martensz, & Tuite, 1989), and blocking of opioid binding through antagonists greatly enhances social motivation (Kalin, Shelton, & Lynn, 1995; Panksepp, Lensing, Leboyer, & Bouvard, 1991). Furthermore, social contact can lead to the pain-reducing benefits of opiate use because of the analgesic properties of opioid release (D'Amato & Pavone, 1993). The broader literature in this area has supported the conceptualization of opioid mechanisms as a consummatory reward in social behavior. It appears to signal satiety, is highly reinforcing, and is released during social contact. Indeed, low levels of opioid binding are associated with increased social motivation, indicating that the organism is out of homeostatic balance and promoting social affiliation to restore that balance.

Stress, pain, and avoidance. One of the key components involved in attachment, but also in caregiving in a vicarious way, is the experience of negative motivational states. As discussed in the empathy section, one of the ways the brain understands others is through vicarious emotional states, which are a major source of motivation for caregiving. However, negative affect is also a potent motivator of attachment behavior. As Simpson and Rholes (2012) noted in their stress-diathesis model of attachment, stress is a critical feature of attachment relationships. Attachment styles often emerge out of the interaction between two people in stressful circumstances (cf. Beckes, Simpson, & Erickson, 2010), and those styles typically manifest themselves primarily in stressful situations (cf. Simpson, Rholes, & Nelligan, 1992). Neurobiological investigations into attachment and related phenomena also indicate a critical role for stress and pain systems, and much is now understood regarding the brain mechanisms that support both the stress response and social behavior.

As Taylor's (2006) tend-and-befriend model suggests, stress and pain are critical pieces of the relationship puzzle. The hypothalamus is an intensively studied stress substrate that marks the beginning of the hypothalamic–pituitary–adrenal axis (Kemeny, 2003). On detection of a stressful stimulus, the hypothalamus receives inputs from various brain regions such as the amygdala (e.g., McEwen, 2007) and produces corticotropin-releasing hormone (Gainer & Wray, 1992). Corticotropin-releasing hormone stimulates the production of adrenocorticotropic hormone in the pituitary gland, which in turns releases cortisol, epinephrine, and norepinephrine in the adrenal cortex. Cortisol then loops through the body back to the hippocampus (Kemeny, 2003), where it stimulates glucocorticoid receptors that inhibit further action of the hypothalamus.

Evidence for the role of social contact and the downregulation of stress circuits has been documented in humans and animal models (cf. DeVries, Glasper, & Detillion, 2003). For example, stable social hierarchies and higher status foster lower basal cortisol in primates (Creel, Creel, & Monfort, 1996; Ray & Sapolski, 1992). Social support in humans lowers blood cortisol (Kirschbaum, Klauer, Filipp, & Hellhammer, 1990) and benefits disease outcomes in both humans and primates (Capitanio, Mendoza, & Lerche, 1998; Uchino et al., 1996). A recent fMRI study (Coan, Schaefer, & Davidson, 2006) indicated that handholding downregulated the hypothalamic response to a threat of electric shock, providing direct evidence in humans for the reduction in hypothalamic activity during social contact.

In addition to the stress circuit, the pain circuit is intimately tied to interpersonal processes. Several lines of theory and research have emerged in social psychology and social neuroscience suggesting that social pain is neurobiologically linked to neural systems involved in the processing of physical pain (Eisenberger, Lieberman, & Williams, 2003; MacDonald & Leary, 2005). Much of this work has been done by Eisenberger and colleagues using the cyberball paradigm. This paradigm uses a virtual ball-tossing game in which participants are first included and then excluded from the game. During the cyberball game, images of the participant's brain are collected via fMRI to identify the regions that are activated by social exclusion. Generally, social exclusion leads to greater activity in the dorsal anterior cingulate cortex and the anterior insular cortex.

Activity in the dorsal anterior cingulate cortex is typically associated with self-reports of distress and is thought to represent a "neural alarm" indicating that a problem or discrepancy has been detected. Furthermore, right ventromedial PFC activity is often negatively correlated with both dorsal anterior cingulate cortex activity and distress. This pattern of activation mirrors what one would expect in a physical pain paradigm, because dorsal anterior cingulate cortex activity and insular activity are usually associated with pain reports and right ventromedial PFC activity is associated with automatic self-regulation of pain. Further evidence for the pain interpretation has been gathered from cyberball studies using acetaminophen (Tylenol) in an experimental group, showing that pain relievers reduce dorsal anterior cingulate cortex activity associated with social rejection (DeWall et al., 2010). Additional studies have shown a moderating role for attachment styles, time spent with friends, and rejection sensitivity in predictable ways (DeWall et al., 2012; Masten et al., 2009; Masten, Telzer, Fuligni, Lieberman, & Eisenberger, 2012).

As it stands, it appears that social contact and positive social interaction downregulate pain and stress systems in the brain, facilitating the health benefits of positive social relationships. By contrast, social rejection and loneliness have the opposite effect, wreaking havoc on the body through increased stress and pain response and chronic activation of these circuits. The reason for the downregulatory effects of social contact are currently unknown, but several prime candidates exist, including oxytocin, opioids, and dopamine systems.

Emotion regulation. Emotion regulation is an important construct in relationships, particularly attachment relationships (cf. Mikulincer & Shaver, 2003). Indeed, it has been argued that emotion regulation is a primary function of attachment in both children and adults. The PFC is integrally involved in emotion and its regulation in a variety of ways (Coan & Allen, 2004; Coan, Allen, & McKnight, 2006). The PFC is highly connected to other brain regions, and its connections are a function of its role in integrating information from other systems and exerting a controlling influence in a top-down

manner on a variety of emotion and motivation systems throughout the brain. Different regions within the PFC, however, are involved in different aspects of emotion regulation (Ochsner & Gross, 2005). For example, the vmPFC and medial OFC appear to be critical in extinction learning and conditioning (Milad et al., 2005; Quirk & Beer, 2006; Sierra-Mercado, Corcoran, Lebrón-Milad, & Quirk, 2006). This type of emotion regulation is relatively quick and automatic. Alternatively, more effortful forms of emotion regulation are associated with the dorsolateral PFC, which is involved in working memory, language processing, and action planning (Ochsner et al., 2002). An example of effortful emotion regulation might involve reappraisal processes. Attachment relationships probably have multiple effects on the functioning of these systems by providing a scaffold to build self-regulation in early life (e.g., Volling, 2001), by associating through conditioning the attachment figure with downregulation of threat responding, or by providing memories of social soothing that can be used in more effortful self-regulation. It is interesting, however, that social contact does not seem to use these neural systems directly to downregulate stress or pain responses (Coan, Schaefer, & Davidson, 2006; Eisenberger, Taylor, Gable, Hilmert, & Lieberman, 2007). In contrast, images of attachment figures seem to act as automatic emotion regulators through the activation of the vmPFC (Eisenberger et al., 2011), which may reflect the fact that social contact acts more directly on emotional systems, possibly through opioid mechanisms (hence, physical contact conditions the brain in this situation), whereas images of attachment figures act on already-conditioned circuits.

Possible modularity in the brain stem. Affective neuroscientist Jaak Panksepp, Moskal, Panksepp, and Kroes (2002) have argued that one of the major "sins" of evolutionary psychology is ignoring brain evidence that homologous brain circuits exist in a variety of species and that most of these circuits have their core in the brain stem. Panksepp (e.g., 1998) argued for the existence of three such modular brain systems that map onto the attachment, sex, and caregiving systems, respectively. First, he argued that attachment is largely undergirded by a separation distress system, termed the *PANIC system,* which is closely related to the pain circuit. The separation distress system has been mapped out most directly through methods using electrical stimulation of the brain in a variety of species (see Panksepp, 1998). Stimulation of the separation distress circuit increases distress vocalizations in a variety of species (see Panksepp, Herman, Vilberg, Bishop, & De Eskinazi, 1980). This circuit emanates from the periaqueductal gray and is projected into the dorsomedial thalamus, ventral septal area, the medial preoptic area, and the bed nucleus of the stria terminalis (Panksepp, 1998). Panksepp (1998) also noted that in "higher species," this circuit extends to the anterior portion of the cingulate cortex, the amygdala, and the hypothalamus. The primary neurotransmitter involved in this system appears to be glutamate, but corticotrophin releasing factor, a stress-related neurochemical, also activates this system strongly.

In addition, Panksepp (1998) argued for a CARE and a SEX circuit, both of which are composed of similar brain structures. He noted that the CARE circuit involves two paths, one that projects down from the medial preoptic area via the habenula into the brain stem and the other that projects upward, starting in the hypothalamus and VTA and continuing into the dopamine strata. The SEX circuit is similarly composed and takes inputs from sensory systems and hormones. The hypothalamus and medial preoptic area are important in hormonal inputs, each of which is reciprocally connected. The medial preoptic area sends information upstream to the amygdala and frontal regions, and it also has projections to the bed nucleus of the stria terminalis and periaqueductal gray. In addition, the hypothalamus projects to the VTA, which then sends information up the dopamine strata.

These modularity claims are hard to verify in humans because imaging techniques cannot investigate neural circuits at a fine-grain level. Panksepp and others usually use animal models. Because they can stimulate individual circuits directly and look at the behavioral and physiological sequelae, animal models can provide much more detailed information on these putatively ancient social brain modules. As such, it is difficult to know exactly how much the PANIC circuit actually organizes attachment behavior, or how much the CARE circuit organizes maternal or paternal behavior. Despite the difficulty, however, it is advisable to consider this perspective when thinking about neural modularity as it relates to interpersonal relationships.

Summary of the Neuroscience of Behavioral Systems

The neuroscience that speaks to the idea of behavioral systems lends evidence to some key ideas inherent in Bowlby's (1969/1982) original work. First, Bowlby's idea that these systems are not monolithic structures at the beginning of life but rather are individual instincts that organize over time, is reasonably consistent with the distributed manner in which the brain represents components of various relational features. Attachment, caregiving, and sexual components appear to be broadly distributed throughout the brain, with different neural constituents involved in various component processes such as person perception, familiarity, anticipatory motivation, behavioral organization, consummatory behavior, emotion regulation, and aversive motivation. Despite this, many of these systems are coherent in adulthood, and the normative processes that undergird these relationship phenomena are consistent across individuals. This suggests that a high level of organization takes place over the course of development. It is still highly debatable whether some core modular circuits form the primary organizing features of these systems. Panksepp and colleagues (e.g., Panksepp, 1998) would almost certainly argue for such modular components in the brain stem, but direct evidence for such components is currently lacking.

Another feature of the neuroscience evidence that relates to behavioral systems in support of Bowlby's (1969/1982) theses is the evidence for anticipatory and consummatory distinctions in the motivational and emotional components of these systems. Although it is not a perfect match, the idea that behavioral systems have activating stimuli (and therefore activation phases) and terminating stimuli (and therefore termination phases) is fairly clear in the current evidence. The fact that dopamine plays a role in reward that roughly corresponds with incentive salience (cf. Berridge, 2007) indicates that desirable stimuli activate behavior to pursue such stimuli. Also, the fact that endogenous opioids are associated with consumption, appear to diminish motivation for social affiliation of all kinds (including sex), but are also associated with successfully getting the rewards of affiliation (e.g., Panksepp et al., 1991; Pfaus & Gorzalka, 1987) indicates that they play a terminating role in relational behavior.

More difficult to map onto Bowlby's (1969/1982) framework is the fact that these relationship-supporting brain systems share a tremendous amount of neural real estate with each other. In this sense, neuroscience might be particularly useful in reconceptualizing many of these processes by identifying the component processes involved in behavioral systems. It may also lead to a better understanding of when behavioral systems act as a monolithic behavioral construct versus when thinking about relationship behavior in a component-focused manner might be more fruitful. Indeed, it seems at this point that conceptualizing Bowlby's behavioral systems as an emergent variable rather than as a traditional latent variable might be a more reasonable measurement strategy (cf. Coan, 2010a). Such an approach might look not only for consistencies in behavior that support the behavioral system approach but inconsistencies as well, further clarifying whether, when, and why covariation among behavioral and physiological systems occurs in relational contexts.

As Ellen Berscheid (2006a) has noted, social psychology is often applied to other fields, but rarely does integration occur in this process, and other fields rarely contribute as much heuristically or conceptually to social psychology as the other way around. We hope that readers are already beginning to see how knowledge of neuroscience can inform the study of interpersonal relationships. In the next section, we describe some overarching principles that social and personality psychologists may find useful heuristically, and we provide an example of how we have applied these principles in the service of our own integrative theory of relationship functioning.

EMERGING PRINCIPLES AND ATTEMPTS AT INTEGRATION

Although the principles we discuss in here do not originate from the neurosciences, they are increasingly implicated in neuroscientific research. In this section, we describe the principles of economy of action, prediction, perception–action links, rerepresentation, and sociality—principles of biology and perception that originated in behavioral ecology, evolutionary biology, cognitive psychology, and modern neuroscience, all of which are highly related to the study of social relationships (e.g., Simpson, Beckes, & Weisberg, 2008; Simpson & Belsky, 2008). We conclude with a description of SBT, which attempts to integrate all of these principles to explain how social relationships function to facilitate survival.

Economy of Action

The economy of action principle states that to survive organisms must consume more energy than they expend. This principle is well documented in behavioral ecology (cf. Krebs & Davies, 1997), and it has been adapted by psychology researchers such as Dennis Proffitt (2006), who has investigated how energy principles affect perception. Evidence for the principle comes from numerous ecological studies of animals. For example, certain crows can calculate the height they need to drop snails to crack their shells and rarely drop them from any higher than necessary (Zach, 1979). Moreover, many animals, particularly birds, forage in groups of an ideal size to maximize the trade-offs between energy intake and demands on resources owing to predator vigilance (cf. Roberts, 1996). Because more eyes and ears mean less energy spent individually on predator detection, foraging in groups affords more time looking for and collecting food (Krebs & Davies, 1997). Indeed, energy-sensitive behavior appears to be nearly universal, and animals seem to have the ability to rapidly calculate the energy trade-offs of any given set of behavioral choices (Krebs & Davies, 1997). In human research, Stefanucci, Proffitt, Banton, and Epstein (2005) have demonstrated that wearing a heavy backpack increases estimates of the perceived steepness of a hill. Such findings suggest that perceptual judgments are sensitive to situational energy demands.

Prediction

In making decisions, the brain reflexively monitors resource use and energy maintenance. Judgments of current resource accessibility bias organisms to make economical decisions in accord with the economy of action. To do so, however, each organism must make accurate predictions about contextual demands and access to future potential resources. Thus, prediction is a core property of the brain, and one can argue that much of its processing power is devoted to predicting how the world will be in the future and how to behave in the present to minimize energy expenditure while maximizing reproductive fitness. Indeed, some have argued that one of the brain's chief functions is to act as a Bayesian predictor (cf. Coan, 2008; Friston, 2010; Knill & Pouget, 2004). More concretely, the brain fills in gaps in perception and calculates prior probabilities (Bayesian priors) to make decisions about how to invest resources, given contextual demands. Friston (2010) has argued that the brain tests an internal model against perceptual inputs to continuously update its predictions. Thus, the brain is always actively perceiving the world and imputing information onto it. In this way, it is constantly making bets as to which action will most benefit the overall well-being of the individual.

Perception–Action Links

Prediction, however, is not enough. The brain must also translate those predictive powers into action plans. At least two principles tap into the idea that thinking is for doing. The first is that the brain seems to be organized on a principle of perception–action linkage. In other words, it is efficiently designed to take perceptual inputs and transform them into behavior to facilitate evolutionary imperatives. The position that cognition is for action (cf. Wilson, 2002) and the principle of perception–action linkage are common among neuroscientists. This idea is based on evidence that the brain processes sensory input and feeds it directly (and very rapidly) to areas of the brain that are responsible for taking action. This feature of brain organization appears to be omnipresent and suggests that the brain is designed with very direct links between perceptual and motor planning systems (cf. Bridgeman & Tseng, 2011).

Rerepresentation

The next principle that reflects the idea that thinking is for doing appears most clearly in humans. This principle emerges out of one of the critical organizational features of how the brain makes decisions and makes sense of an organism's current fit in the environment. This principle, which we call the *rerepresentation principle,* emerges out of the numerous ways in which the brain integrates disparate information that is being processed in parallel and then translates that information into progressively integrated representations of the body and the environmental context that the body is in. The idea that brain structures appear to be composed of circuits that progressively integrate distributed streams of information into rerepresentations of the self, its current state, and its possible behavioral choices is most evident in the somatic marker hypothesis (e.g., Bechara & Damasio, 2004) and Craig's (2009) theory of insula function as a rerepresentation of the material me and its emotional moment. We should note, however, that many regions of the brain integrate tremendous amounts of information even before these higher cortical integrative circuits begin the rerepresentational processes. There is a trend in neuroscience toward thinking about more anterior (e.g., frontal) areas having more integrative function, and this principle may underlie some important features of how psychological phenomena emerge from the brain. The bottom line is that the brain is continuously working with internally modified perceptual models of the self and the world to facilitate rapid prediction and action in the service of economical action

Sociality

The final principle, the principle of sociality, is particularly important for humans. At some point in humans' evolutionary heritage, they adapted to a social niche. This principle is outlined in SBT (Beckes & Coan, 2011; Coan, 2008), which argues that social proximity is critical to the maintenance and successful execution of evolutionary imperatives in human beings. Many of the systems involved in self-related cognition are directly involved in understanding and predicting the behaviors and outcomes of other individuals. Indeed, much of the way in which the brain understands the self is closely related to the way in which it understands others. Huge portions of the human brain are engaged in social cognition, and older aspects of brain function may have been exapted for social purposes (cf. Di Pelligrino et al., 1992; Eisenberger et al., 2003; MacDonald & Leary, 2005; Morris et al., 2008; Taylor, 2006).

Social Baseline Theory

We developed SBT to explain how and why humans use social relationships for the purposes of emotion regulation and energy management (e.g., Beckes & Coan, 2011; Coan, 2008). The theory is most strongly grounded in the principles of economy of action, prediction, and sociality and in many ways is the basis for our argument that sociality is a principle of the human brain. The theory argues that humans make constant predictions about the energy needs and expenditures they are going to make in a way that is sensitive to the availability and proximity of other people along with their determination of others' ability to serve as a resource. The presence of others translates into a net energy savings through two processes: risk distribution and load sharing. The first process, risk distribution, is seen in most social animals; the second, load sharing, is present only in the most social of animals. Load sharing depends on familiarity and interdependence, making it a critical process in close relationships.

Humans are unique from many other species in that "the dominant ecology to which humans are adapted is other humans" (Beckes & Coan, 2011, p. 4; cf. Brewer & Caporael, 1990). SBT emerged out of neuroscience investigations of emotion regulation as a way to understand a somewhat counterintuitive yet reliable finding. Coan, Schaefer, and Davidson (2006) found that women were less responsive to a shock threat when holding their spouse's hand than when alone and that this effect was enhanced if they had higher quality marriages. In and of itself, this finding is not particularly shocking because attachment theory, for one, would have predicted

this outcome. What is less obvious is the specific neural mechanism involved in this process. Whereas the threat matrix was less active during handholding, no neural region seemed to be more active, suggesting that no single region was acting to inhibit the threat response. It was originally believed that the regions of the brain associated with self-regulation, such as the vmPFC and the dorsolateral PFC, should be involved in downregulating the threat response during handholding and thus be more active (or at least that reward-focused regions such as the dopamine strata would be more active during handholding). Neither of these predictions was supported, and many of these regions were, in fact, less active during handholding.

This led us to the conclusion that the social regulation of emotion functions very differently than the self-regulation of emotion (cf. Eisenberger et al., 2007). SBT argues, however, that such results are only surprising if one assumes that the experimental baseline condition for human beings is when they are alone. Another way of thinking about such results is that adding a person removes perceived contextual demands from the situation, and being alone represents an added load that the individual must bear. Thus, SBT argues that being with others decreases the costs associated with engaging in the environment and therefore decreases vigilance and other processes associated with threat responding.

Two mechanisms are theorized to create this decreased cost. The first, risk distribution, involves spreading the risk of predation and negative outcomes over a larger group of individuals (cf. Krebs & Davies, 1997). The old saying that "I don't have to outrun the bear, I just have to outrun you" is an accurate description of this mechanism. One sees this mechanism at work at stoplights on college campuses across the United States. When one person begins to cross the street, a whole group of students begins to cross the street, largely depending on the perceptual judgments of the first crosser rather than actually checking for coming cars. Most social animals engage in risk distribution behavior, as the flock-based foraging behavior of birds suggests (e.g., Roberts, 1996). A large body of research has indicated that the larger a flock is, the less individual birds look up to check for predators, so flock size decreases the vigilance displayed by any given individual in the flock.

By contrast, load sharing is about interdependent and cooperative behavior, and it is more likely to support the most interesting aspects of socially sensitive energy usage in humans (cf. Beckes & Coan, 2012). As people become more interdependent and familiar with someone and their value as a social resource becomes more predictable, they begin to "outsource" (e.g., Fitzsimons & Finkel, 2011) various cognitive and physical tasks to that person. This seems to be particularly true of self-regulation tasks (cf. Beckes & Coan, 2011). When others engage in tasks for one's benefit and one reciprocates, one can expend energy in a more efficient manner, producing a net energy savings for both individuals. Indeed, the energy benefits of cooperative behavior may be a reason that attachment-like processes are seen in various types of adult relationships. This energy-saving and emotion regulatory benefit may have been the evolutionary pressure that exapted infant and pair-bonding attachment mechanisms into other adult human relationships (cf. Hazan & Zeifman, 1999).

It is possible that neurochemistry still supports these effects in the brain. The best candidates might be oxytocin and opioids. Even so, the abundant presence of these neurochemicals, particularly opioids, may indicate relative homeostasis, supporting the conclusion that social contact is a baseline condition and that isolation is, on average, odd and difficult for people. Indeed, standing with a close friend decreases the influence of wearing a heavy backpack on perceptions of hill steepness (Schnall, Harber, Stefanucci, & Proffitt, 2008), an effect that is enhanced by the length of the relationship.

As can be gleaned from this discussion of SBT, the principles of economy of action, prediction, and perception–action linkage are implied in the theory broadly. Moreover, the principle of sociality emerges from the way in which social resources insert themselves on these processes. Indeed, attachment styles can be reconceptualized as Bayesian priors in which the likelihood that any given person will act as a social resource is represented as a prior probability in memory, depending on past experiences with that particular individual. Speculatively, one might also imagine that self–other overlap during threat may index or be a major mechanism representing these prior probabilities. Recent work in our lab has suggested that the degree of self–other overlap evinced during threat and the degree of neural threat regulation during handholding are associated with early social resources, particularly mother responsiveness in the teen years and neighborhood quality between the ages of 12 and 13 (Coan et al., 2013).

SBT is an important attempt to integrate social and neuroscience-based research and theory on social relationships using general principles that are emerging out of neuroscience. We hope that such endeavors will lead to true integration of the fields of neuroscience, social and personality psychology, and relationship science, and we expect that more theory development will occur with time.

FUTURE DIRECTION AND RECOMMENDATIONS

Much remains to be explored in relationship neuroscience, and we look forward to the growth of this infant field of inquiry. To conclude this chapter, we leave the reader with some broad recommendations for future research.

Utilize Relational Contexts

As the principle of sociality suggests, many basic emotional and cognitive processes are strongly influenced by the relational context in which they occur. In line with this observation, we recommend introducing relationship contexts into the social, cognitive, and affective neurosciences. New methods to do so are being invented every year (e.g., Conner et al., 2012; Hasson, Ghazanfar, Galantucci, Garrod, & Keysers, 2012), and such approaches are often punctuated with calls to increase the use of social context within the fMRI environment. Indeed, simply adding a social presence within brain scanning environments might illuminate entirely new ways of thinking about the function of the human brain.

Expand Measurement and Analytical Approaches

Very few neuroscientific studies of human relationships have used methods other than fMRI.

Electroencephalography (EEG) is a good alternative candidate for expanding research in this area. EEG methods—including both the time and the frequency domains—allow for testing of important questions that may be untestable in the fMRI environment. Specifically, EEG can provide information about the timing of various brain processes at the millisecond level, whereas fMRI only scans the brain approximately once every 2 seconds. Moreover, EEG may be more flexibly applied to more ecologically (and hence generalizable) experimental situations, such as interacting face-to-face with a relationship partner.

A second recommendation is for both social psychologists and neuroscientists to become more familiar with the measurement approaches and analytical methods of each field. Whereas both types of scholars are expertly educated in analyzing and understanding their own research cultures and traditions, a trading of knowledge would be very helpful. Social psychologists would be wise to understand the assumptions involved in neuroimaging, such as the ways in which multiple-comparison correction is conducted. Alternatively, social and personality psychology has a long history of theory, measurement, and analytical development, and neuroscientists could benefit from adapting and understanding the theoretical and data analytic approaches used in that field as well. For example, the actor–partner interdependence model, which involves multilevel modeling, has become a critical analytic technique in relationship science. Adapting such methods to neuroimaging research may prove fruitful in future endeavors.

Another possible avenue for future research might be to use fMRI techniques as an endophenotype in genetic and epigenetic studies of genetic involvement in relationship processes (cf. Jack et al., 2012). Functional brain activity can be used to index the phenotypic expression of genetic processes, serving as a bridge between genetic-level analyses and behavioral analyses. Such approaches could be very fruitful in terms of developing a better understanding of genetic influences in relationships and Gene × Environment interaction processes.

Larger Samples and Longitudinal Designs

One of the greatest weaknesses of the current human neuroscience literature is that most of the data have been collected on a small number of participants and at only one time point. These issues may bias the understanding of neuroscience findings in specific ways. For example, researchers may not be able to detect regions of the brain that are critically involved in certain tasks because their effects are relatively small. Without sufficient sample sizes, researchers may be detecting only the most active of neural sites in any given task and missing critical information in the process. Furthermore, much has yet to be learned about brain development and change over time and how social and relationship factors change the way the brain functions. For example, does the pattern of activity associated with holding a lover's hand change from the early relationship stage to later relationship stages? Moreover, very little is known about how early attachment affects the social regulation of emotion in adulthood or the functioning of sex or caregiving-related brain structures in adulthood. Thus, more longitudinal designs with large samples should be pursued.

Collaborate and Cross-Train

Much of this work is only possible in collaborative work environments. It is difficult to find individual investigators who have the background necessary to be an expert in both neuroscience and relationship science. Thus, we urge those who are interested in integrated relationship science and neuroscience to find willing and interested collaborators. Such arrangements are often highly valued by funding agencies, and such efforts should be pursued. Equally important, however, is promoting cross-training in both relationship science and neuroscience among younger investigators. As Berscheid (2006a) noted, true integration of fields may require people who have all the ideas in the same head. Such investigators can theoretically and empirically integrate fields in ways that collaborative relationships may not be able to support. This goal is more difficult because the current incentive structure in science promotes specialization, and the publish-or-perish reality makes extended learning risky in terms of career prospects. Developing expertise in two fields takes time, and it often precludes doing a lot of highly specialized studies that can be published more quickly. As such, cross-training is swimming upstream in terms of the way current academic and funding institutions are structured. Still, we recommend this type of training when possible. We strongly urge those who have influence in funding agencies and hiring committees to consider the enormous investment cross-training often represents and to consider the possible long-term payoffs.

Clinical Application

Finally, we hope researchers will consider the clinical implications and potential applications of relationship neuroscience. For example, the SBT model suggests that social affect regulation is likely to be much less energy intensive than self-regulation. Despite this, most current therapeutic models stress techniques designed to build self-regulation. Thus, our research and the work of others (e.g., Johnson, 2005) might lead to important approaches that use relationship contexts to more effectively deal with relationship issues that center on emotional problems and emotion regulation patterns.

CONCLUSION

The field of relationship neuroscience is still in its early infancy. Along with its recent emergence comes a tremendous amount of possibility. Many relationship theories and ideas have barely been touched on in the neuroscience traditions, and social and personality psychologists are ideally situated to stimulate new ways of thinking and new areas of research. For example, little has been done to date on understanding the relation between commitment or interdependence and brain functioning, despite a long line of behavioral research with a long and distinguished tradition in social psychology (cf. Rusbult, 1983; Thibaut & Kelley, 1959). We hope investigators will take the opportunity to collaborate and cross-train so that the neuroscience of relationships can be fully integrated with the broader relationships research field. With this in mind, we believe that relationship research will be a critical component of neuroscience in the future, and we look forward to its "greening" (cf. Berscheid, 1999) as a critical component of relationship research in social and personality psychology.

References

Acevedo, B. P., Aron, A., Fisher, H. E., & Brown, L. L. (2012). Neural correlates of long-term intense romantic love. *Social Cognitive and Affective Neuroscience, 7,* 145–159. doi:10.1093/scan/nsq092

Adolphs, R. (1999). The human amygdala and emotion. *Neuroscientist, 5,* 125–137. doi:10.1177/107385849900500216

Adolphs, R. (2002). Neural systems for recognizing emotion. *Current Opinion in Neurobiology, 12,* 169–177. doi:10.1016/S0959-4388(02)00301-X

Adolphs, R. (2010). What does the amygdala contribute to social cognition? *Annals of the New York Academy of Sciences, 1191,* 42–61. doi:10.1111/j.1749-6632.2010.05445.x

Allison, T., Puce, A., & McCarthy, G. (2000). Social perception from visual cues: Role of the STS region. *Trends in Cognitive Sciences, 4,* 267–278. doi:10.1016/S1364-6613(00)01501-1

Andersen, S. M., & Chen, S. (2002). The relational self: An interpersonal social-cognitive theory. *Psychological Review, 109,* 619–645. doi:10.1037/0033-295X.109.4.619

Argiolas, A. (1999). Neuropeptides and sexual behaviour. *Neuroscience and Biobehavioral Reviews, 23,* 1127–1142. doi:10.1016/S0149-7634(99)00068-8

Argiolas, A., & Gessa, G. L. (1991). Central functions of oxytocin. *Neuroscience and Biobehavioral Reviews, 15,* 217–231. doi:10.1016/S0149-7634(05)80002-8

Argiolas, A., & Melis, M. R. (2005). Central control of penile erection: Role of the paraventricular nucleus of the hypothalamus. *Progress in Neurobiology, 76,* 1–21. doi:10.1016/j.pneurobio.2005.06.002

Aron, A., & Aron, E. N. (1996). Love and expansion of the self: The state of the model. *Personal Relationships, 3,* 45–58. doi:10.1111/j.1475-6811.1996.tb00103.x

Aron, A., Aron, E. N., & Smollan, D. (1992). Inclusion of Other in the Self scale and the structure of interpersonal closeness. *Journal of Personality and Social Psychology, 63,* 596–612. doi:10.1037/0022-3514.63.4.596

Aron, A., Aron, E. N., Tudor, M., & Nelson, G. (1991). Close relationships as including other in the self. *Journal of Personality and Social Psychology, 60,* 241–253. doi:10.1037/0022-3514.60.2.241

Aron, A., Fisher, H., Mashek, D. J., Strong, G., Li, H., & Brown, L. L. (2005). Reward, motivation, and emotion systems associated with early-stage intense romantic love. *Journal of Neurophysiology, 94,* 327–337. doi:10.1152/jn.00838.2004

Aron, A., & Fraley, B. (1999). Relationship closeness as including the other in the self: Cognitive underpinnings and measures. *Social Cognition, 17,* 140–160. doi:10.1521/soco.1999.17.2.140

Balleine, B. W., Delgado, M. R., & Hikosaka, O. (2007). The role of the dorsal striatum in reward and decision making. *Journal of Neuroscience, 27,* 8161–8165. doi:10.1523/JNEUROSCI.1554-07.2007

Bartels, A., & Zeki, S. (2000). The neural basis of romantic love. *Neuroreport, 11,* 3829–3834. doi:10.1097/00001756-200011270-00046

Bartels, A., & Zeki, S. (2004). The neural correlates of maternal and romantic love. *NeuroImage, 21,* 1155–1166. doi:10.1016/j.neuroimage.2003.11.003

Beckes, L., & Coan, J. A. (2011). Social baseline theory: The role of social proximity in emotion and economy of action. *Social and Personality Psychology Compass, 5,* 976–988. doi:10.1111/j.1751-9004.2011.00400.x

Beckes, L., Coan, J. A., & Allen, J. (2012). Childhood maternal support and neighborhood quality moderate the social regulation of neural threat responding in adulthood. International Journal of Psychophysiology, 88, 224–231.

Beckes, L., Coan, J. A., & Hasselmo, K. (2013). Familiarity promotes the blending of self and other in the neural representation of threat. *Social Cognitive and Affective Neuroscience, 8,* 670–677. doi:10.1093/scan/nss046

Beckes, L., Simpson, J., & Erickson, A. (2010). Of snakes and succor. *Psychological Science, 21,* 721–728. doi:10.1177/0956797610368061

Berridge, K. C. (2007). The debate over dopamine's role in reward: The case for incentive salience. *Psychopharmacology, 191,* 391–431. doi:10.1007/s00213-006-0578-x

Berridge, K. C., & Robinson, T. E. (1998). What is the role of dopamine in reward: Hedonic impact, reward learning, or incentive salience? *Brain Research Reviews, 28,* 309–369. doi:10.1016/S0165-0173(98)00019-8

Berscheid, E. (1995). Help wanted: A grand theorist of interpersonal relationships, sociologist or anthropologist preferred. *Journal of Social and Personal Relationships, 12,* 529–533. doi:10.1177/0265407595124005

Berscheid, E. (1999). The greening of relationship science. *American Psychologist, 54,* 260–266. doi:10.1037/0003-066X.54.4.260

Berscheid, E. (2006a). The difficulty of getting from here to there and back again. In P. A. M. Van Lange (Ed.), *Bridging social psychology: Benefits of transdisciplinary approaches* (pp. 35–40). Mahwah, NJ: Erlbaum.

Berscheid, E. (2006b). Seasons of the heart. In M. Mikulincer & G. S. Goodman (Eds.), *Dynamics of romantic love: Attachment, caregiving, and sex* (pp. 404–422). New York, NY: Guilford Press.

Berscheid, E., Snyder, M., & Omoto, A. M. (1989). The Relationship Closeness Inventory: Assessing the closeness of interpersonal relationships. *Journal of Personality and Social Psychology, 57,* 792–807. doi:10.1037/0022-3514.57.5.792

Berscheid, E., Snyder, M., & Omoto, A. M. (2004). The Relationship Closeness Inventory revisited. In D. J. Mashek & A. Aron (Eds.), *Handbook of closeness and intimacy* (pp. 81–102). Hillsdale, NJ: Erlbaum.

Bechara, A., & Damasio, A. R. (2005). The somatic marker hypothesis: A neural theory of economic decision. *Games and Economic Behavior, 52,* 336–372.

Borman-Spurrell, E., Allen, J. P., Hauser, S. T., Carter, A., & Cole-Detke, H. C. (1995). *Assessing adult attachment: A comparison of interview-based and self-report methods.* Unpublished manuscript, Yale University, New Haven, CT.

Bowlby, J. (1982). *Attachment* (2nd ed.). New York, NY: Basic Books. (Original work published 1969)

Brasted, P. J., Bussey, T. J., Murray, E. A., & Wise, S. P. (2003). A role of the hippocampal system in learning arbitrary associations beyond the spatial domain: Evidence from nonhuman primates. *Brain: A Journal of Neurology, 126,* 1202–1223. doi:10.1093/brain/awg103

Brewer, M. B., & Caporael, L. R. (1990). Selfish genes vs. selfish people: Sociobiology as origin myth. *Motivation and Emotion, 14,* 237–243. doi:10.1007/BF00996182

Brewer, M. B., & Gardner, W. (1996). Who is this "we"? Levels of collective identity and self representations. *Journal of Personality and Social Psychology, 71,* 83–93. doi:10.1037/0022-3514.71.1.83

Bridgeman, B., & Tseng, P. (2011). Embodied cognition and the perception-action link. *Physics of Life Reviews, 8,* 73–85. doi:10.1016/j.plrev.2011.01.002

Bunzl, M., Hanson, S. J., & Poldrack, R. A. (2010). An exchange about localism. In S. J. Hanson & M. Bunzl (Eds.), *Foundational issues in human brain mapping* (pp. 49–54). Cambridge, MA: MIT Press.

Burri, A., Heinrichs, M., Schedlowski, M., & Kruger, T. (2008). The acute effects of intranasal oxytocin administration on endocrine and sexual function in males. *Psychoneuroendocrinology, 33,* 591–600. doi:10.1016/j.psyneuen.2008.01.014

Cahill, L., Prins, B., Weber, M., & McGaugh, J. L. (1994). Beta-adrenergic activation and memory for emotional events. *Nature, 371,* 702–704. doi:10.1038%2F371702a0

Capitanio, J. P., Mendoza, S. P., & Lerche, N. W. (1998). Individual differences in peripheral blood immunological and hormonal measures in adult male rhesus macaques (*Macaca mulatta*): Evidence for temporal and situational consistency. *American Journal of*

Primatology, 44, 29–41. doi:10.1002/(SICI)1098-2345(1998)44:1<29::AID-AJP3>3.0.CO;2-Z

Capuco, A. V., & Akers, R. M. (2009). The origin and evolution of lactation. *Journal of Biology, 8,* 37. doi:10.1186/jbiol139

Carter, C., & Keverne, E. (2002). The neurobiology of social affiliation and pair bonding. In D. W. Pfaff, A. P. Arnold, S. E. Fahrbacj, A. M. Etgen, & R. T. Rubin (Eds.), *Hormones, brain, and behavior* (pp. 299–337). San Diego: Academic Press. doi:10.1016/B978-012532104-4/50006-8

Carter, C. S. (1992). Oxytocin and sexual behavior. *Neuroscience and Biobehavioral Reviews, 16,* 131–144. doi:10.1016/S0149-7634(05)80176-9

Carter, C. S. (1998). Neuroendocrine perspectives on social attachment and love. *Psychoneuroendocrinology, 23,* 779–818. doi:10.1016/S0306-4530(98)00055-9

Carter, C. S. (2003). Developmental consequences of oxytocin. *Physiology and Behavior, 79,* 383–397. doi:10.1016/S0031-9384(03)00151-3

Carter, C. S., Grippo, A. J., Pournajafi-Nazarloo, H., Ruscio, M. G., & Porges, S. W. (2008). Oxytocin, vasopressin and sociality. *Progress in Brain Research, 170,* 331–336. doi:10.1016/S0079-6123(08)00427-5

Cassidy, J., & Shaver, P. (Eds.). (2008). *Handbook of attachment: Theory, research and clinical implications* (2nd ed.). New York, NY: Guilford Press.

Cho, M. M., DeVries, A. C., Williams, J. R., & Carter, C. S. (1999). The effects of oxytocin and vasopressin on partner preference in male and female prairie voles. *Behavioral Neuroscience, 113,* 1071–1079. doi:10.1037/0735-7044.113.5.1071

Coan, J. (2008). Toward a neuroscience of attachment. In J. Cassidy & P. Shaver (Eds.), *Handbook of attachment: Theory, research and clinical implications* (2nd ed., pp. 241–265). New York, NY: Guilford Press.

Coan, J. (2010a). Adult attachment and the brain. *Journal of Social and Personal Relationships, 27,* 210–217. doi:10.1177/0265407509360900

Coan, J. A. (2010b). Emergent ghosts of the emotion machine. *Emotion Review, 2,* 274–285. doi:10.1177/1754073910361978

Coan, J. A., & Allen, J. J. B. (2004). Frontal EEG asymmetry as a moderator and mediator of emotion. *Biological Psychology, 67,* 7–50. doi:10.1016/j.biopsycho.2004.03.002

Coan, J. A., Allen, J. J. B., & McKnight, P. E. (2006). A capability model of individual differences in frontal EEG asymmetry. *Biological Psychology, 72,* 198–207. doi:10.1016/j.biopsycho.2005.10.003

Coan, J. A., Beckes, L., & Allen, J. P. (2013). Childhood maternal support and neighborhood quality moderate the social regulation of neural threat responding in adulthood. *International Journal of Psychophysiology, 88,* 224–231.

Coan, J. A., Schaefer, H. S., & Davidson, R. J. (2006). Lending a hand: Social regulation of the neural response to threat. *Psychological Science, 17,* 1032–1039. doi:10.1111/j.1467-9280.2006.01832.x

Conner, O. L., Siegle, G. J., McFarland, A. M., Silk, J. S., Ladouceur, C. D., Dahl, R. E., . . . Ryan, N. D. (2012). Mom—It helps when you're right here! Attenuation of neural stress markers in anxious youths whose caregivers are present during fMRI. *PLoS ONE, 7*(12), e50680. doi:10.1371/journal.pone.0050680

Costa, V. D., Lang, P. J., Sabatinelli, D., Versace, F., & Bradley, M. M. (2010). Emotional imagery: Assessing pleasure and arousal in the brain's reward circuitry. *Human Brain Mapping, 31,* 1446–1457.

Craig, A. D. (2002). How do you feel? Interoception: The sense of the physiological condition of the body. *Nature Reviews Neuroscience, 3,* 655–666. doi:10.1038/nrn894

Craig, A. D. B. (2009). How do you feel—Now? The anterior insula and human awareness. *Nature Reviews Neuroscience, 10,* 59–70. doi:10.1038/nrn2555

Creel, S., Creel, N. M., & Monfort, S. L. (1996). Social stress and dominance. *Nature, 379,* 212. doi:10.1038/379212a0

Cushing, B. S., & Carter, C. S. (2000). Peripheral pulses of oxytocin increase partner preferences in female, but not male, prairie voles. *Hormones and Behavior, 37,* 49–56. doi:10.1006/hbeh.1999.1558

Cushman, P. (1972). Sexual behavior in heroin addiction and methadone maintenance: Correlation with plasma luteinizing hormone. *New York State Journal of Medicine, 72,* 1261–1265.

Dalton, K. M., Kalin, N., Grist, T. M., & Davidson, R. J. (2005). Neural-cardiac coupling in threat-evoked anxiety. *Journal of Cognitive Neuroscience, 17,* 969–980. doi:10.1162/0898929054021094

Damasio, A. (1994). *Descartes' error: Emotion, reason, and the human brain.* New York, NY: Putnam.

Damasio, A. (1999). *The feeling of what happens: Body and emotion in the making of consciousness.* Orlando, FL: Harcourt.

D'Amato, F. R., & Pavone, F. (1993). Endogenous opioids: A proximate mechanism for kin selection? *Behavioral and Neural Biology, 60,* 79–83. doi:10.1016/0163-1047(93)90768-D

Dantzer, R., & Bluthé, R. M. (1992). Vasopressin involvement in antipyresis, social communication, and social recognition: A synthesis. *Critical Reviews in Neurobiology, 6,* 243–255.

Davis, M. (1992). The role of amygdala in fear and anxiety. *Annual Review of Neuroscience, 15*, 353–375. doi:10.1146/annurev.ne.15.030192.002033

Davis, M., & Whalen, P. J. (2001). The amygdala: Vigilance and emotion. *Molecular Psychiatry, 6*, 13–34. doi:10.1038/sj.mp.4000812

DeCasper, A. J., & Fifer, W. P. (1980). Of human bonding: Newborns prefer their mothers' voices. *Science, 208*, 1174–1176. doi:10.1126/science.7375928

Decety, J., Echols, S., & Correll, J. (2010). The blame game: The effect of responsibility and social stigma on empathy for pain. *Journal of Cognitive Neuroscience, 22*, 985–997. doi:10.1162/jocn.2009.21266

Decety, J., Michalska, K. J., & Akitsuki, Y. (2008). Who caused the pain? An fMRI investigation of empathy and intentionality in children. *Neuropsychologia, 46*, 2607–2614. doi:10.1016/j.neuropsychologia.2008.05.026

Depue, R. A., & Collins, P. (1999). Neurobiology of the structure of personality: Dopamine facilitation of incentive value and extraversion. *Behavioral and Brain Sciences, 22*, 491–517. doi:10.1017/S0140525X99002046

de Vignemont, F., & Singer, T. (2006). The empathic brain: How, when and why? *Trends in Cognitive Sciences, 10*, 435–441. doi:10.1016/j.tics.2006.08.008

DeVries, A. C., Glasper, E. R., & Detillion, C. E. (2003). Social modulation of stress. *Physiology and Behavior, 79*, 399–407. doi:10.1016/S0031-9384(03)00152-5

DeWall, C., MacDonald, G., Webster, G., Masten, C., Baumeister, R., Powell, C., . . . Eisenberger, N. I. (2010). Acetaminophen reduces social pain: Behavioral and neural evidence. *Psychological Science, 21*, 931–937. doi:10.1177/0956797610374741

DeWall, C. N., Masten, C. L., Powell, C., Combs, D., Schurtz, D. R., & Eisenberger, N. I. (2012). Do neural responses to rejection depend on attachment style? An fMRI study. *Social Cognitive and Affective Neuroscience, 7*, 184–192. doi:10.1093/scan/nsq107

di Pellegrino, G., Fadiga, L., Fogassi, L., Gallese, V., & Rizzolatti, G. (1992). Understanding motor events: A neurophysiological study. *Experimental Brain Research, 91*, 176–180.

Dluzen, D. E., Muraoka, S., & Landgraf, R. (1998). Olfactory bulb norepinephrine depletion abolishes vasopressin and oxytocin preservation of social recognition responses in rats. *Neuroscience Letters, 254*, 161–164. doi:10.1016/S0304-3940(98)00691-0

Eisenberger, N. I., Lieberman, M. D., & Williams, K. D. (2003). Does rejection hurt? An fMRI study of social exclusion. *Science, 302*, 290. doi:10.1126/science.1089134

Eisenberger, N. I., Master, S. L., Inagaki, T. I., Taylor, S. E., Shirinyan, D., Lieberman, M. D., & Naliboff, B. (2011). Attachment figures activate a safety signal-related neural region and reduce pain experience. *Proceedings of the National Academy of Sciences, USA, 108*, 11721–11726. doi:10.1073/pnas.1108239108

Eisenberger, N. I., Taylor, S. E., Gable, S. L., Hilmert, C. J., & Lieberman, M. D. (2007). Neural pathways link social support to attenuated neuroendocrine stress responses. *NeuroImage, 35*, 1601–1612. doi:10.1016/j.neuroimage.2007.01.038

Engell, A. D., Haxby, J. V., & Todorov, A. (2007). Implicit trustworthiness decisions: Automatic coding of face properties in the human amygdala. *Journal of Cognitive Neuroscience, 19*, 1508–1519. doi:10.1162/jocn.2007.19.9.1508

Fisher, H. E., Aron, A., & Brown, L. L. (2006). Romantic love: A mammalian brain system for mate choice. *Philosophical Transactions of the Royal Society B: Biological Sciences, 361*, 2173–2186. doi:10.1098/rstb.2006.1938

Fisher, H. E., Brown, L. L., Aron, A., Strong, G., & Mashek, D. (2010). Reward, addiction, and emotion regulation systems associated with rejection in love. *Journal of Neurophysiology, 104*, 51–60. doi:10.1152/jn.00784.2009

Fitzsimons, G. M., & Finkel, E. J. (2011). Outsourcing self-regulation. *Psychological Science, 22*, 369–375. doi:10.1177/0956797610397955

Fleming, A. S., Korsmit, M., & Deller, M. (1994). Rat pups are potent reinforcers to the maternal animal: Effects of experience, parity, hormones and dopamine function. *Psychobiology, 22*, 44–53.

Fodor, J. A. (1983). *Modularity of mind: An essay on faculty psychology.* Cambridge, MA: MIT Press.

Friston, K. (2010). The free-energy principle: A unified brain theory? *Nature Reviews Neuroscience, 11*, 127–138. doi:10.1038/nrn2787

Frith, C. D., & Frith, U. (1999). Interacting minds—A biological basis. *Science, 286*, 1692. doi:10.1126/science.286.5445.1692

Gainer, H., & Wray, S. (1992). Oxytocin and vasopressin. From genes to peptides. *Annals of the New York Academy of Sciences, 652*, 14–28.

Gallese, V., & Goldman, A. (1998). Mirror neurons and the simulation theory of mind-reading. *Trends in Cognitive Sciences, 2*, 493–501.

Gonzalez, A., Atkinson, L., & Fleming, A. S. (2009). Attachment and comparative psychobiology of mothering. In M. DeHaan & M. R. Gunnar (Eds.), *Handbook of developmental social neuroscience* (pp. 225–245). New York, NY: Guilford Press.

Graber, B., Blake, C., Gartner, J., & Wilson, J. (1984). The effects of opiate receptor blockage on male sexual response. In R. T. Seagraves (Ed.), *Emerging dimensions of sexology* (pp. 253–260). New York, NY: Praeger.

Greenberg, A. (1984). Effects of opiates on male orgasm. *Medical Aspects of Human Sexuality, 18*, 207–210.

Grossman, E. D., & Blake, R. (2002). Brain areas active during visual perception of biological motion. *Neuron, 35*, 1167–1175. doi:10.1016/S0896-6273(02)00897-8

Hamann, S. B., Ely, T. D., Hoffman, J. M., & Kilts, C. D. (2002). Ecstasy and agony: Activation of the human amygdala in positive and negative emotion. *Psychological Science, 13*, 135–141. doi:10.1111/1467-9280.00425

Hasson, U., Ghazanfar, A. A., Galantucci, B., Garrod, S., & Keysers, C. (2012). Brain-to-brain coupling: A mechanism for creating and sharing a social world. *Trends in Cognitive Sciences, 16*, 114–121. doi:10.1016/j.tics.2011.12.007

Hatfield, E., Cacioppo, J. T., & Rapson, R. L. (1994). *Emotional contagion.* New York, NY: Cambridge University Press.

Hazan, C., & Shaver, P. (1987). Romantic love conceptualized as an attachment process. *Journal of Personality and Social Psychology, 5*, 511–524.

Hazan, C., & Zeifman, D. (1999). Pair bonds as attachments: Evaluating the evidence. In J. Cassidy & P. R. Shaver (Eds.), *Handbook of attachment theory and research* (pp. 336–354). New York, NY: Guilford Press.

Heinrichs, M., Baumgartner, T., Kirschbaum, C., & Ehlert, U. (2003). Social support and oxytocin interact to suppress cortisol and subjective responses to psychosocial stress. *Biological Psychiatry, 54*, 1389–1398. doi:10.1016/S0006-3223(03)00465-7

Herschkowitz, N. (2000). Neurological bases of behavioral development in infancy. *Brain and Development, 22*, 411–416. doi:10.1016/S0387-7604(00)00185-6

Hofer, M. (2006). Psychobiological roots of early attachment. *Current Directions in Psychological Science, 15*, 84–88. doi:10.1111/j.0963-7214.2006.00412.x

Holister, L. (1975). The mystique of social drugs and sex. In M. Sandler (Ed.), *Sexual behavior: Pharmacology and biochemistry* (pp. 85–92). New York, NY: Raven Press.

Holt-Lunstad, J., Smith, T. B., & Layton, J. B. (2010). Social relationships and mortality risk: A meta-analytic review. *PLoS Medicine, 7*, e1000316. doi:10.1371/journal.pmed.1000316

House, J. S., Landis, K. R., & Umberson, D. (1988). Social relationships and health. *Science, 241*, 540. doi:10.1126/science.3399889

Insel, T. R., & Fernald, R. D. (2004). How the brain processes social information: Searching for the social brain. *Annual Review of Neuroscience, 27*, 697–722. doi:10.1146/annurev.neuro.27.070203.144148

Jabbi, M., Swart, M., & Keysers, C. (2007). Empathy for positive and negative emotions in the gustatory cortex. *NeuroImage, 34*, 1744–1753. doi:10.1016/j.neuroimage.2006.10.032

Jack, A., Connelly, J. J., & Morris, J. P. (2012). DNA methylation of the oxytocin receptor gene predicts neural response to ambiguous social stimuli. *Frontiers in Human Neuroscience, 6*, 280. doi:10.3389/fnhum.2012.00280

Jacob, P. (2008). What do mirror neurons contribute to human social cognition? *Mind and Language, 23*, 190–223. doi:10.1111/j.1468-0017.2007.00337.x

James, W. (1890). *The principles of psychology.* Cambridge, MA: Harvard University Press. doi:10.1037/11059-000

Johnson, S. M. (2005). *Emotionally focused couple therapy with trauma survivors.* New York, NY: Guilford Press.

Jones, H. B., & Jones, H. C. (1977). *Sensual drugs.* New York, NY: Cambridge University Press.

Kalin, N. H., Shelton, S. E., & Lynn, D. E. (1995). Opiate systems in mother and infant primates coordinate intimate contact during reunion. *Psychoneuroendocrinology, 20*, 735–742. doi:10.1016/0306-4530(95)00023-2

Kanwisher, N. (2010). Functional specificity in the human brain: A window into the functional architecture of the mind. *Proceedings of the National Academy of Sciences, USA, 107*, 11163–11170. doi:10.1073/pnas.1005062107

Kaplan, H. S., & Gangestad, S. W. (2005). Life history theory and evolutionary psychology. In D. M. Buss (Ed.), *The handbook of evolutionary psychology* (pp. 68–95). Hoboken, NJ: Wiley.

Karmiloff-Smith, A. (2010). A developmental perspective on modularity. In B. Glatzeder, V. Goel, & A. von Muller (Eds.), *Towards a theory of thinking: Building blocks for a conceptual framework* (pp. 179–187). Heidelberg, Germany: Springer-Verlag. doi:10.1007/978-3-642-03129-8_12

Kealey, G. P. (1995). Opioids and analgesia. *Journal of Burn Care and Rehabilitation, 16*, 363–364. doi:10.1097/00004630-199505001-00005

Keer, S. E., & Stern, J. M. (1999). Dopamine receptor blockade in the nucleus accumbens inhibits maternal retrieval and licking, but enhances nursing behavior in lactating rats. *Physiology and Behavior, 67*, 659–669. doi:10.1016/S0031-9384(99)00116-X

Kemeny, M. E. (2003). The psychobiology of stress. *Current Directions in Psychological Science, 12*, 124–129. doi:10.1111/1467-8721.01246

Kemp, A. H., & Guastella, A. J. (2011). The role of oxytocin in human affect: A novel hypothesis. *Current Directions in Psychological Science, 20*, 222–231. doi:10.1177/0963721411417547

Kennedy, P. J., & Shapiro, M. L. (2004). Retrieving memories via internal context requires the hippocampus. *Journal of Neuroscience, 24,* 6979–6985. doi:10.1523/JNEUROSCI.1388-04.2004

Keverne, E. B., & Kendrick, K. M. (1991). Morphine and corticotrophin-releasing factor potentiate maternal acceptance in multiparous ewes after vagino-cervical stimulation. *Brain Research, 540,* 55–62. doi:10.1016/0006-8993(91)90492-E

Keverne, E. B., & Kendrick, K. M. (1994). Maternal behaviour in sheep and its neuroendocrine regulation. *Acta Paediatrica, 83*(Suppl. s397), 47–56. doi:10.1111/j.1651-2227.1994.tb13265.x

Keverne, E. B., Martensz, N. D., & Tuite, B. (1989). Beta-endorphin concentrations in cerebrospinal fluid of monkeys influenced by grooming relationships. *Psychoneuroendocrinology, 14,* 155–161. doi:10.1016/0306-4530(89)90065-6

Keysers, C., & Gazzola, V. (2009). Expanding the mirror: Vicarious activity for actions, emotions, and sensations. *Current Opinion in Neurobiology, 19,* 666–671. doi:10.1016/j.conb.2009.10.006

Kirschbaum, C., Klauer, T., Filipp, S. H., & Hellhammer, D. H. (1995). Sex specific effects of social support on cortisol and subjective responses to acute psychological stress. *Psychosomatic Medicine, 57,* 23–31.

Knill, D. C., & Pouget, A. (2004). The Bayesian brain: The role of uncertainty in neural coding and computation. *Trends in Neurosciences, 27,* 712–719. doi:10.1016/j.tins.2004.10.007

Koscik, T. R., & Tranel, D. (2011). The human amygdala is necessary for developing and expressing normal interpersonal trust. *Neuropsychologia, 49,* 602–611. doi:10.1016/j.neuropsychologia.2010.09.023

Kosfeld, M., Heinrichs, M., Zak, P. J., Fischbacher, U., & Fehr, E. (2005). Oxytocin increases trust in humans. *Nature, 435,* 673–676. doi:10.1038/nature03701

Krebs, J. R., & Davies, N. B. (1997). *Behavioral ecology.* Malden, MA: Wiley-Blackwell.

Kreek, M. J. (1996). Opiates, opioids and addiction. *Molecular Psychiatry, 1,* 232–254.

Lakoff, G., & Johnson, M. (1999). *Philosophy in the flesh.* New York, NY: Basic Books.

Lal, S., Laryea, E., Thavundayil, J., Nair, N., Negrete, J., & Ackman, D. (1987). Apomorphine-induced penile tumescence in impotent patients—Preliminary findings. *Progress in Neuro-Psychopharmacology and Biological Psychiatry, 11,* 235–242. doi:10.1016/0278-5846(87)90066-2

Lamm, C., Batson, C. D., & Decety, J. (2007). The neural substrate of human empathy: Effects of perspective-taking and cognitive appraisal. *Journal of Cognitive Neuroscience, 19,* 42–58. doi:10.1162/jocn.2007.19.1.42

Lamm, C., Meltzoff, A. N., & Decety, J. (2010). How do we empathize with someone who is not like us? A functional magnetic resonance imaging study. *Journal of Cognitive Neuroscience, 22,* 362–376. doi:10.1162/jocn.2009.21186

LeDoux, J. E. (2000). Emotion circuits in the brain. *Annual Review of Neuroscience, 23,* 155–184. doi:10.1146/annurev.neuro.23.1.155

Le Moal, M., & Simon, H. (1991). Mesocorticolimbic dopaminergic network: Functional and regulatory roles. *Physiological Reviews, 71,* 155–234.

Levine, A. S., Morley, J. E., Gosnell, B. A., Billington, C. J., & Bartness, T. J. (1985). Opioids and consummatory behavior. *Brain Research Bulletin, 14,* 663–672. doi:10.1016/0361-9230(85)90116-9

Light, K. C., Smith, T. E., Johns, J. M., Brownley, K. A., Hofheimer, J. A., & Amico, J. A. (2000). Oxytocin responsivity in mothers of infants: A preliminary study of relationships with blood pressure during laboratory stress and normal ambulatory activity. *Health Psychology, 19,* 560–567. doi:10.1037/0278-6133.19.6.560

Lorenz, K. (1981). *The foundations of ethology.* New York, NY: Springer-Verlag. doi:10.1007/978-3-7091-3671-3

MacDonald, G., & Leary, M. (2005). Why does social exclusion hurt? The relationship between social and physical pain. *Psychological Bulletin, 131,* 202–223. doi:10.1037/0033-2909.131.2.202

Markus, H., & Kunda, Z. (1986). Stability and malleability of the self-concept. *Journal of Personality and Social Psychology, 51,* 858–866. doi:10.1037/0022-3514.51.4.858

Markus, H., & Wurf, E. (1987). The dynamic self-concept: A social psychological perspective. *Annual Review of Psychology, 38,* 299–337. doi:10.1146/annurev.ps.38.020187.001503

Mashek, D. J., Aron, A., & Boncimino, M. (2003). Confusions of self with close others. *Personality and Social Psychology Bulletin, 29,* 382–392. doi:10.1177/0146167202250220

Masten, C. L., Eisenberger, N. I., Borofsky, L. A., Pfeifer, J. H., McNealy, K., Mazziotta, J. C., & Dapretto, M. (2009). Neural correlates of social exclusion during adolescence: Understanding the distress of peer rejection. *Social Cognitive and Affective Neuroscience, 4,* 143. doi:10.1093/scan/nsp007

Masten, C. L., Telzer, E. H., Fuligni, A. J., Lieberman, M. D., & Eisenberger, N. I. (2012). Time spent with friends in adolescence relates to less neural sensitivity to later peer rejection. *Social Cognitive and Affective Neuroscience, 7,* 106–114. doi:10.1093/scan/nsq098

Mattson, B. J., & Morrell, J. I. (2005). Preference for cocaine- versus pup-associated cues differentially activates neurons expressing either Fos or cocaine- and amphetamine-regulated transcript in lactating, maternal rodents. *Neuroscience, 135*, 315–328. doi:10.1016/j.neuroscience.2005.06.045

McEwen, B. S. (2007). Physiology and neurobiology of stress and adaptation: Central role of the brain. *Physiological Reviews, 87*, 873–904. doi:10.1152/physrev.00041.2006

Melis, M. R., Argiolas, A., & Gessa, G. L. (1987). Apomorphine-induced penile erection and yawning: Site of action in brain. *Brain Research, 415*, 98–104. doi:10.1016/0006-8993(87)90272-1

Melis, M. R., Spano, M. S., Succu, S., & Argiolas, A. (1999). The oxytocin antagonist d(CH2)5Tyr(Me)2-Orn8-vasotocin reduces non-contact penile erections in male rats. *Neuroscience Letters, 265*, 171–174. doi:10.1016/S0304-3940(99)00236-0

Mendelson, J. H., Ellingboe, J., Keuhnle, J. C., & Mello, N. K. (1978). Effects of naltrexone on mood and neuroendocrine function in normal adult males. *Psychoneuroendocrinology, 3*, 231–236. doi:10.1016/0306-4530(78)90013-6

Mikolajczak, M., Gross, J. J., Lane, A., Corneille, O., de Timary, P., & Luminet, O. (2010). Oxytocin makes people trusting, not gullible. *Psychological Science, 21*, 1072–1074. doi:10.1177/0956797610377343

Mikulincer, M. (2006). Attachment, caregiving, and sex within romantic relationships: A behavioral systems perspective. In M. Mikulincer & G. S. Goodman (Eds.), *Dynamics of romantic love* (pp. 23–44). New York, NY: Guilford Press.

Mikulincer, M., & Shaver, P. (2003). The attachment behavioral system in adulthood: Activation, psychodynamics, and interpersonal processes. In M. P. Zanna (Ed.), *Advances in experimental social psychology* (Vol. 35, pp. 53–152). San Diego, CA: Academic Press. doi:10.1016/S0065-2601(03)01002-5

Milad, M. R., Quinn, B. T., Pitman, R. K., Orr, S. P., Fischl, B., & Rauch, S. L. (2005). Thickness of ventromedial prefrontal cortex in humans is associated with extinction memory. *Proceedings of the National Academy of Sciences, USA, 102*, 10706–10711. doi:10.1073/pnas.0502441102

Miller, E. K., & Cohen, J. (2001). An integrative theory of prefrontal cortex function. *Annual Review of Neuroscience, 24*, 167–202. doi:10.1146/annurev.neuro.24.1.167

Moriceau, S., & Sullivan, R. M. (2005). Neurobiology of infant attachment. *Developmental Psychobiology, 47*, 230–242. doi:10.1002/dev.20093

Morris, J. P., Pelphrey, K. A., & McCarthy, G. (2008). Perceived causality influences brain activity evoked by biological motion. *Social Neuroscience, 3*, 16–25. doi:10.1080/17470910701476686

Neckameyer, W. S. (1998). Dopamine modulates female sexual receptivity in *Drosophila melanogaster. Journal of Neurogenetics, 12*, 101–114. doi:10.3109/01677069809167259

Nelson, E. E., & Panksepp, J. (1998). Brain substrates of infant-mother attachment: Contributions of opioids, oxytocin, and norepinephrine. *Neuroscience and Biobehavioral Reviews, 22*, 437–452. doi:10.1016/S0149-7634(97)00052-3

Niedenthal, P. M. (2007). Embodying emotion. *Science, 316*, 1002. doi:10.1126/science.1136930

Numan, M., Fleming, A. S., & Levy, F. (2006). Maternal behavior. In J. D. Neill, T. M. Plant, D. W. Pfaff, J. R. G. Challis, D. M. de Kretser, J. S. Richards, & P. M. Wassarman (Eds.), *Knobil and Neill's physiology of reproduction* (3rd ed., pp. 1921–1993). New York, NY: Academic Press. doi:10.1016/B978-012515400-0/50040-3

Numan, M., Numan, M. J., Pliakou, N., Stolzenberg, D. S., Mullins, O. J., & Murphy, J. M. (2005). The effects of D1 or D2 dopamine receptor antagonism in the medial preoptic area, ventral pallidum, or nucleus accumbens on the maternal retrieval response and other aspects of maternal behavior in rats. *Behavioral Neuroscience, 119*, 1588–1604. doi:10.1037/0735-7044.119.6.1588

Ochsner, K. N., Bunge, S. A., Gross, J. J., & Gabrielli, J. D. E. (2002). Rethinking feelings: An fMRI study of the cognitive regulation of emotion. *Journal of Cognitive Neuroscience, 14*, 1215–1229. doi:10.1162/089892902760807212

Ochsner, K. N., & Gross, J. J. (2005). The cognitive control of emotion. *Trends in Cognitive Sciences, 9*, 242–249. doi:10.1016/j.tics.2005.03.010

Ortigue, S., Bianchi-Demicheli, F., de C. Hamilton, A., & Grafton, S. (2007). The neural basis of love as a subliminal prime: An event-related functional magnetic resonance imaging study. *Journal of Cognitive Neuroscience, 19*, 1218–1230. doi:10.1162/jocn.2007.19.7.1218

Panksepp, J. (1981). Brain opioids: A neurochemical substrate for narcotic and social dependence. In S. Cooper (Ed.), *Progress in theory in psychopharmacology* (pp. 149–175). London, England: Academic Press.

Panksepp, J. (1998). *Affective neuroscience.* New York, NY: Oxford University Press.

Panksepp, J., Herman, B. H., Vilberg, T., Bishop, P., & De Eskinazi, F. G. (1980). Endogenous opioids and social behavior, *Neuroscience and Biobehavioral Reviews, 4*, 473–487. doi:10.1016%2F0149-7634%2880%2990036-6

Panksepp, J., Lensing, P., Leboyer, M., & Bouvard, M. P. (1991). Naltrexone and other potential new pharmacological treatments of autism. *Brain Dysfunction, 4*, 281–300.

Panksepp, J., Moskal, J. R., Panksepp, J. B., & Kroes, R. A. (2002). Comparative approaches in evolutionary psychology: Molecular neuroscience meets the mind. *Neuroendocrinology Letters, 23*, 105–115.

Panksepp, J., Nelson, E., & Bekkedal, M. (1997). Brain systems for the mediation of social separation distress and social reward: Evolutionary antecedents and neuropeptide intermediaries. *Annals of the New York Academy of Sciences, 807,* 78–100. doi:10.1111/j.1749-6632.1997.tb51914.x

Pedersen, C. A., Ascher, J. A., Monroe, Y. L., & Prange, A. J. (1982). Oxytocin induces maternal behavior in virgin female rats. *Science, 216,* 648–650. doi:10.1126/science.7071605

Pelphrey, K. A., Morris, J. P., Michelich, C. R., Allison, T., & McCarthy, G. (2005). Functional anatomy of biological motion perception in posterior temporal cortex: An fMRI study of eye, mouth, and hand movements. *Cerebral Cortex, 15,* 1866–1876. doi:10.1093/cercor/bhi064

Pereira, M., Seip, K., Morrell, J., & Bridges, R. S. (2008). Maternal motivation and its neural substrate across the postpartum period. In R. S. Bridges (Ed.), *Neurobiology of the parental brain* (pp. 39–59). Burlington, MA: Academic Press. doi:10.1016/B978-0-12-374285-8.00003-2

Pfaus, J. G. (1996). Frank A. Beach award: Homologies of animal and human sexual behaviors. *Hormones and Behavior, 30,* 187–200. doi:10.1006/hbeh.1996.0024

Pfaus, J. G. (1999). Revisiting the concept of sexual motivation. *Annual Review of Sex Research, 10,* 120–156.

Pfaus, J. G. (2009). Pathways of sexual desire. *Journal of Sexual Medicine, 6,* 1506–1533. doi:10.1111/j.1743-6109.2009.01309.x

Pfaus, J., & Gorzalka, B. (1987). Opioid and sexual behavior. *Neuroscience and Biobehavioral Reviews, 11,* 1–34.

Pfaus, J. G., Kippen, T. E., & Coria-Avila, G. (2003). What can animal models tell us about human sexual response? *Annual Review of Sex Research, 14,* 1–63.

Pfaus, J. G., & Phillips, A. G. (1991). Role of dopamine in anticipatory and consummatory aspects of sexual behavior in the male rat. *Behavioral Neuroscience, 105,* 727–743.

Platek, S. M., Krill, A. L., & Wilson, B. (2009). Implicit trustworthiness ratings of self-resembling faces activate brain centers involved in reward. *Neuropsychologia, 47,* 289–293. doi:10.1016/j.neuropsychologia.2008.07.018

Price, D. D. (2000). Psychological and neural mechanisms of the affective dimension of pain. *Science, 188,* 1769–1772. doi:10.1126/science.288.5472.1769

Proffitt, D. (2006). Embodied perception and the economy of action. *Perspectives on Psychological Science, 1,* 110–122. doi:10.1111/j.1745-6916.2006.00008.x

Quirk, G. J., & Beer, J. S. (2006). Prefrontal involvement in the regulation of emotion: Convergence of rat and human studies. *Current Opinion in Neurobiology, 16,* 723–727. doi:10.1016/j.conb.2006.07.004

Ray, J., & Sapolski, R. (1992). Styles of male social behavior and their endocrine correlates among high-ranking baboons. *American Journal of Primatology, 28,* 231–250. doi:10.1002/ajp.1350280402

Roberts, G. (1996). Why individual vigilance declines as group size increases. *Animal Behaviour, 51,* 1077–1086. doi:10.1006/anbe.1996.0109

Robles, T. F., & Kiecolt-Glaser, J. K. (2003). The physiology of marriage: Pathways to health. *Physiology and Behavior, 79,* 409–416. doi:10.1016/S0031-9384(03)00160-4

Rusbult, C. E. (1983). A longitudinal test of the investment model: The development (and deterioration) of satisfaction and commitment in heterosexual involvements. *Journal of Personality and Social Psychology, 45,* 101–117. doi:10.1037/0022-3514.45.1.101

Saarela, M. V., Hlushchuk, Y., Williams, A. C. D. C., Schürmann, M., Kalso, E., & Hari, R. (2007). The compassionate brain: Humans detect intensity of pain from another's face. *Cerebral Cortex, 17,* 230–237. doi:10.1093/cercor/bhj141

Saxe, R., & Kanwisher, N. (2003). People thinking about thinking people: The role of the temporo-parietal junction in "theory of mind." *NeuroImage, 19,* 1835–1842. doi:10.1016/S1053-8119(03)00230-1

Schnall, S., Harber, K., Stefanucci, J., & Proffitt, D. (2008). Social support and the perception of geographical slant. *Journal of Experimental Social Psychology, 44,* 1246–1255. doi:10.1016/j.jesp.2008.04.011

Schultz, W., Dayan, P., & Montague, P. R. (1997). A neural substrate of prediction and reward. *Science, 275,* 1593–1599. doi:10.1126/science.275.5306.1593

Shah, N. J., Marshall, J. C., Zafiris, O., Schwab, A., Zilles, K., Markowitsch, H. J., & Fink, G. R. (2001). The neural correlates of person familiarity: A functional magnetic resonance imaging study with clinical implications. *Brain: A Journal of Neurology, 124,* 804–815. doi:10.1093/brain/124.4.804

Sierra-Mercado, D., Jr., Corcoran, K. A., Lebrón-Milad, K., & Quirk, G. J. (2006). Inactivation of the ventromedial prefrontal cortex reduces expression of conditioned fear and impairs subsequent recall of extinction. *European Journal of Neuroscience, 24,* 1751–1758. doi:10.1111/j.1460-9568.2006.05014.x

Simpson, J., Beckes, L., & Weisberg, Y. (2008). Evolutionary accounts of individual differences in adult attachment orientations. In J. V. Wood, A. Tesser, & J. G. Holmes (Eds.), *The self and social relationships* (pp. 183–206). New York, NY: Psychology Press.

Simpson, J. A., & Belsky, J. (2008). Attachment theory within a modern evolutionary framework. In J. Cassidy & P. Shaver (Eds.), *Handbook of attachment: Theory, research, and clinical applications* (2nd ed., pp. 131–157). New York, NY: Guilford Press.

Simpson, J. A., & Rholes, W. S. (2012). Adult attachment orientations, stress, and romantic relationships. In P. G. Devine & A. Plant (Eds.), *Advances in experimental social psychology* (Vol. 45, pp. 279–328). San Diego, CA: Academic Press. doi:10.1016/B978-0-12-394286-9.00006-8

Simpson, J. A., Rholes, W. S., & Nelligan, J. S. (1992). Support-seeking and support-giving within couples in an anxiety-provoking situation: The role of attachment styles. *Journal of Personality and Social Psychology, 62,* 434–446. doi:10.1037/0022-3514.62.3.434

Singer, T., & Lamm, C. (2009). The social neuroscience of empathy. *Annals of the New York Academy of Sciences, 1156,* 81–96. doi:10.1111/j.1749-6632.2009.04418.x

Singer, T., Seymour, B., O'Doherty, J., Kaube, H., Dolan, R. J., & Frith, C. D. (2004). Empathy for pain involves the affective but not sensory components of pain. *Science, 303,* 1157–1162. doi:10.1126/science.1093535

Singer, T., Seymour, B., O'Doherty, J. P., Stephan, K. E., Dolan, R. J., & Frith, C. D. (2006). Empathic neural responses are modulated by the perceived fairness of others. *Nature, 439,* 466–469. doi:10.1038/nature04271

Stefanucci, J. K., Proffitt, D. R., Banton, T., & Epstein, W. (2005). Distances appear different on hills. *Perception and Psychophysics, 67,* 1052–1060. doi:10.3758/BF03193631

Sullivan, R. M. (2003). Developing a sense of safety: The neurobiology of neonatal attachment. *Annals of the New York Academy of Sciences, 1008,* 122–131. doi:10.1196/annals.130.013

Szechtman, H., Hershkowitz, M., & Simantov, R. (1981). Sexual behavior decreases pain sensitivity and stimulated endogenous opioids in male rats. *European Journal of Pharmacology, 70,* 279–285. doi:10.1016/0014-2999(81)90161-8

Taylor, S. (2006). Tend and befriend. *Current Directions in Psychological Science, 15,* 273. doi:10.1111/j.1467-8721.2006.00451.x

Taylor, S. E., Klein, L. C., Lewis, B. P., Gruenewald, T. L., Gurung, R. A., & Updegraff, J. A. (2000). Biobehavioral responses to stress in females: Tend-and-befriend, not fight-or-flight. *Psychological Review, 107,* 411–429. doi:10.1037/0033-295X.107.3.411

Thibaut, J. W., & Kelley, H. H. (1959). *The social psychology of groups.* New York, NY: Wiley.

Uchino, B. N., Cacioppo, J. T., & Kiecolt-Glaser, J. K. (1996). The relationship between social support and physiological processes: A review with emphasis on underlying mechanisms and implications for health. *Psychological Bulletin, 119,* 488–531. doi:10.1037/0033-2909.119.3.488

Ungerleider, L. G., & Haxby, J. V. (1994). What and where in the human brain. *Current Opinion in Neurobiology, 4,* 157–165. doi:10.1016/0959-4388(94)90066-3

Uvnäs-Moberg, K. (1998). Oxytocin may mediate the benefits of positive social interaction and emotions. *Psychoneuroendocrinology, 23,* 819–835. doi:10.1016/S0306-4530(98)00056-0

Volling, B. L. (2001). Early attachment relationships as predictors of preschool children's emotion regulation with a distressed sibling. *Early Education and Development, 12,* 185–207. doi:10.1207/s15566935eed1202_2

Walker, C. R. (2010). Study: Conservatives have a larger "fear center." *Salon.* Retrieved from http://www.salon.com/2010/12/29/conservative_brains

Whalen, P. J., Davis, F. C., Oler, J. A., Kim, H., Kim, M. J., & Neta, M. (2009). Human amygdala responses to facial expressions of emotion. In P. J. Whalen & E. A. Phelps (Eds.), *The human amygdala* (pp. 265–288). New York, NY: Guilford Press.

Whipple, B., & Komisaruk, B. (1985). Elevation of pain threshold by vaginal stimulation in women. *Pain, 21,* 357–367. doi:10.1016/0304-3959(85)90164-2

Williams, J. R., Catania, K. C., & Carter, C. S. (1992). Development of partner preferences in female prairie voles (*Microtus ochrogaster*): The role of social and sexual experience. *Hormones and Behavior, 26,* 339–349. doi:10.1016/0018-506X(92)90004-F

Williams, J. R., Insel, T. R., Harbaugh, C. R., & Carter, C. S. (1994). Oxytocin administered centrally facilitates formation of a partner preference in female prairie voles (*Microtus ochrogaster*). *Journal of Neuroendocrinology, 6,* 247–250. doi:10.1111/j.1365-2826.1994.tb00579.x

Wilson, M. (2002). Six views of embodied cognition. *Psychonomic Bulletin and Review, 9,* 625–636. doi:10.3758/BF03196322

Winslow, J. T., Hastings, N., Carter, C. S., Harbaugh, C. R., & Insel, T. R. (1993). A role for central vasopressin in pair bonding in monogamous prairie voles. *Nature, 365,* 545–548. doi:10.1038/365545a0

Winslow, J. T., & Insel, T. R. (2004). Neuroendocrine basis of social recognition. *Current Opinion in Neurobiology, 14,* 248–253. doi:10.1016/j.conb.2004.03.009

Young, L. J., & Wang, Z. (2004). The neurobiology of pair bonding. *Nature Neuroscience, 7,* 1048–1054. doi:10.1038/nn1327

Zach, R. (1979). Shell dropping: Decision-making and optimal foraging in northwestern crows. *Behaviour, 68,* 106–117. doi:10.1163/156853979X00269

Zajonc, R. B. (1968). Attitudinal effects of mere exposure. *Journal of Personality and Social Psychology, 9,* 1–27. doi:10.1037/h0025848

Zajonc, R. B. (1980). Feeling and thinking: Preferences need no inferences. *American Psychologist, 35,* 151–175. doi:10.1037/0003-066X.35.2.151

Zajonc, R. B. (2001). Mere exposure: A gateway to the subliminal. *Current Directions in Psychological Science, 10,* 224–228. doi:10.1111/1467-8721.00154

Zak, P. J., Kurzban, R., & Matzner, W. T. (2005). Oxytocin is associated with human trustworthiness. *Hormones and Behavior, 48,* 522–527. doi:10.1016/j.yhbeh.2005.07.009

Zak, P. J., Stanton, A. A., & Ahmadi, S. (2007). Oxytocin increases generosity in humans. *PLoS ONE, 2,* e1128. doi:10.1371/journal.pone.0001128

Zinkova, M. (2009). Love on the brain. *Wired PR News.* Retrieved from http://www.wiredprnews.com/2009/02/13/love-on-the-brain_200902132353.html

CHAPTER 6

RELATIONSHIPS AND HEALTH

Timothy J. Loving and David A. Sbarra

Scientific study of the idea that high-quality relationships are associated with and might even cause good health dates back more than a century (Farr, 1858). Many disciplines have joined this pursuit, and a large body of evidence (across psychology, family studies, sociology, communications, and epidemiology) has now documented the strong positive association between good relationships and good physical and mental health. It is also known that negative interpersonal interactions (e.g., conflict) and relationship disruptions (e.g., bereavement, divorce) are associated with greater risk for poor health. In the 1960s, Holmes and Rahe (1967) created a measure of the most stressful life events a person can experience. The top five events were all social in nature: death of a spouse, divorce, marital separation, a jail term, and the death of a close family member. Rahe, Meyer, Smith, Kjaer, and Holmes (1964) argued that the psychological stress associated with these events had the potential to heighten risk for a variety of physical and mental health problems. Overwhelming evidence exists for this assertion.

House, Landis, and Umberson (1988) conducted the first quantitative synthesis of research on social integration and mortality and found a robust association between low levels of social integration and risk for early death. Their article spurred a generation of research, and major reviews have now been published on the putative mechanisms linking social support and positive health outcomes (Holt-Lunstad, Birmingham, & Jones, 2008; Uchino, 2004), loneliness and poor health (Cacioppo, Hawkley, et al., 2002), marriage and health (Kiecolt-Glaser & Newton, 2001), bereavement and the risk for early death (Stroebe, 2009), and divorce and the risk for early death (Sbarra, Law, & Portley, 2011; Shor, Roelfs, Bugyi, & Schwartz, 2012). In addition, considerable evidence has indicated that a high level of marital quality is associated with general psychological well-being (Proulx, Helms, & Buehler, 2007) and less risk for clinically significant mental health problems (Whisman, 2007). More generally, high levels of social support are also associated with better psychological well-being (Kessler, 1979).

In a recent meta-analysis, Holt-Lunstad, Smith, and Layton (2010) conducted a qualitative benchmarking analysis comparing the association between social integration and mortality with the magnitude of other well-known public health risks (e.g., light to moderate smoking, excessive alcohol intake, lack of physical exercise, being obese). The connection between social integration and mortality rivaled the effect observed for these other significant public health risk factors. This benchmarking analysis demonstrated that, without question, the quantity and quality of people's relationships are clearly associated with their survival. What remains to be determined is whether the association is causal (Cohen & Janicki-Deverts, 2009), and we address this topic toward the end of the chapter.

The authors contributed to this chapter equally. Preparation of this chapter was supported in part by Grant 1R21HD057432-01A2 awarded to Timothy J. Loving and grants from the National Science Foundation (BCS#0919525) and the National Institute of Aging (AG#036895) to David A. Sbarra.

http://dx.doi.org/10.1037/14344-006
APA Handbook of Personality and Social Psychology: Vol. 3. Interpersonal Relations, M. Mikulincer and P. R. Shaver (Editors-in-Chief)

CHAPTER OVERVIEW

The purpose of this chapter is to summarize the large body of research regarding the link between social relationships and health. In light of the explosion of work on this topic over the past 20 or so years, any such summary necessitates focusing on some lines of work to the exclusion of others. To this end, we have chosen to center our review, broadly, on health-relevant outcomes that have been observed within the context of normative romantic relationship development transitions (e.g., falling in love, breaking up).

Health-Relevant Outcomes

As we noted, scientific investigation of the link between relationships and health has expanded exponentially over the past couple of decades. A number of factors have worked in tandem to contribute to this growth, including, at least within North America, a relatively larger available pool of extramural funding opportunities for relationship researchers who have chosen to study relationship processes in health contexts (see Loving & Campbell, 2011). Simultaneously, the costs for conducting such work have declined significantly; methods for illuminating internal bodily processes have become less invasive, less costly, and more prevalent. For example, only a decade ago the assessment of salivary cortisol (discussed later) was generally reserved for use by mainstream health psychologists and psychoneuroendocrinologists; today, research using salivary assessment of cortisol is found across many disciplines, including most subdisciplines of psychology. The justification for the vast majority of such work is that cortisol (and the biological cascade of events leading to its production) has implications for objective health outcomes. This argument derives from the associations that have been observed between cortisol changes and observable physical health markers in studies using very different research paradigms and stressors (e.g., wound healing; Christian, Graham, Padgett, Glaser, & Kiecolt-Glaser, 2006). In reality, it is very rare for researchers to draw links between cortisol production and more objective markers of health (e.g., immunity; for a notable exception, see Jaremka

et al., 2013), yet the health relevance of acute and chronic cortisol increases is enough to justify these investigations and their funding.

Our review draws a similar distinction. Whenever possible, we focus on research that uses objective health markers (i.e., morbidity and mortality rates), because we contend that it is these lines of work that provide the most compelling case for the relationships–health link. However, we also extensively review research centered on biomarkers of health (i.e., health-relevant biological outcomes). Finally, we also review the compelling evidence that relationship processes and dynamics influence mental health outcomes, such as mental illness and particularly depression.

Normative Romantic Relationship Development

We organize our review around normative romantic relationship development processes. One of the more exciting trends in the study of romantic relationships and health is the recent shift in focus away from a conflict-centered approach (Slatcher, 2010; Wright & Loving, 2011) to one that considers the full life cycle of relationships more broadly, including nonconflict interactions (e.g., support, capitalization) as well as other relationship stages (e.g., initiation, dissolution). Thus, we attempt to give equal weight to the many phases and dynamics that characterize romantic relationships, from early life experiences known to affect later relationship functioning (i.e., epigenetic influences) to relationship initiation and development, maintenance, and, ultimately for many, dissolution.

It is important to note that this focus on normative relationship development generally lumps together findings from studies of marital and nonmarital romantic relationships. We believe such a focus is justified; it has become clear that romantic relationship functioning, and not marriage per se, affects individuals' mental and physical health (Ross, 1995). The focus on normative development also highlights the significance of transitions within romantic relationships. As we noted at the outset, such a focus on transitions is not novel; many of the most stressful life events in the classic Social Readjustment Rating Scale (Holmes & Rahe, 1967) involve transitions in interpersonal relationships. Although Holmes and Rahe (1967) validated their measure on married couples, the transitions that define nonmarital romances are also equally powerful predictors of health outcomes. For example, transitioning into a romance increases life satisfaction (Lee & Gramotnev, 2007), whereas transitioning out of a romance results in physical and mental health outcomes indicative of distress (Lepore & Greenberg, 2002; Mearns, 1991; Monroe, Rohde, Seeley, & Lewinsohn, 1999). Transitions require individuals to adapt to a changing environment (Wheaton, 1990), and the quality of adaptation is a key predictor of stress and physiological reactivity (Selye, 1978). It is therefore no coincidence that the developmental shifts that characterize relationship development have provided a rich context in which to study the link between relationships and health.

Excluded Research

Our organization around normative relationship development necessitates a certain conspicuous omission of research relevant to the broad topic of interpersonal relationships and health (vs. romantic relationships and health). For example, the large literatures on social support and support processes (outside of the romantic context) and on social isolation and integration and loneliness receive only cursory mention in this chapter. Such exclusions reflect nothing other than a concern for parsimony and a desire to highlight basic normative relationship processes and their health consequences. With that caveat, we now offer a very brief review of the relevant biological systems and health outcomes discussed throughout the remainder of the chapter.

RELEVANT BIOLOGICAL SYSTEMS AND HEALTH OUTCOMES

The vast majority of research on the topic has focused on two broad types of outcomes: physiological markers (i.e., autonomic, neuroendocrine, and immune activity) implicated in a range of objective physical health outcomes and objective disease outcomes, including physical and mental illnesses. We begin with a brief overview of the biological systems responsible for autonomic and neuroendocrine outcomes as well as common markers of immune function.

Autonomic, Neuroendocrine, and Immune Activity

References to biomarkers or health-relevant physiological responses generally refer to some assessment of autonomic, neuroendocrine, or immune functioning (Loving, Heffner, & Kiecolt-Glaser, 2006). The autonomic nervous system consists of sensory and motor nerves that innervate the body's organ systems to regulate their activity. It is composed of the sympathetic nervous system, the parasympathetic nervous system, and the enteric nervous system. The enteric branch is responsible for regulation of the digestive tract, but digestion is also controlled by the sympathetic and parasympathetic branches. The sympathetic nervous system, essential for energy mobilization, and the parasympathetic nervous system, responsible for energy conservation, work together to maintain the body's normal functioning by continually making adjustments in response to normal metabolic demands. The sympathetic nervous system is largely responsible for the fight-or-flight response during threat or danger. Its activities promote the transfer of blood to the brain and the muscles, increase sugar levels in the blood, and heighten heart rate and other organ activity in preparation for physical exertion. Conversely, the parasympathetic nervous system plays essential roles in reproduction and energy storage. This system opposes activity of the sympathetic nervous system.

Cardiovascular outcomes make up the majority of research in the romantic relationships and health domain given their links to current or future cardiovascular disease (CVD). Common markers of cardiovascular health include the traditional parameters of heart rate and blood pressure (including both systolic blood pressure and diastolic blood pressure), which serve as indirect markers of autonomic activity as well as sympathetically influenced endocrine activity. Other markers of cardiovascular function include, for example, cardiac output and vascular resistance indexes. Each of these indices provides important information regarding the manner in which the body is responding physiologically, and researchers often choose a subset of these markers to represent overall cardiovascular reactivity.

The endocrine system regulates functioning through the release of hormones that travel through the bloodstream to target organs. These hormones originate from endocrine glands whose activity is under the influence of the brain's pituitary gland as well as the autonomic nervous system. Two endocrine pathways are critical to the stress response: the sympathetic adrenomedullary (SAM) pathway and the hypothalamic–pituitary–adrenocortical (HPA) pathway. Both pathways begin at the hypothalamus, the key structure in the coordination of autonomic and endocrine function, and end at the adrenal glands. The SAM pathway is ultimately responsible for the release of the catecholamines, epinephrine (adrenaline) and norepinephrine, into the bloodstream. Epinephrine acts on many tissues at one time and serves to coordinate metabolic and behavioral responses during stress. Norepinephrine has minimal effects on the body when traveling though the bloodstream, but when released via autonomic nerve pathways, norepinephrine increases general blood vessel constriction essential for blood pressure regulation. During activation of the SAM pathway, the HPA response also occurs; HPA release of adrenocorticotropin hormone into the bloodstream stimulates the adrenal cortex to secrete cortisol. Cortisol is especially important for maintaining normal metabolic function but is also very important during the stress response; cortisol enhances the responses of the sympathetic nervous system and increases the release of glucose and stored fats for energy.

One convenient aspect of neuroendocrine responses is that they can be directly assessed. For example, as noted earlier, cortisol can be measured via saliva (in addition to blood and urine), and some have argued that assay of alpha-amylase, an enzyme found in saliva, provides a marker of sympathetic nervous system activity and bypasses some of the challenges in assessing catecholamine responses (Granger et al., 2006; Rohleder, Wolf, Maldonado, & Kirschbaum, 2006). However, recent reviews have suggested that claims that alpha-amylase

provides an index of epinephrine and norepinephrine levels are premature, although alpha-amylase is likely to be a reliable marker of general autonomic activity (Nater & Rohleder, 2009; Rohleder & Nater, 2009).

Finally, oxytocin and vasopressin are two additional peptide hormones receiving increased attention. In addition to their associations with relationship quality and behaviors (Ditzen et al., 2009; Gonzaga, Turner, Keltner, Campos, & Altemus, 2006; Gouin et al., 2012), both hormones are capable of influencing immune functioning, including inflammation and wound healing (Clodi et al., 2008; Gouin et al., 2010; Palin et al., 2009), and they have hypothesized roles in relationship development and maintenance (Carter, 1998; Fisher, 1998; Marazziti, 2005). Moreover, animal models suggest that oxytocin is capable of buffering organisms from stressful interpersonal contexts (Grippo, Trahanas, Zimmerman, Porges, & Carter, 2009). Thus, each hormone holds promise for shedding additional light on the mechanisms underlying the relationship–health link. That said, despite these known effects, much debate still surrounds the measurement of oxytocin (see Campbell, 2010) and the implications of peripheral measures of oxytocin used in human studies.

The justification for measurement of many biomarkers is their known role in downstream physical effects, such as immunity. For example, cortisol has multiple influences on immune functioning, including the trafficking of immune cells throughout the body and the ability of immune cells to kill antigen-infected cells (A. H. Miller, 1998), as well as the expression of latent viruses, such as the Epstein–Barr virus responsible for mononucleosis (Cacioppo, Kiecolt-Glaser, et al., 2002). However, the multiple counterregulatory mechanisms involved in physiological responses often make it difficult to know exactly how acute or short-term autonomic or endocrine changes affect real-world morbidity and mortality (G. Miller, Chen, & Cole, 2009). As a result, direct assessment of immunity often provides more definitive assessments of potential disease-related outcomes.

The immune system is responsible for (a) distinguishing the "self," the body's normal cells, from the "nonself," foreign invaders or transformed cells, and (b) destroying the latter. These processes are performed through cellular and humoral immune responses operating across two categories of the immune system termed *innate* and *acquired immunity*. Measuring the performance and condition of the immune system typically takes two forms. Functional assays provide information on the ability of immune system cells to perform their job, whereas enumerative assays provide information regarding actual counts or percentages of specific immune cells (see Kiecolt-Glaser & Glaser, 1997). Additionally, increased attention is being given to markers of inflammation, particularly proinflammatory cytokines (e.g., interleukin [IL]-1, IL-6, tumor necrosis factor-α) and C-reactive protein, because the evidence for the link between inflammation and morbidity and mortality continues to mount (see Kiecolt-Glaser, Gouin, & Hantsoo, 2010, for a review).

Disease Outcomes

Physical disease.   Our review also focuses on the role romantic relationships (and relationship processes) play in predicting the incidence of several diseases and disease outcomes. CVD is the leading cause of death in the United States, with roughly one person dying from CVD every 38 seconds (Lloyd-Jones et al., 2010). *CVD* refers to a number of specific diseases that affect the heart or the blood vessel system, including coronary heart disease (CHD) and congestive heart failure. CVD results from atherosclerosis, the thickening of the artery walls resulting from accumulated fatty deposits, which can itself result from a number of high-risk conditions, including hypertension and diabetes. The major outcomes of CVD include angina pectoris (pain resulting from decreased blood flow to the heart), myocardial infarction (a heart attack resulting from an interruption of blood to the heart and yielding permanent damage to the cells of the heart), and stroke (a disturbance of blood supply to the brain). Recent advances in ultrasound technology permit researchers to study intima-media thickness, a measurement of the thickness of the artery walls, which permits noninvasive assessment

of early-stage artherosclerotic processes (Janicki, Kamarck, Shiffman, Sutton-Tyrrell, & Gwaltney, 2005). Metabolic syndrome is a constellation of conditions (including hypertension, elevated waist circumference, elevated fasting glucose, elevated triglycerides, and reduced high-density lipoproteins) that occurs in one in five adults in the United States (Ford, Giles, & Dietz, 2002) and increases risk for CVD and poor CVD outcomes. Thus, increasing attention is being paid to metabolic syndrome in health psychology (Niaura et al., 2002).

Beyond CVD, we also review research on relationships and two other disease processes: cancer and pain. Although *cancer* is the overarching term for more than 100 diseases, all malignant processes involve unregulated cell growth as a function of DNA damage to gene regions that impair proper cell functioning. Interest in the role of relationship processes and cancer outcomes is considerable. For example, Pinquart and Duberstein (2010) conducted a meta-analysis of 87 studies linking perceptions of social support, network size, and marital status with cancer survival and found that longevity is related to all three of these constructs. A great deal of relationship research has also focused on chronic pain, which affects 30 to 50 million people in the United States (Hardt, Jacobsen, Goldberg, Nickel, & Buchwald, 2008) and is associated with considerable functional impairment and disability. As discussed later, one interesting finding in the pain literature is that putatively positive relationship processes, such as caretaking behaviors by a spouse, can unintentionally maintain and sometimes exacerbate the experience of chronic pain.

Mental illness.   Our review also covers mental health outcomes, especially those found in the *Diagnostic and Statistical Manual of Mental Disorders* (4th ed.; American Psychiatric Association, 1994). Among those disorders, the most commonly studied in the context of relationships are mood disorders (e.g., major depressive disorder) and anxiety disorders (e.g., generalized anxiety disorder, posttraumatic stress disorder). The distinction between a diagnosed mental health problem and self-reported measures of psychological distress is important; the former, by definition, reflects considerable functional impairment, whereas the latter can reflect clinical or even practical significance (cf. Jacobson & Truax, 1991). Thus, our review focuses largely on diagnosable mental health problems.

EARLY RELATIONSHIPS CAN SHAPE PHYSIOLOGICAL RESPONDING: PSYCHOSOCIAL EPIGENETICS

A core idea of attachment theory is that people's earliest relationships can set the stage for how they think, feel, and act in later relationships (Bowlby, 1969; Simpson, Collins, & Salvatore, 2011). Across the life span, individual differences in attachment styles guide how both children and adults respond to stressful situations (Simpson & Rholes, 2012), especially (real or perceived) stressors that challenge people's sense of felt security within their relationships. From this perspective, people's earliest-relationships play a critical role in sculpting biological responding by heightening their perceptions of stress in the environment. This process is largely top-down: People's experiences in relationships shape how they perceive the environment, which in turn results in biological responses that, if maintained over time, are harmful for health.

In contrast to this top-down model, emerging evidence from animal research has indicated that a critically important bottom-up process may be operating as well: Early social behaviors can cause molecular changes at the level of the genome; these changes promote or constrain health-relevant biological responses (G. E. Miller, Chen, & Parker, 2011). As a discipline of study, epigenetics investigates how experience can change gene expression without altering the underlying nucleotide structure, and startling evidence has revealed that these changes can alter observable phenotypes across multiple generations (e.g., Robertson & Wolffe, 2000).

How can epigenetics inform the study of relationships and health? G. E. Miller et al. (2011) have recently proposed a model of biological embedding that explains how early adverse experiences alter cellular signals and sculpt biological processes in a manner that increases risk for poor health later in life. One view of these biological changes is a defensive programming hypothesis—the idea that early stress sensitizes biological systems to be highly responsive in order to promote survival; this sensitization, or programming, has adaptive value in the short term, but it can be physiologically destructive through exaggerated neuroendocrine and inflammatory responses (G. Miller, Chen, Fok, et al., 2009).

The most well-developed animal model for the lasting effect of early care is the rat dam–pup dyad. Maternal rats (dams) have natural variability in two caregiving behaviors, licking and grooming and arched-back nursing. These behaviors lead to changes in pups' HPA responses to stress (Meaney, 2001). Pups of mothers high in licking and grooming and arched-back nursing show less fearful behavioral responding and less HPA responding than pups of mothers low in these behaviors (Liu et al., 1997). These differences emerge during the 1st week of life and are maintained into adulthood. Specifically, these maternal behaviors result in changes in DNA methylation and chromatin structures, which are chemical changes to the genome that result in differences in gene expression (Weaver et al., 2004). In effect, these changes represent a genomic imprinting by maternal behavior that has long-term implications for stress responding as a function of hippocampal glucocorticoid receptor gene expression (Zhang et al., 2006).

Research into human epigenetic and gene expression as a function of early psychosocial processes remains nascent, but the work that exists is consistent with the available animal literature (Cole, 2009; G. E. Miller et al., 2011). For example, early social adversity in the form of low socioeconomic status is associated with peripheral blood mononuclear cell gene-expression patterns that heighten risk for disease susceptibility in early midlife (G. Miller, Chen, Fok, et al., 2009). Other evidence has indicated that prenatal exposure to maternal depression is associated with increased methylation of the glucocorticoid receptor gene in infants' cord blood and that this methylation pattern is associated with increased salivary cortisol at age 3 months (Oberlander et al., 2008).

These first human studies are providing vast new insights into how people's earliest relational experiences can become embedded in biological programming in a manner that has long-term health implications (see G. E. Miller et al., 2011). Most of the research on this topic thus far has focused on adverse experiences or the absence of nurturing environments. The next decade should witness a surge of research into precisely how early relationships—of both high and low quality—can set the stage for biological responses that unfold over the remainder of the life span (e.g., Merjonen et al., 2011). Although this work is emerging and many questions remain, it is one of the most exciting and potentially generative lines of inquiry in all of science.

RELATIONSHIP INITIATION AND HEALTH

Study of the biological predeterminants and consequences of relationship initiation also holds promise for shedding light on the health-protective effects of romantic relationships. Perhaps some of the more striking evidence for predetermination has derived from work on major histocompatibility complex alleles and perceived partner attractiveness. Much of this work has built off the good genes hypothesis (Gangestad & Simpson, 2000; Thornhill & Gangestad, 1999)—the idea that individuals seek mates who have high heritable fitness because such pairings create the best possible genotype (all else being equal) for offspring. Indeed, when women are fertile, they are more attracted to short-term (vs. long-term) mates who display traits indicative of greater genetic fitness (e.g., facial symmetry; Gangestad, Garver-Apgar, Simpson, & Cousins, 2007; Thornhill et al., 2003). Interestingly, women (but not men) also report greater sexual desire for current romantic partners to the extent that their male partners' major histocompatibility complex alleles are more dissimilar to their own (Garver-Apgar, Gangestad, Thornhill, Miller, & Olp, 2006). The major histocompatibility complex gene complex essentially instructs the body's innate immune system what to identify as "me" versus "not me." Heterozygosis within the major histocompatibility complex gene complex is adaptive because it results in the immune system's being able to recognize a greater variety of pathogens. These and other studies (e.g., Caryl et al., 2009; Gangestad & Buss, 1993; Perilloux, Webster, & Gaulin, 2010; Thornhill &

Gangestad, 1999) have provided compelling evidence that basic innate mechanisms derived to influence the health of offspring also influence partner choice and relationship behaviors.

Within the normative relationship development model, relationships often proceed from initial attraction to initiation, a period characterized by a high degree of passion, or what some refer to as falling in love or intense or early-stage romantic love (Aron et al., 2005; Emanuele et al., 2006; Marazziti & Canale, 2004). Movement into romantic relationships is associated with many positive outcomes (Lee & Gramotnev, 2007), including reductions in self-reported stress (Bell & Lee, 2008). Moreover, events such as starting a love relationship and beginning to date are considered positive life events in the health literature (Reich & Zautra, 1981), despite the fact that such events require individual adaptations (Loving & Wright, 2012). For example, forming a new relationship requires individuals to adapt affectively (e.g., emotions become linked to a partner; Berscheid, 1983), cognitively (e.g., incorporating a partner's identity; Aron, Aron, Tudor, & Nelson, 1991), and behaviorally (Kelley & Thibaut, 1978). More important, any negative effects of relationship disruption are generally diminished, if not reversed, when individuals begin a new relationship (Wheaton, 1990).

The effects of relationship initiation extend to the physical and physiological domain as well. Falling in love alters a number of physiological outcomes, including chronic and acute cortisol production (Loving, Crockett, & Paxson, 2009; Marazziti & Canale, 2004), nerve growth factor (Emanuele et al., 2006), and serotonin transporter receptors (Marazziti, Akiskal, Rossi, & Cassano, 1999). The former two outcomes are notable for several reasons. First, nerve growth factor may promote production of cortisol (Loving et al., 2009; Otten, Baumann, & Girard, 1979), which provides one explanation of the cortisol effects reported by Marazziti and Canale (2004), or it may desensitize the immune system to the immunosuppressive effects of cortisol (i.e., glucocorticoid resistance; Sheridan, Stark, Avitsur, & Padgett, 2000). The qualifier *may* is deliberate because these suggestions are highly speculative and await additional research, but the potential to provide mechanistic information regarding the interplay and potential downstream health effects of distinct biomarkers is enormous.

Second, Marazziti and Canale (2004) compared cortisol levels in individuals who had recently fallen in love relative to those in long-term relationships or in no relationship at all. Their finding that those who had recently fallen in love had higher circulating levels of plasma cortisol generally goes against many models linking chronic stress to poor health (Baum & Grunberg, 1997; Loving & Wright, 2012). Interestingly, Loving et al. (2009) demonstrated that cortisol could also be increased acutely by having individuals think about falling in love (vs. being in a control condition). Exactly how these chronic and acute effects might interact to influence health outcomes, if at all, remains to be seen, but an interesting study by Schneiderman, Zagoory-Sharon, Leckman, and Feldman (2012) has provided one possible explanation for why observed increases in cortisol during relationship formation may not be associated with poor health. These researchers compared plasma oxytocin levels of two groups of individuals—"new lovers" who had been dating less than 4 months and singles. Consistent with theorizing and empirical evidence supporting a link between the attachment system and oxytocin (Buchheim et al., 2009; Carter, 1998; Diamond, 2001), plasma oxytocin levels of new lovers were significantly higher than those of singles. This finding is noteworthy in light of the evidence that oxytocin is capable of promoting cortisol release (Tops, Van Peer, Korf, Wijers, & Tucker, 2007), although some evidence has also shown that oxytocin buffers or suppresses HPA axis activity (Heinrichs, Baumgartner, Kirschbaum, & Ehlert, 2003; Quirin, Kuhl, & Dusing, 2011). As a result, it is becoming clearer that attempts to isolate the effects of experiences of relationship initiation on health-relevant biomarkers are likely to be most fruitful when multiple markers and systems are assessed over time.

Relationship initiation may also promote physical health via its effect on the occurrence and frequency of physical contact. At least in the early stages, the progression of relationships is marked by an increase in physical contact between romantic partners (Emmers & Dindia, 1995; Guerrero & Andersen,

1994; O'Sullivan, Mantsun, Harris, & Brooks-Gunn, 2007), and affectionate behaviors are a defining feature of most high-quality relationships (Call, Sprecher, & Schwartz, 1995). In addition to communicating important information between partners in a relationship (Gallace & Spence, 2010), physical touch also benefits individuals physiologically and physically. For example, levels of physical touch reduce neuroendocrine and autonomic markers of stress in naturalistic and laboratory-based paradigms (Ditzen et al., 2007; Grewen, Anderson, Girdler, & Light, 2003; Light, Grewen, & Amico, 2005). Much of this work has involved individuals in more established relationships, but there are few reasons to believe that physical touch is not equally beneficial in the early formation of relationships as well.

RELATIONSHIP MAINTENANCE: ONGOING RELATIONSHIP PROCESSES AND HEALTH

The majority of research on the health effects of romantic relationships has focused on dynamics within established relationships, particularly conflict and support processes. Much of this work has been reviewed previously, especially the work on conflict and health, so we offer a brief review of this interaction context next (for more extensive reviews, see Kiecolt-Glaser & Newton, 2001; Robles & Kiecolt-Glaser, 2003; Wright & Loving, 2011).

Conflict

Although the exact topic of conflict varies across couple and relationship types (Kurdek, 1994; Laursen, 1995; Papp, Cummings, & Goeke-Morey, 2009; Solomon, Rothblum, & Balsam, 2005), conflict is a natural part of relationships (Cupach, 2000), with most couples arguing at least once a month (McGonagle, Kessler, & Schilling, 1992). Although simply disagreeing with a romantic partner can increase autonomic activity relative to other interaction contexts (Nealey-Moore, Smith, Uchino, Hawkins, & Olson-Cerny, 2007; Smith & Gallo, 1999), the presence of negativity (or being nasty) often exacerbates these negative outcomes (Ewart, Taylor, Kraemer, & Agras, 1991; Smith et al., 2011), especially in the partner who is most invested in the outcome of the discussion (Kiecolt-Glaser & Newton,

2001; Newton & Sanford, 2003). In contrast, interacting with a supportive partner can buffer individuals from some of the detrimental effects of relationship conflict (e.g., Broadwell & Light, 1999; Heffner, Kiecolt-Glaser, Loving, Glaser, & Malarkey, 2004), and positive behaviors during conflict may do the same (Robles, Shaffer, Malarkey, & Kiecolt-Glaser, 2006).

In line with the cardiovascular effects discussed earlier, negative interactions with a romantic partner also affect individual hormones. For example, Malarkey, Kiecolt-Glaser, Pearl, and Glaser (1994) assessed a range of hormones before, during, and after couples participated in a standard conflict interaction. Although the newlywed couples were all highly satisfied with their marriages, they experienced alterations in five of six hormones assayed, including increases in the catecholamines, epinephrine and norepinephrine, and adrenocorticotrophic hormone (which is a precursor of cortisol). Additional analyses revealed that wives', but not husbands', hormones were especially affected by specific behavioral patterns during the interactions (Kiecolt-Glaser et al., 1996). Such shifts may forecast a host of negative health outcomes down the road. Chronic increases in many of these hormones contribute to the overall wear and tear on the body, leading to sickness and early mortality (McEwen, 1998).

Evidence that these effects on hormones have a negative impact on health is most abundant when one considers the immune consequences of negative marital interactions. In the seminal study on this topic, spouses exhibiting more nasty behaviors during a conflict discussion demonstrated signs of immunological disruption and downregulation, including increased antibody titers to a latent virus (i.e., the Epstein–Barr virus; see Kiecolt-Glaser et al., 1993). Such findings indicate that the body's immune system was challenged to fight off a virus that, under normal conditions, lies dormant. Even more compelling evidence has come from a more recent study. Specifically, in a study of 42 married couples who received eight standardized suction blister wounds on their nondominant forearms before engaging in (during separate visits) a conflict and a support interaction, the wounds of those in highly hostile relationships healed at approximately

60% the rate of those of individuals in less hostile relationships (Kiecolt-Glaser et al., 2005). Moreover, couple members in highly hostile relationships also had higher plasma IL-6 levels the morning after the interaction. IL-6 is one of several proinflammatory cytokines implicated in a host of cardiovascular disorders, osteoporosis, certain cancers, and Alzheimer's disease (e.g., Black, 2006; Swardfager et al., 2010). An interesting finding in this same sample was that more avoidantly attached spouses also had significantly higher IL-6 levels during the conflict discussion than during the supportive interaction (Gouin et al., 2009), as did partners who were less cognitively engaged during the conflict (Graham et al., 2009). These latter sets of findings underscore the importance of considering individual difference moderators in these interaction contexts.

Evidence for a link between marital conflict and mental health is less clear, primarily because studies often use measures that make it difficult to separate the effects of conflict from other features of marital relationships. However, as one would expect, marital conflict does appear to undermine mental health, particularly by increasing depression. For example, in a sample of more than 8,000 women who provided data twice over about a year, women reported fewer depressive symptoms after experiencing a separation from a partner if there was a high level of conflict before the separation (T. G. O'Connor, Cheng, Dunn, & Golding, 2005). Additionally, in a sample of 1,044 individuals from the National Survey of Families and Households, frequency of marital disagreements was positively associated with depressed affect, and marital disagreements also moderated the association between physical disability and depressed affect, such that greater conflict exacerbated the effect of disability on depressed affect (Bookwala & Franks, 2005). Other research has highlighted moderators of the link between marital conflict and distressed mood, which included measures of anxiety, hostility, and depression (Almeida, McGonagle, Cate, Kessler, & Wethington, 2003). In this daily diary study of 166 couples, the association between husbands' and wives' reports of distressed mood and the presence of spousal conflict was moderated by different sets of relationship-specific (e.g., trust, intimacy) and broader social (e.g., acute life events, support from relatives) variables.

Finally, although the work we have reviewed primarily focused on samples of married couples, the effects of conflict on health-relevant parameters have also been studied in nonmarital samples, particularly adolescent and emerging adult dating samples (e.g., Gunlicks-Stoessel & Powers, 2009; Laurent & Powers, 2007; S. I. Powers, Pietromonaco, Gunlicks, & Sayer, 2006). This work is exciting because it highlights the knowledge to be gained when theoretically relevant individual- and couple-level characteristics are considered in the context of conflict. For example, Laurent and Powers (2007) investigated whether individuals' temperament, attachment anxiety, and avoidance moderate heterosexual couple members' cortisol responses to a conflict discussion. The findings underscored the benefits obtained by considering the unique features that characterize relationships and people within them when studying the physiological costs of romantic relationship interaction dynamics.

Support

The literature on social support and health is vast and complex, and a complete review of this topic is beyond the scope of this chapter. Several excellent reviews of the topic exist (Holt-Lunstad et al., 2010; Thoits, 2011; Uchino, 2004; Uchino, Cacioppo, & Kiecolt-Glaser, 1996), so we limit our discussion to findings that address support processes within intact relationships. Readers interested in a more complete discussion of theory and the potential mechanisms of action linking social support processes and physical health are encouraged to consult Uchino's (2004; Uchino et al., 1996) comprehensive reviews.

To begin, what is social support? A common definition of social support includes both structural and functional components (Cassel, 1976; Cobb, 1976; Cohen & Willis, 1985). The structural components of social support are the number of ties people have in their lives and their degree of social integration (e.g., group membership, network density, existence of familial relationships). The functional components are the actions of these relationships (e.g., whether people can get advice or help from others in their lives; see Uchino, 2004). The epidemiological literature on social support and physical health has focused much more squarely on

structural measures, especially social integration (e.g., Holt-Lundstad et al., 2010). In contrast, the psychological literature has focused much more on perceived support and its association with, for example, cardiovascular reactivity in the laboratory (e.g., Uchino & Garvey, 1997). The distinction between perceived and received support is important (Uchino, 2009), with the former construct being associated with positive health-relevant outcomes and the latter construct being associated with inconsistent results and sometimes even negative effects (Bolger, Zuckerman, & Kessler, 2000; Coyne, Wortman, & Lehman, 1988). Research has suggested that in specific circumstances—especially when people are trying to adjust to acute stress—received support can protect against excessive cardiovascular responding (Lepore, Allen, & Evans, 1993).

The field has yet to make a clear distinction between the positive effects of social support and the absence of negative effects that often follow from acrimonious relationships. This issue has proven vexing for many years. For example, Coyne and Downey (1991) wrote, "The apparent benefits of support may in large part represent freedom from the otherwise deleterious effects of relationships that are conflictful, insecure, or otherwise not sustaining" (p. 413). We believe that this distinction matters, especially for revealing the mechanisms of action that link conflict, support, and health. Recently, for example, Whisman and Sbarra (2012) found that, in early midlife, low levels of marital support (not high levels of marital strain) were uniquely associated with elevated rates of IL-6 in married woman. Although the distinction between the absence of support and the presence of conflict is not fully understood, it remains important for researchers to consider these issues.

Social support, physical health outcomes, and health-relevant responding. Berkman and Syme (1979) published one of the first large-scale epidemiological studies linking social and community ties with mortality rates. Their main findings indicated that people in the lowest social connections groups were nearly 2.5 times more likely to die early than people with the largest number of social connections, and these findings held after statistically controlling for participants' sex, socioeconomic status, health behaviors, and health service utilization (Berkman & Syme, 1979). In the time since this report was published, work in this area has flourished. Holt-Lunstad et al.'s (2010) recent meta-analysis included 148 studies that examined the association between functional and structural support variables with mortality. The key finding from this meta-analysis is that measurement matters: Studies that included multidimensional measurement of social relationships (e.g., combining measures of network size, density, diversity, marital status) were most highly predictive of mortality.

Although documenting broad-based associations between social support and both morbidity and mortality is important, epidemiological studies rarely provide the degree of resolution needed to understand precisely how the functional elements of support are associated with health outcomes or health-relevant biological responding within ongoing relationships. In a now classic study, Orth-Gomér et al. (2000) showed that marital stress—defined, in part, by low levels of supportive behaviors in the relationship—was associated with a 2.9-fold increase in the risk for incidence of recurrent cardiac events among married women who were hospitalized for acute myocardial infarction or unstable angina pectoris (also see Lett et al., 2005; Mookadam & Arthur, 2004; Orth-Gomér & Leineweber, 2005). In a sample of healthy adults who had mild hypertension, marital adjustment predicted increased risk for the development of a left ventricular mass over a 3-year period (Baker et al., 2000).

Other research has demonstrated that high levels of marital quality protect against mortality from congestive heart failure, over and above congestive heart failure severity, and that this association is stronger for women than for men (Coyne et al., 2001; Rohrbaugh, Shoham, & Coyne, 2006). Two interesting extensions of this study have provided further evidence of how these marital quality effects might unfold. Rohrbaugh et al. (2004) found that spouse confidence in congestive heart failure patients' efficacy for managing medical regimens was associated with decreased risk for cardiac mortality during the next 4 years, and this effect held after accounting for participants' self-efficacy

and disease severity. Moreover, high levels of communal coping—or the extent to which couples discussed the patient's cardiac problems using words such as *we* (vs. *I, me,* or *my*)—were associated with positive changes in congestive heart failure symptoms and patients' general health over the next 6 months (Rohrbaugh, Mehl, Shoham, Reilly, & Ewy, 2008). Thus, high levels of marital quality, the extent to which spouses actively believe in patients' coping abilities, and the extent to which couples define patients' CVD communally all predict decreased risk for worsening of CVD outcomes.

The association between social support in established relationships and disease outcomes is not limited to CVD. Marital support plays an important role in how patients manage cancer, their psychological responses to cancer, and potentially their cancer outcomes (Manne, 1998; Manne, Taylor, Dougherty, & Kemeny, 1997; Weihs, Enright, & Simmens, 2008), although considerable disagreement surrounds the latter issue (Coyne & Thombs, 2008). Recent evidence has also linked relationship satisfaction and distress with the development of metabolic syndrome. Thus far, however, the association between marital functioning and metabolic syndrome has been observed only in women (Troxel, Matthews, Gallo, & Kuller, 2005; Whisman & Uebelacker, 2011; Whisman, Uebelacker, & Settles, 2010).

In the chronic pain literature, the association between marital functioning and disease outcomes has been equivocal. Leonard, Cano, and Johansen (2006) reported that existing studies have found quite mixed results in terms of the association between pain severity and marital functioning. One of the most influential models in this literature is the behavioral formulation of chronic pain, which stipulates that pain behaviors can come under the control of social contingencies (Fordyce, 1976; Kerns, Haythornthwaite, Southwick, & Giller, 1990). That is, partners' bids to help patients manage pain may unwittingly reinforce pain symptoms, meaning that chronic pain is one disease in which spousal support behaviors can maintain or even exacerbate pain symptoms (Cano, Weisberg, & Gallagher, 2000; Raichle, Romano, & Jensen, 2011; Turk, Kerns, & Rosenberg, 1992). Despite the prominence of the operant model of chronic pain and partners' roles in maintaining it, other models have suggested that displays of pain behaviors can be construed as emotional disclosure. Accordingly, they provide couples with the opportunity to build intimacy, which, in turn, may protect against the worsening of pain symptoms (see Cano & de C. Williams, 2010).

Beyond the study of disease outcomes, laboratory and field investigations have provided more nuanced accounts of how social support processes operate within relationships. The bulk of this research has focused on cardiovascular reactivity. In one study, 120 adults were monitored with ambulatory blood pressure devices over 6 days (Gump, Polk, Kamarck, & Shiffman, 2001). After every social interaction, participants rated their emotional activation, intimacy, and support. Interactions with partners, relative to all other people, were associated with significantly lower blood pressure, and these interactions were characterized by more intimacy and perceived emotional support. Holt-Lunstad et al. (2008) investigated the physiological correlates of marital quality in a study of ambulatory blood pressure among 204 married and 99 single men and women. Relative to their single counterparts, married adults experienced greater dips in ambulatory blood pressure from day to night, and among married participants, those who had greater marital satisfaction evidenced significantly higher 24-hour ambulatory blood pressure than those whose marital satisfaction was less. Of course, marital satisfaction does not speak directly to perceptions of support within relationships, but it does characterize the affective climate of the marriage. In a very interesting comparison, these authors found that participants reporting low marital quality had significantly higher 24-hour ambulatory blood pressure than single participants, suggesting that it is better for one's health to be single than to be in a low-quality marriage.

Social support and mental health. The literature on marital quality and mental health has long served as a proxy for understanding whether and how support processes are linked to psychological well-being and mental health (Coyne & DeLongis, 1986). We now focus on some of the key findings from this area.

Using data from the National Comorbidity Survey, which included more than 2,500 community-dwelling

adults, Whisman (1999) examined the association between marital satisfaction and the 12-month prevalence of a diagnosable mental disorder. Women who reported high levels of marital satisfaction were significantly less likely to be diagnosed with any mood or anxiety disorder, major depression, or posttraumatic stress disorder during the prior year; in contrast, for men, the only significant association involved dysthymia, with more satisfied men demonstrating a decreased likelihood of being diagnosed with dysthymia during the prior year. Whisman (2007) extended these results using data from the National Comorbidity Survey Replication study and found that the association between marital distress and risk for a major depressive disorder increased with age. This finding can also be interpreted to suggest that older adults who have high-quality relationships are protected against depression relative to younger adults involved in high-quality relationships. Thus, as people age, the protective benefits of high-quality relationships increase.

One especially interesting part of the literature on marital quality and mental health is that mental health outcomes can be improved by improving the quality of a couple's relationship. Results from a meta-analysis of eight controlled trials showed no differences between couples therapy and individual psychotherapy in the treatment of depression (measured in terms of either depressive symptoms or persistence of depression) and that couples therapy was more effective than individual psychotherapy in improving relationship discord, particularly among couples who had distressed relationships at the beginning of treatment (Barbato & D'Avanzo, 2008). Furthermore, behavioral couples therapy is an effective treatment for substance use disorders. A meta-analysis of 12 controlled trials found that couples therapy was more effective than individual-based treatments in improving relationship satisfaction, frequency of use, and consequences of substance use (M. B. Powers, Vedel, & Emmelkamp, 2008).

Emerging Themes

We now turn our attention to what we view as key emerging themes relevant to the study of health outcomes within the context of ongoing relationships.

Sleep. Both sleep quality and sleep duration have important implications for morbidity and mortality (Buysse, Reynolds, Monk, Berman, & Kupfer, 1989; Hoevenaar-Blom, Spijkerman, Kromhout, van den Berg, & Verschuren, 2011; Motivala & Irwin, 2007). As such, studying sleep within a dyadic context is critical, especially given that couple members at all relationship stages regularly share a bed (Jamison & Proulx, 2012; Troxel, 2010). More important, both large-scale epidemiological studies and smaller daily diary studies have documented the profound influence that romantic relationships have on sleep duration and quality. For example, those whose romantic relationships were disrupted (e.g., divorce) had more frequent sleep disturbances and poorer sleep quality than those whose relationships remained intact over time (Hale, 2010; Troxel et al., 2010). Additionally, even short-term separations from a romantic partner can negatively affect sleep quality, especially among anxiously attached women (Diamond, Hicks, & Otter-Henderson, 2008), and couple conflict on one day results in smaller cortisol awakening responses the next day (Hicks & Diamond, 2011). The cortisol awakening response is the characteristic rise in cortisol observed immediately after awakening, which is a normal part of cortisol's diurnal rhythm (Fries, Dettenborn, & Kirschbaum, 2009). The health implication of modulated cortisol awakening responses, however, is still a matter of debate (Clow, Hucklebridge, Stalder, Evans, & Thorn, 2010; Fries et al., 2009). Regardless, the strong link between sleep disturbance and quality and morbidity and mortality more than justifies the need for further research on this topic.

Emotional expression. Pennebaker's (1992, 1997) theory of emotional expression is experiencing a revival of sorts in the romantic relationships and health domain. This should come as no surprise; emotional expression and inhibition have unique effects on important health outcomes. For example, as mentioned previously, spouses who used more cognitive words during a conflict discussion had smaller increases in proinflammatory cytokines (Graham et al., 2009). In another study, emotional inhibition (or self-silencing) was associated with

higher 10-year mortality rates in married women (Eaker, Sullivan, Kelly-Hayes, D'Agostino, & Benjamin, 2007). Together, these two studies, and others that have underscored the utility of considering specific features of language during interactions (e.g., Priem & Solomon, 2011), have suggested a pathway through which behavioral and psychological variables (emotional expression and inhibition) affect biological mechanisms (inflammation) that ultimately affect objective health outcomes (mortality).

End of Relationships

The loss of a romantic partner with whom one had intended to spend the rest of one's life is a difficult and sometimes devastating experience. Few other emotional and psychological experiences in life are as potentially devastating as ending a committed romantic relationship (Sbarra et al., 2011). In cases of divorce, those who initiate their romantic separations often experience guilt, uncertainty, and fear, whereas those who are left by their partners may feel acute rejection, loneliness, and shame. For those who miss their former partner, longing can evolve into clinical depression, prolonged grief, and substance abuse. Yet, many people who leave unsatisfying marriages experience positive outcomes (e.g., Amato & Hohmann-Marriott, 2007), and the transition out of an unsatisfying or stress-filled relationship can provide opportunities for growth (Tashiro, Frazier, & Berman, 2006). In this section of the chapter, we review what is known about the mental and physical health correlates of divorce and bereavement. We also discuss the potential mechanisms linking relationship disruptions and more distal outcomes.

Bereavement and divorce: A focus on resilience. Bonanno's (2004) research on human resilience after loss and other traumatic life events is a reminder that most people fare quite well when relationships end. For example, using multilevel modeling, Lucas (2005) reported that divorce predicts lasting decrements in subjective well-being over time. In contrast, Mancini, Bonanno, and Clark (2011) reanalyzed the same panel data using a latent trajectory method and found that nearly

72% of adults experience almost no changes in their subjective well-being leading up to and after their separation and that roughly 20% of people show moderate decreases in well-being that persist after the separation. The latent class analysis illustrates an important point that is obscured in mean-based analyses: After both bereavement and divorce, most people do well over time and can be characterized as resilient in the face of these relationship transitions. Nevertheless, because bereavement and divorce are common experiences, the fact that 10% to 20% of people experience adverse outcomes means that a large percentage of the population is at risk for developing health problems after having experienced one of these relationship transitions. Thus, it is important to understand these risks in light of the fact that most people cope well over time.

Social epidemiology of loss: Broad-based morbidity and mortality. Loss resulting from divorce or death of a romantic partner is associated with increased risk for poor psychological and physical health, sadness, and distress (Sbarra et al., 2011; Shor et al., 2012; Stroebe, 2009; Stroebe, Schut, & Stroebe, 2007). The experience of romantic loss—not simply the lack of a romantic partner—may be responsible for these poorer health outcomes. For example, Pienta, Hayward, and Jenkins (2000) found that the end of a marriage, via either divorce or death, is associated with poorer health outcomes than never having been married at all. In comparison to matched controls, bereaved adults reported more headaches, dizziness, indigestion, and chest pain, as well as higher rates of disability and physical illness (Stroebe et al., 2007). Similar to the case of bereavement, being or becoming divorced (or separated) is associated with increased risks for a variety of poor physical health outcomes, including decreased immune functioning, CVD, respiratory disease, and liver disease, among others (see Sbarra et al., 2011).

Research has suggested that the notion that one can die of a broken heart may be true. The loss of a romantic partner is associated with heightened mortality, even after accounting for several lifestyle and socioeconomic factors (Kposowa, 2000; Parkes, Benjamin, & Fitzgerald, 1969). Mortality risk is greater during the first 6 months after the death of a spouse, with a spike in mortality in the weeks immediately after the loss, although data have also suggested that increased risk can persist beyond this timeframe. This pattern of increased mortality risk has been labeled the *widowhood effect* (Elwert & Christakis, 2008a). Although explanations for the widowhood effect have been debated in the literature (see Stroebe et al., 2007), considerable evidence has supported its existence.

Mortality risk for those who divorce is greater than that for their married counterparts. In a meta-analysis of 32 studies involving more than 6 million people, 755,000 divorces, and 160,000 deaths, Sbarra et al. (2011) recently found significantly elevated risk for early death among divorced adults relative to married adults. Compared with married adults, divorced adults were, on average, 23% more likely to have died at each follow-up period in each of the studies in the meta-analysis. One of the major problems with most of the studies in this meta-analysis is that they are macroscopic—marital status is generally assessed at one period of time, and participants are followed over some extended period during which some of them die. This approach is perfectly fine when considering the effects of a medical condition on mortality—for example, does having a past diagnosis of cancer increase risk for early death?—but the approach becomes problematic when studying something more fluid, such as marital status. To address this issue, Sbarra and Nietert (2009) compared the risk for early death (across a 40-year study) of two marital status classifications: having ever been divorced and becoming and remaining divorced. The former group characterizes many people, whereas the latter group represents only about 25% of people who experience divorce and do not remarry. The comparisons revealed that, relative to married adults, the ever-divorced group experienced no elevation in risk for early death, but the always-divorced group was at substantially elevated risk. Thus, how participants' marital history is defined and studied is an important methodological issue in the study of divorce and death (also see Dupre, Beck, & Meadows, 2009).

When considering the entirety of the literature linking social separations and health, one important question is whether the alleged consequences of a romantic breakup or becoming bereaved are better accounted for by third-variable explanations. For example, hostility may predict divorce and early mortality. This dimension of personality is also associated with health outcomes by virtue of changes in health behaviors and emotional reactivity, which can spur cardiovascular reactivity and prolong physiological stress responses. The widowhood effect may be explained by assortative mating or homogamy (Elwert & Christakis, 2008b), in which similar people marry each other (e.g., two smokers marry, so both have increased risk for early death).

Although poor health can select people out of marriage, two research designs have provided strong evidence that the health correlates of ending a relationship may indeed be consequences of the loss rather than merely being explained by third variables. First, the strongest evidence that divorce and bereavement exert causal effects on consequent mood disturbances comes from cotwin control designs. Osler, McGue, Lund, and Christensen (2008) recently used a cotwin control design to investigate rates of health outcomes between twins who were discordant for widowhood or divorce. The results indicated that depression and rates of smoking may be consequences of ending a marriage, but differences in many other health outcomes (e.g., self-rated health, alcohol use, body mass index) are due to underlying genetic explanations, not the stress of a relationship transition. Using a similar cotwin design in a sample of more than 1,900 pairs of twins discordant for spousal bereavement, Lichtenstein, Gatz, and Berg (1998) found evidence for a causal effect of bereavement on mortality. Of course, divorce and bereavement are different life events, but the results of this work have suggested that the experience of social loss may causally increase risk for early mortality. A cotwin control study focused on divorce and mortality has yet to be conducted. Research of this nature will be a major advance in the study of divorce and health outcomes.

The second approach for addressing potential spuriousness in the association between loss and mortality focuses on the widowhood effect. Elwert and Christakis (2008b) reasoned that if the widowhood effect is best explained by homogamy, men should show increased risk for death after the death

of their ex-wives. Consistent with this explanation, results from a large-scale analysis revealed no elevated risk among men after their ex-spouse's death (Elwert & Christakis, 2008b). Together, these studies have indicated that a large percentage of the variance in mental and physical health outcomes is likely a consequence of the loss experience.

Mechanisms of action. A growing literature has indicated that the psychological stress of divorce and bereavement is also associated with impaired immune responses. For example, in their comparisons of 38 married and 38 divorced or separated women, Kiecolt-Glaser et al. (1987) found that divorced women had significantly higher antibody titers to Epstein–Barr virus and a lower percentage of natural killer cell activity, both of which indicate compromised immune functioning. Among the divorced group, time since separation and continued attachment to a former spouse were associated with poorer immune responses. More recently, Sbarra, Law, Lee, and Mason (2009) designed a laboratory-based study of autonomic nervous system responses to test whether physiological reactivity after marital separation is correlated with the degree of emotion regulatory effort adults need to invoke when thinking about their separation experience. Participants who reported greater divorce-related emotional intrusion (e.g., dreaming about the separation, experiencing waves of sudden emotion about the separation) entered the study with significantly higher levels of resting systolic and diastolic blood pressure. In addition, during a task in which participants mentally reflected on their separation experience, men who reported that the task required a great deal of emotion regulatory effort (i.e., feeling upset combined with a need to exert control over one's emotions to prevent a worsening of distress) experienced the largest increases in blood pressure, and these effects were above and beyond those observed for baseline functioning (Sbarra et al., 2009).

When considering the lasting physiological effects of bereavement, more recent studies have indicated that the distinction between complicated grief and noncomplicated grief is important. Complicated grief is a disorder characterized by chronic longing for the person who has died, intense sadness, intrusive thoughts, and avoidance of reminders that the person has died (Prigerson et al., 2009). In a comparison of 12 women with complicated grief and 12 women without complicated grief, M. F. O'Connor, Willisch, Stanton, Olmstead, and Irwin (2012) found that those with complicated grief evidenced a flatter cortisol slope across the study day. This profile is consistent with dysregulation in the HPA axis. Exaggerated cortisol responses across the day may also lead to glucocorticoid sensitivity, which can result in chronic inflammation (M. F. O'Connor et al., 2011). What remains to be learned is what precise symptoms of complicated grief—yearning, emotional intrusion, self-blame—drive this response profile. If these associations can be revealed, the field will learn a great deal about the psychological pathways linking bereavement and neuroendocrine disruptions.

FUTURE DIRECTIONS

In a recent review of the literature on social relationships and health, Cohen and Janicki-Deverts (2009) wrote,

> The size, consistency, and range of the established relationships between our social networks and morbidity and mortality often lead us to talk about them as if they were causal. However, the truth is, we do not know this. This literature is based on prospective correlational research. . . . These studies also tend to control for spurious "third" factors such as age, sex, ethnicity, and socioeconomic status that could influence both the nature of our social networks and our health. Even so, there are still many psychosocial, environmental, and biological factors that could account for a correlation between a social factor and health outcomes. (p. 376)

Indeed, as we suggested earlier, a substantial literature has indicated that mentally and physically unhealthy people may have difficulty nurturing and maintaining high-quality relationships. With respect

to divorce, for example, the social selection perspective holds that some people possess characteristics that increase risk for both separation and divorce and poor health outcomes. Hostility, depression, and substance abuse are just a few examples of the myriad processes that increase the likelihood of future divorce among married people and are also unique predictors of early death in prospective cohort studies.

Clear evidence exists, for example, that health behaviors such as alcohol and drug use predict the future likelihood of divorce (Fu & Goldman, 2000), which suggests that these problems reliably select adults out of marriage. The perspective that separation or divorce outcomes are nonrandom and can be explained in part by understanding third variables is supported by the well-known existence of Gene × Environment correlations—that is, the observation that environments are shaped by genotypes (Scarr & McCartney, 1983)—and by evidence from behavior genetic studies of marital dissolution. McGue and Lykken (1992), for instance, found greater concordance of divorce in monozygotic twins than in dizygotic twins, indicating that a substantial portion of the risk for marital dissolution is explained by genetic factors. A follow-up study demonstrated that between 30% (in women) and 42% (in men) of heritable divorce risk was attributable to personality differences (Jocklin, McGue, & Lykken, 1996), and other work has shown the genetic association with controllable life events, of which divorce is one, is entirely explained by differences in personality (Saudino, Pedersen, Lichtenstein, McClearn, & Plomin, 1997).

Despite these associations, we have also shown that cotwin control studies (and similar research designs) have indicated that the association between relationship loss and health outcomes is nonspurious and may even be causal. To move closer to determining causality and identifying causal processes, Cohen and Janicki-Deverts (2009) advocated the increased use of randomized clinical trials; experimental methods are desperately needed to establish causality. Although work on this topic is largely lacking in the study of physical health outcomes, we have reviewed evidence indicating that progress is being made on this topic in mental health research. The critical next step for this literature is to study mechanisms. If couples therapy leads to improvements in major depression, what processes get set in motion that ultimately alleviate depressed mood? Plausible candidate mediators include not only decreases in perceived stress, decreases in loneliness, and increases in perceived control, but also the addition of salubrious processes directly related to the relationship itself—increased physical and sexual contact, greater communication, and more nurturance. Thus, to advance the study of relationships and health, we need experimental studies on physical health outcomes and, ultimately, an investigation of plausible mediators in both physical and mental health outcomes.

References

Almeida, D. M., McGonagle, K. A., Cate, R. C., Kessler, R. C., & Wethington, E. (2003). Psychosocial moderators of emotional reactivity to marital arguments: Results from a daily diary study. *Marriage and Family Review, 34,* 89–113.

Amato, P. R., & Hohmann-Marriott, B. (2007). A comparison of high- and low-distress marriages that end in divorce. *Journal of Marriage and Family, 69,* 621–638. doi:10.1111/j.1741-3737.2007.00396.x

American Psychiatric Association. (1994). *Diagnostic and statistical manual of mental disorders* (4th ed.). Washington, DC: Author.

Aron, A., Aron, E. N., Tudor, M., & Nelson, G. (1991). Close relationships as including other in the self. *Journal of Personality and Social Psychology, 60,* 241–253. doi:10.1037/0022-3514.60.2.241

Aron, A., Fisher, H., Mashek, D. J., Strong, G., Li, H., & Brown, L. L. (2005). Reward, motivation, and emotion systems associated with early-stage intense romantic love. *Journal of Neurophysiology, 94,* 327–337. doi:10.1152/jn.00838.2004

Baker, B., Paquette, M., Szalai, J. P., Driver, H., Perger, T., Helmers, K., . . . Tobe, S. (2000). The influence of marital adjustment on 3-year left ventricular mass and ambulatory blood pressure in mild hypertension. *Archives of Internal Medicine, 160,* 3453. doi:10.1001/archinte.160.22.3453

Barbato, A., & D'Avanzo, B. (2008). Efficacy of couple therapy as a treatment for depression: A meta-analysis. *Psychiatric Quarterly, 79,* 121–132. doi:10.1007/s11126-008-9068-0

Baum, A., & Grunberg, N. (1997). Measurement of stress hormones. In S. Cohen, R. C. Kessler, & L. U. Gordon (Eds.), *Measuring stress: A guide for health and social scientists* (pp. 175–192). New York, NY: Oxford University Press.

Bell, S., & Lee, C. (2008). Transitions in emerging adulthood and stress among young Australian women. *International Journal of Behavioral Medicine, 15,* 280–288. doi:10.1080/10705500802365482

Berkman, L. F., & Syme, S. L. (1979). Social networks, host resistance, and mortality: A nine-year follow-up study of Alameda County residents. *American Journal of Epidemiology, 109,* 186–204.

Berscheid, E. (1983). Emotion. In H. H. Kelley, E. Berscheid, A. Christensen, J. H. Harvey, T. L. Huston, G. Levinger, . . . Peterson, D. R. (Eds.), *Close relationships* (pp. 110–168). New York, NY: Freeman.

Black, P. H. (2006). The inflammatory consequences of psychologic stress: Relationship to insulin resistance, obesity, atherosclerosis and diabetes mellitus, type II. *Medical Hypotheses, 67,* 879–891. doi:10.1016/j.mehy.2006.04.008

Bolger, N., Zuckerman, A., & Kessler, R. C. (2000). Invisible support and adjustment to stress. *Journal of Personality and Social Psychology, 79,* 953–961. doi:10.1037/0022-3514.79.6.953

Bonanno, G. A. (2004). Loss, trauma, and human resilience: Have we underestimated the human capacity to thrive after extremely aversive events? *American Psychologist, 59,* 20–28. doi:10.1037/0003-066X.59.1.20

Bookwala, J., & Franks, M. M. (2005). Moderating role of marital quality in older adults' depressed affect: Beyond the main-effects model. *Journals of Gerontology, Series B: Psychological Sciences and Social Sciences, 60,* P338–P341. doi:10.1093/geronb/60.6.P338

Bowlby, J. (1969). *Attachment and loss: Vol. 1. Attachment* (2nd ed.). New York, NY: Basic Books.

Broadwell, S. D., & Light, K. C. (1999). Family support and cardiovascular responses in married couples during conflict and other interactions. *International Journal of Behavioral Medicine, 6,* 40–63. doi:10.1207/s15327558ijbm0601_4

Buchheim, A., Heinrichs, M., George, C., Pokorny, D., Koops, E., Henningsen, P., . . . Gündel, H. (2009). Oxytocin enhances the experience of attachment security. *Psychoneuroendocrinology, 34,* 1417–1422. doi:10.1016/j.psyneuen.2009.04.002

Buysse, D. J., Reynolds, C. F., Monk, T. H., Berman, S. R., & Kupfer, D. J. (1989). Pittsburgh Sleep Quality Index: A new instrument for psychiatric practice and research. *Psychiatry Research, 28,* 193–213. doi:10.1016/0165-1781(89)90047-4

Cacioppo, J. T., Hawkley, L. C., Crawford, E., Ernst, J. M., Burleson, M. H., Kowalewski, R. B., . . . Berntson, G. G. (2002). Loneliness and health: Potential mechanisms. *Psychosomatic Medicine, 64,* 407–417.

Cacioppo, J. T., Kiecolt-Glaser, J. K., Malarkey, W. B., Laskowski, B. F., Rozlog, L. A., Poehlmann, K. M., . . . Glaser, R. (2002). Autonomic and glucocorticoid associations with the steady-state expression of latent Epstein-Barr virus. *Hormones and Behavior, 42,* 32–41. doi:10.1006/hbeh.2002.1801

Call, V., Sprecher, S., & Schwartz, P. (1995). The incidence and frequency of marital sex in a national sample. *Journal of Marriage and the Family, 57,* 639–652. doi:10.2307/353919

Campbell, A. (2010). Oxytocin and human social behavior. *Personality and Social Psychology Review, 14,* 281–295. doi:10.1177/1088868310363594

Cano, A., & de C. Williams, A. C. (2010). Social interaction in pain: Reinforcing pain behaviors or building intimacy? *Pain, 149,* 9–11. doi:10.1016/j.pain.2009.10.010

Cano, A., Weisberg, J. N., & Gallagher, R. M. (2000). Marital satisfaction and pain severity mediate the association between negative spouse responses to pain and depressive symptoms in a chronic pain patient sample. *Pain Medicine, 1,* 35–43. doi:10.1046/j.1526-4637.2000.99100.x

Carter, C. S. (1998). Neuroendocrine perspectives on social attachment and love. *Psychoneuroendocrinology, 23,* 779–818. doi:10.1016/S0306-4530(98)00055-9

Caryl, P. G., Bean, J. E., Smallwood, E. B., Barron, J. C., Tully, L., & Allerhand, M. (2009). Women's preference for male pupil-size: Effects of conception risk, sociosexuality, and relationship status. *Personality and Individual Differences, 46,* 503–508. doi:10.1016/j.paid.2008.11.024

Cassel, J. (1976). The contribution of the social environment to host resistance. *American Journal of Epidemiology, 104,* 107–123.

Christian, L. M., Graham, J. E., Padgett, D. A., Glaser, R., & Kiecolt-Glaser, J. K. (2006). Stress and wound healing. *Neuroimmunomodulation, 13,* 337–346. doi:10.1159/000104862

Clodi, M., Vila, G., Geyeregger, R., Riedl, M., Stulnig, T. M., Struck, J., . . . Luger, A. (2008). Oxytocin alleviates the neuroendocrine and cytokine response to bacterial endotoxin in healthy men. *American Journal of Physiology. Endocrinology and Metabolism, 295,* E686–E691. doi:10.1152/ajpendo.90263.2008

Clow, A., Hucklebridge, F., Stalder, T., Evans, P., & Thorn, L. (2010). The cortisol awakening response: More than a measure of HPA axis function. *Neuroscience and Biobehavioral Reviews, 35,* 97–103.

Cobb, S. (1976). Presidential Address—1976: Social support as a moderator of life stress. *Psychosomatic Medicine, 38,* 300–314.

Cohen, S., & Janicki-Deverts, D. (2009). Can we improve our physical health by altering our social networks? *Perspectives on Psychological Science, 4,* 375–378. doi:10.1111/j.1745-6924.2009.01141.x

Cohen, S., & Willis, T. A. (1985). Stress, social support and the buffering hypothesis. *Psychological Bulletin, 98,* 310–357. doi:10.1037/0033-2909.98.2.310

Cole, S. W. (2009). Social regulation of human gene expression. *Current Directions in Psychological Science, 18,* 132–137. doi:10.1111/j.1467-8721.2009.01623.x

Coyne, J. C., & DeLongis, A. (1986). Going beyond social support: The role of social relationships in adaptation. *Journal of Consulting and Clinical Psychology, 54,* 454–460. doi:10.1037/0022-006X.54.4.454

Coyne, J. C., & Downey, G. (1991). Social factors and psychopathology: Stress, social support, and coping processes. *Annual Review of Psychology, 42,* 401–425. doi:10.1146/annurev.ps.42.020191.002153

Coyne, J. C., Rohrbaugh, M. J., Shoham, V., Sonnega, J. S., Nicklas, J. M., & Cranford, J. A. (2001). Prognostic importance of marital quality for survival of congestive heart failure. *American Journal of Cardiology, 88,* 526–529. doi:10.1016/S0002-9149(01)01731-3

Coyne, J. C., & Thombs, B. D. (2008). Was it shown that "close relationships and emotional processing predict decreased mortality in women with breast cancer?" A critique of Weihs et al. (2008). *Psychosomatic Medicine, 70,* 737–738. doi:10.1097/PSY.0b013e318180f26e

Coyne, J. C., Wortman, C. B., & Lehman, D. R. (1988). The other side of support: Emotional overinvolvement and miscarried helping. In B. H. Gottlieb (Ed.), *Marshaling social support: Formats, processes, and effects* (pp. 305–330). San Diego, CA: Sage.

Cupach, W. R. (2000). Advancing understanding of relational conflict. *Journal of Social and Personal Relationships, 17,* 697–703. doi:10.1177/0265407500174013

Diamond, L. M. (2001). Contributions of psychophysiology to research on adult attachment: Review and recommendations. *Personality and Social Psychology Review, 5,* 276–295. doi:10.1207/S15327957PSPR0504_1

Diamond, L. M., Hicks, A. M., & Otter-Henderson, K. D. (2008). Every time you go away: Changes in affect, behavior, and physiology associated with travel-related separations from romantic partners. *Journal of Personality and Social Psychology, 95,* 385–403. doi:10.1037/0022-3514.95.2.385

Ditzen, B., Neumann, I. D., Bodenmann, G., von Dawans, B., Turner, R. A., Ehlert, U., & Heinrichs, M. (2007). Effects of different kinds of couple interaction on cortisol and heart rate responses to stress in women. *Psychoneuroendocrinology, 32,* 565–574. doi:10.1016/j.psyneuen.2007.03.011

Ditzen, B., Schaer, M., Gabriel, B., Bodenmann, G., Ehlert, U., & Heinrichs, M. (2009). Intranasal oxytocin increases positive communication and reduces cortisol levels during couple conflict. *Biological Psychiatry, 65,* 728–731. doi:10.1016/j.biopsych.2008.10.011

Dupre, M. E., Beck, A. N., & Meadows, S. O. (2009). Marital trajectories and mortality among U.S. adults. *American Journal of Epidemiology, 170,* 546–555. doi:10.1093/aje/kwp194

Eaker, E. D., Sullivan, L. M., Kelly-Hayes, M., D'Agostino, R. B., Sr., & Benjamin, E. J. (2007). Marital status, marital strain, and risk of coronary heart disease or total mortality: The Framingham Offspring Study. *Psychosomatic Medicine, 69,* 509–513. doi:10.1097/PSY.0b013e3180f62357

Elwert, F., & Christakis, N. A. (2008a). The effect of widowhood on mortality by the causes of death of both spouses. *American Journal of Public Health, 98,* 2092–2098. doi:10.2105/AJPH.2007.114348

Elwert, F., & Christakis, N. A. (2008b). Wives and ex-wives: A new test for homogamy bias in the widowhood effect. *Demography, 45,* 851–873. doi:10.1353/dem.0.0029

Emanuele, E., Politi, P., Bianchi, M., Minoretti, P., Bertona, M., & Geroldi, D. (2006). Raised plasma nerve growth factor levels associated with early-stage romantic love. *Psychoneuroendocrinology, 31,* 288–294.

Emmers, T. M., & Dindia, K. (1995). The effect of relational stage and intimacy on touch: An extension of Guerrero and Andersen. *Personal Relationships, 2,* 225–236. doi:10.1111/j.1475-6811.1995.tb00088.x

Ewart, C. K., Taylor, C. B., Kraemer, H. C., & Agras, W. S. (1991). High blood pressure and marital discord: Not being nasty matters more than being nice. *Health Psychology, 10,* 155–163. doi:10.1037/0278-6133.10.3.155

Farr, W. (1858). The influence of marriage on the mortality of French people. In *Transactions of the National Association for the Promotion of Social Science* (pp. 504–513). London, England: John W. Parker.

Fisher, H. E. (1998). Lust, attraction, and attachment in mammalian reproduction. *Human Nature, 9,* 23–52. doi:10.1007/s12110-998-1010-5

Ford, E. S., Giles, W. H., & Dietz, W. H. (2002). Prevalence of the metabolic syndrome among US adults. *JAMA, 287,* 356–359. doi:10.1001/jama.287.3.356

Fordyce, W. E. (1976). *Behavioral methods for chronic pain and illness.* St. Louis, MO: Mosby.

Fries, E., Dettenborn, L., & Kirschbaum, C. (2009). The cortisol awakening response (CAR): Facts and future directions. *International Journal of Psychophysiology, 72,* 67–73. doi:10.1016/j.ijpsycho.2008.03.014

Fu, H., & Goldman, N. (2000). The association between health-related behaviours and the risk of divorce in the USA. *Journal of Biosocial Science, 32,* 63–88. doi:10.1017/S0021932000000638

Gallace, A., & Spence, C. (2010). The science of interpersonal touch: An overview. *Neuroscience and Biobehavioral Reviews, 34,* 246–259. doi:10.1016/j.neubiorev.2008.10.004

Gangestad, S. W., & Buss, D. M. (1993). Pathogen prevalence and human mate preferences. *Ethology and Sociobiology, 14,* 89–96. doi:10.1016/0162-3095(93)90009-7

Gangestad, S. W., Garver-Apgar, C. E., Simpson, J. A., & Cousins, A. J. (2007). Changes in women's mate preferences across the ovulatory cycle. *Journal of Personality and Social Psychology, 92,* 151–163. doi:10.1037/0022-3514.92.1.151

Gangestad, S. W., & Simpson, J. A. (2000). The evolution of human mating: Trade-offs and strategic pluralism. *Behavioral and Brain Sciences, 23,* 573–587. doi:10.1017/S0140525X0000337X

Garver-Apgar, C. E., Gangestad, S. W., Thornhill, R., Miller, R. D., & Olp, J. J. (2006). Major histocompatibility complex alleles, sexual responsivity, and unfaithfulness in romantic couples. *Psychological Science, 17,* 830–835. doi:10.1111/j.1467-9280.2006.01789.x

Gonzaga, G. C., Turner, R. A., Keltner, D., Campos, B., & Altemus, M. (2006). Romantic love and sexual desire in close relationships. *Emotion, 6,* 163–179. doi:10.1037/1528-3542.6.2.163

Gouin, J.-P., Carter, C. S., Pournajafi-Nazarloo, H., Glaser, R., Malarkey, W. B., Loving, T. J., . . . Kiecolt-Glaser, J. K. (2010). Marital behavior, oxytocin, vasopressin, and wound healing. *Psychoneuroendocrinology, 35,* 1082–1090. doi:10.1016/j.psyneuen.2010.01.009

Gouin, J.-P., Carter, C. S., Pournajafi-Nazarloo, H., Malarkey, W. B., Loving, T. J., Stowell, J., & Kiecolt-Glaser, J. K. (2012). Plasma vasopressin and interpersonal functioning. *Biological Psychology, 91,* 270–274. doi:10.1016/j.biopsycho.2012.07.003

Gouin, J.-P., Glaser, R., Loving, T. J., Malarkey, W. B., Stowell, J., Houts, C., & Kiecolt-Glaser, J. K. (2009). Attachment avoidance predicts inflammatory responses to marital conflict. *Brain, Behavior, and Immunity, 23,* 898–904. doi:10.1016/j.bbi.2008.09.016

Graham, J. E., Glaser, R., Loving, T. J., Malarkey, W. B., Stowell, J. R., & Kiecolt-Glaser, J. K. (2009). Cognitive word use during marital conflict and increases in proinflammatory cytokines. *Health Psychology, 28,* 621–630. doi:10.1037/a0015208

Granger, D. A., Kivlighan, K. T., Blair, C., El-Sheikh, M., Mize, J., Lisonbee, J. A., . . . Schwartz, E. B. (2006). Integrating the measurement of salivary alpha-amylase into studies of child health, development, and social relationships. *Journal of*

Social and Personal Relationships, 23, 267–290. doi:10.1177/0265407506062479

Grewen, K. M., Anderson, B. J., Girdler, S. S., & Light, K. C. (2003). Warm partner contact is related to lower cardiovascular reactivity. *Behavioral Medicine, 29,* 123–130. doi:10.1080/08964280309596065

Grippo, A. J., Trahanas, D. M., Zimmerman, R. R., II, Porges, S. W., & Carter, C. S. (2009). Oxytocin protects against negative behavioral and autonomic consequences of long-term social isolation. *Psychoneuroendocrinology, 34,* 1542–1553. doi:10.1016/j.psyneuen.2009.05.017

Guerrero, L. K., & Andersen, P. A. (1994). Patterns of matching and initiation: Touch behavior and touch avoidance across romantic relationship stages. *Journal of Nonverbal Behavior, 18,* 137–153. doi:10.1007/BF02170075

Gump, B. B., Polk, D. E., Kamarck, T. W., & Shiffman, S. M. (2001). Partner interactions are associated with reduced blood pressure in the natural environment: Ambulatory monitoring evidence from a healthy, multiethnic adult sample. *Psychosomatic Medicine, 63,* 423–433.

Gunlicks-Stoessel, M. L., & Powers, S. I. (2009). Romantic partners' coping strategies and partners of cortisol reactivity and recovery in response to relationship conflict. *Journal of Social and Clinical Psychology, 28,* 630–649. doi:10.1521/jscp.2009.28.5.630

Hale, L. (2010). Sleep as a mechanism though which social relationships affect health. *Sleep, 33,* 862–863.

Hardt, J., Jacobsen, C., Goldberg, J., Nickel, R., & Buchwald, D. (2008). Prevalence of chronic pain in a representative sample in the United States. *Pain Medicine, 9,* 803–812. doi:10.1111/j.1526-4637.2008.00425.x

Heffner, K. L., Kiecolt-Glaser, J. K., Loving, T. J., Glaser, R., & Malarkey, W. B. (2004). Spousal support satisfaction as a modifier of physiological responses to marital conflict in younger and older couples. *Journal of Behavioral Medicine, 27,* 233–254. doi:10.1023/B:JOBM.0000028497.79129.ad

Heinrichs, M., Baumgartner, T., Kirschbaum, C., & Ehlert, U. (2003). Social support and oxytocin interact to suppress cortisol and subjective responses to psychosocial stress. *Biological Psychiatry, 54,* 1389–1398. doi:10.1016/S0006-3223(03)00465-7

Hicks, A. M., & Diamond, L. M. (2011). Don't go to bed angry: Attachment, conflict, and affective and physiological reactivity. *Personal Relationships, 18,* 266–284. doi:10.1111/j.1475-6811.2011.01355.x

Hoevenaar-Blom, M. P., Spijkerman, A. M. W., Kromhout, D., van den Berg, J. F., & Verschuren, W. M. M. (2011). Sleep duration and sleep quality in relation to 12-year cardiovascular disease incidence: The MORGEN study. *Sleep, 34,* 1487–1492.

Holmes, T. H., & Rahe, R. H. (1967). The Social Readjustment Rating scale. *Journal of Psychosomatic Research, 11,* 213–218. doi:10.1016/0022-3999(67)90010-4

Holt-Lunstad, J., Birmingham, W., & Jones, B. Q. (2008). Is there something unique about marriage? The relative impact of marital status, relationship quality, and network social support on ambulatory blood pressure and mental health. *Annals of Behavioral Medicine, 35,* 239–244. doi:10.1007/s12160-008-9018-y

Holt-Lunstad, J., Smith, T. B., & Layton, J. B. (2010). Social relationships and mortality risk: A meta-analytic review. *PLoS Medicine, 7,* e1000316. doi:10.1371/journal.pmed.1000316

House, J. S., Landis, K. R., & Umberson, D. (1988). Social relationships and health. *Science, 241,* 540–545. doi:10.1126/science.3399889

Jacobson, N. S., & Truax, P. (1991). Clinical significance: A statistical approach to defining meaningful change in psychotherapy research. *Journal of Consulting and Clinical Psychology, 59,* 12–19. doi:10.1037/0022-006X.59.1.12

Jamison, T. B., & Proulx, C. M. (2012). Stayovers in emerging adulthood: Who stays over and why? *Personal Relationships, 20,* 155–169.

Janicki, D. L., Kamarck, T. W., Shiffman, S., Sutton-Tyrrell, K., & Gwaltney, C. J. (2005). Frequency of spousal interaction and 3-year progression of carotid artery intima medial thickness: The Pittsburgh Healthy Heart Project. *Psychosomatic Medicine, 67,* 889–896. doi:10.1097/01.psy.0000188476.87869.88

Jaremka, L. M., Glaser, R., Loving, T. J., Malarkey, W. B., Stowell, J. R., & Kiecolt-Glaser, J. K. (2013). Attachment anxiety is linked to alterations in cortisol production and cellular immunity. *Psychological Science, 24,* 272–279.

Jocklin, V., McGue, M., & Lykken, D. T. (1996). Personality and divorce: A genetic analysis. *Journal of Personality and Social Psychology, 71,* 288–299. doi:10.1037/0022-3514.71.2.288

Kelley, H. H., & Thibaut, J. W. (1978). *Interpersonal relations: A theory of interdependence.* New York, NY: Wiley-Interscience.

Kerns, R. D., Haythornthwaite, J., Southwick, S., & Giller, E. L. (1990). The role of marital interaction in chronic pain and depressive symptom severity. *Journal of Psychosomatic Research, 34,* 401–408. doi:10.1016/0022-3999(90)90063-A

Kessler, R. C. (1979). Stress, social status, and psychological distress. *Journal of Health and Social Behavior, 20,* 259–272. doi:10.2307/2136450

Kiecolt-Glaser, J. K., Fisher, L. D., Ogrocki, P., Stout, J. C., Speicher, C. E., & Glaser, R. (1987). Marital quality, marital disruption, and immune function. *Psychosomatic Medicine, 49,* 13–34.

Kiecolt-Glaser, J. K., & Glaser, R. (1997). Measurement of immune response. In S. Cohen, R. C. Kessler, & L. U. Gordon (Eds.), *Measuring stress: A guide for health and social scientists* (pp. 213–229). New York, NY: Oxford University Press.

Kiecolt-Glaser, J. K., Gouin, J.-P., & Hantsoo, L. (2010). Close relationships, inflammation, and health. *Neuroscience and Biobehavioral Reviews, 35,* 33–38. doi:10.1016/j.neubiorev.2009.09.003

Kiecolt-Glaser, J. K., Loving, T. J., Stowell, J. R., Malarkey, W. B., Lemeshow, S., Dickinson, S. L., & Glaser, R. (2005). Hostile marital interactions, proinflammatory cytokine production, and wound healing. *Archives of General Psychiatry, 62,* 1377–1384. doi:10.1001/archpsyc.62.12.1377

Kiecolt-Glaser, J. K., Malarkey, W. B., Chee, M., Newton, T., Cacioppo, J. T., Mao, H., & Glaser, R. (1993). Negative behavior during marital conflict is associated with immunological down-regulation. *Psychosomatic Medicine, 55,* 395–409.

Kiecolt-Glaser, J. K., & Newton, T. L. (2001). Marriage and health: His and hers. *Psychological Bulletin, 127,* 472–503. doi:10.1037/0033-2909.127.4.472

Kiecolt-Glaser, J. K., Newton, T., Cacioppo, J. T., MacCallum, R. C., Glaser, R., & Malarkey, W. B. (1996). Marital conflict and endocrine function: Are men really more physiologically affected than women? *Journal of Consulting and Clinical Psychology, 64,* 324–332. doi:10.1037/0022-006X.64.2.324

Kposowa, A. J. (2000). Marital status and suicide in the National Longitudinal Mortality Study. *Journal of Epidemiology and Community Health, 54,* 254–261. doi:10.1136/jech.54.4.254

Kurdek, L. A. (1994). Areas of conflict for gay, lesbian, and heterosexual couples: What couples argue about influences relationship satisfaction. *Journal of Marriage and the Family, 56,* 923–934. doi:10.2307/353603

Laurent, H., & Powers, S. (2007). Emotion regulation in emerging adult couples: Temperament, attachment, and HPA response to conflict. *Biological Psychology, 76,* 61–71. doi:10.1016/j.biopsycho.2007.06.002

Laursen, B. (1995). Conflict and social interaction in adolescent relationships. *Journal of Research on Adolescence, 5,* 55–70. doi:10.1207/s15327795jra0501_3

Lee, C., & Gramotnev, H. (2007). Life transitions and mental health in a national cohort of young Australian women. *Developmental Psychology, 43,* 877–888. doi:10.1037/0012-1649.43.4.877

Leonard, M. T., Cano, A., & Johansen, A. B. (2006). Chronic pain in a couples context: A review and integration of theoretical models and empirical evidence. *Journal of Pain, 7,* 377–390. doi:10.1016/j.jpain.2006.01.442

Lepore, S. J., Allen, K. M., & Evans, G. W. (1993). Social support lowers cardiovascular reactivity to an acute stressor. *Psychosomatic Medicine, 55,* 518–524.

Lepore, S. J., & Greenberg, M. A. (2002). Mending broken hearts: Effects of expressive writing on mood, cognitive processing, social adjustment and health following a relationship breakup. *Psychology and Health, 17,* 547–560. doi:10.1080/08870440290025768

Lett, H. S., Blumenthal, J. A., Babyak, M. A., Strauman, T. J., Robins, C., & Sherwood, A. (2005). Social support and coronary heart disease: Epidemiologic evidence and implications for treatment. *Psychosomatic Medicine, 67,* 869–878. doi:10.1097/01.psy.0000188393.73571.0a

Lichtenstein, P., Gatz, M., & Berg, S. (1998). A twin study of mortality after spousal bereavement. *Psychological Medicine, 28,* 635–643. doi:10.1017/S0033291798006692

Light, K. C., Grewen, K. M., & Amico, J. A. (2005). More frequent partner hugs and higher oxytocin levels are linked to lower blood pressure and heart rate in premenopausal women. *Biological Psychology, 69,* 5–21. doi:10.1016/j.biopsycho.2004.11.002

Liu, D., Diorio, J., Tannenbaum, B., Caldji, C., Francis, D., & Freedman, A., . . . Meaney, M. J. (1997). Maternal care, hippocampal glucocorticoid receptors, and hypothalamic-pituitary-adrenal responses to stress. *Science, 277,* 1659–1662.

Lloyd-Jones, D., Adams, R. J., Brown, T. M., Carnethon, M., Dai, S., De Simone, G., . . . Gillespie, C. (2010). Executive summary: Heart disease and stroke statistics—2010 update: A report from the American Heart Association. *Circulation, 121,* 948–954. doi:10.1161/CIRCULATIONAHA.109.192666

Loving, T. J., & Campbell, L. (2011). Mind–body connections in personal relationships: What close relationships researchers have to offer. *Personal Relationships, 18,* 165–169. doi:10.1111/j.1475-6811.2011.01361.x

Loving, T. J., Crockett, E. E., & Paxson, A. A. (2009). Passionate love and relationship thinkers: Experimental evidence for acute cortisol elevations in women. *Psychoneuroendocrinology, 34,* 939–946. doi:10.1016/j.psyneuen.2009.01.010

Loving, T. J., Heffner, K. L., & Kiecolt-Glaser, J. K. (2006). Physiology and interpersonal relationships. In A. Vangelisti & D. Perlman (Eds.), *Cambridge handbook of personal relationships* (pp. 385–406). New York, NY: Cambridge University Press. doi:10.1017/CBO9780511606632.022

Loving, T. J., & Wright, B. L. (2012). Eustress in romantic relationships. In L. Campbell, J. G. La Guardia, J. M. Olson, & M. P. Zanna (Eds.), *The science of the couple* (Vol. 12, pp. 169–184). New York, NY: Psychology Press.

Lucas, R. E. (2005). Time does not heal all wounds: A longitudinal study of reaction and adaptation to divorce. *Psychological Science, 16,* 945–950. doi:10.1111/j.1467-9280.2005.01642.x

Malarkey, W. B., Kiecolt-Glaser, J. K., Pearl, D., & Glaser, R. (1994). Hostile behavior during marital conflict alters pituitary and adrenal hormones. *Psychosomatic Medicine, 56,* 41–51.

Mancini, A. D., Bonanno, G. A., & Clark, A. E. (2011). Stepping off the hedonic treadmill. *Journal of Individual Differences, 32,* 144–152. doi:10.1027/1614-0001/a000047

Manne, S. (1998). Psychosocial issues: Cancer in the marital context: A review of the literature. *Cancer Investigation, 16,* 188–202. doi:10.3109/07357909809050036

Manne, S. L., Taylor, K. L., Dougherty, J., & Kemeny, N. (1997). Supportive and negative responses in the partner relationship: Their association with psychological adjustment among individuals with cancer. *Journal of Behavioral Medicine, 20,* 101–125. doi:10.1023/A:1025574626454

Marazziti, D. (2005). The neurobiology of love. *Current Psychiatry Reviews, 1,* 331–335. doi:10.2174/157340005774575037

Marazziti, D., Akiskal, H. S., Rossi, A., & Cassano, G. B. (1999). Alteration of the platelet serotonin transporter in romantic love. *Psychological Medicine, 29,* 741–745. doi:10.1017/S0033291798007946

Marazziti, D., & Canale, D. (2004). Hormonal changes when falling in love. *Psychoneuroendocrinology, 29,* 931–936. doi:10.1016/j.psyneuen.2003.08.006

McEwen, B. S. (1998). Stress, adaptation, and disease: Allostasis and allostatic load. *Annals of the New York Academy of Sciences, 840,* 33–44.

McGonagle, K. A., Kessler, R. C., & Schilling, E. A. (1992). The frequency and determinants of marital disagreements in a community sample. *Journal of Social and Personal Relationships, 9,* 507–524. doi:10.1177/0265407592094003

McGue, M., & Lykken, D. T. (1992). Genetic influence on risk of divorce. *Psychological Science, 3,* 368–373. doi:10.1111/j.1467-9280.1992.tb00049.x

Meaney, M. J. (2001). Maternal care, gene expression, and the transmission of individual differences in stress reactivity across generations. *Annual Review of Neuroscience, 24,* 1161–1192.

Mearns, J. (1991). Coping with a breakup: Negative mood regulation expectancies and depression following the end of a romantic relationship. *Journal of Personality and Social Psychology, 60,* 327–334. doi:10.1037/0022-3514.60.2.327

Merjonen, P., Pulkki-Råback, L., Lipsanen, J., Lehtimäki, T., Rontu, R., Viikari, J., . . . Keltikangas-Järvinen, L.

(2011). Development of adulthood hostile attitudes: Childhood environment and serotonin receptor gene interactions. *Personal Relationships, 18,* 184–197. doi:10.1111/j.1475-6811.2010.01321.x

Miller, A. H. (1998). Neuroendocrine and immune system interactions in stress and depression. *Psychiatric Clinics of North America, 21,* 443–463. doi:10.1016/S0193-953X(05)70015-0

Miller, G., Chen, E., & Cole, S. W. (2009). Health psychology: Developing biologically plausible models linking the social world and physical health. *Annual Review of Psychology, 60,* 501–524. doi:10.1146/annurev.psych.60.110707.163551

Miller, G. E., Chen, E., Fok, A. K., Walker, H., Lim, A., & Nicholls, E. F.. . . Kobor, M. S. (2009). Low early-life social class leaves a biological residue manifested by decreased glucocorticoid and increased proinflammatory signaling. *Proceedings of the National Academy of Sciences, USA, 106,* 14716–14721.

Miller, G. E., Chen, E., & Parker, K. J. (2011). Psychological stress in childhood and susceptibility to the chronic diseases of aging: Moving toward a model of behavioral and biological mechanisms. *Psychological Bulletin, 137,* 959–997. doi:10.1037/a0024768

Monroe, S. M., Rohde, P., Seeley, J. R., & Lewinsohn, P. M. (1999). Life events and depression in adolescence: Relationship loss as a prospective risk factor for first onset of major depressive disorder. *Journal of Abnormal Psychology, 108,* 606–614. doi:10.1037/0021-843X.108.4.606

Mookadam, F., & Arthur, H. M. (2004). Social support and its relationship to morbidity and mortality after acute myocardial infarction: Systematic overview. *Archives of Internal Medicine, 164,* 1514–1518. doi:10.1001/archinte.164.14.1514

Motivala, S., & Irwin, M. (2007). Sleep and immunity: Cytokine pathways linking sleep and health outcomes. *Current Directions in Psychological Science, 16,* 21–25. doi:10.1111/j.1467-8721.2007.00468.x

Nater, U. M., & Rohleder, N. (2009). Salivary alpha-amylase as a non-invasive biomarker for the sympathetic nervous system: Current state of research. *Psychoneuroendocrinology, 34,* 486–496. doi:10.1016/j.psyneuen.2009.01.014

Nealey-Moore, J. B., Smith, T. W., Uchino, B. N., Hawkins, M. W., & Olson-Cerny, C. (2007). Cardiovascular reactivity during positive and negative marital interactions. *Journal of Behavioral Medicine, 30,* 505–519. doi:10.1007/s10865-007-9124-5

Newton, T. L., & Sanford, J. M. (2003). Conflict structure moderates associations between cardiovascular reactivity and negative marital interactions. *Health Psychology, 22,* 270–278. doi:10.1037/0278-6133.22.3.270

Niaura, R., Todaro, J. F., Stroud, L., Spiro, A., III, Ward, K. D., & Weiss, S. (2002). Hostility, the metabolic syndrome, and incident coronary heart disease. *Health Psychology, 21,* 588. doi:10.1037/0278-6133.21.6.588

Oberlander, T. F., Weinberg, J., Papsdorf, M., Grunau, R., Misri, S., & Devlin, A. M. (2008). Prenatal exposure to maternal depression, neonatal methylation of human glucocorticoid receptor gene (NR3C1) and infant cortisol stress responses. *Epigenetics, 3,* 97–106. doi:10.4161/epi.3.2.6034

O'Connor, M. F., Wellisch, D. K., Stanton, A. L., Olmstead, R., & Irwin, M. R. (2012). Diurnal cortisol in complicated and non-complicated grief: Slope differences across the day. *Psychoneuroendocrinology, 37,* 725–728.

O'Connor, T. G., Cheng, H., Dunn, J., & Golding, J. (2005). Factors moderating change in depressive symptoms in women following separation: Findings from a community study in England. *Psychological Medicine, 35,* 715–724.

Orth-Gomér, K., & Leineweber, C. (2005). Multiple stressors and coronary disease in women: The Stockholm Female Coronary Risk Study. *Biological Psychology, 69,* 57–66. doi:10.1016/j.biopsycho.2004.11.005

Orth-Gomér, K., Wamala, S. P., Horsten, M., Schenck-Gustafsson, K., Schneiderman, N., & Mittleman, M. A. (2000). Marital stress worsens prognosis in women with coronary heart disease. *JAMA, 284,* 3008–3014. doi:10.1001/jama.284.23.3008

Osler, M., McGue, M., Lund, R., & Christensen, K. (2008). Marital status and twins' health and behavior: An analysis of middle-aged Danish twins. *Psychosomatic Medicine, 70,* 482–487. doi:10.1097/PSY.0b013e31816f857b

O'Sullivan, L. F., Mantsun, M., Harris, K. M., & Brooks-Gunn, J. (2007). I wanna hold your hand: The progression of social, romantic and sexual events in adolescent relationships. *Perspectives on Sexual and Reproductive Health, 39,* 100–107. doi:10.1363/3910007

Otten, U., Baumann, J. B., & Girard, J. (1979). Stimulation of the pituitary-adrenocortical axis by nerve growth factor. *Nature, 282,* 413–414. doi:10.1038/282413a0

Palin, K., Moreau, M. L., Sauvant, J., Orcel, H., Nadjar, A., Duvoid-Guillou, A., . . . Moos, F. (2009). Interleukin-6 activates arginine vasopressin neurons in the supraoptic nucleus during immune challenge in rats. *American Journal of Physiology, Endocrinology and Metabolism, 296,* E1289–E1299. doi:10.1152/ajpendo.90489.2008

Papp, L. M., Cummings, E. M., & Goeke-Morey, M. C. (2009). For richer, for poorer: Money as a topic of marital conflict in the home. *Family Relations: Interdisciplinary Journal of Applied Family Studies, 58,* 91–103. doi:10.1111/j.1741-3729.2008.00537.x

Parkes, C. M., Benjamin, B., & Fitzgerald, R. G. (1969). Broken heart: A statistical study of increased mortality among widowers. *British Medical Journal, 1,* 740. doi:10.1136/bmj.1.5646.740

Pennebaker, J. W. (1992). Inhibition as the linchpin of health. In H. S. Friedman (Ed.), *Hostility, coping, and health* (pp. 127–139). Washington, DC: American Psychological Association. doi:10.1037/10105-009

Pennebaker, J. W. (1997). *Opening up: The healing power of expressing emotions.* New York, NY: Guilford Press.

Perilloux, H. K., Webster, G. D., & Gaulin, S. J. C. (2010). Signals of genetic quality and maternal investment capacity: The dynamic effects of fluctuating asymmetry and waist-to-hip ratio on men's ratings of women's attractiveness. *Social Psychological and Personality Science, 1,* 34–42.

Pienta, A. M., Hayward, M. D., & Jenkins, K. R. (2000). Health consequences of marriage for the retirement years. *Journal of Family Issues, 21,* 559–586. doi:10.1177/019251300021005003

Pinquart, M., & Duberstein, P. R. (2010). Associations of social networks with cancer mortality: A meta-analysis. *Critical Reviews in Oncology/Hematology, 75,* 122–137. doi:10.1016/j.critrevonc.2009.06.003

Powers, M. B., Vedel, E., & Emmelkamp, P. M. G. (2008). Behavioral couples therapy (BCT) for alcohol and drug use disorders: A meta-analysis. *Clinical Psychology Review, 28,* 952–962. doi:10.1016/j.cpr.2008.02.002

Powers, S. I., Pietromonaco, P. R., Gunlicks, M., & Sayer, A. (2006). Dating couples' attachment styles and patterns of cortisol reactivity and recovery in response to a relationship conflict. *Journal of Personality and Social Psychology, 90,* 613–628. doi:10.1037/0022-3514.90.4.613

Priem, J. S., & Solomon, D. H. (2011). Relational uncertainty and cortisol responses to hurtful and supportive messages from a dating partner. *Personal Relationships, 18,* 198–223. doi:10.1111/j.1475-6811.2011.01353.x

Prigerson, H. G., Horowitz, M. J., Jacobs, S. C., Parkes, C. M., Aslan, M., Goodkin, K., . . . Neimeyer, R. A. (2009). Prolonged grief disorder: Psychometric validation of criteria proposed for DSM-V and ICD-11. *PLoS Medicine, 6,* e1000121. doi:10.1371/journal.pmed.1000121

Proulx, C. M., Helms, H. M., & Buehler, C. (2007). Marital quality and personal well-being: A meta-analysis. *Journal of Marriage and Family, 69,* 576–593. doi:10.1111/j.1741-3737.2007.00393.x

Quirin, M., Kuhl, J., & Dusing, R. (2011). Oxytocin buffers cortisol responses to stress in individuals with impaired emotion regulation abilities. *Psychoneuroendocrinology, 36,* 898–904. doi:10.1016/j.psyneuen.2010.12.005

Rahe, R. H., Meyer, M., Smith, M., Kjaer, G., & Holmes, T. H. (1964). Social stress and illness onset. *Journal of Psychosomatic Research, 8,* 35–44. doi:10.1016/0022-3999(64)90020-0

Raichle, K. A., Romano, J. M., & Jensen, M. P. (2011). Partner responses to patient pain and well behaviors and their relationship to patient pain behavior, functioning, and depression. *Pain, 152,* 82–88. doi:10.1016/j.pain.2010.09.015

Reich, J. W., & Zautra, A. (1981). Life events and personal causation: Some relationships with satisfaction and distress. *Journal of Personality and Social Psychology, 41,* 1002–1012. doi:10.1037/0022-3514.41.5.1002

Robertson, K. D., & Wolffe, A. P. (2000). DNA methylation in health and disease. *Nature Reviews Genetics, 1,* 11–19. doi:10.1038/35049533

Robles, T. F., & Kiecolt-Glaser, J. K. (2003). The physiology of marriage: Pathways to health. *Physiology and Behavior, 79,* 409–416. doi:10.1016/S0031-9384(03)00160-4

Robles, T. F., Shaffer, V. A., Malarkey, W. B., & Kiecolt-Glaser, J. K. (2006). Positive behaviors during marital conflict: Influences on stress hormones. *Journal of Social and Personal Relationships, 23,* 305–325. doi:10.1177/0265407506062482

Rohleder, N., & Nater, U. M. (2009). Determinants of salivary α-amylase in humans and methodological considerations. *Psychoneuroendocrinology, 34,* 469–485. doi:10.1016/j.psyneuen.2008.12.004

Rohleder, N., Wolf, J. M., Maldonado, E. F., & Kirschbaum, C. (2006). The psychosocial stress-induced increase in salivary alpha-amylase is independent of saliva flow rate. *Psychophysiology, 43,* 645–652. doi:10.1111/j.1469-8986.2006.00457.x

Rohrbaugh, M. J., Mehl, M. R., Shoham, V., Reilly, E. S., & Ewy, G. A. (2008). Prognostic significance of spouse *we* talk in couples coping with heart failure. *Journal of Consulting and Clinical Psychology, 76,* 781–789. doi:10.1037/a0013238

Rohrbaugh, M. J., Shoham, V., & Coyne, J. C. (2006). Effect of marital quality on eight-year survival of patients with heart failure. *American Journal of Cardiology, 98,* 1069–1072. doi:10.1016/j.amjcard.2006.05.034

Rohrbaugh, M. J., Shoham, V., Coyne, J. C., Cranford, J. A., Sonnega, J. S., & Nicklas, J. M. (2004). Beyond the "self" in self-efficacy: Spouse confidence predicts patient survival following heart failure. *Journal of Family Psychology, 18,* 184–193. doi:10.1037/0893-3200.18.1.184

Ross, C. E. (1995). Reconceptualizing marital status as a continuum of social attachment. *Journal of Marriage and the Family, 57,* 129–140. doi:10.2307/353822

Saudino, K. J., Pedersen, N. L., Lichtenstein, P., McClearn, G. E., & Plomin, R. (1997). Can personality explain genetic influences on life events? *Journal of Personality and Social Psychology, 72,* 196–206. doi:10.1037/0022-3514.72.1.196

Sbarra, D. A., Law, R. W., Lee, L. A., & Mason, A. E. (2009). Marital dissolution and blood pressure reactivity: Evidence for the specificity of emotional intrusion-hyperarousal and task-rated emotional difficulty. *Psychosomatic Medicine, 71,* 532–540. doi:10.1097/PSY.0b013e3181a23eee

Sbarra, D. A., Law, R. W., & Portley, R. M. (2011). Divorce and death: A meta-analysis and research agenda for clinical, social, and health psychology. *Perspectives on Psychological Science, 6,* 454–474. doi:10.1177/1745691611414724

Sbarra, D. A., & Nietert, P. J. (2009). Divorce and death: Forty years of the Charleston Heart Study. *Psychological Science, 20,* 107–113. doi:10.1111/j.1467-9280.2008.02252.x

Scarr, S., & McCartney, K. (1983). How people make their own environments: A theory of genotype environment effects. *Child Development, 54,* 424–435.

Schneiderman, I., Zagoory-Sharon, O., Leckman, J. F., & Feldman, R. (2012). Oxytocin during the initial stages of romantic attachment: Relations to couples' interactive reciprocity. *Psychoneuroendocrinology, 37,* 1277–1285. doi:10.1016/j.psyneuen.2011.12.021

Selye, H. (1978). *The stress of life* (Rev. ed.). New York, NY: McGraw Hill.

Sheridan, J. F., Stark, J. L., Avitsur, R., & Padgett, D. A. (2000). Social disruption, immunity, and susceptibility to viral infection: Role of glucocorticoid insensitivity and NGF. *Annals of the New York Academy of Sciences, 917,* 894–905. doi:10.1111/j.1749-6632.2000.tb05455.x

Shor, E., Roelfs, D. J., Bugyi, P., & Schwartz, J. E. (2012). Meta-analysis of marital dissolution and mortality: Reevaluating the intersection of gender and age. *Social Science and Medicine, 75,* 46–59. doi:10.1016/j.socscimed.2012.03.010

Simpson, J. A., Collins, W. A., & Salvatore, J. E. (2011). The impact of early interpersonal experience on adult romantic relationship functioning. *Current Directions in Psychological Science, 20,* 355–359. doi:10.1177/0963721411418468

Simpson, J. A., & Rholes, W. S. (2012). Adult attachment orientations, stress, and romantic relationships. In P. Devine & A. Plant (Eds.), *Advances in experimental social psychology* (Vol. 45, pp. 279–328). San Diego, CA: Academic Press. doi:10.1016/B978-0-12-394286-9.00006-8

Slatcher, R. B. (2010). Marital functioning and physical health: Implications for social and personality psychology. *Social and Personality Psychology Compass, 4*, 455–469. doi:10.1111/j.1751-9004.2010.00273.x

Smith, T. W., Cribbet, M. R., Nealey-Moore, J. B., Uchino, B. N., Williams, P. G., MacKenzie, J., & Thayer, J. F. (2011). Matters of the variable heart: Respiratory sinus arrhythmia response to marital interaction and associations with marital quality. *Journal of Personality and Social Psychology, 100*, 103–119. doi:10.1037/a0021136

Smith, T. W., & Gallo, L. C. (1999). Hostility and cardiovascular reactivity during marital interaction. *Psychosomatic Medicine, 61*, 436–445.

Solomon, S. E., Rothblum, E. D., & Balsam, K. F. (2005). Money, housework, sex, and conflict: Same-sex couples in civil unions, those not in civil unions, and heterosexual married siblings. *Sex Roles, 52*, 561–575. doi:10.1007/s11199-005-3725-7

Stroebe, M., Schut, H., & Stroebe, W. (2007). Health outcomes of bereavement. *Lancet, 370*, 1960–1973. doi:10.1016/S0140-6736(07)61816-9

Stroebe, M. S. (2009). *Beyond the broken heart: Mental and physical health consequences of losing a loved one.* Utrecht, the Netherlands: Universiteit Utrecht.

Swardfager, W., Lanctôt, K., Rothenburg, L., Wong, A., Cappell, J., & Herrmann, N. (2010). A meta-analysis of cytokines in Alzheimer's disease. *Biological Psychiatry, 68*, 930–941. doi:10.1016/j.biopsych.2010.06.012

Tashiro, T., Frazier, P., & Berman, M. (2006). Stress-related growth following divorce and relationship dissolution. In M. A. Fine & J. H. Harvey (Eds.), *Handbook of divorce and relationship dissolution* (pp. 361–384). Mahwah, NJ: Erlbaum.

Thoits, P. A. (2011). Mechanisms linking social ties and support to physical and mental health. *Journal of Health and Social Behavior, 52*, 145–161. doi:10.1177/0022146510395592

Thornhill, R., & Gangestad, S. W. (1999). The scent of symmetry: A human sex pheromone that signals fitness? *Evolution and Human Behavior, 20*, 175–201. doi:10.1016/S1090-5138(99)00005-7

Thornhill, R., Gangestad, S. W., Miller, R., Scheyd, G., McCollough, J. K., & Franklin, M. (2003). Major histocompatibility complex genes, symmetry, and body scent attractiveness in men and women. *Behavioral Ecology, 14*, 668–678. doi:10.1093/beheco/arg043

Tops, M., Van Peer, J. M., Korf, J., Wijers, A. A., & Tucker, D. M. (2007). Anxiety, cortisol, and attachment predict plasma oxytocin. *Psychophysiology, 44*, 444–449. doi:10.1111/j.1469-8986.2007.00510.x

Troxel, W. M. (2010). It's more than sex: Exploring the dyadic nature of sleep and implications for health.

Psychosomatic Medicine, 72, 578–586. doi:10.1097/PSY.0b013e3181de7ff8

Troxel, W. M., Buysse, D. J., Matthews, K. A., Kravitz, H. M., Bromberg, J. T., Sowers, M., & Hall, M. H. (2010). Marital/cohabitation status and history in relation to sleep in midlife women. *Sleep, 33*, 973–981.

Troxel, W. M., Matthews, K. A., Gallo, L. C., & Kuller, L. H. (2005). Marital quality and occurrence of the metabolic syndrome in women. *Archives of Internal Medicine, 165*, 1022. doi:10.1001/archinte.165.9.1022

Turk, D. C., Kerns, R. D., & Rosenberg, R. (1992). Effects of marital interaction on chronic pain and disability: Examining the down side of social support. *Rehabilitation Psychology, 37*, 259. doi:10.1037/h0079108

Uchino, B. N. (2004). *Social support and physical health: Understanding the health consequences of relationships.* New Haven, CT: Yale University Press.

Uchino, B. N. (2009). Understanding the links between social support and physical health: A life-span perspective with emphasis on the separability of perceived and received support. *Perspectives on Psychological Science, 4*, 236–255. doi:10.1111/j.1745-6924.2009.01122.x

Uchino, B. N., Cacioppo, J. T., & Kiecolt-Glaser, J. K. (1996). The relationship between social support and physiological processes: A review with emphasis on underlying mechanisms and implications for health. *Psychological Bulletin, 119*, 488–531. doi:10.1037/0033-2909.119.3.488

Uchino, B. N., & Garvey, T. S. (1997). The availability of social support reduces cardiovascular reactivity to acute psychological stress. *Journal of Behavioral Medicine, 20*, 15–27. doi:10.1023/A:1025583012283

Weaver, I. C. G., Cervoni, N., Champagne, F. A., D'Alessio, A. C., Sharma, S., Seckl, J. R., . . . Meaney, M. J. (2004). Epigenetic programming by maternal behavior. *Nature Neuroscience, 7*, 847–854. doi:10.1038/nn1276

Weihs, K. L., Enright, T. M., & Simmens, S. J. (2008). Close relationships and emotional processing predict decreased mortality in women with breast cancer: Preliminary evidence. *Psychosomatic Medicine, 70*, 117–124. doi:10.1097/PSY.0b013e31815c25cf

Wheaton, B. (1990). Life transitions, role histories, and mental health. *American Sociological Review, 55*, 209–223. doi:10.2307/2095627

Whisman, M. A. (1999). Marital dissatisfaction and psychiatric disorders: Results from the National Comorbidity Survey. *Journal of Abnormal Psychology, 108*, 701–706. doi:10.1037/0021-843X.108.4.701

Whisman, M. A. (2007). Marital distress and DSM-IV psychiatric disorders in a population-based national survey. *Journal of Abnormal Psychology, 116,* 638. doi:10.1037/0021-843X.116.3.638

Whisman, M. A., & Sbarra, D. A. (2012). Marital adjustment and interleukin-6. *Journal of Family Psychology, 26,* 290–295.

Whisman, M. A., & Uebelacker, L. A. (2011). A longitudinal investigation of marital adjustment as a risk factor for metabolic syndrome. *Health Psychology, 31,* 80–86.

Whisman, M. A., Uebelacker, L. A., & Settles, T. D. (2010). Marital distress and the metabolic syndrome: Linking social functioning with physical

health. *Journal of Family Psychology, 24,* 367–370. doi:10.1037/a0019547

Wright, B. L., & Loving, T. J. (2011). Health implications of conflict in close relationships. *Social and Personality Psychology Compass, 5,* 552–562. doi:10.1111/j.1751-9004.2011.00371.x

Zhang, T.-Y., Bagot, R., Parent, C., Nesbitt, C., Bredy, T. W., Caldji, C., . . . Meaney, M. J. (2006). Maternal programming of defensive responses through sustained effects on gene expression. *Biological Psychology, 73,* 72–89. doi:10.1016/j.biopsycho.2006.01.009

PART III

ATTRACTION AND RELATIONSHIP DEVELOPMENT

Chapter 7

INTERPERSONAL ATTRACTION: IN SEARCH OF A THEORETICAL ROSETTA STONE

Eli J. Finkel and Paul W. Eastwick

Research on interpersonal attraction has a checkered history. It flourished in the 1960s and 1970s before being largely eclipsed by research on established romantic relationships in the 1980s. As the 1990s approached, it reemerged in a barely recognizable form as a major prong of evolutionary psychology, which largely jettisoned the most central research questions from previous decades. Then, in the first decade of the 21st century, broad interest in interpersonal attraction reemerged, inspired in part by the power afforded by major dating innovations in the business world, including online dating and speed dating. This reemergence not only built on the flourishing literature deriving predictions from evolutionary principles, but also revitalized topics that had largely been neglected for decades.

Although we view the nascent reemergence of research on interpersonal attraction with enthusiasm, we fear that the status of this research domain remains precarious and vulnerable to supersession. The primary reason for this fear is that the interpersonal attraction literature, as a whole, lacks the theoretical depth and breadth to prevent it from flagging or splintering.

This concern is not new. Indeed, scholars have long observed that theoretical disorganization has stunted the field's development. In the beginning, Newcomb (1956) observed that "there exists no very adequate theory of interpersonal attraction" (p. 575). Although the 1960s and 1970s witnessed a major surge of research on this topic, Berscheid (1985) concluded from her review of that work that the field "'just grew,' proceeding without the

advantage of a master plan" (p. 417). Finkel and Baumeister (2010), reviewing the interpersonal attraction literature recently—a half-century after Newcomb and a quarter-century after Berscheid—echoed their sentiments, concluding that the field of interpersonal attraction research "remains a theoretical morass" (p. 421).

As an illustration of this point, consider the organization of the extant integrative reviews of this literature. Such reviews tend to be built around one of two organizational structures. Several reviews, including those presented in the major textbooks in the field (e.g., Berscheid & Regan, 2005; Bradbury & Karney, 2010; R. S. Miller, 2012), have organized the literature around the fundamental principles of attraction, such as familiarity, reciprocity, similarity, and the allure of physical attractiveness. Other reviews have organized the literature around the key predictors of attraction (e.g., Finkel & Baumeister, 2010; Simpson & Harris, 1994; see Kelley et al., 1983), typically categorizing them as most relevant to (a) the actor (characteristics of the person who experiences attraction), (b) the target (characteristics of the person to whom the actor is attracted), (c) the relationship (characteristics of the dyad above and beyond actor and partner characteristics), or (d) the environment (characteristics of the physical or social environment). Both of these organizational structures have value, but neither is especially theoretical.

Our goal in this chapter is to take a step toward the theoretical integration of the interpersonal attraction literature. We seek to do so in two ways.

http://dx.doi.org/10.1037/14344-007
APA Handbook of Personality and Social Psychology: Vol. 3. Interpersonal Relations, M. Mikulincer and P. R. Shaver (Editors-in-Chief)

First, we suggest that almost all research on interpersonal attraction has been implicitly or explicitly guided by one of three overarching metatheoretical perspectives—domain-general reward perspectives, domain-specific evolutionary perspectives, and attachment perspectives—and we use this tripartite theoretical structure to review the attraction literature. Second, we argue that this literature coheres around a single core principle, the instrumentality principle, which suggests that people become attracted to others who help them achieve needs or goals that are currently high in motivational priority.

Domain-general reward perspectives emphasize people's fundamental needs (e.g., pleasure, belonging, self-esteem, consistency) that are relevant to diverse life domains (e.g., friendship, work, family, mating). In principle, people can satisfy these needs through diverse nonsocial and social means, including through romantic relationships. For example, people's need to maintain a positive self-view can be satisfied by acing an exam (i.e., nonsocial means) or by receiving a compliment from a friend (i.e., nonromantic social means), and it can also be satisfied by a spouse's sexual overtures (i.e., romantic social means). In contrast, domain-specific evolutionary perspectives emphasize that people possess specific needs that were linked to reproductive success in humans' ancestral past, and these specific needs can be met only through specific means. For example, people's need to reproduce can be satisfied (in a long-term context) by their spouse's exhibiting sexual attraction toward them but not by having their friend compliment them or by acing an exam. Finally, attachment perspectives, which are still in their infancy vis-à-vis understanding interpersonal attraction, are built on the idea that humans are motivated to approach attachment figures in times of distress in an attempt to reestablish a sense of security (Bowlby, 1969). Some elements of the attachment perspective are reminiscent of the domain-general perspective, such as the need for contact comfort, which applies in both parental and mating relationships (Harlow, 1958), yet other elements are reminiscent of the domain-specific perspective, such as the initiation of particular behavioral and physiological patterns (e.g., distress)

in response to particular environmental cues (e.g., loss of an attachment figure; Sbarra & Hazan, 2008). Chronologically, the domain-general reward perspective has guided research since scholars began studying interpersonal attraction in the middle of the 20th century, the domain-specific evolutionary perspective came to prominence in the late 1980s, and the attachment perspective emerged in the early 1990s and has picked up steam over the past several years.

Finally, after concluding our review of the attraction literature, we argue that the instrumentality principle can serve as the central, unifying principle for the interpersonal attraction literature—a theoretical Rosetta Stone. In building this argument, we offer a selective tour through classic and current perspectives on motivation and motivated cognition. In addition, we suggest that the instrumentality principle is more precise, more empirically tractable, more theoretically generative, and more integrative than the reward principle.

REVIEW OF THE INTERPERSONAL ATTRACTION LITERATURE

We now pivot to a review of the interpersonal attraction literature. We organize this literature review around the three overarching metatheoretical perspectives, beginning with domain-general reward perspectives.

Domain-General Reward Perspectives

From the inception of psychological research investigating interpersonal attraction, the single most influential idea has been that people are attracted to others to the degree that those others are rewarding for them. Indeed, Newcomb (1956) asserted that "we acquire favorable or unfavorable attitudes toward persons as we are rewarded or punished by them" (p. 577). Influential scholars frequently echoed this view in the subsequent heyday of research on initial attraction, asserting, for example, that "we like people most whose overall behavior is most rewarding" (Aronson, 1969), that "individuals like those who reward them" (Walster, 1971), and that liking emerges from "the rewards others provide" (Levinger & Snoek, 1972). This view remains dominant today, as illustrated by the assertion, in the interpersonal attraction chapter of a current best-selling textbook on social relationships, that the rewards people experience in the presence of others are "the fundamental basis of attraction" to those others (R. S. Miller, 2012, p. 70).

Much of the research on interpersonal attraction has revolved around a handful of the domain-general needs people can seek to satisfy through interpersonal processes, both romantic and platonic. Because the satisfaction of these needs is rewarding, scholars' explicit or implicit recognition of these needs has influenced their conceptualizations of how interpersonal attraction works. We organize our review of domain-general reward perspectives around five such needs: hedonic pleasure, self-esteem, belonging, consistency, and self-expansion. This review is intended to be neither comprehensive of the literature relevant to any particular domain-general need nor exhaustive of the needs explicitly or implicitly recognized by attraction scholars. Furthermore, it is not intended to imply that a given process promotes attraction by satisfying only one need (indeed, several processes presumably promote attraction by satisfying multiple needs). Rather, it is simply intended to extract some of the domain-general needs that appear to underlie many of the attraction effects scholars have identified since the 1950s. This extraction approach allows us to discuss disparate interpersonal attraction effects as fulfilling the same need.

Pleasure.   People tend to approach physical and psychological pleasure and avoid physical and psychological pain (Atkinson, 1964; Freud, 1920/1952; Gray, 1982; Thorndike, 1935). As applied to the attraction domain, people tend to approach others whom they associate with pleasure and avoid others whom they associate with pain (Clore & Byrne, 1974; Lott & Lott, 1974). Some interpersonal pleasures are normative in that they are enjoyed by all; for example, one of the two core dimensions of interpersonal interaction is warmth (T. Leary, 1957; Wiggins, 1979), and people generally find interactions with warm people to be pleasurable. However, the list of pleasures that people enjoy is, to some extent, also idiographic: "If you like to play piano

duets, or tennis, you are apt to be rewarded by those who make it possible for you to do so" (Newcomb, 1956, p. 576). We illustrate the link from pleasure to attraction by discussing two normatively pleasurable factors—physical attractiveness and sense of humor—and the impact of secondary reinforcers.

Others' physical attractiveness is perhaps the single most robust predictor of people's initial attraction to them (Eastwick & Finkel, 2008b; Feingold, 1990). In a seminal demonstration of this effect, college students attended a dance party with a randomly assigned partner they had not previously met (Walster, Aronson, Abrahams, & Rottman, 1966). The major predictor of attraction was the target's objectively coded physical attractiveness. Neural evidence has spoken to the hedonic value of beholding beautiful people, demonstrating that reward circuitry in the brain (e.g., the nucleus accumbens) activates in response to viewing physically attractive faces (Aharon et al., 2001; Cloutier, Heatherton, Whalen, & Kelley, 2008; O'Doherty et al., 2003). As testimony to the domain generality of this tendency, people tend to be especially attracted to physically attractive others even in platonic contexts (Feingold, 1990; Langlois et al., 2000), and even 3-month-old babies prefer to gaze at the faces of attractive others (Langlois et al., 1987; Slater et al., 1998). Furthermore, this robust tendency to be attracted to physically attractive others appears to be due, at least in part, to a general tendency to be attracted to beautiful, easy-to-process objects, both human and nonhuman (Reber, Winkielman, & Schwarz, 1998).

Moving beyond physical attractiveness, others' sense of humor also predicts attraction to them, presumably because laughter and mirth are inherently pleasurable experiences. For example, a good sense of humor is among the most important qualities that both men and women seek in a potential romantic partner (Buss, 1988; Feingold, 1992). As testimony to the domain generality of this desire for humor, people report that possessing a good sense of humor is a desirable quality not only in diverse romantic contexts (a casual sex partner, a dating partner, a marriage partner), but also in both same-sex and cross-sex friendships (Sprecher & Regan, 2002).

In addition to qualities that are inherently pleasurable, scholars have also investigated qualities that provide for indirect access to pleasurable experiences and can consequently function as secondary reinforcers. One such example is a target's status or resources (Eastwick & Finkel, 2008b; Fletcher, Simpson, Thomas, & Giles, 1999; Pérusse, 1993). For example, people tend to experience attraction to others who are, or who have the potential to be, wealthy or ambitious, presumably in part because interdependence with such others provides people with access to a lifestyle that offers elevated levels of hedonic pleasure.

Self-esteem. Despite their undeniable enthusiasm for the pursuit of hedonic pleasure, people are much more than mere pleasure seekers. For example, people also have a need to possess high self-esteem—to evaluate themselves positively—and many of the most powerful means for meeting this need involve interpersonal processes (M. R. Leary & Baumeister, 2000). We suggest that a broad range of interpersonal attraction effects are due, at least in part, to people's desire to pursue or maintain high self-esteem. We discuss four such effects here.

First, ever since Byrne (1961) and Newcomb (1961) published their landmark studies, scholars have explored the attraction-promoting effects of similarity. Recent research has demonstrated that the link between similarity and attraction is strong for perceived similarity (i.e., subjective assessments of similarity) but sporadic and weak for actual similarity (i.e., objectively determined similarity; Montoya, Horton, & Kirchner, 2008; Tidwell, Eastwick, & Finkel, 2013). Although multiple explanations exist for the link between perceived similarity and attraction (including the reverse-causality explanation that attraction causes people to perceive relatively high levels of similarity; Morry, Kito, & Ortiz, 2011), we find Thibaut and Kelley's (1959) analysis particularly compelling: "If we assume that in many value areas an individual is in need of social support for his opinions and attitudes then another person's agreeing with him will constitute a reward for him" (p. 43). We suggest that others' agreement with people's attitudes or values causes people to like those others and that this link is partially mediated by the bolstering effect of that agreement on people's view of themselves.

Second, ever since Beckman and Secord (1959) published their landmark study, scholars have explored the reciprocity effect—the tendency for people to be attracted to others who like them. This emphasis on the reward potential of being liked by others was underscored by interdependence theory (Thibaut & Kelley, 1959) and social exchange theory (Homans, 1961), with Homans (1961) asserting that the social approval of others is a "generalized reinforcer." In one set of studies, Walster, Walster, Piliavin, and Schmidt (1973) sought to demonstrate that men tend to be attracted to women who play hard to get (an effect that could have contradicted the reciprocity effect), but their conclusion, based on six studies, was that men are attracted to women who are easy for them to get but hard for other men to get (also see Finkel & Eastwick, 2009b). These findings suggest that people tend to be attracted to others who like them but only if this liking makes them feel special. A subsequent speed-dating study yielded compatible conclusions: Speed daters were especially attracted to partners who liked them more than those partners liked other people, but they were not attracted to partners who indiscriminately liked everybody (Eastwick, Finkel, Mochon, & Ariely, 2007; also see Eastwick & Finkel, 2009). Similarly, classic research has suggested that people tend to be more attracted to others who grow to like them over time than to others who have always liked them, who have always disliked them, or who have grown to dislike them over time (Aronson & Linder, 1965). This effect appears to derive from the tendency for people to experience a self-esteem boost from having discerning others like them as they get to know them better. Indeed, people tend to be sufficiently eager for evidence that others like them that they even tend to be attracted to others who ingratiate themselves to win favor (Gordon, 1996; Vonk, 2002).

A third attraction effect inspired, at least in part, by others helping one meet one's self-esteem needs is the pratfall effect. People are more attracted to appealing others (but not to unappealing others) who have committed a pratfall, such as spilling coffee on themselves, than to appealing others who have not (Aronson, Willerman, & Floyd, 1966; see Deaux, 1972). The effect seems to occur because although people like appealing others, this attraction is bolstered to the degree that those others do not make them feel inferior by social comparison (Herbst, Gaertner, & Insko, 2003).

A fourth attraction effect inspired, at least in part, by others' ability to meet a person's self-esteem needs is the tendency for people with a low comparison level, relative to people with a high comparison level, to experience stronger attraction toward others. People who are dispositionally low in self-esteem or high in attachment anxiety, or who have recently been primed to have relatively low romantic expectations, tend to experience greater attraction to specific targets in part because their standards for receiving an ego boost from romantic involvement are lower. In accordance with this perspective, physically unattractive (vs. attractive) people not only tend to have lower standards for a potential partner (Buss & Shackelford, 2008), but they also tend to view particular potential partners as more attractive (Montoya, 2008; but see Lee, Loewenstein, Ariely, Hong, & Young, 2008). Similarly, relative to people whose comparison standards have temporarily been raised, people whose comparison standards have not been altered tend to view others as more attractive. For example, male participants rated a target female as less attractive after watching a television show that depicted gorgeous women than after watching a television show that did not (Kenrick & Gutierres, 1980), and men who had just viewed *Playboy* centerfolds rated their wife as less attractive than did men looking at magazines that did not depict beautiful women (Kenrick, Gutierres, & Goldberg, 1989).

Belonging. A third major need that people can meet through social processes is belonging. We focus on three classic attraction effects that appear to be driven, at least in part, by helping people satisfy their need to belong (Baumeister & Leary, 1995): familiarity, self-disclosure, and the social basis of anxiety reduction. First, people tend to be more attracted to others who are familiar to them than to others who are not. For example, people tend to become attracted to others who live in close

physical proximity to them. In one classic study, people were about twice as likely to become close friends with somebody who lived next door to them (about 20 feet away) than to somebody who lived two doors down (about 40 feet away; Festinger, Schachter, & Back, 1950). This effect has been replicated many times (e.g., Segal, 1974), including in initial attraction contexts (Back, Schmulke, & Egloff, 2008; Reis, Maniaci, Caprariello, Eastwick, & Finkel, 2011a). To be sure, elevated familiarity can sometimes undermine liking (e.g., Ebbesen, Kjos, & Konečni, 1976), but those cases appear to result from the complexities of elevated interdependence rather than from familiarity per se (Reis, Maniaci, Caprariello, Eastwick, & Finkel, 2011b).

Additional evidence in support of the attraction-promoting effects of familiarity has come from research on the mere exposure effect, which suggests that people tend to experience greater attraction to familiar stimuli, including familiar people, than to unfamiliar stimuli (Zajonc, 1968, 2001). This effect cannot be explained by other factors frequently confounded with familiarity, such as the quality of the direct experience, and it emerges even without perceivers being aware they have gained familiarity. In one compelling demonstration, female research assistants posed as students in a lecture course and, by random assignment, attended 0, 5, 10, or 15 of the 40 lectures (Moreland & Beach, 1992). Although these women did not interact with the students in the course, those students rated the women as more attractive as the number of classes the women attended increased, despite having no recollection of having ever seen the women.

A major reason why familiarity tends to promote attraction is that the human psyche is built to bond with others (Hazan & Diamond, 2000; Hazan & Zeifman, 1994). In one study, pairs of unacquainted strangers experienced greater attraction toward each other if they had been randomly assigned to gaze into each other's eyes for 2 minutes than if they had been assigned to gaze at each other's hands or to engage in asymmetric eye contact (Kellerman, Lewis, & Laird, 1989). These results suggest that experiencing brief intimacy with another person causes attraction to that person, even when people did not choose to interact with him or her. In short, it seems that taking two people at random and assigning them to experience increased contact—through physical proximity, mere exposure, or intimate interaction—tends to promote mutual attraction.

Complementing this research on familiarity is a compelling line of research linking self-disclosure to interpersonal attraction. People who disclose intimately tend to be liked more than people who disclose less intimately, and people like others as a result of having disclosed intimately to them (Collins & Miller, 1994; but see Mikulincer & Nachshon, 1991, for individual differences in this effect).

The third line of research differs from the familiarity and self-disclosure work, but it also illustrates that people tend to be attracted to others who meet their belonging needs. Specifically, people experiencing acute anxiety tend to be attracted to others who have the potential to help them manage that anxiety. In a classic series of studies, for example, women who believed that they would soon endure a stressful experience preferred to wait with another person who was also awaiting that experience rather than wait by themselves, presumably because pursuing social contact with that person would help to assuage their anxiety (Schachter, 1959; also see Rofé, 1984; Shaver & Klinnert, 1982).

Consistency. A fourth major need that people frequently seek to meet through interpersonal relationships is consistency, defined in terms of people's motivation to believe that their thoughts and behaviors are internally coherent. An early line of research sought to predict interpersonal attraction by building on Heider's (1958) suggestion that people seek consistency, or balance, in their evaluations and associations. In an influential study (Aronson & Cope, 1968), participants tended to be especially attracted to another person who had punished their enemies and rewarded their friends. This effect could not be explained by participants' beliefs that the other person was similar to them, was trying to help or curry favor with them, or could potentially develop some sort of relationship with them in the future. In another example of the importance of consistency, people often look to others for self-verification—that is, for feedback that their views of

themselves (positive or negative) are accurate, even when doing so causes them distress (Swann, 1983).

Another influential program of research has demonstrated that people not only seek internal consistency—consistent cognitions and self-assessments—but also consistency between the norms they desire for a given relationship and the norms the other person displays. In particular, research on exchange and communal norms has demonstrated that people tend to be especially attracted to others who immediately reciprocate benefits and favors when people desire exchange norms, which are built on principles of reciprocity. In contrast, they tend to be especially attracted to others who do not immediately reciprocate benefits when they desire communal norms, which are built on principles of responsiveness to needs (M. S. Clark & Mills, 1979).

Self-expansion. A fifth need that people frequently seek to meet through interpersonal relationships is the need for self-expansion. According to self-expansion theory, people are fundamentally motivated to expand their potential efficacy, and one important means by which they do so is through social relationships (Aron, Lewandowski, Mashek, & Aron, 2013). People sometimes view themselves as having some degree of ownership over others' resources, perspectives, and identities—the so-called inclusion-of-the-other-in-the-self principle (Aron et al., 2013). For example, participants in one study who expected to initiate a new same-sex relationship preferred somebody who they believed possessed dissimilar interests, presumably because the dissimilarity would provide an opportunity for self-expansion (Aron, Steele, Kashdan, & Perez, 2006).

Incidental association of others with successful goal pursuit. Before concluding our discussion of domain-general reward approaches to understanding interpersonal attraction, we discuss one final issue pertaining to this topic: Incidentally associating others with rewards can promote attraction to them, even when those others have not played any causal role in the presence of the rewards. In a seminal study, grade-school children played a novel game in same-sex groups of three (Lott & Lott, 1960). The experimenter randomly assigned each member of each group either to succeed or to fail in the game. Subsequently, in an unrelated context, the children chose two classmates to join them on a hypothetical vacation to outer space. Children who had (vs. had not) succeeded at the game were almost 4 times more likely to choose a member of their play group to join them (23% vs. 6% likelihood). In another classic study, participants in a comfortable room experienced significantly stronger attraction to an anonymous stranger than did participants in an uncomfortably hot and humid room (Griffitt, 1970; also see Griffitt & Veitch, 1971; May & Hamilton, 1980). Similarly, people who are currently experiencing an incidental happy mood tend to be more attracted to others than people who are currently experiencing an incidental sad mood (Gouaux, 1971; Veitch & Griffitt, 1976).

More recently, several lines of research have demonstrated that such attraction-promoting effects of incidentally associating others with certain psychological states can emerge even when people lack conscious awareness that they are experiencing the relevant psychological state. For example, because people unconsciously associate physical warmth with psychological warmth and physical approach with psychological approach, they tend to be more attracted to others when they have been randomly assigned to hold a cup of hot coffee rather than a cup of iced coffee (Williams & Bargh, 2008) or when they have been randomly assigned to approach those others rather than to be approached by them (Finkel & Eastwick, 2009a). Similarly, consistent with the classic concept of transference (Freud, 1912/1958), people tend to be more attracted to strangers who cosmetically resemble positive rather than negative significant others in their life, an effect that is not a result of the simple positivity or negativity of the stranger's characteristics (Andersen, Reznik, & Manzella, 1996).

Domain-general reward perspectives: Conclusion. The preceding review has illustrated that the domain-general reward perspective can encompass a broad range of important findings regarding the causes of interpersonal attraction. The common thread running through all of the preceding findings is that people's needs can be satisfied not only through various social means (through diverse interactions with a friend, a romantic partner, a sibling, a classmate, etc.), but also through nonsocial means. This review also addressed circumstances under which people can become attracted to others simply by associating them with domain-general need-fulfilling experiences.

Domain-Specific Evolutionary Perspectives

Dominant evolutionary approaches to human attraction challenge the idea that theoretically generative explanations for attraction phenomena can be achieved with appeals to domain-general needs (Buss, 1992; Buss & Reeve, 2003; Tooby & Cosmides, 1992). The evolutionary psychological perspective on mating came into prominence in the late 1980s on the heels of three major developments in evolutionary theory.

Three major developments that led to the emergence of the evolutionary psychology of interpersonal attraction. The first development was the application of the concept of adaptation to human behavior. An adaptation is a feature of an organism that arose through natural selection because of its contributions to the organism's reproductive success (Buss, Haselton, Shackelford, Bleske, & Wakefield, 1998). Although adaptation had been an essential element of evolutionary biology even before Darwin's (1859) theory of natural selection achieved widespread acclaim, it was not until the publication of Wilson's (1975) *Sociobiology* that scholars widely began to use the adaptation concept as a tool to explain human behavior. Wilson applied to *Homo sapiens* the same adaptive logic that had long been applied to animal morphology and behavior; that is, natural selection should have fashioned human behaviors in a manner that promotes reproductive success across a variety of life domains (e.g., altruism, aggression, mating; see also Wilson, 1979). Thus, if human mating behaviors were shaped by natural selection, scholars could use evolutionary concepts to understand and predict how humans navigate the mating domain.

The second development was the publication of Trivers's (1972) theory of differential parental investment. Trivers noted that in most animal species (including *Homo sapiens*), females invest more resources in offspring than males do, and he hypothesized that this difference was the engine that drove sexual selection. When females invest considerably more in offspring than males do, the costs of a poor mating decision for females are especially high, so they should be especially discriminating among sex partners. Under these circumstances, males should compete vigorously for sexual access to many females, because males' reproductive success is limited primarily by the number of partners they can acquire. Among animals in which the sex difference in parental investment is smaller (e.g., monogamous birds), sex differences in mating behaviors should be smaller.

The third development was the concept of domain specificity. Domain specificity, when applied to the mind, refers to the idea that a mental system incorporates specific classes of information in the service of a specific functional outcome (Barrett & Kurzban, 2006). For example, a domain-specific module in the mind of a human male might respond to the presence of a sexual cue (e.g., an attractive young female) by increasing his sexual desire and motivating sexual solicitations; the module would not facilitate these responses to the myriad mating-irrelevant cues that he encounters. Cosmides and Tooby integrated the concept of domain specificity with the emerging discipline of evolutionary psychology in their studies of social exchange (Cosmides, 1985, 1989; Tooby & Cosmides, 1992). Their studies revealed that participants were much better at solving logic problems when the instructions framed the problems in terms of "cheater detection" rather than generic if–then reasoning. Tooby and Cosmides (1992) suggested that this content effect reflected domain-specific, specialized mechanisms in the mind of *Homo sapiens* that had been designed by natural selection to solve the specific problem of cheater detection, not generic logic problems. Broadly speaking, these scholars surmised that natural selection would have fashioned the human psyche to consist largely of domain-specific mechanisms because such a design would have been more efficient and effective than a design consisting largely of content-independent learning or reasoning mechanisms.

First-generation findings from the evolutionary psychology of interpersonal attraction. These three developments laid the foundation for the evolutionary psychological perspective on mating. By the mid- to late 1980s, there was a precedent for the application of adaptationist principles to humans (Wilson, 1975), and there was a strong theoretical basis for predicting that adaptations relevant to men's and women's mating behaviors would have evolved differently (Symons, 1979; Trivers, 1972). Furthermore, if the mind consisted largely of domain-specific modules (Cosmides, 1985, 1989; Tooby & Cosmides, 1992), then natural selection might have fashioned sex-differentiated mental modules to solve particular sex-differentiated adaptive problems in the mating domain. With these tools in hand, Buss revolutionized attraction research with the application of evolutionary psychological principles, starting with an evolutionary analysis of mate preferences.

Mate preferences. This revolution began in the mid-1980s (Buss, 1985; Buss & Barnes, 1986), and it picked up steam soon thereafter with the publication of Buss's (1989) landmark article in *Behavioral and Brain Sciences*. In this article, Buss assessed men's and women's mate preferences in a sample of more than 10,000 participants spanning 37 samples drawn from 33 countries, which came from six continents and five islands. In one sense, Buss's mate preferences research was a straightforward extension of research dating back to the first half of the 20th century (e.g., Hill, 1945), which asked men and women to report the degree to which certain characteristics were important to them in a potential marriage partner. This work had shown, for example, that people desire partners who are kindhearted and exciting, and Buss replicated those findings. In another sense, though, Buss's mate preference research was a radical departure from everything that had preceded it. His emphasis on identifying specific adaptive problems faced by humans' male and female ancestors and on deriving testable predictions regarding sex differences based on these adaptive problems gave his research a level of theoretical innovation and scope that had been absent from the research that preceded it.

Building on Trivers's (1972) differential parental investment theory, Buss (1989) advanced three hypotheses about sex differences in the characteristics people seek in a mate. First, on the basis of the ideas that human males frequently monopolized and defended resources in the evolutionary past and that the survival of females and their offspring had been especially dependent on gaining access to such resources, Buss hypothesized that women should be more likely than men to seek characteristics associated with resource acquisition in a mate. Consistent with this hypothesis, relative to men's preferences in a mate, women valued good financial prospects significantly more in 36 of the 37 samples (with no significant reversals), they valued ambition and industriousness significantly more in 29 of the 37 samples (with one significant reversal), and they valued having a mate older than themselves in all 37 samples (see also Kenrick & Keefe, 1992). Second, on the basis of the idea that that men's reproductive success is constrained by challenges associated with gaining sexual access to fertile women, Buss hypothesized that men should be more likely than women to seek reproductive capacity in a mate. Consistent with this hypothesis, relative to women's preferences in a mate, men valued physical attractiveness significantly more in 34 of the 37 samples (with no significant reversals), and they valued having a mate younger than themselves in all 37 samples. Third, based on the fact that men can never be 100% certain that they are the parent of a given newborn (in contrast to women's 100% certainty) and thus are susceptible to cuckoldry, Buss hypothesized that men should be more likely than women to seek characteristics related to sexual chastity in a mate. Consistent with this hypothesis, relative to women's preferences in a mate, men valued chastity, defined as having had no previous sexual partners, significantly more in 23 of the 37 samples (with no significant reversals).

Various scholars have found such sex differences in representative samples in the United States (Sprecher, Sullivan, & Hatfield, 1994), in participants' evaluations of photographs or descriptions of opposite-sex individuals (e.g., Townsend & Wasserman, 1998), and in early meta-analyses of the existing mate preferences literature (Feingold, 1990, 1992). These findings are consistent with Trivers's (1972) logic, with women desiring earning

prospects, ambition, and age in a mate because such traits suggest that a man can acquire and provide resources and with men desiring physical attractiveness and youth in a mate because such traits suggest that a woman is fertile.

Short-term versus long-term mating strategies.   In the early 1990s, Buss teamed up with Schmitt to build a broader theoretical framework, sexual strategies theory, for understanding the evolutionary psychology of human mating (Buss & Schmitt, 1993). Sexual strategies theory is predicated on four premises: (a) "In human evolutionary history, both men and women have pursued short-term and long-term matings under certain conditions where the reproductive benefits have outweighed the costs"; (b) "different adaptive problems must be solved when pursuing a short-term sexual strategy as opposed to pursuing a long-term sexual strategy"; (c) "because of a fundamental asymmetry between the sexes in minimum levels of parental investment, men devote a larger proportion of their total mating effort to short-term mating than do women"; and (d) "because the reproductive opportunities and reproductive constraints differ for men and women in these two contexts, the adaptive problems that women must solve when pursuing each strategy are different from those that men must solve, although some problems are common to both sexes" (p. 205). According to this theory, men have historically been constrained in their reproductive success by the challenge of procuring sexual access to fertile women, whereas women have historically been constrained by the challenge of procuring access to resources for themselves and their offspring ("and perhaps secondarily by the quality of the man's genes"; Buss & Schmitt, 1993, p. 206). Consequently, men and women developed divergent short-term and long-term mating strategies, with *strategies* defined as "evolved solutions to adaptive problems, with no consciousness or awareness on the part of the strategist implied" (p. 206).

Buss and Schmitt (1993) garnered extensive support for core predictions of sexual strategies theory. For example, men tend to report greater interest in short-term mating than do women, but the sexes report comparable levels of interest in long-term mating. In addition, men tend to desire many more sexual partners in the future than women do, and men report a willingness to engage in sexual intercourse earlier in a relationship than women do. These sex differences are robust; for example, all of them emerged in a subsequent 52-nation study that sampled more than 16,000 participants (Schmitt, 2003).

In one particularly compelling, and particularly famous, demonstration of the sex difference in receptivity to short-term sexual requests, research assistants approached attractive individuals on a college campus and initiated a one-to-one interaction as follows: "I have been noticing you around campus. I find you to be very attractive" (R. D. Clark & Hatfield, 1989). By random assignment, the research assistant concluded these introductory comments with one of three questions: "Would you go out with me tonight?" "Would you come over to my apartment tonight?" or "Would you go to bed with me tonight?" Consistent with Buss and Schmitt's (1993) finding that men and women are equally interested in pursuing long-term mating opportunities, approximately 50% of both sexes were likely to say yes to the simple "go out" request. In contrast, but consistent with sexual strategies theory, men were much more likely than women to say yes to both the "apartment" request (69% vs. 3%) and the "bed" request (72% vs. 0%).

Scholars have complemented this work investigating sex differences in the pursuit of short-term mating opportunities by examining sex differences in sociosexuality, a personality variable representing people's tendency or willingness to have short-term, uncommitted sexual relationships (Simpson & Gangestad, 1991). In the 52-nation study by Schmitt (2005), men exhibited higher levels of sociosexuality in all 52 nations.

Taken together, evolutionary psychologists have procured extensive evidence that men are more interested in short-term mating opportunities than are women, a finding that is consistent with Trivers's (1972) ideas regarding differential parental investment. In addition, consistent with the evidence that sex differences in sexual receptivity appear to be much stronger in short-term than in long-term mating contexts, sex differences in mate preferences also tend to be stronger in short-term

than in long-term mating contexts (Kenrick, Groth, Trost, & Sadalla, 1993).

Critiques of first-generation findings from the evolutionary psychology of interpersonal attraction. Although these first-generation findings have been enormously influential, they are among the most controversial in the field's history, and a brief discussion of some of the critiques of this first-generation work is warranted. Perhaps the most notable critique was offered by Eagly and Wood (1999; Wood & Eagly, 2002), who suggested that alternative theoretical perspectives can readily accommodate the findings. These scholars argued that the sex differences demonstrated by Buss and others (e.g., Buss, 1989) derive not from domain-specific naturally selected mechanisms but from socialization processes that equip men and women for the roles that people of their sex typically occupy. Given that, in most industrialized societies, women are more likely than men to perform the roles of homemaker and caretaker, and men are more likely than women to perform the role of resource provider, social role theory predicts that society will instill nurturance-related characteristics in women and ambition-related characteristics in men. Over time, these sex differences become enshrined in broader gender roles, which in turn shape people's expectations about how the sexes behave (Prentice & Carranza, 2002).

Consistent with their social role theory analysis, Eagly and Wood (1999) reanalyzed the data from Buss's (1989) 37-cultures study, demonstrating that sex differences in the preference for good financial prospects and youth in a mate were smaller in countries with greater gender equality. In other words, as the roles occupied by men and women in a society converged, so did their romantic partner preferences. Subsequent research showed that the sex difference in sociosexuality shows a similar trend, shrinking as a culture becomes more gender equal (Schmitt, 2005).

Other critiques of the first-generation findings involved methodological concerns with important theoretical implications. One such critique observed that the sex differences in preferences for earning prospects and physical attractiveness are robust in methodological paradigms in which attraction is assessed regarding hypothetical or abstract romantic partners but nonexistent in paradigms in which attraction is assessed regarding specific romantic partners whom participants have actually met (Eastwick & Finkel, 2008b; see Feingold, 1992). In an initial attraction context, for example, speed daters tended to be much more attracted to partners who were high rather than low in physical attractiveness and somewhat more attracted to partners who were high rather than low in earning prospects. Crucially, however, men and women did not differ in the degree to which either of these traits inspired their romantic attraction (Eastwick & Finkel, 2008b; Finkel & Eastwick, 2008). These results, which have been replicated in non–speed-dating contexts and among middle-aged adults (Eastwick, Finkel, & Eagly, 2011), suggest that people's stated mate preferences for specific traits may be largely irrelevant to the attraction that they experience for potential romantic partners (see also Eastwick, Eagly, Finkel, & Johnson, 2011).

A second methodological critique applied specifically to R. D. Clark and Hatfield's (1989) "three questions" study. Specifically, Conley (2011) identified a confound in that study: The procedure not only manipulated the sex of the responder (the participant, who either did or did not agree to the request), but also the sex of the proposer (the confederate, who made the request). Manipulating this second variable is not inherently problematic, but it becomes a confound because men believe the female proposer to be much more sexually skilled than women believe the male proposer to be, and the proposer's perceived sexual skill is a strong predictor of agreeing to sexual contact for both men and women. Consequently, relative to the women in the R. D. Clark and Hatfield (1989) study, it is likely that the men were propositioned by a person they perceived to be better in bed. When controlling for both the proposer's sexual skills and the perceived stigma associated with engaging in casual sex, the massive sex difference in receptivity to casual sex disappears (Conley, 2011). Perhaps not surprisingly, evolutionary psychologists have voiced considerable reservations about both the social role (e.g., Gangestad, Haselton, & Buss, 2006) and the methodological (Schmitt, 2012) critiques, and

future research is sure to advance scholars' understanding of these sex differences.

Second-generation findings from the evolutionary psychology of interpersonal attraction. These critiques notwithstanding, the evolutionary psychology of interpersonal attraction has continued to flourish, and the explanatory principles have become increasingly sophisticated over time. These second-generation approaches have doubled down on Buss and Schmitt's (1993) distinction between short-term and long-term mating, investigating how people make strategic trade-offs when allocating their mating-related resources. For example, people can invest various resources in pursuing short-term mating, but, to a large degree, those resources will no longer be available for long-term mating. This idea, too, derives from Trivers (1972), who argued that mating effort (e.g., working to procure access to sexual partners) is frequently in competition with parenting effort (e.g., working to raise healthy offspring).

Strategic pluralism. The most ambitious and influential second-generation approach to the evolutionary psychology of interpersonal attraction is Gangestad and Simpson's (2000) strategic pluralism theory. One of the most important aspects of this theory is that it provides a sophisticated analysis of strategic trade-offs not only between sexes, but also within each sex. For example, some ancestral men might have achieved significant reproductive success by pursuing short-term mating strategies with multiple partners, but most ancestral men were probably unable to pursue this strategy successfully, so such men likely pursued long-term mating strategies with a small number of partners, perhaps only one. From this perspective, men's relatively strong desire for short-term mating (Buss & Schmitt, 1993) might not mean that many men have historically engaged in successful short-term mating. In fact, it is plausible that most men, like most women, achieved the greatest reproductive success from pursuing long-term rather than short-term mating strategies. Consistent with this strategic pluralism analysis that casual sex was historically available only to a select subset of men, men who possess characteristics indicative of biological features such as healthy immune functioning (e.g., possessing a symmetrical face and body; Gangestad & Thornhill, 1997; Thornhill & Gangestad, 1994) and exposure to high levels of prenatal testosterone relative to estrogen (e.g., possessing a long ring finger relative to the index finger; Schwarz, Mustafíc, Hassebrauck, & Jörg, 2011) tend to be especially likely to pursue short-term mating opportunities (see Gangestad & Simpson, 2000).

According to strategic pluralism theory, women, too, faced evolutionary pressures that allowed for multiple reproductive strategies, and women, too, can achieve reproductive success through both short-term and long-term mating strategies. For example, women can extract genetic resources from a casual sexual encounter, and there are circumstances under which these genetic resources might be sufficiently advantageous, in evolutionary terms, to override the disadvantages of being impregnated by a man who will not invest resources in the offspring. For example, girls who received insufficient parental care sometimes grow into women who are pessimistic that they will find a mate who will invest in their offspring (Belsky, Steinberg, & Draper, 1991), and such women might conclude that the best strategy available to them is to procure robust genes.

The most extensive program of research investigating women's strategic pluralism examined how the mating behavior of women who are not taking hormonal contraceptives changes across their ovulatory cycle (Gangestad, Thornhill, & Garver-Apgar, 2005). Women are most likely to conceive just before ovulation, and many evolutionary scholars have argued that, as a result, women at this fertile stage of their ovulatory cycle are especially likely to focus on a potential short-term sexual partner's genetic qualities when deciding whether to have sex with him. Consistent with this hypothesis, women at the fertile (vs. the nonfertile) stage of their ovulatory cycle tend to be more attentive to attractive men (Anderson et al., 2010). In addition, they have a stronger preference for the scent of men who are symmetrical rather than asymmetrical (Gangestad & Thornhill, 1998; also see Thornhill & Gangestad, 1999). Similarly, when considering a short-term sexual partner, they prefer physically attractive,

masculine, muscular, socially respectable, dominant, intersexually competitive men with deep voices (Gangestad, Garver-Apgar, Simpson, & Cousins, 2007; Gangestad, Simpson, Cousins, Garver-Apgar, & Christensen, 2004; Havlicek, Roberts, & Flegr, 2005; Jones et al., 2008; Puts, 2005). Furthermore, women who are currently involved in a serious romantic relationship report greater attraction to, and flirtatious behavior with, other men at the fertile stage of their cycle, but only those women whose current partner is not physically attractive (Haselton & Gangestad, 2006).

Complementing this research demonstrating that women's preferences for a short-term sexual encounter change across their ovulatory cycle is research demonstrating that men's attraction to women for a short-term sexual encounter changes, in a parallel manner, across the women's ovulatory cycle. For example, men find ovulating women to possess more appealing voices and scents than nonovulating women (Pipitone & Gallup, 2008; Thornhill et al., 2003). In addition, they pay ovulating strippers much more money than nonovulating strippers for lap dances (G. Miller, Tybur, & Jordan, 2007), and they are more likely to engage in subtle forms of affiliative behavior (e.g., mimicry) with an ovulating than with a nonovulating research confederate (S. L. Miller & Maner, 2011).

Social cognition. Recent research spearheaded by Maner et al. (2003; Maner, Gailliot, Rouby, & Miller, 2007) has also begun to investigate the intersection of the evolutionary psychology of human mating with the massive literature on social cognition. For example, one study used eye-tracking procedures to test the hypothesis that people, especially those high in sociosexuality, find it more difficult to look away from attractive relative to unattractive faces of opposite-sex targets (Maner et al., 2003). Subsequent research demonstrated that, among participants high in sociosexuality, this attentional adhesion effect was stronger among those who had been primed with sexual thoughts than among those in a control prime condition (Maner et al., 2007).

A follow-up line of research examined whether participants' current relationship status moderates such effects. Whereas single (romantically unattached) participants exhibited greater attentional adhesion to attractive opposite-sex faces when primed with mating words such as *kiss* and *lust* than when primed with mating-irrelevant words such as *talk* and *floor,* romantically attached participants exhibited the opposite pattern (Maner, Gailliot, & Miller, 2009). Similarly, romantically attached participants exhibited less attentional adhesion to attractive opposite-sex faces when primed with love for their partner than when primed with happiness (Maner, Rouby, & Gonzaga, 2008). In a particularly impressive study, romantically attached male participants viewed an attractive female confederate as less appealing after a face-to-face interaction when she was at the fertile rather than the nonfertile phase of her ovulatory cycle (S. L. Miller & Maner, 2010). Such findings are broadly consistent with an extensive line of research demonstrating that romantically involved and psychologically committed people tend to derogate attractive alternative partners and turn their attention away from them (Finkel, Molden, Johnson, & Eastwick, 2009; Johnson & Rusbult, 1989; Lydon, Fitzsimons, & Naidoo, 2003; Lydon, Meana, Sepinwall, Richards, & Mayman, 1999; R. S. Miller, 1997; Simpson, Gangestad, & Lerma, 1990).

Domain-specific evolutionary perspectives: Conclusion.   The preceding review has illustrated that, similar to the domain-general reward perspective, the domain-specific evolutionary perspective can encompass a broad range of important findings regarding the causes of interpersonal attraction. The common thread running through all of the preceding findings is that the relevant needs appear to be domain specific. For example, men's eagerness for short-term relationships is specific to short-term sexual partners rather than relevant to social relationships more generally.

Attachment Perspectives

The third major theoretical approach that scholars have applied to the topic of interpersonal attraction derives from attachment theory. Attachment theory proposes that humans are motivated to seek out attachment figures in times of stress in an attempt to reestablish a sense of security, and people's initial experiences with attachment figures shape how they

approach relationships throughout their lives. Although attachment theory has inspired thousands of studies on established romantic relationships over the past 25 years, the number of applications of the theory to the attraction domain is much more modest, perhaps because one might suspect a priori that attraction might not be an attachment-relevant context. After all, it takes about 2 years to form a full-fledged attachment bond to a romantic partner (Fagundes & Schindler, 2012; Fraley & Davis, 1997; Hazan & Zeifman, 1994). If the attachment behavioral system becomes relevant to an adult romantic relationship only after the bond has been established, then the pursuit of a potential relationship partner would have few attachment-relevant implications. Nevertheless, emerging evidence has suggested that the desire for an attachment bond may be a strong motivator of relationship initiation, and new research deriving from both the individual differences and the normative elements of attachment theory has generated a host of new findings in recent years.

Individual differences attachment perspectives.   The individual differences component of attachment theory posits that people's early experiences with significant caregivers affect how they think, feel, and behave in romantic relationships later in life (Hazan & Shaver, 1987). People's expectations about interactions with attachment figures reside within mental representations called *internal working models;* variability in such expectations causes people to exhibit personality differences, sometimes called *attachment styles,* that affect behavior in attachment-relevant contexts (Bowlby, 1969, 1973). If attachment figures are available and responsive, people develop a sense of attachment security and come to believe that caregivers are dependable sources of support and comfort. However, if people find that attachment figures are unresponsive or erratically responsive, they may develop a sense of attachment-related insecurity.

Current perspectives on the measurement of attachment styles suggest that insecurity can take either or both of two forms: attachment anxiety, which means that an individual is hypervigilant for signs of rejection and highly preoccupied with attaining closeness and protection, and attachment avoidance, which means that an individual is uncomfortable with close relationships and prefers not to depend on others (Brennan, Clark, & Shaver, 1998; Simpson, Rholes, & Phillips, 1996). Individuals who are low on both the anxiety and the avoidance dimensions are secure with respect to attachment; they generally expect romantic partners to be available and responsive, and they are comfortable with closeness and interdependence. Research inspired by the individual differences component of attachment theory has focused largely on two attraction-relevant questions: How does attachment style affect the way people approach relationship initiation (i.e., actor effects), and how much attraction do participants report to people who possess a particular attachment style (i.e., partner effects)? We now review these two lines of research in turn.

Attachment style differences in relationship initiation. People who are high in attachment anxiety are highly motivated to establish relationships (Mikulincer & Shaver, 2007). Their attachment system is hyperactivated, which means that they engage in intense, obsessive acts of proximity seeking as a means of achieving closeness with romantic partners. Furthermore, this hyperactivation interferes with their ability to assess interpersonal threat accurately, causing them to exaggerate the potential for and consequences of rejection. Therefore, individuals who are high in attachment anxiety experience an approach–avoidance conflict in close relationships: They strongly desire close relationships, but they fear that they will be rejected. One recent study provided evidence of the approach-oriented inclinations of anxious individuals by examining their tendency to be receptive or unreceptive to opposite-sex speed-dating partners for a follow-up interaction (McClure, Lydon, Baccus, & Baldwin, 2010). Participants who were high in attachment anxiety were generally more likely to say yes to their speed-dating partners; that is, they tended to be unselective. Furthermore, to the extent that participants were anxious about attachment, they were more likely to report attending the speed-dating event because they were lonely. In short, such individuals appear to be relatively unselective in initial attraction contexts, perhaps

because their strong needs for social connection are unmet, making them willing to view an especially wide swath of potential romantic partners as acceptable.

Given this tendency, it would also make sense for attachment-anxious individuals to communicate more romantic interest in potential partners, on average, than attachment-secure individuals do. In support of this hypothesis, attachment anxiety predicts subtle behaviors (e.g., choosing a colored pen that gives the appearance of working on the same team as a desirable opposite-sex partner; M. S. Clark, 1984) that potentially indicate a desire for a close, communal relationship (Bartz & Lydon, 2006). However, in some situations, fears of rejection may cause anxious individuals to be ineffective at communicating their romantic interest. In one study, participants who were relatively high in attachment anxiety and romantically interested in an opposite-sex interaction partner were especially likely to overestimate the extent to which their behaviors communicated romantic interest (Vorauer, Cameron, Holmes, & Pearce, 2003). This signal amplification bias emerges because anxious individuals mistakenly believe that an interaction partner will take their fears of rejection into account when interpreting the level of romantic interest conveyed in their romantic overtures. In summary, individuals high in attachment anxiety often face the approach–avoidance conflict of strongly desiring connection with potential partners while at the same time fearing rejection and failing to communicate their desire for connection clearly.

The romantic attraction strategies of people who are avoidant with respect to attachment differ markedly from those of attachment-anxious individuals. Attachment-related avoidance is associated with a reduced desire for closeness and intimacy; therefore, avoidant individuals should favor strategies that are unlikely to lead to the formation of a committed relationship. For example, avoidance correlates positively with approval of casual sexual relationships (Brennan & Shaver, 1995; Feeney, Noller, & Patty, 1993) and negatively with the self-reported desire to form an exclusive relationship (Schachner & Shaver, 2002). Furthermore, avoidant individuals are especially likely to report having sex to impress their peers, and they seek out short-term sexual opportunities to avoid the emotional entanglements of long-term relationships (Schachner & Shaver, 2004). Indeed, attachment-related avoidance is negatively associated with the desire to engage in intimate sexual behaviors such as holding hands, mutual gazing, and cuddling (Fraley, Davis, & Shaver, 1998). Finally, avoidantly attached individuals are more likely to be poached and to poach others' mates for short-term relationships (Schachner & Shaver, 2002). Although avoidant individuals do not eschew romantic pursuits entirely, their relationship initiation strategies suggest that they care less than nonavoidant people about the emotionally intimate components of romantic relationships.

Also relevant to the effects of attachment styles on relationship initiation is one study that examined how people's relationship-specific attachment orientations might transfer from one relationship partner to another (Brumbaugh & Fraley, 2006). Participants in this study read descriptions of two potential dating partners: one who resembled a past partner of the participant and one who resembled a past partner of a different participant (i.e., a yoked control). Participants' relationship-specific anxious and avoidant attachment tendencies regarding these new potential partners were significantly associated with their anxious and avoidant attachment tendencies with their past partner, and these associations were especially strong for the potential partner who resembled their own past partner. In other words, participants seem to apply their attachment orientation with a former dating partner to new potential dating relationships, even if they have learned through only minimal descriptive information that the new partner resembles the former partner.

Attachment style differences in romantic desirability. Other research has examined whether people experience differing levels of attraction to potential partners who possess secure, anxious, or avoidant attachment styles. In studies in which people perused descriptions of potential dating partners, participants tended to prefer descriptions of secure individuals the most and descriptions of avoidant individuals the least (Baldwin, Keelan, Fehr, Enns, & Koh-Rangarajoo, 1996; Chappell & Davis, 1998; Klohnen & Luo, 2003; Latty-Mann & Davis, 1996;

Pietromonaco & Carnelley, 1994; for a review, see Holmes & Johnson, 2009). Several studies have also found that people are more attracted to potential partners described as having attachment styles that are similar to their own (Frazier, Byer, Fischer, Wright, & Debord, 1996; Klohnen & Luo, 2003) or that are similar to the style with which they have been recently primed (Baldwin et al., 1996).

However, live dating studies have told a somewhat different story: Participants actually experience less attraction to potential partners to the extent that those partners are anxious with respect to attachment, whereas participants' attraction ratings are not associated with partners' avoidant attachment scores (McClure et al., 2010). In other words, secure potential partners come across as appealing in both scenario and live dating contexts, but the desirability of anxious versus avoidant partners differs between the two contexts. Perhaps avoidant individuals sound less desirable than anxious individuals in the abstract, but in a real-life interaction anxious individuals' neediness may be more apparent than avoidant individuals' discomfort with intimacy. Or perhaps first interactions provide insufficient information to assess relationship liabilities characteristic of attachment-related avoidance, liabilities that are likely to become increasingly relevant as interdependence increases.

Why might attachment security inspire more attraction on average than attachment insecurity? Although only a few studies (reviewed earlier) have examined attachment styles in live initial romantic contexts (e.g., Bartz & Lydon, 2006; McClure et al., 2010; Vorauer et al., 2003), a huge corpus of research has examined the interpersonal consequences of attachment styles more generally. For example, anxious and avoidant attachment scores correlate negatively with extraversion and agreeableness—two appealing interpersonal qualities (McCrae & Costa, 1989)—although these negative correlations emerge more consistently for avoidance than for anxiety (Mikulincer & Shaver, 2007). With regard to emotional communication, avoidance is associated with a reduced likelihood of expressing one's feelings (Mikulincer & Shaver, 2007), whereas attachment anxiety is associated with poorer accuracy in reading others' emotions

(Fraley, Niedenthal, Marks, Brumbaugh, & Vicary, 2006). Relative to secure individuals, anxious and avoidant individuals are also more likely to use ineffective conflict-management strategies (Campbell, Simpson, Boldry, & Kashy, 2005), and they have difficulties coordinating with partners on problem-solving tasks (Mikulincer & Shaver, 2007). Avoidance is also associated with a lower likelihood of expressing gratitude (Mikulincer, Shaver, & Slav, 2006), and anxiety is associated with a greater likelihood of responding with hostility to the provision of support by an interaction partner (Feeney, Cassidy, & Ramos-Marcuse, 2008) and with the perpetration of intimate partner violence (Finkel & Slotter, 2007). In short, individuals with insecure attachment styles exhibit a variety of interpersonal deficits, although it remains unclear which deficits translate to a greater likelihood of being disliked in initial attraction situations.

Normative attachment perspectives. Hazan and Diamond (2000) argued that mainstream evolutionary psychological examinations of mate selection had neglected important elements of the way humans form and maintain mating relationships. Drawing from the normative components of attachment theory, they argued that the species-typical form of long-term mating was not the pairing of young women with resource-rich men (Buss & Schmitt, 1993) but rather the formation of an emotionally close pair-bonded relationship. The pair bond, they argued, was itself an evolved adaptation and reflected natural selection's co-option of the infant–caregiver attachment behavioral system to bond adult mating partners for the purpose of raising costly and vulnerable offspring. Although evolutionary approaches had long recognized humans' use of long-term mating strategies, they tended to emphasize men's ability to provide tangible resources and to guard against rivals for the purpose of achieving paternity certainty. Attachment theory, in contrast, emphasized adaptive couple-level processes such as emotional coregulation (Diamond, Hicks, & Otter-Henderson, 2008; Sbarra & Hazan, 2008), caregiving (Simpson, Rholes, & Nelligan, 1992),

and support of goal strivings (Feeney, 2004). Thus, Hazan and Diamond (2000) posited that normative components of attachment theory could offer a complementary evolutionary perspective on the initiation of close relationships, and an emerging empirical literature has examined how the pair-bonding elements of the human mating psyche shape relationship formation.

Partner-specific attachment anxiety as an engine of relationship initiation. One set of studies tested two hypotheses about the possible functional role of the statelike experience of attachment anxiety (i.e., partner-specific anxiety) in the attraction process (Eastwick & Finkel, 2008a). First, consistent with the idea that fledgling relationships tend to elicit those feelings of uncertainty and the need for reassurance that are core features of attachment anxiety, the researchers predicted that partner-specific anxiety would be a normative experience in the developing phases of potential romantic relationships. In support of this hypothesis, participants reported greater partner-specific attachment anxiety about a desired romantic partner than about an established romantic partner. Second, the researchers proposed that partner-specific anxiety might signal the activation of the attachment system and would therefore predict the presence of attachment-relevant features, such as proximity seeking, support behavior, and passionate love. Indeed, correlational and experimental evidence demonstrated that partner-specific anxiety motivates participants to engage in these behaviors, and partner-specific anxiety was at least as strong a predictor of these behaviors as sexual desire was. In short, partner-specific attachment anxiety seems to be a normative experience in fledgling relationships that motivates people to seek out contact with potential partners and begin forming an attachment bond (Eastwick & Finkel, 2008a).

Situating adaptations for pair bonding within the time course of human evolution. Another set of studies merged normative attachment and evolutionary psychological approaches to examine how developing attachment bonds might intersect with ovulatory cycle adaptations (Eastwick & Finkel, 2012). Ovulatory adaptations have been part of the hominid mating psyche for many millions of years—longer than adult pair bonds—and these adaptations could have destabilized the pair bond if they periodically inspired women to pursue extrapair partners with good genes. However, attachment bonds between adult mating partners emerged more recently in humans' evolutionary lineage (approximately 2 million years ago), and thus they should have evolved the capacity to refocus the effects of prior adaptations to the purpose of strengthening the bond (Eastwick, 2009). Two studies suggested that to the extent that a woman's attachment bond to her sexual partner was strong, she exhibited elevated desire for intimacy-building sexual contact with her partner when she was at the fertile rather than the nonfertile phase of her ovulatory cycle. These results suggest that adaptations for attachment bonds may refocus the effects of ovulatory adaptations to inspire behaviors that might actually strengthen, not destabilize, the pair bond. Consistent with Hazan and Diamond's (2000) suggestion that pair bonds are also part of *Homo sapiens*' adaptive legacy, these studies have suggested that researchers can draw on the time course of human evolution (i.e., phylogeny) to advance predictions about how attachment bonds might intersect with other evolved elements of the human mating psyche (Eastwick & Finkel, 2012).

Several additional findings are broadly consistent with this normative attachment perspective on interpersonal attraction. For example, people consistently rate warmth and kindness as the most important qualities in a romantic partner (Buss & Barnes, 1986), and these are precisely the qualities that would make for a good attachment figure (Hazan & Diamond, 2000). Along these lines, people tend to experience greater attraction to a new acquaintance to the extent that they perceived the acquaintance to exhibit responsiveness (Birnbaum & Reis, 2012; Lemay & Clark, 2008). In addition, attachment theory can shed new light on the tendency for people to become attracted to others with whom they frequently interact (e.g., Festinger et al., 1950). This tendency could reflect the opportunistic operation of the attachment behavioral system, which functions in infancy to bond children to the nearest available and responsive caregiver (Hazan & Diamond, 2000).

Attachment perspectives: Conclusion. The preceding review illustrates that although attachment perspectives on interpersonal attraction are newer and less entrenched than domain-general reward perspectives and domain-specific evolutionary perspectives, they, too, encompass a broad range of important findings regarding interpersonal attraction. Scholars have typically used attachment theory principles to established relationships, but recent research has suggested that these principles also yield novel insights regarding initial attraction.

INTRODUCING INSTRUMENTALITY AS THE CRUCIAL PRINCIPLE UNDERLYING INTERPERSONAL ATTRACTION

Having reviewed many of the major findings in the interpersonal attraction literature from these three overarching perspectives—domain-general reward perspectives, domain-specific evolutionary perspectives, and attachment perspectives—we now turn to our second major task in this chapter: building an argument that instrumentality can serve as the central organizing principle for the attraction literature. In particular, we argue that people's current goal pursuits fundamentally alter their perceptions and evaluations of target objects in their environment, including their perceptions and evaluations of other people, frequently without their awareness. We also argue that the instrumentality principle can help to integrate the attraction literature by providing a language, a theoretical orientation, and a methodological approach that cut across the three overarching metatheoretical perspectives introduced in the Review of the Interpersonal Attraction Literature section.

Motivated Cognition: Active Goals Fundamentally Alter Perception and Evaluation

The view that interpersonal attraction is fundamentally dependent on others' instrumentality for achieving one's goals is steeped in the motivation-relevant theoretical traditions spawned by Bruner and Lewin in the first half of the 20th century. For example, Bruner and Goodman (1947) argued that people's goals function as filters that color their perceptions of the world, causing them to focus their attention on goal-relevant over goal-irrelevant objects and to alter their evaluations of such objects on the basis of the objects' potential to facilitate versus undermine their goal pursuit. In a compelling recent demonstration, research participants who believed that a computer would assign them to drink a delicious beverage by briefly flashing a letter of the alphabet on the screen or to drink a disgusting beverage by briefly flashing a number on the screen systematically interpreted an ambiguous figure as the letter *B* rather than as the number *13* (Balcetis & Dunning, 2006). Indeed, of the participants who saw the briefly flashed figure, 100% of them perceived it as a letter. In contrast, only 28% of participants who were randomly assigned to possess the inverse motivational priorities (letter = disgusting drink; number = delicious drink) interpreted the ambiguous figure as the letter *B*. This huge discrepancy across the two conditions illustrates the sometimes profound biasing effects of motivation on people's perception of reality.

Recent research on automatic attitude activation has examined the biasing effects of motivation on evaluative processes, demonstrating that people's automatic attitudes tend to be more positive toward goal-relevant than toward goal-irrelevant objects. For example, research participants exhibited more positive implicit attitudes toward the letter *C* when they were actively searching for *C*s than when they were not, presumably because people value objects that are immediately usable for the pursuit of a current goal (Ferguson & Bargh, 2004). On the flip side, cigarette smokers who had been deprived of cigarettes valued cash less than cigarette smokers who had not been so deprived, presumably because people devalue objects that are not immediately useful for a current goal pursuit (Brendl, Markman, & Messner, 2003). Such findings caused the authors of the recent chapter on motivation in the *Handbook of Social Psychology* to assert that "the level of proximal control over behavior and higher mental processes may be not the self but, rather, the currently active goal" (Bargh, Gollwitzer, & Oettingen, 2010, p. 289).

Instrumentality: The Crucial Organizing Principle Underlying Interpersonal Attraction

We suggest that a similar analysis applies to interpersonal attraction. As Lewin (1935) argued long ago, people tend to evaluate others positively rather than negatively as a function of the degree to which those others facilitate versus hinder their goal pursuits. Also, as observed previously, Newcomb (1956) observed that people find others rewarding to the degree that those others facilitate their ability to engage in activities they find enjoyable (e.g., piano duets or tennis). This observation that others are rewarding insofar as they help people pursue their idiographic goals underscores the importance of instrumentality for understanding why one person is likely to become attracted to another. However, research on interpersonal attraction has insufficiently appreciated how fundamental instrumentality is to the attraction process. Fortunately, scholars have begun to emphasize the importance of instrumentality for close relationships, an emphasis that served as the inspiration for the present integration of the interpersonal attraction literature around the instrumentality principle.

Instrumentality and relationship closeness.   Given the prominent role that social relationships play in people's everyday lives, scholars have long theorized that people strategically regulate their social life in ways that facilitate their goal achievement (Kelley, 1979; Seeley & Gardner, 2006). Indeed, Berscheid and Ammazzalorso (2001) went so far as to suggest that the interpersonal facilitation of one's goal pursuits is "the *raison d'être* of most close relationships" (i.e., the reason why such relationships exist; p. 319). Building on this insight, and on the observation that "people are in constant pursuit of personal goals" (p. 319), Fitzsimons and Shah (2008) published a seminal article testing the instrumentality principle, which they defined as the tendency for people to "draw closer to instrumental others, evaluate them more positively, and approach them more readily, while distancing themselves from noninstrumental others, evaluating them more negatively, and avoiding them more readily" (p. 320). Across a broad range of elegant experiments, Fitzsimons and Shah (2008) demonstrated that people indeed manifest such preferences for significant others who are instrumental for a currently activated goal (e.g., to achieve academically, to enjoy social activities). Furthermore, this tendency to feel closer to significant others who are instrumental for a given goal than to those who are not disappears once people believe that they have made good progress toward achieving that goal, a social disengagement process that allows them to focus their self-regulatory efforts on goals that require more urgent attention (Fitzsimons & Fishbach, 2010; also see Converse & Fishbach, 2012).

Applying the instrumentality principle to the interpersonal attraction domain. As noted previously, our central thesis is that the fundamental principle underlying almost all interpersonal attraction is that people become attracted to others to the degree that those others help them achieve goals that are currently high in motivational priority. Furthermore, we suggest that people become less attracted to others who are instrumental for a certain goal once people have made substantial progress toward achieving that goal—because people tend to shift their emphasis to other goals at that point. Indeed, because people can fluctuate rapidly in terms of which goals have motivational priority (Bargh, Gollwitzer, Lee-Chai, Barndollar, & Trötschel, 2001; Carver & Scheier, 1998), they will also fluctuate not only in terms of their attraction to a given target person but also in terms of whether (or the degree to which) they continue to be more attracted to one target person over another.

For example, people seeking to satisfy a sexual goal might experience especially strong attraction to others who are physically attractive and sexually skilled—or at least sexually willing. If people are able to satisfy their sexual needs, however, those needs will lose motivational priority for a while, and other needs (e.g., for belonging or consistency) are likely to rise to the fore. This motivational shift will undermine attraction to others who are potentially instrumental for people's sexual needs and bolster attraction to others who are instrumental for those other needs. More concretely, a college freshman who is experiencing strong sexual desire might be especially attracted to the casual sex partner she met when she first arrived on campus a few weeks previously, but the quenching of this sexual desire might lead it to plummet in motivational priority, allowing the stress regarding tomorrow's calculus exam to rise to the fore. With these major, but quite common, shifts in motivational priority, our college student may become less attracted to the casual sex partner who was so appealing 30 minutes earlier and more attracted to her roommate, who serves as her study partner and who was entirely forgotten 30 minutes earlier.

As a second example, people whose need to belong (Baumeister & Leary, 1995) is currently high in motivational priority, perhaps because they are currently backpacking around Europe by themselves, are likely to be especially attracted to others who can potentially be instrumental in fostering emotional intimacy. However, once people's belonging needs have been sated, they tend to prioritize other goals (DeWall, Baumeister, & Vohs, 2008; Kumashiro, Rusbult, & Finkel, 2008). This analysis dovetails with classic theorizing in the attachment literature (Ainsworth, Blehar, Waters, & Wall, 1978; Bowlby, 1969), which suggests that people are only willing to pursue a broad range of exploration-related goals once they have achieved a sense of felt security. No research has yet examined the effects of satiation of one's belonging or attachment needs on interpersonal attraction, but we suggest that people currently experiencing such satiation tend to be less attracted to others with the potential to foster further belonging and more attracted to others with the potential to promote the pursuit of other goals.

In general, we suggest that others are likely to be instrumental to the degree that they possess both the ability and the motivation to help people achieve their goals, where *ability* refers to goal-relevant skills and resources and *motivation* refers to the eagerness or willingness to deploy these skills and resources in a manner that can help people achieve their goals. For example, if a poor young man seeks to advance his financial and psychological well-being by attending cooking school, others who have relevant resources (e.g., money for tuition or skills for tutoring) have the ability to be instrumental, but they will actualize this potential instrumentality only if they are willing to spend these resources on his cooking development.

Three motivational principles relevant to the instrumentality–attraction link.

In crucial ways, the preceding analysis differs radically from prevailing perspectives on interpersonal attraction. For example, it implies that Jason should be more attracted to Scott, the telephone-based tech-support representative who is currently helping him fix a problem with his computer, than to Rachel, his wife of 20 years. Do we, the authors, really believe something so patently absurd?

Yes, we do. To be sure, if researchers interrupted Jason at that moment to ask him whether he is more attracted to Scott or to Rachel, he would almost certainly report greater attraction to his wife. And that report would be accurate. But such reports require cognitive abstractions that synthesize information well beyond Jason's immediate psychological experience. When aggregating across time and motivational domain, as such a report requires Jason to do, there is little doubt that Rachel satisfies his needs better than Scott does. However, consider an alternative dependent measure, one that does not require that Jason remove himself psychologically from the immediate situation. For example, imagine that Rachel, who is feeling frisky, begins to seduce him 45 minutes into the call. Jason's emotional and behavioral responses to her overtures will depend on his current motivational priorities. If his desire to have a properly functioning computer is especially strong, perhaps because he needs to get an important document to his boss within the hour, then he will almost certainly rebuff his wife's advances (perhaps in annoyance) in favor of additional time with Scott. In contrast, if his desire to have his computer fixed is weaker, then he might ask Scott if they can continue their tech-support meeting after a brief, hot delay. In short, from an instrumentality perspective, momentary fluctuations in motivational priority exert profound effects on interpersonal attraction to others who are helpful versus unhelpful for currently activated goals, and scholars have generally neglected these effects because they typically assess attraction with measurement instruments that are largely insensitive to them.

More generally, we suggest that understanding people's attraction to various members of their social network depends on a deeper understanding of motivational principles than the interpersonal attraction literature has recognized. A comprehensive analysis along those lines is beyond the scope of this chapter (for relevant recent discussions, see Bargh et al., 2010; Förster, Liberman, & Friedman, 2007), but we illustrate this approach by discussing three motivational principles. The first is that goals vary in their chronicity—the degree to which a given goal is frequently activated for a given individual (for a related discussion, see Bargh, Bond, Lombardi, & Tota, 1986). Chronicity is determined both by species-typical psychological architecture and by individual-specific ontogeny, and greater chronicity predicts greater frequency of attraction to others who are instrumental for that goal. For example, one reason why Jason tends, at any random moment in time, to be more attracted to Rachel than to Scott is that the needs and goals that she is better at helping him satisfy (e.g., belonging, sexuality) are more chronic than his computer functionality needs.

The second motivational principle is that goals vary in their importance—the degree to which a given goal, when activated, tends to be high in motivational priority for a given individual (Emmons, 1986). In other words, whereas chronicity refers to the frequency with which a given goal is activated, importance refers to the typical motivational priority of that goal when it is activated. For example, although Jason typically values his belonging needs quite highly, he values strong performance on standardized tests even more strongly during those rare occasions when such performance is relevant. Consequently, just as he withdrew from friends and family leading up to the SAT, he may withdraw from Rachel in the weeks preceding his medical board exam. Indeed, during that brief but intense study period, the enormous importance he places on passing the board exam may cause him to become more attracted to his study partner than to his wife.

The third motivational principle is that other people vary in their multifinality—the degree to which those others are instrumental for many rather than few of an individual's goals (Kruglanski et al., 2002). For example, all else equal, if Jason finds

Rachel and his colleague James to be equally instrumental in helping him train for an upcoming marathon, he will ultimately experience greater attraction to Rachel if she is more instrumental to his other goals than James is, especially if those goals are high in chronicity and importance. For example, if he values nightly pillow talk and family dinners more than any goals James can help him achieve, Jason will tend to be more attracted to Rachel. After all, once his fitness goals have been attained (e.g., by running 10 miles), then other goals come to the fore. In general, if another person is instrumental for many of one's goals—that is, if the person is multifinal—then the attainment of one goal for which that person is instrumental is not especially likely to undermine that person's instrumentality for a new goal that has now gained motivational priority.

Advantages of the instrumentality over the reward principle. Although reward-based theories have been influential in the attraction literature since its inception, the reward construct is broad and vague. We share both Berscheid's (1985) assessment that "the major problem with the general reinforcement approach . . . is the determination of what constitutes a reward or a cost to whom and when" (p. 439) and Lott and Lott's (1974) assessment that when considering what serves as a reward, "one must know what that human being needs or wants, what he or she considers valuable, desirable, or positive, and to what conditions the human being has been previously exposed" (pp. 173–174). In short, to understand how others can be rewarding for people, scholars investigating attraction must first understand what people need and want—what their goals are.

To be sure, some of these issues remain challenging when thinking in terms of instrumentality rather than reward, but the instrumentality principle has four crucial advantages over the reward principle. First, instrumentality is the more precise construct. Although strict behaviorists have long conceptualized the term *reward* in precise, behavioral terms, scholars of interpersonal attraction have frequently defined it in broad, intrapsychic ways (e.g., in terms of cognitive consistency or self-esteem maintenance) that would distress John B. Watson and B. F. Skinner.

The reward construct has become sufficiently bloated over time that it is no longer especially useful, especially in terms of deriving novel hypotheses or inspiring innovative empirical investigations. In contrast, as reviewed previously, scholars have defined instrumentality precisely (e.g., Fitzsimons & Shah, 2008).

Second, identifying instrumentality, rather than reward, as the crucial organizing principle underlying interpersonal attraction immediately links the attraction literature to the broad array of innovative and compelling empirical paradigms from the motivation literature, all of which can be retrofitted to the study of interpersonal attraction. The research methods with the greatest immediate relevance for the interpersonal attraction literature are those developed by Fitzsimons and colleagues to examine instrumentality dynamics in close relationship contexts. Scholars could adapt procedures from Fitzsimons and Shah (2008), priming people with certain goals and then studying their attraction to others. For example, scholars could prime some participants (acute goal activation) with a goal to achieve academically and other participants with a goal to have fun socially and then assess the degree to which participants in each experimental condition are attracted to strangers with characteristics associated with each of those goals (e.g., to others who are wearing glasses vs. holding a beer). Similarly, scholars could adapt these procedures to study attraction in stereotype-relevant domains. For example, they could prime the same two goals and then assess attraction to strangers from ethnic or racial groups associated with one of the goals. For example, such participants might be more attracted to Asian Americans, who are stereotypically associated with strong academic achievement, in the academic goal priming condition, whereas they might be more attracted to fraternity members, who are stereotypically associated with partying, in the social goal priming condition. Scholars could also adapt procedures from Fitzsimons and Fishbach (2010), priming participants' self-perception that they either have or have not made good progress toward achieving a certain goal and then assessing the degree to which participants in each experimental condition are attracted to strangers who have the potential to be instrumental for that goal.

Third, identifying instrumentality as the crucial organizing principle underlying interpersonal attraction immediately links the attraction literature to the motivation literature, which is currently witnessing a period of immense theoretical ferment. Not only has the long-standing literature examining people's use of conscious thought in their goal-pursuit efforts exhibited a renaissance over the past 2 decades, but a new literature examining people's use of nonconscious thought in their goal-pursuit efforts has exploded onto the scene in that same timeframe (Bargh et al., 2010). One major development, which is related to the chronicity point discussed previously, is the recognition that goal priorities fluctuate markedly over time, even nonconsciously (Bargh, 1990; Bargh et al., 2001). A second major development is the emergence of goal systems theory, which identifies a range of crucial tenets regarding the cognitive underpinnings of goal pursuit, all of which are relevant to interpersonal attraction (Kruglanski et al., 2002). For example, one tenet is that whichever goal is currently highest in motivational priority dominates a given means, thereby reducing the degree to which that means is used to serve a different goal. In the attraction domain, an intense desire to view the self positively (e.g., after failure on a final examination) might cause people to interpret signs of similarity with another person as evidence that they possess desirable qualities rather than as evidence that they view the world accurately.

Fourth, identifying instrumentality as the crucial organizing principle underlying interpersonal attraction enables scholars to talk in a common language about attraction phenomena from all three overarching metatheories. In that sense, the instrumentality principle can function as a Rosetta Stone for the attraction literature, providing a unifying theoretical framework and establishing a coherent set of empirical methodologies, thereby facilitating intermetatheory communication. To be sure, the specifics of the theoretical analyses and the methodologies will vary from topic to topic, but scholars adopting any of the three metatheoretical orientations can now discuss concepts such as needs and goals, seek to identify which other people are instrumental for which goals under which circumstances, and capitalize on

theoretically powerful methodologies such as goal priming. For example, from a domain-general reward perspective, scholars can investigate whether people tend to be more attracted to others who introduce them to new activities (and can help them pursue self-expansion goals) than to others who do not and whether those effects are strongest among people whose self-expansion motivation is especially strong (either dispositionally or situationally). From a domain-specific evolutionary perspective, scholars can investigate whether men have a stronger preference for women with fertile-looking body shapes (which has historically helped men pursue reproductive goals) when the women are ovulating than when they are not. From an attachment perspective, scholars can investigate whether people tend to be more attracted to responsive others (who can help them pursue bonding goals) when those people are feeling emotionally vulnerable rather than secure.

IMPLICATIONS AND FUTURE DIRECTIONS

People's goals are complex and multiply determined. Regarding interpersonal attraction, goals vary as a function of people's immediate environment (e.g., the physical attractiveness of a stranger at a sporting event), their present life circumstances (e.g., their current lack of a romantic partner), their life course ontogeny (e.g., past successes vs. failures in their romantic overtures toward attractive others), cultural factors (e.g., norms about cross-race romance), species-typical evolutionary pressures (e.g., physical indicators of reproductive viability), and so forth. We suggest that the primary tasks facing scholars who seek to understand interpersonal attraction are (a) to identify which needs are particularly salient and important under which circumstances; (b) to discern which other people (potential targets of attraction) are especially, perhaps uniquely, effective at helping people meet those needs; and (c) to establish the circumstances under which others' instrumentality elicits one form of attraction rather than another (e.g., platonic affection vs. sexual frenzy)—which is almost certainly due in large part to the fundamental nature of the need or goal in question (e.g., a sexual goal vs. a productivity goal). Accomplishing these tasks, we suggest, will allow scholars to account for the lion's share of the variance in predicting whether one person will become attracted to another in a given context.

More immediately, conceptualizing the interpersonal attraction literature from the perspective of the instrumentality principle has many important implications, all of which suggest future research possibilities. We discuss five such implications here. First, this new conceptualization allows for the integration of disparate scholarly literatures underneath a single theoretical umbrella. For example, the literatures on attraction to romantic alternatives (e.g., Johnson & Rusbult, 1989) and on extrarelationship sexuality (Atkins, Baucom, & Jacobson, 2001) have emerged largely independently from the literature on interpersonal attraction, but we suggest that instrumentality dynamics represent a major force in both contexts. In particular, we suggest that attraction to a given romantic alternative, and the likelihood of engaging in extrarelationship sexual activity with him or her, increases to the degree that the alternative in question is instrumental for a goal that is of high motivational priority to the person in question. For example, if a person feels acutely deprived of excitement in his or her relationship, he or she will be especially likely to experience attraction to a romantic alternative who is exciting. The instrumentality perspective can also shed light on why people sometimes engage in extrarelationship behaviors that cause them acute guilt and distress moments later, once the motivational priority of the goal or goals that contributed to those behaviors has been attained by enacting those behaviors.

Other examples of how the instrumentality perspective can link disparate literatures together abound. For example, as noted previously, the instrumentality perspective can help to integrate the massive literature on stereotyping and prejudice with the interpersonal attraction literature (see also Graziano, Bruce, Sheese, & Tobin, 2007). Scholars have long suggested, for example, that people tend to experience diminished liking toward members of ethnic or racial groups whom people perceive to be undermining their pursuit of an important goal, such as competing with them for employment opportunities.

Second, in contrast to the traditional conceptualization of the link between reward and interpersonal attraction, the link between instrumentality and interpersonal attraction is not monotonic. For example, if a given person requires 10 units of social connection to sate a current belonging need, then the association of a target's instrumentality for the person's belonging goal with attraction should be monotonically, albeit nonlinearly, positive from 0 to 9 units. However, that association should be flat or even negative on hitting the 10th unit and progressing behind it. At that point, the person will become less attracted to others who promote social connection and more attracted to others who are instrumental for whichever needs have increased in motivational priority in the wake of the satiation of the belonging need.

Third, people are likely to experience greater interpersonal attraction toward a stranger to the degree that he or she is instrumental to goals for which members of their current social network are not instrumental. For example, when one's current social network does not adequately meet one's need for emotional intimacy (or for cognitive consistency, academic achievement, etc.), one is likely to be especially attracted to others with the potential to meet that need.

Fourth, as discussed previously, the instrumentality principle has the potential to bring substantial explanatory power to the scholarly understanding of the fickleness of interpersonal attraction. As people's motivational priorities change—over the course of years, days, or even seconds—their attraction to others who are more effective at helping them achieve some goals rather than others will change, too (see Fitzsimons & Fishbach, 2010). Interpersonal attraction scholars could fruitfully incorporate some of the major recent advances scholars of self-regulation have made in recent years to understand the nature of motivational fluctuation over time (e.g., Louro, Pieters, & Zeelenberg, 2007).

Fifth, our application of the instrumentality principle has assumed that people's goals emerge and fluctuate independently of their attraction to a given target, but abundant research over the past decade has shown that social processes exert powerful influences on people's self-regulation (see Finkel & Fitzsimons, 2011; Fitzsimons & Finkel, 2010). In other words, targets of attraction might influence not only how people pursue their goals, but also the setting of such goals in the first place. As such, an important direction for future research is to examine the ways in which targets of interpersonal attraction alter people's goals (e.g., triggering the novel goal to learn Japanese) and the ways in which these effects alter the attraction that people experience both toward members of their current social network and toward strangers they will meet going forward.

CONCLUSION

Scholars have explicitly or implicitly adopted one or more of three overarching perspectives to understand interpersonal attraction: domain-general reward perspectives, domain-specific evolutionary perspectives, and attachment perspectives. At their core, all three of these perspectives are dependent on understanding the needs people bring to attraction contexts. In light of this observation, we suggest that the key unifying principle underlying the interpersonal attraction literature is instrumentality—people are attracted to others to the degree that those others help them achieve the goals that are currently high in motivational priority. Linking the attraction literature to the goal-pursuit literature unleashes a torrent of immediately accessible directions for future research. Our hope is that that the theoretical contributions of this chapter—both the theoretical structure for reviewing the extant literature and the novel emphasis on instrumentality—will serve as an important step toward the theoretical integration of the interpersonal attraction literature.

References

Aharon, I., Etcoff, N., Ariely, D., Chabris, C. F., O'Connor, E., & Breiter, H. C. (2001). Beautiful faces have variable reward value: FMRI and behavioral evidence. *Neuron, 32*, 537–551. doi:10.1016/S0896-6273(01)00491-3

Ainsworth, M. D. S., Blehar, M., Waters, E., & Wall, S. (1978). *Patterns of attachment*. Hillsdale, NJ: Erlbaum.

Andersen, S. M., Reznik, I., & Manzella, L. M. (1996). Eliciting facial affect, motivation, and expectancies in transference: Significant-other representations in social relations. *Journal of Personality and Social Psychology, 71*, 1108–1129. doi:10.1037/0022-3514.71.6.1108

Anderson, U. S., Perea, E. F., Becker, D. V., Ackerman, J. M., Shapiro, J. R., Neuberg, S. L., & Kenrick, D. T. (2010). I only have eyes for you: Ovulation redirects attention (but not memory) to attractive men. *Journal of Experimental Social Psychology, 46*, 804–808. doi:10.1016/j.jesp.2010.04.015

Aron, A., Lewandowski, G. W., Jr., Mashek, D., & Aron, E. N. (2013). The self-expansion model of motivation and cognition in close relationships. In J. A. Simpson, & L. Campbell (Eds.), *Oxford handbook of close relationships* (pp. 90–115). New York, NY: Oxford University Press.

Aron, A., Steele, J., Kashdan, T., & Perez, M. (2006). When similars do not attract: Tests of a prediction from the self-expansion model. *Personal Relationships, 13*, 387–396. doi:10.1111/j.1475-6811.2006.00125.x

Aronson, E. (1969). Some antecedents of interpersonal attraction. In W. J. Arnold & D. Levine (Eds.), *Nebraska symposium on motivation* (Vol. 17, pp. 143–173). Lincoln: University of Nebraska Press.

Aronson, E., & Cope, V. (1968). My enemy's enemy is my friend. *Journal of Personality and Social Psychology, 8*, 8–12. doi:10.1037/h0021234

Aronson, E., & Linder, D. (1965). Gain and loss of esteem as determinants of interpersonal attractiveness. *Journal of Experimental Social Psychology, 1*, 156–171. doi:10.1016/0022-1031(65)90043-0

Aronson, E., Willerman, B., & Floyd, J. (1966). The effect of a pratfall on increasing interpersonal attractiveness. *Psychonomic Science, 4*, 227–228.

Atkins, D. C., Baucom, D. H., & Jacobson, N. S. (2001). Understanding infidelity: Correlates in a national random sample. *Journal of Family Psychology, 15*, 735–749. doi:10.1037/0893-3200.15.4.735

Atkinson, J. W. (1964). *An introduction to motivation*. Princeton, NJ: Van Nostrand.

Back, M. D., Schmulke, S. C., & Egloff, B. (2008). Becoming friends by chance. *Psychological Science, 19*, 439–440. doi:10.1111/j.1467-9280.2008.02106.x

Balcetis, E., & Dunning, D. (2006). See what you want to see: Motivational influences on visual perception. *Journal of Personality and Social Psychology, 91*, 612–625. doi:10.1037/0022-3514.91.4.612

Baldwin, M. W., Keelan, J. P. R., Fehr, B., Enns, V., & Koh-Rangarajoo, E. (1996). Social-cognitive conceptualization of attachment working models: Availability and accessibility effects. *Journal of Personality and Social Psychology, 71*, 94–109. doi:10.1037/0022-3514.71.1.94

Bargh, J. A. (1990). Auto-motives: Preconscious determinants of social interaction. In E. T. Higgins & R. M.

Sorrentino (Eds.), *Handbook of motivation and cognition* (Vol. 2, pp. 93–130). New York, NY: Guilford Press.

Bargh, J. A., Bond, R. N., Lombardi, W. J., & Tota, M. E. (1986). The additive nature of chronic and temporary sources of construct accessibility. *Journal of Personality and Social Psychology, 50,* 869–878. doi:10.1037/0022-3514.50.5.869

Bargh, J. A., Gollwitzer, P. M., Lee-Chai, A., Barndollar, K., & Trötschel, R. (2001). The automated will: Unconscious activation and pursuit of behavioral goals. *Journal of Personality and Social Psychology, 81,* 1014–1027. doi:10.1037/0022-3514.81.6.1014

Bargh, J. A., Gollwitzer, P. M., & Oettingen, G. (2010). Motivation. In S. Fiske, D. T. Gilbert, & G. Lindzey (Eds.), *Handbook of social psychology* (5th ed., pp. 268–316). New York, NY: Wiley.

Barrett, H. C., & Kurzban, R. (2006). Modularity in cognition: Framing the debate. *Psychological Review, 113,* 628–647. doi:10.1037/0033-295X.113.3.628

Bartz, J. A., & Lydon, J. E. (2006). Navigating the interdependence dilemma: Attachment goals and the use of communal norms with potential close others. *Journal of Personality and Social Psychology, 91,* 77–96. doi:10.1037/0022-3514.91.1.77

Baumeister, R. F., & Leary, M. R. (1995). The need to belong: Desire for interpersonal attachments as a fundamental human motivation. *Psychological Bulletin, 117,* 497–529. doi:10.1037/0033-2909.117.3.497

Beckman, C. W., & Secord, P. F. (1959). The effect of perceived liking on interpersonal attraction. *Human Relations, 12,* 379–384. doi:10.1177/001872675901200407

Belsky, J., Steinberg, L., & Draper, P. (1991). Childhood experience, interpersonal development, and reproductive strategy: An evolutionary theory of socialization. *Child Development, 62,* 647–670. doi:10.2307/1131166

Berscheid, E. (1985). Interpersonal attraction. In G. Lindzey & E. Aronson (Eds.), *Handbook of social psychology* (3rd ed., pp. 413–484). New York, NY: Random House.

Berscheid, E., & Ammazzalorso, H. (2001). Emotional experience in close relationships. In M. Hewstone & M. Brewer (Eds.), *Blackwell handbook of social psychology: Vol. 2. Interpersonal processes* (pp. 308–330). Oxford, England: Blackwell.

Berscheid, E., & Regan, P. (2005). *The psychology of interpersonal relationships.* New York, NY: Prentice-Hall.

Birnbaum, G. E., & Reis, H. T. (2012). When does responsiveness pique sexual interest? Attachment and sexual desire in initial acquaintanceships. *Personality and Social Psychology Bulletin, 38,* 946–958.

Bowlby, J. (1969). *Attachment and loss: Vol. 1. Attachment.* New York, NY: Basic Books.

Bowlby, J. (1973). *Attachment and loss: Vol. 2. Separation.* New York, NY: Basic Books.

Bradbury, T. N., & Karney, B. R. (2010). *Intimate relationships.* New York, NY: Norton.

Brendl, C. M., Markman, A. B., & Messner, C. (2003). The devaluation effect: Activating a need devalues unrelated choice options. *Journal of Consumer Research, 29,* 463–473. doi:10.1086/346243

Brennan, K. A., Clark, C. L., & Shaver, P. R. (1998). Self-report measurement of adult attachment: An integrative overview. In J. A. Simpson & W. S. Rholes (Eds.), *Attachment theory and close relationships* (pp. 46–76). New York, NY: Guilford Press.

Brennan, K. A., & Shaver, P. R. (1995). Dimensions of adult attachment, affect regulation, and romantic relationship functioning. *Personality and Social Psychology Bulletin, 21,* 267–283. doi:10.1177/0146167295213008

Brumbaugh, C. C., & Fraley, R. C. (2006). Transference and attachment: How do attachment patterns get carried forward from one relationship to the next? *Personality and Social Psychology Bulletin, 32,* 552–560. doi:10.1177/0146167205282740

Bruner, J. S., & Goodman, C. C. (1947). Value and need as organizing factors in perception. *Journal of Abnormal and Social Psychology, 42,* 33–44. doi:10.1037/h0058484

Buss, D. M. (1985). Human mate selection. *American Scientist, 73,* 47–51.

Buss, D. M. (1988). The evolution of human intrasexual competition: Tactics of mate attraction. *Journal of Personality and Social Psychology, 54,* 616–628. doi:10.1037/0022-3514.54.4.616

Buss, D. M. (1989). Sex differences in human mate preferences: Evolutionary hypotheses tested in 37 cultures. *Behavioral and Brain Sciences, 12,* 1–49. doi:10.1017/S0140525X00023992

Buss, D. M. (1992). Mate preference mechanisms: Consequences for partner choice and intrasexual competition. In J. H. Barkow, L. Cosmides, & J. Tooby (Eds.), *The adapted mind: Evolutionary psychology and the generation of culture* (pp. 249–266). New York, NY: Oxford University Press.

Buss, D. M., & Barnes, M. L. (1986). Preferences in human mate selection. *Journal of Personality and Social Psychology, 50,* 559–570. doi:10.1037/0022-3514.50.3.559

Buss, D. M., Haselton, M. G., Shackelford, T. K., Bleske, A. L., & Wakefield, J. C. (1998). Adaptations, exaptations, and spandrels. *American Psychologist, 53,* 533–548. doi:10.1037/0003-066X.53.5.533

Buss, D. M., & Reeve, H. K. (2003). Evolutionary psychology and developmental dynamics: Comment on Lickliter and Honeycutt (2003). *Psychological Bulletin, 129,* 848–853. doi:10.1037/0033-2909.129.6.848

Buss, D. M., & Schmitt, D. P. (1993). Sexual strategies theory: An evolutionary perspective on human mating. *Psychological Review, 100*, 204–232. doi:10.1037/0033-295X.100.2.204

Buss, D. M., & Shackelford, T. K. (2008). Attractive women want it all: Good genes, economic investment, parenting proclivities, and emotional commitment. *Evolutionary Psychology, 6*, 134–146.

Byrne, D. (1961). Interpersonal attraction and attitude similarity. *Journal of Abnormal and Social Psychology, 62*, 713–715. doi:10.1037/h0044721

Campbell, L., Simpson, J. A., Boldry, J., & Kashy, D. A. (2005). Perceptions of conflict and support in romantic relationships: The role of attachment anxiety. *Journal of Personality and Social Psychology, 88*, 510–531. doi:10.1037/0022-3514.88.3.510

Carver, C. S., & Scheier, M. F. (1998). *On the self-regulation of behavior.* Cambridge, England: Cambridge University Press. doi:10.1017/CBO9781139174794

Chappell, K. D., & Davis, K. E. (1998). Attachment, partner choice, and perception of romantic partners: An experimental test of the attachment-security hypothesis. *Personal Relationships, 5*, 327–342.

Clark, M. S. (1984). Record keeping in two types of relationships. *Journal of Personality and Social Psychology, 47*, 549–557. doi:10.1037/0022-3514.47.3.549

Clark, M. S., & Mills, J. (1979). Interpersonal attraction in exchange and communal relationships. *Journal of Personality and Social Psychology, 37*, 12–24. doi:10.1037/0022-3514.37.1.12

Clark, R. D., & Hatfield, E. (1989). Gender differences in receptivity to sexual offers. *Journal of Psychology and Human Sexuality, 2*, 39–55. doi:10.1300/J056v02n01_04

Clore, G. L., & Byrne, D. (1974). The reinforcement-affect model of attraction. In T. L. Huston (Ed.), *Foundations of interpersonal attraction* (pp. 143–170). New York, NY: Academic Press.

Cloutier, J., Heatherton, T. F., Whalen, P. J., & Kelley, W. M. (2008). Are attractive people rewarding? Sex differences in the neural substrates of facial attractiveness. *Journal of Cognitive Neuroscience, 20*, 941–951. doi:10.1162/jocn.2008.20062

Collins, N. L., & Miller, L. C. (1994). Self-disclosure and liking: A meta-analytic review. *Psychological Bulletin, 116*, 457–475. doi:10.1037/0033-2909.116.3.457

Conley, T. D. (2011). Perceived proposer personality characteristics and gender differences in acceptance of casual sex offers. *Journal of Personality and Social Psychology, 100*, 309–329. doi:10.1037/a0022152

Converse, B. A., & Fishbach, A. (2012). Instrumentality boosts appreciation: Helpers are more appreciated while they are useful. *Psychological Science, 23*, 560–566.

Cosmides, L. (1985). *Deduction or Darwinian algorithms? An explanation of the "elusive" content effect on the Wason selection task* (unpublished doctoral dissertation). Harvard University, Cambridge, MA.

Cosmides, L. (1989). The logic of social exchange: Has natural selection shaped how humans reason? Studies with the Wason selection task. *Cognition, 31*, 187–276. doi:10.1016/0010-0277(89)90023-1

Darwin, C. (1859). *On the origin of species by means of natural selection.* London: J. Murray.

Deaux, K. (1972). To err is humanizing: But sex makes a difference. *Representative Research in Social Psychology, 3*, 20–28.

DeWall, C. N., Baumeister, R. F., & Vohs, K. D. (2008). Satiated with belongingness? Effects of acceptance, rejection, and task framing on self-regulatory performance. *Journal of Personality and Social Psychology, 95*, 1367–1382. doi:10.1037/a0012632

Diamond, L. M., Hicks, A. M., & Otter-Henderson, K. D. (2008). Every time you go away: Changes in affect, behavior, and physiology associated with travel-related separations from romantic partners. *Journal of Personality and Social Psychology, 95*, 385–403. doi:10.1037/0022-3514.95.2.385

Eagly, A. H., & Wood, W. (1999). The origins of sex differences in human behavior: Evolved dispositions versus social roles. *American Psychologist, 54*, 408–423. doi:10.1037/0003-066X.54.6.408

Eastwick, P. W. (2009). Beyond the Pleistocene: Using phylogeny and constraint to inform the evolutionary psychology of human mating. *Psychological Bulletin, 135*, 794–821. doi:10.1037/a0016845

Eastwick, P. W., Eagly, A. H., Finkel, E. J., & Johnson, S. E. (2011). Implicit and explicit preferences for physical attractiveness in a romantic partner: A double dissociation in predictive validity. *Journal of Personality and Social Psychology, 101*, 993–1011. doi:10.1037/a0024061

Eastwick, P. W., & Finkel, E. J. (2008a). The attachment system in fledgling relationships: An activating role for attachment anxiety. *Journal of Personality and Social Psychology, 95*, 628–647. doi:10.1037/0022-3514.95.3.628

Eastwick, P. W., & Finkel, E. J. (2008b). Sex differences in mate preferences revisited: Do people know what they initially desire in a romantic partner? *Journal of Personality and Social Psychology, 94*, 245–264. doi:10.1037/0022-3514.94.2.245

Eastwick, P. W., & Finkel, E. J. (2009). Reciprocity of liking. In H. T. Reis & S. Sprecher (Eds.), *Encyclopedia of human relations* (pp. 1333–1336). Thousand Oaks, CA: Sage. doi:10.4135/9781412958479.n433

Eastwick, P. W., & Finkel, E. J. (2012). The evolutionary armistice: Attachment bonds moderate the function of ovulatory cycle adaptations. *Personality and Social Psychology Bulletin, 38*, 174–184. doi:10.1177/0146167211422366

Eastwick, P. W., Finkel, E. J., & Eagly, A. H. (2011). When and why do ideal partner preferences affect the processes of initiating and maintaining romantic relationships? *Journal of Personality and Social Psychology, 101*, 1012–1032. doi:10.1037/a0024062

Eastwick, P. W., Finkel, E. J., Mochon, D., & Ariely, D. (2007). Selective versus unselective romantic desire: Not all reciprocity is created equal. *Psychological Science, 18*, 317–319. doi:10.1111/j.1467-9280.2007.01897.x

Ebbesen, E. B., Kjos, G. L., & Koneîcni, V. J. (1976). Spatial ecology: Its effects on the choice of friends and enemies. *Journal of Experimental Social Psychology, 12*, 505–518. doi:10.1016/0022-1031(76)90030-5

Emmons, R. A. (1986). Personal strivings: An approach to personality and subjective well-being. *Journal of Personality and Social Psychology, 51*, 1058–1068. doi:10.1037/0022-3514.51.5.1058

Fagundes, C. P., & Schindler, I. (2012). Making of romantic attachment bonds: Longitudinal trajectories and implications for relationship stability. *Personal Relationships, 19*, 723–742.

Feeney, B. C. (2004). A secure base: Responsive support of goal strivings and exploration in adult intimate relationships. *Journal of Personality and Social Psychology, 87*, 631–648. doi:10.1037/0022-3514.87.5.631

Feeney, B. C., Cassidy, J., & Ramos-Marcuse, F. (2008). The generalization of attachment representations to new social situations: Predicting behavior during initial interactions with strangers. *Journal of Personality and Social Psychology, 95*, 1481–1498. doi:10.1037/a0012635

Feeney, J. A., Noller, P., & Patty, J. (1993). Adolescents' interactions with the opposite sex: Influence of attachment style and gender. *Journal of Adolescence, 16*, 169–186. doi:10.1006/jado.1993.1015

Feingold, A. (1990). Gender differences in effects of physical attractiveness on romantic attraction: A comparison across five research paradigms. *Journal of Personality and Social Psychology, 59*, 981–993. doi:10.1037/0022-3514.59.5.981

Feingold, A. (1992). Gender differences in mate selection preferences: A test of the parental investment model. *Psychological Bulletin, 112*, 125–139. doi:10.1037/0033-2909.112.1.125

Ferguson, M. J., & Bargh, J. A. (2004). Liking is for doing: The effect of goal pursuit on automatically activated attitudes. *Journal of Personality and Social Psychology, 87*, 557–572. doi:10.1037/0022-3514.87.5.557

Festinger, L., Schachter, S., & Back, K. (1950). *Social pressures in informal groups: A study of human factors in housing.* Stanford, CA: Stanford University Press.

Finkel, E. J., & Baumeister, R. F. (2010). Attraction and rejection. In R. F. Baumeister & E. J. Finkel (Eds.), *Advanced social psychology: The state of the science* (pp. 419–459). New York, NY: Oxford University Press.

Finkel, E. J., & Eastwick, P. W. (2008). Speed-dating. *Current Directions in Psychological Science, 17*, 193–197. doi:10.1111/j.1467-8721.2008.00573.x

Finkel, E. J., & Eastwick, P. W. (2009a). Arbitrary social norms and sex differences in romantic selectivity. *Psychological Science, 20*, 1290–1295. doi:10.1111/j.1467-9280.2009.02439.x

Finkel, E. J., & Eastwick, P. W. (2009b). Hard-to-get phenomenon. In H. T. Reis & S. Sprecher (Eds.), *Encyclopedia of human relations* (pp. 788–790). Thousand Oaks, CA: Sage. doi:10.4135/9781412958479.n251

Finkel, E. J., & Fitzsimons, G. M. (2011). The effects of social relationships on self-regulation. In K. D. Vohs & R. F. Baumeister (Eds.), *Handbook of self-regulation: Research, theory, and applications* (2nd ed., pp. 390–406). New York, NY: Guilford Press.

Finkel, E. J., Molden, D. C., Johnson, S. E., & Eastwick, P. W. (2009). Regulatory focus and romantic alternatives. In J. P. Forgas, R. F. Baumeister, & D. M. Tice (Eds.), *Self-regulation: Cognitive, affective, and motivational processes* (pp. 319–335). New York, NY: Psychology Press.

Finkel, E. J., & Slotter, E. B. (2007). An attachment theory perspective on the perpetration of intimate partner violence. *De Paul Law Review, 56*, 895–907.

Fitzsimons, G. M., & Finkel, E. J. (2010). Interpersonal influences on self-regulation. *Current Directions in Psychological Science, 19*, 101–105. doi:10.1177/0963721410364499

Fitzsimons, G. M., & Fishbach, A. (2010). Shifting closeness: Interpersonal effects of personal goal progress. *Journal of Personality and Social Psychology, 98*, 535–549. doi:10.1037/a0018581

Fitzsimons, G. M., & Shah, J. (2008). How goal instrumentality shapes relationship evaluations. *Journal of Personality and Social Psychology, 95*, 319–337. doi:10.1037/0022-3514.95.2.319

Fletcher, G. J. O., Simpson, J. A., Thomas, G., & Giles, L. (1999). Ideals in intimate relationships. *Journal of Personality and Social Psychology, 76*, 72–89. doi:10.1037/0022-3514.76.1.72

Förster, J., Liberman, N., & Friedman, R. S. (2007). Seven principles of goal activation: A systematic approach to distinguishing goal priming from priming of non-goal constructs. *Personality and Social Psychology Review, 11*, 211–233. doi:10.1177/1088868307303029

Fraley, R. C., & Davis, K. E. (1997). Attachment formation and transfer in young adults' close friendships and romantic relationships. *Personal Relationships, 4*, 131–144. doi:10.1111/j.1475-6811.1997.tb00135.x

Fraley, R. C., Davis, K. E., & Shaver, P. R. (1998). Dismissing-avoidance and the defensive organization of emotion, cognition, and behavior. In J. A. Simpson & W. S. Rholes (Eds.), *Attachment theory and close relationships* (pp. 249–279). New York, NY: Guilford Press.

Fraley, R. C., Niedenthal, P. M., Marks, M. J., Brumbaugh, C. C., & Vicary, A. (2006). Adult attachment and the perception of emotional expressions: Probing the hyperactivating strategies underlying anxious attachment. *Journal of Personality, 74*, 1163–1190. doi:10.1111/j.1467-6494.2006.00406.x

Frazier, P. A., Byer, A. L., Fischer, A. R., Wright, D. M., & Debord, K. A. (1996). Adult attachment style and partner choice: Correlational and experimental findings. *Personal Relationships, 3*, 117–136. doi:10.1111/j.1475-6811.1996.tb00107.x

Freud, S. (1952). *A general introduction to psychoanalysis.* New York, NY: Washington Square Press. (Original work published 1920) doi:10.1037/10667-000

Freud, S. (1958). The dynamics of transference. In J. Strachey (Ed. & Trans.), *The standard edition of the complete psychological works of Sigmund Freud* (Vol. 12, pp. 97–108). London, England: Hogarth Press. (Original work published 1912)

Gangestad, S. W., Garver-Apgar, C. E., Simpson, J. A., & Cousins, A. J. (2007). Changes in women's mate preferences across the ovulatory cycle. *Journal of Personality and Social Psychology, 92*, 151–163. doi:10.1037/0022-3514.92.1.151

Gangestad, S. W., Haselton, M. G., & Buss, D. M. (2006). Evolutionary foundations of cultural variation: Evoked culture and mate preferences. *Psychological Inquiry, 17*, 75–95.

Gangestad, S. W., & Simpson, J. A. (2000). The evolution of human mating: Trade-offs and strategic pluralism. *Behavioral and Brain Sciences, 23*, 573–587. doi:10.1017/S0140525X0000337X

Gangestad, S. W., Simpson, J. A., Cousins, A. J., Garver-Apgar, C. E., & Christensen, P. (2004). Women's preferences for male behavioral displays change across the menstrual cycle. *Psychological Science, 15*, 203–207. doi:10.1111/j.0956-7976.2004.01503010.x

Gangestad, S. W., & Thornhill, R. (1997). The evolutionary psychology of extrapair sex: The role of fluctuating asymmetry. *Evolution and Human Behavior, 18*, 69–88. doi:10.1016/S1090-5138(97)00003-2

Gangestad, S. W., & Thornhill, R. (1998). Menstrual cycle variation in women's preference for the scent of symmetrical men. *Proceedings of the Royal Society B: Biological Sciences, 265*, 927–933. doi:10.1098/rspb.1998.0380

Gangestad, S. W., Thornhill, R., & Garver-Apgar, C. E. (2005). Adaptations to ovulation: Implications for sexual and social behavior. *Current Directions in Psychological Science, 14*, 312–316. doi:10.1111/j.0963-7214.2005.00388.x

Gordon, R. A. (1996). Impact of ingratiation on judgments and evaluations: A meta-analytic investigation. *Journal of Personality and Social Psychology, 71*, 54–70. doi:10.1037/0022-3514.71.1.54

Gouaux, C. (1971). Induced affective states and interpersonal attraction. *Journal of Personality and Social Psychology, 20*, 37–43. doi:10.1037/h0031697

Gray, J. A. (1982). *The neuropsychology of anxiety: An enquiry into the functions of the septo-hippocampal system.* New York, NY: Oxford University Press. doi:10.1017/S0140525X00013066

Graziano, W. G., Bruce, J. W., Sheese, B. E., & Tobin, R. M. (2007). Attraction, personality and prejudice: Liking none of the people most of the time. *Journal of Personality and Social Psychology, 93*, 565–582. doi:10.1037/0022-3514.93.4.565

Griffitt, W. (1970). Environmental effects on interpersonal affective behavior: Ambient effective temperature and attraction. *Journal of Personality and Social Psychology, 15*, 240–244. doi:10.1037/h0029432

Griffitt, W., & Veitch, R. (1971). Hot and crowded: Influences of population density and temperature on interpersonal affective behavior. *Journal of Personality and Social Psychology, 17*, 92–98. doi:10.1037/h0030458

Harlow, H. F. (1958). The nature of love. *American Psychologist, 13*, 673–685. doi:10.1037/h0047884

Haselton, M. G., & Gangestad, S. W. (2006). Conditional expression of women's desires and men's mate guarding across the ovulatory cycle. *Hormones and Behavior, 49*, 509–518. doi:10.1016/j.yhbeh.2005.10.006

Havlicek, J., Roberts, S. C., & Flegr, J. (2005). Women's preference for dominant male odour: Effects of menstrual cycle and relationship status. *Biology Letters, 1*, 256–259. doi:10.1098/rsbl.2005.0332

Hazan, C., & Diamond, L. M. (2000). The place of attachment in human mating. *Review of General Psychology, 4*, 186–204. doi:10.1037/1089-2680.4.2.186

Hazan, C., & Shaver, P. (1987). Romantic love conceptualized as an attachment process. *Journal of Personality and Social Psychology, 52*, 511–524.

Hazan, C., & Zeifman, D. (1994). Sex and the psychological tether. In K. Bartholomew & D. Perlman (Eds.), *Advances in personal relationships: Vol. 5. Attachment processes in adulthood* (pp. 151–177). London, England: Jessica Kingsley.

Heider, F. (1958). *The psychology of interpersonal relations*. New York, NY: Wiley. doi:10.1037/10628-000

Herbst, K. C., Gaertner, L., & Insko, C. A. (2003). My head says yes but my heart says no: Cognitive and affective attraction as a function of similarity to the ideal self. *Journal of Personality and Social Psychology, 84*, 1206–1219. doi:10.1037/0022-3514.84.6.1206

Hill, R. (1945). Campus values in mate-selection. *Journal of Home Economics, 37*, 554–558.

Holmes, B. M., & Johnson, K. R. (2009). Adult attachment and romantic partner preference: A review. *Journal of Social and Personal Relationships, 26*, 833–852. doi:10.1177/0265407509345653

Homans, G. C. (1961). *Social behavior: Its elementary forms*. New York, NY: Harcourt, Brace, & World.

Johnson, D. J., & Rusbult, C. E. (1989). Resisting temptation: Devaluation of alternative partners as a means of maintaining commitment in close relationships. *Journal of Personality and Social Psychology, 57*, 967–980. doi:10.1037/0022-3514.57.6.967

Jones, B. C., DeBruine, L. M., Perrett, D. I., Little, A. C., Feinberg, D. R., & Law Smith, M. J. (2008). Effects of menstrual cycle phase on face preferences. *Archives of Sexual Behavior, 37*, 78–84. doi:10.1007/s10508-007-9268-y

Kellerman, J., Lewis, J., & Laird, J. D. (1989). Looking and loving: The effects of mutual gaze on feelings of romantic love. *Journal of Research in Personality, 23*, 145–161. doi:10.1016/0092-6566(89)90020-2

Kelley, H. H. (1979). *Personal relationships: Their structure and processes*. Hillsdale, NJ: Erlbaum.

Kelley, H. H., Berscheid, E., Christensen, A., Harvey, J. H., Huston, T. L., Levinger, G., . . . Peterson, D. R. (1983). *Close relationships*. New York, NY: Freeman.

Kenrick, D. T., Groth, G. E., Trost, M. R., & Sadalla, E. K. (1993). Integrating evolutionary and social exchange perspectives on relationships: Effects of gender, self-appraisal, and involvement level on mate selection criteria. *Journal of Personality and Social Psychology, 64*, 951–969. doi:10.1037/0022-3514.64.6.951

Kenrick, D. T., & Gutierres, S. E. (1980). Contrast effects and judgments of physical attractiveness: When beauty becomes a social problem. *Journal of Personality and Social Psychology, 38*, 131–140. doi:10.1037/0022-3514.38.1.131

Kenrick, D. T., Gutierres, S. E., & Goldberg, L. L. (1989). Influence of popular erotica on judgments of strangers and mates. *Journal of Experimental Social Psychology, 25*, 159–167. doi:10.1016/0022-1031(89)90010-3

Kenrick, D. T., & Keefe, R. C. (1992). Age preferences in mates reflect sex differences in reproductive strategies. *Behavioral and Brain Sciences, 15*, 75–133.

Klohnen, E. C., & Luo, S. (2003). Interpersonal attraction and personality: What is attractive—Self similarity, ideal similarity, complementarity or attachment security? *Journal of Personality and Social Psychology, 85*, 709–722. doi:10.1037/0022-3514.85.4.709

Kruglanski, A. W., Shah, J. Y., Fishbach, A., Friedman, R., Chun, W. Y., & Sleeth-Keppler, D. (2002). A theory of goal systems. In M. P. Zanna (Ed.), *Advances in experimental social psychology* (pp. 331–378). San Diego, CA: Academic Press.

Kumashiro, M., Rusbult, C. E., & Finkel, E. J. (2008). Navigating personal and relational concerns: The quest for equilibrium. *Journal of Personality and Social Psychology, 95*, 94–110. doi:10.1037/0022-3514.95.1.94

Langlois, J. H., Kalakanis, L., Rubenstein, A. J., Larson, A., Hallam, M., & Smoot, M. (2000). Maxims or myths of beauty? A meta-analytic and theoretical review. *Psychological Bulletin, 126*, 390–423. doi:10.1037/0033-2909.126.3.390

Langlois, J. H., Roggman, L. A., Casey, R. J., Ritter, J. M., Rieser-Danner, L. A., & Jenkins, V. Y. (1987). Infant preferences for attractive faces: Rudiments of a stereotype? *Developmental Psychology, 23*, 363–369. doi:10.1037/0012-1649.23.3.363

Latty-Mann, H., & Davis, K. E. (1996). Attachment theory and partner choice: Preference and actuality. *Journal of Social and Personal Relationships, 13*, 5–23. doi:10.1177/0265407596131001

Leary, M. R., & Baumeister, R. F. (2000). The nature and function of self-esteem: Sociometer theory. In M. P. Zanna (Ed.), *Advances in experimental social psychology* (Vol. 32, pp. 1–62). San Diego, CA: Academic Press. doi:10.1016/S0065-2601(00)80003-9

Leary, T. (1957). *Interpersonal diagnosis of personality: A functional theory and methodology for personality evaluation*. Oxford, England: Ronald Press.

Lee, L., Loewenstein, G., Ariely, D., Hong, J., & Young, J. (2008). If I'm not hot, are you hot or not: Physical attractiveness evaluation and dating preferences as a function of one's own attractiveness. *Psychological Science, 19*, 669–677. doi:10.1111/j.1467-9280.2008.02141.x

Lemay, E. P., Jr., & Clark, M. S. (2008). How the head liberates the heart: Projection of communal responsiveness guides relationship promotion. *Journal of Personality and Social Psychology, 94*, 647–671. doi:10.1037/0022-3514.94.4.647

Levinger, G., & Snoek, J. D. (1972). *Attraction in relationship: A new look at interpersonal attraction*. New York, NY: General Learning Press.

Lewin, K. (1935). *A dynamic theory of personality*. New York, NY: McGraw-Hill.

Lott, B. E., & Lott, A. J. (1960). The formation of positive attitudes toward group members. *Journal of Abnormal*

and *Social Psychology, 61,* 297–300. doi:10.1037/
h0045778

Lott, B. E., & Lott, A. J. (1974). The role of reward in the formulation of positive interpersonal attitudes. In T. L. Huston (Ed.), *Foundations of interpersonal attraction* (pp. 171–192). New York, NY: Academic Press.

Louro, M. J., Pieters, R., & Zeelenberg, M. (2007). Dynamics of multiple-goal pursuit. *Journal of Personality and Social Psychology, 93,* 174–193. doi:10.1037/0022-3514.93.2.174

Lydon, J. E., Fitzsimons, G. M., & Naidoo, L. (2003). Devaluation versus enhancement of attractive alternatives: A critical test using the calibration paradigm. *Personality and Social Psychology Bulletin, 29,* 349–359. doi:10.1177/0146167202250202

Lydon, J. E., Meana, M., Sepinwall, D., Richards, N., & Mayman, S. (1999). The commitment calibration hypothesis: When do people devalue attractive alternatives? *Personality and Social Psychology Bulletin, 25,* 152–161. doi:10.1177/0146167299025002002

Maner, J. K., Gailliot, M. T., & Miller, S. L. (2009). The implicit cognition of relationship maintenance: Inattention to attractive alternatives. *Journal of Experimental Social Psychology, 45,* 174–179. doi:10.1016/j.jesp.2008.08.002

Maner, J. K., Gailliot, M. T., Rouby, D. A., & Miller, S. L. (2007). Can't take my eyes off you: Attentional adhesion to mates and rivals. *Journal of Personality and Social Psychology, 93,* 389–401. doi:10.1037/0022-3514.93.3.389

Maner, J. K., Kenrick, D. T., Becker, D., Delton, A. W., Hofer, B., Wilbur, C. J., & Neuberg, S. L. (2003). Sexually selective cognition: Beauty captures the mind of the beholder. *Journal of Personality and Social Psychology, 85,* 1107–1120. doi:10.1037/0022-3514.85.6.1107

Maner, J. K., Rouby, D. A., & Gonzaga, G. C. (2008). Automatic inattention to attractive alternatives: The evolved psychology of relationship maintenance. *Evolution and Human Behavior, 29,* 343–349. doi:10.1016/j.evolhumbehav.2008.04.003

May, J. L., & Hamilton, P. A. (1980). Effects of musically evoked affect on women's interpersonal attraction toward and perceptual judgments of physical attractiveness of men. *Motivation and Emotion, 4,* 217–228. doi:10.1007/BF00995420

McClure, M. J., Lydon, J. E., Baccus, J. R., & Baldwin, M. W. (2010). A signal detection analysis of chronic attachment anxiety at speed dating: Being unpopular is the only first part of the problem. *Personality and Social Psychology Bulletin, 36,* 1024–1036. doi:10.1177/0146167210374238

McCrae, R. R., & Costa, P. T., Jr. (1989). The structure of interpersonal traits: Wiggins's circumplex and the five-factor model. *Journal of Personality and*

Social Psychology, 56, 586–595. doi:10.1037/0022-3514.56.4.586

Mikulincer, M., & Nachshon, O. (1991). Attachment styles and patterns of self-disclosure. *Journal of Personality and Social Psychology, 61,* 321–331. doi:10.1037/0022-3514.61.2.321

Mikulincer, M., & Shaver, P. R. (2007). *Attachment in adulthood: Structure, dynamics, and change.* New York, NY: Guilford Press.

Mikulincer, M., Shaver, P. R., & Slav, K. (2006). Attachment, mental representations of others, and gratitude and forgiveness in romantic relationships. In M. Mikulincer & G. S. Goodman (Eds.), *Dynamics of romantic love: Attachment, caregiving, and sex* (pp. 190–215). New York, NY: Guilford Press.

Miller, G., Tybur, J. M., & Jordan, B. D. (2007). Ovulatory cycle effects on tip earnings by lap dancers: Economic evidence for human estrus? *Evolution and Human Behavior, 28,* 375–381. doi:10.1016/j.evolhumbehav.2007.06.002

Miller, R. S. (1997). Inattentive and contented: Relationship commitment and attention to alternatives. *Journal of Personality and Social Psychology, 73,* 758–766. doi:10.1037/0022-3514.73.4.758

Miller, R. S. (2012). *Intimate relationships* (6th ed.). New York, NY: McGraw-Hill.

Miller, S. L., & Maner, J. K. (2010). Evolution and relationship maintenance: Fertility cues lead committed men to devalue relationship alternatives. *Journal of Experimental Social Psychology, 46,* 1081–1084. doi:10.1016/j.jesp.2010.07.004

Montoya, R. M. (2008). I'm hot, so I'd say you're not: The influence of objective physical attractiveness on mate selection. *Personality and Social Psychology Bulletin, 34,* 1315–1331. doi:10.1177/0146167208320387

Montoya, R. M., Horton, R. S., & Kirchner, J. (2008). Is actual similarity necessary for attraction? A meta-analysis of actual and perceived similarity. *Journal of Social and Personal Relationships, 25,* 889–922. doi:10.1177/0265407508096700

Moreland, R. L., & Beach, S. R. (1992). Exposure effects in the classroom: The development of affinity among students. *Journal of Experimental Social Psychology, 28,* 255–276. doi:10.1016/0022-1031(92)90055-O

Morry, M. M., Kito, M. I. E., & Ortiz, L. (2011). The attraction–similarity model and dating couples: Projection, perceived similarity, and psychological benefits. *Personal Relationships, 18,* 125–143. doi:10.1111/j.1475-6811.2010.01293.x

Newcomb, T. M. (1956). The prediction of interpersonal attraction. *American Psychologist, 11,* 575–586. doi:10.1037/h0046141

Newcomb, T. M. (1961). *The acquaintance process.* New York, NY: Holt, Rinehart, & Winston. doi:10.1037/13156-000

O'Doherty, J., Winston, J., Critchley, H., Perrett, D., Burt, D. M., & Dolan, R. J. (2003). Beauty in a smile: The role of medial orbitofrontal cortex in facial attractiveness. *Neuropsychologia, 41,* 147–155. doi:10.1016/S0028-3932(02)00145-8

Pérusse, D. (1993). Cultural and reproductive success in industrial societies: Testing the relationship at the proximate and ultimate levels. *Behavioral and Brain Sciences, 16,* 267–322. doi:10.1017/S0140525X00029939

Pietromonaco, P. R., & Carnelley, K. B. (1994). Gender and working models of attachment: Consequences for perceptions of self and romantic relationships. *Personal Relationships, 1,* 63–82. doi:10.1111/j.1475-6811.1994.tb00055.x

Pipitone, R. N., & Gallup, G. G. (2008). Women's voice attractiveness varies across the menstrual cycle. *Evolution and Human Behavior, 29,* 268–274. doi:10.1016/j.evolhumbehav.2008.02.001

Prentice, D. A., & Carranza, E. (2002). What women and men should be, shouldn't be, are allowed to be, and don't have to be: The contents of prescriptive gender stereotypes. *Psychology of Women Quarterly, 26,* 269–281. doi:10.1111/1471-6402.t01-1-00066

Puts, D. A. (2005). Mating context and menstrual phase affect women's preferences for male voice pitch. *Evolution and Human Behavior, 26,* 388–397. doi:10.1016/j.evolhumbehav.2005.03.001

Reber, R., Winkielman, P., & Schwarz, N. (1998). Effects of perceptual fluency on affective judgments. *Psychological Science, 9,* 45–48. doi:10.1111/1467-9280.00008

Reis, H. T., Maniaci, M. R., Caprariello, P. A., Eastwick, P. W., & Finkel, E. J. (2011a). Familiarity does indeed lead to attraction in live interaction. *Journal of Personality and Social Psychology, 101,* 557–570. doi:10.1037/a0022885

Reis, H. T., Maniaci, M. R., Caprariello, P. A., Eastwick, P. W., & Finkel, E. J. (2011b). In live interaction, does familiarity promote attraction or contempt? A reply to Norton, Frost, and Ariely (2011). *Journal of Personality and Social Psychology, 101,* 575–578. doi:10.1037/a0023471

Rofé, Y. (1984). Stress and affiliation: A utility theory. *Psychological Review, 91,* 235–250. doi:10.1037/0033-295X.91.2.235

Sbarra, D. A., & Hazan, C. (2008). Coregulation, dysregulation, self-regulation: An integrative analysis and empirical agenda for understanding adult attachment, separation, loss, and recovery. *Personality and Social Psychology Review, 12,* 141–167. doi:10.1177/1088868308315702

Schachner, D. A., & Shaver, P. R. (2002). Attachment style and human mate poaching. *Nouvelle Revue de Psychologie Sociale/New Review of Social Psychology, 1,* 122–129.

Schachner, D. A., & Shaver, P. R. (2004). Attachment dimensions and sexual motives. *Personal Relationships, 11,* 179–195. doi:10.1111/j.1475-6811.2004.00077.x

Schachter, S. (1959). *The psychology of affiliation: Experimental studies of the sources of gregariousness.* Stanford, CA: Stanford University Press.

Schmitt, D. P. (2003). Universal sex differences in the desire for sexual variety: Tests from 52 nations, 6 continents, and 13 islands. *Journal of Personality and Social Psychology, 85,* 85–104. doi:10.1037/0022-3514.85.1.85

Schmitt, D. P. (2005). Sociosexuality from Argentina to Zimbabwe: A 48-nation study of sex, culture, and the strategies of human mating. *Behavioral and Brain Sciences, 28,* 247–275. doi:10.1017/S0140525X05000051

Schwarz, S., Mustafic, M., Hassebrauck, M., & Jörg, J. (2011). Short- and long-term relationship orientation and 2d:4d finger-length ratio. *Archives of Sexual Behavior, 40,* 565–574. doi:10.1007/s10508-010-9698-9

Seeley, E. A., & Gardner, W. L. (2006). Succeeding at self-control through a focus on others: The roles of social practice and accountability in self-regulation. In K. D. Vohs & E. J. Finkel (Eds.), *Self and relationships: Connecting intrapersonal and interpersonal processes* (pp. 407–425). New York, NY: Guilford Press.

Segal, M. W. (1974). Alphabet and attraction: An unobtrusive measure of the effect of propinquity in a field setting. *Journal of Personality and Social Psychology, 30,* 654–657. doi:10.1037/h0037446

Shaver, P. R., & Klinnert, M. (1982). Schachter's theories of affiliation and emotion: Implications of developmental research. In L. Wheeler (Ed.), *Review of personality and social psychology* (Vol. 3, pp. 37–72). Beverly Hills, CA: Sage.

Simpson, J. A., & Gangestad, S. W. (1991). Individual differences in sociosexuality: Evidence for convergent and discriminant validity. *Journal of Personality and Social Psychology, 60,* 870–883.

Simpson, J. A., Gangestad, S. W., & Lerma, M. (1990). Perceptions of physical attractiveness: Mechanisms involved in the maintenance of romantic relationships. *Journal of Personality and Social Psychology, 59,* 1192–1201. doi:10.1037/0022-3514.59.6.1192

Simpson, J. A., & Harris, B. A. (1994). Interpersonal attraction. In A. L. Weber & J. H. Harvey (Eds.), *Perspectives on close relationships* (pp. 45–66). Boston, MA: Allyn & Bacon.

Simpson, J. A., Rholes, W. S., & Nelligan, J. S. (1992). Support seeking and support giving within couples in an anxiety-provoking situation: The role of attachment styles. *Journal of Personality and Social Psychology, 62,* 434–446. doi:10.1037/0022-3514.62.3.434

Simpson, J. A., Rholes, W. S., & Phillips, D. (1996). Conflict in close relationships: An attachment perspective. *Journal of Personality and Social Psychology, 71*, 899–914. doi:10.1037/0022-3514.71.5.899

Slater, A., Von der Schulenburg, C., Brown, E., Badenoch, M., Butterworth, G., Parsons, S., & Samuels, C. (1998). Newborn infants prefer attractive faces. *Infant Behavior and Development, 21*, 345–354. doi:10.1016/S0163-6383(98)90011-X

Sprecher, S., & Regan, P. C. (2002). Liking some things (in some people) more than others: Partner preferences in romantic relationships and friendships. *Journal of Social and Personal Relationships, 19*, 463–481. doi:10.1177/0265407502019004048

Sprecher, S., Sullivan, Q., & Hatfield, E. (1994). Mate selection preferences: Gender differences examined in a national sample. *Journal of Personality and Social Psychology, 66*, 1074–1080. doi:10.1037/0022-3514.66.6.1074

Swann, W. B., Jr. (1983). Self-verification: Bringing social reality into harmony with the self. In J. Suls & A. G. Greenwald (Eds.), *Social psychological perspectives on the self* (Vol. 2, pp. 33–66). Hillsdale, NJ: Erlbaum.

Symons, D. (1979). *The evolution of human sexuality.* New York, NY: Oxford University Press.

Thibaut, J. W., & Kelley, H. H. (1959). *The social psychology of groups.* New York, NY: Wiley.

Thorndike, E. L. (1935). *The psychology, of wants, interests, and attitudes.* New York, NY: Appleton-Century-Crofts.

Thornhill, R., & Gangestad, S. W. (1994). Human fluctuating asymmetry and sexual behavior. *Psychological Science, 5*, 297–302. doi:10.1111/j.1467-9280.1994.tb00629.x

Thornhill, R., & Gangestad, S. W. (1999). The scent of symmetry: A human sex pheromone that signals fitness? *Evolution and Human Behavior, 20*, 175–201. doi:10.1016/S1090-5138(99)00005-7

Thornhill, R., Gangestad, S. W., Miller, R., Scheyd, G., McCollough, J. K., & Franklin, M. (2003). Major histocompatibility complex genes, symmetry, and body scent attractiveness in men and women. *Behavioral Ecology, 14*, 668–678. doi:10.1093/beheco/arg043

Tidwell, N. D., Eastwick, P. W., & Finkel, E. J. (2013). Perceived, not actual, similarity predicts initial attraction in a live romantic context: Evidence from the speed-dating paradigm. *Personal Relationships, 20*, 199–215.

Tooby, J., & Cosmides, L. (1992). The psychological foundations of culture. In J. H. Barkow, L. Cosmides, & J. Tooby (Eds.), *The adapted mind: Evolutionary psychology and the generation of culture* (pp. 19–136). New York, NY: Oxford University Press.

Townsend, J. M., & Wasserman, T. (1998). Sexual attractiveness: Sex differences in assessment and criteria. *Evolution and Human Behavior, 19*, 171–191. doi:10.1016/S1090-5138(98)00008-7

Trivers, R. L. (1972). Parental investment and sexual selection. In B. G. Campbell (Ed.), *Sexual selection and the descent of man, 1871–1971* (pp. 136–179). Chicago, IL: Aldine.

Veitch, R., & Griffitt, W. (1976). Good news-bad news: Affective and interpersonal effects. *Journal of Applied Social Psychology, 6*, 69–75. doi:10.1111/j.1559-1816.1976.tb01313.x

Vonk, R. (2002). Self-serving interpretations of flattery: Why ingratiation works. *Journal of Personality and Social Psychology, 82*, 515–526. doi:10.1037/0022-3514.82.4.515

Vorauer, J. D., Cameron, J. J., Holmes, J. G., & Pearce, D. G. (2003). Invisible overtures: Fears of rejection and the signal amplification bias. *Journal of Personality and Social Psychology, 84*, 793–812. doi:10.1037/0022-3514.84.4.793

Walster, E. (1971). Passionate love. In B. L. Murstein (Ed.), *Theories of attraction and love* (pp. 85–99). New York, NY: Springer.

Walster, E., Aronson, V., Abrahams, D., & Rottman, L. (1966). Importance of physical attractiveness in dating behavior. *Journal of Personality and Social Psychology, 4*, 508–516. doi:10.1037/h0021188

Walster, E., Walster, G. W., Piliavin, J., & Schmidt, L. (1973). "Playing hard to get": Understanding an elusive phenomenon. *Journal of Personality and Social Psychology, 26*, 113–121. doi:10.1037/h0034234

Wiggins, J. S. (1979). A psychological taxonomy of trait-descriptive terms: The interpersonal domain. *Journal of Personality and Social Psychology, 37*, 395–412.

Williams, L. E., & Bargh, J. A. (2008). Experiencing physical warmth promotes interpersonal warmth. *Science, 322*, 606–607. doi:10.1126/science.1162548

Wilson, E. O. (1975). *Sociobiology: The new synthesis.* Cambridge, MA: Harvard University Press.

Wilson, E. O. (1979). *On human nature.* Cambridge, MA: Harvard University Press.

Wood, W., & Eagly, A. H. (2002). A cross-cultural analysis of the behavior of women and men: Implications for the origins of sex differences. *Psychological Bulletin, 128*, 699–727. doi:10.1037/0033-2909.128.5.699

Zajonc, R. B. (1968). Attitudinal effects of mere exposure. *Journal of Personality and Social Psychology, 9*(2, Pt. 2), 1–27. doi:10.1037/h0025848

Zajonc, R. B. (2001). Mere exposure: A gateway to the subliminal. *Current Directions in Psychological Science, 10*, 224–228. doi:10.1111/1467-8721.00154

CHAPTER 8

RELATIONSHIP INITIATION AND DEVELOPMENT

Susan Sprecher, Diane Felmlee, Sandra Metts, and William Cupach

The initiation stage is arguably the most critical phase of a relationship; what occurs during initial interactions often determines whether two people come to define (or not) their experiences to be the beginning of a close relationship. Many relationships never progress beyond the initiation point; therefore, it is the most frequently experienced stage. In those relationships that are developed, the initiation stage is often vividly recalled years later (Custer, Holmberg, Blair, & Orbuch, 2008). *Relationship initiation* is an elusive term that refers broadly to the period from first mutual awareness between two people to the time when they begin to think of themselves as a couple, a process that may occur over days or weeks. The initiation of a relationship is difficult to distinguish from its development; therefore, we discuss topics related to both the very earliest interactions between two people and what occurs as two people attempt to intensify and clarify their bond.

We begin this chapter by discussing two components necessary for a relationship to begin: the context (e.g., proximity) and the prospective partners' motives (e.g., mutual attraction). In our second section, we discuss the initiation phase as it applies especially to the romantic relationship, which includes various behaviors (flirting, opening gambits, and mating strategies) that might elicit a prospective partner's attention and then a first date. In the third section, we address the important role of self-disclosure in the initiation process. Self-disclosure helps reduce uncertainty and allows rapport and

trust to develop. In the fourth section, we discuss the intensification phase, which for many romantic relationships also includes sexual activity. Relationship initiation does not always go smoothly, and in the fifth section we review problematic initiation experiences, including deception and unwanted relationship pursuit. In our final major section, we focus on third-party assistance in relationship initiation, both from informal social networks and from commercial services such as Internet dating websites.

Although the issues we discuss and much of the research we summarize focus largely on the initiation of romantic relationships, friendship also has a preliminary phase that has some similarity to that of romantic relationships (for a review, see Fehr, 2008). In our conclusion section, we discuss several directions for future research including the further study of same-sex and cross-sex friendship initiation.

INITIATION POTENTIAL: SETTING THE SCENE

Relationships begin in particular interaction contexts and between people who bring certain motives to the interaction. In this section of the chapter, we begin by discussing contextual factors that influence relationship initiation and then turn to a discussion of the various motivations people have that can influence the likelihood that a relationship develops.

http://dx.doi.org/10.1037/14344-008
APA Handbook of Personality and Social Psychology: Vol. 3. Interpersonal Relations, M. Mikulincer and P. R. Shaver (Editors-in-Chief)

Contexts

Relationships do not begin in a vacuum. They begin at workplaces, in classrooms, at parties, in bars, on the Internet, and in many other places. In this section, we discuss the environmental context for relationship initiation, beginning with the role of proximity. Second, we discuss the specific settings in which people meet others, including how these settings might be distinguished on abstract dimensions that could be associated with how the relationship develops.

Role of proximity. Proximity or propinquity is considered to be a necessary, although not sufficient, condition for relationship initiation. As noted by Parks (2007), "Physical proximity has been recognized as a force in relationship initiation for so long, that we rarely review or question the evidence behind the claim" (p. 60). Classic studies that have demonstrated the important role of proximity in forming relationships include Bossard's (1932) finding that most couples who applied for marriage licenses in Philadelphia in 1931 lived within a few blocks of each other and Festinger, Schachter, and Back's (1950) study of the role of proximity in friendship choices in married student housing (see also Newcomb, 1961; Segal, 1974).

Research has also indicated that functional distance, sometimes referred to as *interaction accessibility,* is more important than linear (physical) distance in leading to relationship formation (Festinger et al., 1950), especially when people are diverse in race and age (Nahemow & Lawton, 1975). Several explanations have been provided for the important role of proximity. Proximity makes people accessible and provides opportunities for interaction. As a consequence, rewards can be exchanged without the costs of time, effort, and money that might be associated with interacting over a greater distance. Furthermore, just the anticipation of interaction associated with being proximal to others can increase the likelihood of relationship initiation with others. This can occur through several processes, including that people are often more civil and courteous to those whom they expect to see again (Regan, 2011) and that the anticipation of interaction with someone increases liking (Darley & Berscheid, 1967). Mere

exposure, and the familiarity associated with seeing someone multiple times even if there is no interaction, can also increase attraction and the desire to initiate a relationship (e.g., Zajonc, 1968).

It is often assumed that the Internet has reduced the importance of proximity (Merkle & Richardson, 2000), but it is perhaps more accurate to say that the Internet has expanded the types of proximity that contribute to relationship initiation. Through computer-mediated communication, people can begin relationships with others across the world as easily as they can with those next door; that is, physical proximity is no longer necessary for a relationship to be initiated. A proximity effect, however, manifests itself in the online world, too—just a different type. For two people to meet online, they need the opportunity to communicate, which means they need to be proximal to each other in a virtual way. For example, people need to be part of the same chat room, play the same online games at the same time, write entries to the same blogs, or be a member of the same dating website. Furthermore, fledgling relationships that are able to overcome geographical distance (e.g., one partner moves to be near the other) are more likely to develop into full-fledged relationships than those that cannot overcome geographical distance, the latter of which are likely to dissolve or at best remain online friendships.

Although proximity, either in face-to-face settings or through its virtual equivalent, may be a necessary condition to enter a relationship, it does not explain why a particular choice is made from among an array of people who would be available within a particular geographical area or online venue. Next, we discuss other important factors beyond proximity that lead to attraction.

Types of settings in which relationships begin. People meet romantic partners and friends in a variety of settings. Surprisingly, though, there is little empirical research on this topic, and even less conceptual work that might distinguish the settings in which people meet along dimensions that could have implications for the course of relationship development. In an exception, Murstein (1970), in his stimulus–value–role theory, proposed that interaction settings for relationship initiation can vary on a voluntariness dimension. In some settings, referred to by Murstein as *closed fields,* people are expected or even forced to interact with each other, often on the basis of the roles they play. Examples are small seminars and work settings. Murstein distinguished these interaction settings from those that take place in *open fields*, in which interaction is voluntary, as is the choice of with whom to interact. Bars, large parties, and school classes are examples of open fields. In these settings, people choose to interact because it is intrinsically rewarding (Berscheid & Regan, 2005).

Another and related conceptual distinction is between interaction settings that are designed to be relationship building versus settings that create more naturally occurring involvements. This distinction can be made about both face-to-face (e.g., Sprecher & McKinney, 1987) and online settings (Baker, 2008; McKenna, 2008). In relationship-building contexts, attendance or membership in the setting is an advertisement of one's availability and interest in developing a connection. The major motivation people have for being present is to find a partner, and the intent is explicit and overt. In contrast, in naturally occurring venues, the primary motivation is to accomplish a task or to share with others who have common interests. For example, people frequent particular settings to take a class, complete an activity, play a game, or receive social support. If a relationship develops, it is a by-product of being in the setting and interacting with others (McKenna, 2008).

The process and predictors of attraction may differ as a function of the type of context in which people meet. For example, physical appearance is likely to be important in overt relationship initiation settings and open fields, whereas opportunities for developing interdependence through shared activities are likely to be particularly relevant in closed fields and in those that are more covert in regard to relationship intent. In addition, the process of developing or defining a relationship as romantic is likely to take less time in relationship-building settings, although potential partners may also decide just as quickly that a romantic relationship would not work.

Where, specifically, do people meet partners? A few recent studies have provided data on this topic primarily for the purpose of documenting the increasing role of the Internet in relationship initiation. In 2005, the Pew Internet and American Life Project interviewed a sample of 3,215 adults of diverse ages, 56% who were married or in another form of committed relationship. As reported in Madden and Lenhart (2006), 38% said they met their partner through work or school; 34%, through family or friends; and 13%, at a nightclub, bar, café, or other social gathering. Only 3% met through the Internet.

Although the Internet was not yet a prominent way in which people began relationships in 2005, data collected more recently have revealed the increasing importance of the Internet as a setting for meeting partners, although friends also continued to be important. Rosenfeld and Thomas (2012), in a national study on how couples meet and stay together, surveyed 4,002 adults (3,009 who were partnered) and asked them how they met their partner. Of the participants who met an opposite-sex partner in the 2 years before the administration of the survey, approximately 22% had met on the Internet (the percentage of those meeting a same-sex partner was much higher at 61%). For the entire sample, the Internet was the second most common way to meet partners, only behind friends. In comparison to the 22% who met their opposite-sex partner online in 2008–2010, the percentages were 19.5% for 2004–2006, 10.7% for 1999–2003, and 3.9% for 1994–1998.

Although the particular setting in which a meeting that occurred through family and friends was not specified in these studies, it would presumably be an open-field setting, such as a party or social gathering. Research conducted pre-Internet also found that it was very common to meet new partners through friends and in such contexts as work or school (e.g., Laumann, Gagnon, Michael, & Michaels, 1994).

An interesting question is whether the setting in which a couple meets is associated with the quality of their relationship. Unfortunately, not much research has been done on this topic. In the Rosenfeld and Thomas (2012) study referred to earlier, level of relationship quality was compared among the respondents as a function of how they met their partner, but no significant difference in relationship quality was found. We speculate that the place of first meetings may affect the likelihood that the relationship is initiated and how, but once a relationship is developed, the place of initial meeting may explain little variance in relationship phenomena, such as satisfaction, intimacy, and stability.

Motivations

People are motivated to develop romantic relationships or friendships to varying degrees and for various reasons. First, we discuss a relatively neglected influence on relationship initiation, individuals' readiness to form a new relationship. Second, we discuss the fuel that drives the initiation process—mutual attraction. Finally, we consider other motives for entering relationships such as the need to belong.

Readiness to enter a relationship. Preadolescents and young adolescents are usually not in a serious intimate relationship, although they experience crushes and have intermittent romantic experiences. At some point, however, adolescents may develop the desire to enter a special, romantic relationship. Developmental theorists (e.g., Erickson, 1968) have argued that adolescence is a time of seeking intimacy and companionship. Furthermore, according to attachment theorists, adolescents desire to replace parents with friends and romantic partners as their preferred source of attachment functions, such as proximity seeking and safe haven (Doherty & Feeney, 2004). Therefore, many young people experience a sense of readiness to form a romantic bond, which is likely to be influenced by the onset of puberty, social and cultural expectations, and peers (Collins, Welsh, & Furman, 2009). A representative, national study indicated that approximately 80% of adolescents have experienced a romantic relationship by the time they reach the age of 18 (Carver, Joyner, & Udry, 2003).

Although the first romantic relationship may be a significant transition in adolescence, and one that may be preceded by a period of increasing readiness for the transition, a number of young adults cycle in and out of pairings that can be relatively brief in nature (e.g., Collins et al., 2009). For many, there is a coping and recovery period after a breakup and before there is a state of readiness to enter a new relationship, particularly if the breakup was unexpected and initiated by the other (Sprecher, Felmlee, Metts, Fehr, & Vanni, 1998).

Single adults, too, have intermittent and fluctuating readiness to be part of a couple. Although a widespread belief is that most singles who are currently unattached want to be in a relationship (DePaulo, 2011), evidence has not supported this stereotype. For example, on the basis of the Pew representative sample of Americans referred to earlier, Madden and Lenhart (2006) found that 55% of single adults were not in a relationship and were not looking for a partner. People who have become unpartnered as a result of divorce or death of a spouse may be especially likely to vary in how soon they feel ready to enter a relationship as a function of such factors as encouragement from their social network (Fine, Coffelt, & Olson, 2008).

Only a few studies have included a measure of readiness to enter a relationship as a predictor of its development. Aron, Dutton, Aron, and Iverson (1989) reviewed diverse literatures and identified 11 predictors of falling in love, one of which was the readiness to enter a relationship. In Aron et al.'s Study 1, undergraduate students wrote essays about experiences in which they felt an upsurge of attraction for another; 44% of the accounts mentioned readiness. In a follow-up study, approximately one third of undergraduate respondents rated readiness to enter a relationship as either 8 or 9 on a 9-point positive impact scale in regard to influence on the recent falling-in-love experience (see also Sprecher et al., 1994).

Schindler, Fagundes, and Murdock (2010) conducted a longitudinal study with 90 undergraduate students who were not in a committed relationship at the time and looked at predictors of transitions from not dating to dating and then from either not dating or casual dating to a more committed relationship stage. They examined the influence of dating goals (conceptually similar to readiness), which were assessed by items such as "I want to find someone with whom I can have a serious and committed relationship." They found that dating goals were a marginally significant predictor of the transition from not dating to dating (the major predictor was prior dating involvement).

In sum, readiness to enter a relationship may influence the transition from being unattached to beginning a relationship, but it may not be a necessary condition for at least two reasons. First, people who do not feel they are ready to enter a relationship may still do so because they are successfully pursued by someone who is interested in forming an attachment. In addition, people could be ready but not meet someone who is eligible and interested in them in return. Although the state of readiness may not always lead to the initiation of a relationship, it is likely to affect people's behaviors, such as the settings they frequent and the behaviors in which they engage to make themselves attractive to others.

Attraction. What mysterious process attracts one person to another to form a short-term, or in some cases an enduring, relationship? This question represents one of the most elemental and widely addressed within the broader field of personal relationships, and one that led to the development of relationship science as an area of study. Attraction is typically defined as an attitude toward another that has cognitive, emotional, and behavioral components (Berscheid, 1985). We cannot provide in-depth coverage of this voluminous topic in this chapter (for greater detail, see Chapter 7, this volume). Nevertheless, attraction arguably represents the most basic motive for entering and developing a close bond, and it would be remiss not to give attention to the part it plays in relationship initiation. A host of theories have attempted to account for the process of interpersonal attraction, resulting in a morass of perspectives that could benefit from substantial integration (Finkel & Baumeister, 2010). In this summary, we focus on several empirical findings in the literature.

The causal sources of attraction are located in one or more of the following: the person, the other person or target, the interaction between the two people, and the environment (e.g., Kelley et al., 1983). Factors situated in the environment set the initial stage. People are often in physical proximity,

or in virtual contact, when attraction first occurs, as discussed earlier. Characteristics of the other person who is the target of attraction become important as well, with physical attractiveness a well-established feature (for review, see Hatfield & Sprecher, 1986). Physical appearance has a powerful effect on first impressions, and people often apply the general stereotype that what is beautiful is good, whether correct or not (Langlois et al., 2000). In a classic study of undergraduate students paired for a dance, the best predictor of liking a potential date was physical attractiveness (Walster, Aronson, Abrahams, & Rottman, 1966). More recently, physical appearance was found to strongly predict preferences in a speed-dating service, with men drawn to slender, young, attractive women and women preferring men who were tall, young, and attractive (Kurzban & Weeden, 2005).

In spite of the common adage that opposites attract, the bulk of experimental and survey research has found that similarity between two people strongly influences the attraction process (for a review, see Fehr, 2008). Numerous studies have demonstrated that the extent to which a partner possesses, or is perceived to possess, characteristics closely related to those of the other person promotes attraction (e.g., Byrne, 1971; Caspi, Herbener, & Ozer, 1992). Partner similarity to one another's ideal, rather than actual, selves—that is, the Michelangelo phenomenon—also plays a role in attraction (e.g., Rusbult, Kumashiro, Kubacka, & Finkel, 2009). According to meta-analyses, women value similarity more than do men in attraction to a stranger of the opposite sex, whereas men place more emphasis on physical attractiveness (e.g., Feingold, 1991). A recent meta-analysis by Montoya, Horton, and Kirchner (2008) found that perceived similarity, but not actual similarity, predicts attraction in existing relationships. Actual similarity produces attraction primarily in laboratory settings.

Biology shapes initial attraction as well. For example, women who are nearing ovulation adopt a more short-term mating strategy aimed at masculine and dominant men (Gangestad, Garver-Apgar, Simpson, & Cousins, 2007). The color red, as opposed to blue or green, heightens a woman's attractiveness, presumably because red primes associations with genitalia and reproductive potential (Kayser, Elliot, & Feltman, 2010). On a general level, males place more value on the physical attributes of a partner than do females (e.g., Buss & Barnes 1986), whereas females place greater emphasis on a potential mate's internal qualities (e.g., Buss & Barnes, 1986). Evolutionary psychology, which maintains that the aim of maximizing reproductive success drives attraction, is often used to account for such biological and sex differences (Buss & Barnes, 1986).

Other important personal and social predictors of attraction include the following: familiarity, reciprocal liking, pleasing characteristics of the target, social network approval, and need fulfillment (for reviews, see Aron et al., 1989; Sprecher & Felmlee, 2008). The desirable characteristics of agreeableness, extraversion, attractiveness, and intelligence rate high as initial attractors (Felmlee, Orzechowicz, & Fortes, 2010), although in certain cases, people may eventually become annoyed by these same attracting qualities, a process referred to as *fatal attraction* (Felmlee, 1995). According to cross-cultural research (Sprecher et al., 1994), a number of similar characteristics attract one person to another across several cultures, including desirable personality, physical appearance, and reciprocal liking.

In sum, attraction represents a fundamental element of the process of relationship initiation. Without some sort of positive attraction, a relationship between two people is unlikely to unfold. Scholarly research has made progress in identifying several major components of this process. People tend to be drawn to those with whom they are in contact; those who are attractive; those who possess similar, desirable, or familiar attributes; and those who like them in return and are endorsed by their friends and family. For more information on this topic, see Chapter 7, this volume.

Need to belong and other motives. Although readiness to enter a relationship and attraction catalyze initiation intentions and actions, a more fundamental human motivation predisposes people to seek attachments in general. It is now well-established that individuals are driven by a strong need to belong, also known as belongingness

(Baumeister & Leary, 1995; Gere & MacDonald, 2010). This need impels individuals "to form and maintain at least a minimum quantity of lasting, positive, and significant interpersonal relationships" (Baumeister & Leary, 1995, p. 497). The initiation and cultivation of meaningful connections is therefore grounded in a basic belongingness need held to some degree by virtually all individuals. When belongingness is undermined, such as when someone feels excluded, rejected, or ostracized, that person incurs considerable negative affect and potentially adverse health consequences (Blackhart, Eckel, & Tice, 2007; Leary, Koch, & Hechenbleikner, 2001).

The existence of a fundamental need to belong has been supported by copious research (Baumeister & Leary, 1995; Gere & MacDonald, 2010). It also resonates with various theories of human motivation, such as Deci and Ryan's (1991, 2008; LaGuardia & Patrick, 2008) self-determination theory (i.e., relatedness need) and attachment theory (e.g., Mikulincer & Shaver, 2007). Moreover, Schutz's (1966) theory of interpersonal relations is based on the simple premise that people need people. To elucidate in what ways people need others, Schutz proposed that individuals possess three primary interpersonal needs: inclusion, affection, and control. The needs for inclusion and affection correspond to belongingness. Inclusion is reflected in the desire of people to associate with others, to be recognized, and to attract attention. People achieve social status and prestige when they affiliate with popular individuals and groups. On one hand, the desire for inclusion leads people to seek togetherness rather than intimacy. The need for affection, on the other hand, manifests itself in activity designed to achieve emotional closeness, reciprocal self-disclosure, and mutual love. The need to control others affords one desired power, dominance, and authority over others. At the same time, control promotes perceptions that the self is competent and responsible (Schutz, 1966), which is akin to the needs of competence and autonomy stipulated by Deci and Ryan (1991).

The need for control, as well as other needs commonly represented in the literature, may ultimately be driven by the fundamental need to belong

(Baumeister & Leary, 1995). For example, Baumeister and Leary (1995) contended that "people prefer achievements that are validated, recognized, and valued by other people over solitary achievements, so there may be a substantial interpersonal component behind the need for achievement" (p. 498). People possess a variety of desires that inherently involve connection to other people, including needs for intimacy, approbation, acceptance, approval, affirmation, affiliation, fellowship, membership, power, status, achievement, and so on. Even desires such as escape, relaxation, and pleasure motivate interpersonal communication (e.g., Paulsel & Mottet, 2004; Rubin, Perse, & Barbato, 1988). Consequently, belongingness and its corollary needs motivate individuals to instigate relationships with other people.

INITIATION PHASE

Readiness, attraction, belongingness, and other motives provide the motivation for entering a new relationship, but individuals seeking a new relationship also need to engage in behaviors that elicit the interest of the other and create smooth and rewarding interactions. Although little research has focused specifically on the skills of relationship initiation per se (for a review of interpersonal skills more generally, see Simpson & Harris, 1994; Spitzberg & Cupach, 2011), it is evident that individuals differ in their abilities to enact small talk, proffer credible opening lines, and flirt effectively and appropriately (e.g., Bell, Tremblay, & Buerkel-Rothfuss, 1987). In this section of the chapter, we outline the topography of relationship initiation actions.

First Meetings

In this section, we discuss several relationship-initiating behaviors, including flirting, opening lines, and mating tactics. If these initiation strategies are successful, two people may advance to a first significant interaction. In some cases, this interaction is a concurrent sexual episode that satisfies sexual gratification goals but does not lead to the further development of a dating relationship (i.e., a hookup). In other circumstances, this event is a traditional first date, which occurs at some later point

after the first encounter and provides the opportunity for two people to explore each other's potential. We discuss these initiation behaviors, episodes, and outcomes in this section.

Flirting and attracting attention. One way to communicate attraction to another person is through flirting. Flirting refers to subtle or playful verbal and nonverbal behaviors that indicate a romantic interest in another person. Scholars have identified numerous types or stages of flirting, or courtship readiness. For example, early descriptions of nonverbal "quasi-courting" behavior (Scheflen, 1965) focused on four types: courtship readiness (e.g., high muscle tone), preening (e.g., adjusting clothing), positional cues (e.g., leaning), and actions of invitation (e.g., an open palm). According to Cunningham and Barbee (2008), the flirtation and courtship stages of a relationship consist of the following steps, not necessarily fixed in sequence: attract attention, notice and approach, talk and reevaluate, and, finally, touch and synchronize. A large study of 5,020 adults identified five general styles of attracting attention from a potential mate: traditional, physical, sincere, polite, and playful, with men using the playful approach more often than women and the other styles less often (Hall, Carter, Cody, & Albright, 2010).

Flirtatious behavior plays a central role in human courtship, according to repeated empirical studies (e.g., Moore, 2010). People use flirting for a number of purposes, argued Moore (2010), such as to have fun and to engage in playful, quasi-courtship behavior (Scheflen, 1965), although flirting is usually meant to convey genuine interest in a potential romantic partner and can aid in the maintenance of an ongoing relationship. Women tend to take the initiative in the courting process by displaying nonverbal cues of interest, signaling to a man that he is welcome to approach (e.g., Moore, 2010; Perper, 1985). Women also instigate and control intricate patterns of rhythmic, nonverbal synchronization that develop between a man and a woman when they meet for the first time (Grammer, Kruck, & Magnusson, 1998).

People engage in numerous types of nonverbal behavior to indicate their interest in romance. An observational study of people in bars and restaurants reported the following typical flirting actions: moving close to a potential partner, eye contact, smiling, laughing, and self-grooming (McCormick & Jones, 1989). In flirtatious conversations, people's speech is also more animated and warmer, and they laugh more frequently with fewer periods of silence (Coker & Burgoon, 1987). According to self-reports, the three most frequently used flirtatious behaviors are smiling, extended eye contact, and being attentive (Egland, Spitzberg, & Zormeier, 1996). Touch also communicates attraction, and people rate gentle, informal gestures, such as a soft touch on the face or hugging as embodying the highest level of flirtation and romantic attraction (J. W. Lee & Guerrero, 2001). Similarly, when people flirt, they smile more, move closer, gaze longer, and touch each other relatively frequently (Koeppel, Montagne-Miller, O'Hair, & Cody, 1993). Typical flirtatious expressions include a head cant, pouting mouth, and coyness (Simpson, Gangestad, & Biek, 1993). For men, flirting involves gestures that get women to notice them and imply high status, such as taking up space, an open posture, and unreciprocated touching of other men (Renninger, Wade, & Grammer, 2004).

With the explosion of interaction on the Internet, the topic of "cyberflirting" has gained recent attention. According to a report by the Pew Internet and American Life Project (Madden & Lenhart, 2006), a large proportion (40%) of single or "looking" online users reported flirting online, and approximately 22% of general users of MySpace and Facebook admitted to using these social networking websites to flirt. Some of the most common forms of online flirting included the use of emoticons and acronyms to portray emotion and laughter (Whitty, 2004).

The question remains, however, as to whether flirting is effective. Does moving closer, smiling, and sneaking glances gain attention from a prospective partner? Moore (1985) found that women who engaged in the greatest number of flirting behaviors in a bar were those approached most often by men. Similarly, men who were most successful in establishing romantic contact with women were those who exhibited the greatest number of

nonverbal, flirtatious actions, such as glancing, maximizing personal space, and changing location (Renninger et al., 2004). Certain flirting styles—physical, sincere, and playful—were particularly successful in culminating in attracting a date, and the physical and sincere types led to relationships with the deepest emotional connection (Hall, Carter, et al., 2010). Although general flirting did not determine a person's own choices in a recent speed-dating experiment, flirting did predict how often a person was chosen as a mate (Back et al., 2011). Thus, flirting does appear to work.

Opening lines. Although nonverbal signals of interest, such as the flirting behaviors just described, may gain or reciprocate another person's attention, verbal messages of greeting must at some point be exchanged if an interaction is to occur. Opening lines are a highly ritualized mechanism to accomplish this goal.

In one of the first attempts to systematize opening lines, Kleinke, Meeker, and Staneski (1986) conducted several studies in which college students and employees generated the most common opening lines that men and women might use in a general setting and in five specific situations: bars, restaurants, supermarkets, laundromats, and beaches. Other samples then rated the quality of these lines (i.e., from terrible to excellent) and indicated which they would prefer in each situation. Results indicated that opening lines clustered reliably on three factors, labeled *cute–flippant, innocuous,* and *direct*. Ratings of preferred lines indicated that both men and women found the cute–flippant lines to be the least desirable (e.g., "Is that your hair?" "I'm easy. Are you?"). However, consistent with hypothesized gender scripts, women rated them as less preferred than men and rated the innocuous lines as more preferred than men. Men preferred the direct opening lines more than did women.

Subsequent research, using different methods, has generally been consistent with Kleinke et al.'s (1986) findings (Cunningham & Barbee, 2008; Levine, King, & Popoola, 1994). For example, Cunningham (1989) demonstrated the salience of gender preferences for opening lines in two field experiments in which participants were approached by male or female confederates in Chicago bars. In both studies, women responded more positively and continued interaction when the male confederate used innocuous or direct opening lines. Men, however, displayed interest and continued interaction with the female confederate regardless of the opening line she used.

Recent efforts to elaborate on factors influencing women's responses to opening lines have indicated that women continue to prefer direct approaches. For example, Weber, Goodboy, and Cayanus (2010) assessed women's perceptions of the appropriateness and effectiveness of opening lines displayed in videos of male actors. Consistent with prior research, direct introductions were rated as the most appropriate opening line. In addition, being introduced by a third party was a strategy that women rated as most appropriate and most effective. In addition, research has suggested that the type of relationship desired influences a woman's evaluation of a man's opening line. Senko and Fyffe (2010) varied the nature of the relationship being sought by a woman (short vs. long term), the attractiveness of the male, and the opening lines in hypothetical scenarios. Consistent with evolutionary theory, if a long-term relationship was being sought, women preferred the direct or innocuous lines and associated these with intelligence and trustworthiness, but if a short-term relationship was the goal and the man was attractive, women had no preference for type of opening line.

Although Senko and Fyffe (2010) were among the first scholars to explicitly incorporate the underlying premise of evolutionary theory in women's reactions to opening lines, it is a fundamental element in mate selection practices. We turn now to the broader topic of mating strategies in the initiation of romantic relationships that extend beyond an initial interaction.

Mating strategies and relationship initiation. When people desire to begin a relationship, they engage in a variety of behaviors called *mating strategies, mating or attraction tactics, mating efforts,* and *strategic behaviors* (e.g., Allen & Bailey, 2007; Schmitt & Buss, 1996). Evolutionary theorists have argued that men and women faced different evolutionary opportunities and constraints

in achieving reproductive success and therefore developed gender-specific mating tactics that help them maximize their reproductive opportunities and overcome their constraints by emphasizing characteristics that would be preferred by the opposite sex (Schmitt & Buss, 1996).

Schmitt and Buss (1996) examined behavioral tactics in the two contexts of mating strategies, long term and short term. In a preliminary study, they asked a group of participants to list what behaviors they would do to attract either a long-term or a short-term mating partner. Another group of participants was then asked to judge the behaviors on effectiveness as tactics for men versus women to attract others. The degree to which tactics were perceived to be effective in attracting a partner depended on both the mating context (short term vs. long term) and the gender of the person enacting the behavior. For example, flirtatious and seductive behaviors and sexualizing one's appearance were perceived to be more effective if enacted by women than if enacted by men. Behaviors that suggested sexual availability were judged to be better for short-term mating than for long-term mating. The display of sexual exclusivity was judged to be a more effective tactic for women in a long-term context than in a short-term context. In addition, the tactic of giving resources immediately was judged to be especially effective for men in a short-term mating context, whereas showing resource potential was perceived to be more efficacious for men in a long-term mating context.

Focusing on the strategies that people actually use to initiate relationships, Clark, Shaver, and Abrahams (1999) asked a group of college students to write a narrative of two recent episodes of successful relationship initiation. Through analysis of the narratives, which involved coding the participants' own behaviors and the behaviors they recalled the other partner doing, they identified 19 distinct behaviors, including talking in person, spending time together, using third parties to initiate a relationship, touching, asking directly, manipulating the setting, presenting the self well, nonverbal communication, and gift giving. Clark et al. found that the most frequently mentioned strategies for successful relationship initiation were talking in person, touching the partner, and asking directly. Third-party intervention (e.g., introducing the two) was also mentioned frequently. Men were found to be more active in their strategies to begin relationships; women, more passive, especially when the focus was on the participants' reports of their partner's behaviors. Recent research (MacGregor & Cavallo, 2011) has shown that when women's sense of personal control concerning relationship initiation is increased, they, like men, also engage in direct strategies to initiate a relationship.

First Dates

Relationships with romantic potential may emerge from a first meeting in which flirtatious behaviors and effective opening lines encourage a second meeting or from repeated interactions at work, in classes, or within social networks that bring people together. However, despite variations in origin, most relationships will experience a socially recognized initiation episode—the first date. Of course, the extent to which this date represents a first step in formal dating, and the extent to which it unfolds in a traditional manner, depends on the context from which it emerges.

For example, mixed-gender activities among adolescents in middle school (Connolly, Craig, Goldberg, & Pepler, 2004) and co-ed dorms for college students (Glenn & Marquardt, 2001) facilitate group interactions and social opportunities that make a first date something of a blurry distinction. Indeed, college students use the increasingly common terms *hanging out* or *hooking up* to describe their dating experiences, at least to the point when a discussion of exclusivity or commitment becomes salient (Glenn & Marquardt, 2001). Although hookups, or one-night stands, have traditionally been considered sexual involvement without an intention to develop a romantic relationship (Paul, McManus, & Hayes, 2000), college students, particularly men, report feeling moderately positive reactions after a hookup that they attribute to the possibility of a romantic relationship developing (Owen & Fincham, 2011b). Although the odds are fairly low that a hookup will lead to a romantic relationship, experts have suggested that it may occur in 10% to 12% of cases (Bisson & Levine, 2009; Paul et al., 2000).

To recognize emerging trends in informal and nontraditional dating patterns, however, is not to suggest that traditional dates do not occur. As Gallmeier, Knox, and Zusman (2002) found in their study of university undergraduates, couples who considered themselves to have an exclusive relationship still followed the norms of traditional dating practices. In addition, as evident in the research we discuss next, when asked to describe a recent first date, young adults are able to do so with remarkable consistency.

The consistency found in descriptions of first dates is generally attributed to the presence of a first date script. Scripts are cognitive representations of socially constructed norms for appropriate and expected sequences of behaviors that both constitute and define an event (Schank & Abelson, 1977). Scripts allow participants to generate their own behavior, understand the actions of others, and infer the meaning associated with these actions (Simon & Gagnon, 1986). Thus, first date scripts serve important functions during the initial phase of relationship beginnings. Particularly for dates between relative strangers in which uncertainty is high, knowledge of expected behavioral sequences provides at least a fundamental plan for how the date will unfold. For example, college students expect that dating activities will include "going to the movies, a bar, a party, a sports event, eating, talking, dancing, watching TV, going on walks, and drinking" and that the outcomes of a date will include "goodnight kiss, hug, invite in a for a drink/talk, set up another date, and take date home" (Bartoli & Clark, 2006, pp. 68–69).

Gender expectations are a prominent feature in first date scripts, although the interpersonal enactments of these scripts do reflect some variation. In a comparison of hypothetical first dates and actual first dates in a college student sample, Rose and Frieze (1993) found strong gender role patterns in both situations, as expected. The man displayed a more proactive role (e.g., initiating and planning the date, driving, initiating physical contact and kissing) and the woman a more reactive role (e.g., being concerned with appearance, control of sexual activity). This pattern was subsequently confirmed by Laner and Ventrone (2000), suggesting the enduring stability of gender roles in the first date script. Mongeau, Morr Serewicz, and Therrien (2004) found that both men and women listed the first date goals of reducing uncertainty, relational escalation, fun, and friendship to the same extent and more often than that of sexual activity, although men listed the sexual goal much more often than did women.

Additionally, research has indicated that the basic first date script is adapted to individual and contextual factors. For example, Bartoli and Clark (2006) found that sexual experience and older age among college students are associated with an increased expectation of sexual intercourse on a first date. Morr and Mongeau (2004) found that when alcohol was included in a hypothetical scenario involving friends on an initial date, men envisioned more reluctance to engage in sexual activity, whereas women envisioned a greater likelihood that they would. In similar hypothetical scenarios, Morr Serewicz and Gale (2008) found that men's tendency to include more than kissing on a first date is particularly evident in dates that are initiated by women, perhaps because they assume that the preexisting friendship motivated the woman to take the initiative in advancing the relationship to a more intimate level.

Advancing the Relationship: Phases and Turning Points

Throughout the preceding section, we summarized research on the behavioral and communicative signals people use to initiate conversation with, and elicit interest from, a potential dating partner. We also discussed the more or less explicit indication of a desire to form a relationship manifested in the first date episode. These preliminary relationship events and the phases that often follow have been integrated into relationship development models by scholars. In this section, we summarize two different, but compatible, approaches to relationship development that are noteworthy for their comprehensiveness and utility: the staircase model and the turning points approach. Both serve as reminders that relationships may evolve rapidly, slowly, smoothly, or awkwardly, but they eventually exhibit common patterns and markers of initiation and development.

The staircase model, first proposed by Knapp (1978) and later elaborated by Knapp and Vangelesti (2005), presents five advancing steps of coming together with five comparable steps of coming apart, which are linked by a midsection of stabilizing. The intent is to provide a visual representation of the fact that some dating involvements advance to a certain level of intimacy and commitment and either stabilize at that point or move back down the staircase to termination. The coming-together stages are (a) initiating (superficial communication, polite conversation); (b) experimenting (gaining information about each other's likes and dislikes, small talk); (c) intensifying (increasing breadth and depth of disclosure, using *we* rather than *you* and *I*); (d) integrating (emergence of a relational identity that is recognized by the social network as well as the couple); and (e) bonding (a formal union displayed in a cultural ritual such as marriage).

The turning points perspective (Baxter & Bullis, 1986; Baxter & Pittman, 2001) shifts the focus from progressive developmental stages to specific events or occurrences that prompt partners to evaluate the nature of their relationship. Baxter and her colleagues identified a number of turning points by asking couples to recall events that caused a change in their relationship and indicate on a graph the increase or decrease in commitment associated with that event. Turning points often reported include get-to-know time (e.g., first meeting, first date), quality time (e.g., a deeply meaningful conversation), passion (e.g., first kiss, first sex, saying "I love you"), conflict (e.g., first big fight), relationship talk (e.g., explicit conversations about the dyad), positive psychic change (e.g., realizing strong positive emotions about the relationship), negative psychic change (e.g., realizing negative emotions toward relationship), exclusivity (e.g., agreement to not date others), and serious commitment (e.g., living together, marital plans).

Taken together, both approaches to relationship initiation and development underscore the role of initial interactions as an important first step in assessing relationship potential. Both also underscore the salience of more intimate self-disclosure in advancing the relationship to a more significant level. We turn now to a more detailed discussion of factors associated with this phase of development.

EXPERIMENTING PHASE: SELF-DISCLOSURE

Self-disclosure is a voluntary act in which a person reveals information about him- or herself to another, usually in the form of facts, opinions, personal history, and feelings. Self-disclosure is important for the initiation of relationships because it provides the information that influences judgments about similarity, trustworthiness, character, personality, and other qualities that influence decisions about whether to pursue a relationship (Derlega, Winstead, & Greene, 2008). In this section, we first discuss two theories that address the role of self-disclosure in relationship formation: uncertainty reduction theory and social penetration theory. In addition, we also review individual characteristics (e.g., gender) associated with the tendency to disclose in initial interactions. We end this section by discussing the enhanced role of self-disclosure in the initiation of relationships when it occurs online.

Uncertainty Reduction and Information Seeking

In an effort to systematize the interface among communication, liking, and similarity during initial interactions, Berger and Calabrese (1975) proposed uncertainty reduction theory. The explanatory premise is that uncertainty about another person's values, attitudes, or interests is an uncomfortable state that motivates people to acquire the information necessary to better predict and explain the other person's actions and responses. The process of reducing uncertainty during initial interactions involving strangers moves through three phases. The entry phase relies largely on normative behaviors and seeking demographic information such as asking about someone's hometown, major in college, or place of employment. The personal phase is characterized by more probing questions regarding attitudes, values, beliefs, and personal information and typically follows from one or more entry phases. The exit phase indicates whether future interactions are desired or not (e.g., plans are made to meet again). The fundamental assumption reflected in the theory is that as the degree of communication increases, the intimacy of the self-disclosure also increases, and as a result uncertainty is reduced, leading to greater liking.

In subsequent elaborations of uncertainty reduction theory, Berger (e.g., 1987; Berger & Kellermann, 1994) proposed three broad strategies to reduce uncertainty, particularly when the target other may have relationship potential. Passive strategies include unobtrusive observations to gather information about a target. For example, relationship status might be evident when noticing a wedding ring, or religious values might be inferred from seeing a cross on a necklace. Intellect might be assessed by observing someone's responses in the classroom, and interaction style might be assessed by watching how the target responds to others in informal situations that are not rule guided, for example, in a bar or social gathering. Active strategies include more direct information gathering such as asking friends or family members for details about the target or arranging situations to see how the target reacts. For example, a friend might be recruited during a social gathering to approach a target in a flirtatious manner in order to evaluate the target's responses. Interactive strategies involve asking questions to obtain information and disclosure of increasingly personal information that will presumably be reciprocated.

Uncertainty reduction theory has been critiqued for not recognizing the restraining impact of some disclosure patterns on liking. For example, too much information too soon that is too negative and that appears to be shared indiscriminately violates normative expectations and will more likely lead to avoidance and disliking than to liking (Derlega, Metts, Petronio, & Margulis, 1993). In addition, uncertainty reduction theory has been critiqued for not recognizing the role of predicted outcome value as a key motivation for efforts to reduce uncertainty. These concerns form the basis of Sunnafrank's (1986, 1990) predicted outcome value theory. Sunnafrank argued that reducing uncertainty during initial interactions is secondary to assessing the probability of positive or negative relational outcomes, that is, the costs and rewards associated with pursuing the relationship. This social exchange perspective is reflected in social penetration theory's emphasis on the role of self-disclosure across the phases of relationship development.

Social Penetration Theory

Social penetration theory (Altman & Taylor, 1973; Taylor & Altman, 1987) draws from and builds on social exchange theory (Thibaut & Kelley, 1959). It was proposed as a framework for explaining the temporal development of interpersonal relationships. The basic premise of the theory is that people construct relationships primarily through mutual self-disclosure. By revealing his or her personality to another, the discloser demonstrates openness and vulnerability, thereby permitting the escalation of relational closeness and intimacy. Normally, the disclosure process is systematic, such that facets of personality are revealed gradually over time. Self-disclosures are expected to be mutually exchanged; that is, partners reciprocate disclosures comparably, particularly in the early developing stages of a relationship (see Vanlear, 1987).

Self-disclosures are characterized on two dimensions. First, breadth of information concerns the variety of different facets of personality that are revealed—how many different topics are discussed (e.g., political views, family history, hobbies). Depth refers to the degree of intimacy of disclosures. Information that is relatively more private and riskier to reveal represents enhanced depth of disclosure. Breadth of disclosure is typically greater than depth, but over time both breadth and depth increase as a relationship develops.

To elucidate the dimensions of breadth and depth, Altman and Taylor (1973) conceptualized personality as a set of concentric circles, or layers, of information. Outer circles represent public and superficial information, and inner circles represent increasingly private and unique information. Using the metaphor of an onion to represent personality, the process of social penetration (i.e., revelation of one's personality) involves peeling away layers of the onion. The entire surface area of a layer represents breadth of information about one's personality, and the penetration into deeper layers reflects depth of information. Relationship development is realized in the mutual revelations of personalities over time.

Individual decisions about whether to progress in social penetration are governed by a consideration of costs and rewards. The relative benefits of past and current interactions are assessed, and forecasts are made about the future benefit–cost ratio associated with further social penetration. Favorable assessments increase the likelihood (and sometimes speed) of relationship development. If a point is reached at which costs of penetration exceed (accumulated and projected) rewards, then a process of depenetration ensues whereby interactions are less intimate and less frequent, and fewer topics are discussed. In essence, there is a withdrawal back to more superficial forms of interchange (cf. Baxter, 1983).

Gender and Other Influences on Self-Disclosure in Initiation Interactions

Although most people self-disclose in first interactions with others as a way to become acquainted, there are individual differences in the ability and motivation to do so. One such factor that has received the most attention in the literature is gender (Dindia, 2000). According to Dindia and Allen's (1992) meta-analysis, women generally self-disclose more than do men, although the difference is stronger in interaction with same-sex others.

In early male–female interactions, however, men may actually self-disclose more as a strategy to get to know an attractive opposite-sex partner. In such cases, a man may be more likely than a woman to self-disclose to allow a potential partner to get to know him and also to elicit information from a partner by encouraging reciprocity in self-disclosure. In one early study along these lines, men were more likely to take the initiator role in a series of interactions with the opposite sex, and they selected more intimate topics than did women (Davis, 1978). Similarly, men, as compared with women, disclosed more intimately to an opposite-sex stranger, someone who they thought had an interest in getting to know them (Derlega, Winstead, Wong, & Hunter, 1985).

The expectation of future interaction increases the likelihood of obtaining certain gender differences. Men disclose more intimately when they expect to interact with a partner in the future, whereas women disclose less intimately, as demonstrated in an experiment in which participants either anticipated or did not anticipate future interaction with a confederate (Shaffer & Ogden, 1986). In a similar study, Shaffer, Pegalis, and Bazzini (1996) found that women were more responsive with same-sex, as opposed to opposite-sex, confederates. Highly masculine men, however, disclosed more to an opposite-sex target, although they did so only when they were led to believe that they would be able to further develop the relationship.

Other individual difference factors in addition to gender are likely to influence the likelihood that people freely disclose early in a relationship. Social anxiety, for example, includes an aspect of trait self-disclosure anxiety (Endler, Flett, Macrodimitris, Corace, & Kocovski, 2002). Moreover, socially anxious people tend to be self-protective and less likely to reciprocate the level of intimacy in a conversational partner's self-disclosure; the lack of reciprocity then leads to less liking and more discomfort on the part of the conversational partner (Meleshko & Alden, 1993). Individual attachment styles also manifest variations in willingness to self-disclosure and reciprocate self-disclosure. Mikulincer and Nachshon (1991) concluded from three studies using surveys, hypothetical situations, and actual interactions that secure and ambivalent people disclosed more personal information than avoidant individuals and felt more comfortable with and more attracted to a highly disclosing partner than a low disclosing partner. Secure individuals also demonstrated more responsive self-disclosure than individuals with other attachment styles. According to Mikulincer and Nachshon, "The 'responsive self-disclosure' of secure persons is the best strategy for developing the intimate relationships that the secure person desires" (p. 328). There are also individual differences in ability to elicit self-disclosures from others in initial interactions. For example, those who score high on the Miller, Berg, and Archer (1983) Opener Scale (e.g., "I encourage people to tell me how they are feeling") are more successful than those who score lower in getting low self-disclosers to open up in a get-acquainted interaction (e.g., Miller et al., 1983).

Self-Disclosure in Online Relationship Initiation

As noted elsewhere in this chapter, relationships are increasingly beginning online, through matchmaking sites and other online venues such as Facebook, games, comments sections of blogs, and chat rooms. In addition, even when two people initiate their relationship in a face-to-face setting, they may engage in online communication with each other as part of a get-acquainted process. Although spatial factors (e.g., proximity) and physical attractiveness may be important predictors of attraction in relationship initiation in face-to-face settings, Internet-initiated relationships have been described as involving an inverted developmental sequence that first involves a high level of mutual and sometimes intense self-disclosure and only an initial minimal role for physical attractiveness and physical proximity (e.g., Merkle & Richardson, 2000; Sprecher, 2009).

When initial communication between two potential partners occurs online, through e-mails and instant messages, the two may come to personally know one another better and share intimate knowledge more quickly than if they interacted initially in person (e.g., Merkle & Richardson, 2000). Not only does the intensity of the self-disclosure lead to development of closeness, but closeness can also be enhanced by the ability to present oneself in a strategic way by editing messages. People can come to believe that they are disclosing their authentic self and that the other (on the basis of his or her disclosures) is an ideal partner (e.g., Bargh, McKenna, & Fitzsimons, 2002; McKenna, Green, & Gleason, 2002). Even if true names and contact information are shared, there can be a sense of anonymity in communicating online, where intimate details are shared more easily than would occur in face-to-face communication. People who suffer from shyness may be especially likely to benefit from online interaction as a way to initiate relationships (e.g., Brunet & Schmidt, 2007).

Whether personal information about another person is learned through face-to-face conversations or online exchanges; is learned quickly or slowly over time; or is gathered through observations, manipulations of the environment, or from third parties, it serves a critical function. It either decreases interest in pursuing the relationship further or it moves potential partners toward greater commitment to the emerging relationship. We turn now to the relationship intensification phase of relationship initiation.

INTENSIFICATION PHASE: INCREASING INTIMACY

Assuming that the initiation and experimentation phases lead partners to believe that further relationship development is possible and desirable, couples move to deeper levels of relationship intimacy and eventually more explicit levels of commitment. In this section, we summarize two areas of research on this phase of relationship development: intensification strategies and sexual intimacy.

Intensification Strategies

One of the earliest and still most comprehensive lists of intensification strategies is that offered by Tolhuizen (1989). Tolhuizen's goal of identifying specific intensification strategies was prompted by what he viewed as limitations in phasic models that described general stages of relationship development (e.g., casual dating, serious dating, and engagement) but not the actions that partners undertake to communicate intent and negotiate definitional changes in the status of the relationship.

In a first study designed to generate a list of intensification strategies, college students listed behaviors they would use to move a hypothetical relationship from casual dating to serious and exclusive dating. Tolhuizen (1989) derived 15 strategies from the responses. The five most frequent included increased contact (e.g., more time together and frequent phone calls); relationship negotiation (e.g., direct discussion of the relationship and its future); social support and assistance (e.g., asking for advice, assistance, comfort, or support); increased rewards (e.g., compliments and favors); and direct definitional bid (direct request for a more serious and exclusive relationship such as going steady). In a second study, respondents sorted the strategies into clusters, and analysis yielded four categories: social rewards and attraction, implicitly expressed intimacy, passive and indirect, and verbal directness and intimacy.

Intensification strategies have proven to be a useful tool for relationship scholars. Kunkel,

Wilson, Olufowote, and Robson (2003) have confirmed the underlying assumption that the intensification stage of relationship development does, indeed, pose risks to social identity or face. More specifically, potential threats to positive face (i.e., the desire to be valued by significant others) included appearing too forward or overly dependent, and threats to negative face (i.e., the desire for autonomy) included fears that the partner may feel pressured or that the intensifier might lose the possibility of alternative future relationships. In a more direct incorporation of Tolhuizen's (1989) strategies, Levine, Aune, and Park (2006) confirmed the assumption that individual differences may influence the choice of intensification strategies. Using J. A. Lee's (1977) love styles as the individual differences variable, Levine et al. found a systematic pattern of association. For example, respondents high on eros were more likely to report using increased contact, tokens of affection, and behavioral adaption, whereas respondents high on pragma were more likely to use social enmeshment and personal appearance. For respondents high on ludus, sexual intimacy was the most highly endorsed strategy for intensifying a relationship.

Sex and Relationship Intensification

Although Tolhuizen's (1989) respondents listed sexual intimacy less frequently than intensification strategies that confirmed the relationship's status (e.g., relationship negotiation, direct definitional bid, verbal and nonverbal expressions of affection), this finding does not mean that increasingly intimate sexual behaviors are unimportant. To the contrary, turning points research has indicated that the passion turning point, which includes the first kiss, first sexual intimacy (typically intercourse), first expression of "I love you," and the whirlwind phenomenon of excitement and arousal (Baxter & Bullis, 1986), is a highly salient relationship event that is associated with increased intimacy and commitment (Bullis, Clark, & Sline, 1993).

In addition, however, when explicit communication about the state of the relationship occurs before intercourse, the passion turning point is associated with more positive emotions (e.g., happiness) and fewer negative emotions (e.g., fear, anger, sadness)

as well as perceptions that it was a positive event (Theiss & Solomon, 2007). Likewise, research on the temporal sequencing of the elements contained within the passion turning point has indicated that when "I love you" is verbally expressed before first sex, it is considered to be a much more positive turning point and to more significantly increase commitment and trust than when expressions of love follow the sexual episode (Metts, 2004). Partners may perceive the expression of love after the transition to sex as an obligated manifestation of normative expectations rather than a spontaneous or genuine expression of love. In sum, then, the relatively greater frequency of relationship-defining strategies that emerged in Tolhuizen's (1989) study may reflect their utility as a framing device to set the stage for the highly salient intensification behaviors of sexual intimacy.

Before leaving this discussion of the intensification phase of dating relationships, we should note two important caveats. First, as people enter dating relationships, they differ in how early in the relationship sexual behaviors occur. For example, Peplau, Rubin, and Hill (1977) identified three types of couples: sexual traditionalists who maintained their relationship without engaging in sexual intercourse, sexual moderates who had sex after establishing emotional intimacy, and sexual liberals who had sexual intercourse before emotional intimacy was established. Christopher and Cate (1985), using a more finely discriminated measure of sexual involvement, identified four types of couples. Rapid-involvement couples had high levels of sexual intimacy (typically intercourse) on a first date or within the first few weeks of dating. Gradual-involvement couples increased their levels of sexually intimate behaviors through casual dating and considering becoming a couple but did not have sexual intercourse until they considered themselves to be a couple. Delayed-involvement couples engaged in low levels of sexual intimacy through early stages of dating until the couple stage, when sexual intimacy increased dramatically. Finally, the low-involvement couples engaged in virtually no sexual intimacy throughout the early stages of the relationship (not even kissing on the first date) and by the couple stage limited sexual intimacy to preorgasmic levels (e.g., genital manipulation).

Second, recollections of sexual involvement and relationship definition reflect the sense-making process of partners who seek consistency across events of the past and current status of the relationship. If ambiguity or uncertainty about the nature of the relationship is high when sexual involvement first occurs, the meaning of both the act and relational intensification are open to interpretation or negotiation. For example, very rapid sexual involvement that is not framed by clarification of relationship status may initiate a "booty call" relationship rather than intensify a romantic relationship. A booty call relationship has some degree of investment and may include signs of affection such as kissing (Grello, Welsh, & Harper, 2006), but it is less likely to include talking and displays of emotional intimacy, such as holding hands, than is a dating relationship (Jonason, Li, & Richardson, 2010).

Alternatively, if ambiguity about the nature of the relationship is low because sex emerges within a preexisting friendship that both partners want to retain, a friends-with-benefits relationship may develop. Other than the sexual component, this social tie is comparable to any other close friendship. In fact, the inclusion of sexual intimacy increases the perceived quality of the friendship (Afifi & Faulkner, 2000). The relationship is also associated with more positive (e.g., happy, pleased) than negative (e.g., disappointed, used) emotions, especially for men (Owen & Fincham, 2011b), unless psychological distress and feeling constrained reduces the positive response (Owen & Fincham, 2011a). Consistent with gender role patterns, however, women do seem to be more emotionally involved in the relationship, whereas men are more sexually involved (e.g., desiring sex more often; McGinty, Knox, & Zusman, 2007).

PROBLEMATIC INITIATION EXPERIENCES

Relationship initiation activity would seem to be routine and generally positive. Nevertheless, attempts to initiate and escalate romance carry challenges and risks. In this section, we consider some of the aspects of these processes that are tricky and potentially problematic. We begin with a discussion of the ramifications associated with the use of deception to initiate relationships. We then review strategies ordinarily used to resist unwanted initiations. Next we explain how ambiguities surrounding relationship construction can lead two parties to unknowingly have disjunctive intentions and meanings for an ostensibly shared relationship.

When People Lie to Initiate a Relationship

Lying is remarkably common in everyday interactions, with people reporting telling lies one to two times per day and only a small minority, 5%, reporting no lying (DePaulo, Kashy, Kirkendol, Wyer, & Epstein, 1996). It should come as no surprise, therefore, that people are often untruthful while obtaining a date and beginning a relationship. As noted by Rowatt, Cunningham, and Druen (1999), approximately 46% of men and 36% of women report telling a lie to get a date with an attractive partner.

A central strategy of mate attraction involves using tactics that make oneself more attractive than others of the same sex (Buss, 1988), and deception is one such strategy. Deception refers to giving or creating a misleading, or false, impression. Why would people use deception in the process of initiating a relationship? According to the expectation-discordance model (as discussed in Rowatt, Cunningham, & Druen, 1998), people attempt to deceive someone when they believe that communicating honestly will make it challenging or impossible to meet that person's expectations. They lie to a potential partner presumably because they think that it will enhance their likelihood of attracting that person. More generally, people engage in deceptive acts with a partner to avoid costs associated with telling the truth (Cole, 2001). Costs include failing to have truthfulness reciprocated, the negative reactions of a partner, and concern that the truth will prevent achievement of attachment goals. The most frequently reported reason for deceiving a partner, in one study (Metts, 1989), was to avoid hurting that person, and dating respondents reported more reasons focused on avoiding relationship trauma or termination than did married respondents.

Men and women use a variety of deceptive strategies to attract a mate, with men using them more than women (Tooke & Camire, 1991). Tactics used

more frequently by men include feigning commitment, sincerity, and the ability to acquire resources. Women are more likely than men to engage in deceptive acts that alter their appearance. Both sexes, in particular men, also engage in deception with others of the same sex, presumably to ward off competitors. Another mode of deception used by both men and women is to alter their self-presentation to more closely match the desires of an attractive potential partner, such as describing themselves as more, or less, traditional in sex role orientation (e.g., Zanna & Pack, 1975).

Individual differences exist in the tendency to use deception in relationship initiation. Men and women who are high self-monitors, as compared with low self-monitors, engage in more deceptive self-presentations with a potential date, report using deception more frequently, and have more positive attitudes toward such behavior (Rowatt et al., 1998). Characteristics of a prospective partner also influence the likelihood of lying. Both men and women are more likely to lie to make themselves appear more desirable to attractive potential dates than to less attractive dates, and they are willing to lie about a variety of personal characteristics, such as appearance, personality, and income (Rowatt et al., 1999). Moreover, friends may lie to help friends obtain dates. People who exaggerate or lie about a friend to make an optimal impression on a potential date are liked more than friends who are truthful, although truthful friends are accorded more respect (Pontari & Schlenker, 2006).

Recent research has focused on the use of deception on Internet dating websites, such as in online profile information (for a review, see Sprecher, 2011). For example, an examination of 80 online daters (Toma, Hancock, & Ellison, 2008) found that men lie more about their height, whereas women lie more frequently about their weight, and that photographs tend to be particularly misleading, as compared with personal information. Moreover, deception is used strategically, balancing opportunities presented by an online venue with the risks of possible detection. In a study of 5,020 online dating service users, Hall, Park, Song, and Cody (2010) documented that both men and women sometimes misrepresent their self-portrayals. Men were particularly likely to be untruthful about their personal assets, goals for the relationship, interests, and attributes. Women, however, were more apt to misrepresent their weight. Self-monitoring was a particularly important individual predictor of being untruthful about all categories of personal information (e.g., assets, goals, interests, attributes), with the exception of weight.

In sum, lying appears to be a common tactic used in the initiation of a relationship, whether in person or on the Internet. Some types of deception are likely to be relatively minor (DePaulo, 2004) and may have little visible impact on a relationship, especially because deception can be hard to detect by those involved in a romance (e.g., Levine & McCornack, 1992). Once uncovered, however, deception can result in negative outcomes, especially for significant lies (McCornack & Levine, 1990). Thus, deception represents a risky endeavor for those attempting to establish a rewarding, long-term relationship.

Strategies to Resist Unwanted Initiations

Many flirtations and relationship initiation attempts are met with rejection. Recipients of initiation attempts who do not share the initiator's goal for relating use a variety of behaviors to deflect, rebuff, or ignore unwanted advances. Kellermann, Reynolds, and Chen (1991; Reynolds, 1991), for example, identified a number of conversation retreat strategies people use to unilaterally withdraw from unwanted conversations. These strategies vary in terms of their relative social appropriateness (i.e., polite vs. rude) and efficiency (direct and expedient vs. indirect and effortful). An appropriate and efficient strategy includes offering an excuse for leaving (whether true or not), and an inappropriate and inefficient strategy would be showing cues of impatience or preoccupation. An appropriate and inefficient approach would be changing the topic, and an inappropriate but efficient one would be making curt or abrupt statements that cut off talk. Situational factors determine the influence of preferences for appropriateness and efficiency. For example, the urgency to retreat from a conversation elevates the preferred level of efficiency in retreat tactics (Kellermann & Park, 2001).

Using a variety of qualitative and observational methods, Snow, Robinson, and McCall (1991) investigated the strategies used by women to fend off unwanted approaches by men in bars and nightclubs. The first set of strategies they identified was in response to initial unwanted overtures to dance or converse. These strategies were intended to convey rejection in a cordial and face-saving manner. Among these cordial strategies were polite refusals (e.g., "No, thank you"; "Not right now"), excuses (e.g., "I'm married," "I can't dance in these shoes"), and joking (e.g., "No, I can't dance. My feet are too big and I'd step all over you").

Although polite rebuffs were often successful, in some cases men persisted after the initial refusal, leading women to become more assertive and defensive in their rejection. "In contrast to the initial exchange, typically characterized by seemingly ritualized civility and playfulness, this form of exchange was decidedly somber and potentially combative, as indicated by the interactants' stiffened postures, sharpened voices, and seriousness of expression" (Snow et al., 1991, p. 436). Women's responses were marked by defensive incivility and self-evident justifications (e.g., "Back off!"; "I don't want anything to do with you!").

A third set of strategies (Snow et al., 1991) entailed avoidance behaviors designed to prevent unwanted approaches by conveying disinterest or unavailability. Avoidance was accomplished with tie signs, such as hand and arm holding, occasional embracing, and continuous conversation with male or female friends to signal involvement. In addition, women demonstrated nonverbal cues of disinterest such as frowning, scowling, and avoiding eye contact. Sometimes unwanted contact was avoided by moving to another location within the bar or by simply leaving the premises (similar results were found by Goodboy & Brann, 2010).

Mismatching of Relational Intentions

Even when relationship initiation is apparently successful, partners may unknowingly possess conflicting aspirations and meanings for their encounter. Each partner may have a different conception of the type of relationship that is currently shared, the desired relationship that is being sought, and the type of relationship that can be inferred from enacted behaviors. One person may envision a cordial work-related relationship, whereas the other sees a budding romantic relationship. One person's bid for intimacy may be viewed by the recipient as playful teasing. Gestures intended to convey friendliness may be construed as sexual overture. One person's casual sexual relationship can be viewed by the partner as an intimate bond. Relationship definitions tend not to be explicitly discussed, because such talk is often regarded as taboo (Baxter & Wilmot, 1985). Rather, they are implied and inferred through ordinary interactions involving behaviors that can take on multiple meanings (Baxter, 1987). The interactions that compose emerging relationships are inherently ambiguous in meaning, so it is not surprising that two individuals may view the same relationship somewhat differently. Although such mismatches in meanings and intentions can be discovered after a few encounters, they can also go undetected for a long period of time. On the surface, it appears that a viable relationship has been initiated. Although encounters run smoothly insofar as the mismatch goes undetected, the potential for relational strife is magnified by the mismatch. Indeed, manifest conflict and relationship difficulties are often symptomatic of latent nonmutuality of relationship definition (Morton, Alexander, & Altman, 1976).

A number of factors contribute to misperception of the extent to which relational intentions are shared. First, even when two individuals begin a relationship on similar terms, one of them may gradually change intentions without clearly indicating them to the other, who retains the original intentions. This gap in intentions and interpretations can widen over time, even when neither partner is aware of it. Second, people can sometimes approach a relationship opportunity ambivalently. It is possible to view a potential partner as having both desirable and undesirable features at any given time. It is also possible for individuals to fluctuate in their aspirations: Two days ago I was pretty sure I wanted a relationship with person X, yesterday I didn't want it, and today I am uncertain. Mixed feelings about a potential partner diminish the likelihood of matched orientations to the relationship.

Systematic sex-based misattributions further contribute to mismatching in interpersonal interactions. For example, evidence from studies using both experimental manipulations (Abbey, 1982; Abbey & Melby, 1986; Saal, Johnson, & Weber, 1989) and naturally occurring events (Abbey, 1987; Haselton, 2003) has indicated that men tend to overestimate women's intentions to engage in sexual activity on the basis of observing women's friendly behavior. A number of explanations have been proffered for this phenomenon. One is that men experience greater sexual desire than women and project their own desire when estimating the desire of women (Shotland & Craig, 1988). Another is that men may simply interpret the world in a more sexualized manner than women (Abbey, 1982). Perhaps the most rigorously tested and supported account derives from error management theory (Haselton & Buss, 2000). Error management theory proposes that

> decision-making adaptations have evolved through natural or sexual selection to commit predictable errors. Whenever there exists a recurrent cost asymmetry between two types of errors over the period of time in which selection fashions adaptations, they should be biased toward errors that are less costly. (Haselton & Buss, 2000, p. 81)

In the case of men perceiving women's sexual intent, the error of underestimating sexual interest (a false negative error) and thereby missing sexual opportunities is presumed to be more costly than wasting effort as a result of overestimating sexual interest (a false-positive error). Haselton and Buss (2000) demonstrated that men overestimated women's sexual intent compared with both women's perceptions of other women and women's self-perceived sexual intent. Moreover, women's perception of men's sexual intent did not show a similar bias. Consistent with error management theory, the researchers also predicted and found that men's biased perceptions of sexual intent did not occur when the target was their sister.

Extending the logic of asymmetrical costs associated with decision-making errors, Haselton and Buss

(2000) applied error management theory to perceptual biases in inferring relationship commitment. In this case, women's costs associated with overestimating a potential partner's commitment presumably outweigh the costs of underestimating a partner's commitment, thereby leading to the evolutionary adaptation of women being skeptical about men's commitment. Again using hypothetical scenarios, Haselton and Buss found women's perceptions of men's commitment intent were lower than men's self-perceived commitment intent and men's perceptions of other men's commitment intent. Men's assessments of women's commitment intent did not evidence a similar bias.

Persistent Unwanted Relationship Pursuit

Some relationship initiations are unwelcome and easily rebuffed by recipients. However, other ardent pursuers are particularly pushy. When unwanted pursuit persists, despite explicit rejection by the pursued, it constitutes obsessive relational intrusion (Cupach & Spitzberg, 1998, 2004). Obsessive relational intrusion can occur in the context of initiating a new relationship, escalating the closeness of a current relationship, or reconciling a previously terminated relationship. Milder forms are merely annoying and typically include attempts by the pursuer to initiate frequent contacts, maneuver physical proximity to the target, pester the target for a date, obtain information, and escalate intimacy by acting as though the pursuer shares more closeness than he or she actually does. More serious manifestations of obsessive relational intrusion involve surveillance of the target, unexpected visits, excessive contact, and other forms of harassment. The most severe forms of obsessive relational intrusion entail threatening forms of contact and the experience of fear by the target. These severe cases legally qualify as stalking (Cupach & Spitzberg, 2004; Tjaden & Thoennes, 1998).

Both large-scale epidemiological studies (e.g., Baum, Catalano, Rand, & Rose, 2009) and meta-analyses (e.g., Spitzberg, Cupach, & Ciceraro, 2010) have shown that obsessive relational intrusion and stalking are not rare events. Conservative estimates have indicated that 2% of men and 8% of women in the United States will be stalked during their lifetime (Tjaden & Thoennes, 1998). Although stalking is not always motivated by relationship pursuit, it most often emerges out of attempts to establish or reestablish a relationship, or it represents anger and revenge fueled by relational rejection (Cupach & Spitzberg, 1998; Spitzberg & Cupach, 2007).

Given the ambiguities and misunderstandings surrounding relationship initiation and development noted earlier, the occurrence of unwanted relationship pursuit is not surprising. Additional cultural and contextual factors associated with ordinary courtship serve to fuel the persistence of undesired suitors. For instance, unwanted overtures are usually met with soft and ambiguous rejections (e.g., Bratslavsky, Baumeister, & Sommer, 1998; Emerson, Ferris, & Gardner, 1998; Folkes, 1982). Recipients of relational initiations want to neither appear cruel nor hurt a pursuer's feelings—particularly when pursuit behaviors are prosocial and ingratiating. By responding to unwanted bids in a polite and indirect manner, the pursued individual wards off guilt and saves face for both self and pursuer (Cupach & Metts, 1994). Moreover, relationship initiation attempts can be flattering at the same time as they are annoying or harassing, especially when framed in the context of pursuing romantic connection (Dunn, 1999). The resulting ambivalence in emotional reactions translates into ambiguous behavioral reactions to the unwanted pursuit.

Another cultural factor that promotes excessive relational pursuit, despite some apparent rejection, is the pervasive belief in the importance of persistence when pursuing important goals (Cupach & Spitzberg, 2004). In everyday experience as well as depictions in popular culture, persistence often pays. When goal pursuit meets obstacles, the general tendency is to try harder, and greater effort often ultimately yields success. This is true in attempting all kinds of goals, including relationship goals. In courtship and the pursuit of relationships, a modicum of resistance is expected, and even seen as part of the game of love. When persistence of relational pursuit is unwanted and explicitly rejected, however, it is excessive and reflects distorted and obsessive thinking.

THIRD-PARTY ASSISTANCE IN RELATIONSHIP INITIATION

Many relationships begin without assistance and the knowledge of others; however, the two most common ways that people meet partners is now through friends and on the Internet, including through Internet dating services (Rosenfeld & Thomas, 2012). In addition, eventually all relationships are influenced by the partners' social networks. In this section of the chapter, we discuss how relationship initiation is influenced by social networks and can occur through commercial third-party assistance.

Informal Assistance: Social Networks

The initiation of a relationship takes place within a wider social environment that has a substantial impact on the relationship's trajectory. Yet the influence of the environment has received relatively little attention in the literature (Berscheid, 1999). A person's social ties, in particular, may play either a direct or an indirect role in facilitating a connection between two people in a variety of ways, as we discuss here. In addition, the reactions of social network members to a potential or existing relationship influence the course of that relationship. Online social networks facilitate relationship initiation as well, which we also discuss in this section.

Opportunity and information. Social networks have an impact on close pairs in at least three major ways (Sprecher, Felmlee, Orbuch, & Willetts, 2002), ways that are applicable to the initiation of relationships. The first is opportunity. Social networks aid in providing opportunities for individuals to meet a prospective partner and to develop a budding relationship. Parents originate the process by which the social environment indirectly shapes romantic relationships by structuring the environment in which their children grow up and meet potential mates and dates. Parents, and the wider social network, attempt to control mate selection by choosing the correct schools, neighborhoods, and activities for their progeny and by encouraging young people to develop appropriate companions and dates. Family members also use direct, verbal strategies, encouraging or sometimes threatening, to convince their children to associate with a particular partner. These direct and indirect management attempts are apt to reinforce powerful norms of social homogamy, in which people are encouraged to match up with those who are similar on a variety of characteristics, such as age, race, social class, religion, and educational background (McPherson, Smith-Lovin, & Cook, 2001).

Second, social networks act as a source of information about available partners. A family member or friend who is familiar with a potential partner can reveal information that enhances that person's apparent attractiveness and the level of similarity between the two individuals. Social networks also provide information concerning the appropriateness of various prospective mates, typically emphasizing similarity or homogamy (e.g., Kerckhoff, 1974), although women, in particular, may be encouraged to pair with a more desirable mate. In addition, network members can serve the important function of reducing uncertainty by acting as an important source of information about a partner (e.g., Berger & Calabrese, 1975).

Finally, social networks can provide support for a potential, or beginning, relationship. Support could be practical, such as assisting meeting someone, or financial. Support could also take the form of relationship advice, with friends and family offering suggestions intended to help a person obtain a desired date. Support can be emotional too, which we discuss further later on.

One of the most common ways to meet someone for a new relationship is through a social network member, in particular family members or friends. According to Parks (2007), the number of social ties that connect two people, that is, their social proximity, relates directly to the likelihood of two people meeting; for example, Parks reported that in one study approximately two thirds of 858 people reported having met at least one member of a partner's social network before forming a romantic relationship or a same-sex friendship, with those in romantic relationships knowing about twice as many network members as those in friendships. Multiple studies have also revealed that introductions by a third party are heavily involved in the initiation of intimate adult pairs (Laumann et al., 1994; Parks & Eggert, 1991). In his college student survey, Parks (2007) found that 64% of those in a relationship said that they had received assistance from one or more third parties, and 55% reported helping at least one couple to start a relationship. People were much more likely to date extensively when they were brought together by a third party than when no third party was involved. Finally, several types of strategies were used to help in initiating a romance, and these included attraction manipulations (e.g., said good things about one to the other), direct initiations (e.g., arranged for two people to be in the same place), and direct assists (e.g., coached on methods of approach).

Social network approval and disapproval. Social network approval of existing relationships has been found to be a particularly potent predictor of relationship development over time. Common approving behaviors on the part of parents include asking about the partner and letting the two of them have time alone (Leslie, Huston, & Johnson, 1986). Approval from one's social network is associated with several positive relationship outcomes, such as levels of satisfaction, commitment, and love (Sprecher & Felmlee, 1992), as well as with attachment, closeness, and expectations that the relationship will continue (e.g., Eggert & Parks, 1987; Parks, 2007). Perceptions of social support also predict increases in commitment and other types of attachment over time (e.g., Lewis, 1973; Sprecher & Felmlee, 1992), and they enhance a pair's identity as a couple (Lewis, 1973). Approval from various social network members was also one of the strongest predictors of relationship stability in several longitudinal studies (e.g., Felmlee, 2001; Felmlee, Sprecher, & Bassin, 1990; Parks & Adelman, 1983; Parks, Stan, & Eggert, 1983; Sprecher & Felmlee, 1992). According to some studies, the female member's network, in particular, is relatively successful at predicting couple stability or dissolution (Agnew, Loving, & Drigotas, 2001; Sprecher & Felmlee, 1992). Taken together, the bulk of the findings have suggested that approval from social networks is likely to be a salient factor for people who are initiating a new relationship, enhancing the likelihood that they form a relationship in the first place and maintain a rewarding one once it is started.

The influence of social networks on close relationships is not always benign, however. Instead of providing opportunities, helpful information, and

support, networks can place barriers to the development of a relationship, convey damaging partner information, fail to support, or express disapproval toward, a nascent relationship. Parents may be hesitant to have their teenager form a romance (Leslie et al., 1986), for example, and adult children can be reluctant to have a widowed parent enter into a relationship (Atchley, 1994). Friends and family members may also disapprove of a couple because of the tendency for newly formed pairs to withdraw from their networks as they become more involved (e.g., Huston & Burgess, 1979). Moreover, network members could serve as alternative, or substitutable (Marsiglio & Scanzoni, 1995), sources of companionship or romance and therefore have a deleterious effect on a blossoming romance. Finally, according to a study on the "Romeo and Juliet effect," in cases in which there was network opposition to a couple, it caused pairs to grow, not shrink, in love for each other (Driscoll, Davis, & Lipetz, 1972). Further research has found limited support for the Romeo and Juliet effect, and only under special circumstances, such as when parents' and friends' attitudes differ (Felmlee, 2001) or when personal reactance is high (Sinclair, Denson, Felmlee, & Sprecher, 2011).

Facebook and relationship initiation. Social networking no longer remains limited to face-to-face interaction or communication via "snail mail." Instead, in a 21st-century revolution, millions of people connect with others via the Internet. Social networking websites, such as Facebook, MySpace, and LinkedIn, represent one type of online venue. There is little doubt that these networking sites are stepping in quickly to play an extensive, and expanding, role in the relationship initiation process. Here we focus largely on the most popular of these sites, Facebook. More than 750 million people actively use Facebook, with the average user having about 130 friends (Facebook, 2011). Facebook has grown at an extraordinary rate, with about one half of Americans using the site today. Given Facebook's vast popularity, it remains likely that the potential of this website for instigating romantic ties will expand substantially with time.

How would a person meet someone on Facebook? First and foremost, Facebook provides social connections that link two people. Singles can find out information online about the friends of their friends, and they can ask a friend to introduce the two of them, mimicking one of the most common ways that people meet offline (e.g., Parks, 2007), as discussed earlier. Facebook also leads to the development of people's social capital and weak ties (Ellison, Steinfield, & Lampe, 2007), which can provide additional potential intermediaries. In addition, Facebook includes lists of people's interest groups and clubs, and these lists can be used to locate someone who shares an important common interest. Facebook also allows people to view a friend's events or activities. Event information can point to a relatively comfortable, natural setting that can be used to meet a prospective date while in the company of one's friend. Moreover, people can quickly find out about a friend's or acquaintance's shift in relationship status to single. Such an update can be used to initiate a meeting or date with the newly single individual.

What are the advantages of initiating relationships through Facebook? To begin with, there are practical motivations, such as the fact that unlike common dating venues, Facebook is free and, because of its inordinate popularity, probably provides the largest pool of singles of any online site. Furthermore, as compared with face-to-face interaction, Facebook users have more control over the information they convey, allowing them to selectively present themselves to a prospective partner (e.g., Walther, 1996). According to McKenna (2008), developing a relationship via one's connections online (a "networked relationship"), versus offline, also has the advantage that a search for a partner can be self-initiated and does not involve waiting for an introduction from a mutual friend. Finally, the availability of multiple online applications attached to Facebook, such as Zoosk, Social Connect, and Flirtmaps, can help locate a date, sometimes for a fee, in which case Facebook begins to resemble more traditional matchmaking web locations.

In sum, Facebook and other social networking sites represent the newest frontier for the initiation of romance. The factors that influence relationship formation online resemble in many ways those that form offline, such as meeting through the friend of a friend. Yet, websites such as Facebook also significantly expand the opportunities and options for connecting with a prospective mate (Bargh & McKenna, 2004; McKenna & Bargh, 2000).

Commercial Third-Party Assistance in Relationship Initiation

Friends and family represent informal third-party assistance in the relationship initiation process, but single adults who are seeking a partner also have the option of paying for services that can assist in finding a partner and in the initiation of the relationship. The commercial aspect of relationship initiation is not new. Human matchmakers have existed for centuries (Ahuvia & Adelman 1992), and they are still in business and have active clientele today. Printed personal advertisements, another form of commercial assistance, have existed almost as long as there have been newspapers, although they became more popular in the 1970s and 1980s, both in mainstream publications and in niche magazines and newspapers (Orr, 2004). Video dating services and other types of singles events also became popular in the 1970s and 1980s. With the introduction of the Internet, however, there has been an explosion in third-party commercial assistance in relationship formation. In addition to the widespread adoption of the Internet, other social factors that have likely contributed to the increased use of commercial assistance in the matching process include the growing number of single adults; greater mobility, which can create a need to meet partners; and social change, which makes it more acceptable to use a commercial service to find a partner (Ahuvia & Adelman, 1992; Sautter, Tippett, & Morgan, 2010). Next, we discuss two recent forms of commercial third-party assistance in relationship initiation: Internet dating sites and speed dating.

Internet dating sites. Today, many single adults who are looking for a partner are turning to Internet dating sites. Internet dating services encourage single adults to use their services to find their perfect match or soul mate. Internet dating sites offer various services. Ahuvia and Adelman (1992) introduced a framework referred to as the

233

searching–matching–interaction model to describe the functions offered by commercial marriage-market intermediaries such as Internet dating services. The searching function refers to acquiring information on who is available. The matching stage includes actual decisions about who would make a compatible match. The third stage refers to the transaction, or interaction. Some Internet dating sites focus primarily on providing access to other singles (or the searching function), whereas others, such as eHarmony, offer matching decisions and guided interaction within the site.

Thousands of Internet dating sites now exist that offer one or more of these functions to singles. Some of the dating sites are mainstream, drawing from a large demographic base (e.g., Match.com). Others constitute niche sites for people of particular races (BlackSingles.com), ages (e.g., SeniorPeopleMeet.com), religions (JDate.com), or interests (DateMy-Pet.com). Many of the sites focus primarily on giving users the opportunity to post online profile information and search for potential matches with particular characteristics. These sites have been referred to as "glorified search engines" and "search/sort/match" systems (e.g., Fiore & Donath, 2004). Certain sites have distinguished themselves from others by offering a scientific approach to matching, with personality surveys constructed by academic scientists and proprietary matching algorithms guided by scientific principles used to match pairs. The first of such scientific-based sites was eHarmony, which offers a patented compatibility system that emphasizes 29 dimensions of compatibility. Perfectmatch, which has the Duet Compatibility System based on the famous Myers–Briggs Type indicator, was launched in 2002, followed by Chemistry.com, which offers matching based on a combination of similarity and complementarity on four personality types believed to be associated with hormones and brain chemicals. Members who seek matches on these sites begin by completing lengthy surveys that assess their personality characteristics, interests, and desired characteristics in a partner and then wait to receive the recommended matches (for a review, see Sprecher, 2009; Sprecher, Schwartz, Harvey, & Hatfield, 2008). Although a growing number of people are turning to Internet dating

sites, perhaps with the hope of finding a highly compatible partner, there is currently no evidence that Internet matching sites produce relationships that are more successful than relationships that begin in real-world settings (Houran, Lange, Rentfrow, & Bruckner, 2004). However, they are likely to be an efficient way to find a partner, especially for busy professionals.

Speed dating. Speed dating was developed in the late 1990s to help Jewish singles in Los Angeles find mates (Finkel & Eastwick, 2008), and it has become a popular, commercial way to meet partners in many major cities of the United States and other countries (Eastwick & Finkel, 2008). Typically, people register in advance for the event through a speed-dating organization (e.g., Cupid.com, HurryDate.com) and are notified about upcoming events in their geographical area for their particular age group. In the typical heterosexual speed-dating event, there may be 10 to 20 members of each sex; women are seated, and men change tables every 6 to 8 minutes (Houser, Horan, & Furler, 2008). At the end of the event, the attendees provide ratings of their partners. When there is mutual interest, the organizer then provides contact information to each person (Eastwick & Finkel, 2008). Although speed dating relies on face-to-face interaction, the Internet can be used to organize the event and to provide a way for matches to communicate after the event. There are also online versions of speed dating in which people interact with others over the Internet, including through web chats (SpeedDate.com). Relationship scientists, including Eli Finkel and Paul Eastwick (see Chapter 7, this volume), have recognized speed dating as a context for studying interpersonal attraction and relationship initiation.

FUTURE RESEARCH DIRECTIONS AND CONCLUSIONS

The topic of this chapter is an important one, with implications for a range of social psychological processes, as noted in the preceding discussion. Although typically less vivid, dramatic, and emotionally provocative than other relational events such as the first big fight or a breakup, the initiation of a relationship is a transitional accomplishment no less important. We turn now to a summary of the key points discussed in this chapter and the implications they raise for future research.

We started our chapter by discussing that relationships begin in various settings that differ in the extent to which interaction with others is voluntary and whether relationship initiation is the raison d'être for interaction. Settings vary along other dimensions as well, including the degree to which they attract those similar to each other on demographic and personality characteristics, the extent to which members already feel part of a mutual social network, and the level of legitimatization and encouragement of pairings. Contextual factors are generally the overlooked causal variables in the study of relationships (e.g., Felmlee & Sprecher, 2000), and this may be especially true of the initiation phase. As noted by Berscheid and Regan (2005),

> To understand why others currently are in the relationships they are—and to understand why we ourselves developed the relationships we did—it is usually necessary to retrace the history of the relationship back to its very beginning and to identify the causal conditions that were in force at that time. It is especially important to identify the environmental conditions under which the relationship was established, because their influence is likely to be overlooked. (p. 159)

One particular context for relationship initiation today is the Internet, yet the Internet offers many variants of virtual settings. As we noted, relationships can begin through commercial Internet dating sites but also through social network sites such as Facebook. Relationship initiation also occurs while people play online games, communicate in chat rooms, and otherwise engage in naturally occurring online interactions. Many have speculated about how early attraction and initiation steps differ online versus offline (e.g., Merkle & Richardson, 2000), and some have begun to explore these issues (e.g., McKenna et al., 2002); however, much more research is needed. Future investigations should explore these different trajectories and their respective precursors.

Regardless of the setting in which a relationship is beginning, the initiation requires the involvement of a minimum of two people. Reciprocity and mutuality, whether this is in regard to attraction, flirting, or self-disclosure, is essential for a relationship to be initiated. Although one partner could do more of the work of initiation than the other (Guynn, Brooks, & Sprecher, 2008)—probably because people vary in their degree of readiness, attraction, and other motives for entering a relationship—it takes two to tango. Rejection in the initiation process is painful (e.g., Finkel & Baumeister, 2010). In fact, some people may be overly sensitive to the possibility of rejection to the point that they do not respond to initiation cues of others (Vorauer, Cameron, Holmes, & Pearce, 2003); others are not sensitive or even ignore rejection behaviors and engage in unwanted pursuit, as discussed earlier. This dark side of relationships, borne of nonreciprocity in relationship intent, deserves more attention across diverse contexts.

Most research conducted on processes of relationship initiation has focused on young adults, typically college students who are heterosexual. Although they are a logical population to study because they are often initiating relationships, greater attention is needed to diverse populations, with a focus on how relationship initiation may differ on the basis of past experiences. For example, older adults who are divorced or widowed may use different strategies to initiate a new relationship than college students who frequent social events or bars. Likewise, people who may rekindle a relationship with an old flame from high school, or even reconcile after breaking off an engagement or divorcing, face unique challenges in initiating a "new" relationship with the same person (Bevan, Cameron, & Dillow, 2003). Relationship initiation is also likely to vary as a function of access to resources (e.g., social class), age, and sexual orientation. Personality factors play a role, too. We noted, for example, that attachment styles influence the patterns of openness to relationship initiation and that characteristics such as shyness and social anxiety can inhibit people from engaging in initiating behaviors. Future research focused on how individual differences are manifested in the early interactions of potential partners, whether they occur online or in person, would enhance our understanding of this influence. In other words, unitizing conversational turns or thematizing content would allow researchers to identify types of questions asked, nonverbal responsiveness, avoidance cues, evasive or engaging comments, and so forth.

We also summarized the extensive research on gender differences, including in self-disclosure, mating strategies, and first date scripts. Although a traditional cultural norm encourages men to be initiators of relationships, this may be changing. More research is needed on social norms focused on relationship initiation and the consequences of violating social norms. There are norms about gender roles in relationship initiation (e.g., Finkel & Eastwick, 2009) but also normative expectations about behaviors (regardless of gender) associated with this earliest stage of the relationship, including how appropriate it is to self-disclose and about what topics, how early one should begin having sex in the relationship, and how appropriate it is for a friend to engage in romantic initiation behaviors (e.g., Afifi & Metts, 1998; Felmlee, 1999).

The initiation stage may be more obvious for romantic relationships than for friendships, not only to the prospective partners engaged in the process but also to their social network members who often become aware of a pair's first meetings, first dates, and even first sexual encounters. Although the initiation stage of friendships may not have the same salience or comparable transition points to a first date or first sex, it does occur frequently and, for most people, more often than that of a romantic relationship. We need more work on the initial stages of same-sex and opposite-sex friendships and, in fact, on all types of relationships that bring meaning to life, including collaborators, business partners, and employer–employee, mentor–mentee, and therapist–patient ties.

We also encourage more diverse types of methods to best study relationship initiation. In general, it is difficult to conduct research that assesses participants' reactions to the initiation process as it is naturally occurring. Some studies have involved people who are in a relationship recalling the first stage of involvement (e.g., Clark et al., 1999;

Custer et al., 2008), but there are problems with recall data, and the full range of initiation experiences may not be represented in surviving dyads. Very few studies are prospective, following a group of people who are likely to initiate a relationship while in the study (for an exception, see Schindler et al., 2010); however, such prospective research would be useful for examining predictors of entering a relationship as well as psychological states that occur as a consequence of the initiation of a new relationship (e.g., feelings of well-being). This type of method could be extended further by asking participants (who could provide survey data preinitiation) to go to a website and complete brief (daily) surveys during the process of initiating a relationship.

Moreover, one main reason to examine relationship initiation is the presupposition that it heavily shapes subsequent development and outcomes. Yet relatively little work has been done regarding such associations. A number of relevant questions along these lines exist, such as whether the type of context in which relationships unfold influences their development. Do Internet matches, for example, undertake the same path as those instigated by a mutual friend? Do couples whose relationship began as a hookup develop similar levels of satisfaction as those with more traditional starting points? Can couples learn to survive, or even thrive, when one or both of them is deficient in relational skills, strategies, or self-disclosure? These and other questions that link relationship beginnings to endings or relationship survival deserve additional attention.

Finally, although we recognize the challenge, we encourage scholarly attention to the construction of a model of relationship initiation that is responsive to its complexity, both conceptually and in actual practice. As the turning points approach illustrates, intimacy and commitment over the course of a relationship do not simply increase in a linear fashion. Yet, much of the research on initiation of a relationship implies that intimacy and commitment increase systematically to the point—some point—when, for example, a person says, "I love you" or "I don't want you to see other people." In actual practice, however, cues of commitment are more finely nuanced, intensification intentions sometimes fade without conscious awareness, and partners may not even realize that what they assumed was a connection, best described as a romantic relationship, is nothing more than a casual friendship. In short, the dynamic, cyclical, and ambiguous process of moving from a state of mutual awareness to the explicit, shared recognition of being in a relationship involves the interplay, over time, of all elements (structural, psychological, sociological, and communicative) that we have summarized here. Integration of these factors into a model reflecting the complexity of the process would be beneficial for existing work and motivating future research.

In conclusion, although the breadth of this chapter is evidence that relationship initiation is not an unexplored topic, we believe that relationship initiation is a complex phase that is understudied and needs more research. Furthermore, relationship beginnings are influenced by a host of factors, including their social environment, psychological foundations, and communicative content. We maintain that this topic will benefit particularly from interdisciplinary work that explicitly incorporates this full range of influences, an approach we have attempted to offer here.

References

Abbey, A. (1982). Sex differences in attributions for friendly behavior: Do males misperceive females' friendliness? *Journal of Personality and Social Psychology, 42*, 830–838. doi:10.1037/0022-3514.42.5.830

Abbey, A. (1987). Misperceptions of friendly behavior as sexual interest: A survey of naturally occurring instances. *Psychology of Women Quarterly, 11*, 173–194. doi:10.1111/j.1471-6402.1987.tb00782.x

Abbey, A., & Melby, C. (1986). The effects of nonverbal cues on gender differences in perceptions of sexual intent. *Sex Roles, 15*, 283–298. doi:10.1007/BF00288318

Afifi, W., & Faulkner, S. L. (2000). On being "just friends": The frequency and impact of sexual activity in cross-sex friendships. *Journal of Social and Personal Relationships, 17*, 205–222. doi:10.1177/0265407500172003

Afifi, W. A., & Metts, S. (1998). Characteristics and consequences of expectation violations in close relationships. *Journal of Social and Personal Relationships, 15*, 365–392. doi:10.1177/0265407598153004

Agnew, C. R., Loving, T. J., & Drigotas, S. M. (2001). Substituting the forest for the trees: Social networks and the prediction of romantic relationship state and fate. *Journal of Personality and Social Psychology, 81*, 1042–1057. doi:10.1037/0022-3514.81.6.1042

Ahuvia, A. C., & Adelman, M. B. (1992). Formal intermediaries in the marriage market: A typology and review. *Journal of Marriage and the Family, 54*, 452–463. doi:10.2307/353076

Allen, J. S., & Bailey, K. G. (2007). Are mating strategies and mating tactics independent constructs? *Journal of Sex Research, 44*, 225–232. doi:10.1080/00224490701443601

Altman, I., & Taylor, D. A. (1973). *Social penetration: The development of interpersonal relationships*. New York, NY: Holt, Rinehart, & Winston.

Aron, A., Dutton, D. G., Aron, E. N., & Iverson, A. (1989). Experiences of falling in love. *Journal of Social and Personal Relationships, 6*, 243–257. doi:10.1177/0265407589063001

Atchley, R. C. (1994). Change and continuity in adulthood. *Journal of Religious Gerontology, 9*, 95–97.

Back, M. D., Penke, L., Schmukle, S. C., Sachse, K., Borkenau, P., & Asendorpf, J. B. (2011). Why mate choices are not as reciprocal as we assume: The role of personality, flirting, and physical attractiveness. *European Journal of Personality, 25*, 120–132. doi:10.1002/per.806

Baker, A. (2008). Down the rabbit hole: The role of place in the initiation and development of online relationships. In A. Barak (Ed.), *Psychological aspects of cyberspace: Theory, research, applications* (pp. 163–184). Cambridge, England: Cambridge University Press. doi:10.1017/CBO9780511813740.008

Bargh, J. A., & McKenna, K. Y. A. (2004). The Internet and social life. *Annual Review of Psychology, 55*, 573–590. doi:10.1146/annurev.psych.55.090902.141922

Bargh, J. A., McKenna, K. Y. A., & Fitzsimons, G. M. (2002). Can you see the real me? Activation and expression of the "true self" on the Internet. *Journal of Social Issues, 58*, 33–48. doi:10.1111/1540-4560.00247

Bartoli, A. M., & Clark, M. D. (2006). The dating game: Similarities and differences in dating scripts among college students. *Sexuality and Culture, 10*, 54–80. doi:10.1007/s12119-006-1026-0

Baum, K., Catalano, S., Rand, M., & Rose, K. (2009). *Stalking victimization in the United States* (NCJ 224527). Washington, DC: U.S. Department of Justice, Bureau of Justice Programs.

Baumeister, R. F., & Leary, M. R. (1995). The need to belong: Desire for interpersonal attachments as a fundamental human motivation. *Psychological Bulletin, 117*, 497–529. doi:10.1037/0033-2909.117.3.497

Baxter, L. A. (1983). An examination of the reversal hypothesis. *Western Journal of Speech Communication, 47*, 85–98. doi:10.1080/10570318309374109

Baxter, L. A. (1987). Cognition and communication in the relationship process. In R. Burnett, P. McGhee, & D. D. Clarke (Eds.), *Accounting for relationships* (pp. 192–212). London, England: Methuen.

Baxter, L. A., & Bullis, C. (1986). Turning points in developing romantic relationships. *Human Communication Research, 12*, 469–493. doi:10.1111/j.1468-2958.1986.tb00088.x

Baxter, L. A., & Pittman, G. (2001). Communicatively remembering turning points of relationship development in heterosexual romantic relationships. *Communication Reports, 14*, 1–17. doi:10.1080/08934210109367732

Baxter, L. A., & Wilmot, W. W. (1985). Taboo topics in close relationships. *Journal of Social and Personal Relationships, 2*, 253–269. doi:10.1177/0265407585023002

Bell, R. A., Tremblay, S. W., & Buerkel-Rothfuss, N. L. (1987). Interpersonal attraction as a communication accomplishment: Development of a measure of affinity-seeking competence. *Western Journal of Speech Communication, 51*, 1–18. doi:10.1080/10570318709374249

Berger, C. R. (1987). Communicating under uncertainty. In M. E. Roloff & G. R. Miller (Eds.), *Interpersonal processes: New directions in communication research* (pp. 39–62). Newbury Park, CA: Sage.

Berger, C. R., & Calabrese, R. J. (1975). Some explorations in initial interaction and beyond: Toward a developmental theory of interpersonal communication. *Human Communication Research, 1*, 99–112. doi:10.1111/j.1468-2958.1975.tb00258.x

Berger, C. R., & Kellermann, K. (1994). Acquiring social information. In J. A. Daley & J. M. Weimann (Eds.), *Strategic interpersonal communication* (pp. 1–31). Hillsdale, NJ: Erlbaum.

Berscheid, E. (1985). Interpersonal attraction. In G. Lindzey & E. Aronson (Eds.), *The handbook of social psychology* (pp. 413–484). New York, NY: Random House.

Berscheid, E. (1999). The greening of relationship science. *American Psychologist, 54*, 260–266. doi:10.1037/0003-066X.54.4.260

Berscheid, E., & Regan, P. (2005). *The psychology of interpersonal relationships*. Upper Saddle River, NJ: Pearson Education.

Bevan, J. L., Cameron, K. A., & Dillow, M. R. (2003). One more try: Compliance-gaining strategies associated with romantic reconciliation attempts. *Southern Communication Journal, 68*, 121–135. doi:10.1080/10417940309373255

Bisson, M. A., & Levine, T. R. (2009). Negotiating a friends with benefits relationship. *Archives of Sexual Behavior, 38*, 66–73. doi:10.1007/s10508-007-9211-2

Blackhart, G. C., Eckel, L. A., & Tice, D. M. (2007). Salivary cortisol in response to acute social rejection and acceptance by peers. *Biological Psychology, 75*, 267–276. doi:10.1016/j.biopsycho.2007.03.005

Bossard, J. H. S. (1932). Residential propinquity in marriage selection. *American Journal of Sociology, 38*, 219–224. doi:10.1086/216031

Bratslavsky, E., Baumeister, R. F., & Sommer, K. L. (1998). To love or be loved in vain: The trials and tribulations of unrequited love. In B. H. Spitzberg & W. R. Cupach (Eds.), *The dark side of close relationships* (pp. 307–326). Mahwah, NJ: Erlbaum.

Brunet, P. M., & Schmidt, L. A. (2007). Is shyness context specific? Relation between shyness and online self-disclosure with and without a live webcam in young adults. *Journal of Research in Personality, 41*, 938–945. doi:10.1016/j.jrp.2006.09.001

Bullis, C., Clark, C., & Sline, R. (1993). From passion to commitment: Turning points in romantic relationships. In P. J. Kalbfleisch (Ed.), *Interpersonal communication: Evolving interpersonal relationships* (pp. 213–236). Hillsdale, NJ: Erlbaum.

Buss, D. M. (1988). The evolution of human intrasexual competition: Tactics of mate attraction. *Journal of Personality and Social Psychology, 54*, 616–628. doi:10.1037/0022-3514.54.4.616

Buss, D. M., & Barnes, M. (1986). Preferences in human mate selection. *Journal of Personality and Social Psychology, 50*, 559–570. doi:10.1037/0022-3514.50.3.559

Byrne, D. (1971). *The attraction paradigm*. New York, NY: Academic Press.

Carver, K., Joyner, K., & Udry, J. R. (2003). National estimates of adolescent romantic relationships. In P. Florsheim (Ed.), *Adolescent romantic relations and sexual behavior: Theory, research, and practical implications* (pp. 23–56). Mahwah, NJ: Erlbaum.

Caspi, A., Herbener, E. S., & Ozer, D. J. (1992). Shared experiences and the similarity of personalities: A longitudinal study of married couples. *Journal of Personality and Social Psychology, 62*, 281–291. doi:10.1037/0022-3514.62.2.281

Christopher, F. S., & Cate, R. M. (1985). Premarital sexual pathways and relationship development. *Journal of Social and Personal Relationships, 2*, 271–288. doi:10.1177/0265407585023003

Clark, C. L., Shaver, P. R., & Abrahams, M. F. (1999). Strategic behaviors in romantic relationship initiation. *Personality and Social Psychology Bulletin, 25*, 709–722. doi:10.1177/0146167299025006006

Coker, D. A., & Burgoon, J. K. (1987). The nature of conversational involvement and nonverbal encoding patterns. *Human Communication Research, 13,* 463–494. doi:10.1111/j.1468-2958.1987.tb00115.x

Cole, T. (2001). Lying to the one you love: The use of deception in romantic relationships. *Journal of Social and Personal Relationships, 18,* 107–129. doi:10.1177/0265407501181005

Collins, W. A., Welsh, D. P., & Furman, W. (2009). Adolescent romantic relationships. *Annual Review of Psychology, 60,* 631–652. doi:10.1146/annurev.psych.60.110707.163459

Connolly, J., Craig, W., Goldberg, A., & Pepler, D. (2004). Mixed-gender groups, dating, and romantic relationships in early adolescence. *Journal of Research on Adolescence, 14,* 185–207. doi:10.1111/j.1532-7795.2004.01402003.x

Cunningham, M. (1989). Reactions to heterosexual opening gambits: Female selectivity and male responsiveness. *Personality and Social Psychology Bulletin, 15,* 27–41. doi:10.1177/0146167289151003

Cunningham, M. R., & Barbee, A. P. (2008). Prelude to a kiss: Nonverbal flirting, opening gambits, and other communication dynamics in the initiation of romantic relationships. In S. Sprecher, A. Wenzel, & J. Harvey (Eds.), *Handbook of relationship initiation* (pp. 97–120). New York, NY: Psychology Press.

Cupach, W. R., & Metts, S. (1994). *Facework.* Thousand Oaks, CA: Sage.

Cupach, W. R., & Spitzberg, B. H. (1998). Obsessive relational intrusion and stalking. In B. H. Spitzberg & W. R. Cupach (Eds.), *The dark side of close relationships* (pp. 233–263). Mahwah, NJ: Erlbaum.

Cupach, W. R., & Spitzberg, B. H. (2004). *The dark side of relationship pursuit: From attraction to obsession and stalking.* New York, NY: Routledge.

Custer, L., Holmberg, D., Blair, K., & Orbuch, T. L. (2008). "So how did you two meet?" Narratives of relationship initiation. In S. Sprecher, A. Wenzel, & J. Harvey (Eds.), *Handbook of relationship initiation* (pp. 453–470). New York, NY: Psychology Press.

Darley, J. M., & Berscheid, E. (1967). Increased liking as a result of the anticipation of personal contact. *Human Relations, 20,* 29–40. doi:10.1177/001872676702000103

Davis, J. D. (1978). When boy meets girl: Sex roles and the negotiation of intimacy in an acquaintance exercise. *Journal of Personality and Social Psychology, 36,* 684–692. doi:10.1037/0022-3514.36.7.684

Deci, E. L., & Ryan, R. M. (1991). A motivational approach to self: Integration in personality. In R. Dienstbier (Ed.), *Nebraska symposium on motivation: Vol. 38. Perspectives on motivation* (pp. 237–288). Lincoln: University of Nebraska Press.

Deci, E. L., & Ryan, R. M. (2008). Self-determination theory: A macrotheory of human motivation, development, and health. *Canadian Psychology, 49,* 182–185.

DePaulo, B. (2011). Living single: Lightening up those dark, dopey myths. In W. R. Cupach & B. H. Spitzberg (Eds.), *The dark side of close relationships II* (pp. 409–439). New York, NY: Taylor & Francis.

DePaulo, B. M. (2004). The many faces of lies. In A. G. Arthur (Ed.), *The social psychology of good and evil* (pp. 303–326). New York, NY: Guilford Press.

DePaulo, B. M., Kashy, D. A., Kirkendol, S. E., Wyer, M. M., & Epstein, J. A. (1996). Lying in everyday life. *Journal of Personality and Social Psychology, 70,* 979–995. doi:10.1037/0022-3514.70.5.979

Derlega, V., Winstead, B. A., & Greene, K. (2008). Self-disclosure and starting a close relationship. In S. Sprecher, A. Wenzel, & J. Harvey (Eds.), *Handbook of relationship initiation* (pp. 153–174). New York, NY: Psychology Press.

Derlega, V. J., Metts, S., Petronio, S., & Margulis, S. T. (1993). *Self-disclosure.* London, England: Sage.

Derlega, V. J., Winstead, B. A., Wong, P. T. P., & Hunter, S. (1985). Gender effects in an initial encounter: A case where men exceed women in disclosure. *Journal of Social and Personal Relationships, 2,* 25–44. doi:10.1177/0265407585021002

Dindia, K. (2000). Sex differences in self-disclosure, reciprocity of disclosure, and self-discourse and liking: Three meta-analyses reviewed. In S. Petronio (Ed.), *Balancing the secrets of private disclosures* (pp. 21–36). Mahwah, NJ: Erlbaum.

Dindia, K., & Allen, M. (1992). Sex differences in self-disclosure: A meta-analysis. *Psychological Bulletin, 112,* 106–124. doi:10.1037/0033-2909.112.1.106

Doherty, N. A., & Feeney, J. A. (2004). The composition of attachment networks throughout the adult years. *Personal Relationships, 11,* 469–488. doi:10.1111/j.1475-6811.2004.00093.x

Driscoll, R., Davis, K. E., & Lipetz, M. E. (1972). Parental interference and romantic love: The Romeo and Juliet effect. *Journal of Personality and Social Psychology, 24,* 1–10. doi:10.1037/h0033373

Dunn, J. L. (1999). What love has to do with it: The cultural construction of emotion and sorority women's responses to forcible interaction. *Social Problems, 46,* 440–459. doi:10.2307/3097109

Eastwick, P. E., & Finkel, E. J. (2008). Speed-dating: A powerful and flexible paradigm for studying romantic relationship initiation. In S. Sprecher, A. Wenzel, & J. Harvey (Eds.), *Handbook of relationship initiation* (pp. 217–234). New York, NY: Psychology Press.

Eggert, L. L., & Parks, M. R. (1987). Communication network involvement in adolescents' friendships and romantic relationships. In M. L. McLaughlin (Ed.), *Communication yearbook* (Vol. 10, pp. 283–322). Newbury Park, CA: Sage.

Egland, K. L., Spitzberg, B. H., & Zormeier, M. M. (1996). Flirtation and conversational competence in cross-sex platonic and romantic relationships. *Communication Reports, 9,* 105–117.

Ellison, N. B., Steinfield, C., & Lampe, C. (2007). The benefits of Facebook "friends": Social capital and college students' use of online social network sites. *Journal of Computer-Mediated Communication, 12,* 1143–1168. doi:10.1111/j.1083-6101.2007.00367.x

Emerson, R. E., Ferris, K. O., & Gardner, C. B. (1998). On being stalked. *Social Problems, 45,* 289–314. doi:10.2307/3097188

Endler, N. S., Flett, G. L., Macrodimitris, S. D., Corace, K. M., & Kocovski, N. L. (2002). Separation, self-disclosure, and social evaluation anxiety as facets of trait social anxiety. *European Journal of Personality, 16,* 239–269. doi:10.1002/per.452

Erickson, E. H. (1968). *Identity: Youth and crisis.* London, England: Faber & Faber.

Facebook. (2011). *Facebook statistics.* Retrieved July 25, 2011, from http://www.facebook.com/press/info.php?statistics

Fehr, B. (2008). Friendship formation. In S. Sprecher, A. Wenzel, & J. Harvey (Eds.), *Handbook of relationship initiation* (pp. 29–54). New York, NY: Psychology Press.

Feingold, A. (1991). Sex differences in the effects of similarity and physical attractiveness on opposite-sex attraction. *Basic and Applied Social Psychology, 12,* 357–367. doi:10.1207/s15324834basp1203_8

Felmlee, D. (2001). No couple is an island: A social network perspective on dyadic stability. *Social Forces, 79,* 1259–1287. doi:10.1353/sof.2001.0039

Felmlee, D., Orzechowicz, D., & Fortes, C. (2010). Fairy tales: Attraction and stereotypes in same-gender relationships. *Sex Roles, 62,* 226–240. doi:10.1007/s11199-009-9701-x

Felmlee, D., & Sprecher, S. (2000). Close relationships and social psychology: Intersections and future paths. *Social Psychology Quarterly, 63,* 365–376. doi:10.2307/2695846

Felmlee, D., Sprecher, S., & Bassin, E. (1990). The dissolution of intimate relations: A hazard model. *Social Psychology Quarterly, 53,* 13–30.

Felmlee, D. H. (1995). Fatal attractions: Affection and disaffection in intimate relationships. *Journal of Social and Personal Relationships, 12,* 295–311. doi:10.1177/0265407595122009

Felmlee, D. H. (1999). Social norms in same- and cross-gender friendships. *Social Psychology Quarterly, 62,* 53–67. doi:10.2307/2695825

Festinger, L., Schachter, S., & Back, K. W. (1950). *Social pressures in informal groups: A study of human factors in housing.* Stanford, CA: Stanford University Press.

Fine, M. A., Coffelt, T. A., & Olson, L. N. (2008). Romantic relationship initiation following relationship dissolution. In S. Sprecher, A. Wenzel, & J. Harvey (Eds.), *Handbook of relationship initiation* (pp. 391–407). New York, NY: Psychology Press.

Finkel, E. J., & Baumeister, R. F. (2010). Attraction and rejection. In R. F. Baumeister & E. J. Finkel (Eds.), *Advanced social psychology: The state of the science* (pp. 419–459). New York, NY: Oxford University Press.

Finkel, E. J., & Eastwick, P. W. (2008). Speed-dating. *Current Directions in Psychological Science, 17,* 193–197. doi:10.1111/j.1467-8721.2008.00573.x

Finkel, E. J., & Eastwick, P. W. (2009). Arbitrary social norms and sex differences in romantic selectivity. *Psychological Science, 20,* 1290–1295. doi:10.1111/j.1467-9280.2009.02439.x

Fiore, A. T., & Donath, J. S. (2004, April). *Online personals: An overview.* Paper presented at the Conference on Human Factors in Computing Systems, Vienna, Austria. Retrieved from http://www4.comp.polyu.edu.hk/~csehung/fyp0607/fd04.pdf

Folkes, V. S. (1982). Communicating the reasons for social rejection. *Journal of Experimental Social Psychology, 18,* 235–252. doi:10.1016/0022-1031(82)90052-X

Gallmeier, C. P., Knox, D., & Zusman, M. E. (2002). Going out or hanging out: Couple dating and group dating in the new millennium. *Free Inquiry in Creative Sociology, 30,* 221–225.

Gangestad, S. W., Garver-Apgar, C. E., Simpson, J. A., & Cousins, A. J. (2007). Changes in women's mate preferences across the ovulatory cycle. *Journal of Personality and Social Psychology, 92,* 151–163. doi:10.1037/0022-3514.92.1.151

Gere, J., & MacDonald, G. (2010). An update of the empirical case for the need to belong. *Journal of Individual Psychology, 66,* 93–115.

Glenn, N., & Marquardt, E. (2001). *Hooking up, hanging out, and hoping for Mr. Right: College women on dating and mating today.* New York, NY: Institute for American Values.

Goodboy, A. K., & Brann, M. (2010). Flirtation rejection strategies: Toward an understanding of communicative disinterest in flirting. *Qualitative Report, 15,* 268–278. Retrieved from http://www.nova.edu/ssss/QR/QR15-2/goodboy.pdf

Grammer, K., Kruck, K. B., & Magnusson, M. S. (1998). The courtship dance: Patterns of nonverbal synchronization in opposite-sex encounters. *Journal of Nonverbal Behavior, 22,* 3–29. doi:10.1023/A:1022986608835

Grello, C. M., Welsh, D. P., & Harper, M. S. (2006). No strings attached: The nature of casual sex in college students. *Journal of Sex Research, 43,* 255–267. doi:10.1080/00224490609552324

Guynn, L., Brooks, J. E., & Sprecher, S. (2008). The balance of work in initiating relationships. *Free Inquiry in Creative Sociology, 36,* 83–93.

Hall, J. A., Carter, S., Cody, M. J., & Albright, J. M. (2010). Individual differences in the communication of romantic interest: Development of the Flirting Styles Inventory. *Communication Quarterly, 58,* 365–393. doi:10.1080/01463373.2010.524874

Hall, J. A., Park, N., Song, H., & Cody, M. J. (2010). Strategic misrepresentation in online dating: The effects of gender, self-monitoring, and personality traits. *Journal of Social and Personal Relationships, 27,* 117–135. doi:10.1177/0265407509349633

Haselton, M. G. (2003). The sexual overperception bias: Evidence of a systematic bias in men from a survey of naturally occurring events. *Journal of Research in Personality, 37,* 34–47. doi:10.1016/S0092-6566(02)00529-9

Haselton, M. G., & Buss, D. M. (2000). Error management theory: A new perspective on biases in cross-sex mind reading. *Journal of Personality and Social Psychology, 78,* 81–91. doi:10.1037/0022-3514.78.1.81

Hatfield, E., & Sprecher, S. (1986). *Mirror, mirror: The importance of looks in everyday life.* Albany: State University of New York Press.

Houran, J., Lange, R., Rentfrow, J. P., & Bruckner, K. H. (2004). Do online matchmaking tests work? An assessment of preliminary evidence for a publicized "predictive model of marital success." *North American Journal of Psychology, 6,* 507–526.

Houser, M. L., Horan, S. M., & Furler, L. A. (2008). Dating in the fast lane: How communication predicts speed-dating success. *Journal of Social and Personal Relationships, 25,* 749–768. doi:10.1177/0265407508093787

Huston, T. L., & Burgess, R. L. (1979). The analysis of social exchange in developing relationships. In R. L. Burgess & T. L. Huston (Eds.), *Social exchange in developing relationships* (pp. 3–28). New York, NY: Academic Press.

Jonason, P. K., Li, N. P., & Richardson, J. (2010). Positioning the booty-call relationship on the spectrum of relationships: Sexual but more emotional than one-night standards. *Journal of Sex Research, 48,* 486–495.

Kayser, D. N., Elliot, A. J., & Feltman, R. (2010). Red and romantic behavior in men viewing women. *European Journal of Social Psychology, 40,* 901–908. doi:10.1002/ejsp.757

Kellermann, K., & Park, H. S. (2001). Situational urgency and conversational retreat: When politeness and efficiency matter. *Communication Research, 28,* 3–47. doi:10.1177/009365001028001001

Kellermann, K., Reynolds, R., & Chen, J. B.-S. (1991). Strategies of conversational retreat: When parting is not sweet sorrow. *Communication Monographs, 58,* 362–383. doi:10.1080/03637759109376236

Kelley, H. H., Berscheid, E., Christensen, A., Harvey, J. H., Huston, T. L., Levinger, G., . . . Peterson, D. R. (1983). Analyzing close relationships. In H. H. Kelley (Ed.), *Close relationships* (pp. 20–67). New York, NY: W. H. Freeman.

Kerckhoff, A. C. (1974). The social context of interpersonal attraction. In T. L. Huston (Ed.), *Foundations of interpersonal attraction* (pp. 61–78). New York, NY: Academic Press.

Kleinke, C. L., Meeker, F. B., & Staneski, R. A. (1986). Preference for opening lines: Comparing ratings by men and women. *Sex Roles, 15,* 585–600. doi:10.1007/BF00288216

Knapp, M. L. (1978). *Social intercourse: From greeting to goodbye.* Boston, MA: Allyn & Bacon.

Knapp, M. L., & Vangelesti, A. L. (2005). *Interpersonal communication and human relationships* (5th ed.). Boston, MA: Allyn & Bacon.

Koeppel, L. B., Montagne-Miller, Y., O'Hair, D., & Cody, M. J. (1993). Friendly? Flirting? Wrong? In P. J. Kalbfleisch (Ed.), *Interpersonal communication: Evolving interpersonal relationships* (pp. 13–32). Hillsdale, NJ: Erlbaum.

Kunkel, A. D., Wilson, S. R., Olufowote, J., & Robson, S. (2003). Identity implications of influence goals: Initiating, intensifying, and ending romantic relationships. *Western Journal of Communication, 67,* 382–412. doi:10.1080/10570310309374780

Kurzban, R., & Weeden, J. (2005). HurryDate: Mate preferences in action. *Evolution and Human Behavior, 26,* 227–244. doi:10.1016/j.evolhumbehav.2004.08.012

LaGuardia, J. G., & Patrick, H. (2008). Self-determination theory as a fundamental theory of close relationships. *Canadian Psychology, 49,* 201–209.

Laner, M. R., & Ventrone, N. A. (2000). Dating scripts revisited. *Journal of Family Issues, 21,* 488–500. doi:10.1177/019251300021004004

Langlois, J. H., Kalakanis, L., Rubenstein, A. J., Larson, A., Hallam, M., & Smoot, M. (2000). Maxims or myths of beauty? A meta-analytic and theoretical review. *Psychological Bulletin, 126,* 390–423. doi:10.1037/0033-2909.126.3.390

Laumann, E. O., Gagnon, J. H., Michael, R. T., & Michaels, S. (1994). *The social organization of sexuality: Sexual practices in the United States.* Chicago, IL: University of Chicago Press.

Leary, M. R., Koch, E. J., & Hechenbleikner, N. R. (2001). Emotional responses to interpersonal rejection. In M. R. Leary (Ed.), *Interpersonal rejection* (pp. 145–166). New York, NY: Oxford University Press.

Lee, J. A. (1977). A typology of styles of loving. *Personality and Social Psychology Bulletin, 3*, 173–182. doi:10.1177/014616727700300204

Lee, J. W., & Guerrero, L. K. (2001). Types of touch in cross-sex relationships between coworkers: Perceptions of relational and emotional messages, inappropriateness, and sexual harassment. *Journal of Applied Communication Research, 29*, 197–220. doi:10.1080/00909880128110

Leslie, L. A., Huston, T. L., & Johnson, M. P. (1986). Parental reactions to dating relationship: Do they make a difference? *Journal of Marriage and the Family, 48*, 57–66. doi:10.2307/352228

Levine, T. R., Aune, K. S., & Park, H. S. (2006). Love styles and communication in relationships: Partner preferences, initiation, and intensification. *Communication Quarterly, 54*, 465–486. doi:10.1080/01463370601036515

Levine, T. R., King, G., & Popoola, J. K. (1994). Ethnic and gender differences in opening lines. *Communication Research Reports, 11*, 143–151. doi:10.1080/08824099409359952

Levine, T. R., & McCornack, S. A. (1992). Linking love and lies: A formal test of McCornack and Parks' model of deception detection. *Journal of Social and Personal Relationships, 9*, 143–154. doi:10.1177/0265407592091008

Lewis, R. A. (1973). Social reaction and the formation of dyads: An interactionist approach to mate selection. *Sociometry, 36*, 409–418. doi:10.2307/2786342

MacGregor, J. C. D., & Cavallo, J. V. (2011). Breaking the rules: Personal control increases women's direct relationship initiation. *Journal of Social and Personal Relationships, 28*, 848–867.

Madden, M., & Lenhart, A. (2006). *Online dating.* Retrieved from http://www.pewinternet.org/ Reports/2006/Online-Dating.aspx

Marsiglio, W., & Scanzoni, J. (1995). *Families and friendships.* New York, NY: HarperCollins.

McCormick, N. B., & Jones, A. J. (1989). Gender differences in nonverbal flirtation. *Journal of Sex Education and Therapy, 15*, 271–282.

McCornack, S. A., & Levine, T. R. (1990). When lovers become leery: The relationship between suspicion and accuracy in detecting deception. *Communication Monographs, 57*, 219–230. doi:10.1080/03637759009376197

McGinty, K., Knox, D., & Zusman, M. E. (2007). Friends with benefits: Women want "friends," men want "benefits." *College Student Journal, 41*, 1128–1131.

McKenna, K. Y. A. (2008). Myspace or your place: Relationship initiation and development in the wired and wireless world. In S. Sprecher, A. Wenzel, & J. Harvey (Eds.), *Handbook of relationship initiation* (pp. 235–247). New York, NY: Psychology Press.

McKenna, K. Y. A., & Bargh, J. A. (2000). Plan 9 from cyberspace: The implications of the Internet for personality and social psychology. *Personality and Social Psychology Review, 4*, 57–75. doi:10.1207/ S15327957PSPR0401_6

McKenna, K. Y. A., Green, A. S., & Gleason, M. E. J. (2002). Relationship formation on the Internet: What's the big attraction? *Journal of Social Issues, 58*, 9–31. doi:10.1111/1540-4560.00246

McPherson, M., Smith-Lovin, L., & Cook, J. M. (2001). Birds of a feather: Homophily in social networks. *Annual Review of Sociology, 27*, 415–444. doi:10.1146/annurev.soc.27.1.415

Meleshko, K. G. A., & Alden, L. (1993). Anxiety and self-disclosure: Toward a motivational model. *Journal of Personality and Social Psychology, 64*, 1000–1009. doi:10.1037/0022-3514.64.6.1000

Merkle, E. R., & Richardson, R. A. (2000). Digital dating and virtual relating: Conceptualizing computer mediated romantic relationships. *Family Relations: Interdisciplinary Journal of Applied Family Studies, 49*, 187–192. doi:10.1111/j.1741-3729.2000.00187.x

Metts, S. (1989). An exploratory investigation of deception in close relationships. *Journal of Social and Personal Relationships, 6*, 159–179.

Metts, S. (2004). First sexual involvement in romantic relationships: An empirical investigation of communicative framing, romantic beliefs, and attachment orientation in the passion turning point. In J. H. Harvey, A. Wenzel, & S. Sprecher (Eds.), *The handbook of sexuality in close relationships* (pp. 135–158). Mahwah, NJ: Erlbaum.

Mikulincer, M., & Nachshon, O. (1991). Attachment styles and patterns of self-disclosure. *Journal of Personality and Social Psychology, 61*, 321–331. doi:10.1037/0022-3514.61.2.321

Mikulincer, M., & Shaver, P. R. (2007). *Attachment in adulthood: Structure, dynamics, and change.* New York, NY: Guilford Press.

Miller, L. C., Berg, J. H., & Archer, R. L. (1983). Openers: Individuals who elicit intimate self-disclosure. *Journal of Personality and Social Psychology, 44*, 1234–1244. doi:10.1037/0022-3514.44.6.1234

Mongeau, P. M., Morr Serewicz, M. C. M., & Therrien, L. F. (2004). Goals for cross-sex first dates: Identification, measurement, and the influence of contextual factors. *Communication Monographs, 71*, 121–147. doi:10.1080/0363775042331302514

Montoya, R. M., Horton, R. S., & Kirchner, J. (2008). Is actual similarity necessary for attraction?

A meta-analysis of actual and perceived similarity. *Journal of Social and Personal Relationships, 25,* 889–922. doi:10.1177/0265407508096700

Moore, M. M. (1985). Nonverbal courtship patterns in women: Context and consequences. *Ethology and Sociobiology, 6,* 237–247. doi:10.1016/0162-3095(85)90016-0

Moore, M. M. (2010). Human nonverbal courtship behavior—A brief historical review. *Journal of Sex Research, 47,* 171–180. doi:10.1080/00224490903402520

Morr, M. C., & Mongeau, P. A. (2004). First-date expectations: The impact of sex of initiator, alcohol consumption, and relationship type. *Communication Research, 31,* 3–35. doi:10.1177/0093650203260202

Morr Serewicz, M. C. M., & Gale, E. (2008). First-date scripts: Gender roles, context and relationship. *Sex Roles, 58,* 149–164. doi:10.1007/s11199-007-9283-4

Morton, T., Alexander, J., & Altman, I. (1976). Communication and relationship definition. In G. R. Miller (Ed.), *Explorations in interpersonal communication* (pp. 105–126). Beverly Hills, CA: Sage.

Murstein, B. I. (1970). Stimulus-value-role: A theory of marital choice. *Journal of Marriage and the Family, 32,* 465–481. doi:10.2307/350113

Nahemow, L., & Lawton, M. P. (1975). Similarity and propinquity in friendship formation. *Journal of Personality and Social Psychology, 32,* 205–213. doi:10.1037/0022-3514.32.2.205

Newcomb, T. M. (1961). *The acquaintance process.* New York, NY: Holt. doi:10.1037/13156-000

Orr, A. (2004). *Meeting, mating, and cheating: Sex, love, and the new world of online dating.* Upper Saddle River, NJ: Reuters.

Owen, J., & Fincham, F. (2011a). Effects of gender and psychosocial factors on "friends with benefits" relationships among young adults. *Archives of Sexual Behavior, 40,* 311–320. doi:10.1007/s10508-010-9611-6

Owen, J., & Fincham, F. (2011b). Young adults' emotional reactions after hooking up encounters. *Archives of Sexual Behavior, 40,* 321–330. doi:10.1007/s10508-010-9652-x

Parks, M. R. (2007). *Personal relationships and personal networks.* Mahwah, NJ: Erlbaum.

Parks, M. R., & Adelman, M. B. (1983). Communication networks and the development of romantic relationships: An expansion of uncertainty reduction theory. *Human Communication Research, 10,* 55–79. doi:10.1111/j.1468-2958.1983.tb00004.x

Parks, M. R., & Eggert, L. L. (1991). The role of social context in the dynamics of personal relationships. In W. Jones & D. Perlman (Eds.), *Advances in personal relationships* (Vol. 2, pp. 1–34). London, England: Jessica Kingsley.

Parks, M. R., Stan, C. M., & Eggert, L. L. (1983). Romantic involvement and social network involvement. *Social Psychology Quarterly, 46,* 116–131. doi:10.2307/3033848

Paul, E. L., McManus, B., & Hayes, A. (2000). "Hookups": Characteristics and correlates of college students' spontaneous and anonymous sexual experiences. *Journal of Sex Research, 37,* 76–88. doi:10.1080/00224490009552023

Paulsel, M. L., & Mottet, T. P. (2004). Interpersonal communication motives: A communibiological perspective. *Communication Quarterly, 52,* 182–195. doi:10.1080/01463370409370189

Peplau, L. A., Rubin, Z., & Hill, C. T. (1977). Sexual intimacy in dating relationships. *Journal of Social Issues, 33,* 86–109. doi:10.1111/j.1540-4560.1977.tb02007.x

Perper, T. (1985). *Sex signals: The biology of love.* Philadelphia, PA: ISI Press.

Pontari, B. A., & Schlenker, B. R. (2006). Helping friends manage impressions: We like helpful liars but respect nonhelpful truth tellers. *Basic and Applied Social Psychology, 28,* 177–183. doi:10.1207/s15324834basp2802_7

Regan, P. (2011). *Close relationships.* New York, NY: Routledge.

Renninger, L. A., Wade, T. J., & Grammer, K. (2004). Getting that female glance: Patterns and consequences of male nonverbal behavior in courtship contexts. *Evolution and Human Behavior, 25,* 416–431. doi:10.1016/j.evolhumbehav.2004.08.006

Reynolds, R. A. (1991). Beliefs about conversation abandonment: I do; you don't; we will. *Journal of Language and Social Psychology, 10,* 61–70. doi:10.1177/0261927X91101004

Rose, S., & Frieze, I. H. (1993). Young singles' contemporary dating scripts. *Sex Roles, 28,* 499–509. doi:10.1007/BF00289677

Rosenfeld, M. J., & Thomas, R. J. (2012). Searching for a mate: The rise of the Internet as a social intermediary. *American Sociological Review, 77,* 523–547. doi:10.1177/0003122412448050

Rowatt, W. C., Cunningham, M. R., & Druen, P. B. (1998). Deception to get a date. *Personality and Social Psychology Bulletin, 24,* 1228–1242. doi:10.1177/01461672982411009

Rowatt, W. C., Cunningham, M. R., & Druen, P. B. (1999). Lying to get a date: The effect of physical attractiveness on the willingness to deceive prospective dating partners. *Journal of Social and Personal Relationships, 16,* 209–223. doi:10.1177/0265407599162005

Rubin, R. B., Perse, E. M., & Barbato, C. A. (1988). Conceptualization and measurement of interpersonal communication motives. *Human*

Communication Research, 14, 602–628. doi:10.1111/j.1468-2958.1988.tb00169.x

Rusbult, C. E., Kumashiro, M., Kubacka, K. E., & Finkel, E. J. (2009). "The part of me that you bring out": Ideal similarity and the Michelangelo phenomenon. *Journal of Personality and Social Psychology, 96*, 61–82. doi:10.1037/a0014016

Saal, F. E., Johnson, C. B., & Weber, N. (1989). Friendly or sexy? It may depend on whom you ask. *Psychology of Women Quarterly, 13*, 263–276.

Sautter, J., Tippett, R. M., & Morgan, S. P. (2010). The social demography of Internet dating in the United States. *Social Science Quarterly, 91*, 554–575. doi:10.1111/j.1540-6237.2010.00707.x

Schank, R. C., & Abelson, R. P. (1977). *Scripts, plans, goals, and understanding: An inquiry into human knowledge structures.* Hillsdale, NJ: Erlbaum.

Scheflen, A. E. (1965). Quasi-courtship behavior in psychotherapy. *Psychiatry: Journal of Study of Interpersonal Processes, 28*, 245–257.

Schindler, I., Fagundes, C. P., & Murdock, K. W. (2010). Predictors of romantic relationship formation: Attachment style, prior relationships, and dating goals. *Personal Relationships, 17*, 97–105. doi:10.1111/j.1475-6811.2010.01255.x

Schmitt, D. P., & Buss, D. M. (1996). Strategic self-promotion and competitor derogation: Sex and context effects on the perceived effectiveness of mate attraction tactics. *Journal of Personality and Social Psychology, 70*, 1185–1204. doi:10.1037/0022-3514.70.6.1185

Schutz, W. C. (1966). *The interpersonal underworld.* Palo Alto, CA: Science & Behavior Books.

Segal, M. W. (1974). Alphabet and attraction: An unobtrusive measure of the effect of propinquity in field setting. *Journal of Personality and Social Psychology, 30*, 654–657. doi:10.1037/h0037446

Senko, C., & Fyffe, V. (2010). An evolutionary perspective on effective vs. ineffective pick-up lines. *Journal of Social Psychology, 150*, 648–667. doi:10.1080/00224540903365539

Shaffer, D. R., & Ogden, J. K. (1986). On sex differences in self-disclosure during the acquaintance process: The role of anticipated future interaction. *Journal of Personality and Social Psychology, 51*, 92–101. doi:10.1037/0022-3514.51.1.92

Shaffer, D. R., Pegalis, L. J., & Bazzini, D. G. (1996). When boy meets girl (revisited): Gender, gender-role orientation, and prospect of future interaction as determinants of self-disclosure among same- and opposite-sex acquaintances. *Personality and Social Psychology Bulletin, 22*, 495–506. doi:10.1177/0146167296225007

Shotland, R. L., & Craig, J. M. (1988). Can men and women differentiate between friendly and sexually interested behavior? *Social Psychology Quarterly, 51*, 66–73. doi:10.2307/2786985

Simon, W., & Gagnon, J. H. (1986). Sexual scripts: Permanence and change. *Archives of Sexual Behavior, 15*, 97–120. doi:10.1007/BF01542219

Simpson, J. A., Gangestad, S. W., & Biek, M. (1993). Personality and nonverbal social behavior: An ethological perspective of relationship initiation. *Journal of Experimental Social Psychology, 29*, 434–461. doi:10.1006/jesp.1993.1020

Simpson, J. A., & Harris, B. A. (1994). Interpersonal attraction. In A. L. Weber & J. H. Harvey (Eds.), *Perspectives on close relationships* (pp. 45–66). Boston, MA: Allyn & Bacon.

Sinclair, H. C., Denson, J. K., Felmlee, D., & Sprecher, S. (2011, January). *Searching for the Romeo and Juliet effect: The role of source, trust, and disapproval type.* Paper presented at the annual meeting for the Society for Personality and Social Psychology, San Antonio, TX.

Snow, D. A., Robinson, C., & McCall, P. L. (1991). "Cooling out" men in singles bars and nightclubs: Observations on the interpersonal survival strategies of women in public places. *Journal of Contemporary Ethnography, 19*, 423–449. doi:10.1177/089124191019004003

Spitzberg, B. H., & Cupach, W. R. (2007). The state of the art of stalking: Taking stock of the emerging literature. *Aggression and Violent Behavior, 12*, 64–86. doi:10.1016/j.avb.2006.05.001

Spitzberg, B. H., & Cupach, W. R. (2011). Interpersonal skills. In M. L. Knapp & J. Daly (Eds.), *The Sage handbook of interpersonal communication* (4th ed., pp. 481–524). Newbury Park, CA: Sage.

Spitzberg, B. H., Cupach, W. R., & Ciceraro, L. D. L. (2010). Sex differences in stalking and obsessive relational intrusion: Two meta-analyses. *Partner Abuse, 1*, 259–285. doi:10.1891/1946-6560.1.3.259

Sprecher, S. (2009). Relationship initiation and formation on the Internet. *Marriage and Family Review, 45*, 761–782. doi:10.1080/01494920903224350

Sprecher, S. (2011). Internet matching services: The good, the bad, and the ugly (disguised as attractive). In W. R. Cupach & B. H. Spitzberg (Eds.), *The dark side of close relationships II* (pp. 119–143). New York, NY: Routledge.

Sprecher, S., Aron, A., Hatfield, E., Cortese, A., Potapova, E., & Levitskaya, A. (1994). Love: American style, Russian style, and Japanese style. *Personal Relationships, 1*, 349–369. doi:10.1111/j.1475-6811.1994.tb00070.x

Sprecher, S., & Felmlee, D. (1992). The influence of parents and friends on the quality and stability of romantic relationships: A three-wave longitudinal investigation. *Journal of Marriage and the Family, 54*, 888–900. doi:10.2307/353170

Sprecher, S., & Felmlee, D. (2008). Insider perspectives on attraction. In S. Sprecher, A. Wenzel, & J. Harvey (Eds.), *Handbook of relationship initiation* (pp. 297–313). New York, NY: Psychology Press.

Sprecher, S., Felmlee, D., Metts, S., Fehr, B., & Vanni, D. (1998). Factors associated with distress following the breakup of a close relationship. *Journal of Social and Personal Relationships, 15,* 791–809. doi:10.1177/0265407598156005

Sprecher, S., Felmlee, D., Orbuch, T. L., & Willetts, M. C. (2002). Social networks and change in personal relationships. In A. L. Vangelisti, H. T. Reis, & M. A. Fitzpatrick (Eds.), *Stability and change in relationships* (pp. 257–284). Cambridge, England: Cambridge University Press. doi:10.1017/CBO9780511499876.015

Sprecher, S., & McKinney, K. (1987). Overcoming barriers in the initiation of intimate relationships. In H. Gochros & W. Ricketts (Eds.), *Social work and love* (pp. 77–110). New York, NY: Hayworth Press.

Sprecher, S., Schwartz, P., Harvey, J., & Hatfield, E. (2008). The businessoflove.com: Relationship initiation at Internet matching services. In S. Sprecher, A. Wenzel, & J. Harvey (Eds.), *Handbook of relationship initiation* (pp. 249–265). New York, NY: Psychology Press.

Sunnafrank, M. (1986). Predicted outcome value during initial interactions: A reformulation of uncertainty reduction theory. *Human Communication Research, 13,* 3–33. doi:10.1111/j.1468-2958.1986.tb00092.x

Sunnafrank, M. (1990). Predicted outcome value and uncertainty reduction theories: A test of competing perspectives. *Human Communication Research, 17,* 76–103. doi:10.1111/j.1468-2958.1990.tb00227.x

Taylor, D. A., & Altman, I. (1987). Communication in interpersonal relationships: Social penetration processes. In M. E. Roloff & G. R. Miller (Eds.), *Interpersonal processes: New directions in communication research* (pp. 257–277). Newbury Park, CA: Sage.

Theiss, J. A., & Solomon, D. H. (2007). Communication and the emotional, cognitive, and relational consequences of first sexual encounters between partners. *Communication Quarterly, 55,* 179–206. doi:10.1080/01463370601036663

Thibaut, J., & Kelley, H. (1959). *The social psychology of groups.* New York, NY: Wiley.

Tjaden, P., & Thoennes, N. (1998). *Stalking in America: Findings from the National Violence Against Women Survey* (NCJ 169592). Washington, DC: National Institute of Justice and Centers for Disease Control and Prevention.

Tolhuizen, J. H. (1989). Communication strategies for intensifying dating relationships: Identification, use and structure. *Journal of Social and Personal Relationships, 6,* 413–434. doi:10.1177/0265407589064002

Toma, C. L., Hancock, J. T., & Ellison, N. B. (2008). Separating fact from fiction: An examination of deceptive self-presentation on online dating profiles. *Personality and Social Psychology Bulletin, 34,* 1023–1036. doi:10.1177/0146167208318067

Tooke, W., & Camire, L. (1991). Patterns of deception in intersexual and intrasexual mating strategies. *Ethology and Sociobiology, 12,* 345–364. doi:10.1016/0162-3095(91)90030-T

Vanlear, C. A., Jr. (1987). The formation of social relationships: A longitudinal study of social penetration. *Human Communication Research, 13,* 299–322. doi:10.1111/j.1468-2958.1987.tb00107.x

Vorauer, J. D., Cameron, J. J., Holmes, J. G., & Pearce, D. G. (2003). Invisible overtures: Fears of rejection and the signal amplification bias. *Journal of Personality and Social Psychology, 84,* 793–812. doi:10.1037/0022-3514.84.4.793

Walster, E., Aronson, V., Abrahams, D., & Rottman, L. (1966). The importance of physical attractiveness in dating behavior. *Journal of Personality and Social Psychology, 4,* 508–516. doi:10.1037/h0021188

Walther, J. B. (1996). Computer-mediated communication: Impersonal, interpersonal and hyperpersonal interaction. *Communication Research, 23,* 3–43. doi:10.1177/009365096023001001

Weber, K., Goodboy, A., & Cayanus, J. (2010). Flirting competence: An experimental study on appropriate and effective opening lines. *Communication Research Reports, 27,* 184–191. doi:10.1080/08824091003738149

Whitty, M. T. (2004). Cyber-flirting: An examination of men's and women's flirting behaviour both offline and on the Internet. *Behaviour Change, 21,* 115–126. doi:10.1375/bech.21.2.115.55423

Zajonc, R. B. (1968). Attitudinal effects of mere exposure. *Journal of Personality and Social Psychology, 9,* 1–27. doi:10.1037/h0025848

Zanna, M. P., & Pack, S. J. (1975). On the self-fulfilling nature of apparent sex-differences in behavior. *Journal of Experimental Social Psychology, 11,* 583–591. doi:10.1016/0022-1031(75)90009-8

IDEAL MATE STANDARDS AND ROMANTIC RELATIONSHIPS

Lorne Campbell, Jennifer C. Pink, and Sarah C. E. Stanton

Isabel Burton (née Arundell) was born into an affluent and respected family in London, England, in 1831. She was afforded many luxuries during her upbringing as she grew into a physically attractive and intelligent young woman. As part of the bustling and elite society of London during the Victorian period, she had a bevy of willing suitors. Isabel, however, was not very impressed with the available men of London and was considered foolish by many for not marrying what seemed to be excellent candidates. According to Isabel, however, "The young men of the day passed before me without making the slightest impression. My ideal was not among them" (as cited in Rice, 1999, p. 174). What qualities, then, defined Isabel's ideal partner?

Fortunately, it is possible to answer this question because Isabel kept a very detailed diary. Apparently written before she met her future husband, her ideal partner was

> about six feet in height; he has not an ounce of fat on him; he has broad and muscular shoulders, a powerful deep chest. . . . He has black hair, a brown complexion, a clever forehead, sagacious eyebrows, large black wondrous eyes— those strange eyes you dare not take yours off from them—with long lashes. He is a soldier and a *man*. . . . His religion is like my own, free, liberal, and generous minded. . . . He is a man who owns something more than a body: he has a head and heart, a mind and soul. (as cited in Rice, 1999, pp. 174–175)

In a few short sentences, Isabel provides stunning detail of her ideal partner, covering physical, interpersonal, and spiritual domains. She finally met her ideal partner, Richard Burton, while walking in the streets of Boulogne, France. Burton was an officer in the military, possessed the physical qualities she was looking for, and was a daring and adventurous man. For example, in his lifetime he traveled to Mecca disguised as a Moslem traveler (he spoke the language perfectly, converted to Islam, and knew all the customs), helped find the source of the Nile River (along with John Speke), translated the *Arabian Nights* (10 volumes) as well as the *Kama Sutra* into English, and was awarded a knighthood, among other things (Rice, 1999). Pictures of Burton in his prime also strongly suggest he possessed sagacious eyebrows. Ten years after Isabel first met Burton, a mirror image of her ideal partner, they married and enjoyed a long and adventurous life together.

This fascinating story highlights important features of interpersonal attraction, relationship formation, and relationship maintenance. First, it suggests that individuals possess a mental image of the type of person they would like to meet and form a relationship with (i.e., an image of their ideal partner). Indeed, the content of individuals' ideal standards, or mate preferences, has been the target of a great deal of research. Second, it suggests that ideal standards play an important role in interpersonal attraction and mate selection processes. That is, individuals should be attracted to and enter relationships with others who more closely approximate their ideal standards. Some research has supported

http://dx.doi.org/10.1037/14344-009
APA Handbook of Personality and Social Psychology: Vol. 3. Interpersonal Relations, M. Mikulincer and P. R. Shaver (Editors-in-Chief)

the link between ideal standards and relationship initiation, but recent research has been less conclusive and somewhat controversial. Third, it implies that a close fit between an individual's ideal standards and the qualities of that individual's actual partner predict more positive relationship quality and greater relationship stability, whereas a relatively large discrepancy between ideal standards and partner perceptions should predict lower relationship quality and behaviors targeted to improve, or end, the relationship.

In this chapter, we focus on the role of ideal mate preferences within each of these three broad domains. We feel that a more holistic understanding of ideal standards in a romantic relationship context is best achieved by recognizing what qualities individuals desire in potential mates and why, how these ideal standards are implicated in relationship initiation, and how they shape relationship processes over time. We begin by discussing the diverse literature on interpersonal attraction and ideal partner preferences: How are ideal partner preferences calibrated? Next, we move to a discussion of research assessing links between how closely individuals perceive their partners to match their ideal standards and relationship processes. We do so because ideal standards have been the focus of much research in the fields of interpersonal attraction and relationship processes, whereas less research has focused squarely on relationship initiation. We then discuss the apparent conflicting research testing the role of ideal partner preferences during actual relationship initiation. Finally, we make suggestions for future research.

INTERPERSONAL ATTRACTION AND IDEAL PARTNER PREFERENCES

How do unattached individuals navigate the sea of available, potential romantic partners to eventually select a mate? How do people decide which interested parties they will consider and which ones they will avoid? What do they look for in a prospective mate and why? The amount of research devoted to answering these questions is too voluminous to adequately review here (see also Chapters 7 and 8, this volume), but we want to highlight some important

themes that have emerged from this corpus of research, especially as they relate to the calibration of ideal partner standards and preferences.

Mate preferences have arguably been studied in the greatest detail from the perspective of evolutionary theory. Evolutionary models of mate attraction focus on why certain traits should have been more appealing to men and women during humans' evolutionary history (i.e., questions of ultimate causation), from which hypotheses regarding the similarities and differences between men's and women's current mate preferences are derived (Buss, 1995). The basis of modern evolutionary models of mate attraction is Trivers's (1972) parental investment and sexual selection theory. According to Trivers, differences in minimal parental investment between the sexes of all sexually reproducing species have had a profound influence on mating preferences during evolutionary history (Trivers, 1972; see also Buss & Schmitt, 1993). In the case of humans, the minimal parental investment that a woman must expend on a child involves 9 months of gestation, parturition, and lactation, which can last from several months to a few years. Women are also born with a limited number of ova (eggs), which can be fertilized only during a circumscribed period of time, with fertility peaking in the mid-20s and decreasing significantly to essentially zero in the later 40s. For men, the minimal parental investment can conceivably involve a single sexual encounter, and men are capable of producing sperm from puberty well into old age. Throughout evolutionary history, this disparity in minimal investment should result, on average, in the more investing sex (women) being more selective and discriminating than the less investing sex (men) when deciding with whom to mate.

These dissimilarities in minimal parental investment indicate that men and women have faced somewhat different reproductive problems over evolutionary time, resulting in predictable differences in the contents of their ideal standards to help them solve these problems (Buss, 1995; Kenrick & Trost, 1997; Symons, 1979). One reproductive problem faced by men has been gaining sexual access to healthy and fertile women; therefore, men should evaluate potential mates more closely on physical features that covary with youth and fertility. Indeed, a great deal of research has demonstrated that men focus more attention on physical appeal relative to other cues when assessing the suitability of potential mates (e.g., Buss, 1989; Feingold, 1992; Singh, 1993; Sprecher, Sullivan, & Hatfield, 1994; Symons, 1979; Townsend & Levy, 1990). In addition, men are generally attracted to women younger than themselves, particularly as they grow older (Kenrick & Keefe, 1992). Furthermore, experimental paradigms that force people to make trade-offs in the traits they desire in potential mates have shown that men are particularly likely to trade off status and resources for physical appeal when choosing mates (Fletcher, Tither, O'Loughlin, Friesen, & Overall, 2004; Li, Bailey, Kenrick, & Linsenmeier, 2002).

A reproductive problem faced by women, though, has been securing resources to assist in raising offspring. Women, therefore, should be attracted to men who possess qualities suggesting that they have the ability and willingness to provide resources to their partner and relationship over time (Buss, 1989). Consistent with this theorizing, men who have many resources or the ability to acquire them (e.g., men who are highly ambitious) and are willing to share these resources are more appealing to most women (e.g., Buss, 1989; Ellis, 1992; Graziano, Jensen-Campbell, Todd, & Finch, 1997; Pérusse, 1993; Sadalla, Kenrick, & Vershure, 1987; Sprecher et al., 1994; Symons, 1979). Furthermore, when women are forced to make trade-offs in the traits they desire in potential mates, they are particularly likely to trade off physical appeal for status and resources (Fletcher et al., 2004; Li et al., 2002).

Most evolutionary models of mate preferences have focused more on differences between men and women, but both sexes have also faced the same adaptive challenge of successfully rearing offspring (Geary, 2000; Kenrick & Trost, 1997). Human children require many years of constant care, supervision, and socializing to survive childhood and grow to reproductive age, and children born and raised by pair-bonded parents are more likely to survive to reproductive age and be more socially competitive later in life when they attempt to attract mates (Geary, 2000). Both men and women should thus be attentive to a potential long-term partner's capacity for intimacy and commitment, because this would

increase their chances of finding a cooperative, committed partner who is likely to be a devoted parent (see Gangestad & Simpson, 2000). Consistent with this reasoning, research has indicated that both men and women place high value on warmth, kindness, and a sense of humor in potential mates (Botwin, Buss, & Shackelford, 1997; Buss, 1989, 1994; Buss & Barnes, 1986; Campbell & Wilbur, 2009; Li et al., 2002).

Ideal Preferences for Different Types of Relationships

When individuals are asked to indicate their ideal mate preferences, their responses are sensitive to the type of relationship under consideration. Mate selection criteria differ in short-term versus long-term mating contexts, suggesting that people's preferences and minimum standards differ when choosing a serious relationship partner compared with a mate for a brief sexual encounter (e.g., Buss & Schmitt, 1993; Regan, 1998). Both men and women emphasize cues of sexual appeal (e.g., physical attractiveness, fitness) when choosing a mate for a short-term sexual relationship, but they consider interpersonal qualities (e.g., kindness, trustworthiness) to be more important when selecting long-term partners (Regan, Levin, Sprecher, Christopher, & Cate, 2000; Li & Kenrick, 2006). Interpersonal qualities such as a mate's intelligence and personality may take a back seat to physical characteristics when individuals consider short-term sexual partners because the latter are more relevant to a brief sexual liaison. That is to say, people considering a potential mate for a short-term relationship may be more willing to compromise on traits they consider crucial in a long-term mate (e.g., a sense of humor) because they do not intend for the relationship to progress beyond a sexual relationship. Interpersonal qualities are not completely disregarded, however, because both men and women prefer well-rounded short-term (as well as long-term) mates if given the choice (Li & Kenrick, 2006; Wilbur & Campbell, 2010). Overall, both men and women generally relax their standards (except with respect to physical appearance) when considering someone for a short-term rather than a long-term relationship, although men's ideal standards for a casual sex partner (e.g., a one-night stand) tend to be consistently lower than women's (Kenrick, Groth, Trost, & Sadalla, 1993).

Women's Ideal Partner Preferences Across the Menstrual Cycle

Some of the most interesting and compelling research on mate preferences from an evolutionary perspective has focused on shifts in women's ideal mate preferences across the menstrual cycle. Human females are capable of conceiving a child during only a brief time each month, ranging from several days before the day of ovulation up until the day of ovulation itself (Wilcox, Weinberg, & Baird, 1995). A large body of research has shown that women's mate preferences, particularly for short-term sexual liaisons, differ in important and predictable ways when they are (vs. are not) ovulating, but only in women who are not taking any form of hormonal birth control (Alvergne & Lummaa, 2009; Gangestad & Thornhill, 2008). Hormonal birth control regulates the flow of androgens, including testosterone, and it is believed to even out women's sex drive across the reproductive cycle.

One of the first studies assessing changes in women's mate preferences across the menstrual cycle was conducted by Gangestad and Thornhill (1998). In this research, men who were told to not use any deodorant or cologne wore a new T-shirt for 2 nights while sleeping and then gave it in a sealed bag to the researchers. A physical marker of "good genes" (e.g., body symmetry) was then measured across 10 different body parts (e.g., foot width, finger length) using special calipers for each man.[1] A large group of women were asked to smell each T-shirt and rate the degree to which each shirt had a pleasant and sexy scent. The ratings of women who were not currently ovulating did not correlate with the body symmetry of the men. In contrast, women who were currently ovulating rated the scent of symmetrical men's T-shirts more favorably than the

scent of asymmetrical men's shirts (Gangestad & Thornhill, 1998). They also rated the T-shirts worn by the symmetrical men as smelling more pleasant than fresh, unworn T-shirts. The ratings of women who were taking hormonal birth control, however, did not correlate with the symmetry of the men, regardless of their menstrual phase, which suggests that normal hormonal fluctuations (which are suppressed by the pill) are causing this phenomenon. An identical pattern of results emerged in three other studies (Rikowski & Grammer, 1999; Thornhill & Gangestad, 1999; Thornhill et al., 2003). Thus, women are more attracted to more symmetrical men, but only when they are fertile and potentially able to conceive a child.

Research has also documented that when women are ovulating, compared with when they are not ovulating, they are also more attracted to other traits associated with good genes such as masculine facial features (Penton-Voak & Perrett, 2000; Penton-Voak et al., 1999; Scarbrough & Johnston, 2005); more masculine, lower pitched voices (Feinberg et al., 2006; Puts, 2005); masculine body odor (Grammer, 1993); the scent of men who are socially dominant (Havlicek, Roberts, & Flegr, 2005); socially dominant interpersonal behaviors (Gangestad, Garver-Apgar, Simpson, & Cousins, 2007; Gangestad, Simpson, Cousins, Garver-Apgar, & Christensen, 2004); and more muscular bodies (Gangestad et al., 2007). Again, these effects do not emerge when women are on hormonal birth control.

In sum, only women's preferences for men as short-term sexual partners—not long-term partners—shift across the menstrual cycle (e.g., Gangestad et al., 2004, 2007; Penton-Voak et al., 1999). Because a man's good genes are the sole certain benefits that can result from short-term sexual relationships for women, it is not surprising that women are more attracted to men who display such cues to good genes (e.g., symmetry, testosterone, social

---

[1]"Good genes" models of sexual selection (see Gangestad & Thornhill, 1997) suggest that an individual's degree of genetic fitness might be inferred from specific phenotypic markers. Individuals who have these markers should, on average, be more successful in intrasexual competitions because the traits they possess are valued by opposite-sex individuals (Zahavi, 1975). To be evolutionarily stable, however, these traits must be honest or difficult-to-feign indicators of an individual's true viability. One widely studied indicator is fluctuating asymmetry (i.e., the degree to which individuals deviate from perfect bilateral symmetry). Fluctuating asymmetry should be a good marker of genetic viability for three reasons. First, greater asymmetry is associated with lower survival rates, slower growth rates, and lower rates of reproduction in many different species (Møller & Thornhill, 1998). Second, it is partly heritable. Thus, some of its variance is due to genetic variability, which is likely to be associated with greater fitness and genetic viability (Møller & Thornhill, 1997). Third, the development of symmetry cannot occur unless individuals have efficient immune systems capable of warding off pathogens, which can cause asymmetry (Møller & Swaddle, 1997).

dominance), but only when they are ovulating. Women's ideal standards, therefore, are not static.

The Ideal Standards Questionnaire

Much of the research on mate preferences discussed to this point has shared a similar feature: The traits presented to participants were derived on the basis of theories of what men and women should look for in potential mates. Fletcher, Simpson, Thomas, and Giles (1999) took a different approach—they asked individuals what qualities they were attracted to in potential mates. Specifically, Fletcher et al. asked large groups of women and men to write down items that described their own ideal mates for long-term relationships (i.e., what qualities were important to them in a romantic partner). The hundreds of items that were generated were placed into categories and infrequently mentioned items were removed, leaving 49 items. A new sample of students then rated how much importance they placed on each trait in describing their ideal partner in the context of sexual or romantic relationships. These ratings were factor analyzed, resulting in a tripartite mate preference structure consistent with Fletcher et al.'s speculations and reflecting the types of traits assessed in the research already discussed: warmth–trustworthiness (e.g., understanding, supportive, considerate, kind, a good listener, sensitive), vitality–attractiveness (e.g., adventurous, nice body, outgoing, sexy, attractive, good lover), and status–resources (e.g., good job, financially secure, nice house or apartment, successful, dresses well). These results were the same regardless of whether the samples consisted of men or women and whether or not individuals were currently involved in relationships.

According to Fletcher et al. (1999; see also Simpson, Fletcher, & Campbell, 2001), these three categories of ideal partner preferences make sense when considered from an evolutionary perspective. By being attentive to a partner's capacity for intimacy and commitment, an individual should increase his or her chances of finding a cooperative, committed partner who would be a devoted mate and parent (i.e., someone who is likely to invest in the relationship). By focusing on attractiveness and health, an individual should be more likely to acquire a mate who is younger, healthier, and more fertile. Last, by considering a partner's resources and status, an individual should be more likely to obtain a mate who can ascend social hierarchies and form coalitions with other people who have, or can acquire, valued social status or resources.

Self-Evaluations and Ideal Partner Preferences

Although much research has investigated ideal partner preferences or traits that individuals might use to describe their ideal mate, many people may not be able to secure an ideal mate. Success in the mating market rests not only on finding people who match one's own criteria but also on being a desirable mate (i.e., someone who satisfies the criteria of others). According to Baldwin (1992) and Bowlby (1982), models of the self and models of others are intricately related. Thus, if people have positive self-views, they may be more likely to have positive views of others. Extending this link, past research has shown that individuals' self-perceptions are also tied to images of their ideal partner (Hester, 1996; Murray, Holmes, & Griffin, 1996). Likewise, individuals who view themselves as especially warm attach more importance to warmth–trustworthiness in an ideal partner, those who perceive themselves as more attractive place more weight on the vitality–attractiveness component, and those who believe they have more status and resources rate this corresponding ideal category as more important (Campbell, Simpson, Kashy, & Fletcher, 2001).

Additionally, social exchange perspectives (e.g., Thibaut & Kelley, 1959) suggest that individuals seek the "best" mate they can attain on the basis of the limits imposed by their own mate value, which leads partners who have similar "market value" to pair up. A person's mate value depends on the degree to which he or she possesses culturally valued traits such as beauty, warmth, and status (Kenrick et al., 1993). Realistically, then, individuals can use their list of ideal partner traits as a general guide (vs. a stringent, inflexible checklist) when considering possible partners, and they can seek out individuals who fall above specific minimum values on preferred traits (Regan, 1998). For example, an individual does not have to be strikingly gorgeous or gifted to be considered a desirable mate; he or she simply needs to be deemed attractive or smart enough.

Accurately assessing one's own mate value, and being able to assess the self relative to the standards of potential mates, allows people to accomplish two important aims. First, it avoids wasting time and energy along with the pain and humiliation associated with being rejected by people of higher mate value. Second, it prevents a second kind of mistake by avoiding the formation of relationships with people of much lower mate value, who may constrain their reproductive success (cf. Regan, 1998). In short, people are relatively realistic when choosing mates in terms of the quality of mate they can attract.

Summary

Much of the research on interpersonal attraction focuses on ideal mate preferences or standards: What are people looking for in a mate? Research guided by evolutionary models of mate attraction typically highlight differences between the qualities preferred by men and women by referencing the unique pressures that men and women faced in evolutionary history. Men tend to put a premium on youth and beauty, whereas women tend to evaluate a potential mate's status and resource-accruing potential. Research by Fletcher et al. (1999) asked individuals what they looked for in potential mates and found three broad categories of traits: warmth–trustworthiness, vitality–attractiveness, and status–resources. Ideal standards are associated with self-perceptions of an individual's own mate value and how appealing they are likely to be to potential mates, but ideal standards are relaxed somewhat when individuals consider potential mates for short-term compared with long-term relationships. Presumably, ideal mate preferences play an important role in relationship initiation, a topic we turn our attention to later.

IDEAL STANDARDS AND RELATIONSHIP PROCESSES

In addition to developing scales to assess individual differences in ideal mate standards, Fletcher et al. (1999) and Simpson et al. (2001) introduced the ideal standards model (ISM) to better understand how individuals form and maintain close relationships over time. The development of this model was influenced by interdependence theory (Thibaut & Kelley, 1959), the first major theory to suggest that individuals evaluate the quality of their relationships by assessing the consistency between what they feel they deserve from their relationship and what they are actually getting (called the *comparison level*), as well as between what they feel they could obtain in an alternative relationship and what they are getting from their current relationship (called the *comparison level for alternatives*). Large perceived discrepancies involving the comparison level results in less satisfaction with the partner and relationship, whereas large perceived discrepancies involving the comparison level for alternatives results in less commitment to the relationship (Rusbult, Arriaga, & Agnew, 2001). The ISM was also influenced by Higgins's (1987, 1989) self-discrepancy theory, which suggests that perceived discrepancies between one's actual, ideal, and ought selves should produce unique emotional reactions. According to Higgins, monitoring the size of these self-discrepancies should allow people to (a) regulate their behavior to maintain or reduce discrepancies between actual–ideal and actual–ought selves and (b) evaluate how well they are maintaining or reducing these discrepancies. Unique features of the ISM are that it specifies the content of ideal mate standards and it adopts a dyadic perspective to understanding how perceived discrepancies should influence thoughts, feelings, and behaviors in relationships over time (for a more thorough discussion of the ISM, see Simpson et al., 2001).

The ISM (Fletcher et al., 1999; Simpson et al., 2001) proposes that people possess images of their ideal partner, or an abstract concept of the qualities they would like their potential or current romantic partner to have, which is consistent with the literature reviewed earlier. Ideals consist of three interlocking components: perceptions of the self, partners, and relationships (Baldwin, 1992). That is, individuals' images of their ideal partners reflect their self-perceptions, the qualities they would like their partner to possess, and the type of relationship they would like to have.

According to the model, comparisons between these ideal standards and perceptions of one's current partner or relationship serve three basic functions. The magnitude of the discrepancies between ideal standards and perceptions of the current partner and relationship (hereinafter referred to as *partner discrepancies*) allows individuals to (a) estimate and evaluate the quality of their partners and relationships (e.g., assess the appropriateness of potential or current partners or relationships), (b) explain what happens in relationships (e.g., give causal accounts explaining relationship satisfaction, problems, or conflicts), and (c) regulate and make adjustments in relationships (e.g., to predict and possibly control current partners and relationships). Larger partner discrepancies should indicate to people that they are in a less satisfactory relationship, which may motivate them to make adjustments to it (e.g., either lower their ideals or enhance their view of their partners) or to end the relationship. When people fall short of their partner's ideals, they are in a qualitatively different situation. Such people may have to enact regulatory behaviors to reduce the size of their partner's discrepancy. For instance, an individual may have to avoid conflict and showcase his or her best qualities in an effort to more closely meet his or her partner's elevated standards. To date, the majority of research guided by the ISM has tested the evaluation and regulation functions of partner discrepancies within ongoing relationships.

Partner Discrepancies and Evaluation

To test whether smaller partner discrepancies are associated with more positive relationship evaluations, Fletcher et al. (1999) had people rank the importance of various ideal attributes along with their perceptions of their current partner and relationship on the ideal partner scales. Consistent with ISM, individuals who reported smaller partner discrepancies rated their relationships more favorably. To test and make inferences about possible causal relations, Fletcher, Simpson, and Thomas (2000) then tracked a large sample of individuals in newly formed dating relationships over time and found that comparisons between ideals and perceptions of the current partner had a causal impact on later relationship evaluations. These results suggest that

cognitive comparisons between ideal standards and perceptions of the current partner and relationship influence the way in which partners and relationships are evaluated over time, at least during the early stages of relationship development.

The magnitude of partner discrepancies should affect not only how individuals evaluate their relationships but also how their partners feel about the relationship (Sternberg & Barnes, 1985). Campbell et al. (2001) tested this hypothesis by asking both members of a large sample of dating couples to report their ideal standards, including how closely their partners matched their ideals. Consistent with Fletcher et al. (1999), individuals who reported smaller perceived discrepancies between their partner perceptions and ideal mate standards also reported higher levels of relationship quality than those who reported larger discrepancies. Interestingly, individuals also reported higher levels of relationship quality when they more closely matched their partner's ideal standards (as rated by their partners; see also Overall, Fletcher, & Simpson, 2006).

This partner effect implies that individuals' satisfaction with their relationships may, at least to some degree, be associated with an accurate assessment of how closely they compare with their partner's ideals. Indeed, according to the ISM, one of the main functions of ideal standards is to help individuals evaluate the health of their romantic relationships by identifying areas of strength and weakness in both themselves and their romantic partners (Simpson et al., 2001). Recent research using two large samples of heterosexual dating and married partners found that individuals accurately gauged the extent to which they met their partners' ideal mate standards, and this accuracy mediated the link between how their partners evaluated them and their own relationship satisfaction (Campbell, Overall, Rubin, & Lackenbauer, 2013).

Partner Discrepancies and Regulation

According to the ISM, larger partner discrepancies should motivate individuals to align ideal mate standards and partner perceptions. Specifically, if a gaping discrepancy exists between one's current and one's ideal partner, an individual should try to regulate the partner or the relationship (Fletcher et al.,

2000). For example, a person can attempt to change his or her partner or relationship over time so that the partner more closely matches his or her ideals. Alternatively, an individual can decide that the current situation is unsatisfactory and simply terminate the relationship. In contrast, romantic partners may alter their ideals to more closely match their current relationship situation. A study of newly formed dating relationships indeed found that individuals subtly changed their ideals over time to be more consistent with their perceptions of current partners and relationships, but not vice versa (Fletcher et al., 2000).

Individuals can certainly alter their ideal mate standards to be more in line with their partner perceptions, but recent research by Nickola Overall and colleagues has found that individuals also attempt to motivate their partners to change in a manner that is more consistent with their own ideal mate standards. For example, Overall, Fletcher, Simpson, and Sibley (2009) focused on situations in which individuals seek to improve their relationships by trying to change something they do not like about their partners. These conversations are not always pleasant given that asking a partner to change something about himself or herself implies being dissatisfied with them. Indeed, Overall et al. (2006) found that relationship satisfaction suffered in the short term when partners reported making more strenuous efforts to change things about each other that they did not like.

Nevertheless, an open discussion of what partners like and do not like about each other can have positive long-term effects as partners become aware of each others' needs, wants, and desires. Testing this possibility, Overall et al. (2009) had couples discuss aspects of each other that they wanted to see changed while they were being videotaped. The use of exit, voice, loyalty, and neglect behavioral strategies enacted by each partner was coded by independent raters, and relationship perceptions were obtained from each partner at 3-month intervals for 1 year. Consistent with past research (e.g., Overall et al., 2006), the enactment of more active strategies during the discussion (both positive and negative) was viewed by both partners as less successful in promoting the desired change. Instead, the use of

more positive passive strategies during the discussion (e.g., loyalty) was perceived as more successful at producing change. Remarkably, the results completely reversed when examining reports obtained over the course of the year. Across time, the use of direct strategies (e.g., voice) produced greater change in the targeted features as reported by both partners. Indirect strategies such as loyalty, in contrast, resulted in absolutely no change over time (see also Overall, Sibley, & Travaglia, 2010). It seems, then, that when individuals explicitly express dissatisfaction with their relationship, or ask their partners to change, this may create friction or negative feelings between partners in the short term; however, if the problem is eventually worked through, often via additional voice strategies, the couple may end up being better off and more satisfied over time.

When considering regulation in relationships, it is valuable to distinguish the discrepancy between one's current and one's ideal partner from the discrepancy between oneself and the partner's ideal partner because it matters whether it is an individual or his or her partner who does not measure up to standards. As suggested by Campbell et al. (2001), feeling that a partner falls short of one's ideals may indicate a failure to reach an important relationship goal, whereas falling short of a partner's ideals may indicate that one could face rejection for being a less-than-perfect partner. As a result, the perceived options available to partners when confronted with each type of discrepancy should diverge in important and predictable ways.

Lackenbauer and Campbell (2012) tested the potentially unique outcomes associated with each type of ideal discrepancy. Across a series of five studies, participants who perceived their partners as discrepant from their ideal standards experienced more dejection-related emotions (e.g., dissatisfaction, upset) and a more promotion-focused regulatory style (i.e., focusing on behaviors to enact to achieve a relationship goal), suggesting that such partner discrepancies activate nurturance-related concerns. Consistent with regulatory focus theory (Higgins, 1997), a promotion focus in this instance should generate promotion behaviors intended to reduce the discrepancy to achieve the desired relationship outcomes. These findings are also consistent with those of Overall et al. (2006), who showed that people try to regulate or change their partners to be more in line with their own ideal standards by enacting behaviors aimed at reducing the partner discrepancy to achieve relationship-relevant goals.

Perceiving that one is discrepant from one's partner's ideal standards, however, was associated with agitation-related emotions (e.g., guilt, anxiety) and a prevention focus (i.e., focusing on behaviors to avoid to achieve a relationship goal). This supports the notion that this form of discrepancy leads to concerns about negative outcomes that could occur and, thus, activates security-related concerns (Lackenbauer & Campbell, 2012). This type of discrepancy and resulting regulatory focus may also lead to behavior aimed at preventing feared negative outcomes. For instance, Campbell et al. (2001) suggested that an individual may have to focus on avoiding conflict and emphasizing his or her best qualities to more closely meet his or her partner's standards. Especially for people involved in generally satisfying and committed relationships, this prevention strategy could reduce the partner discrepancy and maintain relationship satisfaction. Alternatively, Murray, Holmes, and Collins (2006) suggested that this form of discrepancy may lead to avoidance behaviors aimed at reducing one's dependency on the partner and relationship to protect against the pain of possible rejection. Campbell et al. and Murray et al. both suggested similar root causes for the adoption of a prevention focus in romantic relationship contexts (i.e., perceived rejection by one's partner), but they differ in terms of the outcomes desired when people adopt a prevention focus. Future research should examine the possible outcomes sought by people when they adopt a prevention focus in this context.

Accuracy and Enhancement Motives

When people enter romantic relationships, they take a leap of faith. Unfortunately, most individuals do not have partners who match their ideals perfectly. This reality can undermine relationship satisfaction and stability as individuals begin to recognize that their partners have faults as well as virtues. Among others, Murray (2001) has suggested that people reduce relationship uncertainties and maintain a sense of conviction by perceiving their partners in an overly positive light. Such positive illusions presumably assuage doubts and fears associated with committing to less-than-perfect partners, and they maintain consistency between ideal standards and partner perceptions. For example, individuals commonly reconstrue their partners' faults as redeeming virtues (Murray & Holmes, 1993). During conflicts, people frequently encode relationship events in a relationship-enhancing manner (McGregor & Holmes, 1999). The ability to construct positive relationship narratives given negative information ought to defuse negative outcomes and sustain confidence about partners and relationships.

Although positive illusions may help to sustain satisfying relationships, relationship well-being should also depend on making accurate appraisals of a partner's virtues and faults at critical junctures. Vorauer and Ross (1996), for example, identified several circumstances in which individuals should seek accurate information about their partners during relationship development. Moreover, when marital partners address potentially threatening relationship problems, they are less likely to enhance their relationships or view themselves as better off than other couples (Frye & Karney, 2002). Even in Murray et al.'s (1996) research, people not only developed idealistic perceptions of their partners, they also perceived their partners in ways that were consistent with their partners' own self-perceptions.

Simpson et al. (2001) proposed that two motives guide how people evaluate, explain, and regulate their relationships: (a) partner–relationship enhancement (idealization) motives and (b) partner–relationship accuracy motives. According to this model (the ISM), idealization goals may occasionally conflict with accuracy goals. Although harboring positive illusions has clear benefits, there should also be situations in which accurately understanding a partner's qualities and motives is more adaptive. Accuracy motives, for instance, should be beneficial when people must make decisions that are likely to affect levels of commitment and interdependence in a relationship, such as when deciding whether to date someone, get married, or have a child. In these situations, a more accurate assessment of how closely a partner matches one's ideals should result in better decision making about the future. Enhancement motives, however, should be more important when partners are maintaining their relationship or when no major relationship-relevant decisions are on the horizon.

Overlapping nicely with this model is research showing that making decisions involves predecisional and postdecisional phases (Gollwitzer & Bayer, 1999). During the predecisional phase, individuals are open to new information as they decide between competing alternatives; during the postdecisional phase, they focus on implementing a choice that has already been made. These phases are associated with different modes of information processing. In the predecisional phase, people in deliberative mindsets often consider all available information relevant to possible response options (Gollwitzer, Heckhausen, & Steller, 1990). They evenhandedly contemplate the positive and the negative aspects of competing goals or decisions (S. E. Taylor & Gollwitzer, 1995), and they remain realistic about the likelihood of achieving each goal or decision. On entering the postdecisional phase, however, people switch to an implemental mindset whereby information is processed in a biased (overly positive) manner, which justifies their choice as they execute a chosen goal or decision (Gollwitzer et al., 1990).

Borrowing ideas from research on decision making, Gagné and Lydon (2001) surmised that individuals in romantic relationships should adopt an accuracy motivation when in a deliberative mindset, whereas they should adopt an enhancement motive when in an implemental mindset. In one study (Study 3), they randomly assigned participants to a deliberative or an implemental mindset condition and then asked them to estimate how long they believed their current romantic relationship would last. A majority of the participants agreed to answer follow-up questions 6 months later. Of those participants, 29% were no longer romantically involved with the person they were with at the initial testing phase. Fascinatingly, individuals in the deliberative mindset condition were much more accurate in predicting the length of their relationship than those in the implemental mindset condition. Consistent with Simpson et al.'s (2001) predictions, when important relationship-relevant decisions must be made, individuals temporarily suspend positive partner–relationship illusions and process information in a less idealistic, more evenhanded manner (see also Gagné & Lydon, 2004).

Bias and accuracy in judgments, however, can coexist. Recent theoretical and empirical work has shown that bias and accuracy (depending on how they are measured) can operate independently, meaning that relationship and partner judgments can simultaneously be both positively biased and reasonably accurate (Fletcher, 2002; Gagné & Lydon, 2004; Kenny & Acitelli, 2001). Taking an example from Fletcher (2002), consider a hypothetical relationship between Jill and Jack. Assume that across a set of four traits, Jack rates himself a 4, 5, 5, and 6 out of 10. Now assume that Jill's perceptions of Jack on the same set of traits are 5, 6, 6, and 7. It is apparent that Jill's perceptions are positively biased, with an overall mean difference between perceptions of one point on the scale. Jill's appraisals, however, also perfectly track Jack's self-perceptions across the four traits, yielding a correlation of +1.0 between the two sets of ratings. Thus, in this example, Jill's perceptions of Jack denote both positive bias (suggesting partner enhancement) and tracking accuracy (suggesting partner verification or profile agreement; Funder & Colvin, 1997). Other combinations of ratings can yield different levels of tracking accuracy and positive bias. According to Gagné and Lydon (2004), people are motivated to be both positively biased and accurate at important choice points in their relationships. They suggested that romantic partners are able to satisfy both enhancement-related and accuracy-related needs by becoming more accurate when making epistemic-related judgments (e.g., to predict or understand their relationships) but more positively biased when making esteem-regulatory judgments (e.g., relationship appraisals; Gagné & Lydon, 2004). In sum, individuals both want their current partners to match their ideals and may be motivated to positively enhance their perceptions of their partner's qualities (Murray, 2001), but they also keep track of the consistency between their ideal standards and less sanguine evaluations of their partner's qualities to make important relationship decisions.

Partner Discrepancies and Ideal Flexibility

Because of the limited existence and availability of ideal partners, most people need to be flexible when considering and choosing potential romantic partners. Flexibility in ideals refers to the degree to which an individual is willing to accept partners or relationships that fall below his or her ideal standards (Campbell et al., 2001). Some degree of willingness to accommodate should allow individuals to be less critical of partners who fall below their ideals and maintain more positive perceptions of their relationships in the process. This implies that an individual's level of ideal flexibility should relate to how large a discrepancy can be tolerated before attempts to regulate the partner or relationship are made (Campbell et al., 2001). In fact, relative to less flexible people, those who are more flexible tend to be more satisfied in relationships with larger partner discrepancies (Campbell et al., 2001).

Consistent with an evolutionary perspective of human mating, sex differences exist in romantic partners' willingness to compromise on different ideal dimensions (Fletcher et al., 2004). Relative to men, women tend to be less willing to concede on the warmth–trustworthiness and status–resources dimensions, but they place less importance on mate vitality–attractiveness. Men, though, tend to be less willing to sacrifice the vitality–attractiveness dimension. In other words, women are more willing to make a compromise in the looks department if a potential mate is kind and successful, whereas men are less forgiving of a potential mate's homeliness.

Additionally, people who have more positive self-perceptions typically hold higher and less flexible ideal standards (Campbell et al., 2001). That is, individuals who view themselves positively tend to expect more from partners and relationships and are less willing to compromise. Presumably, positive self-perceptions give individuals greater confidence in their ability to attract and hold onto an ideal mate. For example, a very attractive person may desire an equally attractive partner and be confident that he or she can secure one without having to settle for a less appealing mate.

Altogether, a person's partner and relationship ideals provide a big picture of their ideal romantic situation, which may or may not be realized. The reality is that people are generally required to make trade-offs because very few perfectly ideal partners exist and those who do are probably reserved for each other. More important, although ideals may serve as a sort of shopping list when individuals initially consider potential romantic partners or evaluate their current partners, a perfect match between a current partner and an ideal partner is not a necessary requirement for a satisfying, committed relationship.

Ideals and Goal Pursuit in Relationships

People do not only use ideal standards when evaluating their relationship partners, they also have an ideal self they wish to become. This ideal self is made up of a person's goals and aspirations, as well as the skills, traits, and resources he or she ideally hopes to possess (Higgins, 1987; Markus & Nurius, 1986). For instance, Jill's ideal self might include goals such as being a good manager in her workplace, becoming more physically fit, and learning to salsa dance. When people perceive a discrepancy between their actual, current self and their ideal self, they experience discomfort, sadness, and frustration. Individuals are thus motivated to bring their actual, current self closer to their ideal self (Higgins, 1987). In our example, Jill might work toward her ideal self by soliciting peer feedback about her management skills, setting up a weekly exercise routine at a nearby gym, and enrolling in dance classes. Although individuals can sometimes achieve their goals on their own, romantic partners can be particularly influential in shaping the self. Specifically, intimates can promote or inhibit each other's pursuits of ideal traits via what has been termed the *Michelangelo phenomenon* (Drigotas, Rusbult, Wieselquist, & Whitton, 1999; Rusbult, Finkel, & Kumashiro, 2009).

Michelangelo Buonarroti viewed sculpting as a process whereby the artist releases an ideal figure from the block of stone in which it slumbers. The artist simply removes the stone covering the figure

(Gombrich, 1995). Romantic partners can similarly shape each other; for example, Jack may help Jill become more physically fit by accompanying her to the gym. Indeed, intimates often adapt to each other over the course of an interaction, responding and adjusting as needed and, over time, such adjustments can become permanently integrated into the self (Rusbult & Van Lange, 2003). In other words, with long-term interaction, individuals can "sculpt" each other by affirming (or disaffirming) certain skills and traits.

The Michelangelo phenomenon is thought to occur through three processes (Drigotas et al., 1999). First, partner perceptual affirmation refers to the extent to which a close partner's perceptions of the target match the target's ideal self. Jack shows greater perceptual affirmation if he holds beliefs about Jill that are congruent with her goals and aspirations. Second, partner behavioral affirmation stems from perceptual affirmation and refers to the extent to which a close partner's behavior toward the target matches the target's ideal self. Jack displays greater behavioral affirmation if he behaves in ways that bring out or encourage Jill's ideal qualities. Finally, partner behavioral affirmation leads to self-movement toward the ideal self, in which the target develops into a closer reflection of the target's ideal self. That is, Jack's behavior may lead Jill to move closer to being the person she dreams of becoming.

Partners may influence each other's movement toward ideal selves in ways that can be beneficial, neutral, or harmful (Drigotas et al., 1999; Rusbult et al., 2009). The most beneficial is when partners affirm qualities that are central to each other's ideal selves. For instance, Jill may help Jack reach his goal of being more sociable by introducing him to her friends and encouraging opportunities for him to tell interesting stories. Alternatively, she may help him more indirectly by responding positively when Jack enacts sociable behaviors, such as initiating conversation with a new group of people. However, partners can also fail to affirm each other's ideal selves by affirming qualities that are irrelevant to the ideal. Jack might ideally desire to become more sociable, but Jill may instead affirm other qualities, such as his handyman skills or his taste in fashion. Finally, and arguably most harmfully, partners can

disaffirm each other's ideal selves by responding negatively to qualities central to the ideal. Jill may not view Jack as sociable (rather, as shy and aloof), which may create situations in which Jack acts shy and aloof, inhibiting his progression toward his ideal self.

When a romantic partner affirms ideal qualities, individuals actually do report greater movement toward their ideal self. This seems to be enhanced when partners are more similar to each other's ideal selves or shared ideal traits (Rusbult, Kumashiro, Kubacka, & Finkel, 2009). However, when intimates fail to affirm or disaffirm ideal qualities, targets do not come to more closely resemble their ideal selves over time (Drigotas et al., 1999). Disaffirmation seems to be especially deleterious because targets are not only inhibited from realizing their aspirations, but they come to realize that their partners do not view them the way they want to be, reducing relationship quality (Drigotas et al., 1999). The Michelangelo phenomenon has a number of implications for goal achievement. Personal growth is central to human development (Deci & Ryan, 2000), and movement toward the ideal self has been linked to greater psychological well-being and better health (e.g., Drigotas, 2002). Additionally, when intimates help each other achieve ideal qualities, the relationship benefits and it is more likely to continue (Kumashiro, Rusbult, Finkenauer, & Stocker, 2007; Rusbult et al., 2009).

Summary

In this section, we highlighted research guided by the ideal standards model (Fletcher et al., 1999; Simpson et al., 2001) on relationship evaluation and regulation. Individuals are more satisfied in their relationships when they perceive their partners as more closely matching their ideal standards. When a discrepancy is perceived to exist between partner perceptions and one's ideal standards, partners are more likely to enact regulatory behaviors aimed at changing each other to more closely align with their own ideals. Individuals are also sensitive to how closely they match their partner's ideal standards, being less satisfied when they fall short of their partner's ideals, largely because they possess an accurate assessment of how their partners view them. Other research has tested how partners help to shape each other's ideal selves (i.e., the Michelangelo phenomenon). Intimates can behave in ways that affirm their partner's ideal self and, over time, they can move toward their ideal selves with the assistance of their partners.

DO IDEAL STANDARDS AND PREFERENCES INFLUENCE ACTUAL MATE CHOICES?

So far, we have shown that individuals have ideal mate standards before entering a romantic relationship, and these standards are associated in a variety of ways with the thoughts, feelings, and behaviors of individuals involved in ongoing romantic relationships. One might assume that the road to actual relationship initiation is paved with ideal mate standards. Indeed, the very purpose of ideal mate preferences seems to be that they guide the mate selection process. However, recent research has suggested that this may not be entirely true.

One topic that is currently being hotly debated in the literature is whether the qualities that individuals say they ideally desire in a romantic partner actually influence their mate selections. That is, do individuals tend to initiate relationships with others who more closely match their ideal preferences? Such a link is implied in research that asks participants to indicate their ideal mate preferences, and if there were no meaningful links between stated ideal mate preferences and actual mate selection, the usefulness of hundreds of published studies would be called into question. For example, knowing that men tend to value physical appeal more than women and that women value status more than men across 37 different cultures (Buss, 1989) might be inconsequential if these preferences are checked at the mate selection door and replaced by other preferences or psychological processes. If so, research would need to focus on actual predictors of mate selection and relationship initiation and move away from simply asking people about their ideal mate standards.

Assessing the Empirical Evidence

Ideal mate standards influence relationship initiation. Lamenting the fact that most studies of human mate choice are based almost exclusively on self-reported preferences, Pérusse (1994; see also 1993) obtained reports of actual recent mating behaviors from a large representative sample of heterosexual men and women (more than 1,100 participants). Guided by evolutionary models of human mating, Pérusse surmised that mating behaviors should be linked with the current mate value of men and women. Consistent with this hypothesis, men of higher social status had more mating partners than did men of lower status, implying that women place considerable importance on status and resources in their ideal mate standards (Pérusse, 1993). The social status of women, however, was not associated with their number of mating partners. The number of mating partners of women, however, did decrease linearly with age, suggesting that reproductive potential may be an importance component of male choice. Men's age was not associated with number of mating partners. Actual mating behaviors, therefore, correspond with some of the known ideal mate standards identified in prior self-report research: Women seem to pursue and choose men who have more resources as mating partners, whereas men seem to pursue and choose women who display cues of youth and fertility as mating partners. We should note that these participants retrospectively reported on their recent mate choices and that the motivations guiding these romantic unions were inferred, not directly assessed.

Two large-scale epidemiological studies have also shown that more physically attractive women tend to marry men of higher occupational status (Elder, 1969; P. A. Taylor & Glenn, 1976). These results suggest that the mating preferences of men with higher status, of more physically attractive women, or both are actualized in real-world marital outcomes. An important limitation of these studies is that they did not assess the link between men's physical attractiveness and the qualities of their spouses. Attractive men may marry women who have relatively more occupational prestige.

More recent research has found that when women prefer more masculine men as romantic partners, they are indeed in relationships with more masculine-looking men (Burriss, Welling, & Puts, 2011; DeBruine et al., 2006). Presumably, women's preferences for romantic partners who have more masculine features influence their mate choices. This possibility is plausible, but to date these studies have assessed women's preferences and the masculinity of their male partners in existing romantic unions. Women's preference for masculinity in these studies, therefore, could have been influenced by the masculinity of their partners after the relationship had started.

Perhaps the most convincing evidence that ideal mate preferences map onto actual mate choices was compiled by Kenrick and Keefe (1992). They tested the idea that men should prefer women around their own age when they (men) were younger, but as they grew older, men should prefer women progressively younger than themselves (i.e., preference for relative youth and fertility). Additionally, they hypothesized that women should prefer men who are slightly older than themselves, regardless of their own age (i.e., a preference for status and resources associated with older men). Kenrick and Keefe (1992) accessed a range of data sources in six studies, including personal advertisements, over 1,000 marriages from two cities in the United States, 100 marriages in 1923, matrimonial advertisements from two European countries and India, more than 1,500 marriages recorded from 1913 to 1939 on a small island in the Philippines, and singles advertisements placed by financially secure men and women in the United States. They consistently found that as men increased in age, men both preferred and married women who were progressively younger than themselves. Women, however, both preferred and married men who were slightly older than themselves, regardless of their own age. This research provides robust support for the notion that ideal preferences (at least with respect to partners' age) correspond closely with actual mate choice.

Ideal mate standards do not influence relationship initiation. Some recent research, however, has challenged the role that ideal preferences play in actual mate selection. Eastwick and Finkel (2008) used a speed-dating approach in which they had equal numbers of men and women engage in 4-minute "dates" with nine to 13 potential dating partners (the number of potential partners depended on event attendance). After each date, participants answered questions about each date. Before the speed-dating event, participants reported their ideal mate preferences, particularly for physical attraction and earning prospects. After the speed-dating event, they answered questions at 10 different times over a 30-day period regarding their desire to form a relationship with each person they met at the event. Consistent with research on self-reported mate preferences, Eastwick and Finkel (2008) found that men and women differed in the importance placed on physical attraction (more important for men) and earning prospects (more important for women) for ideal mates. These stated preferences, however, did not predict participants' romantic attraction to any of the opposite-sex individuals they had dated in the speed-dating event (see also Todd, Penke, Fasolo, & Lenton, 2007). According to Eastwick and Finkel (2008), the link between stated ideal mate preferences and actual mate choice is tenuous at best, suggesting that people lack introspective awareness of what influences their mate choices.

Building on the finding that stated mate preferences do not influence actual mate choices, Eastwick, Finkel, and Eagly (2011) examined the circumstances in which ideal preferences may (or may not) influence romantic attraction across three studies. In the first study, they found that ideal preferences predicted romantic attraction when participants viewed a profile of an opposite-sex person who more closely matched their ideal standards. When the participant then met and had a 4-minute interaction discussing a picture from the Thematic Apperception Test with this opposite-sex stranger (actually a study confederate), no differences in attraction emerged between participants who interacted with a partner who more closely matched their ideals and one who did not. In the second study, Eastwick, Finkel, and Eagly replicated this finding and investigated the mediating role of person perception. After viewing a profile and then interacting with an opposite-sex stranger (a study confederate) who matched or did not match their ideal standards, it seemed as though participants changed the meaning of their ideal preferences to be characteristic of the confederate. Also, although participants inferred more positive meaning for traits presumably possessed by confederates who matched their ideals, this did not influence their attraction to them. In the third study, Eastwick, Finkel, and Eagly once again found that the ideal preferences of single participants did not predict relationship outcomes (e.g., passion). They did, however, find that for participants who were in a current relationship, ideal preferences predicted passion, satisfaction, commitment, and other relationship outcomes. This latter finding supports the idea that individuals in relationships do use ideal standards to evaluate their relationships, as discussed previously. Eastwick, Finkel, and Eagly suggested that ideal preferences do have a role to play in predicting relationship processes and outcomes when considering an actual (current) partner or a hypothetical partner, but not when assessing a potential partner who is interacted with in person. Properties of interactions with potential mates are thought to trump preexisting ideal preferences during relationship initiation.

In another series of studies, Eastwick, Eagly, Finkel, and Johnson (2011) found a distinction between explicit and implicit ideal preferences for physical attractiveness in predicting interpersonal attraction. Implicit attitudes for physical attractiveness in particular did not show sex differences, whereas explicit attitudes did. This research also suggested that explicit and implicit ideal preferences for physical attractiveness are not correlated. Explicit attitudes predicted attraction to hypothetical romantic partners (e.g., photographs of potential partners) but not attraction to speed-dating partners or study confederates. Implicit attitudes, in contrast, predicted attraction to the latter potential partners but not the former. Eastwick, Eagly, et al. reasoned that a preference for individual characteristics such as physical attractiveness can influence romantic interest in certain types of potential mates, but in different ways.

Making Sense of Inconsistent Data

There are some major differences between the two literatures we have discussed that may be important for understanding the inconsistent effects reported between them. For example, in the research showing links between ideal mate preferences and mate choice, participants had already made mate choices that either they reported or government agencies

documented (e.g., marriage records). Pérusse (1994) asked participants about actual recent mating choices, P. A. Taylor and Glenn (1976) assessed the actual physical attractiveness of wives and the social status of their husbands, and Kenrick and Keefe (1992) looked at marriage records to determine the actual ages of men and women when they married. Conversely, in the research that has not demonstrated links between ideal mate preferences and mate choice, mate choices were assessed in participants shortly after they interacted with opposite-sex strangers. The assessment of mate choice in these studies also did not involve actual relationship initiation in that few, if any, long-term romantic relationships were formed between speed-dating participants or between participants and study confederates. Instead, these studies assessed initial attraction and the stated desire to get to know another person better. Although it is true that the outcomes of both bodies of research can be operationalized as mate choice, the types of choices assessed are at very different ends of the mate-choice spectrum and may not be directly comparable.

Moreover, not all of the results from the speed-dating studies are completely inconsistent with the notion that ideal mate preferences influence mate choice. In a speed-dating context, participants have very little time to evaluate the quality of each date as a long-term romantic partner, and the ability to do so in such a short period of time is very constrained. Therefore, such events may be better suited to assessing the desirability of each date as a short-term partner. Li and Kenrick (2006) have found that both men and women desire physical appeal in short-term partners, and speed-dating decisions in the research we have discussed seem to be based more on physical, observable traits (such as attractiveness, body mass index, and height for both men and women) than less directly observable ones. Additionally, on the basis of Trivers's (1972) model of parental investment and sexual selection, women should be choosier than men in a speed-dating context. Indeed, all of the speed-dating studies have found that men want to meet up again with many more dates than do women. Overall, both men and women make speed-dating decisions based on the physical appeal of their dates, which is not surprising given that both men and women value physical attraction highly and equally in short-term mates, and women are more selective than men in speed-dating studies.

The speed-dating or confederate interaction environment may also prime short-term rather than long-term relationship goals. That is, the brief interaction time allowed in such contexts may lead individuals to focus on the extent to which they get along with their interaction partner, a goal that does not necessitate the implementation of ideal standards in judging the interaction partner. In contrast, research conducted in a longitudinal context with individuals currently involved in relationships is more likely to tap into long-term relationship goals. In these cases, ideal preferences may be more important because individuals are emphasizing long-term relationship goals, such as compatibility, similar values, and marriage potential. Indeed, Eastwick, Finkel, and Eagly (2011) found that ideal standards predicted a number of relationship outcomes (e.g., satisfaction) for individuals who were currently involved in romantic relationships. Thus, both men and women are more selective when considering a long-term mate (Regan, 1998), and ideal preferences may be one avenue through which individuals are more selective.

Different research paradigms may also activate the use of minimal standards rather than ideal standards. For instance, Regan (1998) found that individuals were more likely to use minimal standards in a short-term mating context. Other research has demonstrated that, in a long-term mating context, individuals have higher minimal standards and their self-appraisals predict their mate choice and commitment (Kenrick et al., 1993). This phenomenon does not seem to occur in a short-term context. If speed-dating and confederate interaction contexts emphasize short-term relationship goals, individuals may be willing to compromise their ideal standards on the basis of the available partners at hand and instead use minimal standards to inform their choices.

Additionally, ideal preferences may act as a filter at various stages of romantic relationships. For example, an individual may pursue potential mates who do not closely match his or her ideals but be less likely to continue pursuing or to enter a committed relationship with those who are more discrepant from his or her ideals. Stated differently, ideal preferences may fail to strongly influence whom a person is romantically interested in or attracted to, but they may largely dictate the choice of whether or not to enter a committed relationship with someone. Over time, a lack of ideal–perception consistency may arouse doubts regarding the level of compatibility or probability of entering an enduring, satisfying romantic relationship with a nonideal partner.

Admittedly, these explanations for why stated ideal mate preferences did not significantly predict attraction to dates or study confederates who more closely approximated participants' ideals are speculative. An impartial reading of the research might conclude that a definitive answer regarding the role of stated ideal mate standards in relationship initiation and formation does not yet exist. In addition to the fine scholarship of Eastwick and Finkel's (2008) research, they have motivated researchers to assess, instead of infer, actual relationship initiation, which has been good for the field.

Summary

Some extant research has suggested that actual mate choice is guided by ideal mate preferences, whereas other research has shown that features of the social interaction with potential mates influence mate choice, whereas ideal mate preferences do not. A large number of studies have indirectly made conclusions about relationship initiation and mate choice on the basis of self-reports of ideal mate preferences. The usefulness of this body of research may be called into question if these preferences do not influence actual mate choice. Additional research focusing on actual relationship initiation is needed to determine the role, if any, of ideal mate preferences in this process.

FUTURE DIRECTIONS

In our opinion, the most important future direction in the study of ideal mate standards is to determine the nature of the links between ideal preferences and mate choice. As already noted, if ideal preferences do not influence actual mate choice, the implications for the field would be rather large. For example, the voluminous studies assessing mate preferences would seem to be of little value. Given the abundance of research on ideal preferences, however, it would be rather surprising if these preferences did not map onto actual mate choice and relationship initiation in some systematic way. This gap in the literature needs to be, and likely will soon be, addressed by researchers interested in interpersonal attraction and relationship processes.

What might research that addresses this gap in the literature look like? To begin, the focus of the research should be on actual relationship initiation. This focus would require bridging the literatures on interpersonal attraction and relationship processes. That is, ideal mate preferences would need to be assessed in individuals before they entered a relationship. Furthermore, once individuals enter a relationship, the attributes of the new partner need to be assessed as well as how the new relationship progresses over time. This type of research could determine whether people enter relationships with individuals who more closely match their ideal mate preferences (or particular ideal preferences and not others) and whether relationships develop more positively when greater ideal consistency exists. This method could also be altered to focus on different types of relationships (e.g., short-term sexual relationships, dating relationships).

It may be difficult to directly assess the role of ideal standards in relationship initiation in a laboratory setting or over a short period of time. To move beyond measuring attraction or romantic interest, research may need to more closely approximate the complexities of actual relationship initiation. Relationship initiation is a process that unfolds over time, and research thus needs to observe individuals over time to witness the mechanisms involved. Following individuals over time as they enter new relationships is a challenging task, but it may be necessary to convincingly establish how ideal preferences do or do not guide relationship initiation.

Future research should also assess how ideal standards change over time. Fletcher et al. (2000) assessed how individuals change their ideal standards to more closely match their perceptions of their partners in newly established relationships, but ideal standards may change for many different reasons across the life span. If what people ideally prefer in a partner and relationship changes over time, there is the potential to be dissatisfied with a relationship that had previously been fulfilling.

In line with this, future research should also continue to investigate how romantic partners shape each other's ideal selves (e.g., via the Michelangelo phenomenon; Drigotas et al., 1999). Some studies have suggested that partners who affirm each other and help each other move toward their respective ideal selves experience personal and relationship benefits, such as enhanced health and well-being (Drigotas, 2002), and better relationship quality (Kumashiro et al., 2007). What are the implications for the self and relationship, however, when partners disaffirm each other? Drigotas et al. (1999) suggested that disaffirmation leads to negative outcomes as individuals realize that their partners do not see them as they want to be seen. Indeed, Kumashiro et al. (2007) found that disaffirmation led to lower relationship quality. Although this research sets a strong foundation for studies of how partners influence each other's ideals in relationships, the specific nature of the negative outcomes associated with disaffirmation has not been fully explored. It may be, for example, that partners who disaffirm each other experience poorer health (e.g., mental distress) or decreased self-esteem over time.

It is also likely that the importance of the three ideal standard dimensions highlighted in the ISM (Fletcher et al., 1999; Simpson et al., 2001) peaks at different times in relationships. For example, standards of beauty may influence relationship processes more strongly in the early stages of relationship development, and standards of status and resources may become salient in tough economic times or when a partner loses a job. Standards of warmth and trustworthiness could potentially be most salient when partners experience stress or require emotional support. Overall, different stages of relationship development, or the presence of particular contexts, should render some ideal dimensions more important than others.

Thus far, the majority of research on ideal standards, interpersonal attraction, and relationship processes has used self-report methodologies. As is well known, self-report methodologies are subject to various limitations (Stone et al., 2000), including impression management (Crowne & Marlowe, 1960), self-deceptive motivated distortions (Paulhus, 1984), and limits of self-awareness (Nisbett & Wilson, 1977). These limitations may be particularly pronounced in the context of romantic relationships given that it may be difficult for many individuals to access their actual mate preferences (cf. Eastwick & Finkel, 2008) or admit that a current romantic partner does not closely approximate their ideals. In recent years, researchers have developed implicit methods to measure the thoughts and feelings individuals have for their partners. These implicit measures tend not to be correlated with explicit measures of partner evaluations, yet they seem to capture important aspects of partner evaluations that are missed by conscious reports (Murray, Holmes, & Pinkus, 2010). For example, implicit partner evaluations have been linked to a decreased likelihood of breakup in the future, both indirectly (via relationship satisfaction; LeBel & Campbell, 2009) and directly (controlling for relationship satisfaction; Lee, Rogge, & Reis, 2010). Additionally, both explicit and implicit partner evaluations uniquely predict perceptions of relationship quality, and positive behavior enacted toward a romantic partner, over a 21-day diary period (LeBel & Campbell, 2013).

To date, very little research has used implicit measures of ideal mate preferences or of ideal standards in relation to perceptions of a current romantic partner. Recently, Eastwick, Eagly, et al. (2011) assessed implicit and explicit ideal preferences for physical attraction and found that implicit preferences were largely predictive of attraction to an opposite-sex person the participant interacted with in the lab. The small but growing body of relationship research using implicit measures has suggested the unique predictive power of these measures compared with explicit measures, and future research on ideal standards and relationships should make an effort to use implicit measures.

CONCLUDING REMARKS

In conclusion, the study of ideal standards has focused a great deal on ideal preferences and how comparisons of partners with ideal standards influence relationship processes. Much less research has assessed the role of ideal standards in relationship initiation, and the rather preliminary research that does exist provides conflicting conclusions. Perhaps the most important next step in the study of ideal standards and relationships is to bridge the study of preferences and relationship processes by determining what role, if any, ideal preferences play in mate selection and relationship initiation.

References

Alvergne, A., & Lummaa, V. (2009). Does the contraceptive pill alter mate choice in humans? *Trends in Ecology and Evolution, 25,* 171–179. doi:10.1016/j.tree.2009.08.003

Baldwin, M. W. (1992). Relational schemas and the processing of social information. *Psychological Bulletin, 112,* 461–484. doi:10.1037/0033-2909.112.3.461

Botwin, M. D., Buss, D. M., & Shackelford, T. K. (1997). Personality and mate preferences: Five factors in mate selection and marital satisfaction. *Journal of Personality, 65,* 107–136. doi:10.1111/j.1467-6494.1997.tb00531.x

Bowlby, J. (1982). *Attachment and loss: Vol. 1. Attachment.* London, England: Hogarth.

Burriss, R. P., Welling, L. L. M., & Puts, D. A. (2011). Mate-preference drives mate-choice: Men's self-rated masculinity predicts their female partner's preference for masculinity. *Personality and Individual Differences, 51,* 1023–1027. doi:10.1016/j.paid.2011.08.018

Buss, D. M. (1989). Sex differences in human mate preferences: Evolutionary hypotheses tested in 37 cultures. *Behavioral and Brain Sciences, 12,* 1–14. doi:10.1017/S0140525X00023992

Buss, D. M. (1994). *The evolution of desire.* New York, NY: Basic Books.

Buss, D. M. (1995). Evolutionary psychology: A new paradigm for psychological science. *Psychological Inquiry, 6,* 1–30. doi:10.1207/s15327965pli0601_1

Buss, D. M., & Barnes, M. (1986). Preferences in human mate selection. *Journal of Personality and Social Psychology, 50,* 559–570. doi:10.1037/0022-3514.50.3.559

Buss, D. M., & Schmitt, D. P. (1993). Sexual strategies theory: An evolutionary perspective on human mating. *Psychological Review, 100,* 204–232. doi:10.1037/0033-295X.100.2.204

Campbell, L., Overall, N. C., Rubin, H., & Lackenbauer, S. D. (2013). Inferring a partner's ideal discrepancies: Accuracy, projection, and the communicative role of interpersonal behavior. *Journal of Personality and Social Psychology, 105,* 217–233.

Campbell, L., Simpson, J. A., Kashy, D. A., & Fletcher, G. J. O. (2001). Ideal standards, the self, and flexibility of ideals in close relationships. *Personality and Social Psychology Bulletin, 27,* 447–462. doi:10.1177/0146167201274006

Campbell, L., & Wilbur, C. J. (2009). Are the traits we prefer in potential mates the traits they value in themselves? An analysis of sex differences in the self-concept. *Self and Identity, 8,* 418–446. doi:10.1080/15298860802505434

Crowne, D. P., & Marlowe, D. (1960). A new scale of social desirability independent of psychopathology. *Journal of Consulting Psychology, 24,* 349–354. doi:10.1037/h0047358

DeBruine, L. M., Jones, B. C., Little, A. C., Boothroyd, L. G., Perrett, D. I., Penton-Voak, I. S., . . . Tiddeman, B. P. (2006). Correlated preferences for facial masculinity and ideal or actual partner's masculinity. *Proceedings of the Royal Society B: Biological Sciences, 273,* 1355–1360. doi:10.1098/rspb.2005.3445

Deci, E. L., & Ryan, R. M. (2000). The "what" and "why" of goal pursuits: Human needs and the self-determination of behavior. *Psychological Inquiry, 11,* 227–268. doi:10.1207/S15327965PLI1104_01

Drigotas, S. M. (2002). The Michelangelo phenomenon and personal well-being. *Journal of Personality, 70,* 59–77. doi:10.1111/1467-6494.00178

Drigotas, S. M., Rusbult, C. E., Wieselquist, J., & Whitton, S. W. (1999). Close partner as sculptor of the ideal self: Behavioral affirmation and the Michelangelo phenomenon. *Journal of Personality and Social Psychology, 77,* 293–323. doi:10.1037/0022-3514.77.2.293

Eastwick, P. W., Eagly, A. H., Finkel, E. J., & Johnson, S. E. (2011). Implicit and explicit preferences for physical attractiveness in a romantic partner: A double dissociation in predictive validity. *Journal of Personality and Social Psychology, 101,* 993–1011. doi:10.1037/a0024061

Eastwick, P. W., & Finkel, E. J. (2008). Sex differences in mate preferences revisited: Do people know what they initially desire in a romantic partner? *Journal of Personality and Social Psychology, 94,* 245–264. doi:10.1037/0022-3514.94.2.245

Eastwick, P. W., Finkel, E. J., & Eagly, A. H. (2011). When and why do ideal partner preferences affect the process of initiating and maintaining close relationships? *Journal of Personality and Social Psychology, 101,* 1012–1032. doi:10.1037/a0024062

Elder, G. H., Jr. (1969). Appearance and education in marriage mobility. *American Sociological Review, 34,* 519–533. doi:10.2307/2091961

Ellis, B. J. (1992). The evolution of sexual attraction: Evaluative mechanisms in women. In J. H. Barkow, L. Cosmides, & J. Tooby (Eds.), *The adapted mind: Evolutionary psychology and the generation of culture* (pp. 267–288). London, England: Oxford University Press.

Feinberg, D. R., Jones, B. C., Law Smith, M. J., Moore, F. R., DeBruine, L. M., Cornwell, R. E., . . . Perrett, D. I. (2006). Menstrual cycle, trait estrogen level, and masculinity preferences in the human voice. *Hormones and Behavior, 49,* 215–222. doi:10.1016/j.yhbeh.2005.07.004

Feingold, A. (1992). Gender differences in mate selection preferences: A test of the parental investment model. *Psychological Bulletin, 112,* 125–139. doi:10.1037/0033-2909.112.1.125

Fletcher, G. J. O. (2002). *The new science of intimate relationships.* Malden, MA: Blackwell. doi:10.1002/9780470773390

Fletcher, G. J. O., Simpson, J. A., & Thomas, G. (2000). Ideals, perceptions, and evaluations in early relationship development. *Journal of Personality and Social Psychology, 79,* 933–940. doi:10.1037/0022-3514.79.6.933

Fletcher, G. J. O., Simpson, J. A., Thomas, G., & Giles, L. (1999). Ideals in intimate relationships. *Journal of Personality and Social Psychology, 76,* 72–89. doi:10.1037/0022-3514.76.1.72

Fletcher, G. J. O., Tither, J. M., O'Loughlin, C., Friesen, M., & Overall, N. (2004). Warm and homely or cold and beautiful? Sex differences in trading off traits in mate selection. *Personality and Social Psychology Bulletin, 30,* 659–672. doi:10.1177/0146167203262847

Frye, N. E., & Karney, B. R. (2002). Being better or getting better? Social and temporal comparisons as coping mechanisms in close relationships. *Personality and Social Psychology Bulletin, 28,* 1287–1299. doi:10.1177/01461672022812013

Funder, D. C., & Colvin, C. R. (1997). Congruence of other's and self-judgments of personality. In R. Hogan, J. A. Johnson, & S. R. Briggs (Eds.), *Handbook of personality psychology* (pp. 617–647). San Diego, CA: Academic Press. doi:10.1016/B978-012134645-4/50025-1

Gagné, F. M., & Lydon, J. E. (2001). Mind-set and close relationships: When bias leads to (in)accurate predictions. *Journal of Personality and Social Psychology, 81,* 85–96. doi:10.1037/0022-3514.81.1.85

Gagné, F. M., & Lydon, J. E. (2004). Bias and accuracy in close relationships: An integrative overview.

Personality and Social Psychology Review, 8, 322–338. doi:10.1207/s15327957pspr0804_1

Gangestad, S. W., Garver-Apgar, C. E., Simpson, J. A., & Cousins, A. J. (2007). Changes in women's mate preferences across the ovulatory cycle. *Journal of Personality and Social Psychology, 92,* 151–163. doi:10.1037/0022-3514.92.1.151

Gangestad, S. W., & Simpson, J. A. (2000). The evolution of human mating: Trade-offs and strategic pluralism. *Behavioral and Brain Sciences, 23,* 573–587. doi:10.1017/S0140525X0000337X

Gangestad, S. W., Simpson, J. A., Cousins, A. J., Garver-Apgar, C. E., & Christensen, P. N. (2004). Women's preferences for male behavioral displays change across the menstrual cycle. *Psychological Science, 15,* 203–207. doi:10.1111/j.0956-7976.2004.01503010.x

Gangestad, S. W., & Thornhill, R. (1997). Human sexual selection and developmental instability. In J. A. Simpson & D. T. Kenrick (Eds.), *Evolutionary social psychology* (pp. 169–195). Mahwah, NJ: Erlbaum.

Gangestad, S. W., & Thornhill, R. (1998). Menstrual cycle variation in women's preference for the scent of symmetrical men. *Proceedings of the Royal Society B: Biological Sciences, 265,* 927–933. doi:10.1098/rspb.1998.0380

Gangestad, S. W., & Thornhill, R. (2008). Human oestrus. *Proceedings of the Royal Society B: Biological Sciences, 275,* 991–1000. doi:10.1098/rspb.2007.1425

Geary, D. C. (2000). Evolution and proximate expression of human paternal investment. *Psychological Bulletin, 126,* 55–77. doi:10.1037/0033-2909.126.1.55

Gollwitzer, P. M., & Bayer, U. (1999). Deliberative versus implemental mind-sets in the control of action. In S. Chaiken & Y. Trope (Eds.), *Dual-processes theories in social psychology* (pp. 403–422). New York, NY: Guilford Press.

Gollwitzer, P. M., Heckhausen, H., & Steller, B. (1990). Deliberative and implemental mind-sets: Cognitive tuning toward congruous thoughts and information. *Journal of Personality and Social Psychology, 59,* 1119–1127. doi:10.1037/0022-3514.59.6.1119

Gombrich, E. H. (1995). *The story of art* (16th ed.). London, England: Phaidon Press.

Grammer, K. (1993). 5-α-androst-16en-3α-on: A male pheromone? A brief report. *Ethology and Sociobiology, 14,* 201–207. doi:10.1016/0162-3095(93)90006-4

Graziano, W. G., Jensen-Campbell, L. A., Todd, M., & Finch, J. F. (1997). Interpersonal attraction from an evolutionary psychology perspective: Women's reactions to dominant and prosocial men. In J. A. Simpson & D. T. Kenrick (Eds.), *Evolutionary social psychology* (pp. 141–167). Hillsdale, NJ: Erlbaum.

Havlicek, J., Roberts, S. C., & Flegr, J. (2005). Women's preference for dominant males' odour: Effects of menstrual cycle and relationship status. *Biology Letters, 1,* 256–259. doi:10.1098/rsbl.2005.0332

Hester, C. (1996). The relationship of personality, gender, and age to adjective check list profiles of the ideal romantic partner. *Journal of Psychological Type, 36,* 28–35.

Higgins, E. T. (1987). Self-discrepancy: A theory relating self and affect. *Psychological Review, 94,* 319–340. doi:10.1037/0033-295X.94.3.319

Higgins, E. T. (1989). Self-discrepancy theory: What patterns of self-beliefs cause people to suffer? In L. Berkowitz (Ed.), *Advances in experimental social psychology* (Vol. 22, pp. 93–136). New York, NY: Academic Press. doi:10.1016/S0065-2601(08)60306-8

Higgins, E. T. (1997). Beyond pleasure and pain. *American Psychologist, 52,* 1280–1300. doi:10.1037/0003-066X.52.12.1280

Kenny, D. A., & Acitelli, L. K. (2001). Accuracy and bias in the perception of the partner in a close relationship. *Journal of Personality and Social Psychology, 80,* 439–448. doi:10.1037/0022-3514.80.3.439

Kenrick, D. T., Groth, G. E., Trost, M. R., & Sadalla, E. K. (1993). Integrating evolutionary and social exchange perspectives on relationships: Effects of gender, self-appraisal, and involvement level on mate selection criteria. *Journal of Personality and Social Psychology, 64,* 951–969. doi:10.1037/0022-3514.64.6.951

Kenrick, D. T., & Keefe, R. C. (1992). Age preferences in mates reflect sex differences in human reproductive strategies. *Behavioral and Brain Sciences, 15,* 75–91. doi:10.1017/S0140525X00067595

Kenrick, D. T., & Trost, M. R. (1997). Evolutionary approaches to relationships. In S. Duck (Ed.), *Handbook of personal relationships: Theory, research and interventions* (2nd ed., pp. 151–177). New York, NY: Wiley.

Kumashiro, M., Rusbult, C. E., Finkenauer, C., & Stocker, S. L. (2007). To think or to do: The impact of assessment and locomotion orientation on the Michelangelo phenomenon. *Journal of Social and Personal Relationships, 24,* 591–611. doi:10.1177/0265407507079261

Lackenbauer, S. D., & Campbell, L. (2012). Measuring up: The unique emotional and regulatory outcomes of different perceived partner-ideal discrepancies in romantic relationships. *Journal of Personality and Social Psychology, 103,* 472–488. doi:10.1037/a0029054

LeBel, E. P., & Campbell, L. (2009). Implicit partner affect, relationship satisfaction, and the prediction of romantic breakup. *Journal of Experimental*

Social Psychology, 45, 1291–1294. doi:10.1016/j. jesp.2009.07.003

LeBel, E. P., & Campbell, L. (2013). The interactive role of implicit and explicit partner evaluations on ongoing affective and behavioral romantic realities. *Social Psychological and Personality Science, 4,* 167–174. doi:10.1177/1948550612448196

Lee, S., Rogge, R. D., & Reis, H. T. (2010). Assessing the seeds of relationship decay: Using implicit evaluations to detect the early stages of disillusionment. *Psychological Science, 21,* 857–864. doi:10.1177/0956797610371342

Li, N. P., Bailey, J. M., Kenrick, D. T., & Linsenmeier, J. A. W. (2002). The necessities and luxuries of mate preferences: Testing the tradeoffs. *Journal of Personality and Social Psychology, 82,* 947–955. doi:10.1037/0022-3514.82.6.947

Li, N. P., & Kenrick, D. T. (2006). Sex similarities and differences in preferences for short-term mates: What, whether, and why. *Journal of Personality and Social Psychology, 90,* 468–489. doi:10.1037/0022-3514.90.3.468

Markus, H., & Nurius, P. (1986). Possible selves. *American Psychologist, 41,* 954–969. doi:10.1037/0003-066X.41.9.954

McGregor, I., & Holmes, J. G. (1999). How storytelling shapes memory and impression of relationship events over time. *Journal of Personality and Social Psychology, 76,* 403–419. doi:10.1037/0022-3514.76.3.403

Møller, A. P., & Swaddle, J. P. (1997). *Asymmetry, developmental stability, and evolution.* Oxford, England: Oxford University Press.

Møller, A. P., & Thornhill, R. (1997). A meta-analysis of the heritability of developmental stability. *Journal of Evolutionary Biology, 10,* 1–16. doi:10.1007/s000360050001

Møller, A. P., & Thornhill, R. (1998). Bilateral symmetry and sexual selection: A meta-analysis. *American Naturalist, 151,* 174–192. doi:10.1086/286110

Murray, S. L. (2001). Seeking a sense of conviction: Motivated cognition in close relationships. In G. J. O. Fletcher & M. S. Clark (Eds.), *Blackwell handbook of social psychology: Interpersonal process* (pp. 107–126). Oxford, England: Blackwell.

Murray, S. L., & Holmes, J. G. (1993). Seeing virtues in faults: Negativity and the transformation of interpersonal narratives in close relationships. *Journal of Personality and Social Psychology, 65,* 707–722. doi:10.1037/0022-3514.65.4.707

Murray, S. L., Holmes, J. G., & Collins, N. L. (2006). Optimizing assurance: The risk regulation system in relationships. *Psychological Bulletin, 132,* 641–666. doi:10.1037/0033-2909.132.5.641

Murray, S. L., Holmes, J. G., & Griffin, D. W. (1996). The benefits of positive illusions: Idealization and the construction of satisfaction in close relationships. *Journal of Personality and Social Psychology, 70,* 79–98. doi:10.1037/0022-3514.70.1.79

Murray, S. L., Holmes, J. G., & Pinkus, R. T. (2010). A smart unconscious? Procedural origins of automatic partner attitudes in marriage. *Journal of Experimental Social Psychology, 46,* 650–656. doi:10.1016/j.jesp.2010.03.003

Nisbett, R. E., & Wilson, T. D. (1977). Telling more than we can know: Verbal reports on mental processes. *Psychological Review, 84,* 231–259. doi:10.1037/0033-295X.84.3.231

Overall, N. C., Fletcher, G. J. O., & Simpson, J. A. (2006). Regulation processes in intimate relationships: The role of ideal standards. *Journal of Personality and Social Psychology, 91,* 662–685. doi:10.1037/0022-3514.91.4.662

Overall, N. C., Fletcher, G. J. O., Simpson, J. A., & Sibley, C. G. (2009). Regulating partners in intimate relationships: The costs and benefits of different communication strategies. *Journal of Personality and Social Psychology, 96,* 620–639. doi:10.1037/a0012961

Overall, N. C., Sibley, C. G., & Travaglia, L. K. (2010). Loyal but ignored: The benefits and costs of constructive communication behavior. *Personal Relationships, 17,* 127–148. doi:10.1111/j.1475-6811.2010.01257.x

Paulhus, D. L. (1984). Two-component models of socially desirable responding. *Journal of Personality and Social Psychology, 46,* 598–609. doi:10.1037/0022-3514.46.3.598

Penton-Voak, I. S., & Perrett, D. I. (2000). Female preference for male faces changes cyclically: Further evidence. *Evolution and Human Behavior, 21,* 39–48. doi:10.1016/S1090-5138(99)00033-1

Penton-Voak, I. S., Perrett, D. I., Castles, D. L., Burt, D. M., Kobayashi, T., Murray, L. K., & Minamisawa, R. (1999). Menstrual cycle alters face preference. *Nature, 399,* 741–742. doi:10.1038/21557

Pérusse, D. (1993). Cultural and reproductive success in industrial societies: Testing the relationship at proximate and ultimate levels. *Behavioral and Brain Sciences, 16,* 267–322. doi:10.1017/S0140525X00029939

Pérusse, D. (1994). Mate choice in modern society: Testing evolutionary hypotheses with behavioral data. *Human Nature, 5,* 255–278.

Puts, D. A. (2005). Menstrual phase and mating context affect women's preferences for male voice pitch. *Evolution and Human Behavior, 26,* 388–397. doi:10.1016/j.evolhumbehav.2005.03.001

Regan, P. C. (1998). Minimum mate selection standards as a function of perceived mate value, relationship context, and gender. *Journal of Psychology and Human Sexuality, 10,* 53–73. doi:10.1300/J056v10n01_04

Regan, P. C., Levin, L., Sprecher, S., Christopher, F. S., & Cate, R. (2000). Partner preferences: What characteristics do men and women desire in their short-term sexual and long-term romantic partners? *Journal of Psychology and Human Sexuality, 12,* 1–21. doi:10.1300/J056v12n03_01

Rice, E. (1999). *Captain Sir Richard Francis Burton: A biography.* New York, NY: Barnes & Noble.

Rikowski, A., & Grammer, K. (1999). Human body odour, symmetry, and attractiveness. *Proceedings of the Royal Society B: Biological Sciences, 266,* 869–874. doi:10.1098/rspb.1999.0717

Rusbult, C. E., Arriaga, X. B., & Agnew, C. R. (2001). Interdependence in close relationships. In G. Fletcher & M. Clark (Eds.), *The Blackwell handbook of social psychology: Vol. 2. Interpersonal processes* (pp. 359–387). Oxford, England: Blackwell.

Rusbult, C. E., Finkel, E. J., & Kumashiro, M. (2009). The Michelangelo phenomenon. *Current Directions in Psychological Science, 18,* 305–309. doi:10.1111/j.1467-8721.2009.01657.x

Rusbult, C. E., Kumashiro, M., Kubacka, K. E., & Finkel, E. J. (2009). "The part of me that you bring out": Ideal similarity and the Michelangelo phenomenon. *Journal of Personality and Social Psychology, 96,* 61–82. doi:10.1037/a0014016

Rusbult, C. E., & Van Lange, P. A. M. (2003). Interdependence, interaction, and relationships. *Annual Review of Psychology, 54,* 351–375. doi:10.1146/annurev.psych.54.101601.145059

Sadalla, E. K., Kenrick, D. T., & Vershure, B. (1987). Dominance and heterosexual attraction. *Journal of Personality and Social Psychology, 52,* 730–738. doi:10.1037/0022-3514.52.4.730

Scarbrough, P. S., & Johnston, V. S. (2005). Individual differences in women's facial preferences as a function of digit ratio and mental rotation ability. *Evolution and Human Behavior, 26,* 509–526. doi:10.1016/j.evolhumbehav.2005.03.002

Simpson, J. A., Fletcher, G. J. O., & Campbell, L. (2001). The structure and functions of ideal standards in close relationships. In G. J. O. Fletcher & M. S. Clark (Eds.), *Blackwell handbook of social psychology: Interpersonal processes* (pp. 86–106). Oxford, England: Blackwell.

Singh, D. (1993). Adaptive significance of female physical attractiveness: Role of waist-to-hip ratio. *Journal of Personality and Social Psychology, 65,* 293–307. doi:10.1037/0022-3514.65.2.293

Sprecher, S., Sullivan, H., & Hatfield, E. (1994). Mate selection preferences: Gender differences examined in a national sample. *Journal of Personality and Social Psychology, 66,* 1074–1080. doi:10.1037/0022-3514.66.6.1074

Sternberg, R. J., & Barnes, M. L. (1985). Real and ideal others in romantic relationships: Is four a crowd? *Journal of Personality and Social Psychology, 49,* 1586–1608. doi:10.1037/0022-3514.49.6.1586

Stone, A. A., Turkkan, J. S., Bachrach, C. A., Jobe, J. B., Kurtzman, H. S., & Cain, V. S. (2000). *The science of self-report: Implications for research and practice.* Mahwah, NJ: Erlbaum.

Symons, D. (1979). *The evolution of human sexuality.* New York, NY: Oxford University Press.

Taylor, P. A., & Glenn, N. D. (1976). The utility of education and attractiveness for females' status attainment through marriage. *American Sociological Review, 41,* 484–498. doi:10.2307/2094255

Taylor, S. E., & Gollwitzer, P. M. (1995). Effects of mindset on positive illusion. *Journal of Personality and Social Psychology, 69,* 213–226. doi:10.1037/0022-3514.69.2.213

Thibaut, J. W., & Kelley, H. H. (1959). *The social psychology of groups.* New York, NY: Wiley.

Thornhill, R., & Gangestad, S. W. (1999). The scent of symmetry: A human sex pheromone that signals fitness? *Evolution and Human Behavior, 20,* 175–201. doi:10.1016/S1090-5138(99)00005-7

Thornhill, R., Gangestad, S. W., Miller, R., Scheyd, G., Knight, J., & Franklin, M. (2003). MHC, symmetry, and body scent attractiveness in men and women. *Behavioral Ecology, 14,* 668–678. doi:10.1093/beheco/arg043

Todd, P. M., Penke, L., Fasolo, B., & Lenton, A. P. (2007). Different cognitive processes underlie human mate choices and mate preferences. *Proceedings of the National Academy of Sciences, USA, 104,* 15011–15016. doi:10.1073/pnas.0705290104

Townsend, J. M., & Levy, G. D. (1990). Effects of potential partners' costume and physical attractiveness on sexuality and partner selection. *Journal of Psychology: Interdisciplinary and Applied, 124,* 371–389. doi:10.1080/00223980.1990.10543232

Trivers, R. L. (1972). Parental investment and sexual selection. In B. Campbell (Ed.), *Sexual selection and the descent of man* (pp. 136–179). New York, NY: Aldine de Gruyter.

Vorauer, J. D., & Ross, M. (1996). The pursuit of knowledge in close relationships: An informational goals analysis. In G. J. O. Fletcher & J. Fitness (Eds.), *Knowledge structures in close relationships: A social psychological approach* (pp. 369–396). Mahwah, NJ: Erlbaum.

Wilbur, C. J., & Campbell, L. (2010). What do women want? An interactionist account of women's mate preferences. *Personality and Individual Differences, 49*, 749–754. doi:10.1016/j.paid.2010.06.020

Wilcox, A. J., Weinberg, C. R., & Baird, D. D. (1995). Timing of sexual intercourse in relation to ovulation: Effects on the probability of conception, survival of the pregnancy and sex of the baby. *New England Journal of Medicine, 333*, 1517–1521. doi:10.1056/NEJM199512073332301

Zahavi, A. (1975). Mate selection—A selection for handicap. *Journal of Theoretical Biology, 53*, 205–214. doi:10.1016/0022-5193(75)90111-3

PART IV

MOTIVATION, EMOTION, AND INTERSUBJECTIVITY

CHAPTER 10

GOAL PURSUIT IN RELATIONSHIPS

Gráinne M. Fitzsimons and Michelle R. vanDellen

Almost all goal pursuit occurs in relationships. People pursue their life goals—whether those are individual goals such as losing weight and earning a promotion or joint goals such as building a secure nest egg for retirement and raising healthy children—as subparts of larger social structures such as marriages, friendships, work teams, and families. With few exceptions, individuals are part of social relationships. And with few exceptions, important goal pursuits are affected by those relationships. Certainly, goal pursuits can be set independently, pursued independently, and accomplished independently—a person can be thirsty, walk to the vending machine, and buy a bottle of water—but it is rare that any goal pursuit of significance to an individual is independent from start to finish. Instead, most goal pursuits of significance are set, pursued, and accomplished within interdependent social contexts, triggered and shaped and influenced by other people.

Thus, we suggest that no model of self-regulation that starts and ends with the individual goal pursuer is a complete model of self-regulation. If researchers take the individual as the unit of analysis, they miss the interdependent processes of self-regulation. Those processes are the focus of this chapter. We suggest that a more appropriate unit of analysis for the study of goal pursuit is not the individual but the social relationship. Indeed, research in the past couple of decades has begun to uncover many ways in which apparently independent goal pursuits and self-control processes are actually interdependent, shaped by social relationships (see Fitzsimons &

Finkel, 2010, for review). In this chapter, we briefly present a new model of interdependent goal pursuit and then use that model as a framework to review recent research on interdependent goal pursuit from a number of different research perspectives.

TRANSACTIVE SELF-REGULATION: AN INTERPERSONAL MODEL OF GOAL PURSUIT

Building on the theoretical foundation laid by scholars interested in cognitive interdependence of self and other (Agnew, Van Lange, Rusbult, & Langston, 1998; Andersen & Cole, 1990; Aron, Aron, Tudor, & Nelson, 1991; Baldwin, 1992; Cross, Bacon, & Morris, 2000; Gardner, Gabriel, & Lee, 1999; Markus & Kitayama, 1991) and on research suggesting that goals are an important part of the relational self-concept (Fitzsimons & Bargh, 2003; Miller & Read, 1991; Moretti & Higgins, 1999a), we have developed a new model of self-regulation that highlights interdependence among the goal pursuits of close relationship partners (Fitzsimons, Finkel, & vanDellen, 2012). In this model, we suggest that when people are in interdependent relationships, such as those between long-term romantic partners, family members, or close coworkers, their goal pursuits can be conceptualized as one shared system of self-regulation. We suggest that this "coregulation" system has its own collective properties that emerge from the combination of the two interdependent goal pursuers; together, these collective and interdependent processes can fundamentally alter the individual's goal pursuit.

http://dx.doi.org/10.1037/14344-010
APA Handbook of Personality and Social Psychology: Vol. 3. Interpersonal Relations, M. Mikulincer and P. R. Shaver (Editors-in-Chief)

The interpersonal perspective taken by the trans-active self-regulation (TSR) model complements existing models of self-regulation, which have exclusively focused on intrapersonal processes. These models have generated a huge number of important insights about the fundamental processes of self-regulation, but because of their focus on the individual's internal characteristics and tendencies, they have tended to ignore the potential for interpersonal processes. For most people, this solitary, independent kind of goal pursuit—in which they set, choose, and pursue goals without the influence of other people—describes only a subset of their self-regulation. For most people, a more relational, interdependent, social kind of goal pursuit—in which they set, choose, and pursue goals because of other people, in spite of other people, and in cooperation or conflict with other people—describes a greater percentage of their self-regulation. Indeed, all of the goals that self-regulation researchers study, such as academic goals, career goals, power goals, mastery and learning goals, and health and fitness goals, are pursued while people are embedded in close relationships, and all of the psychological processes that self-regulation researchers study, such as willpower, ego depletion, and counteractive self-control, occur while people are embedded in close relationships. For these reasons, we believe that the time has come for researchers to put some serious thought into the interpersonal processes of self-regulation. It was this rationale that motivated the development of the TSR model.

According to the TSR model, interpersonal processes are fundamental to the self-regulation process. Of course, broader social relationships (such as those with social groups, institutions, and systems) are also important to self-regulation (e.g., Fishbach, Henderson, & Koo, 2011; Laurin, Fitzsimons, & Kay, 2011; Laurin, Kay, & Fitzsimons, 2012; Shteynberg & Galinsky, 2011) and are theoretically consistent with the TSR model (see Fitzsimons et al., 2012). However, given the topic of this chapter—goals in relationships—we limit our discussion to the interpersonal processes that occur among members of dyadic relationships. We focus on close relationships—those in which there is substantial behavioral interdependence—but do not

limit our analysis to romantic relationships. We believe that shared systems of self-regulation may exist in other relationship types as well, such as those between close friends, coworkers, or family members.

At the core of the TSR model is the proposal that close relationship partners are best conceptualized as subparts of one larger self-regulatory system rather than as independent agents or even linked agents. That is, we suggest that highly interdependent relationship partners essentially share one system of self-regulation. Construing two partners at this higher order unit or system level has two advantages compared with construing two partners as separate agents. First, this perspective allows the model to better capture the dynamic and multifaceted nature of the associations among partners' self-regulatory processes. In a transactive system, the two partners' self-regulatory processes are inextricably linked. They cannot be cleanly separated, leaving two independent goal pursuers; rather, the two goal pursuers' sequences of cognitions, motivations, and actions are so fully linked and interactive that to pull them apart would leave two incompletely understood agents. Thus, we suggest that in close relationships, the self-regulation of either individual is better understood in light of the myriad associations among the two. The second benefit of seeing both partners as one unit is that it allows for the existence of collective processes and outcomes. When two people work together as part of one system of self-regulation, these shared efforts can produce outcomes at the unit level in terms of efficiency, resource conservation, and, ultimately, success at achieving goals.

At an abstract level, the model echoes the pioneering work on interdependent cognitive processes done by researchers on transactive memory (Wegner, Erber, & Raymond, 1991). Transactive memory is a shared system for encoding, storing, and retrieving knowledge from memory (Wegner, 1987, 1995); it originated in the study of romantic couples (Wegner et al., 1991; also see Hollingshead, 1998) but has since been studied mostly within teams and groups (Austin, 2003; Liang, Moreland, & Argote, 1995). Research has suggested that transactive memory systems in groups promote more efficient individual and group performance. By differentiating memory responsibilities—who is supposed to remember what—groups can decrease redundancy and increase efficiency. Indeed, enhanced performance results from the use of transactive memory systems in both new and mature dyads and groups (Austin, 2003; Hollingshead, 1998; Liang et al., 1995). The TSR model suggests that memory processes and structures are not unique in their potential to be shared across individuals, and it examines the idea that even the broad class of self-regulatory processes can be beneficially construed as a shared, or coregulating, system in close relationships.

As shown in Figure 10.1, the TSR model breaks the process of self-regulation into four main phenomena of interest: goal qualities, goal pursuit, goal outcomes, and collective outcomes. The first three phenomena are linked in a dynamic feedback loop (Carver & Scheier, 1981, 1990) whereby all are theorized to influence each other. The model is designed to reflect two levels of transactive goal processes. Most simply, it represents how interpersonal processes shape individuals' pursuit of one specific goal from start to finish (in this case, it ends at the individual goal outcomes stage of the model). On a more complex level, the model also represents how interpersonal processes shape individuals' pursuit of the many goals they seek to accomplish in their lives more generally. Thus, on the simplest level, imagine that all you know about an individual is that he seeks to lose 5 pounds. That self-regulation process could be represented in our model by the content and value of the individual's goal (goal qualities; Box 1) and would be expressed in his behaviors (goal pursuit; Box 2), both of which predict his

success, failure, or disengagement from the goal (goal outcomes; Box 3).

Of course, the model is not about one individual's goal pursuit. It primarily seeks to advance knowledge of self-regulation by including the second partner in the model. Thus, the model also depicts his wife's feelings about his goal, her behavioral support for his goal, and how her own goals interact with and influence his goal qualities, pursuit, and outcome. On a more complex level, then, the model also describes how the individual's other goals, and his wife's other goals plus the many complex associations among these goal pursuits, combine to influence each of their individual successes and failures, as well as their collective outcomes. These processes are explained in the following discussion of the model.

Goal Qualities

We begin by briefly defining what we have called goal qualities: the cognitive, affective, and motivational qualities of goals. We emphasize five essential qualities, based on classic and current self-regulation research in personality, organizational, clinical, and social psychology (Atkinson, 1964; Bargh, Gollwitzer, Lee-Chai, Barndollar, & Trötschel, 2001; Baumeister, Vohs, & Tice, 2007; Carver & Scheier, 1990; Gollwitzer, 1999; Heckhausen, 1991; Kruglanski et al., 2002; Metcalfe & Mischel, 1999; Vallacher & Wegner, 1987). The five qualities are content, value, style, resources, and standards. By *content*, we mean the substance of a goal end state: What is the individual driven to achieve? Thus, content includes the end states of what are typically called needs or drives or higher order goals, such as

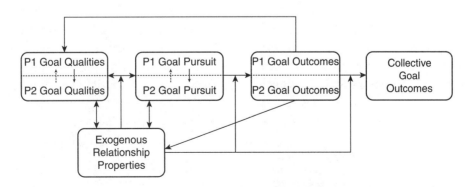

FIGURE 10.1.   Overview of the transactive self-regulation model. P1 = Person 1; P2 = Person 2.

"to feel close to others" or "to be an autonomous person," as well as means or lower order goals, such as "to earn a smile from my grumpy wife" or "to make this decision on my own" (see Vallacher & Wegner, 1987). By *value*, we mean the psychological value placed on the goal; this construct includes concepts such as motivation, commitment, importance, and so on. By *style*, we mean the orientation or manner in which the goal is pursued; this construct includes concepts such as approach versus avoidance orientations, regulatory foci and modes, and deliberative and implemental mindsets. By *resources*, we mean the self-regulatory resources available to the individual to allocate to goal pursuit; this construct includes concepts such as executive control and state and trait self-control resources. By *standards*, we mean both the specific criteria individuals use to evaluate goal progress (e.g., the desired amount of weight loss, the desired test grade) and individuals' efficacy—their sense that they can achieve those standards.

More important, in the TSR model these goal qualities can be directed at both the self and the other. Individuals can hold a given goal content for themselves, and they can also hold it for their partners. For example, a man may want to lose 5 pounds, or he may want his wife to lose 5 pounds. We refer to the latter example as a *partner-directed goal*. The same is true for each of the five basic goal qualities: Individuals may value goals differently for themselves and their partners, approach their own goals with different styles than they approach their partner's goals, have different standards and efficacy beliefs about their own and their partner's goals, and have different amounts of resources allocated for their own versus their partner's goals. Thus, with two partners, there are four categories of each of these qualities: Person 1 (P1)–P1 goal qualities (P1's qualities regarding his or her own goals), P1–Person 2 (P2) goal qualities (P1's qualities regarding his or her partner's goals), P2-P2 goal qualities (P2's qualities regarding her or his own goals), and P2-P1 goal qualities (P2's qualities regarding her or his partner's goals).

Perhaps most important, the TSR model states that all four of these categories of goal qualities are interpersonal: The content, value, style, resources, and standards of one partner both affect and are affected by the self-regulatory processes of the other partner. For example, an individual who cares a lot about his own appearance (P1-P1 goal value) will be more likely to care about his partner's appearance (P1-P2 goal value), and his partner is more likely to grow to care more about her appearance (P2-P2 goal value). As another example, an individual facing illness or stress may have temporarily low energy and self-control (P1-P1 resources), which may cause his partner to allocate more resources to her goals (P2-P1 resources). These influences of one partner's goal qualities on the other's can occur consciously or unconsciously, can be observable or implicit, and can operate entirely via cognitive processes or be mediated through the behavioral phenomena we discuss in the next section.

Goal Pursuit

By *goal pursuit*, we mean the action or volitional component of self-regulation (Heckhausen, 1991; Gollwitzer, 1990)—the behaviors that goal pursuers engage in to move toward their desired goal end states or to reduce the discrepancy between their current and desired end states (Carver & Scheier, 1981, 1990). These include nonobservable cognitive behaviors as well, if they are actions oriented toward making goal progress. For example, if the goal is to be happier, one goal pursuit behavior might be to ruminate less about an ex-boyfriend.

The same basic transactive principles apply to this phase of the model. First, an individual can engage in behaviors directed at his or her own goals (P1-P1 pursuit), or an individual can also engage in behaviors directed at his or her partner's goals (P1-P2 pursuit), such as providing direct or instrumental support for the partner's goals. For example, if the partner sets a goal to keep the house cleaner, the individual can pick up the baby's toys.[1] Second, these pursuits can affect each other, both indirectly in interaction with goal qualities and directly as in

---

[1]Of course, he may have his own motivations for helping her; we discuss these kinds of higher order goal effects throughout the chapter. For now, let's just take him at face value—he is picking up toys because his wife wants a tidier house.

behavioral interdependence. In the indirect route, for example, one partner's pursuit of a goal may make it more attractive or valuable for the other partner to start pursuing the goal (in which case, P1's effect on P2's pursuit is mediated through the P1-P1 goal value). In the direct route, one partner's pursuit may block or obstruct the other's pursuit. For example, it is substantively more difficult to pursue a goal of having a quiet night at home while one's partner pursues a goal of entertaining. In this case, P1's pursuit directly affects P2's pursuit, without changing P2's goal content, value, standards, and so forth.

As illustrated in the indirect route mentioned earlier, these first two phases of TSR can also interact with each other, such that one partner's goal pursuit can influence the other's goal qualities and vice versa.

These transactive self-regulatory processes are further shaped by non–self-regulatory relational processes. These processes are exogenous to the system in that they are not self-regulatory processes themselves but they are nonetheless still important interpersonal influences on self-regulation. In the TSR model, they function as moderating variables of the other key transactive processes. For example, if an individual feels dissatisfied with his or her relationship or has a conflict-prone relationship, that individual is more likely to react differently to his or her partner's goals than if the individual feels satisfied or has a conflict-free relationship.

Goal Outcomes

Ultimately, this model, as with most models of self-regulation, is concerned with predicting progress and attainment of goals. We refer to goal progress, success, failure, and disengagement as goal outcomes, and we include both outcomes for specific goals as well as overall outcomes on multiple goals in this construct. It is very clear from decades of research on self-regulation that individual goal qualities and pursuits have important consequences for goal outcomes. We suggest that the transactive links we have described have predictive power beyond the individual properties themselves. That is, we predict that the likelihood that an individual makes progress toward a goal, succeeds, or disengages is shaped

by transactive self-regulatory processes in addition to individual ones.

Although the focus of the TSR model is on predicting goal outcomes, we secondarily predict that these transactive processes also predict relationship outcomes, which then feed back into predicting goal outcomes. If a partner is instrumental to a given goal outcome, for example, this leads to increased closeness and satisfaction; this satisfaction may then predict an increased likelihood of behaving in a goal-supportive fashion.

Collective Outcomes

Unlike individual models of self-regulation, the TSR model does not end with individual goal attainment. Instead, we argue that the two goal pursuers are part of one system, which has its own outcomes—outcomes that are best understood at the unit or collective level rather than the individual level. Indeed, we further suggest that the combination of two transactive goal pursuers' outcomes is not simply the addition of both partners' individual outcomes. Instead, collective outcomes can be positive even when one partner's individual outcomes are negative. Whether collective outcomes are a simple sum of both partners' outcomes or some modified version depends on exogenous relationship variables. For example, if both partners agree that one person's goals are currently more important than the other's, as when one is preparing for a stressful exam, then collective outcomes should more heavily weight the more important partner's goals.

Evaluating Systems of Transactive Self-Regulation: The Importance of Collective Resources

We propose that transactive systems of self-regulation emerge organically from the high cognitive and behavioral interdependence of close relationship partners. Pursuing goals while being embedded in interpersonal relationships, we suggest, leads to the emergence of a dynamic, multifaceted, messy system of associations among one's pursuits and one's partners. However, it is also useful and valuable to take a functional perspective on these systems and to ask prescriptively how well-functioning and dysfunctional transactive systems work. What does being part of a system accomplish, if anything? If both partners are aiming to accomplish goals, it is logical to conclude that, ultimately, this model, as with all models of self-regulation, should predict goal attainment. Extending that theorizing, one of the unique aspects of this model is that it allows for an examination of the system-level outcomes. One primary outcome, we argue, is efficient use of resources. An effective dyad should be an efficient dyad: Together, partners should be able to increase their pool of self-regulation.

As with other forms of interdependence in close relationships, the extent to which two partners' goal pursuits are linked via these transactive processes varies. Some significant relationships have almost entirely separate goal pursuits, as with two adult siblings. In such relationships, it is more appropriate to describe the two partners as separate, independent goal pursuers, not as two subparts of one shared system of self-regulation. At the other extreme, some relationship partners have some degree of interdependence on nearly all of their goal pursuits. These relationships may most commonly involve romantic partners but may also involve close colleagues or friends. In such relationships, a transactive perspective is likely to be the best-fitting model of self-regulation. Because most individuals belong to at least one of these types of relationships, the TSR model has the potential to be widely useful in understanding goal pursuit.

GOALS IN RELATIONSHIPS: REVIEWING RECENT ADVANCES IN KNOWLEDGE

In this section, we briefly present nine major contributions to research on self-regulation in the context of interpersonal relationships. We first review the main findings of each research program. Next, we briefly discuss how that research can be understood as a transactive self-regulatory process. Finally, we point to missing links and future avenues for research in that area. We hope that taking a transactive systems perspective on these research programs will help draw links among the different research programs, provide structure to this rapidly growing field of research, and highlight exciting new directions for the study of self-regulation in social contexts.

When Partners Instill New Goals: Goal-Priming and Goal Contagion Processes

According to both laypeople and self-regulation scholars, individuals are the masters of their own fates. They choose and set their goals, and their actions and competencies determine their success or failure. In other words, individuals are the sole drivers of goal pursuit—independent agents in a solitary pursuit. Despite the cultural consensus around this somewhat romantic portrayal, we believe that individual goal pursuit is often not as independent as it seems. In many cases, the goals that individuals pursue and believe to be independent (Wegner & Wheatley, 1999) are put in place by others in the social environment. Advances in the understanding of the cognitive nature of goals within the field of social cognition (e.g., Bargh, 1990; Bargh et al., 2001) have made it possible to study these kinds of social influences more easily without having to ask people whether they are so affected and without people even having to recognize that such influences have occurred.

The first such influence occurs because of the repetitive nature of most social interactions. Because individuals tend to repeatedly think about, discuss, and pursue their goals in the presence of their relationship partners—coworkers, friends, romantic partners—it is likely that, over time, cognitive associations develop between those goals and the interpersonal relationships in which they are pursued (Miller & Read, 1991; Moretti & Higgins, 1999b). Once these associations have developed, individuals' behavior is vulnerable to the influence of any activation of the relationship representation in memory, whether that activation is caused by the partner's physical or psychological presence. When a partner representation is activated, the linked goal is automatically activated as well, and it can then go on to guide perception and behavior just like a goal that has purely individual origins (Fitzsimons & Bargh, 2003; Shah, 2003). Through this simple cognitive mechanism, relationship partners can trigger goal pursuit without intending to do so and without the goal pursuers even recognizing the influence (Bargh et al., 2001; Wegner & Wheatley, 1999).

Partners' automatic influence on goal pursuit was first studied by Andersen, Reznik, and Manzella (1996), who found that when an individual met someone new who resembled an existing relationship partner, feelings of motivation toward the partner were transferred to the new person (Andersen et al., 1996). Building on those initial findings, several programs of research have shown that priming or subtly reminding individuals of relationship partners automatically affects their goal-directed behavior (Fitzsimons & Bargh, 2003; Shah, 2003). These studies showed that when participants were primed with relationship partners such as friends, romantic partners, or family members, the goals that they reported pursuing with those partners were also activated and guided behavior. For example, in one study undergraduate students were primed with the representation of their mothers (vs. a control prime) and then completed an academic achievement task. Students who were primed with their mothers outperformed those who received the control prime but only if they had (earlier in the semester) reported a goal to achieve academically to please their mother. Similarly, students subliminally primed with their fathers outperformed control participants but only if they reported a close relationship with their father and felt their father cared about their academic achievement (Shah, 2003).

As suggested by Shah's (2003) early findings, these automatic effects of partners on individual goal pursuit do not happen in every relationship or in every situation. For example, characteristics of the partner matter: When individuals perceive their relationship partners as controlling or bossy, they pursue goals that oppose their partner's wishes (Chartrand, Dalton, & Fitzsimons, 2007). Characteristics of the individual also matter: Individuals high in reactance pursued contrasting goals, whereas individuals high in the need to belong showed stronger assimilative goal-priming effects (Morrison, Wheeler, & Smeesters, 2007).

Interacting with a relationship partner—or thinking of a partner—can thus trigger goal pursuit and shape behavior because of simple associative processes resulting from well-practiced routines in long-term relationships. In addition to these kinds of schema-based processes, another well-documented route exists through which others in the social environment can trigger goals—one that is not dependent on the existence of any kind of relationship whatsoever. According to research on goal contagion, individuals who simply view another person's behavior automatically infer goals underlying that behavior; once those goals are inferred (and more accessible in the mind of the perceiver), they function like all active goals (Bargh, Green, & Fitzsimons, 2008) and guide the individual's behavior (Aarts, Gollwitzer, & Hassin, 2004; Dik & Aarts, 2007). In a number of studies, Aarts and colleagues have shown that being exposed to another person's goal-directed behavior can lead individuals to pursue the same goal, even in an entirely different context and apparently without any awareness of the source of the adopted goal. For example, in one study, heterosexual male participants who read about a character who seemed to be pursuing a goal for sex (vs. a different goal) went on to behave in a more flattering and ingratiating fashion to a female confederate, implying that they too had active sexual motives. Aspects of the goal pursuer have been shown to be influential moderators of goal contagion effects: When the other person appeared to be expending more (vs. less) effort toward the goal, the contagion effect was stronger (Dik & Aarts, 2007); when the partner appeared to have successfully completed the goal, the contagion effect disappeared, suggesting that the observer satiated the goal vicariously (McCulloch, Fitzsimons, Chua, & Albarracin, 2011).

Goal contagion studies have mostly examined the effects of a stranger's behavior. However, because relationship partners commonly witness each other pursuing goals, they have many more opportunities to catch each other's goal pursuits than do strangers; studying goal contagion within romantic partnerships, and determining the consequences for relationship outcomes, are important directions for future research (see Laurin et al., 2012).

Both of these literatures examine incidental influences of the partner on individual goal pursuit. Such influences are likely to be extremely common and may help to explain some of the hugely powerful social network effects on health outcomes such as obesity (Christakis & Fowler, 2007). Also common, however, is the influence of partners who actually intend to directly change an individual's goals. When individuals want to change their partners, they often do not implement goal-priming and contagion processes (although certainly some people do try to inspire their partners via their own goal pursuits). Instead, they more typically try to talk to their partners; motivate their partners with incentives, bribes, and threats; or engage in other kinds of more direct behavior control attempts. These attempts to instill new goals in a relationship partner have varying degrees of success, some of which is predicted by the manner in which the partner approaches the situation (Overall, Fletcher, Simpson, & Sibley, 2009). For example, individuals who were more direct in their initial discussions of how they wanted their partners to change their behaviors were initially seen as less influential by both partners and objective coders, but over the following year, individuals with more direct partners showed more behavior change in line with their partner's wishes (Overall et al., 2009).

Thus, from these disparate lines of research we can conclude that relationship partners seem to exert influence over the goals that their partners pursue. Next, we turn to discussing the likely processes through which these effects occur within a TSR system. From the perspective of the TSR model, straightforward significant-other goal-priming effects (e.g., Fitzsimons & Bargh, 2003; Shah, 2003) can be the result of two processes. In one description of the process, significant others simply prime the goals the individual typically pursues with those others (Fitzsimons & Bargh, 2003); the individual's goals are thus interpersonal goals—"I want to please my mother by succeeding at college" or "I want to help my friend." In the TSR model, those goals are captured by P1-P2 goal content and pursuit—the individual's goals toward the partner. In another description of the process, significant others prime their own goals in the individual's mind (Shah, 2003). This effect is the influence of the goal content and value of one partner on the goal content and value (and subsequent pursuit and outcome) of the other partner. When an individual (P1) is reminded of a relationship partner (P2), the partner's (P2's)

goal content is activated. Whatever the individual was thinking about before the partner arrived on the scene, the arrival (whether physical or mental) automatically activates the partner's goals in the individual's mind. Because individual action is so heavily shaped by whatever is accessible, the individual then behaves as though the activated goals are his or her own. These basic findings have been shown to be further moderated by exogenous (i.e., non–self-regulatory) relationship variables. For example, Shah (2003) showed that individuals show these effects only when they feel close to the primed other. In this case, an aspect of relationship quality moderates the transactive link between P1 and P2 goal content.

Goal contagion findings have also been shown to be moderated by exogenous relationship variables. For example, Laurin et al. (2012) showed that individuals high in relationship power do not show these basic effects. Their goal pursuit is unaffected by the goal content or pursuit of their partners. Similarly, Walton and Cohen (2011) have found that a sense of belonging to the academic community predicts whether a new student will absorb the goals of the community. In both of these examples, a relationship variable moderates the transactive link between P2-P2 pursuit and P1-P1 content and pursuit.

Direct attempts to change the partner, such as those studied by Overall et al. (2009), most likely operate through different transactive processes. In these cases, the influence of one partner on the other's self-regulation is not incidental as it commonly is in the case of goal priming and goal contagion. Instead, in these cases one partner is explicitly attempting to alter the other's goal pursuit. P1 is not influenced by P2's goal for him- or herself (P2-P2 goal content); instead, P1 is influenced by P2's goal for P1 (e.g., to lose weight, to listen more). In the TSR model, this is represented as a P2-P1 goal—a goal that one partner has for the other. What transactive effect does P2's goal have on P1? P1's goal content might change in one of two ways. First, P1 may truly take on the goal as his or her own new goal. Second, P1 may pursue a new goal of engaging in the desired behavior to please or mollify the partner. P1's goal value might change, too: P1 might start caring more about an already-present goal.

Finally, P1 may act in ways that seem consistent with P2's goal but fail to internalize the goal. If so, P1's goal pursuit might change without any real modification of his or her goal content.

This analysis connects to research by self-determination theorists on the internalization of goals: When goals are extrinsic, P2-P1 goal content is altering P1-P1 behavior directly; when they are internalized, that effect is likely mediated by a real change in P1-P1 goal content and value, such that the individual comes to own and care about this goal for him- or herself. In future research, it would be interesting to examine these kinds of process differences and how they play out over time to affect goal and relationship outcomes. For example, if partners succeed in affecting each other's behaviors, does this mean they have successfully altered each other's cognitive goal content as they hoped? Or is one partner pursuing another goal, such as to get the other partner off his or her back? What predicts when people will truly take on the goal as their own versus pursue the behaviors to satisfy a goal to please the partner?

When Partners Are Instrumental to Ongoing Goals

Even if goals are set into motion in a completely independent fashion—the individual, free of influence, chooses to pursue a new goal—the subsequent path between the individual's goal content and his or her eventual success or failure will be greatly shaped by the individual's relationships with others. As explained by interdependence theory (Kelley & Thibaut, 1978; Rusbult & Van Lange, 2003) and the emotions-in-relationships model (Berscheid & Ammazzalorso, 2001) and further elaborated on in work on social support and dependency regulation processes (e.g., Brunstein, Dangelmayer, & Schultheiss, 1996; Feeney, 2004), relationship partners have numerous opportunities to affect each other's goal pursuit, and these effects, in turn, can greatly influence the nature and quality of their relationships.

Research on instrumentality (Fitzsimons & Fishbach, 2010; Fitzsimons & Shah, 2008, 2009) has explored how relationships are affected by partners' positive or negative effects on each other's

goal pursuits. In the typical study examining this topic, participants nominate relationship partners—for example, friends, family members, or romantic partners—who either have positive effects on their progress toward a given goal (i.e., instrumental others) or have no effect on that goal's progress (i.e., noninstrumental others). Instrumentality is defined as "the existence of this person in your life makes it likelier that you will achieve this goal" (Fitzsimons & Shah, 2008). When goals are subsequently brought to mind via standard goal-priming procedures (Bargh et al., 2001), they shape how close individuals feel to their relationship partners, such that individuals tend to feel closer to others whom they perceive as instrumental for activated goals and less close to others whom they perceive as noninstrumental for those goals. For example, when an academic achievement was active, participants reported more closeness to friends as instrumental for achievement and less closeness to friends as not instrumental for achievement. Instrumentality for currently active goals also shapes memory for members of one's social network. For example, after a goal prime, individuals make more memory errors among instrumental others and among noninstrumental others than between members of the two categories (Fitzsimons & Shah, 2009).

In follow-up research, instrumentality was shown to primarily benefit relationships during the period in which a goal has high motivational priority—that is, when it is relatively more important to the individual than other goals (Fitzsimons & Fishbach, 2010). When a goal drops in priority, as it does after the individual makes good progress on the goal, instrumentality for that goal ceases to influence relationship evaluations. In a series of studies, after participants felt they had made good progress on a given goal, they stopped showing an evaluative preference for others who were instrumental for that goal. Instead, they switched allegiances, preferring others who were instrumental for other goals on which less progress has been made and that were thus currently higher in priority. Although this effect may seem to reflect a lack of gratitude for and appreciation of partners (see Converse & Fishbach, 2012, for a very interesting demonstration that individuals feel more grateful to helpful others before—rather than after—a goal is attained), it is also true that many close partners are instrumental to more than one important goal. Evaluations of those partners are less likely to be affected by fluctuations in the priority of any one goal.

From the perspective of the TSR model, instrumentality can be captured by at least three transactive processes or routes:

A. If the instrumentality is truly incidental, as in the case when "my husband has friends in my desired industry," it is likely to be best captured by an exogenous relationship variable strengthening the link between P1's goal content and P1's goal outcome. That is, something non–self-regulatory about the partner—his friend network—shapes the individual's likelihood of turning goal content into goal success.

B. If the instrumentality is intentional, resulting from the partner's direct help, it is captured by a different transactive link. In this case, P2's direct pursuit of P1's goal (P2-P1 pursuit) strengthens the link between P1's content and outcome. That is, P2's direct work on behalf of the individual shapes the individual's likelihood of turning his goal content into goal success.

C. If the instrumentality is caused by the other person sharing the same goal or a compatible goal, making the environment more goal friendly, that is captured by yet another transactive process. In this case, P2-P2 content affects the link between P1-P1 content and P1-P1 outcome, mediated by pursuit. That is, P2's goal content affects P1's likelihood of turning his goal content into goal success.

Research on instrumentality has examined the effects of these processes on relationship and goal outcomes. The finding that instrumentality leads to positive relationship evaluations is captured by the effect of one of the previously mentioned processes on relationship quality. The finding that instrumentality can promote goal success—or, more accurately, that those who draw closer to instrumental others are more successful over time—is a particularly interesting case. It is captured by the moderation of P1 goal content on P1 goal

outcome by the link between instrumentality (one of the previously described processes) and relationship outcomes. That is, whether P1 successfully turns his or her goal content ("I want to get an A") into his or her goal outcome (getting an A) is moderated by the strength of P1's link between instrumentality for this goal and relationship evaluations. If P1 strongly prefers academically instrumental (vs. noninstrumental) others (i.e., if P1's evaluations are strongly dependent on academic instrumentality), P1 has higher goal outcomes.

As the discussion of different types of instrumentality suggests, this research is in its very early phases. At this point, no research has examined different types of instrumentality, which means that little is known about how these different transactive processes may change goal and relationship outcomes. This is one promising avenue for future research. Different ways to be instrumental may produce different outcomes for goal and relationship outcomes. For example, it would be interesting to examine whether partners who are instrumental incidentally (through Route A, described earlier) receive the same relationship benefits as partners who are instrumental intentionally, by directly helping the individual (through Route B).

Examining the link between instrumentality and other goal qualities—such as resources and efficacy—also has the potential to make an interesting contribution to the literature. For example, a partner's instrumentality may increase the individual's efficacy, leading the individual to feel more confident about her or his likely success (e.g., "Now that I have this help, I can do it"). Alternatively, as we discuss in the next section on social support, some types of instrumentality may also decrease efficacy because they imply that the partner does not have high efficacy for the individual (P2-P1 efficacy). Ultimately, instrumentality Route B should also have a direct beneficial impact on an individual's resources; if someone is helping, the individual should need to expend fewer resources on the goal and should thus have more resources available for other pursuits. These ideas are at the core of research on outsourcing, which is reflected in the TSR model by the effect of the instrumental Route B mentioned earlier (i.e., P2's pursuit of P1's goal) on P1's pursuit. The outsourcing effect is partially driven by changes in P1 efficacy ("I feel more optimistic about the future") that lead to an ironic reduction in pursuit and is also known to be moderated by P1's resources (i.e., individuals are more likely to show the effect if resources are low).

Partner Support for Goal Pursuit

Perhaps the clearest way that goals and relationships are connected is that individuals in relationships tend to support their partners' goal pursuits and receive support from their partners for their own goal pursuits. Such goal-relevant social support can be defined as processes by which individuals help others pursue their goals. Social support is one way in which partners can be instrumental, as we have described, although support does not always have positive outcomes for goal pursuit, as we discuss later. Overall, social support research conducted in the domain of health has shown that when individuals have social support, they are more likely to pursue their health goals. For instance, people who have stronger social support are more likely to eat healthy, quit smoking, and engage in physical activity (Allgöwer, Wardle, & Steptoe, 2001; Cohen & Lichtenstein, 1990; Davison, Cutting, & Birch, 2003; Eyler et al., 1999; Novak & Webster, 2011; Reblin & Uchino, 2008).

More broadly speaking, partner support is important for facilitating goal pursuit (Feeney, 2004). Individuals who receive action-oriented and emotional support from their partners for their goal pursuits are more likely to pursue their individual goals (Overall, Fletcher, & Simpson, 2010). Goal-relevant social support enhances intrapersonal goal qualities (e.g., individual commitment to goal pursuit), such that individuals who are both highly committed to their goals and report being supported by their partners are those most likely to engage in goal pursuit (Brunstein et al., 1996). Willingness to accept support from one's partner also seems to be an important component of whether goal-relevant social support produces independent goal pursuit (Feeney,

2007). As an added benefit, receiving support from one's partner enhances feelings of relationship satisfaction and commitment (Brunstein et al., 1996; Overall et al., 2010). Because individuals in better relationships tend to give and receive goal-relevant social support more frequently, such processes can provide an upward cycle for relationship partners who invest in each other's goal pursuits.

The benefits of goal-relevant social support do not necessarily come from explicitly experienced conversations and influences from one's partners (Lakey & Orehek, 2011). In fact, being aware of support from another person may undermine goal qualities such as self-efficacy (Bolger & Amarel, 2007). Indeed, invisible support—support that is provided by one's partner but is not recognized—may actually facilitate adjustment during periods of stress, such as when preparing for an intensive professional exam (Bolger, Zuckerman, & Kessler, 2000). The benefits of invisible goal-relevant social support for goal pursuit are a function of both the provider's skillful support provision and the recipient's lack of awareness that the support occurred (Howland & Simpson, 2010).

Social support is a complex and multifaceted phenomenon, and as such it does not affect self-regulation through one unitary process. Instead, there are likely to be dozens of routes through which different kinds of social support can elicit effects on self-regulatory outcomes. In this chapter, we highlight three such routes. First and most straightforward, partners can provide instrumental assistance to each other's goal pursuit. In the TSR model, this is captured by a link connecting P2-P1 goal pursuit to P1 outcome: When P2 behaviorally pursues P1's goal on P1's behalf, P1 is more likely to succeed at meeting or moving closer to the goal. For instance, if P1 has a goal of getting a good score on the Graduate Record Examination, P2 could pursue this goal by reviewing vocabulary words with P1.[2] P1's outcome on the examination will likely improve thanks to P2's efforts to help him or her learn and review vocabulary words. However, as previously discussed, direct social support in relationships can

[2]Note that P2 is simultaneously pursuing two goals here with one behavior. P2 is pursuing P1's goal of learning vocabulary and also her or his own goal of helping P1.

also backfire. To the extent that P2-P1 goal pursuit is viewed as intrusive (e.g., Bolger et al., 2000; Feeney, 2004; Feeney & Thrush, 2010), P1 may experience a decrease in self-efficacy, which is a fundamental goal quality. Returning to the example of an individual learning vocabulary, if the support the individual receives from his or her partner suggests that the individual needs the partner's help, the individual may feel less able to learn on his or her own. When the individual has opportunities to study on his or her own, the individual may feel less confident in his or her ability and, therefore, not take advantage of independent opportunities for learning. Social support, then, can feed back into the goal system, producing less P1-P1 goal pursuit.

Second, partners can also support goal pursuit by valuing the goals that their partners value. In our transactive model, we suggest that P2-P1 value predicts P1-P1 goal pursuit and ultimately P1 success. For example, if both P1-P1 and P2-P1 value for learning vocabulary is high, P1 will be more likely to engage in studying. A mismatch between P2-P1 value and P1-P1 value can have the opposite effect, however. When individuals do not value a goal that their partner values for them, they often react with less goal pursuit (Ranby & Aiken, 2012).

Third, individuals can provide their partners with opportunities for goal pursuit. Perhaps P1 wants to train for a long-distance bicycling race. To accomplish this goal, P1 needs to train for several hours on the weekends. This goal pursuit could interfere with P2's goal to visit the farmer's market every Saturday morning together. Exogenous factors related to the relationship (e.g., relationship commitment, satisfaction) and factors related to P2 (e.g., the extent to which P2 has a content goal related to P1's being physically fit) should moderate the extent to which P1 content (completing the long-distance race) and P1 goal pursuit (training for the race) can occur. For instance, if P2 is insecurely attached, she or he may be less willing to sacrifice the goal of spending time with P1 to support P1's training needs. However, if P2 has a fitness goal for P1, P2 may encourage P1 to train and instead go to the farmer's market with a friend. Opportunity provision may also occur indirectly. Perhaps P1 usually handles the yard work on Saturday mornings and so

cannot both train and keep up with the yard work. P2 could then provide an opportunity for P1 to complete this training by either hiring someone to do the yard work for P1 or doing it her- or himself.

Partners as Sculptors: The Michelangelo Phenomenon

Individuals pursue goals that are short term and concrete, such as to clean up the backyard, and they also pursue goals that are long term and abstract, such as to be an organized person (Emmons, 1992; Vallacher & Wegner, 1987). They also pursue goals that are ought-directed ("I should" goals, which are oriented toward responsibilities and obligations) and ideal-directed ("I want" goals, which are oriented toward ideals and hopes; Higgins, 1987; Markus & Nurius, 1986). Relationship partners affect the successful pursuit of all different types of goals, and there are likely to be unique predictors and consequences of being instrumental (Fitzsimons & Shah, 2008) for different categories of goals. Research on the Michelangelo phenomenon investigates one such set of unique processes, emphasizing the importance of supporting partners' ideal-self goals. The term refers to Michelangelo Buonarroti's description of sculpture as a process in which the artist's purpose is to reveal the ideal form already existing within the block of marble. Applying that metaphor to close relationships, Rusbult and her colleagues theorized that partners may also "sculpt" each other, helping one another to become the ideal selves they have the potential to be (Drigotas, Rusbult, Wieselquist, & Whitton, 1999; Rusbult, Finkel, & Kumashiro, 2009).

One important individual difference that affects the Michelangelo process is regulatory mode (Kruglanski et al., 2002). Locomotion is the tendency to initiate and sustain movement from state to state; high locomotors want to "just do it." Locomotion tendencies in either the sculptor (the partner) or the sculptee (the individual) facilitate growth toward the ideal self (Kumashiro, Rusbult, Finkenauer, & Stocker, 2007). In contrast, assessment is the tendency to evaluate and appraise goals or to "do it right" (Kruglanski et al., 2002). Assessment tendencies in either the sculptor or the sculptee inhibit growth toward the ideal self (Kumashiro et al., 2007). The Michelangelo phenomenon also appears to be most successful when the sculptor (the partner) already possesses the characteristics that the sculptee (the individual) aspires to achieve (Rusbult, Kumashiro, Kubacka, & Finkel, 2009). When the partner already has these traits, the partner provides more affirmation to the individual, which is a major predictor of ideal-self growth. Affirmation is defined as perceiving—and treating—the target in ways that are compatible with the target's ideal self (Drigotas et al., 1999; Rusbult et al., 2009). This affirmation, in turn, predicts both greater ideal-self growth and better relationship outcomes.

As with most interpersonal goal effects, the Michelangelo phenomenon is complex, and research to date has been inconclusive about its underlying psychological mechanisms. The Michelangelo metaphor suggests that the process involves the sculptor engaging in behavioral pursuit on behalf of the sculptee; that is, the partner works toward the individual's own goal. In the TSR model, the metaphor would thus be captured by P2-P1 goal pursuit: P2 is working toward P1's goal (e.g., being an organized person). The research findings we have described, however, do not operate by the same self-regulatory processes as the metaphor. For example, the phenomenon's key process of perceptual affirmation is captured by P2-P1 efficacy ("I see you as organized, when being organized is your ideal-self goal"). Perceptual affirmation has been hypothesized to affect P1-P1 efficacy ("Now I see myself as more organized"), which then influences P1's pursuit and outcome. Although P1's behavioral goal pursuit has not been directly measured in research, it seems to be the likeliest mediator of the demonstrated link between P2-P1 efficacy (perceptual affirmation) and P1 success. The moderation of this effect by P2 qualities—such as P2's locomotion or to what extent P2 already possesses P1's ideal traits—can also be captured in the model. P2's locomotion would be reflected by a moderating effect of P2's self-regulatory style (one of the model's goal qualities)

on the perceptual affirmation process described earlier. Similarly, the extent to which P2 approximates P1's ideal self would be reflected by P2's goal outcomes moderating the affirmation process.[3]

Examining the Michelangelo phenomenon from the perspective of the transactive processes it reflects points to a number of valuable directions for future research. First, there is as yet no clear evidence for how the basic phenomenon translates into successful goal pursuit. Second, there are interesting new questions that could be asked, for example, are other goal qualities important moderators, beyond the style or manner in which goals are approached (i.e., individuals' regulatory mode)? Resources are also likely to have an important influence: Partners with more self-regulatory resources may be better able to help each other pursue ideal-self goals and be better able to capitalize on partner affirmation and turn it into success. Similarly, content may be important as well: Are some domains of ideal-self goals easier or harder for partners to support? Finally, efficacy also seems important: Are individuals who are lower in efficacy more responsive to affirmation? Or are they harder to sculpt, typically resisting affirming responses from their partners?

When Partners Inspire: Effects of Partner Success on Motivation

By affirming the partner, individuals can inspire the partner to pursue his or her ideal-self goals more successfully. Individuals can also inspire others by acting as role models for successful goal pursuit. For example, being in a relationship with a highly productive person who pursues fulfilling goals in an energized fashion is likely to affect one's own goal pursuit. Of course, inspiration is not the only reaction that individuals are likely to experience when they are interdependent with a highly successful other. Indeed, in some cases, individuals may need to protect themselves from potential social comparison threats that may arise if close others are too successful at reaching high standards. When close others' success is in domains that are perceived as

---

[3]This description of the process requires the assumption that P2 is motivated at least to some degree to possess these desired qualities. If P2 were totally uninterested in being organized, for example, it would not be accurate to depict P2's organization as a goal outcome. Instead, the model would describe that effect as an exogenous relationship variable, much like any other non–self-regulatory trait possessed by either partner.

valuable to the self and represent successes that are possible to attain, individuals tend to demonstrate increased motivation and goal pursuit (Lockwood, Jordan, & Kunda, 2002; Lockwood & Kunda, 1997). However, when social comparison threats are salient, individuals may be less likely to pursue goals that close others have attained (Tesser, Millar, & Moore, 1988; vanDellen, Moon, & Johnson, 2012). In addition, individuals in interdependent relationships may be at risk of perceiving their partners' success in goal pursuit as a substitute for their own efforts. For instance, when individuals witness someone else finishing a goal, they show less accessibility and motivation for that goal pursuit themselves (McCulloch et al., 2011).

In the TSR model, this research represents the link between P1 outcome and P2 goal qualities. Specifically, P2 efficacy and P2 standards may change as a function of the extent to which P1 succeeds at reaching his or her goal. Moderation of this link may occur by P2 goal content (e.g., the match between P2-P2 goal content and P1's outcome) and exogenous variables in the relationship, such as closeness and satisfaction. Whether P1's success has positive or negative effects further depends on content: If P1's success on a goal benefits both members of the couple (e.g., saving money for a vacation), the whole system benefits if P1's success curtails the pursuit of P2 (e.g., P2 is free to pursue other goals). However, if the goal is such that individual pursuit remains important (e.g., both members of a couple need to reach a healthy weight), P1's success could inadvertently reduce the extent to which P2 pursues a goal that she or he has yet to reach.

High-Maintenance Interaction

We have discussed how individuals' goal pursuit is affected by their partners' goals and support; we now discuss how their successful pursuit is further influenced by the quality of their interpersonal interactions. In general, both the quantity and the quality of social interaction improves cognitive functioning (Ybarra et al., 2008; Ybarra, Winkielman, Yeh, Burnstein, & Kavanagh, 2011). Even thinking about loved ones (e.g., family members) can increase self-regulation performance (Stillman, Tice, Fincham, & Lambert, 2009).

However, interpersonal interactions are not always seamless and easy. Building on evidence that when individuals exert self-control their capacity for further self-regulation is attenuated (Baumeister, Bratslavsky, Muraven, & Tice, 1998), research has shown that interpersonal interactions that are draining and require effortful self-regulation impair cognitive functioning and self-regulatory performance. For instance, when interpersonal interactions do not go as expected, individuals perform worse on subsequent self-regulatory tasks (Dalton, Chartrand, & Finkel, 2010). Likewise, when interactions are difficult or frustrating, as when individuals try to complete a task with a partner who is offering unhelpful or unclear advice, individuals lose self-regulatory resources as a result of regulating their emotions, responses, and behaviors during the interaction (Finkel et al., 2006).

Other interpersonal interactions that require effort or self-regulation may likewise impair self-regulation. For instance, when individuals engage in effortful self-presentation, they become less likely to persist on difficult academic problems and tasks that require physical effort (Vohs, Baumeister, & Ciarocco, 2005). Similarly, heterosexual men who are trying to impress attractive women show impairments in cognitive functioning (Karremans, Verwijmeren, Pronk, & Reitsma, 2009). Whereas self-presentational concerns involve regulating the self to promote relationships with others, similar concerns about keeping oneself from offending others can likewise make interpersonal interactions effortful. For instance, individuals who are motivated to appear egalitarian and avoid offending their partner in an interaction with an individual of a different race demonstrate later impairments in executive functioning (Richeson & Shelton, 2003; Richeson & Trawalter, 2005). Thus, although smooth interpersonal interactions can support self-regulation, difficult interpersonal interactions can leave individuals vulnerable to a loss of regulatory resources.

In addition to influences from immediate interpersonal interactions, the salience of specific interpersonal influences can support and hinder self-regulation. When salient close others are good at self-control, individuals' own success at self-control increases; when salient close others are poor at self-control, individuals' own success at self-control decreases (vanDellen & Hoyle, 2010). The influence of salient others on self-regulation is not always so straightforward, however. Research on mental simulation has suggested that imagining behaviors is often enough to produce effects that are consistent with having actually engaged in the imagined behaviors (e.g., Morewedge, Huh, & Vosgerau, 2010). Such mental simulation effects can occur when individuals empathically consider others' behaviors. For instance, when participants in one study merely thought about a hungry waitress resisting food, they demonstrated increased self-control (Ackerman, Goldstein, Shapiro, & Bargh, 2009). However, when individuals engaged in empathy for this hungry waitress, putting themselves in her shoes, they demonstrated decreased self-control. Such decreases may be due to mental simulation facilitating vicarious depletion effects, or they may be due to the fact that taking others' perspectives can at times be difficult (Vorauer, Martens, & Sasaki, 2009).

From a TSR perspective, this research on vicarious depletion is described by the link between P1 resources and P2 resources, subsequent goal pursuit, and goal outcome. In addition, to the extent that P1's reduced resources make P1 unpleasant or difficult as an interaction partner, P2's goal pursuit and likelihood of goal success will suffer. Thus, if both members of a transactive system are aware of the effortful goal pursuit of P1, both will experience a cost in their ability to pursue goals (P1 because his or her resources are depleted from effortful goal pursuit, and P2 because her or his resources are depleted from interacting with P1). Thus, the characteristics of the goal pursuits of one partner directly influence the goal pursuits of the other.

One potential area for interesting future research could be the similarity of partners' goal content and how it affects resources. Clearly, if resources for self-regulation are limited (Baumeister et al., 1998), then if P1 puts many of his or her resources into his or her own (P1-P1) goal pursuit, P1 is likely to have fewer resources to put toward pursuit of his or her partner's goals (P1-P2). Given that, goal compatibility is very important in predicting resource use

(Gere, Schimmack, Pinkus, & Lockwood, 2011). If goals are shared, resources put into one's goals are also by definition put into the other's goals. In addition, as interdependence theory would suggest, if P1's and P2's goal pursuit is dissimilar, this may reduce the couple's overall success because of conflict. To the extent that P1 does not share P2's goals for P2, or to the extent that P1 pursues incompatible goals for him- or herself, then P2's goal pursuits may be weakened because of the conflict P2 experiences as a result of P1's lack of interest in P2's goals. Therefore, a match between the goal pursuits of both partners should prevent regulatory resources from being drained during their interactions and allow for greater resources to be spent on productive goal pursuit, ultimately resulting in greater outcome success for both and the potential to conserve resources for other goal pursuits.

This perspective highlights the importance of accurately understanding and monitoring partners' goals. When partners possess the same goals for each other (P1-P2 and P2-P2 match), they can prevent regulatory resources from being unnecessarily compromised in everyday interactions between partners.

Motivational Strategies in Relationships

Goals vary not only in content—achievement versus intimacy versus power—but also in the style and strategies with which they are pursued. Even if two individuals are pursuing the same goal—say, to have a good relationship—each individual could pursue that goal in many different ways, both in terms of the specific means each can use (e.g., to increase the quality or the quantity of time spent together) and in terms of the broader strategic orientation each adopts (e.g., to be cautious or risky, to focus on relationship positives or negatives). The research we discuss in this section highlights the importance of these general strategic orientations—the style with which individuals pursue their goals—in understanding goals in relationship contexts.

According to one prominent approach, goals can be framed in terms of approach or avoidance, in which individuals seek to move toward a positive outcome (approach) or move away from a negative outcome (avoid; Carver & White, 1994;

Elliot & Covington, 2001; Gray, 1990). Individuals can pursue the same goal end state (save money), but they can do so by approaching positives (clip coupons) or avoiding negatives (avoid splurges). These strategic orientations have been studied within relationship contexts (see Gable, 2006), and they have important implications for relationship processes. For example, for individuals with strong approach goals, the existence of positives—such as passion or intimacy—determines their relationship satisfaction, whereas for individuals with strong avoidance goals, the existence of negatives—such as insecurity or conflict—determines their satisfaction (Gable & Poore, 2008). Approach and avoidance styles of goal pursuit influence relationship quality through a number of different routes, such as affecting how individuals construe making relationship sacrifices (Impett, Gable, & Peplau, 2005) and how they construe sexual behavior and desire (Impett, Peplau, & Gable, 2005; Impett, Strachman, Finkel, & Gable, 2008). Overall, research has suggested that taking an approach goal orientation leads to better outcomes for relationships than does taking an avoidance goal orientation (Impett et al., 2010).

Another goal orientation that has been linked with relationship outcomes is regulatory focus, or the extent to which individuals have a promotion versus a prevention orientation (Higgins, 1997; Molden, Lee, & Higgins, 2008). According to regulatory focus theory, individuals pursue positive and negative end states via two different orientations. Promotion-focused individuals emphasize gains versus nongains; they are oriented toward not missing out on opportunities and tend to pursue opportunities eagerly. Prevention-focused individuals emphasize losses versus nonlosses; they are oriented toward not making mistakes or risking threats to their security; they pursue security vigilantly. Although research has only begun to examine regulatory focus in relationships, it has already been shown to influence relationship processes. First, predominantly promotion-focused individuals pay more attention to romantic alternatives and pursue them more readily (Finkel, Molden, Johnson, & Eastwick, 2009), and they see their partners as more supportive and as less distant (Winterheld &

Simpson, 2011). Regulatory focus orientations also affect emotional reactions, conflict behavior (Winterheld & Simpson, 2011), and trust (Molden & Finkel, 2010).

Research has also examined how the regulatory orientations of both relationship partners can interact. Some research has suggested that fit or matching of regulatory orientations best promotes relationship outcomes (Righetti, Finkenauer, & Rusbult, 2011), whereas other research has suggested that, under some circumstances, complementarity of regulatory focus promotes the best outcomes (Bohns et al., 2009).

From the perspective of the TSR model, the influence of an individual's regulatory focus on relationship outcomes is captured by the link between P1-P1 goal style and non–self-regulatory relationship variables. When individuals pursue approach goals or adopt a promotion focus, they tend to have better relationship outcomes, most likely because of myriad perceptual and behavioral relationship processes. The match between two individuals' motivational orientations can be reflected as a moderation of the effects of one partner's style on his or her relationship outcomes by the other partner's style. Future research examining the interaction of motivational orientations on goal outcomes would be valuable. For example, under what circumstances does having similar or complementary orientations lead to success? In addition, future research should delineate the relationship processes that mediate the influence of these orientations on relationship outcomes. Research is also needed to examine how orientations interact with other aspects of self-regulation, such as resources or content, to affect outcomes.

Regulatory Resources in Pursuing Relationship Goals

The programs of research we have presented, as with most research on self-regulation, have primarily focused on the pursuit of personal or individual goals. However, people also pursue interpersonal or relationship goals—those that are targeted at improving or maintaining the quality of the relationship. For example, people may want to get along better with their partners, stay faithful to them, and have long-lasting relationships. Along with a burgeoning interest in how interpersonal relationships affect self-regulation has come new research highlighting the importance of basic self-regulatory processes for the pursuit of relationship goals.

One important quality of individuals that affects their relationship goal pursuit and success is the degree to which they have regulatory resources available to pursue relationship goals. By regulatory resources, we mean individuals' available energy, time, and effort to put toward goal pursuit. Individuals who have more of these resources—at either a state or a trait level—tend to pursue relationship goals more successfully. Self-regulatory resources help individuals both inhibit behaviors that might thwart relationship goal success and initiate and maintain behaviors that promote relationship goal success (Finkel & Campbell, 2001). For instance, increased executive functioning—a cognitive proxy for trait self-control—is associated with increased inhibition of pursuing romantic alternatives (Pronk, Karremans, & Wigboldus, 2011). Increased conscientiousness—a personality trait related to discipline and self-control—is associated with persisting in relationship-enhancing behaviors across time (Kammrath & Peetz, 2011).

Regulatory resources also predict how individuals will respond to negative relationship events. For example, individuals who are higher in self-control are less likely to respond to partner provocation with violence (Finkel et al., 2012). Likewise, individuals who are higher in self-control are generally more likely to respond to partner transgressions with forgiveness and to overcome self-interest and engage in prorelationship behavior (Balliet, Li, & Joireman, 2011; Pronk, Karremans, Overbeek, Vermulst, & Wigboldus, 2010). Thus, individuals who have higher regulatory resources tend to be better partners. In addition, a dyad's total resources also predict successful attainment of relationship goals. For instance, dyads composed of friends and romantic partners report more satisfaction with their relationship to the extent that their summed self-control scores are high (Vohs, Finkenauer, & Baumeister, 2011).

From a TSR perspective, people are more likely to succeed at relationship goals (such as being satisfied with their relationship) if their partners have self-regulatory resources available to pursue relationship goals. Given that relationship goals may often share goal content (i.e., a match exists among P1-P1, P1-P2, P2-P2, and P2-P1 goals), the extent to which P1 resources are available directly affects the pursuit of not only P1's relationship goals but also P2's relationship goals. Thus, to the extent that P1 has resources available, both P1 and P2 are more likely to succeed at pursuing their relationship goals. Furthermore, if P2 can rely on P1 to contribute to relationship goals, P2 may conserve regulatory resources by engaging in less goal pursuit (vanDellen & Baker, 2011). Because P1's resources influence P1-P2 goal pursuit, P2 is more likely to conserve regulatory resources, resulting in an increased capacity to pursue other goals, including those that may not be shared with P1. Thus, the benefits to P2 of P1's having regulatory resources involve not only increasing the likelihood of P2's relationship goal success but also of P2's individual goal success. Alternatively, exogenous factors that influence only P1 (e.g., stress, the presence of attractive romantic alternatives, relationship uncertainty) may drain P1's resources, reducing both P1-P1 and P1-P2 goal pursuit and ultimately requiring P2 to invest more resources in the pursuit of the relationship goals.

When Dependence and Insecurity Affect Goal Pursuit

In this final section, we describe several programs of research that, taken together, show that feelings of relationship security can profoundly affect the pursuit of both relationship goals and individual goals. We begin by briefly describing the important work by Murray and Holmes and their colleagues on interdependence and risk regulation. A fundamental self-regulatory task faced by close relationship partners is to reconcile two goals—the need to safeguard oneself against rejection or pain and the need to belong to a warm and loving relationship (Murray & Holmes, 2009; Murray, Holmes, & Collins, 2006). These two goals often compete because many actions that promote a happy, healthy relationship—such as disclosing personal feelings and making sacrifices—also put people at risk of being hurt or rejected. According to the risk regulation model (Murray et al., 2006), individuals calibrate their risk taking—their willingness to engage in risky actions that promote their relationship—to current feelings of trust and security in the relationship. When individuals trust that their partners care for and need them, they feel safe, which allows them to overcome worries about risk and goals for self-protection and, thus, to focus on their goals to improve or maintain the quality of their relationship. One way that individuals have been shown to increase this sense of insurance is by making themselves irreplaceable to their partners by taking on many of their partners' daily goals, thus increasing their partners' dependence on them (Murray, Aloni, et al., 2009; Murray, Leder, et al., 2009). If an individual grows to rely on his or her partner for the accomplishment of many of the individual's basic daily tasks, the individual is much less likely to leave that partner and she or he can feel more secure in the relationship.

Although this research program has emphasized interpersonal goals and relationship outcomes, it is very likely that interpersonal risk regulation also shapes goal pursuit in other contexts. Indeed, when individuals' sense of security in a romantic relationship is threatened, this can spill over to influence even the most seemingly individually driven goals. In particular, it seems that feeling insecure about a partner's regard can shift individuals' motivational orientation toward risk aversion, even in contexts unrelated to the partner (Cavallo, Fitzsimons, & Holmes, 2009, 2010). When participants in one series of studies felt unsure of their partner's commitment, they showed greater accessibility of safety-related goals and behaved more cautiously, making, for example, safer but lower paying investment decisions (Cavallo et al., 2009)

Feeling insecure or threatened can thus shape goal pursuit, both inside and outside of the relationship. Conversely, feeling particularly secure and trusting can have a host of self-regulatory benefits. For example, individuals who visualized close, positive relationships (vs. more distant ones) responded less defensively to failure feedback, staying more open to learning diagnostic information that could improve future performance (Kumashiro &

Sedikides, 2005). Similarly, individuals primed with responsive partners (vs. acquaintances and strangers) engaged in less self-handicapping and more persistence in the face of failure (Caprariello & Reis, 2011). According to research on the dependency paradox, individuals who encourage their partners to depend on them—who make their partners feel trusting and secure enough to allow themselves to openly depend on their partners—create a safe environment in which their partners can explore and take risks in their goal pursuits (Feeney, 2004; 2007).

From the perspective of the TSR model, these phenomena related to trust and security in relationships are captured by the interaction of relationship qualities and various transactive processes. For example, the Cavallo et al. (2009, 2010) findings on risk avoidance after threat are likely captured by P1's relationship quality directly affecting P1-P1 style: Insecurity in the relationship leads to a motivational orientation of risk avoidance, which governs goal pursuit broadly across domains. Some of the simpler risk regulation processes can be captured by P1's relationship quality (e.g., "I feel insecure") affecting P1-P2 goal content ("I seek to avoid getting too close to you"), which then affects both P1's and P2's relationship quality. It is also conceivable to describe this process as deriving from P1's efficacy regarding his or her P1-P2 goal to seek closeness: When efficacy is low (because perceived regard is low), P1 disengages from the relationship goal. In a fascinating new program of research, the role of resources was shown to importantly moderate individuals' reactions to insecurity: Only individuals with sufficient self-regulatory resources in the form of working memory capacity were able to override the automatic pull of the interpersonal situation and act in line with their chronic motivational orientation (Murray et al., 2011). In this research, the previously mentioned transactive risk regulation process would then be further moderated by P1's resources.

This research on making oneself indispensable as a strategy to enhance partner reliance can be described in the TSR model as a multistage process: P1 relationship quality to P1 content to P2 resources, means, and goal outcomes to P2 relationship quality. That is, P1 feels insecure so he pursues a relationship goal to make himself indispensable to P2. All the extra assistance that P1 provides P2 for her goal pursuits frees P2's resources, changes the means by which she pursues her goal, and may lead to more success for P2 in her goals. If all goes well for P1, this transactive process then feeds back to influence P2's feelings, making her feel more reliant on and less likely to leave P1.

CONCLUSIONS

According to a recent model of TSR (Fitzsimons et al., 2012), individual goal pursuit is best conceptualized as interdependent with others in the social environment. The TSR framework we have presented in this chapter builds on groundbreaking research in the self and relationships literatures. First and most obviously, it owes a very clear debt to the great strides made in understanding interdependence among relationship partners, and among members of social groups, in the past few decades. Second, the TSR model also very clearly builds on research on individual self-regulation, which has elucidated important fundamental processes of goal pursuit and self-control. Third, the model echoes several key principles from research on transactive memory (e.g., Wegner et al., 1991), which popularized the innovative notion that cognitions can be shared across people.

Fundamentally, the model also reflects a new perspective on self-regulation that has recently emerged in the field of social psychology. Although the first major articles on links between relationships and self-regulation appeared only 10 to 15 years ago (Brunstein et al., 1996; Finkel & Campbell, 2001), and a critical mass of research has emerged only in the past 5 years, this perspective has already been extremely fruitful. The purpose of this chapter was to review this research and point to new directions for future research. We believe that the work we have reviewed holds great potential to complement the standard analysis of self-regulation from the individualistic perspective. We also believe that the new model will allow for more progress in that aim by highlighting new directions for future research and emphasizing that self-regulation models that ignore interdependent relationships are incomplete.

This work is in its infancy. Compared with the thousands of published articles on self-regulation in the mind of the individual, there are merely dozens of published articles on self-regulation in social contexts. We believe there are literally thousands of unanswered questions about how relationship partners can affect goal pursuit, and we hope that the next decade will provide new insights into and answers to some of those questions. We believe that self-regulation is a social process at least as often as, if not more often than, it is an individual process.

References

Aarts, H., Gollwitzer, P. M., & Hassin, R. R. (2004). Goal contagion: Perceiving is for pursuing. *Journal of Personality and Social Psychology, 87*, 23–37. doi:10.1037/0022-3514.87.1.23

Ackerman, J. M., Goldstein, N. J., Shapiro, J. R., & Bargh, J. A. (2009). You wear me out: The vicarious depletion of self-control. *Psychological Science, 20*, 326–332. doi:10.1111/j.1467-9280.2009.02290.x

Agnew, C. R., Van Lange, P. A. M., Rusbult, C. E., & Langston, C. A. (1998). Cognitive interdependence: Commitment and the mental representation of close relationships. *Journal of Personality and Social Psychology, 74*, 939–954. doi:10.1037/0022-3514.74.4.939

Allgöwer, A., Wardle, J., & Steptoe, A. (2001). Depressive symptoms, social support, and personal health behaviors in young men and women. *Health Psychology, 20*, 223–227. doi:10.1037/0278-6133.20.3.223

Andersen, S. M., & Cole, S. W. (1990). "Do I know you?": The role of significant others in general social perception. *Journal of Personality and Social Psychology, 59*, 384–399. doi:10.1037/0022-3514.59.3.384

Andersen, S. M., Reznik, I., & Manzella, L. M. (1996). Eliciting facial affect, motivation, and expectancies in transference: Significant-other representations in social relations. *Journal of Personality and Social Psychology, 71*, 1108–1129. doi:10.1037/0022-3514.71.6.1108

Aron, A., Aron, E. N., Tudor, M., & Nelson, G. (1991). Close relationships as including other in the self. *Journal of Personality and Social Psychology, 60*, 241–253. doi:10.1037/0022-3514.60.2.241

Atkinson, J. W. (1964). *An introduction to motivation.* Princeton, NJ: Van Nostrand.

Austin, J. R. (2003). Transactive memory in organizational groups: The effects of content, consensus, specialization, and accuracy on group performance. *Journal of*

Applied Psychology, 88, 866–878. doi:10.1037/0021-9010.88.5.866

Baldwin, M. W. (1992). Relational schemas and the processing of social information. *Psychological Bulletin, 112,* 461–484. doi:10.1037/0033-2909.112.3.461

Balliet, D., Li, N. P., & Joireman, J. (2011). Relating trait self-control and forgiveness within prosocials and proselfs: Compensatory versus synergistic models. *Journal of Personality and Social Psychology, 101,* 1090–1105. doi:10.1037/a0024967

Bargh, J. A. (1990). Auto-motives: Preconscious determinants of social interaction. In E. T. Higgins & R. M. Sorrentino (Eds.), *Handbook of motivation and cognition: Vol. 2. Foundations of social behavior* (pp. 93–130). New York, NY: Guilford Press.

Bargh, J. A., Gollwitzer, P. M., Lee-Chai, A., Barndollar, K., & Trötschel, R. (2001). The automated will: Nonconscious activation and pursuit of behavioral goals. *Journal of Personality and Social Psychology, 81,* 1014–1027. doi:10.1037/0022-3514.81.6.1014

Bargh, J. A., Green, M., & Fitzsimons, G. (2008). The selfish goal: Unintended consequences of intended goal pursuits. *Social Cognition, 26,* 534–554. doi:10.1521/soco.2008.26.5.534

Baumeister, R. F., Bratslavsky, E., Muraven, M., & Tice, D. M. (1998). Ego depletion: Is the active self a limited resource? *Journal of Personality and Social Psychology, 74,* 1252–1265. doi:10.1037/0022-3514.74.5.1252

Baumeister, R. F., Vohs, K. D., & Tice, D. M. (2007). The strength model of self-control. *Current Directions in Psychological Science, 16,* 351–355. doi:10.1111/j.1467-8721.2007.00534.x

Berscheid, E., & Ammazzalorso, H. (2001). Emotional experience in close relationships. In G. J. O. Fletcher & M. S. Clark (Eds.), *Blackwell handbook of social psychology: Interpersonal processes* (pp. 308–330). Malden, MA: Blackwell.

Bohns, V. K., Lucas, G., Molden, D. C., Finkel, E. J., Coolsen, M. K., Kumashiro, M., . . . Higgins, E. T. (2009). *When opposites fit: Increased relationship strength from partner complementarity in regulatory focus.* Unpublished manuscript, University of Toronto, Toronto, Ontario, Canada.

Bolger, N., & Amarel, D. (2007). Effects of support visibility on adjustment to stress: Experimental evidence. *Journal of Personality and Social Psychology, 92,* 458–475. doi:10.1037/0022-3514.92.3.458

Bolger, N., Zuckerman, A., & Kessler, R. C. (2000). Invisible support and adjustment to stress. *Journal of Personality and Social Psychology, 79,* 953–961. doi:10.1037/0022-3514.79.6.953

Brunstein, J. C., Dangelmayer, G., & Schultheiss, O. C. (1996). Personal goals and social support in close

relationship: Effects on relationship mood and marital satisfaction. *Journal of Personality and Social Psychology, 71,* 1006–1019. doi:10.1037/0022-3514.71.5.1006

Caprariello, P. A., & Reis, H. T. (2011). Perceived partner responsiveness minimizes defensive reactions to failure. *Social Psychological and Personality Science, 2,* 365–372. doi:10.1177/1948550610391914

Carver, C. S., & Scheier, M. F. (1981). The self-attention-induced feedback loop and social facilitation. *Journal of Experimental Social Psychology, 17,* 545–568. doi:10.1016/0022-1031(81)90039-1

Carver, C. S., & Scheier, M. (1990). *Principles of self-regulation: Action and emotion.* New York, NY: Guilford Press.

Carver, C. S., & White, T. L. (1994). Behavioral inhibition, behavioral activation, and affective responses to impending reward and punishment: The BIS/BAS Scales. *Journal of Personality and Social Psychology, 67,* 319–333. doi:10.1037/0022-3514.67.2.319

Cavallo, J. V., Fitzsimons, G. M., & Holmes, J. G. (2009). Taking chances in the face of threat: Romantic risk regulation and approach motivation. *Personality and Social Psychology Bulletin, 35,* 737–751. doi:10.1177/0146167209332742

Cavallo, J. V., Fitzsimons, G. M., & Holmes, J. G. (2010). When self-protection overreaches: Relationship-specific threat activates domain-general avoidance motivation. *Journal of Experimental Social Psychology, 46,* 1–8. doi:10.1016/j.jesp.2009.07.007

Chartrand, T. L., Dalton, A. N., & Fitzsimons, G. J. (2007). Nonconscious relationship reactance: When significant others prime opposing goals. *Journal of Experimental Social Psychology, 43,* 719–726. doi:10.1016/j.jesp.2006.08.003

Christakis, N. A., & Fowler, J. H. (2007). The spread of obesity in a large social network over 32 years. *New England Journal of Medicine, 357,* 370–379. doi:10.1056/NEJMsa066082

Cohen, S., & Lichtenstein, E. (1990). Partner behaviors that support quitting smoking. *Journal of Consulting and Clinical Psychology, 58,* 304–309. doi:10.1037/0022-006X.58.3.304

Converse, B. A., & Fishbach, A. (2012). Instrumentality boosts appreciation: Helpers are more appreciated while they are useful. *Psychological Science, 23,* 560–566.

Cross, S. E., Bacon, P. L., & Morris, M. L. (2000). The relational-interdependent self-construal and relationships. *Journal of Personality and Social Psychology, 78,* 791–808. doi:10.1037/0022-3514.78.4.791

Dalton, A. N., Chartrand, T. L., & Finkel, E. J. (2010). The schema driven chameleon: How mimicry affects executive and self-regulatory resources. *Journal of Personality and Social Psychology, 98*, 605–617. doi:10.1037/a0017629

Davison, K. K., Cutting, T. M., & Birch, L. L. (2003). Parents' activity-related parenting practices predict girls' physical activity. *Medicine and Science in Sports and Exercise, 35*, 1589–1595.

Dik, G., & Aarts, H. (2007). Behavioral cues to others' motivation and goal pursuits: The perception of effort facilitates goal inference and contagion. *Journal of Experimental Social Psychology, 43*, 727–737. doi:10.1016/j.jesp.2006.09.002

Drigotas, S. M., Rusbult, C. E., Wieselquist, J., & Whitton, S. W. (1999). Close partner as sculptor of the ideal self: Behavioral affirmation and the Michelangelo phenomenon. *Journal of Personality and Social Psychology, 77*, 293–323. doi:10.1037/0022-3514.77.2.293

Elliot, A. J., & Covington, M. V. (2001). Approach and avoidance motivation. *Educational Psychology Review, 13*, 73–92. doi:10.1023/A:1009009018235

Emmons, R. A. (1992). Abstract versus concrete goals: Personal striving level, physical illness, and psychological well-being. *Journal of Personality and Social Psychology, 62*, 292–300. doi:10.1037/0022-3514.62.2.292

Eyler, A. A., Brownson, R. C., Donatelle, R. J., King, A. C., Brown, D., & Sallis, J. F. (1999). Physical activity social support and middle- and older-aged minority women: Results from a U.S. survey. *Social Science and Medicine, 49*, 781–789. doi:10.1016/S0277-9536(99)00137-9

Feeney, B. C. (2004). A secure base: Responsive support of goal strivings and exploration in adult intimate relationships. *Journal of Personality and Social Psychology, 87*, 631–648. doi:10.1037/0022-3514.87.5.631

Feeney, B. C. (2007). The dependency paradox in close relationships: Accepting dependence promotes independence. *Journal of Personality and Social Psychology, 92*, 268–285. doi:10.1037/0022-3514.92.2.268

Feeney, B. C., & Thrush, R. L. (2010). Relationship influences on exploration in adulthood: The characteristics and function of a secure base. *Journal of Personality and Social Psychology, 98*, 57–76. doi:10.1037/a0016961

Finkel, E. J., & Campbell, W. K. (2001). Self-control and accommodation in close relationships: An interdependence analysis. *Journal of Personality and Social Psychology, 81*, 263–277. doi:10.1037/0022-3514.81.2.263

Finkel, E. J., Campbell, W. K., Brunell, A. B., Dalton, A. N., Scarbeck, S. J., & Chartrand, T. L. (2006). High maintenance interaction: Inefficient social coordination impairs self-regulation. *Journal of Personality and*

Social Psychology, 91, 456–475. doi:10.1037/0022-3514.91.3.456

Finkel, E. J., DeWall, C. N., Slotter, E. B., McNulty, J. K., Pond, R. S., Jr., & Atkins, D. C. (2012). Using I[3] theory to clarify when dispositional aggressiveness predicts intimate partner violence. *Journal of Personality and Social Psychology, 102*, 533–549.

Finkel, E. J., Molden, D. C., Johnson, S. E., & Eastwick, P. W. (2009). Regulatory focus and romantic alternatives. In J. P. Forgas, R. F. Baumeister, D. M. Tice (Eds.), *Psychology of self-regulation: Cognitive, affective, and motivational processes* (pp. 319–335). New York, NY: Psychology Press.

Fishbach, A., Henderson, M. D., & Koo, M. (2011). Pursuing goals with others: Group identification and motivation resulting from things done versus things left undone. *Journal of Experimental Psychology: General, 140*, 520–534. doi:10.1037/a0023907

Fitzsimons, G. M., & Bargh, J. A. (2003). Thinking of you: Nonconscious pursuit of interpersonal goals associated with relationship partners. *Journal of Personality and Social Psychology, 84*, 148–164. doi:10.1037/0022-3514.84.1.148

Fitzsimons, G. M., & Finkel, E. J. (2010). Interpersonal influences on self-regulation. *Current Directions in Psychological Science, 19*, 101–105. doi:10.1177/0963721410364499

Fitzsimons, G. M., Finkel, E. J., & vanDellen, M. R. (2012). *Transactive self-regulation.* Unpublished manuscript, Duke University, Durham, NC.

Fitzsimons, G. M., & Fishbach, A. (2010). Shifting closeness: Interpersonal effects of personal goal progress. *Journal of Personality and Social Psychology, 98*, 535–549. doi:10.1037/a0018581

Fitzsimons, G. M., & Shah, J. Y. (2008). How goal instrumentality shapes relationship evaluations. *Journal of Personality and Social Psychology, 95*, 319–337. doi:10.1037/0022-3514.95.2.319

Fitzsimons, G. M., & Shah, J. Y. (2009). Confusing one instrumental other for another: Goal effects on social categorization. *Psychological Science, 20*, 1468–1472. doi:10.1111/j.1467-9280.2009.02475.x

Gable, S. L. (2006). Approach and avoidance social motives and goals. *Journal of Personality, 74*, 175–222. doi:10.1111/j.1467-6494.2005.00373.x

Gable, S. L., & Poore, J. (2008). Which thoughts count? Algorithms for evaluating satisfaction in relationships. *Psychological Science, 19*, 1030–1036. doi:10.1111/j.1467-9280.2008.02195.x

Gardner, W. L., Gabriel, S., & Lee, A. Y. (1999). "I" value freedom, but "we" value relationships: Self-construal priming mirrors cultural differences in judgment. *Psychological Science, 10*, 321–326. doi:10.1111/1467-9280.00162

Gere, J., Schimmack, U., Pinkus, R. T., & Lockwood, P. (2011). The effects of romantic partners' goal congruence on affective well-being. *Journal of Research in Personality, 45,* 549–559. doi:10.1016/j.jrp.2011.06.010

Gollwitzer, P. M. (1990). Action phases and mind-sets. In E. T. Higgins & R. M. Sorrentino (Eds.), *Handbook of motivation and cognition: Vol. 2. Foundations of social behavior* (pp. 53–92). New York, NY: Guilford Press.

Gollwitzer, P. M. (1999). Implementation intentions: Strong effects of simple plans. *American Psychologist, 54,* 493–503. doi:10.1037/0003-066X.54.7.493

Gray, J. A. (1990). Brain systems that mediate both emotion and cognition. *Cognition and Emotion, 4,* 269–288. doi:10.1080/02699939008410799

Heckhausen, H. (1991). *Motivation and action.* Berlin: Springer-Verlag. doi:10.1007/978-3-642-75961-1

Higgins, E. T. (1987). Self-discrepancy: A theory relating self and affect. *Psychological Review, 94,* 319–340. doi:10.1037/0033-295X.94.3.319

Higgins, E. T. (1997). Beyond pleasure and pain. *American Psychologist, 52,* 1280–1300. doi:10.1037/0003-066X.52.12.1280

Hollingshead, A. B. (1998). Retrieval processes in transactive memory systems. *Journal of Personality and Social Psychology, 74,* 659–671. doi:10.1037/0022-3514.74.3.659

Howland, M., & Simpson, J. A. (2010). Getting in under the radar: A dyadic view of invisible support. *Psychological Science, 21,* 1878–1885. doi:10.1177/0956797610388817

Impett, E. A., Gable, S. L., & Peplau, L. A. (2005). Giving up and giving in: The costs and benefits of daily sacrifice in intimate relationships. *Journal of Personality and Social Psychology, 89,* 327–344. doi:10.1037/0022-3514.89.3.327

Impett, E. A., Gordon, A. M., Kogan, A., Oveis, C., Gable, S. L., & Keltner, D. (2010). Moving toward more perfect unions: Daily and long-term consequences of approach and avoidance goals in romantic relationships. *Journal of Personality and Social Psychology, 99,* 948–963. doi:10.1037/a0020271

Impett, E. A., Peplau, L. A., & Gable, S. L. (2005). Approach and avoidance sexual motives: Implications for personal and interpersonal well-being. *Personal Relationships, 12,* 465–482. doi:10.1111/j.1475-6811.2005.00126.x

Impett, E. A., Strachman, A., Finkel, E. J., & Gable, S. L. (2008). Maintaining sexual desire in intimate relationships: The importance of approach goals. *Journal of Personality and Social Psychology, 94,* 808–823. doi:10.1037/0022-3514.94.5.808

Kammrath, L. K., & Peetz, J. (2011). The limits of love: Predicting immediate versus sustained caring behaviors in close relationships. *Journal of Experimental Social Psychology, 47,* 411–417. doi:10.1016/j.jesp.2010.11.004

Karremans, J. C., Verwijmeren, T., Pronk, T. M., & Reitsma, M. (2009). Interacting with women can impair men's cognitive functioning. *Journal of Experimental Social Psychology, 45,* 1041–1044. doi:10.1016/j.jesp.2009.05.004

Kelley, H. H., & Thibaut, J. W. (1978). *Interpersonal relations: A theory of interdependence.* New York, NY: Wiley.

Kruglanski, A. W., Shah, J. Y., Fishbach, A., Friedman, R., Chun, W. Y., & Sleeth-Keppler, D. (2002). A theory of goal systems. In M. P. Zanna (Ed.), *Advances in experimental social psychology* (Vol. 34, pp. 331–378). doi:10.1016/S0065-2601(02)80008-9

Kumashiro, M., Rusbult, C. E., Finkenauer, C., & Stocker, S. L. (2007). To think or to do: The impact of assessment and locomotion orientation on the Michelangelo phenomenon. *Journal of Social and Personal Relationships, 24,* 591–611. doi:10.1177/0265407507079261

Kumashiro, M., & Sedikides, C. (2005). Taking on board liability-focused information. *Psychological Science, 16,* 732–739. doi:10.1111/j.1467-9280.2005.01603.x

Lakey, B., & Orehek, E. (2011). Relational regulation theory: A new approach to explain perceived social support's link to mental health. *Psychological Review, 118,* 482–495. doi:10.1037/a0023477

Laurin, K., Fitzsimons, G. M., & Kay, A. C. (2011). Social disadvantage and the self-regulatory function of justice beliefs. *Journal of Personality and Social Psychology, 100,* 149–171. doi:10.1037/a0021343

Laurin, K., Kay, A. C., & Fitzsimons, G. M. (2012). Divergent effects of activating thoughts of God on motivation. *Journal of Personality and Social Psychology, 102,* 4–21. doi:10.1037/a0025971

Liang, D. W., Moreland, R., & Argote, L. (1995). Group versus individual training and group performance: The mediating role of transactive memory. *Personality and Social Psychology Bulletin, 21,* 384–393. doi:10.1177/0146167295214009

Lockwood, P., Jordan, C. H., & Kunda, Z. (2002). Motivation by positive or negative role models: Regulatory focus determines who will best inspire us. *Journal of Personality and Social Psychology, 83,* 854–864. doi:10.1037/0022-3514.83.4.854

Lockwood, P., & Kunda, Z. (1997). Superstars and me: Predicting the impact of role models on the self. *Journal of Personality and Social Psychology, 73,* 91–103. doi:10.1037/0022-3514.73.1.91

Markus, H. R., & Kitayama, S. (1991). Culture and the self: Implications for cognition, emotion, and motivation. *Psychological Review, 98,* 224–253. doi:10.1037/0033-295X.98.2.224

Markus, H. R., & Nurius, P. (1986). Possible selves. *American Psychologist, 41*, 954–969. doi:10.1037/0003-066X.41.9.954

McCulloch, K. C., Fitzsimons, G. M., Chua, S. N., & Albarracin, D. (2011). Vicarious goal satiation. *Journal of Experimental Social Psychology, 47*, 685–688. doi:10.1016/j.jesp.2010.12.019

Metcalfe, J., & Mischel, W. (1999). A hot/cool-system analysis of delay of gratification: Dynamics of willpower. *Psychological Review, 106*, 3–19. doi:10.1037/0033-295X.106.1.3

Miller, L. C., & Read, S. J. (1991). Inter-personalism: Understanding persons in relationships. *Advances in Personal Relationships: A Research Annual, 2*, 233–267.

Molden, D. C., & Finkel, E. J. (2010). Motivations for promotion and prevention and the role of trust and commitment in interpersonal forgiveness. *Journal of Experimental Social Psychology, 46*, 255–268. doi:10.1016/j.jesp.2009.10.014

Molden, D. C., Lee, A. Y., & Higgins, E. T. (2008). Motivations for promotion and prevention. In J. Shah & W. Gardner (Eds.), *Handbook of motivation science* (pp. 169–187). New York, NY: Guilford Press.

Moretti, M. M., & Higgins, E. T. (1999a). Internal representations of others in self-regulation: A new look at a classic issue. *Social Cognition, 17*, 186–208. doi:10.1521/soco.1999.17.2.186

Moretti, M. M., & Higgins, E. T. (1999b). Own versus other standpoints in self-regulation: Developmental antecedents and functional consequences. *Review of General Psychology, 3*, 188–223. doi:10.1037/1089-2680.3.3.188

Morewedge, C. K., Huh, Y. E., & Vosgerau, J. (2010). Thought for food: Imagined consumption reduces actual consumption. *Science, 330*, 1530–1533. doi:10.1126/science.1195701

Morrison, K. R., Wheeler, S. C., & Smeesters, D. (2007). Significant other primes and behavior: Motivation to respond to social cues moderates pursuit of prime-induced goals. *Personality and Social Psychology Bulletin, 33*, 1661–1674. doi:10.1177/0146167207307491

Murray, S. L., Aloni, M., Holmes, J. G., Derrick, J. L., Stinson, D. A., & Leder, S. (2009). Fostering partner dependence as trust insurance: The implicit contingencies of the exchange script in close relationships. *Journal of Personality and Social Psychology, 96*, 324–348. doi:10.1037/a0012856

Murray, S. L., & Holmes, J. G. (2009). The architecture of interdependent minds: A motivation-management theory of mutual responsiveness. *Psychological Review, 116*, 908–928. doi:10.1037/a0017015

Murray, S. L., Holmes, J. G., & Collins, N. L. (2006). Optimizing assurance: The risk regulation system in relationships. *Psychological Bulletin, 132*, 641–666. doi:10.1037/0033-2909.132.5.641

Murray, S. L., Leder, S., MacGregor, J. C. D., Holmes, J. G., Pinkus, R. T., & Harris, B. (2009). Becoming irreplaceable: How comparisons to the partner's alternatives differentially affect low and high self-esteem people. *Journal of Experimental Social Psychology, 45*, 1180–1191. doi:10.1016/j.jesp.2009.07.001

Murray, S. L., Pinkus, R. T., Holmes, J. G., Harris, B., Gomillion, S., Aloni, M., . . . Leder, S. (2011). Signaling when (and when not) to be cautious and self-protective: Impulsive and reflective trust in close relationships. *Journal of Personality and Social Psychology, 101*, 485–502. doi:10.1037/a0023233

Novak, S. A., & Webster, G. D. (2011). Spousal social control during a weight loss attempt: A daily diary study. *Personal Relationships, 18*, 224–241. doi:10.1111/j.1475-6811.2011.01358.x

Overall, N. C., Fletcher, G. J. O., & Simpson, J. A. (2010). Helping each other grow: Romantic partner support, self-improvement, and relationship quality. *Personality and Social Psychology Bulletin, 36*, 1496–1513. doi:10.1177/0146167210383045

Overall, N. C., Fletcher, G. J. O., Simpson, J. A., & Sibley, C. G. (2009). Regulating partners in intimate relationships: The costs and benefits of different communication strategies. *Journal of Personality and Social Psychology, 96*, 620–639. doi:10.1037/a0012961

Pronk, T. M., Karremans, J. C., Overbeek, G., Vermulst, A. A., & Wigboldus, D. H. J. (2010). What it takes to forgive: When and why executive functioning facilitates forgiveness. *Journal of Personality and Social Psychology, 98*, 119–131. doi:10.1037/a0017875

Pronk, T. M., Karremans, J. C., & Wigboldus, D. H. J. (2011). How can you resist? Executive control helps romantically involved individuals to stay faithful. *Journal of Personality and Social Psychology, 100*, 827–837. doi:10.1037/a0021993

Ranby, K. W., & Aiken, L. S. (2012). *Incorporating close others into health behavior models: Husband influences on wives' exercise.* Manuscript submitted for publication.

Reblin, M., & Uchino, B. N. (2008). Social and emotional support and its implication for health. *Current Opinion in Psychiatry, 21*, 201–205. doi:10.1097/YCO.0b013e3282f3ad89

Richeson, J. A., & Shelton, J. N. (2003). When prejudice does not pay: Effects of interracial contact on executive function. *Psychological Science, 14*, 287–290. doi:10.1111/1467-9280.03437

Richeson, J. A., & Trawalter, S. (2005). Why do interracial interactions impair executive function? A resource depletion account. *Journal of Personality and Social Psychology, 88*, 934–947. doi:10.1037/0022-3514.88.6.934

Righetti, F., Finkenauer, C., & Rusbult, C. (2011). The benefits of interpersonal regulatory fit for individual goal pursuit. *Journal of Personality and Social Psychology, 101*, 720–736. doi:10.1037/a0023592

Rusbult, C. E., Finkel, E. J., & Kumashiro, M. (2009). The Michelangelo phenomenon. *Current Directions in Psychological Science, 18*, 305–309. doi:10.1111/j.1467-8721.2009.01657.x

Rusbult, C. E., Kumashiro, M., Kubacka, K. E., & Finkel, E. J. (2009). "The part of me that you bring out": Ideal similarity and the Michelangelo phenomenon. *Journal of Personality and Social Psychology, 96*, 61–82. doi:10.1037/a0014016

Rusbult, C. E., & Van Lange, P. A. (2003). Interdependence, interaction, and relationships. *Annual Review of Psychology, 54*, 351–375. doi:10.1146/annurev.psych.54.101601.145059

Shah, J. (2003). Automatic for the people: How representations of significant others implicitly affect goal pursuit. *Journal of Personality and Social Psychology, 84*, 661–681. doi:10.1037/0022-3514.84.4.661

Shteynberg, G., & Galinsky, A. (2011). Implicit coordination: Sharing goals with similar others intensifies goal pursuit. *Journal of Experimental Social Psychology, 47*, 1291–1294. doi:10.1016/j.jesp.2011.04.012

Stillman, T. F., Tice, D. M., Fincham, F. D., & Lambert, N. M. (2009). The psychological presence of family improves self-control. *Journal of Social and Clinical Psychology, 28*, 498–529. doi:10.1521/jscp.2009.28.4.498

Tesser, A., Millar, M., & Moore, J. (1988). Some affective consequences of social comparison and reflection processes: The pain and pleasure of being close. *Journal of Personality and Social Psychology, 54*, 49–61. doi:10.1037/0022-3514.54.1.49

Vallacher, R. R., & Wegner, D. M. (1987). What do people think they're doing? Action identification and human behavior. *Psychological Review, 94*, 3–15. doi:10.1037/0033-295X.94.1.3

vanDellen, M. R., & Baker, E. (2011). The implicit delegation model: Joint self-control in close relationships. *Social Psychological and Personality Science, 2*, 277–283. doi:10.1177/1948550610389082

vanDellen, M. R., & Hoyle, R. H. (2010). Regulatory accessibility and social influences on state self-control. *Personality and Social Psychology Bulletin, 36*, 251–263. doi:10.1177/0146167209356302

vanDellen, M. R., Moon, P. E., & Johnson, C. (2012). *Too much of a good thing: Anticipated success and effort after exposure to positive exemplars.* Unpublished manuscript, Duke University, Durham, NC.

Vohs, K., Finkenauer, C., & Baumeister, R. F. (2011). The sum of friends' and lovers' self-control scores predicts relationship quality. *Social Psychological and Personality Science, 2*, 138–145. doi:10.1177/1948550610385710

Vohs, K. D., Baumeister, R. F., & Ciarocco, N. J. (2005). Self-regulation and self-presentation: Regulatory resource depletion impairs impression management and effortful self-presentation depletes regulatory resources. *Journal of Personality and Social Psychology, 88*, 632–657. doi:10.1037/0022-3514.88.4.632

Vorauer, J. D., Martens, V., & Sasaki, S. J. (2009). When trying to understand detracts from trying to behave: Effects of perspective-taking in intergroup interaction. *Journal of Personality and Social Psychology, 96*, 811–827. doi:10.1037/a0013411

Walton, G. M., & Cohen, G. L. (2011). A brief social-belonging intervention improves academic and health outcomes of minority students. *Science, 331*, 1447–1451. doi:10.1126/science.1198364

Wegner, D. M. (1987). Transactive memory: A contemporary analysis of the group mind. In B. Mullen & G. R. Goethals (Eds.), *Theories of group behavior* (pp. 185–208). New York, NY: Springer-Verlag. doi:10.1007/978-1-4612-4634-3_9

Wegner, D. M. (1995). A computer network model of human transactive memory. *Social Cognition, 13*, 319–339. doi:10.1521/soco.1995.13.3.319

Wegner, D. M., Erber, R., & Raymond, P. (1991). Transactive memory in close relationships. *Journal of Personality and Social Psychology, 61*, 923–929. doi:10.1037/0022-3514.61.6.923

Wegner, D. M., & Wheatley, T. (1999). Apparent mental causation: Sources of the experience of will. *American Psychologist, 54*, 480–492. doi:10.1037/0003-066X.54.7.480

Winterheld, H. A., & Simpson, J. A. (2011). Seeking security or growth: A regulatory focus perspective on motivations in romantic relationships. *Journal of Personality and Social Psychology, 101*, 935–954. doi:10.1037/a0025012

Ybarra, O., Burnstein, E., Winkielman, P., Keller, M. C., Manis, M., Chan, E., & Rodriguez, J. (2008). Mental exercising through simple socializing: Social interaction promotes general cognitive functioning. *Personality and Social Psychology Bulletin, 34*, 248–259. doi:10.1177/0146167207310454

Ybarra, O., Winkielman, P., Yeh, I., Burnstein, E., & Kavanagh, L. (2011). Friends (and sometimes enemies) with cognitive benefits: What types of social interactions boost executive functioning? *Social Psychological and Personality Science, 2*, 253–261. doi:10.1177/1948550610386808

EMOTIONS IN RELATIONSHIPS

Julie Fitness

There is little about a relationship that can be understood without understanding its affective tenor and the emotions and feelings the partners experience in their association with each other. (Reis, Collins, & Berscheid, 2000, p. 858)

From the time they are born, human beings depend on one another for their physical survival and psychological well-being; they simply cannot survive alone and uncared for. Fortunately, evolution has equipped humans with the mechanisms they need to persuade others to care for them and to assist them in their struggles to survive. These mechanisms are feelings and emotions. Without them, people would experience no preferences, desires, frustrations, or sorrows; they would not care about themselves or others. Only through experiences of joy and love, fear and anger, and shame and grief do humans come to know who, and what, matters to them. In this sense, emotions constitute the currency of human relationships and make life meaningful.

It is somewhat surprising, then, to learn that for much of the 20th century, the study of emotion was a no-go area of psychology (Lazarus, 1991). During the early years under the reign of behaviorism, emotions were regarded as unobservable and therefore unknowable phenomena of little scientific interest. In the second half of the century, social-cognitive psychologists tended to regard emotions as a relatively undifferentiated nuisance variable that disrupted rational thought and interfered with people's capacities to live well-reasoned lives (Fitness & Strongman, 1991; Planalp & Fitness, 1999). Over

the past 30 years, however, a revolution has occurred in the way emotions have been conceptualized, with a growing number of social psychologists in particular arguing that emotions have a long evolutionary history and that they motivate people to behave in ways that facilitate their survival and well-being (Fredrickson, 2001; Panksepp, 1998; Plutchik, 1994). According to this functional view, emotions move people, quite literally, to act in the service of their needs, desires, and goals (Frijda, 2007). Moreover, because so many of these needs, desires, and goals involve other people, emotions are increasingly being regarded as intrinsically interpersonal (Clark, Fitness, & Brissette, 2001). It is within people's personal relationships that they experience the broadest range of emotions, from the mildest feelings of contentment, annoyance, and anxiety to the most profound experiences of love, rage, and despair. It is people's romantic partners, parents, children, siblings, friends, and enemies who possess the greatest power to facilitate or frustrate their needs and desires; hence, they are also the primary source of people's emotions.

The overall aim of this chapter is to elaborate on this functional framework and to provide an empirically informed and theoretically integrative account of what is known—and what still remains to be discovered—about the features and functions of emotions in relationships. I begin with an overview of emotion theory from an evolutionary, social psychological perspective, with an emphasis on the importance of the informational and communicative functions of emotion. I then discuss how emotions

http://dx.doi.org/10.1037/14344-011
APA Handbook of Personality and Social Psychology: Vol. 3. Interpersonal Relations, M. Mikulincer and P. R. Shaver (Editors-in-Chief)

are generated in relationships and consider the ways in which relationship partners' personalities and relationship histories affect their experience and expression of emotions in relationships. The importance of effective emotion communication and regulation for maintaining healthy relationships is then discussed, along with the role of positive emotions in adaptive relationship functioning. Finally, I point the way to further research in this fascinating field.

WHY DO HUMANS EXPERIENCE EMOTIONS?

Of all the questions that may be asked about any kind of psychological phenomenon or process, the "why" question is one of the most interesting and important. This is particularly the case with emotions such as love, joy, anger, jealousy, and many others that serve crucial interpersonal functions in the lives of human beings (Cosmides & Tooby, 2000; Keltner & Haidt, 1999; Niedenthal & Brauer, 2012). According to the social-functionalist view of emotion, the why question can be asked and answered at a number of different levels (see Fitness, Fletcher, & Overall, 2003). At the distal level, the focus is on the evolutionary origins of emotions, such as joy and anger, and on the ways in which these emotions have contributed to human survival over thousands of years of evolutionary history. Anger, for example, is an innate, hard-wired psychological mechanism that serves a critical survival function: It alerts individuals to the fact that their desires or goals have been blocked, and it both motivates and energizes them to attack and remove the perceived source of the obstruction. Ancient humans who had the capacity for anger out-survived humans who neither fought for what they needed nor resisted attempts to exploit or mistreat them. Today's humans are born with the same adaptive capacity (Fitness, 2009). Similarly, the emotion of fear motivates escape and avoidance behaviors that keep people safe; happiness motivates adaptive behaviors that build resources and strengthen social bonds; and parental love motivates nurturing behaviors that ensure the survival of people's offspring.

At a more proximal, here-and-now level, the focus of analysis is on the functions currently served by emotions in people's daily lives and on the ways in which emotions that may have been adaptive during evolutionary history may be less adaptive in the current environmental context. For example, at a distal level, the emotion of jealousy is a powerful motivator of behaviors such as mate guarding and rival attack, both of which may have been highly adaptive in humans' ancestral environment to ensure exclusive access to mating opportunities and parental resources (Panksepp, 2010). However, when cultural norms discourage partner possessiveness and murdering one's siblings, the same feelings of jealousy that may have made good sense in the distal environment may be regarded in the proximal environment as irrational, inappropriate, or dysfunctional. Similarly, although the evolved capacity to feel and respond with anger to perceived obstruction is potentially adaptive, from the time people are born they must learn, according to the rules of their culture, when and where it is appropriate to experience and express anger. They must also learn how to regulate its expression so that, as adults, they do not (typically) throw temper tantrums at the dinner table when dessert is not to their liking (Planalp & Fitness, 1999).

It is important to note that, from this functional perspective, emotions are neither negative nor positive, though emotion scholars tend to label them as such (Lazarus, 1991). Certainly, the experience of joy is more pleasurable than the experience of shame, but too much joy may spill over into mania (Gruber, 2011), and too little shame may result in social rejection (Tangney & Dearing, 2002). Moreover, a so-called negative emotion such as anger may feel empowering and motivate constructive behaviors that change an undesirable situation (Fischer & Roseman, 2007), whereas a so-called positive emotion such as love may be intensely painful at times and can motivate obsessive, dysfunctional behaviors (Mullen, 1994). Thus, emotions are neither good nor bad; rather, they function to help people solve survival and personal welfare–related problems, most of which involve their relationships with others.

Along with motivating potentially adaptive behaviors, emotions play a second, crucial function in the proximal context of people's lives and relationships on the basis of their communicative properties. Specifically, just as the experience of emotions informs one of the status of one's needs, desires, and goals, the expression of emotions also lets others know what is currently going right or wrong for one. In turn, this information enables close others to share one's joys or respond appropriately to one's needs. Expressing anger, for example, lets a relationship partner know that there is a problem, which is the first step toward negotiation and resolution (Fitness & Fletcher, 1993); expressing sadness or fear enables relationship partners to provide comfort or support (Clark, Pataki & Carver, 1996); and expressing love encourages reciprocation, which, in turn, builds trust and intimacy (Berscheid & Ammazzalorso, 2001). In line with this functional approach, a sizable body of research has demonstrated that emotions are most likely to be expressed in communal relationships in which people feel responsible for one another's needs and believe that others will be responsive to their needs (Clark et al., 2001). Moreover, willingness to express a range of emotions is positively associated with adaptive relationship functioning and marital happiness (Feeney, 1999; Graham, Huang, Clark & Helgeson, 2008).

In summary, the social-functionalist account of emotion argues that both the experience and the expression of emotions serve important intrapersonal and interpersonal functions. They inform people and relationship partners about how they are doing in the world as well as the status of their needs, desires, and goals. This information enables relationship partners to help meet each other's needs, further strengthening the bonds between them. In the next section of the chapter, I consider when and how emotions are elicited in relationships, focusing on the role of cognition in determining the kinds of emotions that relationship partners experience.

WHEN DO PEOPLE EXPERIENCE EMOTIONS IN CLOSE RELATIONSHIPS?

One of the most influential accounts of emotion elicitation that has informed researchers' understanding of how and when relationship partners experience emotion was proposed by Mandler (1975). In line with functionalist approaches, Mandler argued that emotion (conceptualized as a state of relatively undifferentiated physiological arousal) functions as an evolved, trouble-shooting system that responds to perceived interruptions to one's expectations—events that capture one's attention because they disrupt the smooth running of one's lives. Such interruptive events may be very serious (e.g., discovering that one has a terminal illness) or relatively minor (e.g., misplacing one's car keys). The critical point is that one perceives the interruptive event as being relevant to one's plans and goals (e.g., losing the car keys matters because one needs to get to work). This appraisal of relevance activates the emotion system, which in turn arouses and motivates one to take remedial action (e.g., frantically searching for one's keys in all the usual places).

Although the different kinds of emotions that might be elicited by interruptive events were not specified in Mandler's (1975) model (e.g., some people may respond to the loss of car keys with anxiety, others with frustration), the model acknowledged the functional nature of the emotion system. It also led to the development of an elegant model of emotion elicitation in relationships, published by Ellen Berscheid in 1983, that provided a coherent framework for understanding when and how emotions are generated within and between relationship partners (see also Berscheid & Ammazzalorso, 2001). Specifically, Berscheid (1983) argued that, during the course of sharing their lives, relationship partners develop an enormous number of interdependent routines, plans, and goals; in a sense, they depend on each other to keep both of their lives running smoothly. Provided that each partner does what the other expects, there are no interruptions, and the relationship is emotionally tranquil. However, when one partner fails to do what is expected or does something unexpected, the impact of such interruptive events may be extremely powerful and generate strong emotional arousal. For example, partners may have developed a child care routine in which they take turns picking up their children from school. If John forgets it is his day and he arrives home without the children, Mary is likely to perceive this as a seriously interruptive event, and Mary (and eventually John) ought to experience a strong emotional response to it.

According to this model, the potential for experiencing emotions in close relationships grows as partners become increasingly interdependent and vulnerable to more and stronger interruptions. Ironically, however, the better meshed and synchronized partners' routines and plans are, the less interruption (and the less emotion) each partner should experience on a daily basis. With respect to the experience of painful or disruptive emotions, this may be a desirable outcome. However, the fact that partners experience only rare instances of anger or hurt does not mean that they are necessarily experiencing frequent instances of love and happiness, because positive emotions do not automatically occur in the absence of negative emotions. Rather, the key to eliciting positive emotions and enhancing relationship quality, according to Berscheid's (1983) model, is for partners to engineer interruptions that either remove existing obstacles to each other's desires, plans, or goals (e.g., Mary finds John's car keys) or facilitate their completion (e.g., Mary agrees that John should buy the car of his dreams). It is these kinds of unexpected, but facilitative, behaviors that generate positive feelings and emotions such as joy.

This model of emotion generation in relationships provides a strong foundation for understanding the basic conditions under which relationship partners respond with relatively undifferentiated feelings of upset or happiness in response to one another's daily behaviors. Essentially, individuals initially appraise interruptive events along two dimensions: motivational relevance ("Does it matter to me?") and motivational congruence ("Is it harmful or helpful to me?"; see also Roseman, 1984). However, to predict the experience of specific kinds of negative and positive emotions such as anger, fear, love, and pride, it is necessary to consider how individuals appraise an event or behavior along a variety of other dimensions, including its novelty, perceived cause (self, other, or external circumstances), legitimacy, and perceived controllability (see Ellsworth & Scherer, 2003). For example, if John notices that a personally relevant, motivationally incongruent event has

occurred (e.g., he will have to look after the children on his own during the coming week) and he appraises it as having been caused by his wife Mary (who is going on another business trip), unjust (this is the third trip in 3 months), and potentially within her control (she volunteered for it), John is likely to feel angry. Moreover, and in line with the functional account of emotion, anger motivates and energizes individuals to oppose or engage with the source of the perceived obstruction to their needs and desires; hence, John may feel an urge to confront Mary and demand that she cancel her trip. However, if Mary notices that a personally relevant, motivationally congruent event has occurred (e.g., she receives flowers at the office) and she appraises it as having been caused by her husband John (who remembered their wedding anniversary), and John intended to make her happy, Mary may feel an urge to express feelings of love to him (Fitness, 1996).

The results of cognitive appraisal studies have helped to elucidate the ways in which individuals' interpretations of events elicit different kinds of emotional responses, including in the context of close relationships. For example, in a study comparing the cognitive appraisals associated with experiences of hurt, sadness, and anger in romantic relationships, the fundamental cause of all three emotions was an interruptive event that was appraised as relevant to both relationship partners and motivationally incongruent (i.e., not what the partners wanted to happen; Fitness & Warburton, 2009). However, in contrast to the kinds of appraisals that characterized anger, which involved perceptions of injustice and partner blame, hurt-eliciting events were associated with appraisals of relationship devaluation and a perceived lack of caring from the partner; moreover, hurtful events were viewed as significantly more unexpected, effortful, and difficult to understand than anger-eliciting events. Sadness, in contrast to both anger and hurt, was associated with appraisals involving perceived loss, low unexpectedness, and low control (e.g., after a relationship breakup). Each of these emotions, in turn, was associated with distinct motivations to confront (anger), cry and withdraw (hurt), and seek comfort (sadness).

People frequently experience several emotions in rapid succession, depending on the focus of their appraisals. For example, jealousy is typically regarded as a mix of more basic emotions such as anger, sadness, and anxiety (Harris & Darby, 2010; Panksepp, 2010). Depending on which aspect of the love triangle is being examined, individuals experiencing jealousy may feel anger toward the partner in response to the appraisal that his or her behavior is unjust and controllable; fear in response to the appraisal that their valued relationship is under threat; and sadness in response to the appraisal that their partner's affections have been lost or that the relationship has been irreparably damaged. Individuals may also experience painful, self-focused emotions such as shame when focusing on their own inadequacies in comparison to a romantic rival and other-focused emotions such as hatred for a rival who is favored by their partner. Each of these emotions may, in turn, instigate urges to take revenge on, or destroy, a rival (Fitness, 1996; Rempel & Burris, 2005; Tangney & Dearing, 2002).

It is important to be explicit about the distinction between motivations and behaviors. As discussed previously, emotions are ancient, evolved systems that prepare and motivate individuals to solve problems of survival and reproduction; however, evolutionary theory cannot predict an individual's likely behavior in response to a particular kind of situation. Such prediction requires an understanding of both how the individual cognitively appraises (interprets) the situation and how she or he has been emotionally socialized, given her or his particular familial and cultural background (Planalp & Fitness, 1999). For example, although many jealous individuals may engage in vengeful fantasies about murdering their hated rivals, very few of them actually do so (Frijda, 1994). In different cultures, however, such behaviors in response to relationship threats or offended honor are regarded as not only appropriate but mandatory (e.g., Vandello, Cohen, Grandon, & Franiuk, 2009). Moreover, although researchers have demonstrated that laypeople can describe prototypical emotion features and rules according to their cultural backgrounds (e.g., understanding what typically causes anger in relationships

and what angry people typically do; see Fehr & Baldwin, 1996), they often behave quite differently in their own relationships, depending on the idiosyncratic emotion rules they have learned within their own families (e.g., "sulk to let people know you're angry" or "never let anyone know you are jealous"; Fitness, 1996).

In summary, emotions are elicited in close relationships when partners perceive an interruptive event that they view as being either congruent or incongruent with their needs, desires, plans, and goals. To the extent that such events are cognitively elaborated along various dimensions such as perceived cause, fairness, controllability, and intentionality, different kinds of emotions are elicited along with their associated motivational features. The question that arises, then, is why individuals' appraisals differ, such that one individual appraises an interruptive event such as a surprise 40th birthday party as motivationally congruent, partner caused, and well intentioned and thus experiences love, whereas another individual appraises the same event as motivationally incongruent, partner caused, and maliciously intentioned and hence experiences anger. In fact, a variety of proximal and distal factors shape individuals' cognitive appraisals and emotions within close relationships, several of which I now discuss.

WHAT SHAPES PARTNERS' APPRAISALS AND EMOTIONS IN RELATIONSHIPS?

As noted previously, the cognitive appraisal process is a sequential one that takes place over time, with even the most subtle shifts in appraisal shaping corresponding shifts in feelings and emotions (Ellsworth, 1991). However, the process is also dynamic, with emotions having the capacity to shape ongoing cognitive appraisals. For example, sadness is elicited by appraisals of a circumstantially caused, uncontrollable loss, whereas anger is elicited by appraisals of a controllable, other-caused unjust behavior. Once elicited, these emotional states may color perceptions and interpretations of future interruptive events, such as discovering a dent in a new car after a partner's trip to the supermarket. Whereas a sad individual might appraise this event as beyond the partner's control and as a reminder of all the other disappointments the partner has experienced in life, an angry individual may appraise the same event as entirely the partner's fault and as a reminder of what a terrible driver the partner is (Keltner, Ellsworth, & Edwards, 1993).

In this sense, and as Sartre (1948/1976) noted, emotions magically transform the world and people's relationships with one another, such that an individual in love perceives the beloved through rose-colored glasses, spends her or his days dreaming about the beloved's wonderful qualities, and either fails to notice the beloved's less-than-ideal traits or reinterprets them as desirable. Of course, once the magic of love wears off, the same traits may be reappraised as irritating or unbearable flaws (Felmlee, 1995). Jealousy, too, colors the world green and drives paranoid ruminations about a partner's potential faithlessness, along with heightening vigilance for betrayal cues, lowering the threshold for detecting them, and motivating behaviors such as spying, arguing, pleading, and revenge (Guerrero & Andersen, 1998).

Such emotion-driven ways of appraising relationship events may also derive from chronic, or dispositional, emotion tendencies. For example, personality researchers have found that individuals differ in the extent to which they habitually experience positive and negative emotions (positive vs. negative affectivity; Watson, 2002). Positive affectivity is associated with optimism, expansiveness, and an approach-related disposition (Gable, Reis, & Elliot, 2000). Individuals who have high positive affectivity are more likely to explore and take advantage of novel and challenging situations, and they display more interest, excitement, and pleasure than individuals who have low positive affectivity. As might be expected, individuals who have optimistic, approach-oriented dispositions tend to have more satisfying marriages (Gordon & Baucom, 2009). In part, this is likely to be a function of their greater optimism and more adaptive coping skills; however, individuals high in positive affectivity also experience negative emotions less intensely than do individuals low in positive affectivity, which may help them resolve relationship conflicts more effectively (see Simpson, Winterheld & Chen, 2006, for a review).

In contrast to individuals who perceive the world through rose-colored spectacles, other individuals tend to experience relatively frequent episodes of anxiety, tension, anger, feelings of rejection, and sadness (high negative affectivity). The motivations of individuals high in negative affectivity tend to be avoidance or prevention focused, and they experience negative emotions more intensely and positive emotions less intensely than do other people (Higgins, 1998). They also overreact to even mildly unpleasant or anxiety-inducing events and ruminate over perceived hurts and injustices wrought by others. Such negative emotional traits often spell disaster for marital happiness in the long term (Beach & Fincham, 1994), partly because such individuals are not much fun to live with but also because their negative emotionality can be contagious (Hatfield, Cacioppo, & Rapson, 1993). Another important reason for the negative impact of high negative affectivity on relationship satisfaction derives from the primary motivation of individuals high in negative affectivity to prevent bad things from happening rather than seeking out and facilitating the kinds of positive events that generate positive relationship emotions (Berscheid, 1983; Simpson et al., 2006). Moreover, the tendency to ruminate in response to perceived relationship threats impairs individuals' abilities to maintain positive feelings for their partners (Jostmann, Karremans, & Finkenauer, 2011).

Along with chronic emotional dispositions, another important influence on partners' appraisals of, and emotional responses to, relationship events derives from what they have learned during their lives, both explicitly and implicitly, about relationships and, in particular, their attachment histories (e.g., Bowlby, 1969, 1973, 1980; Feeney, 1999; Hazan & Shaver, 1987; Shaver, Collins, & Clark, 1996). According to attachment theorists, human infants learn through their relationships with caregivers about the extent to which they are loved and valued and the extent to which others are caring and trustworthy. If all goes well, caregivers effectively fall in love with their infants and provide a safe and caring haven for them. This attachment relationship, in turn, generates strong positive emotions when attachment figures are perceived as being available and strong negative emotions when humans lose, or perceive they may lose, their attachment figures. Ideally, these early relationships are the source of an infant's first powerful experiences of love, trust, and joy, and they enable the child to learn, in a secure and loving relationship, how to regulate emotions such as anger, anxiety, and sadness. However, not every attachment relationship is secure. Some infants learn from their experiences of inconsistent, harsh, or neglectful parenting that they are fundamentally unsafe and uncared for, and their relationships with their caregivers are correspondingly insecure.

As adults, individuals enter relationships with implicit cognitive theories (working models or schemas), derived from earlier attachment experiences, about what to expect from relationships and relationship partners (Mikulincer & Shaver, 2005; Shaver & Mikulincer, 2006). These theories play a powerful role in shaping individuals' appraisals and emotions in adult relationships. Specifically, individuals whose early attachment experiences have been characterized by love, support, and trust have a secure base from which to draw comfort and strength when it is needed. Such securely attached adults believe that they are valued and that their relationship partners are trustworthy. As a result, they are well equipped to solve relationship problems constructively and to manage difficult emotions such as anxiety or anger effectively. In contrast, individuals whose early attachment experiences have been characterized by inconsistent parenting learn that relationships are highly unstable and unsafe. Such anxiously attached individuals hope that they will be loved and cared for, yet they also fear and expect that they could be abandoned. Accordingly, they are hypervigilant for signs of rejection; they tend to appraise their partners' ambiguous behaviors as hostile, and they experience frequent and strong feelings of anger, hurt, and anxiety. These emotions, in turn, motivate responses such as either furious retaliation or clingy, dependent behaviors that damage their relationships. Finally, individuals who have avoidant attachment styles have learned from experiences of harsh and rejecting parenting that relationship partners cannot be relied on for support when it is needed. Avoidant individuals expect that relationship partners will also be rejecting and unhelpful; hence, during times of stress, they reject emotional closeness and favor self-reliance to protect themselves from experiencing further pain.

In summary, cognitive appraisal theorists have argued that emotions are elicited as a function of individuals' appraisals of events; furthermore, emotions themselves color ongoing appraisals in ways that may, over time, become chronic or dispositional. In this sense, cognition and emotion are profoundly intertwined, with beliefs and expectations shaping appraisals and emotions and with emotions, in turn, informing and shaping beliefs and expectations. Attachment schemas are one of the clearest examples of this dynamic cognition–emotion link, with partners' beliefs about their own lovability and trustworthiness shaping their emotional responses to disruptive relationship events and partner behaviors. However, an important distinction must be noted. Specifically, the focus of this chapter has thus far been on the experience of emotions rather than on their expression, and the two are not necessarily congruent. Relationship partners may express emotions they do not feel, and they may feel emotions they do not express; they may also attempt to express the emotions they feel but do so in ways that lead to misunderstandings and distress. In the next section, I discuss the communication of emotion in relationships and consider the role of emotion regulation in adaptive emotion functioning.

EMOTION COMMUNICATION IN CLOSE RELATIONSHIPS

As noted in the first section of this chapter, one of the defining features of close relationships is that partners care about and take responsibility for each others' needs. Emotional expressions of joy, sadness, anger, and love communicate partners' needs and desires to one another and allow for the reciprocal fulfillment of needs (Clark et al., 2001). This process, in turn, strengthens relationship intimacy and connection. For example, in a study of people with osteoarthritis, Monin, Martire, Schulz, and Clark (2009) found that their willingness to express happiness was associated with more sensitive caregiver responses, whereas their willingness to express other-focused emotions, such as compassion, guilt, or worry for their caregivers, predicted less caregiving stress. Caregiving wives, in particular, benefited from their husbands' willingness to express vulnerable emotions such as anxiety and sadness.

Clearly, emotional expressiveness is important for adaptive relationship functioning. However, its effectiveness depends on the extent to which partners are able to accurately express and interpret emotion signals. Research on the features and outcomes of empathic accuracy (e.g., Ickes, Simpson, & Oriña, 2005) has generally confirmed the link between effective emotional communication and positive relationship outcomes. In their study of nonverbal emotional expression in marriage, for example, Koerner and Fitzpatrick (2002) found that the ability to accurately decode nonverbal expressions of relationship-related positive emotions such as love and nonverbal expressions of non–relationship-related negative emotions such as anger about work (and not with the partner) was associated with greater marital satisfaction.

Moreover, the adaptiveness of emotional expressivity in close relationships depends to some extent on the type of emotion being expressed. For example, Kubany, Bauer, Muraoka, Richard, and Read (1995) found that both husbands and wives reacted more negatively to communications of explicit anger than to communications of implicit distress. Feeney, Noller, and Roberts (1998) noted that expressing sadness, but not anger, in response to negative partner behavior was associated with positive relationship outcomes. Similarly, Sanford and Rowatt (2004) found that, after controlling for the overlap between the experience of "soft" (e.g., distress) and "hard" (e.g., anger) emotions during marital conflict, the experience of soft emotion predicted higher satisfaction, lower conflict, and lower avoidance, whereas the unique component of hard emotions predicted poorer relationship outcomes.

These findings do not imply that the expression of anger is never adaptive, because anger communicates an important message about a relationship partner's needs and desires (Fischer & Roseman, 2007; Fitness & Fletcher, 1993). Moreover, Ellis and Malamuth (2000) demonstrated that partners' feelings of love and anger were not mutually exclusive

(i.e., that anger and love coexist in close relationships), and both serve separate, but equally important, goals. However, there is a problem with the frequent expression of anger that derives from the tendency for interacting spouses to reciprocate the emotions they perceive (either accurately or inaccurately) are being expressed to them. Unhappy spouses, who typically expect the worst from one another, tend to perceive even soft, negative emotional messages as hostile and reciprocate with overtly hostile emotional messages. These messages, in turn, are perceived even more negatively than intended by the partner, which triggers even more hostile responses. In this way, destructive tit-for-tat emotion sequences are established from which most couples find it difficult to disengage (Gottman, 1994). Moreover, the frequent reciprocation and escalation of anger in relationships can have a corrosive effect over time, with chronically angry partners appraising each other's behaviors as automatically blameworthy and maliciously motivated.

One important implication of these findings is that if individuals have a clear and coherent understanding of the features and functions of emotions, they may find it easier to both clearly express their own emotions and recognize and empathize with their partners' emotions. Such emotion knowledge derives from childhood, when people learn, both explicitly and implicitly, about the causes and consequences of emotions such as anger, fear, and love from their families and their wider culture (Eisenberg, Cumberland, & Spinrad, 1998). For example, they learn what typically causes different emotions, what different emotions feel like, what people who feel them typically do, and what their short-term and long-term consequences are (e.g., Fehr & Baldwin, 1996; Fitness, 1996; Fitness & Fletcher, 1993; Shaver, Schwartz, Kirson, & O'Connor, 1987). Depending on how differentiated and sophisticated their emotion knowledge is, individuals may be more or less able to perceive, interpret, and respond appropriately to their partners' emotional expressions (or lack thereof). For example, an empathic spouse who has a deep understanding of emotions may readily understand how his or her spouse is feeling after a stressful day at work or may appreciate the underlying insecurity of a partner who demands frequent reassurance that she or he is loved and valued. This empathic spouse may then correctly interpret the causes of his or her ill temper or anxiety and choose not to react defensively but rather to respond with support and affection. This, in turn, ought to soothe and comfort the partner (Fitness, 2006).

Possessing such differentiated emotion knowledge is positively associated with the ability to cope effectively with the emotional ups and downs of marriage. In a study of emotional intelligence in marriage, for example, Fitness and Mathews (1998) found that individuals who reported higher emotion clarity (a measure of emotion understanding) also tended to report greater marital happiness, irrespective of their age or gender. Furthermore, individuals who displayed higher emotion clarity reported significantly less difficulty in forgiving a partner-caused offense than did participants displaying lower emotion clarity, regardless of how serious the offense was, how much hurt and pain it caused, or how happily or unhappily married the individual was. Interestingly, individuals low in emotion clarity were more likely than those high in emotion clarity to experience shame (rather than guilt) in relation to their own marital offenses and believed that their partners hated them more. On one hand, guilt is a constructive emotion that motivates attempts to repair a damaged relationship; shame, on the other hand, frequently motivates displays of defensive anger (Tangney & Dearing, 2002). It is possible, then, that offending individuals who have lower emotion understanding may interpret their partners' hurt as hatred and respond with humiliated fury rather than with remorse and sorrow. These emotions, in turn, would mitigate against relationship repair (Fitness & Peterson, 2008).

It is also interesting to consider the ways in which attachment orientations may affect relationship partners' empathic accuracy. Securely attached individuals are able to acknowledge their own distress and turn to their attachment figures for comfort and support, whereas highly anxious individuals tend to focus their attention on the source of their distress and to make every effort to obtain the responsiveness they fear is not forthcoming. Avoidantly attached individuals tend not to acknowledge

being upset about relational issues and turn away from their attachment figures rather than seeking support (Mikulincer & Shaver, 2005). Consistent with these observations, anxiously attached individuals actually become more empathically accurate under conditions of relationship threat, whereas avoidant individuals show reduced empathic accuracy (Simpson et al., 2011). As Simpson et al. (2011) commented, simply staying "out of the partner's head" is one of the best ways to ensure that painful attachment-related emotions are not activated. Moreover, Sprecher and Fehr (2011) found that avoidantly attached young adults experience significantly less compassionate love for their partners than do securely attached adults. Such emotional distancing and lack of empathic concern means that avoidantly attached individuals may miss out on the rewards of both giving and receiving nurturance.

Finally, it is instructive to note the findings of a recent study on the effects of both empathic accuracy and perceived empathic effort on the relationship satisfaction of partners in committed relationships (Cohen, Schulz, Weiss, & Waldinger, 2012). During a videotaped interaction, these researchers found that partners' perceptions of empathic effort were more strongly linked to relationship satisfaction than empathic accuracy itself. This finding underscores the importance of partners' perceived motivation to care and be responsive to one another, with such responsive behaviors signaling relationship investment. It is also reminiscent of a 14-year longitudinal study of married couples that found it was the absence of any expressed emotion in spouses' coded conversations that was most predictive of later divorce (Gottman & Levenson, 2002). Such emotionally disengaged interactions signal that partners may effectively be living their lives along parallel lines with few, if any, interconnections (Berscheid, 1983); they have simply become irrelevant to one another.

As noted earlier, emotional expressiveness is generally adaptive in close relationships, but there are times when it may be more adaptive not to express one's emotions, or even to express emotions that are not felt (such as gratitude for an unwanted gift or a strategic display of anger to ensure toddler compliance with a safety directive; see Clark et al., 1996). This raises a critically important aspect of emotional communication—the ability to manage and regulate both one's own and sometimes another person's emotions (such as when soothing one's partner).

The results of several studies have confirmed the importance of effective emotion regulation for relationship happiness and stability. For example, and as noted previously, individuals who have high levels of negative affectivity tend to experience more frequent and intense negative emotions, and they have correspondingly more difficult and less satisfying relationships because it is difficult to be married to a chronically bad-tempered, pessimistic, and depressed spouse (Beach & Fincham, 1994). Indeed, a longitudinal study by Caspi, Elder, and Bem (1987) found that nearly 50% of men who had a long-standing history of temper tantrums during childhood had divorced by age 40, compared with only 22% of men without such a history. Similarly, nearly 25% of women who had a history of bad temper had divorced by midlife, compared with only 12% of women who had a history of being more good tempered. In line with these findings, happy spouses are also more likely to inhibit their impulses to react destructively when their spouses express anger or behave unreasonably, and they try to respond instead in a conciliatory or constructive manner (e.g., Rusbult, Bissonnette, Arriaga, & Cox, 1998). However, it is important to consider how people go about inhibiting or regulating their emotions in light of the fact that some strategies are more adaptive than others.

Gross and John (2003) identified two common strategies for regulating emotions: cognitive reappraisal (whereby individuals reinterpret an emotion-eliciting situation in such a way that changes its emotional impact) and expressive suppression (whereby individuals attempt to hide or inhibit the expression of their emotions). There are several intrapersonal costs associated with suppressing emotions, including the more frequent experience of negative emotions and the less frequent experience of positive emotions over time (Gross & John, 2003). Suppressing emotions is also effortful. For example, a study in which romantic partners were instructed to suppress their emotional expressions during a naturalistic interaction found that suppressors showed poorer memory for what was said during the interaction (Richards, Butler, & Gross, 2003). This finding indicates that suppressing emotion reduces the amount of attention an individual can devote to his or her partner's actual behavior, with potentially negative implications for relationship functioning. Furthermore, in a study in which college women were videotaped engaging in a conflict discussion with their partners (Mongrain & Vettese, 2003), women who later reported that they had felt highly ambivalent about expressing their emotions to their partners also reported trying to suppress negative emotions such as anger during the discussion. However, there was some leakage of their negative emotions, with ambivalent women making fewer positive comments and sending more mismatched verbal and nonverbal expressions to their partners. The communication of such contradictory nonverbal emotion signals is reliably associated with greater marital distress (Noller & Ruzzene, 1991).

Another interesting line of research that has demonstrated both the intrapersonal and the interpersonal costs of emotional suppression was reported by Impett et al. (2012). These researchers demonstrated that the connection between emotional suppression (e.g., pretending that one is not annoyed about having to run an inconvenient errand for one's partner) and interpersonal costs (such as relational dissatisfaction) is the perception of inauthenticity; that is, because they are behaving in ways that are incongruent with their actual feelings, suppressors feel less true to themselves. Consistent with this argument, Gross and John (2003) noted that feelings of greater authenticity predict better intrapersonal adjustment and relationship quality. This helps to explain why cognitive reappraisal is a more functional method than suppression for managing and regulating one's emotions. Rather than trying to smile through gritted teeth while wishing he or she could shout at a partner, an individual may reappraise the partner's request to run an errand either as an opportunity to do some shopping along the way or as a reminder of all the errands that the partner ran when the individual was recently ill. These appraisals, in turn, should diminish anger and may even generate positive emotions such as gratitude—emotions that are experienced as authentic and that also send signals of support to the spouse.

In summary, the effective communication of emotions is integral to adaptive relationship functioning. Emotions transmit information about partners' needs and desires, so relationships flounder when partners fail to understand, clearly express, or accurately interpret each other's emotion signals. Maintaining satisfying relationships also depends on the effective management of emotions such as anger and hostility, not only via emotional suppression but also via cognitive reappraisal of disruptive events such that blaming, anger-eliciting cognitions, and emotions are reduced or replaced with more positive cognitions and emotions. This underscores a growing understanding among both relationship researchers and clinicians that simply reducing the frequency and intensity of negative emotions is not sufficient for relationship happiness; partners must actively work to elicit positive emotions such as love, joy, excitement, and gratitude to keep their relationships happy and healthy. I discuss this link between positivity and adaptive relationship functioning next.

ROLE OF POSITIVE EMOTIONS IN ADAPTIVE RELATIONSHIP FUNCTIONING

Traditionally, the focus of researchers interested in relationship emotions has been on the so-called negative emotions such as anger, anxiety, and jealousy—the ones that bring couples to marital therapy. Over the past 10 years, however, there has been an explosion of interest in the so-called positive emotions and the critical role they play in building and maintaining healthy and happy relationships (e.g., Fredrickson, 2001). According to Fredrickson's (2001) broaden-and-build model, positive emotions serve three important functions. First, when individuals experience positive emotions, their perceptions, cognitions, and behaviors become broader and more expansive, and they are motivated to approach and engage more with their environments. Second, as a consequence of this expansion

and engagement, positive emotions help individuals build their intellectual, psychological, and physical resources, which can strengthen their social relationships. Third, when positive emotions are experienced after a stressful event, they help to undo the negative effects of stress and facilitate recovery—in effect, they provide the calm after the storm and facilitate reflection and psychological growth. Moreover, and as Fredrickson (2001) also noted, a major benefit for relationships of having the kind of broad outlook that positive emotions generate is the way they help partners see the big picture and avoid becoming focused on small, transient annoyances. Similarly, positive emotions stimulate creativity, which in turn assists in problem solving and strengthens partners' feelings of strength and solidarity.

Of course, positive emotions are not an amorphous, global entity. As Sauter (2010) noted, there are many ways of feeling good, and positive emotions such as joy, excitement, passion, pride, wonder, relief, and hope should be treated as discrete psychological entities (see also Ekman, 2003). Furthermore, and in line with the functionalist perspective, each of these emotions has its own cognitive and motivational profile and has a potentially important role to play in the formation and maintenance of relationships. Happiness, for example, can be separated into joy (a high-arousal emotion) and contentment (a low-arousal emotion; Fredrickson, 2001). The function of contentment is to enable savoring, whereby one enjoys and mentally integrates the experience of having one's needs met (a process that presumably assists in producing similar experiences in the future). The function of joy, however, is to promote the formation and maintenance of social bonds. It also creates the urge to play, which in turn builds and strengthens friendships and attachment relationships (see also Panksepp, 1998). Tomkins (1962), too, discussed how important it is for social creatures who depend on others for their survival to be motivated to seek one another out, to find pleasure in each other's company, and to enjoy close bodily contact and touch. He also noted how mutual gaze and smiling (the look of love) create a *felicité à deux,* through which individuals become aware of each other's enjoyment, amplifying the experience of their mutual attraction and communion.

However, joy and contentment are not the only positive emotions involved in the formation and maintenance of close relationships: Interest and excitement are also vital, though understudied, aspects. Silvia (2008) noted that, whereas happiness promotes attachments to people, objects, or experiences that have proven rewarding in the past, interest motivates individuals to explore new objects, people, and experiences. The two emotions frequently co-occur (such as when dating partners are first getting to know one another and find each other fascinating) with the experience of joy and happiness as partners play, laugh, and share intimacy together. However, interest and excitement may also occur independently, such as when an individual feels torn between his or her alternating desires for familiar attachments (motivated by joy, contentment, or both) and his or her desire for novelty (motivated by interest). Similarly, within a close relationship, partners may be emotionally attuned to one another with respect to the joy and interest they feel for one another, or they may be out of step, with one partner finding him- or herself bored with the familiar and desiring some novelty and excitement (Planalp, Fitness, & Fehr, 2006).

The importance of interest and excitement in close relationships has also been underscored by research on relational boredom. For example, Harasymchuk and Fehr (2012) found relational boredom was more strongly associated with the lack of positive emotions than with the presence of negative emotions (i.e., it was the perceived absence of facilitative interruptions, rather than the occurrence of motivationally incongruent interruptions, that generated feelings of apathy and discontent). Moreover, the greater the boredom reported by participants, the lower the likelihood that they had engaged in exciting activities with their spouses during the past few weeks, which is consistent with the previous discussion on the role of interest in close relationships. Other studies have also demonstrated that the joint pursuit of novel and exciting activities significantly enhanced spouses' marital satisfaction (e.g., Aron, Norman, Aron, McKenna, & Heyman, 2000).

None of the positive emotions discussed thus far are experienced exclusively within close relationships. Love, however, is a prototypically relationship-oriented emotion; indeed, laypeople report that love is one of most important emotions of all (Shaver, Morgan, & Wu, 1996). Even so, it has only been recently that love has been regarded by researchers as an emotion distinct from other-directed happiness, and some debate still occurs about whether love is a drive or an emotion. Rempel and Burris (2005), for example, defined love as a "motivational state in which the goal is to preserve and promote the well-being of the valued object" (p. 299), suggesting that love is a hunger, or desire, rather than an evolved psychological mechanism with its own physiological, cognitive, motivational, and behavioral features. Romantic love has also been characterized as a motivational state that leads to specific emotions such as euphoria or anxiety (Aron et al., 2005). Other researchers have argued that at least two functionally distinct types of love exist: passionate love and attachment love, both of which frequently co-occur in romantic love relationships. Attachment love, in turn, may be further divided into nurturing or caregiving love and intimate, companionate love (see Berscheid, 2010).

Passionate love has been defined as "a state of intense longing for union with another" (Hatfield, Bensman, & Rapson, 2012, p. 144). Found in more than 140 cultures across the world (Jankowiak & Fischer, 1992), the function of passionate love is to motivate mating behavior; accordingly, the experience of passionate love is associated with a strong desire for sex. Attachment love, however, is believed to derive from the same evolved attachment system that binds infants to their caregivers (Berscheid, 2010). Just as attachment love motivates parents to care for their children as they grow to adulthood, so too does attachment love motivate relationship partners to commit to one another while they (potentially) raise highly dependent children (Fisher, 1994). Both passionate love and attachment love are functionally independent (i.e., one can feel sexual desire without the desire for commitment and emotional closeness, and vice versa; Gonzaga, Turner, Keltner, Campos, & Altemus, 2006), and both are associated with different physiological processes and hormones (i.e., oxytocin and endogenous opioids are associated with attachment love, whereas gonadal estrogens and androgens are associated with sexual desire; Panksepp, 1998).

Although a considerable amount of research has been done on the features and functions of passionate love (Hatfield et al., 2012, published a list of more than 33 measures of this construct), attachment love is what keeps couples together, long after passion has waned. Moreover, attachment love is extremely rewarding in its own right. For example, in a study exploring laypeople's remembered accounts of feeling love rather than lust for their spouses, respondents reported feelings of warmth, positive partner-related appraisals (including daydreaming about their partners and their admirable qualities) and urges to hug and be close to them and give them gifts (Fitness & Fletcher, 1993). These results suggest that partners do experience feelings of love in their close relationships that presumably are functional over time with respect to building trust, intimacy, and relationship happiness. The results of Fitness and Fletcher's (1993) study also confirmed that there is an important difference between sexual desire and romantic love (though the latter may at times include the former). The respondents were asked to think of times when they felt love (rather than lust) for their spouses, and their responses were consistent with the kind of deep and affectionate caring that typifies attachment love, involving such features as caring for the loved one's welfare, mutual understanding, and giving and providing emotional support.

Another area of research that has strong links to attachment love is being carried out by scholars with an interest in compassion (or compassionate love; see Sprecher & Fehr, 2011). Goetz, Keltner, and Simon-Thomas (2010) argued that compassion is a distinct emotion that arises in response to an appraisal of another's suffering, which is associated with subjective feelings of concern and with behaviors designed to alleviate the suffering (including physical soothing). From an evolutionary perspective, Goetz et al. argued that compassion serves various functions, such as motivating care of vulnerable offspring and (most relevant to adult relationships)

signaling kindness and nurturing abilities to prospective mates. Given that a very large cross-cultural study on mate preferences found that kindness is the top priority for both men and women all over the world (Buss, 1989), the capacity for compassion may give individuals a real mating advantage. However, as Goetz et al. noted, many of their hypotheses about the functions of compassion and other kinds of positive, other-oriented emotions (such as tenderness and sympathy; see Lishner, Batson, & Huss, 2011) have yet to be empirically tested.

Gratitude is another important relationship-relevant emotion that is attracting growing attention. According to Kubacka, Finkenauer, Rusbult, and Keijsers (2011), gratitude is triggered when individuals perceive their partners have engaged in costly behaviors that are responsive to their important needs. From a functional perspective, feelings of gratitude are part of an evolved detection-and-response system that helps people to "find, remind, and bind ourselves to attentive others" (Algoe, Haidt, & Gable, 2008, p. 429). Clearly, the emotion of gratitude (which can be overwhelming when a loved one rescues one from a dire situation) strengthens people's relationships with those who care about them. Furthermore, Lambert, Clark, Durtschi, Fincham, and Graham (2010) argued that expressing gratitude sends a positive, relationship-building signal not only to the person who gave the benefit (with its implied promise of reciprocation in the future) but also to the beneficiary, whose feelings of gratitude further reinforce his or her own belief that this is a strong relationship in which the helpful partner can be trusted.

In a longitudinal study of married couples, Kubacka et al. (2011) tested the dyadic effects of gratitude over three time points for approximately 4 years after marriage. They found that feelings of gratitude stem from partners' recognition of each other's relationship maintenance behaviors, such as encouragement and attempts to resolve conflicts and help one another, because such behaviors signal the kind of responsiveness to one's needs that typify close relationships (Clark et al., 2001). In turn, gratitude motivates reciprocal relationship maintenance behaviors, whereby each partner's helpfulness, perceptions of responsiveness, and feelings of gratitude feed back on and influence the other's behaviors, perceptions, and feelings.

Taken together, the research on positive emotions is highly informative with respect to the key emotion-related features that distinguish functional from dysfunctional relationships. First, happy relationships are characterized by the expression of more positive than negative emotions. Carstensen, Gottman, and Levenson (1995) found that spouses in long-term, happy marriages express conflict-related emotions to one another much less frequently than they express affection and good humor. Indeed, they calculated that a ratio of 5 positive emotions to 1 negative emotion is essential for adaptive relationship functioning. Happy spouses are also skilled at deescalating the kinds of destructive negative interaction sequences characteristic of unhappy couples. For example, they tend to react to a spouse's expressions of anger with neutral or caring responses instead of with retaliatory anger.

Second, partners in happy relationships foster a culture of appreciation within their marriages that involves warmth and emotional connectedness (Fitness, 2006; Gottman, 1998). For example, Pinkus, Lockwood, Marshall, and Yoon (2012) found that romantically involved individuals responded positively in situations in which their partners had outperformed them because they were both pleased for, and proud of, their partners (as opposed to being envious or resentful).

Third, happy couples share positive emotions with one another; they enjoy enhancing each other's happiness, including the sharing of good news with one another. For example, Gable, Reis, Impett, and Asher (2004) found that telling others about personal positive events (referred to as *capitalization*) was positively associated with the experience of daily positive emotions and well-being, above and beyond the impact of the positive events themselves. Similarly, Hicks and Diamond (2008) found that participants reported more positive emotional experiences when they or their partners discussed the most positive event they had experienced that day. Moreover, when others were perceived to respond enthusiastically to the sharing of positive events, the beneficial effects on relationship satisfaction and intimacy were even greater (Reis et al., 2010).

In summary, adaptive relationship functioning requires partners to engage with one another in a climate of trust and affection. They need to exceed each other's expectations, delight and surprise each other, plan activities together, help realize each other's hopes and plans, and actively support each other in times of trouble and stress. These are also the requirements for generating the emotions of joy and love, interest and excitement, and compassion and gratitude, emotions that build relationship strengths and enable partners to flourish both individually and together.

DIRECTIONS FOR FUTURE RESEARCH

Although research on emotions has been rapidly increasing over the past few years, many aspects of the features and functions of emotions in explicitly relational contexts are still unexplored and poorly understood. For example, a relatively large body of research now exists on the development and impact of attachment working models on relationship partners' cognitions, emotions, motivations, and behaviors. However, there is still much to learn about the role of emotion schemas in shaping relationship interactions. As noted earlier in this chapter, people acquire knowledge about the causes and consequences of various emotions, including the rules for their expression (or suppression), as they grow up in their families of origin. These knowledge structures (schemas) drive people's expectations, perceptions, judgments, and even memories of emotion-related events in adulthood (Fitness, 1996). For example, an individual's expressions of vulnerability when she or he is growing up may be met with expressions of disgust from the individual's primary caregiver; hence, the individual may be likely as an adult to be vigilant for signs of vulnerability in her or his partner, to appraise any signs of vulnerability as weakness, and to respond to any perceived expressions of vulnerability with disgust. This emotion may, in turn, motivate punishment and rejection of the partner when the partner is actually signaling a need for support. Another individual may have learned from childhood experiences to respond to both his or her own and other people's anger with fear; hence, the individual is likely to notice even mild signs of partner displeasure and to experience anxiety-related urges to appease or escape the situation (Jenkins & Oatley, 1998; Magai & McFadden, 1995; Tomkins, 1962, 1963).

These kinds of emotion schemas have potentially important implications for how people feel about, and respond to, experiences of perceived threat, abandonment, challenge, powerlessness, unjust treatment, or even care and compassion in their close relationships. Moreover, similar to attachment schemas, emotion schemas may frequently operate at a nonconscious level. Consequently, people may fail to realize what it is about their interactions with their relationship partners that presses their buttons and triggers powerful feelings of distress, anger, shame, or disgust. Indeed, people may find such feelings difficult to articulate and make sense of at a conscious level. They may also feel powerless to escape the repetitious cycles and frequently destructive effects of their negative emotion schemas, both on themselves and on their relationships. For example, researchers have demonstrated the powerful effects of dispositional guilt proneness and shame proneness on the ways in which individuals appraise their own and each other's behaviors (e.g., Tangney & Dearing, 2002). Appraising relationship events through a shame-prone lens, in particular, activates feelings of belittlement and humiliation, along with motivating defensive and destructive relationship behaviors. Such behaviors elicit the kinds of reactions from partners that confirm the shame-prone individual's view of him- or herself as defective and without value.

Although they may be powerful and resistant to change, learned emotion schemas are unlikely to be set in stone from early childhood. Rather, over the course of people's lives, these schemas may be modified as a function of people's ongoing emotional experiences with others. Why particular kinds of emotion schemas might be more or less likely to develop, what impact they might have on relationship processes, how such emotion schemas might be changed, or the role of others in mediating such changes remain empirical questions. Clearly, this is a fascinating and important topic that would reward a systematic approach by future relationship researchers (see Consedine & Magai, 2003).

There is also a need for more research on discrete emotions that, to date, have been relatively neglected. Contempt, for example, is a critically important relationship emotion that has attracted little research attention. Oatley and Jenkins (1996) argued that contempt is "the emotion of complete rejection, of unmodulated power, treating the other as a nonperson" (p. 313). In line with this theoretical analysis, Fischer and Roseman (2007) found that anger and contempt frequently occur together, but that there are differences between them. Specifically, the experience of anger is characterized by relatively short-term attack responses with the possibility of reconciliation over time (in line with its function of resolving interpersonal problems). However, contempt is characterized by the rejection and social exclusion of another person, in both the short term and the long term. Contempt may also develop from previously experienced anger, but a key feature involves a lack of connectedness to, intimacy with, and empathy for another, along with a perceived lack of control over their behaviors (i.e., "My partner is no good and will never change!"). The functions of contempt, then, are to isolate and exclude someone bad from one's life, and in this respect, contempt shares features with hatred. For example, Fitness and Fletcher (1993) found spouses' recalled experiences of marital anger to be characterized by powerful urges to do battle with their partners and to convince them of the rightness of their own positions. Experiences of marital hate, though, were characterized by urges to escape, avoid, and be rid of the offending partner (see also Fitness, 2001).

Given its features and functions, contempt is clearly toxic for all relationships. Indeed, Gottman (1994) reported that spouses' expressions of contempt during conflict interactions spell disaster for the marriage. However, relatively little is still known about its origins, its motivations, and its short- to medium-term relational consequences. For example, individuals who are frequently shamed by expressions of contempt from their partners may come to believe that they are less powerful and less worthy than their partners. Other couples may regularly engage in contempt–shame interactions and chronically belittle one another. Retzinger (1991), for example, described how spouses may jockey for position during marital quarrels by trading insults and put-downs. One partner's insult shames the other, who responds with defensive anger and a humiliating remark of his or her own, creating a relational interaction revolving around issues of power and subordination.

This observation underscores the need for more research on power and emotion dynamics within the close relationship context. Power is something of a dirty word in the close relationship context, with its connotations of coercion, manipulation, and exploitation; however, power is an integral and inescapable feature of all social relationships (see Chapter 15, this volume). All people negotiate power with others on a regular basis via their feelings and emotions (see Planalp et al., 2006). Furthermore, Anderson, Keltner, and John (2003) found that high-power individuals tend to shape the emotions of low-power partners (regardless of gender), which has a number of interesting implications for close relationship dynamics. For example, Anderson et al. argued that although it may seem dysfunctional for low-power individuals to adapt emotionally to high-power individuals, the resulting emotional similarity may actually contribute to relationship cohesion and longevity (see also Chapter 15, this volume). However, this is likely to depend on the emotion, with contempt, as noted previously, being a highly dysfunctional emotion for the relationship in the long term.

Relatedly, more longitudinal research is needed on emotions and emotional trajectories over time. For example, in a fascinating longitudinal study, Sbarra and Emery (2005) examined emotional reactions at different points in time after a relationship breakup in former dating partners. Participants recorded their emotions of love, sadness, anger, and relief over 28 days in a daily diary. Compared with still-dating participants, individuals who had broken up with their partners reported significantly more anger and less love over the 28 days, with feelings of love decreasing more slowly than feelings of sadness, which decreased more slowly still than feelings of anger. An important finding was that participants felt more love and sadness on days when they spoke to their ex-partners, either because the contact elicited fresh experiences of these emotions or because

feelings of love and sadness motivated them to contact their partners. In either case, this may clearly constitute a problem for separated and divorced individuals, who need to maintain contact with one another to share childcare or other joint responsibilities.

Individual differences are also an important consideration in understanding emotional responses to relationship breakdown and deattachment. For example, Simpson (1990) found that avoidant attachment was associated with less postbreakup distress for men in dating relationships, and Sbarra and Emery (2005) found in their longitudinal study that attachment security was negatively associated with reported anger and positively correlated with relief. Securely attached participants also experienced significantly faster rates of decline in sadness over time. Moreover, Sbarra (2006) found that more anxiously attached individuals have more difficulty recovering from postbreakup sadness than less anxiously attached individuals. As noted by other attachment theorists (e.g., Mikulincer & Shaver, 2005), anxiously attached individuals tend to become overwhelmed with negative emotions and loss- or rejection-related thoughts in response to relationship threat. In line with these observations, Fagundes (2012) conducted a study looking at postbreakup emotional adjustment and found that reflecting on painful emotions after a breakup predicted poor emotional adjustment immediately after the breakup, regardless of attachment security; however, only anxiously attached individuals suffered maladaptive outcomes from such reflections 1 month later, presumably because they were unable to effectively regulate their painful emotions. One potential antidote to such painful reflections might be self-compassion, involving the ability to engage in positive cognitive reappraisal when thinking about painful experiences (see also Sbarra, Smith, & Mehl, 2012).

Clearly, much more remains to be learned about emotional responses to relationship breakdown and loss, including such relatively understudied emotions as grief, guilt, relief, and hope. Future research should also include the emotional responses of others within a person's social network, including the cultural rules and norms that prescribe and proscribe particular forms of feeling, expression, and suppression (Planalp & Fitness, 1999). Such a consideration will require researchers not only to cross interdisciplinary boundaries but also to accept that the sociocultural aspects of emotions are, like their biological aspects, integral to scientific understanding of them. As social animals, all humans must deal with the same survival-related problems, including frustration, threat, and loss. Furthermore, research has confirmed that humans universally recognize and experience the same basic emotions in response to these situations such as anger, fear, and sadness (e.g., Ekman, 1992). However, there are also historical and cross-cultural differences in beliefs and value systems that shape cognitive appraisals and emotions.

For example, in contrast to Western, individualistic societies, many non-Western societies emphasize the importance of interconnectedness and the relational self (Andersen & Chen, 2002). This means that non-Western cultures have complex rules and systems for avoiding and dealing with emotions that may be considered disruptive to the smooth functioning of relationships. In line with this, Impett et al. (2012) noted the importance of considering potential cross-cultural differences in relation to the costs of emotional suppression, particularly in relational contexts. In Western individualist cultures that value independence and being true to oneself, emotional suppression may be seen as more harmful (less authentic) than in collectivist cultures, which place greater value on interdependence. Here, emotional suppression for the sake of relationship harmony may be less dysfunctional than in independent cultures (see Matsumoto, Yoo, & Nakagawa, 2008).

Finally, strong theory is needed to drive research in this field, and efforts must be made to conceptually integrate research questions and findings into a coherent, integrated body of knowledge and understanding. One of the strengths of emotion research to date is that so much work has been conducted in so many different disciplines, including sociology, neuroscience, anthropology, communication studies, and even history and philosophy. However, this diversity can pose a problem when research is conducted without reference to similar work that has been carried out in different fields or when researchers do not share basic conceptualizations of emotion. As discussed in this chapter, the social-functionalist approach can provide a solid foundation for emotion research at various levels of analysis, from the most distal evolutionary level to the most proximal analysis of real-time emotional experiences and expressions. Clearly, considerable scope exists within this overarching framework to further explore and enrich the understanding of the features and functions of emotions within close relationships.

In summary, many fascinating topics await the attention of researchers with an interest in emotions and the emotional dynamics of close relationships. In particular, there is much to be learned about the emotion schemas, derived from early familial and cultural contexts, that individuals bring to relationships and the impact of these schemas on relationship functioning. There is also more work to be done on the features and functions of discrete emotions and on changes in emotional trajectories from the beginning to the end of close relationships. Finally, researchers in this field need a strong theoretical framework for their studies to build a more coherent body of knowledge about the features and functions of emotions in relationship contexts. As noted throughout this chapter, the social-functionalist approach to emotion provides a potentially useful integrative framework to guide future research in this important field.

CONCLUSION

Emotions are the lifeblood of human relationships. Emotions move people to pursue their dreams, fall in and out of love, fight for what they desire, protect what they value, and mourn what they have lost. It is within people's close relationships that these emotional imperatives are experienced most frequently and urgently, for people cannot survive alone and uncared for. It is my hope that researchers will continue to be inspired and fascinated by emotions and that, over the next few years, we will see even richer and more coherent accounts of the crucial roles that emotions play in the initiation, maintenance, breakdown, and repair of close relationships.

References

Algoe, S. B., Haidt, J., & Gable, S. L. (2008). Beyond reciprocity: Gratitude and relationships in everyday life. *Emotion, 8,* 425–429. doi:10.1037/1528-3542.8.3.425

Andersen, S. M., & Chen, S. (2002). The relational self: An interpersonal social-cognitive theory. *Psychological Review, 109,* 619–645. doi:10.1037/0033-295X.109.4.619

Anderson, C., Keltner, D., & John, O. P. (2003). Emotional convergence between people over time. *Journal of Personality and Social Psychology, 84,* 1054–1068. doi:10.1037/0022-3514.84.5.1054

Aron, A., Fisher, H., Mashek, D., Strong, G., Li, H., & Brown, L. L. (2005). Reward, motivation and emotion systems associated with early-stage intense romantic love. *Journal of Neurophysiology, 94,* 327–337. doi:10.1152/jn.00838.2004

Aron, A., Norman, C. C., Aron, E. N., McKenna, C., & Heyman, R. E. (2000). Couples' shared participation in novel and arousing activities and experienced relational quality. *Journal of Personality and Social Psychology, 78,* 273–284. doi:10.1037/0022-3514.78.2.273

Beach, S., & Fincham, F. (1994). Toward an integrated model of negative affectivity in marriage. In S. Johnson & L. Greenberg (Eds.), *The heart of the matter: Perspectives on emotion in marital therapy* (pp. 227–255). New York, NY: Brunner/Mazel.

Berscheid, E. (1983). Emotion. In H. H. Kelley, E. Berscheid, A. Christensen, J. H. Harvey, T. L. Huston, G. Levinger, . . . Peterson, D. R. (Eds.), *Close relationships* (pp. 110–168). New York, NY: W. H. Freeman.

Berscheid, E. (2010). Love in the fourth dimension. *Annual Review of Psychology, 61,* 1–25. doi:10.1146/annurev.psych.093008.100318

Berscheid, E., & Ammazzalorso, H. (2001). Emotional experience in close relationships. In G. J. O. Fletcher & M. Clark (Eds.), *Blackwell handbook of social psychology: Interpersonal processes* (pp. 308–330). Oxford, England: Blackwell.

Bowlby, J. (1969). *Attachment and loss: Vol. 1. Attachment.* New York, NY: Basic Books.

Bowlby, J. (1973). *Attachment and loss: Vol. 2. Separation—Anxiety and anger.* New York, NY: Basic Books.

Bowlby, J. (1980). *Attachment and loss: Vol. 3. Loss.* New York, NY: Basic Books.

Buss, D. (1989). Sex differences in human mate preferences: Evolutionary hypotheses tested in 37 cultures. *Behavioral and Brain Sciences, 12,* 1–49. doi:10.1017/S0140525X00023992

Carstensen, L. L., Gottman, J. M., & Levenson, R. W. (1995). Emotional behavior in long-term marriage. *Psychology and Aging, 10,* 140–149. doi:10.1037/0882-7974.10.1.140

Caspi, A., Elder, G. H., & Bem, D. J. (1987). Moving against the world: Life-course patterns of explosive children. *Developmental Psychology, 23,* 308–313. doi:10.1037/0012-1649.23.2.308

Clark, M., Fitness, J., & Brissette, I. (2001). Understanding peoples' perceptions of relationships is crucial to understanding their emotional lives. In G. J. O. Fletcher & M. Clark (Eds.), *Blackwell handbook of social psychology: Interpersonal processes* (pp. 253–278). Oxford, England: Blackwell.

Clark, M. S., Pataki, S. P., & Carver, V. H. (1996). Some thoughts and findings on self-presentation of emotions in relationships. In G. J. O. Fletcher & J. Fitness (Eds.), *Knowledge structures in close relationships: A social psychological approach* (pp. 247–274). Mahwah, NJ: Erlbaum.

Cohen, S., Schulz, N. S., Weiss, E., & Waldinger, R. J. (2012). Eye of the beholder: The individual and dyadic contributions of empathic accuracy and perceived empathic effort to relationship satisfaction. *Journal of Family Psychology, 26,* 236–245. doi:10.1037/a0027488

Consedine, N. S., & Magai, C. (2003). Attachment and emotion experience in later life: The view from emotions theory. *Attachment and Human Development, 5,* 165–187. doi:10.1080/1461673031000108496

Cosmides, J., & Tooby, J. (2000). Evolutionary psychology and the emotions. In M. Lewis & J. Haviland-Jones (Eds.), *Handbook of emotions* (pp. 91–115). New York, NY: Guilford Press.

Eisenberg, N., Cumberland, A., & Spinrad, T. (1998). Parental socialization of emotions. *Psychological Inquiry, 9,* 241–273. doi:10.1207/s15327965pli0904_1

Ekman, P. (1992). An argument for basic emotions. *Cognition and Emotion, 6,* 169–200. doi:10.1080/02699939208411068

Ekman, P. (2003). Sixteen enjoyable emotions. *Emotion Researcher, 18,* 6–7.

Ellis, B. J., & Malamuth, N. A. (2000). Love and anger in romantic relationships: A discrete systems model. *Journal of Personality, 68,* 525–556. doi:10.1111/1467-6494.00105

Ellsworth, P. (1991). Some implications of cognitive appraisal theories of emotion. In K. T. Strongman (Ed.), *International review of studies on emotion* (Vol. 1, pp. 143–162). New York, NY: Wiley.

Ellsworth, P., & Scherer, K. R. (2003). Appraisal processes in emotion. In R. J. Davidson, H. Goldsmith, & K. R. Scherer (Eds.), *Handbook of affective sciences* (pp. 572–595). New York, NY: Oxford University Press.

Fagundes, C. (2012). Getting over you: Contributions of attachment theory for postbreakup emotional adjustment. *Personal Relationships, 19,* 37–50. doi:10.1111/j.1475-6811.2010.01336.x

Feeney, J. A. (1999). Adult romantic attachment and couple relationships. In J. Cassidy & P. R. Shaver (Eds.), *The handbook of attachment: Theory, research, and clinical applications* (pp. 355–377). New York, NY: Guilford Press.

Feeney, J. A., Noller, P., & Roberts, N. (1998). Emotion, attachment, and satisfaction in close relationships. In P. A. Anderson & L. Guerrero (Eds.), *Handbook of communication and emotion* (pp. 473–505). San Diego, CA: Academic Press.

Fehr, B., & Baldwin, M. (1996). Prototype and script analyses of laypeople's knowledge of anger. In G. J. O. Fletcher & J. Fitness (Eds.), *Knowledge structures in close relationships: A social psychological approach* (pp. 219–245). Mahwah, NJ: Erlbaum.

Felmlee, D. H. (1995). Fatal attractions: Affection and disaffection in intimate relationships. *Journal of Social and Personal Relationships, 12,* 295–311. doi:10.1177/0265407595122009

Fischer, A. H., & Roseman, I. J. (2007). Beat them or ban them: The characteristics and social functions of anger and contempt. *Journal of Personality and Social Psychology, 93,* 103–115. doi:10.1037/0022-3514.93.1.103

Fisher, H. (1994). The nature of romantic love. *Journal of NIH Research, 6,* 59–64.

Fitness, J. (1996). Emotion knowledge structures in close relationships. In G. J. O. Fletcher & J. Fitness (Eds.), *Knowledge structures in close relationships: A social psychological approach* (pp. 195–218). Mahwah, NJ: Erlbaum.

Fitness, J. (2001). Betrayal, rejection, revenge, and forgiveness: An interpersonal script approach. In M. Leary (Ed.), *Interpersonal rejection* (pp. 73–103). New York, NY: Oxford University Press.

Fitness, J. (2006). The emotionally intelligent marriage. In J. Ciarrochi, J. P. Forgas, & J. Mayer (Eds.), *Emotional intelligence in everyday life: A scientific inquiry* (2nd ed., pp. 129–139). New York, NY: Psychology Press.

Fitness, J. (2009). Anger in relationships. In H. Reis & S. Sprecher (Eds.), *Encyclopedia of human relationships* (pp. 94–97). Thousand Oaks, CA: Sage. doi:10.4135/9781412958479.n32

Fitness, J., & Fletcher, G. J. O. (1993). Love, hate, anger, and jealousy in close relationships: A prototype and cognitive appraisal analysis. *Journal of Personality and Social Psychology, 65,* 942–958. doi:10.1037/0022-3514.65.5.942

Fitness, J., Fletcher, G. J. O., & Overall, N. (2003). Attraction and intimate relationships. In M. Hogg & J. Cooper (Eds.), *The Sage handbook of social psychology* (pp. 258–278). Thousand Oaks, CA: Sage.

Fitness, J., & Mathews, S. (1998). *Emotions, emotional intelligence, and forgiveness in marriage.* Paper presented at the 9th International Conference on Personal Relationships, Saratoga Springs, NY.

Fitness, J., & Peterson, J. (2008). Punishment and forgiveness in close relationships: An evolutionary, social-psychological perspective. In J. P. Forgas & J. Fitness (Eds.), *Social relationships: Cognitive, affective, and motivational processes* (pp. 255–269). New York, NY: Psychology Press.

Fitness, J., & Strongman, K. (1991). Affect in close relationships. In G. J. O. Fletcher & F. Fincham (Eds.), *Cognition in close relationships* (pp. 175–202). Hillsdale, NJ: Erlbaum.

Fitness, J., & Warburton, W. (2009). Thinking the unthinkable: Cognitive appraisals and hurt feelings. In A. L. Vangelisti (Ed.), *Feeling hurt in close relationships* (pp. 34–49). New York, NY: Cambridge University Press. doi:10.1017/CBO9780511770548.004

Fredrickson, B. L. (2001). The role of positive emotion in positive psychology: The broaden-and-build theory of positive emotions. *American Psychologist, 56,* 218–226. doi:10.1037/0003-066X.56.3.218

Frijda, N. H. (1994). The Lex Talionis: On vengeance. In S. H. van Goozen, N. E. van de Poll, & J. Sergeant (Eds.), *Emotions: Essays on emotion theory* (pp. 263–289). Hillsdale, NJ: Erlbaum.

Frijda, N. H. (2007). *The laws of emotion.* New York, NY: Cambridge University Press.

Gable, S. L., Reis, H. T., & Elliot, A. J. (2000). Behavioral activation and inhibition in everyday life. *Journal of Personality and Social Psychology, 78,* 1135–1149. doi:10.1037/0022-3514.78.6.1135

Gable, S. L., Reis, H. T., Impett, E. A., & Asher, E. R. (2004). What do you do when things go right? The intrapersonal and interpersonal benefits of sharing positive events. *Journal of Personality and Social Psychology, 87,* 228–245. doi:10.1037/0022-3514.87.2.228

Goetz, J. L., Keltner, D., & Simon-Thomas, E. (2010). Compassion: An evolutionary analysis and empirical review. *Psychological Bulletin, 136,* 351–374. doi:10.1037/a0018807

Gonzaga, G. C., Turner, R. A., Keltner, D., Campos, B., & Altemus, M. (2006). Romantic love and sexual desire in close relationships. *Emotion, 6,* 163–179. doi:10.1037/1528-3542.6.2.163

Gordon, C. L., & Baucom, D. H. (2009). Examining the individual within marriage: Personal strengths and relationship satisfaction. *Personal Relationships, 16,* 421–435. doi:10.1111/j.1475-6811.2009.01231.x

Gottman, J. M. (1994). *What predicts divorce? The relationship between marital processes and marital outcomes.* Hillsdale, NJ: Erlbaum.

Gottman, J. M. (1998). Psychology and the study of marital processes. *Annual Review of Psychology, 49,* 169–197. doi:10.1146/annurev.psych.49.1.169

Gottman, J. M., & Levenson, R. W. (2002). A two-factor model for predicting when a couple will divorce: Exploratory analyses using 14-year longitudinal data. *Family Process, 41,* 83–96. doi:10.1111/j.1545-5300.2002.40102000083.x

Graham, S. M., Huang, J. Y., Clark, M. S., & Helgeson, V. S. (2008). The positives of negative emotions: Willingness to express negative emotions promotes relationships. *Personality and Social Psychology Bulletin, 34,* 394–406. doi:10.1177/0146167207311281

Gross, J. J., & John, O. P. (2003). Individual differences in two emotion regulation processes: Implications for affect, relationships, and well being. *Journal of Personality and Social Psychology, 85,* 348–362. doi:10.1037/0022-3514.85.2.348

Gruber, J. (2011). Can feeling too good be bad? Positive emotion persistence (PEP) in bipolar disorder. *Current Directions in Psychological Science, 20,* 217–221. doi:10.1177/0963721411414632

Guerrero, L. K., & Andersen, P. (1998). Jealousy experience and expression in romantic relationships. In P. Andersen & L. Guerrero (Eds.), *Handbook of communication and emotion: Research, theory, applications, and contexts* (pp. 155–188). New York, NY: Academic Press.

Harasymchuk, C., & Fehr, B. (2012). Development of a prototype-based measure of relational boredom. *Personal Relationships, 19,* 162–181. doi:10.1111/j.1475-6811.2011.01346.x

Harris, C. R., & Darby, R. S. (2010). Jealousy in adulthood. In S. Hart & M. Legerstee (Eds.), *Handbook of jealousy* (pp. 547–571). New York, NY: Wiley-Blackwell. doi:10.1002/9781444323542.ch23

Hatfield, E., Bensman, L., & Rapson, R. (2012). A brief history of social scientists' attempts to measure passionate love. *Journal of Social and Personal Relationships, 29,* 143–164. doi:10.1177/0265407511431055

Hatfield, E., Cacioppo, J. T., & Rapson, R. L. (1993). *Emotional contagion.* Cambridge, England: Cambridge University Press. doi:10.1017/CBO9781139174138

Hazan, C., & Shaver, P. R. (1987). Romantic love conceptualized as an attachment process. *Journal of Personality and Social Psychology, 52,* 511–524. doi:10.1037/0022-3514.52.3.511

Hicks, A. M., & Diamond, L. M. (2008). How was your day? Couples' affect when telling and hearing daily events. *Personal Relationships, 15,* 205–228. doi:10.1111/j.1475-6811.2008.00194.x

Higgins, E. T. (1998). Promotion and prevention: Regulatory focus as a motivational principle. In M. P. Zanna (Ed.), *Advances in experimental social psychology* (pp. 1–46). New York, NY: Academic Press. doi:10.1016/S0065-2601(08)60381-0

Ickes, W., Simpson, J. A., & Oriña, M. M. (2005). Empathic accuracy and inaccuracy in close relationships. In B. Malle & S. Hodges (Eds.), *Other minds: How humans bridge the divide between self and others* (pp. 310–322). New York, NY: Guilford Press.

Impett, E. A., Kogan, A., English, T., John, O., Oveis, C., Gordon, A. M., & Keltner, D. (2012). Suppression sours sacrifice: Emotional and relational costs of suppressing emotions in romantic relationships. *Personality and Social Psychology Bulletin, 38,* 707–720. doi:10.1177/0146167212437249

Jankowiak, W. R., & Fischer, E. (1992). A cross-cultural perspective on romantic love. *Ethnology, 31,* 149–155. doi:10.2307/3773618

Jenkins, J., & Oatley, K. (1998). The development of emotion schemas in children. In W. Flack, Jr., & J. Laird (Eds.), *Emotions in psychopathology* (pp. 45–56). New York, NY: Oxford University Press.

Jostmann, N. B., Karremans, J., & Finkenauer, C. (2011). When love is not blind: Rumination impairs implicit affect regulation in response to romantic relationship threat. *Cognition and Emotion, 25,* 506–518. doi:10.1080/02699931.2010.541139

Keltner, D., Ellsworth, P., & Edwards, K. (1993). Beyond simple pessimism: Effects of sadness and anger on social perception. *Journal of Personality and Social Psychology, 64,* 740–752. doi:10.1037/0022-3514.64.5.740

Keltner, D., & Haidt, J. (1999). Social functions of emotions at four levels of analysis. *Cognition and Emotion, 13,* 505–521. doi:10.1080/026999399379168

Koerner, A., & Fitzpatrick, M. (2002). Nonverbal communication and marital adjustment and satisfaction: The role of decoding relationship-relevant and relationship-irrelevant affect. *Communication Monographs, 69,* 33–51. doi:10.1080/03637750216537

Kubacka, K. E., Finkenauer, C., Rusbult, C. E., & Keijsers, L. (2011). Maintaining close relationships: Gratitude as a motivator and a detector of maintenance behavior. *Personality and Social Psychology Bulletin, 37,* 1362–1375. doi:10.1177/0146167211412196

Kubany, E., Bauer, G., Muraoka, M., Richard, D., & Read, P. (1995). Impact of labeled anger and blame in intimate relationships. *Journal of Social and Clinical Psychology, 14,* 53–60. doi:10.1521/jscp.1995.14.1.53

Lambert, N. M., Clark, M., Durtschi, J., Fincham, F. D., & Graham, S. M. (2010). Benefits of expressing gratitude: Expressing gratitude to a partner changes one's view of the relationship. *Psychological Science, 21*, 574–580. doi:10.1177/0956797610364003

Lazarus, R. (1991). *Emotion and adaptation.* New York, NY: Oxford University Press.

Lishner, D. A., Batson, C. D., & Huss, E. (2011). Tenderness and sympathy: Distinct empathic emotions elicited by different forms of need. *Personality and Social Psychology Bulletin, 37*, 614–625. doi:10.1177/0146167211403157

Magai, C., & McFadden, S. (1995). *The role of emotions in social and personality development.* New York, NY: Plenum Press.

Mandler, G. (1975). *Mind and emotion.* New York, NY: Wiley.

Matsumoto, D., Yoo, S. H., & Nakagawa, S. (2008). Culture, emotion regulation, and adjustment. *Journal of Personality and Social Psychology, 94*, 925–937. doi:10.1037/0022-3514.94.6.925

Mikulincer, M., & Shaver, P. (2005). Attachment theory and emotions in close relationships: Exploring the attachment-related dynamics of emotional reactions to relational events. *Personal Relationships, 12*, 149–168. doi:10.1111/j.1350-4126.2005.00108.x

Mongrain, M., & Vettese, L. C. (2003). Conflict over emotional expression: Implications for interpersonal communication. *Personality and Social Psychology Bulletin, 29*, 545–555. doi:10.1177/0146167202250924

Monin, J. K., Martire, L. M., Schulz, R., & Clark, M. S. (2009). Willingness to express emotions to caregiving spouses. *Emotion, 9*, 101–106. doi:10.1037/a0013732

Mullen, P. E. (1994). The pathological extensions of love. *British Journal of Psychiatry, 165*, 614–623. doi:10.1192/bjp.165.5.614

Niedenthal, P. M., & Brauer, M. (2012). Social functionality of human emotion. *Annual Review of Psychology, 63*, 259–285. doi:10.1146/annurev.psych.121208.131605

Noller, P., & Ruzzene, M. (1991). The effects of cognition and affect on marital communication. In G. J. O. Fletcher & F. D. Fincham (Eds.), *Cognition in close relationships* (pp. 203–233). Mahwah, NJ: Erlbaum.

Oatley, K., & Jenkins, J. (1996). *Understanding emotions.* Cambridge, MA: Blackwell.

Panksepp, J. (1998). *Affective neuroscience: The foundations of human and animal emotions.* New York, NY: Oxford University Press.

Panksepp, J. (2010). The evolutionary sources of jealousy. In S. Hart & M. Legerstee (Eds.), *Handbook of jealousy* (pp. 101–120). New York, NY: Wiley-Blackwell. doi:10.1002/9781444323542.ch6

Pinkus, R. T., Lockwood, P., Marshall, T., & Yoon, H. M. (2012). Responses to comparisons in romantic relationships: Empathy, shared fate, and contrast. *Personal Relationships, 19*, 182–201. doi:10.1111/j.1475-6811.2011.01347.x

Planalp, S., & Fitness, J. (1999). Thinking/feeling about social and personal relationships. *Journal of Social and Personal Relationships, 16*, 731–750. doi:10.1177/0265407599166004

Planalp, S., Fitness, J., & Fehr, B. (2006). Emotion in theories of close relationships. In D. Perlman & A. Vangelisti (Eds.), *Handbook of personal relationships* (pp. 369–384). New York, NY: Cambridge University Press. doi:10.1017/CBO9780511606632.021

Plutchik, R. (1994). *The psychology and biology of emotion.* New York, NY: HarperCollins.

Reis, H. T., Collins, W. A., & Berscheid, E. (2000). The relationship context of human behavior and development. *Psychological Bulletin, 126*, 844–872. doi:10.1037/0033-2909.126.6.844

Reis, H. T., Smith, S. M., Carmichael, C. L., Caprariello, P. A., Tsai, F. F., Rodrigues, A., & Maniaci, M. R. (2010). "Are you happy for me?" How sharing positive events with others provides personal and interpersonal benefits. *Journal of Personality and Social Psychology, 99*, 311–329. doi:10.1037/a0018344

Rempel, J. K., & Burris, C. T. (2005). Let me count the ways: An integrative theory of love and hate. *Personal Relationships, 12*, 297–313. doi:10.1111/j.1350-4126.2005.00116.x

Retzinger, S. M. (1991). *Violent emotions: Shame and rage in marital quarrels.* Newbury Park, CA: Sage.

Richards, J., Butler, E., & Gross, J. (2003). Emotion regulation in romantic relationships: The cognitive consequences of concealing feelings. *Journal of Social and Personal Relationships, 20*, 599–620. doi:10.1177/02654075030205002

Roseman, I. J. (1984). Cognitive determinants of emotion: A structural theory. In P. Shaver (Ed.), *Review of personality and social psychology* (Vol. 5, pp. 11–36). Beverly Hills, CA: Sage.

Rusbult, C. E., Bissonnette, V., Arriaga, X. B., & Cox, C. (1998). Accommodation processes during the early years of marriage. In T. Bradbury (Ed.), *The developmental course of marital dysfunction* (pp. 74–113). New York, NY: Cambridge University Press. doi:10.1017/CBO9780511527814.005

Sanford, K., & Rowatt, W. C. (2004). When is negative emotion positive for relationships? An investigation of married couples and roommates. *Personal Relationships, 11*, 329–354. doi:10.1111/j.1475-6811.2004.00086.x

Sartre, J. P. (1976). *The emotions: Outline of a theory.* New York, NY: Citadel Press. (Original work published 1948)

Sauter, D. (2010). More than happy: The need for disentangling positive emotions. *Current Directions in Psychological Science, 19*, 36–40. doi:10.1177/0963721409359290

Sbarra, D. A. (2006). Predicting the onset of emotional recovery following nonmarital relationship dissolution: Survival analyses of sadness and anger. *Personality and Social Psychology Bulletin, 32*, 298–312. doi:10.1177/0146167205280913

Sbarra, D. A., & Emery, R. (2005). The emotional sequelae of non-marital relationship dissolution: Analyses of change and intraindividual variability over time. *Personal Relationships, 12*, 213–232. doi:10.1111/j.1350-4126.2005.00112.x

Sbarra, D. A., Smith, H. L., & Mehl, M. R. (2012). When leaving your ex, love yourself: Observational ratings of self-compassion predict the course of emotional recovery following marital separation. *Psychological Science, 23*, 261–269. doi:10.1177/0956797611429466

Shaver, P., Schwartz, J., Kirson, D., & O'Connor, C. (1987). Emotion knowledge: Further explorations of a prototype approach. *Journal of Personality and Social Psychology, 52*, 1061–1086. doi:10.1037/0022-3514.52.6.1061

Shaver, P. R., Collins, N., & Clark, C. L. (1996). Attachment styles and internal working models of self and relationship partners. In G. J. O. Fletcher & J. Fitness (Eds.), *Knowledge structures in close relationships: A social psychological approach* (pp. 25–61). Mahwah, NJ: Erlbaum.

Shaver, P. R., & Mikulincer, M. (2006). Attachment theory, individual psychodynamics, and relationship functioning. In A. Vangelisti & D. Perlman (Eds.), *The Cambridge handbook of personal relationships* (pp. 251–272). New York, NY: Cambridge University Press. doi:10.1017/CBO9780511606632.015

Shaver, P. R., Morgan, H. J., & Wu, S. (1996). Is love a "basic" emotion? *Personal Relationships, 3*, 81–96. doi:10.1111/j.1475-6811.1996.tb00105.x

Silvia, P. (2008). Interest—the curious emotion. *Current Directions in Psychological Science, 17*, 57–60. doi:10.1111/j.1467-8721.2008.00548.x

Simpson, J. A. (1990). Influence of attachment styles on romantic relationships. *Journal of Personality and Social Psychology, 59*, 971–980. doi:10.1037/0022-3514.59.5.971

Simpson, J. A., Kim, J. S., Fillo, J., Ickes, W., Rholes, W. S., Oriña, M. M., & Winterheld, H. A. (2011). Attachment and the management of empathic accuracy in relationship-threatening situations. *Personality and Social Psychology Bulletin, 37*, 242–254. doi:10.1177/0146167210394368

Simpson, J. A., Winterheld, H. A., & Chen, J. Y. (2006). Personality and relationships: A temperament perspective. In A. Vangelisti & D. Perlman (Eds.), *The Cambridge handbook of personal relationships* (pp. 231–250). New York, NY: Cambridge University Press. doi:10.1017/CBO9780511606632.014

Sprecher, S., & Fehr, B. (2011). Dispositional attachment and relationship-specific attachment as predictors of compassionate love for a partner. *Journal of Social and Personal Relationships, 28*, 558–574. doi:10.1177/0265407510386190

Tangney, J. P., & Dearing, R. L. (2002). *Shame and guilt.* New York, NY: Guilford Press.

Tomkins, S. S. (1962). *Affect, imagery, and consciousness: Vol. 1. The positive affects.* New York, NY: Springer.

Tomkins, S. S. (1963). *Affect, imagery, and consciousness: Vol. 2. The negative affects.* New York, NY: Springer.

Vandello, J. A., Cohen, D., Grandon, R., & Franiuk, R. (2009). Stand by your man: Indirect prescriptions for honorable violence and feminine loyalty in Canada, Chile, and the United States. *Journal of Cross-Cultural Psychology, 40*, 81–104. doi:10.1177/0022022108326194

Watson, D. (2002). The disposition to experience pleasurable emotional states. In C. R. Snyder & S. J. Lopez (Eds.), *Handbook of positive psychology* (pp. 106–119). New York, NY: Oxford University Press.

CHAPTER 12

THE MATTER OF OTHER MINDS: EMPATHIC ACCURACY AND THE FACTORS THAT INFLUENCE IT

Sara D. Hodges, Karyn L. Lewis, and William Ickes

When asked which superpower they would most like to have, 28% of Americans put mind reading at the top of the list (Marist Poll, 2011). Apparently, knowing what is going on in other people's heads is seen as being very useful, a point of great curiosity, or both. However, whereas only comic book heroes have x-ray vision or the ability to shoot spiderwebs from their wrists, most ordinary folk have at least some ability to accurately infer another person's thoughts and feelings—a phenomenon called *empathic accuracy*. Still, superhero-level performance on empathic accuracy is rarely, if ever, found among mere mortals (Ickes, 2008). Perhaps having had a small taste of this "superpower" is precisely why people crave more—and why psychologists have conducted research to identify what leads people to be empathically accurate and what outcomes they experience as a result.

In the first section of this chapter, we set the stage by defining key concepts and consider the fundamental components that contribute to humans' ability to be empathically accurate. In the next section, we consider three sources of variance in empathic accuracy performance. First, we consider characteristics of perceivers that predict empathic accuracy, along with other characteristics that would theoretically seem related but have struck out empirically as predictors. Second, we consider factors that contribute to the "readability" of the target whose thoughts are to be read. Third, we nest these two sources of variance in an interaction context,

considering how motives within a particular interaction affect how accurately thoughts are inferred. In the final section of the chapter, we explain where we think empathic accuracy research should go next, raising questions about whether empathic accuracy is critical for successful social outcomes, what additional target variables should be studied, and how the relation between target and perceiver influences empathic accuracy.

WHAT IS EMPATHIC ACCURACY?

Conceptually, empathic accuracy is part of a loosely related family of forms of interpersonal accuracy, including accuracy in making trait judgments and in judging other people's emotional expressions. However, even when limiting consideration solely to constructs that have explicitly been labeled *empathic accuracy*, one finds a variety of constructs answering to this specific name. In this chapter, we are primarily concerned with a form of empathic accuracy that refers to the ability to correctly infer the content of the discrete subjectively perceived mental events of another person as they occur over time.

Some key components of this definition need to be highlighted. First, the goal of these empathic inferences is to understand someone's consciously experienced thoughts. Second, the targets of these empathic inferences—that is, other people's thoughts—change over time, so that the thought to be inferred at one point in a social exchange may be

We thank Devin Howington, Jean Decety, Azim Shariff, Jeff Sherman, and Joann Wu Shortt, who contributed ideas that were useful in writing this chapter, and Patrick Browne, Stephen Frey, and Irina Kuzmina for reading earlier versions of this chapter.

http://dx.doi.org/10.1037/14344-012
APA Handbook of Personality and Social Psychology: Vol. 3. Interpersonal Relations, M. Mikulincer and P. R. Shaver (Editors-in-Chief)
319

quite different from the thought to be inferred a few minutes later, as well as quite distinct from any summary judgment that applies to the entire exchange. For better or worse (mostly for better!), this particular definition has been closely linked with a particular paradigm developed by William Ickes and his colleagues (e.g., Ickes, Stinson, Bissonnette, & Garcia, 1990) to measure empathic accuracy.[1]

Ickes's paradigm involves three phases. In the first, a target person is video recorded while talking, either in conversation with another person or while being interviewed by another person. Later, the target person watches the video recording and is instructed to stop the recording at each point at which he or she remembers having had a thought or feeling and to write down the content of that particular thought or feeling, along with the corresponding time in the recording. In the second phase, a perceiver watches the target's recording. The video recording is stopped at the time points at which the target reported a thought or feeling, and the perceiver is asked to infer the specific contents of the target's mind at those points. Finally, in the third phase, trained coders compare the content of what the target reported at a particular stop point with what the perceiver inferred at the same point and rate how closely the two match.

There are multiple variations on this basic paradigm. For example, the target may be filmed during an unscripted conversation (e.g., Ickes et al., 1990), a counseling session (e.g., Marangoni, Garcia, Ickes, & Teng, 1995), or a structured interview (e.g., Klein & Hodges, 2001). The conversation may be between strangers (e.g., Ickes et al., 1990; Stinson & Ickes, 1992), dating partners (e.g., Simpson, Ickes, & Blackstone, 1995; Thomas & Fletcher, 2003), or married couples (e.g., Kilpatrick, Bissonnette, & Rusbult, 2002; Verhofstadt, Buysse, Ickes, Davis, & Devoldre, 2008). In what Ickes (2001) labeled the *dyadic interaction paradigm,* a conversation between two participants is filmed, and participants serve as both targets and perceivers, first reporting their own thoughts and then inferring the other person's

thoughts. Notably, perceivers in the dyadic interaction paradigm are inferring thoughts the target had during a conversation in which the perceiver took part. In contrast, in the *standard stimulus paradigm* (Ickes, 2001), the same target recording may be shown to many perceivers who have never interacted with or even met the target. In yet other variations, researchers may use designs that involve multiple targets (e.g., Hancock & Ickes, 1996; Lewis, Hodges, Laurent, Srivastava, & Biancarosa, 2012).

Although the initial paradigm had targets identify their own thought stop points, Tipsord (2009) asked perceivers to identify the points at which they believed the target might be having a thought. Verhofstadt et al. (2008) created stop points by arbitrarily dividing the films into equal-sized segments (e.g., 30 seconds long) and asking targets to report what they were thinking at each stop point (see also Gadassi, Mor, & Rafaeli, 2011; Sillars, Koerner, & Fitzpatrick, 2005). In addition, researchers have experimented with having targets record the occurrence of thoughts as they happen in real time and then later report the thought content, rather than identifying retrospectively when they had a thought (Howington, Lewis, & Hodges, 2011).

Ickes and colleagues' (e.g., Ickes et al., 1990) initial coding scheme for accuracy ranged from 0 (the perceiver inferred fully different content than the target's thought) through 1 (the perceiver inferred similar, but not the same, content) to 2 (the perceiver inferred essentially the same content). More recently, researchers interested in using multilevel modeling have adopted a 4-point coding scheme to allow for greater variability and less positive skew in accuracy at the level of individual thoughts (e.g., Lewis et al., 2012; also Sillars et al., 2005). Recent research has also entailed coding targets' thoughts on a variety of dimensions that include their transparency (how easy the thoughts are to guess from context; e.g., Hodges, Kiel, Kramer, Veach, & Villanueva, 2010; Marangoni et al., 1995; Simpson et al., 1995), specific content (e.g., Gesn & Ickes, 1999; Lewis et al., 2012; Schweinle, Ickes &

---

[1]Within Ickes's paradigm, the contents of other people's minds are referred to as their thoughts and feelings. Although people can readily distinguish their thoughts from their feelings (Ickes & Cheng, 2011), no distinction is generally made between the two within the paradigm; thus, throughout this chapter we frequently use the term *thoughts* to encompass both thoughts and feelings.

Bernstein, 2002), and potential to threaten the relationship that exists between interactants (e.g., Simpson, Oriña, & Ickes, 2003).

Empathic accuracy coders are usually independent of the interaction, but the target may also rate how accurate the perceiver's inferences are. Interestingly, when the target's ratings are compared with those of independent coders, the target often gives the highest accuracy ratings and is the least reliable coder in statistical terms, with the independent coders showing higher intercorrelations with each other (Hodges et al., 2010). Of course, the target alone has direct access to what she or he was actually thinking. The target is also the only coder who could rightfully decide that the perceiver has actually done a better job of capturing her or his actual thoughts than the target did when writing them down.

Although much of the work we review in this chapter uses the core Ickes methodology with one or more of the variations we have described, we also occasionally reference studies that have used other methodologies. One of these is a closely related methodology developed by Levenson and Ruef (1992) that has also been called *empathic accuracy* (e.g., Zaki, Bolger, & Ochsner, 2008). This methodology entails having perceivers watch a video recording of a target who has previously provided continuous ratings of the valence of his or her affect. Perceivers use an "affect dial" to continuously rate the valence of the target's affect across the same sequence.

Thus, as with Ickes's paradigm, this technique is temporally dynamic (and in fact allows for a denser array of events within a particular time frame), but it limits the content of mind reading solely to affective responses that differ only in terms of how positive or negative they are. Other researchers (e.g., Haugen, Welsh, & McNulty, 2008; Papp, Kouros, & Cummings, 2010) have had participants rate how much they—and their partners—were feeling specific emotions. Such methods allow for inferences about a wider range of responses than Levenson and Ruef's (1992) affect-labeling method, although the dimensions for describing the content of a person's mind are still quite constrained.

Empathic accuracy research is a cousin of research examining people's accuracy in decoding nonverbal cues. Nonverbal decoding ability is typically measured with a standard set of stimuli, such as the Profile of Nonverbal Sensitivity (Rosenthal, Hall, DiMatteo, Rogers, & Archer, 1979) or the Diagnostic Analysis of Nonverbal Accuracy (Nowicki & Duke, 1994). Participants see short clips or shots of targets and are asked to identify what emotion the target is feeling. Another test of nonverbal sensitivity, the Interpersonal Perception Task (Costanzo & Archer, 1989), presents the participants with video clips of social interactions and asks them to answer factual questions about participants in the clips, such as which of two men near a basketball court just won the game. The test is nonverbal but not solely visual: The audio is left on, although explicit verbal information that would answer the questions is not provided. Still other measures of nonverbal accuracy assess participants' ability to recall another person's appearance (Horgan, Schmid Mast, Hall, & Carter, 2004) or gestures (Hall, Carter, & Horgan, 2001) or to recognize emotions solely on the basis of the muscle configurations around the eye (Reading the Mind in Eyes task; Baron-Cohen, Wheelwright, Hill, Raste, & Plumb, 2001).

These nonverbal sensitivity measures share features with what we call empathic accuracy in this chapter, but they have significant differences, too. The Profile of Nonverbal Sensitivity, Diagnostic Analysis of Nonverbal Accuracy, and Reading the Mind in Eyes task assess only people's ability to identify prespecified categorical emotions (e.g., happy or angry, not blends or degrees of emotion). The items in the Interpersonal Perception Task deal with topics that might be on the minds of the targets, but these topics were not identified as such by the targets. Furthermore, the task requires accuracy about a single fact that will not change during the course of the recorded interaction (e.g., which man won the game?), whereas Ickes's empathic accuracy paradigm requires perceivers to infer the changing content of a target's successive thoughts over the course of a conversation or interview. Thus, we do not consider nonverbal sensitivity scales to be an alternative measure of empathic accuracy, although they do measure sensitivity to specific aspects of a target person's behavior that might contribute to empathic accuracy, a point to which we return later.

We also want to clarify that empathic accuracy should not be confused with the concept of empathy more generally. At worst, *empathy* is a nearly meaningless term because it is used for so many different constructs (see Hodges & Biswas-Diener, 2007; Ickes, 2003). At best, *empathy* is a broad umbrella term for a set of distinguishable constructs that are conceptually (if not always empirically) related to understanding another person's experience and, in many cases, responding sympathetically to it (see Hodges & Myers, 2007). However, empathic accuracy does not guarantee a compassionate response from the perceiver. Indeed, the dark side of empathic accuracy is that accurate inference of another person's thoughts can be used to hurt, embarrass, or even exploit the target. Consider how a soccer player's accurate inference of an opposing team member's strategy may allow the first player to take possession of the ball or score a goal. Also, drawing from a true story, we know of a man whose accurate inference that a rival had romantic intentions toward his girlfriend led him to block the rival's access to her. In close relationships, greater knowledge about one's partner may facilitate greater empathic accuracy (Stinson & Ickes, 1992), which can in turn be applied to soothing—or torturing—that person (Ickes, 2003).

The Challenge of Reading Other Minds

The study of empathic accuracy runs smack into the "other minds" problem. The challenge both in being empathically accurate and in measuring empathic accuracy is that it involves a person's thoughts, which are subjective and directly accessible only to that person. Neuroimaging techniques have advanced in dazzling ways in the past few decades— sometimes even capturing brain signals that predict behavior but of which the brain's owner may not be consciously aware.[2] However, to date, there is still no technique that captures and projects the full, ever-changing Technicolor stream of thoughts that run through another person's head. The contrast between the rich, fluid detail of one's own thoughts

and the impoverished access one has to others' thoughts may be at least partially responsible for the superpower wish that opened this chapter. However, despite the challenges in knowing the subjective contents of another person's mind, people are not totally inept at this task.

Developmentally, one of the major milestones in inferring other people's thoughts is realizing that other people have thoughts that differ from one's own. Children between the ages of 3 and 5 acquire a theory of mind—an understanding that each person has his or her own thoughts and that these thoughts guide the person's behavior. Younger children consistently fail at tasks that require them to take into account the fact that they have access to information that another person does not (e.g., a young child thinks a recipient knows the contents of a wrapped package because the child saw it being wrapped). Furthermore, the developmental course of acquiring a theory of mind is largely unchanged by culture and cannot be rushed before a child is ready (Sabbagh, Xu, Carlson, Moses, & Lee, 2006).

The cognition of very young children can be seen as profoundly egocentric (i.e., they fail to realize that other people even have different thoughts from their own). For older children who have acquired a theory of mind, the challenge in knowing other people's minds increases when there is more information to keep track of. Thus, for very young children, distinctions in mind reading are categorical (i.e., they either do or do not appreciate the unique contents of other people's minds), whereas distinctions in mind reading among older children are continuous and depend on how much information the child can integrate. For example, as children who have acquired a theory of mind progress through childhood, they get better at performing second-order theory-of-mind tasks (see Perner & Wimmer, 1985) that require them to maintain the multiple perspectives needed to keep track of a third person's thoughts about the contents of a second person's mind (e.g., guessing what Brian thinks Devin wants for her birthday).

---

[2]For example, error-related negativity is seen in evoked response potential data that emerge before a person knows he or she has made a mistake (see Holroyd & Coles, 2002).

Even when just one other mind is involved, we suspect that better mind readers are those who are better at collecting and integrating clues to the contents of the other person's mind (M. W. Myers & Hodges, 2009; Thomas & Fletcher, 2003). However, beyond the normal improvements in executive function that occur as children become adults (Moses, 2005), we are unaware of any studies that have compared empathic accuracy performance among other age groups (e.g., adolescents vs. adults) or that have examined whether empathic accuracy is predicted by any cognitive declines associated with aging.

Building Blocks of Empathic Accuracy

Despite the fact that relationship blogs remind people that their partner cannot read their minds and that doing so may be bad for their relationship (Gottman, 1994; Guerrero, Andersen, & Afifi, 2011), most people can infer other people's thoughts at a level much higher than chance would predict (Ickes, 2011). What are the clues that people use to "read" other people's minds?

Verbal cues. The most useful source of clues may be the one obvious one: what the other person is saying (Gesn & Ickes, 1999; Hall & Schmid Mast, 2007). The advanced language and communication skills that have helped secure humans' position at the top of the animal kingdom allow for precise articulation of emotions, opinions, intentions, explanations, motives, and musings. When such articulations are forthcoming, candid, complete, and accurate, the need for mind reading is obviated. However, these qualifications are not always met. The degree to which thoughts are shared verbally is entirely voluntary—people can choose whether or not to tell their thoughts to other people, and if they do verbalize their thoughts they can be selective about what they share. Certain thoughts are disproportionately not shared with others, such as thoughts that would reflect negatively on the thinker (e.g., "I am really bored by these masterpiece paintings in the National Gallery" or "I wonder if I could get away with cheating?") or hurt others (e.g., "She really looks fat in those jeans" or "He'll never be able to land a tenure-track job"). Thoughts that are uncertain ("I was thinking we would spend about

3 nights or so at the coast on our vacation") or not fully developed ("I have a bad feeling about this guy") might also be less frequently shared.

Interestingly, although empathic accuracy researchers have factored the transparency of the target person's thoughts into some of their studies—that is, the extent to which a target's reported thought matches up with what the target is outwardly saying (e.g., Hodges et al., 2010; Marangoni et al., 1995; Simpson et al., 1995)—investigations of empathic accuracy, particularly those using the Ickes paradigm, have not thus far explicitly focused much on manipulating or measuring variables that might be expected to affect how willing the target would be to let others know his or her subjective thoughts. However, when exceptions occur, they tend to be clustered in the domain of romantic relationships. For example, one study (Simpson et al., 1995) introduced a diabolical research technique in which heterosexual individuals were given the task of rating photos of attractive opposite-sex people in the presence of their own dating partner, a situation in which the rater might be slightly less than honest about how attractive he or she finds their partner's rivals, particularly if the relationship is on shaky ground. Several other studies of empathic accuracy in close relationships have required perceivers to infer their partner's thoughts that occurred during a conversation about a relationship issue (e.g., Kilpatrick et al., 2002; Simpson et al., 2003, 2011; Thomas & Fletcher, 2003; Thomas, Fletcher, & Lange, 1997).

In contrast, the study of deception detection (e.g., Bond & DePaulo, 2006; Ekman & O'Sullivan, 1991), which is related to research on both nonverbal behavior and empathic accuracy, has capitalized on varying whether targets are saying out loud what they are thinking or are deliberately trying to shield their true thoughts with their (falsely) spoken words. However, in many deception detection studies, the content of perceivers' inferences is generally limited to assessments of whether the target is telling the truth or telling a lie, whereas in real life spoken lies are often cloaked in a variety of half-truths (DePaulo, 2002), making the job of inferring the true content of another's thoughts somewhat more complicated than making a dichotomous choice between truth and lie.

Nonverbal cues. When perceivers know that targets have thoughts that they are not verbally sharing, or ones that targets are actively trying to prevent others from knowing, perceivers must turn to sources other than verbal cues when they are mind reading. Chief among these sources are nonverbal cues such as body language, facial expressions, and vocal tone. In fact, poets and others might have one believe that nonverbal information is either superior to or somehow "purer" than verbal information. For example, consider Ulysses' description of Cressida in Shakespeare's *Troilus and Cressida* (Act IV, Scene 5):

> There's language in her eye, her cheek, her lip,
> Nay, her foot speaks; her wanton spirits look out
> At every joint and motive of her body.

Indeed, when people intentionally try to send one message while concealing another, information about the concealed thought may "leak" through nonverbal channels, particularly those channels that people usually do not try to pose (e.g., people more often try to control how much they are smiling rather than how much their feet are fidgeting; see Rosenthal & DePaulo, 1979).

However, there is a reason why humans' verbal abilities vaulted them to the top of the animal kingdom: The information conveyed via nonverbal channels is no match for what can be conveyed verbally in terms of shades of meaning or complexity. Furthermore, although people can extract meaningful information from nonverbal cues, their comprehension of these cues—particularly their comprehension of cues leaked when a target is intentionally trying to conceal information (i.e., when he or she is lying)—is not especially impressive (Bond & DePaulo, 2006; Hartwig & Bond, 2011). Thus, perhaps we should not be surprised by the absence of published studies that show positive links between nonverbal decoding performance and empathic accuracy or by the presence of several other studies that have reported null findings (Gesn & Ickes, 1999; Lewis & Hodges, 2009; Zaki, Bolger, & Ochsner, 2009). Still, although communicating nonverbally may be a cruder method than communicating verbally, nonverbal cues can be used to infer others'

thoughts (see Zaki et al., 2009), and they may be particularly useful when people would like to conceal their thoughts, converse in different languages, or say nothing at all (Ickes, 2006).

Social cognition. Verbal and nonverbal cues emerge as obvious cues to what another person is thinking because one thinks of a person's inner mental workings and outer expressions as covarying over time—if nothing else, they both occur in the same person. However, less individuated information may also be useful in inferring other people's thoughts. When it comes to constructing the contents of another person's mind, perceivers may rely on the self as a proxy for others as well as use other social cognitive scaffolds such as social roles and stereotypes.

To illustrate the use of such aids, imagine a couple who has been invited to attend the wedding of the wife's coworker. The wife asks the husband if they should go, and the husband shrugs and says, "It's up to you," leaving the wife to infer his thoughts about the event. She might think how she would feel if he asked her about attending the wedding of one of his coworkers and then project her own simulated reaction as a way of inferring her husband's thoughts. Or perhaps she might rely on the traditional gender stereotype that most men at best consider weddings to be silly romantic events and at worst feel sympathy for the groom who has been trapped. If so, she might infer that her husband does not really want to go. Or she might use her knowledge of their respective social roles to infer that he really has no strong opinion either way and is genuinely leaving the decision up to her because, in their marriage, she plays the role of the couple's social director. Let's examine these strategies in greater depth.

Projection has been widely studied as a useful tool for making a variety of inferences about others, including predictions about their future behavior (L. Ross, Greene, & House, 1977), their perception of sarcasm and sensory stimuli (Epley, Keysar, Van Boven, & Gilovich, 2004), their visceral reactions (Van Boven & Loewenstein, 2003), their reasons for acting (Ames, 2004), and how evident their feelings are to others (Vorauer, 2001). However, as was the case with the deception detection research discussed previously, these demonstrations of projection usually involve short-answer measures in which people are provided with response options about the other person rather than having to generate the content of the other person's mental state on their own. Furthermore, this research has generally used paradigms in which the other person is either a stranger or even a very minimally described other with whom no actual interaction occurs.

Stereotypes may seem a very unlikely tool in comprehending others better. Social stereotypes are often presented as "bad guys" in the field of psychology (especially in social psychology)—a reputation that reflects their close association with prejudice and discrimination. Furthermore, even when an empathic inference based on stereotypes is accurate, the nomothetic nature of the inference may be offensive if the target finds out that the perceiver used a stereotype. Imagine, for example, that a husband tells his wife that he got her jewelry for their anniversary because women like jewelry. It may in fact be true that women on average do like jewelry as gifts, but many wives may be dismayed that their husband was relying on such impersonal knowledge to choose their gift. However, it is exactly the idiographic contents of another person's mind that are obscured by the other-minds problem, and for that reason, stereotypes may be a very valuable tool for achieving empathic accuracy. By the same token, social roles and their accompanying scripts for normative behavior may function similarly, because they can be viewed as situational stereotypes that both the target and the perceiver are likely to share (e.g., both the boss and her subordinate assume that the boss will get the final word in setting the work agenda).

The value of stereotypes was recently demonstrated in a study by Lewis et al. (2012). Perceivers were given the task of inferring the thoughts that new mother targets reported having while talking about their experiences with their new babies. The more the perceivers' inferences were consistent with stereotypes of new mothers, the more empathically accurate the perceivers were. An interesting future direction would be to investigate whether thoughts that are consistent with a particular social role, such

as boss or subordinate (cf. Snodgrass, 1992), or with the roles that sometimes emerge within marriages and close relationships, such as budget manager and date planner, are also inferred more accurately.

Individuated information.   Stereotypes and social roles can be thought of as general knowledge that is useful for inferring another person's thoughts, but when it comes to ongoing relationships, individuated information about known targets also helps people infer their thoughts. Replaying the anniversary example, a wife may be very pleased to hear her husband say, "I got you jewelry because I know it's what you like." Acquaintanceship has been shown to give friends an advantage over strangers in guessing each other's thoughts (Stinson & Ickes, 1992), and established dating partners may be even more advantaged (Thomas & Fletcher, 2003).

This acquaintanceship advantage seems to be a product of previously acquainted pairs of people having more shared past experiences—either ones that they participated in together or ones that they told each other about. Thus, when one partner says, "It's like Nancy's retirement party," the other partner has access to the fact that at that party Nancy's husband got quite drunk, the receptionist made a pass at the tech consultant, and the whole marketing department wore costumes. All of this is information that may help the listener to infer the partner's thoughts beyond what is possible using a more generic schema that involves someone in his or her mid- to late 60s, cake, punch, and the presentation of a gold watch. Indeed, Stinson and Ickes (1992) found that the more a target's thoughts focused on other times and other places, the more close friends were advantaged over strangers in terms of their empathic accuracy.

Even minimal contact with another person may provide background information that can help one to infer the person's thoughts. Indirect evidence has come from empathic accuracy studies (Ickes et al., 1990; Stinson & Ickes, 1992) that have applied a "Cronbachian" (e.g., Cronbach, 1955) componential approach to estimating accuracy. In these studies, baseline accuracy is calculated by randomly pairing a perceiver's inferred thoughts with the target person's actual thoughts and then coding these randomly determined pairs for empathic accuracy. This procedure enables researchers to estimate how much of the perceivers' overall empathic accuracy is attributable to making correct inferences on the basis of the general theme of the target's video or stereotypes about the target and her or his experiences. Baseline accuracy estimates are low but typically greater than zero. This outcome suggests that perceivers rely on (and benefit from) information about that person over and above what is immediately apparent—even in the standard stimulus paradigm, in which the targets are strangers to the perceiver and there is no benefit of past acquaintanceship.

More direct evidence for the benefits of background information comes from a study by Marangoni et al. (1995). They found that perceivers who viewed targets talking about personal problems in pseudopsychotherapy sessions (which lasted about 30 minutes) inferred the targets' thoughts more accurately near the end of the session than near the beginning of the session. In another study that used the same therapy session tapes as stimuli, Gesn and Ickes (1999) found evidence suggesting that perceivers start to develop a person-specific schema quite quickly that can be used in making empathic inferences. In particular, perceivers were more empathically accurate for schema-consistent thoughts than for schema-inconsistent thoughts, suggesting that perceivers were drawing on a target-specific schema to flesh out their inferences. Interestingly, however, when clips from the videos were shown in random order, participants were more accurate at inferring schema-inconsistent thoughts, suggesting that when participants were unable to construct and rely on a schema, they may have paid more attention to idiosyncratic elements of individual thoughts.

In summary, people can consider a variety of cues when trying to infer another person's thoughts: the target's words; the target's nonverbal behavior; social-cognitive constructs such as projection, stereotypes, and roles; and individuating information about the target that the perceiver has collected over time. Although people may rightfully sense that nonverbal cues can sometimes "leak" unintended signals about a person's thoughts, the current

evidence has suggested that verbal cues are a far more valuable source of information in the perceiver's empathic accuracy (Ickes, 2006). Background knowledge—both about people in general and about a specific target person in particular—appears to be a promising tool for achieving empathic accuracy and should be probed in future research.

WHAT PREDICTS EMPATHIC ACCURACY?

Given all of those people pining for mind-reading superpowers, it is not surprising that researchers have devoted a great deal of effort to identifying factors that predict better empathic accuracy. Initially, these efforts were directed largely at identifying the characteristics of good perceivers. Identifying characteristics that explain perceiver variance has proved to be surprisingly difficult, however, and in recent years investigators have expanded their inquiry to explore characteristics of the target and the context in which empathic accuracy occurs.

Perceiver Variables

An early underlying assumption was that empathic accuracy varies substantially across individuals, similar to other talents and skills that involve accuracy (e.g., being good at math, singing in tune, throwing darts). Individual differences in perceivers were expected to explain some amount of variance in empathic accuracy regardless of whether the target was someone the perceiver had a close relationship with or was a stranger to. In this section of the chapter, we review categories of individual differences in perceivers that have been studied as predictors of empathic accuracy.

Other performance measures of interpersonal sensitivity.   Perceivers who show signs of being interpersonally sensitive on other performance measures might be expected to be empathically accurate, and several studies have tested this idea. The results of these studies are at best inconclusive, but in all likelihood they would reveal a null effect if they were combined. The Diagnostic Analysis of Nonverbal Accuracy (Nowicki & Duke, 1994) requires participants to assign one of a set of emotion labels to the facial expressions of people in photographs. The Interpersonal Perceptions Task (Costanzo & Archer, 1989) is designed to assess more naturalistic and contextually embedded nonverbal decoding, with participants asked to watch video clips (that include audio tracks) and then make judgments about the relationships or recent interactions between the people in the videos. The latter might intuitively seem to be a better predictor of empathic accuracy than the former, given that it goes beyond simply reading emotional expressions; however, Lewis and Hodges (2009) found no significant relation between either scale and empathic accuracy using Ickes's paradigm. Notably, both the Interpersonal Perception Task and the Diagnostic Analysis of Nonverbal Accuracy have low internal reliability (Carter & Hall, 2008; Hall, 2001), which could be part of the reason that it is difficult to demonstrate a relation between them and empathic accuracy.

Self-report measures of interpersonal sensitivity.   If we shift our focus from other performance measures of interpersonal sensitivity to personality measures that seem to fall within the same umbrella category of empathy that we outlined in the first section of this chapter, do we find that people who score higher on empathy measures are more empathically accurate? Davis's (1980) Interpersonal Reactivity Index is one of the most widely used self-report measures of empathy. It divides empathy into four components, each with its own subscale: perspective taking (the tendency to consider how things might appear to other people); empathic concern (feelings of compassion and tenderness in response to others); personal distress (arousal and anxiety prompted by other people's experiences); and fantasy (a tendency to be engaged by the fictional worlds represented in movies or books).

Greater perspective-taking tendencies would intuitively seem to predict empathic accuracy, and a case might be made that empathic concern should motivate attention to others and thereby increase empathic accuracy. However, neither perspective taking nor empathic concern was significantly related to empathic accuracy in two studies (Ickes et al., 1990; Stinson & Ickes, 1992). Empathic concern was positively related to empathic accuracy in a third study (Laurent & Hodges, 2009) but only after controlling for socially desirable responding, and in this same study perspective taking was negatively related to empathic accuracy. In a fourth study, male perceivers who reported feeling sympathy for a target were more empathically accurate than those who did not report feeling sympathy (Schweinle & Ickes, 2007).

Further complicating matters, scores from Mehrabian and Epstein's (1972) Balanced Emotional Empathy Scale, which correlates substantially with Davis's (1983) empathic concern and fantasy subscales, predicted greater accuracy in identifying the valence and extremity of a target's emotions in Zaki et al.'s (2008) study but only for targets who were relatively high in expressivity. Together, these results suggest that scores on individual difference measures of empathy are somewhat fickle predictors of empathic accuracy. All of the empathy measures we have cited rely on self-report, which may be partially responsible for their limited ability to predict empathic accuracy.

Measures that distinguish perceivers on the basis of their cognitive style and capacity.   As we have just shown, when researchers attempt to predict empathic accuracy from normal variations in interpersonal sensitivity measures, the general verdict is so far, so bad. However, what do the results look like when distinguishing people on the basis of an index of their more general cognitive abilities? Let's start with a group known for, and in fact partially delineated by, a distinctive cognitive style and fairly dramatic deficits in perceiving other people's thoughts and feelings—that is, people with autism or autism spectrum disorder (ASD; American Psychiatric Association, 2000; Baron-Cohen, 1995).

People with severe autism often have severe language deficits and other behavioral disturbances that make testing their empathic accuracy essentially impossible. However, within samples containing individuals who are high enough in their functioning to be tested using the Ickes paradigm, people diagnosed with ASD show worse empathic accuracy (Demurie, De Corel, & Roeyers, 2011; Ponnet, Buysse, Roeyers, & De Clercq, 2008). The lack of predictable structure in a social interaction appears to be an important moderator of this effect (Ponnet et al., 2008). High-functioning people with autism may be able to understand the gist of what the other person is thinking or feeling if they can learn and apply relevant social schemas or scripts (Grandin, Barron, & Zysk, 2005; Hirschfeld, Bartmess, White, & Frith, 2007; White, Hill, Winston, & Frith, 2006).

Notably, the studies cited in the preceding paragraph make categorical comparisons between people with an ASD diagnosis and "neurotypicals" (those without autism). In contrast, Bartz et al. (2010) examined continuous differences on Baron-Cohen's Autism Quotient, a scale designed more to identify variations in autistic tendencies than to provide cutoff scores for diagnosis, with higher scores indicating more autistic tendencies (Baron-Cohen, Wheelwright, Skinner, Martin, & Clubley, 2001). Bartz et al. found that the Autism Quotient scores of neurotypical male adults inversely predicted their level of performance on the Zaki et al. (2008) emotion-rating task we described earlier. Interestingly, regardless of Autism Quotient scores, a uniformly high level of performance was found on this task when participants were given a dose of the hormone oxytocin—a hormone associated with nurturance and affiliation (H. E. Ross & Young, 2009) and nonverbal acuity (Domes, Heinrichs, Michel, Berger, & Herpertz, 2007).

Another cognitive capacity that might be related to empathic accuracy is IQ.[3] IQ has been found to predict empathic accuracy in a small sample ($N = 22$) of typical adults (Ponnet et al., 2008), and related variables such as college grade-point average have also been found to predict empathic accuracy (Ickes et al., 1990). However, other results have been less conclusive. In a study using a mixed sample of neurotypical participants and participants with Asperger's syndrome, no correlation was found between empathic accuracy and IQ (Ponnet, Roeyers, Buysse, De Clercq, & Van Der Heyden, 2004). Thomas and Fletcher (2003) reported results from a study in which higher IQ predicted greater empathic

accuracy but only when the targets were strangers to the perceivers. Finally, Ickes, Buysse, et al. (2000) discussed an unpublished study that failed to replicate the grade-point average result in Ickes et al. (1990) and another in which verbal IQ was predictive of empathic accuracy for men, but not women, when participants were asked to watch videotapes of women discussing relationship problems. This last finding is perhaps echoed in the results of a study of heterosexual couples in which Thomas et al. (1997) found that more educated men were more empathically accurate when it came to reading their female partners' thoughts about an issue identified by the couple as a problem in their relationship, whereas education level did not predict women's ability to read their male partners' thoughts.

In summary, differences along the autism spectrum appear to be a promising explanation of variance in predicting perceivers' empathic accuracy, although research has not yet examined whether variations in autistic tendencies among those without an ASD diagnosis affect performance on the Ickes paradigm. Intelligence is emerging as an unreliable predictor of empathic accuracy, but the results are slightly more promising among men than women, perhaps especially when men are asked to infer women's thoughts about relationship problems.

Sex and gender.   The last category of perceiver variables we discuss—sex and gender—has the best track record among individual difference variables in terms of predicting empathic accuracy in typically developing adults, but here too the record has been marred by null results and complex interactions. A recent chapter on sex differences in empathic accuracy reviewed several studies in which women's empathic accuracy was better than men's and several studies in which men's and women's performance did not differ significantly, but none in which men performed significantly better than women (Hodges, Laurent, & Lewis, 2011).[4] This specific pattern suggests that there might be

---

[3]In the studies cited earlier that compared participants with and without an ASD diagnosis, the participants with ASD were all high functioning, which among other things meant that they had normal IQs, because major IQ deficits could make the cognitively and verbally challenging task of composing an inference about another person's thoughts nearly impossible.

[4]One exception, a case in which men were more accurate than women, is reported in Simpson, Ickes, and Grich (1999): When perceiving their girlfriends' thoughts during conditions that were highly threatening to their relationship, men were more accurate than women. However, women were more accurate than men in the mildly threatening conditions of the same study, and there was no overall gender difference.

something correlated with gender (the dichotomous categorical variable indicating whether a participant identifies as a man or woman) that is the proximal predictor of empathic accuracy, and this hypothesis was the motivation behind Laurent and Hodges's (2009) study of gender roles and empathic accuracy. Perhaps a communal orientation—a "focus on others and forming connections" (Helgeson, 1994, p. 412), which is considered a hallmark of the feminine gender role—is the key to empathic accuracy, rather than a perceiver's biological sex per se.

Consistent with this hypothesis, Laurent and Hodges (2009) found that how much participants self-reported behaviors that were consistent with the female gender role predicted empathic accuracy in both men and women (but only when differences in socially desirable responding were controlled for). However, as reviewed by Hodges et al. (2011), not all attempts to replicate this finding for communal orientation have been successful, and even when they are the effect sizes are small. Furthermore, even after controlling for communion, biological sex (again, the dichotomous identity variable) still explains a unique portion of the variance in empathic accuracy scores in some samples (e.g., Laurent & Hodges, 2009). Although sex and gender have fared somewhat better than other individual difference variables as occasional predictors of empathic accuracy, predicting empathic accuracy from perceiver sex—similar to other perceiver variables—appears to be more complex than initially thought.

In wrapping up our discussion of perceiver variables, we might ask why researchers have so doggedly pursued the hypothesis that there is something about perceivers that predicts their empathic accuracy. (Indeed, we have asked ourselves that question more than once, especially after examining yet another data set with null or inconsistent results involving perceiver differences.) Beyond the stubborn intuition that empathic accuracy is an ability, and thus has reliable correlates like other abilities, such as verbal fluency or gymnastics, there is a good empirical reason to look for perceiver correlates: A growing number of studies have shown cross-target consistency within perceivers (e.g., Gesn & Ickes; 1999; Lewis et al., 2012; Marangoni et al., 1995; Pham & Rivers, as cited in Ickes, Buysse, et al., 2000; Ponnet et al., 2008; Thomas & Fletcher, 2003). In other words, some of the variance in empathic accuracy does seem to be attributable to the perceiver.

However, cross-target consistency appears to emerge only under some circumstances. Notably, all but one of the studies cited earlier that showed cross-target consistency used targets who were strangers to the perceivers—and people whom the perceivers never actually met. The one exception is Thomas and Fletcher's (2003) study, and even in this study some of the targets were strangers viewed only on videotape, and the highest cross-target consistencies were found among perceivers for whom all the targets were strangers. The strategies a perceiver uses to infer the thoughts of a stranger may be distinct from those a perceiver uses to infer the thoughts of a close other. An unintended but consistent source of variance in cross-target consistency with strangers might be the extent to which perceivers care about being good subjects in the contrived world of psychology studies—an individual difference in perceivers, albeit not one that necessarily affects their empathic accuracy performance in the real world.

Similarly, more than a decade ago, in reviewing several empathic accuracy studies, Ickes, Buysse, et al. (2000) discovered that the only version of the Ickes paradigm that appeared to show substantial perceiver variance was the standard stimulus paradigm. In this paradigm, many perceivers infer the thoughts of the same target person (or set of target people)—targets who are thus also strangers to the perceivers and people with whom the perceivers did not interact. Among studies using the dyadic interaction paradigm, Ickes, Buysse, et al. found little variance attributable to perceivers. To find differences in empathic accuracy that are due to perceiver variables, there must first be significant perceiver variance to be explained, and so we should not be surprised that perceiver variables, such as women's sometimes empathic accuracy advantage, are notably absent in studies using the dyadic interaction paradigm.[5]

---

[5]The one major exception is Thomas and Fletcher's 2003 study, in which they found that female dating partners were better at guessing their partner's thoughts than male dating partners.

Finally, in many of the studies showing cross-target consistency, there have been shared qualities across the multiple targets, such as the targets all being women talking about relationship problems (e.g., Gesn & Ickes; 1999; Marangoni et al., 1995; Pham & Rivers, as cited in Ickes, Buysse, et al., 2000) or new mothers talking about the arrival of their babies in their lives (Lewis et al., 2012). Thus, variance being chalked up to perceivers could in fact be variance that should be attributed to some shared characteristic of targets.

Target Variables

Empathic accuracy is, by definition, an interpersonal phenomenon that involves both a perceiver and a target.[6] Although perceivers and targets are equal players in these interactions, when it comes to empathic accuracy research, perceivers have hogged the limelight. As we showed in the previous section, empathic accuracy researchers have extensively investigated (with varying success) what makes for a good perceiver—that is, the characteristics of a good mind reader. We now turn to a relatively less well-studied aspect of empathic accuracy—the characteristics of an easy-to-read mind.

As was the case for perceiver variables, for characteristics of the target to predict a perceiver's empathic accuracy, there must first be variance in empathic accuracy associated with targets. In Ickes, Buysse, et al.'s (2000) review of several independent studies (discussed previously), the researchers applied the social relations model (Kenny, 1994) to partition the variance in empathic accuracy into perceiver variance, target variance, and residual variance. The average amount of total target variance across the studies examined in that article was roughly 25%. However, this figure differed depending on the type of empathic accuracy study. Variance attributable to targets was lower in studies using the standard stimulus paradigm in which the target person was taped during an interview (11%–14%) but considerably higher in studies in which the targets were taped during live interaction with a partner (23%–41%). A separate study conducted

by Thomas and Fletcher (2003) also computed estimates of variance attributable to targets (who engaged in live interaction with a partner) and found target variance estimates of roughly similar size (23% for male targets and 12% for female targets).

The nonzero target variance accounted for in these studies suggests that there may be variables associated with targets that predict a perceiver's level of empathic accuracy. Two studies have used the Ickes paradigm to investigate the target characteristics that may matter for empathic accuracy (Gesn & Ickes, 1999; Hall & Schmid Mast, 2007). In these studies, target stimuli were manipulated to control the channels of information available to perceivers (e.g., full video, audio only, transcript). Consistent with our earlier discussion of the building blocks of empathic accuracy, these studies found that verbal cues, or what a target said, mattered much more than visual and vocal nonverbal cues. Thus, it seems that one obvious target characteristic that is likely to affect empathic accuracy is the extent to which a target openly expresses information that is diagnostic of his or her current private, subjective mental experience.

Within the empathic accuracy paradigm, researchers have often studied expressivity at the thought level by assessing how readable a given thought is, based on a target's expressive behavior that surrounds the thought. This variable has been referred to as *thought–feeling transparency, readability, inferential difficulty,* or *behavioral diagnosticity.* First introduced by Marangoni et al. (1995), transparency is assessed by asking trained coders to rate how easy it should be to infer the content of each reported thought from the contextual cues (words, eliciting events, etc.) that preceded it on the video recording. The coders have a transcript of the actual reported thoughts in front of them when they make their ratings.

A global measure of transparency can be computed as the average transparency of all of a target's reported thoughts, and this number can then be used as a statistical covariate (Marangoni et al., 1995).

---

[6]In the dyadic interaction paradigm, of course, both dyad members are perceivers and both also occupy the role of each other's target. A special statistical model, the actor–partner interdependence model (Kashy & Donnellan, 2012), is needed to deal with the statistical interdependence of the two dyad members' responses in this case.

In other instances, transparency may be the variable of more focal interest. For example, transparency may not have the same effect on accuracy across all levels of perceiver–target acquaintanceship. Thomas and Fletcher (2003) found that with increasing acquaintanceship between a perceiver and a target, thought transparency and accuracy were less correlated. They suggested that in long-term relationships, target transparency matters less because perceivers have had time to develop a more nuanced personal schema of the target, which they can draw on when making empathic inferences. Similarly, as noted earlier, Gesn and Ickes (1999) found that perceivers start to develop schemas about new targets even at zero acquaintance, and their accuracy in inferring a particular thought or feeling of the target depends on the trade-off between relying on schemas versus relying on behavioral data—and which of these two sources of information is more pertinent for that particular thought or feeling.

Target expressivity may also be an important moderator of the relation between perceiver variables and empathic accuracy. For instance, Thomas and Maio (2008) examined thought transparency in conjunction with perceivers' motivation to be empathically accurate, hypothesizing that greater motivation would result in increased accuracy only for targets with more transparent thoughts. Thomas and Maio confirmed this hypothesis across two studies in which two different motivation manipulations were used. Their results suggest that when targets are very difficult to read, how motivated one is to read them may not matter much. Similarly, Zaki et al. (2008) used the emotion–valence accuracy task and found that perceivers' self-reported empathic concern predicted accuracy only when perceivers made judgments about emotionally expressive targets (measured via target self-report).

Further support for the importance of the target's readability comes from research examining the relation between target variables related to psychopathology and empathic accuracy. Flury, Ickes, and Schweinle (2008) found that in a sample of nonpatient dyads, the participant scoring higher on a scale of borderline personality disorder was harder to read. Gadassi et al. (2011) found that the romantic partners of depressed women achieved less empathic

accuracy. One possible explanation for this effect is that the flat affect that characterizes depression (Berenbaum & Oltmanns, 1992) makes a target a poorer sender of emotional information. Interestingly, though, this effect held only for female targets; the partners of depressed men showed no less empathic accuracy than the partners of men who were not depressed. This may be because men are generally less emotionally expressive than women (Kring & Gordon, 1998) and also tend to self-disclose less (Dindia & Allen, 1992), making them generally less transparent. Thus, compared with women, the different cues men send when they are depressed as opposed to when they are not depressed might be of less consequence.

Given this pattern of gender differences in expressivity-related variables, it seems reasonable to suspect that a target's gender would be related to empathic accuracy. Indeed, research from the related domain of nonverbal communication and decoding accuracy has suggested that women are better "senders" (communicators), at least for nonverbal cues, than are men (Hall, 1984). However, the gender of the target has not consistently been related to empathic accuracy (Ickes, 2003; Thomas & Fletcher, 2003; however, see Simpson et al., 2011, who found that men, not women, were easier to read). An interesting avenue for future research is to examine whether men and women differ in the types of signals they send. Men may make up for their presumed lack of expressivity and self-disclosure with other cues that deserve investigation (e.g., a closer correspondence between verbal cues and mental content).

Although thought transparency has promise in explaining empathic accuracy, this variable is not without flaws. One problem is that because transparency is assessed at the level of individual thoughts, it may not capture general target expressivity as much as it captures whether the thoughts a target reports having are on topic with what a target is saying. Targets sometimes report thoughts that are entirely unrelated to the discussion topic (or what we like to call the *curling iron effect*; i.e., a target who is outwardly talking about a specific topic such as her new baby or her divorce but whose thoughts stray to "Hmm, I wonder if I turned the curling iron off when I left home this morning?"). Such thoughts may stand out more in targets' memory, in part because they are so incongruent, and they are indeed less transparent. However, in these cases, the lack of transparency has little to do with whether that target is generally expressive. Given the multidimensional nature of expressivity (Gross & John, 1997), future research that explores different way to operationalize expressivity will be important.

Taken together, the results of these studies suggest another reason why empathic accuracy researchers have failed to find support for candidate perceiver variables that predict empathic accuracy: Some targets are simply not readable, and they create a perceiver floor effect. What target characteristics besides transparency might affect a perceiver's empathic accuracy? Marangoni et al. (1995) found that a female target who had ambivalent feelings about her marriage was harder to read than two other female targets whose feelings about their marriages were more consistent. Thomas et al. (1997) found a positive relation between a target's level of education and empathic accuracy in heterosexual married couples, but this was true only for wives' level of education. This small handful of studies investigating target variables other than expressivity points directly at what we deem to be a large gap in the current understanding of empathic accuracy. We consider this area ripe for future research, and we return to this point in the Future Directions section.

Motivational Variables

We turn now to how motivation-related variables may influence empathic accuracy. We have given motivation its own section for a couple of reasons. First, the body of research on how motivational variables affect empathic accuracy is growing. In fact, there is more work on this topic than there is on target effects, and the results are more coherent than those coming from studies of perceiver effects. Second, the results we review here do not fit neatly into categories of perceiver or target effects; both perceivers and targets may influence motivational variables in an interaction. Although individual differences may exist in a person's habitual motivation to be

empathically accurate, motivation is not strictly just a perceiver variable because the motivation that helps explain differences in empathic accuracy is often uniquely linked to a particular sort of interaction that perceiver and target have in a particular context.

Motivation is not a simple function of targets either, although at least one study has suggested that people may be more motivated to accurately infer the thoughts of some targets than those of others. Specifically, Ickes et al. (1990) found that university student research participants were more empathically accurate when inferring the thoughts of attractive opposite-sex strangers than of strangers who were less attractive. Presumably, the participants in this study were more interested in an attractive stranger than in a less attractive one, and this greater interest motivated greater attention to the stranger's words and actions as well as a greater effort to infer what the other person was thinking.

The mediating role of motivation in everyday mind-reading accuracy was further explored by Laurent, Hodges, and Lewis (2011), who found that self-reported motivation to accurately infer a target's thoughts predicted empathic accuracy. However, equating better performance with greater motivation can be perilous (see Hall, 2011). Good performance does not necessarily indicate high motivation; good performance may be the result of practice, innate talent, or being given lots of helpful guidance. Motivation is often inferred in studies rather than directly measured (the study by Laurent et al. is an exception), making it difficult to know for sure that motivation was responsible for improvements in performance. Furthermore, even if it is clear that motivation is high, higher motivation may not always improve performance. As Smith, Hall, Hodges, and Ickes (2011) have noted, wanting to be empathically accurate does not necessarily result in more accuracy, any more than simply wanting to spell a word correctly makes one more accurate at spelling. Indeed, a very intense desire to be accurate might actually interfere with performance in some cases, resulting in reduced accuracy (Beilock & Carr, 2001).

We divide our discussion of motivation-related variables into three categories.[7] First are instances in

---

[7]These categories are not meant to be exhaustive, but they do cover a broad swath of motivated empathic accuracy.

which people may be motivated to be accurate because accurate inference of another person's thoughts is useful or rewarding to them. Second are instances in which people are motivated to maintain a relationship, and empathic accuracy—or, in some cases, inaccuracy—is instrumental to that maintenance. Finally are instances in which people are motivated to maintain their worldviews, and the accurate—or again, in some cases, the inaccurate—inference of other people's thoughts can further this goal.

Motivation for personal gain. Accurate inference of other people's thoughts can be rewarding because that knowledge can be used strategically for the perceiver's gain. While on a romantic date, correctly reading another person's thoughts about the ideal next step in the relationship might bring sensual pleasures—or at least prevent one from being slapped or dumped. If subordinates can accurately read their boss's thoughts about their performance, they can pick an ideal time to ask for a raise—or at least avoid asking at a time that might anger the boss. In a very concrete demonstration of how people might be motivated to be more empathically accurate in anticipation of personal gains, Klein and Hodges (2001) showed that people promised monetary payoffs proportionate to their empathic accuracy were indeed more accurate than those in a control condition who were not promised any rewards.

Exploring a different motivator, Thomas and Maio (2008) told some male university student participants that men who were more empathically accurate were more successful at attracting women. Men in this condition were better at reading targets' thoughts than men who were not given this information. Because Thomas and Maio did not run a parallel condition for women (telling them that empathic accuracy would attract men), whether the promise of attention from the opposite sex works only for men is unknown.

Desired rewards other than money and sex have also been shown to motivate empathic accuracy. For example, Pickett, Gardner, and Knowles (2004) found that people who have a habitually higher need for social connectedness (as measured by a Need to Belong Scale) showed greater empathic accuracy. However, an interesting finding was that a manipulation that was designed to temporarily highlight a need to belong did not succeed in improving empathic accuracy. Pickett et al. (2004) asked participants to relive an experience of social rejection, academic failure, or a routine commute to school (with that last condition designed to be the neutral control) before testing their empathic accuracy. The results showed that the lowest empathic scores came from participants who relived a social rejection. Thus, although people who are chronically high in a need to belong may be more motivated to read others' minds more accurately, having to relive feelings of intense rejection may interfere with this ability. These data provide an example of why greater motivation should not always be assumed to result in better performance.

Some of the most interesting findings about the motivation for personal gain and empathic accuracy are specific to a particular close relationship. One might intuitively expect that people would be more motivated to accurately infer the thoughts of relationship partners than those of a random person because a partner's thoughts and actions can have such a big impact on one's own outcomes, and one's partner's well-being would likely concern one. Consistent with this intuition, Stinson and Ickes (1992) found that people were more empathically accurate with friends than with strangers.

The findings from other studies, however, have been mixed. Thomas and Fletcher (2003) found a nonsignificant advantage for friends over strangers, but in their study neither the friends nor the strangers were part of the interactions that formed the stimuli for empathic accuracy—targets were instead filmed while talking with their dating partners. This feature of the study may have reduced the participants' motivation to be accurate, because the thoughts to be inferred may have been less relevant to the friends and their relationship. Consistent with this interpretation, the dating partners in Thomas and Fletcher's study were more empathically accurate perceivers than friends or strangers. Similarly, Hancock and Ickes (1996) found that friends who observed each other having a get-to-know-you conversation with a stranger were no more accurate in their empathic inference than were outside observers. Finally, Clements, Holtzworth-Munroe, Schweinle, and Ickes (2007) found that women and nonviolent men were no better at inferring their partners' thoughts during a conversation about a relationship issue than were objective observers watching the same conversations. In summary, the evidence for acquaintanceship effects is mixed, and if motivational differences underlie these effects, the underlying motivation may not be just relationship dependent but context dependent as well.

Although the motivational account makes a plausible story (i.e., one cares more about what close acquaintances are thinking, particularly when they are interacting with one or talking about their relationship with one), a knowledge-based account may be just as plausible. As noted earlier in the section on using social cognitive constructs to improve empathic accuracy, Stinson and Ickes (1992) found that the acquaintanceship effect appeared to be due to acquaintances' ability to use knowledge about other times and other places to infer targets' thoughts. With this explanation of the relation between acquaintanceship and accuracy, invoking motivation is unnecessary. Recall also that Thomas and Fletcher (2003) found that as acquaintanceship with the target became greater, perceivers' accuracy was less correlated with how transparent targets were. In other words, as acquaintanceship increased, perceivers' empathic inferences appeared to rely less on what the target was outwardly saying or doing, suggesting that they were instead relying on other (insider) knowledge accrued over the course of the relationship. However, as Thomas and Fletcher (2003) noted, "It is difficult to disentangle motivation from ability when analyzing the long-term development of expertise" (p. 1092)—greater motivation could prompt greater interest in the kind of insider knowledge that later helps people to guess a close other's thoughts.

Motivation to maintain a relationship. As we have just shown, people are motivated to be empathically accurate when they think they will be rewarded in specific interactions for that accuracy. However, in the case of empathic accuracy within close relationships, people may also be generally motivated to maintain their relationship (or to avoid its dissolution). Depending on where a couple is in a relationship and how that relationship is going, the partners' motivation for empathic accuracy may change.

At different stages of a relationship, empathic accuracy may count more, with accuracy being particularly important at the beginning of a relationship, when partners may be trying to figure out the other person's commitment to the relationship and interest in furthering it. Later, in a committed relationship that is going reasonably well, accuracy motivation may decline because there is less concern that the relationship will be derailed by a single misapprehended thought and also because after spending a lot of time together in a relationship, the partners may feel like they know the general tenor of each other's thoughts without trying to read their minds at a particular moment. In other words, one may observe "the triumph of habit over scrupulous attention" (Kilpatrick et al., 2002, p. 389) in longer term relationships.

Several empirical findings have supported this hypothesis. In a sample of married couples among whom the mean length of marriage was 15 years, length of marriage was negatively related to the couple's empathic accuracy during a conversation about a relationship issue, especially for men (Thomas et al., 1997). Mediational analysis suggested that couples who had been married longer tended to have less of a shared cognitive focus. That is, they were not thinking about the same topics at the same time in their interactions, which in turn led to lower empathic accuracy. Similarly, Kilpatrick et al. (2002) found that, for recently married couples, empathic accuracy (also while discussing a relationship issue) tended to drop over time.

Again, however, there are some null findings to consider as well. In a sample of married couples, Simpson et al. (2003) found no relation between years married and empathic accuracy. Examining less committed couples, Haugen et al. (2008) asked adolescent heterosexual dating couples to rate their feelings about their relationship at 20-second intervals during a conversation about a relationship issue and also asked them to guess their partner's feelings on the same items. No correlation between relationship length and accuracy was found. Using a sample of older heterosexual dating couples who had been together on average 16.5 months, Thomas and Fletcher (2003) did not report any main effects of relationship length on empathic accuracy but did find that relationship length moderated the link between empathic accuracy and relationship satisfaction.

Time together is not the only variable that may affect the motivation to be accurate in close relationships. If the final goal is to maintain the relationship, then in some cases empathic inaccuracy may be the intermediate goal. In a series of intriguing studies, Simpson, Ickes, and their colleagues developed an empathic accuracy model that predicts when perceivers will be more likely to be accurate versus inaccurate about relationship partners' thoughts (e.g., Ickes & Simpson, 2001). In their first study, Simpson et al. (1995) had members of heterosexual dating couples sit beside each other while they rated aloud the attractiveness and sexual appeal of opposite-sex people depicted in slides. These interactions were videotaped, and the usual video review procedure from Ickes's paradigm was used to first obtain each partner's actual thoughts and feelings and then assess each partner's empathic accuracy for the partner's thoughts and feelings. These researchers also measured how much potential threat this mind-reading activity presented to the partners' relationship on the basis of three possible sources of threat: how attractive the people in the slides were (more attractive targets were more threatening); how secure the couples were about their relationship (less secure couples were under greater threat); and how close the couples were (couples who were closer had more to lose and thus were under greater threat).

Simpson et al.'s (1995) data clearly showed that the greater the threat, the lower the empathic accuracy—with the result that couples experiencing the greatest threat showed empathic accuracy scores that were considerably lower than those seen in most empathic accuracy studies.[8] Thus, the researchers had their first evidence that people might be motivated to be inaccurate under circumstances in

which empathic accuracy might reveal that the target was having thoughts that might threaten the relationship (see also Ickes, Simpson, & Oriña, 2005; Cuperman, Howland, Ickes, & Simpson, 2011). Furthermore, Simpson et al.'s (1995) results suggested that avoiding the truth about these threatening thoughts might have helped the partners to ride out this temporary threat: Participants whose empathic accuracy was lowest under high threat conditions were more likely still to be dating 4 months later.

Further evidence that accurately inferring a partner's true thoughts can sometimes hurt a relationship came in a study by Simpson et al. (2003). In this study, married couples discussed a relationship problem and then inferred each other's thoughts from the videotape of their discussion. Before the discussion and then after inferring their partner's thoughts, participants completed Aron, Aron, and Smollan's (1992) Inclusion of Other in Self Scale as a measure of closeness. In addition, both the participants and the independent coders rated the thoughts in terms of how threatening they were to the relationship. When partners were thinking threatening thoughts and the participants were more empathically accurate, the participants' ratings of closeness declined. However, if the partners were thinking unthreatening thoughts, then participants' increased empathic accuracy predicted increases in closeness.

Simpson et al. (2003) further suggested that the declines in closeness were mediated by the partner's avoidance of discussing a danger-zone relationship issue. To put this in more concrete terms, imagine Brad and Angelina are talking about how having too many children is putting a strain on their relationship. During their conversation, Brad is thinking relationship-threatening thoughts (perhaps about how his life might have been better if he had never hooked up with Angelina and had instead stayed with Jennifer). The better Angelina is at inferring Brad's thoughts, the less close she will feel to Brad, and the mediator of this relation appears to be Brad's attempts to avoid talking about the too-many-children issue. Ironically, however, Simpson et al. would

---

[8]In fact, their scores were lower than the average scores obtained for total strangers in other empathic accuracy studies, suggesting a willful avoidance of the knowledge of what their partners were actually thinking or feeling in this relationship-threatening situation.

suggest that Brad's avoidance is itself a cue to Angelina that Brad is indeed thinking threatening thoughts. Thus, Simpson et al. found another set of circumstances under which greater empathic accuracy for one's partner may have harmful effects on close relationships.

The threat to a relationship that affects empathic accuracy can come from real challenges to the relationship (e.g., attractive rivals), but it is also possible that one or both partners in a relationship dispositionally perceive the relationship to be under chronic threat. For example, individuals who have an anxious attachment style want their partners to be closer to them and fear that their partners will not be there for them (Bartholomew & Horowitz, 1991). This fear leads these individuals to be hypervigilant in regard to their partner's behavior, thoughts, and feelings in relationship-threatening situations. This hypervigilance therefore results in greater, rather than less, accuracy in relationship-threatening situations, contrary to the general trend toward less accuracy under the more relationship-threatening conditions that Simpson et al. (1995) reported.

Consistent with this line of reasoning, Simpson, Ickes, and Grich (1999) found that anxiously attached women were more, rather than less, accurate at inferring their partners' thoughts during the paradigm that required partners to say how attractive they found other opposite-sex people. Furthermore, for both sexes, the interaction of empathic accuracy and anxious attachment predicted reduced closeness—that is, individuals who were more empathically accurate and more anxiously attached were particularly likely to report less closeness at the end of the interaction. For men only, this same interaction also predicted that the relationship was less likely to be intact 4 months later. Once again, accurately perceiving one's partner's thoughts when a relationship is under threat (even when that threat is a perception from within) does not auger well for relationships.

Thus, anxiously attached people perceive greater threats to their relationship and seem to respond by being more vigilant. Certainly, under some threatening circumstances, greater vigilance is helpful (if one lives in a flood plain, vigilance to rising water levels may save one's life, and if one's partner has insulin-dependent diabetes, vigilance to outward signs of low blood sugar may save the partner's life). However, such vigilance often worsens the distress of anxiously attached people, because it appears to have the unfortunate effect of making them more cognizant of what they fear most—that their partner may be having doubtful or unfavorable thoughts about them or the relationship. It is a bit like reading up on all the nasty symptoms that make up a disease after just being diagnosed with that disease. However, to be fair, it is still possible that knowing more—even if it is bad news—still somehow helps anxiously attached individuals to cope. Analogously, defensive pessimists are generally less mentally healthy than optimists, yet depriving them of their preferred strategy in stressful situations by instructing them to think like optimists does not help their performance (Spencer & Norem, 1996).

What about avoidance, the other dimension of insecure adult attachment? Avoidant individuals minimize the importance of close relationships and seek to avoid developing interdependence with their partner (Bartholomew & Horowitz, 1991). Simpson et al. (2011) found that avoidant attachment scores predicted reduced empathic accuracy during relationship-threatening interactions (i.e., discussing relationship problems). These results are consistent with an earlier study by Rholes, Simpson, Tran, Martin, and Friedman (2007), who found that avoidantly attached individuals reported knowing less about their partners and demonstrated less interest in learning more.

Taken together then, these findings suggest that different styles of insecure attachment lead to different strategies for dealing with threatening information: Whereas avoidantly attached individuals withdraw interest and thus are virtually assured lower accuracy, anxiously attached individuals vigilantly attend to their partners. There is a certain irony in the fact that avoidantly attached individuals—who downplay how much they care about their relationships—care enough to avoid knowing their partners' thoughts when those thoughts might be distressing and that anxiously attached individuals—who could be accused of caring too much about their relationships—seem drawn to information that may ultimately unravel the relationship. Furthermore, we have implicitly framed these findings about attachment style and empathic accuracy as strategies, but that raises a question of just how conscious insecurely attached individuals are of what they will find when they infer their partners' thoughts: It is almost as if they would have to first know the gist of the thoughts they will find to execute their preferred strategy of either hypervigilance or avoidance (see Smith et al., 2011).

Motivation to maintain self and worldviews.
Finally, empathic accuracy may be affected by motivation to maintain a particular view of the world and how people within it behave. For example, one of the leading explanations for why women have an advantage—albeit an unreliable one—over men in terms of empathic accuracy is that women see being interpersonally sensitive and attentive to other people's thoughts and feelings as part of their gender role. Although women may generally have a slight edge over men in terms of empathic accuracy (see Hodges et al., 2011; Ickes, 2003, Chapter 5), a significant motivation-based female advantage becomes evident when the female gender role is highlighted, in subtle or indirect ways (e.g., Ickes, Gesn, & Graham, 2000; Klein & Hodges, 2001), or when research participants' skill at empathic accuracy is explicitly questioned (Thomas & Maio, 2008). The assumption underlying these studies is that most women believe that the average woman should excel at understanding others. It remains to be seen, however, whether reminders about or challenges to this aspect of the female gender role have a more powerful effect on women who endorse this belief in women's intuition more than others.

Beliefs and attitudes may affect accuracy in the ways we have described, but they can also bias the content of perceivers' inferences without necessarily affecting their overall accuracy. A powerful set of studies has linked such bias with an important set of outcomes. Schweinle et al. (2002) first investigated the hypothesis that men who were aggressive toward their wives might have deficits or biases in their empathic accuracy. Schweinle et al. specifically examined the idea that men who are aggressive toward their wives may be predisposed (i.e., biased)

to view women as critical and rejecting of men in relationships. These researchers tested men who varied in terms of levels of self-reported aggression toward their wives using the pseudopsychotherapy target tapes developed by Marangoni et al. (1995). For the Schweinle et al. study, the targets' reported thoughts were categorized by research assistants as being critical or rejecting of the target's male romantic partner (or ex-partner) or not critical or rejecting.

The male participants watched the target videotapes and were asked to infer the contents of the female targets' thoughts and feelings. The participants in this standard stimulus study were also asked whether they thought each thought was critical or rejecting. The results painted an interesting picture: Men who were more aggressive toward their wives were biased in terms of rating the content of the targets' thoughts as being critical or rejecting. That is, they were more likely to mischaracterize a noncritical or nonrejecting thought as being critical or rejecting than they were to mischaracterize an actual critical or rejecting thought as being noncritical or nonrejecting. When it came to their overall accuracy—or sensitivity in signal detection terms—the men's level of aggression had no effect. However, the more biased the men were in terms of overattributing critical or rejecting themes to the women's thoughts, the less accuracy they showed using the traditional Ickes measure of empathic accuracy in which the male perceivers guessed the specific content of the targets' thoughts.

The results of follow-up studies are generally consistent with these original results. A study using one of the same targets (Schweinle & Ickes, 2007) identified two mechanisms by which aggressive men maintain this bias: emotional countercontagion, whereby the men demonstrate a contempt for the female target that they then justify by the overattribution to her of critical and rejecting thoughts, and attentional disengagement, whereby men physically looked away from the target on the video screen as she described her relationship troubles. Schweinle, Cofer, and Schatz (2009) found that the bias to view women's thoughts as critical or rejecting was also related to men's self-reported tendency to engage in behaviors related to sexual harassment.

All three of these studies used the standard stimulus paradigm. In fact, all three used one or more of the pseudopsychotherapy targets developed by Marangoni et al. (1995). However, Clements et al. (2007) examined whether men's relationship aggression was related to bias and accuracy when they were inferring their own romantic partners' thoughts, in addition to those of two of the standard stimulus targets used in the study by Marangoni et al. (1995). Clements et al. were also able to investigate whether relationship aggression had parallel effects on women's ability to read their male partners' thoughts. At the between-dyad level (i.e., considering differences between couples in violent and nonviolent relationships), the men in relationships with physical violence displayed impaired empathic accuracy for their female partner's thoughts compared with men in relationships without violence. In addition, the men in violent relationships read their female partners less accurately than did a group of objective male observers who inferred the same thoughts (i.e., from the female partners in violent relationships). Furthermore, within violent dyads (i.e., considering differences between a woman and a man in the same violent relationship), men were worse than women at inferring their partner's thoughts.

Thus, violence in a relationship does not predict reduced empathic accuracy across the board; instead, it appears to be associated with reduced empathic accuracy only for male perceivers, suggesting that beliefs and attitudes may interact with gender roles when it comes to empathic accuracy. Do these violent men lack the motivation to pay attention to women's cues? Actually, the Schweinle and Ickes (2007) data paint a far more troubling picture: Maritally aggressive or abusive men are motivated to actively disattend to a woman's relationship concerns, relying on a cognitive schema that prejudges women's thoughts and feelings as being critical and rejecting of their male partners. (See Crick & Dodge, 1994, for a similar idea about children's social cognition.) Seen from this perspective, maritally aggressive or abusive men appear to have a surfeit of motivation—a motivation to maintain control in their relationship with the use of misattribution and violence (see Clements et al., 2007)—and thus

they are motivated to see women's behavior as provoking such violence. As this example poignantly illustrates, researchers should avoid the easy assumption that stronger motivation will always lead to greater empathic accuracy (Hall, 2011).

A tendency toward relational violence is not the only habitual mindset that can influence empathic accuracy. Using methods similar to those in Schweinle et al.'s (2002) study, Schmid Mast, Hall, and Ickes (2006) asked perceivers to identify whether targets in a persuasive conversation were having thoughts with power-relevant content. They found that men with a preference for high power in social interactions were biased to infer power-related content in other people's thoughts and feelings, relative to men who had a preference for lower power. They did not find this difference among women. Echoing some of Schweinle et al.'s results, they found no effects of gender or power preference on sensitivity scores—that is, on "how accurately a participant inferred that specific thoughts and feelings were power-relevant or non-power-relevant" (Schmid Mast et al., 2006, p. 473).

Thus, men with a high power preference were not making more errors than other people in terms of identifying thoughts as power relevant or not. However, when they did make errors, they were biased in favor of seeing thoughts as being power relevant. Interestingly, accuracy was lower than what is generally found with the original Ickes paradigm—participants in Schmid Mast et al.'s (2006) study did overall no better than chance at identifying whether a thought was power relevant or not.

Sillars, Smith, and Koerner (2010) have documented other examples of biased inference in the context of family relationships, uncovering biases that seem to reflect the roles that family members play. Using methods that vary somewhat from the Ickes paradigm, Sillars et al. had middle school students talk with both of their parents about a family issue, and then everyone in the interaction reported their thoughts at 90-second intervals. They then compared the percentage of target-reported thoughts (*direct perspectives*) falling into certain categories (e.g., positive emotions, agreement, complaints, solutions) with the percentage of inferences (*metaperspectives*) that perceivers put in the same categories. Among other findings, parents overattributed negative thoughts to their middle school–aged children, and children overattributed controlling thoughts to their parents. It is easy to see how these biases are consistent with the stereotypic roles that tweens (think eye-rolling) and their parents (think curfews) play in family interactions.

In summary, research examining the role of motivation has produced some of the most promising—and complicated—results to date in the domain of empathic accuracy. There are clear examples of people who stand to gain something from being empathically accurate showing greater accuracy. There are also more complex results suggesting that a heightened motivation to be empathically accurate does not always result in positive outcomes and that—under some circumstances—people's motivation may lead them to be empathically inaccurate.

FUTURE DIRECTIONS

At this point, we have revealed the thrill of victory and the agony of defeat associated with the study of empathic accuracy. The thrill comes from studying a skill that both showcases the talents that set humans apart from other species and is coveted as a superpower. The agony comes from strings of null or unreplicable findings that defy our theories and intuitions about who should be empathically accurate and when. Somewhere between the two are new findings suggesting that the addition of moderating variables will both complicate models of empathic accuracy and make them more powerful and predictive. In part, these ideas about interactions and moderating variables are emerging because the corpus of empathic accuracy studies is now large enough that it is possible to look for patterns across several studies that have common variables (e.g., sex, motivation, attachment style). We predict that the future study of empathic accuracy will be both robust and challenging. In this final section, we propose three general questions to be tackled in future research.

Does Empathic Accuracy Matter?

Intuitively, it seems that empathic accuracy should matter. As noted previously in the Perceiver Variables section, there does seem to be systematic

variance attributable to perceivers, even if it is statistically significant only in standard stimulus designs in which perceivers infer the thoughts of a stranger. Surely people who are better at empathic accuracy derive benefits from this skill, perhaps having more successful interactions and relationships or using their insights about other people's thoughts to their advantage in negotiations and predicting other people's behavior.

But do they? In a pattern of results that is all too familiar now, studies examining the benefits of empathic accuracy have shown mixed and somewhat unexpected patterns. One of the biggest hits in terms of a demonstration that empathic accuracy matters comes from a study of the social outcomes of young adolescents (Gleason, Jensen-Campbell, & Ickes, 2009). Middle school–aged children's empathic accuracy scores were negatively correlated with peers' reports that they were the targets of relational victimization (e.g., being ostracized by other kids), although empathic accuracy did not appear to protect against overt victimization (e.g., being bullied or harassed). Children who scored higher on empathic accuracy were also less likely to experience both social problems and internalizing problems (e.g., depression and anxiety). Even more interesting, empathic accuracy appeared to serve as a buffer for children who had poor relationships with their peers, and only children with both poor peer relationships and low empathic accuracy had significant behavioral problems.

Verhofstadt et al. (2008) also found that empathic accuracy matters when it is used to predict the social support behaviors of married couples. After first controlling for differences in a couple's marital satisfaction, they found that one partner's empathic accuracy during a discussion about a personal problem identified by the other partner was strongly associated with providing more instrumental support (e.g., advice, practical assistance, a course of action for solving a problem) and less negative support (e.g., criticizing the partner who had the problem). Empathic accuracy was unrelated to emotional support (e.g., encouraging and reassuring the partner with the problem); however, emotional support was predicted by the degree to which participants reported feeling the same emotions as their partner. This dissociation in results led Verhofstadt et al. to speculate that different forms of support in marriage may come from different sources—one's partner may be caring and provide emotional support but not understand the problem well enough to suggest how to help (instrumental support) or one's partner may offer useful instrumental support without providing the warm fuzzies of emotional support—or (if one is really lucky) the partner may offer both.[9]

A person who is empathically accurate may also be perceived more positively by others. In a study in which perceivers tried to infer new mothers' thoughts, the new mother targets were given a chance to read what the perceivers guessed they were thinking as well as the letters that the perceivers had been asked to write to the new mothers, responding to their experiences (Ahnert, Klein, Veach, & Hodges, 2001). The new mother targets rated more empathically accurate perceivers higher on a composite measure of positive regard that included questions about how much they liked the perceivers and how well they thought the perceivers understood them. However, in another study in which targets and perceivers who were previously strangers interacted face to face, greater empathic accuracy did not predict better rapport (J. E. Myers, 2009).

Finally, several major studies of empathic accuracy in close relationships have shown no simple connection between empathic accuracy and relationship quality (Sillars et al., 2005; Simpson et al., 1995, 2003). A few studies have shown such a connection (e.g., Kilpatrick et al., 2002; in addition, Zaki, Bartz, & Ochsner, 2011, found that college students who were better at a continuous emotion-rating task also reported more social interactions and fewer negative emotions). Still others have shown a connection between empathic accuracy and relationship outcomes but only under some circumstances, including the studies of attachment style we reviewed earlier. Thomas and Fletcher (2003) may have uncovered another moderating

variable in their study, finding that greater empathic accuracy was correlated with dating satisfaction in unmarried couples who had been dating longer, but greater empathic accuracy was related to lower satisfaction among couples who had been dating for a shorter period of time (the average amount of time dating across the entire sample was 16.5 months).

Where does this mixed bag of research findings leave people who desire empathic accuracy as a superpower? If granted their wish, might they be disappointed about how little their lives would improve? We think they might be, for three reasons. First, as demonstrated comically in the film *What Women Want,* when Mel Gibson's character can suddenly hear women's thoughts, and as demonstrated empirically in the studies of empathic inaccuracy discussed in this chapter, sometimes the information learned from finely tuned empathic accuracy is unwelcome.

Second, and perhaps of greater importance, instead of attempting mind reading, a highly effective way to find out what another person is thinking is to ask that person. When relationship gurus counsel against mind reading, it is often because they are in favor of more direct means of learning what is on a relationship partner's mind (Guerrero et al., 2011). Humans are gifted with skills that place them at the top of the animal kingdom in terms of sophisticated communication abilities. Because average empathic accuracy scores are usually well below the midpoint of the scale in Ickes's paradigm, it is probably a good thing people are not limited to mind reading for communication—or forced to guess what their conspecifics are thinking and feeling solely on the basis of dramatic nonverbal displays of the kinds used by lions or peacocks. People can sit down and have a chat, conveying and receiving information in a highly efficient, detailed, and unambiguous manner. Mind-reading skills, therefore, may be most important—or at least have the greatest impact—when people are reluctant to share their thoughts, a point that future researchers should note.

---

[9]Zaki and Ochsner (2011) have proposed that different brain systems may underlie empathic accuracy and empathic emotion; indeed, dissociations such as those found in Verhofstadt et al. (2008) have been found in other studies. However, when these dissociations are found, it seems that empathic emotion (and not empathic accuracy) is often more predictive of positive social outcomes, whether the exchange is between newlyweds (Pollmann & Finkenauer, 2009) or strangers (Hodges et al., 2010).

Finally, the third reason why better empathic accuracy might not improve people's lives is that moment-by-moment inference of another person's thoughts may be overkill (M. W. Myers & Hodges, 2009): Much of what passes through another person's mind is of no relevance or strategic value (e.g., curling iron thoughts). Tracking dynamic incremental changes in the contents of another person's thoughts may be of value only in limited—albeit potentially important—settings (e.g., knowing when the other person really has reached the bottom line in a negotiation or knowing when the other person has changed his or her mind about consenting to a sexual act). Many of other people's most important thoughts can easily be read without the aid of advanced mind-reading skills. As is the case in nonhuman species, the messages "I'm really mad at you" and "I think you're sexy" can be communicated with a simple roar or the fanning of one's tail.

Importance of Targets and the Content of Their Thoughts

The evidence for perceiver characteristics that consistently predict empathic accuracy is slim, as is the mere existence of perceiver variance in some studies. These findings highlight the core of our second recommendation for future directions: We suggest that future researchers put more weight on studying characteristics of targets of empathic accuracy and perhaps shift some of the focus away from perceivers. When studying empathic accuracy, choosing to examine target effects rather than perceiver effects may result in more fruitful lines of inquiry, particularly in studies using the dyadic interaction paradigm, in which there is little or no perceiver variance available to predict. Target effects are less limited to a particular type of research design and offer a promising new direction for empathic accuracy research.

Targets and the specific thoughts they express have a lot of power in the current empathic accuracy paradigm. What targets say they are thinking or feeling constitutes the criterion for accuracy, which means that target characteristics may seriously limit the upper boundaries for possible empathic accuracy. To the extent that targets are unable to articulate their thoughts, or perhaps unwilling to do so,

perceivers are in equal proportion doomed to fail in their attempts to be empathically accurate, and thus targets deserve our close and continued attention.

There may be times when a target cannot articulate a thought because it is not something of which he or she is consciously aware. People perceived as being particularly gifted at understanding others, including some psychoanalysts, seem to have the ability to understand aspects of another person's mental state before that person can consciously access it him- or herself. These individuals may be adept at reading nonverbal cues indicating discomfort with a certain topic and are then able to apply the stereotypes and schemas that we have discussed earlier in this chapter to infer the unconscious content that has not bubbled up to the surface with the other person.

However, measuring empathic accuracy is already challenging; things get considerably trickier in terms of establishing the validity of a perceiver's privileged insights when the target is unable to provide a criterion for accuracy. Of course, under some circumstances a target might be privy to hearing a perceiver's inference about his or her unconscious thoughts and say, "Ah, yes! You're right—I hadn't realized it yet, but that is exactly what I was thinking!" Nevertheless, it remains unclear whether the perceiver's inference has truly shepherded the target's unconscious into consciousness or simply given the target a compelling possible account that is compatible with other features of the target's experience. Furthermore, although under some circumstances inferences that guide the target to novel interpretations may have the potential to provide insight and contribute to perceived empathy (Hodges et al., 2010), outside of a psychotherapy context (and perhaps even within it), assertions that someone else knows better than the self what one is thinking are frequently not welcome.

To date, target transparency has been studied in a number of empathic accuracy studies, but targets differ from one another in many other ways that may affect a perceiver's empathic accuracy. Many perceiver characteristics that have been of interest to empathic accuracy researchers may be turned around and examined instead as target characteristics. For example, perceivers' motivation has consistently been shown to affect accuracy. But how is empathic accuracy affected by a target's motivation to be read, or maybe even more interestingly by a target's motivation not to be read? Locks do not exist on diaries by accident—there are some thoughts and feelings people simply do not want others to know and will go to various lengths to hide. Future research that takes into account whether a target wants his or her thoughts to be known is needed.

In addition to giving more attention to the targets of empathic inferences, future research should consider the different thoughts experienced by targets. As we noted early in the chapter, empathic accuracy is distinct from other interpersonal judgments in that it is directed at knowing how the contents of another person's thoughts change dynamically over time, so that a thought to be inferred at one point in a social exchange may be quite different from a thought to be inferred a few minutes later. Exploring and mapping systematic sources of variance in the content of different types of thoughts might also help explain the perceiver's empathic accuracy and, in addition, eliminate a lot of noise from current models, potentially allowing previously obscured effects to become apparent.

Researchers using the empathic accuracy paradigm have typically aggregated accuracy across all of the target's thoughts because the most familiar statistical techniques require independence of observations, a requirement that cannot be guaranteed for a target's multiple thoughts. However, the techniques available to deal with nested data (i.e., multilevel modeling) can now be applied to this problem (see Nezlek, 2011, for an accessible introduction). Using these advanced techniques opens the door to investigating the relation between thought-level content predictors and the perceiver's empathic accuracy. We think this is an important development for empathic accuracy research and one that is likely to uncover many interesting effects as it becomes more widely used.

Importance of Context and the Nature of Relationships

Our final recommended future direction for empathic accuracy research is related to paying more attention to targets but is broader still. While trying to draw generalizations across multiple studies in writing this chapter, we noted that generalizations that could be drawn from studies using targets in face-to-face interactions—targets who were often known to the perceivers in those studies—could not be drawn from studies in which the targets were previously taped strangers (targets whose thoughts likely had low personal relevance to perceivers). We recommend that researchers pay special attention to modeling variables related to context and the nature of the relationship between targets and perceivers in studies of empathic accuracy.

Ickes, Buysse, et al. (2000) laid the groundwork for this advice by noting the absence of perceiver variance in empathic accuracy studies using the dyadic interaction paradigm. This low variance effectively limits the study of perceiver individual difference variables to studies that use the standard stimulus paradigm. They advised empathic accuracy researchers more than a decade ago that it might be a waste of time to look for perceiver individual difference correlates of empathic accuracy in studies not using the standard stimulus paradigm. However, given that reliable estimates of significant variance attributable to perceivers do emerge in the standard stimulus paradigm, it seems plausible that significant perceiver variance disappears in the dyadic interaction paradigm not because of a weakening of the signal but instead because of increased noise.

The standard stimulus paradigm eliminates much of the noise by asking all perceivers to infer the thoughts of a target they have never met face to face and with whom they have no past nor hope of a future. These considerations should serve as a reminder that the dynamic nature of real social interactions is difficult to capture when devising laboratory-friendly methods for measuring empathic accuracy, such as the standard stimulus paradigm. In contrast, the dyadic interaction paradigm is not just a methodology "in which small subsets of perceivers are nested [paired] with similarly small subsets of unique targets" (Ickes, Buysse, et al., 2000, p. 232). In this methodology, when perceivers are asked to guess a target's thoughts, those thoughts are ones that occurred during a conversation in which the perceivers took part. When the dyadic interaction paradigm is used with romantic couples, the thoughts perceivers are inferring are those of the person they are going home with after the study.

Future researchers would do well to identify how differences in relationship and context variables may moderate models of empathic accuracy. Researchers know, for example, that a close other's thoughts are likely to influence a person's outcomes in ways a stranger's thoughts never would, likely increasing the person's motivation to see—or perhaps avoid seeing—certain content. Moreover, if one is part of an interaction, even with a stranger, rather than merely observing another person in an interaction, one can influence where the conversation goes in ways that might help one to better understand the other person's thoughts. Finally, for dyads that continue to exist outside the confines of a laboratory study (e.g., a romantic couple), researchers may need to think more about how the motives and tendencies of both partners interact in a specific situation. For example, a wife's avoidant attachment style may trigger jealous thoughts on the part of her husband at a neighborhood party but not at a family picnic.

The other-minds problem pretty much guarantees that people will be making up quite a bit when they try to read other people's minds (M. W. Myers & Hodges, 2009). Context and relationship variables may have a substantial influence on what people make up as the possible mental contents of various targets. For example, Sillars (2011) noted that target transparency (how much a target's thought resembles what he or she is talking about at the time of the thought) "seems to predict empathic accuracy better for strangers than for friends or couples" (p. 199). With strangers, as Sillars suggested, people pay close attention to what they are outwardly saying and also note their outward appearance (Ickes et al., 1990). People may also be more likely to apply group stereotypes to fill in the gaps in their perceptions of strangers' thoughts (Lewis et al., 2012). In contrast, when inferring the thoughts of known others, people can apply a person-specific stereotype ("what my baby likes"; "how Gavin is"), filling in the gaps with their knowledge of this person in another place and time (Stinson & Ickes, 1992). Thus, future empathic accuracy researchers should question the assumption that the variables

that predict empathic accuracy—and also the outcomes assumed to flow from empathic accuracy—will be the same when empathic accuracy is measured between strangers whose thoughts will have little bearing on one's life and when it is measured between known others.

CONCLUDING THOUGHTS

Despite appearing at the top of the superpowers list, empathic accuracy may be both less elusive—and less valuable—than commonly believed. Although people are rarely very good at guessing another person's thoughts, a broad spectrum of humanity seems to possess some degree of empathic accuracy, muddling along just fine without access to superpower mind-reading skills (Ickes, 2008). Furthermore, research showing that empathic accuracy predicts better outcomes for perceivers is hard to come by (and these studies are generally correlational and cross-sectional, leaving open questions about causal direction).

Empathic accuracy seems to be more a function of targets and their relationship with a perceiver; what the targets are thinking; how much perceivers want (or do not want) to know about it; and, perhaps, how much targets want (or do not want) their thoughts to be known. Without variance in this list of factors, simply studying the transcripts of conversations would tell one pretty much all there is to know about other people's conscious thoughts. In other words, language evolved as the means for people to communicate their thoughts to each other; a separate thought decoder would be largely redundant given the language hardware and software that comes fully loaded on almost every new human, if targets kept nothing to themselves.

And yet, people do have the capacity for private thoughts, and one's curious nature is drawn to them. Would they be better off knowing more precisely and accurately what other people are thinking? Perhaps, in making the occasional business deal or in deciding whether to endure the terror of asking someone to a prom. However, precious little support exists for the idea that boosting empathic accuracy would result in across-the-board improvements in people's relationships with other people, and some evidence has even shown that, in some circumstances, greater empathic accuracy would hurt people's relationships with those they care most about.

The greatest value of studying empathic accuracy may reside not in finding or creating mind-reading super humans but instead in what it reveals about the people striving for it. If one thinks women are critical and judging, it is reflected in the thoughts one attributes to them. If one has a stereotype about new mothers, it is reflected in one's perceptions of what they are thinking about their babies. If one is more empathically accurate, one is perceived as offering more helpful advice to one's spouse. There is much to be learned by studying empathic accuracy—even if it is not what one initially expected to learn.

References

Ahnert, R., Klein, K., Veach, D., & Hodges, S. (2001, February). *Understanding empathic accuracy.* Poster presented at the meeting of the Society of Personality and Social Psychology, San Antonio, TX.

American Psychiatric Association. (2000). *Diagnostic and statistical manual of mental disorders* (4th ed., text revision). Washington, DC: Author.

Ames, D. R. (2004). Inside the mind reader's tool kit: Projection and stereotyping in mental state inference. *Journal of Personality and Social Psychology, 87,* 340–353. doi:10.1037/0022-3514.87.3.340

Aron, A., Aron, E. N., & Smollan, D. (1992). Inclusion of Other in the Self Scale and the structure of interpersonal closeness. *Journal of Personality and Social Psychology, 63,* 596–612. doi:10.1037/0022-3514.63.4.596

Baron-Cohen, S. (1995). *Mindblindness: An essay on autism and theory of mind.* Cambridge, MA: MIT Press.

Baron-Cohen, S., Wheelwright, S., Hill, J., Raste, Y., & Plumb, I. (2001). The "Reading the Mind in the Eyes" test revised version: A study with normal adults, and adults with Asperger syndrome or high-functioning autism. *Journal of Child Psychology and Psychiatry, and Allied Disciplines, 42,* 241–251. doi:10.1111/1469-7610.00715

Baron-Cohen, S., Wheelwright, S., Skinner, R., Martin, J., & Clubley, E. (2001). The Autism-Spectrum Quotient (AQ): Evidence from Asperger syndrome/high-functioning autism, males and females, scientists and mathematicians. *Journal of Autism and Developmental Disorders, 31,* 5–17. doi:10.1023/A:1005653411471

Bartholomew, K., & Horowitz, L. M. (1991). Attachment styles among young adults: A test of a four-category model. *Journal of Personality and Social Psychology, 61,* 226–244. doi:10.1037/0022-3514.61.2.226

Bartz, J. A., Zaki, J., Bolger, N., Hollander, E., Ludwig, N. N., Kolevzon, A., & Ochsner, K. N. (2010). Oxytocin selectively improves empathic accuracy. *Psychological Science, 21,* 1426–1428. doi:10.1177/0956797610383439

Beilock, S. L., & Carr, T. H. (2001). On the fragility of skilled performance: What governs choking under pressure? *Journal of Experimental Psychology: General, 130,* 701–725. doi:10.1037/0096-3445.130.4.701

Berenbaum, H., & Oltmanns, T. F. (1992). Emotional experience and expression in schizophrenia and depression. *Journal of Abnormal Psychology, 101,* 37–44. doi:10.1037/0021-843X.101.1.37

Bond, C. F., & DePaulo, B. M. (2006). Accuracy of deception judgments. *Personality and Social Psychology Review, 10,* 214–234. doi:10.1207/s15327957pspr1003_2

Carter, J. D., & Hall, J. A. (2008). Individual differences in the accuracy of detecting social covariations: Ecological sensitivity. *Journal of Research in Personality, 42,* 439–455. doi:10.1016/j.jrp.2007.07.007

Clements, K., Holtzworth-Munroe, A., Schweinle, W., & Ickes, W. (2007). Empathic accuracy of intimate partners in violent versus nonviolent relationships. *Personal Relationships, 14,* 369–388. doi:10.1111/j.1475-6811.2007.00161.x

Costanzo, M., & Archer, D. (1989). Interpreting the expressive behavior of others: The Interpersonal Perception Task. *Journal of Nonverbal Behavior, 13,* 225–245. doi:10.1007/BF00990295

Crick, N. R., & Dodge, K. A. (1994). A review and reformulation of social information-processing mechanisms in children's social adjustment. *Psychological Bulletin, 115,* 74–101. doi:10.1037/0033-2909.115.1.74

Cronbach, L. (1955). Processes affecting scores on "understanding of others" and "assumed similarity." *Psychological Bulletin, 52,* 177–193. doi:10.1037/h0044919

Cuperman, R., Howland, M., Ickes, W., & Simpson, J. A. (2011). Motivated inaccuracy: Past and future directions. In J. L. Smith, W. Ickes, J. Hall, & S. Hodges (Eds.), *Managing interpersonal sensitivity: Knowing when—and when not—to understand others* (pp. 215–233). New York, NY: Nova Science.

Davis, M. H. (1980). A multidimensional approach to individual differences in empathy. *Catalog of Selected Documents in Psychology, 10,* 85.

Davis, M. H. (1983). Measuring individual differences in empathy: Evidence for a multi-dimensional approach. *Journal of Personality and Social Psychology, 44,* 113–126. doi:10.1037/0022-3514.44.1.113

Demurie, E., De Corel, M., & Roeyers, H. (2011). Empathic accuracy in adolescents with autism spectrum disorders and adolescents with attention-deficit/hyperactivity disorder. *Research in Autism Spectrum Disorders, 5,* 126–134. doi:10.1016/j.rasd.2010.03.002

DePaulo, B. M. (2002). The many faces of lies. In A. G. Miller (Ed.), *The social psychology of good and evil* (pp. 303–326). New York, NY: Guilford Press.

Dindia, K., & Allen, M. (1992). Sex differences in self-disclosure: A meta-analysis. *Psychological Bulletin, 112,* 106–124. doi:10.1037/0033-2909.112.1.106

Domes, G., Heinrichs, M., Michel, A., Berger, C., & Herpetz, S. C. (2007). Oxytocin improves "mind-reading" in humans. *Biological Psychiatry, 61,* 731–733. doi:10.1016/j.biopsych.2006.07.015

Ekman, P., & O'Sullivan, M. (1991). Who can catch a liar? *American Psychologist, 46,* 913–920. doi:10.1037/0003-066X.46.9.913

Epley, N., Keysar, B., Van Boven, L., & Gilovich, T. (2004). Perspective taking as egocentric anchoring and adjustment. *Journal of Personality and Social Psychology, 87,* 327–339. doi:10.1037/0022-3514.87.3.327

Flury, J., Ickes, W., & Schweinle, W. (2008). The borderline empathy effect: Do high BPD individuals have greater empathic ability? Or are they just more difficult to "read"? *Journal of Research in Personality, 42,* 312–332. doi:10.1016/j.jrp.2007.05.008

Gadassi, R., Mor, N., & Rafaeli, E. (2011). Depression and empathic accuracy in couples: An interpersonal model of gender differences in depression. *Psychological Science, 22,* 1033–1041. doi:10.1177/0956797611414728

Gesn, P. R., & Ickes, W. (1999). The development of meaning contexts for empathic accuracy: Channel and sequence effects. *Journal of Personality and Social Psychology, 77,* 746–761. doi:10.1037/0022-3514.77.4.746

Gleason, K. A., Jensen-Campbell, L. A., & Ickes, W. (2009). The role of empathic accuracy in adolescents' peer relations and adjustment. *Personality and Social Psychology Bulletin, 35,* 997–1011. doi:10.1177/0146167209336605

Gottman, J. M. (1994). *What predicts divorce: The relationship between marital processes and marital outcomes.* Hillsdale, NJ: Erlbaum.

Grandin, T., Barron, S., & Zysk, V. (2005). *The unwritten rules of social relationships.* Arlington, TX: Future Horizons.

Gross, J. J., & John, O. P. (1997). Revealing feelings: Facets of emotional expressivity in self-reports, peer ratings, and behavior. *Journal of Personality and Social Psychology, 72,* 435–448. doi:10.1037/0022-3514.72.2.435

Guerrero, L. K., Andersen, P. A., & Afifi, W. A. (2011). *Close encounters: Communication in relationships.* Thousand Oaks, CA: Sage.

Hall, J. A. (1984). *Nonverbal sex differences: Communication accuracy and expressive style.* Baltimore, MD: Johns Hopkins University Press.

Hall, J. A. (2001). The PONS test and the psychometric approach to measuring interpersonal sensitivity. In J. A. Hall & F. J. Bernieri (Eds.), *Interpersonal sensitivity: Theory and measurement* (pp. 143–160). Mahwah, NJ: Erlbaum.

Hall, J. A. (2011). Manipulated motivation and interpersonal accuracy. In J. Smith, W. Ickes, J. A. Hall, & S. D. Hodges (Eds.), *Managing interpersonal sensitivity: Knowing when—and when not—to understand others* (pp. 1–20). New York, NY: Nova Science.

Hall, J. A., Carter, J. D., & Horgan, T. G. (2001). Status roles and recall of nonverbal cues. *Journal of Nonverbal Behavior, 25,* 79–100. doi:10.1023/A:1010797627793

Hall, J. A., & Schmid Mast, M. (2007). Sources of accuracy in the empathic accuracy paradigm. *Emotion, 7,* 438–446. doi:10.1037/1528-3542.7.2.438

Hancock, M., & Ickes, W. (1996). Empathic accuracy: When does the perceiver-target relationship make a difference? *Journal of Social and Personal Relationships, 13,* 179–199. doi:10.1177/0265407596132002

Hartwig, M., & Bond, C. F. (2011). Why do lie-catchers fail? A lens model meta-analysis of human lie judgments. *Psychological Bulletin, 137,* 643–659. doi:10.1037/a0023589

Haugen, P. T., Welsh, D. P., & McNulty, J. K. (2008). Empathic accuracy and adolescent romantic relationships. *Journal of Adolescence, 31,* 709–727. doi:10.1016/j.adolescence.2008.03.003

Helgeson, V. S. (1994). Relation of agency and communion to wellbeing: Evidence and potential explanations. *Psychological Bulletin, 116,* 412–428. doi:10.1037/0033-2909.116.3.412

Hirschfeld, L., Bartmess, E., White, S., & Frith, U. (2007). Can autistic children predict behavior by social stereotypes? *Current Biology, 17,* R451–R452. doi:10.1016/j.cub.2007.04.051

Hodges, S. D., & Biswas-Diener, R. (2007). Balancing the empathy expense account: Strategies for regulating empathic response. In T. F. D. Farrow & P. W. R. Woodruff (Eds.), *Empathy in mental illness and health* (pp. 389–407). Cambridge, England: Cambridge University Press. doi:10.1017/CBO9780511543753.022

Hodges, S. D., Kiel, K. J., Kramer, A. D. I., Veach, D., & Villanueva, B. R. (2010). Giving birth to empathy: The effects of similar experience on empathic accuracy, empathic concern, and perceived empathy. *Personality and Social Psychology Bulletin, 36,* 398–409. doi:10.1177/0146167209350326

Hodges, S. D., Laurent, S. M., & Lewis, K. L. (2011). Specially motivated, feminine, or just female:

Do women have an empathic accuracy advantage? In J. L. Smith, W. Ickes, J. Hall, & S. D. Hodges (Eds.), *Managing interpersonal sensitivity: Knowing when—and when not—to understand others* (pp. 59–73). New York, NY: Nova Science.

Hodges, S. D., & Myers, M. W. (2007). Empathy. In R. F. Baumeister & K. D. Vohs (Eds.), *Encyclopedia of social psychology* (pp. 296–298). Thousand Oaks, CA: Sage. doi:10.4135/9781412956253.n179

Holroyd, C. B., & Coles, M. G. H. (2002). The neural basis of human error processing: Reinforcement learning, dopamine, and the error-related negativity. *Psychological Review, 109*, 679–709. doi:10.1037/0033-295X.109.4.679

Horgan, T. G., Schmid Mast, M., Hall, J. A., & Carter, J. D. (2004). Gender differences in memory for the appearance of others. *Personality and Social Psychology Bulletin, 30*, 185–196. doi:10.1177/0146167203259928

Howington, D. E., Lewis, K. L., & Hodges, S. D. (2011). [You push my buttons: Methodological modifications and empathic accuracy in contentious conversations]. Unpublished raw data.

Ickes, W. (2001). Measuring empathic accuracy. In J. A. Hall & F. J. Bernieri (Eds.), *Interpersonal sensitivity: Theory and measurement* (pp. 219–241). Mahwah, NJ: Erlbaum.

Ickes, W. (2003). *Everyday mind reading: Understanding what other people think and feel.* Amherst, NY: Prometheus Books.

Ickes, W. (2006, November). *Inferring other people's thoughts and feelings: The relative importance of verbal versus nonverbal cues.* Invited talk given at the annual conference of the National Communication Association, San Antonio, TX.

Ickes, W. (2008). Mind reading superheroes: Fiction and facts. In R. S. Rosenberg & J. Canzoneri (Eds.), *The psychology of superheroes* (pp. 119–134). Dallas, TX: BenBella Books.

Ickes, W. (2011). Everyday mind reading is driven by motives and goals. *Psychological Inquiry, 22*, 200–206. doi:10.1080/1047840X.2011.561133

Ickes, W., Buysse, A., Pham, H., Rivers, K., Erickson, J. R., Hancock, M., . . . Gesn, P. R. (2000). On the difficulty of distinguishing "good" and "poor" perceivers: A social relations analysis of empathic accuracy data. *Personal Relationships, 7*, 219–234. doi:10.1111/j.1475-6811.2000.tb00013.x

Ickes, W., & Cheng, W. (2011). How do thoughts differ from feelings? Putting the differences into words. *Language and Cognitive Processes, 26*, 1–23. doi:10.1080/01690961003603046

Ickes, W., Gesn, P. R., & Graham, T. (2000). Gender differences in empathic accuracy: Differential ability

of differential motivation? *Personal Relationships, 7*, 95–109. doi:10.1111/j.1475-6811.2000.tb00006.x

Ickes, W., & Simpson, J. (2001). Motivational aspects of empathic accuracy. In G. J. O. Fletcher & M. S. Clark (Eds.), *Interpersonal processes: Blackwell handbook in social psychology* (pp. 229–249). Oxford, England: Blackwell.

Ickes, W., Simpson, J. A., & Oriña, M. (2005). Empathic accuracy and inaccuracy in close relationships. In B. F. Malle & S. D. Hodges (Eds.), *Other minds: How humans bridge the divide between self and others* (pp. 310–322). New York, NY: Guilford Press.

Ickes, W., Stinson, L., Bissonnette, V., & Garcia, S. (1990). Naturalistic social cognition: Empathic accuracy in mixed-sex dyads. *Journal of Personality and Social Psychology, 59*, 730–742. doi:10.1037/0022-3514.59.4.730

Kashy, D. A., & Donnellan, M. B. (2012). Conceptual and methodological issues in the analysis of data from dyads and groups (pp. 209–238). In K. Deaux & M. Snyder (Eds.), *The Oxford handbook of personality and social psychology.* Oxford, England: Oxford University Press.

Kenny, D. A. (1994). *Interpersonal perception: A social relations analysis.* New York, NY: Guilford Press.

Kilpatrick, S. D., Bissonnette, V. L., & Rusbult, C. E. (2002). Empathic accuracy and accommodative behavior among newly married couples. *Personal Relationships, 9*, 369–393. doi:10.1111/1475-6811.09402

Klein, K. J. K., & Hodges, S. D. (2001). Gender differences, motivation and empathic accuracy: When it pays to understand. *Personality and Social Psychology Bulletin, 27*, 720–730. doi:10.1177/0146167201276007

Kring, A. M., & Gordon, A. H. (1998). Sex differences in emotion: Expression, experience, and physiology. *Journal of Personality and Social Psychology, 74*, 686–703. doi:10.1037/0022-3514.74.3.686

Laurent, S. M., & Hodges, S. D. (2009). Gender and empathic accuracy: The role of communion in reading minds. *Sex Roles, 60*, 387–398. doi:10.1007/s11199-008-9544-x

Laurent, S. M., Hodges, S. D., & Lewis, K. L. (2011). *Trying hard to read your mind: Motivation and empathic accuracy.* Unpublished manuscript, University of Oregon.

Levenson, R. W., & Ruef, A. M. (1992). Empathy: A physiological substrate. *Journal of Personality and Social Psychology, 63*, 234–246. doi:10.1037/0022-3514.63.2.234

Lewis, K. L., & Hodges, S. D. (2009). [Empathic accuracy and nonverbal decoding: Related or distinct constructs?] Unpublished raw data.

Lewis, K. L., Hodges, S. D., Laurent, S. M., Srivastava, S., & Biancarosa, G. (2012). Reading between the minds: The use of stereotypes in empathic accuracy. *Psychological Science, 23*, 1040–1046.

Marangoni, C., Garcia, S., Ickes, W., & Teng, G. (1995). Empathic accuracy in a clinically relevant setting. *Journal of Personality and Social Psychology, 68*, 854–869. doi:10.1037/0022-3514.68.5.854

Marist Poll. (2011, September 11). *Holy super powers, Batman! Mind reading and time travel top list.* Retrieved from http://maristpoll.marist.edu/28-holy-super-powers-batman-mind-reading-and-time-travel-top-list

Mehrabian, A., & Epstein, N. (1972). A measure of emotional empathy. *Journal of Personality, 40*, 525–543. doi:10.1111/j.1467-6494.1972.tb00078.x

Moses, L. J. (2005). Executive functioning and children's theories of mind. In B. F. Malle & S. D. Hodges (Eds.), *Other minds: How humans bridge the divide between self and others* (pp. 11–25). New York, NY: Guilford Press.

Myers, J. E. (2009). *Predicting rapport in dyads: Mattering over mind-reading* (Unpublished master's thesis). University of Oregon, Eugene.

Myers, M. W., & Hodges, S. D. (2009). Making it up and making do: Simulation, imagination and empathic accuracy. In K. Markman, W. Klein, & J. Suhr (Eds.), *The handbook of imagination and mental simulation* (pp. 281–294). New York, NY: Psychology Press.

Nezlek, J. B. (2011). *Multilevel modeling for social and personality psychology.* London, England: Sage.

Nowicki, S., & Duke, M. P. (1994). Individual differences in the nonverbal communication of affect: The Diagnostic Analysis of Nonverbal Accuracy Scale. *Journal of Nonverbal Behavior, 18*, 9–35. doi:10.1007/BF02169077

Papp, L. M., Kouros, C. D., & Cummings, E. M. (2010). Emotions in marital conflict interactions: Empathic accuracy, assumed similarity, and the moderating context of depressive symptoms. *Journal of Social and Personal Relationships, 27*, 367–387. doi:10.1177/0265407509348810

Perner, J., & Wimmer, H. (1985). "John thinks that Mary thinks that . . .": Attribution of second-order beliefs by 5- to 10-year-old children. *Journal of Experimental Child Psychology, 39*, 437–471. doi:10.1016/0022-0965(85)90051-7

Pickett, C. L., Gardner, W. L., & Knowles, M. (2004). Getting a cue: The need to belong and enhanced sensitivity to social cues. *Personality and Social Psychology Bulletin, 30*, 1095–1107. doi:10.1177/0146167203262085

Pollmann, M. M. H., & Finkenauer, C. (2009). Investigating the role of two types of understanding in relationship well-being: Understanding is more important than knowledge. *Personality and Social Psychology Bulletin, 35*, 1512–1527. doi:10.1177/0146167209342754

Ponnet, K., Buysse, A., Roeyers, H., & De Clercq, A. (2008). Mind-reading in young adults with ASD: Does structure matter? *Journal of Autism and Developmental Disorders, 38*, 905–918. doi:10.1007/s10803-007-0462-5

Ponnet, K. S., Roeyers, H., Buysse, A., De Clercq, A., & Van Der Heyden, E. (2004). Advanced mind-reading in adults with Asperger syndrome. *Autism, 8*, 249–266. doi:10.1177/1362361304045214

Rholes, W. S., Simpson, J. A., Tran, S., Martin, A. M., & Friedman, M. (2007). Attachment and information seeking in romantic relationships. *Personality and Social Psychology Bulletin, 33*, 422–438. doi:10.1177/0146167206296302

Rosenthal, R., & DePaulo, B. M. (1979). Sex differences in eavesdropping on nonverbal cues. *Journal of Personality and Social Psychology, 37*, 273–285. doi:10.1037/0022-3514.37.2.273

Rosenthal, R., Hall, J. A., DiMatteo, M. R., Rogers, P. L., & Archer, D. (1979). *Sensitivity to nonverbal communication: The PONS test.* Baltimore, MD: Johns Hopkins University Press.

Ross, H. E., & Young, L. J. (2009). Oxytocin and the neural mechanisms regulating social cognition and affiliative behavior. *Frontiers in Neuroendocrinology, 30*, 534–547. doi:10.1016/j.yfrne.2009.05.004

Ross, L., Greene, D., & House, P. (1977). The false-consensus effect: An egocentric bias in social perception and attribution process. *Journal of Experimental Social Psychology, 13*, 279–301. doi:10.1016/0022-1031(77)90049-X

Sabbagh, M. A., Xu, F., Carlson, S. M., Moses, L. J., & Lee, K. (2006). The development of executive functioning and theory of mind: A comparison of Chinese and U.S. preschoolers. *Psychological Science, 17*, 74–81. doi:10.1111/j.1467-9280.2005.01667.x

Schmid Mast, M. S., Hall, J. A., & Ickes, W. (2006). Inferring power-relevant thoughts and feelings in others: A signal detection analysis. *European Journal of Social Psychology, 36*, 469–478. doi:10.1002/ejsp.335

Schweinle, W., & Ickes, W. (2007). The role of men's critical/rejecting overattribution bias, affect, and attentional disengagement in marital aggression. *Journal of Social and Clinical Psychology, 26*, 173–198. doi:10.1521/jscp.2007.26.2.173

Schweinle, W. E., Cofer, C., & Schatz, S. (2009). Men's empathic bias, empathic inaccuracy, and sexual harassment. *Sex Roles, 60*, 142–150. doi:10.1007/s11199-008-9507-2

Schweinle, W. E., Ickes, W., & Bernstein, I. H. (2002). Empathic inaccuracy in husband to wife aggression:

The overattribution bias. *Personal Relationships, 9,* 141–158. doi:10.1111/1475-6811.00009

Sillars, A. (2011). Motivated misunderstanding in family conflict discussions. In J. L. Smith, W. Ickes, J. Hall, & S. D. Hodges (Eds.), *Managing interpersonal sensitivity: Knowing when—and when not—to understand others* (pp. 193–213). New York, NY: Nova Science.

Sillars, A., Koerner, A., & Fitzpatrick, M. A. (2005). Communication and understanding in parent-adolescent relationships. *Human Communication Research, 31,* 102–128.

Sillars, A. L., Smith, T., & Koerner, A. (2010). Misattributions contributing to empathic (in)accuracy during parent-adolescent conflict discussions. *Journal of Social and Personal Relationships, 27,* 727–747. doi:10.1177/0265407510373261

Simpson, J., Ickes, W., & Blackstone, T. (1995). When the head protects the heart: Empathic accuracy in dating relationships. *Journal of Personality and Social Psychology, 69,* 629–641. doi:10.1037/0022-3514.69.4.629

Simpson, J. A., Ickes, W., & Grich, J. (1999). When accuracy hurts: Reactions of anxious-uncertain individuals to a relationship-threatening situation. *Journal of Personality and Social Psychology, 76,* 754–769. doi:10.1037/0022-3514.76.5.754

Simpson, J. A., Kim, J. S., Fillo, J., Ickes, W., Rholes, S., Oriña, M. M., & Winterheld, H. A. (2011). Attachment and the management of empathic accuracy in relationship threatening situations. *Personality and Social Psychology Bulletin, 37,* 242–254. doi:10.1177/0146167210394368

Simpson, J. A., Oriña, M. M., & Ickes, W. (2003). When accuracy hurts, and when it helps: A test of the empathic accuracy model in marital interactions. *Journal of Personality and Social Psychology, 85,* 881–893. doi:10.1037/0022-3514.85.5.881

Smith, J. L., Hall, J. A., Hodges, S. D., & Ickes, W. (2011). To be, or not to be, accurate: Addressing that and other complicated questions? In J. L. Smith, W. Ickes, J. A. Hall, & S. D. Hodges (Eds.), *Managing interpersonal sensitivity: Knowing when—and when not—to understand others* (pp. 235–254). New York, NY: Nova Science.

Snodgrass, S. E. (1992). Further effects of role versus gender on interpersonal sensitivity. *Journal of Personality and Social Psychology, 62,* 154–158. doi:10.1037/0022-3514.62.1.154

Spencer, S. M., & Norem, J. K. (1996). Reflection and distraction: Defensive pessimism, strategic optimism, and performance. *Personality and Social Psychology Bulletin, 22,* 354–365. doi:10.1177/0146167296224003

Stinson, L., & Ickes, W. (1992). Empathic accuracy in the interactions of male friends versus male strangers.

Journal of Personality and Social Psychology, 62, 787–797. doi:10.1037/0022-3514.62.5.787

Thomas, G., & Fletcher, G. J. O. (2003). Mind-reading accuracy in intimate relationships: Assessing the roles of the relationship, the target, and the judge. *Journal of Personality and Social Psychology, 85,* 1079–1094. doi:10.1037/0022-3514.85.6.1079

Thomas, G., Fletcher, G. J. O., & Lange, C. (1997). On-line empathic accuracy in marital interaction. *Journal of Personality and Social Psychology, 72,* 839–850. doi:10.1037/0022-3514.72.4.839

Thomas, G., & Maio, G. R. (2008). Man, I feel like a woman: When and how gender-role motivation helps mind-reading. *Journal of Personality and Social Psychology, 95,* 1165–1179. doi:10.1037/a0013067

Tipsord, J. M. (2009). *The effects of mindfulness training and individual differences in mindfulness on social perception and empathy* (Unpublished doctoral dissertation). University of Oregon, Eugene.

Van Boven, L., & Loewenstein, G. (2003). Social projection of transient drive states. *Personality and Social Psychology Bulletin, 29,* 1159–1168. doi:10.1177/0146167203254597

Verhofstadt, L. L., Buysse, A., Ickes, W., Davis, M., & Devoldre, I. (2008). Support provision in marriage: The role of emotional similarity and empathic accuracy. *Emotion, 8,* 792–802. doi:10.1037/a0013976

Vorauer, J. D. (2001). The other side of the story: Transparency estimation in social interaction. In G. Moskowitz (Ed.), *Cognitive social psychology: The Princeton Symposium on the legacy and future of social cognition* (pp. 261–276). Mahwah, NJ: Erlbaum.

White, S., Hill, E. L., Winston, J., & Frith, U. (2006). An islet of social ability in Asperger syndrome: Judging social attributes from faces. *Brain and Cognition, 61,* 69–77. doi:10.1016/j.bandc.2005.12.007

Zaki, J., Bartz, J., & Ochsner, K. (2011, January). Interpersonal accuracy, dissociable phenomenon, and their analogues in social life. In J. Zaki & W. Ickes (Chairs), *What it means to get it right, and why it matters: Adventures in accuracy research.* Symposium conducted at the meeting of the Society of Personality and Social Psychology, San Antonio, TX.

Zaki, J., Bolger, N., & Ochsner, K. (2008). It takes two: The interpersonal nature of empathic accuracy. *Psychological Science, 19,* 399–404. doi:10.1111/j.1467-9280.2008.02099.x

Zaki, J., Bolger, N., & Ochsner, K. N. (2009). Unpacking the informational bases of empathic accuracy. *Emotion, 9,* 478–487. doi:10.1037/a0016551

Zaki, J., & Ochsner, K. N. (2011). Reintegrating the study of accuracy into social cognition research. *Psychological Inquiry, 22,* 159–182. doi:10.1080/1047840X.2011.551743

PART V

SUPPORT, COMMUNICATION, AND POWER

CHAPTER 13

SOCIAL SUPPORT

Marci E. J. Gleason and Masumi Iida

Social support has been widely studied by health, clinical, social, developmental, and personality psychologists; communication specialists; sociologists; medical scientists; and those from several other disciplines. Perhaps because of the varying domains in which social support is studied, it is also operationalized in myriad ways. Social support research originated with work on social integration and social networks rooted in Durkheim's (1897/1951) seminal work on the importance of social conditions and suicide, which showed that people who had social relationships were less likely to commit suicide. Following this tradition, the social support literature has focused on social integration (e.g., marital status; Berkman & Breslow, 1983), the perceived availability of support (e.g., Sarason et al., 1991), and community support (e.g., Auerbach & Kilmann, 1977) when investigating the effects of social support. Regardless of its operationalization, social support has been associated with an array of beneficial outcomes, including better health, faster recovery from illness, and lowered anxiety (e.g., Cobb, 1976).

However, the story of social support is not entirely straightforward. In fact, a paradox has emerged showing that enacted social support—that is, supportive behavior performed by close others with the intent of alleviating the distress of the support recipient—is often linked to increased negative mood and health problems (Uchino, 2009). In this chapter, we briefly discuss the history of support research and then focus on work exploring the possible reasons behind this seeming paradox between the benefits of social networks and perceived support and the often negative outcomes associated with enacted support. Specifically, we focus on the motivations behind enacted support, the timeline or sequence of support transactions, the various types of enacted support that have been identified, and the ways in which support can be provided effectively, and we discuss who is likely to provide and receive support. Finally, we discuss more recent work on the benefits of support provision and end with recommendations for the future of social support research.

CONCEPTUALIZATION OF SOCIAL SUPPORT

Beginning in the early 1980s, many researchers started to conceptualize support not as a unitary concept but rather as a mixture of several different concepts (e.g., Barrera, 1986). The social support construct can be thought of as encompassing three components: (a) the existence of social relationships, (b) the structure of one's social networks, and (c) the functions of social support (House, Kahn, McLeod, & Williams, 1985). Barrera (1981) made a further distinction regarding the content of social support: the perceived availability of support and received support. Perceived support is defined as support that is available if needed. Received support refers to the actual occurrence of a socially supportive exchange (Barrera, 1986). Most of our focus in this chapter is on the processes of actual social support exchanges rather than analyses of social networks or perceived support.

http://dx.doi.org/10.1037/14344-013
APA Handbook of Personality and Social Psychology: Vol. 3. Interpersonal Relations, M. Mikulincer and P. R. Shaver (Editors-in-Chief)

Little consensus exists on what to call the receipt of support and therefore it goes by many names, including *received support, enacted support, online support,* or *actual support* (see Dunkel-Schetter & Bennett, 1990). In this chapter, we use the terms *received support* and *enacted support* interchangeably, and we specifically define these behaviors as actions taken by individuals who intend to alleviate the distress of others. These behaviors do not include many actions that may take place naturally in a relationship. For example, if a brother buys coffee for his sister, we would call it an enacted support if he bought the coffee to cheer his sister up after she received a low mark on her exam; however, if the brother bought the coffee because he walked past her favorite coffee shop on the way to her house, we would categorize such behavior as a simple act of kindness rather than as received support.

Many researchers believe that the perception of available support is more important to health than enacted support (e.g., Cutrona, 1996). There are abundant studies of perceived support, but less attention has been paid to actual supportive transactions (Barrera, 1986). However, researchers have recognized the need to investigate enacted support. Dunkel-Schetter and Bennett (1990) noted, "If researchers were to use these current conceptions of support, then the construct of received support would be much more applicable than the construct of available support would be" (pp. 288–289). The lack of studies on the receipt of support may also be attributable to counterintuitive findings in the literature on received support. Barrera (1986) reviewed the effects of the perceived availability of support and received support and found that studies showed that received support was typically positively related to individuals' distress, whereas perceived support was associated with less individual distress. The negative effects of received support may be counterintuitive, but such a relation between distress and received support has been more widely documented and discussed in recent years (Brown, Brown, & Penner, 2012; Maisel & Gable, 2009; Uchino, 2004, 2009).

BENEFITS OF SOCIAL SUPPORT

It is, however, important to acknowledge the wealth of studies that have shown the benefits of being socially integrated and having a high level of perceived support. Among the most convincing research on the benefits of social support, broadly defined, is Uchino, Cacioppo, and Kiecolt-Glaser's (1996) review of 81 studies of social support and physiological benefits. In their review, these authors found consistent evidence that social support was linked to cardiovascular health and immune functioning. In addition, they found evidence that emotional support in particular may be important for positive health outcomes. The studies included in this review operationalized support in many different ways, including, but not limited to, being married, having many social contacts (extensive social networks), perceiving that one has received high levels of support in the past, being in the presence of a close other, and enacted emotional support. Again, this work highlighted the seeming benefits of social support, as well as the variety of ways in which it is defined in the field.

Uchino et al. (1996) also provided evidence that the benefits of social support may occur through a stress-buffering effect. The stress-buffering theory in the support literature suggests that social support is effective in alleviating distress and promoting health not as a main effect but as an interaction between level of stress and social support (Thoits, 1986). The theory proposes that, in high-stress situations, social support protects individuals against stress—that is, individuals who have good support systems suffer less in highly stressful situations. However, when individuals report little to no stress, the presence or absence of a support system is less important because there is nothing to buffer the recipient from. Stress-buffering effects have been found in many studies focusing on social network size and perceived support but, interestingly, the reverse often appears to be true in studies of enacted support: During highly stressful situations, enacted support is often less effective than no support at all (Bolger, Zuckerman, & Kessler, 2000; Grenmore et al., 2011).

This seeming paradox in the social support literature may be attributable, at least in part, to the variety of ways in which researchers have measured and defined social support over the years. Perceived social support and integrated social networks have consistently been related to positive outcomes, whereas received (enacted) support has produced a mixture of positive and negative outcomes that often trend toward negativity (Barrera, 1981; Bolger & Amarel, 2007; Gleason, Iida, Bolger, & Shrout, 2003; Gleason, Iida, Shrout, & Bolger, 2008; Lindorff, 2000; Uchino, 2009). This paradox is well illustrated in Krause's (1997) study of older adults, in which the perceived availability of support predicted a decrease in mortality risk, but actual support transactions predicted an increase in mortality risk.

One common explanation for why support receipt is often associated with negative outcomes is that both the receipt of support and the undesirable effects (e.g., negative mood) may be caused by a third variable. For instance, having a bad day at work might elicit both a negative mood and a support response from one's spouse, resulting in a correlation between the two variables; however, in this hypothetical example, the receipt of support is not causing the negative mood. There are several arguments against this model. Many daily diary studies of social support have protected against the potential explanatory power of third variables by including relevant control variables in the statistical models, such as stressful events that occurred that day and earlier reports of negative mood. Even when controlling for possible third variables, a positive association between support receipt and negative mood has frequently been found (cf. Bolger et al., 2000; Gleason et al., 2008). Moreover, using simulated data in which the third-variable explanations of both the carryover of negative mood and the carryover of stressful events were tested, third variables were not a viable explanation for the association between support receipt and negative mood (Seidman, Shrout, & Bolger, 2006). Additionally, several experimental studies of social support have demonstrated that receiving support leads to increased negative mood and other negative outcomes (Bolger & Amarel, 2007; J. D. Fisher, Nadler, &

Whitcher-Alagna, 1982; Nadler & Fisher, 1976). Given these findings, the idea that support receipt can and often does result in heightened negative outcomes has gained acceptance in the field in recent years.

Uchino (2009) attempted to explain the paradox between perceived support and received support by discussing their potential to differentially affect physiological and psychological outcomes using a life-span perspective that distinguished perceived and received support on the basis of their antecedents. He suggested that the early family environment affects individuals' psychosocial profiles, including their personality, self-esteem, sense of control, and perceived support, all of which have been linked to positive health outcomes. Conversely, received support is a situationally bound experience that occurs in response to a stressor and has the potential to positively or negatively influence subsequent behaviors and outcomes, depending on the context, type, timing, and desirability of the support received.

Rafaeli and Gleason (2009) proposed that these characteristics of received social support (i.e., the type [termed the *what*], timing [termed the *when*], the manner of provision [termed the *how*], and the roles of both provider and receiver [termed the *who*]) are key for support to be provided in a skillful manner and therefore more likely to achieve its intended purpose of alleviating distress and aiding in coping. We have argued that skillful support can be an effective tool, particularly for members of couples, but such support may also be very difficult to implement (Rafaeli & Gleason, 2009). In this chapter, we adapt and modify this organization to understand the enacted support process. Specifically, for support to be effective, we propose that the provider must navigate four aspects of the support process: (a) the when (the timing and temporal process of support), (b) the who (defined here as the characteristics of receivers and providers of support), (c) the what (the types of social support), and (d) the how (defined here as ways in which the effectiveness of received support can be maximized). This framework clarifies the conditions under which support receipt is effective, and it provides a better understanding of the enacted support process. In the following sections, we begin with a discussion of the why—that is, the motivational antecedents of social support—and then review the when, the who, the what, and the how of enacted social support.

THE WHY: MOTIVATIONS FOR SOCIAL SUPPORT

The helping literature has cited two major motivations for providing support: altruistic motivations and egoistic motivations. Regardless of whether one's motivation is altruistic or selfish, individuals have a variety of goals that are associated with different social roles and different aspects of the self (Pervin, 1989). Three goals are of particular interest for this chapter: (a) goals for the self (e.g., to be a competent individual), (b) goals for the partner (e.g., to help one's partner feel better), and (c) goals for the relationship (e.g., to be happily married).

Altruism

The helping behavior literature has a long history of discussing altruism—can human beings act simply to help others without acting on any self-directed motivations? We start from the assumption that altruism is one possible human motivation for helping behavior. If an individual is motivated by altruism, one of the most important determinants for whether that individual provides support is likely to be empathy for his or her partner. More specifically, if an individual empathizes with the predicament of a distressed person, he or she is likely to provide greater support (Trobst, Collins, & Embree, 1994). However, if an individual has empathy for his or her partner's desire for autonomy, he or she may withhold support to preserve the partner's autonomy. For example, a husband may not offer to help his wife write a speech if it is important to her to write it herself.

Although empathy for the partner is rooted in concern for the partner, another determinant of altruistic motivation is a concern for the well-being of one's relationship. Stress that is external to the relationship, such as a cancer diagnosis or chronic job stress, can have a significant influence on both partners and the relationship as a whole (Bolger, DeLongis, Kessler, & Wethington, 1989; Bolger, Foster, Vinokur, & Ng, 1996). Thus, helping one's

partner cope with stressful events may also be rooted in a concern for the quality of the relationship. This is a less "pure" form of altruistic motivation because benefits to the relationship also benefit the provider, making it potentially selfishly motivated.

Egoism

In contrast to altruistic motivation, egoistic motivations are behaviors driven by self-directed interests—acts that are intended to benefit the self rather than other people. Under the assumption of egoistic motivations, negative moods, such as guilt and sadness, promote helping behavior because helping others can attenuate any negative emotions that one is experiencing (e.g., the negative state relief model; see Cialdini et al., 1987). Similarly, positive emotions can promote helping behaviors insofar as helping others sustains a positive mood (Forest, Clark, Mills, & Isen, 1979).

Another egoistic motivation for providing support may be the provider's concern for equity. Equity theory makes clear predictions about how individuals behave in certain interpersonal situations. The basic assumption of equity theory is that individuals try to minimize the discomfort associated with being in an inequitable or "unfair" state (Walster, Berscheid, & Walster, 1973). When the relationship benefits an individual more than his or her partner (i.e., the individual is overbenefited), the individual is more likely to balance the equity by giving back to his or her partner. In the context of social support, proponents of equity theory hypothesize that receiving support disturbs the homeostatic balance of equity within a relationship, motivating the individual to provide support in return to maintain equity in the relationship. When the individual perceives that he or she is underbenefited, he or she devotes less effort to enhancing the relationship. Therefore, when an individual perceives that he or she is providing support but not receiving as much in return, the individual is more likely to withhold support from his or her partner.

Altruism Versus Egoism

We have distinguished between altruistic and egoistic motivations and treated them as separate constructs, but the extent to which any given demonstration of support can be purely altruistic is questionable. Even if the motivation to increase the welfare of another is the driving force behind a given behavior (Batson et al., 1997), the act of helping someone else often benefits the self as well (Cialdini, 1991). In other words, the two sources of motivation are often not entirely separable. This situation becomes more complex when the individual receiving help is a close other, given that intimate others tend to be incorporated into one's own self-concept (Aron & Aron, 1986). As a result, helping one's close other is akin to helping oneself, and empathy toward others is an effective predictor of helping behavior only when the conceptual identities of the self and the other are merged or intertwined (Cialdini, Brown, Lewis, Luce, & Neuberg, 1997). Although we cannot capture the full extent of this debate in this chapter (see replies by Batson, 1997; Batson et al., 1997), we want to acknowledge the implications of the motivations behind social support processes, especially because social support by definition implies a prosocial motive. In the following sections, we discuss specifics of support provision and receipt that have clear ties to these motivations, despite the fact that they have received more attention in the helping behavior literature than in the social support literature.

THE WHEN: THE TIMING OF SOCIAL SUPPORT

Social support is a temporal process, an exchange that unfolds over time. Thus, it is important to consider the when of social support when considering its effects on the recipient. Although situational attributes linked to the provision of help have been extensively investigated in both the helping and the altruistic behavior literatures (see Brown, Brown, & Penner, 2012), situational attributes linked to provision of support have again received relatively little attention from social support theorists and researchers (cf. Iida, Seidman, Shrout, Fujita, & Bolger, 2008; Iida, Stephens, Rook, Franks, & Salem, 2010).

However, several researchers have developed models that describe the course of social support as it unfolds over time (see Rafaeli & Gleason, 2009).

For example, Pearlin and McCall (1990) interviewed 25 couples about providing support to each other and identified a three-stage model of support. According to their model, the need for support must first be communicated either directly or indirectly to the provider. Second, the provider must recognize the need for support in the recipient and determine whether he or she can provide it. Finally, actual support is or is not provided.

For support to be effective, each stage must be recognized and traversed, and the actions taken throughout this process must be appropriate. However, each of these stages is difficult to complete successfully. Consider the first stage, in which the recipient indicates a desire or need for support. Individuals in need of support are often reluctant to ask for it, because asking for support can make the potential recipient feel vulnerable and inefficacious (J. D. Fisher et al., 1982) or indebted (Gleason et al., 2003). These anxieties may lead the individual to indirectly request support by engaging in behaviors such as sighing or moping (Barbee & Cunningham, 1995). Thus, individuals may be unwilling to request support directly even when it is desired, leaving the potential provider to infer that support may be wanted.

Empirical support for the first stage of Pearlin and McCall's (1990) social support model is found in the support mobilization literature, which has shown in retrospective reports that distressed individuals often successfully mobilize support (Eckenrode, 1983). Studies of nondirective support (recipient-guided support, or requested support) and directive support (provider-guided support, or intuited support) have found that nondirective support is associated with positive outcomes, such as increased metabolic control in diabetic patients and decreased depressed mood (E. B. Fisher, La Greca, Greco, Arfken, & Schneiderman, 1997). These findings suggest that requesting support directly, rather than indirectly, is more likely to launch a successful support exchange.

Even without voicing their desire for support, recipients can alert providers to their needs. In a cross-sectional study, Finch et al. (1997) found that higher levels of psychological distress were associated with receiving more support. Other researchers (e.g., Barrera, 1986) have also shown that people who experience higher levels of depressed mood and anxiety tend to receive more support from close others. Iida et al. (2008) have shown that both recipients seeking support and recipients experiencing anxious moods increased the likelihood of support provision in a daily diary study of couples in which one partner was preparing for the bar examination. Similar patterns of daily negative mood mobilizing support were found in couples who were not experiencing a particular stressor (Iida et al., 2008) and in couples in which one partner was diagnosed with Type 2 diabetes (Iida et al., 2010).

The support process can fail during the second stage, which requires the provider to recognize that support is needed. As discussed, support seekers are often indirect in their requests for help, which may result in potential support providers not realizing that support has been requested and is needed. This failure to recognize need is more likely when the potential support providers' resources are limited (Feeney & Collins, 2001, 2003), which impedes their capacity to notice the situation. For example, if a potential provider is preoccupied with his or her own situation or issues, others' distress may go unnoticed. Indeed, some evidence has suggested that support providers' emotional states influence the success or failure of support provision. Iida et al. (2010) have shown that potential providers who are experiencing negative moods are less likely to provide support to their partners the next day.

The support process can also fail during the last stage, when the provider either offers or does not offer support. Interestingly, situations occur when even acknowledged requests for support may go unheeded by a potential provider (Pearlin & McCall, 1990). It is possible that the type of relationship one has with the support seeker plays an important role in whether support is successfully mobilized. For example, in a study of Israeli mothers, relationship satisfaction was a significant predictor of the receipt of support from one's partner (Hobfoll & Lerman, 1989). Iida et al. (2008, 2010) found that, on days when providers felt satisfied in their relationships, they were more likely to provide support to their partners. In addition, the provider may not have sufficient resources to execute the

support that is being requested. For example, a husband may be caught in a meeting when his wife calls and asks him to pick up one of their children from daycare.

Furthermore, given that enacted support is usually conceived of as acts that are intended to reduce distress during a stressful situation (Thoits, 1995), the objective and appraised level of stress associated with a situation should affect both the likelihood of support provision and the quality of that support. If the partner is experiencing a major acute stressor, the provider should be more likely to give support, because the expectation to do so as a good relationship partner is clear (Clark & Mills, 1979). However, if the stressor is minor, the provider may conserve energy by withholding support until more stressful events that call for greater support take place (Hobfoll, 1988). Relatedly, Dunkel-Schetter and Skokan (1990) distinguished between ambiguous and unambiguous stressors. Support provision should be more likely if situations are appraised as stressful by both potential support providers and recipients; therefore, if stressors are ambiguous, they are less likely to be appraised as stressful by both parties and, therefore, they are more likely to result in no support provision.

Other determinants of social support provision include the perceived balance of support within a relationship. Walster et al. (1973) argued that people are motivated to provide support when they perceive they are overbenefited in their relationship. Similarly, reciprocity theory argues that support should be provided as a way to reciprocate the support that was previously given by one's partner (Uehara, 1995), and equity motivations suggest that receiving support should be a precursor to its provision (Walster et al., 1973). For instance, Iida et al. (2008) found that individuals are substantially more likely to provide support on days when they receive support. The tendency to provide support when one has received it is also an effective method of erasing or reversing the possible negative effects of support receipt (Gleason et al., 2003, 2008), which we explore at greater length when we discuss the importance of how support is provided.

Researchers of enacted social support have typically focused on the last step of the support process, the actual receipt of support (Cutrona, 1996). After support is received, researchers ask questions about the type, manner, and so on of the support that is received, and they then measure the effectiveness of that support in alleviating stress, enhancing mood, or minimizing health issues. However, before support can be declared effective or ineffective, it must be communicated. Emphasizing that support occurs along a trajectory or timeline and that it consists of multiple stages may help researchers to identify when the support process is most likely to fail and to pinpoint the mechanisms that reduce this risk. Additionally, viewing the support process as temporal encourages researchers to study all of the steps involved in the provision and receipt of support rather than focusing on only one stage.

THE WHO: CHARACTERISTICS OF THE RECIPIENTS AND PROVIDERS OF SUPPORT

The literatures on helping, social support, and intimate relationships have suggested that certain personality traits and characteristics are more likely to lead to support exchanges than others. For example, certain personality traits of recipients, such as their level of extraversion, make them more likely to receive support (Swickert, Rosentreter, Hittner, & Mushrush, 2002), whereas providers' characteristics, such as their communal orientation, make them more likely to help others in general (Clark & Mills, 1979). In addition, certain types of individuals are more likely to perceive support, or at least report high levels of perceived support in interpersonal exchanges (Lakey et al., 2002). In this section, we discuss the characteristics that are associated with support recipients and providers.

Recipient Characteristics

Perceived support—the perception that support is available if needed—has traditionally been assumed to reflect the actual support provided by others (Sarason, Sarason, & Pierce, 1990), but the empirical evidence for this association is relatively weak. For example, Lakey and Drew (1997) reviewed the literature examining this assumption and found that the average correlation between enacted support

from the recipients' perspective and the perceived availability of support was lower than .30, with many studies reporting correlations approaching zero. The more recent consensus is that perceived support is based on multiple factors, such as characteristics of the recipient (e.g., extraversion; Swickert et al., 2002), characteristics of the relationship (e.g., the recipient's global perception of providers as supportive individuals; Lakey & Drew, 1997), and actual enacted support events.

Extraversion has been an important variable in both the social interaction (e.g., Watson & Clark, 1997) and the support mobilization literatures, and recipients' extraversion has been linked to higher levels of received support (e.g., Swickert et al., 2002). Extraverts seek arousal to compensate for their suboptimal physiological arousal and they are more likely to engage in social interaction (Eysenck, 1967). Because of this tendency, they may have more opportunities to disclose their problems or express their negative emotions to others, leading extraverted people to activate supportive behaviors from those around them. In terms of their coping behavior, extraverts are more likely to seek social support in times of distress than are introverts (Watson & Hubbard, 1996).

Recipients' self-esteem is another characteristic that has been hypothesized to affect whether a potential provider offers support. Some empirical evidence has suggested that people who have high self-esteem are more likely to engage in active coping strategies (e.g., Dunkel-Schetter, Folkman, & Lazarus, 1987), and the active coping strategies engaged in by individuals who are under distress are an important determinant of others' willingness to provide support (Schwarzer & Weiner, 1991). In a community sample of 75 married couples in California, Dunkel-Schetter et al. (1987) found that recipients' self-esteem was positively correlated with their reported use of active coping strategies and that other people were more likely to provide support to people who had higher self-esteem. Dunkel-Schetter and Skokan (1990) posited that individuals are more likely to provide support to those who will benefit the most from support. Findings by Dunkel-Schetter et al. (1987) have suggested that potential providers perceive people who have higher self-esteem as most deserving of support.

Provider Characteristics

Many provider characteristics have been hypothesized to influence support provision behavior. One important characteristic is the provider's attachment style. Attachment security (characterized by low levels of avoidance and anxiety) is associated with more effective and appropriate supportive behaviors (Feeney & Collins, 2001). On one hand, people who are avoidantly attached tend to withhold support when their partners' distress increases (Feeney & Collins, 2001; Fraley & Shaver, 1998; Simpson, Rholes, & Nelligan, 1992), indicating that they are least responsive to their partners when support is most needed. Anxiously attached individuals, on the other hand, exhibit patterns of support provision typical of someone who is emotionally overinvolved with his or her partner. In a study by Feeney and Collins (2001), anxiously attached individuals provided emotional support regardless of how distressed their partners were. Interestingly, anxious individuals exercised discernment when it came to instrumental support, and they provided such support only in the high-need condition.

Providers' communal and exchange orientations might also govern when they engage in support behavior. People who are communally oriented are inclined to watch out for others' welfare and expect others to watch out for their welfare (Mills & Clark, 1994). Individuals who are high in communal orientation are not only more likely to provide help in general but also more responsive to the distress of potential support recipients (Clark, Oullette, Powell, & Milberg, 1987).

Last, the personality of providers should also play an important role in the provision of support, just as recipients' personality characteristics are important determinants. In particular, extraversion and agreeableness should be associated with engaging in more support behavior. Extraverted individuals tend to seek social interactions with others as a form of stimulation (Eysenck, 1967). Because they are more likely to engage in social interactions, the opportunity to provide support to others should also be greater. One of the defining features of agreeableness is social interest, altruism, and concern for others (Costa, McCrae, & Dye, 1991). Therefore, it is easy to imagine an agreeable person providing higher levels of support than one who is less agreeable, but this has yet to be demonstrated empirically.

THE WHAT: THE TYPES OF SUPPORT

For years, support researchers have attempted to classify and demarcate different forms of social support (Cutrona & Russell, 1990). Weiss (1974) named six types of support: advice or guidance, reliable tangible assistance, caring, social integration (i.e., companionship), reassurance of worth (i.e., esteem support), and the fulfillment of others' needs (the provision of support). Cobb (1979) proposed a similar breakdown of social support; specifically, his conceptualization included emotional, network, esteem, material, instrumental, and active support. Barrera and Ainlay's (1983) factor analysis of support types revealed four types of support: tangible support (which includes both material aid and behavioral acts), directive guidance (i.e., advice or information), nondirective support (emotional support), and positive social interaction (i.e., companionship or network support). There have been strong arguments to collapse these various forms of support into two major types of support: emotional and instrumental–practical support (e.g., Carver, Scheier, & Weintraub, 1989), which brings support types in line with the two major coping dimensions: emotion-focused coping and problem-focused coping (see Folkman & Lazarus, 1980).

Unfortunately, none of these categorization schemes has been universally adopted, which has resulted in support being operationalized in a variety of different ways. However, studies of enacted support, particularly when using self-report measures, have been more likely to use a version of the emotional versus practical support dichotomy. For example, in their diary work, Bolger and colleagues (Bolger et al., 2000; Gleason et al., 2003, 2008; Shrout, Herman, & Bolger, 2006) asked participants to indicate whether they had received help for a worry, problem, or difficulty and to indicate whether that help was emotional (e.g., listening or comforting) or practical (e.g., doing something concrete, such as cleaning the house). It is common to see emotional and practical support defined as positive relationship behaviors, so emotional support is captured, in part, by items such as "spouse said something that made you feel loved" (Neff & Karney, 2005, p. 83) or "my partner made me feel cared for" (Maisel & Gable, 2009, p. 929). Perhaps surprisingly, even in studies that have defined support as being largely positive, the daily effects of support are not always positive.

Observational studies in which couples engage in a support discussion have also often coded supportive behaviors as emotional or instrumental–practical but, because it is difficult for a partner to do something concrete, such as wash the dishes or pick up dry cleaning, during a laboratory discussion, the operationalization of practical support emphasizes giving advice, helping the partner develop a plan, and offering to do concrete things in the future (e.g., watch the kids for an afternoon; see Howland & Simpson, 2010; Neff & Karney, 2005). Again, in these coding schemes, attempts at support are often coded as negative or positive. A negative emotional support response might be minimizing a partner's feelings of anxiety by suggesting that she or he is overreacting to an event. In many studies of enacted support, more distinct support categories could be constructed along the Weiss (1974) or Cobb (1979) dimensions, but researchers often collapse items into definitions that parallel Carver et al.'s (1989) emotional and instrumental support categories (e.g., Cutrona, Shaffer, Wesner, & Gardner, 2007).

Researchers often have not distinguished among the many different types of support, and recipients and providers may also not draw distinctions between them. For instance, when a wife comes home after a stressful day at work, her husband may listen to her, offer reassurance, and then cook her dinner. This supportive interaction could be classified both as tangible, instrumental, and practical and as indirect or emotional support, but it is possible that the recipient and the provider of the support will only view certain aspects of these acts as being actual support. For instance, it might be the norm in the relationship for the husband to prepare dinner and so the wife may not consider this act to be supportive, yet the husband believes it is support because it helps his wife cope better with the stress of work. Moreover, what appears to the provider as reassuring may be perceived by the recipient as having negative implications.

This mix of support types during the enacted support process is precisely what makes the strongest argument for adopting a multidimensional framework for understanding support, particularly enacted support. A study of couples' daily support exchanges found that caring, companionship, and esteem support (all of which are aspects of emotional support) as well as tangible assistance, information, and advice (all of which are aspects of practical support) can be differentiated on a daily basis and have unique effects (Rafaeli, Kang, & Bar-Kalifa, 2012). Caring and tangible assistance were beneficial for relationship closeness, whereas esteem and advice were not, suggesting that there may be a hierarchy of preferred supportive behaviors.

If one considers support a monolithic construct, one loses the ability to distinguish which aspects of support lead to either positive or, perhaps more often, negative outcomes. The parsing of social support into its various components or types may lead to insights into what increases the likelihood of support being beneficial to the receiver. In particular, theories advocating for support matching have examined the multidimensionality of support and argued that any particular type of support can have both positive and negative consequences. According to this perspective, whether the effects are desirable or undesirable depends on whether the provided support matches the situation and the desires of the recipient (Cutrona, 1996; Cutrona & Russell, 1990).

Support matching governed by the specificity hypothesis (i.e., Cutrona, 1996) suggests that both stress and support are multidimensional and that these dimensions must be in synchrony for support to be effective at buffering the recipient from the stress he or she is experiencing. Cutrona and Russell (1990) argued for a model of stress consisting of four dimensions: the desirability, the duration, the context or life domain, and the controllability of the stressor.

Desirability makes a distinction between what have often been termed *eustress* and *distress*. Eustress is stress associated with events deemed positive by those experiencing them, such as getting married, having a child, or getting a big promotion at work. Conversely, stressors associated with distress are considered undesirable and include such things as being diagnosed with a chronic illness, going through a divorce, or losing one's job. The duration of the stressor refers to its severity (e.g., how long the stressor is likely to affect an individual), and the life domain of the stressor is the context in which it occurs (e.g., financial assets, relationships, personal achievements). With respect to controllability, controllable events are defined as those in which an individual believes that he or she had a determining role in the occurrence of the stressful event. More important, the controllability of an event does not determine whether it is a positive or negative event; for instance, both marriage and divorce are often controllable, whereas being a victim of crime or winning the lottery are both largely uncontrollable. In this model, controllability is key because it is the dimension that determines which stressors and supportive acts need to be matched; specifically, uncontrollable events require more emotional support, whereas controllable events require more instrumental support. By emphasizing the importance of controllability, this model is in agreement with Folkman and Lazarus's (1980) notion of problem-focused coping and emotion-focused coping, which are viewed as appropriate responses to controllable versus uncontrollable events, respectively. In line with studies discussed earlier and given the centrality of controllability to the matching hypothesis, research investigating support matching theory has tended to group support into emotional and instrumental–practical categories.

The matching hypothesis has received extensive support in the literature (Dehle, Larsen, & Landers, 2001; Horowitz et al., 2001; Peirce, Frone, Russell, & Cooper, 1996; Simpson, Winterheld, Rholes, & Oriña, 2007). For example, a study by Cutrona et al. (2007) found that couple members who engaged in a support discussion during a laboratory visit viewed their partners as more sensitive if the partner responded to the designated support recipient's emotional statements with emotional support; unfortunately, this sensitivity was a relatively uncommon occurrence, taking place only 25% of the time. When information was requested, providers were much more likely to respond with advice or information (53% of the time), but matching informational requests did not increase the support receiver's view of the provider's sensitivity. Cutrona et al. speculated that the benefit of emotional matching might be attributable, in part, to its relative rarity, and the lack of benefit for instrumental matching may be attributable to the fact that advice is often given whether it is desired or not. Even when requested, advice is often viewed negatively by receivers, perhaps because of the perceived uncontrollability of many stressors (Cutrona & Suhr, 1992). The frequency of supportive advice and its tendency to be overused by providers may constitute the most consistent mismatch of support exchanges, possibly helping explain why support attempts often either fail to alleviate stress or, worse yet, exacerbate it. However, recipients may view advice as helpful when they solicit their partners' support to achieve self-improvement goals. For example, Overall, Fletcher, and Simpson (2010) found that tangible support and advice—as well as emotional support—were associated with support providers being viewed as more helpful.

Although the specificity hypothesis allows for stressors to result in positive events, it also focuses on the stressful aspects of those events. Research by Gable and colleagues (Gable, Gonzaga, & Strachman, 2006; Gable & Reis, 2010; Gable, Reis, Impett, & Asher, 2004) has suggested that when support is provided for positive events, it is often not aimed at alleviating distress but rather at enhancing the positive aspects of the events. Such support improves recipients' well-being and promotes positive relationship outcomes, such as greater intimacy and increased relationship satisfaction. Capitalization occurs when an individual shares a positive event and his or her partner responds actively and constructively while avoiding passive and destructive behaviors. For instance, a husband may tell his wife that he has successfully lost 5 pounds after dieting for 2 weeks. An active and constructive response to this good news would be the wife enthusiastically congratulating him and encouraging him to keep up the hard work. If she failed to participate in his excitement and pride (by making a lackluster comment such as, "That's nice, dear") or she negated it (e.g., with a hostile reply such as "Is that all?"), she would be engaging in passive or destructive support, respectively. Given that positive events typically occur more often during a given day than negative events, capitalization attempts and the support that they elicit may be one of the most common types of support exchanged in individuals' lives, suggesting that the ability to celebrate positive events may be as important for both individual and relationship well-being as the ability to help close others through challenges. Furthermore, evidence has shown that successful capitalization attempts might be what drive people's levels of perceived support rather than the support they receive for stressful events (Shorey & Lakey, 2011), and as discussed high levels of perceived support are associated with many emotional, relational, and physical benefits.

The multidimensional nature of social support (or the what of social support, as we have conceptualized it), even if limited to a distinction between emotional and practical support, has proven useful in understanding the effects of receiving social support. The matching hypothesis brings the multidimensional nature of support to the forefront of the literature and suggests several ways for providers to optimize the effectiveness of the support they provide.

THE HOW: THE SKILLFULNESS OF SOCIAL SUPPORT

Unfortunately, understanding the timing and content of social support is not enough to ensure its effectiveness. As discussed, support attempts often backfire or do little to alleviate the negative effects of stressors. Rini and Dunkel-Schetter (2010) suggested a framework, which they called social support effectiveness, to understand the mixed effects of enacted support. They illustrated the many ways in which support attempts can go awry and undermine the best intentions of support providers. Perhaps the simplest reason that support may be ineffective is that it fails to meet the recipient's needs (i.e., the support is not matched to the recipient's needs), but even responsive support can include negative messages by signaling the recipient's incompetence (Bolger et al., 2000; J. D. Fisher et al.,

1982), threatening the recipient's self-esteem (J. D. Fisher & Nadler, 1976) or making the recipient feel indebted to the provider (Walster et al., 1973). All of these potentially negative outcomes can be avoided through the skillful provision of support, shedding light on the importance of the how of social support.

Although support matching was discussed previously in The What: The Types of Support section as it derives from a multidimensional framework of social support, this framework merits further discussion here because it proposes how support can be provided effectively or skillfully. Providers who are able to match the support they provide to the needs and desires of the recipient are much more likely to relieve the recipient's stress, strengthen the relationship with the recipient, and perhaps help the recipient resolve his or her problem. Most providers, however, are not particularly adept at matching support. Work on empathic accuracy has pointed to those providers who may be better at matching support. For example, individuals who understand their partners' thoughts and feelings are better at providing the support desired by their partners and are more effective at alleviating their partners' distress and promoting the well-being of the relationship (Rafaeli & Gleason, 2009). In an observational study of couples providing support to each other, Verhofstadt, Ickes, and Buysse (2010) found that individuals who had a better understanding of what their partners were thinking and feeling during a discussion provided more effective instrumental support and were less likely to engage in negative relationship behaviors.

Such findings have suggested that increasing individuals' empathic accuracy may be an effective way to increase the skillfulness of the support they provide; however, empathic accuracy may be particularly difficult for some individuals to achieve and is likely to vary on the basis of the topic being discussed. For instance, avoidantly attached individuals display almost no empathic accuracy when discussing relationship issues, whereas highly anxious people tend to be more empathically accurate when discussing a topic that is threatening to their relationship (Simpson et al., 2011). Although one might expect securely attached individuals to be particularly empathic, securely attached individuals tend to score fairly low in empathic accuracy when negative relationship issues are discussed. Perhaps being accurate about a partner's unhappiness is threatening to the perceiver and, thus, is unconsciously avoided by those who feel more comfortable with their partners and relationships. However, it is precisely in such discussions that accurately understanding a partner's dissatisfaction may allow individuals to provide support in a manner that ultimately improves marital satisfaction and alleviates tension in the relationship.

Unfortunately, matched support and empathic accuracy are often elusive, which emphasizes the need for other ways to improve the skillfulness of support. Providing support that the recipient is unaware of receiving—a process referred to as invisible support—has also been linked to positive outcomes for recipients, perhaps because recipients who are unaware that support has been provided may be less influenced by the type or content of that support. In a study of couples in which one partner was approaching a stressful event (taking a bar exam), Bolger et al. (2000) found that, on days when partners claimed to have provided support but the recipient did not recognize the support, the recipient's negative mood was lessened (Bolger et al., 2000). These findings suggest that when support is outside of the recipients' awareness, they benefit from the help they receive without a need for it to be matched.

The positive effects of invisible support have also been documented in an observational study (Howland & Simpson, 2010), a diary study of practical support (Shrout et al., 2006), and experimental research (Bolger & Amarel, 2007). Bolger and Amarel (2007) found that students who received practical or emotional support before giving a stressful speech experienced an increase in anxiety compared with those who received no support. However, students who received invisible support (i.e., the same message of support but directed at the experimenter rather than the participant) experienced less anxiety than did students who received a support message directly and those who were in control conditions. Unfortunately, invisible support may be difficult to provide because certain types of support are difficult to hide (i.e., doing extra household chores or pro-

viding reassurance) and because it may be difficult for the provider to resist taking credit for his or her good deeds. A recent study found that, when support provision goes unacknowledged (a necessary component of invisible support), support provision is related to increased anxiety and depression in the provider (Biehle & Mickelson, 2012).

Support reciprocation—when an individual both receives support from and provides support to a partner—may alleviate the negative consequences of support receipt, and it may also be easier to regulate than either matched support or invisible support. The evidence of a norm of reciprocity is ample: People avoid being either overburdened or underburdened (e.g., receiving more than they give) in most support exchanges (Uehara, 1995), preferring equitable relationships. Equity in relationships has long been established as beneficial (Walster et al., 1973), and research on the benefits of equity or reciprocity has suggested that supportive equity is positive for both an individual's mood and relationship closeness. A 4-week diary study involving couples found that on days when emotional support was both given and received, negative mood decreased and positive mood increased (Gleason et al., 2003). This finding was replicated and extended in a larger sample of couples who completed more than 4 weeks of daily diaries while one partner prepared for a stressful event (the state bar exam): Negative mood increased on days when support was received and not reciprocated, but it decreased on days when support was reciprocal (Gleason et al., 2008). These studies show the potential benefits of reciprocal support exchanges in two samples, one of which had distinct support-receiver (one partner preparing for the stressful event) and support-provider roles, indicating that even at moderate to high levels of stress the benefits of reciprocity are measurable.

The importance of avoiding unbalanced support in relationships has received a substantial amount of attention with respect to chronic illness. Perceived equity in couples facing illness is related to higher relationship quality (Kuijer, Buunk, & Ybema, 2001), and patients who disclose more to their partners experience less distress when their partners respond with their own self-disclosures (Manne et al., 2004). It is important to note that patients also respond negatively to a lack of opportunity to provide support—in other words, it is support provision rather than support receipt that is often missing in many support exchanges. For instance, patients who felt that they contributed too little to their intimate relationship were more likely to be depressed (Ybema, Kuijer, Buunk, DeJong, & Sanderman, 2001), and patients who had overprotective partners experienced higher distress (Kuijer et al., 2001). Caregivers, however, seem to suffer from a lack of support receipt as well. Numerous studies have investigated overburden in caregivers and found that caregivers who experience inequitable support in their relationships experience more emotional exhaustion, less personal connection, and fewer feelings of personal accomplishment (Ybema, Kuijer, Hagedoorn, & Buunk, 2002). Caregivers tend to receive less support than cancer survivors (Mellon, Northouse, & Weiss, 2006), and being overburdened has been linked to cognitive and physical declines in caregivers (Christakis & Allison, 2006; George & Gwyther, 1986).

In summary, understanding the enacted support process requires investigating many different aspects of support. We have organized these aspects into why people provide support, who is most likely to receive and provide it, how the support process unfolds over time, what support transactions consist of, and how support is enacted by highlighting effective or skillful ways though which the support process can unfold. By considering all of these aspects, social support researchers may be better able to identify holes in our current understanding of the social support process. For instance, although much of the burden of the support process is placed on the support provider (being sufficiently motivated to provide support, recognizing the need for support, picking a type of support to provide that will work, and then actually providing it), the effect of support provision (outside of caregiving) has until recently been largely neglected by most support researchers.

PROVIDING SUPPORT: IS IT BETTER TO GIVE THAN TO RECEIVE?

There has been a recent surge of interest in the consequences of providing support on the provider.

This new interest has led to several findings suggesting that giving support, at both the aggregate (perceived) and the enacted level, is associated with many positive outcomes (Brown, Brown, & Penner, 2012). As mentioned, social psychology has a long history of studying helping behavior (Batson, 1998), such as work on prosocial behavior (Penner, Dovidio, Piliavin, & Schroeder, 2005) and identifying and investigating the bystander effect (Darley & Latane, 1968). However, the literatures on helping behavior and the provision of support differ in important ways, some of which we have discussed. In particular, helping behavior research has focused on providing aid in times of emergency, primarily to strangers. Support research, conversely, has focused on helpful acts between individuals who typically know each other (e.g., family members and romantic partners) and on situations in which support is expected to be ongoing. In the helping behavior literature, helping behaviors have long been argued to be rewarding, and the reasons for this reward have been debated (see The Why: Motivations for Social Support section). However, the support literature has largely focused on the duties of support providers (i.e., what they need to do to provide support) or on the burdens associated with engaging in the long-term care of another (i.e., caregiver burden).

Although the idea that support provision may often be positive has only recently begun to receive attention in the social support literature, the evidence for this positivity is growing rapidly. Providing social support is associated with many positive outcomes, including reduced depression in bereaved spouses (Brown, Brown, House, & Smith, 2008) and greater well-being in patients with multiple sclerosis (Kleiboer, Kuijer, Hox, Schreurs, & Bensing, 2006). Brown, Nesse, Vinokur, and Smith (2003) found that individuals who reported giving practical support to friends and family or giving emotional support to their spouses had lower mortality risks than those who did not provide support, even after controlling for several variables such as support receipt and dependence. Evidence of the benefits of providing support has also been found in the reward centers of the brain. A study of couples in which the female partner was scanned using an MRI while

(a) offering support to the male partner as he received electric shocks by holding his arm, (b) holding the partner's arm while he did not receive shocks, (c) holding a squeeze ball while the partner received shocks, or (d) holding a squeeze ball while the partner did not receive shocks found that female support providers reported feeling closer to their partners when they were in the support provision condition (Inagaki & Eisenberger, 2012). They also showed more activity in the ventral striatum, an area in the brain associated with reward.

New models attempting to explain the benefits of support provision involving biological systems, neuroscience, and attachment theory have begun to emerge. Brown, Brown, and Preston (2012) argued that the provision of care or support may be driven by a neurobiological system, specifically the medial preoptic area of the hypothalamus, which facilitates caregiving and relationship maintenance with close others. Attachment theory, regardless of the specific biological processes, argues that caregiving is a fundamental aspect of human relationships that serves two basic functions: providing a safe haven (help in times of distress) and providing a secure base (supporting others' exploration). Under this framework, securely attached individuals are most capable of providing both types of support while also benefiting the most from them (Mikulincer & Shaver, 2012). As more is learned about the consequences of support provision on the provider, the mechanisms behind these benefits should be further explored. At this time, though, it is clear that providing support, rather than being a burden, is often a boon to the provider.

FUTURE DIRECTIONS AND CONCLUSIONS

We have discussed several aspects of the support process with the idea of highlighting the role and the consequences of enacted support for both receivers and providers of support. What has become clear is that social support researchers do not work under a unifying theoretical framework but have instead been investigating various aspects of the support process separately. This lack of theoretical unity is, perhaps, a discipline-wide problem, but it is nevertheless limiting to our understanding of support as a process and instead paints a picture of support as a disparate or even random group of relationship behaviors. A promising framework for understanding the social support process, the perceived partner responsiveness model (Reis, Clark, & Holmes, 2004), suggests that feeling responded to by a partner is the key to a healthy relationship. This theory is gaining attention in the social support literature (see Cutrona et al., 2007; Maisel & Gable, 2009; Neff & Karney, 2005; Overall et al., 2010), and there may be no more direct way for a partner to demonstrate responsiveness than to provide support and for the recipient, in turn, to acknowledge it. Continued instances of enacted support between partners may contribute to a perception of responsiveness, which then leads to a global feeling of perceived support that is then linked to positive outcomes. For instance, in our work on enacted support, we found that support receipt was often associated with negative mood, but received support was also associated with increased relationship closeness for the vast majority of the sample (Gleason et al., 2008). The same support act that made an individual feel more anxious also appeared to make an individual feel closer to his or her partner. Perhaps over time the sting or negative consequence of support receipt is forgotten, and only the memory of being helped by one's partner and feeling close to the partner remains.

We do not argue, however, that support would always be a signal of responsiveness by the partner to the receiver. In particular, we caution against including responsiveness in a definition of enacted support. Support may be one way in which individuals demonstrate that they are responsive to their partners, but it is not the only way for partners to do so (see Reis et al., 2004). Furthermore, it is possible that some supportive behaviors are unacknowledged or unrecognized by the support recipients. For instance, invisible support is outside a receiver's awareness and, therefore, unlikely to be experienced as responsive by the recipients. However, it is an effective way in which to alleviate negative mood in recipients (e.g., Bolger et al., 2000). We recommend that support researchers establish social support as a separate construct from responsiveness, which will help to differentiate the aspects of enacted support that are signaling that a provider cares about their needs from those aspects that are detrimental or undermining to the receiver. This would further our understanding of why support attempts so often fail or even backfire, exacerbating stress rather than relieving it. To further this aim, we recommend enacted support be defined as a neutral construct— one that does not explicitly suggest responsiveness or even positivity. Rather, researchers could be more precise by asking whether the recipient received such things as advice, material aid, reassurance, messages of love, and so forth. Many researchers are already obtaining information about specific types of support, but then, as discussed earlier, they collapse the various types into emotional and practical support when analyzing and discussing their data. Both theoretical and measurement justifications exist for this collapsing of categories, but we encourage researchers to consider separating out types of social support, when feasible, to increase our understanding of the underpinnings of recipient reactions.

It is also important to consider types of support that either have yet to be identified or are rarely studied in the literature. For instance, the working definition of enacted social support in this chapter is a behavior that is performed by others with an intention of alleviating distress in the recipient, and it assumes that the provider must engage in an action. Given that enacted support often backfires and increases negative mood, we might consider another kind of behavior within the context of relationships as being supportive, one that does not actually require action by the provider: intentional distancing. The object relations theorist Donald Winnicott proposed that creating a holding environment is crucial for therapeutic settings. The idea is that the therapist should know when to intervene with the client and when to let the client work out the problems for him- or herself. The idea could apply in all relationships, including marital relationships, in which a spouse does not automatically provide support when the partner is in distress but rather allows the partner to feel the distress and work on the problem by giving that person some space to do so. Intentional distancing is often alluded to in open-ended questionnaires that ask individuals to identify ways in which they support

their partners, but it is rarely, if ever, directly measured in social support questionnaires. Another possibly neglected support technique is that of distraction—helping by providing a break from worries or troubles, be it through humor or other means. Distraction and humor have both been studied as methods of coping (Carver et al., 1989) but have received little attention from support researchers. Given that many stressors are intractable (i.e., chronic illness), it seems likely that social networks and partners provide support by interfering with recipients' negative rumination on said stressors. The more we understand the myriad ways in which people engage in supportive behaviors, the more likely we are to gain insight into the paradox of enacted and perceived support by disentangling the effective from the ineffective in the support process.

An area that has been almost completely neglected in the enacted support literature is that of the receiver in the support process. Although social support research has focused almost exclusively on recipient outcomes, it lays very little of the burden of the support process on the recipient. It seems likely that the manner in which a recipient requests support is likely to greatly influence the success of any support received, and some research has investigated the consequences associated with how recipients ask for support (e.g., Barbee & Cunningham, 1995), but otherwise the recipient is often relegated to a passive role in the support process. Receivers' interpretations of support are rarely explored, but they hold the promise of unlocking some of the mysteries of the support process. For instance, when a support recipient hears a message of reassurance— "I'm sure you are going to be fine"—do they experience it as caring or dismissive? It is not only how the support affects outcomes of interest (e.g., mood, health symptoms, relationship satisfaction), but also the recipients' understanding of the support message that may increase our understanding of the support process. Exploring the social cognition of social support receipt would likely add greatly to our understanding of this complex process.

Finally, we believe that social support researchers should make an effort to disseminate their results beyond those who study social support. Many disciplines outside those that traditionally study social support could benefit from knowledge of the support literature's findings. For instance, work in political science and economics is interested in support provision and receipt, but at the group or government level (Le Grand, 2012). Kullberg and Singer (2012) argued that our understanding of the support process or caregiving system can shed light on such political questions as national identity and community organization. A recent article in the *New York Times* (Appelbaum & Gebeloff, 2012) suggested that people who receive benefits from the U.S. government through social benefit programs are also likely to oppose such programs and vote against them. Individuals interviewed in the article stated that they did not like feeling reliant on the government and thought that, although difficult, it would be better if the government provided them with fewer social services. These sentiments echo those of support receipt and provision among close relationship partners—the positives and negatives of support receipt. Just as the science of social support has borrowed from many areas of science, including biology, neuroscience, and evolutionary theory, in the future social support researchers may want to look to economics and political science to gain new insights into this complex process. This process should, of course, be a reciprocal exchange in which social support researchers also share their insights into the why, when, who, what, and how of this fundamental human process.

References

Appelbaum, B., & Gebeloff, R. (2012, February 11). Even critics of safety net increasingly depend on it. *New York Times*. Retrieved from http://www.nytimes.com/2012/02/12/us/even-critics-of-safety-net-increasingly-depend-on-it.html

Aron, A., & Aron, E. N. (1986). *Love and the expansion of self: Understanding attraction and satisfaction.* New York, NY: Hemisphere.

Auerbach, S. M., & Kilmann, P. R. (1977). Crisis intervention: A review of outcome research. *Psychological Bulletin, 84,* 1189–1217. doi:10.1037/0033-2909.84.6.1189

Barbee, A. P., & Cunningham, M. R. (1995). An experimental approach to social support communications: Interactive coping in close relationships. In B. R. Burleson (Ed.), *Communication yearbook* (Vol. 18, pp. 381–413). Thousand Oaks, CA: Sage

Barrera, M. (1981). Social support in the adjustment of pregnant adolescents: Assessment issues. In B. H. Gottlieb (Ed.), *Social networks and social support* (pp. 69–96). Beverly Hills, CA: Sage.

Barrera, M. (1986). Distinctions between social support concepts, measures, and models. *American Journal of Community Psychology, 14,* 413–445. doi:10.1007/BF00922627

Barrera, M., & Ainlay, S. L. (1983). The structure of social support: A conceptual and empirical analysis. *Journal of Community Psychology, 11,* 133–143. doi:10.1002/1520-6629(198304)11:2<133::AID-JCOP2290110207>3.0.CO;2-L

Batson, C. (1997). Self–other merging and the empathy–altruism hypothesis: Reply to Neuberg et al. (1997). *Journal of Personality and Social Psychology, 73,* 517–522. doi:10.1037/0022-3514.73.3.517

Batson, C., Sager, K., Garst, E., Kang, M., Rubchinsky, K., & Dawson, K. (1997). Is empathy-induced helping due to self–other merging? *Journal of Personality and Social Psychology, 73,* 495–509. doi:10.1037/0022-3514.73.3.495

Batson, C. D. (1998). Altruism and prosocial behavior. In D. T. Gilbert, S. T. Fiske, & G. Lindzey (Eds.), *Handbook of social psychology* (Vol. 2, pp. 282–316). Boston, MA: McGraw-Hill.

Berkman, L. F., & Breslow, L. (1983). *Health and ways of living: The Alameda County study.* New York, NY: Oxford University Press.

Biehle, S. N., & Mickelson, K. D. (2012). Provision and receipt of emotional spousal support: The impact of visibility on well-being. *Couple and Family Psychology: Research and Practice, 1,* 244–251. doi:10.1037/a0028480

Bolger, N., & Amarel, D. (2007). Effects of social support visibility on adjustment to stress: Experimental evidence. *Journal of Personality and Social Psychology, 92,* 458–475. doi:10.1037/0022-3514.92.3.458

Bolger, N., DeLongis, A., Kessler, R. C., & Wethington, E. (1989). The contagion of stress across multiple roles. *Journal of Marriage and the Family, 51,* 175–183. doi:10.2307/352378

Bolger, N., Foster, M., Vinokur, A. D., & Ng, R. (1996). Close relationships and adjustment to a life crisis: The case of breast cancer. *Journal of Personality and Social Psychology, 70,* 283–294. doi:10.1037/0022-3514.70.2.283

Bolger, N., Zuckerman, A., & Kessler, R. C. (2000). Invisible support and adjustment to stress. *Journal of Personality and Social Psychology, 79,* 953–961. doi:10.1037/0022-3514.79.6.953

Brown, S. L., Brown, R., House, J. S., & Smith, D. M. (2008). Coping with spousal loss: Potential buffering effects of self-reported helping behavior. *Personality and Social Psychology Bulletin, 34,* 849–861. doi:10.1177/0146167208314972

Brown, S. L., Brown, R. M., & Penner, L. A. (2012). *Moving beyond self-interest: Perspectives from evolutionary biology, neuroscience, and the social sciences.* New York, NY: Oxford University Press.

Brown, S. L., Brown, R. M., & Preston, S. D. (2012). The human caregiving system: A neuroscience model of compassionate motivation and behavior. In S. L. Brown, R. M. Brown, & L. A. Penner (Eds.), *Moving beyond self-interest: Perspectives from evolutionary biology, neuroscience, and the social sciences* (pp. 75–88). New York, NY: Oxford University Press.

Brown, S. L., Nesse, R. M., Vinokur, A. D., & Smith, D. M. (2003). Providing social support may be more beneficial than receiving it: Results from a prospective study of mortality. *Psychological Science, 14,* 320–327. doi:10.1111/1467-9280.14461

Carver, C. S., Scheier, M. F., & Weintraub, J. K. (1989). Assessing coping strategies: A theoretically based approach. *Journal of Personality and Social Psychology, 56,* 267–283. doi:10.1037/0022-3514.56.2.267

Christakis, N. A., & Allison, P. D. (2006). Mortality after the hospitalization of a spouse. *New England Journal of Medicine, 354,* 719–730. doi:10.1056/NEJMsa050196

Cialdini, R. B. (1991). Altruism or egoism? That is (still) the question. *Psychological Inquiry, 2,* 124–126. doi:10.1207/s15327965pli0202_3

Cialdini, R. B., Brown, S. L., Lewis, B. P., Luce, C., & Neuberg, S. L. (1997). Reinterpreting the empathy–altruism relationship: When one into one equals oneness. *Journal of Personality and Social Psychology, 73,* 481–494. doi:10.1037/0022-3514.73.3.481

Cialdini, R. B., Schaller, M., Houlihan, D., Arps, K., Fultz, J., & Beaman, A. L. (1987). Empathy-based helping: Is it selflessly or selfishly motivated? *Journal of Personality and Social Psychology, 52,* 749–758. doi:10.1037/0022-3514.52.4.749

Clark, M. S., & Mills, J. (1979). Interpersonal attraction in exchange and communal relationships. *Journal of Personality and Social Psychology, 37,* 12–24. doi:10.1037/0022-3514.37.1.12

Clark, M. S., Oullette, R., Powell, M. C., & Milberg, S. (1987). Recipient's mood, relationship type, and helping. *Journal of Personality and Social Psychology, 53,* 94–103. doi:10.1037/0022-3514.53.1.94

Cobb, S. (1976). Social support as a moderator of life stress. *Psychosomatic Medicine, 38,* 300–314.

Cobb, S. (1979). Social support and health through the life course. In M. W. Riley (Ed.), *Aging from birth to death: Interdisciplinary perspectives* (pp. 93–106). Boulder, CO: Westview Press.

Costa, P. T., Jr., McCrae, R. R., & Dye, D. A. (1991). Facet scales for agreeableness and conscientiousness:

A revision of the NEO Personality Inventory. *Personality and Individual Differences, 12,* 887–898. doi:10.1016/0191-8869(91)90177-D

Cutrona, C. E. (1996). *Social support in couples: Marriage as a resource in times of stress.* Thousand Oaks, CA: Sage.

Cutrona, C. E., & Russell, D. W. (1990). Type of social support and specific stress: Toward a theory of optimal matching. In B. R. Sarason, I. G. Sarason, & G. R. Pierce (Eds.), *Social support: An interactional view* (pp. 319–366). New York, NY: Wiley.

Cutrona, C. E., Shaffer, P. A., Wesner, K. A., & Gardner, K. A. (2007). Optimally matching support and perceived spousal sensitivity. *Journal of Family Psychology, 21,* 754–758. doi:10.1037/0893-3200.21.4.754

Cutrona, C. E., & Suhr, J. A. (1992). Controllability of stressful events and satisfaction with spouse support behaviors. *Communication Research, 19,* 154–174. doi:10.1177/009365092019002002

Darley, J. M., & Latane, B. (1968). Bystander intervention in emergencies: Diffusion of responsibility. *Journal of Personality and Social Psychology, 8,* 377–383. doi:10.1037/h0025589

Dehle, C., Larsen, D., & Landers, J. E. (2001). Social support in marriage. *American Journal of Family Therapy, 29,* 307–324.

Dunkel-Schetter, C., & Bennett, T. L. (1990). Differentiating the cognitive and behavioral aspects of social support. In B. R. Sarason, I. G. Sarason, & G. R. Pierce (Eds.), *Social support: An interactional view* (pp. 267–296). Oxford, England: Wiley.

Dunkel-Schetter, C., Folkman, S., & Lazarus, R. S. (1987). Correlates of social support receipt. *Journal of Personality and Social Psychology, 53,* 71–80. doi:10.1037/0022-3514.53.1.71

Dunkel-Schetter, C., & Skokan, L. A. (1990). Determinants of social support provision in personal relationships. *Journal of Social and Personal Relationships, 7,* 437–450.

Durkheim, E. (1951). *Suicide.* New York, NY: Free Press. (Original work published 1897)

Eckenrode, J. (1983). The mobilization of social supports: Some individual constraints. *American Journal of Community Psychology, 11,* 509–528. doi:10.1007/BF00896802

Eysenck, H. J. (1967). *The biological basis of personality.* Springfield, IL: Charles C Thomas.

Feeney, B. C., & Collins, N. L. (2001). Predictors of caregiving in adult intimate relationships: An attachment theoretical perspective. *Journal of Personality and Social Psychology, 80,* 972–994. doi:10.1037/0022-3514.80.6.972

Feeney, B. C., & Collins, N. L. (2003). Motivations for caregiving in adult intimate relationships: Influences on caregiving behavior and relationship functioning. *Personality and Social Psychology Bulletin, 29,* 950–968. doi:10.1177/0146167203252807

Finch, J. F., Barrera, M. R., Okun, M. A., Bryant, W. M., Pool, G. J., & Snow-Turek, A. (1997). The factor structure of received social support: Dimensionality and the prediction of depression and life satisfaction. *Journal of Social and Clinical Psychology, 16,* 323–342. doi:10.1521/jscp.1997.16.3.323

Fisher, E. B., La Greca, A. M., Greco, P., Arfken, C., & Schneiderman, N. (1997). Directive and nondirective social support in diabetes management. *International Journal of Behavioral Medicine, 4,* 131–144. doi:10.1207/s15327558ijbm0402_3

Fisher, J. D., & Nadler, A. (1976). Effect of donor resources on recipient self-esteem and self-help. *Journal of Experimental Social Psychology, 12,* 139–150. doi:10.1016/0022-1031(76)90065-2

Fisher, J. D., Nadler, A., & Whitcher-Alagna, S. (1982). Recipient reactions to aid. *Psychological Bulletin, 91,* 27–54. doi:10.1037/0033-2909.91.1.27

Folkman, S., & Lazarus, R. S. (1980). An analysis of coping in a middle-aged community sample. *Journal of Health and Social Behavior, 21,* 219–239. doi:10.2307/2136617

Forest, D., Clark, M. S., Mills, J., & Isen, A. M. (1979). Helping as a function of feeling state and nature of the helping behavior. *Motivation and Emotion, 3,* 161–169. doi:10.1007/BF01650601

Fraley, R., & Shaver, P. R. (1998). Airport separations: A naturalistic study of adult attachment dynamics in separating couples. *Journal of Personality and Social Psychology, 75,* 1198–1212. doi:10.1037/0022-3514.75.5.1198

Gable, S. L., Gonzaga, G. C., & Strachman, A. (2006). Will you be there for me when things go right? Supportive responses to positive event disclosures. *Journal of Personality and Social Psychology, 91,* 904–917. doi:10.1037/0022-3514.91.5.904

Gable, S. L., & Reis, H. T. (2010). Good news! Capitalizing on positive events in an interpersonal context. In M. P. Zanna (Ed.), *Advances in experimental social psychology* (Vol. 42, pp. 195–257). San Diego, CA: Academic Press. doi:10.1016/S0065-2601(10)42004-3

Gable, S. L., Reis, H. T., Impett, E. A., & Asher, E. R. (2004). What do you do when things go right? The intrapersonal and interpersonal benefits of sharing positive events. *Journal of Personality and Social Psychology, 87,* 228–245. doi:10.1037/0022-3514.87.2.228

George, L. K., & Gwyther, L. P. (1986). Caregiver well-being: A multidimensional examination of family caregivers of demented adults. *Gerontologist, 26,* 253–259. doi:10.1093/geront/26.3.253

Gleason, M. E. J., Iida, M., Bolger, N., & Shrout, P. E. (2003). Daily supportive equity in close relationships. *Personality and Social Psychology Bulletin, 29,* 1036–1045. doi:10.1177/0146167203253473

Gleason, M. E. J., Iida, M., Shrout, P. E., & Bolger, N. (2008). Receiving support as a mixed blessing: Evidence for dual effects of support on psychological outcomes. *Journal of Personality and Social Psychology, 94,* 824–838. doi:10.1037/0022-3514.94.5.824

Grenmore, T. M., Baucom, D. H., Porter, L. S., Kirby, J. S., Atkins, D. C., & Keefe, F. J. (2011). Stress buffering effects of daily spousal support on women's daily emotional and physical experiences in the context of breast cancer concerns. *Health Psychology, 30,* 20–30. doi:10.1037/a0021798

Hobfoll, S. E. (1988). *The ecology of stress.* Washington, DC: Hemisphere.

Hobfoll, S. E., & Lerman, M. (1989). Predicting receipt of social support: A longitudinal study of parents' reactions to their child's illness. *Health Psychology, 8,* 61–77. doi:10.1037/0278-6133.8.1.61

Horowitz, L. M., Krasnoperova, E. N., Tatar, D. G., Hansen, M. B., Person, E. A., Galvin, K. L., & Nelson, K. L. (2001). The way to console may depend on the goal: Experimental studies of social support. *Journal of Experimental Social Psychology, 37,* 49–61. doi:10.1006/jesp.2000.1435

House, J. S., Kahn, R. L., McLeod, J. D., & Williams, D. (1985). Measures and concepts of social support. In S. Cohen & S. Syme (Eds.), *Social support and health* (pp. 83–108). San Diego, CA: Academic Press.

Howland, M., & Simpson, J. A. (2010). Getting in under the radar: A dyadic view of invisible support. *Psychological Science, 21,* 1878–1885. doi:10.1177/0956797610388817

Iida, M., Seidman, G., Shrout, P. E., Fujita, K., & Bolger, N. (2008). Modeling support provision in intimate relationships. *Journal of Personality and Social Psychology, 94,* 460–478. doi:10.1037/0022-3514.94.3.460

Iida, M., Stephens, M., Rook, K. S., Franks, M. M., & Salem, J. K. (2010). When the going gets tough, does support get going? Determinants of spousal support provision to type 2 diabetic patients. *Personality and Social Psychology Bulletin, 36,* 780–791. doi:10.1177/0146167210369897

Inagaki, T. K., & Eisenberger, N. I. (2012). Neural correlates of giving support to a loved one. *Psychosomatic Medicine, 74,* 3–7. doi:10.1097/PSY.0b013e3182359335

Kleiboer, A. M., Kuijer, R. G., Hox, J. J., Schreurs, K. G., & Bensing, J. M. (2006). Receiving and providing support in couples dealing with multiple sclerosis: A diary study using an equity perspective. *Personal*

Relationships, 13, 485–501. doi:10.1111/
j.1475-6811.2006.00131.x

Krause, N. (1997). Received support, anticipated support, social class, and mortality. *Research on Aging, 19*, 387–422. doi:10.1177/0164027597194001

Kuijer, R. G., Buunk, B. P., & Ybema, J. F. (2001). Are equity concerns important in the intimate relationship when one partner of a couple has cancer? *Social Psychology Quarterly, 64*, 267–282. doi:10.2307/3090116

Kullberg, J. S., & Singer, J. D. (2012). Bringing neuroscience into political science: The caregiving system and human sociopolitical evolution. In S. L. Brown, R. M. Brown, & L. A. Penner (Eds.), *Moving beyond self-interest: Perspectives from evolutionary biology, neuroscience, and the social sciences* (pp. 246–268). New York, NY: Oxford University Press.

Lakey, B., Adams, K., Neely, L., Rhodes, G., Lutz, C. J., & Sielky, K. (2002). Perceived support and low emotional distress: The role of enacted support, dyad similarity and provider personality. *Personality and Social Psychology Bulletin, 28*, 1546–1555. doi:10.1177/014616702237582

Lakey, B., & Drew, J. B. (1997). *A social-cognitive perspective on social support*. New York, NY: Plenum Press.

Le Grand, J. (2012). Motivation and the delivery of social services. In S. L. Brown, R. M. Brown, & L. A. Penner (Eds.), *Moving beyond self-interest: Perspectives from evolutionary biology, neuroscience, and the social sciences* (pp. 269–279). New York, NY: Oxford University Press.

Lindorff, M. (2000). Is it better to perceive than receive? Social support, stress and strain for managers. *Psychology, Health and Medicine, 5*, 271–286. doi:10.1080/713690199

Maisel, N. C., & Gable, S. L. (2009). The paradox of received social support: The importance of responsiveness. *Psychological Science, 20*, 928–932. doi:10.1111/j.1467-9280.2009.02388.x

Manne, S., Sherman, M., Ross, S., Ostroff, J., Heyman, R. E., & Fox, K. (2004). Couples' support-related communication, psychological distress, and relationship satisfaction among women with early stage breast cancer. *Journal of Consulting and Clinical Psychology, 72*, 660–670. doi:10.1037/0022-006X.72.4.660

Mellon, S., Northouse, L. L., & Weiss, L. K. (2006). A population-based study of the quality of life of cancer survivors and their family caregivers. *Cancer Nursing, 29*, 120–131. doi:10.1097/00002820-200603000-00007

Mikulincer, M., & Shaver, P. R. (2012). Adult attachment and caregiving: Individual differences in providing a safe haven and secure base to others. In S. L. Brown, R. M. Brown, & L. A. Penner (Eds.), *Moving beyond self-interest: Perspectives from evolutionary biology,*

neuroscience, and the social sciences (pp. 39–52). New York, NY: Oxford University Press.

Mills, J., & Clark, M. S. (1994). Communal and exchange relationships: Controversies and research. In R. Erber & R. Gilmour (Eds.), *Theoretical frameworks for personal relationships* (pp. 29–42). Hillsdale, NJ: Erlbaum.

Nadler, A., & Fisher, J. D. (1976). When helping hurts: Effects of donor-recipient similarity and recipient self-esteem on reactions to aid. *Journal of Personality, 44*, 392–409. doi:10.1111/j.1467-6494.1976.tb00129.x

Neff, L. A., & Karney, B. R. (2005). Gender differences in social support: A question of skill or responsiveness? *Journal of Personality and Social Psychology, 88*, 79–90. doi:10.1037/0022-3514.88.1.79

Overall, N. C., Fletcher, G. O., & Simpson, J. A. (2010). Helping each other grow: Romantic partner support, self-improvement, and relationship quality. *Personality and Social Psychology Bulletin, 36*, 1496–1513. doi:10.1177/0146167210383045

Pearlin, L. I., & McCall, M. E. (1990). Occupational stress and marital support: A description of microprocesses. In J. Eckenrode & S. Gore (Eds.), *Stress between work and family* (pp. 39–60). New York, NY: Plenum Press. doi:10.1007/978-1-4899-2097-3_3

Peirce, R. S., Frone, M. R., Russell, M., & Cooper, L. M. (1996). Financial stress, social support, and alcohol involvement: A longitudinal test of the buffering hypothesis in a general population survey. *Health Psychology, 15*, 38–47. doi:10.1037/0278-6133.15.1.38

Penner, L. A., Dovidio, J. F., Piliavin, J. A., & Schroeder, D. A. (2005). Prosocial behavior: Multilevel perspectives. *Annual Review of Psychology, 56*, 365–392. doi:10.1146/annurev.psych.56.091103.070141

Pervin, L. A. (1989). *Goal concepts in personality and social psychology*. Hillsdale, NJ: Erlbaum.

Rafaeli, E., & Gleason, M. E. J. (2009). Skilled support within intimate relationships. *Journal of Family Theory and Review, 1*, 20–37. doi:10.1111/j.1756-2589.2009.00003.x

Rafaeli, E., Kang, N. J., & Bar-Kalifa, E. (2012). *Show, don't tell: Evidence for a hierarchy of support types*. Manuscript submitted for publication.

Reis, H. T., Clark, M. S., & Holmes, J. G. (2004). Perceived partner responsiveness as an organizing construct in the study of intimacy and closeness. In D. J. Mashek & A. P. Aaron (Eds.), *Handbook of closeness and intimacy* (pp. 201–225). Mahwah, NJ: Erlbaum.

Rini, C., & Dunkel Schetter, C. (2010). The effectiveness of social support attempts in intimate relationships. In K. T. Sullivan & J. Davila (Eds.), *Support processes in intimate relationships* (pp. 26–68). New York, NY: Oxford University Press. doi:10.1093/acprof:oso/9780195380170.003.0002

Sarason, B. R., Pierce, G. R., Shearin, E. N., Sarason, I. G., Waltz, J. A., & Poppe, L. (1991). Perceived social support and working models of self and actual others. *Journal of Personality and Social Psychology, 60,* 273–287. doi:10.1037/0022-3514.60.2.273

Sarason, B. R., Sarason, I. G., & Pierce, G. R. (1990). *Social support: An interactional view.* New York, NY: Wiley.

Schwarzer, R., & Weiner, B. (1991). Stigma controllability and coping as predictors of emotions and social support. *Journal of Social and Personal Relationships, 8,* 133–140. doi:10.1177/0265407591081007

Seidman, G., Shrout, P. E., & Bolger, N. (2006). Why is enacted social support associated with increased distress? Using simulation to test two possible sources of spuriousness. *Personality and Social Psychology Bulletin, 32,* 52–65. doi:10.1177/0146167205279582

Shorey, R. C., & Lakey, B. (2011). Perceived and capitalization support arc substantially similar: Implications for social support theory. *Personality and Social Psychology Bulletin, 37,* 1068–1079. doi:10.1177/0146167211406507

Shrout, P. E., Herman, C., & Bolger, N. (2006). The costs and benefits of practical and emotional support on adjustment: A daily diary study of couples experiencing acute stress. *Personal Relationships, 13,* 115–134. doi:10.1111/j.1475-6811.2006.00108.x

Simpson, J. A., Kim, J. S., Fillo, J., Ickes, W., Rholes, W., Oriña, M., & Winterheld, H. A. (2011). Attachment and the management of empathic accuracy in relationship-threatening situations. *Personality and Social Psychology Bulletin, 37,* 242–254. doi:10.1177/0146167210394368

Simpson, J. A., Rholes, W. S., & Nelligan, J. S. (1992). Support seeking and support giving within couples in an anxiety-provoking situation: The role of attachment styles. *Journal of Personality and Social Psychology, 62,* 434–446. doi:10.1037/0022-3514.62.3.434

Simpson, J. A., Winterheld, H. A., Rholes, W., & Oriña, M. (2007). Working models of attachment and reactions to different forms of caregiving from romantic partners. *Journal of Personality and Social Psychology, 93,* 466–477. doi:10.1037/0022-3514.93.3.466

Swickert, R. J., Rosentreter, C. J., Hittner, J. B., & Mushrush, J. E. (2002). Extraversion, social support processes, and stress. *Personality and Individual Differences, 32,* 877–891. doi:10.1016/S0191-8869(01)00093-9

Thoits, P. A. (1986). Social support as coping assistance. *Journal of Consulting and Clinical Psychology, 54,* 416–423. doi:10.1037/0022-006X.54.4.416

Thoits, P. A. (1995). Stress, coping and social support: Where are we? What next? *Journal of Health and Social Behavior, 35*(Extra Issue), 53–79.

Trobst, K. K., Collins, R. L., & Embree, J. M. (1994). The role of emotion in social support provision: Gender, empathy and expressions of distress. *Journal of Social and Personal Relationships, 11,* 45–62. doi:10.1177/0265407594111003

Uchino, B. N. (2004). *Social support and physical health.* New Haven, CT: Yale University Press.

Uchino, B. N. (2009). Understanding the links between social support and physical health: A life-span perspective with emphasis on the reparability of perceived and received support. *Perspectives on Psychological Science, 4,* 236–255. doi:10.1111/j.1745-6924.2009.01122.x

Uchino, B. N., Cacioppo, J. T., & Kiecolt-Glaser, J. K. (1996). The relationship between social support and physiological processes: A review with emphasis on underlying mechanisms and implications for health. *Psychological Bulletin, 119,* 488–531. doi:10.1037/0033-2909.119.3.488

Uehara, E. S. (1995). Reciprocity reconsidered: Gouldner's "moral norm of reciprocity" and social support. *Journal of Social and Personal Relationships, 12,* 483–502. doi:10.1177/0265407595124001

Verhofstadt, L. L., Ickes, W., & Buysse, A. (2010). "I know what you need right now": Empathic accuracy and support provision in marriage. In K. T. Sullivan & J. Davila (Eds.), *Support processes in intimate relationships* (pp. 71–88). New York, NY: Oxford University Press. doi:10.1093/acprof:oso/9780195380170.003.0003

Walster, E., Berscheid, E., & Walster, G. W. (1973). New directions in equity research. *Journal of Personality and Social Psychology, 25,* 151–176. doi:10.1037/h0033967

Watson, D., & Clark, L. A. (1997). *Extraversion and its positive emotional core.* San Diego, CA: Academic Press.

Watson, D., & Hubbard, B. (1996). Adaptational style and dispositional structure: Coping in the context of the five-factor model. *Journal of Personality, 64,* 737–774. doi:10.1111/j.1467-6494.1996.tb00943.x

Weiss, E. R. (1974). The provisions of social relationships. In Z. Rubin (Ed.), *Doing unto others* (pp. 17–26). Englewood Cliffs, NJ: Prentice-Hall.

Ybema, J. F., Kuijer, R. G., Buunk, B. P., DeJong, G., & Sanderman, R. (2001). Depression and perceptions of inequity among couples facing cancer. *Personality and Social Psychology Bulletin, 27,* 3–13. doi:10.1177/0146167201271001

Ybema, J. F., Kuijer, R. G., Hagedoorn, M., & Buunk, B. P. (2002). Caregiver burnout among intimate partners of patients with a severe illness: An equity perspective. *Personal Relationships, 9,* 73–88. doi:10.1111/1475-6811.00005

CHAPTER 14

COMMUNICATION IN PERSONAL RELATIONSHIPS

Anita L. Vangelisti

Communication is integral to human relationships. It affects whether relationships are initiated and how they evolve. What people say when they first meet and how they say it influences whether a romantic relationship develops. Once romantic relationships are established, couples' interaction patterns shape what partners think about each other, how they act toward each other, and how they feel about their relationship. Communication behavior can even serve as an indicator of whether relationships are likely to continue or end. In short, not only is communication a gauge of relational well-being, it also defines relationships.

The purpose of this chapter is to describe the role of communication in romantic relationships. First, to provide a context for the material that is covered, I describe five basic properties of communication (interdependence, reflexivity, complexity, ambiguity, and indeterminacy). Then, I review research on some of the processes that characterize communication in romantic relationships. These processes are examined in terms of both individual characteristics and patterns (e.g., cognition and affect) and dyadic characteristics and patterns (e.g., couple types, behavioral sequences). Finally, I outline several challenges facing researchers and theorists who study the meanings, functions, and outcomes associated with communication in romantic relationships and discuss directions for future research.

BASIC PROPERTIES OF COMMUNICATION

Although communication is studied in a number of different ways and from a variety of perspectives (see Burleson, Metts, & Kirch, 2000), researchers and theorists have generally agreed that it is characterized by several basic properties (Sillars & Vangelisti, 2006). These properties elucidate the ways in which communication creates and sustains relationships as well as the ways in which relationships shape the enactment and interpretation of communication.

Interdependence

One of the most commonly noted qualities of communication is interdependence. Interdependence refers to the fact that verbal and nonverbal messages both influence and are influenced by the messages that precede and follow them. The impact of messages on each other creates coherence between messages and across interactions. It generates the patterns and ongoing processes that define relationships (Rogers, 1998).

Studies examining the development of infants' communication competencies have offered a striking illustration of interdependence. More than 3 decades of research have demonstrated that infants and adults mutually regulate each other's behavior. Infants imitate adults' facial expressions and finger movements (Meltzoff & Moore, 1977), adapt their

I thank Alan L. Sillars and Mark L. Knapp for their contributions to this chapter.

http://dx.doi.org/10.1037/14344-014
APA Handbook of Personality and Social Psychology: Vol. 3. Interpersonal Relations, M. Mikulincer and P. R. Shaver (Editors-in-Chief)

vocalizations and latency of responses to those displayed by their mothers (Beebe, Jaffe, Feldstein, Mays, & Alson, 1985), and change their level of activity to gain the attention of unresponsive adults (Papoušek, Papoušek, & Haekel, 1987). They also structure their own vocalizations to match the phonological patterns of their caregivers (Goldstein & Schwade, 2008). These and other data have suggested that adults' positive, contingent responses to infants influence infants' prelinguistic vocal behavior.

Adults' communication is also affected by infants. As noted by Van Egeren and Barratt (2004), adult caregivers often watch infants until infants make eye contact and then respond by vocalizing, smiling, and touching them. In this way, infants not only influence adults' behavior but also initiate a chain of communication that can, in turn, facilitate language development. Gruenbaum, Depowski, Shaw, and Bortfeld (2013) suggested that infants' ability to actively elicit responses from their caregivers is key to language acquisition. Indeed, research has shown that the number of conversational turns that adult caregivers and children share is positively associated with the children's language development (Zimmerman et al., 2009).

The interdependence illustrated by infants' interactions with their caregivers helps to explain the effort of many communication theorists to focus on patterns of interaction rather than on individual messages. Because messages are interdependent, some theorists have argued that the relations among them are particularly indicative of communication systems (Fisher, 1978). Indeed, patterns of interaction inform the study of communication in personal relationships in several ways. First, they show that relationships are structured and coherent. For instance, people who are unacquainted can carry on conversations because they understand the rules and routines that typically structure initial interactions (Kellermann, 1991). They know that certain topics and questions are appropriate and that topics and questions are usually addressed in a predictable sequence (Berger, Gardner, Clatterbuck, & Schulman, 1976). The notion that relationships are structured does not necessarily imply that they are also static. In fact, interaction patterns are often dynamic

and flexible. They change in response to relational events (Baxter & Bullis, 1986), to external pressures (Karney & Bradbury, 1995), and with the passage of time (Harwood, Rittenour, & Lin, 2013). Even these changes, though, are somewhat patterned and structured. If they were not, researchers would not be able to study the interactions that characterize particular relational experiences, partners' responses to external stressors, or developmental changes in communication.

Second, patterns of interaction reveal the multiple influences on communication. As noted by Duck (2002), communication behaviors are enacted within particular historical contexts. Those contexts can include time and place, relational history, and the history of the current interaction. As such, any given message is affected by the physical and temporal environment as well as the communication behaviors that precede it. For example, the way parents interact with their children is often described in terms of parenting styles (e.g., inductive vs. power-assertive styles of parental discipline). However, these relatively stable styles or patterns of behavior actually represent adaptations to features that emerge as parents and their children interact (Bugental, 2000). Parents of preschool children often mix forms of discipline within a given interaction (Wilson, Cameron, & Whipple, 1997) and use different combinations of induction and power assertion depending on how their child has misbehaved (Wilson, Whipple, & Grau, 1996). Similarly, romantic partnerships are characterized by some researchers as couple types based in part on the patterns of behavior they enact (Fitzpatrick, 1977; Gottman, 1993). Those couple types, however, use a variety of strategies to deal with relational tasks such as seeking compliance (Witteman & Fitzpatrick, 1986) and relational events such as the birth of a child (Fitzpatrick, Vangelisti, & Firman, 1994).

A third way that patterns of interaction inform the study of communication in close relationships is that they reflect behavioral sequences that mediate relational quality. Couples' interaction patterns, in other words, sometimes predict relational outcomes even when overall base rates for communication are controlled. One of the most commonly noted instances of this sort of mediation involves the tendency of couples who are dissatisfied to reciprocate one another's negative affect. Research has indicated that couples' negative affect reciprocity is linked to their relational satisfaction even after the amount of negativity they typically communicate is controlled (Gottman, 1994). Another example involves a sequence of behavior labeled the *demand–withdraw pattern*. This behavioral sequence occurs when one partner demands or tries to engage the other in conversation while the other tries to avoid interaction. The demand–withdraw pattern is associated with marital dissatisfaction (Heavey, Layne, & Christensen, 1993) over and above the amount of negativity in the relationship (Caughlin & Huston, 2002).

Reflexivity

Most researchers who study communication have agreed that communication is reflexive, that it simultaneously creates structure and is constrained by structure. Applied to the study of personal relationships, the principle of reflexivity refers to the idea that communication both shapes and is shaped by relationships. In other words, relational partners are proactive in that they make choices and exert influence over their relational outcomes, and they are also reactive in that their choices and behaviors are affected by "normative and institutionalized practices that establish the boundaries of subsequent communicative moves" (Baxter & Montgomery, 1996, p. 13).

Several lines of research have emphasized the reflexive nature of communication. One of these involves the study of everyday discourse. Duck (1995; Duck & Pond, 1988) argued that everyday, routine conversation functions to create and sustain relationships. He noted that ordinary talk embodies interpersonal associations, reflecting the quality of individuals' relationships. Partners in particular types of relationships tend to discuss certain topics and interpret the discussion of such topics in unique ways. For example, people involved in long-term committed relationships are more likely to converse about a joint future than those who are not, and they are also more likely to interpret conversations about future activities as an indicator of their commitment (Knapp & Taylor, 1994). Duck also noted that everyday talk influences relationships; it is part of an ongoing dialogue between partners that shapes the quality of their tie to each other over time. For instance, partners who routinely express affection toward each other are more likely to maintain a more satisfying relationship over time than those who do not (Huston & Vangelisti, 1991).

Using diary methods with undergraduate students, Duck, Rutt, Hurst, and Strejc (1991) found that most interactions that people have on a day-to-day basis are routine and satisfying. Participants' everyday conversations were usually not linked to major changes in their relationships, but they did differ on the basis of relationship type. For instance, conversations with best friends and lovers were rated as more valuable than conversations with strangers. Goldsmith and Baxter (1996) similarly used diaries and other self-reports to look at the sorts of speech events typically experienced by college students. They found that most of the events were casual and informal and were typically not goal directed. The speech events differed depending on the type of relationship in which they occurred (e.g., small talk was relatively common among acquaintances, gossip was more common between close friends). In short, the routine discourse captured by these two studies appears to reflect the day-to-day quality of relationships and illustrates the way that relationships are constructed through communication.

Another line of study that highlights the principle of reflexivity centers on relationship narratives and accounts. As does everyday discourse, the stories that people tell about their relationships simultaneously reveal and influence relational quality. They offer a portrayal of the relationship, explaining how, when, or why partners behave in particular ways (Harvey, Weber, & Orbuch, 1990). As such, they define relational partners' roles relative to each other and to others in their social network.

A number of studies have indicated that the content of partners' narratives is associated with relational quality. For example, Buehlman, Gottman, and Katz (1992) found that married partners who told stories about overcoming obstacles together had more stable, satisfying relationships than those who did not. Flora and Segrin (2003) similarly found that dating and married couples who described their relationship as fond and affectionate tended to be relatively satisfied, whereas those who appraised their relationship as disappointing or chaotic tended to be relatively dissatisfied. Both studies suggested that people who tell positive stories about their shared history are likely to be happier with their partners.

Individuals' descriptions of their relationship can also affect the way they behave toward their partners. Because people often behave in ways that confirm their views of their relationship (Bruner, 1990), the views reflected in the narratives that individuals tell about their interpersonal affiliations can shape their behavior. People who describe their relationship as affectionate and resilient are likely to interpret their partner's behavior in light of that description and, in turn, are likely to behave in ways that support their portrayal (Sternberg, 1996). Moreover, because people are motivated to support the stories they tell (Murray & Holmes, 1994), stories often represent standards or prescriptions that individuals use to evaluate themselves, their relationship, and their partner (Vangelisti, Crumley, & Baker, 1999). Narratives delineate the rules that define interaction (Jorgenson & Bochner, 2004). When narrators praise certain behaviors or decry the violation of rules, they create and maintain prescriptions for close relationships.

Yet another line of work that exemplifies the reflexive nature of communication is research on relationship cultures. Those who study relationship cultures conceptualize interpersonal affiliations as having their own moral and social order that is enacted, in part, by private codes and interaction rules (e.g., Baxter, 1987). Relationship cultures reside within, and use the conventions of, a larger culture, but they also create routines and practices that mark them as unique (Burleson et al., 2000).

The literature on interpersonal communication has revealed many ways in which relationship cultures are created and sustained through social interaction. Couples may develop personal idioms (Bell & Healey, 1992; Hopper, Knapp, & Scott, 1981) and other private codes and symbols (Baxter, 1987). For instance, some partners generate special nicknames for each other (e.g., Boo, Creampuff) or unique expressions of affection (e.g., pulling on an earlobe

to say "I love you"). They also create routines and rituals (Bruess & Pearson, 1997), keep secrets (Vangelisti, 1994), and establish unique interaction rules (Planalp, 1993) that make them a more cohesive unit and that help them define relationship norms.

Complexity

Complexity refers to the idea, advocated by interactional systems theorists, that communication conveys multiple meanings simultaneously on different levels of analysis (Bateson, 1972; Watzlawick, Beavin, & Jackson, 1967). One of the most basic distinctions made by theorists illustrating this principle involves the difference between the literal content of a given message and its pragmatic meaning. The second level of meaning has been labeled the *command* (Reusch & Bateson, 1951), *relationship* (Watzlawick et al., 1967), *illocutionary* (Searle, 1969), or *episodic* (Frentz & Farrell, 1976) *meaning*. It indicates a particular type of relationship that exists between the speaker and the recipient by denoting an action (e.g., an apology) and the social implications of the action (e.g., whether it displays affection or hostility). In contrast to the literal content of a message, this second level of meaning is typically implicit rather than explicit.

Researchers who conceive communication from a relational perspective (e.g., Rogers & Millar, 1988) have defined this second level of meaning by focusing on the concepts of relationship symmetry and complementarity (dominance). They have noted how symmetry and complementarity are displayed in the features of individual messages (e.g., a question that elaborates on a prior utterance rather than disconfirms it) as well as in the sequences of messages. Other researchers have examined the pragmatic aspects of communication by assessing acts of communication rather than the content of messages. Indeed, most of the literature on couples' conflict looks at how partners negotiate conflict rather than what they fight about (Sillars & Canary, 2013).

The multiple meanings reflected in any given message are further complicated by several other qualities of communication. One of these is that any given message may serve multiple functions simultaneously. Most researchers have agreed that communication can serve informative, expressive, and persuasive functions. Many, however, have advocated for more specific function categories on the basis of the idea that the more specific categories are theoretically useful. For instance, Street and Cappella (1985) argued that messages can serve several functions, such as coherence, intimacy, positive reinforcement, impression management, control, persuasion, and dominance–power. Other scholars have identified functions of particular types of communication, including nonverbal communication (Argyle, 1988), self-disclosure (Derlega & Grzelak, 1979), social support (Wills, 1985), and secrets (Vangelisti, 1994). Although cataloguing the various functions of messages offers an indication of the complexity involved in any interaction, considering the way in which those functions operate together makes the complexity even more apparent. Researchers have yet to decipher whether, for example, the multifunctionality of communication is an additive process or an integrative one (Jacobs, 2002).

In addition to serving multiple functions, any act of communication can, and typically does, address multiple goals. Communication researchers have long acknowledged that messages address multiple goals (Berger, 2004; Wilson & Feng, 2007). As noted by Caughlin (2010), those advocating this position share several assumptions. First, they maintain that communication is purposeful—that is, it is concerned with achieving some desired outcome. Second, they argue that individuals frequently pursue multiple goals simultaneously. For instance, when people seek social support, they may also want to be viewed by others as competent and self-sufficient. Third, they suggest that communication goals often conflict with one another. Individuals' own goals may conflict (e.g., a goal to obtain social support may conflict with a goal to be seen as competent), and individuals' goals may also conflict with the goals of others (e.g., one's goal to obtain social support might conflict with a partner's goal to engage in leisure activity).

The goals and functions of communication are further complicated by the fact that messages—as well as their goals and functions—are interpreted on the basis of the messages that precede and follow them (Duck, 2002). That is, every act of communication is generated in, and interpreted in terms of, a milieu of other communicative acts that can modify its meaning.

Researchers interested in the complex nature of communication are almost invariably confronted with questions about individuals' ability to deal with all the tasks associated with interaction. When people interact with others, they must detect multiple, rapidly changing signals; interpret the various meanings of each signal in terms of multiple messages, functions, and goals; and then respond in an appropriate manner on the basis of their own potentially conflicting goals—all almost instantaneously (Bavelas & Coates, 1992). People manage these various tasks and deal with the complexity of communication in several ways. For instance, they are selective about which messages (or aspects of messages) they attend to (Sperber & Wilson, 1995). Similarly, they conserve their cognitive resources and use mental shortcuts to interpret and respond to others' communication. Indeed, Sillars, Roberts, Leonard, and Dun (2000) found that the demands of communication constrain individuals' cognitions and behavior in very real ways. When they examined the thoughts spouses reported during marital conflict, they found that those thoughts rarely reflected complex cognitive tasks such as perspective taking. In addition, as noted by Kellermann (1991), much of people's communication behavior is automatic. Kellermann argued that although communication is inherently strategic and goal oriented, it is often monitored and adjusted outside individuals' awareness. Many communication strategies, therefore, are tacitly acquired and used.

Ambiguity

Ambiguity in communication involves underdeterminancy in that messages are ambiguous because they only partially encode the meanings they are used to express (Carston, 2002). When people interpret the literal content of a message, they often have to make inferences to understand the speaker's intent. When they interpret the pragmatic or relational aspects of a message, however, ambiguity is much more apparent. For instance, many of the so-called communication "behaviors" that researchers study in the context of personal relationships (e.g., agreement, disconfirmation, validation) actually require observers to make inferences about partners' goals, attitudes, and relational history to deduce their meaning. Communication is ambiguous because any given message can have multiple meanings (e.g., "We haven't talked in a while" can be a descriptive statement, a request, a criticism, or a challenge). In addition, any message can serve multiple functions simultaneously (e.g., "When will you be ready?" can function as a request for information, a suggestion to change one's behavior, or a criticism of the current course of action).

It is tempting to assume that ambiguity in communication is inversely associated with intimacy—that because intimate partners typically have more information about each other than those who are not intimate, their communication is less ambiguous. In fact, several theories are predicated on the idea that long-term relational partners reveal a good deal of information to each other and that the increased information they have in turn often facilitates their relationship by reducing uncertainty, increasing intimacy, or both (Altman & Taylor, 1973; Berger & Calabrese, 1975). Although research has demonstrated that close relationships are characterized by shared knowledge that helps partners understand the implicit meanings in their communication (Planalp & Garvin-Doxas, 1994), studies have also shown that relational partners regularly deal with ambiguous messages and that, in some cases, partners may be more susceptible to ambiguity than would be expected. For instance, because partners tend to have a good deal of information about each other, they may assume they understand each other well (when they do not) or overlook ambiguity (when it is present; Mortensen, 1997). Partners can also encounter events in their relationship that increase their uncertainty (Planalp & Honeycutt, 1985). This increased uncertainty can influence previously held beliefs about the relationship and can create further ambiguity. In addition, partners may use ambiguity strategically in their relationship to obtain some goal. For example, they may be intentionally indirect or vague in an effort to show politeness (e.g., "That's an interesting outfit"), avoid conflict (e.g., "You know how much I care about our relationship"), or maintain personal boundaries (e.g., "I just need a little space"; Bavelas, Black, Chocill, & Mullett, 1990).

Although ambiguity in communication is clearly manifest in the different ways that relational insiders and outsiders interpret partners' behavior (Surra & Ridley, 1991), research has suggested that even insiders to a relationship often see the same behavior differently. For example, parents' and adolescents' reports of family interaction often diverge (e.g., Noller & Callan, 1988). Likewise, husbands and wives involved in conflict tend to perceive each other's communication in different ways. They may, for instance, attribute negative intent to their partners' behavior when none is reported by the partners, or they may make overly positive attributions about their own behavior (Sillars & Canary, 2013).

The incongruity in partners' views of each other's behavior is explicated, in part, by the weak associations between the amount of information that partners disclose to each other and their mutual understanding. Research has suggested that the links between the direct disclosure of information and understanding, if any exist, are weak (Sillars, 1998; Thomas & Fletcher, 1997). Simpson, Ickes, and Blackstone (1995) argued that one reason for the lack of connection between these two variables is that relational partners may be motivated to maintain inaccurate views of each other. They suggested that this "motivated misunderstanding" may serve partners by quelling their fears or alleviating their insecurities—even if only temporarily.

Outcome Indeterminancy

Communication is indeterminant in that the effects of messages on individuals or relationships are variable rather than fixed. In other words, the outcomes of communication are contextual, historical, personal, and cultural. Because any given message can result in varying outcomes and because a variety of outcomes may be linked to a single message, explaining and predicting communication behavior is a challenging task.

The idea that outcomes can be achieved via different means and different starting points—commonly referred to as *equifinality*—is not a new one. Indeed, general systems theorists have long argued that researchers need to attend more closely to processes related to equifinality (Von Bertalanffy, 1968). The literature on communication in close relationships has supported this contention. Studies have indicated that relational partners can use different techniques to persuade each other (Witteman & Fitzpatrick, 1986), provide each other with support (Bolger, Zuckerman, & Kessler, 2000), disagree with each other (Sillars & Canary, 2013), and hurt each other's feelings (Vangelisti, 2007).

Although different strategies or messages can be used to achieve the same outcome, it is also the case that the same message can result in different outcomes. *Multifinality*, another element of general systems theory, is the notion that the same starting point can produce distinct outcomes. For example, a message or sequence of behavior that is interpreted as humorous or affectionate in one relationship may be seen as insulting in another. In line with this idea, researchers have found that the expression of negative affect is detrimental to some relationships but positively associated with satisfaction or unrelated to satisfaction in others (Fincham & Beach, 1999).

Although most researchers and theorists have acknowledged that communication is indeterminant, they have not always examined communication processes in ways that bring indeterminancy to light. In some cases, researchers' tendency to overlook indeterminacy may be related to cultural biases they have brought to their studies. For instance, in the early 1970s, following humanistic traditions in psychology, scholars emphasized the importance of self-disclosure to relational well-being. This overly optimistic view of disclosure was critiqued in the 1980s (e.g., Parks, 1982). After these critiques, researchers began to adopt a different approach to examining disclosure by focusing, for example, on the ways that couples balance disclosure and privacy (Petronio, 2002).

Another reason researchers have overlooked indeterminancy is that they have extensively used relational satisfaction to assess the influence of communication on relationships. Using satisfaction as the only, or the primary, measure of relational well-being is potentially problematic for several reasons (Sillars & Canary, 2013). For instance, it frames communication in clinical terms and encourages a focus on ostensibly high-impact behavior over more mundane behavior. Because the everyday, mundane

aspects of communication provide important information about the way people construct their relationships, discounting such communication is likely to result in a limited view of the links between daily communication and relational well-being. Additionally, dichotomizing relational partners into satisfied versus dissatisfied or adjusted versus maladjusted groups suggests that the communication that differentiates the two groups can be characterized as good versus bad or healthy versus unhealthy. Inasmuch as communication is indeterminant, such characterizations are misleading. Research has demonstrated, for instance, that good or skillful communication does not necessarily predict relationship satisfaction. Burleson and Denton (1997) found that couples they defined as skilled communicators did not differ with regard to marital satisfaction from those whom they defined as unskilled. These researchers suggested that couples who are dissatisfied may use skillful, sophisticated messages to hurt each other. Erbert and Duck (1997) further noted that dissatisfied couples may use positive communication behaviors in harmful ways (e.g., they may engage in excessive accommodation).

Summary

The five basic properties of communication reviewed—interdependence, reflexivity, complexity, ambiguity, and indeterminancy—help to clarify the ways that communication forms relationships as well as the ways relationships affect communication. These properties also provide a context for interpreting the complex and sometimes contradictory research on communication in close relationships, whether that research has emphasized individual or dyadic characteristics and patterns.

INDIVIDUAL CHARACTERISTICS AND PATTERNS

Much of the literature on communication in close relationships has examined the link between partners' thoughts or feelings about their relationship and relational quality. Although, as previously noted, relational quality has been narrowly defined, research has clearly shown that the way people think about themselves, their partners, and their associations with others reflects and shapes relational outcomes such as satisfaction. Similarly, the feelings that individuals express when they interact with their partners offer insights into the quality of their relationship.

Cognition

Three aspects of individuals' cognition in close relationships have received substantial attention from researchers. One of these is descriptive knowledge structures, or thoughts that reflect partners' predictions about the qualities that describe individuals and relationships. The second is evaluative knowledge structures, which reveal partners' beliefs or standards about the qualities that individuals and relationships should have (Baucom, Epstein, Sayers, & Sher, 1989). The third is explanatory knowledge structures, or cognitions that indicate the way in which people interpret behaviors and events associated with their own relationships.

Descriptive knowledge structures. Descriptive knowledge structures influence the way individuals construe information about their partners and the way they behave toward their partners. These "coherent frameworks of relational knowledge" (Planalp, 1985, p. 9) differ from knowledge structures traditionally discussed by psychologists (e.g., Markus, 1977) in that they are inherently social. That is, they define individuals in terms of their relationships with others. For example, relationship partners might have descriptive knowledge that focuses on the self (e.g., I am a good listener), the other (e.g., he is a generous person), or the relationship (e.g., we are kind to each other), but all three types of descriptive knowledge situate individuals within relationships.

Research on descriptive knowledge that is focused on the self has indicated that partners' self-representations affect their romantic relationships. For instance, Swann, Hixon, and De La Ronde (1992) found that people who viewed themselves in relatively negative ways (who had negative self-concepts) tended to be more committed to their marriages when their spouses also evaluated them in relatively negative ways. At the same time, as other researchers have shown, individuals who have

negative views of themselves tend to underestimate the strength of their partner's love for them and have relatively negative perceptions of their partner (Murray, Holmes, Griffin, Bellavia, & Rose, 2001; Murray, Rose, Bellavia, Holmes, & Kusche, 2002). Individuals' negative self-representations, in other words, can foster relationships in which partners view each other in negative ways. Moreover, partners' negative self-conceptions appear to be reinforced by their behavior. Murray, Bellavia, Rose, and Griffin (2003), for example, found that individuals who doubt themselves react to being hurt by behaving badly, and their partners rate them as being more selfish, needy, and overly dependent. Although they behave in ways that may undermine their relationships, those who have low self-esteem also engage in behaviors that often increase their partner's dependence on them (Murray et al., 2009).

Studies examining descriptive knowledge structures that focus on the other rather than the self have similarly indicated that individuals' cognitions can affect their behavior and their relationships. The influence of other-focused knowledge structures on behavior may be best illustrated by the well-known work of Snyder, Tanke, and Berscheid (1977). Snyder et al. conducted a study in which they informed one group of men (by showing them a photograph) that a woman with whom they were about to interact was attractive and informed another group (using another photograph) that the woman was unattractive. The men who believed they were going to interact with an attractive woman rated her more favorably than did those who thought they were going to interact with an unattractive woman. More important, the two groups of women behaved quite differently: The women who were deemed attractive were rated by outside observers as more socially skillful (based on a recording of their phone conversation) than were those deemed unattractive. In short, the men's randomly assigned impression of the women's physical attractiveness influenced the women's behavior, creating a self-fulfilling prophecy.

Another line of work that has illustrated the influence of other-oriented descriptive knowledge structures on relationships is research on rejection sensitivity. Rejection sensitivity occurs when individuals anxiously expect, readily perceive, and overly react to rejection from others (Downey & Feldman, 1996). People who are high in rejection sensitivity consistently view significant others as likely to reject their requests, decline their invitations, and disregard their needs. Downey and Feldman (1996) found that people high in rejection sensitivity more readily perceived rejection in the ambiguous or insensitive behavior of others. Furthermore, Downey, Freitas, Michaelis, and Khouri (1998) found that, during conflict interactions, women high in rejection sensitivity behaved in ways that elicited rejecting responses from their partners. Not surprisingly, both individuals high in rejection sensitivity and their partners were relatively dissatisfied with their relationships. Those who are high in rejection sensitivity also perceive that their partners are relatively dissatisfied (Downey & Feldman, 1996).

Clearly, descriptive knowledge structures focusing on the self or the other affect the way individuals conceive of, and behave in, their relationships. Although the potential impact of these two types of knowledge structures is profound, the influence of descriptive knowledge structures on relationships is more commonly discussed in terms of knowledge structures that focus on individuals' associations with other people. More specifically, a large body of research on adult attachment has articulated consistent associations between the way people represent their relationships and a number of important relational outcomes.

Research on adult attachment can be traced back to the work of Bowlby (1969), who argued that people develop internal working models of relationships on the basis of the interactions they have with attachment figures across the life span. These models have two parts or components. One part denotes the self and construes the self as either worthy or unworthy of love and caring, and the other represents the caregiver and portrays the caregiver as either sensitive or insensitive to the infant's needs.

Since Bowlby's (1969) groundbreaking work, researchers have repeatedly found that people who are secure—those who see themselves as worthy of love and who see others as sensitive to their needs—tend to be relatively well adjusted as individuals and

as relational partners (Cassidy & Shaver, 2008; Feeney & Noller, 1996). For example, those who are secure tend to have relationships that are more committed and satisfying than do those who are insecure. People who are secure also have higher self-esteem and more positive views of others, experience more positive and fewer negative emotions in their close relationships, and tend to be more comfortable expressing their personal feelings to their relationship partners (see Chapter 3, this volume).

Although Bowlby (1969) and many of the researchers who have followed him have suggested that the knowledge structures individuals develop in infancy influence their behavior in adulthood, they also recognize that these knowledge structures are dynamic and mutable (see Simpson, Collins, Tran, & Haydon, 2007). Indeed, Davila, Karney, and Bradbury (1999) noted that people's "past experiences, their current states of mind about relationships, and their experiences with partners all affect how secure they feel in relationships" (p. 798). Studies have shown that individuals' attachment orientations can be influenced by their psychological vulnerabilities, their attitudes toward their relationship (Davila et al., 1999), their perceptions of themselves and their partners (Simpson, Rholes, Campbell, & Wilson, 2003), and their interpersonal behavior (Little, McNulty, & Russell, 2010).

Evaluative knowledge structures. Whereas descriptive knowledge structures such as those that shape attachment orientations reveal individuals' predictions about the qualities that relationships will have, evaluative knowledge structures reflect people's beliefs about or standards for the qualities that individuals and relationships should have (Baucom et al., 1989). Evaluative knowledge structures, like descriptive knowledge structures, have been studied under many different labels, including relationship beliefs, implicit theories of relationships, relational standards, prototype interaction pattern models, and ideal standards. The concepts associated with each of these labels vary, but all involve the notion that individuals hold certain criteria that they use to evaluate their relationships.

The knowledge structures or criteria that people use to evaluate their relationships are central to a number of well-established theories and models, including social exchange theory (Huston & Burgess, 1979), equity theory (Walster, Walster, & Berscheid, 1978), interdependence theory (Thibaut & Kelley, 1959), the ideal standards model (Simpson, Fletcher, & Campbell, 2001), and the investment model (Rusbult, 1983). These perspectives (and others) suggest that individuals compare their current relationship to the evaluative criteria they hold and, on the basis of that comparison, assess the quality of their relationship. When people's criteria are met or exceeded, they tend to be relatively satisfied with their relationship. By contrast, when they perceive their criteria are unmet, they tend to be relatively dissatisfied.

Several studies have examined the link between individuals' evaluations of whether their criteria are met and their relational satisfaction. For instance, Vangelisti and Daly (1997) looked at commonly held relational standards and found that individuals who reported that their standards were fulfilled tended to be relatively satisfied with their relationships. By contrast, those who felt that their standards were unmet tended to be less satisfied. Similarly, Fletcher, Simpson, Thomas, and Giles (1999) studied the standards that people held for their relational partners. They found a positive link between relational satisfaction and individuals' tendency to report that their standards for their partner were fulfilled. Campbell, Simpson, Kashy, and Fletcher (2001) further found that people tend to be happier when they match their partner's ideal standards.

Explanatory knowledge structures. Although evaluative knowledge structures provide an indication of how people assess their associations with others, they do not offer much information about the way people interpret the behaviors and events that take place in their relationships. Explanatory knowledge structures reveal how individuals interpret relationship-relevant behaviors and events. The explanations that people generate to make sense of these behaviors and events are in turn associated with the way they feel about their relationships. For example, a substantial literature on attributions has demonstrated that the explanations individuals

provide for their partner's behavior are linked to their level of relational satisfaction (Bradbury & Fincham, 1990). People who attribute their partner's negative behavior to internal, stable causes (e.g., he was late because he is an inconsiderate person) tend to be relatively dissatisfied with their relationship, whereas those who attribute their partner's negative behavior to external, unstable causes (e.g., he was late because he got stuck in traffic) tend to be more satisfied. More broadly, those who emphasize the impact of their partner's negative behavior and deemphasize the effect of their partner's positive behavior tend to be unhappy with their relationship. Alternatively, individuals who highlight the influence of their partner's positive behavior and minimize the impact of his or her negative behavior tend to be relatively happy. As noted by Holtzworth-Munroe and Jacobson (1985), people who are relationally dissatisfied tend to make distress-maintaining attributions, and those who are satisfied tend to make more positive, relationship-enhancing attributions.

Although the link between partners' attributions and their relational satisfaction is bidirectional (Fincham & Bradbury, 1989), researchers interested in the deterioration of relational quality have studied whether attributions actually contribute to declines in partners' satisfaction over time. Longitudinal evidence has suggested that, indeed, people's explanations for their partner's behavior negatively influence marital satisfaction (Karney & Bradbury, 2000). Moreover, distress-maintaining attributions are associated with higher rates of negative behavior during problem-solving discussions, suggesting that distress-maintaining attributions and negative behavior may operate together to contribute to declines in relational quality (Bradbury, Beach, Fincham, & Nelson, 1996).

Research and theory on accounts of relationship events have similarly indicated that the explanations people generate for the events in their relationships affect the way they feel toward their partners. As noted by Harvey, Orbuch, and Weber (1992; also see Harvey et al., 1990), accounts are storylike narratives that individuals construct to explain certain life events. People are particularly likely to formulate accounts when they have experiences that are extremely stressful and negative. Researchers have examined individuals' explanations for traumatic events such as relationship dissolution (Sorenson, Russell, Harkness, & Harvey, 1993) and incest (Harvey, Orbuch, Chwalisz, & Garwood, 1991). Their findings have demonstrated that people who generate accounts to explain their negative experiences—and who disclose those accounts to close relationship partners—typically reap psychological and physical benefits. Other work has suggested that sharing stressful experiences with others not only affects the quality of people's relationships but can also influence their psychological and physical well-being (Pennebaker, 1990).

Affect

Clearly, the knowledge structures that people bring to their relationships influence, and are influenced by, their affective experiences. When their relationships are threatened, individuals who see themselves as worthy of love are likely to feel different than those who do not (e.g., Murray et al., 2003). People who believe that their standards for a romantic partner are being met probably experience different emotions toward their partner than those who do not (e.g., Fletcher et al., 1999). Similarly, those who explain their partner's behavior in positive, relationship-enhancing ways react differently when they are trying to resolve a problem with their partner than do those who do not (Bradbury et al., 1996).

Research on individuals' affective expressions in romantic relationships has generally indicated that dissatisfied partners communicate more negative affect, less positive affect, and more reciprocated negative affect than do those who are satisfied (Margolin & Wampold, 1981; Noller, 1984; Notarius & Johnson, 1982). Although partners who are dissatisfied often engage in fewer positive behaviors than those who are satisfied (Cutrona, 1996), negative behaviors tend to be the stronger predictor of satisfaction (Gottman & Levenson, 1986; Huston & Vangelisti, 1991; Jacobson, Waldron, & Moore, 1980; Markman, Rhoades, Stanley, Ragan, & Whitton, 2010; Wills, Weiss, & Patterson, 1974). Moreover, the ability of partners' negative behavior to predict their relational satisfaction holds over time. Longitudinal studies have shown that premarital

measures of negative affect are associated with satisfaction later in marriage (Kelly, Huston, & Cate, 1985; Markman, 1981). Expressions of negative affect predict declines in satisfaction over time when initial levels of satisfaction are controlled (Gottman & Krokoff, 1989; Levenson & Gottman, 1983). In addition, more negative communication early in marriage is associated with steeper declines in satisfaction over time (Karney & Bradbury, 1997).

Although the association between negative affective behaviors and relational satisfaction is robust, it is more complex than might be suggested by a cursory review of the literature. In fact, researchers and theorists who study the expression of affect in close relationships have argued that the association is complicated by several issues. One involves the unique function of positive affective behaviors. A number of researchers have noted that the impact of positive behaviors on satisfaction is more difficult to detect than the impact of negative behaviors because positive behaviors function in relatively subtle ways. For example, Fredrickson (2001) argued that the experience and expression of positive emotions functions both to broaden the range of individuals' thoughts and actions and to build resources that people can use to enhance their well-being. For this reason, the link between positive behaviors and relational satisfaction may be less direct than the one between negative behaviors and relational satisfaction. In a similar vein, Gable, Reis, Impett, and Asher (2004) suggested that sharing positive events—or capitalization—increases individuals' enjoyment of those events and builds their personal and social resources. On the basis of this argument, Reis et al. (2010) found that when individuals shared positive events with an enthusiastic listener, they perceived the value of those events as higher. Enthusiastic responses to shared positive events were also associated with more trust in and prosocial attitudes toward others.

Another issue that may complicate the relatively consistent link between negative affective behaviors and satisfaction involves timing. Negative affective behaviors can negatively influence satisfaction almost regardless of when they occur in a relationship. By contrast, positive affective behaviors may contribute to satisfaction only at particular moments in a relationship. For example, Cutrona (1996) argued that positive supportive behaviors tend to affect relational quality when partners experience substantial stress. Positive behaviors may preclude damage to a relationship under such conditions by alleviating the increased isolation and emotional withdrawal typically associated with stress.

The association between partners' negative behaviors and their satisfaction is also complicated when negative behaviors are examined in concert with positive behaviors. A number of studies have suggested that the influence of negative behaviors on satisfaction depends on partners' positive behaviors. For instance, Gottman and Levenson (1992) predicted that the ratio of positive to negative behaviors has a greater impact on couples' satisfaction than does the absolute frequency of either positive or negative behaviors. To test this prediction, they contrasted regulated couples (those in which both partners expressed more positivity than negativity) and unregulated couples (those in which both partners displayed more negativity than positivity). Gottman and Levenson found that regulated couples were more satisfied, less likely to have considered divorce, less likely to have separated, and less likely to have divorced than unregulated couples. In another longitudinal study, Huston and Chorost (1994) found that the link between negative affective behaviors and relational quality was moderated by partners' positive expressions of affection. Partners' expressions of affection, in other words, buffered the impact of negative behaviors on relational quality.

The effect of negative behaviors on satisfaction is further complicated by whether those behaviors are direct or indirect. Overall, Fletcher, Simpson, and Sibly (2009) examined the effectiveness of communication strategies that differed in terms of both valence and directness. They were interested in whether the various strategies produced desired changes in partners over time. Their findings revealed that direct negative strategies were initially perceived as ineffective, but that they were linked to increases in desired change over time as reported by the target of influence. McNulty and Russell (2010) similarly studied direct and indirect negative behaviors and found that direct negative behaviors

interacted with the severity of partners' problems to have an impact on satisfaction. The tendency of partners to engage in direct negative behavior was linked to decreases in satisfaction when couples addressed minor problems but was associated with more stable satisfaction when they addressed severe problems. In contrast, indirect negative behaviors were associated with lower levels of satisfaction, regardless of problem severity. McNulty and Russell noted that, over time, direct negative behaviors may encourage couples to face and resolve problems because they help to clarify the issues at hand.

DYADIC CHARACTERISTICS AND PATTERNS

The associations that have been found between negative and positive affective behaviors and relational satisfaction have enabled researchers to theorize about the ways in which one partner's behavior influences the other's satisfaction and vice versa. Although this type of theorizing has explained the links between individuals' behavior and their satisfaction, it is important to note that couples may interpret and respond to affective behavior in different ways. Some couples may interpret the expression of negative emotions as criticism or hostility (Gottman, 1994), whereas others may see similar expressions as a sign of intimacy or an opportunity for one partner to provide the other with social support (Graham, Huang, Clark, & Helgeson, 2008). In short, couples may develop characteristics and enact patterns together, as a dyad. Those characteristics and patterns may in turn affect the quality of their relationship.

The dyadic characteristics and patterns of interaction that characterize couples have been examined in at least two different ways. First, researchers have looked at partners' behaviors and attitudes and have used those data to classify couples into distinct types. Second, scholars have identified sequences of behavior and have studied the link between those sequences and couples' relationship satisfaction.

Couple Types
On the basis of work by Kantor and Lehr (1975), Fitzpatrick (1977, 1988) identified eight factors that

influence couples' role enactment: (a) conflict avoidance, (b) assertiveness, (c) sharing, (d) ideology of traditionalism, (e) ideology of uncertainty and change, (f) temporal regularity, (g) undifferentiated space, and (h) autonomy. She used these factors to develop a typology for classifying married couples. Fitzpatrick's work emphasized variations in couples' patterns of behavior and beliefs and examined associations between partners' ongoing patterns of interaction and their marital satisfaction.

Fitzpatrick (1977, 1988) identified four different types of couples. Couples who are traditional have relatively conventional ideological values about marriage and are resistant to change. They tend to be highly interdependent and relatively low in autonomy, reporting that they share time, space, and leisure activities together. Traditional partners are not highly assertive, but they do not avoid conflict. Independent couples have fairly nonconventional values about marriage and family life. They accept uncertainty and change, and they value autonomy. Because independent partners do not make assumptions about the roles that men and women should play in relationships, they sometimes have difficulty negotiating their daily schedules. They maintain separate physical spaces but are also quite interdependent and tend to engage in conflict rather than avoid it. In separate couples, partners have a conventional ideology about marriage but a nonconventional ideology toward individual freedom. They usually report less companionship and sharing than do traditional or independent couples, and they need more differentiated space. Separate couples tend to avoid conflict when possible. Finally, mixed couples are those in which each spouse has a different definition of the relationship (e.g., the wife is independent and the husband is traditional).

Rather than emphasizing factors that affect role enactment, Gottman (1993) used partners' behavior during conflict episodes to classify couples. His typology includes three couple types. Partners in validator couples respect each other's point of view on a broad range of topics and try to compromise when they disagree. They tend to display moderate negative affect, moderate positive affect, and a great deal of neutral interaction. Volatile couples, by

contrast, are comfortable with disagreements. They fight openly and often. They typically express a great deal of negative affect but express even more positive affect and relatively little neutral interaction. Finally, avoider couples are uncomfortable with conflict and do what they can to evade it. They may walk away from conflict, placate each other, or give each other the silent treatment. As such, they demonstrate little negative affect, little positive affect, and a great deal of neutral interaction.

Although typologies such as the ones put forth by Fitzpatrick (1977) and Gottman (1993) are limited by the behaviors and attitudes they use to categorize couples, they offer a number of advantages over research that has characterized couples as either high or low in relational satisfaction. For instance, the typologies allow for increased variability because they do not place partners at one of two ends on a continuum of marital satisfaction. That is, they include couples who are moderately satisfied and those who disagree about the extent to which they are satisfied. Similarly, because the typologies are based on characteristics other than partners' satisfaction, they can be used to identify the criteria couples use in evaluating their relationship as happy or unhappy. Finally, the typologies help to identify and explain couples' communication patterns. Rather than focusing on individual communication behaviors and their links to satisfaction, the typologies examine behaviors that typically cluster together and, as a consequence, provide data about how those behaviors operate together to affect various outcomes (Koerner & Fitzpatrick, 2013).

Behavioral Sequences

Using partners' behaviors and attitudes to describe different types of couples is one way to examine the dyadic characteristics and interaction patterns that characterize romantic partnerships. Another way to study couples (as dyads) is to focus on the behaviors that typify partners' interactions and then examine the associations between those behaviors and relational outcomes. Research examining the behavioral patterns of couples has generally suggested that couples who are dissatisfied tend to engage in more negative behaviors and fewer positive behaviors than do those who are satisfied. Dissatisfied couples enact more negative nonverbal cues (Gottman, 1979; Noller, 1982) and engage in fewer supportive behaviors (Pasch & Bradbury, 1998) than do satisfied couples. Those who are unhappy with their relationship also report having more frequent conflict, spending more time in conflict, and trying to avoid conflict more than those who are happy (Schaap, Buunk, & Kerkstra, 1988). When they are engaged in conflict, the behavior of distressed couples is more negative than that of couples who are not distressed. Unhappy partners criticize each other more, complain more, disagree more, and use more sarcasm than do happy partners (Revenstorf, Vogel, Wegener, Hahlweg, & Schindler, 1980; Ting-Toomey, 1983). They also express more contempt, act more defensively, and engage in more avoidance or stonewalling than nondistressed couples (Gottman, 1994). (See Sillars & Canary, 2013, for a review of the couple conflict literature.)

The relatively negative interactions of couples who are dissatisfied hint at how the behavior of one distressed partner may affect the behavior of the other. For instance, when one distressed partner complains, the other is more likely to respond with a complaint than with a compliment or an inquiry about the complaint (Gottman, Markman, & Notarius, 1977). The initial complaint, in other words, sets in motion a cycle of negative behavior. Whether negative behavioral sequences enacted by couples involve complaints or other negative cues, they serve as an indicator of relational satisfaction. In fact, research has suggested that couples who are dissatisfied have a tendency to engage in two sequences of behavior that set them apart from satisfied couples.

Negative affect reciprocity.   One of the behavioral sequences that distinguishes dissatisfied couples from satisfied couples is the reciprocation of negative affect. Studies have indicated that individuals who are relationally dissatisfied respond to their partner's negative behaviors with more negative behaviors in return (Weiss & Heyman, 1990). Dissatisfied partners are often inclined to view negative behaviors as attacks, and consequently they are less likely to respond in positive or neutral ways. Alternatively, those who are dissatisfied might be particularly attuned to their partner's negative behaviors and might thus be more likely to reciprocate them. A study by Gaelick, Bodenhausen, and Wyer (1985) suggested that the latter may more often be true. Gaelick et al. found that people had a tendency to reciprocate the emotion that they thought their partner was conveying. They also found that individuals had difficulty decoding their partner's expressions of love but were more accurate in decoding their partner's expressions of hostility. Because individuals were able to decode hostility more accurately, they reciprocated hostility more frequently than love. In short, the ease with which people were able to interpret expressions of hostility created a situation in which they were more likely to reciprocate hostility than love. Given the tendency of distressed partners to engage in negative, potentially hostile behaviors, this effect may be even stronger in couples who are dissatisfied.

The influence of negative affect reciprocity on relational satisfaction may also depend on whether one partner reciprocates more than the other. Levenson and Gottman (1985), for example, found that declines in marital satisfaction were associated with more reciprocity of husbands' negative affect by wives and less reciprocity of wives' negative affect by husbands. In other words, the negative affect of husbands—and wives' tendency to reciprocate that negative affect in kind—had more impact on their relationship than did wives' affect and husbands' tendency to reciprocate.

Demand–withdraw.   The notion that one partner may be more likely to reciprocate negative affect than the other is relevant to another behavioral sequence that distinguishes satisfied and dissatisfied partners. This sequence—typically labeled the *demand–withdraw pattern*—occurs when one partner attempts to discuss a problem and engage the other in interaction (she or he demands) and the other attempts to avoid the conversation (she or he withdraws). Studies have repeatedly shown that the demand–withdraw pattern is associated with marital dissatisfaction and divorce (e.g., Fogarty, 1976; Heavey, Christensen, & Malamuth, 1995; Noller, Feeney, Bonnell, & Callan, 1994; Schaap et al., 1988).

Research on the demand–withdraw pattern has demonstrated that wives engage in demanding behavior more often than do husbands and that husbands have a greater tendency to withdraw than do wives (Baucom, Notarius, Burnett, & Haefner, 1990; Christensen & Shenk, 1991; Gottman & Levenson, 1988). A number of theorists have argued that this gender difference can be explained by social structural factors (e.g., Christensen & Heavey, 1990; Heavey et al., 1993; Klinetob & Smith, 1996). Those advocating a social structural explanation have suggested that wives usually have less power in their marriages than do husbands, and as a result wives are more likely than husbands to desire changes in their relationship. Wives' greater desire for change may motivate them to discuss their current situation, identify problems, and demand change. Husbands, in contrast, tend to have more power in marriages than do wives. As a consequence, they may not desire as much change in their relationships and may not be motivated to engage in demanding behaviors. In fact, men's greater tendency to withdraw may be a way for them to maintain the status quo.

Studies conducted to examine the social structural explanation for demand–withdraw have looked at couples' interactions when the topic of conversation focused on something that wives wanted to change and contrasted them with interactions when the topic focused on something that husbands wanted to change. When husbands desired more change than wives, the tendency of wives to demand and husbands to withdraw was no longer evident (Christensen & Heavey, 1990; Heavey et al., 1993). In fact, one investigation revealed that the tendency of husbands to demand and wives to withdraw was more evident than the tendency of wives to demand and husbands to withdraw (Klinetob & Smith, 1996).

Although these findings are compelling, some studies have suggested that the demand–withdraw pattern is driven by factors other than individuals' power and their desire for change. For example, Caughlin and Vangelisti (1999) found that partners' desire for change was associated both with wife demand–husband withdraw and with husband demand–wife withdraw. These researchers argued that people's desire for change may be linked to their tendency to engage in both demanding and withdrawing behaviors. Caughlin (2002) also found that couples' tendency to engage in the demand–withdraw pattern was positively associated with

increases in wives' relational satisfaction. He argued that the impact of demand–withdraw on marital outcomes may vary on the basis of how long couples have been together. Caughlin also suggested that couples may engage in demand–withdraw in different ways and that distinctions in the way in which partners enact demanding and withdrawing behaviors may affect their marital satisfaction.

DIRECTIONS FOR FUTURE STUDY

The goal of this chapter was to illustrate the role of communication in romantic relationships. With this aim in mind, I examined five basic properties of communication—interdependence, reflexivity, complexity, ambiguity, and indeterminancy. Using those properties as a backdrop, I reviewed some of the processes that characterize communication in romantic relationships. These processes were discussed with regard to both individual and dyadic characteristics and patterns. More specifically, at the individual level, I described the cognitive and affective patterns that are associated with communication; at the dyadic level, I examined the characteristics of particular couple types and behavioral sequences that affect and are affected by relational outcomes. Although the reviewed literature has clearly illustrated the importance of communication in relationships, it has also raised a number of issues that provide researchers and theorists with several interesting directions for future study.

One of the most obvious directions for future research involves the identification and description of interaction sequences that influence, and are influenced by, relationships. Researchers need to continue to focus their attention on behavioral sequences and patterns of interaction rather than individual behaviors, strategies, or messages. Work on the demand–withdraw pattern (Christensen & Heavey, 1990) and the reciprocity of negative affect (Levenson & Gottman, 1985) has yielded important findings about the effect of communication behaviors on partners' relationships. These findings suggest that communication messages, much like relationships, may be most clearly understood when examined in terms of their connections with each other. Yet, even these well-studied patterns leave a number of issues unaddressed. For instance, as noted by Caughlin (2002), distinctions in the ways in which partners engage in the demand–withdraw pattern may affect their relational satisfaction. Similarly, as suggested by the work of Reis et al. (2010) on sharing positive events, behavioral sequences may influence satisfaction in positive rather than negative ways. Exploring issues such as these would be fruitful.

Another avenue for future study involves examining communication in conjunction with affect and physiology in close relationships. A large body of research has shown that relationships influence people's physical and mental well-being (Berkman, 1995; Myers, 1999). Increasingly, researchers are looking to communication as a possible mechanism linking relationships to physical and mental health. For instance, partners' negative communication during problem-solving interactions has been associated with delays in the healing of wounds (Kiecolt-Glaser et al., 2005) and decreased immune functioning (Kiecolt-Glaser et al., 1997). Affectionate communication from spouses has been linked to lower levels of cortisol (a stress hormone; Floyd & Riforgiate, 2008), whereas hurtful interactions are associated with higher cortisol levels (Priem, McLaren, & Solomon, 2010). Saxbe and Repetti (2010) further found that partners' cortisol levels were linked: The cortisol level of one partner was positively associated with the cortisol level of the other over several days. Although the aforementioned findings have suggested that romantic partners' communication, affect, and physiology operate together to influence well-being, they have also raised important questions about the causal links among these variables and whether other variables, such as relational quality, influence those associations. For instance, Saxbe and Repetti (2010) found that marital satisfaction weakened the association between partners' cortisol levels, but only for wives.

Researchers and theorists also need to consider the influence of relational, historical, and cultural contexts on communication processes. Communication, like relationships, is affected by the environments in which it is situated. The ways in which partners interact are shaped by the quality of their relationship, historical and political events, and each partner's cultural values. Although a substantial literature has examined

communication behavior that is situated in satisfying and dissatisfying relationships, satisfaction is not the only variable that makes up relational contexts. Individuals' history together, their perceptions of each other, and their beliefs about their relationship all create a framework for their partnership. Moreover, social, cultural, and historical contexts affect how partners communicate and the ways in which they interpret communication (Brown, Werner, & Altman, 2006; Gaines, Williams, & Mickelson, 2013). Examining the complex associations between communication and the multiple contexts that affect it will be challenging but will undoubtedly advance the field of personal relationships.

References

Altman, I., & Taylor, D. A. (1973). *Social penetration: The development of interpersonal relationships.* New York, NY: Holt, Rinehart & Winston.

Argyle, M. (1988). *Bodily communication* (2nd ed.). Madison, CT: International Universities Press.

Bateson, G. (1972). *Steps to an ecology of mind.* New York, NY: Ballantine.

Baucom, D. H., Epstein, N., Sayers, S., & Sher, T. G. (1989). The role of cognitions in marital relationships: Definitional, methodological, and conceptual issues. *Journal of Consulting and Clinical Psychology, 57,* 31–38. doi:10.1037/0022-006X.57.1.31

Baucom, D. H., Notarius, C. I., Burnett, C. K., & Haefner, P. (1990). Gender differences and sex-role identity in marriage. In F. D. Fincham & T. N. Bradbury (Eds.), *The psychology of marriage* (pp. 150–171). New York, NY: Guilford Press.

Bavelas, J. B., Black, A., Chocill, N., & Mullett, J. (1990). *Equivocal communication.* Newbury Park, CA: Sage.

Bavelas, J. B., & Coates, L. (1992). How do we account for the mindfulness of face-to-face dialogue? *Communication Monographs, 59,* 301–305.

Baxter, L. A. (1987). Symbols of relationship identity in relationship cultures. *Journal of Social and Personal Relationships, 4,* 261–280. doi:10.1177/026540758700400302

Baxter, L. A., & Bullis, C. (1986). Turning points in developing romantic relationships. *Human Communication Research, 12,* 469–493. doi:10.1111/j.1468-2958.1986.tb00088.x

Baxter, L. A., & Montgomery, B. M. (1996). *Relating: Dialogues and dialectics.* New York, NY: Guilford Press.

Beebe, B., Jaffe, J., Feldstein, S., Mays, K., & Alson, D. (1985). Interpersonal timing: The application of an adult dialogue model to mother-infant vocal and kinesic interactions. In T. M. Field & N. A. Fox (Eds.), *Social perception in infants* (pp. 217–248). Norwood, NJ: Ablex.

Bell, R. A., & Healey, J. G. (1992). Idiomatic communication and interpersonal solidarity in friends' relational cultures. *Human Communication Research, 18*, 307–335. doi:10.1111/j.1468-2958.1992.tb00555.x

Berger, C. R. (2004). Communication: A goal-directed, plan-guided process. In D. R. Roskow-Ewoldsen & J. L. Monahan (Eds.), *Communication and social cognition: Theories and methods* (pp. 47–70). Mahwah, NJ: Erlbaum.

Berger, C. R., & Calabrese, R. J. (1975). Toward a developmental theory of interpersonal communication. *Human Communication Research, 1*, 99–112. doi:10.1111/j.1468-2958.1975.tb00258.x

Berger, C. R., Gardner, R. R., Clatterbuck, G. W., & Schulman, L. S. (1976). Perceptions of information sequencing in relationship development. *Human Communication Research, 3*, 29–469. doi:10.1111/j.1468-2958.1976.tb00502.x

Berkman, L. F. (1995). The role of social relations in health promotion. *Psychosomatic Medicine, 57*, 245–254.

Bolger, N., Zuckerman, A., & Kessler, R. C. (2000). Invisible support and adjustment to stress. *Journal of Personality and Social Psychology, 79*, 953–961. doi:10.1037/0022-3514.79.6.953

Bowlby, J. (1969). *Attachment and loss: Vol. 1. Attachment.* New York, NY: Basic Books.

Bradbury, T. N., Beach, S. R. H., Fincham, F. D., & Nelson, G. (1996). Attributions and behavior in functional and dysfunctional marriages. *Journal of Consulting and Clinical Psychology, 64*, 569–576. doi:10.1037/0022-006X.64.3.569

Bradbury, T. N., & Fincham, F. D. (1990). Attributions in marriage: Review and critique. *Psychological Bulletin, 107*, 3–33. doi:10.1037/0033-2909.107.1.3

Brown, B. B., Wernre, C. M., & Altman, I. (2006). Relationships in home and community environments: A transactional and dialectic analysis. In A. L. Vangelisti & D. Perlman (Eds.), *The Cambridge handbook of personal relationships* (pp. 673–693). New York, NY: Cambridge University Press.

Bruess, C. J. S., & Pearson, J. C. (1997). Interpersonal rituals in marriage and adult friendship. *Communication Monographs, 64*, 25–46. doi:10.1080/03637759709376403

Bruner, J. (1990). *Acts of meaning.* Cambridge, MA: Harvard University Press.

Buehlman, K., Gottman, J. M., & Katz, L. (1992). How a couple views their past predicts their future: Predicting divorce from an oral interview. *Journal of Family Psychology, 5*, 295–318. doi:10.1037/0893-3200.5.3-4.295

Bugental, D. B. (2000). Acquisition of the algorithms of social life: A domain-based approach. *Psychological Bulletin, 126*, 187–219. doi:10.1037/0033-2909.126.2.187

Burleson, B. R., & Denton, W. H. (1997). The relationship between communication skill and marital satisfaction: Some moderating effects. *Journal of Marriage and the Family, 59*, 884–902. doi:10.2307/353790

Burleson, B. R., Metts, S., & Kirch, M. W. (2000). Communication in close relationships. In C. Hendrick & S. S. Hendrick (Eds.), *Close relationships: A sourcebook* (pp. 245–258). Thousand Oaks, CA: Sage. doi:10.4135/9781452220437.n18

Campbell, L., Simpson, J. A., Kashy, D. A., & Fletcher, G. J. O. (2001). Ideal standards, the self, and flexibility of ideals in close relationships. *Personality and Social Psychology Bulletin, 27*, 447–462. doi:10.1177/0146167201274006

Carston, R. (Ed.). (2002). *Thoughts and utterances: The pragmatics of explicit communication.* Cambridge, MA: Blackwell. doi:10.1002/9780470754603

Cassidy, J., & Shaver, P. R. (2008). *Handbook of attachment: Theory, research, and clinical applications* (2nd ed.). New York, NY: Guilford Press.

Caughlin, J. P. (2002). The demand/withdraw pattern of communication as a predictor of marital satisfaction over time: Unresolved issues and future directions. *Human Communication Research, 28*, 49–85.

Caughlin, J. P. (2010). A multiple goals theory of personal relationships: Conceptual integration and program review. *Journal of Social and Personal Relationships, 27*, 824–848. doi:10.1177/0265407510373262

Caughlin, J. P., & Huston, T. L. (2002). A contextual analysis of the association between demand/withdraw and marital satisfaction. *Personal Relationships, 9*, 95–119. doi:10.1111/1475-6811.00007

Caughlin, J. P., & Vangelisti, A. L. (1999). Desire for change in one's partner as a predictor of the demand/withdraw pattern of marital communication. *Communication Monographs, 66*, 66–89. doi:10.1080/03637759909376463

Christensen, A., & Heavey, C. L. (1990). Gender and social structure in the demand/withdraw pattern of marital conflict. *Journal of Personality and Social Psychology, 59*, 73–81. doi:10.1037/0022-3514.59.1.73

Christensen, A., & Shenk, J. L. (1991). Communication, conflict, and psychological distance in nondistressed, clinic, and divorcing couples. *Journal of Consulting and Clinical Psychology, 59*, 458–463. doi:10.1037/0022-006X.59.3.458

Cutrona, C. (1996). *Social support in couples.* Thousand Oaks, CA: Sage.

Davila, J., Karney, B. R., & Bradbury, T. N. (1999). Attachment change processes in the early years of marriage. *Journal of Personality and Social Psychology, 76,* 783–802. doi:10.1037/0022-3514.76.5.783

Derlega, V. J., & Grzelak, J. (1979). Appropriateness of self-disclosure. In G. J. Chelune (Ed.), *Self-disclosure: Origins, patterns, and implications of openness in interpersonal relationships* (pp. 151–176). San Francisco, CA: Jossey-Bass.

Downey, G., & Feldman, S. (1996). The implications of rejection sensitivity for intimate relationships. *Journal of Personality and Social Psychology, 70,* 1327–1343. doi:10.1037/0022-3514.70.6.1327

Downey, G., Freitas, A., Michaelis, B., & Khouri, H. (1998). The self-fulfilling prophecy in close relationships: Rejection sensitivity by romantic partners. *Journal of Personality and Social Psychology, 75,* 545–560. doi:10.1037/0022-3514.75.2.545

Duck, S. (1995). Talking relationships into being. *Journal of Social and Personal Relationships, 12,* 535–540. doi:10.1177/0265407595124006

Duck, S. (2002). Hypertext in the key of G: Three types of "history" as influences on conversational structure and flow. *Communication Theory, 12,* 41–62. doi:10.1111/j.1468-2885.2002.tb00258.x

Duck, S., Rutt, D. J., Hurst, M. H., & Strejc, H. (1991). Some evident truths about conversations in everyday relationships: All communications are not created equal. *Human Communication Research, 18,* 228–267. doi:10.1111/j.1468-2958.1991.tb00545.x

Duck, S. W., & Pond, K. (1988). Friends, Romans, countrymen, lend me your retrospective data: Rhetoric and reality in personal relationships. In C. Hendrick (Ed.), *Review of social psychology and personality: Vol. 10. Close relationships* (pp. 3–27). Newbury Park, CA: Sage.

Erbert, L. A., & Duck, S. W. (1997). Rethinking satisfaction in personal relationships from a dialectical perspective. In R. J. Sternberg & M. Hojjat (Eds.), *Satisfaction in close relationships* (pp. 190–216). New York, NY: Guilford Press.

Feeney, J., & Noller, P. (1996). *Adult attachment.* Thousand Oaks, CA: Sage.

Fincham, F. D., & Beach, S. R. H. (1999). Conflict in marriage: Implications of working with couples. *Annual Review of Psychology, 50,* 47–77. doi:10.1146/annurev.psych.50.1.47

Fincham, F. D., & Bradbury, T. N. (1989). The impact of attributions in marriage: An individual difference analysis. *Journal of Social and Personal Relationships, 6,* 69–85. doi:10.1177/026540758900600105

Fisher, B. A. (1978). *Perspectives on human communication.* New York, NY: Macmillan.

Fitzpatrick, M. A. (1977). A typological approach to communication in relationships. In B. Rubin (Ed.), *Communication yearbook 1* (pp. 263–275). Rutgers, NJ: Transaction Books.

Fitzpatrick, M. A. (1988). *Between husbands and wives.* Newbury Park, CA: Sage.

Fitzpatrick, M. A., Vangelisti, A. L., & Firman, S. M. (1994). Marital communication and change during pregnancy. *Personal Relationships, 1,* 101–122. doi:10.1111/j.1475-6811.1994.tb00057.x

Fletcher, G. J. O., Simpson, J. A., Thomas, G., & Giles, L. (1999). Ideals in intimate relationships. *Journal of Personality and Social Psychology, 76,* 72–89. doi:10.1037/0022-3514.76.1.72

Flora, J., & Segrin, C. (2003). Relational well-being and perceptions of relational history in married and dating couples. *Journal of Social and Personal Relationships, 20,* 515–536. doi:10.1177/02654075030204005

Floyd, K., & Riforgiate, S. (2008). Affectionate communication received from spouses predicts stress hormone levels in healthy adults. *Communication Monographs, 75,* 351–368.

Fogarty, T. F. (1976). Marital crisis. In P. J. Guerin (Ed.), *Family therapy: Theory and practice* (pp. 325–334). New York, NY: Gardner.

Fredrickson, B. L. (2001). The role of positive emotions in positive psychology: The broaden-and-build theory of positive emotions. *American Psychologist, 56,* 218–226. doi:10.1037/0003-066X.56.3.218

Frentz, T. S., & Farrell, T. B. (1976). Language-action: A paradigm for communication. *Quarterly Journal of Speech, 62,* 333–349. doi:10.1080/00335637609383348

Gable, S. L., Reis, T., Impett, E., & Asher, E. R. (2004). What do you do when things go right? The intrapersonal and interpersonal benefits of sharing positive events. *Journal of Personality and Social Psychology, 87,* 228–245. doi:10.1037/0022-3514.87.2.228

Gaelick, L., Bodenhausen, G., & Wyer, R. S. (1985). Emotional communication in close relationships. *Journal of Personality and Social Psychology, 49,* 1246–1265. doi:10.1037/0022-3514.49.5.1246

Gaines, S. O., Jr., Williams, S. L., & Mickelson, K. D. (2013). Support communication in culturally diverse families: The role of stigma. In A. L. Vangelisti (Ed.), *The Routledge handbook of family communication* (2nd ed.; pp. 205–221). New York, NY: Routledge.

Goldsmith, D. J., & Baxter, L. A. (1996). Constituting relationships in talk: A taxonomy of speech events in social and personal relationships. *Human Communication Research, 23,* 87–114. doi:10.1111/j.1468-2958.1996.tb00388.x

Goldstein, M. H., & Schwade, J. A. (2008). Social feedback to infants' babbling facilitates rapid phonological learning. *Psychological Science, 19,* 515–523. doi:10.1111/j.1467-9280.2008.02117.x

Gottman, J. M. (1979). *Marital interaction.* New York, NY: Academic Press.

Gottman, J. M. (1993). The roles of conflict engagement, escalation, and avoidance in marital interaction: A longitudinal view of five types of couples. *Journal of Consulting and Clinical Psychology, 61,* 6–15. doi:10.1037/0022-006X.61.1.6

Gottman, J. M. (1994). *What predicts divorce: The relationship between marital processes and marital outcomes.* Hillsdale, NJ: Erlbaum.

Gottman, J. M., & Krokoff, L. J. (1989). Marital interaction and satisfaction: A longitudinal view. *Journal of Consulting and Clinical Psychology, 57,* 47–52. doi:10.1037/0022-006X.57.1.47

Gottman, J. M., & Levenson, R. W. (1986). Assessing the role of emotion in marriage. *Behavioral Assessment, 8,* 31–48.

Gottman, J. M., & Levenson, R. W. (1988). The social psychophysiology of marriage. In P. Noller & M. A. Fitzpatrick (Eds.), *Perspectives on marital interaction* (pp. 182–200). Philadelphia, PA: Multilingual Matters.

Gottman, J. M., & Levenson, R. W. (1992). Marital processes predictive of later dissolution: Behavior, physiology, and health. *Journal of Personality and Social Psychology, 63,* 221–233. doi:10.1037/0022-3514.63.2.221

Gottman, J. M., Markman, H. J., & Notarius, C. L. (1977). The topography of marital conflict: A sequential analysis of verbal and nonverbal behavior. *Journal of Marriage and the Family, 39,* 461–477. doi:10.2307/350902

Graham, S. M., Huang, J. Y., Clark, M. S., & Helgeson, V. S. (2008). The positives of negative emotions: Willingness to express negative emotions promotes relationships. *Personality and Social Psychology Bulletin, 34,* 394–406. doi:10.1177/0146167207311281

Gruenbaum, B., Depowski, N., Shaw, K., & Bortfeld, H. (2013). Infant communication. In A. L. Vangelisti (Ed.), *The Routledge handbook of family communication* (2nd ed., pp. 241–255). New York, NY: Routledge.

Harvey, J. H., Orbuch, T. L., Chwalisz, K., & Garwood, G. (1991). Coping with sexual assault: The roles of account-making and confiding. *Journal of Traumatic Stress, 4,* 515–531. doi:10.1002/jts.2490040406

Harvey, J. H., Orbuch, T. L., & Weber, A. L. (Eds.). (1992). *Attributions, accounts, and close relationships.* New York, NY: Springer-Verlag.

Harvey, J. H., Weber, A. L., & Orbuch, T. L. (1990). *Interpersonal accounts: A social psychological perspective.* Oxford, England: Basil Blackwell.

Harwood, J., Rittenour, C. E., & Lin, M. C. (2013). Family communication in later life. In A. L. Vangelisti (Ed.), *The Routledge handbook of family communication* (2nd ed., 112–126). New York, NY: Routledge.

Heavey, C. L., Christensen, A., & Malamuth, N. M. (1995). The longitudinal impact of demand and withdrawal during marital conflict. *Journal of Consulting and Clinical Psychology, 63,* 797–801. doi:10.1037/0022-006X.63.5.797

Heavey, C. L., Layne, C., & Christensen, A. (1993). Gender and conflict structure in marital interaction: A replication and extension. *Journal of Consulting and Clinical Psychology, 61,* 16–27. doi:10.1037/0022-006X.61.1.16

Holtzworth-Munroe, A., & Jacobson, N. S. (1985). Causal attributions of married couples: When do they search for causes? What do they conclude when they do? *Journal of Personality and Social Psychology, 48,* 1398–1412. doi:10.1037/0022-3514.48.6.1398

Hopper, R., Knapp, M. L., & Scott, L. (1981). Couples' personal idioms: Exploring intimate talk. *Journal of Communication, 31,* 23–33. doi:10.1111/j.1460-2466.1981.tb01201.x

Huston, T. L., & Burgess, R. L. (1979). Social exchange in developing relationships: An overview. In R. L. Burgess & T. L. Huston (Eds.), *Social exchange in developing relationships* (pp. 3–28). New York, NY: Academic Press.

Huston, T. L., & Chorost, A. F. (1994). Behavioral buffers on the effect of negativity on marital satisfaction: A longitudinal study. *Personal Relationships, 1,* 223–239. doi:10.1111/j.1475-6811.1994.tb00063.x

Huston, T. L., & Vangelisti, A. L. (1991). Socioemotional behavior and satisfaction in marital relationships. *Journal of Personality and Social Psychology, 61,* 721–733. doi:10.1037/0022-3514.61.5.721

Jacobs, S. (2002). Language and interpersonal communication. In M. L. Knapp & J. A. Daly (Eds.), *Handbook of interpersonal communication* (pp. 213–239). Thousand Oaks, CA: Sage.

Jacobson, N. S., Waldron, H., & Moore, D. (1980). Toward a behavioral profile of marital distress. *Journal of Consulting and Clinical Psychology, 48,* 696–703. doi:10.1037/0022-006X.48.6.696

Jorgenson, J., & Bochner, A. P. (2004). Imaging families through stories and rituals. In A. L. Vangelisti (Ed.), *Handbook of family communication* (pp. 513–538). Mahwah, NJ: Erlbaum.

Kantor, D., & Lehr, W. (1975). *Inside the family: Toward a theory of family process.* San Francisco, CA: Jossey-Bass.

Karney, B. R., & Bradbury, T. N. (1995). The longitudinal course of marital quality and stability: A review of theory, method, and research. *Psychological Bulletin, 118,* 3–34. doi:10.1037/0033-2909.118.1.3

Karney, B. R., & Bradbury, T. N. (1997). Neuroticism, marital interaction, and the trajectory of marital satisfaction. *Journal of Personality and Social Psychology, 72,* 1075–1092. doi:10.1037/0022-3514.72.5.1075

Karney, B. R., & Bradbury, T. N. (2000). Attributions in marriage: State or trait? A growth curve analysis. *Journal of Personality and Social Psychology, 78,* 295–309. doi:10.1037/0022-3514.78.2.295

Kellermann, K. (1991). The conversational MOP II: Progression through scenes in discourse. *Human Communication Research, 17,* 385–414. doi:10.1111/j.1468-2958.1991.tb00238.x

Kelly, C., Huston, T. L., & Cate, R. M. (1985). Premarital relationship correlates of the erosion of satisfaction in marriage. *Journal of Social and Personal Relationships, 2*, 167–178. doi:10.1177/0265407585022004

Kiecolt-Glaser, J. K., Glaswer, R., Cacioppo, J. T., MacCallum, R. C., Snydersmith, M., Kim, C., & Malarkey, W. B. (1997). Marital conflict in older adults: Endocrinological and immunological correlates. *Psychosomatic Medicine, 59*, 339–349.

Kiecolt-Glaser, J. K., Loving, T. J., Stowell, J. R., Malarkey, W. B., Lemeshow, S., Dickinson, S., & Glaser, R. (2005). Hostile marital interactions, proinflammatory cytokine production, and wound healing. *Archives of General Psychiatry, 62*, 1377–1384.

Klinetob, N. A., & Smith, D. A. (1996). Demand-withdraw communication in marital interaction: Tests of interspousal contingency and gender role hypotheses. *Journal of Marriage and the Family, 58*, 945–957. doi:10.2307/353982

Knapp, M. L., & Taylor, E. H. (1994). Commitment and its communication in romantic relationships. In A. L. Weber & J. H. Harvey (Eds.), *Perspectives on close relationships* (pp. 153–175). Needham Heights, MA: Allyn & Bacon.

Koerner, A. F., & Fitzpatrick, M. A. (2013). Communication in intact families. In A. L. Vangelisti (Ed.), *The Routledge handbook of family communication* (2nd ed., pp. 177–195). New York, NY: Routledge.

Levenson, R. W., & Gottman, J. M. (1983). Marital interaction: Physiological linkage and affective exchange. *Journal of Personality and Social Psychology, 45*, 587–597. doi:10.1037/0022-3514.45.3.587

Levenson, R. W., & Gottman, J. M. (1985). Physiological and affective predictors of change in relationship satisfaction. *Journal of Personality and Social Psychology, 49*, 85–94. doi:10.1037/0022-3514.49.1.85

Little, K. C., McNulty, J. K., & Russell, V. M. (2010). Sex buffers intimates against the negative implications of attachment insecurity. *Personality and Social Psychology Bulletin, 36*, 484–498. doi:10.1177/0146167209352494

Margolin, G., & Wampold, B. (1981). Sequential analysis of conflict and accord in distressed and nondistressed marital partners. *Journal of Consulting and Clinical Psychology, 49*, 554–567. doi:10.1037/0022-006X.49.4.554

Markman, H. J. (1981). Prediction of marital distress: A 5-year follow-up. *Journal of Consulting and Clinical Psychology, 49*, 760–762. doi:10.1037/0022-006X.49.5.760

Markman, H. J., Rhoades, G. K., Stanley, S. M., Ragan, E. P., & Whitton, S. W. (2010). The premarital communication roots of marital distress and divorce: The first five years of marriage. *Journal of Family Psychology, 24*, 289–298. doi:10.1037/a0019481

Markus, H. (1977). Self-schemata and processing information about the self. *Journal of Personality and Social Psychology, 35*, 63–78. doi:10.1037/0022-3514.35.2.63

McNulty, J. K., & Russell, V. M. (2010). When "negative" behaviors are positive: A contextual analysis of the long-term effects of problem-solving behaviors on changes in relationship satisfaction. *Journal of Personality and Social Psychology, 98*, 587–604. doi:10.1037/a0017479

Meltzoff, A. N., & Moore, M. K. (1977). Imitation of facial and manual gestures by human neonates. *Science, 198*, 75–78. doi:10.1126/science.198.4312.75

Mortensen, C. D. (1997). *Miscommunication*. Thousand Oaks, CA: Sage.

Murray, S. L., Aloni, M., Holmes, J. G., Derrick, J. L., Stinson, D. A., & Leder, S. (2009). Fostering partner dependence as trust insurance: The implicit contingencies of the exchange script in close relationships. *Journal of Personality and Social Psychology, 96*, 324–348. doi:10.1037/a0012856

Murray, S. L., Bellavia, G. M., Rose, P., & Griffin, D. W. (2003). Once hurt, twice hurtful: How perceived regard regulates daily marital interactions. *Journal of Personality and Social Psychology, 84*, 126–147. doi:10.1037/0022-3514.84.1.126

Murray, S. L., & Holmes, J. G. (1994). Storytelling in close relationships: The construction of confidence. *Personality and Social Psychology Bulletin, 20*, 650–663. doi:10.1177/0146167294206004

Murray, S. L., Holmes, J. G., Griffin, D. W., Bellavia, G., & Rose, P. (2001). The mismeasure of love: How self-doubt contaminates relationship beliefs. *Personality and Social Psychology Bulletin, 27*, 423–436. doi:10.1177/0146167201274004

Murray, S. L., Rose, P., Bellavia, G. M., Holmes, J. G., & Kusche, A. G. (2002). When rejection stings: How self-esteem constrains relationship-enhancement processes. *Journal of Personality and Social Psychology, 83*, 556–573. doi:10.1037/0022-3514.83.3.556

Myers, D. G. (1999). Close relationships and the quality of life. In D. Kahneman, E. Diener, & N. Schwartz (Eds.), *Well-being: The foundations of hedonic psychology* (pp. 374–380). New York, NY: Russell Sage Foundation.

Noller, P. (1982). Channel consistency and inconsistency in the communications of married couples. *Journal of Personality and Social Psychology, 43*, 732–741. doi:10.1037/0022-3514.43.4.732

Noller, P. (1984). *Nonverbal communication and marital interaction*. Oxford, England: Pergamon Press.

Noller, P., & Callan, V. J. (1988). Understanding parent-adolescent interactions: Perceptions of family members and outsiders. *Developmental Psychology, 24*, 707–714. doi:10.1037/0012-1649.24.5.707

Noller, P., Feeney, J. A., Bonnell, D., & Callan, V. (1994). A longitudinal study of conflict in early marriage. *Journal of Social and Personal Relationships, 11*, 233–252. doi:10.1177/0265407594112005

Notarius, C. I., & Johnson, J. S. (1982). Emotional expression in husbands and wives. *Journal of Marriage and the Family, 44*, 483–489. doi:10.2307/351556

Overall, N. C., Fletcher, G. J. O., Simpson, J. A., & Sibly, C. G. (2009). Regulating partners in intimate relationships: The costs and benefits of different communication strategies. *Journal of Personality and Social Psychology, 96*, 620–639. doi:10.1037/a0012961

Papoušek, M., Papoušek, H., & Haekel, M. (1987). Didactic adjustments in fathers' and mothers' speech to their 3-month-old infants. *Journal of Psycholinguistic Research, 16*, 491–516. doi:10.1007/BF01073274

Parks, M. R. (1982). Ideology in interpersonal communication: Off the couch and into the world. In M. Burgoon (Ed.), *Communication yearbook 6* (pp. 79–107). Beverly Hills, CA: Sage.

Pasch, L. A., & Bradbury, T. N. (1998). Social support, conflict, and the development of marital dysfunction. *Journal of Consulting and Clinical Psychology, 66*, 219–230. doi:10.1037/0022-006X.66.2.219

Pennebaker, J. (1990). *Opening up.* New York, NY: Morrow.

Petronio, S. (2002). *Boundaries of privacy: Dialectics of disclosure.* Albany, NY: SUNY Press.

Planalp, S. (1985). Relational schemata: A test of alternative forms of relational knowledge as guides to communication. *Human Communication Research, 12*, 3–29. doi:10.1111/j.1468-2958.1985.tb00064.x

Planalp, S. (1993). Friends' and acquaintances' conversations II: Coded differences. *Journal of Social and Personal Relationships, 10*, 339–354. doi:10.1177/0265407593103003

Planalp, S., & Garvin-Doxas, K. (1994). Using mutual knowledge in conversation: Friends as experts on each other. In S. Duck (Ed.), *Dynamics of relationships* (pp. 1–26). Thousand Oaks, CA: Sage.

Planalp, S., & Honeycutt, J. M. (1985). Events that increase uncertainty in personal relationships. *Human Communication Research, 11*, 593–604. doi:10.1111/j.1468-2958.1985.tb00062.x

Reis, H. T., Smith, S. M., Tsai, F., Charmichael, C. L., Caprariello, P. A., Rodrigues, A., & Maniaci, M. R. (2010). Are you happy for me? How sharing positive events with others provides personal and interpersonal benefits. *Journal of Personality and Social Psychology, 99*, 311–329. doi:10.1037/a0018344

Reusch, J., & Bateson, G. (1951). *The social matrix of psychiatry.* New York, NY: Norton.

Revenstorf, D., Vogel, B., Wegener, C., Hahlweg, K., & Schindler, L. (1980). Escalation phenomena in interaction sequences: An empirical comparison of distressed and non-distressed couples. *Behavioral Analysis and Modification, 4*, 97–115.

Rogers, L. E. (1998). The meaning of relationship in relational communication. In R. L. Conville & L. E. Rogers (Eds.), *The meaning of "relationship" in interpersonal communication* (pp. 69–81). Westport, CT: Praeger.

Rogers, L. E., & Millar, F. E. (1988). Relational communication. In S. Duck (Ed.), *Handbook of personal relationships* (pp. 289–305). London, England: Wiley.

Rusbult, C. E. (1983). A longitudinal test of the investment model: The development (and deterioration) of satisfaction and commitment in heterosexual involvements. *Journal of Personality and Social Psychology, 45*, 101–117. doi:10.1037/0022-3514.45.1.101

Saxbe, D., & Repetti, R. L. (2010). For better or worse? Coregulation of couples' cortisol levels and mood states. *Journal of Personality and Social Psychology, 98*, 92–103.

Schaap, C., Buunk, B., & Kerkstra, A. (1988). Marital conflict resolution. In P. Noller & M. A. Fitzpatrick (Eds.), *Perspectives on marital interaction* (pp. 203–244). Philadelphia, PA: Multilingual Matters.

Searle, J. R. (1969). *Speech acts.* London, England: Cambridge University Press.

Sillars, A., Roberts, L. J., Leonard, K. E., & Dun, T. (2000). Cognition during marital conflict: The relationships of thought and talk. *Journal of Social and Personal Relationships, 17*, 479–502. doi:10.1177/0265407500174002

Sillars, A. L. (1998). (Mis)understanding. In B. H. Spitzberg & W. R. Cupach (Eds.), *The dark side of relationships* (pp. 73–102). Mahwah, NJ: Erlbaum.

Sillars, A. L., & Canary, D. J. (2013). Conflict and relational quality in families. In A. L. Vangelisti (Ed.), *The Routledge handbook of family communication* (2nd ed., pp. 338–357). New York, NY: Routledge.

Sillars, A. L., & Vangelisti, A. L. (2006). Communication: Basic properties and their relevance to relationship research. In A. L. Vangelisti & D. Perlman (Eds.), *The Cambridge handbook of personal relationships* (pp. 331–351). New York, NY: Cambridge University Press.

Simpson, J., Ickes, W., & Blackstone, T. (1995). When the head protects the heart: Empathic accuracy in dating relationships. *Journal of Personality and Social Psychology, 69*, 629–641. doi:10.1037/0022-3514.69.4.629

Simpson, J. A., Collins, W. A., Tran, S., & Haydon, K. C. (2007). Attachment and the experience and expression of emotions in adult romantic relationships: A developmental perspective. *Journal of Personality and Social Psychology, 92*, 355–367. doi:10.1037/0022-3514.92.2.355

Simpson, J. A., Fletcher, G. J. O., & Campbell, L. (2001). The structure and function of ideal standards in close relationships. In G. J. O. Fletcher & M. Clark (Eds.), *The*

Blackwell handbook in social psychology: Interpersonal processes (pp. 86–106). Oxford, England: Blackwell.

Simpson, J. A., Rholes, W. S., Campbell, L., & Wilson, C. L. (2003). Changes in attachment orientations across the transition to parenthood. *Journal of Experimental Social Psychology, 39*, 317–331. doi:10.1016/S0022-1031(03)00030-1

Snyder, M., Tanke, E. D., & Berscheid, E. (1977). Social perception and interpersonal behavior: On the self-fulfilling nature of social stereotypes. *Journal of Personality and Social Psychology, 35*, 656–666. doi:10.1037/0022-3514.35.9.656

Sorenson, K. A., Russell, S. M., Harkness, D. J., & Harvey, J. H. (1993). Account-making, confiding, and coping with the ending of a close relationship. *Journal of Social Behavior and Personality, 8*, 73–86.

Sperber, D., & Wilson, D. (1986). *Relevance: Communication and cognition* (2nd ed.). Boston, MA: Blackwell.

Sternberg, R. J. (1996). Love stories. *Personal Relationships, 3*, 59–79. doi:10.1111/j.1475-6811.1996.tb00104.x

Street, R. L., Jr., & Cappella, N. (1985). Sequence and pattern in communicative behavior: A model and commentary. In R. L. Street, Jr., & J. N. Cappella (Eds.), *Sequence and pattern in communicative behavior* (pp. 243–276). London, England: Edward Arnold.

Surra, C. A., & Ridley, C. (1991). Multiple perspectives on interaction: Participants, peers, and observers. In B. M. Montgomery & S. W. Duck (Eds.), *Studying interpersonal interaction* (pp. 35–55). New York, NY: Guilford Press.

Swann, W. B., Jr., Hixon, J. G., & De La Ronde, C. (1992). Embracing the bitter "truth": Negative self concepts and marital commitment. *Psychological Science, 3*, 118–121. doi:10.1111/j.1467-9280.1992.tb00010.x

Thibaut, J. W., & Kelley, H. H. (1959). *The social psychology of groups*. New York, NY: Wiley.

Thomas, G., & Fletcher, G. J. O. (1997). Empathic accuracy in close relationships. In W. Ickes (Ed.), *Empathic accuracy* (pp. 194–217). New York, NY: Guilford Press.

Ting-Toomey, S. (1983). An analysis of verbal communication patterns in high and low marital adjustment groups. *Human Communication Research, 9*, 306–319. doi:10.1111/j.1468-2958.1983.tb00701.x

Van Egeren, L. A., & Barratt, M. S. (2004). The development and origins of communication: Interactional systems in infancy. In A. L. Vangelisti (Ed.), *Handbook of family communication* (pp. 287–310). Mahwah, NJ: Erlbaum.

Vangelisti, A. L. (1994). Family secrets: Forms, functions, and correlates. *Journal of Social and Personal Relationships, 11*, 113–135. doi:10.1177/0265407594111007

Vangelisti, A. L. (2007). Communicating hurt. In B. H. Spitzberg & W. R. Cupach (Eds.), *The dark side of interpersonal communication* (2nd ed., pp. 121–142). Mahwah, NJ: Erlbaum.

Vangelisti, A. L., Crumley, L., & Baker, J. (1999). Family portraits: Stories as standards for family relationships. *Journal of Social and Personal Relationships, 16*, 335–368. doi:10.1177/0265407599163004

Vangelisti, A. L., & Daly, J. A. (1997). Gender differences in standards for romantic relationships. *Personal Relationships, 4*, 203–219. doi:10.1111/j.1475-6811.1997.tb00140.x

Von Bertalanffy, L. (1968). *General system theory: Foundations, development, applications*. New York, NY: Braziller.

Walster, E., Walster, G. W., & Berscheid, E. (1978). *Equity: Theory and research*. Boston, MA: Allyn & Bacon.

Watzlawick, P., Beavin, J., & Jackson, D. D. (1967). *Pragmatics of human communication: A study of interactional patterns, pathologies, and paradoxes*. New York, NY: Norton.

Weiss, R. L., & Heyman, R. E. (1990). Observation of marital interaction. In F. D. Fincham & T. N. Bradbury (Eds.), *The psychology of marriage: Basic issues and applications* (pp. 87–117). New York, NY: Guilford Press.

Wills, T. A. (1985). Supportive functions of interpersonal relationships. In S. Cohen & L. Syme (Eds.), *Social support and health* (pp. 61–82). Orlando, FL: Academic Press.

Wills, T. A., Weiss, R. L., & Patterson, G. R. (1974). A behavioral analysis of the determinants of marital satisfaction. *Journal of Consulting and Clinical Psychology, 42*, 802–811. doi:10.1037/h0037524

Wilson, S. R., Cameron, K. A., & Whipple, E. E. (1997). Regulative communication strategies within mother-child interactions: Implications for the study of reflection-enhancing parental communication. *Research on Language and Social Interaction, 30*, 73–92. doi:10.1207/s15327973rlsi3001_3

Wilson, S. R., & Feng, H. (2007). Interaction goals and message production: Conceptual and methodological developments. In D. R. Roskos-Ewoldsen & J. L. Monahan (Eds.), *Communication and social cognition: Theories and methods* (pp. 71–95). Mahwah, NJ: Erlbaum.

Wilson, S. R., Whipple, E. E., & Grau, J. (1996). Reflection-enhancing regulative communication: How do parents vary across misbehavior types and child resistance? *Journal of Social and Personal Relationships, 13*, 553–569. doi:10.1177/0265407596134005

Witteman, H., & Fitzpatrick, M. A. (1986). Compliance gaining in marital interaction: Power bases, processes, and outcomes. *Communication Monographs, 53*, 130–143. doi:10.1080/03637758609376132

Zimmerman, F. J., Gilkerson, J., Richards, J. A., Christakis, D. A., Xu, D., Gray, S., & Yapanel, U. (2009). Teaching by listening: The importance of adult-child conversations to language development. *Pediatrics, 124*, 342–349. doi:10.1542/peds.2008-2267

CHAPTER 15

POWER AND SOCIAL INFLUENCE IN RELATIONSHIPS

Jeffry A. Simpson, Allison K. Farrell, M. Minda Oriña, and Alexander J. Rothman

The fundamental concept in social science is power, in the same sense in which energy is the fundamental concept in physics.. . . The laws of social dynamics are laws which can only be stated in terms of power. (Russell, 1938)

As the philosopher Bertrand Russell observed, power plays a central role in everyday social interactions, and it serves as an organizing principle in the social and behavioral sciences (Reis, Collins, & Berscheid, 2000). Given its paramount importance, one might expect power would hold a privileged place in the field of social psychology and particularly in the study of relationships. Although there are major theoretical statements on what power is (e.g., French & Raven, 1959; Thibaut & Kelley, 1959) and how it should affect relationship dynamics (e.g., Huston, 1983), and there are isolated pockets of research on how power influences interpersonal outcomes, power has never been a hotbed of theoretical or empirical activity. One overarching goal of this chapter is to begin to change this state of affairs.

There are several reasons why power has not become a central, organizing construct within either social psychology or the field of interpersonal relationships. First, the construct of power has multiple components, making it challenging to define and measure. This, in turn, has made it difficult to interpret the effects that the amount of power wielded by each partner has on important relationship or individual outcomes. Second, most prior studies of power in relationships have been descriptive and have relied on global assessments of power (e.g., "In general, how much power or influence do you have over your partner?"). Partners in established relationships, however, often have and may exert different amounts of power in different decision-making domains (e.g., financial, sexual, future plans), and global conceptualizations and measures of power do not assess—and often may not predict—domain-specific areas of power in relationships, especially in close and committed relationships. In addition, the degree to which people are accurately aware of the power dynamics in their relationships remains unclear. Overreliance on self-report measures may have masked some of the actual processes of power and influence in many relationships. Despite these challenges, understanding power and the influence strategies and tactics that individuals use to get what they want from their relationship partners is essential to understanding a host of important relationship dynamics and outcomes (Reis et al., 2000).

Although power can be (and has been) defined in different ways, we provisionally define power as the ability of one individual in a relationship (the influence agent) to exert influence on another person (the target of influence) so that the influence agent obtains the specific outcomes he or she wants in a given situation while being able to resist influence attempts by the target. We define influence strategies as the higher level goals and interpersonal approaches that influence agents use to try to

http://dx.doi.org/10.1037/14344-015
APA Handbook of Personality and Social Psychology: Vol. 3. Interpersonal Relations, M. Mikulincer and P. R. Shaver (Editors-in-Chief)

persuade targets. Most influence strategies exist along two dimensions: directness (direct vs. indirect) and valence (positive vs. negative). Direct strategies entail overt, visible, and unambiguous attempts to influence another person, whereas indirect strategies involve more covert, less visible, and more subtle forms of influence. Positive strategies entail the use of promises or rewards to engender influence, whereas negative strategies often focus on the use of threats or punishments. These two dimensions, which are fairly orthogonal, result in four basic types of influence: direct–positive, direct–negative, indirect–positive, or indirect–negative approaches (Overall, Fletcher, Simpson, & Sibley, 2009). Influence strategies are conveyed via the use of coordinated sets of influence tactics (e.g., coercion, autocracy, reasoning, manipulation), which are chosen and used to help achieve the influence agent's higher level goals or objectives. As a result, the use and effectiveness of different influence strategies and tactics ought to depend on the type and amount of power that an influence agent holds over a potential target of influence, such as his or her current romantic partner, as well as the target of influence's type and amount of power. As we discuss later, however, the amount of power that an individual holds in relation to his or her partner in a given domain (e.g., financial decision making, household duties) should also affect how both partners think, feel, behave, and attempt to influence each other during their daily interactions. Power differences and the use of specific influence strategies and tactics should also have an impact on short-term and long-term relationship outcomes, ranging from relationship satisfaction and commitment to relationship stability across time. In addition, power differences may affect the cognitive, behavioral, and emotional tendencies of one or both partners within a relationship. As we show, without knowing which relationship partner holds what kind or amount of power in certain decision-making areas, it may be difficult to understand and predict the actions of either partner and the ultimate trajectory of their relationship.

Our chapter is divided into four sections. In the first section, we review six major theoretical perspectives on power: social power theory (French &

Raven, 1959), resource theory (Blood & Wolfe, 1960; Wolfe, 1959), interdependence theory (Kelley & Thibaut, 1978; Thibaut & Kelley, 1959), dyadic power theory (Dunbar & Burgoon, 2005; Rollins & Bahr, 1976), power within relationships theory (Huston, 1983), and power-approach theory (Keltner, Gruenfeld, & Anderson, 2003). While doing so, we discuss each theoretical perspective with respect to five key questions concerning the nature of power and influence in relationships.

In the second section, we review the empirical literature on power and influence, focusing primarily on the use, expression, and consequences of power in close (usually romantic) relationships. We discuss how power and influence have traditionally been measured, how power affects what partners think, feel, and do in different relationship settings, how power is linked to the use of different influence strategies and tactics, and how it relates to gender and being the weak-link (less dependent) partner in a relationship.

In the third section, we present a dyadic model of power and social influence in relationships that incorporates and builds on some of the core principles contained in the six major theoretical perspectives. This model, termed the *dyadic power–social influence model,* specifies how the characteristics of each relationship partner are linked to the type and amount of power that each partner is able to use in the relationship, the influence strategies and tactics that each partner can use, and some of the personal and relational outcomes that are likely to be experienced by each partner as a result of power and influence.

In the final section, we describe a stage model of how power is likely to operate in relationships across time as they develop, grow, and change. We also discuss promising directions for future research on power and influence in relationships, highlighting what makes the study of power particularly challenging to conduct in the context of established relationships.

THEORETICAL PERSPECTIVES

Theoretical perspectives from social psychology, communication studies, and family science have all informed research on power and the use of influence strategies and tactics within relationships. In this first section, we review the six most influential theories of power and influence, both from within and outside the relationship literature. Although these theories vary in which components of power and influence they emphasize, they tend to include related constructs and construe power in fairly similar ways. To clarify how each theoretical perspective complements or contrasts with the others, we have identified five dimensions on which these theories can be compared and contrasted. The following five questions provide an organizing framework for this analysis (see Table 15.1):

1. *What is power?* How does each theory define power? Is power merely the potential to influence others, or does it require intentional action?
2. *Is power dyadic?* Does the conceptualization of power consider the relative degree of power between partners in a relationship?
3. *What are the primary sources of power?* Where does power in relationships come from? Which factors or domains matter the most in determining which partner has greater power within a relationship?
4. *How is power expressed or communicated?* How is power expressed or conveyed during interactions between relationship partners? What specific influence strategies or tactics are displayed?
5. *What are the outcomes of (not) having power?* How does the power dynamic between partners in a relationship affect both each partner individually (e.g., his or her thoughts, emotions, self-esteem) and also the relationship (e.g., its level of commitment, satisfaction, stability) over time?

Social Power Theory

One of the first major theories of power was proposed by French and Raven (1959). According to their social power theory, power is defined as the potential to exert influence on another person, whether it be a stranger, a casual acquaintance, a coworker, a friend, or a romantic partner. Social influence, in turn, is the process through which social power is wielded in interpersonal contexts via the use of different influence strategies and their underlying tactics. Social influence occurs when the presence (either actual or implied) or the actions of one person (the influence agent) produce a change in the beliefs, attitudes, or behavior of another person (the target of influence).

The most important contribution of French and Raven's (1959) theory was the specification of six major bases (sources) of power. Each power base is believed to be associated with the use of different influence strategies and tactics, each of which in turn has unique effects on the targets of influence. Reward power stems from a target's perception that an influence agent has the ability to provide him or her with tangible or intangible objects that the target wants if the target adopts certain beliefs, attitudes, or behaviors the agent desires. This base of power, which tends to be associated with the use of positive reinforcement, is frequently used by parents when they try to cajole their children to engage in desired behaviors (e.g., sitting quietly through a concert) with the promise of an eventual reward (e.g., getting ice cream once it is over). Coercive power exists when a target perceives an agent has the ability to punish him or her for either doing something the agent does not like or not doing something the agent wants. Parents often use this base of power to control undesirable, aversive, or dangerous behaviors with threats of punishment. Reward and coercive power are basic sources of power because they do not require targets to have much understanding of the social norms, relationship status, or information or expertise about a topic to be effective.

The four other bases (sources) of power require greater social understanding and awareness to operate effectively. Legitimate power occurs when the target perceives that an influence agent has the right to affect the target, who then must comply with the agent's request. This type of power is witnessed when one person (a more powerful agent) holds a socially sanctioned role or position that another person (a less powerful target) acknowledges and respects, such as when a boss interacts with an employee about completing a new task. Referent power occurs when a target identifies with (i.e., wants to emulate) an influence agent, who is someone he or she admires greatly. This base of

TABLE 15.1

Major Power Theories

Theory	What is power?	Is power dyadic?	What are the sources or bases of power?	How is power expressed or communicated in interactions?	What are the outcomes of (not) having power?
Social power theory (French & Raven, 1959)	The potential for influence	No	Reward, coercive, legitimate, referent, expert, informational	Through influence processes	—
Resource theory (Blood & Wolfe, 1960)	The ability (potential or actual) of an individual to change the behavior of other members in the social system	Yes; theory considers relative access to resources between partners	Relative access to important or valued resources	—	—
Interdependence theory (Thibaut & Kelley, 1959)	The ability of one person to directly influence the quality of outcomes of another person	Yes; theory considers relative dependence between partners	Relative dependence, fate control, behavior control, expertise	Through power strategies that elevate one's own power and reduce others' power	The more powerful partner can dictate outcomes for both partners
Dyadic power theory (Rollins & Bahr, 1976)	The ability or potential to influence or control the behavior of another person	Yes; theory considers relative power, authority, and control between partners	Perceptions of relative resources and authority	Increased perceived power → increased control attempts → increased power	—
Power within relationships theory (Huston, 1983)	The ability to achieve one's goals by intentionally influencing the partner	Yes; theory considers the traits, relationship norms, and environment of both partners	Reward, coercive, legitimate, referent, expert, informational	Through intentional, deliberate influence tactics	The more powerful partner can dictate outcomes for both partners
Power-approach theory (Keltner et al., 2003)	An individual's relative capacity to modify others' internal states	Yes; theory considers relative access and desire for resources	Holding desired resources, being able to administer punishments	Through providing or withholding resources or administering punishments	Mood expression, threat sensitivity, automaticity of cognition, approach or inhibition, consistency or coherence of behavior

power is often used in TV commercials in which young people are encouraged to buy a product so they will be like the admired celebrity who uses it. Expert power exists when a target perceives that an agent has the ability to provide him or her with special or unique knowledge that is valuable to the target. This type of power is evident when one person (the agent) has considerably more familiarity with a given topic, problem, or issue and the other person (the target) wants or needs to benefit from this expertise. Finally, informational power is evident when an agent has specific information that may be useful to a target but the target must cooperate with the agent to get it. This base of power is frequently seen in business settings in which one person (the agent) has special information that the other person (the target) needs to make a good decision.

In sum, social power theory identifies six fundamental bases (sources) of power, each of which should be linked to specific types of influence strategies, tactics, and interpersonal processes for both the agent and the target of influence (see Table 15.1). The theory, however, does not explain how these bases of power are activated en route to exerting influence in interpersonal contexts or how being a more powerful versus a less powerful agent or target of influence affects personal or relational outcomes. In addition, social power theory says little if anything about how power operates in established dyads, and it is fairly mute on the major outcomes of having versus not having power. This is because the theory tends to focus on individuals rather than individuals within relationships, and it was not designed to address the long-term outcomes and consequences of having versus not having power.

Resource Theory

Resource theory was introduced by Blood and Wolfe (1960) and later extended by Safilios-Rothschild (1976). Wolfe (1959) defined resources as "a property of one person which can be made available to others as instrumental to the satisfaction of their needs or the attainment of their goals" (p. 100), where skills, knowledge, money, and status are considered to be relevant resources. Safilios-Rothschild provided a more comprehensive typology of resources, including socioeconomic (e.g., money, prestige), affective (e.g., affection, love), expressive (e.g., understanding, social support), companionship (e.g., social, leisure), sexual, and service (e.g., housekeeping, childcare) resources. Each of these resources can be possessed to a greater or lesser extent by each relationship partner, and individuals may choose to share or withhold access to a given resource with their partners.

Blood and Wolfe (1960) defined power as an individual's ability—either potential or actual—to change the behavior of other members in his or her social system (see Table 15.1). Imbalances in exchanges of (or access to) resources are the primary sources of power. This consideration of the relative levels of resource access and exchange for both partners in a relationship makes resource theory more dyadic in nature than social power theory because one cannot determine the levels of power within a relationship without knowing the specific resources held by each partner (see Table 15.1). When the levels of resources between partners are imbalanced, the partner who has fewer resources becomes dependent on his or her partner for access to the resources that he or she desires to satisfy his or her needs and achieve important goals. This increased dependence produces less power within the relationship. However, if an individual's situation changes (e.g., he or she gains access to valued resources via something or someone other than his or her romantic partner, such as through family or a career), he or she should become more independent, and the power dynamics within the relationship should shift accordingly.

Determining balance in the exchange of resources, however, can be complicated. Unequal exchanges can be difficult to identify objectively. For example, how can one objectively measure the amount of affection exchanged by each partner? Furthermore, balance in exchanges of resources ought to be based on the value of each resource as well as the total amount exchanged. The value of resources varies depending on the degree to which each partner has access to resources and whether she or he can find other cost-effective ways to gain them. As a result, perceptions of the equality or balance of costs and benefits in exchanges within the relationship primarily determine its power dynamics.

Unlike social power theory, resource theory says little about how power in relationships is expressed (see Table 15.1). Blood and Wolfe (1990) suggested that having relatively less power should lead the more dependent partner to be more willing to accept unequal exchanges of resources in the relationship, which ought to maintain and perhaps increase power imbalances across time. However, Blood and

Wolfe discussed no other avenues for acting on or conveying power. Resource theory also says nothing about the outcomes of power for individuals or the relationship across time.

To illustrate the central tenets of resource theory, imagine that Mary and Richard are involved in a romantic relationship. Mary has little access to money, but she is willing to give Richard a lot of affection and support, and she takes care of the house and family. In return, she expects Richard to support her financially, but she does not require him to return her deep love and affection. Richard is an attractive man, and he could find another romantic partner without much difficulty, but he stays with Mary because he receives so much love and support from her. Thus, Richard has more power in the relationship than Mary does; he probably obtains more tangible rewards in most of their exchanges, he typically sacrifices less, and Mary usually bends to his will to keep their relationship harmonious. However, if Mary suddenly has access to money outside the relationship (perhaps through an inheritance), she may begin to perceive the status quo as imbalanced and may begin to expect more from Richard in return for her resources, which could alter the power dynamics in their relationship.

In sum, resource theory defines power as an ability to change another person's behavior, which stems from imbalances in access to and exchanges of valued resources within a relationship. The theory is dyadic because it considers the degree to which both partners value, hold, and exchange resources with one another. However, resource theory primarily focuses on the sources and bases of power dynamics within relationships; it provides little guidance on how power is expressed or its long-term outcomes.

Interdependence Theory

Interdependence theory (Kelley & Thibaut, 1978; Thibaut & Kelley, 1959) was one of the first social psychological theories of power in dyads. Borrowing concepts from game theory, Thibaut and Kelley (1959) defined power as the ability of one partner in a relationship to directly influence the quality of outcomes (i.e., the amount of rewards vs. costs) that can be obtained by the other partner in a given situation. Individuals who have better alternatives to the current partner or relationship—those who have high comparison levels for alternatives—should typically have greater power within their relationship because they can get better (more rewarding) outcomes outside the relationship than their current partner can. Over time, people who have better alternatives are more likely to leave relationships unless their partners provide them with special or unique outcomes, such as extremely high levels of love and affection.

According to interdependence theory, three types of power can exist when relationship partners make joint decisions, such as deciding whether to do one of two possible activities (e.g., doing yard work vs. going to a movie). Fate control exists when one partner totally determines the outcomes of the other partner, regardless of what the other partner wants to do. For example, if Mary really wants to go see a movie and has fate control over Richard, Richard will most likely end up seeing the movie with her, regardless of his own personal preferences or desires. To the extent that Mary completely dictates the quality of Richard's outcomes across many different situations in their relationship (i.e., she exerts total dominance over him), she has greater fate control over Richard. Individuals who have fate control over others are free to use any of French and Raven's (1959) six bases of power to get what they want in relationships. In its extreme form, fate control is witnessed in abusive relationships in which one partner (the more powerful person) completely dictates what the other, less powerful partner says and does.

A second type of power is behavior control. If Mary can make it more rewarding for Richard to change his behavioral choices in response to what she wants to do, Mary has behavior control over Richard. For example, if Mary can make yard work especially fun and enticing and this leads Richard to choose working in the yard with her instead of going to a movie, she has behavior control over Richard. Individuals who exercise behavior control usually rely on what French and Raven (1959) termed reward power. Most happy, well-adjusted relationship partners rely on behavior control rather than fate control (Thibaut & Kelley, 1959).

Moreover, in long-standing relationships, initial patterns of fate control often shift to behavior control as relationship partners learn more about one another and find ways to approach tasks to ensure that both partners enjoy doing them.

A third type of power is expertise, which comes from one partner' having specialized information or knowledge from which the other partner can benefit. This type of power is similar to French and Raven's (1959) expertise power. Individuals who have expertise can improve their partner's positive outcomes by increasing their partner's rewards or lowering their costs, as when a more knowledgeable partner provides advice or gives information that allows the less knowledgeable partner to complete a task more easily, more quickly, or better. Mary, for example, may have special knowledge and tips about how to complete certain onerous yard work tasks such as weeding the garden that she can share with Richard. These tips then allow Richard to complete the weeding much more quickly and with considerably less effort, allowing him to do other things later that afternoon.

Interdependence theory also proposes that relationship partners can enact different power strategies when interacting and making decisions. For example, an individual can increase his or her power within a relationship by increasing the quality of his or her own alternatives, such as by actively looking for a new partner or by enhancing the desirable features of opposite-sex friends who could eventually become romantic partners. An individual can also increase his or her power by decreasing the apparent quality of his or her partner's alternatives, such as by derogating, denigrating, or downplaying his or her partner's other possible options. Furthermore, an individual can elevate his or her power by improving his or her ability to reward the current partner by reducing his or her partner's perceived qualities, skills, or confidence or by improving the value of the rewards that he or she can uniquely offer to the partner. Finally, an individual can increase his or her power by devaluing what the partner can offer him or her or by concluding that the rewards the partner can provide are not really needed, reducing one's reliance on the partner.

The concept of power in interdependence theory is consistent with the principle of least interest (Waller & Hill, 1951). According to this view, the partner in a relationship who is least interested in continuing the relationship (i.e., the one who has better alternatives and less to lose if the relationship ended) should dictate important decisions made in the relationship, including whether the relationship continues or disbands. The less dependent partner is termed the weak-link partner, whereas the more dependent partner is the strong link. Weak-link partners usually wield greater power than strong-link partners in most relationships (Sprecher & Felmlee, 1997). More powerful partners are also less satisfied and committed to their relationships and believe they have relatively better alternative partners, which suggests how discrepancies in power may develop (Grauerholz, 1987; Lennon, Stewart, & Ledermann, 2013). As we will show, this concept is important because it represents a within-dyad measure of power that indexes how much power one partner has relative to the other within a given relationship.

In sum, as displayed in Table 15.1, interdependence theory directly addresses all five key questions about power. According to this theory, power is the ability of one person to directly influence the quality of outcomes that another person (the partner) experiences. Power is dyadic given the relative levels of dependence that each partner has on the other for good outcomes. The principle sources of power are fate control, behavior control, and expertise, and power is communicated through the use of different power strategies designed to increase one's own power or reduce the partner's power. However, interdependence theory does not address the personal and relational outcomes of power use other than to suggest that the more powerful partner in a relationship should typically dictate the outcomes for both partners.

Dyadic Power Theory

Dyadic power theory (DPT; Rollins & Bahr, 1976) incorporates core elements from several other relationship power theories, resulting in a dyadic model that depicts the primary bases and processes of power dynamics in married couples (see Figure 15.1).

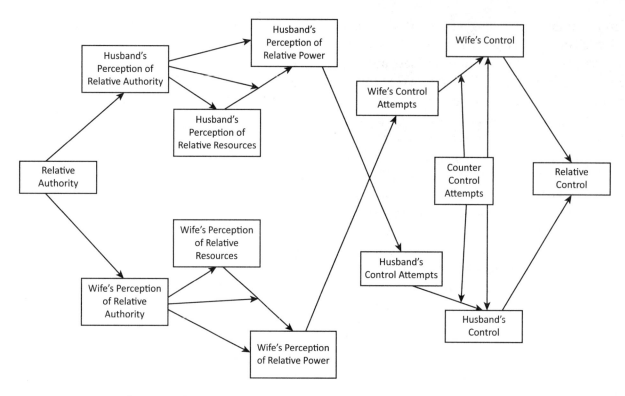

FIGURE 15.1. Dyadic power theory.

Consistent with interdependence theory and resource theory, DPT treats the relative level of resources and authority held by each partner as the basis for power within the relationship. However, DPT focuses on each partner's perceptions of these constructs rather than on each partner's actual levels. DPT also describes how the resulting power affects the behavior and outcomes of each partner within the relationship. According to this theory, power is a dyadic property that depends on the resources and authority that both partners within the dyad believe they hold or have access to (see Table 15.1). Even though an individual may have considerable access to resources or authority compared with most people, he or she can still be the less powerful person in a relationship if his or her partner has even greater resources or authority. Consequently, power is not a characteristic of the individual; it is an emergent property of the relationship.

According to DPT, authority and resources are principle sources of power (see Table 15.1). Power is operationally defined as the relative potential of relationship partners to influence each other's behavior when a conflict arises between them. Authority reflects norms regarding which partner ought to control specific situations, events, or decisions within the relationship, which is similar to French and Raven's (1959) legitimate power base. A resource is defined as anything an individual can make available to his or her partner to satisfy his or her partner's needs and to promote the attainment of his or her partner's goals, as described in resource theory (see earlier discussion). Partners who have greater authority within a given decision domain (e.g., finances, parenting) tend to have more opportunities to gain and control resources relevant to that domain, such as seeking additional knowledge that can then be used to make future decisions relevant to that domain. Perceptions of relative resources and authority, not necessarily actual relative levels, combine to create perceptions of relative relationship power. Thus, even though a partner may have access to many good resources, thereby giving him or her more potential access to power, he or she may not recognize that he or she has access and, as a result, may miss opportunities to use his or her unrecognized power potential. In addition, less powerful partners may sometimes freely confer power on their more powerful partners by accepting that they (their more powerful partners) have greater access to certain resources or authority. DPT also claims that relative authority and resources have cyclically increasing effects on one another. Increases in relative authority produce increases in relative resources, which in turn generate increases in relative power. Authority can also moderate the relation between resources and relationship power, with resources being more predictive of power in egalitarian relationships in which norms call for equality in authority between partners (see Figure 15.1).

Increases in perceived power should also lead people to believe that they can affect or change their partner, which should increase the number of times one partner tries to change the behavior of the other (i.e., control attempts). Such control attempts and their effectiveness are the primary avenues through which power is expressed during daily social interactions (see Table 15.1). Dunbar and Burgoon (2005) proposed that this association is curvilinear, with the most control attempts occurring in relationships in which partners have equal power, given that individuals with low power should change their own behavior to meet their high-power partner's desires without the high-power partner having to control them directly. However, current evidence for this proposal is incomplete. The link between power and control attempts is also believed to be reinforcing, with greater power increasing the likelihood that control attempts will be successful, which in turn should promote greater control. However, the concept of control in DPT refers only to control over behavior; the attitudes underlying a partner's behavior are not necessarily changed by control attempts. The enactment of many successful control attempts typically results in increased power for the individual who is successful (see Figure 15.1).

Relationships, of course, do not exist in a vacuum, and the effectiveness of control attempts is not entirely dependent on the relative power of the partner who typically initiates them. Other members of one's social network, such as family and friends, may initiate countercontrol attempts whereby they try to interfere with or block the control attempts of the influence agent by encouraging the target to resist or behave differently. DPT defines counter-control attempts as coming only from individuals outside the relationship. Countercontrol attempts often have a negative effect on the eventual success of control attempts and resulting partner compliance (see Figure 15.1).

In summary, DPT integrates several major concepts of prior power theories to create a more dyadic model outlining the bases and processes of relational power (see Table 15.1). However, certain features of the theory have constrained it from becoming a central theoretical perspective in the field. First, Rollins and Bahr (1976) defined power as existing or becoming relevant only when a conflict of goals exists between relationship partners. This definition limits power coming into play only when couples have conflict, and it does not explain how power may influence decisions (or either the agent's or the target's behavior) when partners feel neutral or have not established goals. Rollins and Bahr also characterized power as being enacted only in conflict situations that involve control attempts—that is, conscious actions in which one partner has clear intentions of changing the other partner's behavior. However, the enactment of power may also have less direct and less obvious effects on both partners' opinions and behaviors in the absence of any clearly purposeful behavior by the more powerful partner. DPT advances prior theories by incorporating partner effects into the power process in relationships, but partner effects might emerge earlier than DPT suggests, such as when individuals' perceptions of the sources of their or their partner's power affect how decisions are framed and then made. Moreover, the model is very linear. One might expect a more cyclical process, with the success of control attempts then affecting partners' perceptions of their relative power within the relationship as well as their authority, yet such feedback links are not indicated. Finally, DPT describes the sources and processes associated with power, but it says little about the short-term or long-term outcomes of power on individuals (partners) or their relationships.

Power Within Relationships Theory

Huston (1983) proposed a theory of power within relationships grounded in principles of what constitutes a close relationship. Close relationships are those in which both relationship partners have strong and frequent influence on how one another thinks, feels, and behaves over time and across different social contexts (Kelley et al., 1983). According to power within relationships theory, social–interpersonal power reflects the ability of one partner in a relationship to achieve his or her desired goals by intentionally influencing the other partner to facilitate (or at least not block) what he or she wants to achieve. Influence, however, is defined as occurring in situations in which one partner (the influence agent) says or does something that changes how the other partner (the target of influence) actually thinks, feels, or behaves during an interaction. Dominance is evident when influence becomes highly asymmetrical within a relationship over many decision domains, such as when one partner (almost always a much more powerful partner) makes virtually all of the decisions in a relationship. Dominance exists once fate control has been achieved (see Thibaut & Kelley, 1959).

Huston (1983) emphasized that power is the ability to exert influence, yet influence is not always exercised by more powerful partners, sometimes because the less powerful partner in a relationship automatically does what he or she thinks the more powerful partner wants before the more powerful partner even needs to exert influence. Indeed, across time, partners who wield extremely high levels of power and are dominant within a relationship are likely to make relatively few influence attempts, restricting those they do make primarily to the relatively rare occasions when their lower power partner resists or fails to comply with their preferences or desires. Nevertheless, there are bound to be some situations in most relationships when less powerful partners do decide to resist being influenced, at least temporarily. According to this theory, power is dyadic because information about both partners—including what each one is thinking, feeling, or doing in a given interaction—is needed to comprehend how, when, and why power and influence are enacted within a relationship.

Huston (1983) claimed that power and influence emanate from five causal conditions that promote or inhibit each partner's ability to intentionally influence the other or resist being influenced by him or her. These conditions include the personal attributes that each partner brings to the relationship (e.g., his or her personality traits, knowledge, skills, motives, needs), the unique attributes of the relationship (e.g., the relationship norms or rules that govern interactions and decision making), and features of the physical and social environment within which each partner and the relationship are embedded. The primary physical environment features include variables such as where the partners live, each partner's proximity to family and friends, his or her monetary resources, and the many nonsocial opportunities, challenges, and difficulties of everyday life. The primary social environment features include variables such as cultural norms, the quality of social support, access to social resources (e.g., other people to turn to for information, advice, or help), the quality of current friendships, and the structure of the family (e.g., the presence vs. absence of children). These causal conditions set the stage for each partner's power bases (French & Raven, 1959) and, in turn, each partner's ability to influence the other via the deployment of specific tactics (or countertactics) when decisions are being made in the relationship.

Let us return to our example of Richard and Mary. Because Richard entered their relationship with more money and relatively greater attractiveness, the couple may initially have negotiated a relationship norm whereby Richard usually makes most of the important, long-term decisions in the relationship and Mary handles the more routine, somewhat less important daily ones. Mary goes along with this arrangement not only because she has fewer resources and fewer good dating options but also because she loves Richard deeply. This initial arrangement permits Richard to have more power bases (e.g., reward power, coercive power, legitimate power), which allows him to use a wider variety of influence tactics on occasions when Mary does not quickly acquiesce to his preferences. As a result, most of the decision-making outcomes in their relationship, at least during its initial stages, are more in line with Richard's attitudes and preferences than with Mary's.

In sum, power within relationships theory adopts a dyadic view of power in which five causal conditions—features of each partner, their relationship, and the social and physical environment—set the stage for the type (base) and degree of power that each partner has in the relationship (see Table 15.1). These power bases, in turn, affect the degree to which each partner is able to both use and resist (counteract) different influence tactics. As a rule, individuals who have greater power in a relationship (or who have greater power within a given relationship domain) have the ability to exert greater influence on their partners when they want or need to, which allows them to achieve their desired goals more often. The theory says relatively little, however, about the kinds of personal outcomes that should flow from the use or receipt of influence tactics.

Power-Approach Theory

Power-approach theory (Keltner et al., 2003) melds principles from several theoretical perspectives, especially social power theory and interdependence theory, to describe power dynamics in myriad interpersonal interactions and contexts, ranging from close relationships that have less formalized roles (e.g., parent–child, husband–wife, friends) to more impersonal or even exchange-based relationships (e.g., employer–employee, international leader–international leader). Keltner et al. (2003) defined power as an individual's relative capacity to modify another person's state by providing or withholding resources on which that person depends or by administering punishments. Similar to other theoretical perspectives, one does not have power merely because one has resources; one has power because another person needs or depends on those resources. That said, individual characteristics, within-dyad (relationship) characteristics, and the broader social groups to which a person belongs can all affect the amount of power that the person has within a given relationship. Moreover, having versus not having power can have numerous social consequences associated with approach-related and inhibition-related outcomes.

Keltner et al. (2003) identified a broad range of variables linked with having high versus low power. Individual variables such as personality traits (e.g., extraversion, charisma) and physical traits (e.g., height, physical attractiveness) tend to be correlated with having somewhat greater power in many interpersonal contexts. At the dyadic level, dependence and partners' relative levels of commitment should also predict the possession of greater power. Beyond the dyad, more distal variables, such as role relationships, ethnicity, and gender, can also affect power dynamics within relationships.

With respect to the power outcomes for the more versus less powerful partner within a relationship, power-approach theory integrates power principles with motivational theories—especially Higgins's (1997) regulatory focus theory—to generate novel predictions about patterns of affect, cognition, and behavior. For example, having more power, either in absolute terms or within a relationship (i.e., relative to one's partner), should trigger a stronger promotion focus in which individuals concentrate on the positive goals they want to achieve and disregard possible costs. Conversely, not having power should activate a prevention focus in which individuals concentrate on not losing valued things that they already have. Having versus not having power should also influence the experience and expression of emotions in relationships. Indeed, having relatively greater power within a relationship is associated with experiencing more positive emotions such as amusement, enthusiasm, happiness, and love, whereas having less power predicts more negative emotions such as embarrassment, fear, guilt, sadness, and shame (Anderson, Langner, & Keltner, 2001). From a cognitive standpoint, having greater power in a relationship should produce greater attention to rewards, increased reliance on peripheral information processing and heuristic decision rules, and decreased empathic accuracy. Conversely, having less power ought to heighten sensitivity to punishment, facilitate systematic and controlled information processing, and increase empathic accuracy. Behaviorally, more powerful partners should show greater consistency of behavior across different situations, be less inclined to modify or mask their emotional expressions, and display more socially inappropriate behavior than less powerful partners, given that the behavior of more powerful partners should be less socially constrained.

In sum, power-approach theory addresses all five key questions regarding power and power dynamics (see Table 15.1). Similar to resource theory, it adopts a very broad view of the different levels from which power originates and within which it operates, ranging from the individual to the dyad, from social groups to the broader culture.

Comparisons of Power Theories

Viewing the prior theories of power together allows one to identify points of consensus as well as a few disparities. All of the theories conceptualize power as an ability or potential to influence, change, or control another person. Powerful partners can choose whether or not to try to influence their partners in a given situation, but they do not need to actually use their power to be powerful. Indeed, powerful individuals may often influence their partners indirectly without making a conscious, deliberate decision to do so, such as when a low-power partner believes the high-power partner wants him or her to do something that the high-power partner may not necessarily want or desire. The six theories differ somewhat in which specific aspects of the partner can be changed when one holds greater power, ranging from behavior to personal or relational outcomes to emotional states. Interestingly, the influence of power on attitudes and beliefs has not been directly considered by most of these theories, despite the fact that this has been a major focus in the social influence literature (see the next section). In general, however, reasonable consensus appears to exist about what power entails in relationships.

Most of the power theories have focused on the antecedents of power in relationships, and many of them discuss the same individual-level and relationship-level constructs. For example, the relative balance of valued resources between partners, which is discussed in social power theory, resource theory, power-approach theory, and DPT, is uniformly identified as a critical source of power in relationships. Likewise, relative authority is mentioned by both social power theory and DPT as a foundation of power in most relationships. All of the theories also address having control over the partner's outcomes through reward or coercion. Certain aspects of the relationship, such as each partner's level of dependence on one another and the

relationship, have also been proposed as important bases for power in most theories. Interdependence theory, for instance, focuses on these relational constructs quite heavily, and they are also incorporated to some degree into social power theory through the concept of the referent power base. Other relational constructs such as self-expansion (Aron, Aron, & Smollan, 1992) and attachment orientations (Mikulincer & Shaver, 2007) may also be relevant to the use of (or reactions to) power and influence, although they have not been discussed in past power theories. Except for power-approach theory and social power theory, neither of which was introduced as a theory of power in relationships per se, most power theories have a dyadic conceptualization of power and the origins of different power bases. Thus, an individual's absolute level of resources, authority, and dependence do not matter as much in determining his or her power in the relationship as the individual's relative level of these sources in relation to the current partner. For this reason alone, all six of the power theories require information about the partner (or perceptions of the partner) to ascertain which partner has more versus less power within a relationship.

Less has been hypothesized about how power is enacted or communicated during interactions between relationship partners. Resource theory, for example, focuses on antecedents of power but says nothing about how power is expressed or conveyed. The other theories address direct influence or control attempts enacted by more powerful partners, but none of them consider whether or how power should affect interactions when the more powerful partner does not intentionally attempt to exert influence. Interdependence theory and DPT both claim that, by controlling his or her partner, the more powerful partner can gain even greater power in the relationship, amplifying the power imbalance. Surprisingly little is said, however, about the role of the less powerful partner, such as whether or how he or she might resist influence or achieve greater power within the relationship across time.

The most underconsidered topic in prior power theories is the outcomes of power and influence attempts on each partner and their relationship. Power-approach theory addresses this topic fairly extensively, outlining the cognitive, affective, and behavioral tendencies of partners who have more versus less power in a relationship. This theory, however, focuses primarily on power in nonclose relationships (e.g., between strangers or casual acquaintances), so whether or the degree to which these documented effects necessarily transfer to close relationships is unknown. Power-approach theory also says nothing about relationship outcomes based on the power dynamics within a relationship. Interdependence theory provides some guidance on this front, proposing that as the less dependent partner in a relationship gains power or has less to lose if the relationship ends, he or she should be more inclined to terminate the relationship than the more dependent, lower power partner. Nevertheless, most of the prior power theories offer little guidance as to whether, when, or how having more versus less power in a relationship should generate specific personal or relational outcomes.

REVIEW OF THE POWER AND INFLUENCE LITERATURE

In this section, we review the empirical research that has been conducted on power and influence in relationships, focusing primarily on romantic relationships. When possible, we indicate where and how a given finding pertains to one or more of the existing power theories. However, most of the studies we discuss were not designed to test hypotheses derived from specific power theories or models. We begin by discussing how power and influence have been measured to date. Then, we review how the possession or use of power and various influence strategies or tactics are associated with assorted personal and relational outcomes.

Power and Influence Measures

Past research on social power and influence in relationships has been fraught with measurement challenges. Nearly all of this research has used self-report measures that ask relationship partners to make judgments of the relative balance of power in their relationship in general (i.e., across all types of decision domains and interpersonal situations). These measures have typically contained a small

number of face-valid items such as "Indicate your judgment of the overall balance of influence in your marriage," "In your relationship, who has more power?" "How much influence do you have over your partner's actions?" and "How often do you give in to your partner's demands?" (see Dunbar & Burgoon, 2005; Felmlee, 1994; Sprecher & Felmlee, 1997). Other scales have measured power in very specific areas within relationships, such as the sexual domain (e.g., Pulerwitz, Gortmaker, & DeJong, 2000). However, power is likely to vary somewhat between partners across different relationship domains on the basis of the specific resources and power bases that each partner does or does not have with respect to a given domain. As a result, one may not be able to extrapolate findings from domain-specific measures to draw general conclusions about the overall balance of power within a relationship. Furthermore, most of the existing measures of power are rather atheoretical, focusing on face validity rather than directly assessing the processes specified in theories of power. Future theoretically grounded scales assessing power in relationships need to be designed to measure the various power bases and the direct and indirect paths of influence that should affect personal and relational outcomes.

Another strategy for measuring power and influence in relationships that does not rely on subjective perceptions of relationship partners, and can thus circumvent these perceptual biases, is observational coding (see Huston, 1983). Observational coding has been particularly popular in the more recent social influence research. A wide range of coding schemes have been developed to measure the specific influence tactics that partners use when they try to resolve a conflict or attempt to change something about each other (Oriña, Wood, & Simpson, 2002; Overall et al., 2009). Very few studies, however, have assessed the level of power of each partner by coding couple interactions. These isolated studies have treated verbal dominance behaviors, such as interrupting one's partner and the relative amount of time spent talking, as behavioral manifestations of power (Dunbar & Burgoon, 2005; Galliher, Rostosky, Welsh, & Kawaguchi, 1999). Revealed difference tasks, in which couples make a mutually agreed-on rating on a topic or issue that each partner has rated differently, have also been used to assess power but primarily as a more objective outcome measure (i.e., which partner's choice wins out; Huston, 1983).

Priming high-power or low-power roles has become a popular technique in the power literature outside relationships, but most relationship researchers still focus primarily on existing power dynamics in established couples. One exception is work by Fitzsimons (2010), who primed romantic partners to perceive themselves as having either low or high power by writing about a time when their "partner had control of your ability to get something you wanted, or was in a position to evaluate you" (or, for the high-power condition, when "you had control or evaluated your partner"). Future research could also manipulate power subconsciously to tests its effects on how relationship partners communicate and make important decisions. Implicit power motives, such as those measured by the Thematic Apperception Test, have important implications for how friends interact (McAdams, Healy, & Krause, 1984), yet little research has used the Thematic Apperception Test or other subconscious measures or manipulations of power in close relationships.

Desired Versus Actual Power Balance in Relationships

Most romantic couples in Western cultures claim they prefer egalitarian relationships in which both partners have equal power (Caldwell & Peplau, 1984; Galliher et al., 1999; Sprecher & Felmlee, 1997). Approximately half of all romantic relationships, however, show signs of power inequality (Bentley, Galliher, & Ferguson, 2007; Caldwell & Peplau, 1984), and these patterns are fairly stable across time in most relationships (Sprecher & Felmlee, 1997; Sprecher, Schmeeckle, & Felmlee, 2006). When power imbalances exist, both men and women usually indicate that the male partner has greater power in the relationship than the female partner (Felmlee, 1994; for an exception in African American communities, see Davis, Williams, Emerson, & Hourd-Bryant, 2000). However, because most partners divide up roles and duties within their relationship, even the generally less powerful partner often has some decision-making discretion in

certain decision domains, such as how to plan or organize certain household tasks or making certain kinds of financial decisions. As one might expect, relationships in which partners have highly unequal power are characterized by lower satisfaction, less stability, and greater conflict (Caldwell & Peplau, 1984; Sprecher et al., 2006).

Effects of High Versus Low Power in and on Relationships

The bulk of research on social power has investigated how having high versus low power affects interpersonal processes and relationship outcomes. For example, individuals who either are given greater power within a newly formed relationship (with a stranger) or are led to believe they have relatively more power are less likely to adopt their partner's perspective, less inclined to take into account what she or he does and does not know, and are poorer at reading their partner's emotional expressions (Galinsky, Magee, Inesi, & Gruenfeld, 2006). Higher power individuals are also shielded from being influenced by their lower power partners. For example, they are less influenced by the ideas expressed by their partners, less likely to conform to their partner's opinions, and more influenced by their own values and opinions than by their partner's values and opinions (Galinsky, Magee, Gruenfeld, Whitson, & Liljenquist, 2008). Having greater power also makes people more action oriented and leads them to act in line with their own beliefs, attitudes, and preferences rather than those of others (Galinsky, Gruenfeld, & Magee, 2003). There are social contexts, however, in which having greater power can make individuals more interpersonally sensitive and empathic to the wants and needs of those who have less power (Schmid Mast, Jonas, & Hall, 2009).

Keltner et al. (2003) proposed that having more power should also be associated with greater freedom and rewards, which should activate approach-related tendencies, whereas having less power ought to elicit feelings of threat, fear of punishment, and social constraint, which should trigger inhibition-related tendencies. Consistent with these conjectures, more powerful people tend to experience more positive emotions, pay more attention to rewards, process information in a more automatic fashion, and behave in a less inhibited manner (Keltner et al., 2003). Less powerful people, in comparison, usually experience more negative affect; focus more intensely on threats, punishments, and what their partners want to do; process information in a more systematic and controlled way; and inhibit their social behavior. Some of these intrapersonal processes may affect the specific influence tactics that individuals do (or do not) use on their partners as well as how individuals react to specific influence tactics directed at them by their partners. For example, the approach-related tendencies associated with having greater power within a relationship may lead high-power partners to use reward-based influence tactics more often, whereas the avoidance-related tendencies tied to having less power may make low-power partners acutely sensitive to receiving coercive influence attempts from their partners.

In long-term romantic relationships, the more powerful partner usually dominates communications (Dunbar & Burgoon, 2005) and often directs more aggression toward the less powerful partner than vice versa (Bentley et al., 2007). In addition, men who enjoy having greater power in their relationships or who are less happy being the less powerful partner tend to be more abusive toward their female romantic partners, more so than women who like being in the more powerful position (Rogers, Bidwell, & Wilson, 2005). Low-power partners also report having greater difficulty getting their way when making important decisions in the relationship, such as whether to use condoms during sex (Woolf & Maisto, 2008), and they devote greater effort to supporting their partner's goals instead of their own (Fitzsimons, 2010).

Weak-link partners often have comparatively more resources and power in their romantic relationships (Caldwell & Peplau, 1984; Sprecher & Felmlee, 1997). For men, having access to more or better alternative partners is associated with feeling more powerful in romantic relationships (Sprecher, 1985). Weak-link partners also dictate the long-term stability of their relationships more than strong-link (less powerful) partners do (Attridge, Berscheid, & Simpson, 1995).

Power and Influence Strategies

Researchers have tried to identify basic influence strategies (i.e., the general means by which influence agents frame and convey their positions to influence targets) and their underlying structures by empirically clustering different types of influence tactics. Marwell and Schmitt (1967), for example, examined the use of influence tactics in both impersonal and personal dyadic interactions by asking people to rate their use of 16 behavioral tactics (e.g., making promises, threats, moral appeals). From these responses, they identified five types of influence strategies: (a) the use of material and verbal rewards, (b) the use of threats, (c) the use of logic, (d) the activation of impersonal commitments, and (e) the activation of personal commitments. This study was a preliminary step toward identifying the core influence strategies that most people use in relationships. Unfortunately, rather than serving as a starting point on which future research was built, this self-report study became a prototype for later research, which continued to identify influence strategies through empirical means with little theoretical guidance (e.g., Miller, Boster, Roloff, & Seibold, 1977; Raven, Schwarzwald, & Koslowsky, 1998).

Other researchers asked people to write essays on how they typically got their way with close others (e.g., Falbo, 1977; Falbo & Peplau, 1980). These essays were then coded for the use of Marwell and Schmitt's (1967) 16 influence tactics. Multidimensional scaling analyses revealed a two-dimensional structure reflecting higher level influence strategies. The first dimension was labeled *direct tactics* versus *indirect tactics*, and the second one was labeled *bilateral tactics* (e.g., trying to negotiate with the partner) versus *unilateral tactics* (e.g., simply telling the partner what to do). People who claimed to have more power than their partners reported using more direct tactics. Using similar procedures, Cody, McLaughlin, and Jordan (1980) identified four higher level influence strategies: (a) direct–rational (reasoning), (b) manipulation (flattery), (c) exchange (negotiation), and (d) threats.

Early research on influence strategies in relationships was more closely tied to the power literature than recent research has been. Howard, Blumstein, and Schwartz (1986), for instance, examined whether the use of clusters (different sets) of influence tactics depended on a person's control of resources. Specifically, they wanted to determine whether resource control or other factors, such as sex role orientation, were responsible for the different types of power that men and women typically have and use. Howard et al. interviewed people about the strategies and tactics they used on their relationship partners and then categorized these responses into 24 influence tactics. These tactics formed six factors (influence strategies): (a) manipulation, (b) supplication, (c) bullying, (d) autocracy, (e) disengagement, and (f) bargaining. Being female, having more feminine traits, having less power in society, and being relatively more dependent on one's relationship partner predicted the reported use of weaker tactics, such as manipulation and supplication.

Dillard and Fitzpatrick (1985) investigated how influence appeals are verbally constructed, hypothesizing that married couples should use one or more of three general power mechanisms (i.e., influence strategies) to change their partner's behaviors or attitudes. The first general mechanism is previewing expectancies and consequences with the partner, such as emphasizing to the target (the partner) the consequences of performing or failing to perform certain requested or desired behaviors. The second mechanism involves invoking relationship identifications, which includes eliciting compliance on the basis of the target's (the partner's) valuing of the relationship and what is required to maintain it. The third mechanism is appealing to other values and obligations, which can induce behavior change by appealing to the target's core values and beliefs. However, instead of using these three global mechanisms to investigate power in relationships, many marital researchers have subsequently examined how different couple types (e.g., a demanding wife and a withdrawing husband) use the eight tactics that make up these three mechanisms. Research has also studied influence at the level of the dyad, showing that both members of a couple tend to use the same tactics when constructing influence appeals (Fitzpatrick, 1983).

More recent studies have investigated actual influence attempts observed during discussions between romantic partners, such as investigating communication strategies used when individuals are trying to regulate their partner's emotions and behavior. Overall, Fletcher, and Simpson (2006) identified and examined the effects of two partner regulation strategies, valence (positive vs. negative regulation attempts) and directness (direct vs. indirect regulation attempts). Although greater use of direct strategies was perceived by both relationship partners as less effective immediately after discussions of how one partner could change or improve something about himself or herself, direct strategies produced greater self-improvement change across time than did indirect strategies (Overall et al., 2009), with greater use of negative tactics being particularly ineffective (Overall & Fletcher, 2010). The use of regulation strategies also had effects on relationship evaluations. Specifically, receiving more influence attempts from one's partner to change an aspect of the self leads one to believe that he or she does not meet the partner's ideal standards, which in turn predicts poorer relationship evaluations and more negative self-views (Overall & Fletcher, 2010; Overall et al., 2006).

Oriña and her colleagues (e.g., Oriña et al., 2002, 2008) adopted a different theoretical approach based on core social influence processes originally discussed by Kelman (1958, 1961). According to Kelman (1958, 1961), behavior change can be achieved via three different processes, which he labeled *identification, compliance,* and *internalization.* Identification is evident when individuals agree with valued others (i.e., relationship partners) to establish or maintain a satisfying, self-defining relationship with them. Compliance occurs when individuals agree with others to gain favorable outcomes from them or to avoid unfavorable ones. Internalization occurs when individuals agree with others because the attitude position itself (i.e., the quality of its arguments) is intrinsically logical, reasonable, or compelling.

Guided by Kelman's (1958, 1961) model, Oriña et al. (2002) proposed that influence agents should use one or more of these global influence strategies to induce attitude or behavior change in their partners: relationship referencing, coercion, and logic–reasoning. Relationship referencing involves the use of influence tactics that invoke the personal experiences, norms, or rules that define a given relationship, such as mentioning the relationship during influence attempts or emphasizing its importance to both partners. For relationship referencing, the source of power lies in the attractiveness and value of the relationship, the benefits that arise from being in it, and the ability to pursue important relationship-based goals. Coercion involves tactics that highlight the influence agent's ability to deliver contingent consequences. Positive coercion entails the promise of positive rewards and benefits to induce targets to perform certain desired behaviors, whereas negative coercion focuses on the promise of threats of punishment. Logic and reasoning entail influence tactics that involve the presentation of factual, logical, or well-reasoned arguments to induce desired behavior or attitude change in targets. For logic–reasoning, the influence appeals themselves are intrinsically compelling to the target because they appeal to his or her personal belief system.

During observed conflict resolution discussions, romantic partners who report feeling subjectively closer to their partners or relationships are more likely to use relationship-referencing tactics that invoke relationship norms, belongingness, and the importance of the couple as a unit (Oriña et al., 2002, 2008). Furthermore, when subjectively closer men and women are more troubled by the discussion topic than are their partners, their partners are more likely to use relationship-referencing tactics. In terms of effectiveness, relationship referencing is most effective at changing partners' opinions, whereas coercion and logic–reasoning are ineffective, often pushing targets farther away from the influence agents' desired position (Oriña et al., 2002, 2008).

Viewed as a whole, the body of existing influence research does not cohere very well, and it does not permit clear conclusions about (a) which influence tactics underlie specific higher level influence strategies, (b) the major determinants of influence strategy use, or (c) the relationship outcomes associated with these strategies. This lack of coherence stems partly from the fact that most early studies of influence in relationships were not grounded in a firm theoretical base from which to identify and understand influence attempts and processes. To complicate matters, those studies that were theoretically grounded often used different theoretical frameworks and measures that were not integrated. Furthermore, most early models of influence considered the viewpoint of either the influence agent or the target, meaning that they were not truly dyadic in orientation. For example, even though Fitzpatrick's (1983) work was framed dyadically, it did not consider the unique and often divergent goals and motives that each partner often brings to a relationship. However, as we shall show, when some of these power and influence findings are considered from a truly dyadic theoretical perspective, greater integration and coherence begin to emerge.

THE DYADIC POWER–SOCIAL INFLUENCE MODEL

Prior theories of power contain important elements that explain how the characteristics of each partner within a relationship should be related to certain power bases that each partner holds, how these power bases should in turn be associated with the use of specific influence strategies and tactics, and how the use of these strategies and tactics might affect personal or relational outcomes in each partner. Our integrative model, which we call the dyadic power–social influence model (DPSIM), borrows select constructs and principles from each of the power theories we have reviewed and integrates them into a single process model that outlines the individual (partner) and relationship characteristics (dyadic) that should affect the capacity and use of each partner's potential power bases, influence strategies and tactics, and downstream personal or relationship outcomes. The DPSIM is shown in Figure 15.2. Previous power theories have highlighted some, but not all, of the central constructs (boxes) and pathways (lines) contained in this model.

Consistent with prior definitions, we define power as the ability or capacity to change another person's thoughts, feelings, or behavior so they align with one's own desired preferences, along with the ability or capacity to resist influence attempts imposed by another person (see also Galinsky et al., 2008;

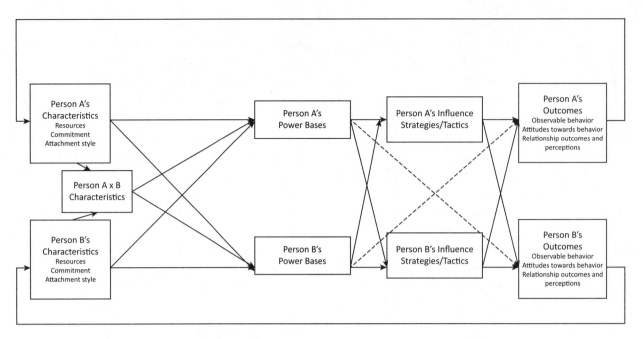

FIGURE 15.2. The dyadic power–social influence model.

Huston, 1983; Thibaut & Kelley, 1959). This definition is more expansive than some prior definitions of power (see Table 15.1) because it suggests that power entails not only the ability or capacity to change the thoughts, feelings, or behavior of another person but also the ability to resist their counterinfluence attempts. The concept of effective resistance has deep roots in the power literature, beginning with how power was originally conceptualized by interdependence theorists (Thibaut & Kelley, 1959).

According to the DPSIM, four sets of constructs are critical to understanding the operation of power and influence within relationships. As shown in Figure 15.2, they include the characteristics of each person in the relationship (see the boxes labeled Person A's Characteristics and Person B's Characteristics), the type of power each person potentially has and can use (see the boxes labeled Person A's Power Bases and Person B's Power Bases), the type of influence strategies and tactics that each person is able to deploy (see the boxes labeled Person A's Influence Strategies and Tactics and Person B's Influence Strategies and Tactics), and the outcomes each person experiences after influence attempts (see the boxes labeled Person A's Outcomes and Person B's Outcomes). Although each construct can be measured in multiple ways, the most important person characteristics are the core attributes that each person brings to the relationship (e.g., his or her attractiveness, status and resources, warmth and trustworthiness; see Fletcher, Simpson, Thomas, & Giles, 1999), each person's personality traits (e.g., his or her standing on the Big Five traits; see McCrae & Costa, 1987), and each person's general orientation toward relationships (e.g., his or her attachment orientation, communal vs. exchange orientation; see Clark & Mills, 1979; Mikulincer & Shaver, 2007). The core power bases are French and Raven's (1959) six bases of power: reward, coercive, legitimate, expert, referent, and informational. The primary influence strategies (and their underlying tactics) exist along two dimensions (Overall et al., 2009): direct versus indirect tactics (e.g., being explicit, overt, and direct vs. being passive or covert to resolve issues or inspire change) and positive versus negative tactics (e.g., using tactics characterized by positive vs. negative affect). The principal outcomes include whether or the degree to which an influence attempt changes the targeted attitudes or behavior of each partner along with his or her more general personal outcomes (e.g., positive well-being, depressive symptoms, anxiety) or relational outcomes (e.g., satisfaction, commitment, trust; see Fletcher, Simpson, & Thomas, 2000).

Though not depicted in Figure 15.2, the DPSIM assumes that each person (each partner) is embedded in a physical and social environment that may affect the personal characteristics that he or she brings to the relationship (Huston, 1983). For instance, the local physical environment in which one has grown up and currently lives is likely to influence the financial and social resources one has (or can develop in the future; Blood & Wolfe, 1960). The local past or present social environment may also shape the orientation one adopts toward relationships, such as whether one is securely or insecurely attached or has a communal or an exchange view of how relationships should operate. The parallel lines running from left to right in the center of the model (see Figure 15.2) reflect actor effects—that is, how an actor's characteristics affect his or her own access to power bases, use of specific influence strategies and tactics, and personal or relational outcomes, statistically controlling for the partner's attributes. The nonparallel lines running from left to right represent partner effects—that is, how the partner's characteristics affect the actor's access to power bases, use of specific influence strategies and tactics, and personal or relational outcomes, statistically controlling for the actor's attributes.

To unpack the DPSIM, let us first consider the actor effects—the pathways depicted in Figure 15.2 by the parallel lines flowing from the box labeled Person A's Characteristics and from the box labeled Person B's Characteristics that then both move to the right. According to the DPSIM, each partner's personal characteristics can affect his or her ability or capacity to utilize certain power bases within the relationship. If, for example, Person A enters the relationship with substantial resources (Blood & Wolfe, 1960) or excellent alternatives to the current relationship (Thibaut & Kelley, 1959), she or he should, on average, be able to leverage more bases (sources) of power to influence his or her partner more effectively and obtain the outcomes that he or she prefers in most of the decisions in the relationship. Consistent with most prior power theories, this should be particularly true if Person A has many more resources or much better alternatives relative to his or her partner. This sort of within-dyad

variable is represented by the box labeled Person A × B Characteristics in the model (see Figure 15.2), which represents the statistical interaction of the two partners' characteristics on a given variable. In the current example, the Person A × Person B interaction indexes the size of the difference between the two partners' levels of resources or quality of alternatives to the current relationship. Other conceivable Person A × Person B interactions might include the magnitude of the discrepancy between partners' personal values, their personality trait scores, or other salient characteristics. Within-dyad variables also index relationship-specific rules or norms that partners develop and follow, such as which partner is responsible for making the decisions in a given domain (e.g., doing the bills, deciding where to go on vacation).

Returning to our earlier example, because Richard entered his relationship with Mary having more money and being a very good catch, he should be able to use different power bases (e.g., reward power, coercive power, legitimate power) to frame better, more convincing, or stronger influence messages that enable him to get his way in most decision-making discussions with Mary. Depending on the specific situation, Richard can leverage one or more of his potential power bases to frame highly effective influence appeals that offer Mary desirable rewards for going along with his preferences, threaten to punish her if she does not do what he prefers, call on her deep commitment to the relationship to see things his way, or use logic and reasoning to convince her to change her opinion or behavior. When certain decisions are important to Richard and Mary is likely to comply, he ought to use direct and positive influence strategies and tactics. When Mary is reluctant to agree with or comply on issues that are important to Richard, he may resort to using direct and negative influence strategies and tactics. When decisions are less consequential to Richard or when Mary needs less of a push to comply, he may use indirect strategies and tactics framed in a more positive fashion because such strategies are less likely to destabilize the relationship (Overall et al., 2009). There are likely to be situations, however, when Richard does not need to exert any direct influence on Mary to get his way because she has learned to anticipate and automatically defer to his preferences before an influence attempt needs to be made. The personal and relational outcomes that Richard experiences after trying to influence Mary are likely to depend on several factors, including how important the issue and decision outcome are to Richard, the degree to which he got what he wanted, how much resistance Mary put up, the extent to which negative influence strategies and tactics were used, and how Mary reacted after the discussion.

Let's now consider the partner effects—the various pathways depicted by the nonparallel lines running from the Person A to the Person B boxes and from the Person B to the Person A boxes in Figure 15.2. According to the DPSIM, the personal characteristics of each individual's (i.e., each actor's) partner may also affect the individual's ability or capacity to use power bases within the relationship. If, for instance, Person B enters the relationship with few resources or poor relationship alternatives, she or he should have fewer and weaker sources of power from which to influence his or her partner. As a result, he or she is less likely to attain the decision outcomes that he or she prefers in most—but not necessarily all—relationship-relevant decision domains. Once again, this should be particularly true if Person B has significantly fewer resources or poorer alternatives than his or her partner, as depicted by the box labeled Person A × Person B Characteristics in the model.

Consider Mary's situation. Because of Richard's comparatively greater resources and ability to find alternative partners more easily, Mary ought to have fewer and weaker power bases from which to generate persuasive influence appeals in the relationship. In most decision-making domains (especially those that are important to Richard), Mary may not be able to offer enticing rewards to get Richard to agree with her preferences, she should find it more difficult to punish him when he fails to do what she prefers, it should be more difficult to appeal to his commitment to their relationship when attempting to persuade him, and her use of logic and reasoning is likely to fall on deaf ears. Mary, in other words, should be less able to act on her personal characteristics and preferences because Richard's

characteristics and preferences restrict what she can say, do, and ultimately accomplish in most relationship-based decisions. When decisions are very important to Mary, she should try to use direct and positive influence strategies and tactics, which may often have minimal or mixed success. In other situations, Mary may simply comply with Richard's preferences unless they are discussing a relationship domain in which Mary has decision-making authority. For example, Mary and Richard may have agreed (i.e., may have developed a relationship norm) that Mary usually makes the decisions in certain domains (e.g., child rearing), perhaps to ensure that both partners have a role in making certain decisions so the relationship runs more smoothly (see Farrell, Simpson, & Rothman, 2013; Huston, 1983). Indeed, as relationships develop, the less powerful partner may gradually assume more domain-specific power, which might eventually increase his or her general power in the relationship as it develops. The personal and relational outcomes that Mary experiences after trying to influence Richard should also depend on myriad factors, including how important the issue and decision outcome are to Mary, how successful she was in getting her way, the extent to which Richard used negative counterinfluence strategies and tactics, and how Richard reacted after the discussion.

As shown in Figure 15.2, two of the partner effect pathways have dashed nonparallel lines that run from the box labeled Person A's Power Bases to the box labeled Person B's Outcomes and from the box labeled Person B's Power Bases to the box labeled Person A's Outcomes. These pathways indicate that, at times, partners who wield greater general or domain-specific power might be able to achieve the outcomes they desire without having to use direct influence strategies or tactics on their partners. For example, because he holds greater overall power in their relationship, Richard (Person A) can get the outcomes he wants from Mary (Person B) because, across time, she has learned to anticipate and automatically abide by his preferences. This highlights an important and underappreciated fact about power and influence in relationships—namely, the most powerful individuals in relationships may often not need to use influence tactics to persuade their less powerful partners because, over time, less powerful partners either acquiesce or eventually change their opinions to be in line with those of the more powerful partner. They may do so to please their more powerful partners, avoid conflicts, maintain the relationship, or circumvent being exposed to direct, negative influence attempts. Although the relation between the capacity for power and the use of influence strategies and tactics should be positive in the early stages of relationship development, it is likely to attenuate as relationships move into the maintenance phase once stable interaction patterns have developed. In relationships in which one partner holds much more power than the other and has little regard for him or her, such as in relationships characterized by dominance (Huston, 1983), the link between power and influence attempts may actually be negative. We return to how power and influence might change across different relationship stages later in the chapter.

Across time, each partner's personal and relational outcomes may loop back to alter some of their personal characteristics (see the solid lines in Figure 15.2 running from the box labeled Person A's Outcomes to the box labeled Person A's Characteristics and from the box labeled Person B's Outcomes to the box labeled Person B's Characteristics). Unlike some power theories, such as DPT, the DPSIM assumes that certain outcomes of the power–influence process may change certain partner features. For example, if the general level of power in Mary and Richard's relationship becomes more equitable over time as Mary takes on more areas of domain-specific power and she provides Richard with better rewards and outcomes (Thibaut & Kelley, 1959), Richard may gradually adopt a more communal orientation toward Mary and their relationship. This, in turn, could increase one or more of Mary's power bases and, therefore, the effectiveness of the influence strategies and tactics she can use to achieve some of her own personal goals and objectives. As most relationships develop and grow, however, partners typically identify new joint, couple-based goals (e.g., buying a house, starting a family) and they merge many of their personal goals with those held by their partners (Aron et al., 1992). This, in turn, should

render the more powerful relationship partner somewhat less powerful within the relationship because what is good for Richard is now also good for Mary as he becomes more dependent on her.

Given its broader definition of power, the DPSIM suggests that the more powerful partner within a relationship should also be more able to resist the influence or counterinfluence attempts enacted by his or her less powerful partner. This greater resistance potential is not shown in Figure 15.2, but it is assumed in the DPSIM. In addition, the DPSIM focuses on both changes in observable behavior and private shifts in underlying attitudes and beliefs. Less powerful partners, therefore, can simply change their behavior to obtain desired results without altering their attitudes to maintain an existing relationship, get rewards, or avoid punishments, or they can change their underlying attitudes in response to partner influence attempts, leading to more permanent, internalization-based behavior change (Kelman, 1961).

Furthermore, similar to DPT, power is highly dependent on the perceptions of each partner in the relationship, according to the DPSIM. For example, even though a partner may have objective access to many good or valuable resources (which should give her or him access to greater power), he or she may not recognize this and, as a result, may miss opportunities to use his or her hidden power potential. Indeed, less powerful partners may at times confer or hand over some of their power to their more powerful partners by perceiving that their high-power partners have greater access to certain resources or power bases than they actually do. As discussed earlier, the DPSIM has recursive links from each person's outcomes back to his or her personal characteristics (see Figure 15.2). However, it is conceivable that the outcomes of a given influence attempt (or a series of influence attempts) may affect perceptions of not only the self's characteristics but perhaps the partner's as well. Moreover, merely having access to power bases may affect perceptions of both the self and the partner.

Consistent with interdependence theory (Thibaut & Kelley, 1959), the DPSIM suggests that the quality of alternative partners, the level of relationship satisfaction, and the amount of dependence on the partner or relationship should all determine which partner has more access to different power bases and which partner should be willing to use her or his power bases to influence the other partner. Furthermore, according to the DPSIM, the less committed partner in a relationship (i.e., the weak-link partner) should hold greater power than the more committed partner (i.e., the strong link partner), and the less committed partner may also be more comfortable using power bases that could potentially harm the stability or well-being of the relationship. However, the more committed partner may sometimes inaccurately perceive that her or his partner has more power than he or she really does in the relationship. If so, the more committed partner's greater perceived dependence on the relationship may lead him or her to succumb to unintentional influence attempts, motivating the more committed partner to preemptively change his or her behavior to appease the less committed partner and forestall negative outcomes.

There may also be important trade-offs between high- and low-power partners in terms of the attributes or resources that are exchanged. For instance, individuals who are physically attractive are likely to have less power in the relationship if their partners place greater weight on other partner attributes, such as earning potential or warmth. In other words, more powerful partners do not inherently have more power because they have resources; their less powerful partners usually confer them with power in part on the basis of the less powerful partner's wants, needs, and desires. Finally, similar to Huston's (1983) power within relationships theory, power-approach theory (Keltner et al., 2003) draws attention to several additional proximal variables that may be relevant to power and influence in relationships, such as the ethnicity, culture, and social class of each partner. Because the DPSIM focuses mainly on the relational aspects of power, it does not directly address these other important distal variables.

CONCLUSIONS AND FUTURE DIRECTIONS

As we have seen, power is a dyadic concept. The DPSIM integrates core elements of each existing power theory into a single dyadic framework. For example, it acknowledges that each partner (Person A and Person B) resides in a physical and social environment, and each partner is likely to bring different resources, goals, needs, motives, and personal characteristics to the relationship. These attributes set the stage for the type of power bases that each partner has and can use, which in turn dictates the specific influence strategies and tactics that each partner uses to get his or her way in decision-making situations. The use of these influence strategies and tactics then affect attitude and behavior change, along with the personal and relational outcomes experienced by each partner. The DPSIM also suggests that power dynamics in a relationship are likely to be fluid processes in which both partners, as well as their unique, interactive characteristics, affect one another's outcomes.

In this final section, we discuss how power and influence may differ depending on the stage a relationship is in (fledging, established, or transitional). We conclude by suggesting some promising and important directions for future research.

Relationship Stage Model of Power

In this chapter, we have argued that theoretical, conceptual, and methodological problems have impeded our understanding of power within established relationships. Part of the reason for this is that our understanding of power and how it is used depends on when power and influence processes are studied in relationships. Relationship partners confront different types of challenges, questions, and issues at different relationship stages, which should have important consequences for the use of power, influence processes, and their ultimate outcomes. By ignoring the stage of the relationship, researchers might not be asking the right questions, studying the appropriate processes and behaviors, and drawing appropriate conclusions.

Let's now consider how power is likely to unfold during three relationship stages: (a) the fledgling relationship stage when partners are just getting to know each other, (b) the established relationship stage when partners are trying to further develop and maintain their relationship, and (c) transitional stages such as the transitions to marriage, parenthood, or retirement when partners must negotiate new roles, new patterns of interaction, and sometimes new identities. As shown in Table 15.2, the key challenges that many partners face at each relationship stage are likely to affect the salience and attention they place on the power dynamics in their relationship, the communal versus exchange orientation displayed by each partner, the degree to which there is role differentiation in how decisions are managed and made, and the degree of automaticity of thought, feeling, and behavior during decision-making discussions.

During the fledgling relationship stage, one key challenge is to establish a power structure in the relationship that satisfies both partners, given the attributes that each one brings to the relationship. As shown in Table 15.2, the enactment of influence attempts and the emerging power dynamics in the relationship should be especially salient and important to both partners during the fledgling stage as partners develop norms and rules for making different decisions in certain domains and negotiate the power dynamics in their developing relationship. To promote equality and equal influence during this stage, most partners may adopt an exchange orientation toward most decisions, regardless of the decision-making domain or their areas of expertise, by exploring, talking about, and making many decisions together. Decision making and influence attempts should be carefully framed and processed by each partner to ensure that neither partner is being taken advantage of or treated unfairly, given what each partner brings to the relationship.

The building of trust should be crucial for the establishment of power dynamics within fledgling relationships and for movement toward the established relationship stage. In fledgling relationships, the degree which an individual can trust his or her partner should be inferred from clear conflicts of interest in which the partner forgos what is best for him or her and instead does what is best for his or her partner or the relationship (Simpson, 2007). Once forged, a basic level of trust allows both partners to feel comfortable relinquishing some decision-making power in certain relationship domains, which should facilitate the differentiation of decision-making roles within the relationship.

During the established relationship stage, a fundamental challenge is to maintain equilibrium and stability in the power structure in the relationship unless the structure is unsatisfactory to one or both partners, especially the more powerful one. Automaticity in decision making and power dynamics should characterize this stage. Relationship roles and expectations should be well established, and partners should act in line with established patterns of influence and power in the relationship (see Table 15.2). By this stage, partners should have divided up specific decision-making domains so that each partner assumes primary responsibility for making certain decisions (e.g., paying the bills, shopping, household decisions). This partitioning of decision making is more efficient than one partner making all the relationship-relevant decisions or both partners

---

TABLE 15.2

Relevance of Relationship Stages for Power and Influence

Stage	Key challenge	Power and influence salience	Processing of decision making	Communal versus exchange orientation	Differentiation across domains
Fledgling relationship stage	Establish a satisfying power structure	High	Effortful	Exchange	No
Established relationship stage	Maintain equilibrium and stability in power structure	Low	Automatic	Communal	Yes
Transitional stages	Rebalance power structures	Higher in relevant domains	Effortful	Exchange (particularly in relevant domains)	Yes (but changing)

being involved in all decisions because it requires less time and less mental energy from both partners. However, if one examines behaviors and decision making within a single decision-making domain rather than across all domains, one could make erroneous conclusions about the actual power dynamics within a relationship.

In established relationships, interactions that involve influence attempts should be fairly routine, and they should not provide much new diagnostic information about each partner's responsiveness to the other's needs because many domains of expertise and decision making have already been partitioned and established. As a result, power and influence processes should be less salient and should not be processed as carefully in light of the fact that decision making has become more automated, routine, and less effortful. In many established relationships, partners should adopt more of a communal orientation, assuming that momentary imbalances in power or influence in the relationship are likely to even out over time or across the different decision-making domains. However, this assumes that sufficient trust has developed between the partners; individuals in established relationships who do not trust their partners should continue to attend closely to the balance of power within their relationship just as they did during the fledgling stage, given their continued concerns that their partners might not be sufficiently responsive to their needs and best interests.

Transitional relationship stages are those in which resources or other power-relevant circumstances change (e.g., the transition to retirement) and decision-making domains are added to or removed from the relationship (e.g., the transition to cohabitation or parenthood). During transitional periods, the key challenges are to redistribute and rebalance the power structure within the relationship as roles change and decision-making domains shift. To regain satisfactory equilibrium in the power structure, couples must often renegotiate the balance of power in the new or changed set of domains. During these transitions, power processes should once again become salient, and decision making should once again become more controlled, systematic, and effortful as partners renegotiate new roles, expectations, and issues in their relationship

(see Table 15.2). However, rather than attending closely to all discussions that might have implications for the allocation of power (as couples do in fledgling relationships), partners in transitional relationships should pay particular attention to decision-making domains that could be taken over by their partners, such as when one partner must stop doing important activities because of declining health. During this stage, partners should once again adopt more of an exchange orientation as they negotiate and gain (or redivide) control over new or revised tasks and issues. Moreover, partners should once again engage in more information processing until new relationship norms and roles have been agreed on and become stable.

In summary, researchers must also consider the possible effects of different relationship stages when studying power and influence in ongoing relationships. Partners in fledgling relationships may be better able to answer questions about the actual power dynamics and influence attempts within their relationships more accurately because these issues are more salient and effortfully processed than they are in established relationships. If one measures power in a single decision-making domain rather than across all domains in a relationship, there are likely to be more decision-making asymmetries in established relationships than in transitional or fledgling relationships because of the greater differentiation in decision-making power across domains within most established relationships. Moreover, if one studies relationships during a major life transition, partners may act very differently in terms of their influence attempts and responses than they would before or after the transition, at least until the power dynamic in their relationships returns to some equilibrium.

Future Directions and Conclusions

There are several important directions in which future research on power and social influence in relationship should head. Perhaps the two most pressing directions are testing the core predictions of the DPSIM model and the stage model of power dynamics within relationships.

Many of the pathways in the DPSIM are based on either theoretical propositions or indirect, preliminary empirical findings. For example, we still do not know whether or how partners trade off the various personal characteristics they contribute to their relationships (such as attractiveness, status, resources, or warmth), or how these trade-offs affect the power structure and influence dynamics within relationships as they develop. We also know little about what happens when the characteristics of one or both partners change during the course of a relationship and how this may alter the power bases or influence tactics deployed by each partner. In addition, remarkably little is known about whether, when, or how each of French and Raven's (1959) power bases lead to the enactment of specific influence strategies and tactics, especially in established relationships in which the repeated use of certain tactics (such as coercion or reward) may become less effective as partners assume more domain-specific decision-making roles and become more interdependent. We also know virtually nothing about how more powerful partners in relationships decide to use certain power bases rather than others and how they intermix different influence strategies and tactics over time to generate optimal attitude or behavior change in their less powerful partners with the fewest negative ramifications for them, their low-power partners, or their relationships.

Furthermore, very little is known about whether or how the use of certain influence strategies and tactics (e.g., direct–positive tactics, indirect–negative tactics) affects the personal or relational well-being of the influence target as well as the influence agent. This is particularly true of the possible long-term effects associated with the consistent use of specific influence strategies and tactics (e.g., direct–negative tactics, indirect–positive tactics). Little if any research has examined whether or how the outcomes of repeated influence attempts across time circle back to change either partner's personal or relational features, such as their personality traits or their broader relationship orientations. Finally, research needs to clarify whether and how Person A × Person B characteristics, such as large discrepancies between partners on certain personal characteristics or the emergence of special relationship norms and rules, affect access to different power bases and the use of different influence strategies and tactics.

Very little research has focused on the developmental stages of relationships, and even less has investigated whether or how they affect power dynamics in relationships. Although grounded in theory, our stage model of power is still speculative and has not been tested. Future researchers need to observe couple interactions and collect both partners' reports of power dynamics in different decision-making domains at different relationship stages to determine the validity of the hypotheses regarding salience, automaticity, differentiation, and communal versus exchange orientation. This developmental perspective on relationships could also be fruitfully applied to other aspects of relationships, and it could clarify how the progression of close relationships in earlier stages influences later outcomes, such as relationship dissolution, stability, or infidelity.

In conclusion, as Bertrand Russell observed nearly 75 years ago, power may be the fundamental concept in the social and behavioral sciences. Although the construct of power is difficult to define, measure, and test, it is far too important to ignore or relegate to mere theoretical speculations. It must be studied and tested, particularly in the context of established relationships. We hope that the DPSIM and the ideas about power dynamics at different relationship stages will stimulate renewed interest and research in power and social influence in ongoing interpersonal contexts.

References

Anderson, C., Langner, C., & Keltner, D. (2001). *Status, power, and emotion.* Unpublished manuscript, University of California, Berkeley.

Aron, A., Aron, E. N., & Smollan, D. (1992). Inclusion of Other in the Self Scale and the structure of interpersonal closeness. *Journal of Personality and Social Psychology, 63,* 596–612. doi:10.1037/0022-3514.63.4.596

Attridge, M., Berscheid, E., & Simpson, J. A. (1995). Predicting relationship stability from both partners versus one. *Journal of Personality and Social Psychology, 69,* 254–268. doi:10.1037/0022-3514.69.2.254

Bentley, C. G., Galliher, R. V., & Ferguson, T. J. (2007). Associations among aspects of interpersonal power and relationship functioning in adolescent romantic relationships. *Sex Roles, 57,* 483–495. doi:10.1007/s11199-007-9280-7

Blood, R. O., & Wolfe, D. M. (1960). *Husbands and wives: The dynamics of married living.* New York, NY: Free Press.

Caldwell, M. A., & Peplau, L. A. (1984). The balance of power in lesbian relationships. *Sex Roles, 10,* 587–599. doi:10.1007/BF00287267

Clark, M. S., & Mills, J. (1979). Interpersonal attraction in exchange and communal relationships. *Journal of Personality and Social Psychology, 37,* 12–24. doi:10.1037/0022-3514.37.1.12

Cody, M. J., McLaughlin, M. L., & Jordan, W. J. (1980). A multidimensional scaling of three sets of compliance-gaining strategies. *Communication Quarterly, 28,* 34–46. doi:10.1080/01463378009369373

Davis, L. E., Williams, J. H., Emerson, S., & Hourd-Bryant, M. (2000). Factors contributing to partner commitment among unmarried African Americans. *Social Work Research, 24,* 4–15. doi:10.1093/swr/24.1.4

Dillard, J. P., & Fitzpatrick, M. A. (1985). Compliance-gaining in marital interaction. *Personality and Social Psychology Bulletin, 11,* 419–433. doi:10.1177/0146167285114008

Dunbar, N. E., & Burgoon, J. K. (2005). Perceptions of power and interactional dominance in interpersonal relationships. *Journal of Social and Personal Relationships, 22,* 207–233. doi:10.1177/0265407505050944

Falbo, T. (1977). Multidimensional scaling of power strategies. *Journal of Personality and Social Psychology, 35,* 537–547. doi:10.1037/0022-3514.35.8.537

Falbo, T., & Peplau, L. A. (1980). Power strategies in intimate relationships. *Journal of Personality and Social Psychology, 38,* 618–628. doi:10.1037/0022-3514.38.4.618

Farrell, A. K., Simpson, J. A., & Rothman, A. J. (2013). *The Relationship Power Inventory: Construction and validation of a self-report measure of power in romantic relationships.* Unpublished manuscript, University of Minnesota, Minneapolis.

Felmlee, D. H. (1994). Who's on top? Power in romantic relationships. *Sex Roles, 31,* 275–295. doi:10.1007/BF01544589

Fitzpatrick, M. A. (1983). Predicting couples' communication from couples' self-reports. In R. N. Bostrom & B. H. Westley (Eds.), *Communication yearbook 7* (pp. 49–82). Beverly Hills, CA: Sage.

Fitzsimons, G. M. (2010, October). *Power and the interdependence of everyday goal pursuits within close relationships.* Invited talk at the Annual Attraction and Close Relationships Pre-Conference, Society of Experimental Social Psychology, Minneapolis, MN.

Fletcher, G. J. O., Simpson, J. A., & Thomas, G. (2000). The measurement of perceived relationship quality components: A confirmatory factor analytic approach. *Personality and Social Psychology Bulletin, 26,* 340–354. doi:10.1177/0146167200265007

Fletcher, G. J. O., Simpson, J. A., Thomas, G., & Giles, L. (1999). Ideals in intimate relationships. *Journal of Personality and Social Psychology, 76,* 72–89. doi:10.1037/0022-3514.76.1.72

French, J. R. P., Jr., & Raven, B. H. (1959). The bases of social power. In D. Cartwright (Ed.), *Studies in social power* (pp. 150–167). Ann Arbor: University of Michigan Press.

Galinsky, A. D., Gruenfeld, D. H., & Magee, J. C. (2003). From power to action. *Journal of Personality and Social Psychology, 85,* 453–466. doi:10.1037/0022-3514.85.3.453

Galinsky, A. D., Magee, J. C., Gruenfeld, D. H., Whitson, J. A., & Liljenquist, K. A. (2008). Power reduces the press of the situation: Implications for creativity, conformity, and dissonance. *Journal of Personality and Social Psychology, 95,* 1450–1466. doi:10.1037/a0012633

Galinsky, A. D., Magee, J. C., Inesi, M. E., & Gruenfeld, D. H. (2006). Power and perspectives not taken. *Psychological Science, 17,* 1068–1074. doi:10.1111/j.1467-9280.2006.01824.x

Galliher, R. V., Rostosky, S. S., Welsh, D. P., & Kawaguchi, M. C. (1999). Power and psychological well-being in late adolescent romantic relationships. *Sex Roles, 40,* 689–710. doi:10.1023/A:1018804617443

Grauerholz, E. (1987). Balancing the power in dating relationships. *Sex Roles, 17,* 563–571. doi:10.1007/BF00287736

Higgins, E. T. (1997). Beyond pleasure and pain. *American Psychologist, 52,* 1280–1300. doi:10.1037/0003-066X.52.12.1280

Howard, J. A., Blumstein, P., & Schwartz, P. (1986). Sex, power, and influence tactics in intimate relationships. *Journal of Personality and Social Psychology, 51,* 102–109. doi:10.1037/0022-3514.51.1.102

Huston, T. L. (1983). Power. In H. H. Kelley, E. Berscheid, A. Christensen, J. H. Harvey, T. L. Huston, G. Levinger, . . . Peterson, D. R. (Eds.), *Close relationships* (pp. 169–219). New York, NY: W. H. Freeman.

Kelley, H. H., Berscheid, E., Christensen, A., Harvey, J. H., Huston, T. L., Levinger, G., . . . Peterson, D. R. (1983). *Close relationships.* New York, NY: W. H. Freeman.

Kelley, H. H., & Thibaut, J. W. (1978). *Interpersonal relationships: A theory of interdependence.* New York, NY: Wiley.

Kelman, H. C. (1958). Compliance, identification, and internalization: Three processes of attitude change. *Journal of Conflict Resolution, 2,* 51–60. doi:10.1177/002200275800200106

Kelman, H. C. (1961). Processes of opinion change. *Public Opinion Quarterly, 25*, 57–78. doi:10.1086/266996

Keltner, D., Gruenfeld, D. H., & Anderson, C. (2003). Power, approach, and inhibition. *Psychological Review, 110*, 265–284. doi:10.1037/0033-295X.110.2.265

Lennon, C. A., Stewart, A. L., & Ledermann, T. (2013). The role of power in intimate relationships. *Journal of Social and Personal Relationships, 30*, 95–114.

Marwell, G., & Schmitt, D. R. (1967). Dimensions of compliance-gaining behavior: An empirical analysis. *Sociometry, 30*, 350–364. doi:10.2307/2786181

McAdams, D. P., Healy, S., & Krause, S. (1984). Social motives and patterns of friendship. *Journal of Personality and Social Psychology, 47*, 828–838. doi:10.1037/0022-3514.47.4.828

McCrae, R. R., & Costa, P. T., Jr. (1987). Validation of the five-factor model of personality across instruments and observers. *Journal of Personality and Social Psychology, 52*, 81–90. doi:10.1037/0022-3514.52.1.81

Mikulincer, M., & Shaver, P. R. (2007). *Attachment in adulthood: Structure, dynamics, and change.* New York, NY: Guilford Press.

Miller, G., Boster, F., Roloff, M., & Seibold, D. (1977). Compliance-gaining message strategies: A typology and some findings concerning effects of situational differences. *Communication Monographs, 44*, 37–51. doi:10.1080/03637757709390113

Oriña, M. M., Simpson, J. A., Ickes, W., Asada, K. J. K., Fitzpatrick, S., & Braz, M. E. (2008). Making it (inter-) personal: Self- and partner-moderated influence in romantic relationships. *Social Influence, 3*, 34–66. doi:10.1080/15534510701774193

Oriña, M. M., Wood, W., & Simpson, J. A. (2002). Strategies of influence in close relationships. *Journal of Experimental Social Psychology, 38*, 459–472. doi:10.1016/S0022-1031(02)00015-X

Overall, N. C., & Fletcher, G. J. O. (2010). Perceiving regulation from intimate partners: Reflected appraisals and self-regulation processes in close relationships. *Personal Relationships, 17*, 433–456. doi:10.1111/j.1475-6811.2010.01286.x

Overall, N. C., Fletcher, G. J. O., & Simpson, J. A. (2006). Regulation processes in intimate relationships: The role of ideal standards. *Journal of Personality and Social Psychology, 91*, 662–685. doi:10.1037/0022-3514.91.4.662

Overall, N. C., Fletcher, G. J. O., Simpson, J. A., & Sibley, C. G. (2009). Regulating partners in intimate relationships: The costs and benefits of different communication strategies. *Journal of Personality and Social Psychology, 96*, 620–639. doi:10.1037/a0012961

Pulerwitz, J., Gortmaker, S. L., & DeJong, W. (2000). Measuring sexual relationship power in HIV/STD research. *Sex Roles, 42*, 637–660. doi:10.1023/A:1007051506972

Raven, B. H., Schwarzwald, J., & Koslowsky, M. (1998). Conceptualizing and measuring a power/interaction model of interpersonal influence. *Journal of Applied Social Psychology, 28*, 307–332. doi:10.1111/j.1559-1816.1998.tb01708.x

Reis, H. T., Collins, W. A., & Berscheid, E. (2000). The relationship context of human behavior and development. *Psychological Bulletin, 126*, 844–872. doi:10.1037/0033-2909.126.6.844

Rogers, W. S., Bidwell, J., & Wilson, L. (2005). Perception of and satisfaction with relationship power, sex, and attachment styles: A couples level analysis. *Journal of Family Violence, 20*, 241–251. doi:10.1007/s10896-005-5988-8

Rollins, B. C., & Bahr, S. J. (1976). A theory of power relationships in marriage. *Journal of Marriage and the Family, 38*, 619–627. doi:10.2307/350682

Russell, B. (1938). *Power: A new social analysis.* New York, NY: Norton.

Safilios-Rothschild, C. (1976). Macro- and micro-examination of family power and love: An exchange model. *Journal of Marriage and the Family, 38*, 355–362. doi:10.2307/350394

Schmid Mast, M., Jonas, K., & Hall, J. A. (2009). Give a person power and he or she will show interpersonal sensitivity: The phenomenon and its why and when. *Journal of Personality and Social Psychology, 97*, 835–850. doi:10.1037/a0016234

Simpson, J. A. (2007). Foundations of interpersonal trust. In A. W. Kruglanski & E. T. Higgins (Eds.), *Social psychology: Handbook of basic principles* (2nd ed., pp. 587–607). New York, NY: Guilford Press.

Sprecher, S. (1985). Sex differences in bases of power in dating relationships. *Sex Roles, 12*, 449–462. doi:10.1007/BF00287608

Sprecher, S., & Felmlee, D. (1997). The balance of power in romantic heterosexual relationships over time from "his" to "her" perspectives. *Sex Roles, 37*, 361–379. doi:10.1023/A:1025601423031

Sprecher, S., Schmeeckle, M., & Felmlee, D. (2006). The principle of least interest: Inequality in emotional involvement in romantic relationships. *Journal of Family Issues, 27*, 1255–1280. doi:10.1177/0192513X06289215

Thibaut, J. W., & Kelley, H. H. (1959). *The social psychology of groups.* New York, NY: Wiley.

Waller, W. W., & Hill, R. (1951). *The family: A dynamic interpretation.* New York, NY: Dryden Press.

Wolfe, D. M. (1959). Power and authority in the family. In D. Cartwright (Ed.), *Studies in social power* (pp. 99–117). Ann Arbor: University of Michigan Press.

Woolf, S. E., & Maisto, S. A. (2008). Gender differences in condom use behavior? The role of power and partner-type. *Sex Roles, 58*, 689–701. doi:10.1007/s11199-007-9381-3

POWER: PAST FINDINGS, PRESENT CONSIDERATIONS, AND FUTURE DIRECTIONS

Adam D. Galinsky, Derek D. Rucker, and Joe C. Magee

Lord Acton had something to say about power. So too did William Shakespeare, Friedrich Nietzsche, Bertrand Russell, and Stan Lee. From playwrights to philosophers to comic book writers, everyone seems to have observed the pervasive and vexing nature of power and constructed their own seemingly unique wisdom regarding its nature and novel insight into its consequences. With enough experiences, any and all proclamations about power may appear to be true. One of the tasks that falls on social scientists, however, is to determine which versions of the folk wisdom surrounding power have stood up to scientific scrutiny and under what conditions they have done so.

Systematic analysis of power in social psychology began at the end of World War II, with a tendency toward cataloging its corruptive lure. In what could be considered the first wave of the social psychological investigation into the effects of power, scholars explored whether positions of power cause the powerful to behave with greater self-interest and in a more antisocial fashion. Set against the backdrop of the extreme contexts of Nazi death camps and prisons, two of the seminal studies in the social psychology canon—Milgram (1963) and Zimbardo (1973; Zimbardo, Pilkonis, & Norwood, 1974)—supported the folk wisdom that power has a negative influence on behavior. Using more ordinary situations and techniques, Kipnis (1972; Kipnis, Castell, Gergen, & Mauch, 1976) documented the selfish and egocentric tendencies that power can incite in individuals. None of these studies, it would be fair to say, suggested that power could be a catalyst for making the world a brighter place.

After a steady interest in power among social psychologists throughout the 1970s and 1980s, a second wave of research explored the topic of power within the dominant paradigm of that period—social cognition. In this work, the methods had changed, but the dim view of power had not. Fiske and colleagues (e.g., Fiske, 1993; Goodwin, Gubin, Fiske, & Yzerbyt, 2000) investigated power's negative effects but departed from prior research on the social psychology of power in two important ways. First, these scholars were interested in attention and stereotyping, phenomena that were not part of the pervasive folk wisdom about power. Second, their predictions were generated from theoretical axioms rather than popular maxims. Throughout the 1990s and the first few years of the 21st century, interest in power rose at a strong and steady rate.

In the middle of the 1st decade of this century, there began a massive surge of empirical work on the topic of power. This wave did not confine itself to the pernicious and nefarious effects of power. Rather, this explosion of research investigated a wide range of effects, both positive and negative. As Figure 16.1 illustrates, the top four journal outlets for social psychological research—the *Journal of Personality and Social Psychology, Psychological Science, Journal of Experimental Social Psychology,* and *Personality and Social Psychology Bulletin*—nearly doubled the number of published articles on power in the past 5 years relative to the preceding 5 years.

Two factors coincided to produce the explosion of power research at the individual level of analysis in the decade before the publication of this chapter.

http://dx.doi.org/10.1037/14344-016
APA Handbook of Personality and Social Psychology: Vol. 3. Interpersonal Relations, M. Mikulincer and P. R. Shaver (Editors-in-Chief)

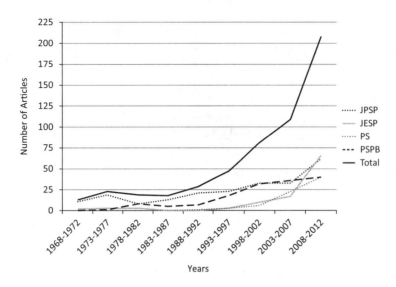

FIGURE 16.1. The rise of research on power: Count of articles about power appearing in the *Journal of Experimental Social Psychology* (JESP), *Journal of Personality and Social Psychology* (JPSP), *Personality and Social Psychology Bulletin* (PSPB), and *Psychological Science* (PS) by 5-year period, 1968–2012. Results were obtained using the Web of Science search engine.

First, Keltner, Gruenfeld, and Anderson (2003) introduced a new theoretical lens—the approach–inhibition theory of power—that reoriented researchers and stimulated new predictions about power in many different domains. Second, Galinsky, Gruenfeld, and Magee (2003) offered a methodological innovation—an episodic recall task that asked people to reflect on an experience with power—that allowed researchers to easily manipulate power in a wide variety of research contexts (e.g., in the laboratory, in the classroom, in surveys).

The subsequent increase in power research demonstrates that a theoretical model and a simple, easy-to-implement method help secure traction for a research topic. Each one can individually stimulate a research area, but the combination of the two—a theory and a simple, flexible, and efficient method—can be a true catalyst for an area of research to explode. Have theory and method, will travel.

In this chapter, we provide a primer on the social psychological study of power and capture emerging themes that we think are likely to develop into the next wave of research on power. To accomplish this objective, we begin the chapter by offering a clear definition of power. We then pay homage to the prior waves of power research by discussing the antecedents (in the form of manipulations and measures) and consequences that bracket the psychological experience of power as well as critical moderators. Figure 16.2 provides a conceptual map for these parts of the chapter. Subsequently, we discuss theories about how power guides and directs behavior. We close by setting an agenda for future research. Our goal is to provide a formative review of new and emerging themes on the study of power, a review that can be used both by individuals new to the domain of power and by more seasoned researchers as they set their future research agendas.

DEFINITION OF POWER

We define social power using the same definition as Magee and Galinsky (2008): asymmetric control over valued resources in a social relationship (for related definitions, see Blau, 1964; Fiske, 2010; Thibaut & Kelley, 1959).

A key reason for using the word *asymmetric* and defining social power in a particular social relationship is that this definition captures the relative state of dependence between two or more parties (individuals or groups; Emerson, 1962) and distinguishes social power from other forms of control (e.g., self-control). Indeed, many power-related theories revolve around this issue of dependency. For example, Thibaut and

Kelley's (1959) interdependence theory makes the comparison level of alternatives a central component of power in close relationships. When power exists between two parties, one party is more dependent on the other party than vice versa. When no power exists between two parties, then either the parties are not dependent on each other (i.e., a state of independence between two parties) or they are equally dependent on each other (i.e., a state of mutual dependence between two parties).

We use the term *valued* because the resource must be important or consequential, objectively or subjectively, to at least one of the two parties. To the extent that an individual has or lacks power in a relationship, one must look both at the value each party assigns to the resources in question and at their alternative routes to acquiring those resources. A high-power person who controls a resource only has power over another individual to the extent that the other person values the resource the first person possesses and has few alternative means to acquire it.

This definition allows one to understand the dynamic and subjective nature of power across situations and contexts. For example, a professor can control a graduate student's career advancement, but the graduate student can have technical expertise on which the professor depends. A teacher controls students' grades, but on the last day of class, students have power over the teacher's evaluations; the students have more power to the extent that the professor's raises or own subjective well-being depends on those evaluations.

Overbeck and Park (2001) distinguished between social and personal power (see also van Dijke & Poppe, 2006). Social power involves control over a resource that others value; the less powerful person is dependent on the powerful person to meet his or her needs. Personal power involves control over one's own access to resources and therefore involves lack of dependence on others. Personal power, it could be said, is equivalent to the concept of autonomy. Lammers, Stoker, and Stapel (2009) have argued that these two types of power can have unique effects on behavior. This distinction is potentially important, but one empirical difficulty is that manipulations of social power often simply involve control over a greater number of valued resources than do manipulations of personal power. Whether social power is different from personal power in magnitude as well as in kind remains to be seen.

The definition of power we present here can be connected to, but also distinguished from, previous definitions of power that involve the constructs influence, resistance, or conflict (for a thorough review, see Magee & Galinsky, 2008). We should also note that three of French and Raven's (1959) famous five bases—reward, coercive, and expert power—relate directly to control over valued resources and thus fall under our definition of power. In contrast to French and Raven, we conceptualize legitimacy not as a base of power but as an independent construct; doing so allows researchers to explore how legitimacy moderates the effects of power. Their final base of power—referent power—can be likened to social status, which we define as respect and admiration in the eyes of others (see also Magee & Galinsky, 2008). More important, status is conceptually orthogonal to power (Fiske, 2010; Fiske & Berdahl, 2007; Magee & Galinsky, 2008), a topic we turn to later in the chapter.

MANIPULATIONS AND MEASURES OF POWER

In this section, we discuss the different ways in which power has been manipulated in social psychological research. In doing so, our objective is to provide a simple guide for how power can be studied empirically. We divide these manipulations into four categories of manipulation that serve to affect one's sense of power. The first category consists of structural manipulations that involve varying control over a resource, typically within the context of a laboratory experiment. The second category involves activating the experience of power via episodic recall or an imagined role manipulation. The third category involves semantically or visually priming the concept of power, using word puzzles, scrambled-sentence tasks, or photos. The final category involves altering an individual's physical posture or nonverbal behavior and builds on work on embodied cognition. In addition to these manipulations, we consider popular individual difference measures that are considered to be related to power and are used in correlational research designs (see Figure 16.2).

Manipulations/Measures　　　　　　　　　　**Consequences**

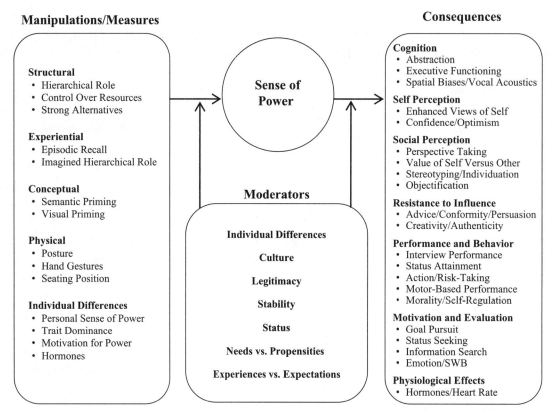

FIGURE 16.2.　Organizing framework for the psychology of power. The manipulations and measures of power create a sense of power that then produces a range of cognitive, behavioral, and physiological consequences. The moderators of power can alter (a) whether power produces a sense of power or (b) whether a sense of power produces a particular outcome.

Structural Manipulations

Hierarchical role. A manipulation of power that has high external validity, personifies our definition of power, and fits with lay conceptualizations of power is the boss–employee manipulation. Kipnis (1972; Kipnis et al., 1976) was one of the first to manipulate power in a lab environment. In the Kipnis studies, everyone played the role of manager, but only some of the participants had reward and coercive power in their role.

Building on this experimental method, Anderson and Berdahl (2002) extensively pretested various components of a boss–employee manipulation and created what is now the gold standard for role-based power manipulations. In their manipulation, participants first complete a Leadership Questionnaire and are told that their responses will be used to assign them to the role of manager–boss or subordinate–employee. The experimenter ostensibly scores the

questionnaire and assigns participants to the high-power or low-power role. The boss is given instructions that emphasize that he or she will have complete control over the work process, the evaluation of the subordinates, and the division of rewards. Thus, the person in this role controls processes, individual outcomes, and the distribution of valuable resources. The employee is told that he or she will have no control over how the work is performed, evaluated, or rewarded.

Control over resources. Although it lacks the multidimensionality of many power dynamics in the real world, the manipulation of power that most personifies our definition of power is to give people asymmetric control over a resource. For example, Galinsky et al. (2003, 2006) had participants take part in a resource allocation task that involved the distribution of tickets for a lottery for a $300 dinner at a local restaurant. In this modified version of a dictator game, high-power participants had power by dictating the distribution of seven lottery tickets between themselves and another participant. Low-power participants had no control over the distribution.

Researchers have also used the ultimatum and dictator games to instantiate power (Roth, 1995; Sivanathan, Pillutla, & Keith Murnighan, 2008). In an ultimatum game, two parties decide how to allocate a resource (e.g., $10). One member (the offerer) suggests a proposed division. If the other participant (the receiver) accepts the offer, then the money is divided according to the proposed proportions. If the receiver rejects the offer, then both parties receive nothing. In the ultimatum game, the offerer has more power than the receiver because the offerer set the terms of the division. However, there is some constraint on the offerer's power because the receiver is able to choose whether to accept the proposed division. The fact that the offerer gets on average significantly more than 50% of the divided money empirically confirms that the offerer has greater power. In the dictator game, the offerer has complete control over the division of a resource. The receiver can reject his or her allocation but cannot affect the offerer's outcome.

Suleiman (1996) created a manipulation that allows researchers to vary the power difference along a continuum from the weaker power of the ultimatum game to the greater power of the dictator game. He did so by adding a discount factor, delta $(0 \leq \delta \leq 1)$. A rejection of the offer by the receiver in a standard ultimatum game produces a 0–0 outcome. In the modified version (the delta game), rejection of the offer leads to a multiplication of the proposed outcomes for the offerer and the recipient by delta. For example, when $\delta = 0.5$, rejection of a 70–30 offer leads to a multiplication of outcomes for both players by 0.5, resulting in a 35–15 division. The delta game covers the entire continuum between a standard ultimatum game and a dictator game. When $\delta = 0$, it is identical to the standard ultimatum game, and when $\delta = 1$ it is identical to the standard dictator game.

Strong alternatives. In the context of negotiations, the strength of two parties' alternatives defines the power relationship between them.

Typically, negotiation power comes from one's best alternative to a negotiated agreement. Having a strong best alternative to a negotiated agreement gives a negotiator power because it makes him or her less dependent on an opponent for acquiring desired resources (Fisher, Ury, & Patton, 1991; Kim, Pinkley, & Fragale, 2005; Mannix & Neale, 1993; Pinkley, Neale, & Bennett, 1994; Sondak & Bazerman, 1991). For example, Magee, Galinsky, and Gruenfeld (2007) manipulated power in an employment negotiation by assigning negotiators a best alternative to a negotiated agreement (e.g., an attractive alternative job offer that gave them power) or by not providing them with an alternative job offer (low power). Pinkley et al. (1994) manipulated not only the presence of an alternative but also the strength of the alternative.

Experiential Manipulations

Episodic recall. Galinsky et al. (2003) introduced a power manipulation in the form of a simple writing task. They asked participants to recall and write about a personally relevant experience with power. Participants assigned to the high-power condition recalled and wrote about an experience in which they had power over another person—power was defined in their original manipulation as "a situation in which you controlled the ability of another person or persons to get something they wanted, or were in a position to evaluate those individuals" (p. 458). In contrast, participants assigned to the low-power condition recalled and wrote about an experience in which someone had power over them. In addition, a variety of instantiations of this manipulation have been shown to activate power. For example, Rucker, Dubois, and Galinsky (2011) subtly embedded the recall task in a print advertisement by simply providing a slogan in the advertisement that read, "Remember a time you felt powerful?"

Galinsky et al. (2003) created the episodic recall task because they were concerned that the structural manipulation of power in which the high-power role directs, evaluates, and distributes rewards would produce confounds and thus alternative explanations for how power affects action tendencies. The powerful could act, not because of their power per se, but because high-power roles require more cognitive resources that otherwise might be deployed to inhibit action or because of prescriptive norms suggesting that people in a high-power role should act. This recall task allows researchers to activate the experience of power in a way that is meaningful to participants without actually altering the objective or structural level of power in a given situation. Thus, this priming procedure allows researchers to activate power without differentially affecting the cognitive capacity or role-based norms of high- and low-power participants. This task is presented as separate from the dependent variable of interest, and very few participants detect any relationship between the tasks or can articulate the hypothesis of interest.

Imagine hierarchical role.   Dubois, Rucker, and Galinsky (2010) have shown that a boss–employee simulation manipulation that is purely hypothetical can also be used to manipulate power. Dubois et al. asked people to simulate being the boss or employee of a hypothetical company and to vividly imagine what it would be like to be in this role (i.e., how they would feel, think, and act). They found that this simple exercise of imagining oneself in a high or low-power role was enough to significantly affect people's sense of power.

Conceptual Manipulations

Semantic priming.   Building off the seminal work on priming by Higgins (1996) and Bargh, Chaiken, Raymond, and Hymes (1996), researchers have also manipulated power by exposing people to power-related words. These manipulations allow researchers to activate the construct of power outside of participants' awareness. One version involves a word-completion task in which participants are presented with word fragments and asked to complete the words by filling in the missing letters (e.g., "P O W _ _" is completed as "P O W E R"; Anderson & Galinsky, 2006; Bargh, Raymond, Pryor, & Strack, 1995; Galinsky, Magee, Gruenfeld, Whitson, & Liljenquist, 2008). Another version involves a scrambled-sentences task in which participants unscramble sentences containing a word

related either to low power (e.g., *subordinate*) or to high power (e.g., *authority*; Smith & Trope, 2006). Researchers have even subliminally primed participants with words related to power (see Bargh et al., 1995). As with the episodic recall manipulation, this task is presented as an task independent from the core dependent measure. Few, if any, participants successfully guess the hypotheses of interest.

Visual priming.   Power can also be primed through visual imagery. For example, Torelli et al. (2012) demonstrated that the concept of power could be successfully activated by showing participants photos (e.g., image of executives disembarking from a private jet). Other research outside the domain of power has established the effectiveness of using visual imagery to prime particular constructs (e.g., Hong, Morris, Chiu, & Benet-Martinez, 2000).

Implications of Priming Power

The experiential and cognitive manipulations demonstrate that power not only resides within social relationships, as a basis of hierarchy, but also that the concept of power is a mental construct that can be primed. Bargh et al. (1995) were the first to conceive of power this way and to suggest that power could have nonconscious, automatic effects on behavior. Research on the priming of power has demonstrated that the tendencies associated with different levels of power are stored in memory, available for activation whenever one's power is made salient in a given situation.

Physical Manipulations

The concept of power can also be manipulated through individuals' physical actions and gestures.

Posture.   Carney, Cuddy, and Yap (2010) demonstrated that power could be activated by one's posture by placing people into an expansive pose (presumed to create a state of high power) or constrictive pose (presumed to create a state of low power). For example, one high-power pose involved participants leaning back in a chair with arms behind their head and legs on the table; one low-power pose involved participants slouching forward with their hands between their legs (see also Huang, Galinsky, Gruenfeld, & Guillory, 2011). Carney et al. (2010) used two posture manipulations: (a) a posture in which people speared their hands and leaned on a desk and (b) a posture in which people leaned back and put their feet on a desk.

Hand gestures. Schubert and colleagues (Schubert, 2004; Schubert & Koole, 2009) have shown that a sense of power can be manipulated by physical gestures with one's hand: Participants in the high-power condition were asked to make a fist with their nonwriting hand throughout the experiment. In the baseline condition, participants were told to keep their nonwriting hands in a relaxed position throughout the study. These subtle physical gestures were shown to affect participants' sense of power and subsequent behavior.

Seating position. Chen, Lee-Chai, and Bargh (2001) have also used a symbolic association with power—seating position—to manipulate power. In their study, the manipulation took place in a professor's office. Participants in the high-power condition sat in the cushioned professor's chair, which was situated behind the desk and raised higher than the other chair. Participants in the low-power condition sat on the other side of the desk in a short and relatively uncomfortable wooden chair (see also Briñol, Petty, Valle, Rucker, & Becerra, 2007). These subtle seating positions were shown to activate the concept of power and either lacking or possessing power.

Manipulating the Moderators of Power

Many of the preceding manipulations allow people to test for moderators of power, a topic we turn to later. For example, a structural manipulation of power can be constructed to be stable and last throughout the experiment or can vary depending on what happens during the experiment (Jordan, Sivanathan, & Galinsky, 2011). The assignment to a hierarchical role can be legitimated, for example, by assigning participants to positions of power according to their responses on a leadership questionnaire (see Anderson & Berdahl, 2002), or it can be assigned illegitimately on the basis of some extraneous factor, such as a demographic characteristic. For example, Lammers, Galinsky, Gordijn, and Otten (2008) told participants they would normally be assigned to be the employee or manager role but

would nonetheless be assigned to the other role because the researchers preferred to have the opposite gender in the other role. The status of the position of power that people are assigned to can also be manipulated; that is, the role can be infused with either respect or disrespect (Fast, Halevy, & Galinsky, 2012).

The experiential primes can also be used to test for moderators. Researchers can have participants recall an incident in which they had power or lacked power but in which this power difference was deemed by them to be stable or unstable, having or lacking status, legitimately or illegitimately acquired, and so forth. Similarly, in the boss–employee simulation task, participants can be asked to simulate the experience of being in a powerful or powerless position that was stable, legitimate, respected, or any other moderator that a researcher is interested in.

Even the semantic priming methods can be used to explore the effects of moderators of power. For example, Lammers, Gordijn, and Otten (2008) embedded words related to high or low power and words related to legitimacy (e.g., *fair, just*) or illegitimacy (e.g., *unfair, unjust*) within a single word puzzle, thereby semantically pairing the two concepts of power and legitimacy.

Individual Differences

In addition to situational factors, myriad individual difference measures are associated with power. These measures are designed to demonstrate that (a) individuals scoring higher on the measure are more likely to hold positions of greater power, (b) individuals in positions of greater power score higher on the measure, or (c) the correlation between the measure and another variable is similar to the pattern of results produced by a manipulation of power. We discuss four such measures that have received significant attention from power researchers.

Personal sense of power. Capitalizing on the notion that power transforms individual psychology and influences individuals' subjective sense of control (Fast, Gruenfeld, Sivanathan, & Galinsky, 2009), Anderson, John, and Keltner (2012) developed the Personal Sense of Power Scale to capture individual variation in one's perceived ability to influence other people. The items can be tailored to reflect one's influence over another individual in a specific relationship, across relationships within a specific context (e.g., in one's workplace), or one's general sense of influence across contexts and relationships. The scale has good external validity because individuals who occupy managerial roles at work and have more power report feeling more powerful than those occupying subordinate roles.

The Personal Sense of Power Scale can also be used to capture a person's current feelings of power, and thus it can also be effectively used as a manipulation check, as a way to understand variation in how people respond to power manipulations (e.g., Chen, Langner, & Mendoza-Denton, 2009), or as a mediating mechanism (Anderson & Berdahl, 2002; Fast, Sivanathan, Mayer, & Galinsky, 2012; see also Shnabel & Nadler, 2008). Indeed, each of the manipulations of power described previously has been shown to affect people's psychological sense of power, that is, how powerful one feels at a given moment in time. By exploring and understanding people's sense of power, researchers can also examine situations in which one objectively has power but does not psychologically feel powerful.

Trait dominance.   Trait dominance is "the tendency to behave in assertive, forceful, and self-assured ways" (Anderson & Kilduff, 2009, p. 491), which can be related to the possession of power. Trait dominance is typically self-reported, although peer reports of targets' dominance could conceivably be used. Regardless of how trait dominance is measured, clarity about what constitutes dominance is critical to the measurement process, because men and women perceive different behaviors as dominant (Buss, 1981; Schmid Mast & Hall, 2004; cf. Carney, Hall, & LeBeau, 2005). Two measures of trait dominance—the dominance scales in Gough's (1987) Personality Research Inventory and in Jackson's (1974) Personality Research Form— have been used extensively (Aries, Gold, & Weigel, 1983; Buss & Craik, 1980; Georgesen & Harris, 2000; Goodwin, Operario, & Fiske, 1998; McClelland, Koestner, & Weinberger, 1989; Operario & Fiske, 2001; Pratto, Sidanius, Stallworth, & Malle, 1994). Anderson and colleagues (Anderson & Berdahl, 2002;

Anderson & Kilduff, 2009) have used dominance items from the Revised Interpersonal Adjective Scales (Wiggins, Trapnell, & Phillips, 1988).

One issue with this measure is that it is important to separate trait dominance, which is stable across contexts, from observable dominance behavior, which can vary across contexts (Dovidio, Ellyson, Keating, Heltman, & Brown,1988). When individuals' dominance behavior is assessed, it ought to be treated primarily as a downstream consequence of a self-report measure. Self-report measures of dominance are typically positively correlated with dominance behavior (Buss & Craik, 1980), but situations in which self-report measures do not predict corresponding behavior are interesting exceptions that demand further study.

Motivation for power.   The power motive captures the extent to which people value having power. Traditional measures include both the desire to influence others and a concern with one's status (McClelland, 1970, 1975, 1985; McClelland & Wilsnack, 1972; Winter, 1973; Winter & Stewart, 1978). Further refinement of the construct has led some researchers to emphasize the importance of teasing apart different types of power motives on the basis of whose interests the individual imagines serving with power (Magee & Langner, 2008). One can desire to have influence over others either for self-serving and antisocial goals (personalized power motive) or for goals that are profitable for others (socialized power motive; McClelland & Wilsnack, 1972; see also Winter & Stewart's [1978] hope of power and fear of power).

An important choice facing power-motive researchers is whether to use an implicit or an explicit measure because they produce empirically independent scores (Brunstein & Maier, 2005; Kehr, 2004; King, 1995; but see Emmons & McAdams, 1991) and effects (e.g., Spangler, 1992; for reviews, see McClelland et al., 1989; Schultheiss, 2001; Woike, Mcleod, & Goggin, 2003). The Thematic Apperception Test has been the most common measure of the implicit power motive (Atkinson, 1958; Schultheiss & Brunstein, 2001; Schultheiss et al., 2005; Winter, 1991), but other written responses to a motive-eliciting stimulus or situation have been used as well (Emmons & McAdams, 1991; Langner & Winter, 2001; Magee & Langner, 2008). Implicit power motive determines the hedonic value derived from situations that satisfy a need to exert influence (Koestner, Weinberger, & McClelland, 1991; McClelland et al., 1989; Pang & Schultheiss, 2005; Schultheiss & Pang, 2007). Explicit power motive is self-reported, as are the other individual differences reviewed here (McClelland et al., 1989), and functions like a value, as a guiding principle in one's life. Power motives can also be manipulated (McClelland et al., 1989; Spangler, 1992). For example, Langner and Winter (2001) manipulated imagery associated with power in one experiment to vary the strength of elicitation of power motives.

Hormones. Both testosterone and cortisol are related to dominance behavior (Mehta, Jones, & Josephs, 2008; Mehta & Josephs, 2010) and to power motives (Schultheiss et al., 2005; Wirth, Welsh, & Schultheiss, 2006), so it is not surprising that they are thought of as biological markers of power. High testosterone and low cortisol appear to be the hormonal profile of high power, whereas low testosterone and high cortisol characterizes people in conditions of low power (Carney et al., 2010; Mehta & Josephs, 2010). These hormones are part of a dynamic neurobiological system sensitized to hierarchical position, responsive both to prospective and to recent changes in rank (Mehta & Josephs, 2010; Schultheiss et al., 2005). However, they are also complicated measures of power because the dynamic nature of testosterone and cortisol requires accounting for diurnal hormone cycles, a pretest and posttest to accurately measure hormone change, and the resources for the requisite medical laboratory analyses.

CONSEQUENCES OF POWER

Research has established that power has profound effects on individuals' cognition, self-perception, social perception, motivation, performance, behavior, and even physiological states. Collectively, this research suggests that one's sense of power is a key proximate variable that predicts behavior.

The fact that the many different manipulations of power reliably alter one's sense of power and that these manipulations have an impact on so many different outcomes raises the question of what

accounts for their robustness. We believe the ease of manipulating power and its panoply of consequences arises, at least in part, because social hierarchy is the predominant form of social organization across cultures and across species. Indeed, several functional theories of hierarchy propose that hierarchy is ubiquitous because hierarchy solves the inherent problems associated with organizing a collection of individuals (Gruenfeld & Tiedens, 2010; Halevy, Chou, & Galinsky, 2011; van Vugt, Hogan, & Kaiser, 2008): It facilitates coordination, reduces conflict, motivates members of a group to contribute to the group, and ultimately fosters goal attainment (Magee & Galinsky, 2008). Remember that power varies from situation to situation, depending on the specific resource and particular relationships in which one is embedded. For hierarchy to function as an organizing principle, it is critical that people quickly and accurately identify their relative power in any situation and within any particular relationship. Therefore, people must be attuned to their level of power and have a range of behavioral repertoires that get activated depending on one's power in a given situation.

In this section, we provide illustrative examples of some of the most provocative effects of power, with a special emphasis on more recent findings. Our goal is not to provide an exhaustive list of all the findings related to power but to provide a primer for researchers less familiar with the construct or with recent advances on the topic.

Cognition Processes

Abstraction. The experience of power is associated with how people mentally represent their world. High power leads people to construe information more abstractly (Magee & Smith, 2013; Smith & Trope, 2006), focusing more on the gist of information (vs. concrete details) and categorizing information and objects at superordinate levels (vs. subordinate levels). For example, Smith and Trope (2006) found that high-power individuals are more prone to identify a behavior or action (e.g., voting) at a higher level (e.g., changing the government), whereas low-power individuals are more prone to identify the behavior at a lower level (e.g., marking a ballot). Similarly, Magee, Milliken, and Lurie (2010) found that individuals in positions of power, such as government officials, described the events during the aftermath of the 9/11 terrorist attacks at a more abstract level than did individuals who had little or no power, such as volunteers or victims. Extending this work, Miyamoto and Ji (2011) found that power promoted the use of analytic cognitive processing: High-power participants, those who had thought about influencing someone else, were more likely to use abstract linguistic categories (i.e., adjectives) than those who had thought about adjusting their behavior to others.

Executive functioning. Smith, Jostmann, Galinsky, and van Dijk (2008) demonstrated that low power tends to impair executive functioning compared with high power. Specifically, they found that powerless participants exhibited impaired performance on executive functioning tasks associated with updating, inhibiting, and planning. In one experiment, Smith et al. found that low-power participants made more errors on incongruent trials of the Stroop task (see Stroop, 1935) than both high-power and baseline participants.

Findings have suggested that power also affects basic cognitive abilities related to mathematics. Much of this work has been studied in the context of sex differences in math performance. For example, Guiso, Monte, Sapienza, and Zingales (2008) found that countries in which women had more power in terms of opportunities to participate in economic and political life also had a smaller gender gap in math ability (see also Hamamura, 2012). Harada, Bridge, and Chiao (2012) manipulated power and replicated this broader finding. Women primed with high power performed better on approximate math calculations; furthermore, this neural response within the left inferior frontal gyrus, a region associated with cognitive interference, was reduced for high-power women (Harada et al., 2012).

Spatial biases. Power has also been linked to differential brain activity and elementary spatial biases. Increases in power have been shown to lead to a heightened activation of the left hemisphere, whereas decreases in power have been shown to lead to a heightened activation of the right hemisphere (see Boksem, Smolders, & De Cremer, 2012). For

example, in one experiment, low power, which is associated with right hemispheric activation, led participants to be more inclined to bisect horizontal lines to the left of center (Wilkinson, Guinote, Weick, Molinari, & Graham, 2010), which occurs because right hemispheric control is accompanied by leftward deviation.

Vocal acoustics. Not only does power affect basic cognitive processes, but it also alters vocal acoustics. Ko, Sadler, and Galinsky (2013) had participants read a baseline passage, then manipulated power before an ostensible negotiation and subsequently had participants read a passage as if they were starting the negotiation. This procedure allowed the researchers to control for baseline acoustics within speakers and therefore capture hierarchy-based acoustics. They used the vocal recording to precisely measure six acoustic cues—the mean and variability in pitch, resonance, and loudness. They found that the voices of high-power speakers were higher pitched, less variable in pitch, and more variable in loudness than low-power voices. They also analyzed Margaret Thatcher's voice before and after she became the British prime minister (Gallafent, 2008). On her election, Thatcher went through extensive voice coaching designed to help her present a more powerful persona. Consistent with Ko et al.'s experimental participants, Thatcher's voice became higher in pitch, less variable in pitch, and more variable in loudness after she became prime minister. Thus, untrained speakers' momentary vocal changes induced by power were similar to those of someone who was trained to express authority in her voice.

These findings contradict lay theories on how power affects the voice, especially with regard to pitch. Indeed, Stel, van Dijk, Smith, van Dijk, and Djalal (2012) found that getting people to lower their voice made them feel more powerful and think more abstractly. Elsewhere, research has found that dominance is associated with lower pitch (Apple, Streeter, & Krauss, 1979; Ohala, 1982). A crucial distinction is that dominance-based pitch captures individual differences in baseline pitch and is tied to physical characteristics of the body. Hierarchy-based pitch is about change in pitch within individuals, independent of baseline pitch.

Self-Perception

Enhanced views of the self. Power has been shown to enhance how positively people view the self. For example, Wojciszke and Struzynska-Kujalowicz (2007) found that experiential and role-based manipulations of power increased state self-esteem and increased the better-than-average effect, and Fast et al. (2009) replicated this effect using the Rosenberg Self-Esteem Scale. Power also leads people to feel more confident in their own knowledge (Fast, Sivanathan, et al., 2012; See, Morrison, Rothman, & Soll, 2011; Tost, Gino, & Larrick, 2012). In Magee et al.'s (2010) examination of how people talked about the 9/11 attacks, they found that power holders expressed more confidence than powerless individuals in the aftermath of the attacks.

The powerful also have enhanced views of themselves physically. Specifically, they see themselves as larger. Duguid and Goncalo (2012) found that manipulating power through experiential primes or roles led people to see themselves as physically taller and to select a taller avatar to represent themselves in a video game. The powerful also tend to underestimate the size of other people (Yap, Mason, & Ames, 2013).

Confidence and optimism. Relative to powerless individuals, powerful individuals also expect better outcomes for themselves in the future. Anderson and Galinsky (2006) found that power was associated with more optimistic perceptions of the future. For example, in one experiment by Anderson and Galinsky, people with a higher chronic sense of power believed they would experience more positive events such as enjoying their job, having the value of their home increase, and having their achievements displayed in a newspaper. Power also exacerbates the planning fallacy; power leads people to be more optimistic and less accurate in predicting how long a task will take to complete (Weick & Guinote, 2010). In sum, the powerful see themselves and their world through rose-colored glasses.

Social Perception

Perspective taking. A variety of research findings have suggested that, compared with lacking power, having power is associated with a reduced ability to take the perspective of others (Galinsky, Magee, Inesi, & Gruenfeld, 2006; Keltner & Robinson, 1997). As one example, Galinsky et al. (2006) instructed participants in a state of high or low power to draw an *E* on their forehead. Compared with low-power participants, high-power participants were more inclined to draw the *E* as if they were reading it, leading to a backward and illegible *E* to other people. This is consistent with the notion that high-power participants were more focused on the self and less focused on the perspective of others, whereas the reverse was true among low-power participants.

Given that powerful individuals tend to be less concerned with taking others' perspectives, Lammers, Gordijn, and Otten (2008) reasoned that the powerful would also be less inclined to activate metastereotypes. Metastereotypes are stereotypes people hold about how out-groups perceive their in-group (e.g., "I think other groups think we are smart."). Accurate metastereotypes can be useful sources of information because they can help groups navigate social interactions. Lammers, Gordijn, and Otten (2008) reasoned, and demonstrated, that powerless individuals, who are typically motivated to understand how others see them, engaged in significantly more metastereotyping than powerful individuals.

Research by Van Kleef et al. (2008) demonstrated that the inclination of power holders to ignore others' perspectives leads powerful individuals to be less empathic toward others' suffering. To test this idea, in one experiment, Van Kleef et al. had participants in same-sex dyads disclose experiences that had caused them personal suffering and pain. Participants with a higher chronic sense of power experienced less distress, experienced less compassion, and exhibited greater autonomic emotion regulation when listening to another participants' suffering than did those with a lower chronic sense of power.

Value of self versus other. Research has also found that states of high and low power have systematic effects on individuals' propensity to allocate resources to themselves versus others. Powerful individuals tend to spend more on themselves, whereas powerless individuals tend to give more to others. For instance, Rucker et al. (2011) found that a state of power led individuals to spend more on a t-shirt purchased for themselves than on a t-shirt purchased for another person. In contrast, a state of powerlessness led individuals to spend more on a t-shirt purchased for others than on the same t-shirt purchased for the self. Similarly, Kraus, Piff, and Keltner (2011) found that individuals higher in socioeconomic status spent a smaller portion of their income on others.

Rucker et al. (2011) discussed how power affects the relative importance of the self versus others. High power essentially provides a signal that one is more important because, by definition, one has more resources and control relative to others. In contrast, low power sends a signal that one is dependent on others. This does not mean, however, that powerful individuals will never spend on others. For example, as illustrated by Chen et al. (2001), goals to serve others may be intensified in high-power individuals (see Rucker, Galinsky, & Dubois, 2012, for further discussion).

Stereotyping and individuation.   Fiske (1993) originally proposed that powerful individuals stereotype others, both by default because they have less incentive to pay close attention to others and by design because stereotyping allows powerful individuals to control and box in others. Goodwin et al. (2000) confirmed that powerful individuals do indeed stereotype others. Participants used stereotypes more than individuating information when evaluating targets. Building on the idea that stereotyping is a building block for prejudice, Guinote, Willis, and Martellotta (2010) found that power led to greater implicit prejudice against out-groups.

Overbeck and Park (2001) also examined the effects of power on individuation and obtained two important findings. First, the effect of power on individuation depended on the target's level of power. High-power perceivers were found to individuate low-power targets more than did low-power perceivers. In addition, high-power perceivers showed greater individuation of low-power targets compared with the amount of individuation low-power perceivers showed for high-power targets. Second,

individuation by powerful individuals was greater when they were focused on interpersonal connections than when they were focused on completing a task.

Objectification.   The finding from Overbeck and Park (2001) that powerful individuals individuated less when task focused speaks to the tendency for powerful individuals to be instrumental in their attention. Those who are powerful are more inclined to attend to the attributes of others that are goal relevant. Gruenfeld, Inesi, Magee, and Galinsky (2008) found that both senior executives and MBA students reported greater objectification in their relationships with a subordinate than with a peer. Furthermore, senior executives, more advanced in the business hierarchy than MBA students, were found to view relationships both with subordinates and with peers in instrumental terms. In another experiment, participants assigned to a high-power condition showed more instrumental views of others than those assigned to a low-power condition.

Resistance to Influence

Power is often conceptualized as the capacity to influence others. A number of research findings have also demonstrated that power psychologically protects people from influence. As a result, power affects the likelihood that people will express their true beliefs.

Advice, conformity, and persuasion.   For example, powerful individuals rely on their knowledge and ignore and reject the advice of others (See et al., 2011; Tost et al., 2012). Tost et al. (2012) found that power led people to discount the advice of both nonexperts and experts. Those who are powerful are also more likely to rely on their own subjective experiences, such as ease of retrieval, when forming judgments (Weick & Guinote, 2008).

Briñol et al. (2007) have shown that powerful individuals are less likely to carefully attend to the beliefs expressed by others and such behavior is especially likely when those beliefs are inconsistent with their own (see Fischer, Fischer, Englich, Aydin, & Frey, 2011). As a result, powerful individuals are able to resist the persuasion attempts of others. Furthermore, Eaton, Visser, Krosnick, and

Anand (2009) found that a sense of power led middle-aged individuals to be more resistant to persuasion than either younger or older people.

Galinsky et al. (2008) found that powerful individuals' attitudes were less susceptible to conformity pressures. Participants in one study completed a relatively boring task and were then presented with other participants' favorable task ratings (that were really bogus). They found power shielded individuals from the influence of others' opinions and led them to express their true attitudes and rate the task less favorably. Those who are powerful can successfully resist the pernicious pressure to act like the rest of the herd.

Powerful individuals are also more likely to express their current feelings and attitudes. Anderson and Berdahl (2002) found that power led people to be more inclined to reveal their own opinion in a group discussion. In negotiations, high-power negotiators' own anger focuses their attention and leads them to claim value, whereas low-power negotiators are more influenced by their counterpart's anger, which derails them from what they are trying to achieve (Overbeck, Neale, & Govan, 2010; see also Anderson & Thompson, 2004; Van Kleef, de Dreu, Pietroni, & Manstead, 2006). Hecht and LaFrance (1998) found that, when in a positive mood, powerful individuals were more likely to smile and reveal their mood than powerless individuals.

The fact that powerful individuals turn a blind eye to other people can protect them in competitive situations. For example, negotiators often quickly concede in the face of an opponent's angry expressions. However, power immunizes negotiators from the influence of their opponents' emotional displays, with high-power negotiators conceding less to an angry opponent than to a baseline or low-power negotiator (Van Kleef et al., 2006). Power protects negotiators from being swayed by the strategic displays of emotions that are designed to induce concessions.

Creativity and authenticity. Because powerful individuals are less influenced by others, they are also able to be more creative. Research on creativity (Osborn, 1953) has found that the ideas of other people limit and constrain one's own imagination. Galinsky et al. (2008) found that powerful individuals

were less influenced by the ideas of others and produced more novel output.

Given that powerful individuals ignore others and the constraints they impose, it is not surprising that power increases authentic expression (Kifer, Heller, Perunovic, & Galinsky, 2013; Kraus, Chen, & Keltner, 2011). In one study, Kifer et al. (2013) used four rounds of surveys, each representing markedly different primary social roles (general, work, romantic relationship, friendship; Study 1) and found that experiencing power in one domain led to greater feelings of authenticity within that same domain. These findings demonstrate that power can induce a subjective correspondence between internal states, and behavior has positive psychological consequences for power holders.

Performance and Behavior

Interview performance. Lammers, Dubois, Rucker, and Galinsky (2013) found that powerful individuals present themselves more effectively, both orally and in writing. In one experiment, participants submitted a written application for a job. Those primed with power before completing the application were more likely to be selected for the job by independent judges. In a second experiment, Lammers et al. (2013) primed high power, low power, and baseline before a practice interview for entrance into business school. Those primed with high power were more than twice as likely to be selected by the expert judges, who were unaware of the power prime, than those primed with low power. The powerful participants were more likely to be selected because they were seen as more persuasive. Similarly, Schmid and Schmid Mast (2013) had participants make speeches in which they described their strengths. Those primed with power were seen as presenting themselves more effectively. The greater performance by the powerful participants was driven by reduced fear of negative evaluation.

Status attainment. As noted earlier, status and power are conceptually distinct but correlated constructs. They are also causally connected. Kilduff and Galinsky (2013) conducted a longitudinal experiment to demonstrate that priming people with power can lead individuals to attain higher status. In their study, three people came to the lab at Time 1. One was primed with high power, one was primed with low power, and one was in a baseline condition. The three people then gathered and participated in a group decision-making task. Two days later, the three people returned to participate in a new group task. Participants primed with power achieved greater status both immediately and 2 days later, long after the primes had worn off. Moreover, these increases in status were driven by increased proactive behavior during the very first few minutes of group interaction. These findings support the notion that the psychological state of power produced greater status by creating initial behaviors that then set off self-reinforcing cycles of group interaction.

Action and risk taking. The experience of power has been associated with greater assertive action across a wide variety of situations (e.g., Fast et al., 2009; Galinsky et al., 2003; Magee et al., 2007). Galinsky et al. (2003) manipulated power through a boss–employee manipulation and found that high-power participants were more likely to take a card in a game of blackjack. Those who are powerful are also more inclined to take action in competitive interactions than those who are powerless. Magee et al. (2007) demonstrated that the experience of power led to nearly a four-fold increase in choosing to make the opening arguments in a debate scenario, increased the likelihood of intending to make a first offer in a negotiation by more than three times, and led people to be twice as likely to actually make first offers in a negotiation. Fast et al. (2009) also provided evidence for the link between power and taking action. In one study, participants were told they would receive a reward if they could correctly predict the outcome of a single roll of a six-sided die. Participants were further told that they could choose to roll the die themselves or could have someone roll the die for them. Objectively, the outcome of a die roll is a random event, so whether the participant or another individual rolls the die should have no effect on the outcome. However, Fast et al. found that whereas 100% of high-power participants chose to roll the die

themselves, only 58% of low-power participants chose to.

Those who are powerful are more likely to engage in risky behavior. Anderson and Galinsky (2006) demonstrated a clear link between power and risk, such that the powerful were more likely to show greater risk preferences, make riskier gambles and choices, find risky sexual activity more attractive, and resort to risky tactics in negotiations. Powerful individuals took greater risks because they did not think negative outcomes would befall them.

Motor-based performance. Burgmer and Englich (2013) found that psychological states of power can also affect individuals' performance on tasks that require motor skills. High-power participants made significantly more golf putts than baseline participants. In a second experiment, participants primed with high versus low power using a scrambled-sentenced task performed better on a dart-throwing task (i.e., threw the dart closer to the bulls-eye). These authors also provided evidence that such motor-based task performance might have roots in how people cognitively represent goals.

Morality and self-regulation. Many popular sentiments about power suggest that it is connected to moral depravity. Research has found that power leads directly to cheating behavior. Lammers, Stapel, and Galinsky (2010) had participants roll a set of dice to determine the number of lottery tickets they would receive. High-power participants were significantly more likely to overreport their outcomes to benefit themselves. Yap, Wazlawek, Lucas, Cuddy, and Carney (2013) found that expansive postures, which are associated with high power, also led to cheating behavior.

Dubois, Rucker, and Galinsky (2014b) found that powerful individuals are more likely to cheat but only when it benefits themselves. They made a critical distinction between unethical behavior and selfish behavior and showed that the powerful act more selfishly. In contrast, low-power people were more likely to cheat and lie to benefit someone else.

Interestingly, powerful individuals cheat more often but condemn the moral deviations of others. Lammers et al. (2010) found that powerful individuals consistently castigated the moral failings of others and punished them for their failure to live up to a higher standard.

Lammers and Stapel (2009) explored how power affected how people resolve moral dilemmas. They found that powerful individuals relied on rule-based moral principles, whereas low power increased focus on outcome-based moral thinking and the consequences of behavior. As a result, powerful individuals stick to the rules, whereas powerless individuals are more likely to make exceptions.

Power has systematic but complex effects on self-regulation. DeWall, Baumeister, Mead, and Vohs (2011) found that power often led people to be more effective at self-regulation, even when their self-regulatory resources were depleted. Given that power creates an increased goal focus, high-power individuals can regulate their behavior toward achieving a goal more effectively than low-power individuals. When self-regulation is not connected to a high-priority goal, however, powerful individuals perform worse than powerless individuals.

Motivation and Evaluation

Goal pursuit. Galinsky et al. (2003) proposed that power leads to goal-directed behavior—in effect, power increases the correspondence between goals on one hand and behavior that would satisfy those goals on the other. They created a situation in which all individuals should want to behave in a particular way—to remove an annoying fan—yet the situation made it ambiguous whether the individuals were allowed to do so. They found that a significantly higher proportion of high-power individuals acted to satisfy their needs by removing the fan compared with low-power individuals.

Guinote (2007) found that power both helps people prioritize their goals and prompts goal-consistent behavior, leading to increases in the speed of responses and performance of tasks related to goal pursuit. Across a number of experiments, having power was associated with requiring less information to make decisions regarding a preferred course of action; initiating goal-directed action sooner; greater task performance and flexibility; and the propensity to take action when opportunities arose to satisfy a goal. Power increases the facilitation

of goal-relevant constructs compared with other constructs, and this facilitation disappears after goal completion (Slabu & Guinote, 2010). Whitson et al. (2013) found that goal-directed behavior is, at least partially, driven by powerful individuals paying less attention to constraints or obstacles in the environment. Similarly, Inesi (2010) found that power reduced loss aversion by decreasing the anticipated threat associated with a loss. Goal directedness can also explain why powerful individuals are more likely to forgive relationship partners, but only when they feel a strong bond with their partner (Karremans & Smith, 2010).

Power can also validate one's goal. That is, power can reinforce, and make people pursue more diligently, whatever goal they currently have. Chen et al. (2001) demonstrated that, for individuals who were naturally focused on the self, having power led people to behave in a more selfish fashion. However, for individuals naturally inclined to focus on others, having power led to greater generosity than low power. Similarly, DeMarree et al. (2012, Experiment 1) found that the effect of power on behavior depended on the goal that had been activated. When individuals had been primed with a goal to compete, high power led to greater competitive responses than low power. In contrast, when primed with the goal to cooperate, high power led to more cooperative responses relative to low power.

Status seeking. Because a state of low power is aversive, people in such states are known to seek opportunities to gain power (Horwitz, 1958; Worchel, Arnold, & Harrison, 1978). Recognizing that status might serve as an input or correlate of power (see French & Raven, 1959), Rucker and Galinsky (2008) proposed that low power may lead individuals to seek status as one means of compensating for a loss of power. In support of this hypothesis, they found that low-power participants, compared with participants in high-power and baseline conditions, were willing to pay more for an object when it was associated with status than when it was not (see also Charles, Hurst, & Roussanov, 2009; Rucker & Galinsky, 2009; Rucker et al., 2012).

The motivated desire for status among those who are powerless has also been shown to affect how people represent symbols associated with status. For example, Bruner and Goodman (1947) found that children from lower socioeconomic backgrounds perceived money as larger than those from richer socioeconomic backgrounds. Bruner and Goodman discussed this increase in size as resulting from the greater value associated with money for those from lower socioeconomic backgrounds. Furthermore, in a systematic effort to demonstrate that the experience of power, decoupled from long-standing differences in economic background, could produce differences in how people represent money, Dubois et al. (2010) manipulated power through an episodic recall task and asked participants to draw a quarter. Conceptually replicating Bruner and Goodman's results, participants in the low-power condition drew a quarter as larger than did those in the high-power condition (see also Dubois, Rucker, & Galinsky, 2012).

Information search. Power influences the search strategies used during negotiations. De Dreu and Van Kleef (2004) found that negotiators with low power asked more diagnostic questions as well as more belief-congruent questions when paired with a competitive versus a cooperative partner. De Dreu and Van Kleef discussed these findings from the perspective of a motivated information-processing model, whereby low-power negotiators have stronger accuracy and impression motivation than more powerful negotiators. Consistent with the notion that low-power negotiators have heightened impression motivation concerns, the asking of belief-congruent questions was also shown to produce more favorable impressions during the negotiation.

Elsewhere, Briñol et al. (2007) have shown that power can reduce the amount of information search. Specifically, because power makes an individual feel confident, powerful individuals are less motivated to engage in processing information carefully.

Power also affects selective exposure to information. Fischer et al. (2011) found that making a fist (one of the physical manipulations of power discussed earlier in this chapter) increased participants' preference for decision-consistent over decision-inconsistent information, in terms of both evaluat-

ing that information and searching for information. This tendency was mediated by decision certainty, indicating that power increased confidence in one's decision.

Emotion and subjective well-being. The two principal components of generalized affect are positive and negative affect, most commonly measured by the Positive and Negative Affect Schedule (Tellegen, Watson, & Clark, 1988). Alertness and enthusiasm indicate high levels of positive affect, and unpleasantness and agitation indicate high levels of negative affect (Watson & Tellegen, 1985). Langner and Keltner (2008) found that individuals high in power reported more positive affect than their partners and individuals low in power reported more negative affect (see also Gonzaga, Keltner, & Ward, 2008; Lücken & Simon, 2005; Wojciszke & Struzynska-Kujalowicz, 2007). Similarly, Berdahl and Martorana (2006) found that participants assigned to a high-power role experienced more positive affect than those assigned to a low-power role (see also Hecht & LaFrance, 1998).

Despite some findings linking power to emotion, many studies have found no relationship between priming manipulations of power and changes in affective states (e.g., Galinsky et al., 2003; Rucker & Galinsky, 2008; Smith & Bargh, 2008; Smith & Trope, 2006; Weick & Guinote, 2008). It appears that emotional effects of power are more likely to emerge in actual dyadic interactions (Anderson & Berdahl, 2002; Berdahl & Martorana, 2006; Langner & Keltner, 2008), but more research is required to understand when power does and does not exert an influence on one's emotions.

Kifer et al. (2013) found that power enhanced subjective well-being (SWB). In one study, Kifer et al. used four rounds of surveys, each representing markedly different primary social roles (general, work, romantic relationship, friendship; Study 1) and found that experiencing power in one domain led to greater SWB in that same domain. They also experimentally manipulated power to demonstrate that the experience of power causes higher SWB. Both the correlational and the experimental data showed that power increased SWB by increasing feelings of authenticity. Anderson, Kraus, Galinsky, and Keltner (2012) demonstrated that the experience of power can also explain why social status leads to greater SWB. People who had status in their face-to-face peer groups had higher SWB because their status made them feel powerful.

Physiological Effects

Hormones. Power affects physiological states. Research by Carney et al. (2010) manipulated power using physical posture and examined participants' testosterone and cortisol levels. Individuals instructed to pose in a manner consistent with having power (e.g., open, expansive postures) exhibited an increase in testosterone and a decrease in cortisol. In contrast, individuals instructed to pose in a manner consistent with low power (e.g., closed, contractive postures) exhibited a decrease in testosterone and an increase in cortisol level.

Power has also been shown to increase tolerance for stress. Carney et al. (2013) examined how power affected people's physiological responses to different types of stress. In one experiment, Carney et al. manipulated participants' power using a series of combined and sequential power manipulations (e.g., role assignment, power poses) and then had participants complete the ice water submersion test (Hines & Brown, 1932). This task involves submerging one's hand in a bucket of ice water for as long as is tolerable. The powerful participants also showed less physiological evidence of stress while their hand was in cold water. In addition, those in the high-power condition kept their hand submerged, on average, for longer than those in the low-power condition. Bohns and Wiltermuth (2012) also found that power led to greater pain tolerance.

Furthermore, Carney et al. (2013) found that high power was a general buffer against the negative physiological effects of telling lies. Specifically, after manipulating participants' power, Carney et al. had participants tell lies and measured their cortisol levels. Past research has shown that telling lies leads to elevated cortisol levels. Compared with their cortisol levels before telling a lie, low-power participants showed elevated cortisol levels, consistent with a stress response. In contrast, attesting to the physiological benefits of high power, high-power participants showed no significant elevation in cortisol levels after telling a lie.

Heart rate and cardiovascular stress. Schmid and Schmid Mast (2013) also found a stress-buffering effect of power. Participants were put in a stressful situation by having them make a speech. These researchers found that priming power led to less stress as measured by heart rate. Power also affects cardiovascular markers of stress. Scheepers, de Wit, Ellemers, and Sassenberg (2012) found that power, either experientially primed or created through strong alternatives, created an efficient cardiovascular pattern that occurs when people feel challenged. In contrast, low power produced an inefficient cardiovascular pattern that occurs when people are under threat.

MODERATORS OF POWER

In describing the consequences of power, we have in the preceding sections clearly laid out the transformative effects that power has on individuals. Power alters cognition, motivation, self- and social perception, behavior, and even hormonal levels. However, this does not mean that power only exerts main effects or operates in a monolithic or invariant fashion. In this section, and as acknowledged in Figure 16.2, we highlight several important moderators that affect the relationship between power and a variety of outcomes. Figure 16.2 denotes two paths for how the moderators affect the experience and consequences of power. First, as represented by the arrow that precedes the sense of power, a variable could moderate whether a manipulation or measure of power affects someone's sense of power. Second, as represented by the arrow that follows the sense of power, a variable could moderate whether a sense of power produces a particular consequence. Understanding the moderators of power not only helps to determine when power has its effects but also begins to shed light on why power has the effects it does.

Power Reveals the Person: Individual Differences Moderate the Effects of Power

> When full power is conferred for any length of time (and I call a year or more

a long time), it is always dangerous, and will be productive of good or ill effects, according as those upon whom it is conferred are themselves good or bad.—Niccoló Machiavelli (1517), *The Discourses*

Here, Machiavelli recognizes that power reveals the person. That is, individual differences interact with power to produce behavioral effects. Thus, the influence of power on behavior is determined in part by the individual characteristics of the power holder. Essentially, power increases the correspondence between individual traits and behavior (Bargh et al., 1995; Chen et al., 2001; Galinsky et al., 2008). That is, the personalities of those who are powerful are better predictors of their thoughts and behaviors than are the personalities of those who are powerless.

As we have already articulated, having power reduces dependence. When people are dependent on others, they are often limited in how they can act, altering their own behavior to fit the whims and tendencies of those on whom they depend. However, with power, the constraints that normally govern thought, expression, and behavior melt away, and people are left with the truest form of themselves.

The past decade of research on power has seen numerous studies that have consistently found that power reveals the person by increasing the correspondence between traits and behavior. In the seminal article in this area, Chen et al. (2001) found that when primed with power, individuals with a communal orientation were more likely to behave generously, whereas those with an exchange orientation behaved in a self-serving manner. In a similar vein, increased power also leads to greater interpersonal accuracy among those who are high in empathy or who are induced to identify with an empathic leadership style (Schmid Mast, Jonas, & Hall, 2009).

As further evidence that power reveals who people are, Bargh et al. (1995) found that priming men with power led them to view female work partners in sexual terms and to flirt more openly with them, but only for those men with a predisposition toward sexual harassment. Here again, the personality of

participants primed with power was a better predictor of their behavior than those not primed with power. Maner and Mead (2010) followed up this work and showed that having power increased expectations of sexual interest from a subordinate, but only when participants had an active mating goal and when their mating goal was attainable because the subordinate was romantically available. Gruenfeld et al. (2008) also found that men in a high-power condition expressed greater desire to work with a mediocre female task partner, but only when she was attractive and they had been primed with sex.

Other work has found that powerful individuals are more likely to act in line with their preexisting value orientations. Galinsky et al. (2008) explored the role of social value orientation (Van Lange, 1999), which identifies preferences for allocations between the self and others and classifies people as either proself or prosocial. They found that social value orientation significantly predicted the extent to which high-power negotiators trusted their opponent, but it did not predict the trust levels of participants in a baseline condition. Thus, power led to different levels of trust by amplifying participants' prior value orientations. In related work, researchers have found that prosocial orientation predicts empathic accuracy but only among those who are powerful (Côté et al., 2011). Even in the uppermost echelon of corporations, power influences the extent to which CEOs' political ideology drives their decision making. Firms with liberal CEOs invest in more corporate social responsibility work than do firms with conservative CEOs, and this difference is greater among CEOs with more power (Chin, Hambrick, & Treviño, 2013).

Powerful individuals are also more likely to act consistently with their emotions. Overbeck et al. (2010) found that the behavior of high-power negotiators was driven by their currently held emotions. In contrast, emotions had little effect on low-power negotiators, who instead were affected by the emotions of others. Similarly, Anderson and Thompson (2004) found that the trait positive affect of powerful negotiators shaped the quality of negotiation processes and outcomes more than the trait positive affect of less powerful negotiators.

The fact that powerful individuals act more in line with their dispositional tendencies helps explain cross-cultural differences in the effects of power. Whereas Western cultures tend to place a premium on understanding power as freedom from external constraints and the capacity to satisfy one's own desires, Eastern cultures highlight the virtue of restraint and responsibility on the part of those who are powerful. Congruent with this view, Zhong, Magee, Maddux, and Galinsky (2006) found that culture affected individuals' associations with power. Westerners (i.e., those from independent cultures) subliminally primed with the word *power* (vs. the word *paper*) responded more quickly to reward-related words but more slowly to responsibility-related words. In contrast, East Asians (i.e., those from interdependent cultures) exhibited greater accessibility of responsibility-related words and weaker accessibility to reward-related words. Kopelman (2009) found that culture affected how power was exercised. She found that managers from Western countries took more resources when they had high versus low power because they felt entitled. In contrast, high power led managers from Hong Kong to voluntarily take fewer resources. Similarly, Torelli and Shavitt (2010) found that vertical individualists conceptualized power in personalized and selfish terms, whereas horizontal collectivists viewed power as a means to benefit and help others.

In all of these studies, the dispositions and current psychological states more strongly predicted the behavior of those with power than of those who lacked power. Guinote et al. (2012) have shown that in the absence of strong current psychological states, the dispositions of powerful individuals predict their behavior. When a counterdispositional construct is made accessible, however, the behavior of high-power individuals corresponds to the accessible construct more than does the behavior of low-power individuals. Building on some of the preceding findings (Côté et al., 2011; Galinsky et al., 2008), Guinote et al. explored the effect of social value orientation and primed prosociality on generosity. They found that when prosociality was not primed, social value orientation predicted how generous the powerful individuals were to an experimental partner, but it did not when prosociality had been primed. These findings suggest that the effects of power depend on whatever construct was most accessible in the mind of the power holder.

Importance of Goals

We have discussed how power both shapes the person by altering cognition and behavior and reveals the person by increasing the correspondence between traits and behavior. Many of these separate effects of power can be synthesized through the robust finding that power increases a focus on goals and facilitates goal-directed behavior. The prominence of goals can elucidate how power transforms people into optimistic, abstract-thinking, action-oriented individuals while also revealing the person's personality and magnifying differences grounded in culture.

Consider social perception as an illustrative example. Overbeck and Park (2006) found that goals play a critical role in how power affects social perception. In their studies, when the powerful were pursuing people-centered goals, they individuated their targets by paying increased attention to and remembering more unique information about them, but if they were pursuing product-centered goals, they recalled less correct unique information about their subordinates. Gruenfeld et al. (2008) established that powerful individuals view others through the lens of their currently held goals. In essence, power increases the tendency to view others through an instrumental lens and focuses one's attention on those aspects of others that serve one's salient goals. The goals of those who are powerful are key directors of their social attention.

Other evidence of the relation between power and goal direction comes from research showing that powerless individuals show decrements in executive functioning (Smith et al., 2008). Proper executive functioning requires effective goal focus, and impairments result from difficulty in actively maintaining a goal (Engle, 2002). As a result, lacking power impairs executive functions: These impairments were not because powerless individuals were less motivated or putting in less effort; instead, they had difficulty maintaining a focus on their current goal (Smith et al., 2008).

Legitimacy

French and Raven (1959) described legitimate power as one of the five bases of power. In contrast, we consider legitimacy to be a moderator or qualifier of power. Legitimacy can refer to how power is acquired or how it is exercised. In terms of acquisition, the question is whether the attainment of power is deserved or undeserved. Illegitimacy also refers to whether the position of power is abused. Power can be exercised in a legitimate, role-appropriate manner, or it can be wielded for the sole benefit of power holders and their associates.

Lammers, Galinsky, et al. (2008) proposed that legitimacy changes the fundamental effects of power and is an important determinant of whether power leads to approach behavior (e.g., action, risk taking). As they noted, legitimate hierarchies are cooperative endeavors where those who are powerful act and those who are powerless follow (Arendt, 1969; Aristotle, 1996). However, illegitimate hierarchies replace this cooperative foundation with resistance from below and defensiveness from above (Lenski, 2006; Mills, 1956; Plato, 1998). Therefore, Lammers and colleagues hypothesized that, when legitimate, power would lead to more behavioral approach than powerlessness. However, when illegitimate, this link between power and approach would be broken and even reversed, with those who are powerless showing more action. Consistent with their reasoning, they found that under conditions of legitimacy, powerful individuals showed more approach, took more action, and accepted more risk than powerless individuals; however, when power was tinged with illegitimacy, powerless individuals acted more than powerful individuals (Lammers, Galinsky, et al. 2008). Lammers, Galinsky, Gordijn, and Otten (2012) found a similar pattern of results with respect to self-sufficiency: Only when power was seen as legitimate did power increase social distance and decrease cooperation and willingness to help. Similarly, Willis, Guinote, and Rodríguez-Bailón (2010) found that illegitimacy improved the ability of powerless individuals to be more goal directed, showing greater persistence in the face of difficulties and more flexibility in achieving their goals. These current findings are consistent with past work showing that illegitimacy motivates those

who are powerless to show in-group favoritism (Brown & Ross, 1982; Commins & Lockwood, 1979).

These findings suggest that the effects of power depend on what being powerless or powerful means in a given relationship. Legitimate hierarchies have a fabric of cooperation—when one is legitimately lacking in power, one should follow the leader (i.e., cooperate) and delay gratifying one's own desires (i.e., inhibition). In a situation of illegitimacy, the tapestry of cooperation is torn and those who are powerless act against the status quo. Under conditions of legitimacy, those who are powerful approach and lead the way. Lacking legitimacy, powerful individuals become more concerned about protecting their position of power. Thus, the effects of power need to be understood through the symbolic value and meaning attached to positions of power or powerlessness.

Stability

Stability refers to the level of actual or perceived constancy in one's currently held position (Cummings, 1980; Tajfel & Turner, 1979, 1986). One of the dynamic aspects of power is the extent to which current power differences in a relationship are expected to endure. Power holders can feel their grip on valued resources tightening or slipping, and those who are powerless can often sense these changes as they are happening. As power becomes unstable, the behavior of high- and low-power individuals can change dramatically. Sligte, de Dreu, and Nijstad (2011) found a reversal of the positive association between power and creativity under conditions of instability. Mead and Maner (2012) found that leaders high in dominance motivation sought proximity to an in-group member who threatened their power when it was unstable. They reasoned that increasing proximity to less powerful group members is a strategy designed to help leaders protect their own power when they are at risk of losing it.

Keltner et al. (2003) suggested that the stability of the power relationship would likely alter the effects of power on behavioral approach. Following this suggestion, much of the research on the stability of power has focused on risk taking. Maner, Gailliot,

Butz, and Peruche (2007) examined the moderating roles of instability and individual differences in power motivation on risk-taking behavior, typically associated with high power (Anderson & Galinsky, 2006) and found that participants in high-power roles took less risk if they were highly motivated by power. Maner et al. explained these findings by proposing that those high in power motivation acted with greater risk aversion because of their desire to maintain their power. In a second study, they explicitly manipulated the stability of power and replicated the interaction between power and power motivation on risk taking, but only when power was unstable. We should note that Maner et al. did not investigate the role of stability among those lacking power.

To understand how stability might affect the relationship between power and risk, Jordan et al. (2011) looked to the literatures on animal hierarchies, childhood hierarchies, and intergroup hierarchies. They noticed that studies with nonhuman populations (e.g., Sapolsky, 2005) and human groups (Scheepers, 2009) have identified stress as a potential process through which power and stability might interact to affect risk taking. In his work with nonhuman primates, Sapolsky (2005) observed that in stable hierarchies, those who are powerless must constantly vie for access to valued resources, and as a result they suffer the greatest stress-related physiological reactions (Barnett, 1955; Sapolsky, 1993). In contrast, when the hierarchy is unstable, it is those who are powerful, faced with the potential loss of access to resources and prospective mates, who experience the greatest stress-related physiology (Manuck, Marsland, Kaplan, & Williams, 1995; Sapolsky & Share, 1994, 2004).

Across four studies, Jordan et al. (2011) found that unstable powerful and stable powerless individuals preferred probabilistic over certain outcomes and engaged in more risky behaviors in an organizational decision-making scenario, a blackjack game, and a balloon-pumping task compared with stable powerful and unstable powerless individuals. Furthermore, they found that these effects were the result of increased stress. Unstable power and stable powerlessness produced more physiological arousal, a direct manipulation of stress led to greater risk

taking, and stress tolerance moderated the interaction between power and stability on risk taking.

One may note that Jordan et al.'s (2011) results seem to contradict the Anderson and Galinsky (2006) findings. However, Jordan et al. offered a parsimonious integration of these seemingly competing findings. Anderson and Galinsky primed power and measured risk taking in an unrelated context. Jordan et al. brought stability to bear on power and linked the risk taking measure to both power and its stability. Integrating these two separate approaches produces the following synthesis: When power or powerlessness is merely primed and risk taking is unrelated to the context of power, the relative activation of the behavioral activation system (BAS) and the behavioral inhibition system (BIS) dominates, leading to a main effect of power on risk taking. However, when power is altered by stability and the risk taking is materially relevant to the stability of power, then the effects of stress resulting from the interaction between stability and power come to bear. The unstable powerful and the stable powerless individuals display the greatest risk-taking behavior.

Status

Power is related to but conceptually distinct from status (i.e., respect and admiration in the eyes of others). Because of the conceptual orthogonality of power and status, researchers have started to explore their interactive effects. Fragale, Overbeck, and Neale (2011) noted that many roles in society afford power but lack status (e.g., airport security, reimbursement administrators, clerks). They found that high-power–low-status individuals were judged the most negatively and seen as dominant and cold. Furthermore, people expected to have the most negative interactions with high-power–low-status individuals.

Fast, Halevy, and Galinsky (2012) provided evidence for why people have these expectations. In their studies, the combination of high power and low status leads people to demean others. Their reasoning is similar to our discussion of how power reveals individuals: Power frees those who lack status to act on the resentment from lacking respect by demeaning others. In contrast, those who lack both power and status are not free to act on this resentment (and high-status people do not have any resentment). Blader and Chen (2012) found that power and status had opposing effects on justice with status positively associated with, and power negatively associated with, justice toward others. They also found an interaction similar to the Fast, Halevy, and Galinsky findings such that the positive effect of status on justice only emerged when power was low but not when it was high.

One final example that connects the three previous moderators of legitimacy, stability, and status is work by Fast and Chen (2009) showing that powerful individuals act in aggressive and demeaning ways toward others when they feel incompetent in their position of power. When one feels unqualified for one's position, it likely no longer feels legitimate, and the future stability is called into question, which may lead people to worry about the level of respect that others have for them.

THEORIES OF POWER

Researchers in the field of social psychology have made a number of theoretical statements about power. Some were taken up immediately and used for years, others have only recently arrived, and still others have yet to be fully proposed or developed. Our goal in this section is not to endorse one explanation of power over another; rather, we seek to summarize the different possible psychological theories that have been hypothesized to underlie power.

Theories Based on the Need for Control

Although there had been theories of power linked to the economic principles of exchange (Blau, 1964; Homans, 1958), an important theoretical shift toward including psychological principles in the study of power occurred when Fiske and Dépret (1996) drew an explicit connection between the notion of dependence and the need for autonomy and control. They argued that having autonomy in one's environment is a basic need that motivates behavior when it has not been satisfied. Specifically, they argued that when people feel a lack of control, they engage in a compensatory process of seeking out information, particularly about the factors

impinging on their autonomy. In the context of power relations, Fiske and Dépret argued that low-power individuals seek to acquire diagnostic information about their high-power counterparts to give them some ability to predict their counterparts' behavior. Information seeking by low-power individuals is, at least in part, motivated by a need to restore control. By contrast, high-power individuals, whose control needs are largely satisfied by their position of power, perceive their counterparts using heuristic strategies, such as attending to expectancy-consistent information and stereotyping. Fiske and Dépret went further, arguing that the attentional strategies of power holders also serve to reinforce their power because if their expectations of subordinates are reinforced, there is no need for the social structure to change.

In outlining their theory, Fiske and Dépret (1996) hoped to find fertile ground for "studying social cognition in its social context" (p. 32). Put another way, they aimed to broaden the view of social cognition by looking at the influence of social structure on social-cognitive phenomena (see also Kipnis, 1972). Ironically, an unintended consequence of this goal was that they also started a trend within social psychology for the study of power to be increasingly about individual social cognition, absent much discussion of social structure.

Guinote (2007) has also argued in her situated focus theory that power operates through the basic need for control. Relying on comparative analyses of hunter-gatherer and agricultural societies showing that hunter-gatherers have fewer constraints on their freedom and are also more selective in their attention (Berry, 1976; Witkin, Dyk, Faterson, Goodenough, & Karp, 1962), Guinote claimed that power holders' autonomy makes them more like hunter-gatherers. Although the leap from hunter-gatherers to power holders is arguably a big one, the core propositions of the situated focus theory—power is positively associated with greater selectivity and flexibility in attention—is supported by Guinote's empirical research.

Approach–Inhibition Theory

By any measure, the most influential theory of power over the past decade has been the approach–inhibition theory (Keltner et al., 2003). Inspired by Kipnis's (1972) idea that power has metamorphic effects on power holders, Keltner et al.'s (2003) model drastically expanded the scope of phenomena that could be caused by power. As did Fiske and Dépret (1996), Keltner et al. tied power to motivation and proposed that people in low-power positions are oriented toward trying to understand and predict the needs of those who are powerful. However, they suggested that people in high-power positions also have salient concerns: They are oriented toward what they want and how to obtain it.

According to Keltner et al. (2003), these different concerns are governed by the relative activation of two neurobiological systems, the BAS and the BIS. They posited that high-power individuals experience greater activation of the BAS relative to the BIS and low-power individuals experience greater activation of the BIS relative to the BAS. These systems have wide-ranging influence on individual psychology, guiding attention, emotion, and action. Broadly speaking, activation of the BAS leads individuals to attend to potential rewards and to engage in behavior that brings them closer to their goals; in contrast, activation of the BIS leads individuals to attend to potential threats, recognize goal conflicts, and interrupt ongoing behavior (Fowles, 1980, 1988; Gray, 1975, 1982; McNaughton & Gray, 2000).

Two points of ambiguity in the approach–inhibition theory require clarification: the intended meaning of the word *inhibition* and the relationship between the BIS–BAS and emotion. In the context of the BIS, *inhibition* refers to processes related to the interruption of ongoing behavior (see Amodio, Master, Yee, & Taylor, 2008; Hirsh, Galinsky, & Zhong, 2011), both checking the environment for the threat of punishment and, if a threat is detected, stopping what one is doing (Avila, 2001; Gray, 1982). It does not refer to the executive control processes related to goal pursuit (Aron, Robbins, & Poldrack, 2004), such as selective attention and suppression of non–goal-facilitating behavioral responses, which are sometimes referred to as *inhibitory control processes*. Amodio et al. (2008) have even speculated that the BAS, rather than the BIS, may govern executive control processes related to the controlled inhibition of a response. Indeed, individuals motivated

by approach-related affect experience a narrowing of attention (Gable & Harmon-Jones, 2008, 2010), which presumably facilitates completion of the goal that triggered approach motivation (Shah, Friedman, & Kruglanski, 2002). Thus, studies demonstrating that high-power individuals outperform low-power individuals at controlled inhibition tasks, such as suppressing goal-defeating behavioral responses (Smith et al., 2008) and avoiding distracting information (Guinote, 2007), are entirely consistent with the approach–inhibition theory.

In their review of the literature on the BIS and BAS, Keltner et al. (2003) described a connection between these systems and the experience of emotion based entirely on the valence of emotions. In their description, the BIS is associated with negative emotion and the BAS with positive emotion. This interpretation was consistent with the evidence at that time, but a series of studies have found that not all approach-oriented emotions (those connected to the BAS) are positive. Anger and guilt, for example, have appetitive properties, suggesting that they are governed by the BAS (Amodio, Devine, & Harmon-Jones, 2007; Carver & Harmon-Jones, 2009). In light of this evidence, the valence of an emotion should be considered orthogonal to whether it is approach or inhibition oriented (Gable & Harmon-Jones, 2010). Accordingly, the propositions regarding emotion in approach–inhibition theory need to be revised along the following lines: High power is associated with approach-oriented emotions, and low power is associated with inhibition-oriented emotions.

General Model of Disinhibition

Hirsh et al. (2011) extended the theorizing of Keltner et al. (2003) and presented a general model of disinhibition. They noted that power, alcohol, and anonymity all led to both prosocial and antisocial effects, and they described how all of these contradictory effects can emerge from a single underlying mechanism—the decreased salience of competing response options prevents activation of the BIS. They reviewed three distinct routes through which power can reduce the salience of competing response options—namely, through BAS activation, cognitive depletion, and reduced social desirability concerns. Keltner et al. (2003) argued that the first of these routes, activation of the BAS, is triggered by having power. Because of increased responsibility, power often carries attentional constraints that can lead to cognitive depletion (Fiske, 1993). Also, powerful individuals have fewer social desirability concerns because they are less dependent on others (Emerson, 1964). Hirsh et al. proposed that BIS activity is the proximal mechanism underlying the effects of power.

The Hirsh et al. (2011) model of disinhibition is consistent with the wide range of research suggesting that powerful individuals are more goal focused (Galinsky et al., 2003; Guinote, 2007; Whitson et al., 2013): Powerful individuals experience less response conflict because of heightened BAS-related activity or greater cognitive load, which narrows goal-focused attention. Through this process of disinhibition, powerful individuals act on their most salient goal regardless of whether it is prosocial or antisocial. Thus, powerful individuals can act more selfishly by cheating (Lammers et al., 2010) and also more generously by helping others (Chen et al., 2001). This model can also explain how power both reveals the person, leading to greater correspondence between underlying dispositions and behavior, and shapes the person by leading individuals to behave more consistently with strong situational cues. Regardless of whether the dominant response emerges from a person's disposition or the situation, power is disinhibiting, producing both prosocial and antisocial behavior by reducing the salience of competing response options.

Agentic–Communal Model of Power

Rucker et al. (2012) recently put forth a new model of power that emphasizes the effects of power through the lens of the self versus others. Specifically, they suggested that states of high power produce an agentic orientation that focuses people on self-expression, self-expansion, and self-protection. In contrast, states of low power produce a communal orientation that focuses people on bonding with others and taking others into consideration in decision making.

Supporting this perspective, past research has shown that high, relative to low, power is associated with agentic behavior such as increased reliance on one's own thoughts (Briñol et al., 2007), increased expression of one's own opinion in a group (Anderson & Berdahl, 2002), and acting as though one is more important (Zimbardo et al., 1974). In contrast, low power, relative to high power, is associated with communal behavior such as greater perspective taking (Galinsky et al., 2006), an enhanced experience of empathy for others (van Kleef et al., 2008), and a desire to work on behalf of others (Dubois, Rucker, & Galinsky, 2014b). In addition, high-power conditions have been shown to increase one's self-importance relative to low-power and baseline conditions, whereas low-power conditions have been shown to increase one's dependence on others relative to high-power and baseline conditions (Rucker et al., 2011).

More important, unlike some theories that use the terms *agentic* and *communal* to reflect only whether the self or another benefits from a behavior (e.g., Abele, 2003), Rucker et al. (2012) used the terms to simply emphasize whether one is focused on the self or others. For example, they suggested that, in some cases, agency can lead to behavior that benefits others, such as when one's natural goal is to help others (Chen et al., 2001). They suggested that a first-order effect of power is to affect one's self–other orientation and that although power may often be associated with differential benefits to the self or others (see previous discussion of Rucker et al., 2011), power need not inevitably do so. As evidence of this, Dubois, Rucker, and Galinsky (2014a) found that states of both power and powerlessness can lead to giving more or less to a charity depending on whether the charity is designed to appeal to people's agentic or communal orientation. Specifically, Dubois et al. found that when charity appeals emphasize competency, which can be linked to agency, high-power individuals donate more than low-power individuals. In contrast, when charity appeals are designed to emphasize warmth, which can be linked to a communal orientation, low-power individuals donate more than high-power individuals.

Two aspects of the agentic–communal model bear additional emphasis. First, power is emphasized to shift the relative degree of agentic versus communal focus in individuals. However, agency and communality are orthogonal constructs that allow for the possibility that power might enhance agency without a cost to communality and that a loss of power might enhance communality without a loss of agency. Consistent with such an idea, Chen et al. (2001) found that increasing power, which is associated with agency, had different effects on the basis of whether individuals were naturally more independent or interdependent. Individuals who were naturally independent became greedier when primed with power, but individuals who were naturally interdependent became more giving. In both cases, this can be understood through the lens of power increasing agency, but it can be critically moderated by whether people have goals related to the self versus others. Second, Rucker et al. (2012) described the agentic–communal shift as one aspect of what power does and recognize that this propensity can interact with other factors such as the power holder's goals and needs. For example, although low power tends to shift people toward being more communal, this tendency might be overridden when being selfish would allow them to escape their low-power state (see Rucker et al., 2012).

Social Distance Theory

Magee and Smith (2013) introduced the social distance theory of power, using Thibaut and Kelley's (1959) theory of interdependence in arguing that whereas mutual dependence tends to make people in a relationship feel closer (Kelley et al., 1983), a lack of dependence makes high-power individuals feel distant from their counterparts. Lammers et al. (2012) found evidence supporting this principle. In their studies, high-power individuals preferred solitary activities over collaborative or joint activities relative to low-power individuals, and their preference for social distance was explained by their perceived lack of dependence on their partners. The experience of social distance among power holders could explain some of the more social and relational phenomena associated with power, such as power holders' resistance to social influence (Anderson & Berdahl, 2002; Berdahl & Martorana, 2006; Galinsky et al., 2008), disinterest in others' mental states (Galinsky et al., 2006; Woltin, Corneille, Yzerbyt, &

Förster, 2011), and empathic inaccuracy (Galinsky et al., 2006; Shirako, Blader, & Chen, 2013). After all, these outcomes are more likely in relationships between individuals who feel distant from each other rather than close to one another.

Social distance is also believed to increase construal level (Trope & Liberman, 2010), which, according to Magee and Smith (2013), could explain many cognitive effects of power beyond the association between power and abstract thinking (Magee et al., 2010; Smith & Trope, 2006). They proposed that high-level construal among power holders could explain their skill at rapidly selecting goals appropriate for the situation (Guinote, 2007, 2008), effective pursuit of goals (Galinsky et al., 2008; Gruenfeld et al., 2008; Guinote, 2007; Smith et al., 2008), and subjective certainty (Briñol et al., 2007; Eaton et al., 2009; Fast, Sivanathan, et al., 2012; Magee et al., 2010). Magee and Smith also argued that power holders' high-level construal could lead to more stereotyping in situations in which a stereotype is applicable (Chen, Ybarra, & Kiefer, 2004; Goodwin et al., 2000), superior individuation in situations in which no stereotype is available (Gruenfeld et al., 2008, Experiment 2; Overbeck & Park, 2001), and more instrumental person perception when a target can be used for a salient goal (Copeland, 1994; Gruenfeld et al., 2008; Kunstman & Maner, 2011; Overbeck & Park, 2001, 2006). Social distance theory provides a unifying account for these diverse, and in some cases apparently contradictory, phenomena linked to power.

Relation Among Various Perspectives on Power

Although the approach–inhibition theory has dominated the field of late, some evidence has supported each one of the theories we have reviewed. These theories are not necessarily in competition with one another. That is, given the breadth of the power construct, we believe it is likely that power often guides and shapes behavior through multiple independent processes. As research in the domain of power intensifies, rather than understand a single process by which power affects behavior, we believe the more relevant endeavor is to understand when the different psychological processes affected by power operate to affect subsequent behavior (see also Magee & Smith, 2013). We discuss this point more thoroughly in our section on setting an agenda for the next wave of power research.

MOVING THE RESEARCH AGENDA FORWARD

In the introduction to this chapter, we recognized several waves of power research have occurred. In this section, we turn to the future and consider the next wave of research and raise a number of ideas that have begun to swell as power-related research has grown. The next wave of research will surely produce more complete models of power. To make the models more comprehensive, the moderators of power's effects will need to be integrated into the theories of power. For example, Magee and Smith (2013) included goals as an important moderator in the social distance theory of power. In many ways, the halcyon days of simply looking at the main effects of power are surely ending. As shown in Figure 16.2, a panoply of direct effects of power have already been discovered. As we embark on the next wave of power research, a deeper exploration into moderators and mechanisms becomes essential.

Integrating and Testing Different Theories of Power

Perhaps one of the most important steps for power research to take with regard to theory development is to make a deeper commitment to understanding and empirically testing when different theories operate. In recent work, Magee and Smith (2013) noted that in some cases the same observed effect of power on an outcome variable can be interpreted through two different theoretical lenses. They noted that a number of effects are compatible both with power operating through approach–inhibition systems (Hirsh et al., 2011; Keltner et al., 2003) and with power operating through social distance (Magee & Smith, 2013). In such cases, researchers might invoke either theory to explain their results. This can lead to the production of an article with a reasonable theoretical process, but one that may fail to consider whether the effects are more strongly linked to an alternative theory.

In the next wave of research, we would encourage researchers both to explicitly tease apart different processes experimentally and to articulate when different processes operate. By paying closer attention to the different models of power, the next wave of research can establish more clearly which model more effectively and more parsimoniously explains the full range of behavior and when it does so.

Meanings Attached to Power

Earlier we mentioned that a sense of power is the key proximate variable that predicts behavior. That is, a manipulation of power has its effects because it makes people feel more powerful. Building on this theme, we propose that the effects of power depend on how it is conceived, acquired, and exercised (Lammers & Galinsky, 2009). Indeed, the Manipulating the Moderators of Power section of this chapter clarified that the effects of power are not invariant but context dependent, determined by personality, culture, legitimacy, and stability. The meaning of power also relates to power motivation and the distinction between whether people want power for personal gain or out of concern for improving the lot of others (Magee & Langner, 2008).

Ultimately, the effects of power are not just about the amount of resources possessed. Rather, the psychological consequences of power depend on its meaning, on how power is conceived and conceptualized by the particular individual under its sway. The effects of power cannot be reduced to quantitative calculations of relative resources but require a qualitative appreciation of how power was acquired, for what purpose, and to what end.

By understanding how an individual conceptualizes power, we can capture not only when power has its effects but also why power has the effects it does. In their approach–inhibition theory of power, Keltner et al. (2003) argued that power produces its effects because powerful individuals have unfettered access to rewards, whereas powerless individuals lack resources and are more subject to social threats. However, our discussion of moderators puts a number of boundaries around their reasoning. It is not just an abstract sense of power that is the proximate cause of behavior but rather the meaning attached to that sense of power. For example, when power is embedded in an interdependent self-construal, powerful individuals lean toward responsibility and cooperation compared with when power is entrenched in an independent self-construal (Torelli & Shavitt, 2010; Zhong et al., 2006). In this case, the sense of power is associated with different meanings, depending on the power holder's culture.

Even expansive postures depend on their symbolic meaning. Park, Streamer, Huang, and Galinsky (2013) found that the seemingly fundamental link between expansive body postures and feelings of power is not universal but depends on people's cultural background. They found that the expansive-feet-on-desk pose (Carney et al., 2010) violated East Asian cultural norms and as a result did not lead to feelings of power or action among East Asians. Because the meaning of different postures varies across cultures, posture does not have a direct effect on power-related behavior and cognition. Instead, posture carries its influence through its culture-specific symbolic meaning.

Future research needs to build models and theories that take into account the meanings attached to power. To predict how power will affect someone, it will be necessary to know how that person conceptualizes and thinks about power.

Fit and Mismatch Effects: Who Benefits From Having Power

In this chapter, we have highlighted the benefits of having, and the costs of lacking, power. However, several lines of research have suggested that the fit between the role and the person determines the extent to which having power is positive. In some situations and for some people, lacking power is preferred to having power.

Josephs, Sellers, Newman, and Mehta (2006) proposed the mismatch effect to describe a situation in which an individual difference makes one uncomfortable in a position of power. They placed high- and low-testosterone individuals into high- or low-ranked positions and found that low-testosterone individuals had a negative physiological reaction to being in the dominant position: They reported greater emotional arousal and showed worse cognitive functioning in a

dominant position. In contrast, high-testosterone individuals showed physiological distress and cognitive deficits when in the subordinate position.

Chen et al. (2009) also found that the degree of fit between an individual's sense of power and hierarchical role influenced authentic self-expression. Earlier, we mentioned that power makes people feel more authentic (Kraus, Piff, & Keltner, 2011) and increases SWB (Kifer et al., 2013). However, Chen et al. found that these effects occurred only when people had a chronically high sense of power. They placed people who had scored high or low on the Sense of Power scale (Anderson, John, & Keltner, 2011) into a high- or low-power role in an interaction with a confederate. When there was a fit between person and role ratings, people's expressions were more congruent with their self-reported emotions and traits. These results bear some resemblance to the finding by Fast and Chen (2009) that when powerful individuals feel incompetent in their role, the psychological benefits of power do not accrue.

The next wave of research will need to capture more precisely who benefits from having power and under what conditions they benefit from it. One potentially promising avenue is for researchers to connect the research on the subjective meaning of power to the research on person–role fit. How people conceptualize power may have critical implications for the degree to which they experience fit in their powerful or powerless role.

Putting Power Back Into a Social Context: Knowing One's Place and Intergroup Competition

In this chapter, we have focused on the psychological experience of power and its many effects. Earlier, we mentioned various manipulations that can make people feel powerful. People can think about a past experience with power or imagine being in a high-power position. They can take on an expansive posture or make a fist. This implies that once people have thought about power or changed their posture, they are now powerful.

However, power is not just an individual property. Power is contextualized in interpersonal relationships, and in most relationships, people are aware of their power vis-à-vis another person. Indeed, Anderson, Srivastava, Beer, Spataro, and Chatman (2006) have shown that people self-enhance in many domains but tend to be accurate in reporting their level of status. This accuracy stems from the fact that people are severely punished if they do not know their place and act with greater authority than they truly have.

Placing the psychological experience of power into the social context raises the question of whether there are interpersonal costs of being primed with power. Will some people accrue more interpersonal benefits from thinking about power or getting into an expansive posture? If a low-power person is primed with power, will he or she rise in the hierarchy or be struck down for acting too powerful? Some initial evidence has come from work on emotional expressions in economic transactions. Lelieveld, Van Dijk, Van Beest, and Van Kleef (2012) found that low-power bargainers were punished for expressing the emotion of anger, a response typically associated with high power.

Expanding the social contexts also brings intergroup considerations into focus. Howard, Gardner, and Thompson (2007) found that powerful individuals primed with interdependence became more generous when resolving a dispute with a low-power opponent. However, in intergroup disputes, powerful teams became less generous when they were primed with interdependence. These results suggest that the construct of interdependence took on a different meaning in the intergroup context. Similarly, Maner and Mead (2010) found that insecure, unstable power led powerful people to withhold valuable information from the group and prevented other skilled group members from having any influence. However, these self-interested actions disappeared when the group was competing against an out-group. In both of these articles, competition that made group goals salient led to different effects when power was experienced individually and within a group. Future research should continue to explore how the intergroup context changes the psychological experience and effects of power as well as its many moderators.

Needs Versus Propensities

The majority of work on the consequences of power has focused on how having versus lacking power alters cognitive and behavioral tendencies. Power leads people to become abstract thinkers, action takers, self-aggrandizers, and so forth. However, states of high and low power can also activate various needs that motivate fulfillment of those needs.

Rucker et al. (2012) proposed that the influence of power on thought and behavior can be governed both by psychological propensities and by needs. They defined psychological propensities as natural inclinations or tendencies. As one example, having power increases the value individuals place on the self, whereas lacking power increases the value people place on others (i.e., the agentic–communal orientation; Rucker et al., 2011). In contrast, psychological needs refer to specific motivations or desires evoked by the state. For instance, lacking power is typically associated with a need to restore one's power, which contributes to a desire for objects related to status (Rucker & Galinsky, 2008, 2009).

Inesi and colleagues have explored how both high and low power can create needs and concerns. Low power is characterized by a dependency on others and diminished influence over one's world. As a result, the need for personal control is threatened by lacking power. Inesi, Botti, Dubois, Rucker, and Galinsky (2011) proposed that when people are in a low-power position, they will seek out ways to regain a sense of control. Because having choice satisfies the need for control, they hypothesized that low-power individuals would want more choice. In their studies, powerless individuals preferred a larger choice set and demonstrated a greater motivation to access a larger choice set.

Inesi, Gruenfeld, and Galinsky (2012) explored the idea that powerful individuals have a fear that others are nice to them only because of their power. They called this the "celebrity's dilemma" in recognition of the concern that celebrities often voice about finding true relatedness: They are haunted by the possibility that someone loves not them but only their celebrity. In their studies, Inesi et al. found that power undermined the quality of relationships by creating instrumental attributions for generous acts. Powerful individuals were more likely to believe that favors they received from low-power individuals were offered for instrumental purposes, and this belief reduced their thankfulness and desire to reciprocate and trust the low-power person. Inesi et al. suggested that power does create a need, a need for true relatedness.

In understanding the relationship between needs and propensities, Rucker et al. (2012) suggested that, given that the propensities of power require little cognitive thought or involvement, propensities should be relatively consistent across contexts. For example, power fosters a propensity to increase action (Galinsky et al., 2003). In contrast, psychological needs are proposed to be more responsive to the context and to guide behavior in a manner consistent with the need. People should be more likely to engage in behavior when that behavior addresses their psychological needs. Thus, lacking power does not lead people to evaluate all objects more favorably; rather, lacking power leads people to evaluate objects associated with status more favorably (Rucker & Galinsky, 2008, 2009). Furthermore, Rucker and Galinsky (2008, 2009) proposed that propensities of power can be overridden by the needs produced by a state of power.

In initial support of the idea that needs can overwhelm propensities, Rucker et al. (2012) reported an experiment in which participants were asked how much they were willing to spend on an object either for themselves or for another person. An important note is that the object was either unrelated to status or related to status. Rucker et al. hypothesized that high power would foster high spending on the self and low power would foster spending on others. They suggested this was consistent with the general notion that a propensity of having power is to increase the value of the self, whereas a propensity of lacking power is to increase the value of others (Rucker et al., 2011). However, they proposed that low-power individuals would spend more on the self: when the object of consumption was related to status and thus fit the psychological need of people lacking power. In other words, they hypothesized that a low-power need could dominate a high-power propensity, leading those lacking power to spend more on a status object for the self than for others. The results of several experiments confirmed their hypothesis.

This recent work provides one example of how different processes associated with power, in this case propensities and needs, can operate in different circumstances and produce different effects. The next wave of power research should seek to further enlighten our understanding of how and when the propensities versus the needs associated with conditions of high and low power drive behavior.

Experiences of Versus Expectations for Power

Recent work has distinguished between the intrapersonal experience of power—the psychological and physiological tendencies that get activated when one has or lacks power—and the interpersonal expectations for power—anticipated or expected behaviors tied to a position of low or high power (Rucker, Hu, & Galinsky, 2014).

Although a large body of research has focused on how the experience of power affects behavior, power is also accompanied by expectations for behavior. Rucker et al. (2014) defined the expectations for power as the cognitive associations people have regarding the anticipated behaviors of people in a position of high versus low power. Rucker et al. demonstrated that a critical determinant of how powerful people will behave depends on whether a person's focus is on the experience of power versus the expectations for power. When focused on the experience of power, those who were powerless engaged in greater information processing and a greater desire for status objects, replicating past findings. However, when focused on the expectations for power, these findings reversed: Those who were powerful exhibited greater information processing and desire for status objects, consistent with the expectations people had for those in positions of power. When the experience of and the expectations for power were consistent with each other, both experience and expectations had the same effect: Power increased action regardless of whether an individual was focused on the experience of power or the expectations for power.

Rucker et al. (2014) also divided expectations into two types—prescriptive and descriptive. They found that in the domain of unethical behavior, people expected that powerful individuals would act more dishonestly than powerless individuals but they thought the former should act more honestly than latter. When they focused participants on the prescriptive expectations for power, the powerful participants cheated less. However, when they focused participants' attention on the descriptive expectations, the powerful participants cheated more.

By distinguishing between the experience of and expectations for power, Rucker et al. (2014) offered a model that can more precisely predict the behavior of powerful and powerless individuals. The goal of this research and the previously discussed work on needs versus propensities is to provide a more comprehensive understanding of when and how power affects behavior and to provide better predictive models. Future research should also establish the conditions, contexts, and situations that alter whether people are focused on the experience of power or expectations for power.

Harnessing the Good and Neutralizing the Bad in Power

We noted that the first wave of power research in social psychology focused on the negative consequences of having power (Milgram, 1963; Zimbardo, 1973; Zimbardo et al., 1974). Since those times, research has begun to recognize that the possession of power can have both desirable and undesirable consequences for people under the direction of power holders and society more generally. Rather than power innately being negative, power affects psychological processes that can have prosocial or antisocial consequences depending on an individual's goals and the situation (see Hirsh et al., 2011; Rucker et al., 2012).

We believe that future research needs to focus on moderating variables that determine (a) when power produces prosocial versus antisocial consequences and (b) when power has distinct effects on the same dependent measure (e.g., generosity). Such efforts will not only paint a more accurate picture of the transformative effects of power but may hold serious policy implications for how society can encourage the use of power for good and deter the use of power for bad.

As we noted, power activates a number of positive psychological processes: It increases action, agency, optimism, and confidence. These processes can make the impossible possible. However, they can also lead people down dead-end alleys. Power also produces a number of effects on social perception, such as diminished perspective taking, that can be more destructive than constructive.

How can the good in power be harnessed without all its potentially deleterious effects? The first obvious idea is to select better people into powerful roles. The numerous findings that power reveals the person, making individual differences better predictors of behavior, clearly suggest that one method to get the good in power is to select the right individual differences for a powerful post. Harnessing the best parts of power will require effective leadership selection. Future research should explore better ways to identify the right people to select for power.

The second method for harnessing power, and one for which we are more hopeful, is creating structural solutions. One potential solution is to make those who are powerful accountable (Tetlock, Skitka, & Boettger, 1989). Some evidence to support the idea that the interaction between power and accountability can produce the most prosocial outcomes comes from a study by Winter and Barenbaum (1985). They found that those with a high need for power—characterized by a desire to have influence and to maintain prestige—generally engaged in self-serving and self-satisfying profligate behaviors, including gambling and sexual promiscuity. However, high need for power was transformed into responsible and socially supportive actions when those individuals faced life events—becoming a parent or having younger siblings—that increased their sense of responsibility. High need for power combined with feelings of responsibility led individuals to both rein in their selfish desires and display community-minded behaviors such as volunteering. To the extent that accountability pressures heighten a sense of responsibility in power holders, they may serve to harness the good in power while neutralizing the bad.

We end this section with a metaphor—driving a car—to understand how the good in power may be harnessed. The agency of power is akin to pressing the gas pedal. Without acceleration, one is left standing still, unable to move forward. But one also needs a steering wheel to avoid crashing into obstacles along the way. Being effective requires acceleration and prudent steering, power with accountability.

CONCLUSION

We wrote this chapter to serve as a guide to the past and present waves of research on power and to chart new waters for the next course of power research. We articulated a precise definition of power, one that can be applied to many different relationships and settings. We catalogued the distinct manipulations and measures that have been used in research on power. Building on the many methods used to study power, we identified and categorized a range of important consequences produced by power. Recognizing that the main effects of power are individually and contextually bound, we also discussed moderators, those variables that alter when people feel powerful and how they act with power. Building off the consequences of power, we also discussed a variety of theories that have been used to explain power's myriad effects. We ended the chapter by offering a few of the many future directions that power research could take over the next few years.

Power has gone through several important and interesting waves of research. We are excited by the fact that the surge in publications on the topic of power suggests that the latest wave of power research has begun to swell. We hope to see many more theoretical and empirical projects in the next wave of power. Ultimately, the rise of research on power, current and future, will help provide an enriched understanding of power and produce a more comprehensive and integrative model for its effects.

References

Abele, A. E. (2003). The dynamics of masculine-agentic and feminine-communal traits: Findings from a prospective study. *Journal of Personality and Social Psychology, 85,* 768–776. doi:10.1037/0022-3514.85.4.768

Amodio, D. M., Devine, P. G., & Harmon-Jones, E. (2007). A dynamic model of guilt: Implications for motivation and self-regulation in the context of prejudice. *Psychological Science, 18,* 524–530. doi:10.1111/j.1467-9280.2007.01933.x

Amodio, D. M., Master, S. L., Yee, C. M., & Taylor, S. E. (2008). Neurocognitive components of the behavioral inhibition and activation systems: Implications for theories of self-regulation. *Psychophysiology, 45,* 11–19.

Anderson, C., & Berdahl, J. L. (2002). The experience of power: Examining the effects of power on approach and inhibition tendencies. *Journal of Personality and Social Psychology, 83,* 1362–1377. doi:10.1037/0022-3514.83.6.1362

Anderson, C., & Galinsky, A. D. (2006). Power, optimism, and risk-taking. *European Journal of Social Psychology, 36,* 511–536. doi:10.1002/ejsp.324

Anderson, C., John, O. P., & Keltner, D. (2012). The personal sense of power. *Journal of Personality, 80,* 313–344. doi:10.1111/j.1467-6494.2011.00734.x

Anderson, C., John, O. P., Keltner, D., & Kring, A. (2001). Social status in naturalistic face-to-face groups: Effects of personality and physical attractiveness in men and women. *Journal of Personality and Social Psychology, 81,* 116–132.

Anderson, C., & Kilduff, G. J. (2009). The pursuit of status in social groups. *Current Directions in Psychological Science, 18,* 295–298. doi:10.1111/j.1467-8721.2009.01655.x

Anderson, C., Kraus, M. W., Galinsky, A. D., & Keltner, D. (2012). The local-ladder effect: Social status and subjective well-being. *Psychological Science, 23,* 764–771. doi:10.1177/0956797611434537

Anderson, C., Srivastava, S., Beer, J. S., Spataro, S. E., & Chatman, J. A. (2006). Knowing your place: Self-perceptions of status in face-to-face groups. *Journal of Personality and Social Psychology, 91,* 1094–1110. doi:10.1037/0022-3514.91.6.1094

Anderson, C., & Thompson, L. L. (2004). Affect from the top down: How powerful individuals' positive affect shapes negotiations. *Organizational Behavior and Human Decision Processes, 95,* 125–139. doi:10.1016/j.obhdp.2004.05.002

Apple, W., Streeter, L. A., & Krauss, R. M. (1979). Effects of pitch and speech rate on personal attributions. *Journal of Personality and Social Psychology, 37,* 715–727. doi:10.1037/0022-3514.37.5.715

Arendt, H. (1969). *On violence.* New York, NY: Harcourt, Brace & World.

Aries, E. J., Gold, C., & Weigel, R. H. (1983). Dispositional and situational influences on dominance behavior in small groups. *Journal of Personality and Social Psychology, 44,* 779–786. doi:10.1037/0022-3514.44.4.779

Aristotle. (1996). *The politics and the Constitution of Athens* (S. Everson, Trans.). Cambridge, England: Cambridge University Press.

Aron, A. R., Robbins, T. W., & Poldrack, R. A. (2004). Inhibition and the right inferior frontal cortex. *Trends in Cognitive Sciences, 8,* 170–177. doi:10.1016/j.tics.2004.02.010

Atkinson, J. W. (1958). *Motives in fantasy, action, and society*. Princeton, NJ: Van Nostrand.

Avila, C. (2001). Distinguishing BIS-mediated and BAS-mediated disinhibition mechanisms: A comparison of disinhibition models of Gray (1981, 1987) and of Patterson and Newman (1993). *Journal of Personality and Social Psychology, 80*, 311–324. doi:10.1037/0022-3514.80.2.311

Bargh, J. A., Chaiken, S., Raymond, P., & Hymes, C. (1996). The automatic evaluation effect: Unconditional automatic attitude activation with a pronunciation task. *Journal of Experimental Social Psychology, 32*, 104–128. doi:10.1006/jesp.1996.0005

Bargh, J. A., Raymond, P., Pryor, J. B., & Strack, F. (1995). Attractiveness of the underling: An automatic power sex association and its consequences for sexual harassment and aggression. *Journal of Personality and Social Psychology, 68*, 768–781. doi:10.1037/0022-3514.68.5.768

Barnett, S. A. (1955). Competition among wild rats. *Nature, 175*, 126–127. doi:10.1038/175126b0

Berdahl, J. L., & Martorana, P. (2006). Effects of power on emotion and expression during a controversial group discussion. *European Journal of Social Psychology, 36*, 497–509. doi:10.1002/ejsp.354

Berry, J. W. (1976). *Human ecology and cognitive style: Comparative studies in cultural and psychological adaptation*. New York, NY: Wiley.

Blader, S. L., & Chen, Y. R. (2012). Differentiating the effects of status and power: A justice perspective. *Journal of Personality and Social Psychology, 102*, 994–1014. doi:10.1037/a0026651

Blau, P. M. (1964). *Exchange and power in social life*. Piscataway, NJ: Transaction.

Bohns, V. K., & Wiltermuth, S. S. (2012). It hurts when I do this (or you do that): Posture and pain tolerance. *Journal of Experimental Social Psychology, 48*, 341–345. doi:10.1016/j.jesp.2011.05.022

Boksem, M. A., Smolders, R., & De Cremer, D. (2012). Social power and approach-related neural activity. *Social Cognitive and Affective Neuroscience, 7*, 516–520. doi:10.1093/scan/nsp006

Briñol, P., Petty, R. E., Valle, C., Rucker, D. D., & Becerra, A. (2007). The effects of message recipients' power before and after persuasion: A self-validation analysis. *Journal of Personality and Social Psychology, 93*, 1040. doi:10.1037/0022-3514.93.6.1040

Brown, R. J., & Ross, G. F. (1982). The battle for acceptance: An exploration into the dynamics of intergroup behavior. In H. Tajfel (Ed.), *Social identity and intergroup relations*. London, England: Cambridge University Press.

Bruner, J. S., & Goodman, C. C. (1947). Value and need as organizing factors in perception. *Journal of Abnormal and Social Psychology, 42*, 33–44. doi:10.1037/h0058484

Brunstein, J. C., & Maier, G. W. (2005). Implicit and self-attributed motives to achieve: Two separate but interacting needs. *Journal of Personality and Social Psychology, 89*, 205–222. doi:10.1037/0022-3514.89.2.205

Burgmer, P., & Englich, B. (2013). Bullseye! How power improves motor performance. *Social Psychological and Personality Science, 4*, 224–232.

Buss, D. M. (1981). Predicting parent-child interactions from children's activity level. *Developmental Psychology, 17*, 59–65. doi:10.1037/0012-1649.17.1.59

Buss, D. M., & Craik, K. H. (1980). The frequency concept of disposition: Dominance and prototypically dominant acts. *Journal of Personality, 48*, 379–392. doi:10.1111/j.1467-6494.1980.tb00840.x

Carney, D. R., Cuddy, A. J., & Yap, A. J. (2010). Power posing brief nonverbal displays affect neuroendocrine levels and risk tolerance. *Psychological Science, 21*, 1363–1368. doi:10.1177/0956797610383437

Carney, D. R., Hall, J. A., & LeBeau, L. S. (2005). Beliefs about the nonverbal expression of social power. *Journal of Nonverbal Behavior, 29*, 105–123. doi:10.1007/s10919-005-2743-z

Carney, D. R., Yap, A. J., Lucas, B., Mehta, P., Ferrero, J. N., McGee, J. A., & Wilmuth, C. (2013). *Power buffers stress: For better and for worse*. Manuscript submitted for publication.

Carver, C. S., & Harmon-Jones, E. (2009). Anger is an approach-related affect: Evidence and implications. *Psychological Bulletin, 135*, 183–204. doi:10.1037/a0013965

Charles, K. K., Hurst, E., & Roussanov, N. L. (2009). Conspicuous consumption and race. *Quarterly Journal of Economics, 124*, 425–467. doi:10.1162/qjec.2009.124.2.425

Chen, S., Langner, C. A., & Mendoza-Denton, R. (2009). When dispositional and role power fit: Implications for self-expression and self-other congruence. *Journal of Personality and Social Psychology, 96*, 710–727.

Chen, S., Lee-Chai, A. Y., & Bargh, J. A. (2001). Relationship orientation as a moderator of the effects of social power. *Journal of Personality and Social Psychology, 80*, 173–187. doi:10.1037/0022-3514.80.2.173

Chen, S., Ybarra, O., & Kiefer, A. K. (2004). Power and impression formation: The effects of power on the desire for morality and competence information. *Social Cognition, 22*, 391–421. doi:10.1521/soco.22.4.391.38296

Chin, M. K., Hambrick, D. C., & Treviño, L. K. (2013). Political ideologies of CEOs: The influence of executives' values on corporate social responsibility. *Administrative Science Quarterly, 58*, 197–232. doi:10.1177/0001839213486984

Commins, B., & Lockwood, J. (1979). The effects of status differences, favoured treatment and equity on intergroup comparisons. *European Journal of Social Psychology, 9,* 281–289. doi:10.1002/ejsp.2420090306

Copeland, J. T. (1994). Prophecies of power: Motivational implications of social power for behavioral confirmation. *Journal of Personality and Social Psychology, 67,* 264. doi:10.1037/0022-3514.67.2.264

Côté, S., Kraus, M. W., Cheng, B. H., Oveis, C., Van der Löwe, I., Lian, H., & Keltner, D. (2011). Social power facilitates the effect of prosocial orientation on empathic accuracy. *Journal of Personality and Social Psychology, 101,* 217. doi:10.1037/a0023171

Cummings, E. M. (1980). Caregiver stability and day care. *Developmental Psychology, 16,* 31. doi:10.1037/0012-1649.16.1.31

de Dreu, C. K., & Van Kleef, G. A. (2004). The influence of power on the information search, impression formation, and demands in negotiation. *Journal of Experimental Social Psychology, 40,* 303–319. doi:10.1016/j.jesp.2003.07.004

DeMarree, K. G., Loersch, L., Briñol, P., Petty, R. E., Payne, B. K., & Rucker. D. D. (2012). From primed construct to motivated behavior: Validation processes in goal pursuit. *Personality and Social Psychology Bulletin, 38,* 1659–1670.

DeWall, C. N., Baumeister, R. F., Mead, N. L., & Vohs, K. D. (2011). How leaders self-regulate their task performance: Evidence that power promotes diligence, depletion, and disdain. *Journal of Personality and Social Psychology, 100,* 47–65. doi:10.1037/a0020932

Dovidio, J. F., Ellyson, S. L., Keating, C. F., Heltman, K., & Brown, C. E. (1988). The relationship of social power to visual displays of dominance between men and women. *Journal of Personality and Social Psychology, 54,* 233. doi:10.1037/0022-3514.54.2.233

Dubois, D., Rucker, D. D., & Galinsky, A. D. (2010). The accentuation bias: Money literally looms larger (and sometimes smaller) to the powerless. *Social Psychological and Personality Science, 1,* 199–205. doi:10.1177/1948550610365170

Dubois, D., Rucker, D. D., & Galinsky, A. D. (2012). Super size me: Product size as a signal of status. *Journal of Consumer Research, 38,* 1047–1062. doi:10.1086/661890

Dubois, D., Rucker, D. D., & Galinsky, A. D. (2014a). *The power matching effect.* Manuscript submitted for publication.

Dubois, D., Rucker, D. D., & Galinsky, A. D. (2014b). *Social class predicts selfish behavior and it does so through power.* Manuscript submitted for publication.

Duguid, M. M., & Goncalo, J. A. (2012). Living large: The powerful overestimate their own height. *Psychological Science, 23,* 36–40. doi:10.1177/0956797611422915

Eaton, A. A., Visser, P. S., Krosnick, J. A., & Anand, S. (2009). Social power and attitude strength over the life course. *Personality and Social Psychology Bulletin, 35,* 1646–1660. doi:10.1177/0146167209349114

Emerson, R. M. (1962). Power-dependence relations. *American Sociological Review, 27,* 31–41. doi:10.2307/2089716

Emerson, R. M. (1964). Power-dependence relations: Two experiments. *Sociometry, 27,* 282–298. doi:10.2307/2785619

Emmons, R. A., & McAdams, D. P. (1991). Personal strivings and motive dispositions: Exploring the links. *Personality and Social Psychology Bulletin, 17,* 648–654. doi:10.1177/0146167291176007

Engle, R. W. (2002). Working memory capacity as executive attention. *Current Directions in Psychological Science, 11,* 19–23. doi:10.1111/1467-8721.00160

Fast, N. J., & Chen, S. (2009). When the boss feels inadequate: Power, incompetence, and aggression. *Psychological Science, 20,* 1406–1413. doi:10.1111/j.1467-9280.2009.02452.x

Fast, N. J., Gruenfeld, D. H., Sivanathan, N., & Galinsky, A. D. (2009). Illusory control: A generative force behind power's far-reaching effects. *Psychological Science, 20,* 502–508. doi:10.1111/j.1467-9280.2009.02311.x

Fast, N. J., Halevy, N., & Galinsky, A. D. (2012). The destructive nature of power without status. *Journal of Experimental Social Psychology, 48,* 391–394. doi:10.1016/j.jesp.2011.07.013

Fast, N. J., Sivanathan, N., Mayer, N. D., & Galinsky, A. D. (2012). Power and overconfident decision-making. *Organizational Behavior and Human Decision Processes, 117,* 249–260. doi:10.1016/j.obhdp.2011.11.009

Fischer, J., Fischer, P., Englich, B., Aydin, N., & Frey, D. (2011). Empower my decisions: The effects of power gestures on confirmatory information processing. *Journal of Experimental Social Psychology, 47,* 1146–1154. doi:10.1016/j.jesp.2011.06.008

Fisher, R., Ury, W., & Patton, B. (1991). *Getting to yes: Negotiating agreement without giving in.* New York, NY: Penguin.

Fiske, S. T. (1993). Controlling other people. *American Psychologist, 48,* 621–628. doi:10.1037/0003-066X.48.6.621

Fiske, S. T. (2010). Interpersonal stratification: Status, power, and subordination. In S. T. Fiske, D. T. Gilbert, & G. Lindzey (Eds.), *Handbook of social psychology* (pp. 941–982). Hoboken, NJ: Wiley.

Fiske, S. T., & Berdahl, J. (2007). Social power. In A. Kruglanski & E. T. Higgins (Eds.), *Social psychology: Handbook of basic principles* (2nd ed., pp. 678–692). New York, NY: Guilford Press.

Fiske, S. T., & Dépret, E. (1996). Control, interdependence, and power: Understanding social cognition in its social context. *European Review of Social Psychology, 7,* 31–61. doi:10.1080/14792779443000094

Fowles, D. C. (1980). The three arousal model: Implications of Gray's two-factor learning theory for heart rate, electrodermal activity, and psychopathy. *Psychophysiology, 17,* 87–104.

Fowles, D. C. (1988). Psychophysiology and psychopathology: A motivational approach. *Psychophysiology, 25,* 373–391.

Fragale, A. R., Overbeck, J. R., & Neale, M. A. (2011). Resources versus respect: Social judgments based on targets' power and status positions. *Journal of Experimental Social Psychology, 47,* 767–775.

French, J. R., & Raven, B. (1959). The bases of social power. In D. Cartwright (Ed.), *Studies in social power* (pp. 150–167). Ann Arbor, MI: Institute for Social Research, University of Michigan.

Gable, P., & Harmon-Jones, E. (2010). The motivational dimensional model of affect: Implications for breadth of attention, memory, and cognitive categorisation. *Cognition and Emotion, 24,* 322–337.

Gable, P. A., & Harmon-Jones, E. (2008). Approach-motivated positive affect reduces breadth of attention. *Psychological Science, 19,* 476–482.

Galinsky, A. D., Gruenfeld, D. H., & Magee, J. C. (2003). From power to action. *Journal of Personality and Social Psychology, 85,* 453–466.

Galinsky, A. D., Magee, J. C., Gruenfeld, D. H., Whitson, J. A., & Liljenquist, K. A. (2008). Power reduces the press of the situation: Implications for creativity, conformity, and dissonance. *Journal of Personality and Social Psychology, 95,* 1450–1466.

Galinsky, A. D., Magee, J. C., Inesi, M. E., & Gruenfeld, D. H. (2006). Power and perspectives not taken. *Psychological Science, 17,* 1068–1074.

Gallafent, A. (Producer). (2008, March 5). *The sound of leadership* [radio broadcast]. Boston, MA: The World, Public Radio International.

Georgesen, J. C., & Harris, M. J. (2000). The balance of power: Interpersonal consequences of differential power and expectancies. *Personality and Social Psychology Bulletin, 26,* 1239–1257.

Gonzaga, G. C., Keltner, D., & Ward, D. (2008). Power in mixed-sex stranger interactions. *Cognition and Emotion, 22,* 1555–1568. doi:10.1080/02699930801921008

Goodwin, S. A., Gubin, A., Fiske, S. T., & Yzerbyt, V. Y. (2000). Power can bias impression processes: Stereotyping subordinates by default and by design. *Group Processes and Intergroup Relations, 3,* 227–256.

Goodwin, S. A., Operario, D., & Fiske, S. T. (1998). Situational power and interpersonal dominance facilitate bias and inequality. *Journal of Social Issues, 54,* 677–698.

Gough, H. G. (1987). *CPI, California Psychological Inventory: Administrator's guide.* Mountain View, CA: Consulting Psychologists Press.

Gray, J. A. (1975). *Elements of a two-process theory of learning.* London, England: Academic Press.

Gray, J. A. (1982). *Neuropsychological theory of anxiety: An investigation of the septal-hippocampal system.* Cambridge, England: Cambridge University Press.

Gruenfeld, D. H., Inesi, M. E., Magee, J. C., & Galinsky, A. D. (2008). Power and the objectification of social targets. *Journal of Personality and Social Psychology, 95,* 111–127.

Gruenfeld, D. H., & Tiedens, L. Z. (2010). Organizational preferences and their consequences. In S. T. Fiske, D. T. Gilbert, & G. Lindzey (Eds.), *Handbook of social psychology* (5th ed., Vol. 2, pp. 1252–1287). Hoboken, NJ: Wiley.

Guinote, A. (2007). Power affects basic cognition: Increased attentional inhibition and flexibility. *Journal of Experimental Social Psychology, 43,* 685–697.

Guinote, A. (2008). Power and affordances: When the situation has more power over powerful than powerless individuals. *Journal of Personality and Social Psychology, 95,* 237–252.

Guinote, A., Willis, G. B., & Martellotta, C. (2010). Social power increases implicit prejudice. *Journal of Experimental Social Psychology, 46,* 299–307.

Guiso, L., Monte, F., Sapienza, P., & Zingales, L. (2008). Culture, gender, and math. *Science, 320,* 1164–1165.

Halevy, N., Chou, E. Y., & Galinsky, A. D. (2011). A functional model of hierarchy: Why, how, and when vertical differentiation enhances group performance. *Organizational Psychology Review, 1,* 32–52.

Hamamura, T. (2012). Power distance predicts gender differences in math performance across societies. *Social Psychological and Personality Science, 3,* 545–548.

Harada, T., Bridge, D. J., & Chiao, J. Y. (2012). Dynamic social power modulates neural basis of math calculation. *Frontiers in Human Neuroscience, 6,* 350.

Hecht, M. A., & LaFrance, M. (1998). License or obligation to smile: The effect of power and sex on amount and type of smiling. *Personality and Social Psychology Bulletin, 24,* 1332–1342.

Higgins, E. T. (1996). Knowledge activation: Accessibility, applicability, and salience. In E. T. Higgins & A. W. Kruglanski (Eds.), *Social psychology: Handbook of basic principles.* New York, NY: Guilford Press.

Hines, E. A., & Brown, G. E. (1932, June). A standard stimulus for measuring vasomotor reactions: Its application in the study of hypertension. In *Proceedings of the Staff Meeting of the Mayo Clinic, 7,* 332–335.

Hirsh, J. B., Galinsky, A. D., & Zhong, C. B. (2011). Drunk, powerful, and in the dark: How general processes of disinhibition produce both prosocial and antisocial behavior. *Perspectives on Psychological Science, 6*, 415–427.

Homans, G. C. (1958). Social behavior as exchange. *American Journal of Sociology, 63*, 597–606.

Hong, Y. Y., Morris, M. W., Chiu, C. Y., & Benet-Martinez, V. (2000). Multicultural minds. *American Psychologist, 55*, 709–720.

Horwitz, M. (1958). The veridicality of liking and disliking. In R. Tagiuri & L. Petrullo (Eds.), *Person perception and interpersonal behavior* (pp. 165–183). Stanford, CA: Stanford University Press.

Howard, E. S., Gardner, W. L., & Thompson, L. (2007). The role of the self-concept and the social context in determining the behavior of power holders: Self-construal in intergroup versus dyadic dispute resolution negotiations. *Journal of Personality and Social Psychology, 93*, 614–631.

Huang, L., Galinsky, A. D., Gruenfeld, D. H., & Guillory, L. E. (2011). Powerful postures versus powerful roles: Which is the proximate correlate of thought and behavior? *Psychological Science, 22*, 95–102.

Inesi, M. E. (2010). Power and loss aversion. *Organizational Behavior and Human Decision Processes, 112*, 58–69.

Inesi, M. E., Botti, S., Dubois, D., Rucker, D. D., & Galinsky, A. D. (2011). Power and choice: Their dynamic interplay in quenching the thirst for personal control. *Psychological Science, 22*, 1042–1048.

Inesi, M. E., Gruenfeld, D. H., & Galinsky, A. D. (2012). How power corrupts relationships: Cynical attributions for others' generous acts. *Journal of Experimental Social Psychology, 48*, 795–803.

Jackson, D. N. (1974). *Personality Research Form manual.* London, Ontario, Canada: Research Psychologists Press.

Jordan, J., Sivanathan, N., & Galinsky, A. D. (2011). Something to lose and nothing to gain: The role of stress in the interactive effect of power and stability on risk taking. *Administrative Science Quarterly, 56*, 530–558.

Josephs, R. A., Sellers, J. G., Newman, M. L., & Mehta, P. H. (2006). The mismatch effect: When testosterone and status are at odds. *Journal of Personality and Social Psychology, 90*, 999–1013.

Karremans, J. C., & Smith, P. K. (2010). Having the power to forgive: When the experience of power increases interpersonal forgiveness. *Personality and Social Psychology Bulletin, 36*, 1010–1023.

Kehr, H. M. (2004). Integrating implicit motives, explicit motives, and perceived abilities: The compensatory model of work motivation and volition. *Academy of Management Review, 29*, 479–499.

Kelley, H. H., Berscheid, E., Christensen, A., Harvey, J. H., Huston, T. L., Levinger, G., & Peterson, D. R. (1983). Analyzing close relationships. In H. H. Kelley, E. Berscheid, A. Christensen, J. H. Harvey, T. L. Huston, G. Levinger, . . . D. R. Peterson (Eds.), *Close relationships* (pp. 20–67). New York, NY: Freeman.

Keltner, D., Gruenfeld, D. H., & Anderson, C. (2003). Power, approach, and inhibition. *Psychological Review, 110*, 265–284.

Keltner, D., & Robinson, R. J. (1997). Defending the status quo: Power and bias in social conflict. *Personality and Social Psychology Bulletin, 23*, 1066–1077.

Kifer, Y., Heller, D., Perunovic, W. Q. E., & Galinsky, A. D. (2013). The good life of the powerful: The experience of power and authenticity enhances subjective well-being. *Psychological Science, 24*, 280–288.

Kilduff, G. J., & Galinsky, A. D. (2013). From the ephemeral to the enduring: Approach-oriented mindsets lead to greater status. *Journal of Personality and Social Psychology, 105*, 816–831. doi:10.1037/a0033667

Kim, P. H., Pinkley, R. L., & Fragale, A. R. (2005). Power dynamics in negotiation. *Academy of Management Review, 30*, 799–822.

King, L. A. (1995). Wishes, motives, goals, and personal memories: Relations of measures of human motivation. *Journal of Personality, 63*, 985–1007.

Kipnis, D. (1972). Does power corrupt? *Journal of Personality and Social Psychology, 24*, 33–41.

Kipnis, D., Castell, J., Gergen, M., & Mauch, D. (1976). Metamorphic effects of power. *Journal of Applied Psychology, 61*, 127–135.

Ko, S. J., Sadler, M. S., & Galinsky, A. D. (2013). *The sound of power: Conveying and detecting hierarchical rank through voice.* Manuscript submitted for publication.

Koestner, R., Weinberger, J., & McClelland, D. C. (1991). Task-intrinsic and social-extrinsic sources of arousal for motives assessed in fantasy and self-report. *Journal of Personality, 59*, 57–82.

Kopelman, S. (2009). The effect of culture and power on cooperation in commons dilemmas: Implications for global resource management. *Organizational Behavior and Human Decision Processes, 108*, 153–163.

Kraus, M. W., Chen, S., & Keltner, D. (2011). The power to be me: Power elevates self-concept consistency and authenticity. *Journal of Experimental Social Psychology, 47*, 974–980. doi:10.1016/j.jesp.2011.03.017

Kraus, M. W., Piff, P. K., & Keltner, D. (2011). Social class as culture: The convergence of resources and rank in the social realm. *Current Directions in Psychological Science, 20*, 246–250.

Kunstman, J. W., & Maner, J. K. (2011). Sexual overperception: Power, mating motives, and biases in social judgment. *Journal of Personality and Social Psychology, 100,* 282–294.

Lammers, J., Dubois, D., Rucker, D. D., & Galinsky, A. D. (2013). Power gets the job: Priming power improves interview outcomes. *Journal of Experimental Social Psychology, 49,* 776–779.

Lammers, J., & Galinsky, A. D. (2009). The conceptualization of power and the nature of interdependency: The role of legitimacy and culture. In D. Tjosvold & B. Wisse (Eds.), *Power and interdependence in organizations* (pp. 67–82). Cambridge, England: Cambridge University Press.

Lammers, J., Galinsky, A. D., Gordijn, E. H., & Otten, S. (2008). Illegitimacy moderates the effects of power on approach. *Psychological Science, 19,* 558–564.

Lammers, J., Galinsky, A. D., Gordijn, E. H., & Otten, S. (2012). Power increases social distance. *Social Psychological and Personality Science, 3,* 282–290.

Lammers, J., Gordijn, E. H., & Otten, S. (2008). Looking through the eyes of the powerful. *Journal of Experimental Social Psychology, 44,* 1229–1238. doi:10.1016/j.jesp.2008.03.015

Lammers, J., & Stapel, D. A. (2009). How power influences moral thinking. *Journal of Personality and Social Psychology, 97,* 279–289.

Lammers, J., Stapel, D. A., & Galinsky, A. D. (2010). Power increases hypocrisy moralizing in reasoning, immorality in behavior. *Psychological Science, 21,* 737–744.

Lammers, J., Stoker, J. I., & Stapel, D. A. (2009). Differentiating social and personal power: Opposite effects on stereotyping, but parallel effects on behavioral approach tendencies. *Psychological Science, 20,* 1543–1548.

Langner, C. A., & Keltner, D. (2008). Social power and emotional experience: Actor and partner effects within dyadic interactions. *Journal of Experimental Social Psychology, 44,* 848–856.

Langner, C. A., & Winter, D. G. (2001). The motivational basis of concessions and compromise: Archival and laboratory studies. *Journal of Personality and Social Psychology, 81,* 711–727.

Lelieveld, G. J., Van Dijk, E., Van Beest, I., & Van Kleef, G. A. (2012). Why anger and disappointment affect other's bargaining behavior differently: The moderating role of power and the mediating role of reciprocal and complementary emotions. *Personality and Social Psychology Bulletin, 38,* 1209–1221.

Lenski, G. E. (2006). *Power and privilege: A theory of social stratification.* New York, NY: McGraw-Hill.

Lücken, M., & Simon, B. (2005). Cognitive and affective experiences of minority and majority members: The role of group size, status, and power. *Journal of Experimental Social Psychology, 41,* 396–413.

Magee, J. C., & Galinsky, A. D. (2008). Social hierarchy: The self-reinforcing nature of power and status. *Academy of Management Annals, 2,* 351–398.

Magee, J. C., Galinsky, A. D., & Gruenfeld, D. H. (2007). Power, propensity to negotiate, and moving first in competitive interactions. *Personality and Social Psychology Bulletin, 33,* 200–212.

Magee, J. C., & Langner, C. A. (2008). How personalized and socialized power motivation facilitate antisocial and prosocial decision-making. *Journal of Research in Personality, 42,* 1547–1559. doi:10.1016/j.jrp.2008.07.009

Magee, J. C., Milliken, F. J., & Lurie, A. R. (2010). Power differences in the construal of a crisis: The immediate aftermath of September 11, 2001. *Personality and Social Psychology Bulletin, 36,* 354–370.

Magee, J. C., & Smith, P. K. (2013). The social distance theory of power. *Personality and Social Psychology Review, 17,* 158–186.

Maner, J. K., Gailliot, M. T., Butz, D. A., & Peruche, B. M. (2007). Power, risk, and the status quo: Does power promote riskier or more conservative decision making? *Personality and Social Psychology Bulletin, 33,* 451–462.

Maner, J. K., & Mead, N. L. (2010). The essential tension between leadership and power: When leaders sacrifice group goals for the sake of self-interest. *Journal of Personality and Social Psychology, 99,* 482–497.

Mannix, E. A., & Neale, M. A. (1993). Power imbalance and the pattern of exchange in dyadic negotiation. *Group Decision and Negotiation, 2,* 119–133.

Manuck, S. B., Marsland, A. L., Kaplan, J. R., & Williams, J. K. (1995). The pathogenicity of behavior and its neuroendocrine mediation: An example from coronary artery disease. *Psychosomatic Medicine, 57,* 275–283.

McClelland, D. C. (1970). The two faces of power. *Journal of International Affairs, 24,* 29–47.

McClelland, D. C. (1975). *Power: The inner experience.* New York, NY: Irvington.

McClelland, D. C. (1985). How motives, skills, and values determine what people do. *American Psychologist, 40,* 812–825.

McClelland, D. C., Koestner, R., & Weinberger, J. (1989). How do self-attributed and implicit motives differ. *Psychological Review, 96,* 690–702.

McClelland, D. C., & Wilsnack, S. C. (1972). The effects of drinking on thoughts about power and restraint. In D. C. McClelland, W. N. Davis, R. Kalin, & E. Wanner (Eds.), *The drinking man* (pp. 123–141). New York, NY: Free Press.

McNaughton, N., & Gray, J. A. (2000). Anxiolytic action on the behavioural inhibition system implies multiple types of arousal contribute to anxiety. *Journal of Affective Disorders, 61,* 161–176.

Mead, N. L., & Maner, J. K. (2012). On keeping your enemies close: Powerful leaders seek proximity to ingroup power threats. *Journal of Personality and Social Psychology, 102,* 576–591.

Mehta, P. H., Jones, A. C., & Josephs, R. A. (2008). The social endocrinology of dominance: Basal testosterone predicts cortisol changes and behavior following victory and defeat. *Journal of Personality and Social Psychology, 94,* 1078–1093.

Mehta, P. H., & Josephs, R. A. (2010). Testosterone and cortisol jointly regulate dominance: Evidence for a dual-hormone hypothesis. *Hormones and Behavior, 58,* 898–906.

Milgram, S. (1963). Behavioral study of obedience. *Journal of Abnormal and Social Psychology, 67,* 371–378.

Mills, C. W. (1956). *The power elite.* New York, NY: Oxford University Press.

Miyamoto, Y., & Ji, L. J. (2011). Power fosters context-independent, analytic cognition. *Personality and Social Psychology Bulletin, 37,* 1449–1458.

Ohala, J. J. (1982). The voice of dominance. *Journal of the Acoustical Society of America, 72,* S66.

Operario, D., & Fiske, S. T. (2001). Ethnic identity moderates perceptions of prejudice: Judgments of personal versus group discrimination and subtle versus blatant bias. *Personality and Social Psychology Bulletin, 27,* 550–561.

Osborn, A. F. (1953). *Applied imagination: Principles and procedures of creative thinking.* New York, NY: Scribner.

Overbeck, J. R., Neale, M. A., & Govan, C. L. (2010). I feel, therefore you act: Intrapersonal and interpersonal effects of emotion on negotiation as a function of social power. *Organizational Behavior and Human Decision Processes, 112,* 126–139.

Overbeck, J. R., & Park, B. (2001). When power does not corrupt: Superior individuation processes among powerful perceivers. *Journal of Personality and Social Psychology, 81,* 549–565.

Overbeck, J. R., & Park, B. (2006). Powerful perceivers, powerless objects: Flexibility of powerholders' social attention. *Organizational Behavior and Human Decision Processes, 99,* 227–243.

Pang, J. S., & Schultheiss, O. C. (2005). Assessing implicit motives in U.S. college students: Effects of picture type and position, gender and ethnicity, and cross-cultural comparisons. *Journal of Personality Assessment, 85,* 280–294. doi:10.1207/s15327752jpa8503_04

Park, L. E., Streamer, L., Huang, L., & Galinsky, A. D. (2013). Stand tall, but don't put your feet up: Universal and culturally-specific effects of expansive postures. *Journal of Experimental Social Psychology, 49,* 965–971.

Pinkley, R. L., Neale, M. A., & Bennett, R. J. (1994). The impact of alternatives to settlement in dyadic negotiation. *Organizational Behavior and Human Decision Processes, 57,* 97–116.

Plato. (1998). *Symposium.* New York, NY: Oxford University Press.

Pratto, F., Sidanius, J., Stallworth, L. M., & Malle, B. F. (1994). Social dominance orientation: A personality variable predicting social and political attitudes. *Journal of Personality and Social Psychology, 67,* 741–763. doi:10.1037/0022-3514.67.4.741

Roth, A. E. (1995). *The handbook of experimental economics* (Vol. 1). Princeton, NJ: Princeton University Press.

Rucker, D. D., Dubois, D., & Galinsky, A. D. (2011). Generous paupers and stingy princes: Power drives consumer spending on self versus others. *Journal of Consumer Research, 37,* 1015–1029.

Rucker, D. D., & Galinsky, A. D. (2008). Desire to acquire: Powerlessness and compensatory consumption. *Journal of Consumer Research, 35,* 257–267.

Rucker, D. D., & Galinsky, A. D. (2009). Conspicuous consumption versus utilitarian ideals: How different levels of power shape consumer behavior. *Journal of Experimental Social Psychology, 45,* 549–555.

Rucker, D. D., Galinsky, A. D., & Dubois, D. (2012). Power and consumer behavior: How power shapes who and what consumers value. *Journal of Consumer Psychology, 22,* 352–368.

Rucker, D. D. Hu, M., & Galinsky, A. D. (2014). *The experience of versus the expectations for power: A recipe for altering the effects of power.* Manuscript submitted for publication.

Sapolsky, R. M. (1993). Endocrinology alfresco: Psychoendocrine studies of wild baboons. *Recent Progress in Hormone Research, 48,* 437–468.

Sapolsky, R. M. (2005). The influence of social hierarchy on primate health. *Science, 308,* 648–652.

Sapolsky, R. M., & Share, L. J. (1994). Rank-related differences in cardiovascular function among wild baboons: Role of sensitivity to glucocorticoids. *American Journal of Primatology, 32,* 261–275.

Sapolsky, R. M., & Share, L. J. (2004). A pacific culture among wild baboons: Its emergence and transmission. *PLoS Biology, 2,* e106.

Scheepers, D. (2009). Turning social identity threat into challenge: Status stability and cardiovascular reactivity during inter-group competition. *Journal of Experimental Social Psychology, 45,* 228–233.

Scheepers, D., de Wit, F., Ellemers, N., & Sassenberg, K. (2012). Social power makes the heart work more efficiently: Evidence from cardiovascular markers of challenge and threat. *Journal of Experimental Social Psychology, 48,* 371–374.

Schmid, P. C., & Schmid Mast, M. (2013). Power increases performance in a social evaluation situation as a result of decreased stress responses. *European Journal of Social Psychology, 43,* 201–211.

Schmid Mast, M., & Hall, J. A. (2004). Who is the boss and who is not? Accuracy of judging status. *Journal of Nonverbal Behavior, 28,* 145–165.

Schmid Mast, M., Jonas, K., & Hall, J. A. (2009). Give a person power and he or she will show interpersonal sensitivity: The phenomenon and its why and when. *Journal of Personality and Social Psychology, 97,* 835–850.

Schubert, T. W. (2004). The power in your hand: Gender differences in bodily feedback from making a fist. *Personality and Social Psychology Bulletin, 30,* 757–769.

Schubert, T. W., & Koole, S. L. (2009). The embodied self: Making a fist enhances men's power-related self-conceptions. *Journal of Experimental Social Psychology, 45,* 828–834.

Schultheiss, O. C. (2001). An information processing account of implicit motive arousal. *Advances in Motivation and Achievement, 12,* 1–41.

Schultheiss, O. C., & Brunstein, J. C. (2001). Assessment of implicit motives with a research version of the TAT: Picture profiles, gender differences, and relations to other personality measures. *Journal of Personality Assessment, 77,* 71–86.

Schultheiss, O. C., & Pang, J. S. (2007). Measuring implicit motives. In R. W. Robins, R. C. Fraley, & R. Krueger (Eds.), *Handbook of research methods in personality psychology* (pp. 322–344). New York, NY: Guilford Press.

Schultheiss, O. C., Wirth, M. M., Torges, C. M., Pang, J. S., Villacorta, M. A., & Welsh, K. M. (2005). Effects of implicit power motivation on men's and women's implicit learning and testosterone changes after social victory or defeat. *Journal of Personality and Social Psychology, 88,* 174–188.

See, K. E., Morrison, E. W., Rothman, N. B., & Soll, J. B. (2011). The detrimental effects of power on confidence, advice taking, and accuracy. *Organizational Behavior and Human Decision Processes, 116,* 272–285.

Shah, J. Y., Friedman, R., & Kruglanski, A. W. (2002). Forgetting all else: On the antecedents and consequences of goal shielding. *Journal of Personality and Social Psychology, 83,* 1261–1280.

Shirako, A., Blader, S., & Chen, Y.-R. (2013) *Looking out from the top: Differential effects of status and power on perspective taking.* Unpublished manuscript.

Shnabel, N., & Nadler, A. (2008). A needs-based model of reconciliation: Satisfying the differential emotional needs of victim and perpetrator as a key to promoting reconciliation. *Journal of Personality and Social Psychology, 94,* 116–132.

Sivanathan, N., Pillutla, M. M., & Keith Murnighan, J. (2008). Power gained, power lost. *Organizational Behavior and Human Decision Processes, 105,* 135–146.

Slabu, L., & Guinote, A. (2010). Getting what you want: Power increases the accessibility of active goals. *Journal of Experimental Social Psychology, 46,* 344–349.

Sligte, D. J., de Dreu, C. K., & Nijstad, B. A. (2011). Power, stability of power, and creativity. *Journal of Experimental Social Psychology, 47,* 891–897.

Smith, P. K., & Bargh, J. A. (2008). Nonconscious effects of power on basic approach and avoidance tendencies. *Social Cognition, 26,* 1–24.

Smith, P. K., Jostmann, N. B., Galinsky, A. D., & van Dijk, W. W. (2008). Lacking power impairs executive functions. *Psychological Science, 19,* 441–447.

Smith, P. K., & Trope, Y. (2006). You focus on the forest when you're in charge of the trees: Power priming and abstract information processing. *Journal of Personality and Social Psychology, 90,* 578–596. doi:10.1037/0022-3514.90.4.578

Sondak, H., & Bazerman, M. H. (1991). Power balance and the rationality of outcomes in matching markets. *Organizational Behavior and Human Decision Processes, 50,* 1–23.

Spangler, W. D. (1992). Validity of questionnaire and TAT measures of need for achievement: Two meta-analyses. *Psychological Bulletin, 112,* 140–154.

Stel, M., van Dijk, E., Smith, P. K., van Dijk, W. W., & Djalal, F. M. (2012). Lowering the pitch of your voice makes you feel more powerful and think more abstractly. *Social Psychological and Personality Science, 3,* 497–502. doi:10.1177/1948550611427610

Stroop, J. R. (1935). *Studies of interference in serial verbal reactions* (Unpublished doctoral dissertation). George Peabody College for Teachers, Nashville, TN.

Suleiman, R. (1996). Expectations and fairness in a modified ultimatum game. *Journal of Economic Psychology, 17,* 531–554.

Tajfel, H., & Turner, J. C. (1979). An integrative theory of intergroup conflict. In W. G. Austin & S. Worchel (Eds.), *The social psychology of intergroup relations* (pp. 33–47). Monterey, CA: Brooks/Cole.

Tajfel, H., & Turner, J. C. (1986). The social identity theory of intergroup behaviour. In S. Worchel & W. G. Austin (Eds.), *Psychology of intergroup relations* (pp. 7–24). Chicago, IL: Nelson Hall.

Tellegen, A., Watson, D., & Clark, L. A. (1988). Development and validation of brief measures of positive and negative affect: The PANAS scales. *Journal of Personality and Social Psychology, 54,* 1063–1070.

Tetlock, P. E., Skitka, L., & Boettger, R. (1989). Social and cognitive strategies for coping with accountability: Conformity, complexity, and bolstering. *Journal of Personality and Social Psychology, 57,* 632–640.

Thibaut, J. W., & Kelley, H. H. (1959). *The social psychology of groups.* New York, NY: Wiley.

Torelli, C. J., & Shavitt, S. (2010). Culture and concepts of power. *Journal of Personality and Social Psychology, 99,* 703–723.

Torelli, C. J., Shavitt, S., Johnson, T. P., Holbrook, A., Cho, Y., Chavez, N., . . . Beebe, T. (2012). Culture, concepts of power, and attitudes toward powerholders: Consequences for consumer satisfaction in ongoing service interactions. *Advances in Consumer Psychology, 4,* 221–222 .

Tost, L. P., Gino, F., & Larrick, R. P. (2012). Power, competitiveness, and advice taking: Why the powerful don't listen. *Organizational Behavior and Human Decision Processes, 117,* 53–65.

Trope, Y., & Liberman, N. (2010). Construal-level theory of psychological distance. *Psychological Review, 117,* 440–463.

van Dijke, M., & Poppe, M. (2006). Striving for personal power as a basis for social power dynamics. *European Journal of Social Psychology, 36,* 537–556.

Van Kleef, G. A., de Dreu, C. K., Pietroni, D., & Manstead, A. S. (2006). Power and emotion in negotiation: Power moderates the interpersonal effects of anger and happiness on concession making. *European Journal of Social Psychology, 36,* 557–581.

Van Kleef, G. A., Oveis, C., Van der Löwe, I., LuoKogan, A., Goetz, J., & Keltner, D. (2008). Power, distress, and compassion: Turning a blind eye to the suffering of others. *Psychological Science, 19,* 1315–1322.

Van Lange, P. A. (1999). The pursuit of joint outcomes and equality in outcomes: An integrative model of social value orientation. *Journal of Personality and Social Psychology, 77,* 337–349.

van Vugt, M., Hogan, R., & Kaiser, R. B. (2008). Leadership, followership, and evolution. *American Psychologist, 63,* 182–196. doi:10.1037/0003-066X.63.3.182

Watson, D., & Tellegen, A. (1985). Toward a consensual structure of mood. *Psychological Bulletin, 98,* 219–235.

Weick, M., & Guinote, A. (2008). When subjective experiences matter: Power increases reliance on the ease of retrieval. *Journal of Personality and Social Psychology, 94,* 956–970.

Weick, M., & Guinote, A. (2010). How long will it take? Power biases time predictions. *Journal of Experimental Social Psychology, 46,* 595–604.

Whitson, J. A., Liljenquist, K. A., Galinsky, A. D., Magee, J. C., Gruenfeld, D. H., & Cadena, B. (2013). The blind leading: Power reduces awareness of constraints. *Journal of Experimental Social Psychology, 49,* 579–582.

Wiggins, J. S., Trapnell, P., & Phillips, N. (1988). Psychometric and geometric characteristics of the Revised Interpersonal Adjective Scales (IAS-R). *Multivariate Behavioral Research, 23,* 517–530.

Wilkinson, D., Guinote, A., Weick, M., Molinari, R., & Graham, K. (2010). Feeling socially powerless makes you more prone to bumping into things on the right and induces leftward line bisection error. *Psychonomic Bulletin and Review, 17,* 910–914.

Willis, G. B., Guinote, A., & Rodríguez-Bailón, R. (2010). Illegitimacy improves goal pursuit in powerless individuals. *Journal of Experimental Social Psychology, 46,* 416–419.

Winter, D. G. (1973). *The power motive.* New York, NY: Free Press.

Winter, D. G. (1991). A motivational model of leadership: Predicting long-term management success from TAT measures of power motivation and responsibility. *Leadership Quarterly, 2,* 67–80.

Winter, D. G., & Barenbaum, N. B. (1985). Responsibility and the power motive in women and men. *Journal of Personality, 53,* 335–355.

Winter, D. G., & Stewart, A. J. (1978). The power motive. In H. London & J. Exner (Eds.), *Dimensions of personality* (pp. 391–447). New York, NY: Wiley.

Wirth, M. M., Welsh, K. M., & Schultheiss, O. C. (2006). Salivary cortisol changes in humans after winning or losing a dominance contest depend on implicit power motivation. *Hormones and Behavior, 49,* 346–352.

Witkin, H. A., Dyk, R. B., Faterson, H. F., Goodenough, D. R., & Karp, S. A. (1962). Psychological individuality. In H. A. Witkin, R. B. Dyk, H. F. Faterson, D. R. Goodenough, & S. A. Karp (Eds.), *Differentiation: Studies of development* (pp. 381–389). Hoboken, NJ: Wiley.

Woike, B., Mcleod, S., & Goggin, M. (2003). Implicit and explicit motives influence accessibility to different autobiographical knowledge. *Personality and Social Psychology Bulletin, 29,* 1046–1055.

Wojciszke, B., & Struzynska-Kujalowicz, A. (2007). Power influences self-esteem. *Social Cognition, 25,* 472–494.

Woltin, K. A., Corneille, O., Yzerbyt, V. Y., & Förster, J. (2011). Narrowing down to open up for other people's concerns: Empathic concern can be enhanced by inducing detailed processing. *Journal of Experimental Social Psychology, 47,* 418–424.

Worchel, S., Arnold, S. E., & Harrison, W. (1978). Aggression and power restoration: The effects of identifiability and timing on aggressive behavior. *Journal of Experimental Social Psychology, 14,* 43–52.

Yap, A. J., Mason, M. F., & Ames, D. R. (2013). The powerful size others down: The link between power and estimates of others' size. *Journal of Experimental Social Psychology, 49,* 591–594.

Yap, A. J., Wazlawek, A. S., Lucas, B. J., Cuddy, A. J. C., & Carney, D. R. (2013). The ergonomics of dishonesty: The effect of incidental expansive posture on stealing, cheating and traffic violations. *Psychological Science, 24,* 2281–2289.

Zhong, C. B., Magee, J. C., Maddux, W. W., & Galinsky, A. D. (2006). Power, culture, and action: Considerations in the expression and enactment of power in East Asian and Western societies. *Research on Managing Groups and Teams, 9,* 53–73.

Zimbardo, P. G. (1973). On the ethics of intervention in human psychological research: With special reference to the Stanford prison experiment. *Cognition, 2,* 243–256.

Zimbardo, P. G., Pilkonis, P. A., & Norwood, R. M. (1974). *The silent prison of shyness* (Office of Naval Research Technical Report No. 2–17). Ft. Belvoir, VA: Defense Technical Information Center.

PART VI

FRIENDSHIP, LOVE, AND SEXUALITY

CHAPTER 17

FRIENDSHIP

Daniel Perlman, Nan L. Stevens, and Rodrigo J. Carcedo

Alone bad; friend, good.
— *Bride of Frankenstein* (Laemmle & Whale, 1935)

I found out what the secret to life is— friends. Best friends.
— *Fried Green Tomatoes* (Lear & Avenet, 1991)

Remember, George, no man is a failure who has friends.
— *It's a Wonderful Life* (Capra, 1946)

If you really want to be someone's friend, it takes time, doesn't it?
— *Mobsters* (Roth & Karbelnikoff, 1991)

It's an insane world but in it there is one sanity, the loyalty of old friends.
— *Ben Hur* (Zimbalist & Wyler, 1959)

True friends are always together in spirit.
— *Anne of Green Gables* (Sullivan, 1985)

Men and women can't be friends because the sex part always gets in the way.
— *When Harry Met Sally* (Reiner, Scheinman, & Reiner, 1989)

Friends come in and out of our lives like busboys in a restaurant.
— *Stand by Me* (Evans, Gideon, Scheinman, & Reiner, 1986)

A friend in need is a pest.
— *The Wedding Crashers* (Abrams, Levy, Panay, & Dobkin, 2005)

I never had any friends later on like the ones I had when I was 12.
— *Stand by Me* (Evans et al., 1986)

What will I do without a best friend?
— *Beaches* (Bruckheimer-Martell, Midler, Smith, & Marshall, 1988)

The preceding quotes reflect views of friendship found in American movies. One sees that friendship is good and leads to success. Friendships take time to develop. Friendships have properties such as loyalty. Friends are together in spirit, if not in body. However, perhaps not everyone can be friends, and friends come and go in one's life like busboys. If they are in need, friends can be a pain. Friendships change over the life cycle. They also come to an end through dissolution or, as in the movie *Beaches*, via death.

During the preparation of this chapter, Nan Stevens was a professor at both the Radboud University Nijmegen and the VU University Amsterdam, the Netherlands.

http://dx.doi.org/10.1037/14344-017
APA Handbook of Personality and Social Psychology: Vol. 3. Interpersonal Relations, M. Mikulincer and P. R. Shaver (Editors-in-Chief)

In this chapter, we synthesize knowledge on friendships. In doing so, we shed light on whether movie views of friendship hold a kernel of truth or are mere fiction. The philosophical analysis of friendship has a long history (see Blieszner & Adams, 1992; Pakaluk, 1991; Reisman, 1979). In this chapter, however, we emphasize work done in the past 40 years, especially work done in the 21st century. As other books and reviews have testified, research on friendship has flourished, especially in the past 25 years (e.g., Adams & Allan, 1998; Bagwell & Schmidt, 2011; Blieszner & Adams, 1992; Fehr, 1996; Hartup & Stevens, 1997; Rawlins, 2009; Spencer & Pahl, 2006; Ueno & Adams, 2006). As a preview, the chapter is divided into several main sections:

1. the nature of friendships, including how they have been defined and categorized into types;
2. the arc of friendships, including their development, maintenance, and demise;
3. the nature of friendships at different points in the life cycle;
4. the role of gender in friendships;
5. friendship and well-being; and
6. the changing nature of friendship in a postmodern world.

Movies often focus on romantic relationships, but friendships are also important, not only in films but also in people's daily lives. Here are a few reasons why. First, people spend a lot of time in the presence of others, probably more than half their waking lives. A considerable amount of the time spent with other people is spent with friends. For example, a sample of employed Texas women estimated that they spent 2.6 hours per day with friends (compared with 2.7 hours per day with their spouses and 2.3 hours per day with their children; Kahneman, Krueger, Schkade, Schwarz, & Stone, 2004). Adolescents attending a suburban Chicago high school spent 30% of their time—close to 5 hours a day—with friends (in comparison with only 18% of their time with family; Larson, 1983). Second, friendship, in some form, is arguably a universal phenomenon. Lothar Krappman (1996) noted that "a term for friendship seems to be available in every language of the world" (p. 22).

Third, people value friendships. In a recent survey, 60% of Americans rated friends as a very important aspect of life (Fischer, 2011). This fell short of how much they valued family and health, but it was comparable to how much they valued money and work, and it surpassed other prominent aspects of life such as religion, leisure, hobbies, and community activity (Gallup Poll News Service, 2005). Fourth, as we will show, friendships also influences people's moods, well-being, attitudes, and behaviors.

FRIENDSHIP: WHAT IS IT?

In her highly regarded examination of the literature on friendship, Fehr (1996) wrote, "Everyone knows what friendship is—until asked to define it. Then, it seems, no one knows. There are virtually as many definitions of friendship as there are social scientists studying the topic" (p. 5). There is not even total agreement on whether friendship should be defined in terms of an absolutely necessary set of characteristics or a proto-typical, fuzzy set of attributes (see also Chapter 18, this volume). Given both the variability in the definitions researchers have used and the variability in whom lay-people call friends, we believe that a less absolute, pro-totypical conceptualization of what friendship is—and is not—is more realistic at this time.

Key Properties of Friendships

Fehr (1996) discussed five different scholarly definitions of friendship. Key qualities captured in these definitions are that friendships are voluntary, they involve companionship (e.g., friends seeking one another's company and engaging in social activities), and they exist over some period of time. Fehr's set of definitions also depict friends as liking one another and caring for each other's well-being. When community members are asked what they mean by friendship, some variability occurs by gender, age, sexual orientation, and nationality, but properties akin to those given in scholarly definitions repeatedly emerge (de Vries & Megathlin, 2009).

Hartup and Stevens (1997) said that "a friendship consists mainly of being attracted to someone who is attracted in return, with parity governing the social exchanges between the individuals involved" (p. 355). They believed that friendships have both a deep and a surface structure. For Hartup and Stevens, the deep structure is reciprocation, giving and taking. They contended that this reciprocation characterizes friendship across the life cycle. The surface aspect of friendship involves the various things that are exchanged, which change over the life cycle.

Some efforts at defining friendship include statements of what friendships are not. For instance, P. H. Wright (1984) stated that friendships are not individuals relating to one another merely as role occupants; instead, friendships involve partners responding to each other personally as unique individuals. Kinship is another exclusionary criterion that is sometimes mentioned. Armstrong (1985) began his definition with "friendship is a non-sexual relationship" (p. 215).

Measurement

Moving from a conceptual to an operational level of definition of who is a friend, many investigators have left it to research participants to define what they mean by friendship. In research with both children and adults, investigators have sometimes had participants refer to their friends collectively as a group without individually identifying them. Other times, researchers have had participants name specific individuals who are their current friends. Asking for specific names has an advantage in that this approach provides data needed to address questions that researchers want to answer (Berndt & McCandless, 2009).

Illustrative of the collective approach, the Gallup organization uses the question "Not counting your relatives, about how many close friends would you say you have?" When polled between 1990 and 2003, the average (median) number of close friends Americans said they had was five to six (Carroll, 2004).

Claude Fischer's (1982) study of the social networks of Northern Californians is a classic example of the approach of asking participants to identify specific friends. He used six questions to elicit names: (a) who would take care of the respondent's home when he or she was away, (b) with whom does the respondent spend leisure time, (c) with whom does the respondent get together, (d) with

whom does the respondent discuss a hobby or personal problem, (e) to whom does the person turn for advice, and (f) from whom could the respondent borrow money. After participants made a list of these individuals, Fischer then asked, "Is there anyone who is important to you who doesn't show up on this list?"

On average, respondents listed 18.5 key members of their social networks. They classified 59% of the individuals they identified as friends, which translated to 11 friends per respondent (Fischer, 1982). Friendship, however, was not an exclusive category. Friends often occupied multiple roles. For example, more than two thirds of coworkers and neighbors were called friends.

Besides techniques to identify and map friendships, a number of scales have been developed to measure attributes of children's and adults' friendship (see Berndt & McCandless, 2009; Davis & Todd, 1985; Furman, 1996; Mendelson & Aboud, 1999). Parker and Asher's (1993) Friendship Quality Questionnaire is illustrative of instruments developed for children. The six features it assesses, along with a sample item for each, are

- validation and caring ("Makes me feel good about my ideas"),
- help and guidance ("Helps me so I can get done quicker," "Gives advice"),
- companionship and recreation ("Do fun things together a lot"),
- intimate exchange ("Always tell each other our problems"),
- conflict and betrayal ("Argue a lot"), and
- conflict resolution ("Make up easily when we fight").

As a way of validating these scales, Parker and Asher demonstrated that they correlated in the expected way with children's satisfaction with their friendships and with their experiencing loneliness.

Multidimensional friendship instruments vary in both the number and the specific qualities they assess. Predominantly, however, they assess positive features of friendships (Furman, 1996). Furthermore, the various subscales often correlate with one another. Some instruments have been factor analyzed to identify a positive or warmth dimension to friendship and a separate negative or conflict dimension (Berndt & McCandless, 2009; Furman, 1996). In terms of validation, comparisons among various friendship groups have been performed (e.g., best friends, close friends, acquaintances). Overall, the findings have suggested that a general factor permeates friendship. However, despite the significant associations among friendship properties, assessing specific features is also useful.

Types of Friendships

Relationships can be categorized at multiple levels. Within the friendship category are subvarieties of friendships. In turn, friendship can be placed as a subcategory within the larger terrain of interpersonal relationships. We consider both, starting with different varieties of friendships. Two approaches to classifying friendships are (a) identifying varieties of friendships on the basis of categories widely used in people's everyday discussions and (b) more formally specifying typologies of friendships.

People categorize their friendships in a plethora of ways. For example, laypeople as well as social scientists classify friendships along a dimension of intimacy or closeness. As illustrated by the validation studies mentioned previously, relations with best friends are more enjoyable, provide more support, and are more stable than relationships with close friends or acquaintances (Davis & Todd, 1985). Friendships are also classified along gender and age lines (men's vs. women's, children's vs. adults'), as we discuss later in the Gender Differences and Similarities in Friendship section of this chapter. Lesbians' and gay men's relationships have also been examined (Nardi, 1999; Rumens, 2010; Weinstock & Rothblum, 1996), as have online friendships (Chan & Cheng, 2004) and imaginary friends (M. Taylor, Shawber, & Mannering, 2009). In the past decade or so, the notion of "friends with benefits"—engaging in sexual activities in platonic relationships—has gained prominence and is quite prevalent among young adults (e.g., Bisson & Levine, 2009). Attention has also focused on the friendships of individuals belonging to specific historical (Adams & Blieszner, 1998), ethnic (e.g., Azmitia, Ittel, & Brenk, 2006), disability (Bauminger et al., 2008),

socioeconomic (Walker, 1995), occupational (Blackbird & Wright, 1985), and service provider–client (e.g., hairstylist–client) groups (Price & Arnould, 1999).

Turning to more formally derived typologies, Vanlear, Koerner, and Allen (2006) recently reviewed typologies in different kinds of relationships. What is most noteworthy about their discussion of friendship typologies is how few they identified. Thus, the full potential of the use of typologies of friendships has not been reached. Nonetheless, typological thinking about friendships dates back more than 2,300 years. Aristotle identified three different kinds of friendships (see Books VIII and IX of his *Nicomachean Ethics*): relationships based on utility, in which people are attracted to others because of the help they provide; relationships based on pleasure, in which people are attracted to others because they find them pleasant and engaging; and relationships based on virtue, in which people are attracted to others because of their virtuous character. Aristotle believed relationships based on utility and pleasure will evaporate if the benefits provided by one's partner stop, so they tend to be shorter lived. He saw relationships based on virtue as being the longest lasting. In these relationships, partners are liked for themselves rather than as merely a means to an end. Friendships based on virtue should endure as long as the partner remains pure.

More recently, Grief (2009) has offered a typology of adult men's friendships with the names *must, trust, rust,* and *just. Must* friends are one's closest friendships. These are the friends one must call if something very good or very bad happens, the friends on whom one can count and who one seeks out to discuss personal problems. *Must* friends can be trusted to not gossip about one's personal affairs, and they make life more fulfilling and fun. *Trust* friends will also keep confidences, but they are not as close as *must* friends. Engaging in personal conversations with them depends on running into them and the circumstances being right. *Trust* friends are also likable and enjoyable. *Rust* friends are long-time friends with whom one has long-standing patterns of interaction and at least a modicum of shared history. Long-time acquaintances can also be in other categories, but *rust* friendships are typically not intense.

Just friends are new relationships or enjoyable company with whom one engages in a particular activity or hobby (e.g., poker buddies). These are not friends with responsibility for one another or friends who are likely to disclose intimate information.

Friendship Compared With Other Relationships

Friendships have been compared with various other types of relationships. In a taxonomic analysis, Robert Weiss (1998) distinguished friendships as a form of affiliation from other forms of affiliation (such as work relationships and kin ties) and other attachment relationships (such as pair bonds, parental relationships, and guidance-obtaining relationships). He viewed friendships as distinct in terms of what leads them to be maintained (if they are gratifying) and what they provide (such as opportunities for companionship, receiving or exchanging information and services, responding to one's thoughts, and reassurance of worth). Turning to illustrative empirical investigations, P. H. Wright's (1985) early work using the Acquaintance Description Form showed that in their friendships, compared with their romantic or marital relationships, adult community members were less likely to commit free time to one another, less exclusive in the sense of feeling they were the only person entitled to interact with their partner in certain ways, and less overt in the expression of affection and positive emotion but more likely to believe they could easily dissolve their relationships. As we have noted, members of the general public believe there is overlap between friendships and other types of relationships, and they sometimes classify friendships as friendships plus another relational form. Nonetheless, at both a conceptual and an empirical level, differences between friendships and other types of relationships have been profitably identified.

ARC OF FRIENDSHIP

In the 1950s, 1960s, and 1970s, the central question that many social psychologists (e.g., Berscheid & Walster, 1969) asked with regard to friendships was "What determines who likes whom?" What factors cause interpersonal attraction? By the late 1970s,

however, social psychologists began taking a more developmental approach to the study of relationships as signified by Huston and Levinger's 1978 *Annual Review* chapter. As Finkel and Eastwick testified in Chapter 7 of this volume, attraction has remained a key question, but in this section we focus on the developmental arc of friendships, discussing how and why friendships form, are maintained, persist over time, and end.

Beginnings of Friendships

Work on the way friendships start and progress is sparse in comparison to research on the way romantic relationships begin. Nonetheless, there are generic analyses of relationship development that offer some insights into friendship (e.g., Levinger & Snoek, 1972). Berscheid and Regan (2005) succinctly synthesized work on friendship formation by saying it "is believed to involve: (1) identification of another as a potential friend; (2) attraction to the other; (3) increasing interaction, especially daily contact; and (4) exchange of information through self-disclosure and other means" (p. 205). We look at this process, building on Levinger and Snoek's (1972) analysis of three relational levels: awareness, surface contact, and mutuality.

Awareness. The beginnings of a relationship can take root when one becomes aware of another person, even before contact occurs. Awareness can be one sided, with one person knowing something about a potential friend but the potential friend not knowing about the person. At this stage, Levinger and Snoek (1972) believed people form generally positive or negative reactions to the other person on the basis of what they know about him or her. In an open-field choice situation in which people can decide what they want to do, Levinger and Snoek believed that the decision to interact with the person will depend not only on people's evaluative reactions but also on a host of other factors, such as people's need for affiliation, their satisfaction with existing relationships, and their appraisal of whether the other person is available and potentially interested.

Whether one has advanced information about the other person, a key beginning step in building friendships is meeting and interacting with that person. At least three contexts are important for starting friendships. First, many relationships are formed in specific settings. When a representative sample of Dutch adults was asked where they formed their friendships, they most frequently reported at work (17.8%), at a club or association (14.2%), in their neighborhood (14%), or at school (13.2%). Going-out places (e.g., cafes) were sometimes mentioned, but less frequently (5.1%; Mollenhorst, Völker, & Flap, 2008). These are places people go regularly in their daily lives where they often cross paths with strangers and interaction is feasible. Second, social networks are also important. Before people start relationships, they often have friends in common (Parks, 2007). In the Dutch study, respondents indicated 17.7% of their friendships were originally formed via mutual friends (11.7%) or family members (6%). Be it incidentally or purposely, overlapping network members are often a bridge through which new friends meet. Third, people today also meet via the Internet. In a survey in which 77% of a national sample of U.S. adults said they used the Internet, 20% of Internet users had friends whom they met via the Internet and with whom they only communicated via the Internet. In this survey, 15% reported establishing friendships online that subsequently included offline contacts (Wang & Wellman, 2010).

Surface contact. Once two people begin relating, they establish what Levinger and Snoek (1972) called *surface contact*. These initial interactions tend to be very socially prescribed or role bound. A good deal of what one learns about the other person is likely to come from his or her public self-presentation, the social categories in which she or he belongs, and whatever is unique or different about the way she or he presents her- or himself. What is crucial about this stage is that people can evaluate the outcomes of their interactions. They can compare the satisfaction of their new relationship with what they expect in relationships and the level of outcomes available in other relationships (Thibaut & Kelley, 1959). If the person's expectations are met and the new relationship compares favorably with

existing relationships, the person will want continued development of the friendship.

Over the course of people's lives, they are exposed to thousands of people and have casual interactions with hundreds of them. Thus, contact is a necessary but not sufficient condition for friendships to develop. Proximity, repeatedly seeing the other person, and external characteristics of the other person such as physical attractiveness are widely discussed aspects of friendship formation (Fehr, 2008) that are likely to be important aspects of moving relationships ahead in their early stages.

Rodin (1982) argued that, when it comes to friendships, people have a set of eligible individuals, people with whom they are willing to have friendships. They also have ineligibles, people they do not consider suitable as friends. Rodin believed that before people decide with whom they want to establish friendships, they first decide who they do not want as friends. Elimination of possible friends probably occurs in the awareness and surface contact stages.

Once people have consciously or unconsciously decided the desired trajectory of their relationships, they treat potential friends differently. A study by Duck and Miell (1986) illustrated this. They asked first-semester university students what they did to intensify or restrict the development of a friendship. For relationships they wanted to advance, students said they would plan meetings, see their partner frequently, discuss a wide range of topics, engage in intimate discussions, and check new information against existing knowledge. To restrict the development of a friendship, students said they would see their partner infrequently, be reserved and polite, limit the range of topics discussed, keep discussions at a general level, avoid being forthcoming or responsive, and avoid asking questions.

Mutuality. As relationships progress, they reach what Levinger and Snoek (1972) called the *mutuality level*. At this level, partners "have shared knowledge of one another, assume some responsibility for each other's outcomes, and at least begin to regulate their association upon a mutually agreed basis" (p. 8). Levinger and Snoek argued that transitions from surface contact to mutuality are facilitated by (a) partners' satisfaction with the outcomes of their interactions, especially interactions beyond those required by their roles; (b) accommodation between partners, so that each receives pleasure and esteem; and (c) similarity in attitudes and values.

Illustrative studies.   Hays (1985) conducted an illustrative study of friendship development. Two weeks into the school year, he had university students identify individuals with whom they felt they might become friends. Hays then followed these relationships throughout the academic year to see how close they became. For some analyses, the relationships were divided into those who did become close versus those who did not. The results were as follows:

- Students who were motivated to form new friendships at the beginning of the year were more likely to do so.
- The shorter the physical distance between the residences of individuals and their potential friends, the closer their friendships became.
- Consistent with expectations based on social penetration theory (Altman & Taylor, 1973), friends' interactions started with more superficial topics and later began including more intimate exchanges.
- Dyads who became close showed an initial increase in the breadth of topics they discussed, whereas dyads who did not become close decreased the breadth of their interactions from the first assessment onward.
- Increases in closeness were strongest during the first 6 weeks of the study.
- From the start of the study, how often partners interacted predicted the closeness of their friendship, but as the semester progressed, the intimacy level of the partners' interactions added to the prediction of how close they felt.
- In relationships in which partners became closer over the semester, partners rewarded one another more frequently and increased their level of rewards over time more than did partners in relationships that did not progress. Costs in friendships increased slightly over the semester, with

costs showing a weak association with closeness, suggesting that as relationships become more interdependent, some negatives come along with the benefits.

- Companionship was the most frequently mentioned benefit of friendship, but having a confidant and receiving emotional support were the two things that most clearly distinguished the development of close versus nonclose relationships.

Other, more recent studies have looked at the development of friendships in work settings (Sias & Cahill, 1998), online (Chan & Cheng, 2004), and with members of another race (Shelton, Trail, West, & Bergsieker, 2010). In a work setting, the transition from acquaintance to friend took a year, somewhat longer than in a university setting. Employees considered communication factors as important to the development of their friendships, but work-related factors were mentioned as significant, too (e.g., sharing work tasks, discussing work problems). In Chan and Cheng's (2004) study, online friendships initially grew more slowly than face-to-face friendships, but "after passing a critical period (about 6 months to 1 year in our sample), online friendships grow quickly and the difference between these two types of relationships decrease" (p. 317). Shelton et al. (2010) found support for the importance that being responsive to one another has in the development of intimacy in both interracial and intraracial friendships.

In her synthesis of the literature on friendship formation, Fehr (2008) identified four key classes of variables that promote friendship: environmental (e.g., proximity), situational (e.g., the probability of future interaction), individual (e.g., physical attractiveness, social skills), and dyadic (e.g., reciprocity of liking, similarity). Each of these categories of variables is clearly important. What a developmental approach to the beginning of friendships underscores, however, is that it is not only knowing what predicts who will like whom that matters; the predictors may vary as a function of the relationship stage. Beyond the predictors of attraction, social scientists studying relationships need to know the phases of friendship development, including the characteristics of friendships at various stages of development. Transitions are crucial: How do relationships move from one phase to the next? Which forces foster each transition occurring? It is tempting to think of the degree of liking between friends or their degree of closeness as synonymous with the level of a relationship's development. It is important to remember, however, that friendships differ both in the functions they serve and in their developmental trajectories, with some reaching higher levels of liking and closeness than others (Johnson, Wittenberg, Villagran, Mazur, & Villagran, 2003). Accordingly, social scientists need to know why some trajectories reach higher levels of closeness than others. Relationship scholars also need to realize that the trajectories of friendships are not always a continuous upward movement toward ever greater closeness; they can have downturns along the way. Why are there downturns, and how do some friends develop their friendships beyond them? A developmental perspective on the formation of relationships goes well beyond the question of who likes whom. In any case, once friendships are established, the next step is to maintain them.

How Do Friends Maintain Their Relationships?

Once psychologists and others began analyzing friendships from a more developmental perspective, they began thinking more about the continuation and maintenance of relationships. One approach to identifying maintenance strategies has been to start by asking people what they do to sustain their relationships (e.g., Canary, Hause, Stafford, & Wallace, 1993). A second approach has been for researchers to identify the thoughts and behaviors partners use, regardless of whether they are strategies partners claim they use (e.g., Rusbult, Olsen, Davis, & Hannon, 2004). Apropos of maintenance strategies specifically used by friends, Oswald, Clark, and Kelly (2004) empirically identified a typology of four key strategies: positivity, supportiveness, openness, and interaction (see Table 17.1). In studying friendships per se, other researchers have identified comparable strategies labeled with relatively similar names.

Other important maintenance strategies, less cited in the literature, include (a) avoidance of particular topics or people (e.g., "We don't talk about sensitive issues"; Canary et al., 1993), (b) antisocial strategies such as coercion or deception (Canary et al., 1993), (c) use of humor and teasing (e.g., "We try to make each other laugh"; Canary et al., 1993), (d) social network support (e.g., getting network members to help friends resolve problems; Canary et al., 1993), and (e) conflict management (Burleson & Samter, 1994).

In terms of the correlates of the use of maintenance strategies, best friends engage in more maintenance behaviors than close or casual friends (Oswald et al., 2004). In cross-sex friendships in which both partners would like the relationship to turn into a romance, use of maintenance behaviors

---

TABLE 17.1

Friendship Maintenance Strategies

Strategy	Description	Sample item
Positivity	Behaviors that make the friendship enjoyable and rewarding	Try to be upbeat and cheerful when together.
Supportiveness	Provision of emotional support and assurances	Try to make the other person "feel good" about who they are.
Openness	Meaningful conversations, sharing private thoughts, self-disclosure	Share your private thoughts with each other.
Interaction	Doing things together	Make an effort to spend time together even when you are busy.

Note. Data from Oswald, Clark, and Kelly (2004).

is generally higher than in other cross-sex friendships. Use of maintenance strategies is also associated with the degree to which friends are committed to their relationships (Oswald & Clark, 2006). In this instance, the causality may be bidirectional, with commitment leading to greater use of maintenance strategies and greater use of maintenance strategies leading to higher commitment. Commitment should produce greater stability (Rusbult et al., 2004).

Using maintenance strategies does appear to predict the stability of relationships, however. For example, as Dainton, Zelley, and Langan (2003) pointed out, the lack of maintenance activities (i.e., the absence of time together and having interactions) is a major reason why friendships end. Bowker's (2004) longitudinal study of early adolescents' friendships is also relevant here. For boys in that investigation, using minimization as a way of responding to conflicts was associated with the stability of their friendships. For girls, however, the use of confrontational and assertive techniques was associated with higher friendship stability. Although there were gender differences, for both genders the types of coping strategies that individuals used to deal with conflict were predictive of their relationships persisting across the school year.

Stability and Duration of Friendships

When partners try to maintain their friendships, they can last a long time. Nonetheless, one vision of friendship networks is that they are like a swimming pool, with water constantly entering and leaving. How long do people's friends stay in their networks?

Poulin and Chan (2010) reviewed more than 35 studies that assessed the stability of children's and adolescents' friendships. Regarding early elementary school–age children, they indicated that stability increases over time. First-graders keep about 50% of their friendships across a school year, whereas fourth-graders keep around 75%. Among early adolescents, Poulin and Chan emphasized the instability of friendships. They characterized friendship stability as increasing during the rest of adolescence, with older adolescents keeping between 50% and 75% of their friendships over a school year.

During the transition to college, high school friendships become vulnerable, especially as the freshman year progresses. This is illustrated in a study in which college students provided data on their best friend in high school during the 1st week of college and again at the end of their freshman year. During Week 1, 95.6% of 1st-year college students still considered their high school best friend as their current best friend, and 4.3% considered him or her a close friend. In the spring, only 54.7% of students still considered their high school best friend their current best friend; 29.2% now classified him or her as a close friend, and 14.6% considered him or her a casual friend (Oswald & Clark, 2003). One factor that slows—but does not stop—the decline in high school friendships is the use of social media and communication technology (Cummings, Lee, & Kraut, 2006). With the greater use of this technology, students now and in the future may be more likely than past generations of freshman to retain their preuniversity friendships.

Various factors have been associated with the stability of children's and adolescents' friendships (Poulin & Chan, 2010). Some factors shown to foster stability include (a) higher relationship quality, (b) higher levels of prosociality, (c) moving from one grade to the next with the same classmates, (d) being friends in both school and nonschool contexts rather than in just one or the other, and (e) maintaining high levels of phone contact and engaging in maintenance behaviors during the 1st year of university. Some factors found to undermine the stability of relationships include (a) changing schools, (b) cross-sex and cross-race friendships, (c) attention deficit/hyperactivity disorder, (d) elevated levels of depression, (e) higher levels of loneliness, (f) having been victimized by peers or having used aggression against peers, and (g) engaging in antisocial behaviors.

Not all studies have found gender differences in the stability of children's and adolescents' friendships, but when they are found it is generally boys whose relationships last longer (Poulin & Chan, 2010). Some have argued that greater intimacy, sharing, and self-disclosure of girls' relationships may be more satisfying but also more prone to cause personal distress and more important conflicts that can lead to relationship termination.

Less research has examined the stability of friendships in adulthood. In one study of working- and middle-class Canadians, Wellman, Wong, Tindall, and Nazer (1997) followed the intimate ties of community residents for a decade. Over that time span, roughly 40% of originally close friendship ties persisted, with about half of those remaining intimate and half becoming less close.

The older one becomes, the longer one's friendships can possibly have lasted. Not surprisingly, people's age and the duration of their friendships are closely related. In a study that asked U.S. men to identify their three closest friends, roughly 25% of the friendships of younger adults (ages 21–35) had lasted 13 or more years. This percentage rose to nearly 50% for men ages 35 to 49 and 68% for those ages 50 to 65 (Stueve & Gerson, 1977). In a binational study of adults ages 55 to 91, the mean duration of close friendships among older Dutch adults was more than 28 years, and among Americans it was 18 years (de Jong Gierveld & Perlman, 2006).

In sum, the stability of friendship seems to increase with age during the early school years, decrease during the transition to middle school and the early adolescent years, then become more stable as adolescence advances. During the transition to college, these relationships become less stable and substitution with new friends occurs. Although evidence during adulthood is less available, the duration of people's key friendships seems to increase as they age. Of course, the exact duration of one's friendships depends on various methodological and substantive factors, such as the definition of friendship used and longitudinal studies versus retrospective recall. Older adults have long-standing friendships, although—as we note later—older adults appear to have decreased involvement with their friends.

Deterioration and Ending of Friendships

Although some friendships are sustained for very long periods of time, all relationships ultimately end and most deteriorate beforehand. Compared with the ending of a marriage or cohabitation, the demise of a friendship is less likely to have public trappings such as moving out or getting a legal separation. Friendships often just fade away. Most endings come while both friends are still alive. Others, however, end because of death.

Some have viewed the deterioration of relationships as a reversal of the factors that contribute to interpersonal attraction and the development of relations. Thus, factors such as decreasing rewards, the emergence of dissimilar attitudes, or a shrinking in the depth and breadth of disclosure have been considered factors leading to the decline of friendships. In reviewing the evidence, especially the evidence from self-disclosure studies, Fehr (1996) concluded that there was some, but not complete, evidence to support the idea of a reversal. As relationships deteriorate, friends are less willing to disclose, especially on high-intimacy topics. However, reversal is not complete. In aspects of communication pertaining to knowledge of the other person, reversal effects are less pronounced. One's knowledge of one's former friend does not vanish.

Reasons friendships end. Researchers have been interested in why friendships end. In a seminal early study, S. M. Rose (1984) identified four reasons given by college students: physical separation (47.2%), friends growing to dislike each other (22.5%), the development of new friendships (18%), and dissolving friendships because of their incompatibility with one or both friends' romantic relations (12.4%). S. M. Rose reflected that "many friendships seemed to deteriorate past the point of being salvaged without the subjects noting their decline" (p. 273).

Not all research, however, has painted such a placid picture. In a more recent investigation of the reasons college students gave for the ending of their relationships, McEwan, Babin Gallagher, and Farinelli (2008) found that only 13.5% of students cited distance as a key reason why their friendships ended. Another 14.3% cited competing relationships, but the majority cited more negative factors such as betrayal (22.6%), disapproving of their friend's behavior (17.3%), or personality trait problems (20.3%). McEwan et al. summarized various additional reasons that have been suggested for why friendships dissolve, including decreased affection; change in friend or self, discovery of dissimilarity, or both; discontinuation of a shared activity;

conflict, criticism, gossiping, or spreading rumors; disloyalty; lack of social support; aggression; and substance abuse.

Friendships ending because of death.   The ending of friendships as a result of death is rare in the early stages of life, but as people age the loss of friends because of death becomes more common. De Vries and Johnson (2002) reported that a third of adults older than 65 and half of those older than 85 lose a close friend through death each year.

De Vries and Johnson (2002) summarized the available literature, saying that the experiences of midlife and older adults who lose a friend are "mostly comparable to those found in family bereavement" (p. 302), although they noted that some studies have shown the intensity of reactions (e.g., depression) after the death of a friend to be less severe. In the narratives they collected from seniors about the death of a friend, de Vries and Johnson found three prominent themes: (a) sensitivity to the number of friends who have died, (b) the loss of instrumental and expressive activities and support, and (c) the survivors' awareness of the relative longevity of their own lives. Thus, the death of a friend engenders feelings of sadness, despair, loss, and aloneness, as well as an appreciation for life and an awareness of one's own longevity and mortality.

Final thoughts on endings.   Earlier, we mentioned the analogy of friendships being like water in a swimming pool that stays for awhile and then flows away. In this section, we have considered the ending of friendships. Some friendships end because friends are no longer in geographical proximity, but the ending of friendships can also be triggered by aversive events or by discovering a friend's negative attributes. In any case, many friendships end via a fairly tranquil process of withdrawal or fading away. And, lest one forget, sometimes long-lost friends suddenly reappear in one's life via the Internet or other means.

In depicting the ending of relationships, we have largely ignored two topics. The first is the steps that people go through in ending friendships. Various models of the processes involved in the termination of romantic relationships (or relationships in general) have been identified. Rollie and Duck (2006) suggested that five general stages or processes occur. In Stage 1, a partner grows dissatisfied. In Stage 2, the unhappy partner reveals his or her discontent—confrontation, negotiation, accommodation, and so on may ensue. In Stage 3, the partners publicize their distress to others outside their relationship. In Stage 4, partners begin getting over their loss and create an account meaningful to themselves that they can discuss with others for the course of the relationships. In Stage 5, the ex-partners reenter their social lives separately.

Second, we have not fully examined the aftermath of friendship terminations. We know that the death of friends can cause grief. In work organizations, Sias, Heath, Perry, Silva, and Fix (2004) found that employees sometimes leave their jobs because a friendship ends and they experience spillover from work to their family life. Both of these topics—the steps in the termination of relationships and the aftermath of relationships ending—warrant further examination.

FRIENDSHIP ACROSS THE LIFE CYCLE

Friendship is an important peer relationship from early childhood through old age. Its most fundamental, enduring characteristic is symmetrical reciprocity. The actual social exchanges and expectations within friendships vary across the life cycle as cognitive, emotional, and interpersonal skills develop and developmental tasks change (Blieszner & Roberto, 2004; Hartup & Stevens, 1997).

Childhood

In early childhood, toddlers express a preference for interacting with certain peers. The word *friend* enters children's vocabularies around age 3. Friendships among preschoolers develop during time spent in play and concrete sharing of toys or food as rudimentary forms of reciprocity (Hartup & Stevens, 1997). In preschool and kindergarten, behavior with friends, as identified by mothers and teachers, differs from behavior with acquaintances. Friends are more expressive; they laugh, talk to, and look at each other more' and they exhibit more complexity in play behavior (Bukowski, Motzoi, & Meyer, 2009). Spending more time together involves more conflicts between preschool friends, yet they tend to resolve these conflicts cooperatively and continue interacting (Hartup, Laursen, Stewart, & Eastenson, 1988).

Friendship facilitates the transition to school, because starting school with a friend improves one's attitude toward school. Adaptation is also easier if a close friendship is formed during the 1st year (Ladd, Kochenderfer, & Coleman, 1996; Dunn, Cutting, & Fisher, 2002). Early development of cognitive and emotional skills enables friends to share their interests and beliefs. Also, children become aware of personal qualities that they like in friends. By ages 8 to 10, prosocial behavior between friends becomes more common as friends respond to one another's needs and provide assistance to each other.

In sociometric studies in school classrooms, friendship is often defined by high levels of reciprocated liking and mutual identification as best friends (Bukowski et al., 2009). A meta-analysis of studies on the behavior of mutual best friends has indicated that best friends demonstrate higher levels of positive engagement as well as more effective conflict management and task activity than do acquaintances (Newcomb & Bagwell, 1995). Friends better coordinate their activities when trying to solve problems or engage in a task, and they demonstrate more exploration during joint tasks than do nonfriends (Bukowski et al., 2009). Friends also demonstrate more similarity, equality, mutual liking, closeness, and loyalty in their interactions and in their descriptions of their relationships, as well as less dominance, than nonfriends in childhood (Newcomb & Bagwell, 1995).

The influence that friends have on development depends on friends' characteristics. Kind and compassionate friends tend to support the development of prosocial tendencies, and regular interaction with aggressive friends leads to involvement in more antisocial acts (Güroğlu, Van Lieshout, Haselager, & Scholte, 2007).

Adolescence

In adolescence, friends spend more time together than in childhood as they seek independence from parents and family. In addition to serving as companions, friends provide a sense of belonging in the larger peer group (Berndt, 1996). Adolescents become more particular about whom they call their best friends, nominating fewer friends than in childhood. Self-disclosure is increasingly important in friendship as adolescents work on the task of establishing their identity in conversations with friends. Gossip becomes more common between friends as adolescents critically examine peers' behavior to clarify how they are similar and different (Hartup & Stevens, 1997). The focus on the self gradually shifts to a focus on the self and the friend by middle adolescence (Shulman & Knafo, 1997).

Improvement in perspective taking enables friends to understand one another better and become more effective in providing mutual support as adolescence progresses. In a longitudinal study across 4 years of high school, perceptions of friendship quality increased for closest friends and friends in general. For some students, there was a positive association between quality of family ties and quality of friendship, indicating an attachment-like pattern. However, the greatest improvements in friendship quality were among those reporting low quality of family ties, indicating a compensatory pattern of influence for friendship (Way & Greene, 2006).

Not all friendships in adolescence are characterized by closeness and mutuality, however. In problem-solving tasks involving pairs of friends, researchers have distinguished disengaged friends (46%) who worked independently (and even competed with one another) and interdependent friends (54%) who collaborated on tasks (Shulman & Knafo, 1997). Interdependent friends are better able to manage conflicts in ways that preserve harmony and mutuality, whereas disengaged friends are more focused on individual gain (Shulman & Laursen, 2002). Adolescents in disengaged friendships are also less close and report less companionship, satisfaction, and commitment than those in other types of friendship (Way, Cowal, Gingold, Pahl, & Bissessar, 2001).

Transition to Adulthood

During the phase of emerging adulthood, young people undergo diverse transitions in educational, occupational, and social domains. These transitions often entail moving away from old friendship networks and developing new ones. During the 1st year of college, friendship networks among students become increasingly cohesive within 3 months and then stabilize. Friendships often develop through other friends (in triads), leading to a network of new friends. Personality traits influence who becomes friends as friends are often selected to have similar levels of agreeableness, extraversion, and openness (Selfhout et al., 2010).

In addition to supporting identity development, interaction with friends also supports the development of intimacy. Originally, this occurs within same-sex friendships, though cross-sex friendships and romantic involvements gradually become more important for development of intimacy. Daily diary studies on social interactions in college (during the 1st and the final year) and 6 to 9 years later in adulthood have revealed that intimacy increases overall in social interactions and specifically in same-sex and cross-sex best friendships between college and adulthood. Both men and women reduce the number of people with whom they interact regularly and increase the amount of time they spend in interaction with specific people in adulthood, suggesting a preference for spending time with a smaller number of close friends as adults (Reis, Lin, Bennett, & Nezlek, 1993). Other studies have confirmed that many emerging adults have both close friends and romantic partners, and spending time with them contributes to happiness (Barry, Madsen, Nelson, Carroll, & Badger, 2009).

Adulthood

Friendship is often studied as a distinct relationship type within social networks in adulthood. It varies in importance as a source of companionship and support depending on the partner and parental status of adults. Carbery and Buhrmester (1998) examined how social provisions by friends varied within three contexts—single and married with and without children—among those ages 20 to 35. Their results indicated that reliance on friends for social provisions such as companionship and emotional support is greatest during the single phase. In the two marital phases, friends played a secondary role along with parents, whereas the spouse provided the most support and companionship. Children joined

the spouse as primary providers of affection, companionship, and opportunities for nurturance. Other studies on married adults in middle and old age have confirmed this pattern. For example, among married adults aged 40 to 85, friends ranked third as providers (and receivers) of emotional support and as companions in leisure activities, following only spouses and children (Stevens & Westerhof, 2006). Other studies of single adults and those in nonheterosexual partnerships have shown frequent contact with friends who are primary sources of support, intimacy, and companionship compared with those not involved in traditional partner relationships (Allan, 2008).

Although friendship in middle age is understudied, a few studies exist in which friendship in middle age has been compared with friendship in younger and older age groups. Heyl and Schmitt (2007) examined whether personality traits differentially influenced the intensity of friendship involvement at ages 43 to 46 and ages 61 to 64. Predictions based on socioemotional selectivity theory were confirmed (Carstensen, Isaacowitz, & Charles, 1999). Specifically, openness to new experiences, indicating interest in knowledge acquisition, predicted greater friendship involvement among middle-aged respondents, whereas agreeableness predicted greater friendship involvement among older respondents, reflecting a priority for emotionally positive interactions.

K. B. Wright and Patterson (2006) compared friendship styles, length of friendship, emotional support, and quality of talk within friendships in groups of young, middle-aged, and older people. Those who identified their friendship style as discerning, with only one or two close friends, reported a longer duration of friendships than those identified as independent, who use the term *friends* loosely and switch friends easily, or as acquisitive, who have both old and new friends of varying degrees of closeness (Matthews, 1986). Younger people were more often acquisitive, younger and middle-aged people were more often independent, and middle-aged and older people were more often discerning in friendship, as predicted by socioemotional selectivity theory. A recent study that examined these friendship patterns in a large, representative sample of people aged 40 to 85 identified discerning and independent styles, as well as unconditionally acquisitive and selectively acquisitive, thus adding a fourth style to Matthews' (1986) classification (Miche, Huxhold, & Stevens, 2013).

Late Adulthood

The amount of time spent with friends is lowest in middle age when family, work, and community roles are very time consuming (Larson & Bradney, 1988). On retirement, there is only a slight increase in time spent with friends. However, closeness to friends remains high in later life for those used to having friends (Field, 1999). Friends continue to fulfill relational needs that are distinct from those fulfilled by family in late adulthood (Blieszner & Roberto, 2004; Pinquart & Sorensen, 2001). Friends are important for reaffirmation of worth and companionship, contributing to social integration when other roles are lost. As in other life phases, friends support one another in dealing with transitions in late adulthood such as retirement, widowhood, and changes in health. They do so by sharing relevant information and personal experience, giving advice, and suggesting or modeling alternative ways of understanding and dealing with new situations (Hartup & Stevens, 1997; Stevens, 2009). When family members are unable to provide instrumental help to older relatives, friends may step in to provide necessary aid, usually on a short-term basis (Barker, 2002; Himes & Reidy, 2000).

In addition to individual characteristics such as personality and friendship style, marital status also influences the availability of friends in late adulthood. Married couples often have more friends in their social networks because of the inclusion of other couples as friends. However, they tend to spend less time with their friends and exchange less support with friends than widowed, divorced, and never-married older adults (Guiaux, van Tilburg, & Broese Van Groenou, 2007).

There are many challenges to maintaining friendship in old age, because health status, marital status, location of friends, interests and activities, and social needs undergo change, leading some to focus more on family. Longitudinal studies of large representative samples of older adults have shown a decrease in having friends in personal networks as individuals age (Ajrouch, Blandon, & Antonucci, 2005; van Tilburg, 1998). However, a recent study of adults aged 55 to 85 who were followed for 17 years found no decline in having friends in personal networks among the youngest cohort, in contrast to two older cohorts (Stevens & van Tilburg, 2011), suggesting that younger cohorts of aging people may be better able and more inclined to maintain friendships or replace them as they age.

Friendship is a dynamic type of relationship during the life cycle, subject to many personal and situational influences. When asked about the importance of friendship in their lives, the majority of older adults describe this type of relationship as very important. The efforts that are made to maintain or revive old friendships and to develop new ones attest to the significance of friendship in late adulthood, as in earlier phases of life (Stevens, 2009).

GENDER DIFFERENCES AND SIMILARITIES IN FRIENDSHIP

Gender differences in friendship are the subject of an ongoing discussion with two prominent positions. The first position emphasizes that clear gender differences indicate fundamentally different orientations in friendships for men and women (Fehr, 1996, 2004; Miller & Perlman, 2009; P. H. Wright, 1989). Evolutionary psychology proposes that, to ensure their own and their offspring's survival in their partner's kinship group, women developed greater interpersonal sensitivity, relationship maintenance behaviors, and investment in smaller social groups in contrast to men, who remained in their own large kinship groups. Social constructionists assume that men and women are raised in separate, sex-segregated cultures in which they learn different forms of social relationships and different styles of communication (Burleson, 2003). Another approach emphasizes the different social roles that focus on communion for women and agency for men. These roles are internalized to form personal dispositions and also serve as norms for expected behavior (Eagly, 2009). Thus, diverse theoretical perspectives that operate at different levels of analysis explain gender differences in behavior in friendship.

The other position is that gender differences are exaggerated, with more actual similarities in the friendships of men and women than differences (Dindia, 2006; Duck & Wright, 1993; P. H. Wright, 2006). This position is based primarily on methodological criticism of many studies that have identified gender differences in friendship. Proponents have pointed out that often, effect sizes are not reported, only significant differences. When effect sizes of gender differences are examined, they are often small, indicating considerable overlap (85% or more) in the nature of men's and women's friendships (Dindia, 2006; P. H. Wright, 2006).

Early Gender Differences in Friendship

If there are gender differences in friendship, they probably originate in childhood and adolescence. Boys and girls interact most frequently with same-sex peers, so different relationship styles develop within male and female peer groups by middle childhood. Boys engage in more group interactions and in larger play groups. However, they do not necessarily interact less frequently in dyads than do girls. The duration of dyadic interaction is longer for girls, with more extended contact between particular girls. Boys tend to have more integrated social networks, which means that their friends or playmates are more likely to be friends of one another than is true of girls (A. J. Rose & Rudolph, 2006).

The content of interactions between peers indicates gender differences, with girls responding more prosocially with helping, sharing, and comforting. Self-reports and observational studies have revealed that girls engage in self-disclosure and social conversations with peers more often than do boys. Boys are more often involved in rough play and competitive games, enabling them to develop more clear dominance hierarchies than do girls (A. J. Rose & Rudolph, 2006).

Most studies have found that girls and boys report similar amounts of conflict in friendship. Girls tend to report higher levels of certain types of friendship stress (e.g., a friend betrays her or stops being her friend), and girls' friendships tend to be of shorter duration. Girls also seek support in response to stress more often than do boys, a difference that increases with age (A. J. Rose & Rudolph, 2006). By adolescence, girls are much more likely to talk about problems and seek emotional and instrumental support from their friends. Girls also develop more empathy for others, with gender differences greatest in adolescence (Olweus & Endresen, 1998).

Various studies on relationship provisions available in friendship have also demonstrated differences (A. J. Rose & Rudolph, 2006). Girls are more likely to experience higher levels of closeness, affection, nurturance, trust, security, validation, acceptance, and enhancement of worth in friendship. Effect sizes are small in childhood and larger in adolescence, indicating that there is temporal development in gender differences in experiencing these provisions. Despite these differences, there are no differences in friendship satisfaction between boys and girls. A. J. Rose and Rudolph (2006) suggested that the relational provisions (e.g., fun, excitement) that contribute to satisfaction in boys' friendships are understudied.

Gender and Friendship in Adulthood

Reviews of research on gender differences in friendship in adulthood are scarce. Fehr (1996) has reviewed gender issues in friendship, with many studies based on samples of college students. For many topics, the evidence regarding gender differences in friendship is mixed; some studies have reported gender differences, and others have reported similarities. Male and female college students have similar numbers of same-sex and cross-sex friends (Sheets & Lugar, 2005), though male students reported having more close friends in one study (Vigil, 2007). Young adult men and women have similar numbers of same-sex friends, but young men are slightly more likely to have cross-sex friends (Kalmijn, 2003). Friends are often studied as part of social networks in adulthood. Married men and women ages 40 to 85 have a similar number of friends in the core networks of their eight most important relationships (Stevens & Westerhof, 2006). Among a representative group of adults ages 55 to 90, women had more friends than men in their larger social networks (Dykstra, 1995; Stevens & van Tilburg, 2011).

Fehr (1996) reported similarities for men and women in the amount of time spent with casual, good, and close friends among college students and young adults. Some evidence has shown that women spend more time talking on the phone with their best friends. Some studies have found that women spend more time with friends in middle age, whereas others have found no gender difference. By late adulthood, women see their friends more often than do men (Field, 1999), which may be due to differences in partner status or differential losses of same-sex and cross-sex friends for men and women in later life resulting from men's lower life expectancy (Field, 1999; Stevens & van Tilburg, 2011).

Modal Patterns in Friendship in Adulthood

The notion of different patterns of friendship for men and women arises from research on interaction goals and activities of men and women with friends. For women, talking is the central activity and goal, even when friends are involved in doing a joint activity. For men, enjoyment of shared activity (sports or a hobby) is the focus of the friendship (Fehr, 1996). These differences led P. H. Wright (1989) to characterize men's friendships as side by side and women's as face to face; others have described the distinction as agentic versus communal or instrumental versus expressive.

However, the distinction between men's and women's friendships may be exaggerated. Walker (1994) revealed that men talk more with friends and women do more with friends than the modal patterns indicate. Duck and Wright (1993) reanalyzed diary data on interactions with same-sex friends to examine within-gender as well as between-gender tendencies. For both women and men, the main purpose of getting together with friends was just to talk; they met less often to engage in a task or to deal with a relationship issue (Duck & Wright, 1993). In another study, almost 70% of men and women classified their interactions with friends as conversations (Reis et al., 1993). What men and women talk about may differ, however.

Fehr (1996) reported that women are more likely to talk about personal matters, such as relationships

and personal problems with friends, whereas men are more likely to talk about sports, hobbies, and shared activities. Both men and women discuss the opposite sex with their same-sex friends. The majority (90%) of men and women in middle age talked about daily activities, community affairs, and family activities with friends (Aries & Johnson, 1983).

A meta-analysis of 205 studies on self-disclosure has indicated that, in interactions with others, women disclose slightly more than men do, but the effect size is small (Dindia & Allen, 1992). Gender differences in self-disclosure are greater when same-sex and female conversation partners are involved. Other studies have shown that explicit self-disclosure in conversations with friends is less common than expected. In a daily diary study, women classified only 12% of their interactions as involving self-disclosure, whereas for men it was only 3% (P. H. Wright, 2006).

Expectations of Friendships

In his review of expectations in friendship, Hall (2011) distinguished four dimensions of expectations. The first, *symmetrical reciprocity*, includes loyalty, mutual regard, authenticity, trustworthiness, and support. Because reciprocity is the "deep structure" of friendship, one might expect no gender differences (Hartup & Stevens, 1997). However, because of their evolved greater involvement in relational maintenance, women should have higher expectations of reciprocal altruism in friendship. Both overall expectations and symmetrical reciprocity showed small differences favoring females. However, less than 3% of the variance in reciprocity was explained by gender.

The second dimension, *communion*, includes emotional availability and self-disclosure. Hall (2011) predicted higher communion expectations among females as a result of evolved mechanisms for managing stress and found a medium-sized gender difference favoring females with no moderation by age or ethnicity. *Solidarity*, the third dimension, refers to expectations of sharing companionship and mutual activities. The meta-analysis revealed no gender differences; thus, as P. H. Wright (2006) has also argued, sharing activities is important for both male and female friendships (P. H. Wright, 2006).

Finally, agency expectations refer to the provision of resources that contribute to personal success. Hall (2011) predicted higher agency expectations among males. Because Hall included only nine studies, the results indicating greater agency in males should be treated with caution.

One study included in Hall's (2011) meta-analysis demonstrated that

> while men and boys rely on their male friendships to increase their social prominence more than do their female counterparts, they do not do so at the expense of friendship closeness. Male participants desire both agentic and communal support from their close male friends. (Zarbatany, Conley, & Pepper, 2004, p. 308)

Considerable consensus was found in the meaning and significance of close friendship; both males and females ranked communal friendship needs higher than agentic needs in this particular study.

Fehr (2004) reported similar results from several studies on a prototype model for intimacy expectations in same-sex friendships. She elicited descriptions of friendship behavior related to intimacy from two samples. The majority of her respondents claimed that self-disclosure and emotional support are central to intimacy in friendship. When asked to rate the likelihood that prototypical statements would produce intimacy, women rated interaction patterns higher, especially those referring to self-disclosure and emotional support. This may represent a gender difference in ways of experiencing intimacy in friendship. However, it may also be related to a developmental lag. Young men may need more time to develop similar levels of intimacy in social interactions, including those with friends. Evidence has shown that men catch up in the levels of intimacy they experience in social interactions and friendships (Reis et al., 1993; Way & Greene, 2006).

Social Support in Friendship

In friendship, there is one type of support exchange for which gender differences are very clear: emotional support. Women are more likely than men to provide emotional support and to seek it in friendships (Burleson & Kunkel, 2006; Fehr, 1996; Stevens & Westerhof, 2006). Burleson and Kunkel (2006) concluded that gender differences in emotionally supportive behavior are substantial, often accounting for more than 10% of the variance in dependent variables. When the effect size is calculated for gender differences in providing emotional support to and receiving it from friends, the effects favoring women are small to medium in married adults ages 40 to 85 (Stevens & Westerhof, 2006).

Women's greater role in emotional support provision does not mean that male friends do not provide this support. In a Canadian study, men reported that 56% of their male friends provided emotional support compared with 73% of their female friends (Wellman, 1992). For women, emotional support was available from 82% of their female friends and 27% of their male friends. Men, however, relied more on male friends for other types of support such as companionship and small and large services.

Quality of Friendship

Quality of friendship is measured by relationship satisfaction or direct ratings of quality (Fehr, 1996). Various questionnaires also allow respondents to rate quality of friendships along dimensions that represent important functions (e.g., companionship, closeness, help, emotional security, self-validation) or negative qualities (conflict, maintenance problems; Bukowski, Hoza, & Boivin, 1994; Duck & Wright, 1993; Mendelson & Aboud, 1999). A rather consistent finding is that men's ratings of same-sex friendships tend to be lower than women's, whether it be by a direct rating (Fehr, 1996), a rating of provisions available in best friendships (Zarbatany et al., 2004), or a rating of positive feelings for a friend (Mendelson & Aboud, 1999). However, ratings of satisfaction with a best friend did not differ for male and female students.

In their reanalysis of data on best friends from 350 adults ages 20 to 65, Duck and Wright (1993) found that women scored more positively on almost all measures of the Acquaintance Description Form, including friendship strength. To compare similar levels of friendship, they then controlled for differences in friendship strength. Women indicated higher levels of emotional expression, permanence, and general favorability in their friendships. Their mean scores for ego support value, self-affirmation value, and security value in same-sex friendships were also higher than those of men. Men and women did not differ on the stimulation or utility value of friendship or on maintenance difficulty. Thus, in studies in which individuals describe the quality of close same-sex friendships, women may be describing better or stronger friendships than are the men (Duck & Wright, 1993).

A trend in research on social relationships is to focus on dyads of mutually identified best friends rather than on individual perceptions of friendships. One study that did this found few gender differences in predictors of friendship quality in adolescence. However, there were twice as many female dyads of mutually nominated best friends among adolescent girls than among boys in a sample in which the sexes were equally represented (Cillessen, Jiang, West, & Laszkowski, 2005), perhaps because of girls' preference for more exclusive friendship dyads and boys' preference for larger groups of less intimate friends (Kirke, 2009; Vigil, 2007).

Another study of dyads of young adult friends used concordance on positive and negative features of the friendship as a proxy measure for friendship quality (Bagwell et al., 2005). Rather striking was the significant agreement among male friends on five friendship features that included companionship, reliable alliance, relative power, conflict, and antagonism. For female friends, there was no concordance on conflict and antagonism, suggesting less openness regarding negative experiences in friendship. On five measures of friendship engagement, significant concordance was found for male and female friends, with women scoring especially high on concordance regarding affection and nurturance.

Conclusion

Although there are many gender similarities in friendship (e.g., values of intimacy, interaction goals, satisfaction with friendship), there are also clear gender differences in behavior in same-sex friendships such as self-disclosure, support seeking, and openness regarding conflict. However, these are differences in degree, not in the kind of behavior in which individuals engage with friends. Effect sizes, when reported, are small to medium.

To explain these differences and similarities, we need theory that integrates important concepts from biological and evolutionary perspectives as well as sociocultural perspectives. An approach involving multicausality may be more fruitful than adhering to a single perspective as an explanation for the complex behavioral patterns associated with friendship.

FRIENDSHIP, HEALTH, AND WELL-BEING

The influence of personal relationships such as friendship on physical and mental health is widely recognized (Baumeister & Leary, 1995; Berkman, Glass, Brisette, & Seeman, 2000). In a classic study, Berkman and Syme (1979) demonstrated that lack of regular interaction with close family and friends was associated with higher risk of mortality, even when baseline health, socioeconomic status, and health practices (e.g., smoking, obesity, alcohol consumption, physical activity) were controlled. More recently, Litwin (2007) examined the social network–mortality association to identify what really matters in social networks. A lack of social ties with friends was the only network characteristic that increased mortality risk. This effect was significant when indicators of psychobiological pathways to increased mortality (e.g., physical activity, smoking, morbidity, depression) were included. In this section, we review research on the influence of friendship on health and well-being (e.g., happiness, life satisfaction, loneliness). We also describe the possible mechanisms involved.

Friendship as a "Behavioral Vaccination"

Various features of friendship may promote health and well-being: mutual affection and validation, companionship, emotional support, and the security derived from a history of reciprocity (Hartup & Stevens, 1997).

Sias and Bartoo (2007) referred to friendship as a "behavioral vaccination" that protects individuals against the aversive effects of stress. They based this notion on the tend-and-befriend response to stress (S. E. Taylor et al., 2000) in which threatened people—especially women—turn to trusted companions to talk about stressful events, reducing the physical and biochemical effects of stress. Laboratory studies have shown that receiving support during a stressful task blunts cardiovascular responses that are detrimental to health. Although support from a stranger also has this effect, support from a friend is even more protective (Christenfeld et al., 1997). The mere presence of a friend—who is not offering explicit support—is sometimes sufficient to reduce cardiovascular reactions to stressful tasks in the laboratory (Ertel, Glymour, & Berkman, 2009). Explanatory mechanisms include the satisfaction of the need for affiliation (Schachter, 1959), which reduces anxiety, and social comparison processes (Festinger, 1954). In novel and stressful situations, people rely on social comparisons to evaluate their own functioning. Comparisons with friends have a more powerful effect than those with strangers. In the presence of a friend who remains calm and supportive, it is easier to remain calm. These interpretations apply to laboratory situations. In a natural environment, friends may also help provide distraction from negative events, whereas isolated people spend more time ruminating, exacerbating their stress rather than reducing it (Christenfeld & Gerin, 2000).

These examples concern targeted social support aimed at a specific stressful situation. Friends also provide general social support during everyday conversations in which being able to vent about routine stressors or seek advice prevents the stressors from escalating and becoming detrimental to health (Sias & Bartoo, 2007). An exception is when friends engage in corumination about stressful events, which increases stress hormones, anxiety, and depressive symptoms. This has been demonstrated among female friends in childhood, adolescence, and young adulthood (Byrd-Craven, Geary, Rose, & Ponzi, 2008).

"Contagion" Between Friends

Not only does social support reduce stress, but person-to-person contact and social influence also explain associations between social contacts and health (Berkman et al., 2000). Unhealthy conditions (e.g., obesity) and healthy behaviors (e.g., cessation of smoking) appear to be contagious in that they spread within social networks of adults. Using network data from the longitudinal Framingham Heart Study, Christakis and Fowler (2007) found that a person's chances of becoming obese increased by 57% if someone identified as a friend became obese. This effect is even stronger when a close, mutually identified friend becomes obese, surpassing the influence of a sibling or a spouse.

When a friend stops smoking, a person's chances of smoking decrease by 36%. Only the spousal relationship has a stronger influence on smoking (Christakis & Fowler, 2008). The higher the education level of friends, the more likely focal people are to emulate their behavior. Apparently, social niches of mutual influence emerge within networks in which self-reinforcing social norms, such as acceptance of overweight and disapproval of smoking, spread among people who are in regular contact with one another. The fact that a time lag is involved in identifying these effects indicates that change is a result of social influence or person-to-person contact, not the selection of friends who share similar characteristics.

Friendship and Happiness

Another form of contagion between friends involves happiness (Fowler & Christakis, 2008). In the social networks of study members, clusters of happy and unhappy people were identified. Those who were surrounded by many happy people were more likely to become happier in the future. The number of happy friends had a more reliable effect than the number of unhappy friends. Living near friends was also an important condition. Mutual friends living within a mile had the strongest effect on happiness among all types of relationships. These results are consistent with evolutionary theories of emotions and how they spread. Happiness appears to serve the adaptive purpose of enhancing human bonds that contribute to survival. Happy people may share their good fortune by being generous or helpful to others. In addition, happiness may be genuinely contagious, with contagion lasting longer than previous studies have demonstrated.

A slightly different perspective on friendship and happiness is found in work by Demir and colleagues on college students. Demir, Ozdemir, and Weitekamp

(2007) found that individuals were happier when they experienced a high-quality close friendship in addition to a high-quality best friendship. In these studies, individuals ranked their friends in closeness in terms of their feelings toward them. Demir and Ozdemir (2010) demonstrated that the association between the quality of best (or close) friendships and happiness is mediated by the satisfaction of their basic needs for relatedness, autonomy, and competence. Two studies of student dyads indicated that other possible mediators of the friendship–happiness connection are the degree of balance in the net benefit-to-contribution ratios that dyads perceive in their friendships (Mendelson & Kay, 2003) and the degree of concordance in the perception of friendship quality between dyads of friends (Bagwell et al., 2005).

Comparing Family and Friends

A popular topic in research involves a comparison of the influence that friends and family have on well-being. In well-known studies, Larson, Mannell, and Zuzanek (1986; see also Larson & Bradbury, 1988) examined in whose company people between the ages of 18 and 85 were most happy and excited. At all ages, respondents were happiest and most excited when they were with friends. Even though family may provide a stable, supportive background, friends seem to offer more intense enjoyment, a conclusion that may explain the greater spread of happiness among friends than among family members (Fowler & Christakis, 2008).

The influence that family and friends have on life satisfaction has also been examined. In early adolescence, parent and peer (or friend) attachment both contribute to life satisfaction, with slightly more influence by parents (Ma & Huebner, 2008). Peer attachment also contributes to satisfaction with friends, whereas parent attachment contributes to satisfaction with family, and satisfaction with each domain contributes to overall life satisfaction (Nickerson & Nagle, 2004). Other studies have emphasized how family environments and the friendships of adolescents interact to influence young people's well-being. Family has a stronger influence on well-being in the absence of close friendships, whereas close friendships have more

influence on well-being among young people with less cohesive families (Gauze, Bukowski, Aquan-Assee, & Sippola, 1996).

Others studies have focused on older adults. A meta-analysis of the factors that influence subjective well-being in later life examined the influence of the amount of contact and quality of relationships with family and friends (Pinquart & Sorensen, 2000). Contact with friends is often more reciprocal, more enjoyable, and generally of higher quality than contact with family, given that unsatisfactory friendships can be terminated (and most unsatisfactory family relationships cannot). Indeed, the frequency of contact with friends shows higher associations with subjective well-being than the frequency of contact with adult children or family members in general, as hypothesized. This association was confirmed when subjective well-being was measured as life satisfaction, self-esteem, and happiness. The second hypothesis was that the quality of relationships with friends and relatives should be of equal importance in determining subjective well-being. This hypothesis was not supported. The associations between quality of relationships with children (or with other relatives) and life satisfaction were stronger than those between quality of relationship with friends and life satisfaction. There is probably more variability in the quality of ties with children and with other relatives than with friends, which may explain this result.

In another meta-analysis on factors explaining loneliness in later life, Pinquart and Sorensen (2001) compared the influence of family and friends on loneliness, testing a hypothesis that predicted greater influence of friends. In studies on the frequency of contact, contact with friends explained 3.3 times as much variance in loneliness as did contact with family. Among studies of contact quality, contact with friends explained 4.1 times as much variance in loneliness as did contact with family. Because of the small number of studies on quality of contact with children, however, these results should be interpreted with caution. The greater influence of friendship on loneliness compared with family, including adult children, may be attributed to differences in the quality of these relationships. Given the greater likelihood of shared biographical experiences, lifestyle, and attitudes between friends, they should offer better protection against loneliness later in life.

Social Network Types

Another approach to studying the influence of friendship on well-being involves examining different social network types. The association between network type and various measures of well-being among older adults has been studied in Israel (Litwin, 2001), the United States (Fiori, Antonucci, & Cortina, 2006; Litwin & Shiovitz-Ezra, 2011), Germany (Fiori, Smith, & Antonucci, 2007), and Japan (Fiori, Antonucci, & Akiyama, 2008). These studies have indicated that diverse networks, consisting of family, friends, and neighbors, and friend-focused networks, consisting of friends (and family in some cases), are associated with higher levels of morale and happiness along with lower levels of depression, anxiety, and loneliness. They also indicated that those in restricted networks or family-focused networks are more vulnerable to negative well-being, that is, lower morale and higher levels of anxiety, depression, and loneliness. Thus, a lack of friends seems to increase vulnerability to various negative states in later life. An exception is Japan, where no associations between network types and well-being were found. In sum, the importance for well-being of having friends in social networks may hold for Western, individualistic societies, but not necessarily for Asian and other collectivistic cultures.

Conclusions

A lack of regular contact with friends has disadvantages that range from vulnerability to depression, anxiety, and loneliness to increased risk of mortality. Friends offer protection through mechanisms that include stress reduction; fulfillment of basic needs for relatedness, autonomy, and competence; and contagion of happiness and health-promoting behaviors. However, friends can also have a negative influence on health through contagion of obesity or on well-being when friends engage in corumination. Thus, who one's friends are, how healthy their behavior is, and how happy they are determine the effect that friendships have on health and well-being.

FUTURE OF FRIENDSHIP

During the first decades of the 21st century, rapid developments in technology and increased globalization will continue to influence people's daily lives and personal relationships through factors such as declines in stable, full-time employment and greater mobility in working life (Allan, 2001). Some have decried the loss of social embedding in the community that began in the previous century, whereas others have emphasized that social embedding has changed but still exists (Pescosolido & Rubin, 2000; van Tilburg & Thomése, 2010). Demographic developments such as increases in cohabitation, divorce, single households, reconstituted families, and registered homosexual partnerships are indications of greater diversity in forms of partnership and family life in society. The underlying processes of detraditionalization (Giddens, 1990) and individualization (Beck, 1992) have resulted in greater freedom of choice in lifestyles, as well as greater individual responsibility for the construction and maintenance of personal networks across the life span (Stevens & van Tilburg, 2011).

There has been both popular and scholarly debate on the effects of these developments for individuals' social lives and for social connectivity in society (Budgeon, 2006; Wang & Wellman, 2010). Two schools of thought regarding the effects of social change on friendship have been identified. One approach has emphasized the increase in uncertainty that accompanies an increase in freedom and choice regarding one's personal relationships (Budgeon, 2006). The emphasis on flexibility and individual responsibility for relationships has made it more difficult to achieve and maintain stable personal relationships (Bauman, 2000). Adherents of this view have argued that informal relationships such as friendships have become more superficial and transient; they are maintained as long as they serve goals of personal fulfillment, as in the case of networking for one's career. An example of empirical evidence for this position concerns change in core discussion networks; the number of confidants with whom people discuss personal matters has declined in the United States during the past 2 decades (McPherson, Mith-Lovin, & Brashers,

2006). Whereas friends and neighbors used to be included as confidants, there has been a shift toward relying only on close kin and spouses for this role, suggesting that the range of intimates in personal networks is now more constricted.

Others have argued that friendship has increased in importance as a source of support and continuity in individuals' lives because other relationships no longer automatically serve these functions (Adams & Allan, 1998; Budgeon, 2006). When jobs and partnerships become more transitory and families more dispersed, people rely on friends for support and confirmation of their identities. Not that friendships are necessarily stable—as social and economic situations change, people often develop new friendships or renew older, latent ones with those in similar situations to replace social ties with people with whom they have less in common (Allan, 2001).

Some have argued that "families of choice"—that is, friends, ex-partners, and other close nonkin—are gradually replacing "families of fate" that include all relatives. This may apply especially to those who are not conventionally partnered (Budgeon, 2006). However, others have claimed that family ties are still important and concluded that the evidence that friends are replacing family is insufficient (Pahl & Spencer, 2004; van Tilburg & Thomése, 2010). In modern society, individuals develop personal communities of important relationships that include friends and family in varying degrees. In a qualitative study of personal communities in the United Kingdom, Pahl and Spencer (2004) distinguished six types of personal communities: two in which friends outnumber family members, two in which family members predominate, and partner-focused and professional-dependent personal communities. Their findings illustrate the heterogeneity of personal communities in this century.

In a longitudinal study of friendship choice using a large British representative sample, Pahl and Pevalin (2005) tested the increasing salience of chosen over given ties. Among those aged 16 to 25, 46 to 55, 56 to 65, and 66 and older at the first measurement point, there was an increase in the number of relatives named as close friends during 10 years. Only in the 36 to 45 age group was there a greater

increase in nonkin named as close friends compared with kin. The importance attached to nonkin friendship seems to vary with the importance attached to the partner relationship in different life phases. Pahl and colleagues (Pahl & Pevalin, 2005; Pahl & Spencer, 2004) may have identified an important process in modern social life, namely the process of suffusion between roles of family and friends, with family members serving as close friends and friends becoming more similar to family. They have also contributed clarity to this discussion by distinguishing given and chosen relationships that may involve either low or high commitment.

In analyzing late-20th-century social trends in the United States, Robert Putnam (2000) advanced his thesis that Americans are "bowling alone"; that is, becoming less socially connected. His widely cited work was also controversial. Among other points, critics claimed that he was primarily concerned with a broader concept of social capital including civic engagement rather than friendship per se. In a test of Americans' connectedness, Fischer (2011) analyzed 40 years of survey data on various measures of social bonds (e.g., number of friends, average frequency of contact). He concluded, "For all the 'lonely, friendless' chatter in the media the evidence suggests that friendship was as healthy in America in the 2000s as in the 1970s" (p. 60).

One trend during the past 3 decades is that individuals have increasingly developed less dense social networks whose members are geographically more dispersed than they were in the past (Boase & Wellman, 2006). The rise in worldwide electronic communication has contributed to this development by making the maintenance of long-distance relationships easier. There are conflicting visions regarding the influence of the Internet on personal relationships. One view is that online relationships are by definition impersonal, shallow, or even hostile, with important social cues missing from interactions. The Internet tends to create an illusion of community. The other position is that communication online liberates personal relationships from the constraints of physical location and creates new opportunities for developing personal relationships and even communities (Parks & Floyd, 1996).

Early research examined the degree to which friendships developed among participants in news groups and other online forums. One study found that 30% of the participants had developed full friendships through newsgroup contacts and 30% had less well-developed friendships (Parks & Floyd, 1996). In two large surveys, only about 10% of Internet users reported that they had met someone new online and had also developed offline contact with these people (Boase & Wellman, 2006; Parks & Floyd, 1996). These authors concluded that the progression of friendship that begins online is similar to that of offline friendships.

A second line of research has focused on the consequences of involvement in social relationships that develop online for relationships with family and friends offline (Boase & Wellman, 2006). In an early study on this topic, Kraut et al. (1998) reported that within a year, new Internet users maintained lower levels of communication within their family than they did before going online. Greater Internet use was also associated with a decline in the size of local and more distant social circles. Those who used the Internet more frequently also experienced more symptoms of depression, stress, and loneliness after going online. These results received much publicity and reinforced the notion that going online for social contact was detrimental both for oneself and for one's existing relationships. However, when the authors did follow-up studies of the same respondents during the next 3 years, the negative effects disappeared. Internet use appeared to have mainly positive effects on social relationships and on psychological well-being in the long run (Kraut et al., 2002).

In their review of relationships on and off the Internet, Boase and Wellman (2005) concluded that there is little evidence that Internet use detracts from socializing in person. Few differences are found between personal contacts of Internet and non-Internet users (Robinson, 2002), and statistical associations between Internet activity and regular social engagements have been few (Katz & Rice, 2002). Occasionally, a positive effect of Internet use is reported, for example, that Internet users are more likely to visit with family and friends (Katz & Rice, 2002). A meta-analysis of 16 studies on Internet use and contact with family and friends between

1995 and 2003 included both longitudinal and cross-sectional studies (Shklovski, Kiesler, & Kraut, 2006). The results from the two types of designs were contradictory. Although cross-sectional studies found a negative association between Internet use and interaction with friends, longitudinal studies found a positive association for Internet use and interaction with friends (but not with family). Shklovski et al. (2006) concluded that e-mail is used to reaffirm friendships and to schedule face-to-face meetings with friends, both of which are important for active maintenance of friendships. The Internet has less influence on actual interactions with family members because these tend to be stable and require less maintenance.

Styles of Internet use also appear to be tied to personal dispositions to engage in social contacts, such as extraversion and introversion (Boase & Wellman, 2006). One study demonstrated that extraverted adolescents self-disclosed and communicated more online, which contributed to the formation of online friendships. However, the Internet also helped introverted adolescents self-disclose more easily than in face-to-face situations, helping them make new friends online (Peter, Valkenburg, & Schouten, 2005). Thus, the Internet appears to be a flexible medium with friendship benefits for those who have different dispositions.

Another approach to positive or negative effects of Internet use on friendship is to study the size of friendship networks over time among those with varying intensities of Internet use. In their study of two national surveys on adult friendship networks in the United States, Wang and Wellman (2010) reported that the average number of offline friends increased between 2002 and 2007 for heavy, moderate, and light Internet users and for nonusers as well. Friendship networks increased the most for heavy Internet users; also, growth in friendship networks was generally greater for Internet users than nonusers. The various new tools in social media foster preexisting ties and lead to the development of new ties. Yet the influence is reciprocal: Internet use leads to growth in friendship networks, which in turn leads to more intense Internet use. Concern about a possible decline in social connectivity seems unnecessary on the basis of these results.

Boase and Wellman (2006) proposed a theory of networked individualism that encompasses development in modern social life, including friendships. This theory states that (a) relationships are currently both local and long distance, (b) personal networks are sparsely knit as a whole but include densely knit groups, and (c) relationships are more easily formed and abandoned. Thus, people tend to belong to personal, individualized communities that often include both local and long-distance friends, other nonkin relationships, and family. Some ties are strong, but many are weak. This networked individualism represents neither a utopia nor a dystopia, but it is well suited to the demands of modern life.

AND THE ANSWER IS . . .

And the answer is, yes, movies do hold a kernel of truth regarding friendship. Although friendships can lead people into risky or unhealthy behavior and be problematic (a pain), for the most part they enhance people's lives ("friend good"). Best friends can be especially important. Are the friendships of 12-year-olds unique? Yes, in the sense that the nature of people's friendships, especially their surface structure, changes over the life course. Friendships have a developmental arc, and they take time to develop. Not all men are like Harry in thinking they cannot be friends with a woman, but most people have a set of ineligibles whom they exclude from their friendship circle. Being together in spirit in the sense of having similar attitudes fosters friendships. Loyalty is a key element of friendship. Yet, similar to busboys or water in a swimming pool, friends come into one's life, stay for a period of time, and often leave. Throughout one's life, however, friends play a crucial role. To paraphrase a Beatles song, people manage in their lives with help from their friends.

References

Abrams, P., Levy, R. L., & Panay, A. (Producers), & Dobkin, D. (Director). (2005). *The wedding crashers* [Motion picture]. United States: New Line Cinema.

Adams, R. G., & Allan, G. A. (1998). *Placing friendship in context*. Cambridge, England: Cambridge University Press.

Adams, R. G., & Blieszner, R. (1998). Baby boomer friendships. *Generations, 22,* 70–75.

Ajrouch, K. J., Blandon, A. Y., & Antonucci, T. C. (2005). Social networks among men and women: The effects of age and socioeconomic status. *Journals of Gerontology, Series B: Psychological Sciences and Social Sciences, 60,* S311–S317.

Allan, G. A. (2001). Personal relationships in late modernity. *Personal Relationships, 8,* 325–339. doi:10.1111/j.1475-6811.2001.tb00043.x

Allan, G. A. (2008). Flexibility, friendship and family. *Personal Relationships, 15,* 1–16. doi:10.1111/j.1475-6811.2007.00181.x

Altman, I., & Taylor, D. (1973). *Social penetration: The development of interpersonal relationships.* New York, NY: Holt, Rinehart & Winston.

Aries, J. E., & Johnson, F. L. (1983). Close friendship in adulthood: Conversational content between same-sex friends. *Sex Roles, 9,* 1183–1196. doi:10.1007/BF00303101

Armstrong, R. L. (1985). Friendship. *Journal of Value Inquiry, 19,* 211–216. doi:10.1007/BF00172509

Azmitia, M., Ittel, A., & Brenk, C. (2006). Latino-heritage adolescents' friendships. In X. Chen, D. C. French, & B. H. Schneider (Eds.), *Peer relationships in cultural context* (pp. 426–451). New York, NY: Cambridge University Press. doi:10.1017/CBO9780511499739.019

Bagwell, C. L., Bender, S. E., Andreassi, C. L., Kinoshita, T. L., Montarello, S. A., & Muller, J. G. (2005). Friendship quality and perceived relationship changes predict psychosocial adjustment in early adulthood. *Journal of Social and Personal Relationships, 22,* 235–254. doi:10.1177/0265407505050945

Bagwell, C. L., & Schmidt, M. E. (2011). *Friendship in childhood and adolescence.* New York, NY: Guilford Press.

Barker, J. C. (2002). Neighbors, friends and other nonkin caregivers of community-living dependent elders. *Journals of Gerontology, Series B: Psychological Sciences and Social Sciences, 57,* S158–S167. doi:10.1093/geronb/57.3.S158

Barry, C., Madsen, S. D., Nelson, L. J., Carroll, J. S., & Badger, S. (2009). Friendship and romantic relationship qualities in emerging adulthood: Differential associations with identity development and achieved adulthood criteria. *Journal of Adult Development, 16,* 209–222. doi:10.1007/s10804-009-9067-x

Bauman, Z. (2000). *Liquid modernity.* Cambridge, England: Polity.

Baumeister, R. F., & Leary, M. R. (1995). The need to belong: Desire for interpersonal attachments as a fundamental human motivation. *Psychological Bulletin, 117,* 497–529. doi:10.1037/0033-2909.117.3.497

Bauminger, N., Solomon, M., Aviezer, A., Heung, K., Gazit, L., Brown, J., & Rogers, S. J. (2008). Children with autism and their friends: A multidimensional study of friendship in high-functioning autism spectrum disorder. *Journal of Abnormal Child Psychology, 36,* 135–150. doi:10.1007/s10802-007-9156-x

Beck, U. (1992). *Risk society: Towards a new modernity.* London, England: Sage.

Berkman, L. F., Glass, T., Brisette, I., & Seeman, T. E. (2000). From social integration to health: Durkheim in the new millennium. *Social Science and Medicine, 51,* 843–857. doi:10.1016/S0277-9536(00)00065-4

Berkman, L. F., & Syme, S. L. (1979). Social networks, host resistance and mortality: A nine-year follow-up of Alameda County residents. *American Journal of Epidemiology, 109,* 186–204.

Berndt, T. J. (1996). Friendships in adolescence. In N. Vanzetti & S. Duck (Eds.), *A lifetime of relationships* (pp. 181–212). Pacific Grove, CA: Brooks/Cole.

Berndt, T. J., & McCandless, M. A. (2009). Methods for investigating children's relationships with friends. In K. H. Rubin, W. M. Bukowski, & B. Laursen (Eds.), *Social, emotional, and personality development in context. Handbook of peer interactions, relationships, and groups* (pp. 63–81). New York, NY: Guilford Press.

Berscheid, E., & Regan, P. (2005). *The psychology of interpersonal relationships.* Upper Saddle River, NJ: Pearson.

Berscheid, E., & Walster, E. H. (1969). *Interpersonal attraction.* Reading, MA: Addison-Wesley.

Bisson, M. A., & Levine, T. R. (2009). Negotiating a friends with benefits relationship. *Archives of Sexual Behavior, 38,* 66–73. doi:10.1007/s10508-007-9211-2

Blackbird, T., & Wright, P. H. (1985). Pastors' friendships: I. Project overview and an exploration of the pedestal effect. *Journal of Psychology and Theology, 13,* 274–283.

Blieszner, R., & Adams, R. G. (1992). *Adult friendship.* Newbury Park, CA: Sage.

Blieszner, R., & Roberto, K. A. (2004). Friendship across the life span: Reciprocity in individual and relationship development. In F. R. Lang & K. L. Fingerman (Eds.), *Growing together: Personal relationships across the life span* (pp. 159–182). Cambridge, England: Cambridge University Press.

Boase, J., & Wellman, B. (2006). Personal relationships: On and off the Internet. In A. L. Vangelisti & D. Perlman (Eds.), *Handbook of personal relationships* (pp. 709–724). Oxford, England: Blackwell. doi:10.1017/CBO9780511606632.039

Bowker, A. (2004). Predicting friendship stability during early adolescence. *Journal of Early Adolescence, 24,* 85–112. doi:10.1177/0272431603262666

Bruckheimer-Martell, B., Midler, B., & Smith, M. J. (Producers), & Marshall, G. (Director). (1988). *Beaches* [Motion picture]. United States: Touchstone Pictures.

Budgeon, S. (2006). Friendship and formations of sociality in late modernity. *Sociological Research Online, 11*(3). doi:10.5153/sro.1248

Bukowski, W. M., Hoza, B., & Boivin, M. (1994). Measuring friendship quality during pre- and early adolescence: The development and psychometric properties of the friendship qualities scale. *Journal of Social and Personal Relationships, 11,* 471–484. doi:10.1177/0265407594113011

Bukowski, W. M., Motzoi, C., & Meyer, F. (2009). Friendship as process, function and outcome. In K. H. Rubin, W. M. Bukowski, & B. Laursen (Eds.), *Handbook of peer interactions, relationships and groups* (pp. 217–231). New York, NY: Guilford Press.

Burleson, B. R. (2003). The experience and effects of emotional support: What the study of cultural and gender differences can tell us about close relationships, emotion, and interpersonal communication. *Personal Relationships, 10,* 1–23. doi:10.1111/1475-6811.00033

Burleson, B. R., & Kunkel, A. W. (2006). Revisiting the different cultures thesis: An assessment of sex differences and similarities in supportive communication. In K. Dindia & D. J. Canary (Eds.), *Sex differences and similarities in communication* (2nd ed., pp. 137–159). Mahwah, NJ: Erlbaum.

Burleson, B. R., & Samter, W. (1994). The social skills approach to relationship maintenance: How individual differences in communication skills affect the achievement of relationship functions. In D. J. Canary & L. Stafford (Eds.), *Communication and relational maintenance* (pp. 61–90). San Diego, CA: Academic Press.

Byrd-Craven, J., Geary, D. C., Rose, A. J., & Ponzi, D. (2008). Co-ruminating increases stress hormone levels in women. *Hormones and Behavior, 53,* 489–492. doi:10.1016/j.yhbeh.2007.12.002

Canary, D. J., Hause, K. S., Stafford, L., & Wallace, L. A. (1993). An inductive analysis of relational maintenance strategies: Comparisons among lovers, relatives, friends, and others. *Communication Research Reports, 10,* 3–14. doi:10.1080/08824099309359913

Capra, F. (Producer & Director). (1946). *It's a wonderful life* [Motion picture]. United States: RKO Radio Pictures.

Carbery, J., & Buhrmester, D. (1998). Friendship and need fulfillment during three phases of young adulthood. *Journal of Social and Personal Relationships, 15*, 393–409. doi:10.1177/0265407598153005

Carroll, J. (2004). *Americans satisfied with number of friends, closeness of friendships*. Retrieved from http://www.gallup.com/poll/10891/americans-satisfied-number-friends-closeness-friendships.aspx

Carstensen, L. L., Isaacowitz, D. M., & Charles, S. R. (1999). Taking time seriously: A theory of socioemotional selectivity. *American Psychologist, 54*, 165–181. doi:10.1037/0003-066X.54.3.165

Chan, D. K.-S., & Cheng, G. H.-L. (2004). A comparison of offline and online friendship qualities at different stages of relationship development. *Journal of Social and Personal Relationships, 21*, 305–320. doi:10.1177/0265407504042834

Christakis, N. A., & Fowler, J. H. (2007). The spread of obesity in a large social network over 32 years. *New England Journal of Medicine, 357*, 370–379. doi:10.1056/NEJMsa066082

Christakis, N. A., & Fowler, J. H. (2008). The collective dynamics of smoking in a large social network. *New England Journal of Medicine, 358*, 2249–2258. doi:10.1056/NEJMsa0706154

Christenfeld, N., & Gerin, W. (2000). Social support and cardiovascular reactivity. *Biomedicine and Pharmacotherapy, 54*, 251–257. doi:10.1016/S0753-3322(00)80067-0

Christenfeld, N., Gerin, W., Linden, W., Sanders, M., Mathur, J., Diech, J. D., & Pickering, T. G. (1997). Social support effects on cardiovascular reactivity: Is a stranger as effective as a friend. *Psychosomatic Medicine, 59*, 388–398.

Cillessen, A. H. N., Jiang, X. L., West, T. V., & Laszkowski, D. K. (2005). Predictors of dyadic friendship quality in adolescence. *International Journal of Behavioral Development, 29*, 165–172. doi:10.1080/01650250444000360

Cummings, J., Lee, J., & Kraut, R. (2006). Communication technology and friends during the transition from high school to college. In R. Kraut, M. Brynin, & S. Kiesler (Eds.), *Computers, phones, and the Internet: Domesticating information technology* (pp. 265–278). New York, NY: Oxford University Press.

Dainton, M., Zelley, E., & Langan, E. (2003). Maintaining friendships throughout the lifespan. In D. J. Canary & M. Dainton (Eds.), *Maintaining relationships through communication: Relational, contextual, and cultural variations* (pp. 79–102). Mahwah, NJ: Erlbaum.

Davis, K. E., & Todd, M. J. (1985). Assessing friendship: Prototypes, paradigm cases and relationship description. In S. W. Duck & D. Perlman (Eds.), *Understanding personal relationships* (pp. 17–38). London, England: Sage.

de Jong Gierveld, J., & Perlman, D. (2006). Longstanding nonkin relationships of older adults in the Netherlands and the United States. *Research on Aging, 28*, 730–748. doi:10.1177/0164027506291873

Demir, M., & Ozdemir, M. (2010). Friendship, need satisfaction and happiness. *Journal of Happiness Studies, 11*, 243–259. doi:10.1007/s10902-009-9138-5

Demir, M., Ozdemir, M., & Weitekamp, L. A. (2007). Looking to happy tomorrows with friends: Best and close friendships as they predict happiness. *Journal of Happiness Studies, 8*, 243–271. doi:10.1007/s10902-006-9025-2

de Vries, B., & Johnson, C. (2002). The death of friends in later life. In R. A. Settersten, Jr., & T. J. Owens (Eds.), *Advances in life course research* (Vol. 7, pp. 299–324). New York, NY: Elsevier. doi:10.1016/S1040-2608(02)80038-7

de Vries, B., & Megathlin, D. (2009). The meaning of friends for gay men and lesbians in the second half of life. *Journal of GLBT Family Studies, 5*, 82–98. doi:10.1080/15504280802595394

Dindia, K. (2006). Men are from North Dakota, women are from South Dakota. In K. Dindia & D. J. Canary (Eds.), *Sex differences and similarities in communication* (2nd ed., pp. 3–20). Mahwah, NJ: Erlbaum.

Dindia, K., & Allen, M. (1992). Sex differences in self-disclosure: A meta-analysis. *Psychological Bulletin, 112*, 106–124. doi:10.1037/0033-2909.112.1.106

Duck, S., & Miell, D. E. (1986). Charting the development of personal relationships. In R. Gilmour & S. Duck (Eds.), *The emerging field of personal relationships* (pp. 133–143). Hillsdale, NJ: Erlbaum.

Duck, S., & Wright, P. H. (1993). Re-examining gender differences in same-gender friendships: A close look at two kinds of data. *Sex Roles, 28*, 709–727. doi:10.1007/BF00289989

Dunn, J., Cutting, A. L., & Fisher, N. (2002). Old friends, new friends: Predictors of children's perspective on their friends at school. *Child Development, 73*, 621–635. doi:10.1111/1467-8624.00427

Dykstra, P. (1995). Network composition. In C. P. M. Knipscheer, J. de Jong Gierveld, T. G. Van Tilburg, & P. A. Dykstra (Eds.), *Living arrangements and social networks of older adults* (pp. 97–114). Amsterdam, the Netherlands: VU University Press.

Eagly, A. H. (2009). The his and hers of prosocial behavior: An examination of the social psychology of gender. *American Psychologist, 64*, 644–658. doi:10.1037/0003-066X.64.8.644

Ertel, K. A., Glymour, M. M., & Berkman, L. F. (2009). Social networks and health: A life course perspective integrating observational and experimental evidence. *Journal of Social and Personal Relationships, 26*, 73–92. doi:10.1177/0265407509105523

Evans, B. A., Gideon, R., & Scheinman, A. (Producers), & Reiner, R. (Director). (1986). *Stand by me* [Motion picture]. United States: Columbia Pictures.

Fehr, B. (1996). *Friendship processes.* Newbury Park, CA: Sage.

Fehr, B. (2004). Intimacy expectations in same-sex friendships: A prototype interaction-pattern model. *Journal of Personality and Social Psychology, 86,* 265–284. doi:10.1037/0022-3514.86.2.265

Fehr, B. (2008). Friendship formation. In S. Sprecher, A. Wenzel, & J. Harvey (Eds.), *Handbook of relationship initiation* (pp. 29–54). New York, NY: Psychology Press.

Festinger, L. (1954). A theory of social comparison processes. *Human Relations, 7,* 117–140. doi:10.1177/001872675400700202

Field, D. (1999). Continuity and change in friendships in advanced old age: Findings from the Berkeley Older Generation Study. *International Journal of Aging and Human Development, 48,* 325–346. doi:10.2190/J4UJ-JAU6-14TF-2MVF

Fiori, K. L., Antonucci, T. C., & Akiyama, H. (2008). Profiles of social relations among older adults: A cross-cultural approach. *Ageing and Society, 28,* 203–231. doi:10.1017/S0144686X07006472

Fiori, K. L., Antonucci, T. C., & Cortina, K. S. (2006). Social network typologies and mental health among older adults. *Journals of Gerontology, Series B: Psychological Sciences and Social Sciences, 61,* P25–P32. doi:10.1093/geronb/61.1.P25

Fiori, K. L., Smith, J., & Antonucci, T. C. (2007). Social network types among older adults: A multidimensional approach. *Journals of Gerontology, Series B: Psychological Sciences and Social Sciences, 62,* P322–P330. doi:10.1093/geronb/62.6.P322

Fischer, C. S. (1982). *To dwell among friends: Personal networks in town and city.* Chicago, IL: University of Chicago Press.

Fischer, C. S. (2011). *Still connected: Family and friends in America since 1970.* New York, NY: Russell Sage Foundation.

Fowler, J. H., & Christakis, N. A. (2008). The dynamic spread of happiness in a large social network. *British Medical Journal, 337,* a2338. doi:10.1136/bmj.a2338

Furman, W. (1996). The measurement of friendship perceptions: Conceptual and methodological issues. In W. M. Bukowski, A. F. Newcomb, & W. W. Hartup (Eds.), *The company they keep: Friendships in childhood and adolescence* (pp. 41–65). Cambridge, England: Cambridge University Press.

Gallup Poll News Service. (2005, December). *Gallup Poll social series: Lifestyle.* Retrieved from http://brain.gallup.com/documents/questionnaire.aspx?STUDY=P0512059&p=3

Gauze, C., Bukowski, W. M., Aquan-Assee, J., & Sippola, L. K. (1996). Interactions between family environment and friendship and associations with self-perceived well-being during early adolescence. *Child Development, 67,* 2201–2216. doi:10.2307/1131618

Giddens, A. (1990). *The consequences of modernity.* Cambridge, England: Polity.

Grief, G. L. (2009). *Buddy system: Understanding male friendships.* New York, NY: Oxford University Press.

Guiaux, M., Van Tilburg, T., & Broese Van Groenou, M. B. (2007). Changes in contact and support exchange in personal networks after widowhood. *Personal Relationships, 14,* 457–473. doi:10.1111/j.1475-6811.2007.00165.x

Güroğlu, B., Van Lieshout, C. F. M., Haselager, G. J. T., & Scholte, R. H. J. (2007). Similarity and complementarity of behavioral profiles of friendship types and types of friends: Friendships and psychosocial adjustment. *Journal of Research on Adolescence, 17,* 357–386. doi:10.1111/j.1532-7795.2007.00526.x

Hall, J. A. (2011). Sex differences in friendship expectations: A meta-analysis. *Journal of Social and Personal Relationships, 28,* 723–747. doi:10.1177/0265407510386192

Hartup, W. W., Laursen, B., Stewart, M. I., & Eastenson, A. (1988). Conflict and the friendship relations of young children. *Child Development, 59,* 1590–1600. doi:10.2307/1130673

Hartup, W. W., & Stevens, N. (1997). Friendships and adaptation in the life course. *Psychological Bulletin, 121,* 355–370. doi:10.1037/0033-2909.121.3.355

Hays, R. B. (1985). A longitudinal study of friendship development. *Journal of Personality and Social Psychology, 48,* 909–924. doi:10.1037/0022-3514.48.4.909

Heyl, V., & Schmitt, M. (2007). The contribution of adult personality and recalled parent–child relations to friendships in middle and old age. *International Journal of Behavioral Development, 31,* 38–48. doi:10.1177/0165025407073539

Himes, C. L., & Reidy, E. B. (2000). The role of friends in caregiving. *Research on Aging, 22,* 315–336. doi:10.1177/0164027500224001

Huston, T. L., & Levinger, G. (1978). Interpersonal attraction and relationships. *Annual Review of Psychology, 29,* 115–156. doi:10.1146/annurev.ps.29.020178.000555

Johnson, A. J., Wittenberg, E., Villagran, M. M., Mazur, M., & Villagran, P. (2003). Relational progression as a dialectic: Examining turning points in communication among friends. *Communication Monographs, 70,* 230–249. doi:10.1080/0363775032000167415

Kahneman, D., Krueger, A. B., Schkade, D. A., Schwarz, N., & Stone, A. A. (2004). A survey method for characterizing daily life experience: The day reconstruction method. *Science, 306*, 1776–1780. doi:10.1126/science.1103572

Kalmijn, M. (2003). Shared friendship networks and the life course: An analysis of survey data on married and cohabiting couples. *Social Networks, 25*, 231–249. doi:10.1016/S0378-8733(03)00010-8

Katz, J. E., & Rice, R. E. (2002). *Social consequences of internet use: Access, involvement, and interaction.* Cambridge, MA: MIT Press.

Kirke, D. M. (2009). Gender clustering in friendship networks: Some sociological implications. *Methodological Innovations Online, 4*, 23–36.

Krappman, L. (1996). Amicitia, drujba, shin-yu, philia, freundschaft, friendship: On the cultural diversity of human relationship. In W. M. Bukowski, A. F. Newcomb, & W. W. Hartup (Eds.), *The company they keep: Friendship in childhood and adolescence* (pp. 19–40). Cambridge, England: Cambridge University Press.

Kraut, R., Kiesler, S., Boneva, B., Cummings, J., Helgeson, V., & Crawford, A. (2002). Internet paradox revisited. *Journal of Social Issues, 58*, 49–74. doi:10.1111/1540-4560.00248

Kraut, R., Patterson, M., Lundmark, V., Kiesler, S., Mukhodpadhyay, T., & Scherlis, W. (1998). Internet paradox: A social technology that reduces social involvement and psychological well-being. *American Psychologist, 53*, 1017–1031. doi:10.1037/0003-066X.53.9.1017

Ladd, G. W., Kochenderfer, B. J., & Coleman, C. C. (1996). Friendship quality as a predictor of young children's early school adjustment. *Child Development, 67*, 1103–1118. doi:10.2307/1131882

Laemmle, C., Jr. (Producer), & Whale, J. (Director). (1935). *Bride of Frankenstein* [Motion picture]. United States: Universal Pictures.

Larson, R., Mannell, R., & Zuzanek, J. (1986). The daily experience of older adults with family and friends. *Psychology and Aging, 1*, 117–126. doi:10.1037/0882-7974.1.2.117

Larson, R. W. (1983). Adolescents' daily experience with family and friends: Contrasting opportunity systems. *Journal of Marriage and the Family, 45*, 739–750. doi:10.2307/351787

Larson, R. W., & Bradney, N. (1988). Precious moments with family members and friends. In R. M. Milardo (Ed.), *Families and social networks* (pp. 107–126). London, England: Sage.

Lear, N. (Producer), & Avenet, J. (Director). (1991). *Fried green tomatoes* [Motion picture]. United States: Universal Pictures.

Levinger, G., & Snoek, J. D. (1972). *Attraction in relationships: A new look at interpersonal attraction.* Morristown, NY: General Learning Press.

Litwin, H. (2001). Social network type and morale in old age. *Gerontologist, 41*, 516–524. doi:10.1093/geront/41.4.516

Litwin, H. (2007). What really matters in the social network–mortality association? A multivariate examination among older Jewish-Israelis. *European Journal of Ageing, 4*, 71–82. doi:10.1007/s10433-007-0048-2

Litwin, H., & Shiovitz-Ezra, S. (2011). Social network type and subjective well-being in a national sample of older Americans. *Gerontologist, 51*, 379–388. doi:10.1093/geront/gnq094

Ma, C. Q., & Huebner, E. S. (2008). Attachment relationships and adolescents' life satisfaction: Some relationships matter more to girls than boys. *Psychology in the Schools, 45*, 177–190. doi:10.1002/pits.20288

Matthews, S. H. (1986). *Friendships through the life course: Oral biographies in old age.* Beverly Hills, CA: Sage.

McEwan, B. L., Babin Gallagher, B., & Farinelli, L. J. (2008, November). *The end of a friendship: Friendship dissolution reasons and methods.* Paper presented at the annual meeting of the NCA 94th Annual Convention, San Diego, CA. Retrieved from http://www.allacademic.com/meta/p257393_index.html

McPherson, M., Mith-Lovin, L., & Brashers, M. (2006). Social isolation in America. *American Sociological Review, 71*, 353–375. doi:10.1177/000312240607100301

Mendelson, M. J., & Aboud, F. E. (1999). Measuring friendship quality in late adolescents and young adults: McGill friendship questionnaires. *Canadian Journal of Behavioural Science, 31*, 130–132. doi:10.1037/h0087080

Mendelson, M. J., & Kay, A. C. (2003). Positive feelings in friendship: Does imbalance in the relationship matter? *Journal of Social and Personal Relationships, 20*, 101–116.

Miche, M., Huxhold, O., & Stevens, N. L. (2013). A latent class analysis of friendship network types and their predictors in the second half of life. *The Journals of Gerontology Series B: Psychological Sciences and Social Sciences, 68*, 644–652. doi: 10.1 093/geronb/gbt041

Miller, R., & Perlman, D. (2009). *Intimate relationships* (5th ed.). New York, NY: McGraw Hill.

Mollenhorst, G., Völker, B., & Flap, H. (2008). Social contexts and personal relationships: The effect of meeting opportunities on similarity for relationships of different strength. *Social Networks, 30*, 60–68. doi:10.1016/j.socnet.2007.07.003

Nardi, P. M. (1999). *Gay men's friendships: Invincible communities.* Chicago, IL: University of Chicago Press.

Newcomb, A. F., & Bagwell, C. F. (1995). Children's friendship relations: A meta-analytic review. *Psychological Bulletin, 117*, 306–347. doi:10.1037/0033-2909.117.2.306

Nickerson, A. B., & Nagle, R. J. (2004). The influence of parent and peer attachments on life satisfaction in middle childhood and early adolescence. *Social Indicators Research, 66*, 35–60. doi:10.1023/B:SOCI.0000007496.42095.2c

Olweus, D., & Endresen, I. M. (1998). The importance of sex-of-stimulus object: Age trends and sex differences in empathetic responsiveness. *Social Development, 7*, 370–388. doi:10.1111/1467-9507.00073

Oswald, D. L., & Clark, E. M. (2003). Best friends forever? High school best friendships and the transition to college. *Personal Relationships, 10*, 187–196. doi:10.1111/1475-6811.00045

Oswald, D. L., & Clark, E. M. (2006). How do friendship maintenance behaviors and problem-solving styles function at the individual and dyadic levels? *Personal Relationships, 13*, 333–348. doi:10.1111/j.1475-6811.2006.00121.x

Oswald, D. L., Clark, E. M., & Kelly, C. M. (2004). Friendship maintenance: An analysis of individual and dyad behaviors. *Journal of Social and Clinical Psychology, 23*, 413–441. doi:10.1521/jscp.23.3.413.35460

Pahl, R., & Pevalin, D. J. (2005). Between family and friends: A longitudinal study of friendship choice. *British Journal of Sociology, 56*, 433–450. doi:10.1111/j.1468-4446.2005.00076.x

Pahl, R., & Spencer, L. (2004). Personal communities: Not simply families of "fate" or "choice." *Current Sociology, 52*, 199–221. doi:10.1177/0011392104041808

Pakaluk, M. (Ed.). (1991). *Other selves: Philosophers on friendship*. Indianapolis, IN: Hackett.

Parker, J. G., & Asher, S. R. (1993). Friendship and friendship quality in middle childhood: Links with peer group acceptance and feelings of loneliness and social dissatisfaction. *Developmental Psychology, 29*, 611–621. doi:10.1037/0012-1649.29.4.611

Parks, M. R. (2007). *Personal relationships and personal networks*. Mahwah, NJ: Erlbaum.

Parks, M. R., & Floyd, K. (1996). Making friends in cyberspace. *Journal of Communication, 46*, 80–97. doi:10.1111/j.1460-2466.1996.tb01462.x

Pescosolido, B. A., & Rubin, B. A. (2000). The web of group affiliations revisited: Social life, postmodernism, and sociology. *American Sociological Review, 65*, 52–76. doi:10.2307/2657289

Peter, J., Valkenburg, P. M., & Schouten, A. P. (2005). Developing a model of adolescent friendship formation on the internet. *CyberPsychology and Behavior, 8*, 423–430. doi:10.1089/cpb.2005.8.423

Pinquart, M., & Sorensen, S. (2000). Influences of socioeconomic status, social network and competence on subjective well-being in later life: A meta-analysis. *Psychology and Aging, 15*, 187–224. doi:10.1037/0882-7974.15.2.187

Pinquart, M., & Sorensen, S. (2001). Influence on loneliness in older adults: A meta-analysis. *Basic and Applied Social Psychology, 23*, 245–266.

Poulin, F., & Chan, A. (2010). Friendship stability and change in childhood and adolescence. *Developmental Review, 30*, 257–272. doi:10.1016/j.dr.2009.01.001

Price, L. L., & Arnould, E. J. (1999). Commercial friendships: Service–provider–client relationships in context. *Journal of Marketing, 63*, 38–56. doi:10.2307/1251973

Putnam, R. (2000). *Bowling alone*. New York, NY: Simon & Schuster.

Rawlins, W. K. (2009). *The compass of friendship: Narratives, identities and dialogues*. Los Angeles, CA: Sage.

Reiner, R., & Scheinman, A. (Producers), & Reiner, R. (Director). (1989). *When Harry met Sally* [Motion picture]. United States: Columbia Pictures.

Reis, H. T., Lin, Y., Bennett, M. E., & Nezlek, J. B. (1993). Change and consistency in social participation during early adulthood. *Developmental Psychology, 29*, 633–645. doi:10.1037/0012-1649.29.4.633

Reisman, J. M. (1979). *Anatomy of friendship*. New York, NY: Irvington.

Robinson, J. P. (2002). Introduction to Issue 2: Mass media and other activity. *IT and Society, 1*, i–viii.

Rodin, M. J. (1982). Non-engagement, failure to engage, and disengagement. In S. Duck (Ed.), *Personal relationships: Vol. 4. Dissolving personal relationships* (pp. 31–49). London, England: Academic Press.

Rollie, S. S., & Duck, S. (2006). Divorce and dissolution of romantic relationships: Stage models and their limitations. In M. Fine & J. Harvey (Eds.), *Handbook of divorce and dissolution of romantic relationships* (pp. 223–240). Mahwah, NJ: Erlbaum.

Rose, A. J., & Rudolph, K. D. (2006). A review of sex differences in peer relationship processes: Potential trade-offs for the emotional and behavioral development of girls and boys. *Psychological Bulletin, 132*, 98–131. doi:10.1037/0033-2909.132.1.98

Rose, S. M. (1984). How friendships end: Patterns among young adults. *Journal of Social and Personal Relationships, 1*, 267–277. doi:10.1177/0265407584013001

Roth, S. J. (Producer), & Karbelnikoff, M. (Director). (1991). *Mobsters* [Motion picture]. United States: Universal Pictures.

Rumens, N. (2010). Firm friends: Exploring the supportive components in gay men's workplace friendships. *Sociological Review, 58*, 135–155. doi:10.1111/j.1467-954X.2009.01879.x

Rusbult, C. E., Olsen, N., Davis, J. L., & Hannon, P. A. (2004). Commitment and relationship maintenance mechanisms. In H. T. Reis & C. E. Rusbult (Eds.), *Close relationships: Key readings* (pp. 287–303). Philadelphia, PA: Taylor & Francis.

Schachter, S. (1959). *The psychology of affiliation: Experimental studies of the sources of gregariousness.* Stanford, CA: Stanford University Press.

Selfhout, M., Burk, W., Branje, S., Denissen, J., Van Aken, M., & Meeus, W. (2010). Emerging late adolescent friendship networks and Big Five personality traits: A social network approach. *Journal of Personality, 78*, 509–538. doi:10.1111/j.1467-6494.2010.00625.x

Sheets, V. L., & Lugar, R. (2005). Friendship and gender in Russia and the United States. *Sex Roles, 52*, 131–140. doi:10.1007/s11199-005-1200-0

Shelton, J. N., Trail, T. E., West, T. V., & Bergsieker, H. B. (2010). From strangers to friends: The interpersonal process model of intimacy in developing interracial friendships. *Journal of Social and Personal Relationships, 27*, 71–90. doi:10.1177/0265407509346422

Shklovski, I., Kiesler, S., & Kraut, R. L. (2006). Effects of using the Internet on interaction with family and friends: A meta-analysis and critique of studies, 1995–2003. In R. Kraut, M. Brynis, & S. Kiesler (Eds.), *Computers, phones, and the internet: Domesticating information technology* (pp. 251–264). Oxford, England: Oxford University Press.

Shulman, S., & Knafo, D. (1997). Balancing closeness and individuality in adolescent close relationships. *International Journal of Behavioral Development, 21*, 687–702. doi:10.1080/016502597384622

Shulman, S., & Laursen, B. (2002). Adolescent perceptions of conflict in interdependent and disengaged friendships. *Journal of Research on Adolescence, 12*, 353–372. doi:10.1111/1532-7795.00037

Sias, P. M., & Bartoo, H. (2007). Friendship, social support, and health. In L. L. Abate (Ed.), *Low-cost approaches to promote physical and mental health* (pp. 455–472). New York, NY: Springer. doi:10.1007/0-387-36899-X_23

Sias, P. M., & Cahill, D. J. (1998). From coworkers to friends: The development of peer friendships in the workplace. *Western Journal of Communication, 62*, 273–299. doi:10.1080/10570319809374611

Sias, P. M., Heath, R. G., Perry, T., Silva, D., & Fix, B. (2004). Narratives of workplace friendship deterioration. *Journal of Social and Personal Relationships, 21*, 321–340. doi:10.1177/0265407504042835

Spencer, L., & Pahl, R. (2006). *Rethinking friendship: Hidden solidarities today.* Princeton, NJ: Princeton University Press.

Stevens, N. L. (2009). Friendship in late adulthood. In H. T. Reis & S. Sprecher (Eds.), *Encyclopedia of human relationships* (Vol. 2, pp. 726–730). Thousand Oaks, CA: Sage.

Stevens, N. L., & van Tilburg, T. G. (2011). Cohort differences in having and retaining friends in personal networks in later life. *Journal of Social and Personal Relationships, 28*, 24–43. doi:10.1177/0265407510386191

Stevens, N. L., & Westerhof, G. J. (2006). Partners and others: Social provisions and loneliness among married Dutch men and women in the second half of life. *Journal of Social and Personal Relationships, 23*, 921–941. doi:10.1177/0265407506070474

Steuve, C. A., & Gerson, K. (1977). Personal relations across the life-cycle. In C. S. Fisher, R. M. Jackson, C. A. Stueve, K. Gerson, & L. M. Jones (Eds.), *Networks and places: Social relationships in the urban setting* (pp. 79–98). New York, NY: Free Press.

Sullivan, K. (Producer & Director). (1985). *Anne of Green Gables* [Motion picture]. United States: Anne of Green Gables Productions.

Taylor, M., Shawber, A. B., & Mannering, A. M. (2009). Children's imaginary companions: What is it like to have an invisible friend? In K. D. Markman, W. M. P. Klein, & J. A. Suhr (Eds.), *Handbook of imagination and mental simulation* (pp. 211–224). New York, NY: Psychology Press.

Taylor, S. E., Cousino Klein, L., Lewis, B. P., Gruenewald, T. L., Gurung, R. A. R., & Updegraff, J. A. (2000). Biobehavioral responses to stress in females: Tend-and-befriend, not fight-or-flight. *Psychological Review, 107*, 411–429.

Thibaut, J. W., & Kelley, H. H. (1959). *The social psychology of groups.* New York, NY: Wiley.

Ueno, K., & Adams, R. G. (2006). Adult friendship: A decade review. In P. Noller & J. A. Feeney (Eds.), *Close relationships: Functions, forms and processes* (pp. 151–169). Hove, England: Psychology Press.

Vanlear, A., Koerner, A. F., & Allen, D. (2006). Relationship typologies. In A. L. Vangelisti & D. Perlman (Eds.), *The Cambridge handbook of personal relationships* (pp. 91–110). Cambridge, England: Cambridge University Press. doi:10.1017/CBO9780511606632.007

van Tilburg, T. (1998). Losing and gaining in old age: Changes in personal network size and social support in a four-year longitudinal study. *Journals of Gerontology, Series B: Psychological Sciences and Social Sciences, 53*, S313–S323. doi:10.1093/geronb/53B.6.S313 van Tilburg, T. G., & Thomése, G. C. F. (2010). Societal dynamics in personal networks. In D. Dannefer & C. R. Phillipson (Eds.), *The Sage handbook of social gerontology* (pp. 215–225). London, England: Sage. doi:10.4135/9781446200933.n16

Vigil, J. M. (2007). Asymmetries in the friendship preferences and social styles of men and women. *Human Nature, 18*, 143–161. doi:10.1007/s12110-007-9003-3

Walker, K. (1994). Men, women and friendship: What they say, what they do. *Gender and Society, 8*, 246–265. doi:10.1177/089124394008002007

Walker, K. (1995). "Always there for me": Friendship patterns and expectations among middle- and working-class men and women. *Sociological Forum, 10*, 273–296. doi:10.1007/BF02095961

Wang, H., & Wellman, B. (2010). Social connectivity in American: Changes in adult friendship network size from 2002 to 2007. *American Behavioral Scientist, 53*, 1148–1169. doi:10.1177/0002764209356247

Way, N., Cowal, K., Gingold, R., Pahl, K., & Bissessar, N. (2001). Friendship patterns among African American, Asian American and Latino adolescents from low-income families. *Journal of Social and Personal Relationships, 18*, 29–53. doi:10.1177/0265407501181002

Way, N., & Greene, M. L. (2006). Trajectories of perceived friendship quality during adolescence: The patterns and contextual predictors. *Journal of Research on Adolescence, 16*, 293–320. doi:10.1111/j.1532-7795.2006.00133.x

Weinstock, J. S., & Rothblum, E. D. (Eds.). (1996). *Lesbian friendships: For ourselves and each other.* New York, NY: New York University Press.

Weiss, R. S. (1998). A taxonomy of relationships. *Journal of Social and Personal Relationships, 15*, 671–683. doi:10.1177/0265407598155006

Wellman, B. (1992). Men in networks: Private communities, domestic friendships. In P. Nardi (Ed.), *Men's friendships* (pp. 74–114). Newbury Park, CA: Sage.

Wellman, B. L., Wong, R. Y., Tindall, D., & Nazer, N. (1997). A decade of network change: Turnover, persistence and stability in personal communities. *Social Networks, 19*, 27–50. doi:10.1016/S0378-8733(96)00289-4

Wright, K. B., & Patterson, B. R. (2006). Socioemotional selectivity theory and the macrodynamics of friendship: The role of friendship style and communication in friendship across the lifespan. *Communication Research Reports, 23*, 163–170. doi:10.1080/08824090600796377

Wright, P. H. (1984). Self-referent motivation and the intrinsic quality of friendship. *Journal of Social and Personal Relationships, 1*, 115–130. doi:10.1177/0265407584011007

Wright, P. H. (1985). The Acquaintance Description Form. In S. Duck & D. Perlman (Eds.), *Understanding personal relationships: An interdisciplinary approach* (pp. 39–62). London, England: Sage.

Wright, P. H. (1989). Gender differences in adults' same- and cross-gender friendships. In R. G. Adams & R. Blieszner (Eds.), *Older adult friendships* (pp. 197–221). London, England: Sage.

Wright, P. H. (2006). Toward an expanded orientation to the comparative study of women's and men's same-sex friendships. In K. Dindia & D. J. Canary (Eds.), *Sex differences and similarities in communication* (2nd ed., pp. 37–57). London, England: Erlbaum.

Zarbatany, L., Conley, R., & Pepper, S. (2004). Personality and gender differences in friendship needs and experiences in preadolescence and young adulthood. *International Journal of Behavioral Development, 28*, 299–310. doi:10.1080/01650250344000514

Zimbalist, S. (Producer), & Wyler, W. (Director). (1959). *Ben Hur* [Motion picture]. United States: Metro-Goldwyn-Mayer.

CHAPTER 18

LOVE: CONCEPTUALIZATION AND EXPERIENCE

Beverley Fehr

In his presidential address at the 1958 American Psychological Association convention, Harry Harlow decried psychologists' lack of interest in love, accusing them of being "unaware of its very existence" (p. 673). He also pointed out that "the apparent repression of love by modern psychologists stands in sharp contrast with the attitude taken by many famous and normal people" (p. 673). More than a half century later, articles and chapters on love typically begin with Harlow's observation that the topic of love has long captured the imagination of poets, philosophers, and the person on the street. These days, however, rather than lament psychologists' lack of interest in love, scholars remark on the great strides in understanding that have been made in the past few decades (while, at times, bemoaning how much still remains to be discovered).

The purpose of this chapter is to document what is currently known about love, based on social science research, with an emphasis on social psychological contributions. In the first half of the chapter, I focus on the fundamental question "What is love?" Experts' answers to this question are presented, followed by a discussion of lay conceptions of love. Next, I turn to research on gender and cultural differences in conceptions of love. Then, I consider the relationship implications of conceptions of love. I examine two important relationship outcome variables: satisfaction and relationship stability. In the second half of the chapter, the spotlight is on the experience of love in relationships. Topics include the neurological correlates of the experience of love and the course of love over time. I also discuss gender and cultural differences. In the final section, I explore relationship implications of the experience of love, including relationship satisfaction, relationship commitment, and the deterioration and dissolution of relationships. The chapter ends with a discussion of future directions for research on love.

CONCEPTIONS OF LOVE

Until relatively recently, social scientists had little to say in response to the fundamental question "What is love?" posed by Shakespeare in *Twelfth Night*. In social psychology, the topic of love did not receive serious conceptual or empirical attention until the 1970s when Zick Rubin (1970) and Ellen Berscheid and Elaine Hatfield (1974) blazed the trail. Their definitions and taxonomies and those of other experts are presented next, followed by research on laypeople's conceptions of love.

Experts' Definitions and Taxonomies

Rubin's (1970, 1973) analysis focused on the concept of love, as distinct from the concept of liking. He defined love as an attitude that predisposes one to think, feel, and act in particular ways toward a love object. He also specified three components of love: intimacy, need–attachment, and caring. Research conducted by Steck, Levitan, McLane, and Kelley (1982) showed that people regard caring as more indicative of love than need–attachment.

Berscheid and Hatfield (1974; Hatfield & Walster, 1978) argued that love is not a single entity but is best conceptualized in terms of two basic kinds:

http://dx.doi.org/10.1037/14344-018
APA Handbook of Personality and Social Psychology: Vol. 3. Interpersonal Relations, M. Mikulincer and P. R. Shaver (Editors-in-Chief)
Copyright © 2015 by the American Psychological Association. All rights reserved.

passionate love and companionate love. *Passionate love* is defined as a wildly emotional state characterized by emotional extremes, physiological arousal, and sexual attraction. This kind of love is typically experienced for only one, rather than multiple, targets. *Companionate love* is defined as "friendly affection and deep attachment to someone" (Hatfield & Walster, 1978, p. 2). This kind of love is characterized by caring, trust, honesty, respect, and the like. It can be experienced for a number of people, such as close friends, family members, and romantic partners.

These early writings inspired a plethora of theories and models of love. On the basis of work by sociologist John Lee (1973), C. Hendrick and Hendrick (1986) articulated a typology of six different love styles: eros (romantic, passionate love), storge (friendship-based love), agape (altruistic, selfless love), ludus (game-playing love), mania (obsessive, dependent love), and pragma (practical love). Around the same time, Sternberg (1986) developed the triangular theory of love in which love was conceptualized as a triangle, with passion, intimacy, and decision–commitment as the vertices. The various combinations of these elements produce eight different kinds of love (e.g., companionate love is the combination of the intimacy and decision–commitment components). Another influential development during this period was Hazan and Shaver's (1987) application of attachment theory to adult romantic relationships. They found evidence that adults' patterns of attachment to their romantic partners mirrored the infant attachment patterns documented by developmental psychologists (secure, anxious–ambivalent, and avoidant). Although attachment theory is not specifically a theory of love (nor do attachment styles constitute a love taxonomy), a monumental body of research exists on how people with different attachment orientations approach love and relationships (see Chapter 2, this volume; Simpson & Rholes, 2012).

The quadrumvirate model. More recently, Berscheid (2006, 2010) proposed a quadrumvirate model in which two kinds of love were added to the original passionate–companionate love typology— namely, attachment love and compassionate love.

In this model, romantic love is regarded as synonymous with passionate love, eros, and being in love. Companionate love is synonymous with friendship love, storge, and strong liking. *Compassionate love* is the umbrella term for types of love such as altruistic love, selfless love, agape, and communal responsiveness. *Attachment love* refers to a strong affectional bond with an attachment figure. (Attachment as a kind of love is considered different from the extensively studied individual differences in attachment style.)

Berscheid (2006, 2010) made the bold claim that these four are basic, fundamental kinds of love that subsume all of the other varieties, in the same way that the Big Five personality traits are basic and fundamental. She acknowledged that these varieties of love are likely to co-occur in romantic relationships but argued that they can—and should—be distinguished. In fact, points of differentiation between these kinds of love are carefully delineated. More specifically, Berscheid maintained that these kinds of love differ in terms of their antecedents or causal conditions, associated behaviors, and temporal course. Concerning antecedents, Berscheid posited that romantic–passionate love is triggered by desirable qualities in the other (e.g., physical attraction), sexual desire, and the perception that one is liked by the other. Companionate love arises from proximity, familiarity, and similarity—variables that facilitate the formation of friendships (see Fehr, 1996). The key antecedent of compassionate love is the perception that the other is in distress or in need. Finally, the cause of attachment love is a threatening situation.

Turning to behaviors, Berscheid (2006, 2010) specified that the acts that are associated with romantic love are those that encourage another person to pursue sexual relations with one. Behaviors of companionate love are those that make it enjoyable for the other to interact with one, which includes spending time together so that familiarity can develop, pursuing similar interests, and expressing liking. The behaviors that are characteristic of compassionate love vary, depending on the nature of the distress that is perceived. Behaviors that are characteristic of attachment love are those that promote proximity (Berscheid, 2006, 2010).

In this chapter, I use the quadrumvirate model as framework within which extant research on love is situated. As will be apparent throughout the chapter, research in the close relationships field has focused overwhelmingly on romantic–passionate love. The three other kinds of love delineated by Berscheid (2006, 2010) have, by comparison, received very little research attention. Companionate (friendship-based) love has long been recognized as an important theoretical construct, but it has not received extensive empirical study. Compassionate love is beginning to receive empirical attention (Fehr, Sprecher, & Underwood, 2009), although much of this work has examined nonintimate contexts (e.g., toward strangers [Mikulincer, Shaver, & Gillath, 2009], physician–patient relationships [Graber & Mitcham, 2009]). Finally, as already mentioned, the literature on attachment styles or orientations is voluminous (see Mikulincer & Shaver, 2007; Simpson & Rholes, 2012), but attachment has not been researched as a kind of love. Thus, in this chapter, my focus is on the three kinds of love that have been examined in empirical investigations: romantic–passionate love, companionate love, and compassionate love.

Integration of models of love.   Several attempts have been made to integrate models of love by conducting factor analyses of love scales. C. Hendrick and Hendrick (1989) led the way in their factor analysis of the Love Attitudes Scale (which assesses the six love styles—eros, storge, agape, ludus, mania, and pragma), the Triangular Love Scale (Sternberg, 1987, as cited in C. Hendrick & Hendrick, 1989), Hazan and Shaver's (1987) attachment scale, the Passionate Love Scale (Hatfield & Sprecher, 1986), and the Relationship Rating Form (Davis & Todd, 1982, 1985), which measures six components of relationships: viability, intimacy, passion, care, conflict, and satisfaction. A number of passion scales loaded on Hendrick and Hendrick's first factor, suggesting that passion is a major dimension of love. However, measures of commitment, satisfaction, and intimacy loaded on this factor as well. Intimacy scales loaded on the second factor too, along with two scales that had negative loadings, namely the Ludus (game-playing) love-style

scale and the Conflict scale. Hendrick and Hendrick described this factor as representing "closeness and an absence of either conflict or game-playing" (p. 791). The three remaining factors included an attachment anxiety factor, an attachment security–avoidance factor, and a factor that captured a pragmatic, friendship orientation to love. This factor structure has been replicated in other research (Tzeng, 1993). In reflecting on these findings, S. S. Hendrick and Hendrick (1997) concluded that their results were best summarized in terms of the companionate–passionate distinction originally proposed by Berscheid and Hatfield (1974).

Fehr (1994) also factor analyzed a number of love scales, including the Love Attitudes Scale, Rubin's (1970) Love and Liking Scales, and several measures of romantic beliefs. Four factors were extracted. The first factor, Romantic Beliefs, consisted of measures of romantic beliefs. Rubin's Love and Liking Scales loaded on the second factor, along with the Ludus love-style scale (negatively). This factor was labeled Companionate Love. Measures of the experience of love (e.g., Passionate Love Scale, Mania love-style scale) loaded on the third factor, which was labeled the Experience of Passionate Love. Finally, the fourth factor, Pragmatic Love, included the Pragma love-style scale, along with a scale of romantic idealism that loaded negatively. In this study, Fehr also concluded that the passionate–companionate love taxonomy best captured the results.

Recently, Graham (2011) conducted a meta-analytic factor analysis of love scales, which included Rubin's Love and Liking Scales, the Love Attitudes Scale, the Passionate Love Scale, and the Triangular Love Scale. A three-factor solution emerged. The first factor was interpreted as a general love factor. Most of the scales loaded on it, including Rubin's Liking Scale, the Passionate Love Scale, all three components of the Triangular Love Scale, and three love-style scales (Eros, Agape, and Ludus; the latter loaded negatively). The second factor was labeled Romantic Obsession, with the Mania love-style scale having the highest loadings. This factor was interpreted in light of Acevedo and Aron's (2009) distinction between romantic love and romantic obsession. The third factor was labeled Practical Friendship. The Storge and Pragma love-style scales loaded on this factor. In Graham's view, neither practical friendship nor romantic obsession qualify as love, leaving only the first factor. He concluded that standard scales that purportedly measure different kinds of love (e.g., passionate love, companionate love) actually tap one general love factor.

Thus, factor analyses of many of the same measures have produced somewhat different results. One limitation of all of these studies is that few measures of companionate love were included. The most commonly used measure is the Storge love-style scale, which tends to behave differently from other measures of companionate love (Masuda, 2003). Given the recent extension of Berscheid's (2006, 2010) model to include compassionate love and attachment love, it will be important in future factor analytic studies to administer scales that measure these kinds of love as well.

In conclusion, psychologists have constructed a number of definitions, models, and taxonomies of love. What is most striking is the lack of consensus, which, as many experts have observed, poses a significant obstacle to progress in this area (Berscheid, 2010; Felmlee & Sprecher, 2006). According to Berscheid (2010), scholars' definitions and models will remain fragmented and disparate so long as love is assumed to be a single entity. In her view, the task for scholars is to articulate and understand the four basic forms that love takes. An analogy can be drawn with personality psychology, a field in which theoretical and empirical energies are directed toward understanding and elucidating the predictive power of the Big Five rather than attempting to reach consensus on a definition of the concept of personality.

Another explanation for the lack of agreement on a definition of love is that this concept may not be amenable to classical definition in terms of a necessary and sufficient set of criterial features. Instead, as discussed next, analyses of lay conceptions suggest that love may be best conceptualized as a prototype concept rather than as a concept that can be precisely defined.

Laypeople's Conceptions of Love

The most extensive, in-depth analyses of laypeople's answers to the question "What is love?" have been conducted from a prototype perspective. Lay conceptions of love have also been explored using the social categorization approach.

Prototype approach. From a prototype perspective, the failure of experts to reach consensus on a definition of love is not surprising. Eleanor Rosch (1973a, 1973b), a cognitive psychologist, made the revolutionary claim that many natural language concepts are not amenable to classical definition (i.e., defined in terms of singly necessary and jointly sufficient criterial features). Rather, such concepts are organized around their clearest cases, or best examples, which she referred to as prototypes. Members of a category can be ordered in terms of their degree of resemblance to the prototypical cases, with members shading gradually into nonmembers. Boundaries between categories, therefore, are blurry rather than clearly demarcated. In empirical tests of the theory, Rosch focused on object categories, such as vegetables, fruit, furniture, and birds (see Mervis & Rosch, 1981, for a review). She demonstrated that some instances of these concepts were considered prototypical, whereas others were regarded as nonprototypical. For example, robins were rated as representative of the concept of bird; turkeys were seen as nonrepresentative. Moreover, this internal structure affected the cognitive processing of category-relevant information. In a reaction time study, for example, the category membership of prototypical cases was confirmed more quickly than that of nonprototypical cases (e.g., robins were verified as a kind of bird more quickly than were turkeys; Rosch, 1973a).

Fehr and colleagues (Fehr, 1988; Fehr & Russell, 1984, 1991; see Fehr, 2001, 2006, 2013, for reviews) explored the possibility that more abstract concepts that had defied classical definition in the past, such as love, might also be better conceptualized as prototypes. To test this possibility, Fehr and Russell (1991) conducted a prototype analysis of types of love. In a series of studies, they found that companionate kinds of love (e.g., familial love, parental love, friendship love) were considered prototypical of the concept; passionate kinds of love (e.g., romantic love, passionate love, sexual love) were considered nonprototypical. This internal structure was validated using different methodologies. For example, in a reaction time study, participants were faster to verify that maternal love is a kind of love than they were to verify that sexual love is a kind of love. Participants also agreed that the prototypical instances were, in fact, types of love, but they disagreed on the category membership of nonprototypical instances.

In a subsequent series of studies, Fehr (1994) conducted a cluster analysis of 15 types of love taken from Fehr and Russell's (1991) research. Types of companionate love clustered together (e.g., familial love, friendship love, maternal love), as did types of passionate love (e.g., romantic love, passionate love, sexual love). Fehr concluded that lay conceptions of types of love are best summarized in terms of Berscheid and Hatfield's (1974) distinction between passionate love and companionate love.

The prototype approach was taken one step further by Fehr (1988), who hypothesized that the attributes or features of concepts might also be organized as prototypes, such that some features would be considered more representative of the concept than others. This idea was tested in a series of studies that focused on the concepts of love and commitment.[1] In the first study, laypeople (university students) were asked to list features or attributes of the concept of love. Coding of these responses resulted in a final set of 68 features listed by more than one participant, suggesting that laypeople have rich, complex knowledge of this concept. Features such as honesty, trust, and caring were listed with high frequency. Features such as dependency, sexual passion, and physical attraction were listed relatively infrequently. In the next study, a new group of participants was asked to rate these features in terms of their prototypicality. Features such as trust, caring, intimacy, and friendship were considered central to love, whereas sexual passion, gazing at the other, and heart rate increases were considered peripheral. Thus, people regarded features portraying companionate love as the essence of love; features depicting passionate love were regarded as nonprototypical of the concept. Once again, this prototype structure was confirmed using a variety of methods. In a study of natural language use, it sounded peculiar to hedge on prototypical, but not nonprototypical, features. For example, given information that Pat loved Chris, it sounded peculiar to state that "Pat sort of trusts Chris"; it was less peculiar sounding to state that "Pat is sort of dependent on Chris." Prototypical features of love were also found to be more salient in memory than were nonprototypical features. Overall, the findings converged with those obtained in the analyses of types of love: Lay conceptions of love encompass both companionate love and passionate love. However, people consider companionate love to be the essence of love, whereas passionate love is seen as peripheral.[2]

Fehr's (1988) research was conducted on the west coast of Canada. Researchers subsequently examined whether the prototype of love would be replicable (see Fehr, 1993, for a review). For example, Button and Collier (1991) sought to replicate Fehr's prototype of love using samples of university students and community participants living on the east coast of Canada. Luby and Aron (1990) explored whether Americans living on the West Coast of the United States would hold a similar prototype of love. Their research was conducted with students at the University of California, Santa Cruz, as well as with members of the public enrolled in music appreciation classes. The findings across these studies were remarkably consistent. Consensus across data sets was especially strong for those features of love identified as prototypical by Fehr (1988). More specifically, five features of love were listed frequently and received the highest prototypicality ratings in each of these data sets: trust, caring, honesty, friendship, and respect. Intimacy also received high ratings in each study. Thus, at least within North America, among university students and nonstudents alike, there appears to be agreement that the companionate features of love capture the true meaning of the concept of love.

---

[1]Only the findings for love are reported here.

[2]Aron and Westbay (1996) factor analyzed the features of love identified by Fehr (1988). They obtained a three-factor solution, which they interpreted as corresponding to the components of Sternberg's (1986) triangular theory of love.

Prototype analyses of the features of love spawned prototype analyses of the features of specific kinds of love. For example, Regan, Kocan, and Whitlock (1998) undertook a prototype analysis of the concept of romantic love (treated as synonymous with being in love). They extracted 119 features from participants' open-ended responses. The features of romantic love that were generated most frequently were trust, sexual attraction–desire, acceptance and tolerance, spend time together, and share thoughts and secrets. Features that were generated with the lowest frequency were adoration, caress, submission–obedience to the other, and controlling. Interestingly, the features that were rated as most prototypical of love (in general) in Fehr's (1988) analysis were also rated as most prototypical of romantic love—namely, trust, honesty, happiness, caring, and intimacy. Intermediate typicality ratings were assigned to the features that are emphasized in experts' definitions of romantic love, such as sexual attraction–desire, spend time together, touching–holding, passion, and miss other–want to be together. Still lower prototypicality ratings were given to features that portrayed the challenges of love (e.g., time consuming–hard work, challenging–stressful, dependent on other, frustration). Finally, the features that received the lowest prototypicality ratings portray the dark side of romantic love (e.g., selfishness, controlling, depression, lies–deception, submission–obedience). Thus, there is evidence that one of the kinds of love identified in Berscheid's (2006, 2010) quadrumvirate model—namely romantic love—is organized as a prototype concept.

Fehr and Sprecher (2003, 2009) tested the hypothesis that compassionate love is also structured as a prototype concept. In their first study, participants were asked to list the features or characteristics of compassionate love. Lay conceptions of compassionate love included feelings and emotions (e.g., feel happiest when with the person), cognitions (e.g., think about the other all the time), motivation (e.g., want to make the other happy), and behaviors (e.g., do anything for the other). In their second study, a new sample of participants rated these features in terms of prototypicality. The features that received the highest prototypicality ratings were trust, honesty, caring, understanding, and

support. Once again, these are features that are central to the concept of love itself (Fehr, 1988). The lowest prototypicality ratings were given to such features as do anything for the other, put other ahead of self, and make sacrifices for the other. Interestingly, these are the kinds of features that experts use to define compassionate love (Shacham-Dupont, 2003). This prototype structure was confirmed using a variety of methods (e.g., reaction time, memory biases).

It is noteworthy that in prototype analyses of romantic love and compassionate love, the features that receive the highest ratings are those that are considered most prototypical of the concept of love in general. This suggests that in the minds of ordinary people, romantic and compassionate love are, first and foremost, kinds of love. The nonprototypical features seem to specify which kind of love it is. In the case of romantic love, the less prototypical features indicate that this is the kind of love that involves sexual attraction and desire, wanting to spend time with the other, touching–holding, and so on. In the case of compassionate love, the nonprototypical features (e.g., sacrifice, put the other first) specify that this kind of love involves giving of oneself for the good of another.

Other prototype-based approaches. Several other researchers have conducted prototype-based analyses of love. Buss (1988) conducted a prototype analysis of the behavioral indicators of love. In this research, participants were asked to list acts or behaviors that exemplify love. These behaviors were then rated for prototypicality by a different sample. As prototype theory would predict, some behaviors of love were regarded as more prototypical than others. For example, behaviors indicative of commitment (e.g., "She agreed to marry him") received high prototypicality ratings. Other acts (e.g., "He made love to her") received low ratings.

Others have elicited laypeople's accounts of particular experiences of love (rather than asking them to describe the meaning of the concept, as in Fehr's research). For example, Shaver, Schwartz, Kirson, and O'Connor (1987) asked participants to describe an episode of love (along with other emotions). A prototype was then derived from these accounts.

More specifically, features were extracted and classified as antecedents (e.g., feeling wanted–needed by the other, finding the other attractive), responses (e.g., wanting to be physically close to the other, kissing, sex), physiological reactions (e.g., high energy, fast heartbeat), behaviors (e.g., gazing, smiling), and so on. A variation of this methodology was used by Fitness and Fletcher (1993) in their analysis of love (and other emotions) as experienced in the context of a marital relationship. They asked married couples to describe the most typical incident that would elicit feelings of love for one's spouse. The respondents reported that love experiences were triggered by events such as thinking about one's partner, receiving support from him or her, sharing happy times, and so on. Their accounts also included low-arousal physiological responses such as feelings of warmth and relaxed muscles. Behaviors included the desire to be physically close to one's partner, giving presents, hugging and kissing, or doing nothing.

Although not billed as a prototype study, Lamm and Wiesmann (1997) asked university students in Germany to answer the question, "How can you tell that you love someone?" Other participants were asked about liking and still others about being in love. The responses were coded, and a feature list was derived for each concept. For love, the responses that were generated with the highest frequency were positive mood when thinking about or being with the other, trust, desire to be with the other, altruistic behavior toward the other, and self-disclosure. For the concept of being in love (which was treated as synonymous with romantic and passionate love), the most frequent attribute was arousal when thinking about or being with the other, positive mood, thinking about the other, desire for the other's presence, and the like. Lamm and Wiesmann concluded that considerable overlap existed between the indicators of love identified in this research and the features generated with the highest frequency in Fehr's (1988) prototype analysis.

Finally, Kline, Horton, and Zhang (2008) asked American university students and Asian students attending university in the United States to report on their attitudes and beliefs about love in marriage.

Some of the responses can be taken as features of the concept of love. These features were remarkably similar in the two samples, particularly those that were listed with the highest frequency. For example, in the American sample, features such as trust, going out together, respect, and honesty were generated with high frequency. In the Asian sample, trust, caring, and respect were also among the most frequently listed responses. As these examples illustrate, the features that were paramount reflected a companionate conception of love more so than a passionate conception. Kline et al. concluded that "these findings parallel and validate Fehr's (1988) prototype analysis of love . . . and extend the prototype findings to East Asians" (p. 211).

In conclusion, prototype analyses of love have taken different forms. It seems likely that each of these approaches is accessing a different kind of relational knowledge. As has been suggested elsewhere (e.g., Fehr, 2005; Surra & Bohman, 1991), there are probably different levels, or at least different storehouses, of knowledge for concepts such as love. Socially shared conceptions reside at the most general level. Presumably, this is the kind of knowledge that is being tapped when people are asked to describe what the concept means or to list the behaviors that are typical of love. People are also likely to hold relationship-specific representations of love based on their experiences. This kind of knowledge may well be what is accessed when participants are asked to describe specific experiences or episodes of love.

Social categorization approach. Meyers and Berscheid (1997) developed the social categorization approach as an indirect way of assessing lay conceptions of love. In this research, the meanings of the terms *love* and *in love* were elucidated by having participants list the names of people in their lives who belonged in each category. The results showed that love is a much broader category (i.e., more names were listed) than in love. Moreover, the concept of love subsumed the concept of in love. Meyers and Berscheid also found that people who were listed for the in-love category were generally listed for a sexual attraction–desire category as well, suggesting that the type of love referred to by the term *in love* contains a sexual element. Thus, another approach to understanding love and types of love is to have laypeople nominate the members of these social categories. This approach holds considerable promise as a subtle or indirect method for assessing people's conceptions of love and related constructs.

GENDER DIFFERENCES IN CONCEPTIONS OF LOVE

Harry Harlow (1958) mused that "thoughtful men, and probably all women, have speculated on the nature of love" (p. 673). Are men and women on the same page when they think about love? As I will show, the answer depends on which kind of love is being speculated on.

Romantic–Passionate Love

There has been a long-standing assumption that women are more concerned with romance than are men. When social scientists began to conduct research on this issue, however, it became apparent that men are actually the more romantic sex. For example, men are more likely than women to subscribe to romantic beliefs such as true love lasts forever; when you meet the right person, you will just know it; and it is possible to fall in love at first sight (e.g., Rubin, Peplau, & Hill, 1981; Sprecher & Metts, 1989). There are some exceptions. For example, Sprecher and Toro-Morn (2002) did not find a gender difference in scores on the Romantic Beliefs Scale (Sprecher & Metts, 1989) in an American sample, but they did find that men scored higher than women in a Chinese sample. It is also the case that men generally do not score higher than women on the Eros love-style scale (see Fehr & Broughton, 2001; S. S. Hendrick & Hendrick, 1997, for reviews). However, the general pattern in the literature is one of gender differences, with men holding a more romantic–passionate conception of love than women. Consistent with this pattern, Fehr and Broughton (2001) found that men rated prototypes of various passionate kinds of love (e.g., romantic love, passionate love, sexual love) as depicting their own view of love to a greater extent than did women.

The converse is also true, namely, that women hold a more pragmatic (nonromantic) orientation to love than do men. Indeed, substantial evidence has shown that women are more likely than men to believe that a satisfying relationship can be had with a number of potential partners, socioeconomic resources should be given consideration in partner selection, and one should choose a partner with a similar background (see S. S. Hendrick & Hendrick, 1997, for a review).

Companionate Love

Women hold a more companionate conception of love than do men. For example, women generally score higher than men on the Storge love-style scale (e.g., C. Hendrick & Hendrick, 1990; S. S. Hendrick & Hendrick, 1997; Worobrey, 2001), although there are some exceptions. For example, in studies conducted in Australia (Heaven, Da Silva, Carey, & Holen, 2004) and the United States (Sprecher & Toro-Morn, 2002), no gender difference was found. Sprecher and Toro-Morn (2002) found that men actually scored higher than women in a Chinese sample.

Fehr and Broughton (2001) found that women rated the prototype of friendship love as representing their view of love to a greater extent than did men. However, there was no gender difference on ratings of a companionate love cluster that included prototypes of familial kinds of love (e.g., maternal, parental) and affection, in addition to friendship love.

Compassionate–Altruistic Love

When conceptions of compassionate–altruistic love are assessed with the Agape scale, gender differences are generally not found (S. S. Hendrick & Hendrick, 1997). However, in several recent studies, men have scored higher on this scale than women, as documented in American (Sprecher & Toro-Morn, 2002; Worobrey, 2001), Australian (Heaven et al., 2004), and Chinese samples (Sprecher & Toro-Morn, 2002). The reason for this shift is unclear. In Fehr and Sprecher's (2009) prototype analysis of compassionate love, women and men held similar conceptions of this kind of love.

Overall, the evidence has suggested that men have a more passionate, romantic orientation to love, whereas women have a more companionate orientation. Consequently, the conclusion has been that, when it comes to love, women and men inhabit different worlds or even different planets (e.g., Gray, 1992). Such a conclusion seems unwarranted, however, given that researchers have generally assessed only romantic–passionate love or only companionate love. Those who measure both kinds of love typically conduct between-, not within-, gender analyses. Thus, the relative emphasis that women and men place on each of these kinds of love is typically not investigated. In a series of studies designed to address this issue, Fehr and Broughton (2001) presented women and men with prototypes depicting passionate and companionate love. Participants were asked to rate the extent to which the view of love portrayed in each prototype corresponded to their own view of love. Both women and men assigned significantly higher ratings to companionate love than to passionate love prototypes. In other words, by assessing both companionate and passionate love and comparing ratings of these kinds of love within each gender, a rather different picture emerged—one in which the sexes appear to exhibit much greater agreement than disagreement. Finally, it appears that women and men also hold similar conceptions of compassionate love. Gender similarity has also been found in prototype analyses and in early studies using the Agape love-style scale.

Cultural Differences in Conceptions of Love

Another question that has intrigued social scientists is whether people in different cultures view love differently. Comparisons are generally made between collectivistic and individualistic cultures.

Romantic–passionate love. According to K. K. Dion and Dion (1993, 1996, 2001), romantic love holds less importance in collectivistic societies than in individualistic societies. In individualistic societies, romantic love is a highly personal experience in which people immerse themselves in the new relationship and withdraw from friends and family. In collectivistic cultures, however, people must take into account the family and other group members. In fact, marriages are often by arrangement, with the respective families choosing marriage

partners (Adams, Anderson, & Adonu, 2004; Fiske, Kitayama, Markus, & Nisbett, 1998; Kline et al., 2008; Levine, Sato, Hashimoto, & Verma, 1995). For example, in West Africa, relationships with one's parents, siblings, and relatives are considered more important and influential than the more recent relationship one has formed with one's spouse. In many areas of West Africa, happily married couples do not even live in the same house, nor do they expect to sleep together every night. In stark contrast to the pattern of intimate relationships in individualistic cultures, their connection and obligation to extended family takes precedence over their connection and obligation to their spouse (Adams et al., 2004).

Cultural differences such as these have implications for how people conceptualize love. For example, studies on mate selection have shown that in individualistic cultures, people believe that romantic–passionate love should be the primary criterion for choosing a mate. In an early influential study, Kephart (1967) posed the following question to more than 1,000 university students: "If a boy (girl) had all the qualities you desired, would you marry this person if you were not in love with him (her)?" Marrying for love was found to be important for men (64.5% said "no") but not nearly as important for women (24.3% said "no"). Simpson, Campbell, and Berscheid (1986) asked the same question of university students in 1976 and again in 1984 ("boy/girl" was replaced with "man/woman"). The belief that love should be the basis for marriage was held even more strongly than in Kephart's study, with 86.2% of men and 80% of women responding "no" in 1976 and 85.6% of men and 84.9% of women responding "no" in 1984 (see Wiederman & Allgeier, 1992, for similar findings).

Other researchers have gathered cross-cultural data on the question of whether romantic love should be the basis for marriage. For example, Levine et al. (1995) presented Kephart's (1967) question to university students in 11 different countries. They found that marrying for love was most important to participants in Western and Westernized countries (e.g., the United States, Brazil, England, Australia) and least important to participants in less developed Eastern countries (e.g., India, Pakistan, Thailand).

Consistent with these findings, Sprecher and Toro-Morn (2002) found that although Chinese university students agreed that marriage should be based on love, they did not endorse this belief as strongly as did American university students (see Kline et al., 2008; Simmons, vom Kolke, & Shimizu, 1986, for similar findings). In contrast, when Sprecher et al. (1994) asked the Kephart question of university students in the United States, Russia, and Japan, more than 80% of women and men in the United States and in Japan responded that they would not marry someone unless they were in love with him or her. The percentages were somewhat lower in Russia (70% of men and 59% of women responded "no"; Sprecher et al., 1994). Thus, people in individualistic cultures are more likely to believe that love should be the basis for marriage than are people in collectivistic cultures.

Another approach to examining cultural differences in conceptions of love is to ask people to rank order a list of qualities that they desire in a mate. Such studies have tended to find evidence of cultural similarity, at least in terms of the top-ranked qualities. For example, in the 37 cultures examined by Buss et al. (1990), mutual attraction–love emerged as the quality most desired in a mate by both women and men. The qualities that were ranked lower (e.g., chastity) were more likely to differ by culture (Buss et al., 1990). These findings were recently replicated in an Arab Jordanian cultural context (Khallad, 2005). Once again, mutual attraction–love received the highest rating. Ratings of other characteristics valued in that culture (e.g., religiosity, neatness, refinement) received lower ratings. Thus, across cultures, people seem to agree that mutual attraction–love is the most important quality that one would want in a mate. However, the qualities that are lower on the list show cultural specificity.

Finally, researchers have also explored cultural differences in love styles. In Sprecher et al.'s (1994) study of university students in the United States, Russia, and Japan, Eros was the most strongly endorsed love style in each country. However, comparisons by culture showed that Americans scored higher on this scale than Russians or Japanese, with Russians scoring higher than the Japanese. Consistent with these findings, Goodwin and Findlay (1997) found that British students scored higher on the Eros scale than did Hong Kong Chinese students. Cho and Cross (1995) administered the relationship-specific Love Attitudes Scale (C. Hendrick & Hendrick, 1990) to Taiwanese students living in the United States. In a factor analysis, Eros and Agape items loaded on the same factor. According to these researchers, in Taiwanese culture, there is a kind of love that is best described as romantic–considerate love, which explains why Eros and Agape formed a single factor in their analysis. However, in a study conducted with university students in Japan, Eros was distinguishable from Agape (Kanemasa, Taniguchi, Daibo, & Ishimori, 2004).

Neto et al. (2000) administered the Love Attitudes Scale to university students in eight countries on four continents. The Eros love style received the highest rating in six of the eight countries. Although they found a significant main effect for culture, follow-up tests revealed only one difference, namely, that respondents from Macao scored lower on the Eros love-style scale than did respondents from Portugal (Neto et al., 2000).

Finally, some researchers have examined whether love styles differ as a function of cultural heritage. C. Hendrick and Hendrick (1986) found that American university students whose ethnic background was Asian scored lower on the Eros love-style scale than did students from Black, White non-Hispanic, or White Hispanic ethnic backgrounds. However, they found no differences when Anglo Americans and Mexican Americans living in the southwestern United States were compared (Contreras, Hendrick, & Hendrick, 1996). Similarly, Sprecher and Toro-Morn (2002) failed to find significant differences in Eros love-style scores among American university students whose ethnic group was classified as White, Black, or Hispanic/Latino. K. L. Dion and Dion (1973) administered love-style scales to an ethnically diverse sample of students attending the University of Toronto. Participants were classified as Anglo Celtic, European, Chinese, or other Asian on the basis of reports of their ethnicity/cultural background. These groups did not vary significantly in terms of endorsement of the Eros love style.

In sum, it appears that people from all over the world are more likely to endorse the romantic, passionate love style than the other love styles. When cultures are compared, people in Asian cultures tend to have lower mean ratings on Eros than people from Western countries. The few studies focused on other cultural groups (e.g., African Americans, Hispanics) have tended to rely on within-country comparisons. These studies tend not to find differences, perhaps because of acculturation.

Companionate love.   It has been suggested that people in collectivistic cultures value and identify with companionate love to a greater extent than those in individualistic cultures. As K. L. Dion and Dion (1993) pointed out, "This style of love would not disrupt a complex network of existing family relationships" (p. 465). Most of the empirical research on cultural differences in conceptions of companionate love has been conducted using the Storge love-style scale. Cross-cultural studies and studies in which ethnic/racial groups within countries are compared have generally found that people from collectivistic cultures score higher on the Storge love-style scale than people from individualistic cultures. For example, Neto et al. (2000) found that Angolans, Cape Verdeans, and Mozambicans were more storgic than the French and Swiss. K. L. Dion and Dion (1993) found that Canadian university students from Chinese and other Asian backgrounds scored higher on the Storge scale than did students from Anglo Celtic and European backgrounds. Similarly, C. Hendrick and Hendrick (1986) found that Asian students scored higher than students from other ethnic backgrounds (Black, White, and Hispanic). In contrast to these findings, in Sprecher et al.'s (1994) study, Americans scored higher on the Storge scale than did Russians or Japanese.

In their comparison of different racial/ethnic groups in the United States, Sprecher and Toro-Morn (2002) found that Black Americans scored significantly higher on Storge than did White Americans, with the scores of Hispanic/Latino participants falling between these two groups. However, Contreras et al. (1996) did not find differences in Storge scores of Anglo Americans and Mexican Americans living in the southwestern United States.

The most consistent finding in these studies was that Asians tend to score higher on the Storge love-style scale than North Americans. Studies that have compared White Americans, Black Americans, and Hispanics have produced inconsistent findings.

Compassionate love.   The Agape love-style scale has also been administered cross-culturally. Participants from the eight countries examined in Neto et al.'s (2000) study did not differ in terms of the Agape love style. However, in Sprecher et al.'s (1994) cross-cultural study, Russians scored higher on the Agape scale than did Americans or Japanese. Turning to within-country comparisons, K. L. Dion and Dion (1993) found that female university students in Canada whose background was other Asian scored higher on the Agape scale than those whose background was Anglo Celtic. However, C. Hendrick and Hendrick (1986) found that the scores of American students of Asian ancestry did not differ significantly from the scores of Black or Hispanic American university students. Black students scored significantly lower on the Agape scale than did Hispanic students. Sprecher and Toro-Morn (2002) found that White Americans scored higher on the Agape love-style scale than did either Black Americans or Hispanic/Latino Americans. Contreras et al. (1996) did not find differences in Agape among samples of Anglo Americans and Mexican Americans living in the southwestern United States. In short, research on cultural differences in conceptions of compassionate–altruistic love, as assessed by the Agape love-style scale, has produced mixed results.

In conclusion, cultural differences have been found in beliefs about whether love should be the basis for marriage. People in collectivistic cultures, particularly cultures in which marriages are arranged, are less likely to subscribe to these beliefs than those in individualistic cultures. Similarly, although people in collectivistic cultures are more likely to endorse the passionate, romantic Eros love style than the other love styles, comparisons across cultures have revealed that people from Asian cultures generally score lower on this scale than people from individualistic cultures (e.g., North America). In contrast to these cultural differences, there appears to be nearly universal agreement that love–attraction is the most desirable quality in a mate.

Turning to companionate love, despite some inconsistencies in the findings, it is generally the case that people in or from Asian countries are more likely to subscribe to a companionate conception of love (as assessed by the Storge love-style scale) than people from North America. According to K. L. Dion and Dion (1993), the powerful role of the family in the formation and maintenance of romantic relationships explains why people in collectivistic cultures are more likely to embrace companionate love than those in individualistic cultures.

Finally, whether cultures differ in compassionate–altruistic love is unclear. Findings using the Agape love-style scale have varied widely from one study to the next. People in individualistic cultures might be expected to endorse a less altruistic conception of love, given the emphasis on gratification of the self. However, it has also been shown that as a relationship develops, the partner becomes part of oneself (Aron, Lewandowski, Mashek, & Aron, 2013). One might therefore expect greater emphasis on compassionate love because altruism directed at the partner is, in a sense, altruism extended to the self. On the other hand, people in collectivistic cultures are less focused on the fulfillment of their own needs, which might translate into a more altruistic conception of love toward one's partner. However, the emphasis on preserving group harmony in such cultures could mean that altruism toward one's group (e.g., family) supersedes altruism toward the partner. In short, people from different cultures may receive the same scores on the Agape love-style scale, but perhaps for different reasons.

RELATIONAL IMPLICATIONS OF CONCEPTIONS OF LOVE

What are the implications of different conceptions of love for the dynamics of people's relationships? As I show, the way in which people construe love plays an important role in predicting how satisfied they are in their relationship and, ultimately, whether it endures.

Conceptions of Love and Relationship Satisfaction

The outcome variable that has most frequently been correlated with conceptions of love is satisfaction. It turns out that conceptions of romantic–passionate love, companionate love, and compassionate love are all linked to the level of satisfaction in a relationship.

Romantic–passionate love.   Fehr (2013) reviewed findings from approximately 30 studies in which measures of romantic–passionate love were correlated with various measures of satisfaction. The Eros scale was the scale most frequently used to measure conceptions of romantic–passionate love. Across these studies, the correlations tended to be moderate to strong in magnitude, most often in the .50s. Some studies obtained higher correlations for men than for women, whereas others found just the opposite; researchers generally did not test whether these correlations differed significantly.

Companionate love.   The measure of companionate love that has been most frequently correlated with relationship satisfaction is the Storge love-style scale. Conceptions of companionate love assessed in this way are largely unrelated to relationship satisfaction. In most studies, correlations fall in the range of 0 to .26, with the majority hovering around the low end of this range (Fehr, 2013). Thus, it would appear that whether or not one agrees with statements such as "It is hard to say exactly where friendship ends and love begins" has little bearing on how happy one is in one's current romantic relationship.

Compassionate love.   The relation between conceptions of compassionate love (assessed by the Agape love-style scale) and satisfaction has also been tested. Correlations vary widely, ranging from .07 to .57 (see Fehr, 2013, for a review), with most falling in the .20s. When coefficients vary by gender, there is generally a stronger link between Agape and satisfaction for women than for men.

Thus, there is evidence that the way in which people construe love is associated with relationship happiness. People who hold a romantic, passionate conception of love are likely to be satisfied in their romantic relationships. Those who hold an altruistic, compassionate conception are also likely to be satisfied, although this relation is not particularly strong. So far, there is little evidence that a companionate conception of love is associated with relationship satisfaction. It is unclear whether the Storge love-style scale does not fully capture a companionate conceptualization of love, or whether thinking about love in friendship-based terms actually has little to do with relational happiness.

Conceptions of Love and the Deterioration and Dissolution of Relationships

People's beliefs about and conceptions of love play an important role in relational decline. For example, Simpson et al. (1986) asked respondents whether the disappearance of love was a sufficient reason for ending a marriage. In their 1976 data set, nearly two thirds of women and men believed so. In their 1984 data set, the numbers were lower. Nevertheless nearly half of the participants agreed that the loss of love was grounds for ending a marriage. In Levine et al.'s (1995) cross-cultural replication of Simpson et al.'s research, there was evidence that people in Western cultures were more likely to hold this belief than people in Eastern cultures, although the differences between cultures were not particularly clear or strong.

Other researchers have examined whether the kind of love matters. Fehr (1988) conducted a scenario study to explore the implications of conceptions of companionate and passionate love for the deterioration and dissolution of relationships. She found that violations of companionate features (e.g., failures of trust or respect) were seen as undermining the level of love in a relationship more so than violations of passionate features (e.g., no longer experiencing sexual attraction). In line with these findings, Sprecher and Toro-Morn (2002) found that the disappearance of passionate love was not regarded by American university students as grounds for ending a marriage if the relationship was still high in companionate love.

Thus, the loss of love is often seen as a reason to end a relationship. It appears that people are especially likely to regard the loss of companionate love as leading to relationship decline—more so than the loss of passionate love.

EXPERIENCE OF LOVE

People not only think about love; they feel it. Research on the experience of love has focused on a wide range of topics: the course of love over time, the neurological correlates of love, gender differences, and cultural differences. How love is experienced also has important implications for relationship satisfaction, commitment, and stability.

Course of Love Over Time

In fleshing out her model of love, Berscheid (2010) spelled out the temporal course of each of the four basic kinds. She described the course of romantic–passionate love as follows: "Uncertainty and facilitative surprises wane, predictability grows, erotic satisfaction becomes readily available, and thus, the emotional experiences that are associated with Romantic Love should wane" (p. 15). The decline of passionate love over time has been a prominent theme in social psychological writings on love (e.g., Baumeister & Bratslavsky, 1999; Sternberg, 1986). Right from the start, Hatfield and Walster (1978) claimed that the intensity of passionate love fades over time. They went on to argue that passionate love is eventually replaced with the more solid, stable companionate love. The idea that passionate love is supplanted by companionate love was revised in later writings (e.g., Traupmann, Eckels, & Hatfield, 1982), although the assumption remained that companionate love develops later in a relationship and, once developed, is more stable than passionate love. Recently, Berscheid (2010) challenged this assumption, arguing that companionate love may be important at the outset of the relationship and may change as the partners and their life circumstances change. In her view, compassionate love may also develop early on, but the true test of this kind of love comes when support and sacrifices are required over a sustained period of time. Empirical research has focused on the course of romantic–passionate love and, to a lesser extent, the course of companionate love. This work generally takes the form of comparisons of people at different stages of relationships, people's retrospective accounts of their experience of love at the beginning of their relationship, or, most commonly, correlations between relationship length and the experience of love. The kind of labor-intensive, long-term longitudinal studies that are required to provide definitive answers about the course of love over time are rare. Nevertheless, the studies that have been conducted provide valuable insights into how the experience of love changes over time.

Turning to romantic–passionate love, Hatfield and Sprecher (1986) found that passionate love scores increased from the occasional–regular dating stage to the exclusive dating stage and then leveled off at the cohabiting–engaged stage. Acker and Davis (1992) administered a number of measures of passionate love to adults in relationships ranging from casually dating to married. Mean relationship length in this sample was 9.5 years. Relationship stage was not a significant predictor of passionate love. However, relationship length was negatively associated with passionate love, especially for women. Acker and Davis speculated that their findings differed from those of Hatfield and Sprecher (1986) because the participants in that study were much younger, on average, and in relationships of much shorter duration. In their words, "An argument can be made that the romantic relationships of most 18-20 year olds are simply too short to reveal any significant decline in passion" (Acker & Davis, 1992, p. 43).

Tucker and Aron (1993) administered the Passionate Love Scale to couples before and after three major life transitions: marriage, parenthood, and empty nest. Passionate love scores were highest for the just-married group, lower for the new parents group, and still lower for the empty nest group. However, even in the empty nest group, levels of passionate love remained relatively high. They concluded that "passionate love appears to remain fairly high over much of the course of marriage, although there is a pattern of lower scores at subsequent transition points and of small declines from before to after each transition" (p. 144).

In the most extensive longitudinal analysis of the course of relationships over time, Huston and colleagues (e.g., Huston, Caughlin, Houts, Smith, & George, 2001; see Huston, 2009, for a review) administered a variety of individual (e.g., personality) and relationship measures to a large sample of recently married couples. Data were gathered from these participants over a 13-year period. Feelings of love were assessed using Braiker and Kelley's (1979) scale. After 2 years of marriage, couples expressed love and affection half as often as they had at the newlywed stage.

Turning to studies that have included measures of passionate love and companionate love, Traupmann et al. (1982) assessed these two kinds of love in a sample of married women ranging in age from 50 to 82 years. Most had been married for 30 years. Participants reported high levels of companionate love for their husbands ($M = 4.1$ on a 5-point scale) and relatively high levels of passionate love ($M = 3.1$). Moreover, both kinds of love were significantly associated with relationship satisfaction ($r = .43$ for companionate love; $r = .39$ for passionate love). The authors concluded that the idea that passionate love dies and is replaced by companionate love may be mistaken, given that in their sample, "the level of passionate love expressed is quite high . . . *and* is strongly correlated with the satisfaction and happiness women feel in their marital relationship" (p. 497).

In another analysis of this data set, Hatfield, Traupmann, and Sprecher (1984) divided the sample into women who had been married for less than 33 years and those who had been married for more than 33 years. The mean passionate love score was 3.27 (on a 5-point scale) in the group that had been married for less than 33 years compared with 2.98 for the longest-married group. Companionate love scores were also higher for women who had been married for less than 33 years than for those who had been married longer ($Ms = 4.24$ vs. 3.98). Once again, the passage of time was no more destructive for passionate love than for companionate love. Moreover, even though both kinds of love were lower in the longest-married group, mean levels remained quite high.

Sprecher and Regan (1998) administered multi-and single-item measures of passionate and companionate love to a sample of dating and young married couples. The average length of relationship was 32 months. Although scores on all of these measures were high, mean levels of companionate love were significantly higher than mean levels of passionate love. Correlations with relationship length were negative for both kinds of love, although most were nonsignificant (ranging from −.06 to −.15).[3] When analyses were conducted by relationship stage, occasional–regular daters reported the lowest levels of both kinds of love, whereas exclusive and engaged couples had the highest scores. Engaged and married couples had intermediate scores. Thus, at least for women, there was evidence that passionate love, but not companionate love, declined over time. However, the analyses of relationship stage suggested that the course of both kinds of love may be curvilinear, at least from the early dating to the newlywed stages.

Finally, Grote and Frieze (1998) examined the course of three kinds of love over time—romantic–passionate, companionate, and compassionate–altruistic. They assessed married women's and men's memories of love for their spouse at the beginning of their relationship and their current perceptions of marital love. More than 500 middle-aged adults (ages 45–47) completed measures of passionate love (a revised Eros love style), companionate love (a friendship-based love scale), and a revised Agape scale. The average length of marriage was 18 years. For women, relationship length (specifically, number of years married) was not correlated with perceptions of passionate love and companionate love at the beginning of their relationship nor with the current experience of these kinds of love. However, the longer a woman had been married, the greater the compassionate–altruistic love she perceived existed at the beginning of the relationship and the greater the compassionate–altruistic love she reported currently experiencing. For men, relationship length was also unrelated to perceptions of early romantic–passionate love and companionate love as well as current perceptions of companionate love. However, contrary to the findings for women, relationship length was significantly negatively correlated with men's current experience of romantic–passionate love, although the association was rather weak. Relationship length

was positively but weakly associated with perceptions of compassionate–altruistic love at the beginning of the relationship, but it was unrelated to current levels of this kind of love.

Grote and Frieze (1998) also compared mean levels of these kinds of love reported at the beginning of the relationship and currently. Women reported higher levels of romantic–passionate love when reflecting on the beginning of the relationship than when reporting on the current experience of this kind of love. However, perceptions of beginning and current levels of companionate love and compassionate–altruistic love did not differ. Men also perceived higher levels of romantic–passionate love early in the relationship than currently. Also, as with women, perceptions of companionate love did not vary. However, men perceived higher levels of compassionate–altruistic love currently than at the beginning of the relationship.

In a provocatively titled article, "Does a Long-Term Relationship Kill Romantic Love?" Acevedo and Aron (2009) suggested that romantic, passionate love can endure in long-term relationships if assessment of this kind of love does not include an obsessive component. To test this idea, they combined a number of data sets in which the Passionate Love Scale had been administered. A factor analysis of the scale items resulted in a Romantic Love factor and an Obsession factor. Neither factor was correlated with relationship length, which Acevedo and Aron interpreted as support for the idea that romantic love can exist in long-term relationships. They also conducted a meta-analysis of studies that have examined the relation between romantic–passionate love and satisfaction. This kind of love was substantially correlated with satisfaction for people in short-term and long-term relationships (although the association was slightly stronger in short-term relationships), reinforcing the conclusion that romantic, passionate love (without the obsessive component) can endure. Obsessive love was not associated with satisfaction, but in relatively new relationships, the direction of the correlation was positive, whereas in more established relationships,

---

[3]The one exception was for women, for whom the correlations between passionate love and relationship length did reach statistical significance (ranging from –.19 to –.30, depending on the measure; these correlations differed significantly from the near-zero correlations found for companionate love).

it was negative. Acevedo and Aron's meta-analysis also revealed that companionate love was more strongly correlated with satisfaction in long-term relationships than in short-term ones.

Overall, little support has been found for the idea that romantic–passionate love gets replaced with companionate love as a relationship matures. Both kinds of love decrease somewhat over the course of a relationship. However, at least in intact relationships, mean levels of these kinds of love remain relatively high. The course of compassionate–altruistic love over time has received very little research attention. An exception is Grote and Frieze's (1998) research, which suggests that this kind of love may increase over time.

In conclusion, as stated earlier, most of the research on the course of love over time is limited to cross-sectional comparisons, correlations with relationship length, or people's recall of love experienced at various stages of their relationship. Huston's (2009) extensive longitudinal study is a notable exception. An important next step will be to conduct similar kinds of longitudinal investigations in which measures for each of the specific types of love (i.e., romantic–passionate, companionate, compassionate) are included.

Neurological Correlates of Love

Initial research on the neurological correlates of love focused on brain activity during the early falling-in-love stage of relationships. More recent research has examined the neurological correlates of romantic, passionate love in longer term relationships as well (see Aron et al., 2013, for a review). The most common paradigm is for researchers to show participants a photograph of their loved one (vs. a nonromantic other, such as a friend) in an functional MRI scanner while the scanner records changes in blood flow to various regions of the brain. For example, Bartels and Zeki (2000) examined the brain activation of people who reported being truly, deeply, and madly in love. They found greater activity in the caudate nucleus, the dopamine-rich reward center of the brain, when participants looked at a photograph of their loved one than when they looked at a photograph of a friend. Aron et al. (2005) replicated these results with a sample of participants who had recently and very intensely fallen in love. These

researchers also found evidence of activation of the right ventral tegmental area, the region of the brain involved in manufacturing and distributing dopamine (Aron et al., 2005).

Gender Differences in the Experience of Love

Do women and men experience love differently? The answer depends on the kind of love.

Romantic–passionate love. In a recent study, Ackerman, Griskevicius, and Li (2011) approached women and men on the street and asked them two questions: "Who normally says they are in love *first* in romantic relationships?" and "In a new relationship, who thinks about getting serious first?" Nearly two thirds of participants (64.4%) responded "women" to the first question; 84.4% of participants responded "women" to the second question. In a follow-up study, the researchers asked participants (undergraduates) to recall a heterosexual romantic relationship in which love was expressed and to indicate who had done so first and at what point in the relationship. Nearly two thirds (61.2%) of the sample reported that the man had expressed love first. Men also reported having thought about confessing love significantly earlier in the relationship (on average, 42 days earlier) than did women (Ackerman et al., 2011). Findings in other studies have been mixed. For example, Galperin and Haselton (2010) did not find gender differences in reports of who fell in love first when the question was asked of an online sample. However, men reported a greater number of love-at-first-sight experiences than did women (although this effect became nonsignificant when controlling for sex drive). These researchers also examined whether men would report having fallen in love more quickly than women. They found this gender difference only for the subset of men who valued physical attractiveness and had managed to find a highly attractive partner.

In another program of research, Riela, Rodriguez, Aron, Xu, and Acevedo (2010) asked university students in the United States and China to describe a recent falling-in-love experience. Overall, few gender differences were found in these accounts. K. L. Dion and Dion (1973; see also K. K. Dion & Dion, 1973) found that women were more likely than men to report having experienced romantic love, but the sexes did not differ in the frequency of romantic love experiences (see Galperin & Haselton, 2010, for other examples of mixed findings).

When the experience of love is assessed with the Passionate Love Scale, gender differences are generally not significant (e.g., Aron & Henkemeyer, 1995; Fehr, Gouriluk, & Harasymchuk, 2010; Hatfield & Sprecher, 1986; Sprecher & Regan, 1998). There are a few exceptions. For example, Grote and Frieze (1994, Study 2) found that men in dating relationships scored lower on the Passionate Love Scale than did women. Ng and Cheng (2010) found just the opposite when they administered Sternberg's (1997) Passion scale to a Chinese sample—namely, that men scored higher than did women.

Thus, studies that have examined gender differences in the experience of romantic–passionate love have either found that men are more prone to falling in love and do so more quickly or that there are no gender differences. Similarly, studies assessing the experience of this kind of love using the Passionate Love Scale have usually not found gender differences. Thus, the stereotype that women are more caught up with passion and romance than are men does not seem to contain a kernel of truth. Nevertheless, as Ackerman et al.'s (2011) findings show, the stereotype continues to persist.

Companionate love.   In a study by Sprecher and Regan (1998), women in dating and marital relationships reported experiencing greater companionate love than did men. Grote and Frieze (1994) found that married women scored higher on their Friendship-Based Love Scale than did married men. However, no gender difference was obtained in a dating sample (Grote & Frieze, 1994, Study 2). Consistent with this latter finding, Fehr et al. (2010) did not find a gender difference on Sprecher and Regan's measure of companionate love in a dating sample. In short, when gender differences are found, they are generally in the direction of women

experiencing higher levels of companionate love for their partner.

Compassionate love.   Fehr and colleagues have administered the Compassionate Love Scale (completed with respect to one's partner) to participants in dating relationships (Fehr et al., 2010) and in marital relationships (Fehr & Harasymchuk, 2010). Women and men did not differ significantly in these samples.

To return to the question of whether women and men experience love differently, if the kind of love the questioner has in mind is romantic–passionate love, the answer is generally no, but when differences occur, it is men who are the more romantic sex. If the question is asked with respect to companionate love, the answer is yes, with women experiencing this kind of love to a greater extent than men when gender differences are found. Finally, if the question is whether women and men differ in the experience of compassionate love, the research conducted so far suggests that the answer is no.

Culture and the Experience of Love

The culture in which people are raised has important implications for how they experience love. In most studies, comparisons have been made between collectivistic and individualistic cultures.

Romantic–passionate love.   In a recent review and analysis of measures of romantic–passionate love, Hatfield, Bensman, and Rapson (2012) pointed out that in early research, it was assumed that passionate love was a Western phenomenon. However, that assumption has been called into question. For example, when Jankowiak and Fischer (1992; Jankowiak, 1995) reviewed anthropological data (e.g., songs and folklore) gathered from 166 societies, they found evidence for romantic love in 147 of them. Turning to sociological and psychological studies, in Sprecher et al.'s (1994) cross-cultural investigation, more Russian participants reported being currently in love than either American or Japanese participants. However, when asked how many times they had been in love, Japanese participants reported a significantly higher number than either the American or the Russian participants. To further complicate matters, the percentage of Japanese participants who reported that they had never been in love was also significantly higher than in the other two groups. In a more recent study, Fisher, Tsapelas, and Aron (2008) found that more American university students (71%) responded that they were currently in love than did Japanese university students (53%). However, slightly more Japanese (96%) than Americans (89%) reported having been in love in the past. In another recent study, White and Asian university students in the United States and university students in China did not differ significantly in reports of the number of times they had fallen in love (Riela et al., 2010, Study 2).

Riela et al. (2010) also asked White Americans and Asian Americans (Study 1) and, in a second study, university students in the United States and in China to describe their most recent experience of falling in love. These accounts were coded in terms of 12 precursors of falling in love gleaned from the literature (e.g., arousal, familiarity, reciprocal liking, filling needs, personality, social influence). In Study 1, only one significant difference was found—namely, that White Americans were more likely to mention arousal than were Asian Americans. A number of cultural differences were found in the second study. However, in that study, the effect for arousal reversed, such that participants in China were more likely to mention this precursor than participants in the United States. The Chinese were also more likely to refer to reciprocal liking, personality, and filling needs than were Americans. Americans were more likely than Chinese to mention personality. Riela et al. suggested that the findings can be interpreted in terms of the individualism that characterizes the United States versus the collectivism that characterizes China. In other research by Reila and colleagues, falling-in-love accounts generated by European Americans, Mexican Americans, and Asian Americans were also coded in terms of these precursors. Few differences were found between these ethnic groups, consistent with the notion of acculturation (Aron et al., 2008).

Cultural differences have not been found when the experience of passionate love is assessed with the Passionate Love Scale. For example, Hatfield and Rapson (1987) found that the scores of European Americans (living in the mainland United States and in Hawaii) and Americans of Filipino and Japanese ancestry did not differ significantly on this scale. Similar results were obtained when University of Hawaii students of various ethnicities (European American, Japanese American, Pacific Islander, and Chinese American) completed the Passionate Love Scale, even though these groups differed in individualism–collectivism (Doherty, Hatfield, Thompson, & Choo, 1994; Kim & Hatfield, 2004).

Companionate love. Doherty et al. (1994) measured the experience of companionate love by combining Sternberg's (1997) Intimacy and Commitment scales. They did not find ethnocultural differences in samples of European Americans, Japanese Americans, Pacific Islanders, and Chinese Americans living in Hawaii.

Compassionate love. Whether the experience of compassionate love for one's romantic partner differs by culture has not received empirical attention. It is unclear whether cultural differences would be expected.

In conclusion, there are striking inconsistencies in findings when people in different cultures are asked questions about whether they are currently in love or how frequently they have been in love in the past. However, the felt experience of romantic–passionate love may be universal, as suggested by research showing that scores on the Passionate Love Scale tend not to vary cross-culturally. At the same time, there may be cultural specificity in terms of the extent to which obligations to family and other cultural factors affect this experience. On the basis of his review of cross-cultural literature, Goodwin (1999) reached the conclusion that "many aspects of 'Western' love are important in African and West Indian societies, but . . . the particular constellation of love beliefs and behaviors adopted is likely to be a complex synthesis of traditional beliefs, local considerations, and outside forces" (p. 65).

Relationship Implications of the Experience of Love: Satisfaction

The way in which people experience love plays an important role in determining how satisfied they are with their relationships. Once again, empirical investigations have focused on mainly romantic–passionate love.

Romantic–passionate love. The association between the experience of romantic–passionate love and relationship satisfaction has received extensive research attention (see Acevedo & Aron, 2009, and Fehr, 2013, for reviews). In studies that have used the Passionate Love Scale, correlations with satisfaction range from .02 to .65; correlations tend to be moderate to strong in magnitude when other measures of passionate love are administered (Fehr, 2013). Acevedo and Aron (2009) partitioned studies on the link between passionate love and satisfaction into those that examined short-term (mostly dating) relationships versus long-term relationships (conducted with middle-aged participants, typically married 10 years or more). Correlations between romantic–passionate love and satisfaction fell in the .40 to .69 range for both short-term and long-term relationships. Overall, it seems clear that the greater the romantic–passionate love experienced for a partner, the greater the happiness with the relationship.

Companionate love. In the few studies that have assessed the experience of companionate love (e.g., Sprecher et al., 1994; Sprecher & Regan, 1998; Traupmann et al., 1982), correlations with satisfaction vary widely ranging from .01 to .78 (see Fehr, 2013). Grote and Frieze (1994) obtained higher correlations between satisfaction and the experience of companionate love (assessed by their Friendship-Based Love Scale) than between satisfaction and passionate love (assessed by a revised Eros love-style scale and the Passionate Love Scale) in both married and dating samples. In Acevedo and Aron's (2009) meta-analysis, the average correlation between companionate love and satisfaction was .26 for people in short-term relationships and increased to .48 for those in long-term relationships. Thus, the association between companionate love and satisfaction seems especially strong for those whose relationships have stood the test of time.

Compassionate love. Fehr and colleagues obtained moderate to strong correlations between scores on the Compassionate Love Scale (completed with respect to one's partner) and measures of relationship satisfaction ($r = .52$ in a dating sample [Fehr et al., 2010]; $r = .67$ in a married sample [Fehr & Harasymchuk, 2010]).

To summarize, the more romantic–passionate love people experience for their partner, the happier they are in their relationship, regardless of its duration. Furthermore, higher levels of companionate and compassionate love are associated with greater relationship satisfaction. The relation between these latter kinds of love and satisfaction tends to be stronger for those in longer term marital relationships. It must be acknowledged that these findings are correlational. Relationship satisfaction may enhance love rather than the other way around. It is, of course, very likely that love and relationship satisfaction are reciprocally causal.

In their discussion of what makes for a satisfying relationship, S. S. Hendrick and Hendrick (1997) suggest that passionate love fuels sexual union and is likely to serve a short-term courtship function and to play a role in longer term bonding. They see companionate love as contributing to long-term bonding and the development of intimacy in a relationship (see Reis & Aron, 2008, for a similar view). Finally, "a touch of the all-giving unselfish love that is Agape would seem to lend potency" (p. 75) to both romantic–passionate love and companionate love as predictors of satisfaction.

Relationship Implications of the Experience of Love: Commitment

Surprisingly few studies have been conducted on the relation between love and commitment. However, the scant research that exists suggest that how much people love their partner plays an important role in how committed they are to him or her.

Romantic–passionate love. Sprecher and Regan (1998) obtained moderate correlations between scores on the Passionate Love Scale and a measure of commitment. Correlations were slightly weaker when passionate love was assessed using a single item. In a recent study by Gonzaga, Turner, Keltner, Campos, and Altemus (2006), dating couples' reports of romantic love and commitment were also moderately correlated. Similarly, scores on the Passion and Commitment scales of the Triangular Love Scale are usually moderately to strongly correlated (e.g., Acker & Davis, 1992; Overbeek, Ha, Scholte, de Kemp, & Engels, 2007; Sternberg, 1997), although these scales have been criticized for a high degree of item overlap.

Companionate love. The relation between companionate love and commitment has rarely been investigated. An exception is a study by Sprecher and Regan (1998), who obtained moderate correlations between companionate love and commitment ($r = .57$ for men; $r = .52$ for women). However, the magnitude of the correlations decreased, especially for women, when companionate love was assessed with a single item ($r = .40$ for men; $r = .14$ for women).

Compassionate love. The relation between the experience of compassionate love for one's partner and commitment has also been underresearched. Fehr, Harasymchuk, and Sprecher (2014) obtained a correlation of .71 between compassionate love experienced for a dating partner and commitment to him or her.

In summary, the literature on the link between love and commitment is sparse. However, the research conducted so far has suggested that the greater the romantic–passionate love, companionate love, and compassionate love experienced for a partner, the greater the commitment to the relationship.

Experience of Love and Relationship Deterioration and Dissolution

The loss of love is a commonly given reason for the deterioration and dissolution of relationships (Berscheid, 2010). Once again, most of the research has focused on romantic–passionate love.

The Boston Couples Study (Hill, Rubin, & Peplau, 1976; Rubin et al., 1981) was perhaps the first to empirically examine the role of romantic love in relationship dissolution. In this investigation, more than 200 dating couples completed Rubin's Love Scale in Spring 1972 and again in Spring 1973. By then, approximately one third of the couples had experienced the dissolution of their relationship. The love scores of the couples who remained together were high at both time points. The couples whose relationships ended started out virtually as

high on the measure of love as did the intact couples, but their scores were dramatically lower at Time 2 (when the Love Scale was completed with respect to their former partner).

The power of love, relative to other relationship qualities, in predicting relationship dissolution was tested by Attridge, Berscheid, and Simpson (1995). In this study, 120 dating couples provided assessments of 16 relationship dimensions (e.g., investment, commitment, closeness), including love (assessed with Rubin's Love Scale). Six months later, the participants reported on their relationship status and, if the relationship had dissolved, on the degree of emotional distress experienced. Love was a significant predictor of relationship stability for both women and men. For those whose relationships had ended, the greater the feelings of love for their partner, the greater the emotional distress experienced after the breakup (although this effect was significant only for men). Similar findings were obtained in a recent program of research in which participants in ongoing dating relationships were compared with those who had recently experienced the dissolution of a dating relationship (Sbarra, 2006; Sbarra & Emery, 2005). All participants completed daily diaries of their moods and other states over a 27-day period. Those in intact dating relationships had higher love scores (on Rubin's scale) throughout the study than those whose relationships had ended. The latter showed a linear decrease in love over time. Those whose relationships ended also displayed more within-person variability in love and other emotional states, particularly during the 1st week after the breakup. Consistent with Attridge et al.'s findings, participants who experienced high levels of love for their former partner reported more emotional intrusion of the breakup experience and less relief and acceptance of the breakup. These feelings persisted over the course of the study.

In a recent meta-analysis of 137 studies on nonmarital romantic dissolution, Le, Dove, Agnew, Korn, and Mutsu (2010) examined a plethora of relationship, individual difference, and external factors as predictors of dissolution. They found the largest effects for three variables: love, positive illusions, and commitment. More specifically, the greater the love, the more positive the illusions, and the greater the commitment to the partner, the lower the likelihood of a relationship ending. Thus, love is among a short list of variables that robustly predicts the dissolution of dating relationships.

In one of the most ambitious investigations of predictors of marital dissolution, Huston et al. (2001) conducted a 13-year longitudinal study in which 168 recently married couples provided extensive data on the nature of their courtship, self and partner's personalities, and the nature of their relationship. Feelings of love were assessed by the Love subscale of Braiker and Kelley's (1979) Relationship Questionnaire. Spouses who were happily married 13 years later had been more deeply in love as newlyweds than those who were not happily married. Interestingly, feelings of love were a less reliable predictor of marital dissolution. The happily married couples did report more love as newlyweds than those who got divorced early in the marriage (between 2 and 7 years). However, those who divorced later (after 7 years of marriage) were indistinguishable from the happily married group as newlyweds. Further analyses revealed that the later-divorcing group had whirlwind courtships that declined in intensity over the 1st year of marriage (Huston et al., 2001; see Huston, 2009, for a review).

Turning to studies that included measures of romantic–passionate love and companionate love, Grote and Frieze (1994) found that middle-aged adults who were married (or currently dating) reported more romantic–passionate love (assessed with a revised Eros scale) and companionate love (assessed with the Friendship-Based Love Scale) than those who were separated or divorced. In a subsequent study, the researchers had university students complete two measures of romantic–passionate love (a revised Eros scale and the Passionate Love Scale) and a measure of companionate love (Friendship-Based Love Scale) with respect to either a current partner or, for those who were not currently in a relationship, their most recent partner. Participants in intact relationships scored higher on all of these scales than those who responded with respect to a former partner (Grote & Frieze, 1994, Study 2).

To summarize, a loss of love—both romantic–passionate and companionate—is associated with the deterioration and dissolution of relationships, especially premarital relationships. More important, love holds its own as a predictor of the dissolution of premarital relationships, even when other important relationship variables such as closeness and commitment are taken into account. In the realm of marital relationships, love is a stronger predictor of a couple's relational happiness than whether they stay together. Considerable research has shown that external factors such as family pressure and investments such as having children or buying a house keep people in marriages, even if the relationship is highly dissatisfying (Johnson, Caughlin, & Huston, 1999). Presumably, this explains why love is a stronger predictor of marital satisfaction than marital dissolution.

FUTURE DIRECTIONS

As is evident from the research presented in this chapter, there is now an impressive body of work on love. Nevertheless, much still remains to be learned about this complex interpersonal emotion. As discussed next, Berscheid's (2006, 2010) quadrumvirate model holds great promise as a grand theory that can not only integrate extant research on love but also guide future research.

Integration of Models of Love

Despite attempts at integration, research on models or theories of love continues to feel somewhat scattered. Factor analyses of love scales tend to produce different results. This is due, in part, to different investigators including different measures in their analyses. Granted, in a few studies, the researchers concluded that there was evidence of a passionate love factor and a companionate love factor, consistent with Berscheid and Hatfield's (1974) original typology. However, Graham's (2011) recent factor analysis pointed to a general love factor. This finding runs counter to Berscheid's (2010) claim that love is not a single entity but comes in four basic forms. Until researchers begin to include measures of all four of these kinds of love in their analyses, it will not be possible to choose between these competing accounts. Unfortunately, there are barriers that prevent researchers from conducting such analyses. One obstacle is that the field still needs a well-validated companionate love scale. Some researchers use items from Rubin's Love Scale to assess this kind of love; others use his Liking Scale, and still others have combined Sternberg's Intimacy and Commitment scales. There has also been a paucity of scales that assess altruistic–compassionate love. The main measure has been the Agape love-style scale, which has been criticized because some items refer to extreme levels of self-sacrifice (Fehr, 2013). Sprecher and Fehr's (2005) Compassionate Love Scale is being used in more recent studies. Scores on the Agape love style scale and the Compassionate Love Scale are correlated in the .50 range, indicating that these are not identical measures (see Fehr et al., 2014). Finally, the need for a measure of attachment love is urgent. The scale that Berscheid and Beckes developed to assess this kind of love remains unpublished.

Graham's (2011) finding that measures of love loaded on a single factor has other sobering implications. When researchers administer the Passionate Love Scale, for example, they assume that they are measuring a different construct than when they administer Rubin's Liking scale or the Agape love-style scale. The fact that these scales load on the same factor raises the question of whether researchers are actually measuring distinguishable constructs. Given that different kinds of love tend to go together in people's relationship experience, it is extremely difficult to devise measurement instruments that are able to disentangle them. Berscheid (2010) articulated specific ways in which the kinds of love specified in her quadrumvirate model differ. However, these ideas cannot be tested until psychometrically strong measures of all four kinds of love are available.

Addressing an Imbalance

If research on love were portrayed as a produce farm, an aerial view would show a massive plot of corn, some potatoes, a narrow row of carrots, and a tiny band of beans. A chef looking to purchase vegetables for his or her "buy local" restaurant might be pleased to see the abundance of corn but worry about offering a menu that featured few other vegetables. Research on love has overwhelmingly focused on romantic–passionate love to the exclusion of the other varieties. Companionate love has received some attention since the beginning, but much less than passionate love. Compassionate love is a relative newcomer to the field. Research on attachment love is virtually nonexistent. This imbalance has important implications. To give just one example, there is compelling evidence that romantic–passionate love plays an important role in the deterioration and dissolution of relationships. However, Fehr (1988) found that people regard the loss of companionate aspects of love as more damaging to a relationship than a loss of passionate love. Although her research relied on scenario methodology, the findings suggest that the deterioration of other kinds of love may be even more crucial in predicting relationship stability.

It will also be important in future research to flesh out lay conceptions of all four kinds of love in Berscheid's (2006, 2010) typology. As discussed in this chapter, prototype analyses have been conducted for the concepts of romantic love and compassionate love. It would be beneficial to undertake prototype analyses of the other two kinds of love—namely, companionate love and attachment love. In addition to completing the picture, such analyses might be useful in illuminating areas of similarity as well as the features that are unique to each kind of love (at least as represented in the minds of ordinary people). The social categorization approach to love should also be extended to the other kinds of love in Berscheid's taxonomy. This approach holds promise as another means of differentiating between kinds of love. Meyers and Berscheid (1997) found that people listed fewer names for the in-love category than for the love category. The set of people for whom one feels attachment love, for example, might also be small but might not necessarily overlap with the in-love category. Given that compassionate love can be experienced for strangers, all of humanity, and close others (Fehr & Sprecher, 2013), this might be the largest social category. Once again, research along these lines would contribute to a more balanced study of love and potentially elucidate areas of overlap and differentiation between the kinds of love articulated in the quadrumvirate model.

Culture and Love

It is difficult to extract a clear bottom line from the research on cultural differences in love. When the Passionate Love Scale is administered, it appears that the experience of passionate love is universal. However, when this kind of love is assessed by asking participants whether they are currently in love, whether they have ever been in love, or how many times they have fallen in love, the findings are highly inconsistent from one study to the next. It is possible that these sorts of questions are interpreted differently in different cultures. It is also possible that only people in individualistic cultures keep a tally of how many times they have been in love. Even within a culture, some people might answer such a question by recounting childhood crushes; others may assume that the question refers to experiences in late adolescence or early adulthood.

The focus on romantic–passionate love in this area of research seems particularly shortsighted given that people in collectivistic cultures may place the greatest emphasis on companionate love (K. L. Dion & Dion, 1993). It therefore seems imperative that cross-cultural research expand beyond the current emphasis on romantic–passionate love to examine companionate love and the other two kinds of love identified in Berscheid's (2006, 2010) typology.

In conclusion, presidents of the American Psychological Association can no longer lament, as Harry Harlow did, that psychologists seem unaware of love. Indeed, the fact that this *APA Handbook of Personality and Social Psychology* contains a chapter on love is a testament to the phenomenal progress that has been made since Harlow's 1958 address. Psychologists and other social scientists are now in a position to give informed answers to fundamental questions regarding what love is and why it matters.

References

Acevedo, B. P., & Aron, A. (2009). Does a long-term relationship kill romantic love? *Review of General Psychology, 13,* 59–65. doi:10.1037/a0014226

Acker, M., & Davis, M. H. (1992). Intimacy, passion and commitment in adult romantic relationships: A test of the triangular theory of love. *Journal of Social and Personal Relationships, 9,* 21–50. doi:10.1177/0265407592091002

Ackerman, J. M., Griskevicius, V., & Li, N. P. (2011). Let's get serious: Communicating commitment in romantic relationships. *Journal of Personality and Social Psychology, 100,* 1079–1094. doi:10.1037/a0022412

Adams, G., Anderson, S. L., & Adonu, J. K. (2004). The cultural grounding of closeness and intimacy. In D. J. Mashek & A. P. Aron (Eds.), *Handbook of closeness and intimacy* (pp. 321–339). Mahwah, NJ: Erlbaum.

Aron, A., Fisher, H., Mashek, D. J., Strong, G., Li, H., & Brown, L. L. (2005). Reward, motivation, and emotion systems associated with early-stage intense romantic love. *Journal of Neurophysiology, 94,* 327–337. doi:10.1152/jn.00838.2004

Aron, A., Fisher, H. E., Strong, G., Acevedo, B., Riela, S., & Tsapelas, I. (2008). Falling in love. In S. Sprecher, A. Wenzel, & J. Harvey (Eds.), *Handbook of relationship initiation* (pp. 315–336). New York, NY: Psychology Press.

Aron, A., & Henkemeyer, L. (1995). Marital satisfaction and passionate love. *Journal of Social and Personal Relationships, 12,* 139–146. doi:10.1177/0265407595121010

Aron, A., Lewandowski, G. W., Mashek, D., & Aron, E. (2013). The self-expansion model of motivation and cognition in close relationships. In J. A. Simpson & L. Campbell (Eds.), *Oxford handbook of close relationships* (pp. 90–115). New York, NY: Oxford University Press. doi:10.1002/9780470998557.ch19

Aron, A., & Westbay, L. (1996). Dimensions of the prototype of love. *Journal of Personality and Social Psychology, 70,* 535–551. doi:10.1037/0022-3514.70.3.535

Attridge, M., Berscheid, E., & Simpson, J. A. (1995). Predicting relationship stability from both partners versus one. *Journal of Personality and Social Psychology, 69,* 254–268. doi:10.1037/0022-3514.69.2.254

Bartels, A., & Zeki, S. (2000). The neural basis of romantic love. *NeuroReport, 11,* 3829–3834. doi:10.1097/00001756-200011270-00046

Baumeister, R. F., & Bratslavsky, E. (1999). Passion, intimacy, and time: Passionate love as a function of change in intimacy. *Personality and Social Psychology Review, 3,* 49–67. doi:10.1207/s15327957pspr0301_3

Berscheid, E. (2006). Searching for the meaning of "love." In R. J. Sternberg & K. Weis (Eds.), *The new psychology of love* (pp. 171–183). New Haven, CT: Yale University Press.

Berscheid, E. (2010). Love in the fourth dimension. *Annual Review of Psychology, 61,* 1–25. doi:10.1146/annurev.psych.093008.100318

Berscheid, E., & Hatfield, E. (1974). A little bit about love. In T. L. Huston (Ed.), *Foundations of interpersonal attraction* (pp. 157–215). New York, NY: Academic Press.

Braiker, H. B., & Kelley, H. H. (1979). Conflict in the development of close relationships. In R. L. Burgess & T. L. Huston (Eds.), *Social exchange in developing relationships* (pp. 135–168). New York, NY: Academic Press.

Buss, D. M. (1988). Love acts: The evolutionary biology of love. In R. J. Sternberg & M. L. Barnes (Eds.), *The psychology of love* (pp. 100–118). New Haven, CT: Yale University Press.

Buss, D. M., Abbott, M., Angleitner, A., Asherian, A., Biaggio, A., Blanco-Villasenor, A., . . . Yang, K. (1990). International preferences in selecting mates: A study of 37 cultures. *Journal of Cross-Cultural Psychology, 21*, 5–47. doi:10.1177/0022022190211001

Button, C. M., & Collier, D. R. (1991, June). *A comparison of people's concepts of love and romantic love.* Paper presented at the Canadian Psychological Association Conference, Calgary, Alberta, Canada.

Cho, W., & Cross, S. E. (1995). Taiwanese love styles and their association with self-esteem and relationship quality. *Genetic, Social, and General Psychology Monographs, 121*, 281–309.

Contreras, R., Hendrick, S. S., & Hendrick, C. (1996). Perspectives on marital love and satisfaction in Mexican American and Anglo-American couples. *Journal of Counseling and Development, 74*, 408–415. doi:10.1002/j.1556-6676.1996.tb01887.x

Davis, K. E., & Todd, M. J. (1982). Friendship and love relationships. In K. E. Davis & T. O. Mitchell (Eds.), *Advances in descriptive psychology* (Vol. 2, pp. 79–122). London, England: Jessica Kingsley.

Davis, K. E., & Todd, M. J. (1985). Assessing friendship: Prototypes, paradigm cases and relationship description. In S. Duck & D. Perlman (Eds.), *Understanding personal relationships: An interdisciplinary approach* (pp. 17–38). Thousand Oaks, CA: Sage.

Dion, K. K., & Dion, K. L. (1993). Individualistic and collectivistic perspectives on gender and the cultural context of love and intimacy. *Journal of Social Issues, 49*, 53–69. doi:10.1111/j.1540-4560.1993.tb01168.x

Dion, K. K., & Dion, K. L. (1996). Cultural perspectives on romantic love. *Personal Relationships, 3*, 5–17. doi:10.1111/j.1475-6811.1996.tb00101.x

Dion, K. K., & Dion, K. L. (2001). Gender and cultural adaptation in immigrant families. *Journal of Social Issues, 57*, 511–521. doi:10.1111/0022-4537.00226

Dion, K. L., & Dion, K. K. (1973). Correlates of romantic love. *Journal of Consulting and Clinical Psychology, 41*, 51–56. doi:10.1037/h0035571

Dion, K. L., & Dion, K. K. (1993). Gender and ethnocultural comparisons in styles of love. *Psychology of Women Quarterly, 17*, 463–473. doi:10.1111/j.1471-6402.1993.tb00656.x

Doherty, W. R., Hatfield, E., Thompson, K., & Choo, P. (1994). Cultural and ethnic influences on love and attachment. *Personal Relationships, 1*, 391–398. doi:10.1111/j.1475-6811.1994.tb00072.x

Fehr, B. (1988). Prototype analysis of the concepts of love and commitment. *Journal of Personality and Social Psychology, 55*, 557–579. doi:10.1037/0022-3514.55.4.557

Fehr, B. (1993). How do I love thee . . . ? Let me consult my prototype. In S. Duck (Ed.), *Understanding personal relationships: Vol. 1. Individuals in relationships* (pp. 87–120). Newbury Park, CA: Sage.

Fehr, B. (1994). Prototype-based assessment of laypeople's views of love. *Personal Relationships, 1*, 309–331. doi:10.1111/j.1475-6811.1994.tb00068.x

Fehr, B. (1996). *Friendship processes.* Thousand Oaks, CA: Sage.

Fehr, B. (2001). The status of theory and research on love and commitment. In G. J. O. Fletcher & M. S. Clark (Eds.), *Blackwell handbook of social psychology: Interpersonal processes* (pp. 331–356). Oxford, England: Blackwell.

Fehr, B. (2005). The role of prototypes in interpersonal cognition. In M. Baldwin (Ed.), *Interpersonal cognition* (pp. 180–205). New York, NY: Guilford Press.

Fehr, B. (2006). A prototype approach to studying love. In R. J. Sternberg & K. Weis (Eds.), *The new psychology of love* (pp. 225–246). New Haven, CT: Yale University Press.

Fehr, B. (2013). The social psychology of love. In J. A. Simpson & L. Campbell (Eds.), *Oxford handbook of close relationships* (pp. 201–233). New York, NY: Oxford University Press.

Fehr, B., & Broughton, R. (2001). Gender and personality differences in conceptions of love: An interpersonal theory analysis. *Personal Relationships, 8*, 115–136. doi:10.1111/j.1475-6811.2001.tb00031.x

Fehr, B., Gouriluk, J., & Harasymchuk, C. (2010, June). *Validation of the quadrumvirate model of love.* Paper presented at the Social Psychology Faculty Symposium on Romantic Relationships, Canadian Psychological Association Conference, Winnipeg, Manitoba, Canada.

Fehr, B., & Harasymchuk, C. (2010, June). *Love.* Invited paper presented at the Canadian Psychological Association Conference, Winnipeg, Manitoba, Canada.

Fehr, B., Harasymchuk, C., & Sprecher, S. (2014). *Compassionate love in romantic relationships: A review and some new findings.* Manuscript submitted for publication.

Fehr, B., & Russell, J. A. (1984). Concept of emotion viewed from a prototype perspective. *Journal of Experimental Psychology: General, 113*, 464–486. doi:10.1037/0096-3445.113.3.464

Fehr, B., & Russell, J. A. (1991). The concept of love viewed from a prototype perspective. *Journal of Personality and Social Psychology, 60*, 425–438. doi:10.1037/0022-3514.60.3.425

Fehr, B., & Sprecher, S. (2003, May). *Prototype analysis of compassionate love*. Paper presented at the Conference on Compassionate Love, Normal, IL.

Fehr, B., & Sprecher, S. (2009). Prototype analysis of compassionate love. *Personal Relationships, 16*, 343–364. doi:10.1111/j.1475-6811.2009.01227.x

Fehr, B., & Sprecher, S. (2013). Compassionate love: What we know so far. In M. Hojjat & D. Cramer (Eds.), *Positive psychology of love* (pp. 106–120). New York, NY: Oxford University Press.

Fehr, B., Sprecher, S., & Underwood, L. (Eds.). (2009). *The science of compassionate love: Theory, research, and applications*. Malden, MA: Wiley-Blackwell.

Felmlee, D., & Sprecher, S. (2006). Love: Psychological and sociological perspectives. In J. E. Stets & J. H. Turner (Eds.), *Handbook of sociology of emotions* (pp. 389–409). New York, NY: Springer. doi:10.1007/978-0-387-30715-2_18

Fisher, H. E., Tsapelas, I., & Aron, A. (2008). *Romantic love in the United States and Japan*. Manuscript in preparation.

Fiske, A., Kitayama, S., Markus, H., & Nisbett, R. E. (1998). The cultural matrix of social psychology. In D. T. Gilbert, S. T. Fiske, & G. Lindzey (Eds.), *The handbook of social psychology* (4th ed., Vols. *1 & 2*, pp. 915–981). New York, NY: McGraw-Hill.

Fitness, J., & Fletcher, G. J. O. (1993). Love, hate, anger, and jealousy in close relationships: A prototype and cognitive appraisal analysis. *Journal of Personality and Social Psychology, 65*, 942–958. doi:10.1037/0022-3514.65.5.942

Galperin, A., & Haselton, M. (2010). Predictors of how often and when people fall in love. *Evolutionary Psychology, 8*, 5–28.

Gonzaga, G. C., Turner, R. A., Keltner, D., Campos, B., & Altemus, M. (2006). Romantic love and sexual desire in close relationships. *Emotion, 6*, 163–179. doi:10.1037/1528-3542.6.2.163

Goodwin, R. (1999). *Personal relationships across cultures*. London, England: Routledge.

Goodwin, R., & Findlay, C. (1997). "We were just fated together": Chinese love and the concept of yuan in England and Hong Kong. *Personal Relationships, 4*, 85–92. doi:10.1111/j.1475-6811.1997.tb00132.x

Graber, D. R., & Mitcham, M. D. (2009). Compassionate clinicians: Exemplary care in hospital settings. In B. Fehr, S. Sprecher, & L. G. Underwood (Eds.), *The science of compassionate love: Theory, research, and applications* (pp. 345–372). Malden, MA: Wiley-Blackwell. doi:10.1002/9781444303070.ch12

Graham, J. M. (2011). Measuring love in romantic relationships: A meta-analysis. *Journal of Social and Personal Relationships, 28*, 748–771. doi:10.1177/0265407510389126

Gray, J. (1992). *Men are from Mars, women are from Venus: A practical guide for improving communication and getting what you want in your relationships*. New York, NY: HarperCollins.

Grote, N., & Frieze, I. (1994). The measurement of friendship-based love in intimate relationships. *Personal Relationships, 1*, 275–300. doi:10.1111/j.1475-6811.1994.tb00066.x

Grote, N. K., & Frieze, I. H. (1998). "Remembrance of things past": Perceptions of marital love from its beginnings to the present. *Journal of Social and Personal Relationships, 15*, 91–109. doi:10.1177/0265407598151006

Harlow, H. F. (1958). The nature of love. *American Psychologist, 13*, 673–685. doi:10.1037/h0047884

Hatfield, E., Bensman, L., & Rapson, R. (2012). A brief history of social scientists' attempts to measure passionate love. *Journal of Social and Personal Relationships, 29*, 143–164.

Hatfield, E., & Rapson, R. L. (1987). Passionate love/sexual desire: Can the same paradigm explain both? *Archives of Sexual Behavior, 16*, 259–278. doi:10.1007/BF01541613

Hatfield, E., & Sprecher, S. (1986). Measuring passionate love in intimate relationships. *Journal of Adolescence, 9*, 383–410. doi:10.1016/S0140-1971(86)80043-4

Hatfield, E., Traupmann, J., & Sprecher, S. (1984). Older women's perception of their intimate relationships. *Journal of Social and Clinical Psychology, 2*, 108–124.

Hatfield, E., & Walster, G. W. (1978). *A new look at love*. Lanham, MD: University Press of America.

Hazan, C., & Shaver, P. (1987). Romantic love conceptualized as an attachment process. *Journal of Personality and Social Psychology, 52*, 511–524. doi:10.1037/0022-3514.52.3.511

Heaven, P. L., Da Silva, T., Carey, C., & Holen, J. (2004). Loving styles: Relationships with personality and attachment styles. *European Journal of Personality, 18*, 103–113. doi:10.1002/per.498

Hendrick, C., & Hendrick, S. (1986). A theory and method of love. *Journal of Personality and Social Psychology, 50*, 392–402. doi:10.1037/0022-3514.50.2.392

Hendrick, C., & Hendrick, S. S. (1989). Research on love: Does it measure up? *Journal of Personality and Social Psychology, 56*, 784–794. doi:10.1037/0022-3514.56.5.784

Hendrick, C., & Hendrick, S. S. (1990). A relationship-specific version of the Love Attitudes Scale. *Journal of Social Behavior and Personality, 5*, 239–254.

Hendrick, S. S., & Hendrick, C. (1997). Love and satisfaction. In R. J. Sternberg & M. Hojjat (Eds.), *Satisfaction in close relationships* (pp. 56–78). New York, NY: Guilford Press.

Hill, C. T., Rubin, Z., & Peplau, L. A. (1976). Breakups before marriage: The end of 103 affairs. *Journal of Social Issues, 32,* 147–168.

Huston, T. L. (2009). What's love got to do with it? Why some marriages succeed and others fail. *Personal Relationships, 16,* 301–327. doi:10.1111/j.1475-6811.2009.01225.x

Huston, T. L., Caughlin, J. P., Houts, R. M., Smith, S. E., & George, L. J. (2001). The connubial crucible: Newlywed years as predictors of marital delight, distress, and divorce. *Journal of Personality and Social Psychology, 80,* 237–252. doi:10.1037/0022-3514.80.2.237

Jankowiak, W. (1995). Introduction. In W. Jankowiak (Ed.), *Romantic passion: A universal experience* (pp. 1–19). New York, NY: Columbia University Press.

Jankowiak, W. R., & Fischer, E. F. (1992). A cross-cultural perspective on romantic love. *Ethnology, 31,* 149–155.

Johnson, M. P., Caughlin, J. P., & Huston, T. L. (1999). The tripartite nature of marital commitment: Personal, moral, and structural reasons to stay married. *Journal of Marriage and the Family, 61,* 160–177. doi:10.2307/353891

Kanemasa, Y., Taniguchi, J., Daibo, I., & Ishimori, M. (2004). Love styles and romantic love experiences in Japan. *Social Behavior and Personality, 32,* 265–282. doi:10.2224/sbp.2004.32.3.265

Kephart, W. M. (1967). Some correlates of romantic love. *Journal of Marriage and the Family, 29,* 470–474. doi:10.2307/349585

Khallad, Y. (2005). Mate selection in Jordan: Effects of sex, socio-economic status, and culture. *Journal of Social and Personal Relationships, 22,* 155–168. doi:10.1177/0265407505050940

Kim, J., & Hatfield, E. (2004). Love types and subjective well-being: A cross-cultural study. *Social Behavior and Personality, 32,* 173–182. doi:10.2224/sbp.2004.32.2.173

Kline, S. L., Horton, B., & Zhang, S. (2008). Communicating love: Comparisons between American and East Asian university students. *International Journal of Intercultural Relations, 32,* 200–214. doi:10.1016/j.ijintrel.2008.01.006

Lamm, H., & Wiesmann, U. (1997). Subjective attributes of attraction: How people characterize their liking, their love, and their being in love. *Personal Relationships, 4,* 271–284. doi:10.1111/j.1475-6811.1997.tb00145.x

Le, B., Dove, N. L., Agnew, C. R., Korn, M. S., & Mutsu, A. A. (2010). Predicting nonmarital romantic relationship dissolution: A meta-analytic synthesis. *Personal Relationships, 17,* 377–390. doi:10.1111/j.1475-6811.2010.01285.x

Lee, J. A. (1973). *The colors of love: An exploration of the ways of loving.* Don Mills, Ontario, Canada: New Press.

Levine, R., Sato, S., Hashimoto, T., & Verma, J. (1995). Love and marriage in eleven cultures. *Journal of Cross-Cultural Psychology, 26,* 554–571. doi:10.1177/0022022195265007

Luby, V., & Aron, A. (1990, July). *A prototype structuring of love, like, and being-in-love.* Paper presented at the Fifth International Conference on Personal Relationships, Oxford, England.

Masuda, M. (2003). Meta-analyses of love scales: Do various love scales measure the same psychological constructs? *Japanese Psychological Research, 45,* 25–37. doi:10.1111/1468-5884.00030

Mervis, C. B., & Rosch, E. (1981). Categorization of natural objects. *Annual Review of Psychology, 32,* 89–115. doi:10.1146/annurev.ps.32.020181.000513

Meyers, S. A., & Berscheid, E. (1997). The language of love: The difference a preposition makes. *Personality and Social Psychology Bulletin, 23,* 347–362. doi:10.1177/0146167297234002

Mikulincer, M., & Shaver, P. R. (2007). *Attachment in adulthood: Structure, dynamics, and change.* New York, NY: Guilford Press.

Mikulincer, M., Shaver, P. R., & Gillath, O. (2009). A behavioral systems perspective on compassionate love. In B. Fehr, S. Sprecher, & L. G. Underwood (Eds.), *The science of compassionate love: Theory, research, and applications* (pp. 225–256). New York, NY: Wiley.

Neto, F., Mullet, E., Deschamps, J., Barros, J., Benvindo, R., Camino, L., . . . Machado, M. (2000. Cross-cultural variations in attitudes toward love. *Journal of Cross-Cultural Psychology, 31,* 626–635. doi:10.1177/0022022100031005005

Overbeek, G., Ha, T., Scholte, R., de Kemp, R., & Engels, R. C. M. E. (2007). Brief report: Intimacy, passion, and commitment in romantic relationships—Validation of a "triangular love scale" for adolescents. *Journal of Adolescence, 30,* 523–258. doi:10.1016/j.adolescence.2006.12.002

Regan, P. C., Kocan, E. R., & Whitlock, T. (1998). Ain't love grand! A prototype analysis of the concept of romantic love. *Journal of Social and Personal Relationships, 15,* 411–420. doi:10.1177/0265407598153006

Reis, H. T., & Aron, A. (2008). Love: What is it, why does it matter, and how does it operate? *Perspectives on Psychological Science, 3,* 80–86.

Riela, S., Rodriguez, G., Aron, A., Xu, X., & Acevedo, B. P. (2010). Experiences of falling in love: Investigating culture, ethnicity, gender, and speed. *Journal of Social and Personal Relationships, 27,* 473–493. doi:10.1177/0265407510363508

Rosch, E. H. (1973a). Natural categories. *Cognitive Psychology, 4,* 328–350. doi:10.1016/0010-0285(73)90017-0

Rosch, E. H. (1973b). On the internal structure of perceptual and semantic categories. In T. E. Moore (Ed.), *Cognitive development and the acquisition of language* (pp. 111–144). New York, NY: Academic Press.

Rubin, Z. (1970). Measurement of romantic love. *Journal of Personality and Social Psychology, 16,* 265–273. doi:10.1037/h0029841

Rubin, Z. (1973). *Liking and loving.* New York, NY: Holt, Rinehart & Winston.

Rubin, Z., Peplau, L. A., & Hill, C. T. (1981). Loving and leaving: Sex differences in romantic attachments. *Sex Roles, 7,* 821–835.

Sbarra, D. A. (2006). Predicting the onset of emotional recovery following nonmarital relationship dissolution: Survival analyses of sadness and anger. *Personality and Social Psychology Bulletin, 32,* 298–312. doi:10.1177/0146167205280913

Sbarra, D. A., & Emery, R. E. (2005). The emotional sequelae of nonmarital relationship dissolution: Analysis of change and intraindividual variability over time. *Personal Relationships, 12,* 213–232. doi:10.1111/j.1350-4126.2005.00112.x

Shacham-Dupont, S. (2003). Compassion and love in relationships—Can they coexist? *Relationship Research News, 2,* 13–15.

Shaver, P., Schwartz, J., Kirson, D., & O'Connor, C. (1987). Emotion knowledge: Further exploration of a prototype approach. *Journal of Personality and Social Psychology, 52,* 1061–1086. doi:10.1037/0022-3514.52.6.1061

Simmons, C. H., vom Kolke, A., & Shimizu, H. (1986). Attitudes toward romantic love among American, German, and Japanese students. *Journal of Social Psychology, 126,* 327–336.

Simpson, J. A., Campbell, B., & Berscheid, E. (1986). The association between romantic love and marriage: Kephart (1967) twice revisited. *Personality and Social Psychology Bulletin, 12,* 363–372. doi:10.1177/0146167286123011

Simpson, J. A., & Rholes, W. S. (2012). Adult attachment orientations, stress, and romantic relationships. In P. Devine & A. Plant (Eds.), *Advances in experimental social psychology* (Vol. 45, pp. 279–328). San Diego, CA: Academic Press.

Sprecher, S., Aron, A., Hatfield, E., Cortese, A., Potapova, E., & Levitskaya, A. (1994). Love: American style, Russian style and Japanese style. *Personal Relationships, 1,* 349–369. doi:10.1111/j.1475-6811.1994.tb00070.x

Sprecher, S., & Fehr, B. (2005). Compassionate love for close others and humanity. *Journal of Social and Personal Relationships, 22,* 629–651. doi:10.1177/0265407505056439

Sprecher, S., & Metts, S. (1989). Development of the "Romantic Beliefs Scale" and examination of the effects of gender and gender-role orientation. *Journal of Social and Personal Relationships, 6,* 387–411.

Sprecher, S., & Regan, P. C. (1998). Passionate and companionate love in courting and young married couples. *Sociological Inquiry, 68,* 163–185.

Sprecher, S., & Toro-Morn, M. (2002). A study of men and women from different sides of earth to determine if men are from Mars and women are from Venus in their beliefs about love and romantic relationships. *Sex Roles, 46,* 131–147. doi:10.1023/A:1019780801500

Sprecher, S., Zimmerman, C., & Abrahams, E. M. (2010). Choosing compassionate strategies to end a relationship: Effects of compassionate love and the reason for the breakup. *Social Psychology, 41,* 66–75. doi:10.1027/1864-9335/a000010

Sprecher, S., Zimmerman, C., & Fehr, B. (2014). The influence of compassionate love on strategies used to end a relationship. *Journal of Social and Personal Relationships.* Advance online publication. doi:10.1177/0265407513517958

Steck, L., Levitan, D., McLane, D., & Kelley, H. H. (1982). Care, need, and conceptions of love. *Journal of Personality and Social Psychology, 43,* 481–491. doi:10.1037/0022-3514.43.3.481

Sternberg, R. J. (1986). A triangular theory of love. *Psychological Review, 93,* 119–135. doi:10.1037/0033-295X.93.2.119

Sternberg, R. J. (1997). Construct validation of a triangular love scale. *European Journal of Social Psychology, 27,* 313–335.

Surra, C. A., & Bohman, T. (1991). The development of close relationships: A cognitive perspective. In G. O. Fletcher & F. D. Fincham (Eds.), *Cognition in close relationships* (pp. 281–305). Hillsdale, NJ: Erlbaum.

Traupmann, J., Eckels, E., & Hatfield, E. (1982). Intimacy in older women's lives. *Gerontologist, 22,* 493–498. doi:10.1093/geront/22.6.493

Tucker, P., & Aron, A. (1993). Passionate love and marital satisfaction at key transition points in the family life cycle. *Journal of Social and Clinical Psychology, 12,* 135–147.

Tzeng, O. S. (1993). *Measurement of love and intimate relations: Theories, scales, and applications for love development, maintenance, and dissolution.* Westport, CT: Praeger.

Wiederman, M. W., & Allgeier, E. R. (1992). Gender differences in mate selection criteria: Sociobiological or socioeconomic explanation? *Ethology and Sociobiology, 13,* 115–124. doi:10.1016/0162-3095(92)90021-U

Worobrey, J. (2001). Sex differences in associations of temperament with love-styles. *Psychological Reports, 89,* 25–26. doi:10.2466/PR0.89.5.25-26

CHAPTER 19

SEXUALITY AND SAME-SEX SEXUALITY IN RELATIONSHIPS

Lisa M. Diamond

Over the past 30 years, the field of relationship science has witnessed explosive growth with regard to both the breadth of topics studied and the increase in conceptual and methodological sophistication. Practically every aspect of coupled life has been scrutinized in the laboratory and in the field, including the initial spark of romantic attraction, scripts for relationship initiation, the time course of deepening intimacy, decisions about marriage and commitment, the day-to-day nuts and bolts of relationship maintenance, the dynamics and implications of conflict, and even the immediate and cumulative consequences of positive and negative relationship experiences for autonomic, neuroendocrine, and immunological functioning (see Diamond, Fagundes, & Butterworth, 2010, for a review).

Sexuality within intimate relationships, however, has not received the same exhaustive and rigorous attention. Although there is a long history of detailed, rigorous research on sexual processes and functioning in the fields of clinical psychology, sexology, and sexual medicine, most of this research has focused on individual experiences of sexuality rather than sexuality as a fundamentally dyadic phenomenon that shapes—and is shaped by—the underlying dynamics of a couple's relationship. Yet clearly, sexuality serves diverse and critical functions at every stage of coupledom. Early on, sexuality fosters the development of intimacy and attachment between new partners (Hazan & Zeifman, 1994). As a relationship develops, sexuality provides a means for expressing vulnerability, reassurance, responsiveness, reconciliation, and mutual

dependence; for enjoying and playing with one another; for dissipating tension and stress; for providing care and nurturance; for enacting and negotiating gender roles; and even for negotiating dominance and interdependence (Ridley, Ogolsky, Payne, Totenhagen, & Cate, 2008; Sprecher & McKinney, 1993).

Furthermore, the growing body of research on the health benefits of well-functioning close relationships has suggested that sexuality plays a key role here as well. As noted by David Satcher in his groundbreaking call to action on sexual health in 2001,

> Sexuality is an integral part of human life. . . . It can foster intimacy and bonding as well as shared pleasure in our relationships. It fulfills a number of personal and social needs. . . . Sexual health is inextricably bound to both physical and mental health. (p. 1)

This endorsement of the health-promoting aspects of sexuality stands in sharp contrast to historical public health perspectives that emphasized the risks and problems associated with sexuality, including sexually transmitted infections, unplanned pregnancies, and sexual assault and abuse. Hence, we appear to be in the midst of an emerging paradigm shift in perspectives on sexuality within intimate relationships, in which the importance, the predictors, and the benefits of healthy sexual functioning are finally receiving their due. In short, research on sexuality in intimate relationships is

http://dx.doi.org/10.1037/14344-019
APA Handbook of Personality and Social Psychology: Vol. 3. Interpersonal Relations, M. Mikulincer and P. R. Shaver (Editors-in-Chief)

finally catching up to research on other fundamental relationship processes.

In this chapter, I provide a comprehensive overview of this burgeoning area of inquiry and identify some of the most provocative and important directions for future research. The first half of the chapter focuses on sexuality in heterosexual couples (on whom the vast majority of research has focused), and the second half of the chapter turns attention to the unique issues and dynamics facing same-sex couples, with respect to both sexuality and other key relationship dynamics that are affected by marginalized sexual minority status.

NEGOTIATING SEXUAL SCRIPTS: THE ROLE OF GENDER

Critical to the understanding of sexuality within intimate relationships is an appreciation of sexual scripts (Simon & Gagnon, 1986), which can be thought of as blueprints or guidelines that structure an individual's sexual wishes, behaviors, fears, habits, fantasies, expectations, and modes of expression. Sexual scripts are influenced by parental socialization, social and community norms, cultural and religious beliefs, and idiosyncratic personal experiences. One of the chief developments in the sexual life of a new couple is the gradual negotiation of a shared sexual script, specifying appropriate and desirable sexual roles and practices that reflect and incorporate each partner's values and needs. Unfortunately, few couples engage in the sort of comprehensive and open self-disclosure about their sexual needs that is necessary for this negotiation to proceed smoothly (Byers, 2011). For example, one study found that even partners who had been together as long as 14 years had not completely disclosed their sexual desires and preferences to one another (MacNeil & Byers, 2009). As a result, misperceptions were common: Partners reported understanding only 62% of what their partner found pleasing and only 26% of what their partner found displeasing. In short, sex is not a "natural act," no matter how long a couple has been together. The development and maintenance of a mutually satisfying sexual script does not happen automatically for couples but involves considerable investments of time, patience, skill, generosity, accommodation, and communication.

Script negotiation becomes especially important—and especially difficult—when one or both partners struggle with sexual problems. Contrary to the notion that sexual problems are usually the domain of older individuals, studies have increasingly indicated that many young, unmarried men and women report experiencing periodic problems with sexual arousal, orgasm, premature ejaculation, and pain during sexual activity (O'Sullivan & Majerovich, 2008). For such individuals, script negotiation with a new partner—as well as script renegotiation with a long-standing partner, as needs and abilities change—is a delicate and difficult business. The introduction of any new activity, or any change in practice, necessarily involves "a certain amount of transgression" (Bozon, 2001, p. 3), leaving each partner vulnerable to rejection and disapproval. For this reason, individuals may prefer to accommodate to unsatisfying scripts rather than attempt changes.

For heterosexual couples, gender differences in sexual scripts pose additional challenges. Men tend to initiate sexual activity more often than women (Byers & Heinlein, 1989; Laumann, Gagnon, Michael, & Michaels, 1994), and men report wanting more frequent and varied sexual activities (Simms & Byers, 2009). Although some would argue that these differences reflect biologically based differences in sex drive (Baumeister, Catanese, & Vohs, 2001), they also reflect the fact that women receive persistent messages from parents, schools, and the media suggesting that women are less interested in sex than men and that their role is to be the sexual gatekeeper in a relationship (Tolman, 2002). Women also suffer more stigmatization than men for engaging in casual and premarital sexual contact, for contracting sexually transmitted infections, and for engaging in nontraditional sexual practices (such as threesomes; Jonason & Marks, 2009; G. Smith, Mysak, & Michael, 2008). These factors undoubtedly influence the development of women's sexual scripts.

Notably, some research has indicated that women do not want less sexual activity than their male partners but rather different types of sexual activities: Specifically, although both men and women rate foreplay as an important part of their sexual interactions (S. A. Miller & Byers, 2004), women report wanting more foreplay than men and (perhaps more important) more foreplay than they are actually having (Witting et al., 2008). This finding underscores the point raised earlier, which is that partners rarely have identical sexual desires, preferences, and expectations (S. A. Miller & Byers, 2004; Simms & Byers, 2009). Achieving a mutually satisfying sexual script (or series of scripts) that makes the most of partners' similarities and works around their discrepancies can be especially difficult if their respective expectations and desires are bound up in cultural conceptions of what it means to be a "good" or "normal" man or woman. For example, if a woman wants more frequent sexual activity than her male partner (thereby violating conventional expectations that men are more sexual than women), both partners may struggle with cultural stereotypes positing that such a woman is somehow indecent and dirty or that her male partner is not a real man. Hence, in interpreting contemporary patterns of sexual behavior in heterosexual couples, one must remain mindful of the multiple interacting forces—cultural, psychological, biological, interpersonal, emotional, and so forth—that shape the development and maintenance of a couple's own unique pattern of sexual expression.

WHAT DO MOST COUPLES DO? AND HOW OFTEN?

Perhaps the most important change in sexual scripts since the 1960s and 1970s concerns the increased acceptability of premarital sex. Today, the vast majority of married couples engage in sexual activity before getting married, and this practice is no longer roundly stigmatized (Laumann et al., 1994; Willets, Sprecher, & Beck, 2004). Once couples are married, studies have suggested that most couples engage in sexual contact one to two times a week, usually consisting of penile–vaginal intercourse (Call, Sprecher, & Schwartz, 1995; Laumann et al., 1994). Laumann et al. (1994) found that 95% of respondents reported having vaginal sex the last time they had sex, and 80% reported having vaginal sex every time they had partnered sexual contact in the past year.

Although a majority of individuals have engaged in oral sex at some point in their lifetime, fewer than 30% of individuals reported that their most recent sexual experience involved oral sex, and fewer than 2% reported that their most recent sexual experience involved anal sex (these percentages are higher among younger and more educated individuals).

Laumann et al. (1994) detected few differences in couples' rates of sexual activity on the basis of demographic factors such as ethnicity, geography, income, education, or religion. Yet two demographic variables have reliably predicted a couple's sexual frequency in every single study conducted: age and relationship duration. Quite simply, older individuals engage in less sexual activity than younger individuals, and long-standing relationships involve less sexual activity than new relationships (Call et al., 1995; Gagnon, Giami, Michaels, & Colomby, 2001; Laumann et al., 1994; Willets et al., 2004; Yabiku & Gager, 2009). Although age and relationship duration are of course confounded, each demonstrates unique predictive utility in studies in which they can be reliably disentangled (i.e., in studies of older individuals in new relationships). The decline in sexual activity associated with relationship duration is particularly stark and immediate: The average couple has more frequent sexual activity during the 1st year of their relationship than they will ever have again (Call et al., 1995). Although these declines have been observed for both married and cohabitating couples, their implications may be more serious for the latter. As summarized by Yabiku and Gager (2009), cohabitation is a narrower institution than marriage, involving fewer structural ties between partners and fewer barriers to dissolution. Hence, sharp declines in one of the chief rewards of an intimate relationship—sexual fulfillment—take on greater significance for cohabiting couples.

Given the obvious pleasures of sexual activity, why does it decline so precipitously over time? Habituation appears to be the best explanation for the declines associated with relationship length (Call et al., 1995). Both men and women report less frequent feelings of sexual desire and arousal in longer term relationships (Dürr, 2009). Some have interpreted this as evidence that a primary function of sexual activity within developing relationships is the establishment of emotional intimacy and attachment, such that the subjective perception of increasing emotional intimacy serves as a potent erotic stimulus in and of itself. Once the relationship solidifies and emotional intimacy stabilizes, this particular stimulus wanes in intensity, resulting in less frequent sexual motivation and behavior (see Dürr, 2009). Having children can dramatically accelerate this decline (Serati et al., 2010). In addition to the discomfort and fatigue that many women experience during pregnancy, some women report finding sex less satisfying after pregnancy and indicate that reestablishing their previous level of sexual intimacy is less important to them than it is to their male partner. In other cases, postpartum depression exacerbates women's low sexual motivation, low sexual self-esteem, or relationship tensions (Huang & Mathers, 2006). After the immediate postpartum period has passed, couples with children face a host of new and ongoing stressors, and the resulting fatigue and stress can significantly dampen sexual motivation (Leiblum, 2003). Advancing age brings a host of additional hurdles, such as declines in overall health and fitness and common age-related health conditions (Laumann, Paik, & Rosen, 1999). Hence, with each advancing decade, individuals pursue progressively less sexual activity. In one national study, the average rate of sexual activity among individuals aged 50 to 54 years was 5.5 times per month compared with 2.4 times per month among individuals 65 to 69 years of age and less than once a month among individuals older than 75 (Call et al., 1995). Yet closer inspection of these data reveals that these declines vary in magnitude from couple to couple. In other words, not all couples undergo a uniform, progressive drop in sexual activity from year to year. Rather, with each passing decade, a greater proportion of couples stop having sex altogether, whereas the remaining couples continue engaging in sexual activity at relatively stable rates. For example, Call et al. (1995) found that among individuals older than 75 who were still sexually active, the average sexual frequency was approximately 3 times per month. Hence, when considering age-related declines in sexual activity, researchers must differentiate older couples who are having any sexual activity from those who are not.

Although such declines are often experienced negatively by couples, this is not always the case. As argued by Bozon (2001), longer term couples might have less frequent and more routine sex, but this should not be presumed to indicate boredom and dissatisfaction. To the contrary, a relatively routine sexual script may allow partners to develop a certain degree of expertise, confidence, comfort, and relaxation. As for issues of frequency, Bozon noted that in the early stages of a relationship, frequent sexual activity serves a relationship-building function that becomes less important as time goes on. Once the bond between partners is well established, couples may find less frequent episodes of sexual behavior—and in some cases, different types of sexually intimate acts that may or may not result in mutual orgasm—to be sufficient for maintaining and nurturing their tie. For all of these reasons, Bozon has argued for greater focus on couples' sexual life histories, including a comprehensive, process-oriented perspective on how couples develop, maintain, and change their sexual scripts over the entire course of their relationship. Supporting this perspective, studies have found that many older couples simply adjust their repertoire of sexual behaviors with advancing age instead of eliminating sexual intimacy altogether. For example, couples contending with physical limitations that interfere with vaginal intercourse may gravitate toward oral stimulation or manual stimulation and may come to place greater priority on physically affectionate behaviors such as cuddling and kissing (Hurd Clarke, 2006). Such adaptive and flexible attitudes and expectations may be far more predictive of later life sexual frequency than physical limitations.

SEXUAL SATISFACTION

Extensive research has focused on identifying predictors of couples' sexual satisfaction, typically defined as "an affective response arising from one's subjective evaluation of the positive and negative dimensions associated with one's sexual relationship" (Lawrance & Byers, 1995, p. 268). One influential perspective on sexual satisfaction has been the social exchange perspective applied by Byers and colleagues (Byers, 2005; Byers & Wang, 2004;

Lawrance & Byers, 1992, 1995). Social exchange theory conceptualizes interpersonal behavior as a function of each partner's motives to maximize his or her rewards and minimize his or her costs, as well as to achieve relative equity in each partner's respective inputs and outcomes. Applied to the domain of sexuality, Lawrance and Byers (1992, 1995) argued that an individual's sexual satisfaction in a relationship is determined by (a) the overall balance of one's sexual rewards and costs, (b) how these rewards and costs compare with one's expectations, (c) perceptions of equity between one's own rewards and costs and those of one's partner, and (d) the quality of the nonsexual dimensions of the relationship. The rewards associated with sexuality in a specific relationship might include such factors as physical pleasure, release of tension, emotional expression, and feelings of closeness; costs associated with sexuality might include dislike of certain practices, embarrassment, or sexual dysfunction (Lawrance & Byers, 1992). The key contribution of the exchange perspective is that these rewards and costs are not conceived as independent and isolated predictors of sexual satisfaction. Rather, their relevance derives from how individuals appraise the overall ratio of sexual rewards to costs.

Numerous studies have confirmed that individuals' perceptions of a high ratio of sexual rewards to sexual costs (regardless of the specific nature of each reward and cost) reliably predict their sexual satisfaction (Lawrance & Byers, 1995). The social exchange perspective is also particularly useful for understanding discrepancies between partners' sexual satisfaction, as partners may assign different values to certain aspects of their sexual relationship. Such discrepancies are particularly notable in heterosexual relationships because they tend to align with traditional gender differences regarding the valuation of physical versus emotional intimacy. For example, relationship dynamics such as emotional closeness, security, and open communication play a larger role in women's sexual arousal and sexual satisfaction than is the case for men (Basson, 2001; Lawrance & Byers, 1992).

Among the most reliable findings in research on sexuality in couples is that sexual satisfaction and overall relationship satisfaction are strongly related,

and changes in one domain predict changes in the other (Byers, 2005; Sprecher, 2002; Yeh, Lorenz, Wickrama, Conger, & Elder, 2006). Sexual satisfaction is positively correlated with partners' feelings of love for one another (Aron & Henkemeyer, 1995; Sprecher, 2002), their respective levels of attachment security (Birnbaum, Reis, Mikulincer, Gillath, & Orpaz, 2006; Hazan & Zeifman, 1994), commitment (Sprecher, 2002; Waite & Joyner, 2001), intimacy (Haning et al., 2007), and relationship stability (Sprecher, 2002; Yeh et al., 2006). Longitudinal studies have yielded a mixed pattern of findings on whether sexual satisfaction influences relationship satisfaction or vice versa. Using cross-lagged analysis of longitudinal data, Yeh et al. (2006) found that sexual satisfaction influenced marital quality, which in turn increased marital stability. Yet another longitudinal study (Byers, 2005) found limited evidence for a strong causal push in either direction, arguing that both forms of satisfaction probably change concurrently as a function of couples' communication dynamics. Specifically, Byers noted that couples who started out with poor communication reported declines in both sexual and relationship satisfaction over an 18-month period, whereas couples who started out with good communication reported increases in both domains. Cupach and Metts (1991) argued that good communication enhances a couple's sexual satisfaction through two mechanisms, which MacNeil and Byers (2009) called the *instrumental pathway* and the *expressive pathway*. The instrumental pathway refers to the fact that good communication allows partners to understand one another's sexual needs and preferences and to make appropriate modifications to their sexual practices (Cupach & Metts, 1991; Purnine & Carey, 1997). The expressive pathway refers to the fact that open disclosure of partners' respective sexual needs and preferences tends to enhance relational intimacy, which in turn enhances sexual satisfaction (Cupach & Metts, 1991; MacNeil & Byers, 1997).

Effective communication may prove particularly important for preventing a couple's sexual hurdles from influencing their overall relationship functioning. For example, one study found that low levels of sexual satisfaction were related to low marital quality only among couples with poor communication skills (Litzinger & Gordon, 2005). Unfortunately, many couples with otherwise strong communication skills may fail to communicate effectively about sexual matters, given that societal taboos and personal discomfort may make it difficult for couples to discuss such issues openly. For example, Kelly, Strassberg, and Turner (2004, 2006) compared the communication skills of couples with a female nonorgasmic partner with the communication skills of couples without a female nonorgasmic partner. The couples with a female nonorgasmic partner had significantly poorer communication overall, but especially when discussing sexual matters. Specifically, partners in these couples assigned more blame to the female partner and showed more discomfort when discussing the very sexual practice (clitoral stimulation) that might actually remedy the problem.

This example is an apt one, given that women's difficulties in reaching orgasm through penile–vaginal penetration alone represent a common hurdle for sexual satisfaction in heterosexual couples, yet one about which many couples find difficult to communicate openly. The vast majority of women do not achieve orgasm through penile–vaginal penetration unless such penetration is combined with clitoral stimulation (Lloyd, 2005). As shown by Wallen and Lloyd (2011), the ease with which a woman achieves orgasm through vaginal penetration is strongly predicted by anatomical variability. For a minority of women, the clitoris and the vagina are close enough together that vaginal penetration ends up simultaneously stimulating the clitoris, greatly increasing the likelihood of orgasm; for women with a greater anatomical distance between the clitoris and the vagina, orgasm almost never occurs through penile–vaginal intercourse, and additional stimulation of the clitoris is necessary for orgasm. As a result of such anatomical variability (along with variability in women's degrees of sexual experience, comfort, self-knowledge, etc.), women show considerable variability in the degree to which different sexual behaviors reliably lead to orgasm. This variability has important implications for relationship research: Specifically, couples seeking mutual experiences of orgasm must engage in some degree of mutual discovery and negotiation (whether implicit

or explicit) regarding the specific combination of sexual practices most likely to achieve this result. In some cases, these negotiations proceed smoothly: A recent representative study found that 40% of heterosexual women, 69% of lesbians, and 66% of bisexual women (the majority of whom were currently involved with male partners) reported having used a vibrator during partnered sexual activity to achieve orgasm (Herbenick et al., 2010). Notably, nearly a third of women reported that they had been the one to initiate vibrator use, and an additional one quarter of women reported that their partner had recommended vibrator use. However, relationship dynamics also appear to play a significant role in women's vibrator use. The vast majority of women who had ever used a vibrator reported believing that their partner liked the fact that they did so, raising the possibility that, for many women, vibrator use (or the use of other toys or techniques for facilitating orgasm during partnered sexual activity) is partially dependent on the partner's approval (Herbenick et al., 2010). Supporting this view, some heterosexual women who used vibrators during masturbation reported hiding this fact from their partner to avoid hurting his feelings or making him feel inadequate. The issue of female orgasm provides one of the most clear-cut examples of how couples' comfort with communication can yield direct benefits with regard to the establishment of a satisfying sexual repertoire.

SEXUALITY IN COUPLES COPING WITH ILLNESS OR DISABILITY

Couples coping with chronic illness or disability face special challenges when it comes to sexual functioning, most commonly precipitous declines in sexual frequency and satisfaction (Gilbert, Ussher, & Perz, 2010). Studies have also found clinically significant levels of sexual dysfunction among men and women with (or showing risk factors for) numerous chronic health conditions (Derogatis & Burnett, 2008; Lewis et al., 2010), most notably cardiovascular disease (Meuleman, 2011). Yet research and rehabilitative practice with such couples has typically focused on psychological adjustment to the physical challenges posed by illness or disability and less often on strategies for maintaining sexual intimacy (L. Miller, 1994; Rolland, 1994), which creates the potential for long-term health risks, given that untreated sexual problems tend to amplify relationship problems and erode partners' capacity to give and receive support, eventually hindering the couples' ability to cope with the demands of treatment and recovery (Günzler, Kriston, Harms, & Berner, 2009). Accordingly, researchers and clinicians have called for a more integrative approach to the simultaneous management of chronic illness and sexual problems, most notably in the realm of cancer and cardiovascular disease (Jackson, Rosen, Kloner, & Kostis, 2006; Meuleman, 2011). Evidence has suggested that such approaches must adopt a dyadic approach, taking both partners' responses into account (Gilbert et al., 2010). For example, one recent study found that just as a man's sexual dysfunction is significantly related to his own cardiovascular risk, his perception of low or absent sexual desire on the part of his partner is also uniquely predictive of his cardiovascular risk (Corona et al., 2010).

Numerous studies have found greater sexual and relationship satisfaction among couples who manage to communicate openly and clearly about sexual needs and limits; who adopt broader, more flexible definitions of sexual intimacy and satisfaction; and who are willing to experiment with new and different sexual practices to cope with the changes posed by physical limitations (L. Miller, 1994; Milligan & Neufeldt, 1998). This may help to explain why couples who initiated their relationship after the onset of illness or disability tend to have higher sexual and relationship satisfaction than couples for whom the illness or disability interrupted their preexisting intimate life (Kreuter, Sullivan, & Siosteen, 1994). For couples in which the illness or disability was present from the very beginning of the relationship, creative adjustments to physical limitations are part and parcel of their sexual repertoire rather than substitutes for what couples did before. Hence, such couples are not plagued by the feelings of loss or regret that often accompany couples for whom the illness or disability necessitated a stark change in their sexual routine (Kreuter et al., 1994). It is important to note that making such changes need not be experienced negatively: Some couples find that the process of

reframing and reimagining their sexual scripts provides a new source of intimacy and meaning to their mutual connection (Gilbert et al., 2010).

Another challenge faced by couples coping with illness and disability is that the more able-bodied partner typically takes on a significant caregiving role, which may interfere with both partners' perceptions of themselves as lovers (Milligan & Neufeldt, 1998; Yoshida, 1994). In fact, studies have suggested that the longer a spouse takes on significant caregiving duties, the more difficulty these couples face in returning to the levels of sexual intimacy they had before the illness or disability (L. Miller, 1994). This may be why Taleporos and McCabe (2003) found that individuals with physical disabilities reported more depressive symptoms if they were cohabitating with their romantic or sexual partner than if they maintained separate residences. Specifically, living together necessarily blurs the boundaries between a sexual partnership and a caretaking relationship, whereas living apart allows partners to maintain clearer boundaries between those functions, along with a greater sense of autonomy and choice regarding the maintenance of the relationship. The type and severity of impairment also proves important. Couples typically report more difficulty coping with cognitive impairments than physical impairments (Sandel, 1997), because deficits in cognition and communication have more direct implications for couples' ability to exchange meaningful and interpretable expressions of emotional intimacy (Rolland, 1994). In some of these cases, sexual intimacy may be discontinued entirely in favor of a greater emphasis on companionship and comfort (L. Miller, 1994).

Much research remains to be done investigating the long-term interpersonal processes through which couples successfully renegotiate sexual intimacy in the wake of illness or disability. Given that many of these issues are similar to those faced by couples coping with age-related declines in physical and sexual functioning, research in this area would profit from more substantive integration of research findings from these two domains. This is not to suggest that aging should be equated with disability when it comes to sexuality but rather that the core interpersonal processes necessary for managing these life transitions require similar core skills and face similar challenges. Longitudinal, dyadic research is particularly critical, given that couples may need to continue revisiting and readjusting their sexual script to accommodate ongoing changes in each partner's physical capacities and expectations.

SEXUAL DYSFUNCTION

Among the most obvious and important physical conditions that potentially impairs a couple's sexual relationship is sexual dysfunction, which affects more than 40% of women and more than 30% of men in the United States (Laumann et al., 1999). The most common dysfunctions among men include difficulty achieving or maintaining an erection, with prevalence estimates ranging from 10% to 50%, and premature ejaculation, with prevalence estimates ranging from 28% to 30% (Heiman, 2002; Laumann et al., 1999; Simons & Carey, 2001). Among women, the most common dysfunctions include difficulty reaching orgasm, with prevalence estimates ranging from 10% to 24%, and low or absent (hypoactive) sexual desire, with prevalence estimates ranging from 15% to 58% (Hayes, Dennerstein, Bennett, & Fairley, 2008; Heiman, 2002; Laumann et al., 1999; Simons & Carey, 2001). The wide range in prevalence estimates is due to discrepancies in the criteria and populations assessed in different studies. The etiology of sexual dysfunction is complex, involving a diverse range of biological, psychosocial, and interpersonal factors that interact in different ways for different individuals (Derogatis & Burnett, 2008; Hayes, Dennerstein, Bennett, Sidat, et al., 2008; Heiman, 2002; Lewis et al., 2010).

In some cases, sexual problems develop abruptly, often in response to specific events such as major illnesses or injuries (Barsky, Friedman, & Rosen, 2006; Corona et al., 2010; Jackson et al., 2006; Meuleman, 2011), major life transitions such as the birth of a child (Heiman, 2002) or job loss (Morokqff & Gillilland, 1993), or experiences of acute psychological trauma (Hirsch, 2009). In other cases, the problem emerges more gradually or sporadically, sometimes in association with generalized stress (Morokqff & Gillilland, 1993) or

developmental transitions such as menopause (Hayes, Dennerstein, Bennett, Sidat, et al., 2008). Predisposing factors such as early traumatic experiences, family dysfunction, sexual victimization, or internalization of negative and stigmatizing messages about sexuality often play a role, even when such events occurred long in the past (Aubin & Heiman, 2004). A formal clinical diagnosis of sexual dysfunction depends on meeting *Diagnostic and Statistical Manual of Mental Disorders* (4th ed.; American Psychiatric Association, 1994) criteria regarding frequency and severity, as well as (and perhaps most important) the experience of psychological distress owing to the problem (Aubin & Heiman, 2004). Yet many individuals with sexual problems that are frequent and severe enough to meet diagnostic criteria for sexual dysfunction do not report significant psychological distress (Hayes, Dennerstein, Bennett, & Fairley, 2008) and are able to maintain satisfying sexual relations despite the dysfunction (Heiman, 2000; Heiman & Meston, 1997). Even couples who experience significant distress and dissatisfaction often wait many years before seeking treatment (Trudel et al., 2001), often after trying a variety of unsuccessful strategies to avoid or work around the problem. Hence, the implications of sexual dysfunction depend on each partner's appraisal of the problem and their combined ability to confront and communicate about its potential antecedents and implications (Barsky et al., 2006).

Notably, partners often have starkly different perceptions of their sexual problems, and these differences often fall out along gender lines. In one study, 69% of men with erectile dysfunction perceived it as an important problem compared with only 45% of women with orgasmic disorder (Fugl-Meyer & Fugl-Meyer, 1999). This may reflect gender-based socialization that emphasizes the centrality of penile–vaginal intercourse for healthy adult sexuality and especially for men's sexual self-esteem. Hence, men often show heightened concern about dysfunctions that affect penile–vaginal intercourse, even when their female partners report being highly physically and emotionally satisfied by nonpenetrative sexual activities (Aubin & Heiman, 2004). In contrast, women are often more distressed by the relationship strains introduced by sexual dysfunction (Fugl-Meyer & Fugl-Meyer, 1999; Heiman & Meston, 1997), such as increased resentment, anger, criticism, or blame; poor communication; emotional distancing; reduced physical affection; and diminished expression of positive and loving feelings toward one another (Pridal & LoPiccolo, 2000; Rosen & Leiblum, 1995).

Historically, such relationship issues have received little clinical attention. Conventional diagnosis and treatment of sexual dysfunction has focused on treating the individual with the problem, and relationship issues have been considered ancillary effects of the dysfunction rather than as potential contributing or exacerbating causes (Aubin & Heiman, 2004). This, however, has changed significantly over the past decade, and relationship-centered approaches to both diagnosing and treating sexual dysfunctions have become widespread and have shown significant clinical success (Heiman, 2000; Leiblum & Rosen, 2000; Pridal & LoPiccolo, 2000). Among the relationship issues that have proven particularly relevant to sexual dysfunction are problems with excessively low or high intimacy, emotion regulation, adaptation to stressful life events, transition to parenthood, insecurity about the status of a relationship, fear of disappointing the partner, and preexisting history of trauma or abuse (Aubin & Heiman, 2004). Relationship distress and conflict play a particularly pronounced role in the development and exacerbation of female sexual dysfunction, especially hypoactive sexual desire (Hayes, Dennerstein, Bennett, Sidat, et al., 2008; Rosen & Leiblum, 1995; Trudel et al., 2001; Witting et al., 2008).

Yet at the same time as clinicians are becoming increasingly aware of, and responsive to, the contributions of interpersonal factors to sexual dysfunction, there is a corresponding push toward ever greater medicalization of sexual dysfunction (Leiblum & Rosen, 2000; Tiefer, 2002) sparked by the Viagra revolution, which has electrified the search for quick fixes that might obviate the need for visiting a therapist and confronting uncomfortable, potentially embarrassing topics with one's partner. The task for contemporary clinicians is to craft the best of both worlds, making use of contemporary biomedical treatment options without neglecting the long-standing interpersonal issues that are known to make fundamental contributions to the emergence and maintenance of couples' sexual problems (Aubin & Heiman, 2004).

Another important topic for future research is sexual dysfunction in younger populations. As noted earlier, although sexual dysfunction is often stereotyped as a problem of older individuals, recent research has found surprisingly high rates of sexual dysfunction among men and women in their late teens and early 20s (Fisher & Boroditsky, 2000; O'Sullivan & Majerovich, 2008). Such problems warrant close attention, given that sexual and romantic experiences during adolescence and young adulthood can set the stage for later sexual scripts and expectations. Also, younger couples may have more difficulty coping with sexual problems than older couples, given that their shorter sexual and relationship histories leave them with less direct experience in negotiating difficult relationship issues and less advanced communication skills (Abel & Fitzgerald, 2006).

SEX AS A MECHANISM THROUGH WHICH RELATIONSHIPS PROMOTE HEALTH

One of the most robust findings to emerge from health psychology over the past 30 years is that individuals in enduring, committed romantic relationships have longer, healthier, and happier lives than unmarried individuals (Diamond et al., 2010). Considerable research has investigated the mechanisms responsible for such findings. Thus far, research on the physical health benefits of well-functioning relationships has focused predominantly on the social and emotional support provided by such relationships, which is known to downregulate a range of physiological processes directly linked to physical health, such as cardiovascular, neuroendocrine, and immune functioning (Uchino, 2006). Hundreds of studies over the past several decades have been designed to capture these health-promoting processes in action to identify which aspects of couple functioning appear to have the largest, most immediate, or most lasting consequences for cardiovascular functioning, neuroendocrine activity, and immunological responses (e.g., Kiecolt-Glaser,

Malarkey, Chee, & Newton, 1993; Powers, Pietromonaco, Gunlicks, & Sayer, 2006; T. W. Smith et al., 2011).

Given the rigor and specificity of such studies, it is somewhat surprising that little research has investigated the potentially unique contribution of couples' sexual interactions to health-related physiological processes. After all, several large-scale observational studies have shown that individuals who engage in regular sexual activity have better health (e.g., Lindau & Gavrilova, 2010). Although these studies do not typically assess whether the sexual activity in question is pursued with a long-term romantic partner or with a casual partner, other studies have shown that approximately 90% of sexual activity occurring in Western industrialized countries takes place within established romantic relationships (Gagnon et al., 2001; Laumann et al., 1994; Willets et al., 2004). This finding is particularly notable given that most individuals hold stereotypes portraying single individuals as leading more voracious and satisfying sex lives than married individuals. This stereotype is clearly false: Married individuals engage in far more sexual activity than single individuals and experience greater emotional and physical satisfaction with their sex lives (Laumann et al., 1994; Lawrance & Byers, 1995; Waite & Joyner, 2001).

This raises the intriguing question of whether coupled sexual activity can be viewed as a significant health behavior in its own right. A handful of longitudinal cohort studies have suggested that this is the case. Persson (1981), for example, followed 219 married Swedish men and women from ages 70 to 75. Men (but not women) who reported ongoing sexual activity at age 70 were less likely to die during the ensuing 5 years. In a similar investigation, the Duke Longevity Study followed 270 older individuals (median age = 70) until death and found greater longevity among men with more frequent sexual activity (Palmore, 1982). Among women, greater enjoyment of sexual activity predicted longevity, even after controlling for numerous health-related covariates. Together, these two early studies suggested that sexual activity promotes health and well-being for both men and women, although potentially for different reasons.

More recently, two large studies with long follow-up periods have yielded even more compelling evidence for the health-promoting qualities of sexual behavior. One study of nearly 3,000 Welsh men between the ages of 45 and 59 found that men who reported a greater frequency of orgasm at baseline had lower all-cause mortality over the 10-year follow-up (Davey Smith, 1997). Adding further support for a possible causal link, the association between orgasmic frequency and death showed a dose–response relationship (i.e., more frequent orgasms were linearly related to lower mortality), and the effects persisted after controlling for a host of health-relevant covariates assessed both via self-report and through physical exam. Finally, Chen, Tsend, Wu, Lee, and Chen (2007) reported findings from a 14-year prospective study of more than 2,000 Taiwanese individuals older than age 65. Being sexually active at baseline was negatively associated with all-cause mortality over the next 14 years for both men and women. Controlling for most possible confounds diminished the effect somewhat for women but not for men.

Of course, given that most adult sexual activity occurs in the context of ongoing romantic relationships, and given the aforementioned correlations between sexual satisfaction and relationship satisfaction, it is difficult to disentangle the health benefits of sexual activity from the health benefits of other positive features of well-functioning close relationships. Yet it remains a provocative and testable possibility that some of the widely appreciated associations between close relationships and health are actually attributable (at least in part) to sexual activity. Consider, for example, the extensive body of research showing that a climate of positivity, acceptance, responsiveness, accommodation, and support in a relationship provides a powerful buffer against stress and may play a critical role in establishing and maintaining health-relevant interpersonal and physiological processes (Fincham, Hall, & Beach, 2006; Gable & La Guardia, 2007; Gottman, 1994; Rusbult, Bissonnette, Arriaga, Cox, & Bradbury, 1998). Satisfying sexual contact might be among the fastest, most reliable, and most effective routes to achieving and maintaining such a health-promoting climate. When partners regularly set aside time to exchange intense physical pleasure in a climate of warmth, excitement, playfulness, mutuality, and positive regard, this arguably provides one of the best possible manifestations of support, responsiveness, emotional engagement, sensitivity, and acceptance. Positive sexual interactions might also help to compensate for problems in other domains. For example, couples with a partner who is high in neuroticism or high in attachment insecurity tend to have lower relationship satisfaction, but this association is significantly attenuated among couples who report engaging in highly frequent sexual activity (Little, McNulty, & Russell, 2010; V. M. Russell & McNulty, 2011). Biological processes might contribute to the potential stress-reducing and stress-buffering effects of couples' sexual activity. Research has documented a cascade of neuroendocrine and autonomic changes associated with partnered sexual activity (Brody & Kruger, 2006; Exton et al., 2001), most notably a pronounced increase in prolactin after orgasm, which may be specifically implicated in feelings of satiety and which reflect inhibitory central dopaminergic processes (Brody, 2003). These findings suggest that sexual activity may play a unique role in day-to-day processes of affect regulation within couples.

Of course, not all sexual interactions are alike: It is a reasonable and testable hypothesis that couples' sexual interactions need to involve high levels of mutual satisfaction, trust, intimacy, and positive regard if they are to confer these benefits. To the degree that one partner feels underbenefited (i.e., feels that he or she is contributing more to the partner's satisfaction than the partner is contributing in return; see Byers & Wang, 2004), regular sexual activity may not have these beneficial effects and might instead reinforce problematic dynamics in the relationship. The aforementioned health benefits associated with sexual activity are unlikely to occur when couples pursue sexual activity as a means of avoiding verbal intimacy or asserting power or control over one another. They are also unlikely to occur when one partner goes along with unwanted sexual activity. Such episodes are fairly common. Using a diary methodology, O'Sullivan and Allgeier (1998) found that about half of young adults (ages 21–30) in committed relationships reported at least

one occasion of unwanted sex in a 2-week period, with an average lifetime prevalence of 12 occasions. Women were more likely to consent to unwanted activity than men, similar to prior research (Impett & Peplau, 2002), but no gender differences were found in retrospective reports of lifetime and 1-year incidence estimates. Notably, studies that have focused on longer term couples (Vannier & O'Sullivan, 2010) have tended to find fewer gender differences, suggesting that the longer individuals have been a couple, the more they may be adhering to an implicit contract of mutual sexual availability (Shotland & Goodstein, 1992). Further supporting this view, individuals who periodically consent to unwanted sexual contact report believing that their partners occasionally did the same.

Men and women report similar reasons for complying with unwanted sexual activity, most commonly to satisfy the partner's needs, promote intimacy, and avoid tension (O'Sullivan & Allgeier, 1998; Vannier & O'Sullivan, 2010). Unwanted sexual contact is particularly likely when there are large desire discrepancies between partners combined with poor communication (Træen & Skogerbø, 2009). Perhaps most interesting, individuals often report that the positive outcomes of consenting to unwanted sex (such as increased intimacy and avoidance of tension or conflict) often outweigh the negative outcomes (such as emotional discomfort and feelings of disappointment; O'Sullivan & Allgeier, 1998). Such findings demonstrate the complexity of sexual interactions in established couples and the importance of carefully discerning each partner's motives for engaging in both mutually desired and one-sided (or otherwise unsatisfying or uncomfortable) sexual interactions to understand the immediate and long-term mental and physical health consequences of such interactions. Clearly, future research on the health consequences of coupled sexual behavior will require comprehensive, rigorous analyses of the specific behaviors that couples pursue, the degree to which each partner appraises these behaviors as satisfying and valued, and the larger interpersonal context in which these behaviors occur, with respect to both day-to-day couple interactions and partners' broader perceptions, expectations, and feelings about their relationship.

SAME-SEX INTIMATE RELATIONSHIPS

I now turn attention to the unique issues and dynamics facing same-sex couples, including their overall relationship processes as well as their sexual norms and practices. Research on same-sex relationships has increased dramatically over the past several decades, with regard to the sheer number of empirical studies as well as the sophistication of the research. Whereas early studies were characterized by small, homogeneous samples; collection of data from only one member of the couple; the use of measures with unknown psychometric properties; exclusive reliance on self-report data; and lack of long-term longitudinal assessment, all of these weaknesses have been remedied in more recent work. This has made it possible for researchers to move beyond the early focus on basic differences between same-sex and heterosexual couples to more complex investigations of why same-sex couples resemble and differ from heterosexual couples and from one another.

Before launching into a review of the major findings, definitional issues require attention. Although discussions of same-sex couples are usually couched as discussions of gay, lesbian, and bisexual couples, such terminology is misleading, because the majority of individuals experiencing same-sex attractions and behavior do not, in fact, openly identify as being lesbian, gay, or bisexual (Chandra, Mosher, Copen, & Sionean, 2011; Laumann et al., 1994). Some of these individuals are actively hiding their same-sex sexuality; others, however, find that the gay–lesbian–bisexual terminology is irrelevant to their own self-concept, that it provides too restrictive a model of sexuality, or that it conflicts with their religious or ethnic identity (see Diamond, 2008). In growing acknowledgment of these issues, researchers increasingly use the term *sexual minorities* to refer to all men and women whose same-sex attractions or behaviors place them outside conventional heterosexual norms. This terminology is used in this chapter, but I have nonetheless retained the descriptors *lesbian, gay,* and *bisexual* when summarizing studies or research traditions that specifically recruited research participants on the basis of lesbian, gay, or bisexual identification.

Between 40% and 60% of gay men and 50% to 80% of lesbians are partnered (Peplau & Spalding, 2000), and the majority of lesbian, gay, and bisexual individuals would like the option of formalizing their relationships through marriage (Kaiser Family Foundation, 2001). In fact, 27% of the country's 581,000 cohabiting same-sex couples consider themselves spouses, even if U.S. law does not (National Center for Family & Marriage Research, 2010). An increasingly sophisticated body of multi-method research has investigated whether same-sex couples meet, fall in love, and maintain their relationships through substantially different processes than heterosexual couples, and the answer is largely no. Same-sex couples show similar communication and conflict resolution skills as heterosexual couples; similar degrees of interpersonal empathy; similar appraisals of intimacy, autonomy, equality, and mutual trust; similar day-to-day cognitive and behavioral strategies for maintaining their relationships; similar struggles over equity, housework, and fairness; and even similar strategies for deciding how to cope with the birth of a new child (Conley, Roesch, Peplau, & Gold, 2009; Roisman, Clausell, Holland, Fortuna, & Elieff, 2008; Solomon, Rothblum, & Balsam, 2005). They have even been found to fight about the same core issues as heterosexual couples—finances, affection, sex, criticism, and household tasks (Kurdek, 2004; Solomon et al., 2005)—and to show similar levels of physiological reactivity to conflict (Gottman, Levenson, Swanson, et al., 2003; Roisman et al., 2008).

What, then, distinguishes same-sex from heterosexual couples? First, their social stigmatization and invalidation—manifested most clearly by the lack of opportunities for legal formalization—introduces an insidious source of strain that may gradually erode relationship quality and commitment (Green, 2008; Lehmiller & Agnew, 2006). Second, the simple fact of combining two individuals of the same gender produces distinctive relationship dynamics.

Sexual Stigmatization and Marginalization

Perhaps the most important defining characteristic of individuals with same-sex attractions and relationships is their marginalized status in contemporary society. Although attitudes toward same-sex sexuality have grown more tolerant in recent years (Loftus, 2001), stigma and intolerance remain pervasive. A national survey by the Kaiser Family Foundation found that three fourths of lesbian, gay, and bisexual adults report some form of prejudice or discrimination as a result of their sexuality, one third of gay men and one half of lesbians report experiencing rejection by a friend or family member, and one third said that they had actually suffered violence against them or their property (Kaiser Family Foundation, 2001). This consistent stigmatization, rejection, and legal disenfranchisement produces a phenomenon called *minority stress,* defined as the unique strain experienced as a result of occupying a socially marginalized category (Meyer, 2003). As reviewed by Meyer (2003), the fundamental tenet underlying the conceptualization of minority stress is that individuals learn about themselves and develop their self-concepts on the basis of how they are treated and perceived by others. Hence, chronic negative evaluations, at the level of both concrete interpersonal interactions and broad-based cultural norms, have detrimental implications for sexual minorities' self-evaluations and well-being. Meyer's formulation of sexual minority stress distinguishes between distal and proximal stressors. Distal stressors include relatively objective forms of marginalization and discrimination, such as straightforward harassment and victimization. Proximal stressors include those that are more subjective and depend more heavily on the individual's perception and appraisal of the experience. For example, if a sexual minority individual does not receive a promotion or if a same-sex couple receives rude treatment at a hotel or restaurant, it may be difficult to discern objectively whether it was or was not attributable to their sexual minority status. According to Meyer, both proximal and distal stressors take a toll on the well-being of sexual minority individuals. Meyers also posited a number of stress processes that are specifically relevant to sexual minorities: (a) expectation of rejection, such that sexual minority individuals become hypervigilant to cues of rejection in their interactions with others, owing to a chronic expectation that their stigmatized sexual minority status makes them undesirable; (b) concealment, in which sexual minority individuals must chronically

hide their sexual minority status (and, in particular, their intimate relationships) to avoid harm and rejection; and (c) internalized homophobia, such that individuals come to adopt (often without their own conscious awareness) negative views and stereotypes about sexual minorities and their relationships, leading them to struggle with chronic shame and negative emotions.

Minority stress has been advanced as an explanation for the fact that sexual minority individuals often show disproportionately high rates of anxiety, depression, suicidality, self-injurious behavior, substance use, and use of mental health services (Institute of Medicine, 2011). In particular, sexual minorities with greater levels of stigmatization and victimization tend to have poorer mental health outcomes (Balsam, Rothblum, & Beauchaine, 2005; D'Augelli, Grossman, & Starks, 2006). However, all of the extant research on minority stress is correlational and based on self-reports. Hence, it is also possible that individuals with higher levels of anxiety or depression are more likely to perceive, remember, and report day-to-day experiences of marginalization and to attribute these experiences to their sexual minority status.

Although most research on minority stress has focused on its implications for sexual minority individuals, researchers have begun to extend the minority stress perspective to explain the distinctive dynamics of same-sex couples (Fingerhut, 2010; Riggle, Rostosky, & Horne, 2010). Although minority stress began as a theory of intrapsychic functioning, it is increasingly being used to understand and explain interpersonal processes and cognitions. Much of this work has focused on the detrimental implications of internalized homophobia, the phenomenon by which sexual minority individuals gradually internalize societal denigration and stigmatization, developing a negative sense of self and a chronic sense of conflict between their same-sex sexuality and their desire for social validation and affirmation (Herek, 2004). Meyer and Dean (1998) described internalized homophobia as the most insidious form of minority stress because although it originates with external social marginalization, the gradual internalization of stigma, negativity, and stereotyping makes these stressors impossible to escape. Hence, even in the absence of objective forms of social stigma and rejection, individuals with high levels of internalized homophobia continue to suffer from feelings of illegitimacy and shame, expectations of rejection, and low self-esteem. Internalized homophobia has been linked to a number of negative mental health outcomes, such as depression, risky sexual behavior, eating disorders, and suicidality (Meyer, 2003; Meyer & Dean, 1998; Remafedi, French, Story, Resnick, & Blum, 1998). It is also related to same-sex relationship quality: Sexual-minority men with higher levels of internalized homophobia have lower rates of romantic relationship participation (Meyer & Dean, 1998), and their romantic relationships are shorter, more problematic, and more conflict ridden (Meyer & Dean, 1998). More important, sexual minority individuals with high levels of internalized homophobia also report lower quality in their nonromantic relationships, such as those with friends, family, and colleagues, suggesting that internalized shame and negativity might have a more general negative effect on core interpersonal processes and cognitions (Otis, Rostosky, Riggle, & Hamrin, 2006). Investigating the processes by which marginalization and stigmatization gradually get under the skin to erode individuals' own well-being and the quality of their social ties is a provocative and important direction for the next generation of research applying minority stress theory to the study of same-sex couples.

One particularly elegant line of research has taken advantage of the natural experiment provided by statewide ballot initiatives outlawing same-sex marriage to investigate how sexual minority individuals and their relationships are affected by living in communities that take active, visible steps to deny legitimacy to their partnerships. These studies have found that sexual minority individuals living in states that have passed laws against same-sex marriage experience significantly higher levels of psychological distress, consistent with minority stress theory (Rostosky, Riggle, Horne, & Miller, 2009) and also have heightened fears about the status of their relationships (Rostosky, Riggle, Horne, Denton, & Huellemeier, 2010). Furthermore, studies have found that sexual minority stress can spill over from one partner to another, magnifying the

negative repercussions for the couple as a whole (Rostosky & Riggle, 2002).

Before leaving this discussion of minority stress theory, however, it is important to note that researchers have increasingly begun to investigate the flip side of stigma and marginalization—social support—as an important moderator of minority stress. Specifically, sexual minority individuals who have access to friends, family members, and colleagues who specifically support their sexuality and who affirm and validate their same-sex relationships appear to be less vulnerable to mental health problems (Grossman, D'Augelli, & Hershberger, 2000) as well as relationship problems (Blair & Holmberg, 2008). Unfortunately, many sexual minority individuals face difficulty obtaining such support, especially from family members. Even when family members do not explicitly reject them, sexual minority individuals often report that their sexual orientation is quietly tolerated but never openly acknowledged (D'Augelli, Grossman, & Starks, 2005) and that their families never formally acknowledge their romantic partners.

However, such instances of family disapproval often serve to strengthen the tie between same-sex partners by drawing them together against a common challenge (LaSala, 1998), fostering the development of adaptive coping strategies and prompting them to develop strong chosen families of supportive friends (Nardi, 1999; Weston, 1991). One unique dynamic of sexual minority social networks is that these chosen families often include previous lovers (Nardi & Sherrod, 1994; Weinstock, 2004). To some extent, this reflects the fact that the boundaries between friend and lover are often somewhat ambiguous within sexual minority communities. Especially in small communities, many sexual minorities report developing romantic relationships out of existing friendships; pursuing periodic sexual contact with close, trusted friends; and maintaining highly emotionally significant ties with former lovers (Nardi & Sherrod, 1994; Peplau & Amaro, 1982). The latter practice runs counter to conventional heterosexual norms, which prescribe relatively rigid boundaries between the categories of friend and lover and which tend to treat ex-lover relationships with some suspicion (Weinstock, 2004). Yet among sexual minorities, this practice appears to represent a common strategy for maximizing access to social support and nurturance in light of the disapproval commonly faced at the hands of colleagues, family members, and society at large.

Lack of Opportunities for Legal Formalization

Currently in the United States, 17 states recognize same-sex marriage. Three states have recognized same-sex marriage by popular vote (Maine, Maryland, and Washington), eight states have recognized same-sex marriage through state legislative action (Delaware, Hawaii, Illinois, Minnesota, New Hampshire, New York, Rhode Island, and Vermont), and six states have recognized same-sex marriages as a result of court decisions (California, Connecticut, Iowa, Massachusetts, New Jersey, and New Mexico). The 1996 Defense of Marriage Act outlawed federal recognition of same-sex marriage and also allowed states to deny recognition of same-sex marriages performed in other states. Yet the landmark 2013 Supreme Court ruling, *United States v. Windsor* (2013), struck down the Defense of Marriage Act and extended federal recognition to same-sex marriages. However, the obligation of states to recognize same-sex marriages performed in other states remains unresolved: Currently, no state which prohibits same-sex marriage recognizes same-sex marriages performed elsewhere. Same-sex marriages performed in other countries are also denied recognition (currently, same-sex marriage is legal in Argentina, Belgium, Canada, Denmark, France, Brazil, Uruguay, New Zealand, Great Britain, Iceland, the Netherlands, Norway, Portugal, Spain, South Africa, and Sweden). In addition, 33 American states have explicitly banned gay marriages, either through state laws or constitutional amendments.

Increasing evidence has suggested that the lack of opportunities for formal recognition of same-sex relationships has implications for the stability and satisfaction of same-sex couples. For example, several studies have directly compared same-sex cohabiting couples in civil unions with same-sex cohabiting couples without civil unions and also with the married heterosexual siblings of couples in a civil union (Solomon, Rothblum, & Balsam, 2004;

Solomon et al., 2005; Todosijevic, Rothblum, & Solomon, 2005). These couples started out quite similar to each other in overall satisfaction or functioning, yet a 3-year follow-up assessment found that the same-sex couples in civil unions were less likely to have broken up than same-sex couples who had not pursued civil unions (Balsam, Beauchaine, Rothblum, & Solomon, 2008), supporting the notion that barriers to relationship dissolution can enhance couples' perceptions of their relationship and bolster their motivation to resolve problems (Kurdek, 1998).

Along the same lines, same-sex couples have reported that formalizing their relationships makes them feel more "real" (Lannutti, 2007) and enhances their sense of commitment, even if they had already been committed to one another beforehand (Alderson, 2004). Perhaps for this reason, Solomon et al. (2005) found that 54% of same-sex couples reported increased love and commitment to one another after having had a civil union. One question that awaits future longitudinal research is whether other methods of legally acknowledging and formalizing same-sex relationships, such as naming one another as insurance beneficiaries or legal heirs, purchasing property together, giving one another power of attorney, designating one another as medical proxies, legally taking the same last name, or merging finances, have the same repercussions for couple functioning, commitment, and stability as more official forms of recognition, such as civil unions and domestic partnerships.

Such investigations call for careful attention to the specific mechanisms through which relationship formalization relates to relationship functioning, and in this respect it is important to distinguish between symbolic and legal formalization. Fingerhut (2010) found that couples who had formalized their relationships symbolically (through commitment ceremonies or weddings with no legal bearing) reported greater life satisfaction and relationship satisfaction, whereas those who formalized their relationships legally (through registered domestic partnerships) reported greater investments in their relationship (which is known to promote relationship stability and commitment; Rusbult, Olsen, Davis, & Hannon, 2004). This suggests that symbolic formalization has particularly strong implications for personal and moral aspects of commitment (consistent with findings regarding the wearing of rings and the changing of last names; Suter & Daas, 2007), whereas legal formalization has relatively stronger implications for structural aspects of commitment (Johnson, 1999). Some same-sex couples, however, desist from symbolic formalization, claiming that rituals such as commitment ceremonies lack meaning if they do not have legal standing (Reczek, Elliott, & Umberson, 2009).

Both symbolic and legal formalization, however, appear to play a role in reducing what Green (2008) has called *relational ambiguity,* or the lack of standard cultural "rules" by which partners can gauge the progress and future status of their relationship, as well as their own responsibilities and duties at different stages of development. Green noted that heterosexual marriage comes with a set of cultural expectations that partners can rely on to guide their behavior, such as cohabitation, pooled property and finances, and caring for one another (and one another's extended families) in times of illness. Without the clear demarcation of marriage, same-sex couples must make such decisions on a case-by-case basis and must openly and repeatedly revisit questions—and conflicts—about whether their relationship is serious or long term enough to warrant certain commitments and sacrifices (such as giving up a job opportunity or allowing elderly parents to share the household). In some cases, same-sex couples cannot even identify a reliable marker of when their relationship began (Reczek et al., 2009). Hence, pursuing either symbolic or legal formalization may help to decrease relational ambiguity and create a set of shared expectations about the status and future of the relationship.

Perhaps most important, relationship formalization may help to buffer couples from the day-to-day stress of their social marginalization. Fingerhut (2010) found that the association between internalized homophobia and psychosocial adjustment (life and relationship satisfaction) was attenuated among individuals who had either legally or symbolically formalized their relationship. Similarly, Riggle et al. (2010) found that same-sex couples in legally recognized relationships reported significantly less psychological distress than those in committed—but not legally recognized—relationships. This does not, however, suggest that formal recognition for same-sex relationships would provide a magic buffer against the stress of social stigmatization. In their study of same-sex couples who entered into civil unions in Vermont, Todosijevic et al. (2005) found that many of these couples continued to struggle with familial rejection of their relationship. Similarly, Eskridge and Spedale (2006) noted that same-sex married couples in Denmark and other Scandinavian countries (which have significantly more accepting attitudes toward same-sex sexuality than does the United States) continue to confront daily prejudice and social rejection. The often vociferous debates over same-sex marriage have been observed to take a notable toll on same-sex couples' views of themselves and their relationships (Rostosky et al., 2009).

This raises the broader question of how same-sex couples' formalization practices are related to their other familial ties. As argued by Cohler and Hammack (2007), sexual minority individuals live linked lives, such that all of their social relationships are intrinsically interbraided. Accordingly, the decision to legally formalize a same-sex relationship—and the preceding changes in the day-to-day experience of that relationship—have ripple effects across each couple's entire social network. These effects deserve more research attention. As eloquently argued by Smart (2007), same-sex couples who decide to formalize their relationship enter into a protracted period of relationship renegotiation with all of their important social ties, which may be extended over many years. The quality of any specific relationship in an individual's network of intimate social ties is not static but dynamic, constantly evolving and adjusting to a changing set of interpersonal and environmental conditions (Finch & Mason, 1993). Currently, little is understood about how these dynamic processes of renegotiation unfold over the course of many years within the social lives of sexual minority individuals, particularly those whose close friends and family members initially express ambivalence, confusion, or even hostility regarding same-sex sexuality. Longitudinal research should examine how same-sex couples' decisions about marriage, cohabitation, and parenthood reverberate through all of their intimate social ties, sometimes enhancing and sometimes eroding the quality of these relationships (Smart, 2007). For example, parents who otherwise disapprove of their child's same-sex orientation might soften in response to their child's same-sex wedding or the birth of their first grandchild. The manner in which these shifts unfold over time, adjusting and readjusting to progressive life course transitions, is a critical area for future research. Smart (2007) noted that marriage is a "fateful moment" during which sexual minority individuals must confront, make sense of, and potentially resolve complicated family ties.

Yet marriage is obviously not the only such fateful moment. Consider, for example, the dissolution of a long-term same-sex relationship. Do the parents of sexual minority individuals treat such changes as equivalent to a conventional heterosexual divorce, or do they inadvertently discount the emotional ramifications? When same-sex couples have children, how does the grandparents' behavior depend on the circumstances of the child's birth (i.e., adoption, surrogacy, birth) and on the status of their child as a biological versus nonbiological parent? What are the long-term ramifications for their roles and contributions (both materially and emotionally) as grandparents? These are some of the important questions that deserve attention in future research.

Magnification of Gender-Related Emotional Dynamics

Gender differences in interpersonal attitudes, cognitions, and behaviors have long been fruitful topics of relationship research. One of the signature characteristics of same-sex couples is that both partners have the same gender role and same history of gender-related socialization, unlike heterosexual couples. Contrary to stereotypes portraying gay men and lesbians as "inverted" with respect to gender (such that gay men are expected to resemble heterosexual women, and lesbian women are expected to resemble heterosexual men), research has consistently shown that sexual minority men and women exhibit largely the same gender-related patterns of relationship behavior that have been observed among heterosexuals (e.g., Bailey, Gaulin, Agyei, &

Gladue, 1994). To some degree, this should not be surprising: Not only have sexual minority men and women received the same gender-related socialization regarding intimate relationships as have their heterosexual counterparts, but the vast majority have had extensive romantic experience (and sometimes their earliest and most formative experiences) in conventional heterosexual relationships (Chandra et al., 2011; Laumann et al., 1994). As a result, they have internalized the same heteronormative cultural scripts regarding gender-related interpersonal behavior as have heterosexuals. The end result appears to be that same-sex relationships provide for a double dose of gender-typed attitudes and behavior.

More important, similarity with respect to gender-related roles and skills appears to facilitate effective communication, support, and negotiation (Gottman, Levenson, Swanson, et al., 2003; Roisman et al., 2008), and similarity in day-to-day experiences also appears to facilitate relationship functioning. For example, one study found that lesbian women suffering from premenstrual syndrome reported high levels of responsiveness, understanding, open communication, and responsibility sharing by their female partners, which contrasts with the findings from research on heterosexual women, who typically report that male partners fail to understand, support, or validate their symptoms (Ussher & Perz, 2008).

Although both male–male and female–female couples appear to benefit from gender similarity at the level of day-to-day communication and functioning, female–female couples appear to have an additional advantage owing to women's relationally oriented socialization: Women are encouraged from an early age to seek and to prioritize high levels of connectedness and intimacy within their close interpersonal relationships (Cross & Madson, 1997). As a result, they tend to surpass men with respect to interpersonal sensitivity, empathy, emotional awareness, and emotional expressivity, especially in their romantic relationships (Barrett, Lane, Sechrest, & Schwartz, 2000; Thomas & Fletcher, 2003). They are also more skilled and more comfortable with emotion work in relationships (Duncombe & Marsden, 1998) and more successful in achieving relational mutuality (Jordan, 1991). In contrast, men are socialized to emphasize autonomy, independence, and self-reliance, which has historically been observed to interfere with intimacy and expressiveness in romantic relationships (Green, Bettinger, & Zacks, 1996).

Consequently, lesbian couples tend to exhibit more emotional connectedness, cohesion, and intimacy than gay male or heterosexual couples (Green et al., 1996; Kurdek, 1998), greater capacity for mutual empathy (Ussher & Perz, 2008), more egalitarianism and more shared and flexible decision making (Eldridge & Gilbert, 1990; Green et al., 1996), and more adaptability in dealing with emotional needs and household tasks (Connolly, 2006). Observational research has found that they show more effective patterns of conflict resolution characterized by more positive emotional tone and more effective negotiation (Gottman, Levenson, Gross, et al., 2003; Roisman et al., 2008). Initially, investigators critiqued the heightened connectedness of female–female couples as evidence of problematic fusion or merger (Hill, 1999; Krestan & Bepko, 1980), yet more recent work has suggested that female–female couples manage to balance emotional expressiveness and sharing with boundary setting and autonomy, suggesting successful resolution of the competing demands of individual emotion regulation and dyadic empathy and emotional sensitivity (Ussher & Perz, 2008). More important, more evidence has been found for interpersonal strengths in female–female couples than for interpersonal deficits in male–male couples. Initially, researchers expected that because men are socialized to value independence and autonomy over connectedness and intimacy, male–male couples would be characterized by distance and disengagement (Krestan & Bepko, 1980). Yet this does not appear to be the case. Most studies have detected no differences (or trivial differences) between levels of support, intimacy, cohesion, and satisfaction between male–male and male–female couples (Kurdek, 2001, 2004, 2006; Means-Christensen, Snyder, & Negy, 2003).

Clearly, research on how each partner's gender—and gender socialization—shapes same-sex relationship dynamics has important implications for understanding such dynamics in all couples. Yet future investigations of these topics must be paired with more systematic assessments of individual differences other than gender to specify more clearly the mechanisms through which gender-related effects operate. For example, how might individual difference dimensions such as locus of control (Kurdek, 1997), attachment style (Birnbaum et al., 2006), rejection sensitivity (Downey & Feldman, 1996), and sociosexuality (Simpson, Wilson, & Winterheld, 2004) and affective states such as anxiety and depression (Kurdek, 1997) mediate or moderate the effects of each partners' gender on couple functioning? Future research along these lines will enable researchers to explain not only differences between female–female, male–male, and heterosexual couples but also to identify and explain differences within each relationship type.

Norms and Practices Regarding Sexuality

In many ways, sexual behavior might appear to be the most distinctive aspect of same-sex couples, given that their basic sexual practices are so different. Whereas penile–vaginal intercourse is the single most common sexual act among heterosexual individuals, manual, oral, and anal contact are the most common sexual behaviors among same-sex couples (Blumstein & Schwartz, 1983; Laumann et al., 1994; Lever, 1994, 1995). Yet, it is important to note that none of these acts uniformly "stands in" for penile–vaginal intercourse as the primary form of sexual contact in male–male or female–female couples. Rather, all same-sex couples must engage in some degree of open and explicit negotiation with their sexual partners about their respective sexual likes and dislikes. As far back as 1979, Masters and Johnson noted that this was most likely responsible for the fact that same-sex couples often reported more satisfying sexual interactions than did heterosexual couples, and this supposition has been borne out by later studies on the importance of communication for sexual satisfaction (MacNeil & Byers, 1997; Purnine & Carey, 1997).

One difference between the sexual practices of same-sex and heterosexual couples is that same-sex couples are more likely to trade off between active and passive sexual roles with respect to both initiating sexual activity and performing certain sexual behaviors (Blumstein & Schwartz, 1983; Lever, 1994, 1995). This is notably consistent with the fact that same-sex couples tend to have more equitable role distributions than heterosexual couples in a variety of nonsexual domains, such as household labor, decision making, and general influence, and they tend to divide up responsibilities on a case-by-case basis according to each partner's respective interests and desires (Kurdek, 1993; Solomon et al., 2004). Furthermore, studies have found that even when one partner in a same-sex couple tends to consistently adopt a stereotypically male or female activity in one domain, it does not typically carry over to other domains (Blumstein & Schwartz, 1983). For example, the partner who is the primary breadwinner in a same-sex couple is not necessarily the partner who takes the more active role in sexual activity. Because same-sex couples cannot default to conventional male and female roles in their relationships, they engage in more active and ongoing negotiation about each partner's respective contributions to both sexual and nonsexual aspects of their relationship, and they tend to adopt more diverse and idiosyncratic patterns of roles, responsibilities, and behaviors.

Studies assessing global sexual satisfaction (as opposed to satisfaction with the progress and outcome of specific sexual episodes) have found no overall differences between same-sex and heterosexual couples, and the primary predictors of sexual satisfaction are also the same, most notably relationship satisfaction (Bryant & Demian, 1994; Eldridge & Gilbert, 1990; Holmberg, Blair, & Phillips, 2010). Yet one unique predictor of sexual satisfaction and sexual dysfunction among sexual minorities is internalized homophobia (Meyer & Dean, 1998; Szymanski, Kashubeck-West, & Meyer, 2008), which is also related to lower romantic relationship satisfaction more generally (Meyer & Dean, 1998; Szymanski et al., 2008). Hence, sexual minorities who have difficulty feeling positive about their sexual orientation and identity have difficulty expressing and enjoying sexual intimacy with their partners.

Sexual Frequency: The Case of Lesbian Bed Death

Sexual satisfaction in same-sex couples is also significantly related to sexual frequency (Blumstein

& Schwartz, 1983; Deenen, Gijs, & van Naerssen, 1994), similar to the case with heterosexual couples (McNulty & Fisher, 2008; Simms & Byers, 2009; Yabiku & Gager, 2009). Rates of sexual frequency among male–male couples are largely similar to those found among heterosexual couples, including the propensity for sexual frequency to decline over time. New male–male couples typically engage in sexual activity three or more times per week, and sometimes as often as every day, whereas sexual frequency in longer term male–male couples drops to one to two times a week, similar to the rates found among heterosexual couples (Blumstein & Schwartz, 1983; Bryant & Demian, 1994; Deenen et al., 1994; Laumann et al., 1994). Female–female couples, however, represent a notable exception when it comes to sexual frequency. Although their rates of sexual frequency are comparable (although slightly lower) to those of heterosexual and male–male couples at the beginning of a new relationship, averaging several times per week (Blumstein & Schwartz, 1983; Lever, 1995), female couples show a much steeper decline in sexual frequency as a function of relationship duration.

In fact, some long-term female couples stop engaging in genital sexual contact altogether, a phenomenon that has been denoted *lesbian bed death* (Iasenza, 2002) and that has generated extensive controversy both among sex researchers and members of the lesbian–bisexual community (Fassinger & Morrow, 1995). Some of the controversy concerns the prevalence of bed death, which is difficult to ascertain reliably because of long-standing problems with measurement and with cultural definitions of sex. Surveys that assess sexual frequency often fail to specify exactly which behaviors "count" as sex and, therefore, women who engage in sexual contact that does not involve mutual genital stimulation to orgasm may not report this behavior on such surveys (Frye, 1990). Numerous researchers have argued that the conventional definition of sex as requiring genital contact represents a malecentric conceptualization of sexual activity and fails to represent the fact that many women gain sexual satisfaction from a broader range of erotic nongenital activities (Fassinger & Morrow, 1995). Hence, it is not clear how many female–female couples who appear to be experiencing bed death are actually engaging regularly in a broad range of erotic, physically intimate activities that simply fail to meet conventional definitions of sex (Peplau, Fingerhut, & Beals, 2004).

Even if the term *bed death* overstates the case, studies have demonstrated that female–female couples in long-term relationships have lower rates of sexual activity than male–male or heterosexual couples. Why is this so? Is it a dysfunctional consequence of excessive intimacy, a side effect of women's socialization toward sexual passivity and shame, or a consequence of the fact that women have lower sex drives than men? In wading through these issues, it becomes clear that research on the causes and consequences of this phenomenon would benefit greatly from more systematic integration with the research literature on heterosexual female sexuality. As noted earlier, nearly a third of U.S. women report difficulties with sexual arousal and sexual desire (Laumann et al., 1999). Given that men do most of the sexual initiation in heterosexual couples (Byers & Heinlein, 1989), low sexual desire on the part of a heterosexual woman may never manifest itself as low sexual frequency; rather, she may simply go along with male-initiated sexual activity despite her lack of interest (O'Sullivan & Allgeier, 1998). Yet if the very same woman had a female sexual partner, sexual activity might be unlikely to occur, given that female–female couples often report that the initiation of sex is mutually negotiated and depends on clear-cut signs of reciprocal interest from both partners (Blumstein & Schwartz, 1983). Hence, one partner's occasional reticence has a much stronger influence on overall sexual frequency in female–female couples than in heterosexual or male–male couples. Given this fact, one might question whether most long-term heterosexual couples might also experience lesbian bed death if they did not have a reliably interested and initiatory male partner.

Another controversy regarding bed death concerns its implications for relationship quality. Historically, clinicians have argued that infrequent sexual contact in female–female couples might indicate deep-seated problems in the relationship or serious sexual dysfunction on the part of one or both

partners (Fassinger & Morrow, 1995). Yet there is little reliable evidence to suggest that this is the case. Some have argued that as long as both partners are satisfied with their sexual relationship and with the overall degree of sensual, affectionate, and nongenital intimacy in their day-to-day lives, the lack of genital contact need not raise concerns, and the persistent preoccupation with sexual frequency represents reliance on male-defined models of sexuality that privilege genital contact and orgasm over the more sensual and emotional aspects of sexual intimacy (Fassinger & Morrow, 1995; Rothblum & Brehony, 1993). Clearly, researchers need to maintain a critical perspective on contemporary definitions of—and proposed clinical treatments for—female sexual problems in general to understand the causes and consequences of diminished sexual activity in female–female couples.

It is also important, as noted earlier, to keep in mind that the phenomenon of diminished (or absent) sexual activity is not unique to female–female couples and that attempts to discern the causes and consequences of this pattern should make relevant comparisons to male–male and male–female couples. Although the Viagra revolution was widely heralded for initiating the rebirth of sexual intimacy in many older heterosexual couples, many clinicians have noted that it subsequently triggered significant relationship problems for many couples who discovered, once sex was a possibility again, that the female partner was no longer interested (Shifren & Hanfling, 2010). As discussed by Donnelly and Burgess (2008), the healthfulness and satisfaction of celibate couples depends largely on the reasons for the decline in sexual activity, whether both partners are satisfied with the current state of affairs, and the strategies they adopt to cope with discrepancies in sexual interest. These issues deserve more attention with regard to all couples.

Sexual Nonexclusivity in Male–Male Couples

One notable area in which male–male couples prove distinct from both female–female and heterosexual couples is sexual exclusivity. Male–male couples are more likely than either male–female or female–female couples to engage in extradyadic sexual activity, usually with the explicit knowledge of their partner (see also Bonello, 2009; Solomon et al., 2004). Estimates have varied from study to study, but data have suggested that between one third and two thirds of male–male couples have open (i.e., sexually nonmonogamous) relationships (Bryant & Demian, 1994; Crawford et al., 2003; LaSala, 2004). Sexual minority men rate monogamy as less important to their relationship satisfaction and sexual satisfaction than do female–female and heterosexual couples (Blumstein & Schwartz, 1983), and studies comparing open with closed relationships have found no differences in satisfaction or stability (Bonello, 2009).

Historically, nonmonogamy among sexual minority men was viewed as a dysfunctional outgrowth of stigmatization, leading them to compartmentalize sexual and emotional intimacy and to avoid long-term committed relationships. Yet this view has been critiqued as inappropriately applying heterocentrist standards (in which monogamy is paramount) to male–male couples (Green et al., 1996). Some have argued, instead, that open relationships among sexual minority men represent adaptive solutions to their combined desire for emotional intimacy and for sexual variety and a means of coping with the declines in sexual frequency that typically occur in long-term relationships (LaSala, 2004). Given that men (regardless of sexual orientation) appear better able than women to separate sexual from emotional intimacy (Banfield & McCabe, 2001), male–male couples appear particularly well suited to maintaining arrangements that permit both partners to pursue recreational sexual activity without threatening their primary partnership (Bonello, 2009). Such couples explicitly distinguish emotional monogamy from sexual monogamy (LaSala, 2004).

More important, the fact that nonmonogamy is so much more common among male–male couples than female–female or heterosexual couples does not suggest that this is the preferred pattern for all gay men (Blumstein & Schwartz, 1983; Bryant & Demian, 1994; Lever, 1994). Personality, ideological factors, and preferences for sexual variety appear to predict which sexual minority men seek open relationships (Crawford et al., 2003). Furthermore, most sexual minority men engaged in open

relationships also have experience with conventional monogamous relationships (Ramirez & Brown, 2010), suggesting that the decision to pursue nonmonogamy depends on the specific features of the relationship in question (such as whether both partners share the same views and expectations regarding monogamy). Couple-level characteristics are also important. Longer term relationships are more likely to be nonmonogamous (Ramirez & Brown, 2010), although the causal mechanism underlying this association is not clear. One possibility is that sexual minority men may not be comfortable establishing nonmonogamy in a relationship until after it has progressed to a sufficient level of commitment and trust. Alternatively, sexual minority men may be motivated to seek extradyadic sexual activity only after the honeymoon phase characterizing the first few years of a new relationship winds down and sexual frequency declines. Finally, it is possible that the decision to open up a relationship stabilizes male–male relationships by circumventing the potential obstacle of sexual boredom, obviating the need for infidelity, and prompting both partners to make explicit their emotional investment and commitment to one another.

Openness and good communication appear to be critical for the successful maintenance of open relationships. Couples without clear agreements about the boundaries regarding these relationships have lower levels of satisfaction and affection than those who establish and maintain clear parameters regarding extradyadic activity (Bonello, 2009; Ramirez & Brown, 2010). The specific types of rules that couples establish vary widely, although most are aimed at protecting the emotional primacy of the relationship, preventing either partner from feeling hurt or left out, and also preventing the acquisition and transmission of sexually transmitted infections (Hoff & Beougher, 2010; Ramirez & Brown, 2010). For example, some couples pursue extradyadic sex only in the form of threesomes; other rules specify that mutual friends and former lovers are off limits or that new friendships or emotional connections cannot be formed with outside sexual partners; some couples agree not to discuss outside sexual partners with one another, whereas other couples specifically request that details be provided afterward (for more examples, see Hoff & Beougher, 2010). Regardless of the rules that couples establish, many find that these rules must be continually updated and revisited over time to account for unanticipated reactions and situations (LaSala, 2001), further underscoring the value of good communication.

Given recent historical changes regarding attitudes toward, recognition of, and men's participation in committed same-sex partnerships, rates of—and rules about—extradyadic sexual activity may change, and they deserve closer attention. For example, one notable topic for future research is whether contemporary cohorts of young gay men, who are exposed to a far greater number of positive images of successful gay male couples than previous cohorts have been, might have significantly more optimistic expectations for forming stable and satisfying long-term relationships and, hence, different attitudes about sexual exclusivity.

Emerging Directions

The first several decades of research on same-sex couples focused considerable attention on comparing them with heterosexual couples and documenting their similarities and differences. Although this research has made important contributions to the understanding of same-sex relationships, it may be time to move beyond the comparative approach and focus more attention on variability among same-sex couples. One important reason for such a shift is to escape the presumption—still implicitly underlying much comparative research—that heterosexual relationships set the standard for normal, healthy functioning (Bonello & Cross, 2009). According to this implicit standard, same-sex couples appear healthy and normal to the extent that they resemble heterosexual couples. When differences between same-sex and heterosexual couples are observed, researchers generally question why same-sex couples think and behave the way they do instead of asking why heterosexual couples think and behave the way they do. Of course, it is perfectly reasonable to use heterosexual relationships as the normative standard on the basis of their overwhelming prevalence in society. Yet normative should not be taken to imply healthful. Rather, one of most important potential contributions of future research on same-sex

couples is to demonstrate the wide range of alternative practices through which individuals might adaptively meet needs for emotional and physical intimacy. The healthfulness of both heterosexual and same-sex practices should be treated as ongoing empirical questions, and researchers should continually challenge and test assumptions about the optimal form and function of intimate relationships.

The institution of legal marriage provides a productive example. As reviewed earlier, most same-sex couples would like the option of formalizing their relationships through marriage, and the lack of legal formalization has negative implications for the satisfaction and stability of same-sex relationships. Yet little research has focused on the subset of sexual minorities (roughly one fourth) who do not want the option of legal marriage. What might their resistance reveal about the potential downsides of legal formalization more generally? Many scholars have responded to the historical exclusion of sexual minority individuals from the institution of marriage with critical reflection about the political, social, legal, and personal meaning of marriage and marriagelike relationships. Some have come away from such reflections strongly critical of the patriarchal underpinnings of traditional marriage and the specter of religious or governmental regulation of personal relationships. Others, more provocatively, have argued that an even more dangerous problem is the hegemonic notion that exclusive, monogamous sexual or romantic partnerships are those most healthy, desirable, and worthy of legal recognition (Ettelbrick, 2001). In light of these debates, some have argued that instead of focusing so much attention on same-sex marriage, researchers should document the potential benefits of alternative relationship practices that are commonly observed in same-sex couples, such as maintaining separate residences from a primary partner (Hess & Catell, 2001); pursuing multiple or nonmonogamous partnerships (Rust, 1996; West, 1996); developing romantic, emotionally primary but nonsexual relationships (Rothblum & Brehony, 1993); or forgoing primary ties altogether in favor of chosen families of close friends (Nardi, 1999). Such investigations can enrich researchers' understanding of same-sex and heterosexual relationships.

Fluidity in sexual attractions and behavior constitutes another emerging direction for future research. Researchers have long noted that some sexual minority individuals—especially women—appear to experience same-sex desires only in the context of a single, unexpectedly intense emotional relationship (Diamond, 2003), and this phenomenon now appears to be related to the broader phenomenon of situation dependence or plasticity in sexuality (Baumeister, 2000). Given that intimate relationships are among the most common triggers for sexual fluidity, future research should systematically investigate how common such experiences are among men and women, the mechanisms through which they operate, and their long-term implications for sexual experience and identity. Another fascinating topic with regard to fluidity concerns how same-sex and other-sex couples manage either partner's periodic experience—and potential expression—of desires that contradict one's self-described sexual orientation. Some research in this vein has been conducted on bisexually attracted individuals in heterosexual relationships (Reinhardt, 2001), but much more could be gained by a broader perspective that treats incongruencies among love, desire, and identity as the central focus and that does not presume impermeable boundaries between heterosexual and sexual minority identities and life histories.

CONCLUSION

The past several decades have witnessed an enormous change in how psychologists study and conceptualize sexuality. Historically, disproportionate attention has been devoted to the negative repercussions of sexual behavior, but numerous scholars within various subdisciplines of psychology have argued for greater study of the positive and normative dimensions of sexual functioning, particularly within the contexts of intimate relationships. Individuals with well-functioning intimate relationships are known to have superior physical and mental health over the life span, including more positive day-to-day emotional functioning and lower morbidity and mortality. The quality of a couple's sexual functioning undoubtedly contributes to these effects. As shown in this chapter, the sexual dynamic between members of a couple reflects dynamics that characterize other nonsexual aspects of their relationship but also provides unique information about their enactment and management of intimacy, comfort, pleasure, power, gender, love, and attachment. The next generation of relationship research will undoubtedly advance the understanding of the multiple psychological, behavioral, and biological mechanisms through which sexuality shapes—and is shaped by—people's experiences in intimate relationships and their physical and mental well-being more generally.

References

Abel, G., & Fitzgerald, L. (2006). "When you come to it you feel like a dork asking a guy to put a condom on": Is sex education addressing young people's understandings of risk? *Sex Education, 6*, 105–119. doi:10.1080/14681810600578750

Alderson, K. G. (2004). A phenomenological investigation of same-sex marriage. *Canadian Journal of Human Sexuality, 13*, 107–122.

American Psychiatric Association. (1994). *Diagnostic and statistical manual of mental disorders* (4th ed.). Washington, DC: Author.

Aron, A. P., & Henkemeyer, L. (1995). Marital satisfaction and passionate love. *Journal of Social and Personal Relationships, 12*, 139–146. doi:10.1177/0265407595121010

Aubin, S., & Heiman, J. R. (2004). Sexual dysfunction from a relationship perspective. In J. H. Harvey, A. Wenzel, & S. Sprecher (Eds.), *The handbook of sexuality in close relationships* (pp. 477–517). Mahwah, NJ: Erlbaum.

Bailey, J. M., Gaulin, S., Agyei, Y., & Gladue, B. (1994). Effects of gender and sexual orientation on evolutionarily relevant aspects of human mating psychology. *Journal of Personality and Social Psychology, 66*, 1081–1093. doi:10.1037/0022-3514.66.6.1081

Balsam, K. F., Beauchaine, T. P., Rothblum, E. D., & Solomon, S. E. (2008). Three-year follow-up of same-sex couples who had civil unions in Vermont, same-sex couples not in civil unions, and heterosexual married couples. *Developmental Psychology, 44*, 102–116. doi:10.1037/0012-1649.44.1.102

Balsam, K. F., Rothblum, E. D., & Beauchaine, T. P. (2005). Victimization over the life span: A comparison of lesbian, gay, bisexual, and heterosexual siblings. *Journal of Consulting and Clinical Psychology, 73*, 477–487. doi:10.1037/0022-006X.73.3.477

Banfield, S., & McCabe, M. P. (2001). Extra relationship involvement among women: Are they different from men? *Archives of Sexual Behavior, 30*, 119–142. doi:10.1023/A:1002773100507

Barrett, L. F., Lane, R. D., Sechrest, L., & Schwartz, G. E. (2000). Sex differences in emotional awareness. *Personality and Social Psychology Bulletin, 26*, 1027–1035. doi:10.1177/01461672002611001

Barsky, J. L., Friedman, M. A., & Rosen, R. C. (2006). Sexual dysfunction and chronic illness: The role of flexibility in coping. *Journal of Sex and Marital Therapy, 32*, 235–253. doi:10.1080/00926230600575322

Basson, R. (2001). Using a different model for female sexual response to address women's problematic low sexual desire. *Journal of Sex and Marital Therapy, 27*, 395–403. doi:10.1080/713846827

Baumeister, R. F. (2000). Gender differences in erotic plasticity: The female sex drive as socially flexible and responsive. *Psychological Bulletin, 126*, 347–374. doi:10.1037/0033-2909.126.3.347

Baumeister, R. F., Catanese, K. R., & Vohs, K. D. (2001). Is there a gender difference in strength of sex drive? Theoretical views, conceptual distinctions, and a review of relevant evidence. *Personality and Social Psychology Review, 5*, 242–273. doi:10.1207/S15327957PSPR0503_5

Birnbaum, G. E., Reis, H. T., Mikulincer, M., Gillath, O., & Orpaz, A. (2006). When sex is more than just sex: Attachment orientations, sexual experience, and relationship quality. *Journal of Personality and Social Psychology, 91*, 929–943. doi:10.1037/0022-3514.91.5.929

Blair, K. L., & Holmberg, D. (2008). Perceived social network support and well-being in same-sex versus mixed-sex romantic relationships. *Journal of Social and Personal Relationships, 25*, 769–791. doi:10.1177/0265407508096695

Blumstein, P., & Schwartz, P. (1983). *American couples: Money, work, sex.* New York, NY: Morrow.

Bonello, K. (2009). Gay monogamy and extra-dyadic sex: A critical review of the theoretical and empirical literature. *Counselling Psychology Review, 24*, 51–65.

Bonello, K., & Cross, M. C. (2009). Gay monogamy: I love you but I can't have sex with only you. *Journal of Homosexuality, 57*, 117–139. doi:10.1080/00918360903445962

Bozon, M. (2001). Sexuality, gender, and the couple: A sociohistorical perspective. *Annual Review of Sex Research, 12*, 1–32.

Brody, S. (2003). Alexithymia is inversely associated with women's frequency of vaginal intercourse. *Archives of Sexual Behavior, 32*, 73–77. doi:10.1023/A:1021897530286

Brody, S., & Kruger, T. H. C. (2006). The post-orgasmic prolactin increase following intercourse is greater than following masturbation and suggests greater satiety. *Biological Psychology, 71*, 312–315. doi:10.1016/j.biopsycho.2005.06.008

Bryant, A. S., & Demian. (1994). Relationship characteristics of American gay and lesbian couples: Findings from a national survey. *Journal of Gay and Lesbian Social Services, 1*, 101–117. doi:10.1300/J041v01n02_06

Byers, E. S. (2005). Relationship satisfaction and sexual satisfaction: A longitudinal study of individuals and long-term relationships. *Journal of Sex Research, 42*, 113–118. doi:10.1080/00224490509552264

Byers, E. S. (2011). Beyond the birds and the bees and was it good for you? Thirty years of research on sexual communication. *Canadian Psychology, 52*, 20–28.

Byers, E. S., & Heinlein, L. (1989). Predicting initiations and refusals of sexual activities in married and cohabiting heterosexual couples. *Journal of Sex Research, 26*, 210–231. doi:10.1080/00224498909551507

Byers, E. S., & Wang, A. (2004). Understanding sexuality in close relationships from a social exchange perspective. In J. H. Harvey, A. Wenzel, & S. Sprecher (Eds.), *The handbook of sexuality in close relationships* (pp. 203–234). Mahwah, NJ: Erlbaum.

Call, V., Sprecher, S., & Schwartz, P. (1995). The incidence and frequency of marital sex in a national sample. *Journal of Marriage and the Family, 57*, 639–652. doi:10.2307/353919

Chandra, A., Mosher, W. D., Copen, C., & Sionean, C. (2011). *Sexual behavior, sexual attraction, and sexual identity in the United States: Data from the 2006–2008 National Survey of Family Growth* (National Health Statistics Report No. 36). Hyattsville, MD: National Center for Health Statistics.

Chen, H. K., Tsend, C. D., Wu, S. C., Lee, T. K., & Chen, H. H. (2007). A prospective cohort study on the effect of sexual activity, libido and widowhood on mortality among the elderly people: 14-year follow-up of 2453 elderly Taiwanese. *International Journal of Epidemiology, 36*, 1136–1142. doi:10.1093/ije/dym109

Cohler, B. J., & Hammack, P. L. (2007). The psychological world of the gay teenager: Social change, narrative, and "normality." *Journal of Youth and Adolescence, 36*, 47–59. doi:10.1007/s10964-006-9110-1

Conley, T. D., Roesch, S. C., Peplau, L. A., & Gold, M. S. (2009). A test of positive illusions versus shared reality models of relationship satisfaction among gay, lesbian, and heterosexual couples. *Journal of Applied Social Psychology, 39*, 1417–1431. doi:10.1111/j.1559-1816.2009.00488.x

Connolly, C. M. (2006). A feminist perspective of resilience in lesbian couples. *Journal of Feminist Family Therapy, 18*, 137–162. doi:10.1300/J086v18n01_06

Corona, G., Monami, M., Boddi, V., Cameron-Smith, M., Lotti, F., de Vita, G., . . . Maggi, M. (2010). Male sexuality and cardiovascular risk. A cohort study in patients with erectile dysfunction. *Journal of Sexual Medicine, 7*, 1918–1927. doi:10.1111/j.1743-6109.2010.01744.x

Crawford, I., Hammack, P. L., McKirnan, D. J., Ostrow, D., Zamboni, B. D., Robinson, B., & Hope, B. (2003). Sexual sensation seeking, reduced concern about HIV and sexual risk behaviour among gay men in primary relationships. *AIDS Care, 15*, 513–524. doi:10.1080/0954012031000134755

Cross, S. E., & Madson, L. (1997). Models of the self: Self-construals and gender. *Psychological Bulletin, 122*, 5–37. doi:10.1037/0033-2909.122.1.5

Cupach, W. R., & Metts, S. (1991). Sexuality and communication in close relationships. In K. McKinney & S. Sprecher (Eds.), *Sexuality in close relationships* (pp. 93–110). Hillsdale, NJ: Erlbaum.

D'Augelli, A. R., Grossman, A. H., & Starks, M. T. (2005). Parents' awareness of lesbian, gay, and bisexual youths' sexual orientation. *Journal of Marriage and the Family, 67*, 474–482. doi:10.1111/j.0022-2445.2005.00129.x

D'Augelli, A. R., Grossman, A. H., & Starks, M. T. (2006). Childhood gender atypicality, victimization, and PTSD among lesbian, gay, and bisexual youth. *Journal of Interpersonal Violence, 21*, 1462–1482. doi:10.1177/0886260506293482

Davey Smith, G. (1997). Sex and death: Are they related? Findings from the Caerphilly Cohort Study. *British Medical Journal, 315*, 1641. doi:10.1136/bmj.315.7123.1641

Deenen, A. A., Gijs, L., & van Naerssen, A. X. (1994). Intimacy and sexuality in gay male couples. *Archives of Sexual Behavior, 23*, 421–431. doi:10.1007/BF01541407

Defense of Marriage Act, Pub.L. 104–199, 110 Stat. 2419 (1996).

Derogatis, L. R., & Burnett, A. L. (2008). The epidemiology of sexual dysfunctions. *Journal of Sexual Medicine, 5*, 289–300.

Diamond, L. M. (2003). What does sexual orientation orient? A biobehavioral model distinguishing romantic love and sexual desire. *Psychological Review, 110*, 173–192. doi:10.1037/0033-295X.110.1.173

Diamond, L. M. (2008). *Sexual fluidity: Understanding women's love and desire.* Cambridge, MA: Harvard University Press.

Diamond, L. M., Fagundes, C. P., & Butterworth, M. R. (2010). Intimate relationships across the lifespan. In M. E. Lamb, L. White, & A. Freund (Eds.), *Handbook of lifespan development* (Vol. 2, pp. 379–433). New York, NY: Wiley. doi:10.1002/9780470880166.hlsd002011

Donnelly, D. A., & Burgess, E. O. (2008). The decision to remain in an involuntarily celibate relationship. *Journal of Marriage and Family, 70*, 519–535. doi:10.1111/j.1741-3737.2008.00498.x

Downey, G., & Feldman, S. I. (1996). Implications of rejection sensitivity for intimate relationships. *Journal of Personality and Social Psychology, 70*, 1327–1343. doi:10.1037/0022-3514.70.6.1327

Duncombe, J., & Marsden, D. (1998). Stepford wives and hollow men? Doing emotion work, doing gender and authenticity in heterosexual relationships. In G. Bendelow & S. Williams (Eds.), *Emotions in social life: Critical themes and contemporary issues* (pp. 34–47). London, England: Routledge.

Dürr, E. (2009). Lack of "responsive" sexual desire in women: Implications for clinical practice. *Sexual and Relationship Therapy, 24*, 292–306. doi:10.1080/14681990903271228

Eldridge, N. S., & Gilbert, L. A. (1990). Correlates of relationship satisfaction in lesbian couples. *Psychology of Women Quarterly, 14*, 43–62. doi:10.1111/j.1471-6402.1990.tb00004.x

Eskridge, W. N., & Spedale, D. R. (2006). *Gay marriage: For better or for worse? What we've learned from the evidence.* New York, NY: Oxford University Press.

Ettelbrick, P. (2001). Domestic partnership, civil unions, or marriage: One size does not fit all. *Albany Law Review, 64*, 905–914.

Exton, M. S., Kruger, T. H. C., Koch, M., Paulson, E., Knapp, W., Hartmann, U., & Schedlowski, M. (2001). Coitus-induced orgasm stimulates prolactin secretion in healthy subjects. *Psychoneuroendocrinology, 26*, 287–294. doi:10.1016/S0306-4530(00)00053-6

Fassinger, R. E., & Morrow, S. L. (1995). Overcome: Repositioning lesbian sexualities. In L. Diamant & R. D. McAnulty (Eds.), *The psychology of sexual orientation, behavior, and identity: A handbook* (pp. 197–219). Westport, CT: Greenwood Press.

Finch, J., & Mason, J. (1993). *Negotiating family responsibilities.* London, England: Tavistock.

Fincham, F. D., Hall, J., & Beach, S. R. H. (2006). Forgiveness in marriage: Current status and future directions. *Family Relations: Interdisciplinary Journal of Applied Family Status, 55*, 415–427. doi:10.1111/j.1741-3729.2005.callf.x-il

Fingerhut, A. W. (2010). Relationship formalization and individual and relationship well-being among same-sex couples. *Journal of Social and Personal Relationships, 27*, 956–969. doi:10.1177/0265407510376253

Fisher, W. A., & Boroditsky, R. (2000). Sexual activity, contraceptive choice, and sexual and reproductive health indicators among single Canadian women aged 15–29: Additional findings from the Canadian Contraception Study. *Canadian Journal of Human Sexuality, 9*, 79.

Frye, M. (1990). Lesbian "sex." In J. Allen (Ed.), *Lesbian philosophies and cultures* (pp. 305–316). Albany: State University of New York Press.

Fugl-Meyer, A. R., & Fugl-Meyer, K. S. (1999). Sexual disabilities, problems and satisfaction in 18–74 year old Swedes. *Scandinavian Journal of Sexology, 2*, 79–105.

Gable, S. L., & La Guardia, J. G. (2007). Positive processes in close relationships across time, partners, and context: A multilevel approach. In A. D. Ong & M. H. M. van Dulmen (Eds.), *Oxford handbook of methods in positive psychology* (pp. 576–590). New York, NY: Oxford University Press.

Gagnon, J. H., Giami, A., Michaels, S., & Colomby, P. (2001). A comparative study of the couple in the social organization of sexuality in France and the United States. *Journal of Sex Research, 38*, 24–34. doi:10.1080/00224490109552067

Gilbert, E., Ussher, J. M., & Perz, J. (2010). Renegotiating sexuality and intimacy in the context of cancer: The experiences of carers. *Archives of Sexual Behavior, 39*, 998–1009. doi:10.1007/s10508-008-9416-z

Gottman, J. M. (1994). *What predicts divorce?* Hillsdale, NJ: Erlbaum.

Gottman, J. M., Levenson, R. W., Gross, J. J., Frederickson, B. L., McCoy, K., Rosenthal, L., . . . Yoshimoto, D. (2003). Correlates of gay and lesbian couples' relationship satisfaction and relationship dissolution. *Journal of Homosexuality, 45*, 23–43. doi:10.1300/J082v45n01_02

Gottman, J. M., Levenson, R. W., Swanson, C., Swanson, K., Tyson, R., & Yoshimoto, D. (2003). Observing gay, lesbian and heterosexual couples' relationships: Mathematical modeling of conflict interaction. *Journal of Homosexuality, 45*, 65–91. doi:10.1300/J082v45n01_04

Green, R.-J. (2008). Gay and lesbian couples: Successful coping with minority stress. In M. McGoldrick & K. V. Hardy (Eds.), *Re-visioning family therapy: Race, culture, and gender in clinical practice* (2nd ed., pp. 300–310). New York, NY: Guilford Press.

Green, R.-J., Bettinger, M., & Zacks, E. (1996). Are lesbian couples fused and gay male couples disengaged? Questioning gender straightjackets. In J. Laird & R.-J. Green (Eds.), *Lesbians and gays in couples and families: A handbook for therapists* (pp. 185–230). San Francisco, CA: Jossey-Bass.

Grossman, A. H., D'Augelli, A. R., & Hershberger, S. L. (2000). Social support networks of lesbian, gay, and bisexual adults 60 years of age and older. *Journals of Gerontology, Series B: Psychological Sciences and Social Sciences, 55*, P171–P179. doi:10.1093/geronb/55.3.P171

Günzler, C., Kriston, L., Harms, A., & Berner, M. M. (2009). Association of sexual functioning and quality of partnership in patients in cardiovascular rehabilitation: A gender perspective. *Journal of Sexual Medicine, 6*, 164–174. doi:10.1111/j.1743-6109.2008.01039.x

Haning, R. V., O'Keefe, S. L., Randall, E. J., Kommor, M. J., Baker, E., & Wilson, R. (2007). Intimacy, orgasm likelihood, and conflict predict sexual satisfaction in heterosexual male and female respondents. *Journal of Sex and Marital Therapy, 33*, 93–113. doi:10.1080/00926230601098449

Hayes, R. D., Dennerstein, L., Bennett, C. M., & Fairley, C. K. (2008). What is the "true" prevalence of female sexual dysfunctions and does the way we assess these conditions have an impact? *Journal of Sexual Medicine, 5*, 777–787. doi:10.1111/j.1743-6109.2007.00768.x

Hayes, R. D., Dennerstein, L., Bennett, C. M., Sidat, M., Gurrin, L. C., & Fairley, C. K. (2008). Risk factors for female sexual dysfunction in the general population: Exploring factors associated with low sexual function and sexual distress. *Journal of Sexual Medicine, 5*, 1681–1693. doi:10.1111/j.1743-6109.2008.00838.x

Hazan, C., & Zeifman, D. (1994). Sex and the psychological tether. In D. Perlman & K. Bartholomew (Eds.), *Advances in personal relationships* (Vol. 5, pp. 151–178). London, England: Jessica Kingsley.

Heiman, J. R. (2000). Orgasmic disorders in women. In S. R. Leiblum & R. C. Rosen (Eds.), *Principles and practice of sex therapy* (3rd ed., pp. 118–153). New York, NY: Guilford Press.

Heiman, J. R. (2002). Sexual dysfunction: Overview of prevalence, etiological factors, and treatments. *Journal of Sex Research, 39*, 73–78. doi:10.1080/00224490209552124

Heiman, J. R., & Meston, C. M. (1997). Evaluating sexual dysfunction in women. *Clinical Obstetrics and Gynecology, 40*, 616–629. doi:10.1097/00003081-199709000-00021

Herbenick, D., Reece, M., Sanders, S. A., Dodge, B., Ghassemi, A., & Fortenberry, J. D. (2010). Women's vibrator use in sexual partnerships: Results from a nationally representative survey in the United States. *Journal of Sex and Marital Therapy, 36*, 49–65. doi:10.1080/00926230903375677

Herek, G. M. (2004). Beyond "homophobia": Thinking about sexual prejudice and stigma in the twenty-first century. *Sexuality Research and Social Policy, 1*, 6–24.

Hess, J., & Catell, P. (2001). Dual dwelling duos: An alternative for long-term relationships. In B. J. Brothers (Ed.), *Couples, intimacy issues, and addiction* (pp. 25–31). New York, NY: Haworth Press. doi:10.1300/J036v10n03_04

Hill, C. A. (1999). Fusion and conflict in lesbian relationships? *Feminism and Psychology, 9*, 179–185. doi:10.1177/0959353599009002010

Hirsch, K. A. (2009). Sexual dysfunction in male Operation Enduring Freedom/Operation Iraqi Freedom patients with severe post-traumatic stress disorder. *Military Medicine, 174*, 520–522.

Hoff, C. C., & Beougher, S. C. (2010). Sexual agreements among gay male couples. *Archives of Sexual Behavior, 39*, 774–787. doi:10.1007/s10508-008-9393-2

Holmberg, D., Blair, K. L., & Phillips, M. (2010). Women's sexual satisfaction as a predictor of well-being in same-sex versus mixed-sex relationships. *Journal of Sex Research, 47*, 1–11. doi:10.1080/00224490902898710

Huang, Y. C., & Mathers, N. J. (2006). A comparison of sexual satisfaction and post-natal depression in the UK and Taiwan. *International Nursing Review, 53*, 197–204. doi:10.1111/j.1466-7657.2006.00459.x

Hurd Clarke, L. (2006). Older women and sexuality: Experiences in marital relationships across the life course. *Canadian Journal on Aging, 25*, 129–140. doi:10.1353/cja.2006.0034

Iasenza, S. (2002). Beyond "lesbian bed death": The passion and play in lesbian relationships. *Journal of Lesbian Studies, 6*, 111–120. doi:10.1300/J155v06n01_10

Impett, E. A., & Peplau, L. A. (2002). Why some women consent to unwanted sex with a dating partner: Insights from attachment theory. *Psychology of Women Quarterly, 26*, 360–370. doi:10.1111/1471-6402.t01-1-00075

Institute of Medicine. (2011). *The health of lesbian, gay, bisexual, and transgender people: Building a foundation for better understanding.* Washington, DC: National Academies Press.

Jackson, G., Rosen, R. C., Kloner, R. A., & Kostis, J. B. (2006). The second Princeton consensus on sexual dysfunction and cardiac risk: New guidelines for sexual medicine. *Journal of Sexual Medicine, 3*, 28–36. doi:10.1111/j.1743-6109.2005.00196.x

Johnson, M. P. (1999). Personal, moral, and structural commitment to relationships: Experiences of choice and constraint. In J. M. Adams & W. H. Jones (Eds.), *Handbook of interpersonal commitment and relationship stability* (pp. 73–87). Dordrecht, the Netherlands: Kluwer Academic. doi:10.1007/978-1-4615-4773-0_4

Jonason, P. K., & Marks, M. J. (2009). Common vs. uncommon sexual acts: Evidence for the sexual double standard. *Sex Roles, 60*, 357–365. doi:10.1007/s11199-008-9542-z

Jordan, J. V. (1991). The meaning of mutuality. In A. G. Kaplan, J. B. Miller, I. Stiver, & J. Surrey (Eds.), *Women's growth in connection: Writings from the Stone Center* (pp. 81–96). New York, NY: Guilford Press.

Kaiser Family Foundation. (2001). *Inside-out: Report on the experiences of lesbians, gays and bisexuals in America and the public's view on issues and policies related to sexual orientation.* Menlo Park, CA: Kaiser Family Foundation.

Kelly, M. P., Strassberg, D. S., & Turner, C. M. (2004). Communication and associated relationship issues in female anorgasmia. *Journal of Sex and Marital Therapy, 30*, 263–276. doi:10.1080/00926230490422403

Kelly, M. P., Strassberg, D. S., & Turner, C. M. (2006). Behavioral assessment of couples' communication in female orgasmic disorder. *Journal of Sex and Marital Therapy, 32*, 81–95. doi:10.1080/00926230500442243

Kiecolt-Glaser, J. K., Malarkey, W. B., Chee, M., & Newton, T. (1993). Negative behavior during marital conflict is associated with immunological down-regulation. *Psychosomatic Medicine, 55*, 395–409.

Krestan, J., & Bepko, C. S. (1980). The problem of fusion in lesbian relationships. *Family Process, 19*, 277–289. doi:10.1111/j.1545-5300.1980.00277.x

Kreuter, M., Sullivan, M., & Siosteen, A. (1994). Sexual adjustment after spinal cord injury—Comparison of partner experiences in pre- and post-injury relationships. *Paraplegia, 32*, 759–770. doi:10.1038/sc.1994.122

Kurdek, L. A. (1993). The allocation of household labor in gay, lesbian, and heterosexual married couples. *Journal of Social Issues, 49*, 127–139. doi:10.1111/j.1540-4560.1993.tb01172.x

Kurdek, L. A. (1997). The link between facets of neuroticism and dimensions of relationship commitment: Evidence from gay, lesbian, and heterosexual couples. *Journal of Family Psychology, 11*, 503–514. doi:10.1037/0893-3200.11.4.503

Kurdek, L. A. (1998). Relationship outcomes and their predictors: Longitudinal evidence from heterosexual married, gay cohabiting, and lesbian cohabiting couples. *Journal of Marriage and the Family, 60*, 553–568. doi:10.2307/353528

Kurdek, L. A. (2001). Differences between heterosexual-nonparent couples and gay, lesbian, and heterosexual-parent couples. *Journal of Family Issues, 22*, 727–754. doi:10.1177/019251301022006004

Kurdek, L. A. (2004). Are gay and lesbian cohabiting couples really different from heterosexual married couples? *Journal of Marriage and Family, 66*, 880–900. doi:10.1111/j.0022-2445.2004.00060.x

Kurdek, L. A. (2006). Differences between partners from heterosexual, gay, and lesbian cohabiting couples. *Journal of Marriage and Family, 68*, 509–528. doi:10.1111/j.1741-3737.2006.00268.x

Lannutti, P. J. (2007). The influence of same-sex marriage on the understanding of same-sex relationships. *Journal of Homosexuality, 53*, 135–151. doi:10.1300/J082v53n03_08

LaSala, M. C. (1998). Coupled gay men, parents, and in-laws: Intergenerational disapproval and the need for a thick skin. *Families in Society, 79*, 585–595. doi:10.1606/1044-3894.862

LaSala, M. C. (2001). Monogamous or not: Understanding and counseling gay male couples. *Families in Society, 82*, 605–611. doi:10.1606/1044-3894.155

LaSala, M. C. (2004). Extradyadic sex and gay male couples: Comparing monogamous and nonmonogamous relationships. *Families in Society, 85*, 405–412. doi:10.1606/1044-3894.1502

Laumann, E. O., Gagnon, J. H., Michael, R. T., & Michaels, F. (1994). *The social organization of sexuality: Sexual practices in the United States*. Chicago, IL: University of Chicago Press.

Laumann, E. O., Paik, A., & Rosen, R. C. (1999). Sexual dysfunction in the United States: Prevalence and predictors. *JAMA, 281*, 537–544. doi:10.1001/jama.281.6.537

Lawrance, K.-A., & Byers, E. S. (1992). Development of the interpersonal exchange model of sexual satisfaction in long term relationships. *Canadian Journal of Human Sexuality, 1*, 123–128.

Lawrance, K.-A., & Byers, E. S. (1995). Sexual satisfaction in long-term heterosexual relationships: The interpersonal exchange model of sexual satisfaction. *Personal Relationships, 2*, 267–285. doi:10.1111/j.1475-6811.1995.tb00092.x

Lehmiller, J. J., & Agnew, C. R. (2006). Marginalized relationships: The impact of social disapproval on romantic relationship commitment. *Personality and Social Psychology Bulletin, 32*, 40–51. doi:10.1177/0146167205278710

Leiblum, S. R. (2003). Sex-starved marriages sweeping the US. *Sexual and Relationship Therapy, 18*, 427–428. doi:10.1080/14681990310001609769

Leiblum, S. R., & Rosen, R. C. (2000). Introduction: Sex therapy in the age of Viagra. In S. R. Leiblum & R. C. Rosen (Eds.), *Principles and practice of sex therapy* (3rd ed., pp. 1–13). New York, NY: Guilford Press.

Lever, J. (1994, August 23). Sexual revelations. *Advocate*, 17–24.

Lever, J. (1995, August 22). Lesbian sex survey. *Advocate*, 21–30.

Lewis, R. W., Fugl-Meyer, K. S., Corona, G., Hayes, R. D., Laumann, E. O., Moreira, E. D., Jr., . . . Segraves, T. (2010). Definitions/epidemiology/risk factors for sexual dysfunction. *Journal of Sexual Medicine, 7*, 1598–1607. doi:10.1111/j.1743-6109.2010.01778.x

Lindau, S. T., & Gavrilova, N. (2010). Sex, health, and years of sexually active life gained due to good health: Evidence from two US population based cross sectional surveys of ageing. *BMJ, 340*, c810. doi:10.1136/bmj.c810

Little, K. C., McNulty, J. K., & Russell, V. M. (2010). Sex buffers intimates against the negative implications of attachment insecurity. *Personality and Social Psychology Bulletin, 36*, 484–498. doi:10.1177/0146167209352494

Litzinger, S., & Gordon, K. C. (2005). Exploring relationships among communication, sexual satisfaction, and marital satisfaction. *Journal of Sex and Marital Therapy, 31*, 409–424. doi:10.1080/00926230591006719

Lloyd, E. A. (2005). *The case of the female orgasm: Bias in the science of evolution*. Cambridge, MA: Harvard University Press.

Loftus, J. (2001). America's liberalization in attitudes toward homosexuality. *American Sociological Review, 66*, 762–782. doi:10.2307/3088957

MacNeil, S., & Byers, E. S. (1997). The relationships between sexual problems, communication, and sexual satisfaction. *Canadian Journal of Human Sexuality, 6*, 277–283.

MacNeil, S., & Byers, E. S. (2009). Role of sexual self-disclosure in the sexual satisfaction of long-term heterosexual couples. *Journal of Sex Research, 46*, 3–14. doi:10.1080/00224490802398399

Masters, W. H., & Johnson, V. E. (1979). *Homosexuality in perspective*. Boston, MA: Little, Brown.

McNulty, J. K., & Fisher, T. D. (2008). Gender differences in response to sexual expectancies and changes in sexual frequency: A short-term longitudinal study of sexual satisfaction in newly married couples. *Archives of Sexual Behavior, 37*, 229–240. doi:10.1007/s10508-007-9176-1

Means-Christensen, A. J., Snyder, D. K., & Negy, C. (2003). Assessing nontraditional couples: Validity of the Marital Satisfaction Inventory–Revised with gay, lesbian, and cohabiting heterosexual couples. *Journal of Marital and Family Therapy, 29*, 69–83. doi:10.1111/j.1752-0606.2003.tb00384.x

Meuleman, E. J. H. (2011). Men's sexual health and the metabolic syndrome. *Journal of Sex Research, 48*, 142–148. doi:10.1080/00224499.2011.558646

Meyer, I. H. (2003). Prejudice, social stress, and mental health in lesbian, gay, and bisexual populations: Conceptual issues and research evidence. *Psychological Bulletin, 129*, 674–697. doi:10.1037/0033-2909.129.5.674

Meyer, I. H., & Dean, L. (1998). Internalized homophobia, intimacy, and sexual behavior among gay and bisexual men. In G. M. Herek (Ed.), *Stigma and sexual orientation: Understanding prejudice against lesbians, gay men, and bisexuals* (pp. 160–186). Thousand Oaks, CA: Sage. doi:10.4135/9781452243818.n8

Miller, L. (1994). Sex and the brain-injured patient: Regaining love, pleasure, and intimacy. *Journal of Cognitive Rehabilitation, 12,* 12–20.

Miller, S. A., & Byers, E. S. (2004). Actual and desired duration of foreplay and intercourse: Discordance and misperceptions within heterosexual couples. *Journal of Sex Research, 41,* 301–309. doi:10.1080/00224490409552237

Milligan, M. S., & Neufeldt, A. H. (1998). Post-injury marriage to men with spinal cord injury: Women's perspectives on making a commitment. *Sexuality and Disability, 16,* 117–132. doi:10.1023/A:1023080009783

Morokqff, P. J., & Gillilland, R. (1993). Stress, sexual functioning, and marital satisfaction. *Journal of Sex Research, 30,* 43–53. doi:10.1080/00224499309551677

Nardi, P. M. (1999). *Gay men's friendships.* Chicago, IL: University of Chicago Press.

Nardi, P. M., & Sherrod, D. (1994). Friendship in the lives of gay men and lesbians. *Journal of Social and Personal Relationships, 11,* 185–199. doi:10.1177/0265407594112002

National Center for Family and Marriage Research. (2010). *Same-sex couple households in the U.S., 2009* (NCFMR Family Profiles FP-10-08). Retrieved from http://ncfmr.bgsu.edu/pdf/family_profiles/file87414.pdf

O'Sullivan, L. F., & Allgeier, E. R. (1998). Feigning sexual desire: Consenting to unwanted sexual activity in heterosexual dating relationships. *Journal of Sex Research, 35,* 234–243. doi:10.1080/00224499809551938

O'Sullivan, L. F., & Majerovich, J. (2008). Difficulties with sexual functioning in a sample of male and female late adolescent and young adult university students. *Canadian Journal of Human Sexuality, 17,* 109–121.

Otis, M. D., Rostosky, S. S., Riggle, E. D. B., & Hamrin, R. (2006). Stress and relationship quality in same-sex couples. *Journal of Social and Personal Relationships, 23,* 81–99. doi:10.1177/0265407506060179

Palmore, E. B. (1982). Predictors of the longevity difference: A 25-year follow-up. *Gerontologist, 22,* 513–518. doi:10.1093/geront/22.6.513

Peplau, L. A., & Amaro, H. (1982). Understanding lesbian relationships. In W. Paul, J. D. Weinrich, J. C. Gonsiorek, & M. E. Hotvedt (Eds.), *Homosexuality: Social, psychological, and biological issues* (pp. 233–248). Beverly Hills, CA: Sage.

Peplau, L. A., Fingerhut, A., & Beals, K. P. (2004). Sexuality in the relationships of lesbians and gay men. In J. H. Harvey, A. Wenzel, & S. Sprecher (Eds.), *Handbook of sexuality in close relationships* (pp. 349–369). Mahwah, NJ: Erlbaum.

Peplau, L. A., & Spalding, L. R. (2000). The close relationships of lesbians, gay men, and bisexuals. In C. Hendrick & S. S. Hendrick (Eds.), *Close relationships: A sourcebook* (pp. 110–123). Thousand Oaks, CA: Sage. doi:10.4135/9781452220437.n9

Persson, G. (1981). Five-year mortality in a 70-year-old urban population in relation to psychiatric diagnosis, personality, sexuality and early parental death. *Acta Psychiatrica Scandinavica, 64,* 244–253. doi:10.1111/j.1600-0447.1981.tb00780.x

Powers, S. I., Pietromonaco, P. R., Gunlicks, M., & Sayer, A. (2006). Dating couples' attachment styles and patterns of cortisol reactivity and recovery in response to a relationship conflict. *Journal of Personality and Social Psychology, 90,* 613–628. doi:10.1037/0022-3514.90.4.613

Pridal, C. G., & LoPiccolo, J. (2000). Multielement treatment of desire disorders: Integration of cognitive, behavioral, and systemic therapy. In S. R. Leiblum & R. C. Rosen (Eds.), *Principles and practice of sex therapy* (3rd ed., pp. 57–81). New York, NY: Guilford Press.

Purnine, D. M., & Carey, M. P. (1997). Interpersonal communication and sexual adjustment: The roles of understanding and agreement. *Journal of Consulting and Clinical Psychology, 65,* 1017–1025. doi:10.1037/0022-006X.65.6.1017

Ramirez, O. M., & Brown, J. (2010). Attachment style, rules regarding sex, and couple satisfaction: A study of gay male couples. *Australian and New Zealand Journal of Family Therapy, 31,* 202–213. doi:10.1375/anft.31.2.202

Reczek, C., Elliott, S., & Umberson, D. (2009). Commitment without marriage: Union formation among long-term same-sex couples. *Journal of Family Issues, 30,* 738–756. doi:10.1177/0192513X09331574

Reinhardt, R. U. (2001). Bisexual women in heterosexual relationship. *Journal of Bisexuality, 2,* 163–171. doi:10.1300/J159v02n02_11

Remafedi, G., French, S., Story, M., Resnick, M. D., & Blum, R. (1998). The relationship between suicide risk and sexual orientation: Results of a population-based study. *American Journal of Public Health, 88,* 57–60. doi:10.2105/AJPH.88.1.57

Ridley, C., Ogolsky, B., Payne, P., Totenhagen, C., & Cate, R. (2008). Sexual expression: Its emotional context in heterosexual, gay, and lesbian couples. *Journal of Sex Research, 45,* 305–314. doi:10.1080/00224490802204449

Riggle, E. D. B., Rostosky, S. S., & Horne, S. G. (2010). Psychological distress, well-being, and legal recognition in same-sex couple relationships. *Journal of Family Psychology, 24,* 82–86. doi:10.1037/a0017942

Roisman, G. I., Clausell, E., Holland, A., Fortuna, K., & Elieff, C. (2008). Adult romantic relationships as contexts of human development: A multimethod comparison of same-sex couples with opposite-sex dating, engaged, and married dyads. *Developmental Psychology, 44*, 91–101. doi:10.1037/0012-1649.44.1.91

Rolland, J. S. (1994). In sickness and in health: The impact of illness on couples' relationships. *Journal of Marital and Family Therapy, 20*, 327–347. doi:10.1111/j.1752-0606.1994.tb00125.x

Rosen, R. C., & Leiblum, S. R. (1995). Hypoactive sexual desire. *Psychiatric Clinics of North America, 18*, 107–121.

Rostosky, S. S., & Riggle, E. D. B. (2002). "Out" at work: The relation of actor and partner workplace policy and internalized homophobia to disclosure status. *Journal of Counseling Psychology, 49*, 411–419. doi:10.1037/0022-0167.49.4.411

Rostosky, S. S., Riggle, E. D. B., Horne, S. G., Denton, F. N., & Huellemeier, J. D. (2010). Lesbian, gay, and bisexual individuals' psychological reactions to amendments denying access to civil marriage. *American Journal of Orthopsychiatry, 80*, 302–310. doi:10.1111/j.1939-0025.2010.01033.x

Rostosky, S. S., Riggle, E. D. B., Horne, S. G., & Miller, A. D. (2009). Marriage amendments and psychological distress in lesbian, gay, and bisexual (LGB) adults. *Journal of Counseling Psychology, 56*, 56–66. doi:10.1037/a0013609

Rothblum, E. D., & Brehony, K. A. (Eds.). (1993). *Boston marriages.* Amherst: University of Massachusetts Press.

Rusbult, C. E., Bissonnette, V. L., Arriaga, X. B., Cox, C. L., & Bradbury, T. N. (1998). Accommodation processes during the early years of marriage. In T. N. Bradbury (Ed.), *The developmental course of marital dysfunction* (pp. 74–113). New York, NY: Cambridge University Press. doi:10.1017/CBO9780511527814.005

Rusbult, C. E., Olsen, N., Davis, J. L., & Hannon, P. A. (2004). Commitment and relationship maintenance mechanisms. In H. T. Reis & C. E. Rusbult (Eds.), *Close relationships: Key readings* (pp. 287–303). New York, NY: Taylor & Francis.

Russell, V. M., & McNulty, J. K. (2011). Frequent sex protects intimates from the negative implications of neuroticism. *Social Psychological and Personality Science, 2*, 220–227. doi:10.1177/1948550610387162

Rust, P. C. R. (1996). Monogamy and polyamory: Relationship issues for bisexuals. In B. A. Firestein (Ed.), *Bisexuality: The psychology and politics of an invisible minority* (pp. 127–148). Thousand Oaks, CA: Sage.

Sandel, M. E. (1997). Traumatic brain injury. In M. L. Sipski & C. J. Alexander (Eds.), *Sexual function in people with disability and chronic illness: A health professional's guide* (pp. 221–245). Gaithersburg, MD: Aspen.

Satcher, D. (2001). *The Surgeon General's call to action to promote sexual health and responsible sexual behavior.* Washington, DC: U.S. Department of Health and Human Services. doi:10.1080/19325037.2001.10603498

Serati, M., Salvatore, S., Siesto, G., Cattoni, E., Zanirato, M., Khullar, V., . . . Bolis, P. (2010). Female sexual function during pregnancy and after childbirth. *Journal of Sexual Medicine, 7*, 2782–2790. doi:10.1111/j.1743-6109.2010.01893.x

Shifren, J. L., & Hanfling, S. (2010). *Sexuality in midlife and beyond* (K. C. Allison, Ed.). Cambridge, MA: Harvard Medical School.

Shotland, R. L., & Goodstein, L. (1992). Sexual precedence reduces the perceived legitimacy of sexual refusal: An examination of attributions concerning date rape and consensual sex. *Personality and Social Psychology Bulletin, 18*, 756–764. doi:10.1177/0146167292186012

Simms, D. C., & Byers, E. S. (2009). Interpersonal perceptions of desired frequency of sexual behaviours. *Canadian Journal of Human Sexuality, 18*, 15–25.

Simon, W., & Gagnon, J. H. (1986). Sexual scripts: Permanence and change. *Archives of Sexual Behavior, 15*, 97–120. doi:10.1007/BF01542219

Simons, J. S., & Carey, M. P. (2001). Prevalence of sexual dysfunctions: Results from a decade of research. *Archives of Sexual Behavior, 30*, 177–219. doi:10.1023/A:1002729318254

Simpson, J. A., Wilson, C. L., & Winterheld, H. A. (2004). Sociosexuality and close relationships. In J. H. Harvey, A. Wenzel, & S. Sprecher (Eds.), *The handbook of sexuality in close relationships* (pp. 87–112). Mahwah, NJ: Erlbaum.

Smart, C. (2007). Same-sex couples and marriage: Negotiating relational landscapes with families and friends. *Sociological Review, 55*, 671–686. doi:10.1111/j.1467-954X.2007.00747.x

Smith, G., Mysak, K., & Michael, S. (2008). Sexual double standards and sexually transmitted illnesses: Social rejection and stigmatization of women. *Sex Roles, 58*, 391–401. doi:10.1007/s11199-007-9339-5

Smith, T. W., Cribbet, M. R., Nealey-Moore, J. B., Uchino, B. N., Williams, P. G., MacKenzie, J. J., & Thayer, J. F. (2011). Matters of the variable heart: Respiratory sinus arrhythmia response to marital interaction and associations with marital quality. *Journal of Personality and Social Psychology, 100*, 103–119.

Solomon, S. E., Rothblum, E. D., & Balsam, K. F. (2004). Pioneers in partnership: Lesbian and gay male couples in civil unions compared with those not in civil unions and married heterosexual siblings. *Journal of Family Psychology, 18*, 275–286. doi:10.1037/0893-3200.18.2.275

Solomon, S. E., Rothblum, E. D., & Balsam, K. F. (2005). Money, housework, sex, and conflict: Same-sex couples in civil unions, those not in civil unions, and heterosexual married siblings. *Sex Roles, 52,* 561–575. doi:10.1007/s11199-005-3725-7

Sprecher, S. (2002). Sexual satisfaction in premarital relationships: Associations with satisfaction, love, commitment, and stability. *Journal of Sex Research, 39,* 190–196. doi:10.1080/00224490209552141

Sprecher, S., & McKinney, K. (1993). *Sexuality.* Newbury Park, CA: Sage.

Suter, E. A., & Daas, K. L. (2007). Negotiating heteronormativity dialectically: Lesbian couples' display of symbols in culture. *Western Journal of Communication, 71,* 177–195. doi:10.1080/10570310701518443

Szymanski, D. M., Kashubeck-West, S., & Meyer, J. (2008). Internalized heterosexism: Measurement, psychosocial correlates, and research directions. *Counseling Psychologist, 36,* 525–574. doi:10.1177/0011000007309489

Taleporos, G., & McCabe, M. P. (2003). Relationships, sexuality and adjustment among people with physical disability. *Sexual and Relationship Therapy, 18,* 5–6.

Thomas, G., & Fletcher, G. J. O. (2003). Mind-reading accuracy in intimate relationships: Assessing the roles of the relationship, the target, and the judge. *Journal of Personality and Social Psychology, 85,* 1079–1094. doi:10.1037/0022-3514.85.6.1079

Tiefer, L. (2002). Beyond the medical model of women's sexual problems: A campaign to resist the promotion of "female sexual dysfunction." *Sexual and Relationship Therapy, 17,* 127–135. doi:10.1080/14681990220121248

Todosijevic, J., Rothblum, E. D., & Solomon, S. E. (2005). Relationship satisfaction, affectivity, and gay-specific stressors in same-sex couples joined in civil unions. *Psychology of Women Quarterly, 29,* 158–166. doi:10.1111/j.1471-6402.2005.00178.x

Tolman, D. L. (2002). *Dilemma of desire: Teenage girls and sexuality.* Cambridge, MA: Harvard University Press.

Træen, B., & Skogerbø, A. (2009). Sex as an obligation and interpersonal communication among Norwegian heterosexual couples. *Scandinavian Journal of Psychology, 50,* 221–229. doi:10.1111/j.1467-9450.2008.00698.x

Trudel, G., Marchand, A., Ravart, M., Aubin, S., Turgeon, L., & Fortier, P. (2001). The effect of a cognitive-behavioral group treatment program on hypoactive sexual desire in women. *Sexual and Relationship Therapy, 16,* 145–164. doi:10.1080/14681990120040078

Uchino, B. N. (2006). Social support and health: A review of physiological processes potentially underlying links to disease outcomes. *Journal of Behavioral Medicine, 29,* 377–387. doi:10.1007/s10865-006-9056-5

United States v. Windsor, 570 U.S. ___ (2013).

Ussher, J. M., & Perz, J. (2008). Empathy, egalitarianism and emotion work in the relational negotiation of PMS: The experience of women in lesbian relationships. *Feminism and Psychology, 18,* 87–111. doi:10.1177/0959353507084954

Vannier, S. A., & O'Sullivan, L. F. (2010). Sex without desire: Characteristics of occasions of sexual compliance in young adults' committed relationships. *Journal of Sex Research, 47,* 429–439. doi:10.1080/00224490903132051

Waite, L. J., & Joyner, K. (2001). Emotional satisfaction and physical pleasure in sexual unions: Time horizon, sexual behavior, and sexual exclusivity. *Journal of Marriage and Family, 63,* 247–264. doi:10.1111/j.1741-3737.2001.00247.x

Wallen, K., & Lloyd, E. A. (2011). Female sexual arousal: Genital anatomy and orgasm in intercourse. *Hormones and Behavior, 59,* 780–792. doi:10.1016/j.yhbeh.2010.12.004

Weinstock, J. S. (2004). Lesbian ex-lover relationships: Under-estimated, under-theorized and under-valued? In J. S. Weinstock & E. D. Rothblum (Eds.), *Lesbian ex-lovers: The really long-term relationships* (pp. 1–8). Binghamton, NY: Harrington Park Press. doi:10.1300/J155v08n03_01

West, C. (1996). *Lesbian polyfidelity.* San Francisco, CA: Bootlegger.

Weston, K. (1991). *Families we choose: Lesbians, gays, kinship.* New York, NY: Columbia University Press.

Willets, M. C., Sprecher, S., & Beck, F. D. (2004). Overview of sexual practices and attitudes within relational contexts. In J. H. Harvey, A. Wenzel, & S. Sprecher (Eds.), *The handbook of sexuality in close relationships* (pp. 57–86). Mahwah, NJ: Erlbaum.

Witting, K., Santtila, P., Varjonen, M., Jern, P., Johansson, A., von der Pahlen, B., Sandnabba, K. (2008). Female sexual dysfunction, sexual distress, and compatibility with partner. *Journal of Sexual Medicine, 5,* 2587–2599. doi:10.1111/j.1743-6109.2008.00984.x

Yabiku, S. T., & Gager, C. T. (2009). Sexual frequency and the stability of marital and cohabiting unions. *Journal of Marriage and Family, 71,* 983–1000. doi:10.1111/j.1741-3737.2009.00648.x

Yeh, H.-C., Lorenz, F. O., Wickrama, K. A. S., Conger, R. D., & Elder, G. H., Jr. (2006). Relationships among sexual satisfaction, marital quality, and marital instability at midlife. *Journal of Family Psychology, 20,* 339–343. doi:10.1037/0893-3200.20.2.339

Yoshida, K. K. (1994). Intimate and marital relationships: An insider's perspective. *Sexuality and Disability, 12,* 179–189. doi:10.1007/BF02547904

PART VII

MAINTENANCE, STRIFE, AND DISSOLUTION

CHAPTER 20

WHY MARRIAGES CHANGE
OVER TIME

Benjamin R. Karney

If finding an intimate connection is, as it has been described, a fundamental human goal (Baumeister & Leary, 1995), then most adults pursue that goal within the institution of marriage. In survey after survey, the vast majority of people express a desire to get married at some point in their lives (Lichter, Batson, & Brown, 2004; Trail & Karney, 2012). Indeed, about 90% of people in the United States do get married, a figure that has remained constant for decades (Goldstein & Kenney, 2001).

On their wedding day, as they make a public, legal, and often religious commitment to a lifelong relationship, newlyweds uniformly hope that their intimate bond will persist and flourish. But the odds are against them. Marriages often change, sometimes drastically, with about half of all first marriages ending in divorce or permanent separation (Cherlin, 2010). The poignancy of marriage is that the vast majority of those who dissolve their marriages will marry again (Sweeney, 2010), approaching their new relationships with all of the hope and optimism they brought to their prior one. Yet these remarriages are at even greater risk of dissolving (Bumpass & Raley, 2007).

How does this happen? How do marital relationships change so often and so severely, especially given spouses' fervent desire to preserve their initial happiness and given the social consensus that this is a change to be avoided at all costs?

The goal of this chapter is to review research addressing these questions. To this end, the chapter is organized into three parts. In the first section, I discuss the nature of change in marriage, examining what it is that actually changes and reviewing research describing how different elements of marriage change over time. In the second section, I address why change in marriage comes about and, in particular, why spouses' evaluations of their marriages can decline despite their strong desire to maintain their initial feelings about their relationships. In the final section, I suggest specific directions for future research that moves work on these questions forward. Throughout this chapter, I emphasize research published over the past 15 years, although influential older studies and theoretical articles are addressed where appropriate.

DESCRIBING HOW MARRIAGES CHANGE OVER TIME

When a marriage changes over time, what is actually changing? Careful consideration of this question offers three answers. First, spouses may experience a change in their marital status, that is, the marital relationship may dissolve through divorce or permanent separation. Second, spouses may experience a change in the way they evaluate the marriage. These evaluations have been discussed using a wide range of terms such as *marital adjustment, marital quality,* and *marital happiness*. In this chapter, I use the term *marital satisfaction*, defined as spouses' global judgment of the extent to which they find their marital

Preparation of this chapter was supported by National Institute for Child Health and Human Development Grants R01HD053825 and R01HD061366 awarded to Benjamin R. Karney.

http://dx.doi.org/10.1037/14344-020
APA Handbook of Personality and Social Psychology: Vol. 3. Interpersonal Relations, M. Mikulincer and P. R. Shaver (Editors-in-Chief)

relationships fulfilling (Fincham & Bradbury, 1987). Third, independent of the way spouses evaluate their relationships, their day-to-day experiences within the relationship may change over time. The way couples communicate, the amount of time spouses spend together, and what spouses do when they are together are all likely to change over the course of the marriage, and these changes may or may not correspond with changes in marital satisfaction or changes in marital status. In the rest of this section, I review research describing how each of these aspects of marriage is known to change over time.

Changes in Marital Status

The decision to marry represents a major life transition, altering the legal and social status of both partners. The decision to end a marriage, therefore, represents a dramatic and costly shift in partners' motivations, moving from the desire to pursue and maintain the relationship to the desire to escape it. In most domains of life, such reversals of intention are rare (e.g., avowed Republicans seldom become Democrats). Yet, in the domain of marriage, these reversals are the norm. Across multiple studies of the most recent data available, the lifetime risk that a first-married couple in the United States will voluntarily end their marriage hovers at around 45% (e.g., Schoen & Canudas-Romo, 2006). That figure typically addresses legal divorces only. If one factors in permanent separations that never progress to legal divorce, then the total risk that a first marriage will dissolve is a little more than 50%. As noted earlier, the risk for remarriages is even higher (Bumpass & Raley, 2007). It is also worth noting that the United States has the highest divorce rate of any Western nation (Amato & James, 2010).

Those figures reflect widespread reversals in spouses' intentions toward their marriage, but the risk for experiencing these reversals is not distributed equally across the population. On the contrary, rates of marital dissolution in the United States are substantially higher among the poor and non-White than among more affluent Whites, and the gap has been widening for the past several decades. For example, among women with college degrees, rates of marital dissolution in the United States have declined since their peak in 1980, but they have remained stable for women with less than a college degree, and they have increased steadily for women without a high school diploma (Martin, 2006). With respect to race and ethnicity, the chance of a Black woman's first marriage ending in divorce is currently estimated at 70%, compared with 47% for a White woman (Raley & Bumpass, 2003), a gap that is also increasing and is only partially explained by education and income differences between Blacks and Whites (Sweeney & Phillips, 2004). Rates of marital dissolution for Hispanics generally depend on their country of birth. Hispanics who have immigrated to the United States experience lower divorce rates than Whites, but those born in the United States have higher divorce rates than Whites, and third- and higher generation Hispanics have divorce rates that approach the rates for Blacks (Bean, Berg, & Hook, 1996).

In sum, although couples experience the transition from commitment to dissolution in all segments of the population, some segments are at far greater risk of experiencing this transition than others. Unfortunately, very little is known about how this transition plays out in the groups in which it occurs most frequently. Whereas demographic and sociological research has documented the widening socioeconomic and racial/ethnic disparities in marital status, almost no psychological research has been done on these transitions in diverse or disadvantaged populations (Fein & Ooms, 2006; Johnson, 2012). Instead, research on how and why marriages change is based almost exclusively on samples composed primarily of White, middle-class, college-educated couples, that is, the segment of the population at lowest risk (Karney & Bradbury, 2005). Of necessity, that is the research that informs most of what follows in this chapter, but the ability of this research to explain marital dissolution in other segments of the population remains an open question.

Changes in Marital Satisfaction

The decision to begin or end a marriage is more or less categorical. A couple is either married or not; the marriage either dissolves or remains intact. In contrast, change in how spouses evaluate their relationships has been described as continuous (Huston, Caughlin, Houts, Smith, & George, 2001; Karney, Bradbury, & Johnson, 1999). Each day of their marriage, spouses have occasion to reflect on how their relationship is going; across days, their evaluations can remain stable, they can become consistently more positive or negative to varying degrees, or they can fluctuate.

What is the normative course of marital satisfaction over time? The fact that so many initially happy marriages end in divorce suggests that many couples experience a process of gradual disaffection. Indeed, influential theories of marriage have long assumed that marital satisfaction on average declines gradually and steadily as the result of accumulated experiences with conflict, disagreement, and irritation between spouses. Social exchange models, for example, propose that "relationships grow, develop, deteriorate, and dissolve as a consequence of an unfolding social-exchange process, which may be conceived as a bartering of rewards and costs both between the partners and between members of the partnership and others" (Huston & Burgess, 1979, p. 4). Behavioral theories of marriage similarly emphasize incremental declines, suggesting that "unresolved negative feelings start to build up, fueling destructive patterns of marital interaction and eventually eroding and attacking the positive aspects of the relationship" (Markman, 1991, p. 422).

Yet evidence for this characterization of marital satisfaction over time was not always easy to find. The first attempts to describe the normative course of marital satisfaction did not even observe a steady decline over time. On the contrary, early research suggested that marital satisfaction declines only in the early years of marriage (after the end of the honeymoon period), remains generally stable during the child-rearing years, and then returns to nearly newlywed levels in the later years, presumably when children have left home and spouses have an empty nest in which to enjoy each other again (Rollins & Cannon, 1974; Rollins & Feldman, 1970). This was a narrative with considerable resonance among members of the public, and it is still frequently repeated as fact (Miller, 2000).

However, there are several good reasons to question whether it is true. First, the primary evidence

for a U-shaped course for marital satisfaction came from cross-sectional surveys of marital satisfaction across spouses of widely varying marital duration. As marital researchers have been noting for decades (e.g., Spanier, Lewis, & Cole, 1975), couples with the longest marital duration in such samples include only the most successful marriages, the less successful ones having long since exited the population of married couples through divorce. Thus, the longest lasting couples in a cross-sectional sample may report higher marital satisfaction only because they represent a different population, not because marital satisfaction increases in the later years of marriage.

Second, when longitudinal studies have followed couples over time to evaluate how their marital satisfaction actually changes, no evidence for a U-shaped curve has emerged. Instead, the consistent message from longitudinal research on marriage is that, on average, marital satisfaction declines monotonically over time, just as social exchange and behavioral theories of marriage predict. Drawing on 40 years of marital satisfaction data from a sample of Harvard graduates and their wives, Vaillant and Vaillant (1993) showed that, although spouses believed that their satisfaction had followed a U-shaped curve, it had actually declined linearly over time. Since then, numerous other longitudinal studies have documented the same pattern: Marital satisfaction starts high among newlyweds and then declines over time (Karney & Bradbury, 1997; Kurdek, 1999; Umberson, Williams, Powers, Chen, & Campbell, 2005). Perhaps the most thorough demonstration examined change in marital satisfaction over 17 years in a diverse sample of more than 1,500 couples participating in the Marital Instability Over the Life Course study (VanLaningham, Johnson, & Amato, 2001). Across the entire sample, marital satisfaction declined monotonically on average. Moreover, when the authors divided their sample into seven cohorts (i.e., examining the youngest marriages separately from the oldest marriages), average reports of marital satisfaction declined monotonically within each of them.

In all of these studies, change in marital satisfaction was examined as a function of time and marital duration. The idea that satisfaction might increase in the later years of marriage, however, is linked specifically to a particular life event—the departure of children from the home. Yet longitudinal research that has directly examined changes in satisfaction across the transition to an empty nest has been hard put to find a normative increase in marital satisfaction. One recent study that did report such an increase examined a sample of 123 women participating in the Mills College Longitudinal Study (Gorchoff, John, & Helson, 2008). Among the women in this study who were married or in marriage-like relationships, average marital satisfaction increased over time, especially for women who transitioned to an empty nest. These results stand in striking contrast to the results of research on larger and more diverse samples of couples, and they may speak to the unique experiences of this relatively affluent and well-educated sample. Cross-cultural research has failed to find any evidence for late increases in marital satisfaction among more diverse populations of couples (Mitchell & Lovegreen, 2009).

Thus, as far as broad generalizations go, the statement "marital satisfaction declines monotonically on average" is about as reliable and well supported as one can find in this literature. Nevertheless, recent studies have revealed overlooked but important nuances even within this reliable conclusion. Marital satisfaction may decline reliably on average, but across studies the variability around the mean trajectory is always substantial. A recent series of longitudinal analyses from multiple independent scholars has begun to examine this variability directly, using cluster analyses (Belsky & Hsieh, 1998) and group-based mixed modeling (Nagin, 1999) to determine whether the shape of spouses' marital satisfaction trajectories varies continuously across members of a sample or whether distinct groups of marital satisfaction trajectories can be identified. The results are consistent across several studies that have used a range of samples, assessment instruments, and measurement intervals, and they suggest two important modifications to the generalization that marital satisfaction starts high and then declines over time (Anderson, Van Ryzin, & Doherty, 2010; Kamp Dush, Taylor, & Kroeger, 2008; Lavner & Bradbury, 2010). First, although newlyweds may indeed be as satisfied with their marriages as they will ever be, not all newlyweds are

equally satisfied. Even in the early years of marriage, studies have revealed meaningful variability in initial satisfaction, and these are almost certainly underestimates of the true variability in the population that includes those who do not volunteer to participate in marital research. Second, even though average marital satisfaction declined significantly in each of these studies, this pattern characterizes only a minority of couples. For example, Anderson et al. (2010) used the group-based approach to reanalyze the same longitudinal data that VanLaningham et al. (2001) had used to demonstrate average declines in marital satisfaction. The newer study, focusing on the variability around the mean trajectory, found that, for nearly two thirds of the respondents, marital satisfaction actually remained high and stable across time; the mean declines were driven entirely by the one third of the sample for whom which satisfaction began low and then declined. Lavner and Bradbury (2010) found a similar pattern in a sample of first-married newlyweds assessed multiple times across the first 4 years of their marriages: 81% of husbands and 82% of wives experienced no or minimal declines in their marital satisfaction over time, but the fewer than 20% of couples that did decline contributed to an average trajectory that was significantly negative. In all of these studies, membership in a trajectory group was strongly associated with initial levels of marital satisfaction, such that the spouses most likely to maintain their satisfaction were those with the highest initial satisfaction, whereas spouses who experienced the greatest declines were those who reported the lowest initial satisfaction. In other words, just as no family actually has the average of 2.5 children, few couples actually experience the average trajectory of initially high satisfaction followed by gradual declines over time. On the contrary, in couples who remain married, marital satisfaction declines modestly when it declines at all, and differences between couples are far larger and more reliable than differences within couples over time.

Both kinds of differences significantly predict which marriages will end in divorce and which will remain intact. That is, divorce rates vary across the trajectory groups, such that couples in the low and declining group are at highest risk for divorce, and couples in the high and stable group are at the lowest risk, although their risk is still above zero (Lavner & Bradbury, 2012). However, it is not simply the fact that some couples are less happy than others that predicts which ones will divorce. When between-couple differences in marital satisfaction are controlled, rates of change in marital satisfaction continue to predict divorce, such that the couples experiencing the steepest declines are at greatest risk (Huston et al., 2001; Karney & Bradbury, 1997).

All of these results await further replication. Because longitudinal research on marriage has focused on relatively affluent, primarily White couples, generalizations to more diverse or more vulnerable populations should be made with caution. Nevertheless, given the high rates at which marriages dissolve, the observation of relative stability in most couples' satisfaction raises provocative questions about the relation between change in marital satisfaction and the decision to divorce. Specifically, is the decision to divorce sensitive to the relatively modest, gradual changes that have been observed in longitudinal research? An affirmative answer would support the incremental models of change that are prevalent in the existing marital literature. Or does divorce follow from a drastic reevaluation of the relationship that may follow years of relative stability? An affirmative answer here would support a model of catastrophic change in marital satisfaction, when it occurs. At present, the evidence to compare these contrasting views does not exist because longitudinal research on marriage, relying on assessments separated by intervals of months to years, has not yet been sensitive enough to measure how spouses' evaluations of their marriage may be changing immediately before the decision to divorce.

Changes in Marital Experiences

Even if most spouses' global evaluations of their marriage remain relatively stable, their experiences within the marriage can and do change over time. Newlywed couples mature, they graduate and take up careers, they bear and raise children, and all of these developmental milestones alter the daily experience of the relationship for both partners. Because there are so many facets of that daily experience—from the way spouses divide household chores, to

their communication, to their sex life—attempts to plot the normative course of marital experiences have reached no consensus on what the most relevant domains of those experiences should be. Instead, this research has tended to focus at a very broad level on normative changes in positive, relationship-promoting experiences (e.g., successful communication, sex, shared activities) or negative, relationship-weakening experiences (e.g., conflict, physical aggression).

As diverse as it is, evaluating this literature is worthwhile for the insight it may offer into the way that global evaluations of marriage change over time. If spouses' global evaluations are the product of their accumulated experiences in the marriage, as many theories of change in marital satisfaction suggest (e.g., Bradbury & Fincham, 1991; Markman, 1991), the fact that global marital satisfaction declines over time on average should correspond with a decline in positive experiences and an increase in negative experiences within the relationship. Some evidence from longitudinal research on marriage has been consistent with this view, but the results have varied widely depending on the type of measures used. Moreover, this variability suggests that the relation between specific marital experiences and global evaluations of the marriage may be more complex than has generally been acknowledged.

With respect to changes in positive experiences within marriage, research using self-report measures has painted a consistent picture of gradual declines in positivity over time. For example, when Huston et al. (2001) asked newlywed spouses to report on the frequency of their expressions of affection and feelings of love for each other across the first 2 years of their marriage, reports of these positive behaviors declined significantly and did so whether or not couples were satisfied and whether or not they went on to divorce. The frequency of sexual intimacy also declines over time, especially in the early years of marriage (Call, Sprecher, & Schwartz, 1995). Some of these declines may be the result of the transition to parenthood, an event that is likely to occur early in marriage and one that is reliably associated with decreases in couples' shared leisure time (Claxton & Perry-Jenkins, 2008) and increases in wives' household responsibilities (Nomaguchi & Milkie, 2003). With more time taken up by the demands of parenting, less time for sex and other forms of affectionate exchange is almost inevitable.

Yet this cannot be the whole explanation for declines in positivity, for two reasons. First, these declines are observed at all stages of the life course. Although they seem to be more pronounced in the early years of marriage, analyses of survey data collected over 8 years from a national sample of more than 1,000 individuals found that reports of positive experiences within the marriage decline at all stages of marriage (Umberson et al., 2005). Second, and more difficult to explain, these declines have not been found in research that has observed what couples are actually doing. Lindahl, Clements, and Markman (1998), in a 9-year study of 36 couples, conducted annual assessments of couples' problem-solving interactions. In contrast to the changes observed in comparable studies using self-reports, observed positivity within these interactions increased significantly over time. This was a small convenience sample, but the results raise the possibility that the declines in positive behavior reported in other longitudinal studies reflect differences in perception and interpretation rather than differences in experience over time. Aron and Aron (1996) acknowledged this possibility when they highlighted the importance of novelty in intimate relationships. Over time, these scholars argued, the human brain acclimates to repeated stimuli. The scent of fresh bread is salient on entering a bakery, but minutes later one can no longer detect it. Similarly, the same behaviors that register as positive and affectionate early in marriage (e.g., checking in to say hello during the day, preparing each other's favorite meals) may over time develop into routines that are no longer processed as affection. Support for this alternative view would suggest that changes in global evaluations of a marriage could result not only from changes in the quality of spouses' experiences within the marriage but also from changes in the way spouses process those experiences, regardless of how the experiences are changing.

Research on longitudinal changes in negative marital experiences has revealed similar complexity. Both self-report (Huston et al., 2001; Umberson

et al., 2005) and observational research (Lindahl et al., 1998) have indicated that negativity and negative experiences either remain stable or increase over time for most married couples. The convergence of the two types of data suggests that these trends are not solely the result of changes in spouses' sensitivity to negative behaviors; spouses do seem more likely to engage in interactions that even outside observers recognize as more negative. This could be the result of greater investment in the marriage over time: As constraints to leaving the marriage increase with shared offspring and shared property, the opportunities for conflict increase, even as the motivation to avoid conflict decreases (Frye, McNulty, & Karney, 2008).

However, with respect to change over time, all negativity is not created equal. Although rates of daily upsets and negative exchanges seem to remain stable or increase, several longitudinal studies have indicated that rates of intimate partner violence decline. Across longitudinal studies of self-reported marital violence, this has been a remarkably consistent finding, emerging across intervals ranging from as short as 3 or 4 years (Lawrence & Bradbury, 2001; Lorber & O'Leary, 2011) to as long as 10 years (Fritz & O'Leary, 2004). Across these studies, the declines cannot be attributed to more violent couples leaving the sample: The analyses have clearly shown that couples who engage in physical violence initially engage in less violence as their marriages endure. The Fritz and O'Leary (2004) study further indicated that this trend is unique to physical aggression. When they examined psychological aggression, a construct that overlaps greatly with the sorts of negative exchanges observed by Lindahl et al. (1998) and reported by spouses in Umberson et al. (2005), they found no average changes over time.

Viewed together, these findings suggest a potentially important distinction between the dramatic negative behaviors represented by physical aggression and the more mundane conflicts and irritations of married life. If the more dramatic events had a greater impact on spouses' global marital satisfaction, average declines in the frequency of marital violence should be associated with average increases in marital satisfaction. That is not the case: Even as marital violence declines, so too does marital satisfaction on average. The implication is that spouses respond more strongly or attend more closely to their mundane conflicts, which are the experiences that characterize their daily experience of the relationship.

One caveat worth highlighting is that longitudinal research on change in marital experiences, similar to most longitudinal research on global marital satisfaction, has focused almost exclusively on describing average trends and accounting for variability in change as a continuous variable. Whereas some research has probed variability around the mean trajectory of marital satisfaction, no research has done so for trajectories of specific experiences. Thus, it remains unclear whether the trends reported so far describe the way most spouses actually experience their marriage or whether the mean trends are driven by a few spouses in each sample who change drastically.

The overall picture of marriage that emerges from this brief review is that different facets of marriage change over time at different rates and in different directions and that changes in different facets of marriage do not always hold together in intuitive ways. The occasional lack of correspondence between changes in marital experiences and changes in spouses' global evaluations of the marriage points toward some flexibility in the way that spouses decide whether their marriages are satisfying. In the next section, I present a model that describes how spouses assemble their marital experiences into a coherent evaluation of their marriage, and I then use the model to explain how spouses' evaluations of their marriage may change or remain stable over time.

UNDERSTANDING HOW MARRIAGES CHANGE OVER TIME

Being married involves two individuals interacting with each other and with their environment. Being satisfied with a marriage, in contrast, is ultimately the result of a cognitive process that occurs within individuals. When judging whether their marriage is fulfilling or not, spouses must integrate an accumulation of specific experiences to arrive at a global conclusion about the relationship, which then

informs their decisions about whether to persist in the relationship and make efforts to maintain it or whether to leave. If newlyweds are, on average, as happy with their marriages as they are ever likely to be (Karney & Bradbury, 1997; Lavner & Bradbury, 2010), most newlyweds should be strongly invested in resisting change and should seek to maintain or enhance their initial satisfaction with the relationship. To the extent that perceiving decline in the marriage is emotionally painful (Karney & Frye, 2002), evaluating one's marriage should therefore invoke motivated reasoning, that is, a review of the facts biased toward a particular, desired conclusion (Kunda, 1990). Indeed, satisfied couples manifest all sorts of cognitive biases designed to preserve and strengthen their positive feelings about each other and their relationship (e.g., Murray, Holmes, & Griffin, 1996; Neff & Karney, 2003; Simpson, Oriña, & Ickes, 2003). Yet, despite these mechanisms and the powerful incentives for using them, spouses' evaluations of their marriage change anyway, with most couples who initially declare their intention to remain together ending up dissolving their relationship. The prevalence of this unwanted transformation highlights poorly understood limits to motivated reasoning within the context of intimate relationships. In this section, I review research relevant to understanding these limits and then develop a model of how marriages often change despite spouses' best efforts to keep them stable.

The Structure of Marital Satisfaction

Within a marriage, as within any long-term close relationship, each partner develops a wealth of information and opinions about the other. One might view one's partner as dependable, a lousy cook, a fan of mystery novels, and someone who regularly leaves the cap off the toothpaste. One might have separate evaluations of different aspects of one's relationship, such as being satisfied with the way one coparents, being thrilled with one's sex life, or being dissatisfied with the way one communicates and solves problems. The fact that spouses can easily provide global evaluations of their marriages when asked to do so suggests that all of this information is structured into a coherent representation of the partner and the relationship (Karney,

McNulty, & Bradbury, 2004). Research on person perception (e.g., Funder, 1999; Gilbert, 1998) and on the self-concept (e.g., McConnell, 2011) has examined the structure of these representations in detail, and the results of this work can also be fruitfully applied to understanding representations of marriage. In particular, this work offers two premises that any model of marital satisfaction must acknowledge.

First, beliefs about a marriage vary in their level of abstraction. Even within a set of beliefs and opinions that all reflect positive evaluations of a marriage, the belief that one's partner is skilled at chess is not the same as the belief that she or he is a suitable and rewarding spouse. Some beliefs about a marriage (such as one's spouse's skill at chess) are specific and concrete, describing a relatively narrow range of behaviors and experiences, whereas others (such as her or his suitability as a spouse) are global and abstract, subsuming within them a wide range of specific behaviors and experiences (Neff & Karney, 2002a, 2002b). Between these extremes, all of spouses' beliefs and opinions about their marriage can be arrayed along a continuum, ranging from the relatively specific to the relatively global, with the belief that the marriage is worth maintaining perhaps being the most global of all.

Second, beliefs about a marriage are organized hierarchically. Research on cognitive structures in other domains has suggested that cognitions not only vary in their level of abstraction but also function at more global levels to organize and give meaning to cognitions at lower, more specific levels (e.g., John, Hampson, & Goldberg, 1991). Models of cognition in close relationships have made the same claim (Fletcher & Thomas, 1996; Neff & Karney, 2002a), as illustrated in Figure 20.1. As the figure shows, beliefs about a spouse at any particular level of abstraction integrate beliefs and knowledge at lower levels of abstraction. Thus, in this example, the belief that "my spouse is a great parent" subsumes the more specific beliefs "my spouse treats our children with love" and "my spouse devotes time to our children," each of which in turn integrates memories of specific experiences related to each statement. With respect to representations of an enduring marriage, the belief that "this marriage is worth sustaining" sits atop the hierarchy, integrating and giving meaning to all of the more specific beliefs and evaluations that lie beneath.

Although the structure described in Figure 20.1 is static, representations of an ongoing relationship are dynamic. Each new experience with a spouse presents new information to be integrated within the existing structure, a process that can be automatic (Smith, Ratliff, & Nosek, 2012). Thus, representations of a marriage evolve over time as they assimilate some experiences and accommodate others. One implication of the hierarchical structure of marital satisfaction is that changes at one level of abstraction need not necessarily require changes at higher levels of abstraction. For example, one might view one's spouse as a talented person on the basis of one's experience of her as a skilled chess player, a great dancer, and a highly paid executive. Even if one of these beliefs should change (e.g., one's spouse begins to lose at chess), it is still possible to maintain the general belief that she is a talented person, as long as other specific beliefs support that general one.

FIGURE 20.1. Cognitive representations of a marriage are organized hierarchically.

Cognitive Structure and Motivated Reasoning in Marriage

Although spouses may be motivated to maintain positive views of their partner and their marriage, there is no reason to expect spouses to be equally motivated to maintain their positive views at every level of abstraction. Global beliefs, because they subsume a greater number and range of behaviors and experiences, tend to be more evaluative than specific beliefs. For example, the global belief "My partner is dependable" has a far greater evaluative range than the more specific belief "My partner is punctual," because being dependable encompasses a greater range of behaviors than being punctual. It follows that spouses should be more invested in maintaining the belief that their partners are dependable than the belief that their partners are punctual and even more invested in maintaining beliefs if those beliefs are more general. In other words, spouses care more about their global beliefs about the marriage than about their specific ones.

Support for this premise comes from research on newlyweds, whose representations of each other tend to be quite positive and whose motivations to protect and preserve those positive evaluations tend to be quite strong (Neff & Karney, 2005). In a sample of 82 first-married newlywed couples, spouses within a few months of their wedding were asked to rate each other on two different scales. One assessed views of the partner's global worth using a version of Rosenberg's (1979) Self-Esteem Scale, modified to refer to the partner rather than the self and including items such as "On the whole, I am satisfied with my spouse" and "My spouse has a number of good qualities." The other scale assessed views of the partner's standing on a set of more specific dimensions (e.g., intelligence, physical appearance, social skills) adapted from Swann's Self-Attributes Questionnaire (Swann, De La Ronde, & Hixon, 1994). The distribution of spouses' scores on the two scales is presented in Figure 20.2. As Panel A of the figure reveals, scores on the global measure were highly skewed, such that the modal response of both husbands and wives was the highest possible score on the scale. In fact, 46% of husbands and 53% of wives gave their partners the highest possible rating. Yet, as Panel B of the figure reveals, these globally

positive views did not correspond to equally positive views about their partners' specific attributes. Whereas the global ratings were positively skewed, the more specific ratings were more or less normally distributed. About half of the spouses gave each other a perfect score on the global measure, but only about 20% of them reported a score of 100 or higher (out of 114) on the specific measure. In other words, among the spouses who were unwilling to admit to having less than a perfect partner in general were a large number of spouses who were willing to admit that their "generally perfect" partners were not perfect in every way.

If spouses are to maintain a coherent representation of their relationships (i.e., if their feelings about their marriages are to make sense), recognizing their partners' imperfections represents a challenge. How can one reconcile the positive global belief "I was right to marry this person" with the specific experience of an emotional conflict, a betrayal, or the mundane irritations and disappointments that are likely to arise in any long-term relationship? Most of what has been described as motivated reasoning in intimate relationships involves the use of cognitive mechanisms for meeting this challenge. That is, processes of motivated reasoning in intimate relationships allow partners to recognize specific negative information about their relationships while protecting or enhancing their positive global evaluations of their relationship.

Research on attributions in relationships (e.g., Karney & Bradbury, 2000) has offered a clear example of these processes at work. Spouses are most likely to think about and seek causal explanations for each other's behaviors when those behaviors are either negative or unexpected, such as when they represent experiences that are not easily reconciled with existing representations of the relationship (Holtzworth-Munroe & Jacobson, 1985). In terms of the hierarchical diagram in Figure 20.1, making an attribution represents linking a specific experience with some higher order global perception. An attribution of blame, in this view, is drawing a link between a specific transgression (e.g., he was 30 minutes late for our date) and a more global statement about the transgressor (e.g., he is a thoughtless person). In terms of relationship maintenance, an

565

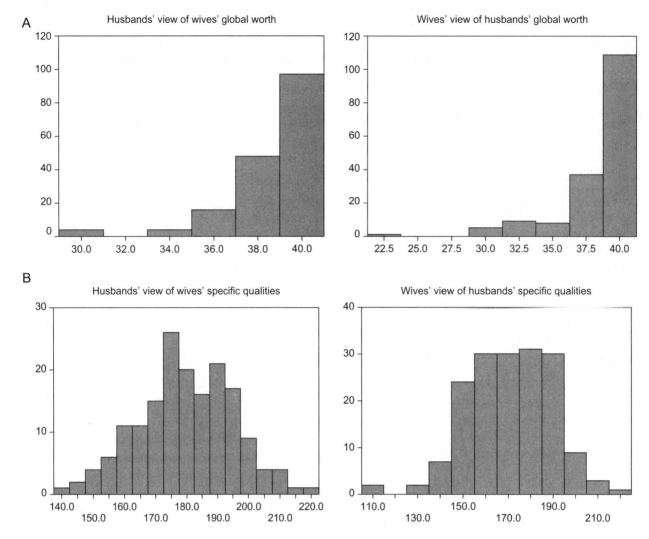

FIGURE 20.2. Distribution of global versus specific partner evaluations among newlyweds. A: Spouses' global esteem for each other, assessed via a version of the Rosenberg (1979) Self-Esteem Scale. B: Spouses' ratings of each other's specific traits, assessed via Swann's Specific Attributes Scale (Swann, De La Ronde, & Hixon, 1994).

adaptive attribution is one that severs this link, allowing the perceiver to recognize the transgression without acknowledging that it may have more global implications for understanding the partner or the relationship (Bradbury & Fincham, 1990). Something such as "Oh, he must be struck in traffic" does the job nicely. By attributing blame for the transgression to an external and uncontrollable source, the specific negative experience can be acknowledged while its implications for more global representations of the relationship are defused. With respect to positive behaviors, adaptive attributions serve the opposite agenda, drawing and strengthening the links between specific positive behaviors ("He bought me my favorite perfume!") and their

global implications ("He is such a thoughtful husband, and he knows my taste so well").

McNulty and Karney (2001) directly linked the nature of newlyweds' attributions to the way spouses integrate their global and specific perceptions of their marriage. In that study, spouses were asked to complete a 7-day nightly diary in which they rated the day's experience of several specific domains of the relationship (e.g., our communication, my spouse's intelligence, my spouse's appearance) and then rated their global feelings at the end of the day (e.g., "How satisfied are you with your marriage today?"). Diary reports have been an especially powerful research method to address these issues, because multiple repeated assessments of both specific experiences and global evaluations allow researchers to evaluate how fluctuations in specific experience across days covary with the variability of global evaluations of the relationship across days (e.g., Gable & Reis, 1999; Neff & Karney, 2009). A strong within-subject covariance between these reports implies that an individual's global feelings about the relationship are sensitive to changes in his or her specific experiences, whereas a weak covariance implies that the individual is able to maintain stable global evaluations despite fluctuations in specific experience. Across this study, the covariance between spouses' global and specific ratings of the marriage varied significantly across spouses, and the quality of their attributions accounted for part of this variance. For spouses who tended to blame their partners, the covariance between global and specific ratings was relatively high, consistent with the idea that blame helps to link specific experience to global implications for the marriage. For spouses who tended to forgive their partners, the covariance between global and specific ratings was relatively low, consistent with the idea that forgiveness helps to sever or weaken links between specific and global perceptions.

Other cognitive processes in close relationships may serve similar functions. In their ideal standards model, for example, Fletcher and Simpson (2000) suggested that the association between a specific experience of a relationship and its global evaluation is moderated by whether the specific experience is consistent with the perceiver's standards and ideals. In terms of the hierarchical model in Figure 20.1, the ideal serves as a decision rule for linking specific experiences with more global judgments. For example, being unsatisfied with one's sex life (a specific judgment) is only a problem for global evaluations of the relationship as a whole if one holds standards that a satisfying sex life is a requirement for a good relationship. Indeed, for people who hold that standard, sexual satisfaction and relationship satisfaction are strongly correlated, but for people who do not endorse that standard, they are not (Fletcher & Kininmonth, 1992). When specific experiences in the relationship vary across domains, or when they change over time, the adaptive response for motivated spouses is to adjust their standards, such that

whatever aspects of the relationship are positive at the moment are also deemed crucial for successful relationships, and whatever aspects are lacking are deemed irrelevant or unnecessary (cf. Fletcher, Simpson, & Thomas, 2000).

Neff and Karney (2003) observed exactly this pattern in newlyweds who had been asked to rate 20 different relationship domains in terms of their importance for successful relationships generally and then later evaluated their own relationships on the same 20 domains. Consistent with the view of standards as decision rules, global satisfaction with the marriage was highest among spouses with the strongest positive correlation between perceiving that a specific domain was important and perceiving that the same domain was positive in their own relationships. For these couples, their standards highlighted the global implications of positive domains and minimized the global implications of negative domains. Furthermore, as spouses' perceptions of specific domains of the marriage evolved over the next 2 years, global satisfaction was most stable among spouses whose standards proved most flexible. When a particular aspect of the relationship deteriorated over that period, these spouses declared that this aspect was not as important to successful relationships as they once believed it to be, thus severing the link between that domain and their global judgments of the relationship.

Further examples abound. Gable and Poore (2008) used experience sampling techniques to examine links between specific positive and negative thoughts about a relationship and global satisfaction with it. Partners' motives affected how these levels of evaluation were linked: Global satisfaction covaried more strongly with positive thoughts for those with approach goals but covaried more strongly with negative thoughts for those with avoidance goals.

In addition, Murray and Holmes (1999) observed that satisfied partners compartmentalize negative perceptions of each other with "Yes, but" refutations, finding reasons to deny that specific failings in the partner have global implications for the relationship. Frye and Karney (2002) also observed that satisfied spouses recalled that specific marital problems were improving over time, even when longitudinal data indicated that they were not; the more spouses demonstrated this bias, the less perceptions of specific problems affected their global satisfaction with the marriage.

What do all of these cognitive processes have in common? In each of them, motivated spouses process specific experiences in ways that protect or enhance desired global evaluations of the relationship. For specific experiences that are consistent with their global evaluations (i.e., positive experiences), the links between the experience and the evaluation can be strengthened through processes that focus more attention on those experiences or highlight their broader implications. For specific experiences that are inconsistent with global evaluations (i.e., negative experiences), the links between the experience and the evaluation can be weakened through processes that deflect attention from those experiences or minimize their broader implications. In all cases, motivated reasoning is a process of assimilating new information into the existing representation of the relationship.

Limits on Adaptive Cognitive Processing in Marriage

Research on cognitive processes in marriage and other intimate relationships has been very successful at identifying mechanisms through which motivated partners protect their positive feelings about their relationships. This research has been less successful at addressing the undeniable fact that these cognitive processes often fail. Despite all of these mechanisms for assimilating specific experiences, people's representations of their marriages and intimate relationships usually accommodate to them in the long run.

How does motivated reasoning fall short? The hierarchical model of marital satisfaction in Figure 20.1 suggests two routes by which global evaluations may change despite spouses' desire to preserve them. First, negative experiences and perceptions may accumulate beyond the individual's ability to assimilate them. Second, spouses may lose the motivation or capacity to engage in motivated reasoning, even if their concrete experiences in the relationship remain relatively constant. Considerable research has supported each of these routes.

Route 1: Negative experiences accumulate. In a marriage or long-term relationship, the beginning of the relationship provides abundant positive experiences to support desirable global evaluations of the relationship, and negative or inconsistent experiences can be rationalized or explained away. However, when spouses forgive their partners for transgressions, declare that an unmet standard is no longer important, or state that a relationship problem is improving, the global implications of a negative experience are minimized, but the experience does not disappear. Negative experiences may remain in memory. More negative inputs require more effort to assimilate into positive views of the relationship, and eventually even the most motivated spouses may not be able to sustain a positive evaluation of the marriage any longer.

Classic models of marriage emphasize this gradual accumulation of specific negative experiences as the mechanism driving change in global marital satisfaction over time. Behavioral models of marriage, for example, explicitly argue that, "to the extent that normal marital disagreements are not handled well, unresolved negative feelings start to build up, fueling destructive patterns of marital interaction and eventually eroding and attacking the positive aspects of the relationship" (Markman, 1991, p. 422). Social ecological models draw attention to the way external contexts affect marital outcomes (e.g., Hill, 1949), but still the effects of external stress are usually described as a gradual process such that "minor stresses originating outside the relationship and spilling over into marriage . . . lead to mutual alienation and slowly decrease relationship quality over time" (Randall & Bodenmann, 2009, p. 108). The view that negative experiences can build up over time is a common feature of several other prominent theoretical frameworks as well, including Aron and Aron's (1986) self-expansion model, Bradbury and Fincham's (1988) contextual model, and Reis and Shaver's (1988) intimacy process model.

These perspectives are perfectly consistent with a motivated reasoning account of marital satisfaction. As Kunda (1990) noted in her original description of motivated reasoning, the motivated perceiver needs to find some basis for reaching a desired conclusion; without that basis, even the most desired conclusion may be impossible to sustain over time. These incremental models of marriage highlight different sources of negative experience—stress, unresolved conflict, boredom—that can shrink the available sample of positive experiences on which positive global views of the marriage can be based.

Kelley's (1967) covariance model of attributions made the links between experience and cognition even more explicit. In that seminal model, Kelley explained that the way people understand a specific behavior from someone they know well (e.g., whether or not they blame a long-term partner for a particular transgression) rests on how the individual's current behavior matches their memories of his or her prior behavior. A unique transgression (e.g., my spouse is late for a date but is usually on time) is easy to explain as the product of a temporary, external cause, and therefore has no bearing on our relationship. A frequent transgression (e.g., my spouse is always late) is harder for the motivated perceiver to reconcile with a positive global view of the partner's punctuality. According to Kelley, a strong covariance between an individual and an observed behavior trumps people's motives to decouple their perceptions of the individual from that behavior.

Whereas some specific marital problems may be hard to assimilate because they occur too frequently, other marital problems may be hard to assimilate because they are too severe. Motivated reasoning may be an effective means of preventing minor issues from escalating within a marriage, but some issues are not minor. Addressing those issues with purely cognitive responses may lessen their sting in the short run but may not motivate any direct action to resolve those issues, leaving couples vulnerable to deteriorating relationships in the long run. McNulty, O'Mara, and Karney (2008) demonstrated these risks in the early years of marriage by examining how the severity of couples' marital problems moderated the well-known effects of adaptive attributions on the development of their marital satisfaction over time. For couples who rated their marital problems as relatively mild, adaptive attributions predicted more satisfying and more stable marriages, consistent with prior research (Bradbury & Fincham, 1990). For couples who rated their marital problems as relatively severe, however, the

traditional effect was reversed: Couples who were willing to blame each other for transgressions maintained more stable satisfaction over time, whereas those who refrained from blame experienced steeper declines. Changes in the problems themselves mediated these effects, such that severe problems got worse for couples who refrained from blame, and these changes accounted for the steeper declines experienced by that group. In other words, the motivated reasoning that worked well for spouses in generally healthy relationships allowed more serious problems to fester in couples with issues that needed to be addressed directly.

In an independent sample, McNulty (2008) made a similar point about forgiveness, showing that couples who demonstrate skill at communicating effectively in a laboratory interaction task benefit from forgiving each other, but couples who are less effective at communication experience more declines when they are more forgiving. A subsequent daily diary study (McNulty, 2010) identified a potential mechanism for this effect: Forgiving a partner's negative behavior on a given day was associated with a greater likelihood that the behavior would recur on subsequent days. When marital problems are severe, it appears that the poet Shel Silverstein was right: "THINKING you can just ain't enough!" (Silverstein, 1974, p. 158). Rather, resolving serious marital problems requires direct confrontation and communication, actions that motivated reasoning may inhibit rather than promote.

In sum, motivated reasoning may fall short as a mechanism of relationship maintenance when (a) too many negative experiences accumulate, (b) the covariance between negative experiences and one's partner is strong, or (c) negative experiences are severe and require attention. With respect to promoting long-term happiness in marriage, one obvious (but still nontrivial) implication of this work is that global marital satisfaction should be easier to sustain when spouses maximize positive inputs into their representations of the marriage and minimize negative inputs. Put another way, spouses with plenty of material with which to support positive views of their marriage should have an easier time doing so, and spouses with many experiences inconsistent with positive views of the marriage will eventually have a harder time supporting those views. Behaviorally oriented marital therapies and interventions (e.g., Christensen & Jacobson, 2002; Jacobson & Margolin, 1979; Markman, Stanley, & Blumberg, 1994) are grounded in this point, asserting that if couples could be taught to behave better and interact with each other more effectively, they would have more positive experiences with which to support positive views of the marriage and fewer negative experiences to detract from those views.

Route 2: Capacity for motivated processing declines. Motivated reasoning takes ability and effort. Some people, owing to their personal history or personality (e.g., Bolger & Zuckerman, 1995), may have limits on their capacity to process specific experiences in ways that support desired conclusions. Others may temporarily lack this capacity, owing to distraction (Gilbert, Pelham, & Krull, 1988), exhaustion (Baumeister, 2002), or inebriation (Steele & Josephs, 1990). For all of these reasons, the likelihood that spouses will effectively assimilate negative experiences within a generally positive evaluation of the marriage varies across individuals and can vary within individuals over time. If the way spouses process their specific experiences changes over the course of the marriage, global marital satisfaction may change over time even if spouses' specific experiences within the marriage remain relatively constant.

Several individual difference variables account for variability in the tendency for spouses and partners to respond to specific relationship experiences in ways that support positive global views of their relationship. Anxious attachment, for example, is an enduring model of the social world that views close relationships as highly desirable but also highly dangerous. Individuals characterized by anxious attachment should be vigilant to signs of risk and should, therefore, be more likely to interpret negative behaviors from their spouses as confirmation of their global fears and concerns. Indeed, in a 14-day daily diary study, anxiously attached individuals were more reactive to specific relationship experiences than were more secure individuals (Campbell, Simpson, Boldry, & Kashy, 2005). Whereas secure individuals maintained optimism about their

relationships and felt equally close to their partners regardless of the specific events of each day, anxious individuals were more optimistic about the relationship and felt closer to their partners on days when their partners had been supportive than when they had experienced conflict with their partners.

The closely related construct of rejection sensitivity, defined as a dispositional tendency to perceive and react strongly to signs of social rejection, similarly operates to strengthen links between specific experiences and global perceptions of social situations (Downey, Freitas, Michaelis, & Khouri, 1998). Research with rejection-sensitive individuals in romantic relationships has shown that they are significantly more likely to ascribe hurtful intent to their partners' negative behaviors than individuals who are less rejection sensitive, who are more likely to seek out external causes to excuse their partners' negative behaviors (Downey & Feldman, 1996). Low self-esteem is another well-studied individual difference that has this effect. Diary studies have revealed that partners with low self-esteem evaluate their relationships positively only on days on which positive events occurred but evaluate their relationships negatively on days on which negative events occurred. These links are significantly weaker among partners with high self-esteem (Murray, Bellavia, Rose, & Griffin, 2003; Murray, Rose, Bellavia, Holmes, & Kusche, 2002). If maintaining marital satisfaction requires that spouses assimilate the inevitable disappointments of married life into a favorable view of the marriage as a whole, these studies indicate that some individuals are better at doing this than others. Over time, then, these individuals should be more vulnerable to declines in marital satisfaction and, in fact, each of these individual differences has been linked to poorer marital outcomes longitudinally (Collins, 2003; Downey et al., 1998; Murray, Griffin, Rose, & Bellavia, 2003).

Whereas individual differences exert stable effects on the way spouses process their specific experiences, situations external to the marriage may also temporarily constrain spouses' capacity for motivated reasoning. To the extent that motivated reasoning takes effort, demands outside the marriage that interfere with spouses' capacity to exert that effort should increase the likelihood that negative experiences in the marriage will affect spouses' global sentiments toward their relationships. This prediction aligns closely with models of self-regulation, which describe self-regulatory capacity as a limited resource that can be depleted, making subsequent efforts at self-regulation more difficult (Baumeister, 2002; Finkel & Campbell, 2001).

For couples, one prominent source of depletion is exposure to chronic and acute stress. Stressors such as financial strain, health problems, or interpersonal conflicts outside the home drain energy from spouses, leaving them with less energy to devote to the marriage (Greenhaus & Beutell, 1985; McCubbin & Patterson, 1983). It follows that, during periods of elevated stress, spouses should be less able to make allowances for each other's negative behaviors than during periods of relative calm. Multiwave longitudinal research examining how the attributions that couples make for each other's transgressions covaries with the amount of stress in their lives has supported this prediction (Neff & Karney, 2004). Within-couples analyses have revealed that the same couples who give each other the benefit of the doubt during periods of relatively low stress are significantly more likely to blame each other for the same transgressions during periods of relatively high stress, even after controlling for the direct effects of stress on marital satisfaction and the kinds of problems that couples face. In other words, couples who can assimilate negative behaviors when stress is low may no longer do so as effectively when stress is high. Subsequent research has drawn on daily diary assessments to reveal the same patterns in the way spouses integrate specific and global perceptions of the marriage across days (Neff & Karney, 2009). During periods of low stress, the covariance between specific perceptions of the marriage and global evaluations of the marriage is relatively low, suggesting that spouses are effective at protecting their global feelings about the marriage from the vicissitudes of daily life. During periods of high stress, however, the links between specific and global ratings are significantly higher in these same couples.

These findings suggest that, consistent with models of self-regulation, spouses' capacity to maintain their relationships fluctuates as a function of the other demands they face in their lives. For couples whose lives become more stressful over time, marital satisfaction should decline, all else being equal, as the demands external to the marriage make it harder and harder for spouses to do the work required to protect their global feelings about the relationship. Indeed, couples under stress do experience lower marital satisfaction, as well as satisfaction that declines more steeply over time (Karney, Story, & Bradbury, 2005). Identifying the ways in which stress affects relationships helps to explain the elevated divorce rates observed in lower income communities as compared with more affluent communities (Bramlett & Mosher, 2002). To the extent that financial strain represents a chronic demand on coping resources for poorer couples, their marital satisfaction should be especially strongly linked to their specific experiences in the marriage. In fact, survey research has indicated that associations between marital satisfaction and acute stressful events are significantly stronger for poorer couples than for more affluent ones (Maisel & Karney, 2012).

Thus far, this section has addressed limits to spouses' ability to engage in motivated processing of marital experiences, assuming throughout that spouses are highly motivated to preserve positive global views of their marriage. Not all spouses are equally motivated, however. As early social exchange theories recognized (Kelley & Thibaut, 1978), some partners are more dependent on their relationships than others and, therefore, some partners have more to lose if the relationship no longer proves satisfying. Variability in spouses' dependence on the marriage should not affect their ability to engage in motivated reasoning but rather the effort they expend on doing so, such that spouses who are highly invested in the marriage should be willing to assimilate more negative experiences into a positive view of the marriage than spouses who are less invested. Research drawing on the investment perspective on relationship commitment (Rusbult, 1980, 1983) has confirmed these predictions. For example, among college students in dating relationships, those reporting greater commitment to their relationships are more willing to forgive serious transgressions (e.g., infidelity) than is true of partners less committed to their relationships (Finkel,

Rusbult, Kumashiro, & Hannon, 2002). In other words, the committed partners assimilated betrayals that less committed partners could not assimilate. Moreover, the link between commitment and forgiveness was mediated by partners' cognitions about the event, such that commitment directly predicted the effort that partners expended on explaining and understanding the transgression, which in turn predicted greater willingness to forgive the transgression. Other research has made similar points: The more that partners depend on their relationships, the more they are willing to do to maintain them (e.g., Rusbult, Bissonette, Arriaga, & Cox, 1998; Van Lange et al., 1997). Although far less attention has been paid to how commitment itself may change over time, this work identifies another route through which marital satisfaction may change: Spouses who grow less committed to or invested in their marriage should expend less effort on maintaining it and thus should experience stronger associations between their specific negative experiences and the global evaluations of their relationships.

In sum, when spouses begin to pay more attention and ascribe more global meaning to their negative experiences in the marriage (and less to their positive experiences), global evaluations of the marriage are likely to decline even if spouses' specific experiences within the marriage remain relatively stable. Research on cognitive processing in marriage and intimate relationships has highlighted three factors that can constrain the way spouses support their initially positive views of their relationships: (a) stable individual differences in the tendency to process specific experiences effectively, (b) demands arising from chronic and acute stress outside the marriage, and (c) changes in spouses' motives to preserve the marriage.

Conclusions. Given all of the pain associated with declines in marital satisfaction, why do initially satisfying marriages decline so frequently? In this section, I have described two routes through which initially positive evaluations of a marriage may change despite the proven ability of spouses to reconcile negative experiences of the marriage with a globally positive view of the relationship as a whole. The first route emphasizes the changing content

of marital experiences. In some couples, negative experiences become so prevalent, so frequent, or so severe that they overwhelm spouses' ability to integrate them with a positive view of the relationship, and the positive view eventually crumbles. The second route emphasizes changes in the cognitive processes spouses use to draw global conclusions about their marriage. In some couples, spouses' capacity to engage in motivated reasoning about the marriage is constrained by stable individual differences in the partners, by external demands that tax spouses' finite cognitive resources, or by changes in spouses' motives to preserve the relationship. These two routes are independent but not mutually exclusive. That is, changes in the content of the marriage need not imply changes in the processes spouses use to understand the marriage, but these changes can coincide. Stress, for example, tends to increase the specific problems spouses must confront and resolve (a change in the content of marital experiences), even as it constrains spouses' ability to address problems effectively (a change in the processes spouses use to understand those experiences; Karney & Neff, 2013).

These two routes to explaining change in marital satisfaction imply two routes for efforts to preserve it. The first, as noted earlier, is to maximize positive experiences within marriage and to minimize negative ones. An alternative, however, is to promote environments that nurture spouses' capacity to process the events of their marriage more effectively. If spouses' capacity to reconcile daily irritations and disappointments within a globally positive view of their marriage can be diminished by distraction or exhaustion, any treatment that minimizes distractions and prevents exhaustion may promote a happier marriage (Karney & Bradbury, 2005). Programs may not need to target marriages directly to have a big impact on the lives of married couples. Researchers in Norway made this point in their analyses of the effects of a 1999 law that subsidized parents who chose to stay home with their children in the first years after their birth (Hardoy & Schøne, 2008). The law made no mention of marriage or marital outcomes, but it did make life easier for families who took advantage of it. A natural experiment that compared families that were and were not affected by the new policy revealed an immediate decline in divorce rates for families affected by the new law. If spouses are generally motivated to maintain their relationship, policies that make it easier for them to do so may be as effective an intervention strategy as programs that teach them how to do so.

FUTURE DIRECTIONS

Despite great strides over the past several decades of research on marriage, important questions about how marriages change over time remain unanswered. In this final section, I highlight directions for future research that would move the field forward.

We Still Need to Describe How Marriages Change

Although scholarship on change in marital satisfaction is nearly 80 years old, descriptions of how marital satisfaction changes over time remain pretty crude. Researchers know that newlyweds are generally satisfied and optimistic (Neff & Karney, 2005), and they know that divorced couples are generally angry and disappointed (e.g., Cleek & Pearson, 1985; Goode, 1956; Kitson & Raschke, 1981), but the course between these two poles has been sketched only vaguely. For example, change in marital satisfaction has frequently been described as a gradual process of deterioration and erosion. Yet, as noted earlier, evidence for this gradual process has been hard to identify (Lavner & Bradbury, 2010), leaving open the possibility that marital satisfaction actually changes suddenly and drastically if and when it changes. The hierarchical view of marital satisfaction described in this chapter raises the further possibility that change in marital satisfaction may follow different trajectories at different levels of abstraction. That is, changes in perceptions of specific domains of the marriage may accumulate gradually, whereas global evaluations of a marriage may be relatively stable until some threshold of specific negativity is reached, whereupon global evaluations may deteriorate rapidly.

To date, two obstacles have prevented the development of more refined views of change in marriage. First, assessments of marital satisfaction in longitudinal research have generally not been sensitive to possible differences in how specific versus global perceptions of the marriage may change over time. Future longitudinal research on marriage would benefit from assessing different levels of evaluation separately. Second, the resolution offered by most longitudinal designs is extremely low. For example, the picture of change that emerges from longitudinal research depends greatly on the frequency and duration of data collection, yet choices about how often and how long to assess couples are generally driven by practical rather than theoretical considerations. The result is research that often goes months or years between assessments, leaving large gaps wherein unknown changes in the marriage may be occurring. The move toward daily diary assessments of married couples (e.g., Murray, Bellavia, et al., 2003; Thompson & Bolger, 1999) is a welcome complement to long-term longitudinal studies, but daily measurements of marital satisfaction are as arbitrary in their way as annual or biannual measurements. When are no researchers are pestering them, how frequently spouses evaluate their marital satisfaction or how salient those evaluations are in their daily lives is not known. Qualitative studies that describe the role of marital satisfaction in spouses' emotional lives would be a first step toward developing an empirical foundation to guide the design of future longitudinal research.

Emphasize Systems, Not Variables

Psychological research on marriage has identified numerous individual differences, cognitive processes, and external stressors that each account for variance in marital outcomes over time. Yet lists of significant predictors do not by themselves accumulate to inform or elaborate on existing models of marriage. As this review I hope has made clear, many variables that have been studied in parallel lines of research may actually operate in very similar ways (e.g., attachment models, self-esteem, and rejection sensitivity). Advancing the understanding of marriage will require not more variables but more research that draws links between variables and compares their relative or combined influence on developing relationships. This goal is especially important as policymakers seek out marital research to inform their efforts to improve the lives of couples and families. To guide their efforts, program developers will need more than merely significant results; they will also need to know which potential targets of their interventions have substantial effects on marital outcomes. Providing that guidance requires research that includes multiple domains of marital functioning, that examines how different domains interact as a system, and that reports and gives proper attention to effect sizes.

Do Not Take Generalizability for Granted

Marital research has identified many contextual variables, such as socioeconomic status, income, and country of residence, that are strongly associated with marital outcomes but are impossible to manipulate experimentally. The size of these effects is often substantial, suggesting that, even though human beings across the planet want more or less the same things from intimacy (Jankowiak & Fischer, 1992), different determinants of successful intimacy may prove more or less important for different couples in different cultures and contexts. Addressing this variability will require efforts to improve the sampling in marital research, which has to date relied heavily on White, college-educated, middle-class samples of convenience (Karney, Kreitz, & Sweeney, 2004). Ironically, these samples have been drawn from segments of the population with the lowest risk of divorce, whereas those couples at highest risk (e.g., less affluent and non-White) have been underrepresented, prompting comparisons to the drunk who, having lost his keys in an alley, searches for them under a streetlight because the light is better there. The time is past due for research on marriage that obtains large, diverse, representative samples, so that the generalizability of models of marital development may be examined directly.

Get Interdisciplinary

The centrality of marriage to adult development ensures that it will be a phenomenon of enduring interest to multiple fields of study outside of psychology. Indeed, what is known about the prevalence of marriage and divorce comes from research by demographers and sociologists (e.g., McNamee &

Raley, 2011; Sweeney & Phillips, 2004). The best work on the effects of employment on marital outcomes has been conducted by economists (e.g., Roy, 2011). Some of the most exciting research on the effectiveness of marital interventions is being conducted not by clinical psychologists but by policy analysts (Wood, McConnell, Moore, Clarkwest, & Hsueh, 2012). The need to build bridges between psychological research and these other disciplines is as acute today as it was when Berscheid (1995) expressed it nearly two decades ago. By placing spouses' psychological and behavioral processes within their cultural, economic, and historic contexts, interdisciplinary research on marriage offers the best hope for advancing the understanding of how marriages and other long-term intimate relationships develop over time.

References

Amato, P. R., & James, S. (2010). Divorce in Europe and the United States: Commonalities and differences across nations. *Family Science, 1,* 2–13. doi:10.1080/19424620903381583

Anderson, J. R., Van Ryzin, M. J., & Doherty, W. J. (2010). Developmental trajectories of marital happiness in continuously married individuals: A group-based modeling approach. *Journal of Family Psychology, 24,* 587–596. doi:10.1037/a0020928

Aron, A., & Aron, E. N. (1986). *Love as expansion of self: Understanding attraction and satisfaction.* New York, NY: Hemisphere.

Aron, A., & Aron, E. N. (1996). Self and self-expansion in relationships. In G. J. O. Fletcher & J. Fitness (Eds.), *Knowledge structures in close relationships: A social psychological perspective* (pp. 325–344). Mahwah, NJ: Erlbaum.

Baumeister, R. F. (2002). Ego depletion and self-control failure: An energy model of the self's executive function. *Self and Identity, 1,* 129–136. doi:10.1080/152988602317319302

Baumeister, R. F., & Leary, M. R. (1995). The need to belong: Desire for interpersonal attachment as a fundamental human motivation. *Psychological Bulletin, 117,* 497–529. doi:10.1037/0033-2909.117.3.497

Bean, F. D., Berg, R. R., & Hook, J. V. W. V. (1996). Socioeconomic and cultural incorporation and marital disruption among Mexican Americans. *Social Forces, 75,* 593–617.

Belsky, J., & Hsieh, K. H. (1998). Patterns of marital change during the early childhood years: Parent personality, coparenting, and division-of-labor correlates. *Journal of Family Psychology, 12,* 511–528. doi:10.1037/0893-3200.12.4.511

Berscheid, E. (1995). Help wanted: A grand theorist of interpersonal relationships, sociologist or anthropologist preferred. *Journal of Social and Personal Relationships, 12,* 529–533. doi:10.1177/0265407595124005

Bolger, N., & Zuckerman, A. (1995). A framework for studying personality in the stress process. *Journal of Personality and Social Psychology, 69,* 890–902. doi:10.1037/0022-3514.69.5.890

Bradbury, T. N., & Fincham, F. D. (1988). Individual difference variables in close relationships: A contextual model of marriage as an integrative framework. *Journal of Personality and Social Psychology, 54,* 713–721. doi:10.1037/0022-3514.54.4.713

Bradbury, T. N., & Fincham, F. D. (1990). Attributions in marriage: Review and critique. *Psychological Bulletin, 107,* 3–33. doi:10.1037/0033-2909.107.1.3

Bradbury, T. N., & Fincham, F. D. (1991). A contextual model for advancing the study of marital interaction. In G. J. O. Fletcher & F. D. Fincham (Eds.), *Cognition in close relationships* (pp. 127–147). Hillsdale, NJ: Erlbaum.

Bramlett, M. D., & Mosher, W. D. (2002). Cohabitation, marriage, divorce, and remarriage in the United States. *Vital and Health Statistics, 23*(22).

Bumpass, L., & Raley, K. (2007). Measuring separation and divorce. In S. L. Hofferth & L. M. Casper (Eds.), *Handbook of measurement issues in family research* (pp. 125–143). Mahwah, NJ: Erlbaum.

Call, V., Sprecher, S., & Schwartz, P. (1995). The incidence and frequency of marital sex in a national sample. *Journal of Marriage and the Family, 57,* 639–652. doi:10.2307/353919

Campbell, L., Simpson, J. A., Boldry, J., & Kashy, D. A. (2005). Perceptions of conflict and support in romantic relationships: The role of attachment anxiety. *Journal of Personality and Social Psychology, 88,* 510–531. doi:10.1037/0022-3514.88.3.510

Cherlin, A. J. (2010). Demographic trends in the United States: A review of research in the 2000s. *Journal of Marriage and Family, 72,* 403–419. doi:10.1111/j.1741-3737.2010.00710.x

Christensen, A., & Jacobson, N. S. (2002). *Reconcilable differences.* New York, NY: Guilford Press.

Claxton, A., & Perry-Jenkins, M. (2008). No fun anymore: Leisure and marital quality across the transition to parenthood. *Journal of Marriage and Family, 70,* 28–43. doi:10.1111/j.1741-3737.2007.00459.x

Cleek, M. G., & Pearson, T. A. (1985). Perceived causes of divorce: An analysis of interrelationships. *Journal of Marriage and the Family, 47,* 179–183.

Collins, W. A. (2003). More than myth: The developmental significance of romantic relationships during adolescence. *Journal of Research on Adolescence, 13,* 1–24. doi:10.1111/1532-7795.1301001

Downey, G., & Feldman, S. (1996). Implications of rejection sensitivity for intimate relationships. *Journal of Personality and Social Psychology, 70,* 1327–1343. doi:10.1037/0022-3514.70.6.1327

Downey, G., Freitas, A. L., Michaelis, B., & Khouri, H. (1998). The self-fulfilling prophecy in close relationships: Rejection sensitivity and rejection by romantic partners. *Journal of Personality and Social Psychology, 75,* 545–560. doi:10.1037/0022-3514.75.2.545

Fein, D., & Ooms, T. (2006). *What do we know about couples and marriage in disadvantaged populations? Reflections from a researcher and a policy analyst.* Washington, DC: Center for Law and Social Policy.

Fincham, F. D., & Bradbury, T. N. (1987). The assessment of marital quality: A reevaluation. *Journal of Marriage and the Family, 49,* 797–809. doi:10.2307/351973

Finkel, E. J., & Campbell, W. K. (2001). Self-control and accommodation in close relationships: An interdependence analysis. *Journal of Personality and Social Psychology, 81,* 263–277. doi:10.1037/0022-3514.81.2.263

Finkel, E. J., Rusbult, C. E., Kumashiro, M., & Hannon, P. A. (2002). Dealing with betrayal in close relationships: Does commitment promote forgiveness? *Journal of Personality and Social Psychology, 82,* 956–974. doi:10.1037/0022-3514.82.6.956

Fletcher, G. J. O., & Kininmonth, L. (1992). Measuring relationship beliefs: An individual differences scale. *Journal of Research in Personality, 26,* 371–397. doi:10.1016/0092-6566(92)90066-D

Fletcher, G. J. O., & Simpson, J. A. (2000). Ideal standards in close relationships: Their structure and functions. *Current Directions in Psychological Science, 9,* 102–105. doi:10.1111/1467-8721.00070

Fletcher, G. J. O., Simpson, J. A., & Thomas, G. (2000). Ideals, perceptions, and evaluations in early relationship development. *Journal of Personality & Social Psychology, 79,* 933–940.

Fletcher, G. J. O., & Thomas, G. (1996). Close relationship lay theories: Their structure and function. In G. J. O. Fletcher & J. Fitness (Eds.), *Knowledge structures in close relationships: A social psychological perspective* (pp. 3–24). Mahwah, NJ: Erlbaum.

Fritz, P. A., & O'Leary, K. D. (2004). Physical and psychological partner aggression across a decade: A growth curve analysis. *Violence and Victims, 19,* 3–16. doi:10.1891/088667004780842886

Frye, N. E., & Karney, B. R. (2002). Being better or getting better? Social and temporal comparisons as coping mechanisms in close relationships. *Personality and Social Psychology Bulletin, 28,* 1287–1299. doi:10.1177/01461672022812013

Frye, N. E., McNulty, J. K., & Karney, B. R. (2008). How do constraints on leaving a marriage affect behavior within the marriage? *Journal of Family Psychology, 22,* 153–161. doi:10.1037/0893-3200.22.1.153

Funder, D. C. (1999). *Personality judgment: A realistic approach to person perception.* New York, NY: Academic Press.

Gable, S. L., & Poore, J. (2008). Which thoughts count? Algorithms for evaluating satisfaction in relationships. *Psychological Science, 19,* 1030–1036. doi:10.1111/j.1467-9280.2008.02195.x

Gable, S. L., & Reis, H. T. (1999). Now and then, them and us, this and that: Studying relationships across time, partner, context, and person. *Personal Relationships, 6,* 415–432. doi:10.1111/j.1475-6811.1999.tb00201.x

Gilbert, D. T. (1998). Ordinary personology. In D. T. Gilbert & S. T. Fiske (Eds.), *The handbook of social psychology* (4th ed., Vol. 2, pp. 89–150). New York, NY: McGraw-Hill.

Gilbert, D. T., Pelham, B. W., & Krull, D. S. (1988). On cognitive busyness: When person perceivers meet persons perceived. *Journal of Personality and Social Psychology, 54,* 733–740. doi:10.1037/0022-3514.54.5.733

Goldstein, J. R., & Kenney, C. T. (2001). Marriage delayed or marriage forgone? New cohort forecasts of first marriage for U.S. women. *American Sociological Review, 66,* 506–519. doi:10.2307/3088920

Goode, W. J. (1956). *After divorce.* Glencoe, IL: Free Press.

Gorchoff, S. M., John, O. P., & Helson, R. (2008). Contextualizing change in marital satisfaction during middle age: An 18-year longitudinal study. *Psychological Science, 19,* 1194–1200. doi:10.1111/j.1467-9280.2008.02222.x

Greenhaus, J. H., & Beutell, N. (1985). Sources of conflict between work and family roles. *Academy of Management Review, 10,* 76–88.

Hardoy, I., & Schøne, P. (2008). Subsidizing "stayers"? Effects of a Norwegian child care reform on marital stability. *Journal of Marriage and Family, 70,* 571–584. doi:10.1111/j.1741-3737.2008.00506.x

Hill, R. (1949). *Families under stress.* New York, NY: Harper & Row.

Holtzworth-Munroe, A., & Jacobson, N. S. (1985). Causal attributions of married couples: When do they search for causes? What do they conclude when they do? *Journal of Personality and Social Psychology, 48,* 1398–1412. doi:10.1037/0022-3514.48.6.1398

Huston, T. L., & Burgess, R. L. (1979). Social exchange in developing relationships: An overview. In R. L. Burgess & T. L. Huston (Eds.), *Social exchange in developing relationships* (pp. 3–28). New York, NY: Academic Press.

Huston, T. L., Caughlin, J. P., Houts, R. M., Smith, S. E., & George, L. J. (2001). The connubial crucible: Newlywed years as predictors of marital delight, distress, and divorce. *Journal of Personality and Social Psychology, 80,* 237–252. doi:10.1037/0022-3514.80.2.237

Jacobson, N. S., & Margolin, G. (1979). *Marital therapy: Strategies based on social learning and behavior exchange principles.* New York, NY: Brunner/Mazel.

Jankowiak, W. R., & Fischer, E. F. (1992). A cross-cultural perspective on romantic love. *Ethnology, 31,* 149–155. doi:10.2307/3773618

John, O. P., Hampson, S. E., & Goldberg, L. R. (1991). The basic level in personality-trait hierarchies: Studies of trait use and accessibility in different contexts. *Journal of Personality and Social Psychology, 60,* 348–361. doi:10.1037/0022-3514.60.3.348

Johnson, M. D. (2012). Healthy marriage initiatives: On the need for empiricism in policy implementation. *American Psychologist, 67,* 296–308.

Kamp Dush, C. M., Taylor, M. G., & Kroeger, R. A. (2008). Marital happiness and psychological well-being across the life course. *Family Relations: Interdisciplinary Journal of Applied Family Studies, 57,* 211–226. doi:10.1111/j.1741-3729.2008.00495.x

Karney, B. R., & Bradbury, T. N. (1997). Neuroticism, marital interaction, and the trajectory of marital satisfaction. *Journal of Personality and Social Psychology, 72,* 1075–1092. doi:10.1037/0022-3514.72.5.1075

Karney, B. R., & Bradbury, T. N. (2000). Attributions in marriage: State or trait? A growth curve analysis. *Journal of Personality and Social Psychology, 78,* 295–309. doi:10.1037/0022-3514.78.2.295

Karney, B. R., & Bradbury, T. N. (2005). Contextual influences on marriage—Implications for policy and intervention. *Current Directions in Psychological Science, 14,* 171–174. doi:10.1111/j.0963-7214.2005.00358.x

Karney, B. R., Bradbury, T. N., & Johnson, M. D. (1999). Deconstructing stability: The distinction between the course of a close relationship and its endpoint. In J. M. Adams & W. H. Jones (Eds.), *Handbook of interpersonal commitment and relationship stability* (pp. 481–499). Dordrecht, the Netherlands: Kluwer. doi:10.1007/978-1-4615-4773-0_28

Karney, B. R., & Frye, N. E. (2002). "But we've been getting better lately": Comparing prospective and retrospective views of relationship development. *Journal of Personality and Social Psychology, 82,* 222–238. doi:10.1037/0022-3514.82.2.222

Karney, B. R., Kreitz, M. A., & Sweeney, K. E. (2004). Obstacles to ethnic diversity in marital research: On the failure of good intentions. *Journal of Social and Personal Relationships, 21,* 509–526. doi:10.1177/0265407504044845

Karney, B. R., McNulty, J. K., & Bradbury, T. N. (2004). Cognition and the development of close relationships. In M. B. Brewer & M. Hewstone (Eds.), *Social cognition* (pp. 194–221). Malden, MA: Blackwell.

Karney, B. R., & Neff, L. A. (2013). Couples and stress: How demands outside a relationship affect intimacy within the relationship. In J. A. Simpson & L. Campbell (Eds.), *Handbook of close relationships* (pp. 664–684). Oxford, England: Oxford University Press.

Karney, B. R., Story, L. B., & Bradbury, T. N. (2005). Marriages in context: Interactions between chronic and acute stress among newlyweds. In T. A. Revenson, K. Kayser, & G. Bodenmann (Eds.), *Couples coping with stress: Emerging perspectives on dyadic coping* (pp. 13–32). Washington, DC: American Psychological Association. doi:10.1037/11031-001

Kelley, H. H. (1967). Attribution theory in social psychology. In D. Levine (Ed.), *Nebraska symposium on motivation* (Vol. 15, pp. 192–238). Lincoln: University of Nebraska Press.

Kelley, H. H., & Thibaut, J. W. (1978). *Interpersonal relations: A theory of interdependence.* New York, NY: Wiley-Interscience.

Kitson, G. C., & Raschke, H. J. (1981). Divorce research: What we know; what we need to know. *Journal of Divorce, 4,* 1–37. doi:10.1300/J279v04n03_01

Kunda, Z. (1990). The case for motivated reasoning. *Psychological Bulletin, 108,* 480–498. doi:10.1037/0033-2909.108.3.480

Kurdek, L. A. (1999). The nature and predictors of the trajectory of change in marital quality for husbands and wives over the first 10 years of marriage. *Developmental Psychology, 35,* 1283–1296. doi:10.1037/0012-1649.35.5.1283

Lavner, J. A., & Bradbury, T. N. (2010). Patterns of change in marital satisfaction over the newlywed years. *Journal of Marriage and Family, 72,* 1171–1187. doi:10.1111/j.1741-3737.2010.00757.x

Lavner, J. A., & Bradbury, T. N. (2012). Why do even satisfied newlyweds eventually go on to divorce? *Journal of Family Psychology, 26,* 1–10. doi:10.1037/a0025966

Lawrence, E., & Bradbury, T. N. (2001). Physical aggression and marital dysfunction: A longitudinal analysis. *Journal of Family Psychology, 15,* 135–154. doi:10.1037/0893-3200.15.1.135

Lichter, D. T., Batson, C. D., & Brown, J. B. (2004). Welfare reform and marriage promotion: The marital expectations and desires of single and cohabiting mothers. *Social Service Review, 78,* 2–25. doi:10.1086/380652

Lindahl, K., Clements, M., & Markman, H. (1998). The development of marriage: A 9-year perspective. In T. N. Bradbury (Ed.), *The developmental course of marital dysfunction* (pp. 205–236). Cambridge, England: Cambridge University Press. doi:10.1017/CBO9780511527814.009

Lorber, M. F., & O'Leary, K. D. (2011). Stability, change, and informant variance in newlyweds' physical aggression: Individual and dyadic processes. *Aggressive Behavior, 38,* 1–15. doi:10.1002/ab.20414

Maisel, N. C., & Karney, B. R. (2012). Socioeconomic status moderates associations among stressful events, mental health, and relationship satisfaction. *Journal of Family Psychology, 26,* 654–660. doi:10.1037/a0028901

Markman, H. J. (1991). Backwards into the future of couples therapy and couples therapy research: A comment on Jacobson. *Journal of Family Psychology, 4,* 416–425. doi:10.1037/0893-3200.4.4.416

Markman, H. J., Stanley, S. M., & Blumberg, S. L. (1994). *Fighting for your marriage: Positive steps for preventing divorce and preserving a lasting love.* San Francisco, CA: Jossey-Bass.

Martin, S. P. (2006). Trends in marital dissolution by women's education in the United States. *Demographic Research, 15,* 537–560. doi:10.4054/DemRes.2006.15.20

McConnell, A. R. (2011). The multiple self-aspects framework: Self-concept representation and its implications. *Personality and Social Psychology Review, 15,* 3–27. doi:10.1177/1088868310371101

McCubbin, H. I., & Patterson, J. M. (1983). Family transitions: Adaptation to stress. In H. I. McCubbin & C. R. Figley (Eds.), *Stress and the family: Coping with normative transitions* (Vol. 1, pp. 5–25). New York, NY: Brunner/Mazel.

McNamee, C., & Raley, K. (2011). A note on race, ethnicity and nativity differentials in remarriage in the United States. *Demographic Research, 24,* 293–312. doi:10.4054/DemRes.2011.24.13

McNulty, J. K. (2008). Forgiveness in marriage: Putting the benefits into context. *Journal of Family Psychology, 22,* 171–175. doi:10.1037/0893-3200.22.1.171

McNulty, J. K. (2010). Forgiveness increases the likelihood of subsequent partner transgressions in marriage. *Journal of Family Psychology, 24,* 787–790. doi:10.1037/a0021678

McNulty, J. K., & Karney, B. R. (2001). Attributions in marriage: Integrating specific and global evaluations of a relationship. *Personality and Social Psychology Bulletin, 27,* 943–955. doi:10.1177/0146167201278003

McNulty, J. K., O'Mara, E. M., & Karney, B. R. (2008). Benevolent cognitions as a strategy of relationship maintenance: "Don't sweat the small stuff" . . . But it is not all small stuff. *Journal of Personality and Social Psychology, 94,* 631–646. doi:10.1037/0022-3514.94.4.631

Miller, R. B. (2000). Misconceptions about the U-shaped curve of marital satisfaction over the life course. *Family Science Review, 13,* 60–73.

Mitchell, B. A., & Lovegreen, L. D. (2009). The empty nest syndrome in midlife families: A multimethod exploration of parental gender differences and cultural dynamics. *Journal of Family Issues, 30,* 1651–1670. doi:10.1177/0192513X09339020

Murray, S. L., Bellavia, G. M., Rose, P., & Griffin, D. W. (2003). Once hurt, twice hurtful: How perceived regard regulates daily marital interactions. *Journal of Personality and Social Psychology, 84,* 126–147. doi:10.1037/0022-3514.84.1.126

Murray, S. L., Griffin, D. W., Rose, P., & Bellavia, G. M. (2003). Calibrating the sociometer: The relational contingencies of self-esteem. *Journal of Personality and Social Psychology, 85,* 63–84. doi:10.1037/0022-3514.85.1.63

Murray, S. L., & Holmes, J. G. (1999). The (mental) ties that bind: Cognitive structures that predict relationship resilience. *Journal of Personality and Social Psychology, 77,* 1228–1244. doi:10.1037/0022-3514.77.6.1228

Murray, S. L., Holmes, J. G., & Griffin, D. W. (1996). The benefits of positive illusions: Idealization and the construction of satisfaction in close relationships. *Journal of Personality and Social Psychology, 70,* 79–98. doi:10.1037/0022-3514.70.1.79

Murray, S. L., Rose, P., Bellavia, G. M., Holmes, J. G., & Kusche, A. G. (2002). When rejection stings: How self-esteem constrains relationship-enhancement processes. *Journal of Personality and Social Psychology, 83,* 556–573. doi:10.1037/0022-3514.83.3.556

Nagin, D. S. (1999). Analyzing developmental trajectories: A semiparametric, group-based approach. *Psychological Methods, 4,* 139–157. doi:10.1037/1082-989X.4.2.139

Neff, L. A., & Karney, B. R. (2002a). Judgments of a relationship partner: Specific accuracy but global enhancement. *Journal of Personality, 70,* 1079–1112. doi:10.1111/1467-6494.05032

Neff, L. A., & Karney, B. R. (2002b). Self-evaluation motives in close relationships: A model of global enhancement and specific verification. In P. Noller & J. A. Feeney (Eds.), *Understanding marriage: Developments in the study of couple interaction* (pp. 32–58). New York, NY: Cambridge University Press. doi:10.1017/CBO9780511500077.004

Neff, L. A., & Karney, B. R. (2003). The dynamic structure of relationship perceptions: Differential importance as a strategy of relationship maintenance.

Personality and Social Psychology Bulletin, 29, 1433–1446. doi:10.1177/0146167203256376

Neff, L. A., & Karney, B. R. (2004). How does context affect intimate relationships? Linking external stress and cognitive processes within marriage. *Personality and Social Psychology Bulletin, 30,* 134–148. doi:10.1177/0146167203255984

Neff, L. A., & Karney, B. R. (2005). To know you is to love you: The implications of global adoration and specific accuracy for marital relationships. *Journal of Personality and Social Psychology, 88,* 480–497. doi:10.1037/0022-3514.88.3.480

Neff, L. A., & Karney, B. R. (2009). Stress and reactivity to daily relationship experiences: How stress hinders adaptive processes in marriage. *Journal of Personality and Social Psychology, 97,* 435–450. doi:10.1037/a0015663

Nomaguchi, K. M., & Milkie, M. A. (2003). Costs and rewards of children: The effects of becoming a parent on adults' lives. *Journal of Marriage and Family, 65,* 356–374. doi:10.1111/j.1741-3737.2003.00356.x

Raley, R. K., & Bumpass, L. (2003). The topography of the divorce plateau: Levels and trends in union stability in the United States after 1980. *Demographic Research, 8,* 245–260. doi:10.4054/DemRes.2003.8.8

Randall, A. K., & Bodenmann, G. (2009). The role of stress on close relationships and marital satisfaction. *Clinical Psychology Review, 29,* 105–115. doi:10.1016/j.cpr.2008.10.004

Reis, H. T., & Shaver, P. (1988). Intimacy as an interpersonal process. In S. W. Duck (Ed.), *Handbook of personal relationships: Theory, research and interventions* (pp. 367–389). Chichester, England: Wiley.

Rollins, B. C., & Cannon, K. L. (1974). Marital satisfaction over the family life cycle: A reevaluation. *Journal of Marriage and the Family, 36,* 271–282. doi:10.2307/351153

Rollins, B. C., & Feldman, H. (1970). Marital satisfaction over the family life cycle. *Journal of Marriage and the Family, 32,* 20–28. doi:10.2307/349967

Rosenberg, M. (1979). *Conceiving the self.* New York, NY: Basic Books.

Roy, S. (2011). Unemployment rate and divorce. *Economic Record, 87,* 56–79. doi:10.1111/j.1475-4932.2011.00746.x

Rusbult, C. E. (1980). Commitment and satisfaction in romantic associations: A test of the investment model. *Journal of Experimental Social Psychology, 16,* 172–186. doi:10.1016/0022-1031(80)90007-4

Rusbult, C. E. (1983). A longitudinal test of the investment model: The development (and deterioration) of satisfaction and commitment in heterosexual involvements. *Journal of Personality and Social Psychology, 45,* 101–117. doi:10.1037/0022-3514.45.1.101

Rusbult, C. E., Bissonette, V. L., Arriaga, X. B., & Cox, C. L. (1998). Accommodation processes during the early years of marriage. In T. N. Bradbury (Ed.), *The developmental course of marital dysfunction* (pp. 74–113). New York, NY: Cambridge University Press. doi:10.1017/CBO9780511527814.005

Schoen, R., & Canudas-Romo, V. (2006). Timing effects on divorce: 20th century experience in the United States. *Journal of Marriage and Family, 68*, 749–758. doi:10.1111/j.1741-3737.2006.00287.x

Silverstein, S. (1974). *Where the sidewalk ends*. New York, NY: Harper & Row.

Simpson, J. A., Oriña, M. M., & Ickes, W. (2003). When accuracy hurts, and when it helps: A test of the empathic accuracy model in marital interactions. *Journal of Personality and Social Psychology, 85*, 881–893. doi:10.1037/0022-3514.85.5.881

Smith, C. T., Ratliff, K. A., & Nosek, B. A. (2012). Rapid assimilation: Automatically integrating new information with existing beliefs. *Social Cognition, 30*, 199–219. doi:10.1521/soco.2012.30.2.199

Spanier, G. B., Lewis, R. A., & Cole, C. L. (1975). Marital adjustment over the family life cycle: The issue of curvilinearity. *Journal of Marriage and the Family, 37*, 263–275. doi:10.2307/350960

Steele, C. M., & Josephs, R. A. (1990). Alcohol myopia: Its prized and dangerous effects. *American Psychologist, 45*, 921–933. doi:10.1037/0003-066X.45.8.921

Swann, W. B., De La Ronde, C., & Hixon, J. G. (1994). Authenticity and positivity strivings in marriage and courtship. *Journal of Personality and Social Psychology, 66*, 857–869. doi:10.1037/0022-3514.66.5.857

Sweeney, M. M. (2010). Remarriage and stepfamilies: Strategic sites for family scholarship in the 21st century. *Journal of Marriage and Family, 72*, 667–684. doi:10.1111/j.1741-3737.2010.00724.x

Sweeney, M. M., & Phillips, J. A. (2004). Understanding racial differences in marital disruption: Recent trends and explanations. *Journal of Marriage and Family, 66*, 639–650. doi:10.1111/j.0022-2445.2004.00043.x

Thompson, A., & Bolger, N. (1999). Emotional transmission in couples under stress. *Journal of Marriage and the Family, 61*, 38–48. doi:10.2307/353881

Trail, T. E., & Karney, B. R. (2012). What's (not) wrong with low-income marriages? *Journal of Marriage and Family, 74*, 413–427. doi:10.1111/j.1741-3737.2012.00977.x

Umberson, D., Williams, K., Powers, D. A., Chen, M. D., & Campbell, A. M. (2005). As good as it gets? A life course perspective on marital quality. *Social Forces, 84*, 493–511. doi:10.1353/sof.2005.0131

Vaillant, C. O., & Vaillant, G. E. (1993). Is the U-curve of marital satisfaction an illusion? A 40-year study of marriage. *Journal of Marriage and the Family, 55*, 230–239. doi:10.2307/352971

Van Lange, P. A. M., Rusbult, C. E., Drigotas, S. M., Arriaga, X. B., Witcher, B. S., & Cox, C. L. (1997). Willingness to sacrifice in close relationships. *Journal of Personality and Social Psychology, 72*, 1373–1395. doi:10.1037/0022-3514.72.6.1373

VanLaningham, J., Johnson, D. R., & Amato, P. (2001). Marital happiness, marital duration, and the U-shaped curve: Evidence from a five-wave panel study. *Social Forces, 79*, 1313–1341. doi:10.1353/sof.2001.0055

Wood, R. G., McConnell, S., Moore, Q., Clarkwest, A., & Hsueh, J. (2012). The effects of building strong families: A healthy marriage and relationship skills education program for unmarried parents. *Journal of Policy Analysis and Management, 31*, 228–252. doi:10.1002/pam.21608

CHAPTER 21

RELATIONSHIP MAINTENANCE AND DISSOLUTION

Christopher R. Agnew and Laura E. VanderDrift

The study of relationship maintenance has a long and rich history, largely flowing from the traditional view of relationships as having a set beginning and a set end. Maintenance is held to be whatever takes place psychologically and behaviorally in between that beginning and end. Voluminous research has catalogued factors related to a relationship's initiation (e.g., Sprecher, Wenzel, & Harvey, 2008), its maintenance (e.g., Canary & Dainton, 2003; Gaines & Agnew, 2003), and its dissolution (e.g., Fine & Harvey, 2006).

Rather than characterizing maintenance by such discrete phases, however, we take the view that a relationship at any given point in time is more fruitfully conceptualized as being on an independence–interdependence continuum, with complete independence of partners on one end and complete interdependence between partners on the other. Relationship maintenance can be thought of as processes that help to keep involved actors relatively interdependent with one another. One benefit of such a conceptualization is that it does not rely on certain assumptions in previous approaches that do not match the reality of how relationships can change over time. For instance, such a conceptualization does not characterize all relationships of one type as equivalent (e.g., a romantic relationship can be more or less interdependent). Moreover, relationship initiation and termination are not considered to be discrete events. A dissolved relationship, for example, does not necessarily mean that no relationship exists; rather, the degree of interdependence may have changed. This is fundamentally different

than an approach that views different relationship types (e.g., romances, friendships, sexual relationships, kin relationships) as characterized by unique processes. Such a conceptualization also provides a useful framework for reviewing past relationship research that has been conducted under the rubric of relationship maintenance. In this chapter, we review that work, as well as findings relevant to failing to maintain a relationship, from this perspective.

We begin by reviewing past work on relationship maintenance, characterizing the processes investigated by researchers as (a) serving to keep partners who are content with their current place on the independence–interdependence continuum stable (stability promotion processes), (b) aiding in increasing partners' interdependence (greater interdependence promotion processes), or (c) coming online when a threat to the current position on the continuum is confronted (threat-induced processes). Despite the bevy of relationship maintenance processes that may be at play, there are, of course, cases in which partners fail to maintain their relationships. We conclude the chapter by reviewing both the positive and the negative consequences for individual partners of failing to maintain, the predictors of maintenance failure, and some suggested avenues for future research.

RELATIONSHIP MAINTENANCE PROCESSES

Some relationship maintenance processes are characteristic of partners who are content with their

http://dx.doi.org/10.1037/14344-021
APA Handbook of Personality and Social Psychology: Vol. 3. Interpersonal Relations, M. Mikulincer and P. R. Shaver (Editors-in-Chief)

place on the continuum of relative independence–interdependence and serve to keep them stable, some aid in increasing partners' interdependence, and others come online when a threat to the current position on the continuum is confronted.

Processes that promote greater interdependence involve the entwinement of personal and relational gain. Those that promote stability can prevent interdependence from either sliding down or sliding up. Those that prevent it from sliding down buffer partners from the deleterious effects of constant reappraisal, as well as assist partners in their attempts to not transgress. Those that prevent it from sliding up have received less research, but what has been done has suggested that these mechanisms limit some component of the relationship to prevent interdependence (e.g., intimacy, amount of contact).

The majority of research to date has been on those mechanisms that come online when a threat is confronted. These threat-induced processes are in service of promoting stability in position on the continuum, but they tend to be reactionary rather than preventive.

Threat-Induced Maintenance Processes

When considering relationship maintenance, it is most common to describe those processes that arise to protect a relationship when a threat is encountered. These processes serve to keep the state of the relationship constant when an event is encountered that threatens to place a wedge between the two partners' personal goals and the goals of the relationship more broadly (Rusbult & Agnew, 2010). Threats to the relationship can take many forms but can be broadly categorized into three classes: (a) noncorrespondence of outcomes, (b) threats internal to the relationship, and (c) threats external to the relationship. It is in dealing with these three classes of threats that the relationship maintenance activities that we broadly call threat-induced processes come online with the goal of holding the state of the relationship constant.

Noncorrespondent outcomes. When in an interdependent relationship, an individual's own behavior affects his or her own well-being, as well as the well-being of his or her partner and relationship.

The extent to which both partners' well-being is similarly affected by the actions that are available to them is known as correspondence of outcomes (Kelley & Thibaut, 1978). Often, the two partners in a relationship are equivalently affected by the available actions (i.e., an action that benefits one partner benefits the other similarly). A threat to the relationship arises in the exception to this, in which the actions that benefit one partner do not benefit the other. If threat-induced maintenance processes do not come online during times of noncorrespondence of outcomes, individuals may act in self-interested ways to the detriment of their relationships. Several processes are available to counter such a threat, including transformation of motivation and willingness to sacrifice.

Transformation of motivation. Transformation of motivation involves considering and placing the broader interests of a relationship ahead of immediate, self-interested instincts (Kelley & Thibaut, 1978). As such, it is a process that protects a relationship against the threat associated with noncorrespondence of outcomes. In the first empirical examination of this process, participants were asked to give their reactions to a hypothetical situation in which their partner and they were trying to decide which of two movies to view on a particular evening (as described in Kelley et al., 2003). There were four possible events for an individual in this situation: (a) see own preferred movie with partner, (b) see own preferred movie without partner, (c) see another movie with partner, and (d) see another movie without partner. Participants were presented with these options and asked to rate their preferences. When they believed their partner had no preference, they rated going together to see their preferred movie as very desirable, going together to the other movie as slightly positive, and going alone to different movies as quite negative. In this situation, there was no transformation of motivation because there was no clear preference incompatibility between partners. However, when participants believed their partner had a preference for the other movie, their view of their own outcomes was sharply modified to take into account the partner's preference: Going together to one's own preferred movie was less attractive than before and going together to the other movie (i.e., the partner's perceived preferred movie) became more desirable. In this case, there was transformation of motivation, and taken together, the total pattern of results shows the influence of transformation of motivation: Individuals who transform motivation take account of both their own and their partners' outcomes when making decisions. Because a partner's happiness affects one's own happiness, the outcomes that are associated with getting one's way versus giving in are not as would be expected when an individual acts alone (Kelley et al., 2003).

The mechanism of transformation of motivation involves individuals attending to the aspects of the situation that are relevant to their own and their partners' outcomes and interpreting and reacting to those aspects in ways that are explained by their own social person factors. When transformation of motivation occurs, individuals act not on the given situation (i.e., the situation as objectively presented) but instead on the transformed effective situation (i.e., how the individual interprets the situation given the outcome implications and his or her social person factors; Kelley et al., 2003; Rusbult & Van Lange, 2003). How this works is twofold.

First, increases in interdependence are frequently accompanied by increases in situation-relevant attention, cognition, and affect (Kelley et al., 2003). In interdependent situations, individuals' attention is diverted to the features of interaction situations that are relevant to their own personal well-being as well as to the well-being of others. Individuals can recognize the ways in which their own outcomes may be affected by others' actions, as well as the ways in which others' outcomes may be affected by their own actions. Second, in interdependent situations, the importance of social person factors (i.e., the abilities, needs, and goals that are relevant to the interaction; Holmes, 2002; Kelley et al., 2003) is high. These factors influence individuals' behavior when they are cognizant and responsive to an interdependent situation, including both their own and their partner's outcomes. Accordingly, individuals in interdependent situations can act in ways that cannot be explained simply by the given situation but instead are attributable to a combination of the situation and the properties of the individual.

Transformation of motivation provides a procedural explanation for why, when faced with noncorrespondent outcomes, relationship partners do not always act in self-interested ways. However, it is also possible for individuals to not act on their self-interests without any perceptual shifts occurring. That is, there are cases in which individuals will inhibit their desired response or engage in an undesired response for the betterment of their relationship.

Willingness to sacrifice. Willingness to sacrifice involves the individual forfeiting his or her own self-interest to promote the well-being of a partner or the relationship (Van Lange et al., 1997). This can be done by passively forfeiting behaviors that would otherwise be desirable, actively engaging in behaviors that would otherwise be undesirable, or both.

The earliest explanations for willingness to sacrifice revolved around the notion of relationship commitment (Rusbult, Agnew, & Arriaga, 2012). Committed individuals are dependent on their relationships and are likely to sacrifice self-interest to maintain their relationship. They have a long-term orientation toward the relationship that promotes sacrifice because patterns of reciprocal cooperation are likely to yield better outcomes long term than behaving in line with immediate self-interest. They are also psychologically attached to their partners (A. Aron, Aron, & Smollan, 1992) and have developed a communal orientation toward their partner (Agnew, 2000; Agnew & Etcheverry, 2006; Agnew, Van Lange, Rusbult, & Langston, 1998), both of which suggest that a departure from one's self-interest that benefits a partner may not be subjectively experienced as a departure from self-interest (Rusbult & Agnew, 2010). This explanation for willingness to sacrifice is akin to transformation of motivation, but it is distinct with regard to the exact mechanism. During cases of transformation of motivation, individuals perceive their behavioral options differently as a function of their partners' preferences, but there is no assumption that they reap benefits for acting in line with their partners' preferences. A commitment-based explanation for sacrifice, however, makes no assumption about whether individuals actually perceive their behavioral options differently as a function of their partners' preferences, but it does suggest that individuals receive benefits from acting in non–self-centered ways. Certainly the two processes share a degree of similarity, but because they differ in whether the mechanism is perceptual (i.e., transformation) or evaluative (i.e., commitment), distinguishing between the two has implications for who will use which mechanism when and what outcomes for the self and the relationship are likely to result.

Other explanations for sacrifice do not rely on transformation of motivation or being high in commitment, but rather on the fact that sacrificing for a partner can yield benefits for the individual. For instance, sacrifice is beneficial for impression management concerns (McCullough et al., 1998), can lead to short-term reciprocity in exchange relationships (Clark & Mills, 1979), and can even yield a boost in positive affect that is associated with behaving prosocially (Batson, 1987). These explanations for sacrifice explain why, when the cost of the sacrifice is low, even individuals low in commitment are willing to sacrifice (Powell & Van Vugt, 2003). Additionally, attachment motives can explain some sacrificial behavior, because sacrifice can promote proximity, love, and support between partners. When these outcomes are perceived to be viable, individuals higher in attachment anxiety exhibit greater willingness to sacrifice than do those lower in anxiety or higher in avoidance (Impett & Gordon, 2010). Whatever the explanation, ample evidence has suggested that willingness to sacrifice is associated with positive outcomes for the relationship, including greater dyadic adjustment and relationship persistence (Mattingly & Clark, 2010; Van Lange et al., 1997; Wieselquist, Rusbult, Foster, & Agnew, 1999), and is thus considered a powerful maintenance mechanism that comes online to protect relationships against the threat of noncorrespondent outcomes.

Threats internal to the relationship. Not all threats to a relationship can be explained as natural consequences of sharing outcome interdependence with another, as the noncorrespondence of outcomes threats can be. Relationship partners, even highly committed and satisfied ones, may act destructively on occasion by engaging in behaviors such as putting their own needs before those of their partners or relationships, acting critically, or being unsupportive. This bad behavior presents a threat to the relationship. How individuals react to their partners' bad behavior has implications for the relationship. Several maintenance mechanisms exist that hold the potential to combat the threat, including accommodation and forgiveness.

Accommodation. When a partner behaves destructively, an individual has numerous behavioral options available to him or her, each associated with different outcomes for the relationship. The individual can choose to retaliate in kind, which has negative implications for the relationship (e.g., Gottman, 1998), or can suppress his or her own destructive behavior and behave prosocially toward the partner. Researchers have examined what reactions are typical in such situations and have formulated a typology of four behaviors (i.e., exit, voice, loyalty, and neglect) that differ along two dimensions (i.e., passive–active and constructive–destructive). The passive–active dimension refers to the influence of the response on the original problem, whereas the constructive–destructive dimension refers to the influence of the response on the relationship (Rusbult, Zembrodt, & Gunn, 1982). Exit, an active destructive reaction, involves behavior such as ending or threatening to end the relationship and abusing, criticizing, or derogating the partner. Neglect is also destructive but differs from exit in being passive. It involves behaviors such as allowing the relationship to deteriorate, avoiding discussing problems, and criticizing the partner regarding unrelated issues. Loyalty is passive and constructive, involving behaviors such as passively waiting for improvement, maintaining faith in the partner in the face of hurtful actions, and forgiving and forgetting an offense. Finally, the active and constructive response of voice encompasses discussing problems, suggesting solutions, and engaging in efforts to change problematic behavior (Rusbult et al., 1982). This range of behavioral options is encompassed in the construct of accommodation.

Accommodation refers to an individual's willingness to inhibit tendencies to react destructively when a partner behaves destructively (i.e., inhibit exit and neglect responses) and instead engage in constructive reactions (i.e., use voice and loyalty responses; Rusbult, Verette, Whitney, Slovik, & Lipkus, 1991). Much research has examined the benefits of accommodation, with the overwhelming majority of the empirical support suggesting a "good manners" rule: Avoiding destructive acts is more beneficial to maintaining a satisfying and enduring relationship than is attempting to maximize constructive acts. Constructive acts are beneficial because they interrupt a spiral of negativity that can result from a partner behaving badly (Holmes & Murray, 1996; Rusbult, Johnson, & Morrow, 1986), but reacting negatively to a partner's destructive behavior by deploying retaliatory criticism or withdrawing, for instance, can lead to a greater likelihood that the threat will indeed harm the relationship (Gottman, 1998) and promote a spiral of negativity that presents more opportunities for the relationship to suffer harm (Rusbult et al., 1986).

Given the benefits for maintaining relationship status associated with accommodating in the face of a partner behaving destructively, it is logical to question why individuals might ever choose to retaliate instead of accommodate. According to interdependence theory, an individual's initial reaction to his or her partner's destructive behavior (i.e., his or her given preference) will be to react in a self-centered way rather than a relationship-centered way (Kelley & Thibaut, 1978). The processes that give rise to accommodation, then, are ones that enable individuals to suppress the initial, automatic destructive impulses they experience. Commitment promotes the ability to accommodate, with the evidence suggesting that not only is accommodation beneficial for maintaining a committed relationship, but it is also more common among those high in commitment to their relationships (Perunovic & Holmes, 2008; Rusbult & Agnew, 2010). However, people also engage in accommodation when they are low in commitment, which suggests that a procedural explanation beyond commitment also exists. Research has suggested that self-regulatory strength is a component of this process. Indirect evidence for this can be found by examining the conditions under which individuals are most likely to react badly, such as when the partner's destructive behavior has evoked strong negative emotions

(Kelley & Thibaut, 1978) or when under time pressure (Yovetich & Rusbult, 1994). Strong negative emotions and time pressure are both known to limit an individual's self-regulatory ability to override basic impulses (Baumeister & Heatherton, 1996), so one can infer that the ability to self-regulate is a key component of a procedural explanation for accommodation that does not rest on commitment level. Indeed, those individuals who have lower dispositional self-regulatory ability or have had their self-regulatory ability experimentally depleted engage in less accommodation than do those with higher self-regulatory ability and those who have not been depleted (Finkel & Campbell, 2001). These differences are robust to the influence of commitment level, suggesting that self-regulation is an important part of accommodation that occurs regardless of commitment. We should note, however, that having the ability to self-regulate and accommodate does not necessarily suggest that an individual also has the desire to do so. For that, an individual must desire his or her relationship to continue or see other benefits in accommodating.

Forgiveness. Accommodation is a maintenance mechanism that explains in-the-moment reactions to destructive partner behavior broadly, but when the destructive partner behavior is extreme, a more considered, pointed response may be required to protect the relationship. Specifically, relationship norm violations and betrayals present some of the largest threats to a relationship, and thus they require a powerful maintenance mechanism to come online to protect relationship status (Finkel, Rusbult, Kumashiro, & Hannon, 2002). That mechanism is forgiveness, which is defined in many ways but most commonly described as the willingness to forgo resentment, condemnation, and subtle revenge toward a partner while simultaneously bolstering feelings of generosity and love that may not be deserved given the transgression (Enright, 1996). This definition has elements suggesting that it is both intrapersonal (i.e., a within-forgiver mental phenomenon) and interpersonal (i.e., a forgiver–betrayer interaction phenomenon). When a betrayal occurs or a relationship norm is violated, the empirical evidence has suggested that forgiveness is often an effective mechanism for protecting the state of the relationship (Fincham, Beach, & Davila, 2007), except when partners frequently engage in betrayals and norm violations, in which cases forgiveness is associated with steep declines in relationship satisfaction for the forgiver (McNulty, 2008). The benefits of forgiveness after a betrayal are not limited to the relationship, as demonstrated by findings that forgiving can benefit the forgiver's mental health (Coyle & Enright, 1997; Karremans, Van Lange, Ouwerkerk, & Kluwer, 2003) and physical health (McCullough, Orsulak, Brandon, & Akers, 2007; van Oyen Witvliet, Ludwig, & van der Laan, 2001). As with accommodation, given the benefits associated with forgiveness of a betrayal for the relationship and the individual, it is reasonable to question why individuals ever fail to forgive. Because forgiveness can entail one partner's making a large concession for the relationship, there are also instances in which negative consequences result for the forgiver. Specifically, when the forgiver's partner has failed to indicate that he or she will be safe and valued in a continued relationship after providing forgiveness, the forgiver's self-respect is likely to be diminished (Luchies, Finkel, McNulty, & Kumashiro, 2010), which may reduce the incentive to forgive in the future. Additionally, individuals may fail to forgive for procedural reasons. As with accommodation, forgiveness involves overriding an impulse to act in a retaliatory or otherwise destructive manner in favor of acting in a more prorelationship manner. Thus, forgiveness of large transgressions is less likely insofar as the potential forgiver's self-regulatory resources have been depleted (Stanton & Finkel, 2012). Other explanations for when individuals will or will not forgive have been examined. Some predictors of forgiveness reside at the individual level (e.g., agreeableness, narcissism, neuroticism; Exline, Baumeister, Bushman, Campbell, & Finkel, 2004), some at the relationship level (e.g., commitment, attachment anxiety; Finkel, Burnette, & Scissors, 2007; Finkel et al., 2002), and others at the level of the betrayal event itself (e.g., apologies, concessions, severity; Folger & Cropanzano, 1998; McCullough et al., 1998). Results from these examinations have indicated that predictors at all

three levels influence how likely forgiveness is for a specific betrayal.

Threats external to the relationship. Relationships do not exist in a vacuum, devoid of social surroundings. Thus far, we have discussed threats to the relationship that originate in the relationship, either as a natural consequence of interdependence (i.e., noncorrespondence of outcomes) or as a consequence of the actions of one of the partners (i.e., destructive partner behavior). It is also possible that a source beyond the dyad can introduce a threat. One of the most commonly encountered threats that originates external to the relationship is that of an attractive other who may materialize and tempt one of the partners to engage in an extradyadic relationship.

Alternatives. One of the most significant hazards to interdependence in relationships is an attractive alternative who might tempt an individual to leave or alter the nature of the current relationship (e.g., Agnew, Arriaga, & Wilson, 2008; Le & Agnew, 2003; Rusbult, 1983). Not all alternatives are equally threatening. Desirable alternatives are those that have greater physical attractiveness and social status (Lydon, Meana, Sepinwall, Richard, & Mayman, 1999) or, in the case of female alternatives, are in their period of peak fertility (S. L. Miller & Maner, 2010). These are the alternatives that most evoke relationship maintenance from the perceiver.

Through two processes, individuals in committed relationships may derogate their alternatives. The first process is motivated, in which partners in committed relationships devalue the quality of possible relationship alternatives to maintain cognitive consistency (i.e., they perceive alternatives to be less physically and emotionally attractive than they objectively are to maintain their image of themselves as a reliable partner; Johnson & Rusbult, 1989). This process is dependent on having the resources necessary to derogate; individuals with greater self-regulatory resources display less interest in attractive members of the desired sex than do individuals whose self-regulatory resources have been depleted (Ritter, Karremans, & Van Schie, 2010).

The literature also supports a perceptual bias against alternatives (Johnson & Rusbult, 1989;

R. J. Miller, 1997; Simpson, Gangestad, & Lerma, 1990), based on the construct of comparison level (see Kelley et al., 2003). A comparison level is the collective set of expectations individuals hold regarding what outcomes they believe they should receive from their relationships. The expectations can come from modeled behavior (e.g., parents' relationship), media (e.g., television depictions of relationships), and personal experience. If the relationship outcomes received surpass the comparison level, an individual is said to be satisfied within his or her relationship. If the outcomes surpass the comparison level over an extended period of time, the comparison level can shift up (i.e., the quality of positive outcomes that are expected increases). In assessing whether an alternative is attractive, individuals compare what they believe they could receive from the alternative with their comparison level. If their current relationship is satisfying, and thus the comparison level is high, fewer alternatives will seem attractive than when the comparison level is low. In this way, individuals perceive alternatives of equal quality differently depending on the perceived satisfaction in their current relationship (Johnson & Rusbult, 1989).

Additional support for the existence of a perceptual bias against alternatives holds that partners simply fail to notice that they have alternatives or ignore the alternatives they encounter (R. J. Miller, 1997). Social life is so complex that individuals often pursue numerous goals at one time. Because of the limited nature of cognitive resources, however, these goals must be hierarchically stacked so that only the most salient goal at any given time receives conscious attention and the rest operate in the background (Schlenker, Britt, & Pennington, 1996). Ongoing goal pursuits are most typically guided by features of automaticity (notably lack of effortful control; Bargh, Gollwitzer, Lee-Chai, Barndollar, & Trotschel, 2001) until a situation arises in which the goal is thrust into conscious awareness (e.g., when a problem in implementation arises). When processing automatically, individuals' attention focuses on goal-relevant stimuli to the exclusion of goal-irrelevant stimuli (see Gollwitzer & Sheeran, 2006). For partners in relationships, the implication is that the goal of maintaining the relationship most

often operates via automatic processing (unless problems have arisen) and, when in this mode, goal-irrelevant distractions (i.e., alternatives) are not attended to. In other words, partners in ongoing relationships may simply ignore their alternatives, or deem them irrelevant, to preserve cognitive resources for ongoing goal pursuits.

Summary. Throughout this section, we have summarized some of the most empirically supported relationship maintenance processes that come online when a threat to relationship status is encountered. Potential threats to the relationship originate in different places, ranging from within the very nature of interdependence to completely external to the relationship, but are similar in that they are all commonly encountered and potentially deleterious to the continued success of the relationship. These mechanisms and processes are important tools available to partners to ensure their relationship status remains constant.

Threat-induced processes are unique from the other classes of processes that will be described in that they are initiated in response to a problem rather than because the partners desired a specific outcome. Because of this, it is important to briefly consider the underlying motivation behind the use of these processes. A perspective on what compels interpersonal behavior that has received support as an explanation for what motivates individuals to use maintenance mechanisms in the face of relationship threat was proposed by Gray (1981), who suggested that two behavioral systems underlie personality: the behavioral approach system and the behavioral inhibition system. The behavioral approach system promotes approach motivation, in which behavior is enacted to achieve rewards and positive outcomes, whereas the behavioral inhibition system promotes avoidance motivation, in which behavior is enacted to avoid punishments and negative outcomes. Research has suggested that which of these motivations drives an individual to use a threat-induced maintenance mechanism plays a significant role in whether that mechanism is beneficial for the relationship or not (Impett, Gable, & Peplau, 2005; Mattingly & Clark, 2012). Only those acts that are engaged in for approach-motivated reasons are beneficial for the relationship; those instances in which individuals engage in maintenance for avoidance-motivated reasons are negatively associated with individual and relational well-being.

The motivation underlying threat-induced maintenance processes is not the only similarity between them worth emphasizing. Each of the threats to the relationship described here involves an individual having to navigate personal and relational concerns. In some cases, an individual must forgo individual desires for the betterment of the relationship (e.g., willingness to sacrifice, derogation of alternatives), whereas in others an individual must suppress an automatic response to act in a self-interested way for the betterment of the relationship (e.g., accommodation, forgiveness). Indeed, the theme of personal concerns and relational concerns requiring reconciliation is not unique to threat-induced maintenance. Theorists have argued that achieving equilibrium between personal and relational concerns is a primary goal of individuals in relationships (Kumashiro, Rusbult, & Finkel, 2008).

Personal and relational concerns can compete for an individual's attention and resources to greater or lesser degrees (VanderDrift & Agnew, in press). As we have alluded to, times of high threat are especially likely to pit personal goals against relational ones. Another instance that is especially likely to have this quality is when the relationship is characterized by a low level of interdependence. For relationships characterized by high interdependence at times of low threat, however, personal and relational concerns are nearly synonymous, and what an individual does for the betterment of one domain has positive implications for both domains. Accordingly, a key characteristic of highly interdependent relationships can be thought of as the enmeshment of personal and relational concerns. Thus, a powerful tool available to partners who want to increase their level of interdependence with their partners is to combine personal and relational concerns.

Interdependence-Promoting Maintenance Processes

Interdependence-promoting maintenance processes are those that involve entwining personal and relational concerns. Research has indicated that some of these interdependence-promoting mechanisms are more commonly used in the beginning stages of relationships to develop relationships characterized initially by low interdependence (e.g., self-disclosure, self-expansion), whereas others are commonly used in already developed relationships to increase moderate or high interdependence levels (e.g., capitalization, investment). These differentiations are normative but not necessary, because each of these mechanisms can theoretically be used at any level to create greater interdependence.

Self-disclosure. Self-disclosure was among the first processes examined to understand how relationships move from relatively low amounts of interdependence to relationships characterized by greater interdependence. In their social penetration theory, Altman and Taylor (1973) theorized that the reciprocal exchange of self-relevant information is the primary means through which relationships develop. As with the majority of relationship phenomena, a pattern of mutual cyclical growth exists with self-disclosure: People disclose more to those whom they initially like, and people like others more as a result of having disclosed to them (Collins & Miller, 1994). Additionally, there is cross-partner cyclical growth in which an individual's disclosure is likely to elicit disclosure from his or her partner (L. C. Miller & Kenny, 1986). In fact, compared with the amount of variability attributable to individual factors (e.g., some people disclose more than others, some people receive more disclosures than others), the variability in frequency of self-disclosure that is attributable to relationship factors (e.g., reciprocity) is exceedingly high (more than 86%; Kenny, 1994).

In terms of self-disclosure content, research has suggested that partners tend to match both in topical content and in depth of their self-disclosures to each other (Derlega, Metts, Petronio, & Margulis, 1993). Typically, the exchange of information begins with relatively nonintimate topics and progresses to more personal and private aspects of the self as interdependence increases (Altman & Taylor, 1973). Longitudinal studies of the influence of self-disclosure on interdependence have suggested that self-disclosure is high in the early stages of relationship formation (Hays, 1985), but after a relatively short period of time, dating couples have exhausted the majority of the factual disclosures they have to make, and most conversations tend to be nondisclosing (Rubin, Hill, Peplau, & Dunkel-Schetter, 1980). In sum, self-disclosure seems to be a means by which relationship partners increase interdependence in the early stages of a relationship, but it is less characteristic of long-term everyday discourse.

Capitalization.   Capitalization, which can be thought of as a special case of self-disclosure, refers to the process by which an individual shares a positive personal life event with a partner and derives additional benefit from it (Gable, Reis, Impett, & Asher, 2004). Empirical evidence has supported the notion that when people share their good news with others they experience enhanced positive affect, beyond the increases expected from the news itself (Langston, 1994), and that this benefit stems from the partners' reaction. The extent to which partners respond actively and constructively to individuals' capitalization disclosures (vs. passively or destructively), as measured by both the individuals' general perception of their partners' enthusiasm during capitalization interactions (Gable et al., 2004) and actual partners' responses provided during a specific capitalization interaction (Gable, Gonzaga, & Strachman, 2006), is associated with increased individual and relationship well-being. These benefits derive from two mechanisms: (a) sharing good news with enthusiastic others increases the perceived value of that news and (b) partners' enthusiastic responses during capitalization interactions promote the development of trust and a prosocial orientation toward the partner (Reis et al., 2010). That is, capitalization is beneficial to the individual and the relationship, and this benefit stems from increases in interdependence between the partners.

Investment.   Other mechanisms for increasing interdependence in a relationship do not rely on information sharing but instead suggest other means by which personal and relational concerns are entwined. Investments in a relationship are the resources that are attached to a relationship that would diminish in value or be lost if the relationship were to end (Rusbult, 1980; Rusbult, Martz, & Agnew, 1998). These resources can be extrinsic (i.e., previously extraneous resources become linked to the relationship) or intrinsic (i.e., resources directly put into the relationship), tangible (i.e., resources that physically exist) or intangible (i.e., resources without material being), and made in the past or planned for the future (Goodfriend & Agnew, 2008). The construct is broad, and whereas some notable differences in relationship outcomes exist depending on the type of investments held by the partners (i.e., intangible investments are more strongly associated with commitment than are tangible investments; Goodfriend & Agnew, 2008), the similarities are more notable. Across all types of investment, investing leads to greater commitment and relationship stability (Le & Agnew, 2003).

Michelangelo phenomenon.   Thus far, each of the interdependence-promoting mechanisms discussed has focused on how personal concerns are folded into relationships. With self-disclosure and capitalization, personal information is shared with another to deepen a relationship, and with investment, personal resources are tied to the relationship. Relational processes also contribute to personal goals, however, which can yield benefits for both the individual and the relationship. One of the most prominent interpersonal models of how close partners promote individuals' pursuit of ideal self-goals has been titled the *Michelangelo phenomenon* (Drigotas, Rusbult, Wieselquist, & Whitton, 1999). Like the sculptor Michelangelo Buonarroti once said regarding blocks of stone, humans possess ideal forms waiting to be released. These ideal forms describe individuals' aspirations, or the skills and traits that they want to acquire that provide direction to personal growth strivings (Higgins, 1987).

Through interactions, individuals adapt to their partners, changing their behavior to coordinate with what their partner needs and expects from them. Whereas this can occur between interaction partners with any amount of shared interdependence, the mutual dependence that characterizes highly interdependent relationships affords opportunities for exerting frequent, benevolent influence across diverse behavioral domains. For that reason, it is in interactions with partners characterized by great interdependence that adaptation is most powerful, probable, and enduring (Rusbult, Finkel, & Kumashiro, 2009). Through processes of partner perceptual affirmation (i.e., the extent to which a partner consciously or unconsciously perceives the individual in ways that are compatible with the individual's ideal self) and partner behavioral affirmation (i.e., the extent to which a partner consciously or unconsciously behaves in ways that elicit ideal-congruent behaviors from the individual), the individual moves toward his or her ideal self. This movement, in turn, has been found to be associated with beneficial individual outcomes such as enhanced personal well-being (e.g., life satisfaction; Drigotas, 2002) and, also important, positive relationship outcomes such as enhanced adjustment and greater probability of relationship persistence (Drigotas et al., 1999).

Self-expansion.   Another instance in which a relationship contributes to an individual's personal goals that yields benefits for both the self and the relationship is with respect to self-expansion. Self-expansion, or the notion that individuals have a fundamental need to expand their sense of self, including their physical influence, cognitive complexity, social identity, and global awareness, can be applied to understanding interpersonal relationship processes (E. N. Aron & Aron, 1996). Early in relationships, opportunities to achieve self-expansion abound because of the high levels of novelty and arousal associated with forming relationships and getting to know a new partner (A. Aron, Norman, Aron, McKenna, & Heyman, 2000). Consistent with the notion that self-expansion is a motivating force for individuals, this experience is imbued with positive affect, leading individuals to continue to develop those relationships that offer self-expansion. Once the novelty of a new relationship ebbs, self-expansion opportunities take a different form but nevertheless still promote greater interdependence. Engaging in shared self-expansion experiences with a romantic partner (i.e., those that are novel and arousing to both partners) can promote greater relationship functioning by increasing positive affect and excitement and decreasing boredom in the

relationship (A. Aron et al., 2000). Furthermore, in close relationships, individuals come to view their partners as extensions of the self (Agnew et al., 1998; A. Aron, Aron, Tudor, & Nelson, 1991), and thus they treat the others' resources, perspectives, identities, and accomplishments as their own (Mashek, Aron, & Boncimino, 2003). The benefits of this process for the self are robust, but there are also notable benefits of self-expansion for the relationship. To the extent that another is included in the self, especially when this is made salient, individuals' immediate responses in conflicts of interest with the partner give equal weight to the concerns and desires of both the partner and the self (A. P. Aron, Mashek, & Aron, 2004).

Risk regulation.   Increasing interdependence does not come without risk. To be highly interdependent, as alluded to by the discussion of entwining personal and relational concerns, involves individuals behaving in ways that give a partner power over their outcomes and emotions (Gagné & Lydon, 2004; Kelley, 1979). Additionally, being interdependent with another is associated with disclosing self-doubts and seeking social support from them during times of vulnerability (Collins & Feeney, 2000). Thus, the mechanisms that promote interdependence also increase the likelihood of rejection in the short term (e.g., because of the sharing of vulnerabilities) and the perception of how much losing the relationship would hurt (e.g., because of idealized perceptions of the relationship). For this reason, a process to manage that risk is necessary. This process, referred to as *risk regulation,* explains how individuals balance the goal of seeking closeness to a partner with the goal of minimizing the likelihood and pain associated with rejection (Murray, Holmes, & Collins, 2006).

Risk regulation entails using confidence in a partner's regard as a gauge of whether it is safe to put self-protection concerns aside to promote the relationship (Murray, Holmes, & Griffin, 2000). To facilitate this process, three systems come online in service of risk regulation: (a) a cognitive system (i.e., the appraisal system), (b) an affective system (i.e., the signaling system), and (c) a behavioral system (i.e., the behavioral response system; Murray et al., 2006). The first system that comes online in the process of risk regulation is the appraisal system, wherein individuals evaluate their partner's perceptions of their qualities and the regard they have for those qualities. Individuals derive confidence from believing that their partner perceives that they have qualities worth valuing that are not readily available in other potential partners. Next, the signaling system comes online and detects discrepancies between the appraisal of their partner's regard and the appraisal they desire from their partner. Discrepancies are experienced emotionally, as either positive (e.g., when the partner's appraisal is higher than desired) or negative (e.g., when the partner's appraisal is lower than desired). Finally, a behavioral response system comes online as either a direct result of the experience of approval or disapproval (as generated by the appraisal system) or an indirect result of that experience through the resulting emotions (as generated by the signaling system). This behavioral response system acts to proactively minimize the likelihood and pain of potential future rejection experiences by allowing interdependence to increase with a partner only as far as the appraisal and signaling systems have indicated the partner will accept. Together, the three systems that make up the risk regulation process help individuals detect and react to their partner's regard for them in ways that promote a safe balance of connectedness and the risk of pain.

Summary. The interdependence-promoting processes summarized are certainly not the only mechanisms an individual can use to deepen the state of his or her relationship, but they were selected to showcase the breadth of activities that can achieve this outcome. Mechanisms are available to increase interdependence from any starting level, which means that increasing interdependence is a form of relationship maintenance that is possible among relative strangers as well as among relationship partners who have been together for decades. All of these mechanisms suggest that combining personal and relational concerns is a primary means to increasing interdependence, but how those concerns are combined differs. Some of the mechanisms described involve personal information or resources

being linked to the relationship, whereas others entail relational processes becoming linked to personal concerns. In both scenarios, there are benefits for both the relationship and the individuals that result in increased interdependence.

Not all individuals and situations lend themselves equally well to using these interdependence-promoting mechanisms. Using capitalization as an example, individuals high in attachment avoidance are less responsive when their partners share positive news and underestimate their partners' enthusiasm regarding their own sharing of positive news (Shallcross, Howland, Bemis, Simpson, & Frazier, 2011). Furthermore, those whose partners have low self-esteem are less likely to disclose positive events than those whose partners have high self-esteem, citing fear that the interaction will go poorly for themselves as the primary reason (MacGregor & Holmes, 2011). Examples such as these can be found for each interdependence-enhancing process. For example, those who are high in avoidant attachment would be expected to be reticent to become highly interdependent with another. Similarly, being in a relationship with a partner with low self-esteem is less likely to be conducive to the development of high interdependence.

It is not just in these cases that individuals may fail to use an interdependence-promoting mechanism. Sometimes, the partners may be satisfied with their current level of interdependence and simply want it to remain constant. Several processes are known to do just that, categorized here as stability-promoting maintenance processes.

Stability-Promoting Maintenance Processes

Early in relationships—perhaps because of concerns about impression management, contact restricted to nearly exclusively positive settings, or the abundant self-expansion opportunities—individuals are overwhelmed by attraction to their partners, seeing primarily virtues in them (E. N. Aron & Aron, 1996; Brickman, 1987; Holmes, 2000). This attraction can be threatened as relationships develop, as impression management efforts ebb, as partners begin interacting across a wider range of domains, and as self-expansion opportunities begin to slow. Additionally, and somewhat ironically, individuals may notice their partners' more serious faults only once the barriers to leaving the relationship are great. Maintenance processes that promote stability of interdependence are, thus, important tools that must be used as relationships persist.

Unlike the previously discussed processes, the processes that promote stability operate continuously and tend to operate outside of individuals' conscious awareness, and by and large they are outside of conscious control (Holmes, 2000). These processes can occur via automatic activation, in which the interpersonal goals that unconsciously guide perception and behavior become activated for an individual by the mere psychological presence of the partner (Fitzsimons & Bargh, 2003). They can also occur via a form of motivated cognition, in which the dissonance associated with feeling dependent on an imperfect other leads to individuals making biased appraisals of their partner and relationship, which leads to relationship-maintaining behavior (Holmes, 2000). Regardless, despite not being consciously enacted to serve a relationship function, each of the mechanisms described here has a profound effect in promoting stability of interdependence in relationships.

Positive illusions.   Because few life decisions have as much impact as choosing to become committed to an imperfect individual, in which the likelihood of being let down by his or her behavior at some point is nearly inevitable given the amount of dependence and emotional vulnerability associated with romantic relationships (Brickman, 1987; Holmes & Rempel, 1989), individuals are motivated to make certain cognitive appraisals that support their decision to maintain their relationship. Indeed, committed individuals see their partners as superior to the average partner (Van Lange & Rusbult, 1995), their relationships as less vulnerable to divorce (Helgeson, 1994), and after relationship trials or hard times, they experience a bolstered sense of commitment (Lydon & Zanna, 1990). Further evidence has suggested that these effects are specific to the amount of interdependence within a relationship; the more central a partner is to the individual's identity, the more favorably the individual perceives

that partner (Martz et al., 1998). A partner's faults and virtues are subject to an observer's subjective biases, which gives individuals latitude with which to make impressions regarding their characteristics and in interpreting their behavior (Griffin & Ross, 1991; Holmes, 2000). This latitude is often used by individuals to become more secure in their partners' dependability, as evidenced by the fact that their partners' negative behavior is more often than not attributed to unstable situational forces rather than stable dispositional ones (Bradbury & Fincham, 1990). Individuals also use this latitude to feel more positive about their choice of partner; individuals' assessments of their ideal partners are highly associated with their perceptions of their actual partners (Fletcher, Simpson, Thomas, & Giles, 1999; Murray, Holmes, & Griffin, 1996). Together, this evidence suggests that people are motivated and do indeed find ways to achieve a sense of security in a relationship, often by seeing their partners in an idealized way. This idealization, referred to as *positive illusions*, entails individuals seeing their partners in more positive ways than even their partners themselves or their other close friends do (Murray et al., 1996). Early research on positive illusions focused on detailing whether holding inaccurate perceptions of one's partner was a detriment or a benefit to the relationship. The majority of the evidence has suggested that not only are positive illusions beneficial, but they "may be a romantic necessity" (Murray et al., 1996, p. 1155), allowing individuals to make a leap of faith and believe that their relationship future is certain, despite evidence stemming from both their own relationship woes and witnessing the relationship woes of others that such confidence is unwarranted. The benefits of positive illusions for relationships are robust. Those who hold strong positive illusions, relative to those who do not, are more satisfied and less distressed and have fewer conflicts in their relationships, and their relationships are less likely to dissolve (Murray et al., 1996). Additionally, spouses who idealized each other as newlyweds were more in love at that time and experienced smaller declines in love over a 13-year span (P. J. Miller, Niehuis, & Huston, 2006). Thus, positive illusions are important to maintaining relationships. Even Japanese individuals, who do not show the self-enhancement characteristic of Western cultures (Kitayama, Takagi, & Matsumoto, 1995), exhibit positive illusions in their relationships (Endo, Heine, & Lehman, 2000), providing further evidence that positive illusions are integral to relationship success. Despite the relational benefits associated with positive illusions, however, there is risk associated with allowing perceptions of one's partner to become biased in this way. Specifically, positive illusions compromise self-protection concerns by increasing the perception of how much losing the relationship would hurt (Simpson, 1987). As such, individuals must have a certain amount of trust in their partner to allow these positive illusions to color their perceptions and decisions.

Trust. Definitions of trust abound (e.g., Deutsch, 1973; Rotter, 1980; Scanzoni, 1979), but the first empirical analyses of the construct as applied to interpersonal relationships found it to be multidimensional (Rempel, Holmes, & Zanna, 1985). This analysis revealed that the most central dimension of trust is faith, defined as "the belief that one's partner will act in loving and caring ways whatever the future holds" (Rempel et al., 1985, p. 109). Also important are the dimensions of dependability (i.e., believing that a partner can be relied on in immediate, objective ways) and predictability (i.e., believing a partner will not act in inconsistent ways). Today, most theorists have agreed that, within the context of close relationships, trust can be considered an internal gauge of the extent and reliability of a partner's motivation to act in ways that promote, rather than hinder, the relationship (Simpson, 2007; Wieselquist et al., 1999).

Having trust in one's partner has many beneficial consequences for a relationship. Notably, trust serves as a filter through which relationship events are perceived and interpreted (Rempel et al., 1985). In problem-solving discussions, for instance, trust in a partner is positively associated with making consistently positive, benevolent attributions for the partner's behavior (Holmes & Rempel, 1989) and expressing these attributions during their discussions (Rempel, Ross, & Holmes, 2001). Furthermore, individuals become increasingly likely to defer immediate gratification and allow themselves to be vulnerable to a partner's influence as they become more trusting (Kelley et al., 2003). Perhaps not surprising in light of the benefits, trust is considered by many to be one of the most desired attributes in an ideal close relationship, on par with love and commitment (Hendrick & Hendrick, 1983).

Given that trust plays a central role in many of the processes necessary to maintain close relationships, a great deal of research has focused on the means through which trust develops. From an interdependence perspective, trust in a relationship is enhanced when an individual witnesses his or her partner behave in a prorelationship manner (e.g., accommodate, be willing to sacrifice; Rusbult & Agnew, 2010; Wieselquist et al., 1999). In addition to the trust an individual can build in interaction with a specific other, individuals may develop relatively stable levels of trust across partners and people more generally. Attachment theory suggests that, because of early childhood experiences, individuals differ dispositionally in the ability and willingness to trust others (Hazan & Shaver, 1994). The amount of trust individuals exhibit toward close others is a key feature that separates those who are securely attached from those who are not (Mikulincer & Shaver, 2007; Simpson, 2007). Notably, individuals high in attachment insecurity find it difficult to trust others, with "fearful avoidants" (i.e., those high in both anxiety and avoidance) being the least trusting (Shaver & Clark, 1994).

Summary. The mechanisms that promote stability in interdependence are more likely than mechanisms used for other purposes to occur automatically, outside of conscious awareness and control. They operate continuously to influence the perceptions and behaviors of involved individuals in ways that promote the level of interdependence shared between the individuals remaining constant. The differentiation between the processes that are stability promoting and those that are interdependence enhancing described in this chapter is normative, but it is not absolute. That is, the mechanisms categorized as stability promoting typically function to promote stability but can promote interdependence enhancement, and vice versa.

Many of the mechanisms discussed as interdependence enhancing (e.g., investing, self-disclosure) serve double functions in relationships. Not only do they promote greater interdependence between partners, but because they represent personal resources that become "sunk" into the relationship and cannot easily be removed, they also promote stability. Indeed, the extent to which an individual feels he or she has invested heavily in the relationship is negatively associated with leaving that relationship (Le & Agnew, 2003; Le, Dove, Agnew, Korn, & Mutso, 2010). In this way, these are barriers to exiting the relationship that need to be considered and navigated before the interdependence level of a relationship can be reduced.

Additionally, many of the mechanisms discussed as stability promoting (e.g., positive illusions, trust) can also contribute to greater interdependence in the relationship. Holding positive illusions, for example, can serve as an interdependence-enhancing mechanism akin to the Michelangelo phenomenon. By treating one's partner as if he or she is ideal and opting to give the benefit of the doubt when necessary, positive illusions can increase esteem and attachment security in the partner, thus facilitating the partner becoming closer to the ideal partner (Murray et al., 1996).

Our categorization of mechanisms, then, is based on the most normative situation in which each process is used, but it is imperfect. This imperfection reflects the reality of relationships, in which processes of mutual cyclical growth or decline characterize the trajectories of interdependence (Agnew et al., 1998; Wieselquist et al., 1999). *Mutual cyclical growth* refers to the process by which prorelationship motives and behavior can influence each other, yielding tendencies toward greater interdependence. The cycle was first described with regard to cognitive interdependence and trust, holding that (a) dependence on a relationship promotes strong commitment, (b) commitment promotes prorelationship thinking and actions, (c) prorelationship acts are perceived by the partner, (d) the perception of prorelationship acts enhances the partner's sense of cognitive interdependence and trust, and (e) cognitive interdependence and trust increase the partner's willingness to become dependent on the relationship, and so on (Agnew et al., 1998; Wieselquist et al., 1999). It is in a shared pattern of interactions

over time that cycles of this nature can develop in ongoing relationships, and thus whether a particular mechanism promotes stability or growth in interdependence is a normative, but not necessary, distinction.

Failing to Maintain a Relationship

Despite the bevy of relationship maintenance processes that promote relationship stability, there are, of course, cases in which partners fail to maintain their relationships. Whether by allowing a threat to affect the relationship without using the necessary maintenance mechanism or by simply failing to engage in sufficient stability-promoting maintenance, the instances in which relationships are not maintained are associated with (sometimes sharp) decreases in interdependence. These drops are often described as breakups, but we have argued that this language and way of thinking (i.e., that relationships are either on or off) does not mirror reality (Agnew et al., 2008). Instead, relationship partners may shift the status of their relationship to one characterized by less interdependence. Nevertheless, because of a shared history and the potential for recurring contact, they are still interdependent relationships.

Consequences of Failing to Maintain

Failing to maintain a romantic relationship has been shown to have many consequences for the individual partners. In the context of stressful life events, divorce and marital separation have been ranked as the second and third most stressful events an individual can undergo, respectively, higher, even, than death of a close family member or being in jail (death of a spouse, which could be considered the dissolution of a romantic relationship as well, was rated the most stressful event; Holmes & Rahe, 1967). It is counterintuitive, then, that some of the consequences of romantic relationship dissolution are positive.

Compared with empirical examinations of the negative consequences of dissolution, relatively few studies have detailed the positive consequences of dissolution. Those that have, however, suggested that it is at least as common to experience positive outcomes after dissolution as it is to experience negative ones, be they independent positive outcomes or positive outcomes that are experienced simultaneously with the negatives (Tashiro, Frazier, & Berman, 2006). Several positive emotions can be experienced by individuals after the dissolution of a relationship, including relief (Spanier & Thompson, 1983), freedom (Reissman, 1990), autonomy (Marks & Lambert, 1998), and enjoyment of life (Nelson, 1982). There are also more global positive outcomes, such as that found in one study in which a majority of women (75%) report being happier 3 years after marital dissolution than they were during the final year of their marriage (Hetherington, 1993). These benefits are hypothesized to stem from stress relief and personal growth (Tashiro et al., 2006). When the relationship itself was stressful, the benefits of its dissolution are likely at least in part to be a result of the relief of the stress being removed. Regardless of whether the relationship was a stressor, however, personal growth can result from dissolution. This growth has been reported to be experienced in many domains, including in the self, one's personal philosophies, and other relationships (Tashiro et al., 2006).

Despite the potential for positive outcomes after dissolution, there are nevertheless a host of negative consequences. After dissolution, individuals report great emotional upheaval, including longing for their ex-partners, anger, and sadness (Sbarra & Ferrer, 2006). For those who are left by their partners, these emotions can be devastating (Amato, 2000; Sprecher, 1994). Those who leave their partners are not exempt from feeling negative emotions. Leavers often feel guilt, regret, and shame (Emery, 1994). After dissolution, individuals often behave in ways that are self-destructive to cope with these emotions, including making exaggerated attempts to reestablish the relationship, engaging in angry or vengeful behavior, and using drugs and alcohol to cope (Davis, Shaver, & Vernon, 2003). Arguably the most negative of the consequences associated with dissolution is with respect to health: Those whose relationships dissolve experience decreased physical health in the form of decreased immunologic functioning (Kiecolt-Glaser et al., 1987).

Perhaps because of the host of negative consequences for individuals whose romantic relationships dissolve, much research has examined predictors of dissolution. Procedurally, evidence has suggested that (a) individuals' commitment to maintaining the relationship ebbs, then (b) commitment to ending the romantic relationship (i.e., dissolution consideration) increases, and finally (c) the individual engages in the behaviors necessary to decrease the amount of interdependence he or she shares with the partner to a desired level (VanderDrift, Agnew, & Wilson, 2009). When an individual has high dissolution consideration, he or she is more likely to take immediate action to reduce his or her interdependence. Thus, dissolution consideration is one of the most proximal precursors to failing to maintain a relationship; it assesses whether individuals are experiencing increasing commitment to end their romantic relationship and making incremental progress toward that outcome (VanderDrift et al., 2009). When examining predictors of romantic relationship dissolution that are more distal to dissolution, there is greater variety both in the nature of the predictor and in how strongly each has been found to be associated with dissolution.

Predictors of Relationship Dissolution

Throughout this chapter, we have described processes that are important for relationship maintenance. Each of these processes is associated with benefits for the relationship, but the outcome most telling with regard to how integral a process is to relationship maintenance is whether it is associated with maintaining the relationship. Examining how strongly these processes contribute to a relationship's failing to be maintained provides additional information about the importance or centrality of the process to relationship maintenance.

The predictors of dissolution are often categorized by whether they are individual level, relationship level, or external (Cate, Levin, & Richmond, 2002; Le et al., 2010; Rodrigues, Hall, & Fincham, 2006). In meta-analytic work, there is robust support for the importance of relationship-level characteristics on dissolution, with the influence of individual-level and external characteristics being less strongly associated with dissolution (Le et al., 2010).

Relationship-level predictors. Some of the predictors of romantic dissolution are relationship-level characteristics, such as relationship quality, interactions between the partners, the affect experienced within the relationship, and the cognitive representations of the relationship (Le et al., 2010). Each of the processes detailed as a maintenance mechanism in this chapter becomes a predictor of romantic dissolution when absent (e.g., willingness to sacrifice is a relationship maintenance process, and failing to be willing to sacrifice is a predictor of romantic dissolution). Among the most robust predictors of dissolution are positive illusions, commitment, and love (Le et al., 2010), each of which evidences a large effect size in predicting dissolution. Also associated with maintaining the relationship, but moderately so, are the previously described processes of trust, self-disclosure, perceived quality of alternatives, and investments. In addition, closeness level, satisfaction level, dependence level, and ambivalence each predict dissolution. Not all relationship-level constructs are highly associated with failing to maintain a relationship. The presence of conflict, for example, evidences a small effect size in predicting dissolution. We should note that the strategies used during conflict (e.g., accommodation, stonewalling) can be highly predictive of later dissolution, but the presence of conflict itself evidences only a small effect size (Gottman, 1998; Le et al., 2010; Rusbult et al., 1991).

Individual-level predictors. Individual factors are characteristics, traits, or dispositions of the individual partners in the relationship. These can be either general (e.g., the Big Five personality traits) or specific to relationships (e.g., attachment orientation). Early research on such individual-level predictors suggested that they are weak predictors of dissolution (Huston & Levinger, 1978). Indeed, neither self-esteem nor positive self-beliefs are associated with dissolution (Felmlee, Sprecher, & Bassin, 1990; Helgeson, 1994), and the Big Five personality dimensions (i.e., agreeableness, conscientiousness, extraversion, neuroticism, and openness) have garnered mixed support as predictors of dissolution. In nonmarital relationships, none of the Big Five dimensions predict dissolution (Le et al., 2010), and

in marital relationships, agreeableness, extraversion, and conscientiousness only predict dissolution in specific circumstances (e.g., high levels of extraversion are weakly associated with dissolution for husbands only; Bentler & Newcomb, 1978). Some evidence has shown that emotional stability predicts dissolution in marital relationships (Kelly & Conley, 1987; Kurdek, 1993), yet other evidence has suggested that it is associated with satisfaction but not dissolution (Bentler & Newcomb, 1978; Karney & Bradbury, 1997).

Individual differences that are specific to relationships are more predictive of dissolution than are broad personality dimensions, but still the support is largely weak or mixed. Implicit theories of relationships refer to the beliefs individuals hold regarding the nature of relationships (Knee, 1998). There is a small effect for destiny beliefs (i.e., the belief that partners are either meant for each other or not), with those who hold strong destiny beliefs being more likely to dissolve their relationships (Le et al., 2010). Attachment, which refers to the nature of the affectual bond between partners (Hazan & Shaver, 1994), has received mixed support as a predictor of dissolution. In an early examination of attachment style and dissolution, researchers found that avoidant men and women had the highest likelihood of dissolution (Feeney & Noller, 1992), whereas subsequent research found avoidant men's relationships and anxious women's relationships were just as stable as the relationships of those who were securely attached after 3 years (Kirkpatrick & Davis, 1994). Meta-analytic results of the attachment–dissolution association found small effects for both avoidance and anxiety, such that higher levels of each is associated with greater likelihood of dissolution (Le et al., 2010). Taken together, the support for individual-level predictors of dissolution is weak, characterized by mixed findings and small effect sizes.

Despite being poor predictors of failing to maintain a relationship on their own, many of the dispositions examined function in tandem with relationship-level predictors to predict dissolution. For example, under some circumstances, attachment anxiety is positively associated with being willing to sacrifice (Impett & Gordon, 2010), and destiny beliefs are positively associated with forgiveness (Finkel et al., 2007). Thus, these dispositions are important to relationship maintenance, but in and of themselves, they do not constitute important relationship maintenance processes.

AVENUES FOR FUTURE RESEARCH

Although an enormous amount of research has been conducted over the years on relationship maintenance and dissolution, areas remain that are particularly ripe for additional work. We highlight several such areas here.

Successful Balancing of Personal and Relational Concerns

As mentioned earlier, an important characteristic of highly interdependent relationships is the enmeshment of personal and relational concerns. Those seeking to increase their interdependence with a partner should work to successfully combine satisfying both personal and relational goals simultaneously. What is less clear is how to do so, particularly in Western societies in which individual goal attainment is so strongly stressed within the larger culture. The message that "one can't have it all" is often broadcast (e.g., Slaughter, 2012) and, if a sacrifice is perceived as necessary, it more often than not tends to be a relationship that is sacrificed. Increasing trends toward solo living testify to rising problems in balancing individual and relational concerns (Klinenberg, 2012). Research that investigates success stories—instances in which individuals are able to achieve a happy balance between personal and partner concerns—may provide insight into particularly effective approaches to getting the balancing act right.

This issue is complicated by the very nature of goal pursuits. Cognitive adaptations arise to help individuals achieve goals that could derail the relationship maintenance processes described previously. For instance, individuals who are pursuing a goal draw closer to others who can facilitate the pursuit (Fitzsimons & Fishbach, 2010), which may make individuals reticent to engage in interdependence-promoting processes with their romantic partners unless they promote their goals. Additionally, while undertaking personal goal pursuits, individuals adopt mindsets that promote closed-minded, one-sided focus on that goal (i.e., they selectively attend away from distractions from the goal pursuit and process incoming information and store it in a biased fashion that supports continuing the goal pursuit; Gollwitzer, 1990). This mindset may make individuals less likely to engage in the stability-promoting mechanisms described previously (VanderDrift & Agnew, in press). Future research examining how goal pursuits and other daily activities influence individuals' willingness and ability to engage in relationship maintenance would be useful, as it may illuminate ways in which people can learn to achieve a balance between personal and relationship concerns.

Shifts Over Time in Interdependence With a Given Partner

Research on the dynamic nature of shifts on the independence–interdependence continuum between given partners is sorely needed (Agnew et al., 2008). For example, it is abundantly clear that people often continue in a relationship featuring a different degree of interdependence after the dissolution of a romantic relationship. How that process unfolds and what predicts the relative satisfaction experienced in latter relationships that feature lower interdependence is an understudied area. Such research requires long-term longitudinal work, involving the vagaries attendant to such efforts (e.g., need for continuous flow of research support, participant attrition), but it is critical to capture the true dynamics at work over time in a given dyadic relationship. The framework offered here, one that situates relationship maintenance on a continuum of relative independence–interdependence, is ideally suited to the task.

Understanding Postdissolution Resilience

More research could also be directed toward understanding what circumstances in a given relationship are more likely to promote a more positive outcome after relationship dissolution. Both person and situational factors require attention. Some individuals are better at coping with the aftermath of a downward shift in interdependence than are others. What dispositional factors account for adaptive coping in a relationship context? What individual differences are associated with particularly poor postdissolution personal outcomes? What predissolution relationship dynamics are associated with optimal individual functioning postrelationship? Such questions deserve attention.

CONCLUSION

Relationship maintenance can be thought of as processes that help to keep involved actors relatively interdependent with one another. Such a conceptualization provides a useful framework for reviewing past research conducted under the rubric of relationship maintenance. In this chapter, we reviewed past work from this perspective, characterizing the processes investigated by researchers as (a) stability promoting, (b) interdependence promoting, or (c) threat induced. We look forward to future work that continues to further our understanding of processes that keep relationships going.

References

Agnew, C. R. (2000). Cognitive interdependence and the experience of relationship loss. In J. H. Harvey & E. D. Miller (Eds.), *Loss and trauma: General and close relationship perspectives* (pp. 385–398). Philadelphia, PA: Brunner-Routledge.

Agnew, C. R., Arriaga, X. B., & Wilson, J. E. (2008). Committed to what? Using the bases of relational commitment model to understand continuity and changes in social relationships. In J. P. Forgas & J. Fitness (Eds.), *Social relationships: Cognitive, affective and motivational processes* (pp. 147–164). New York, NY: Psychology Press.

Agnew, C. R., & Etcheverry, P. E. (2006). Cognitive interdependence: Considering self-in-relationship. In K. D. Vohs & E. J. Finkel (Eds.), *Self and relationships: Connecting intrapersonal and interpersonal processes* (pp. 274–293). New York, NY: Guilford Press.

Agnew, C. R., Van Lange, P. A. M., Rusbult, C. E., & Langston, C. A. (1998). Cognitive interdependence: Commitment and the cognitive representation of close relationships. *Journal of Personality and Social Psychology, 74*, 939–954. doi:10.1037/0022-3514.74.4.939

Altman, I., & Taylor, D. (1973). *Social penetration: The development of interpersonal relationships.* New York, NY: Holt, Rinehart & Winston.

Amato, P. R. (2000). The consequences of divorce for adults and children. *Journal of Marriage and the Family, 62*, 1269–1287. doi:10.1111/j.1741-3737.2000.01269.x

Aron, A., Aron, E. N., & Smollan, D. (1992). Inclusion of Other in the Self Scale and the structure of interpersonal closeness. *Journal of Personality and Social Psychology, 63*, 596–612. doi:10.1037/0022-3514.63.4.596

Aron, A., Aron, E. N., Tudor, M., & Nelson, G. (1991). Close relationships as including other in the self. *Journal of Personality and Social Psychology, 60*, 241–253. doi:10.1037/0022-3514.60.2.241

Aron, A., Norman, C. C., Aron, E. N., McKenna, C., & Heyman, R. M. (2000). Couples' shared participation in novel and arousing activities and experienced relationship quality. *Journal of Personality and Social Psychology, 78*, 273–284. doi:10.1037/0022-3514.78.2.273

Aron, A. P., Mashek, D. J., & Aron, E. N. (2004). Closeness as including other in the self. In D. J. Mashek & A. Aron (Eds.), *Handbook of closeness and intimacy* (pp. 27–41). Mahwah, NJ: Erlbaum.

Aron, E. N., & Aron, A. (1996). Love and the expansion of the self: The state of the model. *Personal Relationships, 3*, 45–58. doi:10.1111/j.1475-6811.1996.tb00103.x

Bargh, J. A., Gollwitzer, P. M., Lee-Chai, A., Barndollar, K., & Trotschel, R. (2001). The automated will: Nonconscious activation and pursuit of behavioral goals. *Journal of Personality and Social Psychology, 81*, 1014–1027. doi:10.1037/0022-3514.81.6.1014

Batson, C. D. (1987). Prosocial motivation: Is it ever truly altruistic? In L. Berkowitz (Ed.), *Advances in experimental social psychology* (Vol. 20, pp. 65–122). San Diego, CA: Academic Press. doi:10.1016/S0065-2601(08)60412-8

Baumeister, R. F., & Heatherton, T. F. (1996). Self-regulation failure: An overview. *Psychological Inquiry, 7*, 1–15. doi:10.1207/s15327965pli0701_1

Bentler, P. M., & Newcomb, M. D. (1978). Longitudinal study of marital success and failure. *Journal of Consulting and Clinical Psychology, 46*, 1053–1070. doi:10.1037/0022-006X.46.5.1053

Bradbury, T. N., & Fincham, E. D. (1990). Attributions in marriage. *Psychological Bulletin, 107*, 3–33. doi:10.1037/0033-2909.107.1.3

Brickman, P. (1987). *Commitment, conflict, and caring.* Englewood Cliffs, NJ: Prentice-Hall.

Canary, D. J., & Dainton, M. (Eds.). (2003). *Maintaining relationships through communication: Relational, contextual, and cultural variations.* Mahwah, NJ: Erlbaum.

Cate, R. M., Levin, L. A., & Richmond, L. S. (2002). Premarital relationship stability: A review of recent research. *Journal of Social and Personal Relationships, 19*, 261–284. doi:10.1177/0265407502192005

Clark, M. S., & Mills, J. (1979). Interpersonal attraction in exchange and communal relationships. *Journal of Personality and Social Psychology, 37*, 12–24. doi:10.1037/0022-3514.37.1.12

Collins, N. L., & Feeney, B. C. (2000). A safe haven: Support-seeking and caregiving processes in intimate relationships. *Journal of Personality and Social Psychology, 78*, 1053–1073. doi:10.1037/0022-3514.78.6.1053

Collins, N. L., & Miller, L. (1994). Self-disclosure and liking: A meta-analytic review. *Psychological Bulletin, 116*, 457–475. doi:10.1037/0033-2909.116.3.457

Coyle, C. T., & Enright, R. D. (1997). Forgiveness intervention with postabortion men. *Journal of Consulting and Clinical Psychology, 65*, 1042–1046. doi:10.1037/0022-006X.65.6.1042

Davis, D., Shaver, P. R., & Vernon, M. L. (2003). Physical, emotional, and behavioral reactions to breaking up: The roles of gender, age, environmental involvement, and attachment style. *Personality and Social Psychology Bulletin, 29*, 871–884. doi:10.1177/0146167203029007006

Derlega, V. J., Metts, S., Petronio, S., & Margulis, S. T. (1993). *Self-disclosure.* Newbury Park, CA: Sage.

Deutsch, M. (1973). *The resolution of conflict.* New Haven, CT: Yale University Press.

Drigotas, S. M. (2002). The Michelangelo phenomenon and personal well-being. *Journal of Personality, 70*, 59–77. doi:10.1111/1467-6494.00178

Drigotas, S. M., Rusbult, C. E., Wieselquist, J., & Whitton, S. (1999). Close partner as sculptor of the ideal self: Behavioral affirmation and the Michelangelo phenomenon. *Journal of Personality and Social Psychology, 77*, 293–323. doi:10.1037/0022-3514.77.2.293

Emery, R. E. (1994). *Renegotiating family relationships: Divorce, child custody, and mediation.* New York, NY: Guilford Press.

Endo, Y., Heine, S. J., & Lehman, D. R. (2000). Culture and positive illusions in close relationships: How my relationships are better than yours. *Personality and Social Psychology Bulletin, 26*, 1571–1586. doi:10.1177/01461672002612011

Enright, R. D. (1996). Counseling within the forgiveness triad: On forgiving, receiving forgiveness, and self-forgiveness. *Counseling and Values, 40*, 107–126. doi:10.1002/j.2161-007X.1996.tb00844.x

Exline, J. J., Baumeister, R. F., Bushman, B. J., Campbell, W. K., & Finkel, E. J. (2004). Too proud to let go: Narcissistic entitlement as a barrier to forgiveness. *Journal of Personality and Social Psychology, 87*, 894–912. doi:10.1037/0022-3514.87.6.894

Feeney, J. A., & Noller, P. (1992). Attachment style and romantic love: Relationship dissolution.

Australian Journal of Psychology, 44, 69–74. doi:10.1080/00049539208260145

Felmlee, D. H., Sprecher, S., & Bassin, E. (1990). The dissolution of intimate relationships: A hazard model. *Social Psychology Quarterly, 53*, 13–30. doi:10.2307/2786866

Fincham, F. D., Beach, S. R. H., & Davila, J. (2007). Longitudinal relations between forgiveness and conflict resolution in marriage. *Journal of Family Psychology, 21*, 542–545. doi:10.1037/0893-3200.21.3.542

Fine, M., & Harvey, J. (Eds.). (2006). *Handbook of divorce and relationship dissolution.* Mahwah, NJ: Erlbaum.

Finkel, E. J., Burnette, J. L., & Scissors, L. E. (2007). Vengefully ever after: Destiny beliefs, state attachment anxiety, and forgiveness. *Journal of Personality and Social Psychology, 92*, 871–886. doi:10.1037/0022-3514.92.5.871

Finkel, E. J., & Campbell, W. K. (2001). Self-control and accommodation in close relationships: An interdependence analysis. *Journal of Personality and Social Psychology, 81*, 263–277. doi:10.1037/0022-3514.81.2.263

Finkel, E. J., Rusbult, C. E., Kumashiro, M., & Hannon, P. A. (2002). Dealing with betrayal in close relationships: Does commitment promote forgiveness? *Journal of Personality and Social Psychology, 82*, 956–974. doi:10.1037/0022-3514.82.6.956

Fitzsimons, G. M., & Bargh, J. A. (2003). Thinking of you: Nonconscious pursuit of interpersonal goals associated with relationship partners. *Journal of Personality and Social Psychology, 84*, 148–164. doi:10.1037/0022-3514.84.1.148

Fitzsimons, G. M., & Fishbach, A. (2010). Shifting closeness: Interpersonal effects of personal goal progress. *Journal of Personality and Social Psychology, 98*, 535–549. doi:10.1037/a0018581

Fletcher, G. J. O., Simpson, J. A., Thomas, G., & Giles, T. (1999). Ideals in intimate relationships. *Journal of Personality and Social Psychology, 76*, 72–89. doi:10.1037/0022-3514.76.1.72

Folger, R., & Cropanzano, R. (1998). *Organizational justice and human resource management.* Beverly Hills, CA: Sage.

Gable, S. L., Gonzaga, G. C., & Strachman, A. (2006). Will you be there for me when things go right? Supportive responses to positive event disclosures. *Journal of Personality and Social Psychology, 91*, 904–917. doi:10.1037/0022-3514.91.5.904

Gable, S. L., Reis, H. T., Impett, E. A., & Asher, E. R. (2004). What do you do when things go right? The intrapersonal and interpersonal benefits of sharing positive events. *Journal of Personality and*

Social Psychology, 87, 228–245. doi:10.1037/0022-3514.87.2.228

Gagné, F. M., & Lydon, J. E. (2004). Bias and accuracy in close relationships: An integrative review. *Personality and Social Psychology Review, 8*, 322–338. doi:10.1207/s15327957pspr0804_1

Gaines, S. O., Jr., & Agnew, C. R. (2003). Relationship maintenance in intercultural couples: An interdependence analysis. In D. J. Canary & M. Dainton (Eds.), *Maintaining relationships through communication: Relational, contextual, and cultural variations* (pp. 231–253). Mahwah, NJ: Erlbaum.

Gollwitzer, P. M. (1990). Action phases and mindsets. In E. T. Higgins & R. M. Sorrentino (Eds.), *Handbook of motivation and cognition: Vol. 2. Foundations of social behavior* (pp. 53–92). New York, NY: Guilford Press.

Gollwitzer, P. M., & Sheeran, P. (2006). Implementation intentions and goal achievement: A meta-analysis of effects and processes. In M. P. Zanna (Ed.), *Advances in experimental social psychology* (Vol. 38, pp. 69–119). San Diego, CA: Academic Press. doi:10.1016/S0065-2601(06)38002-1

Goodfriend, W., & Agnew, C. R. (2008). Sunken costs and desired plans: Examining different types of investments in close relationships. *Personality and Social Psychology Bulletin, 34*, 1639–1652. doi:10.1177/0146167208323743

Gottman, J. M. (1998). Psychology and the study of marital processes. *Annual Review of Psychology, 49*, 169–197. doi:10.1146/annurev.psych.49.1.169

Gray, J. A. (1981). A critique of Eysenck's theory of personality. In H. J. Eysenck (Ed.), *A model of personality* (pp. 246–276). New York, NY: Springer. doi:10.1007/978-3-642-67783-0_8

Griffin, D. W., & Ross, L. (1991). Subjective construal, social inference, and human misunderstanding. In M. Zanna (Ed.), *Advances in experimental social psychology* (Vol. 24, pp. 319–359). New York, NY: Academic Press. doi:10.1016/S0065-2601(08)60333-0

Hays, R. B. (1985). A longitudinal study of friendship development. *Journal of Personality and Social Psychology, 48*, 909–924. doi:10.1037/0022-3514.48.4.909

Hazan, C., & Shaver, P. R. (1994). Attachment as an organizational framework for research on close relationships. *Psychological Inquiry, 5*, 1–22. doi:10.1207/s15327965pli0501_1

Helgeson, V. S. (1994). The effects of self-beliefs and relationship beliefs on adjustment to a relationship stressor. *Personal Relationships, 1*, 241–258. doi:10.1111/j.1475-6811.1994.tb00064.x

Hendrick, C., & Hendrick, S. (1983). *Liking, loving, and relating*. Monterey, CA: Brooks/Cole.

Hetherington, E. M. (1993). An overview of the Virginia Longitudinal Study of Divorce and Remarriage with a focus on early adolescence. *Journal of Family Psychology, 7*, 39–56. doi:10.1037/0893-3200.7.1.39

Higgins, E. T. (1987). Self-discrepancy: A theory relating self and affect. *Psychological Review, 94*, 319–340. doi:10.1037/0033-295X.94.3.319

Holmes, J. G. (2000). Social relationships: The nature and function of relational schemas. *European Journal of Social Psychology, 30*, 447–495. doi:10.1002/1099-0992(200007/08)30:4<447::AID-EJSP10>3.0.CO;2-Q

Holmes, J. G. (2002). Interpersonal expectations as the building blocks of social cognition: An interdependence theory analysis. *Personal Relationships, 9*, 1–26. doi:10.1111/1475-6811.00001

Holmes, J. G., & Murray, S. (1996). Interpersonal conflict in close relationships. In E. T. Higgins & A. Kruglanski (Eds.), *Social psychology: Handbook of basic mechanisms and processes* (pp. 622–654). New York, NY: Guilford Press.

Holmes, J. G., & Rempel, J. K. (1989). Trust in close relationships. In C. Hendrick (Ed.), *Close relationships: Review of personality and social psychology: Vol. 10. Close relationships* (pp. 187–220). Newbury Park, CA: Sage.

Holmes, T. H., & Rahe, R. H. (1967). The Social Readjustment Rating Scale. *Journal of Psychosomatic Research, 11*, 213–218. doi:10.1016/0022-3999(67)90010-4

Huston, T. L., & Levinger, G. (1978). Interpersonal attraction and relationships. *Annual Review of Psychology, 29*, 115–156. doi:10.1146/annurev.ps.29.020178.000555

Impett, E. A., Gable, S. L., & Peplau, L. A. (2005). Giving up and giving in: The costs and benefits of daily sacrifice in intimate relationships. *Journal of Personality and Social Psychology, 89*, 327–344. doi:10.1037/0022-3514.89.3.327

Impett, E. A., & Gordon, A. M. (2010). Why do people sacrifice to approach rewards versus to avoid costs? Insights from attachment theory. *Personal Relationships, 17*, 299–315. doi:10.1111/j.1475-6811.2010.01277.x

Johnson, D. J., & Rusbult, C. E. (1989). Resisting temptation: Devaluation of alternative partners as a means of maintaining commitment in close relationships. *Journal of Personality and Social Psychology, 57*, 967–980. doi:10.1037/0022-3514.57.6.967

Karney, B. R., & Bradbury, T. N. (1997). Neuroticism, marital interaction, and the trajectory of marital satisfaction. *Journal of Personality and Social Psychology, 72*, 1075–1092. doi:10.1037/0022-3514.72.5.1075

Karremans, J. C., Van Lange, P. A. M., Ouwerkerk, J. W., & Kluwer, E. S. (2003). When forgiving enhances psychological well-being: The roles of interpersonal commitment. *Journal of Personality and Social Psychology, 84*, 1011–1026. doi:10.1037/0022-3514.84.5.1011

Kelley, H. H. (1979). *Personal relationships: Their structure and processes.* Hillsdale, NJ: Erlbaum.

Kelley, H. H., Holmes, J. G., Kerr, N., Reis, H. T., Rusbult, C. E., & Van Lange, P. A. M. (2003). *An atlas of interpersonal situations.* New York, NY: Cambridge University Press.

Kelley, H. H., & Thibaut, J. (1978). *Interpersonal relations: A theory of interdependence.* New York, NY: Wiley.

Kelly, E. L., & Conley, J. J. (1987). Personality and compatibility: A prospective analysis of marital stability and marital satisfaction. *Journal of Personality and Social Psychology, 52*, 27–40. doi:10.1037/0022-3514.52.1.27

Kenny, D. A. (1994). *Interpersonal perception: A social relations analysis.* New York, NY: Guilford Press.

Kiecolt-Glaser, J. K., Fisher, L. D., Ogrocki, P., Stout, J. C., Speicher, C. E., & Glaser, R. (1987). Marital quality, marital disruption, and immune function. *Psychosomatic Medicine, 49*, 13–34.

Kirkpatrick, L. A., & Davis, K. E. (1994). Attachment style, gender, and relationship stability: A longitudinal analysis. *Journal of Personality and Social Psychology, 66*, 502–512. doi:10.1037/0022-3514.66.3.502

Kitayama, S., Takagi, H., & Matsumoto, H. (1995). Causal attribution of success and failure: Cultural psychology of the Japanese self. *Japanese Psychological Review, 38*, 247–280.

Klinenberg, E. (2012). *Going solo: The extraordinary rise and surprising appeal of living alone.* New York, NY: Penguin.

Knee, C. R. (1998). Implicit theories of relationships: Assessment and prediction of romantic relationship initiation, coping, and longevity. *Journal of Personality and Social Psychology, 74*, 360–370. doi:10.1037/0022-3514.74.2.360

Kumashiro, M., Rusbult, C. E., & Finkel, E. J. (2008). Navigating personal and relational concerns: The quest for equilibrium. *Journal of Personality and Social Psychology, 95*, 94–110. doi:10.1037/0022-3514.95.1.94

Kurdek, L. A. (1993). Predicting marital dissolution: A 5-year prospective longitudinal study of newlywed couples. *Journal of Personality and Social Psychology, 64*, 221–242. doi:10.1037/0022-3514.64.2.221

Langston, C. A. (1994). Capitalizing on and coping with daily life events: Expressive responses to positive events. *Journal of Personality and Social Psychology, 67*, 1112–1125. doi:10.1037/0022-3514.67.6.1112

Le, B., & Agnew, C. R. (2003). Commitment and its theorized determinants: A meta-analysis of the investment model. *Personal Relationships, 10*, 37–57. doi:10.1111/1475-6811.00035

Le, B., Dove, N. L., Agnew, C. R., Korn, M. S., & Mutso, A. A. (2010). Predicting nonmarital romantic relationship dissolution: A meta-analytic synthesis. *Personal Relationships, 17*, 377–390. doi:10.1111/j.1475-6811.2010.01285.x

Luchies, L. B., Finkel, E. J., McNulty, J. K., & Kumashiro, M. (2010). The doormat effect: When forgiving erodes self-respect and self-concept clarity. *Journal of Personality and Social Psychology, 98*, 734–749. doi:10.1037/a0017838

Lydon, J. E., Meana, M., Sepinwall, D., Richard, N., & Mayman, S. (1999). The commitment calibration hypothesis: When do people devalue attractive alternatives? *Personality and Social Psychology Bulletin, 25*, 152–161. doi:10.1177/0146167299025002002

Lydon, J. E., & Zanna, M. P. (1990). Commitment in the face of adversity: A value-affirmation approach. *Journal of Personality and Social Psychology, 58*, 1040–1047. doi:10.1037/0022-3514.58.6.1040

MacGregor, J. C. D., & Holmes, J. G. (2011). Rain on my parade: Perceiving low self-esteem in close others hinders positive self-disclosure. *Social Psychological and Personality Science, 2*, 523–530. doi:10.1177/1948550611400098

Marks, N. F., & Lambert, J. D. (1998). Marital status continuity and change among young and midlife adults: Longitudinal effects on psychological well-being. *Journal of Family Issues, 19*, 652–686. doi:10.1177/019251398019006001

Martz, J. M., Verette, J., Arriaga, X. B., Slovik, L. F., Cox, C. L., & Rusbult, C. E. (1998). Positive illusion in close relationships. *Personal Relationships, 5*, 159–181. doi:10.1111/j.1475-6811.1998.tb00165.x

Mashek, D. J., Aron, A., & Boncimino, M. (2003). Confusions of self with close others. *Personality and Social Psychology Bulletin, 29*, 382–392. doi:10.1177/0146167202250220

Mattingly, B. A., & Clark, E. M. (2010). The role of activity importance and commitment on willingness to sacrifice. *North American Journal of Psychology, 12*, 51–66.

Mattingly, B. A., & Clark, E. M. (2012). Weakening the relationship we are trying to preserve? Motivated sacrificial behavior as a mediator between attachment anxiety and avoidance and relationship satisfaction. *Journal of Applied Social Psychology, 42*, 373–386.

McCullough, M. E., Orsulak, P., Brandon, A., & Akers, L. (2007). Rumination, fear, and cortisol: An in vivo study of interpersonal transgressions. *Health Psychology, 26*, 126–132. doi:10.1037/0278-6133.26.1.126

McCullough, M. E., Rachal, K., Sandage, S. J., Worthington, E. R., Brown, S., & Hight, T. L. (1998). Interpersonal forgiving in close relationships: II.

Theoretical elaboration and measurement. *Journal of Personality and Social Psychology, 75*, 1586–1603. doi:10.1037/0022-3514.75.6.1586

McNulty, J. K. (2008). Tendencies to forgive in marriage: Putting the benefits into context. *Journal of Family Psychology, 22*, 171–175. doi:10.1037/0893-3200.22.1.171

Mikulincer, M., & Shaver, P. R. (2007). *Attachment patterns in adulthood: Structure, dynamics, and change.* New York, NY: Guilford Press.

Miller, L. C., & Kenny, D. A. (1986). Reciprocity of self-disclosure at the individual and dyadic levels: A social relations analysis. *Journal of Personality and Social Psychology, 50*, 713–719. doi:10.1037/0022-3514.50.4.713

Miller, P. J., Niehuis, S., & Huston, T. L. (2006). Positive illusions in marital relationships: A 13-year longitudinal study. *Personality and Social Psychology Bulletin, 32*, 1579–1594. doi:10.1177/0146167206292691

Miller, R. J. (1997). Inattentive and contented: Relationship commitment and attention to alternatives. *Journal of Personality and Social Psychology, 73*, 758–766. doi:10.1037/0022-3514.73.4.758

Miller, S. L., & Maner, J. K. (2010). Scent of a woman: Men's testosterone responses to olfactory ovulation cues. *Psychological Science, 21*, 276–283. doi:10.1177/0956797609357733

Murray, S. L., Holmes, J. G., & Collins, N. L. (2006). Optimizing assurance: The risk regulation system in relationships. *Psychological Bulletin, 132*, 641–666. doi:10.1037/0033-2909.132.5.641

Murray, S. L., Holmes, J. G., & Griffin, D. W. (1996). The benefits of positive illusions: Idealization and the construction of satisfaction in close relationships. *Journal of Personality and Social Psychology, 70*, 79–98. doi:10.1037/0022-3514.70.1.79

Murray, S. L., Holmes, J. G., & Griffin, D. W. (2000). Self-esteem and the quest for felt security: How perceived regard regulates attachment processes. *Journal of Personality and Social Psychology, 78*, 478–498. doi:10.1037/0022-3514.78.3.478

Nelson, G. (1982). Coping with the loss of father: Family reaction to death or divorce. *Journal of Family Issues, 3*, 41–60. doi:10.1177/019251382003001004

Perunovic, M., & Holmes, J. G. (2008). Automatic accommodation: The role of personality. *Personal Relationships, 15*, 57–70. doi:10.1111/j.1475-6811.2007.00184.x

Powell, C., & Van Vugt, M. (2003). Genuine giving or selfish sacrifice? The role of commitment and cost level upon willingness to sacrifice. *European Journal of Social Psychology, 33*, 403–412. doi:10.1002/ejsp.154

Reis, H. T., Smith, S. M., Carmichael, C. L., Caprariello, P. A., Tsai, F., Rodrigues, A., & Maniaci, M. R.

(2010). Are you happy for me? How sharing positive events with others provides personal and interpersonal benefits. *Journal of Personality and Social Psychology, 99*, 311–329. doi:10.1037/a0018344

Reissman, C. K. (1990). *Divorce talk: Men and women make sense of personal relationships.* New Brunswick, NJ: Rutgers University Press.

Rempel, J. K., Holmes, J. G., & Zanna, M. P. (1985). Trust in close relationships. *Journal of Personality and Social Psychology, 49*, 95–112. doi:10.1037/0022-3514.49.1.95

Rempel, J. K., Ross, M., & Holmes, J. G. (2001). Trust and communicated attributions in close relationships. *Journal of Personality and Social Psychology, 81*, 57–64. doi:10.1037/0022-3514.81.1.57

Ritter, S., Karremans, J. C., & Van Schie, H. (2010). The role of self-regulation in derogating attractive alternatives. *Journal of Experimental Social Psychology, 46*, 631–637. doi:10.1016/j.jesp.2010.02.010

Rodrigues, A., Hall, J., & Fincham, F. D. (2006). Divorce and relationship dissolution: Theory, research and practice. In M. Fine & J. Harvey (Eds.), *Handbook of divorce and relationship dissolution* (pp. 85–112). Mahwah, NJ: Erlbaum.

Rotter, J. B. (1980). Interpersonal trust, trustworthiness and gullibility. *American Psychologist, 26*, 1–7. doi:10.1037/0003-066X.35.1.1

Rubin, Z., Hill, C. T., Peplau, L. A., & Dunkel-Schetter, C. (1980). Self-disclosure in dating couples: Sex roles and the ethic of openness. *Journal of Marriage and the Family, 42*, 305–317. doi:10.2307/351228

Rusbult, C. E. (1980). Commitment and satisfaction in romantic associations: A test of the investment model. *Journal of Experimental Social Psychology, 16*, 172–186. doi:10.1016/0022-1031(80)90007-4

Rusbult, C. E. (1983). A longitudinal test of the investment model: The development (and deterioration) of satisfaction and commitment in heterosexual involvements. *Journal of Personality and Social Psychology, 45*, 101–117. doi:10.1037/0022-3514.45.1.101

Rusbult, C. E., & Agnew, C. R. (2010). Prosocial motivation and behavior in close relationships. In M. Mikulincer & P. R. Shaver (Eds.), *Prosocial motives, emotions, and behavior: The better angels of our nature* (pp. 327–345). Washington, DC: American Psychological Association. doi:10.1037/12061-017

Rusbult, C. E., Agnew, C. R., & Arriaga, X. B. (2012). The investment model of commitment processes. In P. A. M. Van Lange, A. W. Kruglanski, & E. T. Higgins (Eds.), *Handbook of theories of social psychology* (Vol. 2, pp. 218–231). Los Angeles, CA: Sage.

Rusbult, C. E., Finkel, E. J., & Kumashiro, M. (2009). The Michelangelo phenomenon. *Current Directions* in *Psychological Science, 18*, 305–309. doi:10.1111/ j.1467-8721.2009.01657.x

Rusbult, C. E., Johnson, D. J., & Morrow, G. D. (1986). Impact of couple patterns of problem solving on distress and nondistress in dating relationships. *Journal of Personality and Social Psychology, 50*, 744–753. doi:10.1037/0022-3514.50.4.744

Rusbult, C. E., Martz, J. M., & Agnew, C. R. (1998). The Investment Model Scale: Measuring commitment level, satisfaction level, quality of alternatives, and investment size. *Personal Relationships, 5*, 357–387. doi:10.1111/j.1475-6811.1998.tb00177.x

Rusbult, C. E., & Van Lange, P. A. M. (2003). Interdependence, interaction, and relationships. *Annual Review of Psychology, 54*, 351–375. doi:10.1146/annurev.psych.54.101601.145059

Rusbult, C. E., Verette, J., Whitney, G. A., Slovik, L. F., & Lipkus, I. (1991). Accommodation processes in close relationships: Theory and preliminary empirical evidence. *Journal of Personality and Social Psychology, 60*, 53–78. doi:10.1037/0022-3514.60.1.53

Rusbult, C. E., Zembrodt, I. M., & Gunn, L. K. (1982). Exit, voice, loyalty, and neglect: Responses to dissatisfaction in romantic involvements. *Journal of Personality and Social Psychology, 43*, 1230–1242. doi:10.1037/0022-3514.43.6.1230

Sbarra, D. A., & Emery, R. E. (2005). The emotional sequelae of non-marital relationship dissolution: Analysis of change and intraindividual variability over time. *Personal Relationships, 12*, 213–232. doi:10.1111/j.1350-4126.2005.00112.x

Sbarra, D. A., & Ferrer, E. (2006). The structure and process of emotional experience following nonmarital relationship dissolution: Dynamic factor analyses of love, anger, and sadness. *Emotion, 6*, 224–238. doi:10.1037/1528-3542.6.2.224

Scanzoni, J. (1979). Social processes and power in families. In W. Burr, R. Hill, F. Nye, & I. Reiss (Eds.), *Contemporary theories about the family: Vol. 1. Research-based theories* (pp. 295–316). New York, NY: Free Press.

Schlenker, B. R., Britt, T. W., & Pennington, J. W. (1996). Impression regulation and management: A theory of self-identification. In R. M. Sorrentino & E. T. Higgins (Eds.), *Handbook of motivation and cognition: Vol. 3. The interpersonal context* (pp. 118–147). New York, NY: Guilford Press.

Shallcross, S. L., Howland, M., Bemis, J., Simpson, J. A., & Frazier, P. (2011). Not "capitalizing" on capitalization interactions: The role of attachment insecurity. *Journal of Family Psychology, 25*, 77–85. doi:10.1037/a0021876

Shaver, P. R., & Clark, C. L. (1994). The psychodynamics of adult romantic attachment. In J. M. Masling

& R. F. Bornstein (Eds.), *Empirical perspectives on object relations theories* (pp. 105–156). Washington, DC: American Psychological Association. doi:10.1037/11100-004

Simpson, J. A. (1987). The dissolution of romantic relationships: Factors involved in relationship stability and emotional distress. *Journal of Personality and Social Psychology, 53*, 683–692. doi:10.1037/ 0022-3514.53.4.683

Simpson, J. A. (2007). Psychological foundations of trust. *Current Directions in Psychological Science, 16*, 264–268. doi:10.1111/j.1467-8721.2007.00517.x

Simpson, J. A., Gangestad, S. W., & Lerma, M. (1990). Perception of physical attractiveness: Mechanisms involved in the maintenance of romantic relationships. *Journal of Personality and Social Psychology, 59*, 1192–1201. doi:10.1037/0022-3514.59.6.1192

Slaughter, A. M. (2012, July–August). Why women still can't have it all. *The Atlantic*. Retrieved from http:// www.theatlantic.com/magazine/archive/2012/07/ why-women-still-can-8217-t-have-it-all/9020/1

Spanier, G. B., & Thompson, L. (1983). Relief and distress after marital separation. *Journal of Divorce, 7*, 31–49. doi:10.1300/J279v07n01_04

Sprecher, S. (1994). Two sides of the breakup of dating relationships. *Personal Relationships, 1*, 199–222. doi:10.1111/j.1475-6811.1994.tb00062.x

Sprecher, S., Wenzel, A., & Harvey, J. (Eds.). (2008). *Handbook of relationship initiation*. Mahwah, NJ: Erlbaum.

Stanton, S. C. E., & Finkel, E. J. (2012). Too tired to take offense: When depletion promotes forgiveness. *Journal of Experimental Social Psychology, 48*, 587– 590. doi:10.1016/j.jesp.2011.11.011

Tashiro, T., Frazier, P., & Berman, M. (2006). Stress-related growth following divorce and relationship dissolution. In M. A. Fine & J. H. Harvey (Eds.), *Handbook of divorce and relationship dissolution* (pp. 361–384). Mahwah, NJ: Erlbaum.

VanderDrift, L. E., & Agnew, C. R. (in press). Relational consequences of personal goal pursuits. *Journal of Personality and Social Psychology*.

VanderDrift, L. E., Agnew, C. R., & Wilson, J. E. (2009). Romantic relationship commitment and stay/leave behavior: The mediating role of dissolution consideration. *Personality and Social Psychology Bulletin, 35*, 1220–1232. doi:10.1177/0146167209337543

Van Lange, P. A. M., & Rusbult, C. E. (1995). My relationship is better than—and not as bad as—yours is: The perception of superiority in close relationships. *Personality and Social Psychology Bulletin, 21*, 32–44. doi:10.1177/0146167295211005

Van Lange, P. A. M., Rusbult, C. E., Drigotas, S. M., Arriaga, X. B., Witcher, B. S., & Cox, C. L. (1997).

Willingness to sacrifice in close relationships. *Journal of Personality and Social Psychology, 72*, 1373–1395. doi:10.1037/0022-3514.72.6.1373

van Oyen Witvliet, C., Ludwig, T. E., & van der Laan, K. L. (2001). Granting forgiveness or harboring grudges: Implications for emotion, physiology, and health. *Psychological Science, 12*, 117–123. doi:10.1111/1467-9280.00320

Wieselquist, J., Rusbult, C. E., Foster, C. A., & Agnew, C. R. (1999). Commitment, pro-relationship behavior, and trust in close relationships. *Journal of Personality and Social Psychology, 77*, 942–966. doi:10.1037/0022-3514.77.5.942

Yovetich, N. A., & Rusbult, C. E. (1994). Accommodative behavior in close relationships: Exploring transformation of motivation. *Journal of Experimental Social Psychology, 30*, 138–164. doi:10.1006/jesp.1994.1007

CHAPTER 22

ESTABLISHED AND EMERGING PERSPECTIVES ON VIOLENCE IN INTIMATE RELATIONSHIPS

Kim Bartholomew, Rebecca J. Cobb, and Donald G. Dutton

Violence against partners is alarmingly common in heterosexual marital relationships (e.g., 16% prevalence in a year's time; Straus & Gelles, 1990) and even more common in dating, same-sex, and cohabiting relationships (e.g., Statistics Canada, 2005; Straus, 2004). The most common forms of partner violence (PV) are occasional pushing and shoving during an argument; the most severe and fortunately least common forms of PV are acts of injurious violence, such as beating up or attacking a partner with a weapon (e.g., Archer, 2002; Statistics Canada, 2005). We define PV as any nonconsensual physical aggression against a romantic partner.

We review two broad theoretical perspectives that have guided most previous empirical work on PV. Feminist perspectives focus on the patriarchal system in which violence against women occurs, conceptualizing PV as a means by which men maintain domination over women. Psychological perspectives focus on background and personality factors that put some individuals at risk for becoming violent toward their intimate partners. We examine the basic principles underlying these perspectives and, where relevant, question their validity. Next, we describe recent interactional perspectives that focus on dyadic and situational contexts in which PV arises. We then describe several multifactor models that integrate multiple perspectives on PV and provide guidelines for future research. We emphasize the need for researchers to consider how cultural factors are linked to individual, dyadic, and situation mediators of PV. Finally, we consider the implications of the various

perspectives on PV for prevention and treatment, and we highlight promising directions for future research.

ESTABLISHED PERSPECTIVES ON PARTNER VIOLENCE

Feminist Perspectives

Feminist perspectives on PV focus on the patriarchal structure of society—in which men control resources and women are systematically kept in a subordinate position—as the fundamental cause of male violence against women (Bograd, 1988; Dobash & Dobash, 1979; Dragiewicz & Lindgren, 2009). The patriarchal structure is reflected in traditional gender attitudes and roles that affirm the dominance of men over women in a range of social institutions, including the institution of marriage. Men are socialized to believe that they are entitled to assert control over their female partners and, moreover, that violence is an acceptable means of enforcing that control. This gender-based analysis of PV was originally formulated in the 1970s on the basis of qualitative interviews with women in domestic violence shelters. Feminist perspectives were instrumental in generating awareness of violence against women, and they continue to be highly influential in forming societal views of PV and in guiding public policy and domestic violence services. Adherents of this perspective refer to it as the feminist perspective on PV, emphasizing that feminist principles guide their analysis. However, some researchers in the PV field have pointed out that this label has sometimes

http://dx.doi.org/10.1037/14344-022
APA Handbook of Personality and Social Psychology: Vol. 3. Interpersonal Relations, M. Mikulincer and P. R. Shaver (Editors-in-Chief)

been used to brand those who question the premises or conclusions of the perspective as antifeminist (e.g., Dutton, 2012; Ross & Babcock, 2010). Therefore, this perspective also has been referred to as the patriarchal model or the gender paradigm (Dutton, 2010; Dutton & Nicholls, 2005) or more simply as traditional theories on PV (e.g., Ehrensaft, 2008).

There are multiple forms of feminist thought and research, many of which acknowledge that patriarchy is not the only cause of PV (DeKeseredy, 2011). However, "all feminists prioritize gender" (DeKeseredy, 2011, p. 299), and this perspective is guided by the assumption that PV is primarily a gender-based sociological problem rather than a psychological or relationship problem. Thus, PV is viewed as men's abuse of women to maintain and enforce women's subjugation. This perspective further assumes distinct perpetrator and victim roles in relationships that involve violence. Moreover, PV is considered to be just one tactic in a general relationship dynamic in which male perpetrators coercively control their female partners. Thus, PV is viewed as an instrumental behavior aimed at asserting and maintaining control over a partner.

Feminist perspectives on PV are problematic, particularly as applied in Western contexts, in which the vast majority of research has been conducted. Contrary to the assumption that patriarchal values structure all gender relations, most marriages are relatively equal in power (e.g., Coleman & Straus, 1990). In fact, recent evidence has suggested that women are more likely than men to dominate decision making in marriage, even in marital relationships in which men make more money (Morin & Cohn, 2008). Furthermore, contrary to the assumption that male violence enforces male domination of women, a growing body of research has suggested that male violence against women is more likely when men lack equal power in their intimate relationships (e.g., Anderson, 1997; Babcock, Waltz, Jacobson, & Gottman, 1993; Sagrestano, Heavey, & Christensen, 1999). Thus, PV may be an ineffective means of trying to compensate for a perceived lack of equal relationship influence. Other research has suggested that relationships in which either partner dominates decision making, regardless of gender, are prone to violence by both partners, suggesting

that lack of equity contributes to marital distress and perhaps to a struggle for influence (Coleman & Straus, 1990).

Contrary to the feminist perspective, the assumption that violence against women is a societal norm lacks empirical support in Western societies. Rather, condemnation of male violence against women, regardless of context, is the norm (e.g., Simon et al., 2001). Moreover, only a minority of men are violent, which would not be the case if violence against women were normative (Dutton, 1994). In contrast, women and men are much more accepting of women's violence against men than the converse (Simon et al., 2001). There is, however, an association between attitudes relatively more accepting of PV and men's perpetration of PV (Stith, Smith, Penn, Ward, & Tritt, 2004), but whether these attitudes are causally related to PV or are an attempt at justifying past violence is not clear. Additionally, the research linking traditional or patriarchal gender attitudes and roles with PV perpetration has been mixed at best (Sugarman & Frankel, 1996). Moreover, male violence against partners is negatively associated with masculine gender schemas (e.g., Sugarman & Frankel, 1996) and with traditionally masculine traits of self-confidence and independence (e.g., Murphy, Meyer, & O'Leary, 1994).

Overall, there has been limited empirical support in Western societies for the proposition that men internalize and then act on social norms asserting men's entitlement to dominate their female partners through force; however, there has been cross-cultural support for this proposition. The most compelling evidence in support of the feminist perspective has been data indicating that rates of women's victimization are associated with lower levels of women's empowerment in a society relative to men's, stronger societal endorsement of traditional gender roles, and greater societal acceptance of husbands hitting wives (Archer, 2006). When available, the data have suggested that women's attitudes are at least as predictive as men's of levels of PV against women, suggesting the importance of societal norms shared by both genders.

Not only do some of the assumptions and predictions of the feminist perspective fail to hold up under empirical scrutiny, but this conceptualization of PV cannot easily account for much of the established data describing the nature of PV in Western societies. In unselected samples, women are as likely as men to be violent in their intimate relationships (Archer, 2000; Fiebert, 2010), including perpetrating severe forms of violence (Straus, 2011). Only a small percentage of women's violence can be ascribed to self-defense against abusive male partners (e.g., Carrado George, Loxam, & Jones, 1996; DeKeseredy & Schwartz, 1998), women are at least as likely as men to initiate PV (e.g., Fergusson, Horwood, & Ridder, 2005), and somewhat more women than men aggress against nonviolent partners (e.g., Straus, 2011; Whitaker, Haileyesus, Swahn, & Saltzman, 2007). Although the data on motives for violence are complex and at times contradictory (in part because of different methods and samples), there is no consistent evidence that women's motives for violence differ systematically from men's motives. Rather, women and men report a broad range of motives for violence, including anger, retaliation, to get through to a partner, and to make a partner do, or stop doing, something (e.g., Carrado et al., 1996; Fiebert & Gonzalez, 1997; Follingstad, Wright, Lloyd, & Sebastian, 1991).

Also problematic for the feminist perspective is a large body of evidence indicating that in at least half of relationships with violence, both partners report acting violently (e.g., Anderson, 2002; Whitaker et al., 2007). Furthermore, the higher the level of one partner's violence (and abuse more generally), the higher the level of the other partner's violence (e.g., Bartholomew, Regan, White, & Oram, 2008; Fergusson et al., 2005; Magdol et al., 1997). Moreover, the most severe violence and the greatest risk of injury occur in relationships with bidirectional abuse (e.g., Anderson, 2002; Whitaker et al., 2007). The pattern of PV identified by the original feminist perspective—one-sided and severe male-to-female violence—is actually the least common pattern of PV in Western societies (Stets & Straus, 1992). Finally, perspectives that focus on the gendered nature of PV cannot explain the high rates of violence in same-sex relationships (e.g., Bartholomew

et al., 2008; Lie, Schilit, Bush, & Montagne, 1991). If gender inequality and men's subjugation of women underlie PV, why would same-sex romantic partners act violently toward one another?

Women are more likely than men to be severely affected by PV in heterosexual relationships. In adult samples, women are more likely than men to report fearing a violent partner (e.g., Tjaden & Thoennes, 2000) and suffering psychological distress as a result of PV (e.g., Anderson, 2002; Williams & Frieze, 2005). Women are also about twice as likely as men to report being injured by PV (Archer, 2000). Although these gender differences are meaningful, men also experience fear and negative psychological effects from PV, and about a third of victims of severe PV are men victimized by women. Additionally, the gender differences in fear and injury shrink and even disappear in samples of young adults, the group with the highest rate of PV (e.g., Capaldi & Owen, 2001; Fergusson et al., 2005). The reasons for the gender difference in consequences of PV are unclear; however, there is no compelling evidence that women are more negatively affected by PV because their victimization takes place in a relationship context in which they are systematically threatened and controlled. Given the data indicating that severe PV and injury are most common in mutually violent relationships, a plausible alternative explanation is that men are larger and stronger on average than women and therefore more capable of inflicting harm.

To reconcile the feminist analysis of PV with conflicting data from large-scale community samples, Johnson (1995) proposed two distinct forms of PV. The first, patriarchal terrorism (relabeled *intimate terrorism*), found primarily in agency samples, conforms to the feminist image of PV—men subjugating female partners with severe, unilateral violence as part of a general pattern of patriarchal control. The second, common couple violence, is primarily reported in community samples—lower level, often mutual PV that is equally perpetrated by both genders and reflects problematic conflict management.[1] Thus, Johnson concluded that women are

---

[1]Johnson and Ferraro (2000) subsequently added two additional patterns of PV: mutual violent control (consisting of two violent and controlling partners) and violent resistance (primarily women violently resisting abusive male partners).

the victims in the large majority of the most egregious cases of PV.

Johnson's (1995) typology has been helpful in highlighting that PV takes a variety of forms. However, the original empirical work supporting these distinctions was based only on women's reports, even when men were included in the samples (e.g., Johnson & Leone, 2005). Though subsequent studies have confirmed that different samples have different patterns of abuse, they have suggested a more complex picture that does not break down along the gender lines proposed by Johnson. In general population studies applying Johnson's criteria for intimate terrorism (a spouse who is both violent and controlling), about as many women as men qualify as intimate terrorists (Graham-Kevan, 2007b; Laroche, 2005). In agency samples of abused women, the patterns of abuse often fail to conform to the patriarchal pattern. Even in samples identified for high rates of female victimization, the majority of women also report perpetrating severe PV against their male partners (e.g., McDonald, Jouriles, Tart, & Minze, 2009), and the more severe the male PV, the more severe the female PV (Straus, 2011). Finally, contrary to Johnson's expectations, community samples have included significant numbers of individuals who report severe PV, which is equally perpetrated by women and men, most often in relationships with mutual abuse (e.g., Ehrensaft, Moffitt, & Caspi, 2004).

In summary, the feminist perspective on PV has been important in identifying the problem of PV and in highlighting the potential role of gender in understanding such violence. The perspective continues to be influential, but many of the perspective's basic premises have not withstood empirical scrutiny and the feminist perspective fails to account adequately for most of the violence occurring in Western intimate relationships. Unfortunately, researchers working from this perspective have not always been quick to adapt their thinking in response to new data or to incorporate into their models other factors that may play a role in PV. However, in the past decade acknowledgment of data that are inconsistent with the traditional feminist perspective on PV has been growing (Frieze, 2008). See Dutton and Corvo (2006), Dutton and Nicholls (2005), and Dutton (2006) for more detailed critiques of the feminist perspective on PV.

Individual Psychological Perspectives

Sociocultural explanations may be helpful in identifying broad social contexts that foster or inhibit aggression in close relationships. However, they cannot explain why, in a given society, only a minority of men aggress violently against female partners (Dutton, 1994). In all demographic groups studied (e.g., based on ethnicity, class, or education level), a relatively small minority of men commit PV (Straus & Gelles, 1990). Therefore, researchers working from individual psychological perspectives reject the assumption that the cause of PV is primarily situated in social structure and norms. Although they acknowledge the potential role of the broader cultural context, these researchers seek to identify and understand background, personality, and social-cognitive factors that put individuals more or less at risk for perpetrating PV. Informed by the experience of clinicians working with violent individuals, PV is considered a dysfunctional behavior stemming from individual vulnerabilities. The hypothesis guiding much of the individually focused research on PV is that socialization experiences, in conjunction with dispositional tendencies, affect adult social-emotional functioning and, in turn, individuals' risk for PV perpetration. Initial work from an individual perspective did not question the traditional framing of PV as being male violence toward women. Thus, much of this research has addressed why, in the same cultural context, some men aggress against their female partners and other men do not. Over time, as the data indicated that PV was not the sole purview of men in spousal relationships, the question expanded to include why members of both genders perpetrate PV.

Individual factors related to PV perpetration can be grouped into family background, personality or dispositional factors, and psychopathology. A large body of research has indicated that individuals who observe or experience violence in their families of origin are at increased risk for future PV (e.g., Kwong, Bartholomew, Henderson, & Trinke, 2003), although the magnitude of these associations is generally small. Similarly, problematic parenting and various forms of child maltreatment modestly predict future PV (for a review, see Ehrensaft, 2009). Associations between childhood experiences and adult PV may reflect, at least in part, social learning processes whereby children learn to use aggression to deal with conflicts of interest. As expected from social learning principles, PV is associated with more accepting attitudes regarding violence in close relationships (Stith et al., 2004) and with poor communication and problem-solving skills (e.g., Anglin & Holtzworth-Munroe, 1997). Additionally, less than ideal early experiences may adversely affect children's emotional and social development, thus increasing subsequent difficulties in regulating negative affect and developing close, trusting relationships. Consistent with this hypothesis, PV is associated with individual difference variables indicative of emotional vulnerability and reactivity, especially in the context of close relationships. Established dispositional correlates of PV include low self-esteem, interpersonal dependency, anxious attachment, aggressive tendencies, and hostile attribution biases (Dutton, 2006). Not surprisingly, PV perpetration is also associated with various psychological disorders, including personality disorders (notably borderline and antisocial), mood disorders (notably depression and anxiety), and substance use disorders (Dutton, 2006; Stith et al., 2004).

Much of this body of work has continued the traditional focus on male aggression toward female partners, providing considerable insight into the backgrounds and psychological makeup of male perpetrators of PV. However, researchers working from this perspective are increasingly considering the characteristics of both genders in various relationship contexts. Although much work remains to be done, preliminary findings have suggested similarities in the predictors of men's and women's PV, dating and marital PV, and perpetration and receipt of PV (this is not surprising, given the strong cross-partner associations on violence perpetration; e.g., Charles, Whitaker, Le, Swahn, & DiClemente, 2011; Medeiros & Straus, 2007; Robertson & Murachver, 2007; White, Merrill, & Koss, 2001). For example, initial studies applying an attachment perspective to PV demonstrated links between male partners' anxious attachment and aggression toward female partners in samples identified for severe spousal violence (e.g., Dutton, Saunders, Starzomski, & Bartholomew, 1994; Holtzworth-Munroe, Stuart, & Hutchinson, 1997). Subsequent studies suggested that this pattern holds for dating couples, community samples, women's violence against male partners, men's violence toward male partners, and perpetration and receipt of PV (Bartholomew & Allison, 2006).

However, some gender differences are emerging in two areas. First, prospective studies have suggested that young men who perpetrate PV may have higher levels of psychopathology than young female perpetrators (e.g., Ehrensaft et al., 2004), as might be expected given that men's PV is less socially acceptable than women's PV. Second, initial research has suggested that women arrested for domestic violence may be somewhat higher on psychopathology, personality risk factors for PV, and tolerance for their own violence than men arrested for domestic violence (Simmons, Lehmann, & Cobb, 2008). Again, we believe that such findings stem from gendered attitudes regarding violence: Women's violence is treated as less serious; therefore, the threshold for arrest is likely considerably higher for women than for men, resulting in a more extreme group of female compared with male offenders.

Research that has indicated associations between retrospective reports of childhood experiences, dispositional vulnerabilities, and perpetration of PV cannot establish the direction of effects. Some factors that are conceptually understood as predictors of PV may actually be consequences of involvement in abusive relationships. For example, dysfunctional relationships characterized by abuse may undermine attachment security, rather than preexisting attachment insecurity acting as a risk factor for PV perpetration and receipt. Moreover, causal interpretations of cross-sectional findings tend to reflect untested assumptions about the role of gender in the construction of violent relationships. For example, insecurity, social skills deficits, and problem drinking in men are typically interpreted as contributing to PV, whereas these same psychological variables in women are typically interpreted as resulting from their experiences of abuse (Anglin & Holtzworth-Munroe, 1997; Bartholomew & Allison, 2006).

A handful of prospective longitudinal studies have confirmed modest associations between childhood adversity and perpetration and receipt of PV in adult relationships (e.g., Ehrensaft et al., 2003). However, the strongest and most consistent predictors of later PV are childhood and adolescent indicators of emotional vulnerability (including neuroticism, depression, and negative emotionality) and conduct problems (e.g., Ehrensaft et al., 2004; Moffitt, Krueger, Caspi, & Fagan, 2000; Woodward, Fergusson, & Horwood, 2002). Although the specific findings of these prospective studies vary (as do the samples and methods), it is striking that early vulnerabilities tend to be equally predictive of men's and women's later experiences of PV, whether as perpetrators or victims.

Researchers have proposed various typologies of individuals who exhibit PV (for a review, see Graham-Kevan, 2007c). In contrast to initial feminist models that provided a fairly uniform image of men who aggress against women—men with traditional gender roles and attitudes who feel entitled to aggress against spouses to maintain their position of dominance—typology research focuses on the considerable heterogeneity of perpetrators of PV. For example, Holtzworth-Munroe and Stuart (1994) identified three subtypes of male batterers on the basis of different profiles of background characteristics, personality dimensions, psychopathology, and violence-related attitudes: those who are family-only violent, those who are dysphoric or borderline, and those who are generally antisocial and violent. More recently, researchers have extended this approach to identify subtypes of women identified as perpetrating severe PV (e.g., Babcock, Miller, & Siard, 2003; Henning & Feder, 2004). Typological approaches highlight the heterogeneity in background and individual characteristics among PV perpetrators, in some cases incorporating proposed trajectories leading to violence perpetration.

Although typological approaches have been popular in the field of PV, they suffer from a number of limitations: Typologies are difficult to replicate across samples, they imply qualitative differences between subtypes that are not always justified, they fail to account for variability within subtypes, and they generally fail to account for change in violence patterns over time. Additionally, most perpetrator typologies more or less explicitly link types of offenders with distinct forms of aggression. For instance, antisocial perpetrators engage in instrumental or controlling aggression, whereas borderline perpetrators engage in hostile, reactive aggression. Such simple distinctions are conceptually flawed (Bushman & Anderson, 2001) and obscure the multiple and changing motives that come into play in violent interactions (Capaldi & Kim, 2007). Moreover, typologies of PV perpetrators maintain a focus on the individual, failing to take into account the dyadic context of PV. Variability in PV predictors is more appropriately reflected by dimensional models that can also accommodate a dyadic focus (cf. Capaldi & Kim, 2007; Holtzworth-Munroe & Meehan, 2004). For a more detailed critique of violence typologies, see Capaldi and Kim (2007).

Individual psychological perspectives on PV have provided insight into why only some people are violent toward their intimate partners despite similar normative environments. Although research from this perspective has overwhelmingly focused on male perpetration of PV and female victimization, researchers are beginning to address this limitation by examining whether and how the psychological predictors of PV differ by gender of perpetrator and by relationship form. However, psychological perspectives are inherently incomplete because they fail to consider the relational context of PV.

CURRENT AND EMERGING PERSPECTIVES ON PARTNER VIOLENCE

Dyadic Perspectives

Feminist and psychological approaches to PV have typically focused on either perpetrators or victims of PV in isolation; they have not taken into account that abuse occurs in a relational context and that there is strong mutuality of abuse in many intimate relationships. The single strongest predictor of PV by one partner is psychological or physical aggression by the other partner (e.g., K. D. O'Leary & Slep, 2003; White et al., 2001). Dyadic, interactional perspectives on PV are based on the premise that relationships arise from the interaction of enduring characteristics of both partners and that these interactions unfold over time (Kelley et al., 1983). From this perspective, no relational behavior, be it a positive behavior such as support provision or a negative behavior such as PV, can be fully understood without considering the couple system (cf. Reis, Capobianco, & Tsai, 2002). Thus, researchers with dyadic perspectives seek to understand why some relationships are at risk for PV. Some researchers may also take into consideration the psychological makeup of individuals, but they consider both partners in a relationship and examine how individual vulnerabilities predict PV through their effect on relational functioning.

Relationship distress is a consistent correlate of PV (e.g., Stith et al., 2004; Williams & Frieze, 2005), although some couples in relationships with violence are not dissatisfied (Bauserman & Arias, 1992; K. D. O'Leary et al., 1989), and the association between distress and PV is likely to be reciprocal (e.g., Lawrence & Bradbury, 2007). Contrary to the stereotype that abusive partners meet their relational needs at the expense of victimized partners, both partners in relationships with PV tend to be dissatisfied (e.g., Williams & Frieze, 2005). In a large sample of men in the U.S. military, marital distress was the strongest predictor of male PV: For every 20% increase in marital distress, the odds of severe PV increased by almost 200% (Pan, Neideg, & O'Leary, 1994). Other relationship factors related to PV are marital discord (e.g., Coleman & Straus, 1990), problem-solving skill deficits (e.g., Anglin & Holtzworth-Munroe, 1997), and nonegalitarian decision making (regardless of gender), which probably contributes to marital conflict (e.g., Coleman & Straus, 1990). Intrapersonal indicators of relational insecurity and distrust are also associated with PV. Notably, a tendency to make negative attributions for partners' behavior and to view partners as critical and intentionally hurtful is associated with PV perpetration (e.g., Scott & Straus, 2007).

The dispositions of both partners may interact in predicting PV. For example, Roberts and Noller (1998) found that PV was most common in couples in which one partner reported high attachment anxiety and the other reported high attachment avoidance. They speculated that anxious partners' demands for closeness and avoidant partners' withdrawal from these demands are mutually reinforcing, setting the stage for anxious partners to use violence in a desperate attempt to gain a partner's attention. Moreover, the relationship context may moderate and mediate the effect of individual PV risk factors. For example, husbands' hostility and alcohol abuse predict partner abuse, but only in distressed marriages (Leonard & Senchak, 1993), and the effect of individual dispositions on PV tends to be mediated by relationship variables such as marital satisfaction and conflict (e.g., K. D. O'Leary, Slep, & O'Leary, 2007).

Correlational studies linking characteristics and feelings of both partners to PV outcomes cannot rule out the possibility that one partner is driving the couple system, and the other partner responds to and is affected by the primary instigator. However, evidence is growing that both partners' background characteristics predict future involvement in violent relationships. Negative emotionality (assessed at age 18) predicted PV perpetration and receipt 3 years later in established heterosexual relationships in a New Zealand birth cohort (Moffitt, Robins, & Caspi, 2001). Moreover, individuals tend to select romantic partners who share risk factors for PV, and then the two partners mutually reinforce each other's aggressive tendencies. In particular, longitudinal studies have indicated a moderate degree of assortative mating on antisocial behavior (H. K. Kim & Capaldi, 2004; Krueger, Moffitt, Caspi, Bleske, & Silva, 1998). Moreover, in this same New Zealand cohort study, each partner's abuse was equally strongly predicted by their own and their partners' negative emotionality (Moffitt el al., 2001), and the most severely violent relationships at ages 24 to 26 consisted of two partners characterized by adolescent risk factors (Ehrensaft et al., 2004). Research on the stability of PV across relationships has also indicated the importance of the relational context of PV. In young adulthood, the rate at which individuals perpetrate PV is more stable within a given relationship than it is when they enter a new relationship (Capaldi & Owen, 2001; Capaldi, Shortt, & Crosby, 2003; Robins, Caspi, & Moffitt, 2002).

Perhaps the most direct evidence of the dyadic context of PV has come from research examining interaction and communication processes in violent relationships. With few exceptions (see Capaldi & Crosby, 1997), these studies have focused on spousal relationships characterized by significant male-to-female violence. However, most of the women in these couples are also likely to have perpetrated at least moderately high levels of PV (e.g., Cordova, Jacobson, Gottman, Rushe, & Cox, 1993). This is not surprising given the high mutuality of PV and the difficulty of finding couples in which only male partners are violent (presumably because this is the least common pattern of PV in Western cultures). Across a range of methods—including self-reports, observations of at-home and laboratory interactions, and analyses of descriptions of conflict interactions—the findings are remarkably consistent. Couples identified for male violence are distinguished by high levels of hostility by both partners and by high reciprocity of negative affect such as anger, criticism, contempt, and belligerence (e.g., Burman, Margolin, & John, 1993; Cordova et al., 1993; Jacobson et al., 1994). In contrast, satisfied couples tend not to reciprocate negative partner behavior during conflict, thereby avoiding escalation and containing conflict (e.g., Cordova et al., 1993).

Extrapolating from the research reviewed here, it appears that PV is most likely to occur when (a) both members of a couple bring vulnerabilities for aggression to their relationship, (b) the relationship becomes conflictual and distressed, and (c) the partners reciprocate hostile behavior, leading to escalation. This dyadic account of PV is consistent with a large body of research examining patterns of aggression in couples' relationships. Of note, severity of psychological and physical aggression is strongly positively associated across relationship partners (e.g., Bartholomew et al., 2008; Fergusson et al., 2005; Follingstad & Edmundson, 2010); in short-term longitudinal studies, aggression by one partner tends to elicit aggression by the other (e.g., K. D. O'Leary & Slep, 2003; Schumacher & Leonard, 2005); and PV is more severe in mutually abusive relationships than in relationships in which only one partner is abusive (e.g., Anderson, 2002; Whitaker et al., 2007). It is striking that these patterns hold in couples selected for severe male-to-female violence. Thus, most women identified as battered report engaging in severe violence

(e.g., McDonald et al., 2009), and the female partners of young men arrested for PV report just as high levels of PV perpetration as their male partners (Capaldi et al., 2009).

Dyadic perspectives provide insight into a key factor in understanding PV: the relationship context in which violence arises. However, the body of work applying dyadic perspectives to PV is still very limited compared with the decades of work guided by the more established perspectives, and some major gaps exist in the research base on dyadic processes. Notably, almost no information is available on dyadic processes in couples selected for severe female-to-male violence or in same-sex couples. In addition, dyadic perspectives yield limited insight into the conditions under which PV actually occurs within relationships.

Situational Perspectives

Situational perspectives on PV focus on the contextual and interactional factors that affect the chances of partners acting violently toward one another. The basic assumption underlying this perspective is that a full understanding of PV must address the specific situations in which PV is enacted. A couple may live in a culture that is tolerant of PV, one or both partners may have individual risk factors for engaging in PV, and their relationship may be characterized by distress, insecurity, and entrenched patterns of hostility. However, even in such a scenario, PV does not occur randomly. Even the most frequently and severely violent partner is not violent in all situations. Thus, the unit of analysis becomes specific episodes of violence, including the events and conditions leading up to incidents, the interpersonal process culminating in violence, and the outcomes of violent episodes (Wilkinson & Hamerschlag, 2005).

Data have suggested that individual vulnerabilities and situations interact to give rise to aggressive impulses. Traits indicating vulnerability to interpersonal provocation, such as emotional sensitivity and impulsivity, predict aggression only under provoking conditions (Bettencourt, Talley, Benjamin, & Valentine, 2006). For instance, in laboratory studies, partner provocation consistently predicted aggression toward romantic partners only for participants high on dispositional aggressiveness (DeWall et al., 2011; Finkel et al., 2012). Moreover, some of the most robust individual correlates of PV—such as attachment anxiety, sensitivity to rejection, proneness to jealousy, and borderline personality organization—suggest that aggression might be especially likely when vulnerable individuals are faced with the prospect of partner rejection or loss (Leary, Twenge, & Quinlivan, 2006). Consistent with this speculation, Dutton and Browning (1988) found that violent husbands were especially likely to respond with anger to videotaped arguments related to wife abandonment (relative to controls), but not to other forms of couple conflict. Similarly, Holtzworth-Munroe and Anglin (1991) found that violent husbands were distinguished by their inability to provide competent responses to scenarios involving wife rejection.

Qualitative studies of participants' descriptions of violent incidents have also suggested that attachment-related threats are often key in setting the stage for PV (Allison, Bartholomew, Mayseless, & Dutton, 2008; Stanley, Bartholomew, Taylor, Oram, & Landolt, 2006). For instance, for men in same-sex relationships, most violent conflicts involved either perceived partner rejection or incompatible desires for relational closeness versus autonomy (Stanley et al., 2006). In our collective experience of interviewing hundreds of individuals about their experiences with relationship violence, there always appears to be a precipitating event, most often involving perceptions of emotional threat for one or both partners. The content of the initial conflict may be serious, such as concerns about sexual fidelity, or it may be mundane, such as one partner trying to get the other to do some household duty or to refrain from a perceived unacceptable activity such as watching pornography. Regardless of the precipitating issue, there is generally an underlying theme related to fundamental emotional needs, such as feeling that one's partner is inattentive and uncaring or that she or he does not respect one's feelings and contributions.

PV is typically preceded by arguments, suggesting that PV occurs when verbal attempts to resolve couple conflict have failed (e.g., Capaldi, Kim, & Shortt, 2007; Cascardi & Vivian, 1995; Hydén,

1995). The relationship context is likely to affect the occurrence and nature of conflict situations. Distressed insecure partners are more likely to engage in conflict and to find conflict situations threatening than are more satisfied secure partners. Furthermore, couples with established patterns of negative communication will find it especially challenging to deal constructively with conflicts. Unfortunately, relatively little is known about the interactional processes in which PV is embedded. Consistent with work indicating that problematic communication patterns are common in couples in which PV occurs, the few studies of interaction processes leading to PV have suggested that violence typically follows an escalating pattern of negativity by both partners. In home reenactments of previous conflicts, aggressive couples show high levels of hostile affect and patterns of hostile reciprocity (Burman et al., 1993). Moreover, individuals overwhelmingly report that their violent behavior follows verbal or physical abuse or other negative behavior perpetrated by their partner (S. G. O'Leary & Slep, 2006). As described by Winstok and Eisikovits (2008), as conflict escalates couples often shift their focus from the precipitating issue to the inappropriate actions of their partner in the conflict and to how to end the conflict situation. Often, couples are unable to recall the specific disagreement that led to the conflict. Needless to say, such conflicts fail to address the inevitable issues that arise in intimate relationships and are likely to further undermine relational trust and security.

In relationships in which both partners are violent compared with relationships with only one partner who perpetrates PV, the frequency and severity tends to be greater (e.g., Whitaker et al., 2007). Even when couples have been selected for severe male-to-female violence, partners view their behavior as reactions to each other, and mutual escalation precedes violence (Winstok & Eisikovits, 2008). Women who report severe PV by their partners rarely comply with their partner's wishes in violent altercations, and most report fighting back physically (e.g., Gondolf & Beeman, 2003; Goodman, Dutton, Weinfurt, & Cook, 2003). Thus, PV generally arises in a context of mutual conflict. Winstok (2007; Winstok & Eisikovits, 2008) argued that labeling one party as perpetrator and the other as victim artificially imposes individual roles on an interactional process. Rather, he suggested shifting the focus from individual roles to how both partners escalate or deescalate aggression over the course of an interaction.

When feeling provoked, many more individuals experience the impulse to strike out violently against a romantic partner than act upon those impulses (Finkel, DeWall, Slotter, Oaten, & Foshee, 2009). Therefore, Finkel (2007) argued that theory and research should focus on factors that inhibit aggressive impulses in addition to those that impel PV. In particular, attitudes about the unacceptability of PV and expectations about the negative consequences of PV for the self, the partner, and the relationship may inhibit the expression of PV in conflict situations. We speculate that these inhibiting factors differ by gender. Men may be more likely than women to inhibit PV, and therefore to avoid initiating PV in a conflict situation, because of stronger internalized prohibitions and stronger social and legal sanctions against male PV toward women (e.g., Miller & Simpson, 1991; Sorenson & Taylor, 2005). Consistent with this expectation, in heterosexual relationships women are more likely than men to initiate PV (e.g., Fergusson et al., 2005), to report that they would be violent in response to unacceptable partner behavior (e.g., Fold & Robinson, 1998; Winstok, 2006), and to be the perpetrators of PV when only one partner is violent (e.g., Whitaker et al., 2007). In contrast, one might predict that women would be more likely than men to inhibit PV out of fear of retaliatory violence by a physically stronger male partner. However, contrary to this expectation, some women report being violent because they know their partner will not reciprocate (Fiebert & Gonzales, 1997), and the majority of women with severely violent partners report fighting back physically (Gondolf & Beeman, 2003; Goodman et al., 2003). Individual differences in PV attitudes and outcome expectations based on experiences in childhood, in previous relationships, and in the current relationship likely also play a role in inhibiting (or failing to inhibit) individuals' expressions of violent impulses.

Self-regulatory failure may undermine individuals' capacity to inhibit violent impulses toward intimate partners (Finkel et al., 2009). Various dispositional, relational, and situational factors affect self-regulation. In particular, self-control may be compromised by strong negative emotions in couple conflict (Winstok & Eisikovits, 2008) and by alcohol consumption. A diary study of men in PV treatment indicated that the men's drinking was strongly associated with the likelihood of PV by both partners on a given day (Fals-Stewart, 2003). In a marital conflict laboratory study, couples in which male partners received alcohol were more verbally negative than couples in which male partners received a placebo (Leonard & Roberts, 1998). These studies not only suggest that alcohol disinhibits aggressive impulses but also demonstrate the power of the interactional system: a change in husbands' level of intoxication predicts increased negativity by both partners. Other laboratory research has suggested that alcohol may increase relational insecurity and hostile partner attributions in men with low esteem, which then exacerbates conflict (MacDonald, Zanna, & Holmes, 2000). Also, individuals high in dispositional aggressiveness are especially likely to exhibit aggression toward a romantic partner when their self-regulatory capacity is depleted in an experimental paradigm (Finkel et al., 2012). Thus, the likelihood of PV is affected by the interaction between disinhibiting situational factors and individual and relational factors (Slotter & Finkel, 2011).

Situational perspectives on PV hold great potential for providing insight into the specific contexts in which PV is most likely to occur. Consistent with dyadic perspectives, situational perspectives indicate that individual risk factors for PV do not operate in a vacuum. Individuals direct violence against partners only in particular relational contexts and in particular situational contexts. A major challenge of work from this perspective is acquiring valid information on the situations in which PV arises. Qualitative studies of individuals' and couples' detailed descriptions of violent episodes, although subject to the limitations of retrospective reports, can provide insight into the contexts of actual violent episodes (e.g., Allison et al., 2008). Moreover, researchers are developing innovative approaches to examining situational factors, including the use of daily diaries and of experimental analogue studies (e.g., Fals-Stewart, 2003; Finkel et al., 2009).

MULTIFACTOR MODELS

Multifactor theories of PV incorporate and integrate sociocultural, dyadic, individual, and situational influences on PV. Though models differ in emphasis, all acknowledge that understanding PV requires consideration of multiple levels of analysis, from individual dispositions to the cultural context. Additionally, multifactor models allow for variables at different levels of analysis to interact. Given the number and complexity of factors related to PV, rather than specifying specific predictors of PV across social contexts, forms of relationships, and individuals, multifactor models are heuristic frameworks that provide theoretical coherence to the range of approaches in the PV field and provide guidelines for future research.

The earliest systematic integrative model was Dutton's (1985) application of Bronfenbrenner's (1979) nested ecological theory to PV. PV risk factors are conceptualized as falling into four nested levels of analysis. The ontogenetic level addresses characteristics that make individuals more or less prone to violence, such as the capacity for emotional regulation and particular learning history. The ontogenetic level is nested within the microsystem, which captures the dyadic and family relationships in which ontogenetic factors are embedded. For example, trust and patterns of communication in a given relationship will interact with an individual's propensity to jealousy to influence the probability of violence under threatening circumstances. Next, the microsystem is nested within the exosystem, which includes social structures, social networks, and economic conditions within which the family operates. Finally, at the broadest level, the macrosystem refers to the cultural context, including societal norms for gender relations and family violence. As previously reviewed, factors representing each level of the nested ecological theory have relevance for PV. However, variables from the microsystem level and, to a lesser extent, the ontogenetic level are most strongly related to PV (K. D. O'Leary et al., 2007; Stith et al., 2004), indicating that more distal factors may influence violence through their effect on more proximal factors.

In another early model of PV, Riggs and O'Leary (1989) distinguished between background factors that influence an individual's propensity toward aggressive behavior and situational factors that influence the likelihood of conflict and aggressive episodes in a relationship. Background factors include cultural factors such as social norms and individual characteristics such as an individual's history of violence and personality dispositions. Situational factors that set the stage for violence include relationship problems, substance use, and a partner's use of violence. The model further proposes that the interaction between background and situational risk factors may affect the risk of PV. For example, individuals high in impulsivity (a background factor) may be at risk for violence, or may be especially at risk of violence, only under provoking conditions such as in response to a partner's aggression. The background–situational model has guided research predicting men's and women's PV in various populations, although the sets of background and situational variables assessed have differed across studies. Findings have generally indicated that background and situational factors predict PV, with situational factors more strongly predictive (e.g., White et al., 2001) and mediating the indirect effect of background factors (e.g., K. D. O'Leary et al., 2007). Thus, background variables influence PV primarily through their effect on, and perhaps their interaction with, situational variables. However, research based on this framework has not considered how background and situational variables may interact to predict PV perpetration.

Three recent multifactor models further develop how various predictor variables across levels of analysis work together to predict PV. Finkel's (2008; Slotter & Finkel, 2011) I³ theory identifies three processes through which risk factors affect PV perpetration: *instigation,* or factors that trigger an urge to aggress; *impellance,* or factors that influence the degree to which instigating factors lead to urges to aggress; and *inhibition,* or factors that counteract the urge to aggress. Individuals are most likely to enact violence in a given social interaction when instigating and impelling forces are strong and inhibiting forces are weak. As shown in Figure 22.1, the major risk factors for PV identified in previous literature are organized in terms of these three processes. For example, in response to strong partner

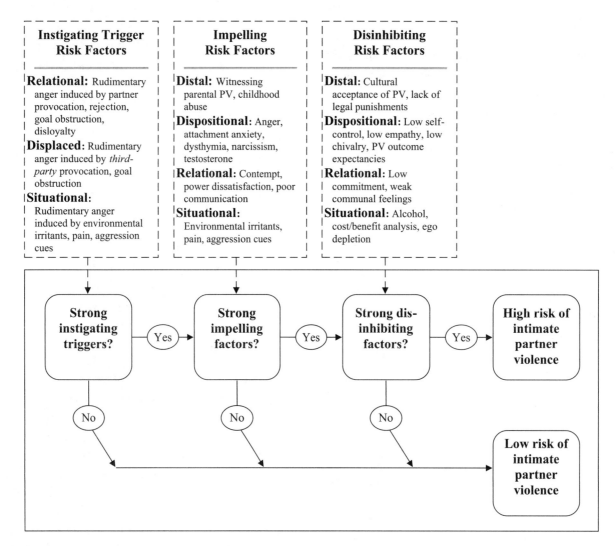

FIGURE 22.1.   The I³ model of partner violence (PV) perpetration. From *Social Relationships: Cognitive, Affective, and Motivational Processes* (p. 276), by J. P. Forgas and J. Fitness, 2008, New York, NY: Psychology Press. Copyright 2008 by the Taylor & Francis Group. Adapted with permission.

provocation such as an insult or threat to leave the relationship (relational instigators), highly insecure partners who lack trust in their partners' regard (dispositional and relational impelling factors) may resort to violence if they lack the ability to control their behavior because of high impulsivity and intoxication (dispositional and situational disinhibiting factors). I³ theory thus incorporates interactions among the three processes. Initial research assessing components of the model is promising. For instance, when provoked by a partner (but not when unprovoked), individuals responded more aggressively when their self-regulatory resources were depleted (an interaction between instigating

and inhibiting factors; Finkel et al., 2009). I³ theory focuses on the forces at work in specific interpersonal situations, although it also incorporates distal variables that affect behavior in the situation. Perhaps the most novel aspect of the theory is the inclusion of disinhibiting factors. Although the importance of restraining violent impulses is implicit in anger management training for PV (Bowen, 2011; Murphy & Eckhardt, 2005), theory and research in the PV field have focused on factors that motivate PV rather than factors that inhibit urges to aggress.

Capaldi, Shortt, and Kim (2005) have proposed a dynamic developmental systems (DDS) model of PV (see Figure 22.2). This model is based on findings from longitudinal studies indicating the developmental and dyadic origins of risk for PV. Although previous models have included background variables such as exposure to violence during childhood, they have not considered these variables in a broader developmental context. This model takes into consideration risk factors for less-than-optimal parenting, parenting deficits that may set the stage for children to develop conduct and emotional problems, at-risk individuals' choice of at-risk relationship partners, and relationship development over time, which potentially changes the risk for PV. Although previous models have acknowledged the dyadic context of partner aggression and may include partner and dyadic variables, they have generally maintained a focus on predicting PV at the individual level. The DDS model focuses on the dyad as the key to understanding PV. It emphasizes that both members of a couple influence the development of abusive dynamics, that partners affect one another over time, and that PV arises out of reciprocal interaction patterns. Moreover, the bidirectional nature of much PV is explicitly acknowledged. Finally, the model includes the proximal context of violent incidents, such as substance use

and relationship events that precipitate abusive conflict. Some of the tenets of the DDS model have been examined in the Oregon Youth Study, a longitudinal study of at-risk boys and their partners. For example, antisocial young men are likely to pair with antisocial young women, and female partners' antisocial behavior and depressive symptoms predict men's aggressiveness over and above the men's own risk factors (H. K. Kim & Capaldi, 2004). Other longitudinal cohort studies have also confirmed various components of the DDS model (e.g., Ehrensaft et al., 2003; Robins et al., 2002; Woodward et al., 2002).

Finally, we have proposed a dyadic model for integrating theory and research on PV (Bartholomew & Cobb, 2011; see Figure 22.3). The model incorporates individual background and dispositional characteristics of both partners (Partner 1 and Partner 2), the ways in which the relationship context is established by the interaction between partners' predispositions, and the situational contexts in which relational patterns give rise to patterns of PV. We expect partners to influence each other at each stage of the model. We also expect that subsequent steps in the model will mediate the effect of earlier factors on the risk of PV. For instance, background and dispositional variables

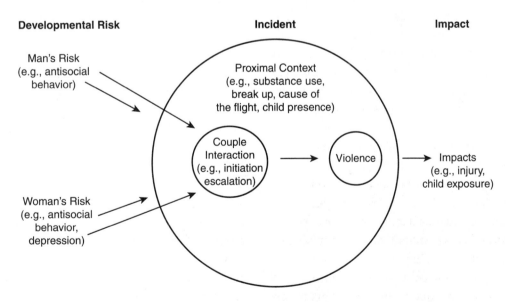

FIGURE 22.2. Dynamic developmental systems model of partner violence. From "Typological Approaches to Violence in Couples: A Critique and Alternative Conceptual Approach," by D. M. Capaldi and H. K. Kim, 2007, *Clinical Psychology Review, 27*, p. 259. Copyright 2007 by Elsevier. Reprinted with permission.

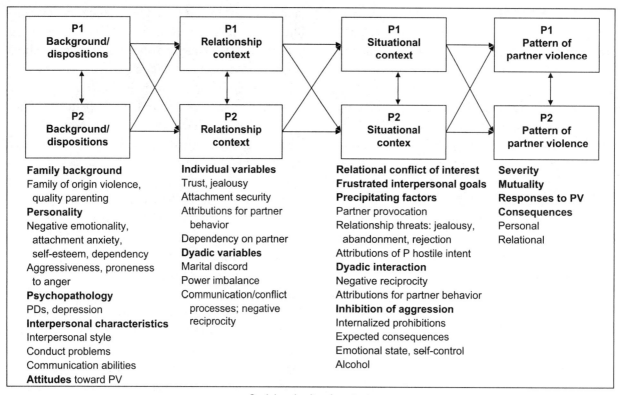

Social and cultural context

FIGURE 22.3.   A dyadic model of partner violence. PD = personality disorder; P1 = Partner 1; P2 = Partner 2; PV = partner violence. From *Handbook of Interpersonal Psychology: Theory, Research, Assessment, and Therapeutic Interventions* (p. 234), by L. M. Horowitz and S. Strack, 2011, Hoboken, NJ: Wiley. Copyright 2011 by John Wiley & Sons Inc. Adapted with permission.

will influence PV primarily through their effect on relationship and situational contexts. Thus, partners whose relationships are characterized by mutual satisfaction, trust, benevolent partner attributions, and constructive communication are not at risk for PV, despite any individual dispositions toward violence. However, we do recognize that individuals who enter into relationships with vulnerabilities and risk factors for PV may find it challenging to establish and maintain a positive relationship. Moreover, PV does not occur randomly, even in distressed relationships with entrenched patterns of hostility. PV occurs when the situational and interactional context triggers and fails to inhibit violent impulses by one or both partners. Finally, relationships are embedded in social and cultural communities that provide an important context for all steps in the process leading to PV. Although not depicted in Figure 22.3, we do not conceive of the model of PV as linear and unidirectional. Rather, we expect that later

stages may feed back to earlier stages. For instance, involvement in a conflictual and distressing relationship may reinforce dispositional risk factors over time, such as attachment anxiety and depression, contributing to further relationship dysfunction and an escalating cycle of couple conflict and abuse. Though research has not specifically assessed this model of PV, most links in the model have received empirical support (for a review, see Bartholomew & Cobb, 2011).

Each of the models of PV described (and there are others) attempts to organize the large and unwieldy research literature on PV. Although these models differ in focus, they are consistent in their inclusion of the key predictors of PV. The later models build on the earlier models, indicating an encouraging movement in the field toward greater integration of the disparate approaches to thinking about PV. These models all take a dimensional rather than a typological approach, thereby allowing for diverse paths to different patterns of PV and for interactions between PV risk factors (dispositional, relational, and situational; cf. Capaldi & Kim, 2007; Holtzworth-Munroe & Meehan, 2004). The I³ model is especially useful for examining the forces at work in a particular situation and how, in interaction, various forces affect the likelihood of violence. Although the focus remains on the individual and on perpetration of PV, the model does accommodate partner and dyadic variables. The DDS (Capaldi et al., 2005) and dyadic (Bartholomew & Cobb, 2011) models identify the dyad, rather than the individual, as the appropriate unit of analysis. Both allow for various patterns of PV, including mutual and unidirectional abuse, rather than focusing exclusively on violence perpetration. They differ in that DDS provides a more clearly articulated developmental framework, especially as applied to the developmental context in which individual risk factors or dispositions arise. The dyadic model, in contrast, more clearly indicates the meditational paths linking individual variables to the relationship context to the specific situational context in which violence may arise.

The models presented share some limitations. Given their complexity and breadth, they cannot realistically be evaluated as a whole; rather, at best, particular components of these models can be assessed. All five models presented here acknowledge the importance of the cultural context in which individuals and their relationships are embedded. Nevertheless, perhaps because psychologists rather than sociologists have formulated these models, an analysis of the cultural context is lacking. In spite of these limitations, multifactor models contribute to researchers' understanding by integrating diverse perspectives on PV, and these models have the potential to provide the basis for a number of productive research directions.

CULTURAL CONTEXT OF PARTNER VIOLENCE

The social and cultural communities in which relationships are embedded provide an overarching context for the individual, relational, and situational factors affecting the development of PV. However, the vast majority of cross-cultural research examining PV has been guided by feminist perspectives and, as such, has focused almost exclusively on male violence against women and on attitudinal predictors. Some of this work has considered how patriarchal societal structures may foster violence against women and how the link between patriarchal structures and violence against women may be mediated by men's sexist attitudes and tolerance of wife abuse. Consistent with expectations from a feminist analysis of PV, the lower the status of women in a society, the higher the society's rate of violence against women, in absolute terms and relative to the rate of violence against men. Additionally, the higher the proportion of men in a society who hold traditional gender role attitudes and find it acceptable for a husband to slap his wife, the higher the rate of violence against women (Archer, 2006).

Further consideration of the cross-cultural data on PV generates a more complex picture. First, women's parallel attitudes are at least as predictive, and in some cases more predictive, of their victimization as are men's attitudes, suggesting that women play a role in maintaining traditional gender roles. In some traditional societies (e.g., Jordan and Egypt), the large majority of women believe that wife beating is justified in at least some situations (e.g., El-Zanty, Hussein, Shawky, Way & Kishor, 1995; Linos, Khawaja, & Al-Nsour, 2010). Second, the higher the level of women's empowerment in a society, the higher the level of their violence toward men; in societies in which women's social power is approaching that of men's, rates of women's PV surpass those of men (Archer, 2006). Third, a strong positive association exists between acceptance of men's violence toward women and women's violence toward men (Archer, 2006). Fourth, even in societies with the highest rates of violence against women (such as Papua New Guinea), a substantial number of women also engage in nondefensive PV, and most marriages with violence do not conform to the feminist stereotype of severe, controlling, one-sided male-to-female violence. The traditional feminist analysis cannot account for these findings because it focuses only on men's aggression toward women. Archer (2006) suggested that social role theory (Eagly, 1987), which considers the social roles of both genders and how they mutually reinforce one another, is a more appropriate framework for understanding these cross-cultural patterns.

As convincingly argued by Bond (2004), it is individuals, not cultures, who aggress against one another. Therefore, it is essential to consider how cultural factors are linked to individual-level psychological mediators of aggressive behavior. We further suggest the need to add dyadic and situational mediators. Unfortunately, very little cross-cultural research has considered psychological, dyadic, or situational correlates of PV. The little research available has suggested that at least some processes appear to operate similarly cross-culturally. Of note, there is evidence that a childhood history of family violence is associated with perpetration and receipt of PV cross-culturally (Krahé, Bieneck, & Möller, 2005). Additionally, PV appears to arise in the relational context of conflicts of interest between partners in different cultural contexts (e.g., J. Kim & Emery, 2003; Winstok & Eisikovits, 2008). However, researchers need to consider the possibility that the individual, dyadic, and situational processes associated with PV may differ cross-culturally (Bond, 2004).

IMPLICATIONS FOR INTERVENTION AND PREVENTION

Intervention programs stemming from the feminist analysis of PV aim to reeducate violent men by challenging their patriarchal attitudes, including their belief that they have the right to dominate and control their female partners. In particular, the Duluth model (Pence & Paymar, 1993) has been used extensively with groups of court-mandated men across the Western world. Psychosocial understandings of PV are generally rejected because they are seen as reducing men's responsibility for their violence and as potentially holding women partially responsible for their victimization. Despite widespread application, little evidence of the effectiveness of these programs has been found (Babcock, Green, & Robie, 2004; Feder & Wilson, 2005), perhaps because they generally fail to consider the individual, dyadic, and interactional dimensions of PV

(Dutton & Corvo, 2006, 2007; Graham-Kevan, 2007a). Additionally, psychoeducational programs train facilitators to take a punitive, confrontational approach to perpetrators, which may undermine the development of a positive working alliance with clients (cf. Dutton & Corvo, 2006). Feminist perspectives have also hindered the development of programs for abused men and for violent women because of their focus on men's violence against women.

Cognitive–behavioral therapy (CBT) programs for male perpetrators, stemming primarily from individually based, psychological perspectives on PV, fare somewhat better than strictly psychoeducational programs (Babcock et al., 2004; Dutton, Bodnarchuk, Kropp, Hart, & Ogloff, 1997; Feder & Wilson, 2005; Murphy & Eckhardt, 2005). Moreover, many current programs based on the Duluth model now incorporate CBT interventions (Babcock et al., 2004). CBT addresses cognitive processes associated with PV (e.g., attitudes toward PV, minimization of abuse) and teaches perpetrators skills such as stress management, assertive communication, anger management, and recognition of the relational situational triggers of PV. Thus, CBT addresses, at least in part, the situational contexts in which PV is most likely to arise. However, this treatment approach is limited by focusing on only one member of dyads with violence and by targeting a relatively narrow subset of the factors that contribute to PV.

In recent years, researchers and clinicians have advocated for a broader range of PV treatments informed by the current research base on PV (Hamel, 2005; Hamel & Nicholls, 2007). Multifactor models may prove helpful by providing inclusive and accessible frameworks for understanding the complex problem of PV, thereby encouraging the development of intervention programs to target risk factors at different levels of analysis (e.g., individual factors, couple factors, situational factors). For instance, blended behavioral therapy holds promise by expanding the therapeutic targets of CBT to include attachment disorders, borderline personality traits, trauma symptoms, and shame (Dutton, 2008). Emerging from dyadic perspectives on PV, couples therapy also offers promise (D. O'Leary,

2001; Stith & McCollum, 2011; Stith, Rosen, & McCollum, 2003). Couples therapy, whether as a stand-alone intervention or in conjunction with other interventions such as individual CBT, can help couples deal with relational issues that give rise to conflict and to learn constructive means of dealing with conflicts that inevitably arise in intimate relationships. Stith et al. (2003) have also developed multicouple treatment groups for PV in which couples learn from the experiences of other couples facing similar challenges. Additionally, interest in incorporating alcohol treatment in PV treatments is growing (Murphy & Ting, 2010), given that alcohol (and other substance abuse) may undermine the capacity to control violent impulses. For example, Fals-Stewart, Kashdan, O'Farrell, and Birchler (2002) have developed an effective PV intervention that combines couples therapy and individual substance use treatment for the male perpetrator. Although these various alternative treatments (and there are others beyond those described here) to the established programs for male perpetrators are encouraging, treatment outcome research is lacking. Thus, the efficacy or effectiveness of these alternative treatments has yet to be clearly demonstrated, especially in head-to-head comparisons to establish whether any particular approach or adjunct to PV treatments yields an advantage (Gondolf, 2011).

Although the development of effective services and treatments for individuals and couples struggling with PV is essential, the goal of preventing PV before it occurs is just as important. Feminist perspectives focus on the need to create gender equity and change patriarchal attitudes on a societal level. Although these are laudable goals, the high rates of PV in countries that have made the most progress toward these goals suggest that societal-level changes in social roles are unlikely to eliminate PV. In Western countries, a number of school-based programs for preventing dating violence have been implemented. These programs generally focus on knowledge about PV, often with a component addressing communication and conflict skills. Many of these programs are based on feminist and social learning perspectives, although the theoretical basis of some programs is unclear (Whitaker et al., 2006).

Unfortunately, there are few well-designed outcome studies of these programs, making it difficult to draw conclusions about their effectiveness. However, a few, such as the Safe Dates program, have shown encouraging results (Foshee et al., 2005; Whitaker et al., 2006).

K. D. O'Leary and Slep (2012) have argued that effective PV prevention programs must be based on four premises. First, PV is most common among young women and men, which requires intervention before dating begins. Second, the behavior of both partners must be targeted (as asserted by dyadic perspectives). Third, PV is quite stable from adolescence through young adulthood, underscoring the need for early prevention. Fourth, PV may be easier to prevent than to treat, given that entrenched and severe problems are generally harder to treat. We add that prevention programs need to be based on empirically derived understandings of PV. Prevention programs given to all youths in a given setting may be helpful in changing attitudes regarding PV (especially the current acceptance of women's PV) and may help some youths to avoid becoming involved in abusive dating relationships. However, prospective studies have indicated that a minority of adolescents are at high risk for PV on the basis of their family backgrounds, personal vulnerabilities (such as conduct problems), and tendencies toward assortative mating on risk factors. Brief, universal prevention programs that focus on attitudes and, to a lesser extent, communication skills are unlikely to be sufficient to intervene in a meaningful way with these high-risk youths. Therefore, some researchers have advocated for more intensive programs for this select group of at-risk children and youths (Ehrensaft, 2008; Whitaker et al., 2006). Given that child maltreatment is a risk factor for later problem behaviors and PV, effective prevention programs will ultimately need to target parenting skills and children's individual risk factors. Such programs can be informed by the literature on preventing youth antisocial behavior (Ehrensaft, 2008; Moffitt, 1993; Moffitt, Caspi, Rutter, & Silva, 2001) and programs to promote better family functioning and prevent child maltreatment (MacLeod & Nelson, 2000).

FUTURE DIRECTIONS

Researchers and theoreticians in the field of partner abuse have made remarkable strides in the past couple of decades. The development and application of dyadic and situational perspectives have greatly contributed to our understanding of partner abuse. Researchers have also developed multifactor models that integrate individual, dyadic, situational, and cultural influences on PV, thereby attempting to grapple with the complexity of the factors that play a role in the development of abuse in intimate relationships. New models of treatment and prevention based on these new, more complex perspectives are under development, but there is still considerable work to do.

The majority of PV research continues to focus on male perpetration of abuse against female partners—the legacy of the feminist analysis of PV. Increasingly, researchers are including both genders and considering PV in a range of relationship forms, including same-sex relationships. However, further work is required to establish whether and how the predictors of PV differ by gender of perpetrator and victim. Moreover, the majority of published research has continued to examine either perpetrators or victims of PV in isolation. As highlighted by the dyadic and situational perspectives, it is essential for researchers to consider both partners in understanding the development of abusive dynamics and to acknowledge the possibility of mutual abuse. In particular, there is a pressing need for the study of dyadic and situational processes in same-sex couples and in couples selected for severe female-to-male violence. Not only do these forms of violent relationships deserve attention in their own right, but such study may provide insight into the role of gender in PV more generally.

Overwhelmingly, research in the PV field has relied on self-reports of individual characteristics, relational feelings, and perpetration and receipt of abusive acts. This reliance reflects the individual, rather than dyadic, focus of most research and is influenced by the fact that abuse typically takes place in private settings and therefore is not directly observable. Although self-report measures will always be required to assess individuals' abuse-related experiences, it is time to broaden methods to better capture the processes leading to partner abuse. Research from dyadic perspectives has demonstrated the value of including reports from both members of couples with violence (e.g., Ehrensaft et al., 2004; Roberts & Noller, 1998) and the value of observing interactional processes in couples with violence (e.g., Cordova et al., 1993). Researchers exploring the situational contexts in which abuse arises have been especially creative in devising new research approaches. For instance, daily diaries can be used to examine situational factors associated with PV in samples with frequent abuse (e.g., Fals-Stewart, 2003). Similar methods could be applied to higher frequency outcomes associated with PV, such as acts of emotional abuse. Additionally, laboratory analogue studies (e.g., Dutton & Browning, 1988; Finkel et al., 2009) and couple interaction studies (Leonard & Roberts, 1998) are useful for identifying situational triggers of PV. We especially encourage the further application of experimental social-cognitive methods such as priming (e.g., Dutton, Lane, Koren, & Bartholomew, 2012) and manipulation of self-regulatory resources (e.g., Finkel et al., 2012) to explore the cognitive and emotional processes that facilitate and inhibit acts of partner abuse.

Perhaps the most pressing and greatest challenge in the field of PV is for a more sophisticated analysis of the cultural context of partner abuse. A high priority should be put on research examining how cultural factors are linked to individual, dyadic, and situational mediators of partner abuse. In some cases, cultural factors may influence the mean level of a psychological construct in a population, in turn influencing mean levels of PV. For example, the patriarchal structure of a society is associated with societal endorsement of patriarchal attitudes and with levels of men's violence against women. However, even in the seemingly straightforward case of patriarchal attitudes, the mechanisms of influence are unclear. Is it the case that patriarchal attitudes actually encourage men's PV, as suggested by the traditional feminist analysis? Or do such attitudes weaken inhibitions against men's violent impulses (impulses that may result from nongendered psychological vulnerabilities and relationship frustrations) and foster women's greater tolerance of men's violence? What is the role of external societal sanctions, or lack of sanctions, for PV? And how might traditional gender attitudes affect spousal relationships? Perhaps marriages in societies with more traditional attitudes are more conflictual and less satisfying. Or perhaps the lack of availability of divorce in many traditional societies plays an important role: If marital conflict escalates over time with no possibility of ending the marriage, women may come to bear an increasing burden of abuse because of men's greater physical strength. A similar analysis could be applied to the data indicating that national rates of corporal punishment of children are strongly associated with national rates of dating PV (Douglas & Straus, 2006). This link could be mediated through personality dispositions (such as higher levels of insecure attachment because of coercive parenting) or through individuals failing to learn effective conflict management skills. Or perhaps a general societal acceptance of interpersonal violence fails to inhibit individuals' violent impulses, whether toward children or relationship partners.

The role of culture in understanding PV is further complicated by the possibility that different psychological and interpersonal processes may lead to PV in different cultural contexts (Bond, 2004). Some general processes are likely to be similar cross-culturally. For example, conflicts of interest between partners likely set the dyadic context for PV cross-culturally (e.g., J. Kim & Emery, 2003; Winstok & Eisikovits, 2008), although the content of conflicts may vary. Some inhibitors (e.g., social sanctions) and disinhibitors (e.g., alcohol) of PV are also likely to operate in similar ways across cultures. Other processes may vary substantially. For instance, assortative mating that matches partners' dispositions toward violence may be less likely in cultures in which marriages are arranged. Additionally, attachment-related personal dispositions and dyadic conflicts may be less relevant in societies in which a close attachment relationship between spouses is not expected or encouraged. Unfortunately, there is little research on psychological, dyadic, or situational correlates of PV cross-culturally, and even less that considers both genders together (for a notable exception, see J. Kim & Emery, 2003). Research

incorporating multiple levels of analysis is essential to understand the etiology of PV in other cultural contexts, and such research may provide insight into societal-level predictors in Western society.

In conclusion, PV is common, and even though it is not always severe, it has serious consequences for individuals and their intimate relationships. To develop better interventions to reduce or eliminate this harmful relationship behavior, models that account for the multifaceted and complex nature of violence in relationships are required. The multifactor models presented here highlight the need to consider not only the psychological factors that put some individuals at risk for PV, but also the dyadic factors that put some relationships at risk, the situational factors that precipitate violence in at-risk relationships, and the broader sociocultural context within which all relationships are embedded.

References

Allison, C. J., Bartholomew, K., Mayseless, O., & Dutton, D. G. (2008). Love as a battlefield: Attachment and relationship dynamics in couples identified for male partner violence. *Journal of Family Issues, 29,* 125–150. doi:10.1177/0192513X07306980

Anderson, K. L. (1997). Gender, status and domestic violence: An integration of feminist and family violence approaches. *Journal of Marriage and the Family, 59,* 655–669. doi:10.2307/353952

Anderson, K. L. (2002). Perpetrator or victim? Relationships between intimate partner violence and well-being. *Journal of Marriage and Family, 64,* 851–863. doi:10.1111/j.1741-3737.2002.00851.x

Anglin, K., & Holtzworth-Munroe, A. (1997). Comparing the responses of maritally violent and nonviolent spouses to problematic marital and nonmarital situations: Are the skill deficits of physically aggressive husbands and wives global? *Journal of Family Psychology, 11,* 301–313. doi:10.1037/0893-3200.11.3.301

Archer, J. (2000). Sex differences in aggression between heterosexual partners: A meta-analytic review. *Psychological Bulletin, 126,* 651–680. doi:10.1037/0033-2909.126.5.651

Archer, J. (2002). Sex differences in physically aggressive acts between heterosexual partners: A meta-analytic review. *Aggression and Violent Behavior, 7,* 313–351. doi:10:1016/S1359-1789(01)00061-1

Archer, J. (2006). Cross-cultural differences in physical aggression between partners: A social-role analysis.

Personality and Social Psychology Review, 10, 133–153. doi:10.1207/s15327957pspr1002_3

Babcock, J. C., Green, C. E., & Robie, C. (2004). Does batterers' treatment work? A meta-analytic review of domestic violence treatment. *Clinical Psychology Review, 23,* 1023–1053. doi:10.1016/j.cpr.2002.07.001

Babcock, J. C., Miller, S. A., & Siard, C. (2003). Toward a typology of abusive women: Differences between partner-only and generally violent women in the use of violence. *Psychology of Women Quarterly, 27,* 153–161. doi:10.1111/1471-6402.00095

Babcock, J. C., Waltz, J., Jacobson, N. S., & Gottman, J. M. (1993). Power and violence: The relation between communication patterns, power discrepancies, and domestic violence. *Journal of Consulting and Clinical Psychology, 61,* 40–50. doi:10.1037/0022-006X.61.1.40

Bartholomew, K., & Allison, C. J. (2006). An attachment perspective on abusive dynamics in intimate relationships. In M. Mikulincer & G. S. Goodman (Eds.), *Romantic love: Attachment, caregiving, and sex* (pp. 102–127). New York, NY: Guilford Press.

Bartholomew, K., & Cobb, R. J. (2011). Conceptualizing relationship violence as a dyadic process. In L. M. Horowitz & S. Strack (Eds.), *Handbook of interpersonal psychology: Theory, research, assessment, and therapeutic interventions* (pp. 233–248). Hoboken, NJ: Wiley.

Bartholomew, K., Regan, K. V., White, M. A., & Oram, D. (2008). Patterns of abuse in male same-sex relationship. *Violence and Victims, 23,* 617–636. doi:10.1891/0886-6708.23.5.617

Bauserman, S. A., & Arias, I. (1992). Relationships among marital investment, marital satisfaction, and marital commitment in domestically victimized and nonvictimized wives. *Violence and Victims, 7,* 287–296.

Bettencourt, B. A., Talley, A., Benjamin, A. J., & Valentine, J. (2006). Personality and aggressive behavior under provoking and neutral conditions: A meta-analytic review. *Psychological Bulletin, 132,* 751–777. doi:10.1037/0033-2909.132.5.751

Bograd, M. (1988). Feminist perspectives on wife abuse: An introduction. In M. Bograd & K. Yllo (Eds.), *Feminist perspectives on wife abuse* (pp. 11–26). Beverly Hills, CA: Sage.

Bond, M. H. (2004). Culture and aggression: From context to coercion. *Personality and Social Psychology Review, 8,* 62–78. doi:10.1207/s15327957pspr0801_3

Bowen, E. (2011). *The rehabilitation of partner violent men.* Chichester, England: Wiley. doi:10.1002/9780470978603

Bronfenbrenner, U. (1979). Contexts of child rearing: Problems and prospects. *American Psychologist, 34,* 844–850. doi:10.1037/0003-066X.34.10.844

Burman, B., Margolin, G., & John, R. S. (1993). America's angriest home videos: Behavioral contingencies observed in home reenactments of marital conflict. *Journal of Consulting and Clinical Psychology, 61,* 28–39. doi:10.1037/0022-006X.61.1.28

Bushman, B. J., & Anderson, C. A. (2001). Is it time to pull the plug on hostile versus instrumental aggression dichotomy? *Psychological Review, 108,* 273–279. doi:10.1037/0033-295X.108.1.273

Capaldi, D. M., & Crosby, L. (1997). Observed and reported psychological and physical aggression in young, at-risk couples. *Social Development, 6,* 184–206. doi:10.1111/j.1467-9507.1997.tb00101.x

Capaldi, D. M., & Kim, H. K. (2007). Typological approaches to violence in couples: A critique and alternative conceptual approach. *Clinical Psychology Review, 27,* 253–265. doi:10.1016/j.cpr.2006.09.001

Capaldi, D. M., Kim, H., & Shortt, J. (2007). Observed initiation and reciprocity of physical aggression in young, at-risk couples. *Journal of Family Violence, 22,* 101–111. doi:10.1007/s10896-007-9067-1

Capaldi, D. M., & Owen, L. D. (2001). Physical aggression in a community sample of at-risk young couples: Gender comparisons for high frequency, injury, and fear. *Journal of Family Psychology, 15,* 425–440. doi:10.1037/0893-3200.15.3.425

Capaldi, D. M., Shortt, J. W., & Crosby, L. (2003). Physical and psychological aggression in at-risk young couples: Stability and change in young adulthood. *Merrill-Palmer Quarterly, 49,* 1–27. doi:10.1353/mpq.2003.0001

Capaldi, D. M., Shortt, J., & Kim, H. K. (2005). A life span developmental systems perspective on aggression toward a partner. In W. M. Pinsof & J. L. Lebow (Eds.), *Family psychology: The art of the science* (pp. 141–167). New York, NY: Oxford University Press.

Capaldi, D. M., Shortt, J., Kim, H. K., Wilson, J., Crosby, L., & Tucci, S. (2009). Official incidents of domestic violence: Types, injury, and associations with non-official couple aggression. *Violence and Victims, 24,* 502–519. doi:10.1891/0886-6708.24.4.502

Carrado, M., George, M. J., Loxam, E., & Jones, L. L. (1996). Aggression in British heterosexual relationships: A descriptive analysis. *Aggressive Behavior, 22,* 401–415. doi:10.1002/(SICI)1098-2337(1996)22:6<401::AID-AB1>3.0.CO;2-K

Cascardi, M., & Vivian, D. (1995). Context for specific episodes of marital violence: Gender and severity of violence differences. *Journal of Family Violence, 10,* 265–293. doi:10.1007/BF02110993

Charles, D., Whitaker, D. J., Le, B., Swahn, M., & DiClemente, R. J. (2011). Differences between perpetrators of bidirectional and unidirectional physical intimate partner violence. *Partner Abuse, 2,* 344–364. doi:10.1891/1946&U8211;6560.2.3.344

Coleman, D. H., & Straus, M. A. (1990). Marital power, conflict, and violence in a nationally representative sample of American couples. In M. A. Straus & R. J. Gelles (Eds.), *Physical violence in American families: Risk factors and adaptations to violence in 8,145 families* (pp. 287–304). New Brunswick, NJ: Transaction.

Cordova, J. V., Jacobson, N. S., Gottman, J. M., Rushe, R., & Cox, G. (1993). Negative reciprocity and communication in couples with a violent husband. *Journal of Abnormal Psychology, 102,* 559–564. doi:10.1037/0021-843X.102.4.559

DeKeseredy, W. S. (2011). Feminist contributions to understanding woman abuse: Myths, controversies, and realities. *Aggression and Violent Behavior, 16,* 297–302. doi:10.1016/j.avb.2011.04.002

DeKeseredy, W. S., & Schwartz, M. D. (1998). *Woman abuse on campus: Results from the Canadian National Survey.* Thousand Oaks, CA: Sage.

DeWall, C. N., Finkel, E. J., Lambert, N. M., Slotter, E. B., Bodenhausen, G. V., Pond, R. S., & Fincham, F. D. (2011). *The voodoo doll task: Introducing and validating a novel method for studying aggression.* Unpublished manuscript, University of Kentucky.

Dobash, R. E., & Dobash, R. (1979). *Violence against wives: A case against the patriarchy.* New York, NY: Free Press.

Douglas, E. M., & Straus, M. A. (2006). Assault and injury of dating partners by university students in 19 countries and its relation to corporal punishment experienced as a child. *European Journal of Criminology, 3,* 293–318. doi:10.1177/1477370806065584

Dragiewicz, M., & Lindgren, Y. (2009). The gendered nature of domestic violence: Statistical data for lawyers considering equal protection analysis. *American University Journal of Gender, Social Policy, and the Law, 17,* 229–268.

Dutton, D., & Browning, J. (1988). Power struggles and intimacy anxieties as causative factors of wife assault. In G. W. Russell (Ed.), *Violence in intimate relationships* (pp. 163–175). Costa Mesa, CA: PMA.

Dutton, D. G. (1985). An ecologically nested theory of male violence towards intimates. *International Journal of Women's Studies, 8,* 404–413.

Dutton, D. G. (1994). Patriarchy and wife assault: The ecological fallacy. *Violence and Victims, 9,* 167–182.

Dutton, D. G. (2006). *Rethinking domestic violence.* Vancouver, British Columbia, Canada: UBC Press.

Dutton, D. G. (2008). Blended behavior therapy for intimate violence. In A. C. Baldry & F. W. Winkel (Eds.), *Intimate partner violence prevention and intervention: The risk assessment and management approach* (pp. 133–146). Hauppauge, NY: Nova Science.

Dutton, D. G. (2010). The gender paradigm and the architecture of anti-science. *Partner Abuse, 1,* 5–25. doi:10.1891/1946-6560.1.1.5

Dutton, D. G. (2012). The case against the role of gender in intimate partner violence. *Aggression and Violent Behavior, 17,* 99–104. doi:10.1016/j.avb.2011.09.002

Dutton, D. G., Bodnarchuk, M., Kropp, R., Hart, S., & Ogloff, J. (1997). Wife assault treatment and criminal recidivism: An eleven year follow-up. *International Journal of Offender Therapy and Comparative Criminology, 41,* 9–23. doi:10.1177/0306624X9704100102

Dutton, D. G., & Corvo, K. (2006). Transforming a flawed policy: A call to revive psychology and science in domestic violence research and practice. *Aggression and Violent Behavior, 11,* 457–483. doi:10.1016/j.avb.2006.01.007

Dutton, D. G., & Corvo, K. C. (2007). The Duluth model: A data-impervious paradigm and a flawed strategy. *Aggression and Violent Behavior, 12,* 658–667. doi:10.1016/j.avb.2007.03.002

Dutton, D. G., Lane, R. A., Koren, T., & Bartholomew, K. (2012). *Secure base priming diminishes conflict-based anger and anxiety.* Manuscript submitted for publication.

Dutton, D. G., & Nicholls, T. L. (2005). The gender paradigm in domestic violence research and theory: Part 1—The conflict of theory and data. *Aggression and Violent Behavior, 10,* 680–714. doi:10.1016/j.avb.2005.02.001

Dutton, D. G., Saunders, K., Starzomski, A. J., & Bartholomew, K. (1994). Intimacy-anger and insecure attachment as precursors of abuse in intimate relationships. *Journal of Applied Social Psychology, 24,* 1367–1386. doi:10.1111/j.1559-1816.1994.tb01554.x

Eagly, A. H. (1987). *Sex differences in social behavior: A social-role interpretation.* Hillsdale, NJ: Erlbaum.

Ehrensaft, M. K. (2008). Intimate partner violence: Persistence of myths and implications for intervention. *Children and Youth Services Review, 30,* 276–286. doi:10.1016/j.childyouth.2007.10.005

Ehrensaft, M. K. (2009). Family and relationship predictors of psychological and physical aggression. In K. O'Leary & E. M. Woodin (Eds.), *Psychological and physical aggression in couples: Causes and interventions* (pp. 99–118). Washington, DC: American Psychological Association. doi:10.1037/11880-005

Ehrensaft, M. K., Cohen, P., Brown, J., Smailes, E., Chen, H., & Johnson, J. G. (2003). Intergenerational transmission of partner violence: A 20-year prospective study. *Journal of Consulting and Clinical Psychology, 71,* 741–753. doi:10.1037/0022-006X.71.4.741

Ehrensaft, M. K., Moffitt, T. E., & Caspi, A. (2004). Clinically abusive relationships in an unselected birth cohort: Men's and women's participation and developmental antecedents. *Journal of Abnormal Psychology, 113,* 258–270. doi:10.1037/0021-843X.113.2.258

El-Zanty, F., Hussein, E. M., Shawky, G. A., Way, A. A., & Kishor, S. (1995). *Egypt demographic and health survey 1995*. Cairo, Egypt: National Population Council.

Fals-Stewart, W. (2003). The occurrence of partner physical aggression on days of alcohol consumption: A longitudinal diary study. *Journal of Consulting and Clinical Psychology, 71*, 41–52. doi:10.1037/0022-006X.71.1.41

Fals-Stewart, W., Kashdan, T. B., O'Farrell, T. J., & Birchler, G. R. (2002). Behavioral couples therapy for drug-abusing patients: Effects on partner violence. *Journal of Substance Abuse Treatment, 22*, 87–96. doi:10.1016/S0740-5472(01)00218-5

Feder, L., & Wilson, D. B. (2005). A meta-analytic review of court-mandated batterer intervention programs: Can courts affect abusers' behavior? *Journal of Experimental Criminology, 1*, 239–262. doi:10.1007/s11292-005-1179-0

Fergusson, D. M., Horwood, L. J., & Ridder, E. M. (2005). Partner violence and mental health outcomes in a New Zealand birth cohort. *Journal of Marriage and Family, 67*, 1103–1119. doi:10.1111/j.1741-3737.2005.00202.x

Fiebert, M. (2010). References examining assaults by women on their spouses or male partners: An annotated bibliography. *Sexuality and Culture, 14*, 49–91. doi:10.1007/s12119-009-9059-9

Fiebert, M. S., & Gonzalez, D. M. (1997). College women who initiate assaults on their male partners and the reasons offered for such behavior. *Psychological Reports, 80*, 583–590. doi:10.2466/pr0.1997.80.2.583

Finkel, E. J. (2007). Impelling and inhibiting forces in the perpetration of intimate partner violence. *Review of General Psychology, 11*, 193–207. doi:10.1037/1089-2680.11.2.193

Finkel, E. J. (2008). Intimate partner violence perpetration: Insights from the science of self-regulation. In J. P. Forgas & J. Fitness (Eds.), *Social relationships: Cognitive, affective, and motivational processes* (pp. 271–288). New York, NY: Psychology Press.

Finkel, E. J., DeWall, C., Slotter, E. B., McNulty, J. K., Pond, R. S., Jr., & Atkins, D. C. (2012). Using I³ theory to clarify when dispositional aggressiveness predicts intimate partner violence perpetration. *Journal of Personality and Social Psychology, 102*, 533–549. doi:10.1037/a0025651

Finkel, E. J., DeWall, C. N., Slotter, E. B., Oaten, M., & Foshee, V. A. (2009). Self-regulatory failure and intimate partner violence perpetration. *Journal of Personality and Social Psychology, 97*, 483–499. doi:10.1037/a0015433

Fold, S. L., & Robinson, D. T. (1998). Secondary bystander effects on intimate violence: When norms of restraint reduce deterrence. *Journal of Social and Personal Relationships, 15*, 277–285. doi:10.1177/0265407598152010

Follingstad, D. R., & Edmundson, M. (2010). Is psychological abuse reciprocal in intimate relationships? Data from a national sample of American adults. *Journal of Family Violence, 25*, 495–508. doi:10.1007/s10896-010-9311-y

Follingstad, D. R., Wright, S., Lloyd, S., & Sebastian, J. A. (1991). Sex differences in motivations and effects in dating violence. *Family Relations, 40*, 51–57. doi:10.2307/585658

Foshee, V. A., Bauman, K. E., Ennett, S. T., Suchindran, C., Benefield, T., & Linder, G. (2005). Assessing the effects of the dating violence prevention program "Safe Dates" using random coefficient regression modeling. *Prevention Science, 6*, 245–258. doi:10.1007/s11121-005-0007-0

Frieze, I. H. (2008). Social policy feminism, and research on violence in close relationships. *Journal of Social Issues, 64*, 665–684. doi:10.1111/j.1540-4560.2008.00583.x

Gondolf, E. W. (2011). The weak evidence for battered program alternatives. *Aggression and Violent Behavior, 16*, 347–353. doi:10.1016/j.avb.2011.04.011

Gondolf, E. W., & Beeman, A. K. (2003). Women's accounts of domestic violence versus tactics-based outcome categories. *Violence Against Women, 9*, 278–301. doi:10.1177/1077801202250072

Goodman, L., Dutton, M. A., Weinfurt, K., & Cook, S. (2003). The Intimate Partner Violence Strategies Index: Development and application. *Violence Against Women, 9*, 163–186. doi:10.1177/1077801202239004

Graham-Kevan, N. (2007a). Domestic violence: Research and implications for batterer programmes in Europe. *European Journal on Criminal Policy and Research, 13*, 213–225. doi:10.1007/s10610-007-9045-4

Graham-Kevan, N. (2007b). Johnson's control-based domestic violence typology: Implications for research and treatment. *Issues in Forensic Psychology, 6*, 109–115.

Graham-Kevan, N. (2007c). Partner violence typologies. In J. Hamel & T. L. Nicholls (Eds.), *Family interventions in domestic violence* (pp. 145–163). New York, NY: Springer.

Hamel, J. (2005). *Gender inclusive treatment of intimate partner abuse: A comprehensive approach*. New York, NY: Springer.

Hamel, J., & Nicholls, T. L. (Eds.). (2007). *Family interventions in domestic violence*. New York, NY: Springer.

Henning, K., & Feder, L. (2004). A comparison of men and women arrested for domestic violence: Who presents the greater threat? *Journal of Family Violence, 19,* 69–80. doi:10.1023/ B:JOFV.0000019838.01126.7c

Holtzworth-Munroe, A., & Anglin, K. (1991). The competency of responses given by maritally violent versus nonviolent men to problematic marital situations. *Violence and Victims, 6,* 257–269.

Holtzworth-Munroe, A., & Meehan, J. C. (2004). Typologies of men who are maritally violent. *Journal of Interpersonal Violence, 19,* 1369–1389. doi:10.1177/0886260504269693

Holtzworth-Munroe, A., & Stuart, G. (1994). Typologies of male batterers: Three subtypes and the differences among them. *Psychological Bulletin, 116,* 476–497. doi:10.1037/0033-2909.116.3.476

Holtzworth-Munroe, A., Stuart, G. L., & Hutchinson, G. (1997). Violent versus nonviolent husbands: Differences in attachment patterns, dependency, and jealousy. *Journal of Family Psychology, 11,* 314–331. doi:10.1037/0893-3200.11.3.314

Hydén, M. (1995). Verbal aggression as prehistory of woman battering. *Journal of Family Violence, 10,* 55–71. doi:10.1007/BF02110537

Jacobson, N. S., Gottman, J. M., Waltz, J., Rushe, R., Babcock, J., & Holtzworth-Munroe, A. (1994). Affect, verbal content, and psychophysiology in the arguments of couples with a violent husband. *Journal of Consulting and Clinical Psychology, 62,* 982–988. doi:10.1037/0022-006X.62.5.982

Johnson, M. P. (1995). Patriarchal terrorism and common couple violence: Two forms of violence against women. *Journal of Marriage and the Family, 57,* 283–294. doi:10.2307/353683

Johnson, M. P., & Ferraro, K. J. (2000). Research on domestic violence in the 1990s: Making distinctions. *Journal of Marriage and the Family, 62,* 948–963. doi:10.1111/j.1741-3737.2000.00948.x

Johnson, M. P., & Leone, J. M. (2005). The differential effects of intimate terrorism and situational couple violence: Findings from the National Violence Against Women Survey. *Journal of Family Issues, 26,* 322–349. doi:10.1177/0192513X04270345

Kelley, H. H., Berscheid, E., Christensen, A., Harvey, J., Huston, T., Levinger, G., . . . Peterson, D. (1983). Analyzing close relationships. In H. H. Kelley, E. Berscheid, A. Christensen, J. H. Harvey, T. L. Huston, G. Levinger, . . . D. R. Peterson (Eds.), *Close relationships* (pp. 20–64). New York, NY: Freeman.

Kim, H. K., & Capaldi, D. M. (2004). The association of antisocial behavior and depressive symptoms between partners and risk for aggression in romantic relationships. *Journal of Family Psychology, 18,* 82–96. doi:10.1037/0893-3200.18.1.82

Kim, J., & Emery, C. (2003). Marital power, conflict, and marital violence in a nationally representative sample

of Korean couples. *Journal of Interpersonal Violence, 18,* 197–219. doi:10.1177/0886260502238735

Krahé, B., Bieneck, S., & Möller, I. (2005). Understanding gender and intimate partner violence from an international perspective. *Sex Roles, 52,* 807–827. doi:10.1007/s11199-005-4201-0

Krueger, R. F., Moffitt, T. E., Caspi, A., Bleske, A., & Silva, P. A. (1998). Assortative mating for antisocial behavior: Developmental and methodological implications. *Behavior Genetics, 28,* 173–186. doi:10.1023/A:1021419013124

Kwong, M. J., Bartholomew, K., Henderson, A. Z., & Trinke, S. J. (2003). The intergenerational transmission of relationship violence. *Journal of Family Psychology, 17,* 288–301. doi:10.1037/0893-3200.17.3.288

Laroche, D. (2005). *Aspects of the context and consequences of domestic violence—Situational couple violence and intimate terrorism in Canada in 1999.* Quebec City, Quebec, Canada: Government of Quebec.

Lawrence, E., & Bradbury, T. N. (2007). Trajectories of change in physical aggression and marital satisfaction. *Journal of Family Psychology, 21,* 236–247. doi:10.1037/0893-3200.21.2.236

Leary, M. R., Twenge, J. M., & Quinlivan, E. (2006). Interpersonal rejection as a determinant of anger and aggression. *Personality and Social Psychology Review, 10,* 111–132. doi:10.1207/s15327957pspr1002_2

Leonard, K. E., & Roberts, L. J. (1998). The effects of alcohol on the marital interactions of aggressive and nonaggressive husbands and their wives. *Journal of Abnormal Psychology, 107,* 602–615. doi:10.1037/0021-843X.107.4.602

Leonard, K. E., & Senchak, M. (1993). Alcohol and premarital aggression among newlywed couples. *Journal of Studies on Alcohol, 11*(Suppl.), 96–108.

Lie, G. Y., Schilit, R., Bush, J., & Montagne, M. (1991). Lesbians in currently aggressive relationships: How frequently do they report aggressive past relationships? *Violence and Victims, 6,* 121–135.

Linos, N., Khawaja, M., & Al-Nsour, M. (2010). Women's autonomy and support for wife beating: Findings from a population-based survey in Jordan. *Violence and Victims, 25,* 409–419. doi:10.1891/0886-6708.25.3.409

MacDonald, G., Zanna, M. P., & Holmes, J. G. (2000). An experimental test of the role of alcohol in relationship conflict. *Journal of Experimental Social Psychology, 36,* 182–193. doi:10.1006/jesp.1999.1412

MacLeod, J., & Nelson, G. (2000). Programs for the promotion of family wellness and the prevention of child maltreatment: A meta-analytic review. *Child Abuse and Neglect, 24,* 1127–1149. doi:10.1016/ S0145-2134(00)00178-2

Magdol, L., Moffitt, T. E., Caspi, A., Newman, D. L., Fagan, J., & Silva, P. A. (1997). Gender differences in partner violence in a birth cohort of 21-year-olds: Bridging the gap between clinical and epidemiological approaches. *Journal of Consulting and Clinical Psychology, 65,* 68–78. doi:10.1037/0022-006X.65.1.68

McDonald, R., Jouriles, E. N., Tart, C. D., & Minze, L. C. (2009). Children's adjustment problems in families characterized by men's severe violence toward women: Does other family violence matter? *Child Abuse and Neglect, 33,* 94–101. doi:10.1016/j.chiabu.2008.03.005

Medeiros, R. A., & Straus, M. A. (2007). Risk factors for physical violence between dating partners: Implications for gender-inclusive prevention and treatment of family violence. In J. Hamel & T. L. Nicholls (Eds.), *Family interventions in domestic violence* (pp. 59–86). New York, NY: Springer.

Miller, S. L., & Simpson, S. S. (1991). Courtship violence and social control: Does gender matter? *Law and Society Review, 25,* 335–365. doi:10.2307/3053802

Moffitt, T. E. (1993). Adolescence-limited and life-course-persistent antisocial behavior: A developmental taxonomy. *Psychological Review, 100,* 674–701. doi:10.1037/0033-295X.100.4.674

Moffitt, T. E., Caspi, A., Rutter, M., & Silva, P. A. (2001). *Sex differences in antisocial behavior: Conduct disorder, delinquency, and violence in the Dunedin Longitudinal Study.* Cambridge, England: Cambridge University Press. doi:10.1017/CBO9780511490057

Moffitt, T. E., Krueger, R. F., Caspi, A., & Fagan, J. (2000). Partner abuse and general crime: How are they the same? How are they different? *Criminology, 38,* 199–232. doi:10.1111/j.1745-9125.2000.tb00888.x

Moffitt, T. E., Robins, R. W., & Caspi, A. (2001). A couples analysis of partner abuse with implications for abuse-prevention policy. *Criminology and Public Policy, 1,* 5–36. doi:10.1111/j.1745-9133.2001.tb00075.x

Morin, R., & Cohn, D. (2008). *Women call the shots at home; Public mixed on gender roles in jobs.* Retrieved from http://pewresearch.org/pubs/967/gender-power

Murphy, C. M., & Eckhardt, C. I. (2005). *Treating the abusive partner.* New York, NY: Guilford Press.

Murphy, C. M., Meyer, S., & O'Leary, K. (1994). Dependency characteristics of partner assaultive men. *Journal of Abnormal Psychology, 103,* 729–735. doi:10.1037/0021-843X.103.4.729

Murphy, C. M., & Ting, L. (2010). The effects of treatment for substance use problems on intimate partner violence: A review of empirical data. *Aggression and Violent Behavior, 15,* 325–333. doi:10.1016/j.avb.2010.01.006

O'Leary, D. (2001). Conjoint therapy for partners who engage in physically aggressive behavior: Rationale and research. *Journal of Aggression, Maltreatment, and Trauma, 5,* 145–164. doi:10.1300/J146v05n02_09

O'Leary, K. D., Barling, J., Arias, I., Rosenbaum, A., Malone, J., & Tyree, A. (1989). Prevalence and stability of physical aggression between spouses: A longitudinal analysis. *Journal of Consulting and Clinical Psychology, 57,* 263–268. doi:10.1037/0022-006X.57.2.263

O'Leary, K. D., & Slep, A. M. (2003). A dyadic longitudinal model of adolescent dating aggression. *Journal of Clinical Child and Adolescent Psychology, 32,* 314–327. doi:10.1207/S15374424JCCP3203_01

O'Leary, K. D., Slep, A. M., & O'Leary, S. G. (2007). Multivariate models of men's and women's partner aggression. *Journal of Consulting and Clinical Psychology, 75,* 752–764. doi:10.1037/0022-006X.75.5.752

O'Leary, K. D., & Slep, A. M. S. (2012). Prevention of partner violence by focusing on behaviors of both young males and females. *Prevention Science, 13,* 329–339. doi:10.100-7/S1121-011-0237-2

O'Leary, S. G., & Slep, A. M. (2006). Precipitants of partner aggression. *Journal of Family Psychology, 20,* 344–347. doi:10.1037/0893-3200.20.2.344

Pan, H. S., Neideg, P. H., & O'Leary, K. D. (1994). Predicting mild and severe husband-to-wife physical aggression. *Journal of Consulting and Clinical Psychology, 62,* 975–981. doi:10.1037/0022-006X.62.5.975

Pence, E., & Paymar, M. (1993). *Education groups for men who batter: The Duluth model.* New York, NY: Springer.

Reis, H. T., Capobianco, A., & Tsai, F. (2002). Finding the person in personal relationships. *Journal of Personality, 70,* 813–850. doi:10.1111/1467-6494.05025

Riggs, D. S., & O'Leary, K. D. (1989). A theoretical model of courtship aggression. In M. A. Pirog-Good & J. E. Stets (Eds.), *Violence in dating relationships: Emerging social issues* (pp. 53–71). New York, NY: Praeger.

Roberts, N., & Noller, P. (1998). The associations between adult attachment and couple violence: The role of communication patterns and relationship satisfaction. In J. A. Simpson & W. S. Rholes (Eds.), *Attachment theory and close relationships* (pp. 317–350). New York, NY: Guilford Press.

Robertson, K., & Murachver, T. (2007). It takes two to tangle: Gender symmetry in intimate partner violence. *Basic and Applied Social Psychology, 29,* 109–118. doi:10.1080/01973530701331247

Robins, R. W., Caspi, A., & Moffitt, T. E. (2002). It's not just who you're with, it's who you are: Personality and relationship experiences across multiple relationships. *Journal of Personality, 70*, 925–964. doi:10.1111/1467-6494.05028

Ross, J. M., & Babcock, J. C. (2010). Gender and intimate partner violence in the United States: Confronting the controversies. *Sex Roles, 62*, 194–200. doi:10.1007/s11199-009-9677-6

Sagrestano, L. M., Heavey, C. L., & Christensen, A. (1999). Perceived power and physical violence in marital conflict. *Journal of Social Issues, 55*, 65–79. doi:10.1111/0022-4537.00105

Schumacher, J. A., & Leonard, K. E. (2005). Husbands' and wives' marital adjustment, verbal aggression, and physical aggression as longitudinal predictors of physical aggression in early marriage. *Journal of Consulting and Clinical Psychology, 73*, 28–37. doi:10.1037/0022-006X.73.1.28

Scott, K., & Straus, M. (2007). Denial, minimization, partner blaming, and intimate aggression in dating partners. *Journal of Interpersonal Violence, 22*, 851–871. doi:10.1177/0886260507301227

Simmons, C. A., Lehmann, P., & Cobb, N. (2008). A comparison of women versus men charged with intimate partner violence: General risk factors, attitudes regarding using violence, and readiness to change. *Violence and Victims, 23*, 571–585. doi:10.1891/0886-6708.23.5.571

Simon, T. R., Anderson, M., Thompson, M. P., Crosby, A. E., Shelley, G., & Sacks, J. J. (2001). Attitudinal acceptance of intimate partner violence among U.S. adults. *Violence and Victims, 16*, 115–126.

Slotter, E. B., & Finkel, E. J. (2011). I³ theory: Instigating, impelling, and inhibiting factors in aggression. In P. R. Shaver & M. Mikulincer (Eds.), *Human aggression and violence: Causes, manifestations, and consequences* (pp. 35–52). Washington, DC: American Psychological Association. doi:10.1037/12346-002

Sorenson, S. B., & Taylor, C. A. (2005). Female aggression towards male intimate partners: An examination of social norms in a community-based sample. *Psychology of Women Quarterly, 29*, 78–96. doi:10.1111/j.1471-6402.2005.00170.x

Stanley, J. L., Bartholomew, K., Taylor, T., Oram, D., & Landolt, M. (2006). Intimate violence in male same-sex relationships. *Journal of Family Violence, 21*, 31–41. doi:10.1007/s10896-005-9008-9

Statistics Canada. (2005). *Family violence in Canada: A statistical profile, 2005.* Ottawa, Ontario, Canada: Canadian Centre for Justice Statistics.

Stets, J. E., & Straus, M. A. (1992). The marriage license as a hitting license. In M. A. Straus & R. J. Gelles (Eds.), *Physical violence in American families* (pp. 227–244). New Brunswick, NJ: Transaction.

Stith, S. M., & McCollum, E. E. (2011). Conjoint treatment of couples who have experienced intimate partner violence. *Aggression and Violent Behavior, 16*, 312–318. doi:10.1016/j.avb.2011.04.012

Stith, S. M., Rosen, K. H., & McCollum, E. E. (2003). Effectiveness of couples treatment for spouse abuse. *Journal of Marital and Family Therapy, 29*, 407–426. doi:10.1111/j.1752-0606.2003.tb01215.x

Stith, S. M., Smith, D. B., Penn, C. E., Ward, D. B., & Tritt, D. (2004). Intimate partner physical abuse perpetration and victimization risk factors: A meta-analytic review. *Aggression and Violent Behavior, 10*, 65–98. doi:10.1016/j.avb.2003.09.001

Straus, M. (2004). Prevalence of violence against dating partners by male and female university students worldwide. *Violence Against Women, 10*, 790–811. doi:10.1177/1077801204265552

Straus, M. A. (2011). Gender symmetry and mutuality in perpetration of clinical-level partner violence: Empirical evidence and implications for prevention and treatment. *Aggression and Violent Behavior, 16*, 279–288. doi:10.1016/j.avb.2011.04.010

Straus, M. A., & Gelles, R. J. (1990). *Physical violence in American families: Risk factors and adaptations to violence in 8,145 families.* New Brunswick, NJ: Transaction.

Sugarman, D. B., & Frankel, S. L. (1996). Patriarchal ideology and wife-assault: A meta-analytic review. *Journal of Family Violence, 11*, 13–40. doi:10.1007/BF02333338

Tjaden, P., & Thoennes, N. (2000). Prevalence and consequences of male-to-female and female-to-male intimate partner violence as measured by the National Violence Against Women Survey. *Violence Against Women, 6*, 142–161. doi:10.1177/10778010022181769

Whitaker, D. J., Haileyesus, T., Swahn, M., & Saltzman, L. S. (2007). Differences in frequency of violence and reported injury between relationships with reciprocal and nonreciprocal intimate partner violence. *American Journal of Public Health, 97*, 941–947. doi:10.2105/AJPH.2005.079020

Whitaker, D. J., Morrison, S., Lindquist, C., Hawkins, S. R., O'Neil, J. A., Nesius, A. M., . . . Reese, L. (2006). A critical review of interventions for the primary prevention of perpetration of partner violence. *Aggression and Violent Behavior, 11*, 151–166. doi:10.1016/j.avb.2005.07.007

White, J. W., Merrill, L. L., & Koss, M. P. (2001). Predictors of premilitary courtship violence in a Navy recruit sample. *Journal of Interpersonal Violence, 16*, 910–927. doi:10.1177/088626001016009004

Wilkinson, D. L., & Hamerschlag, S. J. (2005). Situational determinants in intimate partner violence. *Aggression and Violent Behavior, 10*, 333–361. doi:10.1016/j.avb.2004.05.001

Williams, S. L., & Frieze, I. H. (2005). Patterns of violent relationships, psychological distress, and marital satisfaction in a national sample of men and women. *Sex Roles, 52,* 771–784. doi:10.1007/s11199-005-4198-4

Winstok, Z. (2006). Gender differences in the intention to react to aggressive action at home and in the workplace. *Aggressive Behavior, 32,* 433–441. doi:10.1002/ab.20143

Winstok, Z. (2007). Toward an interactional perspective on intimate partner violence. *Aggression and Violent Behavior, 12,* 348–363. doi:10.1016/j.avb.2006.12.001

Winstok, Z., & Eisikovits, Z. (2008). Motives and control in escalatory conflicts in intimate relationships. *Children and Youth Services Review, 30,* 287–296. doi:10.1016/j.childyouth.2007.10.006

Woodward, L. J., Fergusson, D. M., & Horwood, L. J. (2002). Romantic relationships of young people with childhood and adolescent onset antisocial behavior problems. *Journal of Abnormal Child Psychology, 30,* 231–243. doi:10.1023/A:1015150728887

Index

relationship-specific, as
adaptations, 75
for social support, 354–355
transformation of, 102, 582–583
Motivational congruence, in appraisal of
interruptive events, 300
Motivational relevance, in appraisal of
interruptive events, 300
Motivational strategies, and goal pursuit
in relationships, 287–288
Motivational variables, and empathic
accuracy
overview, 332–333
personal gain motivation, 333–334
relationship maintenance motivation,
334–337
self and worldview maintenance motivation, 337–339
Motor-based performance, effect of power
on, 434
Multidimensional friendship instruments,
465–466
Multidimensionality of support, 359–361
Multifactor models of partner violence,
615–619
Multifinality, 198–199, 377
Multifunctionality of communication,
374–375
Muraoka, M., 304
Murdock, K. W., 214–215
Murray, S. L., 255, 289–290, 378, 567
Murstein, B. I., 212–213
Must friends, 466
Mutsu, A. A., 514–515
Mutual attraction–love, role in mate
choice, 504
Mutual conflict, partner violence in situa-
tions of, 613–614
Mutual cyclical growth, 594
Mutual dependence, in interdependence
theory, 70, 71
Mutuality level, friendship formation,
468–469
Mutual violent control, 607n

Nachshon, O., 224
Narratives, relationship
and explanatory knowledge structures,
380–381
and reflexive nature of communication, 373–374
Naturally occurring venues, relationship
initiation in, 213

Nazer, N., 472
Neale, M. A., 441
Needs
versus propensities, in power research,
448–449
related to relationship initiation,
216–217
in reward perspectives on interpersonal attraction, 181–184
Neff, L. A., 567
Negative affective behaviors, and relational satisfaction, 381–382
Negative affectivity, 302, 306
Negative affect reciprocity, and communication, 373, 384
Negative coercion, 409
Negative emotions
effect of power on, 436
elicitation of in close relationships,
300
in social-functionalist account, 298
Negative experiences within marriage
accumulation of, 568–570
and changes in marital satisfaction,
562–563
Negative influence strategies, 394, 408,
410
Negative mood, received support and, 353
Negative motivational states, in relation-
ship neuroscience, 132
Negative noise, in interdependence the-
ory, 81
Negative self-representations, effect on
romantic relationships, 378
Neglect, as reaction to destructive partner
behavior, 584
Negotiation power, 425, 433, 436
Nelson, G., 121
Nerve growth factor, and relationship–
health link, 157
Nesse, R. M., 363
Nested ecological theory, application to
partner violence, 615
Neto, F., 504, 505
Networked individualism, 486
Networked relationships, 233
Networks, social. *See* Social networks
Neural systems, versus behavioral sys-
tems, 127–128
Neuroendocrine activity, and relation-
ship–health link, 154, 166
Neurological correlates of love, 510
Neuroscience, relationship. *See*
Relationship neuroscience

Newcomb, T. M., 179, 180, 196
Newlyweds, motivated reasoning in, 565,
566, 567. *See also* Marriage
Newman, M. L., 447
Nietert, P. J., 164
Nijstad, B. A., 440
Noise, in interdependence theory, 81
Noller, P., 304, 611
Nonbiological kin care, 19–20
Noncorrespondent outcomes, threat-
induced maintenance processes
due to, 582–584
Nondirective support, 355
Nonexclusivity in male–male couples,
542–544
Nonmutual dependence, in interdepen-
dence theory, 70
Nonromantic orientation to love, in
women, 502
Nonverbal behavior, flirtatious, 217–218
Nonverbal cues, and empathic accuracy,
324
Nonverbal decoding ability, 321
Nonverbal emotional expression, 304
Non–zero-sum view of relationships,
95, 96
Norepinephrine
neuroscience of familiarity, 128
and relationship–health link, 154
Normative attachment perspectives on
interpersonal attraction, 194–195
Normative course of marital satisfaction,
559–560
Normative features of attachment
processes, 34–35
Normative processes in partner
preference, 45–46
Normative romantic relationship
development, and health,
152–153
Norms
and interpersonal attraction, 184
same-sex sexuality, 540–541
social, as adaptations, 75
Novelty, in intimate relationships, 562

Oatley, K., 311
Objectification, effect of power on, 432
Objective health markers, 152. *See also*
Relationship–health link
Obligations, appealing to, as influence
strategy, 408
Observation, of social interactions, 74